SOCIAL DEVELOPMENT IN CHILDHOOD AND ADOLESCENCE

A Contemporary Reader

EDITED BY
MELANIE KILLEN AND
ROBERT J. COPLAN

WILEY-BLACKWELL

A John Wiley & Sons, Ltd., Publication

Blackwell Publishing was acquired by John Wiley & Sons in February 2007. Blackwell's publishing program
has been merged with Wiley's global Scientific, Technical, and Medical business to form Wiley-Blackwell.

Registered Office
John Wiley & Sons Ltd, The Atrium, Southern Gate, Chichester, West Sussex, PO19 8SQ, United Kingdom

Editorial Offices
350 Main Street, Malden, MA 02148-5020, USA
9600 Garsington Road, Oxford, OX4 2DQ, UK
The Atrium, Southern Gate, Chichester, West Sussex, PO19 8SQ, UK

For details of our global editorial offices, for customer services, and for information about how
to apply for permission to reuse the copyright material in this book please see our website at
www.wiley.com/wiley-blackwell.

The right of Melanie Killen and Robert J. Coplan to be identified as the editors of the editorial material in
this work has been asserted in accordance with the UK Copyright, Designs and Patents Act 1988.

Library of Congress Cataloging-in-Publication Data

Social development in childhood and adolescence : a contemporary reader / edited by Melanie Killen
and Robert J. Coplan.
    p. cm.
  Includes bibliographical references and index.
  ISBN 978-1-4051-9756-4 (hardback) – ISBN 978-1-4051-9757-1 (paperback)
1. Child development. 2. Adolescence–Social aspects. 3. Socialization. 4. Developmental
psychology. I. Killen, Melanie. II. Coplan, Robert J., 1967–
  HQ767.9.S657 2011
  305.231–dc22

                      2010053060

A catalogue record for this book is available from the British Library.

Set in 10/12pt Bembo by SPi Publisher Services, Pondicherry, India

Printed and bound in Singapore by Ho Printing Singapore Pte Ltd

1   2011

BRIEF CONTENTS

Preface   ix

PART I   INTRODUCTION   1

  1   Social Development: Concepts, Theory, and Overview   3

PART II   FOUNDATIONS AND EARLY BEGINNINGS   11

  2   Biological and Social–Cognitive Bases of Emotions   13

  3   Parent–Child Attachment Relationships   64

  4   Mental States and Theory of Mind   116

PART III   SELF, RELATIONSHIPS, AND SOCIAL GROUPS   151

  5   Children's Peer Relationships   153

  6   The Development of Morality   202

  7   Self Identity and Group Identity   254

PART IV   PEER REJECTION AND EXCLUSION   313

  8   Shyness and Social Withdrawal   315

  9   Aggression and Bullying   365

  10   Stereotyping, Prejudice, and Exclusion   405

PART V   FAMILY, COMMUNITY, AND CULTURE   455

  11   Parenting Attitudes and Beliefs   457

  12   Culture, Ethnicity, and Rights   515

Acknowledgments   576
Name Index   580
Subject Index   591

CONTENTS

Preface   ix

PART I INTRODUCTION   1

1 Social Development: Concepts, Theory, and Overview   3
Melanie Killen and Robert J. Coplan

PART II FOUNDATIONS AND EARLY BEGINNINGS   11

2 Biological and Social-Cognitive Bases of Emotions   13

Introduction   14

Temperament and Social Behavior in Childhood   15
Mary K. Rothbart, Stephan A. Ahadi, and Karen L. Hershey

The Development of Concern for Others in Children with Behavior Problems   26
Paul D. Hastings, Carolyn Zahn-Waxler, JoAnn Robinson, Barbara Usher, and Dana Bridges

Sympathy Through Affective Perspective Taking and Its Relation to Prosocial Behavior in Toddlers   48
Amrisha Vaish, Malinda Carpenter, and Michael Tomasello

A Closer Look 1   Is Biology Destiny? The Contributions of Genetics to Social Development   62

3 Parent–Child Attachment Relationships   64

Introduction   65

The Nature of the Child's Ties   66
Jude Cassidy

Attachment Security in Infancy and Early Adulthood: A Twenty-Year Longitudinal Study   86
Everett Waters, Susan Merrick, Dominique Treboux, Judith Crowell, and Leah Albersheim

The Effects of Infant Child Care on Infant–Mother Attachment Security: Results of the NICHD Study of Early Child Care   91
NICHD Early Child Care Research Network

A Closer Look 2   How Do I Love Thee? Attachment and Romantic Relationships   114

4 Mental States and Theory of Mind   116

Introduction   117

Mind-Reading, Emotion Understanding, and Relationships   118
Judy Dunn

Twelve-Month-Old Infants Interpret Action in Context   122
Amanda L. Woodward and Jessica A. Sommerville

Scaling of Theory-of-Mind Tasks   129
Henry M. Wellman and David Liu

A Closer Look 3   Autism and Theory of Mind: Understanding Others' Beliefs, Desires, and Emotions   149

PART III SELF, RELATIONSHIPS, AND SOCIAL GROUPS   151

5 Children's Peer Relationships   153

Introduction   154

The Power of Friendship: Protection Against
an Escalating Cycle of Peer Victimization   155
Ernest V. E. Hodges, Michel Boivin,
Frank Vitaro, and William M. Bukowski

Children's Social Constructions of Popularity   165
A. Michele Lease, Charlotte A. Kennedy,
and Jennifer L. Axelrod

Group Status, Group Bias, and Adolescents'
Reasoning About the Treatment of Others
in School Contexts   184
Stacey S. Horn

A Closer Look 4   Leaders and Followers:
Peer Pressure in Adolescence   200

6 The Development of Morality   202

Introduction   203

The Development of Children's Orientations
toward Moral, Social, and Personal Orders:
More than a Sequence in Development   204
Elliot Turiel

Consistency and Development of Prosocial
Dispositions: A Longitudinal Study   218
Nancy Eisenberg, Ivanna K. Guthrie,
Bridget C. Murphy, Stephanie A. Shepard,
Amanda Cumberland, and Gustavo Carlo

Children's Thinking About Diversity
of Belief in the Early School Years:
Judgments of Relativism, Tolerance,
and Disagreeing Persons   233
Cecilia Wainryb, Leigh A. Shaw,
Marcie Langley, Kim Cottam, and Renee Lewis

A Closer Look 5   Learning the Moral of
the Story: Education in the Moral Domain   252

7 Self Identity and Group Identity   254

Introduction   255

Changes in Children's Self-Competence
and Values: Gender and Domain Differences
Across Grades One through Twelve   256

Janis E. Jacobs, Stephanie Lanza,
D. Wayne Osgood, Jacquelynne S. Eccles,
and Allan Wigfield

Ethnic Identity and the Daily Psychological
Well-Being of Adolescents From Mexican
and Chinese Backgrounds   278
Lisa Kiang, Tiffany Yip, Melinda Gonzales-Backen,
Melissa Witkow, and Andrew J. Fuligni

The Development of Subjective Group
Dynamics: Children's Judgments of Normative
and Deviant In-Group and Out-Group
Individuals   292
Dominic Abrams, Adam Rutland,
and Lindsey Cameron

A Closer Look 6   Who Am I and What
Group Do I Belong to? Self Identity in
the Context of Social Interactions   311

PART IV PEER REJECTION AND EXCLUSION   313

8 Shyness and Social Withdrawal   315

Introduction   316

Don't Fret, Be Supportive! Maternal
Characteristics Linking Child Shyness
to Psychosocial and School Adjustment
in Kindergarten   317
Robert J. Coplan, Kimberley A. Arbeau,
and Mandana Armer

Trajectories of Social Withdrawal from
Middle Childhood to Early Adolescence   332
Wonjung Oh, Kenneth H. Rubin, Julie
C. Bowker, Cathryn Booth-LaForce,
Linda Rose-Krasnor, and Brett Laursen

Social Functioning and Adjustment
in Chinese Children: The Imprint
of Historical Time   348
Xinyin Chen, Guozhen Cen, Dan Li,
and Yunfeng He

A Closer Look 7   But I Like to
Be Alone! Unsociability and the Benefits
of Solitude   363

9 Aggression and Bullying   365

Introduction   366

An Integrated Model of Emotion
Processes and Cognition in Social
Information Processing　　　　　　367
Elizabeth A. Lemerise and William F. Arsenio

A Short-Term Longitudinal Study of
Growth of Relational Aggression during
Middle Childhood: Associations with
Gender, Friendship Intimacy, and
Internalizing Problems　　　　　　379
*Dianna Murray-Close, Jamie M. Ostrov,
and Nicki R. Crick*

A Peek Behind the Fence: Naturalistic
Observations of Aggressive Children with
Remote Audiovisual Recording　　　395
Debra J. Pepler and Wendy M. Craig

A Closer Look 8　A Slap in the "Facebook":
The Study of Cyber-Bullying　　　403

10　Stereotyping, Prejudice, and Exclusion　405
　Introduction　　　　　　　　　406

Children's Social Reasoning About
Inclusion and Exclusion in Gender
and Race Peer Group Contexts　　407
Melanie Killen and Charles Stangor

The Development and Consequences
of Stereotype Consciousness in
Middle Childhood　　　　　　　421
Clark McKown and Rhona S. Weinstein

In-group and Out-group Attitudes
of Ethnic Majority and Minority
Children　　　　　　　　　　441
Judith A. Griffiths and Drew Nesdale

A Closer Look 9　Stereotyping
and Discrimination: What Factors Help
to Reduce Prejudice?　　　　　　451

**PART V　FAMILY, COMMUNITY,
AND CULTURE**　　　　　　　**455**

11　Parenting Attitudes and Beliefs　457
　Introduction　　　　　　　　　458

The Company They Keep: Relation
of Adolescents' Adjustment and Behavior
to Their Friends' Perceptions of Authoritative
Parenting in the Social Network　　459
*Anne C. Fletcher, Nancy E. Darling, Laurence
Steinberg, and Sanford M. Dornbusch*

Individual Differences in Adolescents'
Beliefs About the Legitimacy of Parental
Authority and Their Own Obligation
to Obey: A Longitudinal Investigation　476
*Nancy Darling, Patricio Cumsille,
and M. Loreto Martínez*

Domain-Specific Antecedents of Parental
Psychological Control and
Monitoring: The Role of Parenting
Beliefs and Practices　　　　　　493
Judith G. Smetana and Christopher Daddis

A Closer Look 10　Bridging the Generation
Gap: Promoting Healthy Parent–Adolescent
Relationships　　　　　　　　513

12　Culture, Ethnicity, and Rights　515
　Introduction　　　　　　　　　516

Parents' Goals for Children: The Dynamic
Coexistence of Individualism
and Collectivism in Cultures and Individuals　517
*Catherine S. Tamis-LeMonda, Niobe Way,
Diane Hughes, Hirokazu Yoshikawa,
Ronit Kahana Kalman, and Erika Y. Niwa*

Muslim and Non-Muslim Adolescents'
Reasoning About Freedom of Speech
and Minority Rights　　　　　　537
Maykel Verkuyten and Luuk Slooter

Chinese Adolescents' Reasoning About
Democratic and Authority-Based
Decision Making in Peer, Family,
and School Contexts　　　　　　554
*Charles C. Helwig, Mary Louise Arnold,
Dingliang Tan, and Dwight Boyd*

A Closer Look 11　African-American
Culture: Understanding the Past to
Make Predictions About Development　574

Acknowledgments　　　　　　　576
Name Index　　　　　　　　　580
Subject Index　　　　　　　　591

PREFACE

Social development refers to how children become members of families, peer groups, communities, and cultures. Over the past several decades the field of social development has greatly expanded, reflecting biological, social-relational, social-cognitive, and social-emotional changes in development. This broadening scope of social development research has led to accompanying increases in student motivation to learn about this area. In particular, the wide range of topics encompassing multiple disciplines appeals to a breadth of interests, and encourages an understanding of the interrelations between psychological and social sciences. Moreover, student interest is heightened by the centrality of these issues for understanding everyday life. The readings in this volume were selected to represent both classic and current articles on social development from early childhood to adolescence, and which connect to the foundations of what it means to be a social being. To accomplish this goal, five sections were created that reflect topical cross-cutting approaches and include the foundations of development, the self, relationships, and groups, along with specific foci on the family, community, and culture, including both normative and non-normative development. For each of these areas of social life, we have featured different chapters to provide a rich perspective on what social developmental change entails.

Our goal is that reading this book will demonstrate the centrality of social development for understanding psychology and human behavior. No single volume can capture the wealth of information that now exists about social development from infancy to adulthood.

What we have done in this volume is to highlight key findings that will engage readers about the importance of social development as a fundamental aspect of what it means to be human as well as a member of a social species. We selected succinct theoretical articles to provide the landscape and accessible empirical studies to form the core reading list. We also developed a number of supplements to guide readers through the articles.

An introductory chapter written by the editors offers a historical and theoretical overview of social development. Introductory comments by the editors are then provided at the beginning of each section to serve as a guide for instructors and students; these commentaries highlight important points and controversial issues. In addition, chapters include "boxes" with up-to-date "new issues" pertinent to the topic, with a citation for further reading. Each chapter concludes with discussion questions, debate topics, and in-class exercises as well as a short list of recommended readings related to the topic, referred to as "A Closer Look..." in the table of contents. This Reader was designed to serve as a comprehensive text that reflects a coherent collection of articles, serving the pressing needs of college and university faculty members and instructors. It is intended for advanced undergraduate or graduate student courses in the area of "Social Development," which are most often offered in departments of Psychology and Human Development, but can also be found in other departments and programs including Child and Family Studies, Criminology, Sociology, Social Work, and Education.

The origins of this Reader began almost a decade ago with conversations between the editors and Ken Rubin, Adam Rutland, and Paul Hastings. We discussed the need for a new Reader in social development. We gratefully thank Ken, Adam, and Paul, who are each leaders in the field of social development, for their ideas and input, and we hope that this Reader addresses the needs that we identified in our fruitful discussions. Kelly Lynn Mulvey has provided exceptional feedback on all phases of the project, and her assistance is very much appreciated. As associate editor (*Child Development*) and editor (*Social Development*), respectively, of current journals in the field, we have been privileged and fortunate to read cutting-edge research from a wide range of topics in social development, and we are appreciative of the unique opportunities that these positions have provided, and which contributed to our reach for selecting articles for this Reader.

We are extremely indebted to our many respective mentors, colleagues, and graduate students for discussions and collaborations on the topics in this book, and to our social developmental colleagues for generously providing permission to reprint their articles. We acknowledge the feedback and assistance from our summer undergraduate intern students, Naomi Heilweil and Aliya Mann.

We thank our respective universities for support during the preparation of this Reader, the University of Maryland, College Park, and Carleton University. We thank Christine Cardone and Matt Bennett at Wiley-Blackwell publishers for their editorial support and guidance throughout the project. We hope that this collection of articles and supplementary materials leaves the reader motivated to search for more information about how, why, and what makes social development fundamental to the psychological development of individuals, and for understanding the complexity of social life.

Melanie Killen and Robert J. Coplan
August, 2010

Part I

INTRODUCTION

1

SOCIAL DEVELOPMENT
Concepts, Theory, and Overview

Social development is the study of how children become members of the social world. This involves developing social relationships with peers and adults, acquiring morality, figuring out how groups work, developing an identity, understanding others' perspectives, learning about emotions, and interacting with others in a range of social contexts. How do these changes come about and what sources of influence facilitate or hinder these processes? In essence, social development is about how children come to think, feel, and behave towards the people that surround them and how they understand social interactions, relationships, and culture. The developmental changes that occur from infancy to adulthood in the area of social behaviors, social cognitions, and social relationships are tremendous and complex. These changes are related to cognitive, emotional, motivational, and psychopathological development within and between family, community, and cultural contexts.

Debates about the social nature of humans, the origins of morality, the nature of prejudice in childhood, the dilemma of bullying and victimization, the role of emotions in development and communication, and what contributes to healthy peer and parent–child relationships all fall under the topic of social development. Children acquire the fundamentals of social development over thousands of social exchanges and opportunities for reflection, abstraction, inference, evaluation, and interpretation. Acquiring this knowledge is essential for children's survival, and much of this rich database of information about social development is necessary for professionals working with children, such as educators, psychologists, medical experts, and teachers. Children grow up interacting and forming relationships with people who are important in their lives, and they develop beliefs and form attitudes about the nature of humans and how individuals fit (or do not fit) together. Individualized experiences also provide each person with unique perspectives on social development.

The study of social development involves answering (at least) seven important questions: (1) How is social knowledge and competence acquired?; (2) What underlies and promotes change over time?; (3) What types of social influences are important?; (4) What aspects of social development change as a function of the context of social interaction?; (5) What differentiates normative and psychopathological development?; (6) How do institutions promote healthy social development?; and (7) What is universal and culturally specific about social development? These basic questions are explored in this volume, which is focused on the study of social development.

Social Development in Childhood and Adolescence: A Contemporary Reader, First Edition. Edited by Melanie Killen and Robert J. Coplan.
Editorial material and organization © 2011 Blackwell Publishing Ltd. Published 2011 by Blackwell Publishing Ltd.

One central assumption of the approach taken in this Reader is that social development is a multifaceted, multileveled process that entails complex interactions that change over time and across settings (i.e., home, school, neighborhood, and culture). This conceptual approach is applied in answering the above-mentioned questions through the exploration of a wide range of topics, including: (1) the foundations of early social development; (2) how children's self-system develops in the context of social relationships and groups; (3) what happens when children are vulnerable and excluded; and (4) the role of the family, community, and culture in making children become healthy members of their worlds. Each chapter in this Reader addresses one of these fundamental issues about what it means to become a social being, and how this process occurs from infancy to adulthood.

Accordingly, in this Reader, we will cover this wide range of topics related to children's social development from infancy to adolescence through the compilation of carefully selected current research papers, which delve into these aspects of development. The study of social development involves "real world topics" and the findings have implications for policy and practice. Theories guide research questions. Knowing the theoretical basis of a study is central and necessary for evaluating the robustness of a finding, and for giving it meaning. Theories answer the "so what?" question. Methodologies, which answer the "how do you know?" question, are the crux of the phenomenon, and help determine how the behavior, attitudes, judgment, belief, or value was recorded, analyzed, and interpreted.

"Legacies" of the Foundational Theories of Social Development

As the field of social development has advanced and expanded over the past several decades, contemporary researchers rarely provide models to explain all of social behavior and development as part of one global stage sequence. Instead, current researchers, drawing on multiple theoretical perspectives, take a domain specificity approach in which different areas of social development are studied using criteria to identify a phenomenon and its related components. Multiple

levels of theory bear on understanding children's social development, from the biological to the societal levels of analysis. Despite the expansion of theory and research foci, most of the "classic theories" of social development remain extremely influential, and form the building blocks for most of the contemporary research on children's development. In the following sections, we provide a very brief overview of these major historical theories, with a specific focus on their continuing legacies.

Psychoanalytic theories. Freud's (1910) psychoanalytic theory, and its later incarnations (e.g., Erikson, 1950), remains largely influential across numerous domains in psychology. Freud was trained in medical school in the area of neurology, where he studied psychological disorders. In terms of social development, Freud's legacy is particularly noteworthy because he was among the first to promote some "core principles" of psychological development that are widely held today, but were considered "radical new ideas" at the time. For example, Freud argued that human development is predictable and understandable, and that it could be understood and explained through science. Moreover, Freud theorized that emotions and thoughts as unconscious processes had a role in determining behaviors. In fact, Freud was the first psychologist to propose a theoretical framework for understanding unconscious processes to explain mental illness. He outlined dynamic, structural, and sequential theories of development. Freud's dynamic theory postulated that humans were basically driven by sexual and aggressive instincts and the desire to reduce stimulation (contrary to most current theories which have demonstrated that humans seek cognitive, social, and emotional stimulation). This part of his theory was largely disconfirmed with the onset of the cognitive revolution in psychology, which demonstrated that humans actively seek cognitive activity and to understand their world.

Freud's structural theory of the id (instincts), ego (rationality), and superego (morality) provided the developmental model for the onset of social and moral development, which occurred with the formation of the superego in early childhood. Through the resolution of the Oedipal conflict for males or the Electra conflict for females, which required a positive identification with the same-sex parent, children internalized parental values, and became capable of socially oriented behavior and judgments, developing a superego. Thus, in Freud's system, the internalization of parental values was the catalyst for social development (and guilt, as a product of the negative desires for the same-sex parent, provided the motivation to be moral). Freud drew on Kantian philosophy to define morality as a version of the categorical imperative (act in such a way as you would will your act to be universal). He then theorized that this was a principle held by parents who provide the role models for children to become social.

Freud also postulated psychosexual stages of development, which reflected a sequence of resolutions and culminated in adolescence. These stages were later modified by Erikson (1950) who focused on psychosocial rather than psychosexual resolution of conflicts throughout life. The levels of consciousness that Freud proposed, including the unconscious, the preconscious, and the subconscious, were proposed to play a role in how humans interpret, process, and filter information and social experiences in their world, and much evidence suggests that these levels are reflected in how individuals store and interpret information. Perhaps most important for social development, Freud emphasized and promoted the lasting importance and influence of early social relationships (particularly between mother and young child) in the development of children's personalities. As represented in this Reader, these concepts are evident in the exploration of the topics of temperament, attachment, behavior problems, aggression, and personality development.

Behaviorism and social learning theory. In response to the unconscious processes described by psychoanalytic theories, behaviorism emerged as a theory that focused on observable and recordable behaviors. Behaviorists viewed Freud's constructs as mostly speculation. According to the most basic tenets of behaviorism (e.g., Skinner, 1935; Watson, 1913), human development is influenced primarily by emerging associations between external stimuli and observable responses (habits). In this regard, behaviorism introduced the concepts of *reinforcement* and *punishment* as mechanisms that would lead to the increase or decrease of displayed behaviors. By the 1960s, however, the "cognitive revolution" in psychological

research largely challenged the notion that only observable behavior is of interest. From the cognitive perspective, the mind was viewed as a rich part of who we are as human beings, providing the basis for motivation, intention, judgments, attitudes, beliefs, and values. Accordingly, it was argued that observations of behaviors can provide only a part of the information necessary to understand what makes an action social.

Thus, psychologist Alfred Bandura (Bandura, 1977; Bandura & Walters; 1963) adapted learning principles to propose a social-learning theory which accounts for aspects of children's social development that include reflection, thought, interpretation, and mental states. Essentially, his theory purported that children can learn novel social behaviors by attending to "important" others through modeling of their behaviors (e.g., parents, teachers, peers). Social learning theory also described how core constructs of reinforcement and punishment might function within the realm of social development. For example, Bandura suggested that children observe the *consequences* of their own (and others') social behaviors and that the outcomes serve to reinforce or inhibit the future display of these same behaviors.

Among the general legacy of behaviorism, however, is the focus on scientific methodology, controlling variables, and the need for carefully designed experimental protocols. In particular, social learning theory has influenced the study of social development by drawing attention to the critical influence both of parents and of peers as "models" for children's social behaviors. These ideas are depicted in the sections of this Reader that explore such topics as peer pressure, parenting styles, and the development of aggression.

Cognitive- and social-cognitive developmental theories. Piaget (1929, 1932, 1952) was a genetic epistemologist, dedicated to the study of the "origins of knowledge." He studied how infants, children, and adolescents solve problems and understand the physical, logical, and social world. Drawing on multiple disciplines (including biology, philosophy, and psychology), Piaget proposed that children actively construct knowledge about their world through interaction and reflection upon these interactions. Although Piaget is perhaps best known for his research on how children develop concepts such as number, space, time, causality, and logic, he also explored the development of social knowledge, including moral judgment, communication, and the role of peer relationships in fostering development.

In one line of research, Piaget interviewed children about social dilemmas, the rules of their games, their knowledge of social rules, and their conceptions of authority, autonomy, and fairness. Based on these extensive interviews, Piaget formulated a theory of moral judgment in which young children were initially authority-oriented (holding unilateral respect for authority). Through peer interaction, however, children constructed notions of equality and fairness, leading to a mutual respect for both peers and adults. Peer conflict provided children the opportunity to develop perspective-taking, negotiation, and social exchange skills, which provided the experiential basis for developing an understanding of reciprocity, mutuality, and respect for others. As with his logical theory, in which children constructed knowledge of math by interacting with physical objects, Piaget's social theory was based on the assumption that children constructed knowledge of the social world (and morality) by interacting with others, specifically peers.

Thus, the basic tenets of Piaget's theory of social development were that early social interactions enable children to construct social concepts, and that children's reasoning about what is "fair" evolves from early to middle childhood. Moreover, Piaget documented the ways in which children's schemes (organizing structures for assimilating information) and templates for making social decisions (e.g., allocation of resources, turn-taking, sharing, cooperation, avoiding harm to others, conflict resolution strategies, and demonstrating empathy) changed dramatically over the course of 5–10 years. The research that Piaget conducted in a few decades in the early 1900s led to many expansive areas of research in social development, including the development of morality, cooperation, theory of mind, the role of peer interaction in development, and social cognition in childhood.

A foundational aspect of Piaget's theory was that the tenets of social development are universal. From his view, developing social orientation to others is a basic aspect of being human (and today, some researchers would extend this notion to primates).

Although the way that sharing and cooperation emerge will differ across cultures, the fundamentals are the same because the focus of the acquisition is on peer interaction, not adult–child interaction. Thus, while adult–child interaction styles vary dramatically within and across cultures, peer interaction has adaptive properties that reflect an emerging mutuality and cooperation. This part of Piaget's theory has been tested and examined in many parts of the world, providing a rich understanding of early social development. The legacy of Piaget's theory is pervasive across most areas of social development and is demonstrated throughout the sections of this Reader.

Cultural communication theories. Vygotsky's (1978) theory of development was focused on problem solving, communication, cultural tools, and the role of peer tutoring in facilitating children's development. Although Vygotsky died at the young age of 37 in 1934, in his short life he produced important papers that generated many subsequent research programs. His primary focus was on children's consciousness and how thinking is an active and cooperative process. Indeed, Vygotsky theorized that knowledge is *social* in origin and referred to "cultural tools" (such as language) which help children move from one stage to the next. The phrase "zone of proximal development" referred to the time period from one point in development to the next in which children are most ready to learn and to benefit from teaching and tutoring. Identifying this point in children's development promotes their growth and change. The notion that cultural tools enable children to think in more complex ways has been tested in many cultures, providing a rich evidential basis for the universal nature of the role of culture in development. The theory has spawned research on communication and thought, language, cultural tools, play, and socialization.

George Herbert Mead (1934) proposed that "role-taking" (the mental task of putting oneself in another's position) was the foundation of human social intelligence. Being able to take another's perspective enables humans to relate to one another and to engage in symbolic communication. Mead also proposed a "social looking glass" theory about the development of self-knowledge, asserting that we learn about ourselves by observing the effect that our behavior has on others. Mead's theory provided evidence that contributed to the notion that children develop a self-concept early on and that their concept changes over time. Mead also emphasized autonomy and self-identity as primary aspects of social development. His notions of self-awareness, and the "mirror" image that individuals learn to recognize, particularly children as they are developing a self-concept, led to a generation of research on self-understanding, self-concept, and self-development.

Ethology and sociobiological theories. Ethology and other sociobiology theories focus on the biological bases of human behaviors and are derived from Darwin's (1877) theory of evolution. Whereas classic evolutionary theory describes processes that may alter the structural characteristics of species, ethology explores how evolutionary processes may shape species-specific *behaviors*. Early ethologists such as Konrad Lorenz (1937, 1950) focused on the study of "biologically programmed" (i.e., instinctual) animal behaviors that evolved because of naturalistic selection (e.g., imprinting in birds).

John Bowlby was among the most influential human ethologists and charted his foundational theory of attachment. Bowlby (1969, 1973) extensively observed interactions between infants and their mothers. He proposed a theory that interpreted specific infant behaviors and maternal responses within an evolutionary framework. For example, infant crying was viewed as a "distress signal" that mothers were "biologically-programmed" to respond to. Additionally, close proximity and physical contact between mother and infant were thought to serve the adaptive function of promoting the formation of attachment. Bowlby also echoed Freud's idea that early parent–child relationships provide a model for future relationships outside of the family.

A central tenet of ethology is the use of a comparative framework for understanding human development. This is accomplished through a comparative study of similarities and differences across species (Hinde, 1974). Indeed, the study of cross-species behaviors has yielded unique insights into social behaviors of children. For example, many different animal species form strict within-group dominance hierarchies (e.g., wolves, chimpanzees, chickens—hence the term "pecking order"). The adaptive function of these dominancy rankings is to reduce intra-group aggression by "predetermining" the outcome of most within-group conflicts, typically pertaining to the allocation of resources (i.e., food, mating partners). Drawing upon these animal models, Strayer and Strayer (1976) conducted extensive observations of children's conflicts over toys in the preschool playroom and demonstrated that a stable dominance hierarchy was established fairly early in the school year and its appearance was accompanied by an overall reduction in classroom aggression.

Comparative research has provided important findings for many areas of social development, including morality, theory of mind, and communication. As one example, Frans de Waal (2005), a prominent primatologist, studied the origins of morality in non-human primates and demonstrated that non-human primate species engage in a number of behaviors that are related to morality in humans, such as sympathy, empathy, non-aggressive means of conflict resolution, sharing of norms, and allocation of resources. De Waal and other comparative researchers have provided extensive evidence for an evolutionary basis of social predispositions in humans.

Ethology remains an influential theory in social development, particularly in terms of its associated methodological approach. Ethologists argue that behaviors can be understood only when considered within context and advocate the use of direct observations in naturalistic settings. Observational methods derived from ethologists have been used extensively in empirical studies on social behavior, conflict resolution, and play patterns with preschool-aged children in day care and preschool settings. Ethological theory also disputes the rigid distinctions between innate and learned behaviors by demonstrating the interaction of environmental and genetic/biological influences, and has accordingly influenced modern behavioral genetics theory and research. The legacy of ethology can be seen in the Reader in the discussion of topics such as child temperament, parent–child attachment, and aggression.

Summary. A summary of the "legacies" of each of the foundational theoretical perspectives just described is displayed in Figure 1.1. As can be determined by the information in Figure 1.1 each major theory has a domain of focus, an explanation about the social acquisition mechanisms, and other enduring ideas. What most of these theories share is a theoretically

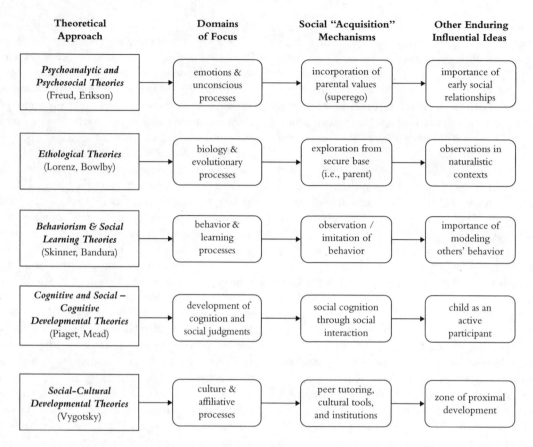

Theoretical Approach	Domains of Focus	Social "Acquisition" Mechanisms	Other Enduring Influential Ideas
Psychoanalytic and Psychosocial Theories (Freud, Erikson)	emotions & unconscious processes	incorporation of parental values (superego)	importance of early social relationships
Ethological Theories (Lorenz, Bowlby)	biology & evolutionary processes	exploration from secure base (i.e., parent)	observations in naturalistic contexts
Behaviorism & Social Learning Theories (Skinner, Bandura)	behavior & learning processes	observation / imitation of behavior	importance of modeling others' behavior
Cognitive and Social – Cognitive Developmental Theories (Piaget, Mead)	development of cognition and social judgments	social cognition through social interaction	child as an active participant
Social-Cultural Developmental Theories (Vygotsky)	culture & affiliative processes	peer tutoring, cultural tools, and institutions	zone of proximal development

Figure 1.1 Legacies of foundational theories of social development.

rich framework for understanding the origins and emergence of social thought, belief, judgment, behavior, and attitudes, and different methodologies for analyzing social development from infancy to adulthood. The focus of development from the "child's perspective" is essential, along with hypothesis-testing theories that provide information about the science of child development. These theories are also multidisciplinary in that most of the scholars drew from multiple disciplines, such as biology, anthropology, sociology, economics, and philosophy. The related disciplines provide ways to think about how to define constructs and how to measure social development.

The theories differ most on the positive or negative view of human nature, as well as the role that culture plays in social development, as evidenced in the articles in this Reader. Most of the research collected by these foundational theorists, however, relied on homogeneous samples, sometimes only boys (not girls), often only middle-income children, with diversity viewed as an inconvenience, not a focus of study. Further, the cultural expectations about who "counts" as members of societies were very restricted, and this was often reflected in the expectations about gender, with race and ethnicity not even discussed. Current research has focused more centrally on how issues of culture, diversity, and hierarchies within cultures contribute to the trajectory of children's social development.

Structure of the Reader

Social development has become a complex and expansive field. To understand the different levels of development, it is important to understand its social-

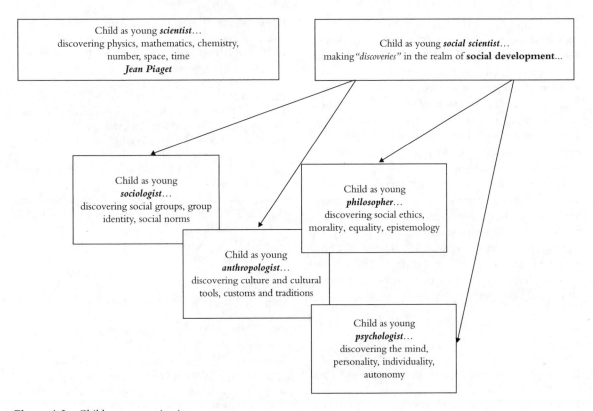

Figure 1.2 Child as young scientist.

cognitive, social-emotional, social-cultural, social-neuro-scientific, and social-personality bases. This is not an easy undertaking as many researchers use different terminology and methods. Reading current theory and research in social development across cognitive, emotional, cultural, neuro-scientific, and personality areas provides a strong foundation for understanding human development. Students of social development have many goals, including becoming scholars, researchers, teachers, medical professionals, childcare practitioners, policy experts, and applying theory to practice in other ways. Contemporary research in social development provides information that is essential, necessary, and of great importance for these many different goals and levels of inquiry.

The articles in this volume enable its readers to delve into the fascinating and engaging world of how humans become social beings and members of societies and cultures. The story of human evolution is always changing and always astounding. In this Reader we have created a selective window for understanding ontogenetic human evolution, the story of social development within the life of an individual from birth to adulthood.

This Reader is designed with a typical 14–15-week academic semester in mind and consists of five sections: (I) Introduction (overview of the foundational theories); (II) Foundations and Early Beginnings; (III) Self, Relationships, and Social Groups; (IV) Peer Rejection and Exclusion; and (V) Family, Community, and Culture. In each section there are three chapters that reflect its themes. For each chapter, three empirical articles were selected that represent the chapter topic. A short introduction is provided for each chapter to orient and guide the Reader, and to provide a framework for interpreting the findings described in the articles. In addition, at the end of each chapter, is a section entitled "A Closer Look..." which includes a list of discussion questions and classroom exercises to provide discussion, debate, dialogue, and reflection on the week's reading. Finally, 11 boxes with information about current interests are inserted, one for each chapter, which provide a brief overview of a current application of the theory or set of new and provocative findings about the topic. These various venues provide multiple ways to be immersed in both foundational and current research in social development from infancy to adulthood.

Jean Piaget famously proposed the analogy of the child as a "young scientist" whose active and explorative nature allows him/her to "discover" physics, mathematics, chemistry, space, and time. To conclude this chapter, we leave you with an "expansion" of this Piaget-inspired metaphor in Figure 1.2, which also serves to highlight many of the underlying themes in this Social Development Reader.

References

Bandura, A. (1977). *Social learning theory*. Englewood Cliffs, NJ: Prentice-Hall.

Bandura, A., & Walters, R. H. (1963). *Social learning and personality development*. New York: Holt, Rinehart, & Winston.

Bowlby, J. (1969). *Attachment and loss: Vol. 1. Attachment*. London: Hogarth Press.

Bowlby, J. (1973). *Attachment and loss: Vol. 2. Separation, anxiety and anger*. New York: Basic Books.

Darwin, C. (1877). A biographical sketch of an infant. *Mind*, *2*, 285–294.

de Waal, F. B. M. (2005). *Our inner ape: A leading primatologist explains why we are who we are*. Riverhead Books: New York.

Erikson, E. (1950). *Childhood and society*. New York: Norton.

Freud, S. (1910). The origin and development of psychoanalysis. *American Journal of Psychology*, *21*, 181–218.

Hinde, R. A. (1974). *Biological bases of human social behaviour*. New York: McGraw-Hill.

Lorenz, K. Z. (1937). The companion in the bird's world. *Auk*, *54*, 254–273.

Lorenz, K. Z. (1950). The comparative method in studying innate behaviour patterns. *Symposium of the Society for Experimental Biology*, *4*, 221–268.

Mead, G. H. (1934). *Mind, self, and society*. Chicago: University of Chicago Press.

Piaget, J. (1929). *The child's conception of the world*. New York: Harcourt, Brace.

Piaget, J. (1932). *The moral judgment of the child*. Glencoe, IL: Free Press.

Piaget, J. (1952). *The psychology of intelligence*. San Diego, CA: Harcourt Brace.

Skinner, B. F. (1935). Two types of conditioned reflex and a pseudo type. *Journal of General Psychology*, *12*, 66–77.

Strayer, F. F., & Strayer, J. (1976). An ethological analysis of social agonism and dominance relations among preschool children. *Child Development*, *47*, 980–989.

Vygotsky, L. S. (1978). *Mind in society: The development of higher psychological processes*. Cambridge, MA: Harvard University Press.

Watson, J. B. (1913). Psychology as the behaviorist views it. *Psychological Review*, *20*, 158–177.

Part II

FOUNDATIONS AND EARLY BEGINNINGS

2

BIOLOGICAL AND SOCIAL-COGNITIVE BASES OF EMOTIONS

Introduction   14

Temperament and Social Behavior in Childhood   15

Mary K. Rothbart, Stephan A. Ahadi, and Karen L. Hershey

    Method   18

    Results   20

    Discussion   22

The Development of Concern for Others in Children with Behavior Problems   26

Paul D. Hastings, Carolyn Zahn-Waxler, JoAnn Robinson, Barbara Usher, and Dana Bridges

    Development of Empathy and Concern for Others   27

    Concern for Others in Children With Disruptive Behavior Problems   27

    Psychophysiology and Concern for Others   27

    Socialization and Concern for Others   28

    Concern for Others as a Moderator of Stability of Externalizing Problems   29

    Summary and Hypotheses   29

    Method   29

    Results   33

    Discussion   41

Sympathy Through Affective Perspective Taking and Its Relation to Prosocial Behavior in Toddlers   48

Amrisha Vaish, Malinda Carpenter, and Michael Tomasello

    Method   49

    Results   53

    Discussion   57

A Closer Look 1   Is Biology Destiny? The Contributions of Genetics to Social Development   62

Introduction

Watching a toddler in the throes of a temper-tantrum provides firsthand evidence that young children have "big feelings." Even in infancy, however, there are notable differences in children's emotional expressions and responses. For example, there is wide variation in the degree to which some children become angry and frustrated (e.g., when they cannot reach a particular object), display fear and wariness (e.g., when meeting a new person), experience joy and exuberance (e.g., when playing with a new toy), or feel empathy and concern (e.g., when a friend is upset and crying). Historically, emotions were viewed as trivial or fleeting responses in childhood, with little systematic and empirical investigation. More recently, emotional development has come to be understood as a core component of children's social development, reflecting changes in temperament, empathy, sympathy, and affective responding.

Temperament can be generally defined as biologically based individual differences in children's reactivity and self-regulation. Temperamental traits (i.e., attention, activity, emotionality, shyness) are evident in infancy, relatively stable across time, and form the building blocks of later personality. Early temperament researchers Thomas and Chess (1977) coined the term "goodness of fit" to describe the "match" between children's temperament and the demands, expectations, and opportunities of the environment. This influential concept has been utilized to help explain children's social functioning in many diverse environments, including the family, the peer group, childcare, and at school.

Although children may come into the world with a predisposition to respond emotionally in different ways to different situations, social interaction with parents and peers also makes an important contribution to children's emotional development. *Empathy* refers to an emotional state that matches another person's emotional state, and its appearance in early childhood is related to the emergence of morality. Related to empathy is the construct of *affective perspective-taking*, which concerns children's ability to understand that others have emotional responses to experiences and social interactions. Through peer interaction in particular, children's emotional responses, as well as their understanding of emotions, develop through childhood.

In this chapter, the articles pertain to both the social-biological and social-cognitive dimensions of emotions and emotional development. The first reading concerns links between temperament and children's social development. Rothbart and colleagues (1994) explored associations between infant temperamental characteristics (e.g., attention, negative affect, fear) and their later display of prosocial (e.g., empathetic) and antisocial (e.g., aggressive) behaviors with peers at age 6–7 years. The second study explores the longitudinal development of empathy in early childhood. Hastings et al. (2000) examined changes in "concern for others" over time and as a function of parental socialization approaches in children with and without behavior problems. Finally, the last study addresses the early emergence of young children's affective perspective-taking skills. Vaish and colleagues (2009) explored whether toddlers displayed signs of sympathy towards an adult whom they observed being "harmed" (i.e., having a possession taken away) and how these early signs of affective perspective-taking might contribute towards the development of early prosocial behaviors. These three studies provide a window into how important emotions are for all aspects of children's social development.

Reference

Thomas, A., & Chess, S. (1977). *Temperament and development*. New York: Brunner/Mazel.

Temperament and Social Behavior in Childhood

Mary K. Rothbart, Stephan A. Ahadi, and Karen L. Hershey

With recent developments in the conceptualization and measurement of temperament (Bates, 1987; Goldsmith et al., 1987; Kohnstamm, Bates, & Rothbart, 1989), it has become increasingly feasible to explore the interaction between the child's temperament and care giver's child-rearing practices in the development of personality and social behavior. Some of the first models and research in this area have emerged for the period of infancy, with relationships between temperament and attachment a major focus of study (Grossman, Grossman, Spangler, Suess, & Unzner, 1985; Miyake, Chen, & Campos, 1985; van den Boom, 1989). More recently, however, work has addressed childhood social development of empathy (Bryant, 1987; Eisenberg, 1988; Hoffman, 1983), conscience and guilt (Dienstbier, 1984; Hoffman, 1983, 1988; Kochanska, 1991), and aggression or conduct disorder (Lytton, 1990; Quay, Routh, & Shapiro, 1987).

At the same time, research on the assessment of temperament has been developing much closer connections to the factor analytic tradition of personality assessment (Halverson, Martin, & Kohnstamm, 1994). Higher-order factors of temperamental variability in children have been identified showing remarkable similarity to some of the "Big Five" factors of adult personality (Digman, 1990). In our own work, we have found evidence for three higher-order temperament factors, which we have labeled Surgency, Negative Affectivity, and Effortful Control (Ahadi & Rothbart, 1994; Ahadi, Rothbart, & Ye, 1993). These factors bear a strong resemblance to the superfactors of Extraversion/Positive Emotionality, Neuroticism/Negative Emotionality, and (to a lesser extent) Psychoticism/Constraint in the models of Eysenck (Eysenck, 1967; Eysenck & Eysenck, 1985) and Tellegen (1985). To the extent that identification of basic dimensions of temperament defines a domain of inquiry, psychological processes underlying these dimensions and their role in social development can be studied. In this paper, we investigate relationships

between individual differences in social behavior patterns and temperament as reported by parents of 6- and 7-year-old children. In addition, for a small subset of subjects, predictions are reported from laboratory temperament assessments in infancy to the children's social characteristics at age 7 years as reported by the parent.

We first briefly define the construct of temperament and outline the processes whereby temperament may mediate social learning generally. Temperamental processes are examined next that may underly the development of more specific social behavior patterns, including individual differences in the tendency to experience guilt/shame, to respond empathically, to act aggressively, to engage in help-seeking behaviors, and to negatively evaluate or to oppose new activities.

We define *temperament* as constitutionally based individual differences in reactivity and self-regulation, with the term *constitutional* referring to the person's relatively enduring biological makeup, influenced over time by heredity, maturation, and experience (Rothbart, 1989; Rothbart & Derryberry, 1981). *Reactivity* refers to arousability of affect, motor activity, and related responses, assessed by threshold, latency, intensity, time to peak intensity, and recovery time of the reaction. *Self-regulation* refers to processes such as attention, approach-withdrawal, behavioral inhibition, and self-soothing, serving to modulate reactivity. Dimensions of temperament constitute a subset of individual differences in personality. Temperamental processes provide a substrate for the development of a variety of personality traits, but other processes also are importantly related to personality development, and emerging traits are likely to be differentially related to temperament.

Temperament can be seen to interact with experience in the development of social outcomes in a number of ways. In 1968, Escalona noted that if children vary in temperamental reactivity, then even in identical situations, they will differ in their "effective experience." Thus, an intrusive approach by a stranger will be a positive event for some infants, distressing for others; failed expectations will lead to strong frustration reactions for some children, others will not be bothered. A similar construct of "organismic specificity" has been more recently put forward by Wachs and Gandour (1983). If children's experiences in social situations can be seen to vary depending upon their temperament, then it will be likely also that the affective meaning of present, past, and future events will be colored by the child's temperament. These biases will influence in turn the "working models" developed by the child reflecting expectations about others, the child's optimistic versus pessimistic views of future events, and the child's perception of self in relation to others.

Temperamental processes are strongly implicated in the social learning process (Eysenck, 1967; Gray, 1981, 1982). They involve, in part, the individual's sensitivity to reward and punishment, leading to different learned reactions to objectively identical social reinforcements (Gray, 1981, 1982). Our temperamental characteristics thus may lead us to construe our environments differently and to learn different things in ostensibly identical situations. A child high in Negative Affectivity, punished for performing an undesirable act, may be more likely to inhibit future performance of the act because memory of the aversive consequence overrides the immediate reward of performing the act. Temperament also involves children's approach and withdrawal tendencies, including the child's tendency to choose risky or dangerous situations, and also can be seen to specify the upper and lower bounds for tolerable excitement, as described by Bell (1974). In his view, when children's or caregivers' upper limit for stimulation is reached, they engage in activities to reduce the intensity of stimulation they experience from the other person or the situation. When their lower limit for stimulation (boredom) is reached, they will attempt "to stimulate, prime, or in other ways to increase the insufficient or nonexistent behavior..." (Bell, 1974, p. 13).

In a previous review we suggested some of the ways in which temperament might predispose a child to "high risk" conditions or to the development of psychopathology (Rothbart, Posner, & Hershey, 1995), and some of these considerations are appropriate to

thinking more generally about socialization. One temperamental characteristic, for example, may moderate or control another. Thus, both fear and effortful control may moderate risky, impulsive, and aggressive behaviors in the child. A very young child may inhibit an aggressive response due to fear of retaliation, whereas an older child also may inhibit the response following a parent's instruction to do so. The child's reactive displays also may influence others' evaluative reactions to the child, especially in situations where the child's behavior does not match care givers' or peers' views of what is appropriate. Thomas and Chess have labeled this construct the "goodness-of-fit" between temperament and environment. When there is a poor fit, the child may be seen as unmotivated by parents or be rejected by peers, and the child's feelings of self-worth may suffer.

Temperament, in part, influences the "learnability" of social behaviors and explicit social knowledge. Theories of social development that either take temperament explicitly into account or refer to emotions as eliciting conditions for social behavior have provided hypotheses for our research. The first of these relate to the development of guilt and conscience. Dienstbier (1984) has proposed that the internalization of moral behavior will be strongly influenced by a person's susceptibility to conditioned fear or anxiety. Lower thresholds for experiencing these internal cues of discomfort also will be associated with a greater likelihood of perceiving the cause of those feelings as being internal, further promoting internalization of moral standards.

Dienstbier suggests that individuals high in fear and anxiety will be more influenced by lower power approaches to the socialization of conscience than individuals low in fear and anxiety. Kochanska (1991) has found support for an interaction between parental child-rearing methods and children's fearfulness in the development of guilt and conscience as would be predicted by Dienstbier's model. A main effect of a relationship between fear and the development of guilt and conscience, however, was not found in her data. In this paper, we hope to provide further information, including developmental data, on the relation between temperamental fearfulness and guilt proneness, although our data do not allow us to study socialization-temperament interactions.

Kochanska (1993) has proposed two factors likely to be associated with the development of conscience, both important aspects of temperament. The first is the child's proneness to distress in connection with wrongdoing; the second is the child's capacity for inhibitory control. Kochanska notes that two kinds of temperament-related control processes relevant to socialization of guilt and conscience have been identified: passive control, associated with fear; and active inhibitory control, related to attentional mechanisms (see also Rothbart, 1989; Rothbart & Posner, 1985). Temperament may be seen then to interact with socialization in the development of conscience by means of individual differences in distress proneness and in both of these control mechanisms.

Zahn-Waxler and her colleagues have noted associations between empathic experience and guilt, and indicated that early socialization of conscience may work through parents' dramatization of the effects of a child's acts in hurting others (Zahn-Waxler, Radke-Yarrow, & King, 1979). As in the development of conscience, greater sensitivity to affective experience, particularly to negative affect, would be expected to give these children greater preparation for empathic responding and related behavior. In research on prosocial behavior, however, distinctions have been made between the elicitation of feelings of concern for others (sympathy) and direct vicarious distress to the distress of others, with the former more highly associated with altruistic behavior and the latter with attempts to alleviate one's own distress (Batson, 1987; Eisenberg, McCreath, & Ahn, 1988). This view suggests there may be an important cognitive aspect of empathy that focuses attention upon the plight of the other person and how to alleviate it.

In aggression, which can be seen as both a reactive behavior and the result of a failure to control its occurrence, recent models by Lytton (1990) and Quay (Quay et al., 1987) implicate temperament in the development of aggressive problems and conduct disorder. Quay et al. (1987) have suggested that aggressive individuals have lower levels of Behavioral Inhibition System (Gray, 1982) functioning, as well as strongly reactive reward or approach systems. Lytton (1990) notes, however, that to date there is little support for this position. Our study allows this research question to be addressed. We expect that aggression

might be modulated not only by passive control related to fear and anxiety but also by active inhibitory control as discussed by Kochanska (1991), and perhaps by control related to empathy and guilt as well (Zahn-Waxler et al., 1979).

We also wished to address the relation between temperament and children's strategies for relating to others. *Help-seeking* refers to behaviors directed toward others with the goal of enlisting their assistance. Sears (1963) has identified the emotion of frustration as an important elicitor of these requests. Once a child becomes frustrated, if the care giver is able to help in relieving the child's frustration, the child will become more likely to call upon the care giver for help. Maccoby and Masters (1970) have suggested that fear and anxiety can lead the child to turn to others. To the extent that emotion-eliciting conditions provide the opportunity for learning of help-seeking, temperamentally more easily frustrated and fearful children will have more opportunities for help-seeking behavior patterns to be reinforced.

Finally, the role of temperament in the tendency to negatively evaluate or to resist or oppose new activities is considered. We expect individuals to oppose engaging in activities that they perceive will have negative outcomes. Two sources of negative outcome expectancies are prior failures and perceived lack of control over outcomes (Carver & Scheier, 1981). Negative Affectivity could contribute to negativity in at least two ways. First, novel stimuli will be more likely to elicit anxiety for individuals high in Negative Affectivity, motivating avoidance of the novel activity. Second, individuals high in Negative Affectivity may be more likely to experience "failure" in novel or challenging activities (e.g., finding them stressful, becoming anxious or discouraged), thereby learning to avoid such activities in the future. Effortful Control may also be related to negativity, with individuals low in Effortful Control perceiving they lack control over "success" in new activities and therefore negatively evaluating and/or avoiding them.

In summary, our review has suggested that (a) internalization of moral behavior leading to guilt and conscience should be mediated by Negative Affectivity and Effortful Control, (b) appreciation of and sensitivity to the emotional experiences of others should be mediated by Effortful Control, (c) individual differences in aggression may be mediated by Negative Affectivity and by reactive approach systems thought to underlie Surgency, (d) individual differences in help-seeking behavior patterns may be influenced by temperamental Negative Affectivity and Effortful Control, and (e) the tendency to negatively evaluate or oppose new or current activities may be influenced by Negative Affectivity and low Effortful Control.

For a subset of the children in this study, tendencies toward the expression of fear, anger/frustration, smiling and laughter, activity level and behavioral wariness have been assessed in a laboratory study of temperament in infancy. In addition, mothers have reported to us the early gestures and words used by the children when they were 10 months of age. These data were used to predict the social behavior patterns of the children at age 7 years, to get at the early matrix from which both later temperament and social behavior will develop. To the extent that these infant measures have predictive validity for temperamental variation at age 7, we can view them as early markers of these underlying temperament systems. For example, Rothbart, Hershey, and Derryberry (1994) found that, in this small sample of 26 children, infant latency to approach small objects in the laboratory predicted age 7-year approach and impulsivity as well as (negatively) inhibitory control and attentional focusing (see also Ahadi & Rothbart, 1994). In presenting these data, however, we stress caution regarding their interpretation. First, the sample is small and thus results may be due to sampling characteristics. Second, as the earlier example illustrates, what may be viewed as a relatively pure measure of approach in infancy appears to be implicated in two of the basic temperament systems in that it correlated with components of both Surgency and Effortful Control at age 7.

Method

Subjects

Subjects were 80 6- to 7-year-old children (40 girls) from the Eugene-Springfield area. Subjects were recruited for the project in three ways: (a) children who had previously participated in a longitudinal research project on temperament when they were infants, and had remained in the area, were asked to participate in the project; (b) parents participating in studies of infants were asked if they had older children who might be involved in this study; and (c) a classified advertisement was placed in a local newspaper. Subjects represented a range of socioeconomic backgrounds, but were all white, reflecting the racial homogeneity of the Eugene-Springfield community.

Measures

Parents were administered the Children's Behavior Questionnaire (CBQ; Rothbart, Ahadi, Hershey and Fisher, in preparation) a parent-report instrument assessing temperament in children aged 3–8 years. The CBQ has 15 scales with alpha coefficients ranging from .67 to .94. In the instrument, parents are instructed to read each item and decide whether a statement is a "true" or "untrue" description of their child's reactions within the past 6 months. Ratings are made on a 7-point scale: *extremely untrue of your child* (1), *quite untrue of your child* (2), *slightly untrue* (3), *neither true nor false* (4), *slightly true* (5), *quite true* (6), *extremely true of your child* (7). Parents may also indicate that the statement is not applicable if, for example, they have not seen their child in the situation described in the item.

Ahadi et al. (1993) factor-analyzed the 15 CBQ scales from a sample of 468 6- and 7-year-old children in the People's Republic of China. We identified a three-factor solution, similar to that obtained in a U.S. sample, which appeared to correspond to the broad temperamental dimensions of Surgency/Extraversion, Negative Affectivity/Neuroticism, and Effortful Control/Constraint. Because the Chinese sample was the largest sample for which CBQ protocols have been administered, it is likely the most reliable index of the CBQ's latent structure. Moreover, the derived Chinese solution is completely independent from the current sample. Consequently, scales were assigned unit weights to the factor they loaded most highly on to compute three broad measures of temperamental variation (i.e., scales assigned to each factor were weighted equally). Table 2.1 presents the CBQ scales and sample items with respect to their second-order factor structure. Scales on the Surgency measure

Table 2.1 Temperament scale definitions: Children's Behavior Questionnaire (CBQ)

Behavior	Definition
	Surgency
Approach	Amount of excitement and positive anticipation for expected pleasurable activities (becomes very excited before an outing such as a picnic, party).
High intensity pleasure	Amount of pleasure or enjoyment related to situations involving high stimulus intensity, rate, complexity, novelty, and incongruity (enjoys being in crowds of people).
Smiling and laughter	Amount of positive affect in response to changes in stimulus intensity, rate, complexity, and incongruity (laughs a lot at jokes and silly happenings).
Activity level	Level of gross motor activity including rate and extent of locomotion (is full of energy, even in the evening).
Impulsivity	Speed of response initiation (usually rushes into an activity without thinking about it).
Shyness	Slow or inhibited approach in situations involving novelty or uncertainty (often prefers to watch rather than join other children playing).
	Negative Affectivity
Discomfort	Amount of negative affect related to sensory qualities of stimulation, including intensity, rate or complexity of light, movement, sound, texture (is quite upset by a minor cut or bruise).
Fear	Amount of negative affect, including unease, worry, or nervousness related to anticipated pain or distress and/or potentially threatening situations (is afraid of the dark).
Anger/frustration	Amount of negative affect related to interruption of ongoing tasks or goal blocking (gets angry when told s/he has to go to bed).
Sadness	Amount of negative affect and lowered mood and energy related to exposure to suffering, disappointment, and object loss (sometimes appears downcast for no reason).
Falling reactivity and soothability	Rate of recovery from peak distress, excitement, or general arousal (is easy to soothe when s/he is upset).
	Effortful Control
Inhibitory control	The capacity to plan and to suppress inappropriate approach responses under instructions or in novel or uncertain situations (is good at games like "Simon Says," "Mother, May I?").
Attentional focusing	Tendency to maintain attentional focus upon task-related channels (when drawing or coloring in a book, shows strong concentration).
Low intensity pleasure	Amount of pleasure or enjoyment related to situations involving low stimulus intensity, rate, complexity, novelty and incongruity (enjoys looking at picture books).
Perceptual sensitivity	Amount of detection of slight, low intensity stimuli from the external environment (notices the smoothness or roughness of objects s/he touches).

included (positively) approach, high intensity pleasure (stimulation-seeking), smiling and laughter, impulsivity, and (negatively) shyness. Scales on the Negative Affectivity measure included (positively) discomfort, fear, anger, sadness, and (negatively) falling reactivity/ soothability. Scales on the Effortful Control measure included (positively) inhibitory control, attentional focusing, low intensity pleasure, and perceptual sensitivity. Scores on these three temperament measures

were then correlated with the social behavior patterns.

For this study, we also developed a set of scales designed to assess the social behavior patterns of aggressiveness, empathy, guilt/shame, help-seeking, and negativity. For each of these scales, 13 or 14 new items were developed. Internal consistency estimates and sample items for each of these scales are the following: aggression ($\alpha = .88$), "Takes toys away from

Table 2.2 Correlations between big-three temperament dimensions and socialization-relevant traits

Temperament dimensions	Socialization-relevant traits				
	Aggression	Empathy	Guilt	Help-seeking	Negativity
Surgency	.54***	−.12	−.24*	.18	.07
Negative affect	.35**	−.01	.22*	.36**	.56***
Effortful control	−.38***	.48***	.36**	−.23	−.36**

*p < .05. **p < .01. ***p < .001.

other children"; empathy (α = .81), "Is upset by stories in which the characters are hurt or die"; guilt/ shame (α = .84), "Doesn't act very upset when s/he has done something wrong" (reversed); negativity (α = .62), "Often reacts to a suggested new activity with 'no'."

Infant assessments

For 26 of the children (42% of the original infant sample), data were available from infant laboratory assessments of temperament taken at 13 months of age (for the anger/frustration measure and parent reports of children's vocabulary and gesture usage, at 10 months of age). Ten-month data were used for anger/frustration because the anger/frustration measure at 13 months had proved to be negatively related to concurrent parent reports of temperament, unlike the measure taken at the younger age (Rothbart et al., in preparation).

Three measures of emotionality were made in the laboratory for an original sample of 62 infants: fear, anger/frustration, and smiling and laughter. In these assessments, infants sat in a three-sided gray enclosure, where stimuli were presented from one of three curtained windows. Multiple stimuli designed to elicit each of the reactions were presented and infants' responses to the stimuli were videotaped. Emotional reactions were coded for latency to onset, highest intensity, and duration of emotional reaction, with levels of intercoder reliability maintained at .85 agreement or greater. Scores for the parameters of latency, intensity, and duration were standardized and combined for each stimulus presentation (episode). When the combined measures proved to be positively

correlated across episodes, scores from the multiple episodes were standardized and a composite score formed, yielding an overall score for fear, anger/frustration, and smiling and laughter.

Latency-to-grasp scores involved averaging infants' latencies to grasp a set of both simple and more complex and exciting toys, with the latter including sound and movement producing mechanical toys. Activity level was assessed by placing infants on a carpet marked with grid lines, and with toys distributed across the floor space. Activity level was measured by the number of grid lines crossed by the infant within a period of 3 min. Mothers also were interviewed by telephone and asked questions about the words and gestures their children were using. A simple sum of the numbers of words in the child's vocabulary and the number of gestures used by the child was further entered into the analysis.

Results

Table 2.2 presents the zero-order correlations between the measures of temperament and social behavior patterns. Surgency correlated positively with aggression and negatively with guilt/shame. Negative Affectivity correlated positively with aggression, guilt/shame, help-seeking, and negativity. Effortful Control correlated positively with empathy and guilt/shame, and negatively with aggression, help-seeking, and negativity.

There are, however, moderate intercorrelations among the temperament scales that may contribute to redundancies in the zero-order effects just described. Specifically, Effortful Control correlated negatively

Table 2.3 Standardized regression coefficients for predicting socialization-relevant traits

Social traits	Temperament dimensions		
	Surgency	Negative affect	Effort
Aggression	.48★★★	.25★	−.14
Empathy	.02	.27★	.57★★★
Guilt/shame	−.14	.44★★★	.50★★★
Help-seeking	.13	.32★★	−.06
Negativity	−.02	.49★★★	−.17

★$p < .05$. ★★$p < .01$. ★★★$p < .001$.

with both Surgency ($r = −.29, p < .01$) and Negative Affectivity ($r = −.40, p < .001$). Consequently, multiple regression models were employed to determine the unique effects of temperamental variation on social behavior patterns and the magnitude of those effects. Each of the five social traits were regressed onto the three temperament variables. The three temperament variables were entered into the model simultaneously.

Table 2.3 presents the standardized regression coefficients for the five regression models. Aggression was related to high levels of both Surgency and Negative Affectivity. Effortful Control did not account for unique variance in the prediction of aggression. The overall model was significant ($R^2 = .40, F(3, 76) = 17.17, p < .0001$). Empathy and guilt/shame were both positively related to Effortful Control and Negative Affectivity. The overall models were significant, ($R^2 = .27, F(3, 76) = 9.24, p < .0001$) and ($R^2 = .31, F(3, 76) = 11.60, p < .0001$), for empathy and guilt/shame, respectively. Help-seeking and negativity were both positively related to Negative Affectivity. Neither Surgency nor Effortful Control accounted for unique variance in the prediction of these traits. The overall models were significant, ($R^2 = .15, F(3, 76) = 4.56, p < .01$) and ($R^2 = .33, F(3, 76) = 12.74, p < .0001$) for help-seeking and negativity, respectively.[1]

That Negative Affectivity contributed to both pro- and anti-social traits led us to consider whether analysis of the component first-order factors or primary traits would clarify the situation somewhat. For example, analysis of the zero-order correlations between the primary traits of Negative Affectivity and social traits shows that whereas anger is corre-

lated with aggression ($r = .60, p < .0001$), it is unrelated to empathy [$r = −.17$, not significant (n.s.)] and guilt/shame ($r = .05$, n.s.). Conversely, although sadness is correlated with empathy ($r = .37, p < .001$) and guilt/shame ($r = .52, p < .001$), it is unrelated to aggression ($r = .15$, n.s.).

To identify unique effects of the Negative Affectivity component traits, we again employed multiple regression techniques. In this case models were specified where the component traits underlying Negative Affectivity were allowed to enter the regression model in a stepwise (SAS, 1982) fashion with the constraint that they explain variation beyond that already accounted for by the Surgency and Effortful Control variables. Anger accounted for significant variance beyond Surgency and Effortful Control in the prediction of aggression (partial $R^2 = .14, F(1, 76) = 20.36, p < .0001$) and negativity (partial $R^2 = .28, F(1, 76) = 35.84, p < .0001$), and also predicted, negatively, empathy (partial $R^2 = .04, F(1, 76) = 4.91, p < .05$). Beyond the effects of Surgency and Effortful Control, the primary factor of discomfort accounted for significant variation in help-seeking (partial $R^2 = .15, F(1, 76) = 14.26, p < .001$). Finally, sadness was positively related to both empathy (partial $R^2 = .20, F(1, 76) = 26.58, p < .0001$) and guilt/shame (partial $R^2 = .32, F(1, 76) = 45.83, p < .0001$).

As noted previously, a subset of these children had been assessed in the laboratory during infancy. Table 2.4 presents correlations between infant measures of temperament and the social behavior patterns for these 26 children. Infant activity level, assessed by locomotion across a grid, and smiling/laughter, assessed by positive reactivity to novel objects and auditory stimuli, and to interaction with the experimenter (both thought to reflect individual differences in infantile Surgency), correlated positively with later aggression. Infant activity level also correlated with later negativity.

Infant anger/frustration, assessed through negative affective reactions to objects placed out of reach (behind a Plexiglas barrier) or removed from infants, and fear (assessed by negative affective reactions to stimuli that were both novel and intense) were thought to reflect individual differences in infantile Negative Affectivity. Infant anger correlated positively with later aggression, guilt/shame, and help-seeking. Infant

Table 2.4 Correlations between infant laboratory measures of temperament and childhood socialization-relevant traits

Infant temperament	Socialization-relevant traits				
	Aggression	Empathy	Guilt	Help-seeking	Negativity
Activity	.55**	−.23	.16	.12	.37*
Smiling	.38*	−.32	−.27	.16	−.11
Anger/ frustration	.45*	.05	.42*	.34*	.14
Fear	−.34*	.42*	.37*	−.17	−.21
Grasp latency	−.32	.34*	−.12	−.34*	−.25
Early gestures	−.08	.41*	.43*	.16	−.10
Early words	−.24	.55**	.44*	−.10	−.44*

*$p < .05$. **$p < .01$.

levels of fear correlated negatively with later aggression, and positively with later empathy and guilt/shame. Latency to grasp small, interesting objects (thought to reflect infantile individual differences in Effortful Control) correlated positively with later empathy and negatively with childhood help-seeking. The use of early gesturing and words, assessed at age 10 months, also may be indicative of early appearing Effortful Control. The early uses of gestures and words both correlated positively with later empathy and guilt/shame, and the early use of words correlated negatively with negativity.

Discussion

These results support the idea that temperament is strongly implicated in the socialization process in ways that have been predicted by other researchers. Our goal was to examine relationships between temperament and social development within the framework of a global temperament systems model. In mapping the structure of childhood temperament onto the temperament models of researchers such as Eysenck (1967), Gray (1981), and Tellegen (1985), access is gained to previously identified dimensions that may help us to better understand the dynamics of interactions between individual differences and social factors in social development. We also found, however, that

limiting inquiry to a global model can be too constraining and that, despite commonalities among components of the temperament dimensions, it is often necessary to apply more fine-grained analyses to understand the role of temperament in social development. Our interpretations must be limited due to our reliance on mothers' perceptions of their children's behavior. However, to the extent that these findings converge with results obtained employing other measures, some confidence can be maintained in our interpretations.

With respect to aggressive tendencies, zero-order correlations were found indicative of unregulated behavior (low Effortful Control), approach (high Surgency), and Negative Affectivity. The Surgency findings confirm Quay et al.'s (1987) prediction that aggressiveness would be related to more reactive approach tendencies. Although this pattern of correlations is quite consistent with, and descriptive of, aggressive behavior, when a multiple regression model was employed, only Surgency and Negative Affectivity explained significant variation, with Negative Affectivity accounting for relatively little of the variation in aggressive tendencies. Although the scales that make up the Negative Affectivity factor are structurally related, they were differentially related to aggression. Whereas the irritable components of Negative Affectivity, such as anger, are related to aggression, internalizing components, such as sadness, are not.

Although we can only speculate as to why Effortful Control did not account for unique variance in aggressive tendencies, we (Rothbart & Posner, 1985) have postulated that individual differences in attentional self-regulation (Effortful Control) can serve as a superordinate self-regulatory system that, in addition to its direct effects, can modulate the reactivity of other temperament systems. Given the negative correlations between Effortful Control and Negative Affectivity and Surgency, Effortful Control may operate to regulate the reactive tendencies underlying Negative Affectivity and Surgency, thereby controlling aggressive tendencies.

Consistent with Dienstbier's (1984) and Kochanska's (1991) conceptualizations of the social development of guilt, Negative Affectivity accounted for substantial variation in our measure of guilt proneness. Importantly, it was the internalized components of Negative Affectivity that were related to individual differences in guilt. Our small sample follow-up data are equivocal on this matter, however, with both infantile anger and fear predicting later guilt. As predicted by Kochanska (1991), individual differences in Effortful Control also accounted for substantial variation in guilt proneness, indicating the importance of self-regulatory controls in the development of guilt and conscience.

To a degree, variability in Effortful Control may be represented by individual differences in attentional capacities. For the development of guilt to occur, individuals may need to develop the ability to disengage attention from signals of immediate personal reward in the environment (e.g., the positive outcomes of taking a playmate's toy) to the consequences of one's behaviors (e.g., a verbal rebuke, the playmate's distress). To the extent that children low in Effortful Control are less able to shift attention from immediate impulse gratification to its likely consequences, they will be less able to regulate harmful or antisocial behavior.

We have speculated elsewhere that individual differences in Effortful Control may be developmentally related to the "Big Five" dimensions of Agreeableness and Conscientiousness (Ahadi & Rothbart, 1994). It is interesting in this respect that Robins, John, and Caspi (1994) have found these two personality dimensions to be strongly correlated with antisocial personality in an ethically diverse sample of inner-city adolescents. Recent work by Harpur and Hare (1990) also suggests an attentional deficit in psychopaths leading to an "over-focus" of attention on events that interest them.

Attentional self-regulation also appears to be central to the development of empathy, a strongly cognitive trait. Our measures thought to assess infantile Effortful Control, latency to grasp toys and mothers' reports of early use of words and gestures, all predicted later empathy. The ability to disengage attention from one's own perspective to attend to another's, the hallmark of empathy, is an operation that, in theory, could serve to regulate behavior without reference to the negative affects. The social development of the empathy we have studied does appear, however, to be related to the negative affects as well. The internalizing, and not externalizing, components of Negative Affectivity are related to individual differences in empathy. This relationship also holds in our small sample follow-up with infantile fear, but not anger, predicting childhood empathy.

It is interesting to note that although Negative Affectivity predicted empathy in the regression models, there was no zero-order relationship between Negative Affectivity and empathy. We have speculated elsewhere that individuals high in Negative Affectivity and Effortful Control may be predisposed to repressive or defensive tendencies (Ahadi & Rothbart, 1994; Rothbart et al., 1995). If this is the case, Effortful Control may serve as a suppressor variable, hiding the effects of Negative Affectivity in the zero-order analysis.

As suggested by Sears (1963) and by Maccoby and Masters (1970), help-seeking was related to the Negative Affectivity superfactor. Specifically, it was largely related to discomfort, the tendency to experience distress to sensory stimulation. In the small sample follow-up laboratory assessment of infant behavior, anger/frustration, as predicted by Sears, but not fear, predicted later help-seeking tendencies. Children prone to frustration and distress may more readily elicit helping behaviors from care givers, reinforcing help-seeking behaviors. Conceptually, help-seeking would seem to be related to low Effortful Control, but no evidence was found for this relationship in the primary sample. Infant latency to grasp toys was negatively correlated with later help-seeking tendencies, but neither of the other two infant measures thought to indicate Effortful Control was correlated with later help-seeking.

Negativity not only correlated positively with Negative Affectivity, but also correlated negatively with Effortful Control. The latter finding is consistent with Carver and Scheier's (1981) construct of dispositional optimism, which reflects individual differences in the degree to which people will persevere, despite difficulty or even pain, in order to attain goals (Scheier et al., 1989). However, Effortful Control did not account for significant variation in negativity beyond that explained by Negative Affectivity. Again, however, effects of Effortful Control may be nondirect. Individual differences in Effort Control may serve, for example, to decrease the effects of Negative Affectivity by maintaining attention on goal-relevant stimuli and away from goal-irrelevant stimuli. Though all correlated negatively, only one of three infant markers of Effortful Control was significantly related to later negativity.

In summary, temperamental characteristics of children are related in predictable ways to social development. Because individual differences in temperament have consequences for how individuals perceive and react to their environments, they must necessarily have consequences for learning, child-rearing practices, and the effective socialization of children. Interestingly, the least well-understood of the three major dimensions of temperament in adulthood, Effortful Control, may prove to be most important in effective social development. In Eysenck's adult model a related dimension, labeled "Psychoticism," reflects, in its extreme, attitudes and behavior patterns indicative of "poor socialization" and even psychopathy. Although our focus, reflected by the label of Effortful Control, is on processes of attentional self-regulation, the strong relationships between this dimension and social traits of guilt proneness and empathy suggest that lack of attentional self-regulation may predispose a child to problems in socialization.

Negative Affectivity was found to be related to all the social traits examined in this study. However, we found it necessary to abandon a global temperament model and to analyze separately the components of Negative Affectivity and their possible role in social development. In general, the irritable negative affects such as anger and discomfort proneness were related to antisocial traits, whereas the internalizing negative affects of sadness and fear were related to prosocial traits. It is interesting that the two distress-related superfactors emerging from infant temperament assessment differentiate fear from anger/irritable affect as well (Rothbart & Mauro, 1990). It is therefore important in the study of social development to take a more fine-grained approach to the role of the negative affects, despite the common factor that binds these traits in superfactor models for childhood and beyond.

Finally, we again caution that our findings on concurrent relationships are limited to parent report measures and that the predictive findings were obtained with a very small sample of children. We hope that future work on temperament and social development will determine the generality of these results.

Note

1   There appear to be gender differences in these relationships, but space restrictions prevent us from presenting them in detail. Surgency appears to be primarily related to aggression in girls. Negative Affectivity appears to be primarily related to the externalizing social behavior pattern of aggression in boys, whereas it appears to be related primarily to the internalizing social behavior patterns of empathy and guilt/shame in girls. Effortful Control is negatively related to aggression in girls but not boys. Also Effortful Control appears to be primarily related to guilt/shame in girls. Results concerning these gender differences can be obtained from the authors.

References

Ahadi, S. A., & Rothbart, M. K. (1994). Temperament, development and the Big Five. In C. F. Halverson, G. A. Kohnstamm & R. P. Martin (Eds.), *The developing structure of temperament and personality from infancy to adulthood.* Hillsdale, NJ: Erlbaum.

Ahadi, S. A., Rothbart, M. K., & Ye, R. (1993). *Child temperament in the U.S. and China: Similarities and differences. European Journal of Personality, 7*, 359–77.

Bates, J. E. (1987). Temperament in infancy. In J. D. Osofsky (Ed.), *Handbook of infant development*. New York: Wiley.

Batson, C. D. (1987). Prosocial motivation: Is it ever truly altruistic? In L. Berkowitz (Ed.), *Advances in experimental social psychology*. New York: Academic Press.

Bell, R. Q. (1974). Contributions of human infants to caregiving and social interaction. In M. Lewis & L. A. Rosenblum (Eds.), *The effect of the infant on its caregiver*. New York: Wiley.

Bryant, B. K. (1987). Mental health, temperament, family, and friends: Perspectives on children's empathy and social perspective taking. In N. Eisenberg & J. Strayer (Eds.), *Empathy and its development*. Cambridge, UK: Cambridge University Press.

Carver, C. S., & Scheier, M. F. (1981). *Attention and self-regulation: A control theory approach to human behavior*. New York: Springer-Verlag.

Dienstbier, R. A. (1984). The role of emotion in moral socialization. In C. Izard, J. Kagan, & R. B. Zajonc (Eds.), *Emotions, cognition, and behavior*. New York: Cambridge University Press.

Digman, J. M. (1990). Personality structure: Emergence of the five-factor model. *Annual Review of Psychology, 41*, 417–440.

Eisenberg, N. (1988). The development of prosocial and aggressive behavior. In M. H. Bornstein & M. E. Lamb (Eds.), *Developmental psychology: An advanced textbook*. Hillsdale, NJ: Erlbaum.

Eisenberg, N., McCreath, H., & Ahn, R. (1988). Vicarious emotional responsiveness and prosocial behavior: Their interrelations in young children. *Personality and Social Psychology Bulletin, 14*, 298–311.

Escalona, S. K. (1968). *The roots of individuality: Normal patterns of development in infancy*. Chicago: Aldine.

Eysenck, H. J. (1967). *The biological basis of personality*. Springfield, IL: Thomas.

Eysenck, H. J., & Eysenck, M. W. (1985). *Personality and individual differences: A natural science approach*. New York: Plenum.

Goldsmith, H. H., Buss, A. H., Plomin, R., Rothbart, M. K., Thomas, A., Chess, S., Hinde, R. A., & McCall, R. B. (1987). Roundtable: What is temperament? Four approaches. *Child Development, 58*, 505–529.

Gray, J. A. (1981). A critique of Eysenck's theory of personality. In J. H. Eysenck (Ed.), *A model for personality*. Berlin: Springer-Verlag.

Gray, J. A. (1982). *The neuropsychology of anxiety*. New York: Oxford University Press.

Grossman, K., Grossman, K. E., Spangler, G., Suess, G., & Unzner, L. (1985). Maternal sensitivity and newborn orientation responses as related to quality of attachment in Northern Germany. In I. Bretherton & E. Waters (Eds.), Growing points of attachment theory and research. *Monographs of the Society for Research in Child Development, 50*(1–2, Serial No. 209).

Halverson, C., Martin, R., & Kohnstamm, G. (Eds.). (1994). *The developing structure of temperament and personality from infancy to adulthood*. Hillsdale, NJ: Erlbaum.

Harpur, T. J., & Hare, R. D. (1990). Psychopathy and attention. In J. T. Enns (Ed.), *The development of attention: Research and theory*. New York: North-Holland.

Hoffman, M. L. (1983). Affective and cognitive processes in moral internalization. In E. T. Higgins, D. Ruble, & W. Hartup (Eds.), *Social cognition and social development: A sociocultural perspective*. New York: Cambridge University Press.

Hoffman, M. L. (1988). Moral development. In M. H. Bornstein & M. E. Lamb (Eds.), *Developmental psychology: An advanced textbook*. Hillsdale, NJ: Erlbaum.

Kochanska, G. (1991). Socialization and temperament in the development of guilt and conscience. *Child Development, 62*, 1379–1392.

Kochanska, G. (1993). Towards a synthesis of parental socialization and child temperament in early development of conscience. *Child Development, 64*, 325–347.

Kohnstamm, G., Bates, J., & Rothbart, M. K. (Eds.). (1989). *Temperament in childhood*. Chichester, England: Wiley.

Lytton, H. (1990). Child and parent effects in boys' conduct disorder: A reinterpretation. *Developmental Psychology, 26*, 683–697.

Maccoby, E. E., & Masters, J. C. (1970). Attachment and dependency. In P. H. Mussen (Ed.), *Carmichael's manual of child psychology* (Vol. 2, 3rd ed.). New York: Wiley.

Miyake, K., Chen, S., & Campos, J. J. (1985). Infant temperament, mother's mode of Interaction, and attachment in Japan: An interim report. In I. Bretherton & E. Waters (Eds.), Growing points of attachment theory and research. *Monographs of the Society for Research in Child Development, 50*(1–2, Serial No. 209).

Quay, H. C., Routh, D. K., & Shapiro, S. K. (1987). Psychopathology of childhood: From description to validation. *Annual Review of Psychology, 38*, 491–532.

Robins, R. W., John, O. P., & Caspi, A. (1994). Major dimensions of personality in early adolescence: The Big Five and beyond. In C. F. Halverson, G. A. Kohnstamm, & R. P. Martin (Eds.), *The developing structure of temperament and personality from infancy to adulthood*. Hillsdale, NJ: Erlbaum.

Rothbart, M. K. (1989). Temperament and development. In G. Kohnstamm, J. Bates, & M. K. Rothbart (Eds.), *Temperament in childhood*. Chichester, England: Wiley.

Rothbart, M. K., & Derryberry, D. (1981). Development of Individual differences in temperament. In M. E. Lamb &

A. L. Brown (Eds.), *Advances in developmental psychology* (Vol. 1). Hillsdale, NJ: Erlbaum.

Rothbart, M. K., Ahadi, S. A., Hershey, K., & Fisher, P. (in preparation). *Temperament in children 4–7 years as assessed in the Children's Behavior Questionnaire.*

Rothbart, M. K., & Mauro, J. A. (1990). Questionnaire measures of infant temperament. In J. W. Fagen & J. Colombo (Eds.), *Individual differences in Infancy: Reliability, stability and prediction.* Hillsdale, NJ: Erlbaum.

Rothbart, M. K., & Posner, M. (1985). Temperament and the development of self-regulation. In L. C. Hartlage & C. F. Telzrow (Eds.), *The neuropsychology of individual differences: A developmental perspective.* New York: Plenum Press.

Rothbart, M. K., Posner, M. I., & Hershey, K. (1995). Temperament, attention and psychopathology. In D. Cicchetti & D. Cohen (Eds.), *Manual of developmental psychopathology.* New York: Wiley.

SAS, User's Guide: Statistics. (1982). Cary, NC: SAS Institute, Inc.

Scheier, M. F., Matthews, K. A., Owens, J. F., Magovern, G. J., SR., Lefebvre, R. C., Abbott, R. A., & Carver, C. S. (1989). Dispositional optimism and recovery from coronary artery bypass surgery: The beneficial effects on physical and psychological well-being. *Journal of Personality and Social Psychology, 57,* 1024–1040.

Sears, R. R. (1963). Dependency motivation. In M. Jones (Ed.), *Nebraska symposium on motivation.* Lincoln: University of Nebraska Press.

Tellegen, A. (1985). Structures of mood and personality and their relevance to assessing anxiety, with an emphasis on self-report. In A. H. Turna & J. D. Maser (Eds.), *Anxiety and the anxiety disorders.* Hillsdale, NJ: Erlbaum.

Van den Boom, D. (1989). Neonatal irritability and the development of attachment. In G. Kohnstamm, J. Bates, & M. K. Rothbart (Eds.), *Temperament in childhood.* Chichester, England: Wiley.

Wachs, T. D., & Gandour, M. J. (1983). Temperament, environment, and six-month cognitive-intellectual development: A test of the organismic specificity hypothesis. *International Journal of Behavioural Development, 6,* 135–152.

Zahn-Waxler, C., Radke-Yarrow, M., & King, R. A. (1979). Child rearing and children's prosocial initiations toward victims of distress. *Child Development, 50,* 319–330.

....

The Development of Concern for Others in Children with Behavior Problems

Paul D. Hastings, Carolyn Zahn-Waxler, JoAnn Robinson, Barbara Usher, and Dana Bridges

Oppositional, aggressive children are characterized by a tendency to act on their negative impulses, often without apparent attention to any effects upon the well-being of others. Deficits in empathy and remorse are recognized as common in children with disruptive behavior disorders (American Psychiatric Association, 1994). Perspective-taking and affective arousal in response to others in distress can promote interpersonal responsibility and inhibit harmful acts (Eisenberg & Mussen, 1989; Feshbach, 1975; Hoffman, 1982). Perhaps owing to the marked stability of externalizing problems over the life span (Mealey, 1995; Olweus, 1979), it has even been suggested that lowered empathy is an inherent part of antisocial individuals (Schacter & Latane, 1964). However, it is not clear when such deficits in concern for others first become evident, or what role deficits play in the development of externalizing behaviors.

In this investigation, we tracked the development of concern for others from preschool age to the early elementary school years in children at varying levels of risk for disruptive behavior disorders. *Concern for others* was used as a broad, inclusive term for the coordinated and correlated behavioral, affective, and cognitive factors associated with empathic and prosocial reactions (see also Grusec, 1991b; Grusec, Goodnow, & Cohen, 1996). We attempted to determine when children with and without externalizing problems begin to manifest reliable differences in their concern for others. We also examined whether the early presence of greater concern for others served as a protective factor against the development or maintenance of disruptive behaviors. Finally, we examined the relations between children's concern for others at 6–7 years of age and their cardiac responses to depictions of sadness and distress and their mothers' socialization approaches at preschool age.

Development of Empathy and Concern for Others

Humans are thought to have a biological preparedness to attend to and recognize the emotional needs of others (Hoffman, 1975). Empathy functions as a social emotion, effectively bridging the affective states of one individual with another (Levenson & Ruef, 1992). Evolutionary perspectives suggest that this empathic awareness has been adaptive for allowing humans to predict each other's behaviors and, in the case of altruistic, helpful, or cooperative acts, for forging lasting bonds of trust and reciprocity within their social groups (Nesse, 1991; Soher & Wilson, 1998). Studies of twins—both children and adults—have identified heritable, genetic components for empathy and prosocial acts (Matthews, Batson, Horn, & Rosenman, 1981; Rushton, Fulker, Neale, Nias, & Eysenck, 1986; Zahn-Waxler, Robinson, & Emde, 1992; Zahn-Waxler, Schiro, Robinson, Emde, & Schmitz, 2001).

The most commonly found group difference in concern for others is between the sexes. Girls show more concern than do boys from the second year of life through adolescence (Eisenberg & Fabes, 1998; Grusec et al., 1996; Zahn-Waxler, Radke-Yarrow, Wagner, & Chapman, 1992). In addition, individual differences in concerned responses to distress in others are moderately stable over the first 2 decades of life (Cummings, Hollenbeck, Iannotti, Radke-Yarrow, & Zahn-Waxler, 1986; Eisenberg et al., 1987, 1999; Zahn-Waxler et al., 2001). Interestingly, there are no published longitudinal observations of children's concern for others over the transition from preschool to the early elementary school years. One might expect both overall increases and moderate individual stability in concern for others over this period.

Concern for Others in Children With Disruptive Behavior Problems

The lack of concern for others in many antisocial adolescents has been well documented (Chandler & Moran, 1990; Cohen & Strayer, 1996; Ellis, 1982). The few studies done with younger children do not mirror these results. Examinations of the children in the present sample (Zahn-Waxler, Cole, Welsh, & Fox, 1995) and in

an independent study (MacQuiddy, Maise, & Hamilton, 1987) have shown that, at preschool age, children with and without disruptive behavior problems do not differ in their concern for others. However, Kochanska (1991) found that more disobedient toddlers were less likely, 6 to 8 years later, to report prosocial responses to vignettes depicting transgressions against others than were less disobedient toddlers. She suggested that early poor behavioral self-regulation, as indexed by disobedience, might predict future problems in conscience development through either biological or environmental pathways. In addition, Zahn-Waxler (1993, 2000) has described social and biological contributors to the widely recognized gender differences in both concern for others and externalizing problems. Compared with boys, girls' greater orientation toward the needs and well-being of others may be involved in their decreased risk for the development of disruptive behavior disorders.

Concurrent negative associations between concern for others and aggressive or disruptive behavior typically become detectable in children in the early elementary school years (Feshbach & Feshbach, 1969; Tremblay, Vitaro, Gagnon, Piche, & Royer, 1992). The inverse relation between concern for others and antisocial behavior may increase with age (Miller & Eisenberg, 1988). Early aggression and externalizing problems in children may therefore be expected to coexist with normal levels of concern for others. The empathic deficits of aggressive individuals emerge over time, either through arrested development of concern at a relatively immature stage or by an actual decrease from earlier levels. In addition, antisocial children may not only lack concern but may also actively disregard or be callous toward others in need. These possibilities suggest not only the need for longitudinal analysis of this issue but also for examination of both constitutional and environmental factors that may be implicated in suboptimal patterns of the development of concern for others.

Psychophysiology and Concern for Others

Because empathic concern for the well-being of others may be a heritable, biologically based response system, some researchers have attempted to identify physiological components of such responses. Sympathetic activation or parasympathetic inhibition lead to changes in cardiac functioning, which can be interpreted as bodily cues of discomfort or distress and a need for action. Empathy may be associated with such autonomic changes in response to others' experiencing distress, as their needs are attended to, recognized, and to some degree shared. If one is the cause of the distress, this heightened arousal may serve as negative physiological feedback, such that the aggression or harmful acts are not continued or increased (Miller & Eisenberg, 1988). Further, prosocial and reparative behavior may become more likely, because one is cued to the presence of distress in another that could be alleviated. Thus, more empathic children are expected to be more physiologically aroused by distress in others and to display more concern for others.

Antisocial behavior is associated with, and predictable from, low resting heart rate (HR) in children, adolescents, and adults (Lahey, Hart, Pliszka, Applegate, & McBurnett, 1993; Raine, Venables, & Sarnoff, 1997). Because low HR is associated with greater aggression, and aggression and concern for others are inversely related, it may be that high HR should predict greater concern for others. Examining the current sample at preschool age, Zahn-Waxler et al. (1995) found that HR was positively correlated with concerned responses toward adults who were simulating injuries. Eisenberg and her colleagues (e.g., Eisenberg, Fabes, Murphy, et al., 1996; Fabes, Eisenberg, & Miller, 1990), however, have generally not found measures of HR to relate strongly to children's reports of their empathy or sympathy.

Vagal tone ($\hat{V}$), a measure of HR variability, was used to index the efficiency of the autonomic nervous system (Porges & Byrne, 1992) in terms of general arousal thresholds and the ability to regulate arousal. Because higher resting $\hat{V}$ has been associated with better self-regulation (e.g., Fox & Field, 1989), it has been hypothesized to relate positively to showing concern for others in distress (Eisenberg et al., 1995). However, there is little support for this in the literature. As $\hat{V}$ may also mark the threshold for arousal, it is plausible that the opposite relation should be expected: Children with high $\hat{V}$ may be unresponsive to distress in others because such distress is not a strong-enough stimulus to evoke empathy. This inverse relation has been shown in this sample at preschool age (Zahn-Waxler et al., 1995) and in independent studies (Eisenberg et al.,

1995; Eisenberg, Fabes, Karbon, et al., 1996; Eisenberg, Fabes, Murphy, et al., 1996).

Socialization and Concern for Others

Several aspects of parental socialization have been implicated in children's expressions of concern for others (see review by Eisenberg & Fabes, 1998), including authoritative parenting, authoritarian parenting, and parents' negative affect (Baumrind, 1971; Grusec, 1991a; Janssens & Dekovic, 1997). These dimensions encompass, and are related to independent measures of, parental behaviors, emotional experiences and expressions, and cognitions and attitudes regarding child rearing (Hastings & Rubin, 1999; Kochanska, Kuczynski, & Radke-Yarrow, 1989). Authoritative parenting includes being warm, responsive, and supportive, establishing guidelines for behavior, and using reasoning in conjunction with controlled discipline. Authoritarianism centers on harsh, restrictive, punitive, and inappropriately controlling parenting. Negative affect within the context of child rearing includes the extent to which parents feel and show anger, frustration, and disappointment with their children (Block, 1981; Kochanska et al., 1989).

More than 3 decades ago, Baumrind (1967) found that preschoolers who behaved in prosocial ways with their peers most often had parents who used an authoritative rather than an authoritarian or a permissive style of parenting. Many studies have replicated the pattern. Maternal parenting that reflects authoritative approaches and de-emphasizes authoritarianism and negative affect has been linked to children's concern for others at home (Robinson, Zahn-Waxler, & Emde, 1994; Zahn-Waxler, Radke-Yarrow, & King, 1979), in school settings (Krevans & Gibbs, 1996), in the laboratory (Eisenberg et al., 1992; Eisenberg, Fabes, & Murphy, 1996; Eisenberg, Fabes, Schaller, Carlo, & Miller, 1991), and across cultures (Dekovic & Janssens, 1992; Janssens & Dekovic, 1997). Most studies have considered only contemporaneous associations. However, Robinson and her colleagues (1994) found that maternal warmth predicted high levels of empathic responding from 14 to 20 months of age, and maternal negative control predicted decreases in empathic responding over this period. Kochanska (1991) also found that authoritative and nonpunitive parenting by mothers of toddlers predicted more prosocial responses to vignettes when children were 8 to 10 years of age. Additional longitudinal work is necessary to determine whether these aspects of parenting contribute to stability or change in children's concern for others over time.

Concern for Others as a Moderator of Stability of Externalizing Problems

The presence or maintenance of concern for others may function as a protective factor against the stability of externalizing problems. Empathy should provide immediate, proximal feedback that discourages aggressive acts by making the perpetrator of the aggression aware of, and possibly sympathetic toward, the pain suffered by the victim. There is some evidence for this line of reasoning. Tremblay and his colleagues (1992) found that disruptive 6-year-old boys who also were highly prosocial engaged in fewer disruptive behaviors 3 years later than did boys who were disruptive and less prosocial. Following individuals from middle childhood into adulthood, Hamalaimen and Pulkkinen (1995) found that adult men and women who had been more prosocial as children were less likely to have been arrested or convicted of repeat offenses; criminality was greatest among adults who had been high in aggression and low in prosocial behavior as children. Concern for others is thus expected to moderate the stability of children's externalizing problems over time. That is, young children who have both externalizing problems and great concern for others may be less likely to maintain their levels of externalizing problems over time, compared with children who have externalizing problems and relatively little concern for others.

Summary and Hypotheses

We followed three groups of children from preschool into the elementary school years who varied in their risk for the development of disruptive behavior

disorders. On the basis of mothers' and teachers' reports, children of preschool age had low, moderate, or high rates of externalizing problems. We used behavioral observations, physiological assessments, self-reports, and the reports of mothers and teachers to test the following predictions.

First, observed concern for others was expected to increase from 5 to 7 years of age. Second, in comparison to children with fewer problems, children with moderate and greater problems were expected to develop deficits in their concern for others by 7 years of age. Third, children with more behavior problems were expected to show more disregard for others than children with fewer problems. We also expected to find sex differences; consistent with the majority of studies in the literature, we predicted that boys would score lower than girls on all measures of concern. Fourth, we expected to find moderate individual stability in concern for others from 5 to 7 years of age, as well as consistency in the measures of concern within each age. Fifth, concern for others was expected to moderate the development of externalizing behavior problems, acting as a protective factor against the maintenance or exacerbation of problems over time. Sixth, cardiac measures of children's autonomic arousal to sadness and distress in others were expected to be associated with children's concern for others in preschool and 2 years later. Finally, we predicted that concern for others would be positively associated with mothers' reports of authoritative parenting and negatively associated with their authoritarian parenting and negative affect. Disregard for others was expected to share opposite relations with psychophysiology and socialization variables than were expected for the measures of concern for others.

Method

Sample and recruitment

This investigation was based on data collected as part of an ongoing study of children at varying levels of risk for the development of disruptive behavior disorders. The initial sample consisted of 51 male and 31 female 4–5-year-old children (mean age = 54.68 months, SD = 3.28) living in a major urban community, the parents of whom were contacted through newspaper announcements and flyers to preschools and daycare providers (see Cole, Zahn-Waxler, Fox, Usher, & Welsh, 1996, for further details). Children with mental or physical challenges (e.g., hearing impairment, autism) that were outside the purview of the investigation or who scored in the subaverage range on the McCarthy Scales of Children's Abilities (McCarthy, 1970) were excluded from participation. Participating families were predominantly Caucasian ($n = 67$), two-parent ($n = 73$), and of middle to upper-middle socioeconomic status (SES) on the Hollingshead (1965) index (mean SES = 54.5).

GENERAL RISK CLASSIFICATION

Children were classified as being at low, moderate, or high risk for developing disruptive behavior disorders. Risk designation was determined by mothers' use of the Child Behavior Checklist (CBCL; Achenbach & Edelbrock, 1983) and the Eyberg Child Behavior Inventory (ECBI; Eyberg & Robinson, 1983) to report on their children, and teachers' use of the Teacher Report Form (TRF; Achenbach & Edelbrock, 1986) and the Preschool Behavior Questionnaire (PBQ; Behar & Stringfield, 1974). High risk was defined by CBCL total behavior problem T scores greater than or equal to 70, or TRF behavior problem scores at or above the 85th percentile.[1] Moderate risk was defined by CBCL T scores greater than 60 but below 70, or TRF scores between the 70th and 85th percentile, or scores on the ECBI or PBQ that were more than one standard deviation above published norms. Children with lower scores on the CBCL, TRF, ECBI, and PBQ were determined to be at low risk.

The final distribution of children at Time 1 (T1) was 31 children at high risk (20 boys, 11 girls), 28 at moderate risk (20 boys, 8 girls), and 23 at low risk (11 boys, 12 girls). Analyses of variance (ANOVAs) and comparisons of means confirmed that all three groups differed from each other on the externalizing scores of both the CBCL and TRF (high > moderate > low, all $ps < .0001$). Boys and girls did not differ on their externalizing symptoms. Extensive documentation of the norming procedures, reliability, and validity of the CBCL and TRF is contained in Achenbach's (1991) guide.

SAMPLE RETENTION AT TIMES 2 AND 3

Two years after T1, 77 families, including 29 children at high risk (18 boys, 11 girls), 26 at moderate risk (19 boys, 7 girls), and 22 at low risk (10 boys, 12 girls), agreed to continue participation. Mean age at Time 2 (T2) was 84.48 months ($SD = 4.2$). The five families who withdrew did not differ significantly from the 77 who continued in terms of T1 demographic variables or variables examined in the present investigation. Two to 3 years later, CBCL and TRF data were again obtained for 72 children: 27 children at high risk (16 boys, 11 girls), 24 at moderate risk (19 boys, 5 girls), and 21 at low risk (10 boys, 11 girls); mean age at Time 3 (T3) was 116.40 months ($SD = 5.04$). No T1 or T2 variables distinguished the five families who withdrew after T2 from the 72 families who continued, nor did the families who withdrew at either T1 or T2 differ from the 72 families who continued.

Procedure at T1

Children made five visits to the laboratory at T1. This investigation includes data obtained in three of these sessions. In Session 1, observations were made of children's responses to a female experimenter who was simulating distress. In Session 3, children's cardiac responses (HR, $\hat{V}$) to a mood-induction paradigm were assessed. In Session 4, children's responses to their mother's simulation of distress were observed. On average, 2–3 months separated each session. Detailed descriptions of these procedures are described in Zahn-Waxler et al. (1995).

DISTRESS SIMULATIONS

In both simulations, pain and emotional distress were portrayed in the presence of the child by inserting scripted depictions of minor accidents into the ongoing activities. Both the experimenter and the mother pretended to injure her foot while also dropping some objects on the floor. In each case, the adult winced or grimaced, vocally expressed pain, and rubbed the injured area, according to a specified script.

PSYCHOPHYSIOLOGICAL ASSESSMENT

Measures of cardiac function were taken while children viewed a 12-min videotape depicting a child experiencing eight emotionally charged events (Cole, Jordan, & Zahn–Waxler, 1990). Two vignettes showed the child experiencing sadness in response to distressing events: losing his or her dog, and a grandfather being ill and possibly near death. Each vignette started with a 15-s story lead-in, followed by 30 s of emotional display, and ending with a 15-s pleasant resolution. Each vignette was preceded by a starfield, shown for 15 s.

The cardiac variables were collected via three disposable electrocardiogram (ECG) electrodes on the child's chest, under the shirt. A Coulbourn ECG amplifier and filter module (Coulbourn, Allentown, PA, Model S75-38) transmitted the ECG signal, which was recorded on one channel of a Vetter Model CFM instrumentation recorder (A.R. Vetter, Redensburg, PA). Digitization of this recorded signal at 512 Hz was performed by means of an RTA 815 Analog Devices A/D board (Analog Devices, Cambridge, MA) and HEM acquisition software (HEM DataCorp., Southfield, MI). Interbeat intervals (IBIs) were calculated from the lag between R spikes. IBI data during the 30 s depictions of sadness were examined with MXEDIT software (Porges, 1985) to calculate the measures of HR and $\hat{V}$.

Similar cardiac responses were obtained for both vignettes. Mean HR and $\hat{V}$ during the first depiction of sadness were 92.91 and 6.67, respectively; during the second, they were 93.96 and 6.56, respectively. Cardiac measures were significantly correlated across the vignettes, $r(78) = .97$ for HR and .94 for $\hat{V}$ (both $ps < .0001$). Because of the similarity of cardiac responses to the distress vignettes and the utility of decreasing the number of correlations to be calculated, average scores across the two distress vignettes were taken. The average HR and $\hat{V}$ scores were examined for risk and sex differences in separate 3×2 ANOVAs. There were no significant effects.

MATERNAL REPORT ON PARENTING

Mothers completed the Child Rearing Practices Report (CRPR; Block, 1981) 6 months after the T1 laboratory procedures. The CRPR was completed at home and returned by mail (see Denham et al., 2000, for administration details). The CRPR comprises a set of 91 index cards, each with a statement describing a possible parenting practice or attitude. Mothers were instructed to sort the 91 cards into 7 separate piles

containing 13 cards each and to put each pile into an envelope that labeled how well the cards described her socialization approaches, from 1 (*most undescriptive*) to 7 (*most descriptive*).

Three dimensions of maternal socialization were extracted from responses to the CRPR. The measures of maternal authoritative and authoritarian parenting were identical to those identified by Kochanska and her colleagues (1991; Kochanska et al., 1989). The authoritative dimension reflected the use of reasoning and guidance, encouragement of independence, and support for open expression of affect ($\alpha = .67$). The authoritarian dimension included mothers' discouragement of expressivity, issuing of prohibitions and reprimands, control by anxiety inductions, strict supervision, and corporal punishment ($\alpha = .61$). Authoritarian and authoritative scores were substantially negatively correlated, $r(77) = -.53$, $p < .001$. Therefore, to reduce the number of variables being examined, we standardized the scales and subtracted authoritative scores from authoritarian scores (as has been done in previous studies; e.g., Hastings & Rubin, 1999). The resulting scores constituted a dimension of parenting style that ranged from low authoritarianism/high authoritativeness (low) to high authoritarianism/low authoritativeness (high). Maternal affect with her child was based on the Negative Affect factor described by Block (1981) and reflected feelings of anger, disappointment, and conflict ($\alpha = .79$).

Mothers' authoritarian child-rearing and Negative Affect scores were examined in separate Risk × Sex (3×2) ANOVAs to determine if there were any relevant group differences. There were main effects of risk for both variables: $Fs(2, 72) = 4.92$ and 5.07 for authoritarian child rearing and negative affect, respectively, $ps < .01$. Mothers of high-risk children described their parenting as significantly more authoritarian and involving more negative affect ($Ms = 0.65$ and 10.48, $SDs = 2.10$ and 5.05, respectively), compared with mothers of low-risk children ($Ms = -0.88$ and 6.41, $SDs = 1.13$ and 3.81, respectively). Scores for mothers of moderate-risk children were intermediate to, and nonsignificantly different from, these extremes ($Ms = 0.03$ and 8.33, $SDs = 1.46$ and 4.02, respectively). These group differences are consistent with a previous examination of mothers' restrictiveness and nurturance (Rickel & Biasatti, 1982) as measured by the CRPR (Denham et al., 2000).

Procedure at T2

Observations of the children's responses to the mother's and experimenter's distress simulations, children's self-reported empathy, and mothers' reports of children's empathy and conscience all were assessed during one visit to the laboratory. Mothers completed the CBCL during a separate visit. Teachers completed the TRF and reported on the children's prosocial behavior and social competence in a package of questionnaires that were sent and returned by mail.

DISTRESS SIMULATIONS

The simulations were conducted in a fashion similar to those at Time 1, in the context of the child's ongoing activities. The simulated injuries of the mother and experimenter occurred in different rooms and more than an hour apart. Observations were made of 74 children's responses. However, two mothers did not perform the simulation as requested, and therefore data were only available on their children's responses to the experimenter's simulation of injury. Equipment failure caused the loss of data for 3 other children's responses to both simulations.

CHILDREN'S SELF-REPORTED EMPATHY

Children were administered the Bryant Empathy Scale (Bryant, 1982). The Bryant Scale is a widely used measure of children's empathic tendencies and comprises 22 statements answered in a true–false format. Each statement—for example, "Seeing a boy who is crying makes me feel like crying" and "It's hard for me to see why someone else gets upset" (reverse scored)—was printed on a separate index card. Two boxes, one labeled "Me" and one labeled "Not Me," were placed in front of the child. The experimenter read each statement and then asked the child to put the card into the "Me" box if it described the child or into the "Not Me" box if it did not. This procedure was completed successfully by 73 children; the mean score was 11.96 ($SD = 2.83$, range = 6–19), and the coefficient alpha for the present sample was .69.

MOTHERS' REPORTS OF CHILDREN'S EMPATHY AND CONSCIENCE

To obtain mothers' descriptions of their children's empathy and other behavioral and affective aspects of conscience development, mothers completed the My Child measure (Kochanska, 1992; Kochanska, DeVet, Goldman, Murray, & Putman, 1994). The My Child comprises 100 statements that are rated from 1 (*extremely untrue*) to 7 (*extremely true*)—for example, "Acts upset when s/he sees a hurt animal" and "After having done something naughty, asks to be forgiven." The subscales of the My Child include Empathy (13 items), Affective Discomfort After Wrongdoing (18), Apology (6), Concern About Others' Transgressions (7), Concern Over Good Feelings With Parent (8), Confession (7), Internalized Conduct (20), Reparation (9), Sensitivity to Flawed Objects (7), and Symbolic Reproduction of Wrongdoing (5). This measure was completed by 71 mothers; the mean scores for the subscales ranged from 3.62 ($SD = 1.18$) for Symbolic Reproduction of Wrongdoing to 5.36 ($SD = 0.71$) for Empathy. The coefficient alpha for Sensitivity to Flawed Objects was moderate (.54), but all other scales showed very good internal consistency, with alphas ranging from .74 for Concern About Others' Transgressions to .91 for Internalized Conduct (mean $\alpha = .81$).

Mothers' scores on the 10 scales of the My Child measure were examined in a factor analysis to detect underlying latent variables. A two-factor solution was reached. Scores on the Empathy scale loaded above .40 on both factors; therefore, children's scores on this scale were examined separately rather than aggregated into a factor (for Empathy, $\alpha = .79$). All other scale scores loaded highly onto only one of two factors. The first factor (eigenvalue = 3.87) comprised Confession, Apology, Reparation, Concern About Others' Transgressions, and Internalized Conduct. As these scales all reflected aspects of addressing transgressions and understanding appropriate behavior, scores were standardized and aggregated to form the Interpersonal Responsibility factor (overall $\alpha = .82$). The second factor (eigenvalue = 1.45) comprised Affective Discomfort After Wrongdoing, Concern Over Good Feelings With Parent, Sensitivity to Flawed Objects, and Symbolic Reproduction of Wrongdoing. This factor was less relevant to the current research questions and hence was dropped from further analyses.

TEACHERS' REPORTS OF CHILDREN'S PROSOCIAL BEHAVIOR AND SOCIAL COMPETENCE

Teachers completed a set of measures assessing aspects of children's helpful and positive behaviors in the classroom. These measures included 3 items from the

Assessment of School Behavior (Cassidy & Asher, 1992; e.g., "This child is helpful toward other children"), 6 items from the Teacher Child Rating Scale (Hightower et al., 1986; e.g., "Sensitive to other children's feelings"), and 13 items from the Peer Relationships and Social Skills Ratings (Dodge & Somberg, 1987; e.g., "Other children like this child and seek him or her out for play" and "Is understanding of others' feelings"). The questionnaires were completed and returned by 69 teachers. Separate factor analyses on the 22 individual items and on the subscales derived from the different measures both supported a single-factor solution, with strong positive loadings (all > .55) for all scores. The coefficient alpha for a summary measure of the 22 items was .97. Therefore, a single overall score was computed for teachers' reports of children's Prosocial Behaviors With Peers at School.

Children's behavior problems at T3

At T3, mothers completed the CBCL, and teachers completed the TRF. The CBCL was completed by 70 mothers. The TRF was completed and returned in the mail by 56 teachers. Reports on behavior problems from one or both informants were available for 72 children.

Coding of children's responses to distress simulations

Two aspects of children's responses to the simulated accidents of mother and experimenter were coded: *concern for others* and *disregard for others*. A prior coding scheme assessing multifaceted aspects of concern had been applied to these data (Zahn-Waxler et al., 1995). For the current research questions, however, a new code of concern for others was developed. Concern for others scores were based on ratings, from 1 (*absent*) to 7 (*strong*), of the global concerned responding of children, incorporating facial, vocalic, and behavioral expressions of empathy, sympathy, and helpfulness (see Table 2.5 for descriptions of each point on the scale). Observed concern for others was coded by Paul Hastings and a research assistant. Intraclass correlations were used to examine coder agreement across

59 simulations (21% of the data); ratings of concern corresponded at .77.

Dana Bridges and another research assistant were responsible for coding the behaviors included in the disregard for others scores. Children's disregard for others to the simulated distress was coded from 1 (*absent*) to 4 (*strong*), with one point being assigned for the display of each of three responses: (a) anger toward the victim, (b) amusement or derisiveness, and (c) avoidance of or withdrawal from the victim. These behaviors were grouped on the conceptual basis that each could imply callousness or an unwillingness to acknowledge the needs of others, and they have proven to be an effective measure in a prior, independent study (Zahn-Waxler, Robinson, & Emde, 1992). Each specific behavior occurred with low frequency, limiting the internal consistency for the aggregate ($\alpha = .50$), but the aggregate provided sufficient variability to permit analyses. As coders were able to distinguish the presence or absence of each behavior, kappa coefficients were used to calculate reliability. The coders had extensive training and experience coding children's reactions to simulations of injuries and had demonstrated high reliability with a large, independent sample (Zahn-Waxler et al., 2001). Their reliability for the current sample was tested on 18 cases ($\kappa = 0.88$). All coders were blind to children's risk-group status.

Results

First, we examined whether children with high, moderate, and low levels of behavior problems differed in their development of observable concern and disregard for others from 4–5 to 6–7 years of age. Second, we considered whether teachers, mothers, and the children themselves perceived differences in empathy and prosocial behavior when the children were 6–7 years of age, depending on their level of behavior problems at 4–5 years of age. Third, the consistency between different measures of concern and the stability of concern for others from 4–5 to 6–7 years of age were examined. Fourth, regression analyses were used to determine if concerned responding moderated the stability of externalizing problems from preschool to middle childhood. Fifth, we examined whether children's

Table 2.5   Rating scale for children's global concern for others in distress

Scale point	Description
1	No concern evident
2	Interested, some attention but little evidence of concern. Any questions or statements are factual, for gathering information (e.g., "What happened?").
3	Child sobers, sustains attention for at least 10 s; or mild or brief expression of facial concern; or isolated act of assistance (e.g., picking up dropped object, without accompanying expression of concern, although may look "pleasant" [e.g., small smile]).
4	Sustained attention *with* some expression of concern (facial [e.g., eyebrows raised and drawn together], vocalic [e.g., "Ooooh!" or "Are you okay?"], or physical [e.g., approach or touch] concern); or mild concern combined with single act of assistance.
5	Displays a variety of responses indicating concern (e.g., coordinated assistance [more than single act]); or moderate concern with a single act of helping; or combined expressions of moderate concern (e.g., vocalic and physical).
6	Combined expressions of strong concern; or strong concern with a single helpful act; or multiple helpful acts with some accompanying concern. *Absence* of any selfish, callous, or angry responses.
7	Strong displays of concern *with* very helpful acts; or very high concerned prosocial responses and verbalizations of reassurance (e.g., approach, hug, say "You'll be okay," and stay in proximity). *Absence* of any selfish, callous, or angry responses.

physiological reactions to distress and mothers' socialization approaches when children were 4–5 years of age were associated with children's concern for others at 4–5 years of age and predictive of their concern at 6–7 years of age.

Table 2.6 presents the means and standard deviations for observations of children's responses to distress simulations at T1 and T2 and for children's self-reported empathy, mother-reported Empathy and Interpersonal Responsibility, and teacher-reported Prosocial Behavior With Peers at T2. Means are presented by risk group and sex of child.

Observations of responses to distress at T1 and T2

CONCERN FOR OTHERS

A four-way (3 × 2 × 2 × 2) repeated measures ANOVA was used to examine the ratings of children's observed concerned responses to injuries simulated by mothers and a female experimenter at T1 and T2. Between-groups factors were risk group and child sex; within-groups factors were target (mother vs. experimenter) and time. Children were not included in this analysis if any observational data were missing (e.g., if mother did not perform the simulation at T2), resulting

in a total sample size of 71 for this ANOVA. There were main effects of sex, $F(1, 65) = 10.00, p < .01$, and time, $F(1, 65) = 4.89, p < .05$, and a Risk × Time interaction, $F(2, 65) = 3.80, p < .05$. Overall, girls were observed to show more concern for others ($M = 4.67$, $SD = 1.29$) than were boys ($M = 3.77, SD = 1.06$). Counter to our expectations, the strength of concerned responses decreased from T1 ($M = 4.42, SD = 1.47$) to T2 ($M = 3.82, SD = 1.61$). However, the significant interaction term indicated that this decrease in concern was moderated by children's initial risk status. Paired t tests, with alpha corrected for number of tests, revealed that ratings of concern for others did not change significantly from T1 to T2 for children at low risk or moderate risk but dropped significantly for those at high risk. Least significant difference (LSD) tests did not show significant risk-group differences within either time point (previously reported at T1 in Zahn-Waxler et al., 1995).

DISREGARD FOR OTHERS

The four-way ANOVA for the observations of children's disregard for others revealed main effects of target, $F(1, 65) = 8.05, p < .01$, and sex, $F(1, 65) = 17.34, p < .001$, and an interaction of Risk × Sex, $F(2, 65) = 4.18, p < .05$. Across both time points,

Table 2.6 Means and standard deviations for observed measures of children's concern at 5 years of age and observed and reported measures of concern at 7 years of age, presented by risk group and sex of child

Concern measure	Risk group			Sex of child	
	Low	Moderate	High	Boys	Girls
5-year-olds					
Observed concern for others					
M	4.25	4.21	4.80	4.16$_b$	4.84$_b$
SD	1.36	1.38	1.62	1.46	1.42
Observed disregard for others					
M	1.25	1.25	1.40	1.44$_b$	1.09$_b$
SD	0.37	0.42	0.50	0.49	0.20
7-year-olds					
Observed concern for others					
M	4.07	3.96	3.46	3.37$_b$	4.50$_b$
SD	1.75	1.74	1.32	1.31	1.80
Observed disregard for others					
M	1.09	1.23	1.20	1.23$_b$	1.09$_b$
SD	0.20	0.36	0.35	0.37	0.20
Child: Empathy					
M	12.41	12.75$_a$	10.89$_a$	11.20$_b$	13.18$_b$
SD	3.07	2.69	2.49	2.95	2.14
Mother: Empathy					
M	5.47	5.36	5.26	5.16$_b$	5.68$_b$
SD	0.57	0.90	0.65	0.74	0.55
Mother: Interpersonal Responsibility					
M	0.36$_a$	−0.03	−0.28$_a$	−0.12	0.20
SD	0.56	0.92	0.65	0.82	0.63
Teacher: Prosocial Behavior With Peers					
M	0.56$_{ac}$	−0.29$_a$	−0.16$_c$	−0.28$_b$	0.49$_b$
SD	0.81	0.84	0.85	0.84	0.79

Note. Risk group means that share the same subscript differ at *p* < .05. Sex-of-child means that share the same subscript differ at *p* < .01.

children directed more disregard to their mothers than to the experimenters (*M*s = 1.34 and 1.14, *SD*s = 0.45 and 0.26, respectively). Examining the interaction term with LSD tests revealed that, across both time points, high-risk boys showed more disregard for others (*M* = 1.48, *SD* = 0.26) than did all other children, and moderate-risk boys (*M* = 1.28, *SD* = 0.26) showed more disregard for others than did high-risk girls (*M* = 1.03, *SD* = 0.08; for low-risk boys, low-risk girls, and moderate-risk girls, *M*s = 1.23, 1.13, and 1.13, *SD*s = 0.30, 0.13, and 0.21, respectively). Examinations within time points showed that

high-risk boys had the highest levels of disregard for others at both T1 and T2.

Reports of children's concern at T2

CHILDREN'S SELF-REPORTED EMPATHY
Children's scores on the Bryant Empathy Scale were examined in a Risk Group × Child Sex (3 × 2) ANOVA. There were main effects of both sex, $F(1, 67) = 11.43, p < .01$, and risk, $F(2, 67) = 4.39, p < .05$. Girls described themselves as more empathic than boys. LSD tests revealed that high-risk children

described themselves as significantly less empathic than did moderate-risk children and tended to describe themselves as less empathic than low-risk children ($p < .10$).

MOTHERS' REPORTS OF CHILDREN'S EMPATHY AND INTERPERSONAL RESPONSIBILITY

Two Risk × Sex (3 × 2) ANOVAs were used to examine mothers' reports of child Empathy and Interpersonal Responsibility. For Empathy, there was a main effect of sex, $F(1,65) = 9.56$, $p < .01$. Daughters were described as more empathic than sons. For Interpersonal Responsibility, there was a main effect of risk, $F(2, 65) = 4.07$, $p < .05$. Mothers of low-risk children described their children as significantly more interpersonally responsible than did mothers of high-risk children and as somewhat more interpersonally responsible than did mothers of moderate-risk children ($p < .10$).

TEACHERS' REPORTS OF CHILDREN'S POSITIVE SOCIAL BEHAVIORS WITH PEERS

Examination of the Prosocial Behavior With Peers scores in a Risk Group × Sex of Child ANOVA revealed main effects of sex, $F(1, 63) = 8.69$, $p < .01$, and risk, $F(2,63) = 3.67$, $p < .05$. Girls were described as more prosocial than boys. Low-risk children were described by their teachers as more prosocial than either moderate- or high-risk children.

Consistency and stability of concern

Because there were no interactions between the target and risk group factors in the preceding repeated measures ANOVAs, children's scores for their observed concern for others and disregard for others were averaged across mother and experimenter.[2] This technique has been used effectively in other investigations of concern (e.g., Zahn-Waxler, Robinson, & Emde, 1992) to reduce the number of variables and create more stable assessments of behavior. Three mothers did not perform the simulation at T1, and two mothers did not perform it at T2. In these cases, the ratings of concern and disregard were based on the experimenter simulation only ($n = 82$ at T1, 74 at T2). The intercorrelations of children's observed, self-reported, mother-reported, and teacher-reported

indices of concern at T1 and T2 are presented in Table 2.7. There was moderate consistency across modes of assessment of children's concern at T2 and significant but limited stability over time. Observed concern at T1 was predictive of observed concern at T2. Disregard for others was not stable over time, but children who showed more disregard at T1 were seen by their teachers as less prosocial at T2. Children at T2 who showed more concern also tended to be seen by their teachers as more prosocial ($p < .06$), whereas disregard for others was associated with lower Empathy and Interpersonal Responsibility scores from mothers. Children's reports of their own empathy also correlated with mothers' reports of their empathy and responsibility.

The moderating role of concern in the development of externalizing problems

DATA REDUCTION

Stepwise forward regression analyses were used to test for the moderating effects of concern in the development of externalizing problem behaviors. First, factor analysis and aggregation of variables were used to reduce the numbers of variables necessary for analyses and to create more stable constructs through multiple-source variables. At each age, mothers' and teachers' reports of children's externalizing problems were averaged; when one report was missing, the existing report was used as the sole indicator of externalizing problems. Externalizing problem scores were available for 82 children at T1, 76 children at T2, and T2 children at T3 (9–10 years; $Ms = 58.52, 54.77$, and 54.22; $SDs = 8.08, 9.18, 9.81$; ranges = 43–76, 30–81.50, and 37–76, respectively); correlations between mothers' and teachers' reports were $r(76) = .24, p < .05, r(69) = .32, p < .01$, and $r(57) = .47, p < .001$, respectively.

Observed concern for others, averaged across mother and experimenter, was used as the sole index of concern at T1. The measure of concern at T2 was based on observed concern for others and reported measures. First, mother-reported Empathy and Interpersonal Responsibility were aggregated into a single score. This was done so that mothers would not contribute proportionally more information to an overall aggregate measure of concern at T2 than would other sources of information (observers' ratings,

Table 2.7 Intercorrelations of the measures of concern at 5 and 7 years of age

Concern measure	1	2	3	4	5	6	7	8
Age 5								
1. Concern for others	—	−.27**	.29**	−.13	.16†	.12	.10	.15
		(78)	(73)	(73)	(72)	(70)	(70)	(68)
2. Disregard for others		—	−.08	.02	.02	.01	−.06	−.24*
			(73)	(73)	(72)	(70)	(70)	(68)
Age 7								
3. Concern for others			—	−.42***	.17†	.14	.13	.20†
				(73)	(72)	(70)	(70)	(65)
4. Disregard for others				—	−.09	−.34**	−.24*	.01
					(72)	(70)	(70)	(65)
5. Child: Empathy					—	.31**	.23*	.15
						(70)	(70)	(64)
6. Mother: Empathy						—	.45***	.18
							(70)	(63)
7. Mother: Interpersonal Responsibility							—	.19
8. Teacher: Prosocial Behavior With Peers								(63)
								—

Note. Numbers in parentheses are degrees of freedom.
†$p < .10$. *$p < .05$. **$p < .01$. ***$p < .001$.

children's self-report, teachers' reports). The combination of the maternal scores was supported by the original factor analysis, which showed that the Empathy subscale of the My Child measure had a loading of .42 on the Interpersonal Responsibility measure, and by the significant correlation between Empathy and Interpersonal Responsibility (see Table 2.7).

The average observed concern for others score, the single index of mother-reported empathy and responsibility, children's Bryant Empathy Scale scores, and teacher-reported Prosocial Behavior With Peers were standardized and examined in a factor analysis. All of the variables loaded highly and positively on a single dimension (loadings ranged from .59 to .67; eigenvalue = 1.60, accounting for 40% of the variance). Therefore, the standardized variables were weighted by their factor loadings and combined into a single aggregate concern index at T2 ($\alpha = .49$). If one measure was missing (e.g., seven teachers did not complete the ratings of children's Prosocial Behavior With Peers), the aggregate concern index was computed from the other three scores; scores were computed for a total of 72 children.

THE DEVELOPMENT OF EXTERNALIZING PROBLEMS FROM T1 TO T2

Because the test of the moderating effect of concern on the stability of externalizing problems required the use of interaction terms in the regressions, the method of analysis recommended by Aiken and West (1991) was used. All variables were centered by standardizing, thus decreasing potential collinearity, and the interaction term was calculated from the centered scores. Centered variables were entered into the regression predicting externalizing problem behavior scores at T2 in three steps (see Table 2.8). In Step 1, externalizing problems at T1 were found to predict externalizing problems at T2 (the stability of externalizing scores in this sample has been reported previously in Denham et al., 2000). Despite this stability, Step 2 showed that the independent contribution of observed concern for others at T1 to the variance accounted for in externalizing problems at T2 approached statistical significance. Children who showed more concern toward their mothers or an experimenter simulating injury were reported to have fewer behavior problems 2 years later. In Step 3, the interaction of concern for others and

Table 2.8 Regression analyses of the moderating role of concern in the development of externalizing behaviors

Variable	ΔR^2	p	β	R
Prediction of problems at Age 7				
Step 1				
5-year externalizing problems	.342	<.001	.59	.584
Step 2				
5-year observed concern	.029	<.10	−.17	.609
Step 3				
5-year observed concern × Externalizing	.040	<.05	−.20	.641
Adjusted R^2 = .386				
$F(3, 72) = 16.70, p < .0001$				
Prediction of problems at Age 9				
Step 1				
7-year externalizing problems	.425	<.001	.66	.652
Step 2				
7-year aggregate concern index	.00	ns	.01	.652
Step 3				
7-year aggregate concern index × Externalizing	.052	<.02	−.29	.691
Adjusted R^2 = .453				
$F(3, 64) = 19.47, p < .0001$				

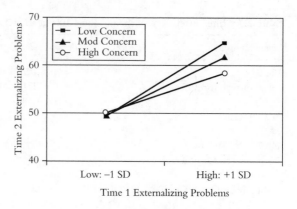

Figure 2.1 The moderating role of children's concern at 5 years of age on development of externalizing problems from 5 to 7 years of age.

externalizing problems at T1 was also shown to account for a significant, unique portion of the variance in externalizing problems at T2.

The interaction was plotted to compare the stability of externalizing problems from T1 to T2 for low (−1 SD), moderate (at the mean), and high (+1 SD) values of observed concern at T1 (see Figure 2.1) in order to examine whether the hypothesized moderator role for children's concerned responding was supported. Externalizing problems were most stable from T1 to T2 for low, $t(72) = 6.01, p < .0001$ (slope = .85), and moderate, $t(72) = 7.00, p < .0001$ (slope = .66), values of observed concern at T1. The stability of externalizing problems was moderately attenuated when T1 concern was higher, $t(72) = 4.03, p < .001$ (slope = .46). As shown in Figure 2.1, the moderating influence of concern for others was evidenced by the decreased ability to predict externalizing scores at early elementary school age years from externalizing

scores at preschool age when observed concern for others was higher at preschool age.

To determine whether the significant interaction term also reflected a moderating influence of concern on changes in mean level of externalizing problems from T1 to T2, a median split was performed on concern for others at T1. Paired t tests were used to compare externalizing T scores at T1 vs. T2 for children who were relatively low in concern and for children who were relatively high in concern. For children who were higher in concern, the actual number of externalizing problems decreased significantly from T1 ($M = 58.60, SD = 8.31$) to T2 ($M = 54.06, SD = 8.34$), $t(38) = 3.56, p < .05$, whereas the problem scores of children lower in concern did not change significantly over this period ($Ms = 57.66$ and $56.41, SDs = 7.40$ and 9.46, respectively), $t(36) = 1.07$ (ns). Thus, concern for others moderated both the stability and the severity of children's externalizing problems from the preschool to the early elementary school years.

THE DEVELOPMENT OF EXTERNALIZING PROBLEMS FROM T2 TO T3

A parallel regression analysis was performed to predict externalizing problems at T3 (see Table 2.8). Externalizing problems were again shown to be highly stable from T2 to T3, but the aggregate concern index at T2 was not a significant predictor of problems at T3. The interaction of the aggregate concern index and externalizing problems at T2, however, did

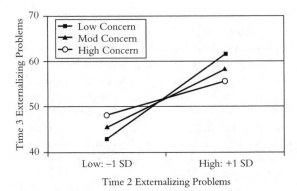

Figure 2.2   The moderating role of children's concern at 7 years of age on development of externalizing problems from 7 to 10 years of age.

account for a significant, unique portion of the variance in externalizing problems at T3.

Again, the interaction was plotted to compare the stability of externalizing problems from T2 to T3 for low (-1 SD), moderate (at the mean), and high ($+1$ SD) values of the aggregate concern index at T2 (see Figure 2.2). Externalizing problems at T3 were most predictable from T2 problem scores for low, $t(64) = 6.07$, $p < .0001$ (slope = .97), and moderate, $t(64) = 6.33$, $p < .0001$ (slope = .68), levels of aggregated concern at T2. The slope was markedly reduced when scores on the T2 aggregate concern index were higher, $t(64) = 2.54$, $p < .01$ (slope = .39). Figure 2.2 shows that the moderating influence of concern on the stability of the development of severe externalizing problems in children persisted from 6–7 years to 9–10 years.[3]

To determine whether the moderating influence of the aggregate concern index at T2 also contributed to mean level changes in externalizing problems from T2 to T3, a median split was used to create two groups of children who were relatively high versus relatively low on the T2 aggregated concern index. Paired t tests were used to examine changes in externalizing problems within each group. On average, the more concerned group had few externalizing problems at T2, and this did not change (mean t scores = 51.12 and 51.43, SDs = 8.49 and 8.75, respectively), $t(33) = -0.21$ (ns). There was a nonsignificant decrease in behavior problems over this period for the less concerned group (Ms = 58.90 and 56.16, SDs = 8.09

and 10.59, respectively), $t(33) = 2.30$, $p < .12$. Thus, although concern continued to moderate the stability of externalizing problems after 6–7 years of age, it did not appear to continue moderating the severity of problems into middle childhood.

Predicting children's concern from psychophysiological variables

Correlations between children's cardiac responses to the distress vignettes and the observed and reported measures of concern at T1 and T2 are presented in Table 2.9. We examined the correlations between cardiac responses and the measures of concern separately for responses to the first and second vignettes. In general, the magnitude of correlations was slightly higher for responses to the second vignette than for responses to the first, but overall, very similar patterns of results were obtained. This consistency supported the decision to use cardiac scores averaged across the two vignettes for the correlational analyses.

First the concurrent associations between psychophysiology and observed responses to injury simulations at T1 were examined. Two-tailed t tests were used, because the literature was not considered consistent enough to make directional hypotheses about the relations between cardiac reactivity and concern for others. Separate analyses conducted for responses to the mother's and the experimenter's simulations of injury revealed similar patterns; therefore, correlations for the composite scores are reported. As previously reported (Zahn-Waxler et al., 1995), children who had higher HR and lower $\hat{V}$ during the vignettes were observed to show more concern for others when their mothers or an experimenter simulated an injury.

The relations between cardiac responses to depictions of sadness at T1 and observed behaviors in response to adults' simulations of injury at T2 also were examined. To ensure that obtained relations were not due to stability in the children's behavior, we used partial correlations to control for the levels of observed behavior at T1. Thus, any significant results would suggest that early patterns of psychophysiological responding predicted the development of concerned and callous behavior. However, there were no significant partial correlations indicating a link between

Table 2.9 Correlations between psychophysiological responses at 5 years of age and measures of children's concern at 5 and 7 years of age[a]

Concern measure		Physiological responses		
	df	Heart rate	Vagal tone
Age 5			
1. Concern for others	78	.25★	−.19[†]
2. Disregard for others	78	−.03	−.09
Age 7			
3. Concern for others	70	.00	.06
4. Disregard for others	70	.16	−.12
5. Child: Empathy	69	.14	−.05
6. Mother: Empathy	67	.06	−.16
7. Mother: Interpersonal Responsibility	67	.02	−.02
8. Teacher: Prosocial Behavior With Peers	66	.22★	−.30★★

[a]Partial correlations were used to predict observed behaviors at 7 years of age, controlling for the level of observed behavior at 5 years of age.
[†]$p < .10$. ★$p < .05$. ★★$p < .01$.

children's earlier physiological responding and their observed behavior at T2. There were also few indications that physiological responses were associated with later reports of the children's empathy and prosocial behavior. Only two of eight correlations (25%) involving self-reports, mothers' reports, and teacher's reports were significant: Children who had higher HR and lower V̂ during the vignettes were described by teachers as more prosocial. These relations are consistent with the T1 results, but given the number of nonsignificant correlations, the present findings should be regarded as tentative and in need of replication.

Relations between psychophysiological responses and measures of concern might not have been equivalent across risk or sex groups. Therefore, regression analyses including Group × Predictor Variable interaction terms were conducted. For each regression, the main-effect predictors of risk, sex, and cardiac response were entered first, and then the two-way interactions of Risk × Cardiac Response and Sex × Cardiac Response were entered. For prediction of observed variables at T2, the corresponding T1 observed variables were also controlled by entry on the first step. After controlling for main effects, none of the 32 interaction terms for HR or V̂ was significant.

The general message extracted from the regression analyses was that the few obtained relations between psychophysiology and concern are consistent for children at low, moderate, and high risk for developing disruptive behavior disorders and also for boys and girls. Although centering variables improves the chances of detecting significant interaction effects in regression analyses (Jaccard, Wan, & Turrisi, 1990), it should still be recognized that our sample size offered relatively low power to detect significant interactions.

Predicting children's concern from socialization variables

Children's concern was also examined in relation to mothers' reported approaches to parenting at T1. Because of the risk-group differences in maternal socialization scores, we used an additional analytical approach. After examining the correlations for the full sample, we also examined partial correlations controlling for risk group for all concern measures. Regressions were then conducted to determine if risk group or gender interacted with maternal parenting in the prediction of concern.

The correlations are presented in Table 2.10. Mother-reported socialization variables at T1 were predictive of observations of children's concern and disregard for others at T2 but were not concurrently associated with observed behavior at T1. In total, 6 of the 12 predictive correlations (50%) reported in Table 2.10 were significant, one additional correlation approached significance, and all were in the predicted directions. Mothers with relatively more authoritarian child-rearing approaches had children who, 2 years later, were more likely to show disregard for others and tended to be less likely to show concern for others. In addition, mothers and teachers described the children at T2 as more empathic, interpersonally responsible, and prosocial when, 2 years earlier, mothers had described their parenting as predominantly authoritative and involving less negative affect.

Risk-group differences both in mothers' reported parenting and in most T2 measures of concern could have contributed to the appearance of relations between maternal socialization and children's concern. To examine this possibility, we used partial correlations to control for children's risk status. All of

Table 2.10 Correlations between maternal socialization approaches at 5 years of age and measures of children's concern at 5 and 7 years of age[a]

Concern measure	df	Maternal socialization approach	
		Authoritarian	Negative affect
Age 5			
1. Concern for others	77	.14	.04
2. Disregard for others	77	−.02	.05
Age 7			
3. Concern for others	72	−.19†	−.11
4. Disregard for others	72	.23★	.18
5. Child: Empathy	71	−.05	.00
6. Mother: Empathy	69	−.27★	−.22★
7. Mother: Interpersonal Responsibility	69	−.32★★	−.40★★★
8. Teacher: Prosocial Behavior With Peers	67	−.34★★	−.09

[a]Partial correlations were used to predict observed behaviors at 7 years of age, controlling for the level of observed behavior at 5 years of age.

†$p < .10$. ★$p < .05$. ★★$p < .01$. ★★★$p < .001$.

the correlations were reduced in magnitude, but four remained significant at $p < .05$. These were the relations between mothers' child-rearing style and mothers' reports of children's Empathy, $r(68) = −.24$, mothers' reports of children's Interpersonal Responsibility, $r(68) = −.23$, and teachers' reports of children's Prosocial Behavior With Peers, $r(66) = −.25$, and the relation between negative affect and mothers' reports of children's Interpersonal Responsibility, $r(68) = −.28$. In addition, the correlation between child-rearing style and observed disregard for others at T2 still approached significance, $r(71) = .20, p = .09$. Thus, independently of children's earlier behavior problems, mothers' socialization practices predicted reports of children's concern 2 years later.

Regression analyses were also used to examine whether there were any moderating influences of sex or risk group for the relations between socialization measures and concern. Of the 32 two-way interactions examined for negative affect and authoritarian child-rearing, only 2 were significant (Risk × Authoritarianism; Sex × Negative Affect), no more than would be expected by chance.

Discussion

Deficits in concern for others' well-being have long been held as one of the hallmarks of antisocial personality disorders, which by definition include a history of disruptive behavior (American Psychiatric Association, 1994). Studies with adolescents and adults have supported this characterization. However, the existence of these deficits early in the development of antisocial individuals heretofore has been presumed rather than documented. Consistent with other studies of young children (e.g., MacQuiddy et al., 1987), our initial investigation demonstrated that such deficits are not readily detectable in preschool-aged children with externalizing problems (Zahn–Waxler et al., 1995). More specifically, at least in the early years of life, concern for the welfare of others can exist in conjunction with behaviors that violate the rights of others and garner the displeasure of adults.

The current investigation showed that observable deficits in concern for others develop after the preschool years for children with clinical levels of behavior problems. These children actually decreased in the strength of their concerned responses over the transition from preschool to elementary school. Kochanska (1991) has suggested that early disruptiveness and later deficits in concern could be age-dependent manifestations of a common underlying predisposition for weak conscience. However, it is equally possible that deficits in concern and disruptive behavior disorders may reflect two distinct systems with etiologies that only overlap in part.

This is not to suggest that no early differences in how the children responded to adults' simulations of injuries were detected. Indeed, despite being just as prosocial as other preschool-aged children, moderate- and high-risk boys displayed more active disregard for others (e.g., anger, avoidance, amusement by another's distress), a negatively toned response pattern that differs markedly from the simple absence of concern. Mothers were the most frequent targets of disregard. The at-risk boys' displays of disregard toward their mothers' distress may have been fostered by the more authoritarian and negative parenting experiences they had. These boys may have experienced more emotional, and possibly physical, pain in their maternal relationships than had the other children. Their angry or detached stance when their mothers were in need may have reflected an effort to distance themselves or decrease their own arousal in distressing interactions. Whatever the principal cause, the stronger displays of disregard by boys at risk may serve as early indicators of differences in their affective responsiveness. Further attention to ways in which young children with behavior problems blend positive and negative responses during emotionally charged social interactions may be important for understanding the children's self-regulatory abilities, their perceptions of social cues and context, and their contributions to interpersonal exchanges.

Not all high-risk children decreased in their observed concern for others between preschool and early elementary school. Eight of the 25 high-risk children for whom there were observed data at both times maintained or increased their concern for others, which might serve to protect these children against stable, severe problems of aggression or disruptiveness. Even more pronounced heterogeneity appeared to characterize the moderate-risk group of children, who had quite disparate levels of self-reported empathy, teacher-reported prosocial behavior, and mother-reported empathy and concern for others. Within-group variability was also apparent when gender was considered. As expected, at all levels of risk and across most measures used, girls had higher concern scores than boys. It would be valuable to replicate these results with a larger sample of children at varying levels of risk for disruptive behavior disorders in order to determine whether identifiable subgroups follow divergent developmental trajectories.

Counter to our expectations, observed concern for others did not increase in the low-risk children from preschool age to the elementary school years. This inconsistency with existing literature may be due to methodological differences. This was the first investigation, to our knowledge, that used direct observations to examine the development of concerned responses toward others in distress in a group of children over this period. Most prior studies of this age range have been cross-sectional in design. Even the few longitudinal studies have assessed concerned responses by means of reports from parents and teachers or by placing children in situations requiring such abstract decision-making processes as

choosing to donate earned prizes to sick children in a local hospital (e.g., Eisenberg & Shell, 1986; Grusec, 1972). The transition from 4–5 years to 6–7 years of age may be a period when responses to adults' needs do not change markedly for children without significant behavior problems. However, responsiveness to peers in need may increase, and levels of prosocial reasoning definitely develop over this time (Eisenberg, Lennon, & Roth, 1983).

One of the most salient results of this investigation was the demonstration of the protective role that concern for others may play in the development of children's externalizing behavior problems. Externalizing behavior problems were less stable from the preschool years to the early elementary school years, and also from the early- to mid-elementary school years, when children demonstrated more concern for others. In addition, the actual level of externalizing problems decreased from 4–5 to 6–7 years when the children had also displayed relatively more concern for others at 4–5 years (although concern at 6–7 years was not associated with further decreases in the actual level of problems from 6–7 to 9–10 years). These are important results, particularly given that, at preschool age, the high-risk children showed just as much concern in their responses to adults simulating injuries as did children with fewer problems. Fostering young children's attention to and concern for the needs of others may be an effective avenue of intervention for improving the developmental trajectories of children with early-appearing externalizing problems.

We found support for the potential of environmental factors to play such a role in the development of children's concern for others. Mothers' approaches to socialization were predictive of several measures of children's concern, even when children's initial risk status and the stability in children's levels of observed concern and disregard for others were controlled statistically. This is an important extension to the literature associating parenting with children's prosocial development, which contains relatively few longitudinal studies. The present results clearly suggest that mothers who are overly strict and harshly punitive, who do not tend to reason or establish reasonable and consistent rules, and who strongly show their anger or disappointment with their children, are likely to impede their children's prosocial development. These relations were as true for children with behavior problems as for children without, suggesting that the development of concern in highly difficult young children is not less subject to influence by maternal socialization. However, the group differences in socialization suggest that the actual experiences of the three risk groups might contribute to divergent pathways of development.

Previous work with data from this investigation has demonstrated that mothers of high-risk children are more likely to act in angry, authoritarian ways than are mothers of low- or moderate-risk children, and that in turn, these negative approaches to parenting can exacerbate the externalizing problems of high-risk children (Denham et al., 2000; also see Dishion, Andrews, Kavanagh, & Soberman, 1996, for supporting evidence). The current analyses show that this negative parenting impacts other aspects of social behavior and affect as well and thus may have indirect effects upon aggression by undermining related competent behaviors. Experiencing more forceful and angry socialization, disruptive and aggressive children are less likely to maintain or develop their concern for others, and thus their aggressive tendencies may be further disinhibited.

There are several possible processes that could account for this pattern of relations. Angry, authoritarian parenting could be interpreted by the children as a lack of care or concern on the part of their parents. Modeling of this behavior, or internalization of parental messages that the child is bad, could then discourage the disruptive children's ability or willingness to consider and sympathize with the needs of others. Alternatively, the children may have experienced negative effects from a relative absence of opportunities to emulate a more reasoned and considerate approach to parent–child interactions. However, it should be emphasized that the present sample constituted a fairly homogeneous and economically privileged group. The relations between socialization and children's characteristics can be expected to vary across ethnic, cultural, and social groups (e.g., Chen et al., 1998; Deater-Deckard, Dodge, Bates, & Pettit, 1996). It also should be recognized that this study was conducted over the children's transition from preschool to the elementary school environment. Aggressive and disruptive children are known to elicit aggression and rejection from peers in elementary school (Coie, Belding, & Underwood, 1988). The high-risk children probably engaged in more frequent conflicts and were more regularly exposed to distress in others. Such experiences could have a desensitizing effect that would negatively impact the children's concerned responses. It will be necessary to explore further how contexts and social interactions function together to shape the development of children.

The predominantly nonsignificant relations between cardiac responses to depictions of distress and children's concern at 6–7 years of age were somewhat surprising. It is important to note that the concurrent significant relations at 4–5 years of age were consistent with our earlier report (Zahn-Waxler et al., 1995), despite our having recoded all injury simulations in order to obtain a global, Gestalt measure of concerned responding. However, the lack of predictive value for the cardiac measures may suggest that the integration of affective, behavioral, and physiological response systems is specific to developmental periods or that there is a transition in the functional significance of cardiac reactivity over time. Our assessment of cardiac responses may have been too brief to serve as an effective measure of enduring cardiac function, although brief measures of HR have proven effective in other longitudinal studies (e.g., Raine et al., 1997). Alternatively, age-dependent increases in behavioral self-regulation and understanding of social standards for concerned behavior may come to contribute more to concerned responses than do physiological reactions. Finally, it may simply be the case that autonomic reactivity does not contribute as much to the development of concern for others as do socialization factors.

Despite the lack of association between earlier cardiac responses and later indices of concern, the present results do not rule out the possibility that late-maturing, biological factors could contribute to the changes in concern observed in the high-risk children. Given that genetics play a significant role in empathic and prosocial development (Zahn-Waxler et al., 2001), it is reasonable to search for biological correlates and components of concern for others. It may be necessary to broaden assessments of potential physiological correlates (e.g., hormonal assays, EEGs, functional MRIs, and genetic analyses) or to refine the precision of the more commonly used measures of autonomic functions. One pertinent question is the relative value of examining indicators of arousal versus indicators of regulatory abilities, two aspects of autonomic function that were confounded in this investigation. Arousal and regulation are not completely independent, but they are likely to have different meanings for, and associations with, social behavior. The negative relation between vagal tone and a school-based measure of prosocial behavior that we observed has been found in at least two prior investigations (Eisenberg et al., 1995; Eisenberg, Fabes, Karbon, et al., 1996). This finding is more compatible with regarding vagal tone as a marker of threshold for arousal rather than as an index of dispositional regulatory ability. Disentangling these components of functioning from psychophysiological measures will be important in future work.

In conclusion, it is apparent that concern for others is an important aspect of young aggressive and disruptive children's interpersonal repertoires and that it undergoes dynamic and worrisome changes as they begin to enter middle childhood. Examining the responses of children at risk for disruptive behavior disorders in contexts in which one would not normally expect to see displays of aggression and disruptiveness, per se, extends our understanding of these children. First, they are capable of showing concern for others in distress and they can respond in caring ways. Children with externalizing problems and high concern for others are most likely to show decreases in their aversive behaviors over time. Interventions to protect those concerned responses from the general pattern of decreasing concern over time might be effective in guiding children with early-appearing aggressive and disruptive behaviors toward more desirable developmental pathways; parent-training techniques seem promising in this regard. Second, disruptive children's concern for others decreases as they enter the elementary school years. Further work will be necessary to determine whether disruptive children truly decrease in their abilities to feel and show concern for others as they develop or whether these abilities are retained but selectively inhibited. Third, we detected patterns of blended positive and negative affective responses to distress in others in boys with behavior problems. These patterns may be indicative of particular forms of emotional dysregulation or social cognitive biases that contribute to negative trajectories. Using a longitudinal approach to the study of concern for others has revealed that models of aggressive and antisocial problems must be developmentally informed in order to understand the etiology and trajectories of, and possible interventions for, these aversive behavior patterns.

Notes

1 At the time the sample was recruited, the TRF had not been standardized for this age group. The 85th percentile was used as the high-risk cutoff and the 70th percentile as the moderate-risk cutoff on the basis of the recommendations of T. M. Achenbach (personal communication, August 15, 1988).

2 The ratings of observed concern for others toward mother and experimenter were positively but nonsignificantly correlated at both T1 and T2. Examination of the stability correlations separately for mother and experimenter revealed similar patterns of correlations. The correlations for concern for mother were slightly stronger than the correlations for concern for experimenter, but all correlations were in the same direction. For disregard for others, the relations between responses to mother and experimenter were similar to those for concern. However, as noted previously, there were far fewer instances of disregard directed to experimenter than to mother. The stability correlations for disregard for mother alone were almost identical to the correlations for the combined mother and experimenter disregard scores.

3 Although these analyses show that concern for others served to moderate the stability of externalizing problems over time, it is also possible that externalizing problems could play a similar role in the development of concern for others, serving to moderate the stability of concern. Therefore, we performed two regression analyses, in which we used observed concern at 5 years, externalizing problems at 5 years, and the interaction of these variables to predict (a) observed concern at 7 years and (b) the aggregate index of concern at 7 years. The analyses did not support a moderating role for externalizing problems, as neither interaction term approached significance (both $ps > .70$).

References

Achenbach, T. M. (1991). *Integrative guide for the 1991 CBCL/4–18, YSR, and TRF profiles.* Burlington: University of Vermont, Department of Psychiatry.

Achenbach, T. M., & Edelbrock, C. S. (1983). *Manual for the Child Behavior Checklist and Revised Child Behavior Profile.* Burlington, VT: University Associates in Psychiatry.

Achenbach, T. M., & Edelbrock, C. S. (1986). *Manual for the Teacher's Report Form.* Burlington: University of Vermont.

Aiken, L. S., & West, S. G. (1991). *Multiple regression: Testing and interpreting interactions.* Newbury Park, CA: Sage.

American Psychiatric Association. (1994). *Diagnostic and statistical manual of mental disorders* (4th ed.). Washington, DC: Author.

Baumrind, D. (1967). Child care practices associated with three patterns of preschool behavior. *Genetic Psychology Monographs, 75,* 43–88.

Baumrind, D. (1971). Current patterns of parental authority. *Developmental Psychology Monographs, 4*(1, Pt. 2).

Behar, L., & Stringfield, S. (1974). A behavior rating scale for the preschool child. *Developmental Psychology, 10,* 601–610.

Block, J. H. (1981). *The child-rearing practices report (CRPR): A set of Q-sort items for the description of parental socialization attitudes and values.* Berkeley: University of California, Institute of Human Development.

Bryant, B. (1982). An index of empathy for children and adolescents. *Child Development, 53,* 413–425.

Cassidy, J., & Asher, S. R. (1992). Loneliness and peer relations in young children. *Child Development, 63,* 350–365.

Chandler, M., & Moran, T. (1990). Psychopathy and moral development: A comparative study of delinquent and nondeliquent youth. *Development and Psychopathology, 2,* 227–246.

Chen, X., Hastings, P. D., Rubin, K. H., Chen, H., Cen, G., & Stewart, S. L. (1998). Child-rearing attitudes and behavioral inhibition in Chinese and Canadian toddlers: A cross-cultural study. *Developmental Psychology, 34,* 677–686.

Cohen, D., & Strayer, J. (1996). Empathy in conduct-disordered and comparison youth. *Developmental Psychology, 32,* 988–998.

Coie, J. D., Belding, M., & Underwood, M. (1988). Aggression and peer rejection in childhood. In B. B. Lahey & A. E. Kazdin (Eds.), *Advances in clinical child psychology* (Vol. 11, pp. 125–158). New York: Plenum Press.

Cole, P. M., Jordan, P. R., & Zahn-Waxler, C. (1990). *Mood induction stimulus for children.* Bethesda, MD: National Institute of Mental Health.

Cole, P. M., Zahn-Waxler, C., Fox, N. A., Usher, B. A., & Welsh, J. D. (1996). Individual differences in emotion regulation and behavior problems in preschool children. *Journal of Abnormal Psychology, 105,* 518–529.

Cummings, E. M., Hollenbeck, B., Iannotti, R., Radke-Yarrow, M., & Zahn-Waxler, C. (1986). Early organization of altruism and aggression: Developmental patterns and individual differences. In C. Zahn-Waxler, M. Cummings, & R. Iannotti (Eds.), *Altruism and aggression* (pp. 165–188). New York: Cambridge University Press.

Deater-Deckard, K., Dodge, K. A., Bates, J. E., & Pettit, G. S. (1996). Physical discipline among African American and European American mothers: Links to children's externalizing problems. *Developmental Psychology, 32,* 1065–1072.

Dekovic, M., & Janssens, J. M. A. M. (1992). Parents' child-rearing style and child's sociometric status. *Developmental Psychology, 28,* 925–932.

Denham, S. A., Workman, E., Cole, P. M., Weissbrod, C., Kendziora, K. T., & Zahn-Waxler, C. (2000). Prediction of behavior problems from early to middle childhood: The role of parental socialization and emotion expression. *Development and Psychopathology, 12,* 23–45.

Dishion, T. J., Andrews, D. W., Kavanagh, K., & Soberman, L. (1996). Preventive interventions for high-risk youth: The Adolescent Transitions Program. In R. D. Peters & R. J. McMahon (Eds.), *Preventing childhood disorders, substance abuse, and delinquency* (pp. 184–214). Thousand Oaks, CA: Sage.

Dodge, K. A., & Somberg, D. R. (1987). Hostile attribution biases among aggressive boys are exacerbated under conditions of threat to the self. *Child Development, 58,* 213–224.

Eisenberg, N., & Fabes, R. A. (1998). Prosocial development. In W. Damon (Series Ed.) & N. Eisenberg (Vol. Ed.), *Handbook of child psychology: Vol. 3. Social, emotional, and personality development* (5th ed., pp. 701–778). New York: Wiley.

Eisenberg. N., Fabes, R. A., Carlo, G., Troyer, D., Speer, A. L., Karbon, M., & Switzer, G. (1992). The relations of maternal practices and characteristics to children's vicarious emotional responsiveness. *Child Development, 63,* 583–602.

Eisenberg, N., Fabes, R. A., Karbon, M., Murphy, B. C., Wosinski, M., Polazzi, L., Carlo, G., & Juhnke, C. (1996). The relations of children's dispositional prosocial behavior to emotionality, regulation, and social functioning. *Child Development, 67,* 974–992.

Eisenberg, N., Fabes, R. A., & Murphy, B. C. (1996). Parents' reactions to children's negative emotions: Relations to children's social competence and comforting behavior. *Child Development, 67,* 2227–2247.

Eisenberg, N., Fabes, R. A., Murphy, B., Karbon, M., Smith, M., & Maszk, P. (1996). The relations of children's dispositional empathy-related responding to their emotionality, regulation, and social functioning. *Developmental Psychology*, *32*, 195–209.

Eisenberg, N., Fabes, R. A., Murphy, B., Maszk, P., Smith, M., & Karbon, M. (1995). The role of emotionality and regulation in children's social functioning: A longitudinal study. *Child Development*, *66*, 1360–1384.

Eisenberg, N., Fabes, R. A., Schaller, M., Carlo, G., & Miller, P. A. (1991). The relations of parental characteristics and practices to children's vicarious emotional responding. *Child Development*, *62*, 1393–1408.

Eisenberg, N., Guthrie, I. K., Murphy, B. C., Shepard, S. A., Cumberland, A., & Carlo, G. (1999). Consistency and development of prosocial dispositions: A longitudinal study. *Child Development*, *70*, 1360–1372.

Eisenberg, N., Lennon, R., & Roth, K. (1983). Prosocial development: A longitudinal study. *Developmental Psychology*, *19*, 846–855.

Eisenberg, N., & Mussen, P. H. (1989). *The roots of prosocial behavior in children*. New York: Cambridge University Press.

Eisenberg, N., & Shell, R. (1986). The relation of prosocial moral judgement and behavior in children: The mediating role of cost. *Personality and Social Psychology Bulletin*, *12*, 426–433.

Eisenberg, N., Shell, R., Pasternack, J., Lennon, R., Beller, R., & Mathy, R. M. (1987). Prosocial development in middle childhood: A longitudinal study. *Developmental Psychology*, *23*, 712–718.

Ellis, P. L. (1982). Empathy: A factor in antisocial behavior. *Journal of Abnormal Child Psychology*, *10*, 123–134.

Eyberg, S. M., & Robinson, E. A. (1983). Conduct problem behavior: Standardization of a behavioral rating scale. *Journal of Clinical Child Psychology*, *12*, 347–354.

Fabes, R. A., Eisenberg, N., & Miller, P. A. (1990). Maternal correlates of children's vicarious emotional responsiveness. *Developmental Psychology*, *26*, 639–648.

Feshbach, N. D. (1975). Empathy in children: Some theoretical and empirical considerations. *The Counseling Psychologist*, *4*, 25–30.

Feshbach, N., & Feshbach, S. (1969). The relationship between empathy and altruism in two age groups. *Developmental Psychology*, *1*, 102–107.

Fox, N. A., & Field, T. M. (1989). Individual differences in preschool entry behavior. *Journal of Applied Developmental Psychology*, *10*, 527–540.

Grusec, J. E. (1972). Demand characteristics of the modeling experiment: Altruism as a function of age and aggression. *Journal of Personality and Social Psychology*, *27*, 91–128.

Grusec, J. E. (1991a). The socialization of altruism. In M. S. Clark (Ed.), *Prosocial behavior: Review of personality and social psychology* (Vol. 12, pp. 9–33). Newbury Park, CA: Sage.

Grusec, J. E. (1991b). Socializing concern for others in the home. *Developmental Psychology*, *27*, 338–342.

Grusec, J. E., Goodnow, J. J., & Cohen, L. (1996). Household work and the development of concern for others. *Developmental Psychology*, *32*, 999–1007.

Hamalaimen, M., & Pulkkinen, L. (1995). Aggressive and non-prosocial behavior as precursors of criminality. *Studies on Crime and Crime Prevention*, *4*, 6–21.

Hastings, P. D., & Rubin, K. H. (1999). Predicting mothers' beliefs about preschool-aged children's social behavior: Evidence for maternal attitudes moderating child effects. *Child Development*, *70*, 722–741.

Hightower, A. D., Work, W. C., Cowen, E. L., Lotyczewski, B. S., Spinell, A. P., Guare, J. C., & Rohrbeck, C. A. (1986). The teacher–child rating scale: A brief objective measure of elementary children's school problem behaviors and competencies. *School Psychology Review*, *15*, 393–409.

Hoffman, M. L. (1975). Developmental synthesis of affect and cognition and its interplay for altruistic motivation. *Developmental Psychology*, *11*, 607–622.

Hoffman, M. L. (1982). Development of prosocial motivation: Empathy and guilt. In N. Eisenberg (Ed.), *The development of prosocial behavior* (pp. 281–313). New York: Academic Press.

Hollingshead, A. B. (1965). *Four Factor Index of Social Status*. Unpublished manuscript, Yale University, Department of Sociology.

Jaccard, J., Wan, C. K., & Turrisi, R. (1990). The detection and interpretation of interaction effects between continuous variables in multiple regression. *Multivariate Behavioral Research*, *25*, 467–478.

Janssens, J., & Dekovic, M. (1997). Child rearing, prosocial moral reasoning, and prosocial behaviour. *International Journal of Behavioral Development*, *20*, 509–527.

Kochanska, G. (1991). Socialization and temperament in the development of guilt and conscience. *Child Development*, *62*, 1379–1392.

Kochanska, G. (1992). *My Child, version 2: A preliminary manual*. Iowa City: University of Iowa, Department of Psychology.

Kochanska, G., DeVet, K., Goldman, M., Murray, K., & Putman, S. P. (1994). Maternal reports of conscience development and temperament in young children. *Child Development*, *65*, 852–868.

Kochanska, G., Kuczynski, L., & Radke-Yarrow, M. (1989). Correspondence between mothers' self-reported and observed child-rearing practices. *Child Development*, *60*, 56–63.

Krevans, J., & Gibbs, J. C. (1996). Parents' use of inductive discipline: Relations to children's empathy and prosocial behavior. *Child Development, 67*, 3263–3277.

Lahey, B. B., Hart, E. L., Pliszka, S., Applegate, B., & McBurnett, K. (1993). Neurophysiological correlates of conduct disorder: A rationale and a review of research. *Journal of Clinical Child Psychology, 22*, 141–153.

Levenson, R. W., & Ruef, A. M. (1992). Empathy: A physiological substrate. *Journal of Personality and Social Psychology, 63*, 234–246.

MacQuiddy, S. L., Maise, S. J., & Hamilton, S. B. (1987). Empathy and affective perspective-taking skills in parent-identified conduct-disordered boys. *Journal of Child Clinical Psychology, 16*, 260–268.

Matthews, K. A., Batson, C. D., Horn, J., & Rosenman, R. H. (1981). "Principles in his nature which interest him in the fortune of others…": The heritability of empathic concern for others. *Journal of Personality, 49*, 237–247.

McCarthy, D. (1970). *McCarthy Scales of Children's Abilities*. New York: Psychological Corporation.

Mealey, L. (1995). The sociobiology of sociopathy: An integrated evolutionary model. *Behavioral and Brain Sciences, 18*, 523–599.

Miller, P. A., & Eisenberg, N. (1988). The relation of empathy to aggressive and externalizing/antisocial behavior. *Psychological Bulletin, 103*, 324–344.

Nesse, R. M. (1991). Psychiatry. In M. Maxwell (Ed.), *The sociobiological imagination: SUNY series in philosophy and biology* (pp. 23–40). Albany: State University of New York Press.

Olweus, D. (1979). Stability of aggressive reaction patterns in males: A review. *Psychological Bulletin, 86*, 852–875.

Porges, S. W. (1985). Spontaneous oscillations on heart rate: A potential index of stress. In P. Mogberg (Ed.), *Animal stress: New directions in defining and evaluating the effects of stress* (pp. 97–111). Bethesda, MD: American Psychological Society.

Porges, S. W., & Byrne, E. A. (1992). Research methods for measurement of heart rate and respiration. *Biological Psychology, 34*, 93–130.

Raine, A., Venables, P. H., & Sarnoff, M. A. (1997). Low resting heart rate at age 3 predisposes to aggression at age 11 years: Evidence from the Mauritius Child Health Project. *Journal of the American Academy of Child & Adolescent Psychiatry, 36*, 1457–1464.

Rickel, A. U., & Biasatti, L. I. (1982). Modification of the Block Child Rearing Practices Report. *Journal of Clinical Psychology, 38*, 129–134.

Robinson, J., Zahn-Waxler, C., & Emde, R. (1994). Patterns of development in early empathic behavior: Environmental and child constitutional influences. *Social Development, 3*, 125–145.

Rushton, J. P., Fulker, D. W., Neale, M. C., Nias, D. K., & Eysenck, H. J. (1986). Altruism and aggression: The heritability of individual differences. *Journal of Personality and Social Psychology, 50*, 1192–1198.

Schacter, S., & Latane, B. (1964). Crime, cognition, and the autonomic nervous system. In D. Levine (Ed.), *Nebraska Symposium on Motivation* (Vol. 12, pp. 221–275). Lincoln: University of Nebraska Press.

Sober, E., & Wilson, D. S. (1998). *Unto others: The evolution and psychology of unselfish behavior*. Cambridge, MA: Harvard University Press.

Tremblay, R. E., Vitaro, F., Gagnon, C., Piche, C., & Royer, N. (1992). A prosocial scale for the preschool behaviour questionnaire: Concurrent and predictive correlates. *International Journal of Behavioral Development, 15*, 227–245.

Zahn-Waxler, C. (1993). Warriors and worriers: Gender and psychopathology. *Development and Psychopathology, 5*, 79–89.

Zahn-Waxler, C. (2000). The early development of empathy, guilt, and internalization of responsibility: Implications for gender differences in internalizing and externalizing problems. In R. Davidson (Ed.), *Wisconsin Symposium on Emotion: Vol. 1. Anxiety, depression, & emotion* (pp. 222–265). Oxford, England: Oxford University Press.

Zahn-Waxler, C., Cole, P. M., Welsh, J. D., & Fox, N. A. (1995). Psychophysiological correlates of empathy and prosocial behaviors in preschool children with behavior problems. *Development and Psychopathology, 1*, 27–48.

Zahn-Waxler, C., Radke-Yarrow, M., & King, R. A. (1979). Child rearing and children's prosocial initiations toward victims of distress. *Child Development, 50*, 319–330.

Zahn-Waxler, C., Radke-Yarrow, M., Wagner, E., & Chapman, M. (1992). Development of concern for others. *Developmental Psychology, 28*, 126–136.

Zahn-Waxler, C., Robinson, J., & Emde, R. N. (1992). The development of empathy in twins. *Developmental Psychology, 28*, 1038–1047.

Zahn-Waxler, C., Schiro, K., Robinson, J., Emde, R. N., & Schmitz, S. (2001). Empathy and prosocial patterns in young MZ and DZ twins: Development, genetic, and environmental influences. In R. N. Emde & J. K. Hewitt (Eds.), *Infancy to early childhood: Genetic and environmental influences on developmental change* (pp. 141–162). New York: Oxford University Press.

Sympathy Through Affective Perspective Taking and Its Relation to Prosocial Behavior in Toddlers

Amrisha Vaish, Malinda Carpenter, and Michael Tomasello

Sympathy (feeling concern for the other) and empathy (feeling as the other feels) regulate much of human social interaction. They are thought to lead to prosocial behaviors such as helping and lead away from antisocial behaviors such as aggression (Batson, 1991, 1998; Eisenberg & Miller, 1987; Hoffman, 1982, 2000; Miller & Eisenberg, 1988). Human infants from soon after birth show reactions to crying or distress that might be considered empathy, or at least some precursor to empathy such as emotional contagion (e.g., Sagi & Hoffman, 1976). Around 14–18 months, as children more clearly differentiate self from other, they show more varied and more other-directed empathic and sympathetic responses to others' distress (see Eisenberg, Spinrad, & Sadovsky, 2006, for a review).

Virtually all research on sympathy and empathy has assessed children's responses to conspicuous emotional cues such as crying or distress, thus tapping children's ability to sympathize either via emotional contagion or by identifying emotional signals. While this route to sympathy and empathy is certainly indispensable and commonly used, it could be entirely based upon reading the victim's overt emotional cues. There has, however, been much discussion in the literature about the possibility of sympathizing and empathizing in the absence of overt emotional cues, such as by affective perspective taking, that is, by imagining or inferring what the other person is feeling based on various nonemotional and situational cues and by putting oneself in the other's place (Eisenberg, Shea, Carlo, & Knight, 1991; Feshbach, 1978; Hoffman, 1984; Smith, 1759/2006; Thompson, 1987). Moreover, adults have been shown to engage in this latter form of sympathy or empathy in both behavioral and neuroscience work (see Batson et al., 1997; Ruby & Decety, 2004; see Blair, 2005; Decety & Jackson, 2006, for reviews). The question addressed here is whether young children, too, can sympathize in the absence of emotional cues. Despite the rele-

vance of this ability to the understanding of others' minds and experiences, and despite the extensive discussion of this issue in the literature, the development of this route to sympathy has received little attention in research with young children.

The developmental research relevant to this question has been conducted in two areas. First is the assessment of children's affective perspective-taking skills (e.g., Dunn & Hughes, 1998; Harwood & Farrar, 2006; Wellman, Phillips, & Rodriguez, 2000), and second is the investigation of empathy-related responding using picture and story tasks (e.g., Eisenberg-Berg & Lennon, 1980; Feshbach & Roe, 1968; Iannotti, 1985). In both paradigms, children are told or shown stories about protagonists in emotion-eliciting situations and are asked how the protagonists or the children themselves feel. Children from around 3 years of age pass some versions of these tasks. However, both lines of research are limited because they require relatively sophisticated cognitive and linguistic skills, which limits the ages that can be tested (see Eisenberg et al., 2006).

To our knowledge, only one recent study has assessed sympathy without emotion reading. Hobson, Harris, García-Pérez, and Hobson (2009) tested 11-year-olds with autism, 11-year-olds with learning disabilities, and typically developing 6-year-olds (all groups had verbal mental ages of around 6 years). In their task, participants and two experimenters each drew a picture; then one experimenter (the perpetrator) unexpectedly tore up the other experimenter's (the victim's) drawing (experimental condition) or else tore up a blank sheet of paper (control condition). In both cases, the victim observed the perpetrator neutrally. Children's looks to and concern for the victim were analyzed. In the experimental condition, a significantly higher percentage of children without autism than children with autism looked immediately and spontaneously to the victim and showed concern for the victim. These differences did not emerge in the control condition.

To assess sympathy without emotion reading in toddlers, we adapted Hobson and colleagues' (2009) task for two reasons: First, it does away with the affective cues typically provided in work on sympathy, thus allowing for a test of sympathy in the absence of emotional cues, and second, since the task is nonlinguistic and nonhypothetical, it does away with the difficult task demands placed on children in picture-story and the existing affective perspective-taking tasks. We extended the task by introducing several further scenarios in addition to the drawing situation (hereafter called *sympathy situations*).

Like Hobson and colleagues (2009), along with measuring patterns of children's looks to the victim, we also examined children's concern for the victim. One potential problem with measuring concern is that perhaps children look concerned about the generally negative situation (e.g., someone tearing someone else's picture) without really being concerned for the victim. To address this issue, we took two steps. First, like Hobson and colleagues, we only coded those concerned looks that were directed toward the victim. Second, extending Hobson and colleagues' work, we assessed children's prosocial behavior toward the victim in a subsequent task (hereafter called *prosocial situation*). This step was taken because sympathy is thought to play an important role in motivating altruistic prosocial behavior. Early in the second year, children display prosocial behaviors such as comforting or making helpful suggestions (e.g., Young, Fox, & Zahn-Waxler, 1999; Zahn-Waxler, Robinson, & Emde, 1992), and their empathic and sympathetic responses to victims who show overt emotional cues relate moderately with their prosocial behaviors (e.g., Eisenberg et al., 1989; Eisenberg & Miller, 1987). Thus, to test whether children's expressions of concern represented sympathy for the victim rather than more general concern, we examined whether children's prosocial behavior toward the victim was greater after they had witnessed situations that aroused sympathy for the victim than after situations that were neutral in nature. Finally, to better compare our study with prior work, we also assessed associations between children's concern and their subsequent prosocial behavior.

We predicted that toddlers would show more concern toward an adult when she had been harmed than when she had not. Note that although the victim showed no emotional response, we nevertheless assessed children's emotional response (concern for the victim). Our aim was thus not to assess children's cognitive skills per se but rather to assess whether children could arrive at an affective response without any overt affective input (and thus without emotion reading or emotional contagion). Based upon past work, we also predicted that toddlers would subsequently help the victim more and that there would be an association between concern for and prosocial behavior toward the victim.

Since prior work has mostly been conducted with children in the second postnatal year, we too tested 1.5- and 2-year-olds to assess whether at these ages, children can sympathize with a victim not only when she shows overt emotions but even when she does not. We also piloted the procedure with a few 14-month-olds but found that they did not fully grasp the sympathy situations. We therefore did not further test this age group. Finally, given that sympathy and prosocial behavior have sometimes been found to vary by gender, we assessed the effects of gender, but we did not have any specific predictions regarding this variable due to the mixed results from prior work (e.g., Holmgren, Eisenberg, & Fabes, 1998; Eisenberg & Lennon, 1983; Zahn-Waxler, Radke-Yarrow, Wagner, & Chapman, 1992).

Method

Participants

Participants were 18-month-olds ($n = 32$, 16 girls) between 17 months 1 day and 18 months 28 days ($M = 18; 2; SD = 11.7$ days) and 2-year-olds ($n = 32$, 16 girls) between 23 months 15 days and 26 months 28 days ($M = 25; 16; SD = 31.8$ days) from a medium-sized German city. The sample was predominantly White, and all participants were native German speakers. Thirty participants had no siblings, 17 had one or more siblings, and no information was available regarding siblings of the remaining 17. No information concerning parents' education, occupation, or socioeconomic status was collected. Five additional children were tested but were excluded due to fussiness or inattentiveness during the sympathy situations (two 2-year-olds and two 18-month-olds) and equipment failure (one 18-month-old). All participants were tested by the same two female experimenters playing the same role each time.

Materials

Each child saw four sympathy situations in which the following materials were used: two similar-looking necklaces with large, colorful beads; two similar-looking black belts with large, colorful beads; blank sheets of white paper and a color pencil; and a blue and a red ball of clay. Before each sympathy situation, children and one experimenter (E1, who would later play the victim) played together with one of two filler toys; an age-appropriate puzzle or a "climber" toy (consisting of a ladder and a wooden man). During the prosocial situation, three similar-looking colorful balloons were used, one filled with helium and the others filled with air. The helium balloon was E1's balloon and was tied to a piece of string, whereas the two air balloons were the children's and were tied to plastic yellow sticks that were easy for children to hold. Between the last sympathy situation and the prosocial situation, a ball and a stuffed toy served as filler toys.

Setting

During the sympathy situations, children sat on their parent's lap at a $120 \times 70 \times 75$-cm table, facing E1, while a second experimenter (E2, who played the perpetrator) sat beside the children on their right. For the prosocial situation, the child and E1 moved to a red carpet (200×140 cm) in the same room while the parent sat on a chair close by.

Procedure

E1 and E2 first played with children in a waiting room for about 10 min, and E1 obtained parents' informed consent. Throughout, E1 wore one of the necklaces and belts described above (in order to make it seem as though these really belonged to her and she enjoyed wearing them). When children were judged to be comfortable, parents and children were taken to the testing room, where everyone took their designated seat. Parents were asked not to provide the children with cues and to look away if children looked at them during the study. The overall experimental procedure was as follows: All children saw four sympathy situations, but half of the children saw them in the harm condition and half saw them in the neutral condition. After the sympathy situations, all children took part in the same prosocial situation.

To get started, E1 and the children played with the climber toy for 2 or 3 min, after which E1 put the toy away and the first of four sympathy situations began. Each situation (in both conditions) began with a phase (45 s) in which E1 acted on one of the four target objects (which, in the harm condition, would later be taken or destroyed by E2). The four situations were as follows:

Necklace. E1 admired and showed off her necklace. This involved looking admiringly at it, taking it off to examine it, commenting on the different beads, stating how much she liked it, and so on. The second, similar-looking necklace lay on a tray to the right of E2, visible but inaccessible to the children.

Belt. E1 admired and showed off her belt in a similar way as with her necklace. The second, similar-looking belt lay on the tray to the right of E2.

Picture. E1 happily and proudly drew a picture of a house and an apple tree, commenting the entire time about what a pretty picture it was, how much she liked it, and how happy it made her. To begin drawing, E1 picked up a stack of blank paper that had been lying out of the children's view, took one sheet for herself, and left the remainder of the stack on the table, visible but inaccessible to the children.

Clay. E1 happily and proudly made a clay bird using either the blue or the red clay ball and commenting as in the picture situation. To begin this task, E1 picked up a small tray that had thus far been lying out of the children's view and that held both balls of clay; she took one of the balls of clay for herself and left the other ball on the tray, visible but inaccessible to the children.

The necklace and belt comprised possession situations, and the picture and clay comprised effort situations. Since this was the first study of its kind with young children, we were unsure about what kinds of situations might elicit sympathy when the victim provided no emotional cues. We thus used two different kinds of situations in order to increase the chances that children would show sympathy in at least one kind. We did not have any predictions about which (if any) type of situation might elicit more sympathy.

In each case, E1 acted on the object for 45 s, during which time she occasionally looked to the child to share her excitement or to reengage the child but was mostly focused on the objects and her actions. During these 45 s, E2 watched E1's actions with mild interest but did not speak and did not look at the child. For each situation, when the 45 s were over, E1 placed the target object (her necklace, belt, picture, or bird) in front of her on the table while still looking admiringly at it. At this point, the experimental manipulation began.

Half of the children in each age group were randomly assigned to the harm condition, and the other half were assigned to the neutral condition. In the harm condition, E2 grabbed the target object as soon as E1 had put it down, said in a mildly aggressive tone, "I'm going to take/tear/break this now," and proceeded to do so mildly aggressively for 15 s. Specifically, E2 put on the necklace or belt and looked at it admiringly, or tore up the picture or broke apart the bird into small bits and threw the bits into a bin lying to her right on the ground. In the neutral condition, E2 said the same words in a neutral tone of voice and produced the same actions in a more neutral way upon the second (similar) object. That is, in the necklace and belt situations, E2 put on the necklace or belt lying on the tray; in the picture situation, E2 tore up a blank sheet of paper; and in the clay situation, E2 broke apart the second ball of clay. Critically, regardless of E2's action or the condition, E1 silently watched E2's actions with a neutral face; she neither spoke to nor looked at the child or anywhere else during this time. E2 also only watched her own actions; she did not look at E1 or at the child during this time. Children's looks to E1 (the victim) were coded during these 15-s periods (see below). After 15 s, E2 stopped acting upon the target object, which indicated the end of the trial to E1; E1 then neutrally picked up a filler toy and engaged children with it for approximately 1 min while E2 neutrally looked away (e.g., at the bin lying near her) and did not engage in the play.

A manipulation check was conducted on a random 25% of participants ($n = 16$; 8 in each age group and in each condition) to ensure that E1 maintained a neutral expression during the 15-s intervals in which E2 acted. A coder who was blind to condition coded E1's facial expression on a 5-point scale, consisting of −2 (*very negative*), −1 (*somewhat negative*), 0 (*neutral*), 1 (*somewhat positive*), and 2 (*very positive*). The scores were 0 in 62 of 64 instances, and 1 in the remaining two instances ($M = 0.03$, $SD = 0.18$), indicating that E1 did indeed maintain a neutral expression.

Each child saw all four situations in counterbalanced order, alternating between possession and effort situations, after which E1 and the children moved to the floor to play with filler toys while parents moved to a chair near the carpet and were given something to read. Parents were told that if children offered them a balloon, they could take it but then should put it on the floor and go back to reading.

After 2 or 3 min of play, E2 took out the three balloons and said excitedly, "Look [name of child], look what I found! Balloons!" She handed the two air balloons to the child and the helium balloon to E1. E1 played happily with her balloon and did not engage with the children, and children generally played with their own balloons. About 1 min later, E1 "accidentally" let go of her balloon (which floated to the ceiling), gasped, pointed to her balloon, and said in a shocked voice, "Oh no, my balloon!" She then "attempted" to bring it down, failed, and sat back down. She was then vocally and facially obviously sad. During the next 2 min (from the moment E1's balloon hit the ceiling), children's behavior was coded (see below).

During these 2 min, E1 never looked at children's hands or at their balloons and only very rarely looked at them at all so as to prevent giving them hints or pressuring them to help. After the 2 min, E1 stood on a chair, brought her balloon down, and was obviously happy. The prosocial situation did not last the full 2 min (a) if children became very upset, in which case the study was cut short and E1 brought down her balloon, or (b) if children handed one or both of their balloons to E1, in which case E1 gratefully took and then handed back the balloon(s) before bringing down her own balloon. For children who had seen the harm sympathy situations, after the entire procedure was completed, E2 apologized to E1 while the children were paying attention, and E1 accepted the apology. This was done so as not to end the session on a negative note, and in order to show children that E2's behavior had been wrong.

Coding and reliability

In the sympathy situations, the four 15-s intervals during which E2 acted upon the objects were coded. The primary coder (Amrisha Vaish, who was not blind to condition) used Interact (Mangold International GmbH, 2007) to code looks to E1's face, E2's face, E2's actions, and away. (However, looks to E2's face, E2's actions, and away were not analyzed and will not be discussed further.) Reliability was assessed on a randomly selected 25% of children (8 in each age group) by two secondary coders who were blind to condition, one of whom coded 6 children in each age group (3 in each condition), and the other of whom coded 4 children in each age group (2 in each condition). Agreement with the primary coder was excellent: $\kappa = .81$ for 2-year-olds and $\kappa = .80$ for 18-month-olds.

The primary coder also coded the quality of all looks to E1 using three categories (based partially on Hobson et al.'s, 2009, categories): concerned, checking, and other looks. Concerned looks were those expressing concern for E1. For a look to be coded as concerned, children's facial expression while looking to E1 had to involve either a furrowing or raising of the brow and sadness or concern in the eyes. In addition, their expression had to be different from that just before they turned to look to E1 as well as different from the overall facial expression that they had shown during E1's presentation. Counting only those looks of concern that were directed at E1 made our measure of concerned looks rather conservative since, of course, a child might experience concern for the victim even when she is looking away from the victim. However, since a concerned expression not directed at the victim might be the result of a general worry or confusion about the situation, we thought it safer to count only those concerned looks specifically directed at the victim.

Checking looks were looks meant to evaluate the situation, E1's response, and what might happen next (somewhat similar to the hypothesis-testing category used by Zahn-Waxler, Radke-Yarrow, et al., 1992). These looks were accompanied by neutral facial expressions or facial expressions that were no differ-

ent from those just before the children turned to look to E1 and from the children's overall facial expression during E1's presentation. Checking looks were coded to gauge children's expectation of a reaction from E1. We predicted that even if children did not show concern, they would show more checking looks in the harm than in the neutral condition because they perceived the harm condition as affecting E1 more. Finally, other looks were any looks that were not coded as concerned or checking (e.g., looks during which children smiled at E1). However, as almost no significant differences emerged with regard to other looks, and as these looks were not theoretically interesting, they will not be discussed further.

Due to the subjective nature of the coding of quality of looks, two secondary coders who were blind to condition assessed reliability on 100% of children: One secondary coder coded 24 children in each age group (12 in each condition), and the other coded 8 in each age group (4 in each condition). Agreement with the primary coder was excellent: $\kappa = .82$ for 2-year-olds and $\kappa = .80$ for 18-month-olds. Despite the high reliability, we used the blind coders' coding of quality of looks in analyses to avoid any bias in the primary coder's coding.

In the prosocial situation, the primary coder coded the 2 min or, if the trial was shorter, the full trial length, using the following categories, with their associated scores in parentheses (ordered from the highest to lowest level of prosocial or emotional response): helps/shares (3), shows distress (2); describes situation for self or E1 (2), attends to situation (1), or ignores situation (0; see Table 2.11 for details). *Shows distress* and *describes situation for self or E1* were assigned scores of 2 because we took these to be greater emotional responses to or involvement in the other's situation than *attends to situation* or *ignores situation*. These categories were based partially on prior work (Zahn-Waxler, Radke-Yarrow, et al., 1992).

Although children could show any or all of these prosocial behaviors, for analyses, children's prosocial score consisted of each child's highest score. Since no child's prosocial score was 0 (ignores situation), this category was not included in analyses. Two coders who were blind to condition assessed reliability on 25% of children: One coded 6 children in each age group (3 in each condition), and

Table 2.11   Coding scheme for prosocial situation

Prosocial score	Category	Behaviors
3	Helps/shares	Gives own balloon to E1: Fully approaches E1 and clearly offers her one or both balloons
		Puts balloon near E1 or throws it toward E1; may then move away: Tosses balloon(s) in E1's direction or places it/them near her and then retreats, usually still watching her. If it was clear during testing that the child intended to give the balloon(s) to E1. E1 picked up the balloon(s) and the 2 minutes were cut short, but if E1 was unsure about what the child intended, she continued displaying sadness
		Comforts E1: Hugs or pats E1
		Describes the situation to parent: verbal or gestural descriptions about the situation (e.g., "The balloon is gone") directed to parent in an effort to draw the parent's attention to the situation; akin to Zahn-Waxler, Radke-Yarrow, et al.'s (1992, p. 129) "indirect helping"
		Makes suggestions to E1: Suggests ways to retrieve balloon (e.g., "ladder") or to cheer E1 up (e.g., "ball," referring to the ball that E1 had previously enjoyed playing with)
2	Shows distress	Shows distress: including whimpering or crying
	Describes situation for self or E1	Describes situation verbally (e.g., "Balloon is up") or gestures (e.g., pointing to balloon at ceiling), while looking not to parent but to situation or E1; akin to Zahn-Waxler, Radke-Yarrow, et al.'s (1992, p. 129) "hypothesis testing"
		Points out to self or E1 that s/he has balloon(s): Verbal (e.g., "I have a balloon") or gestural communication (e.g., pointing to own balloon[s]) while looking not to parent but to situation or E1
1	Attends to situation	Watches E1 and situation in a serious way; stops play
		Goes to parent or moves away but continues watching E1
0	Ignores situation	Shows no involvement or interest in the situation
		Goes to parent and tries to engage him/her

the other coded 4 children in each age group (2 in each condition). Agreement on the prosocial scores was excellent: $\kappa = .80$ for 2-year-olds and $\kappa = .81$ for 18-month-olds.

Results

We first report results from the sympathy situations, followed by results from the prosocial situation, and finally the correlations between the two. Effect sizes were calculated using partial eta-squared (η_p^2).

Sympathy situations: Patterns of looks

To assess patterns of children's looks to E1, we used four dependent measures: number of the four trials in which children looked to E1, average latency of first look to E1, average total duration of all looks to

E1, and average number of looks to E1. Average latency and duration were obtained by averaging across only those trials in which children looked to E1.

As a preliminary analysis, we compared patterns of looks in possession versus effort situations and found two significant effects: Children looked to E1 in a significantly higher number of possession than effort trials, $F(1, 60) = 13.74, p < .0005, \eta_p^2 = .186$, and children also directed a greater number of looks to E1 in possession than effort trials, $F(1, 60) = 8.65, p = .005, \eta_p^2 = .126$. However, these variables did not interact with condition or age group. Furthermore, average latency and duration of looks did not differ across possession versus effort situations, nor did they interact with condition or age group (all $ps > .095$). Thus, for analysis of these four dependent measures, we collapsed data across possession and effort situations.

Table 2.12   Means and standard deviations for various measures of children's looks in the sympathy situations

Dependent measure	Neutral condition		Harm condition		η_p^2
	M	SD	M	SD	
Number of trials child looked to E1	2.13	1.14	3.16	1.0**	.20
Average latency to look to E1	9.67 s	2.71	6.19 s	2.94***	.28
Average duration of looks to E1	1.40 s	0.54	1.71 s	0.66***	.29
Average number of looks to E1	0.79	0.64	1.44	0.83**	.17

Note. E1 = Experimenter 1, who played the victim.
**$p < .005$. ***$p < .0005$.

The main analysis consisted of a multivariate analysis of variance using the same four dependent measures. The fixed factors were condition (harm, neutral), age group (18 months, 2 years), and gender. There was a significant multivariate effect of condition, Wilks's $\lambda = .520$, $F(4, 50) = 11.53$, $p < .0005$, $\eta_p^2 = .480$. Univariate tests revealed striking condition differences in all four variables: Compared to the neutral condition, children in the harm condition looked to E1 in a significantly higher number of trials, more quickly, for longer, and more often (see Table 2.12).

The multivariate analysis of variance also revealed a nearly significant Condition × Gender interaction, Wilks's $\lambda = .833$, $F(4, 50) = 2.50$, $p = .054$, $\eta_p^2 = .167$. Univariate tests revealed that this interaction was only significant for average duration of looks, $F(1, 53) = 8.77$, $p = .005$, $\eta_p^2 = .142$. Simple main effects (Bonferroni corrected) showed that girls in the harm condition looked to E1 for a significantly longer duration ($M = 2.32$ s, $SD = 0.75$) than did girls in the neutral condition ($M = 1.05$ s, $SD = 0.47$), $F(1, 53) = 31.0$, $p < .001$, whereas duration of boys' looks did not differ across conditions (harm: $M = 1.93$ s, $SD = 0.76$; neutral: $M = 1.59$ s, $SD = 0.56$, $p = .48$). The multivariate analysis of variance did not reveal any other significant main effects or interactions (all $ps > .288$).

Sympathy situations: Quality of looks

To assess the quality of looks to E1, we analyzed (a) the number of children who showed concerned and checking looks, (b) the number of the four sympathy situations in which children showed concerned and

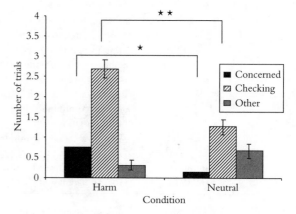

Figure 2.3   Mean number of trials ($\pm SE$, denoted by the error bars) in which children showed each type of look. *$p < .05$. **$p < .0005$.

checking looks, and (c) the proportion of individuals' looks that were concerned and checking looks. The means for the second measure (the number of situations) are presented in Figure 2.3.

CONCERNED LOOKS

As predicted, children showed more concern for E1 in the harm than in the neutral condition. Specifically, more children showed concerned looks in the harm (13 of 32, or 40.6%) than in the neutral (4 of 32, or 12.5%) condition, $\chi^2(1, N = 64) = 6.49$, $p = .011$, with no difference between type of situation (possession vs. effort), age group, or gender (all $ps > .395$). Children also showed concerned looks in a significantly greater number of the four harm situations ($M = 0.75$, $SD = 1.11$) than the four neutral situations ($M = 0.16$,

$SD = 0.45$), independent-samples $t(62) = 2.81, p = .008$. However, this difference might be explained by the fact that children simply looked to E1 much more in the harm than in the neutral conditions. To control for this difference, for each child we calculated the number of situations in which the child showed concern as a proportion of the number of situations in which the child looked to E1. Thus, if a child looked to E1 in two of the four situations and showed concern in one of those situations, the child received a proportion of 50. Using these proportions revealed the same result: Children showed concerned looks in a greater proportion of harm ($M = 20.97$, $SD = 29.57$) than neutral ($M = 7.22, SD = 21.3$) situations, $t(59) = 2.09, p = .041$. Finally, analyses of the proportion of individuals' looks that were concerned looks revealed a similar albeit nonsignificant pattern (harm: $M = 15.70$, $SD = 23.23$; neutral: $M = 6.44$, $SD = 20.23$), $t(59) = 1.66, p = .102$. Note that 3 children (1 in the harm condition and 2 in the neutral condition) were excluded from the last two analyses because they did not look to E1 in any of the four trials.

Given that children were presented with four sympathy situations in succession, it is conceivable that children's concern was primarily evident in the first few harm situations and faded with repeated presentation. However, a repeated-measures analysis indicated no significant difference across the four harm situations ($p = .985$): In all four situations, the proportion of looks that were concerned looks ranged between 15.56% and 18.89%. Thus, children's concerned looks did not fade across the four harm situations despite E1's lack of response.

CHECKING LOOKS

As with concerned looks, and as would be expected, more children showed checking looks toward E1 in the harm (97%) than in the neutral (75%) condition ($p = .026$, using Fisher's exact test because of low expected count in some cells). However, this effect was mediated by situation type and age. That is, significantly more children showed checking looks to E1 in the possession (77%) than in the effort (55%) situations, McNemar test, $\chi^2(1, N = 64) = 6.50, p = .009$. Still, in both types of situations, more children showed checking looks in the harm than in the neutral condition (possession: 28 of 32 in harm vs. 21 of 32 in

neutral, $\chi^2[1, N = 64] = 4.27, p = .039$; effort: 22 of 32 in harm versus 13 of 32 in neutral, $\chi^2[1, N = 64] = 5.11, p = .024$).

In addition, more 18-month-olds (97%) than 2-year-olds (75%) showed checking looks ($p = .026$, Fisher's exact test). Analyzing the age groups separately revealed that among the 2-year-olds, whereas 15 of 16 (94%) showed checking looks in the harm condition, only 9 of 16 (56%) did so in the neutral condition ($p = .037$, Fisher's exact test). There was no difference between conditions for the 18-month-olds (16 of 16 in the harm condition and 15 of 16 in the neutral condition showed checking looks; $p = 1.000$, Fisher's exact test). The number of children who showed checking looks did not differ by gender ($p = .148$).

Children in the harm condition also showed checking looks in a significantly greater number of the four sympathy situations ($M = 2.69$, $SD = 1.23$) than did children in the neutral condition ($M = 1.28$, $SD = 1.05$), $t(62) = 4.91, p < .0005$. To control for the baseline difference in amount of looking to E1 across conditions, we again calculated proportion scores (i.e., the number of situations in which a child showed checking looks as a proportion of the number of situations in which the child looked to E1). This more conservative measure revealed the same result (harm: $M = 88.17$, $SD = 21.17$; neutral: $M = 64.72$, $SD = 40.69$), $t(59) = 2.84$, $p = .007$. Finally, a similar pattern emerged in the proportion of individuals' looks that were checking looks (harm: $M = 79.22$, $SD = 25.53$; neutral: $M = 66.54$, $SD = 39.43$), but this difference was not significant, $t(59) = 1.50$, $p = .14$. Again, the 3 children who did not look to E1 in any of the four trials were excluded from the last two analyses.

The effect of condition on subsequent prosocial behavior

The distribution of children's prosocial scores across condition, age group, and gender are presented in Table 2.13. As expected, significantly more children helped or shared with E1 (i.e., received a prosocial score of 3) if they had previously experienced the harm rather than the neutral condition (harm: 21 of 32, or 65.6%; neutral: 12 of 32, or 37.5%), $\chi^2(1, N = 64) = 5.07, p = .024$. The number of children who helped or shared did not differ by age group or gender (both ps $= .802$).

Table 2.13   Percentage of children who received each score as their highest prosocial score

Category	Score	Condition previously experienced		Age group		Gender	
		Harm	Neutral	18 months	2 years	Girls	Boys
Helps/shares	3	65.6	37.5	53.1	50.0	53.1	50.0
Shows distress or describes situation	2	15.6	25.0	15.6	25.0	25.0	15.6
Attends to situation	1	18.8	37.5	31.3	25.0	21.9	34.4
Ignores situation	0	0	0	0	0	0	0

An additional analysis of the effect of condition on prosocial behavior consisted of a univariate analysis of variance using prosocial scores as the dependent measure and condition, age group, and gender as fixed factors. This revealed a main effect of condition, $F(1, 56) = 5.16, p = .027, \eta_p^2 = .084$: Children who had previously seen E1 in the harm condition had higher prosocial scores toward her ($M = 2.47, SD = 0.80$) than did children who had seen her in the neutral condition ($M = 2.00, SD = 0.88$). The analysis of variance also revealed a nearly significant Age Group × Gender interaction, $F(1, 56) = 3.88, p = .054$, but simple main effects (Bonferroni corrected) revealed no significant gender differences in prosocial scores in either age group (both $ps > .117$). There were no further main effects or interactions (all $ps > .100$).

Relations between individual children's concerned looks and prosocial behavior

To assess the association between degree of concern in the sympathy situations and subsequent prosocial behavior, we conducted nonparametric correlations using the number of the four sympathy situations in which children showed concern and children's prosocial scores. As predicted, the two factors were positively correlated (Kendall's $\tau = .24, p = .036$). This correlation was specific to concerned looks; a similar analysis conducted using children's checking looks was not significant ($p = .514$).

Since prosocial scores varied by condition (see above), the correlations between concerned looks and prosocial scores were also conducted separately for each condition. As predicted, in the harm condition,

the correlation between number of situations with concerned looks and prosocial scores was positive (Kendall's $\tau = .26$), although this was a nonsignificant trend ($p = .097$). In the neutral condition, the number of situations with concerned looks was not associated with prosocial scores (Kendall's $\tau = .015, p = .928$). Note that correlational analyses conducted using the more conservative measure of proportion of situations (i.e., number of situations in which a child showed concerned looks divided by the number of situations in which the child looked to E1) revealed very similar results, as did correlational analyses using proportions of individuals' looks that involved concern.

One possible alternative interpretation of this correlation is that what we coded as concern actually indexed emotional arousal caused by the perpetrator's aggressive behavior in the harm condition (since, in order for the conditions to be believable, the perpetrator did behave mildly aggressively in the harm but not in the neutral condition). Furthermore, perhaps those children who experienced this emotional arousal were then more susceptible to the victim's distress cues in the prosocial situation. This is potentially problematic given that children received a higher prosocial score for showing distress (a score of 2) than for only attending to the situation (1) or showing no response (0). Thus, perhaps the increased emotional arousal during sympathy situations and the resulting increased distress in the prosocial situation created a spurious correlation that does not index a sympathy–prosocial behavior link at all. However, this alternative interpretation of the correlation does not hold because, even when showing distress was excluded from the coding scheme and those 3 children who showed distress were assigned their next highest score (they all received a 1 for attending to the situation), the correlation between the number of trials in which children showed concerned looks and children's prosocial behavior persisted (Kendall's $\tau = .23, p = .045$).

Discussion

We examined whether children can, even in the absence of emotional cues, sympathize with a victim. Extending the study by Hobson and colleagues (2009), we tested significantly younger children in multiple situations and, in addition, examined the relation between children's sympathy and prosocial behavior. We found that as early as 18 months of age, children show concern for an adult stranger who is in a hurtful situation but shows no emotion. What is striking about these results is not that such young children showed sympathy, which was to be expected given past work (e.g., Bischof-Köhler, 1991; Young et al., 1999; Zahn-Waxler, Radke-Yarrow, et al., 1992); what is striking is that this is, to our knowledge, the first demonstration that such young children can sympathize with a sufferer even in the absence of overt emotional cues. This study thus also extends past work on sympathy in toddlers, which had, up to this point, mostly focused on children's empathy and sympathy in response to a sufferer's overt emotional signals.

Our claim that children were concerned for the sufferer (rather than, say, about the generally negative situation or the victim's potentially angry response) gains support from two additional findings. First, children in the harm condition later helped E1 significantly more than did children in the neutral condition. Our interpretation of this finding is that observing someone experiencing negative situations increases the likelihood of children helping that person, presumably by inducing sympathy, which has been both theoretically and empirically linked to prosocial behavior (see, e.g., Batson, 1991; Eisenberg & Miller, 1987). This proposal is strengthened by a second finding: the correlation between children's concerned looks and their subsequent prosocial behavior toward the sufferer, which indicates that individual children who expressed concern for E1 were also more likely to help E1. Together, these findings substantiate our

claim that we have measured sympathy and support our conclusion that the early ability to sympathize does not require overt emotional cues: In the absence of such cues, children can use situational cues to sympathize with another person.

One open question concerns the mechanism(s) children employed to arrive at sympathy. Obviously, sympathy in the present study did not result directly from exposure to the victim's affective cues (e.g., via mechanisms such as mimicking the emotional cues, emotional contagion, etc.), as such cues were not provided. We thus argue that sympathy in our study resulted at least partially from cognitive processes.[1] Several cognitive processes can contribute to empathy-related responses (see Eisenberg et al., 2006; Feshbach, 1978; Hoffman, 1982, 1984). Simpler processes include direct association (e.g., seeing another's blood elicits distress in the observer due to blood being linked to the observer's own past distress) and classical conditioning. However, sympathy results from more sophisticated processes that involve an analysis of the source of the vicarious feeling and therefore a focus on the other (Eisenberg et al., 1991).

One such sophisticated cognitive process is affective perspective taking, that is, making inferences about the other's affective state by putting oneself in the other's place and basing one's responses on those inferences (Eisenberg et al., 1991; Hoffman, 1984). In the absence of emotional cues, one way to make this inference is via simulation, which involves imagining oneself in another's situation (e.g., Decety & Sommerville, 2003; Harris, 1995). An alternative but related possibility (and the one preferred by Hobson et al., 2009) is that the observer can feel her way into the experience of and feel for the other person because she identifies with that person's attitudes. According to Hobson and colleagues (2009), in their study, children with autism did not identify with the victim's attitudes and could therefore not experience concern for the way the victim would be expected to feel, whereas children with learning disabilities and typically developing children did not have difficulties with identification and could thus experience concern for the victim. Importantly, whether via simulation, identification, or some other mechanism(s), one eventually takes the other's perspective and apprehends the other's affective state, which can activate affective responses such as sympathy and can thereby motivate prosocial behavior (Batson, Fultz, & Schoenrade, 1987; Feshbach, 1978; Krebs & Russell, 1981). Plausibly, then, in our study, children apprehended the victim's state by taking her affective perspective, which stimulated their sympathy and prosocial behavior.

This might be surprising given that thus far, affective perspective taking has only been demonstrated in the 3rd year and beyond (Denham, 1986; Wellman et al., 2000). However, tasks used in prior work required children to display relatively sophisticated cognitive and linguistic skills, such as comprehending hypothetical situations and answering questions about their own feelings. These skills might not amply develop until the 3rd year. It is thus possible that children younger than 3 years possess some affective perspective-taking abilities, but the methods used in prior work have not been sensitive enough to tap these abilities. Relevant here is recent work on children's theory of mind, in which the use of sensitive, implicit measures shows that, rather than emerging around 4 years of age, as previously believed, a basic theory of mind is already present during the 2nd year (Onishi & Baillargeon, 2005; Southgate, Senju, & Csibra, 2007). We thus believe that when appropriate measures are used, children in their 2nd year could well demonstrate some affective perspective-taking skills as well.

Depending on how familiar children were with situations like our sympathy situations, they might additionally have relied on their past experiences to infer the victim's affect. That is, if children had previously directly or vicariously experienced such situations on multiple occasions, perhaps they had formed scripts about people's responses to such situations and, in our study, were partially relying on these scripts to infer the victim's affect. On the other hand, if the situations were novel for children, then children likely engaged in perspective taking (see Blair, 2005; Eisenberg et al., 1991; Karniol, 1982). It is possible that our sympathy situations were somewhat familiar to children, especially to those with siblings and those in day care. Thus, perhaps some children in the harm condition (those familiar with such situations) relied less on affective perspective taking and more on scripts than did children who were unfamiliar with such situations. However, even if the situations were to some degree familiar to children, it is highly unlikely that children

had ever witnessed precisely the situations that they witnessed in our study (e.g., an adult tearing up another adult's drawing), and so although they might have had some scripts to rely on, they also had to engage in some affective perspective taking. In any case, children did sympathize, indicating that they can arrive at sympathy without expression reading or emotional contagion.

It is noteworthy that in our harm condition, only some children (40%) showed concerned looks (although this proportion is similar to proportions reported in studies in which the victim provided emotional signals; e.g., Zahn-Waxler, Radke-Yarrow, et al., 1992). One possible explanation for this might be that the degree of sympathy aroused is related to the level of observer–sufferer attachment (Batson, 1987). As E1 was a relative stranger, fewer children may have experienced sympathy than they would have if the sufferer had been their parent (van der Mark, van IJzendoom, & Bakermans-Kranenburg, 2002; Young et al., 1999). There are also likely differences in individuals' tendency to outwardly express sympathy. Thus, some children might have experienced sympathy but not expressed it facially. Indeed, given that all but 1 child in the harm condition showed checking looks, perhaps some checking looks were in fact sympathetic looks but without the accompanying overt expressions. However, concerned but not checking looks correlated with prosocial behavior, indicating that the two kinds of looks tapped into distinct responses and that checking looks were not simply sympathetic looks without the overt expressions.

A related possibility for why more children did not show concern might have to do with the fact that concerned looks were only coded as such when they were directed at the victim. Our measure of concern was thus quite conservative, and perhaps some children experienced concern for the victim but were not coded as doing so because they did not meet our conservative criterion. One way to get around this problem in the future might be to use physiological measures such as heart rate and skin conductance, which are less vulnerable to such coding decisions (see, e.g., Eisenberg & Fabes, 1990, 1998; Hastings, Zahn-Waxler, & McShane, 2006).

Even so, we found a correlation between sympathy and prosocial behavior, the strength of which is comparable to some prior work in which the victim presented emotional cues (e.g., .20 in Zahn-Waxler, Robinson & Emde, 1992) and is consistent with the general finding that the relation between sympathy and prosocial behavior exists but is not very strong (see Eisenberg & Miller, 1987; Eisenberg et al., 2006). This correlation could represent a causal link such that sympathy for a person leads to prosocial behavior toward that person, but it could also be due to a third variable such as temperament or emotion regulation (see Batson, 1998; Eisenberg & Miller, 1987; Hoffman, 1976, 1982). For instance, Young and colleagues (1999) found that inhibited children show less prosocial behavior and less empathy toward an unfamiliar experimenter (see also Eisenberg, 2005; Radke-Yarrow & Zahn-Waxler, 1984; van der Mark et al., 2002). A similar factor might also partially explain our correlation. Along similar lines, it could be argued that the correlation between children's concern and their subsequent prosocial behavior was actually a spurious correlation between the increased emotional arousal during sympathy situations and the resulting increased distress in the prosocial situation. However, this alternative interpretation of the correlation does not hold since we obtained the correlation even when showing distress was excluded from the coding scheme.

An interesting aspect of our results was that 4 of the 32 children in the neutral condition showed concern for E1. At first glance, this seems strange considering that E1 was in no way affected by E2's actions in this condition, but our sense during testing was that some children nevertheless worried that E2's behavior might be threatening to E1. For instance, after E1 had just finished drawing a picture, E2 tore up a blank piece of paper for no reason, and perhaps some children perceived this as a threat to E1's drawing, which was lying within easy reach of E2. Our aim in designing the neutral condition was to make it as similar as possible to the harm condition. This might, however, have led some children in the neutral condition to interpret E2's actions as negative for E1.

It is worth mentioning that we found almost no gender differences in our dependent measures and only one age difference in checking looks. Importantly, there were no age differences in children's show of concern, which suggests that the ability to sympathize without overt emotional cues from the sufferer is

present by 18 months. On the one hand, this is striking considering the kinds of cognitive and affective experiences and abilities that are likely needed to sympathize in the absence of emotional signals. On the other hand, it is unsurprising given that even 14-month-olds have been shown to sympathize when a sufferer displays emotions (e.g., Zahn-Waxler, Radke-Yarrow, et al., 1992). Future work could further simplify our sympathy situations to test whether 14-month-olds also show concern without the aid of the victim's emotional signals.

One caveat about our findings is that children might have been influenced by their parents. Parents were instructed not to provide any cues and they were generally very good at following these instructions. Nevertheless, future work might have parents sit to the children's side to prevent them from potentially subtly influencing their children's responses. A more fundamental caveat concerns the generalizability of our findings. What, for example, is the range of situations within which young children can sympathize without emotion reading? We found that children sympathized in two kinds of situations: possession and effort. These categories cover many of the situations that children experience regularly. However, it is implausible that young children would sympathize in entirely novel categories of situations that they had no way to understand and in which they had no affective cues to guide them (e.g., hearing that someone did not get the job that he wanted). Clearly, the ability to sympathize, especially in the absence of emotional cues from the sufferer, rests on one's knowledge and understanding of the world, both of which develop with age. There might also be cultural variation in the kinds of situations that elicit sympathy. Our possession situations, for instance, might not elicit sympathy in a culture in which belongings tend to be shared and not to be the sole property of one person. Finally, sympathy might vary depending on children's attachment to the victim or the victim's gender and race (see, e.g., Eisenberg & Lennon, 1983; Young et al., 1999). Thus, our findings certainly do not generalize to all situations and all cultures. How and why children's sympathy varies are fascinating questions that deserve much more attention.

In sum, even 18-month-old children can sympathize with someone who is in a negative situation but shows no affective cues. Moreover, the sympathy thus experienced follows the patterns that true sympathy is expected to follow: It increases the likelihood of prosocial behavior and, within individuals, it correlates with prosocial behavior. These findings show that we feel for and help people who are in hurtful situations, and we do so robustly and flexibly from very early in development.

Note

1   Our claim is not that cognitive processes are entirely distinct and separable from affective processes. On the contrary, our claim would be that cognitive and affective processes are interdependent such that a cognitive construal of someone else's situation or state can arouse an affective response (such as the sympathy aroused in our study), affective appraisal can give rise to cognitive construal, and that the two work closely together to jointly give rise to behavior (see Pessoa, 2008).

References

Batson, C. D. (1987). Prosocial motivation: Is it ever truly altruistic? In L. Berkowitz (Ed.), *Advances in experimental social psychology* (Vol. 20, pp. 65–122). San Diego, CA: Academic Press.

Batson, C. D. (1991). *The altruism question: Toward a social-psychological answer*. Hillsdale, NJ: Erlbaum.

Batson, C. D. (1998). Altruism and prosocial behavior. In D. T. Gilbert, S. T. Fiske, & G. Lindzey (Eds.), *The handbook of social psychology* (Vol. 2, pp. 282–316). Boston: McGraw-Hill.

Batson, C. D., Fultz, J., & Schoenrade, P. A. (1987). Adults' emotional reactions to the distress of others. In N. Eisenberg & J. Strayer (Eds.), *Empathy and its development* (pp. 163–185). Cambridge, England: Cambridge University Press.

Batson, C. D., Sager, K., Garst, E., Kang, M., Rubchinsky, K., & Dawson, K. (1997). Is empathy-induced helping due to self–other merging? *Journal of Personality and Social Psychology, 73*, 495–509.

Bischof-Köhler, D. (1991). The development of empathy in infants. In M. E. Lamb & H. Keller (Eds.), *Infant development: Perspectives from German speaking countries* (pp. 245–273). Hillsdale, NJ: Erlbaum.

Blair, R. J. R. (2005). Responding to the emotions of others: Dissociating forms of empathy through the study of

typical and psychiatric populations. *Consciousness and Cognition, 14*, 698–718.

Decety, J., & Jackson, P. L. (2006). A social-neuroscience perspective on empathy. *Current Directions in Psychological Science, 15*, 54–58.

Decety, J., & Sommerville, J. A. (2003). Shared representations between self and other: A social cognitive neuroscience view. *Trends in Cognitive Sciences, 7*, 527–533.

Denham, S. A. (1986). Social cognition, prosocial behavior, and emotion in preschoolers: Contextual validation. *Child Development, 57*, 194–201.

Dunn, J., & Hughes, C. (1998). Young children's understanding of emotions within close relationships. *Cognition and Emotion, 12*, 171–190.

Eisenberg, N. (2005). The development of empathy-related responding. In G. Carlo & C. P. Edwards (Eds.), *Nebraska symposium on motivation: Vol. 51. Moral motivation through the life span* (pp. 73–117). Lincoln: University of Nebraska Press.

Eisenberg, N., & Fabes, R. A. (1990). Empathy: Conceptualization, measurement, and relation to prosocial behavior. *Motivation and Emotion, 14*, 131–149.

Eisenberg, N., & Fabes, R. A. (1998). Prosocial development. In N. Eisenberg (Ed.), *Handbook of child psychology: Vol. 3. Social, emotional, and personality development* (5th ed., pp. 701–778). New York: Wiley.

Eisenberg, N., Fabes, R. A., Miller, P. A., Fultz, J., Shell, R., Mathy, R. M., et al. (1989). Relation of sympathy and personal distress to prosocial behavior: A multimethod study. *Journal of Personality and Social Psychology, 57*, 55–66.

Eisenberg, N., & Lennon, R. (1983). Sex differences in empathy and related capacities. *Psychological Bulletin, 94*, 100–131.

Eisenberg, N., & Miller, P. A. (1987). The relation of empathy to prosocial and related behaviors. *Psychological Bulletin, 101*, 91–119.

Eisenberg, N., Shea, C. L., Carlo, G., & Knight, G. P. (1991). Empathy-related responding and cognition: A "chicken and the egg" dilemma. In W. Kurtines & J. Gewirtz (Eds.), *Handbook of moral behavior and development: Vol. 2. Research* (pp. 63–88). Hillsdale, NJ: Erlbaum.

Eisenberg, N., Spinrad, T. L., & Sadovsky, A. (2006). Empathy-related responding in children. In M. Killen & J. G. Smetana (Eds.), *Handbook of moral development* (pp. 517–549). Mahwah, NJ: Erlbaum.

Eisenberg-Berg, N., & Lennon, R. (1980). Altruism and the assessment of empathy in the preschool years. *Child Development, 51*, 552–557.

Feshbach, N. D. (1978). Studies of empathic behavior in children. In B. A. Maher (Ed.), *Progress in experimental personality research* (Vol. 8, pp. 1–47). New York: Academic Press.

Feshbach, N. D., & Roe, K. (1968). Empathy in six- and seven-year-olds. *Child Development, 39,* 133–145.

Harris, P. L. (1995). From simulation to folk psychology: The case for development. In M. Davies & T. Stone (Eds.), *Folk psychology: The theory of mind debate* (pp. 207–231). Oxford, England: Blackwell.

Harwood, M. D., & Farrar, M. J. (2006). Conflicting emotions: The connection between affective perspective taking and theory of mind. *British Journal of Developmental Psychology, 24,* 401–418.

Hastings, P. D., Zahn-Waxler, C., & McShane, K. (2006). We are, by nature, moral creatures: Biological bases of concern for others. In M. Killen & J. G. Smetana (Eds.), *Handbook of moral development* (pp. 483–516). Mahwah, NJ: Erlbaum.

Hobson, J. A., Harris, R., García-Pérez, R., & Hobson, P. (2009). Anticipatory concern: A study in autism. *Developmental Science, 12,* 249–263.

Hoffman, M. L. (1976). Empathy, role taking, guilt, and development of altruistic motives. In T. Liekona (Ed.), *Moral development and behavior* (pp. 124–143). New York: Holt, Rinehart, & Winston.

Hoffman, M. L. (1982). Development of prosocial motivation: Empathy and guilt. In N. Eisenberg (Ed.), *The development of prosocial behavior* (pp. 281–338). New York: Academic Press.

Hoffman, M. L. (1984). Interaction of affect and cognition in empathy. In C. E. Izard, J. Kagan, & R. B. Zajonc (Eds.), *Emotion, cognition, and behavior* (pp. 103–131). Cambridge, England: Cambridge University Press.

Hoffman, M. L. (2000). *Empathy and moral development: Implications for caring and justice.* Cambridge, England: Cambridge University Press.

Holmgren, R. A., Eisenberg, N., & Fabes, R. A. (1998). The relations of children's situational empathy-related emotions to dispositional prosocial behavior. *International Journal of Behavioral Development, 22,* 169–193.

Iannotti, R. J. (1985). Naturalistic and structural assessments of prosocial behavior in preschool children: The influence of empathy and perspective taking. *Developmental Psychology, 21,* 46–55.

Karniol, R. (1982). Settings, scripts, and self-schemata: A cognitive analysis of the development of prosocial behavior. In N. Eisenberg (Ed.), *The development of prosocial behavior* (pp. 251–278). New York: Academic Press.

Krebs, D., & Russell, C. (1981). Role-taking and altruism: When you put yourself in the shoes of another, will they take you to their owner's aid? In J. P. Rushton & R. M. Sorrentino (Eds.), *Altruism and helping behavior* (pp. 137–165). Hillsdale, NJ: Erlbaum.

Mangold International GmbH. (2007). Interact (Version 8.0) [Computer software]. Arnstorf, Germany: Author.

Miller, P. A., & Eisenberg, N. (1988). The relation of empathy to aggressive and externalizing/antisocial behavior. *Psychological Bulletin, 103,* 324–344.

Onishi, K. H., & Baillargeon, R. (2005, April 8). Do 15-month-old infants understand false beliefs? *Science, 308,* 255–258.

Pessoa, L. (2008). On the relationship between emotion and cognition. *Nature Reviews Neuroscience, 9,* 148–158.

Radke-Yarrow, M., & Zahn-Waxler, C. (1984). Roots, motives, and patterns in children's prosocial behavior. In E. Staub, D. Bar-Tal, J. Karylowski, & J. Reykowski (Eds.), *Development and maintenance of prosocial behavior: International perspectives on positive behavior* (pp. 81–99). New York: Plenum Press.

Ruby, P., & Decety, J. (2004). How would *you* feel versus how do you think *she* would feel? A neuroimaging study of perspective-taking with social emotions. *Journal of Cognitive Neuroscience, 16,* 988–999.

Sagi, A., & Hoffman, M. L. (1976). Empathic distress in newborns. *Developmental Psychology, 12,* 175–176.

Smith, A. (2006). *The theory of moral sentiments.* Mineola, NY: Dover Publications. (Original work published 1759)

Southgate, V., Senju, A., & Csibra, G. (2007). Action anticipation through attribution of false belief in two-year-olds. *Psychological Science, 18,* 587–592.

Thompson, R. A. (1987). Empathy and emotional understanding: The early development of empathy. In N. Eisenberg & J. Strayer (Eds.), *Empathy and its development* (pp. 119–143). New York: Cambridge University Press.

van der Mark, I. L., van IJzendoorn, M. H., & Bakermans-Kranenburg, M. J. (2002). Development of empathy in girls during the second year of life: Associations with parenting, attachment, and temperament. *Social Development, 11,* 451–468.

Wellman, H. M., Phillips, A. T., & Rodriguez, T. (2000). Young children's understanding of perception, desire, and emotion. *Child Development, 71,* 895–912.

Young, S. K., Fox, N. A., & Zahn-Waxler, C. (1999). The relations between temperament and empathy in 2-year-olds. *Developmental Psychology, 35,* 1189–1197.

Zahn-Waxler, C., Radke-Yarrow, M., Wagner, E., & Chapman, M. (1992). Development of concern for others. *Developmental Psychology, 28,* 126–136.

Zahn-Waxler, C., Robinson, J. L., & Emde, R. N. (1992). The development of empathy in twins. *Developmental Psychology, 28,* 1038–1047.

A Closer Look 1   Is Biology Destiny? The Contributions of Genetics to Social
Development

In recent years, advances in medical technology have made the study of behavioral genetics a very hot topic. Genetic contributions to aspects of social development have just begun to receive research attention. This is a particularly challenging area of inquiry because the pathways that may link genetics to social behaviors are complex and multifaceted (i.e., one gene does not account for a specific behavior) and must also take into account environmental influences. Thus, despite newspaper headlines declaring the discovery of the "gene for aggression" or "gene for altruism," this avenue of research is still at its earliest stages.

Bakermans-Kranenburg and van IJzendoorn (2006) explored genetic and environmental contributions to the development of behavior problems. They took cheek swabs of 47 young children and found that some had a particular genetic marker that has been implicated in the expression of aggression (7-repeat DRD4 polymorphism). They also assessed children's behavior problems and observed maternal parenting behaviors. The results indicated significant gene by environment interaction effects. Children with the DRD4 genetic marker were more likely to display behavior problems only if they also experienced more insensitive parenting. That is, the genetic predisposition appeared to create a vulnerability that was only manifested under certain environmental conditions.

Bakermans-Kranenburg, M. J., & van IJzendoorn, M. H. (2006). Gene–environment interaction of the dopamine D4 receptor (DRD4) and observed maternal insensitivity predicting externalizing behavior in preschoolers. *Developmental Psychobiology, 48*, 406–409.

Classroom Exercises, Debates, and Discussion Questions

- *Classroom exercise.* Contemporary temperament researchers are interested in the dynamic interplay between children's temperamental traits and their environments. One context in which this might occur is in early child–parent interactions. Divide into groups and discuss how young children with the following different temperamental characteristics might "evoke" different responses from parents: (1) fussy, irritable, difficult to soothe; (2) fearful, cautious; (3) highly active; and (4) excitable, exuberant.
- *Classroom discussion.* Research into the possible genetic contributions to children's social development is still at its earliest stages. Notwithstanding, what are some of the possible moral, ethical, and societal implications of finding a genetic link with the development of child aggression or altruism? How might parents respond to this information?
- *Classroom discussion.* Studies show that toddlers will spontaneously help others even when they do not benefit from the gesture towards others. Researchers have debated whether this behavior reflects an early form of morality or something else. What would make this behavior a form of early morality? Can someone feel empathetic or sympathetic without acting in a kind or fair way towards others?
- *Classroom discussion.* A young child showing sympathy towards someone in distress has been characterized as a result of reciprocal experience. That is, the child is behaving sympathetically because he or she knows what sadness feels like and responds to another person in a manner that he or she would want to be treated. Based on personal observations of young children, what types of behaviors have you observed that appear to be reflecting sympathy or empathy?

- *Classroom discussion.* Young children who do *not* show sympathy or empathy for others are viewed as at increased risk for being maladjusted. Why is this lack of an emotional response a problem, and what might it signify that makes it a social deficit?
- *Classroom exercise.* Observe a preschool classroom for signs of empathy, sympathy, and affective responses (positive and negative) to others. Note the following information: (1) the recipient of the emotional display; (2) the target of the emotion; (3) the source of the exchange (what happened that led to the emotional reaction?); (4) the role of the teacher (did the teacher respond and if so, how?); and (5) the outcome. What are the most frequent types of emotional reactions (positive or negative)? How do teachers react most often, and what is the most common outcome?

Additional Resources

For more about biological and social-cognitive bases of emotions, see:

Calkins, S. D., Gill, K. L., Johnson, M. C., & Smith, C. L. (1999). Emotional reactivity and emotional regulation strategies as predictors of social behavior with peers during toddlerhood. *Social Development, 8*(3), 310–334.

De Schipper, J. C., Tavecchio, L. W. C., IJzendoorn, M. H.V., & Zeijl, J. V. (2004). Goodness-of-fit in center day care: Relations of temperament, stability, and quality of care with the child's adjustment. *Early Childhood Research Quarterly, 19,* 257–272.

Eisenberg, N., Fabes, R. A., & Spinrad, T. L. (2006). Prosocial development. In W. Damon & R. M. Lerner (Series Eds.), *Handbook of child psychology: Social, emotional, and personality development* (Vol. 3, pp. 646–718). New York: John Wiley & Sons.

Masten, C., Gillen-O'Neel, C., & Brown, C. S. (2010). Children's intergroup empathic processing: The roles of novel ingroup identification, situational distress, and social anxiety. *Journal of Experimental Child Psychology, 106,* 115–128.

Sanson, A. S., Hemphill, S. A., & Smart, D. (2004). Connections between temperament and social development: A review. *Social Development, 13,* 142–170.

Thompson, R. A. (2006). The development of the person: Social understanding, relationships, conscience, self. In W. Damon & R. M. Lerner (Series Eds.), *Handbook of child psychology: Social, emotional, and personality development* (Vol. 3, pp. 24–98). New York: John Wiley & Sons.

3 PARENT–CHILD ATTACHMENT RELATIONSHIPS

Introduction   65

The Nature of the Child's Ties   66

Jude Cassidy

Biological Bases of Attachment
Behavior   67

Attachment in Relation to Other
Behavioral Systems   70

The Attachment Bond   75

Multiple Attachments   77

Summary   80

Attachment Security in Infancy
and Early Adulthood: A Twenty-Year
Longitudinal Study   86

*Everett Waters, Susan Merrick, Dominique Treboux,
Judith Crowell, and Leah Albersheim*

Introduction   86

Method   87

Results   88

Discussion   89

The Effects of Infant Child Care on
Infant–Mother Attachment Security:
Results of the NICHD Study of Early
Child Care   91

NICHD Early Child Care Research Network

Introduction   91

Method   94

Results   99

Discussion   107

A Closer Look 2   How Do I Love
Thee? Attachment and Romantic
Relationships   114

Social Development in Childhood and Adolescence: A Contemporary Reader, First Edition. Edited by Melanie Killen
and Robert J. Coplan.
Editorial material and organization © 2011 Blackwell Publishing Ltd. Published 2011 by Blackwell Publishing Ltd.

Introduction

Sigmund Freud once wrote that the infant–mother relationship was "unique, without parallel, established unalterably for a whole lifetime as the first and strongest love-object and as the prototype for all later love-relations" (Freud, 1940, p. 45). Although few psychologists today would agree with the finality of this deterministic approach, subsequent research and theory support the notion that the early relationships established between infants and their primary caregivers (e.g., mothers, fathers, adoptive parents) have enduring implications for children's social development. Indeed, as described by influential attachment theorist and researcher Bowlby (1969, 1973), early relationship experiences with the primary caregiver lead to more generalized expectations about the self, others, and the world. Influenced by both Freud (1940) and Darwin (1877), Bowlby's writings have been central to most of what we know today about the parent–child attachment relationship.

Following from Bowlby, Ainsworth (1967) demonstrated the importance of infants' "secure" (i.e., positive) attachment relationships with their parents. A secure attachment relationship allows the infant to feel safe and protected during ambiguous or threatening situations. The infant also learns that they can rely on parents to comfort them when they are feeling upset. As a result, the attachment figure serves as a "secure base" from which the infant can explore and learn about their environment. Secure attachment relationships are thought to promote children's confidence, independence, agency, and foster the development of positive "internal working models." Internal working models are cognitive representations of oneself and other people used to interpret events and form expectations about the character of human relationships. However, relationships between infants and their parents can sometimes be characterized by anger, fear, or indifference. Such "insecure" attachment relationships may lead the child to develop more negative internal working models and come to view the world through a lens "distorted" by mistrust or anxiety.

Attachment relationships are thought to have "emergent properties"—that is, their properties are not predictable based on the individual characteristics of the individuals involved. In support of this notion, proponents of attachment theory cite research suggesting that it is not uncommon for a child to form quite different attachment relationships with his/her mother versus father. Notwithstanding, the establishment of a secure parent–child attachment relationship is predicted by warm and responsive parenting and an infant temperament that is not overly fussy or difficult to soothe.

The first reading in this chapter provides an overview of the theoretical bases for the study of attachment. Cassidy (2008) reviews the historical, conceptual, and methodological underpinnings of attachment relationships. As well, the enormous and continuing influence of attachment theory and research on the contemporary study of social development is highlighted. The second study concerns the long-term implications of attachment. In a 20-year longitudinal study, Waters et al. (2000) examined the prospective links between infant–mother attachment and young adults' internal representations of themselves and others. Finally, the last study addresses the controversial topic of attachment security and childcare. In response to earlier findings suggesting that children placed in childcare may be more likely to develop insecure attachment relationships with mothers, the *NICHD Early Childcare Research Network* conducted a national study of the effects of early childcare (i.e., during the first year of life) on children's emerging attachment relationships with mothers. Taken together, these three articles provide a window into the profound effects of attachment theory on the study of children's social development.

References

Ainsworth, M. D. S. (1967). *Infancy in Uganda: Infant care and the growth of love.* Baltimore: Johns Hopkins University Press.

Bowlby, J. (1969). *Attachment and loss: Vol. 1. Attachment.* London: Hogarth Press.

Bowlby, J. (1973). *Attachment and loss: Vol. 2. Separation, anxiety and anger.* New York: Basic Books.

Darwin, C. (1877). A biographical sketch of an infant. *Mind, 2,* 285–294.

Freud, S. (1940). *An outline of psychoanalysis.* London: Hogarth Press.

The Nature of the Child's Ties

Jude Cassidy

John Bowlby's work on attachment theory can be viewed as starting shortly after his graduation from Cambridge University, with the observations he made when he worked in a home for maladjusted boys. Two boys, both of whom had suffered disruptions in their relationships with their mothers, made important impressions on him. Bowlby's more systematic retrospective examination, published over a decade later as "Forty-Four Juvenile Thieves: Their Characters and Home Life" (Bowlby, 1944), as well as the observations of others (Bender & Yarnell, 1941; Goldfarb, 1943), convinced him that major disruptions in the mother–child relationship are precursors of later psychopathology. Bowlby's observations led not only to his belief that the child's relationship with the mother is important for later functioning, but also to a belief that this relationship is of critical immediate importance to the child. Bowlby, along with his colleague James Robertson, observed that children experienced intense distress when separated from their mothers, even if they were fed and cared for by others. A predictable pattern emerged—one of angry protest followed by despair (Robertson & Bowlby, 1952). Bowlby came to wonder why the mother is so important to the child.

At the time, the two widely accepted theories that offered explanations for the child's tie to the mother were both secondary-drive theories. Psychoanalytic and social learning theorists alike proposed that an infant's relationship with the mother emerges because she feeds the infant (e.g., Freud, 1910/1957; Sears, Maccoby, & Levin, 1957), and that the pleasure experienced upon having hunger drives satisfied comes to be associated with the mother's presence. When Bowlby was first developing attachment theory, he became aware of evidence from animal studies that seriously called this perspective into question. Lorenz (1935) noted that infant geese became attached to parents—even to objects—that did not feed them. Harlow (1958) observed that infant rhesus monkeys, in times of stress, preferred not the wire-mesh "mother"

that provided food, but the cloth-covered "mother" that afforded contact comfort. Soon systematic observations of human infants were made, and it became evident that babies too became attached to people who did not feed them (Ainsworth, 1967; Schaffer & Emerson, 1964). Years later, Bowlby recalled that

> this [secondary-drive] theory did not seem to me to fit the facts. For example, were it true, an infant of a year or two should take readily to whomever feeds him, and this clearly is not the case. But, if the secondary drive dependency theory was inadequate, what was the alternative? (1980b, p. 650)

Because he found himself dissatisfied with traditional theories, Bowlby sought a new explanation through discussion with colleagues from such fields as evolutionary biology, ethology, developmental psychology, cognitive science, and control systems theory (Bowlby, 1969/1982). He drew upon all of these fields to formulate the innovative proposition that the mechanisms underlying the infant's tie to the mother originally emerged as a result of evolutionary pressures. For Bowlby, this strikingly strong tie, evident particularly when disrupted, results not from an associational learning process (a secondary drive), but rather from a biologically based desire for proximity that arose through the process of natural selection. Bowlby (1958, 1960a, 1960b) introduced attachment theory in a series of papers, the first of which was "The Nature of the Child's Tie to His Mother." All of the major points of attachment theory were presented there in at least rudimentary form, providing, as Bretherton (1992) noted, "the first basic blueprint of attachment theory" (p. 762). These ideas were later elaborated in Bowlby's trilogy, *Attachment and Loss* (1969/1982, 1973, 1980a).

A member of Bowlby's research team during this period of initial formulation of attachment theory was a developmental psychologist visiting from Canada, Mary Salter Ainsworth. Her serendipitous connection with Bowlby—a friend had shown her a newspaper advertisement for a developmental research position—proved fortunate for the development of attachment theory. Ainsworth conducted two pioneering naturalistic observation studies of mothers and infants in which she applied the ethological principles of attachment theory as a framework. One of these investigations was conducted in the early 1950s in Uganda; the other was carried out in the early 1960s in Baltimore. These inquiries provided the most extensive home observation data to date and laid the foundation for Ainsworth's contributions to attachment theory, as well as for Bowlby's continued formulations. Ainsworth later created an assessment tool, the "Strange Situation," that triggered the productive flowering of the empirical study of individual differences in attachment quality—the research that is largely responsible for the place of attachment theory in contemporary developmental psychology.

The present chapter summarizes Bowlby's initial ethological approach to understanding the child's tie to the mother, along with elaborations based on more recent research and theorizing. First, I discuss the biological bases of attachment, describing the evolutionary roots of attachment behavior, the attachment behavioral system and its organization, the role of context in the system's operation, the role of emotion, the role of cognition, and individual differences in attachment. Next, I examine the attachment system in relation to other behavioral systems: the exploratory, fear, sociable, and caregiving systems. Third, I consider the nature of the child's attachment bond to his or her attachment figures, and describe how attachments differ from other affectional bonds. Finally, I discuss multiple attachments. Although Bowlby's idea that attachment is a lifespan phenomenon was present in his earliest writings (e.g., Bowlby, 1956), his principal focus was the tie to the mother during childhood, and I maintain that focus in this chapter.

Biological Bases of Attachment Behavior

The most fundamental aspect of attachment theory is its focus on the biological bases of attachment behavior (Bowlby, 1958, 1969/1982). "Attachment

behavior" has the predictable outcome of increasing proximity of the child to the attachment figure (usually the mother). Some attachment behaviors (smiling, vocalizing) are signaling behaviors that alert the mother to the child's interest in interaction, and thus serve to bring her to the child. Other behaviors (crying) are aversive, and bring the mother to the child to terminate them. Some (approaching and following) are active behaviors that move the child to the mother.

An evolutionary perspective

Bowlby proposed that during the time in which humans were evolving, when they lived in what he called "the environment of evolutionary adaptedness," genetic selection favored attachment behaviors because they increased the likelihood of child–mother proximity, which in turn increased the likelihood of protection and provided survival advantage. In keeping with the evolutionary thinking of his time, Bowlby emphasized survival of the species in his earliest theoretical formulations. By the time he revised *Attachment* (Volume 1 of his trilogy, *Attachment and Loss*; Bowlby, 1969/1982), he noted that advances in evolutionary theory necessitated a framework within which for all behavioral systems, including attachment, "the ultimate outcome to be attained is always the survival of the genes an individual is carrying" (p. 56).

Many predictable outcomes beneficial to the child are thought to result from the child's proximity to the parent (Bowlby, 1969/1982). These include feeding, learning about the environment, and social interaction, all of which are important. In the environment of evolutionary adaptedness, infants who were biologically predisposed to stay close to their mothers were less likely to be killed by predators, and it was for this reason that Bowlby referred to protection from predators as the "biological function" of attachment behavior.[1] Because of this biological function of protection, Bowlby considered infants to be predisposed particularly to seek their parents in times of distress. In a basic Darwinian sense, then, the proclivity to seek proximity is a behavioral adaptation in the same way that a fox's white coat on the tundra is an adaptation. Within this framework, attachment is considered a normal and healthy characteristic of humans throughout the lifespan, rather than a sign of immaturity that needs to be outgrown.

The attachment behavioral system

Attachment behaviors are thought to be organized into an "attachment behavioral system." Bowlby (1969/1982) borrowed the behavioral system concept from ethology to describe a species-specific system of behaviors that leads to certain predictable outcomes, at least one of which contributes to reproductive fitness. The concept of the behavioral system involves inherent motivation. There is no need to view attachment as the by-product of any more fundamental processes or "drive." Children are thought to become attached whether their parents are meeting their physiological needs or not. This idea is supported by evidence indicating that in contrast to what secondary-drive theories lead one to expect (e.g., Freud, 1910/1957; Sears et al., 1957), attachment is not a result of associations with feeding (Ainsworth, 1967; Harlow, 1962; Schaffer & Emerson, 1964). Furthermore, findings that infants become attached even to abusive mothers (Bowlby, 1956) suggest that the system is not driven by simple pleasurable associations. Bowlby's notion of the inherent motivation of the attachment system is compatible with Piaget's (1954) formulation of the inherent motivation of the child's interest in exploration.

Central to the concept of the attachment behavioral system is the notion that several different attachment behaviors are organized within the individual in response to a particular history of internal and external cues. Sroufe and Waters (1977) emphasized that the attachment behavioral system is "not a set of behaviors that are constantly and uniformly operative" (p. 1185). Rather, the "functional equivalence" of behaviors is noted, with a variety of behaviors having similar meanings and serving similar functions. As Bowlby (1969/1982) noted, "whether a child moves toward a mother by running, walking, crawling, shuffling or, in the case of a thalidomide child, by rolling, is thus of very little consequence compared to the set-goal of his locomotion, namely proximity to mother" (p. 373). The behaviors chosen in a particular context are the ones the infant finds most useful at that moment. With development, the child gains access to a greater variety of ways of achieving proximity, and learns which ones are most effective in which circumstances. Indeed, as Sroufe and Waters pointed out, this organizational perspective helps to explain stability within the context of both developmental and contextual changes. Thus an infant may maintain a stable internal organization of the attachment behavioral system in relation to the mother over time and across contexts, yet the specific behaviors used in the service of this organization may vary greatly. Thus, whereas a nonmobile infant may be expected to cry and reach out to the mother for contact, a mobile child may achieve the same goal of establishing contact by crawling after her.

This emphasis on the organization of the attachment behavioral system also helps to explain its operation in a "goal-corrected" manner. Unlike certain reflexes that, once activated, maintain a fixed course (e.g., sneezing, rooting), the attachment behavioral system enables the individual to respond flexibly to environmental changes while attempting to attain a goal. Bowlby used the analogy of a heat-seeking missile: Once launched, the missile does not remain on a preset course; rather, it incorporates information about changes in the target's location and adjusts its trajectory accordingly. Similarly, the infant is capable of considering changes in the mother's location and behavior (as well as other environmental changes) when attempting to maintain proximity to her. And the flexible use of a variety of attachment behaviors, depending on the circumstances, affords the infant greater efficiency in goal-corrected responses. For instance, an infant may see the mother starting to leave in an unfamiliar environment and may desire to increase proximity to her. The infant may begin by reaching for her and then following her (changing course as she moves); if this fails, calling or crying may be initiated.

Bowlby's approach to the organization of attachment behavior involves a control systems perspective. Drawing on observations of ethologists who described instinctive behavior in animals as serving to maintain them in a certain relation with the environment for long periods of time, Bowlby proposed that a control systems approach could also be applied to attachment behavior. He described the workings of a thermostat as an example of a control system. When the room gets too cold, the thermostat activates the heater; when the desired temperature is reached, the thermostat turns the heater off. Bowlby described children as wanting to maintain a certain proximity to their mothers. When a separation becomes too great in distance or time, the attachment system becomes activated, and when sufficient proximity has been achieved, it is terminated. Bowlby (following Bretherton, 1980; see Bowlby, 1969/1982) later described the attachment system as working slightly differently from a thermostat—as being continually activated (with variations of relatively more or less activation), rather than being completely turned off at times. According to Bowlby, the child's goal is not an object (e.g., the mother), but rather a state—a maintenance of the desired distance from the mother, depending on the circumstances. Bowlby described this idea of behavioral homeostasis as similar to the process of physiological homeostasis, whereby physiological systems (e.g., blood pressure and body temperature) are maintained within set limits. Like physiological control systems, a behavioral control system is thought to be organized within the central nervous system. According to Bowlby, the distinction between the two is that the latter is "one in which the set-limits concern the organism's relation to features of the environment and in which the limits are maintained by behavioral rather than physiological means" (p. 372).

The role of context

The child's desired degree of proximity to the parent is thought to vary under differing circumstances, and Bowlby (1969/1982) was interested in understanding how these different circumstances contribute to relative increases and decreases in activation of the attachment system. Thus he described two classes of factors that contribute to activation of the attachment system, both of which are conditions indicating danger or stress. One relates to conditions of the child (such as illness, fatigue, hunger, or pain). The other relates to conditions of the environment (such as the presence of threatening stimuli); particularly important are the location and behavior of the mother (such as her absence, withdrawal, or rejection of the child).

Interaction among these causal factors can be quite complex: Sometimes only one needs to be present, and at other times several are necessary. In regard to relative deactivation of the attachment system, Bowlby made it clear that his approach had nothing in common with a model in which a behavior stops when its energy supply is depleted (e.g., Freud, 1940/1964). In Bowlby's view, attachment behavior stops in the presence of a terminating stimulus. For most distressed infants, contact with their mothers is an effective terminating stimulus. Yet the nature of the stimulus that serves to terminate attachment behavior differs according to the degree of activation of the attachment system. If the attachment system is intensely activated, contact with the parent may be necessary to terminate it. If it is moderately activated, the presence or soothing voice of the parent (or even of a familiar substitute caregiver) may suffice. In either case, the infant is viewed as using the mother as a "safe haven" to return to in times of trouble. In sum, proximity seeking is activated when the infant receives information (from both internal and external sources) that a goal (the desired distance from the mother) is exceeded. It remains activated until the goal is achieved, and then it stops.

The role of emotion

According to Bowlby (1979), emotions are strongly associated with attachment:

> Many of the most intense emotions arise during the formation, the maintenance, the disruption, and the renewal of attachment relationships. The formation of a bond is described as falling in love, maintaining a bond as loving someone, and losing a partner as grieving over someone. Similarly, threat of loss arouses anxiety and actual loss gives rise to sorrow; whilst each of these situations is likely to arouse anger. The unchallenged maintenance of a bond is experienced as a source of joy. (p. 130)

It is likely that these affective responses originally resulted from evolutionary pressures. An infant predisposed to experience positive emotions in relation to an attachment and sadness with its loss may actively work to maintain attachments, which contribute in turn to the infant's enhanced reproductive fitness.

Bowlby also viewed emotions as important regulatory mechanisms within attachment relationships, noting, for instance, that anger and protest, as long as they do not become excessive and destructive, can serve to alert the attachment figure to the child's interest in maintaining the relationship (Bowlby, 1973). More recently, attachment theorists have noted the ways in which the regulation of emotions is used in the service of maintaining the relationship with the attachment figure, and they have noted that individual differences in attachment security have much to do with the ways in which emotions are responded to, shared, communicated about, and regulated within the attachment relationship (Cassidy, 1994; Cassidy & Berlin, 1994; Cassidy & Kobak, 1988; Kobak & Duemmler, 1994; Thompson & Meyer, 2007).

The role of cognition

Drawing on cognitive information theory, Bowlby (1969/1982) proposed that the organization of the attachment behavioral system involves cognitive components—specifically, mental representations of the attachment figure, the self, and the environment, all of which are largely based on experiences. Bretherton (1991) suggested that repeated attachment-related experiences could become organized as scripts, which would in turn become the building blocks of broader representations (see also Vaughn et al., 2006). (This emphasis on the importance of an individual's actual experiences was another way in which Bowlby's theory differed from that of Freud, who emphasized instead the role of internal fantasies.) Bowlby referred to these representations as "representational models" and as "internal working models." According to Bowlby, these models allow individuals to anticipate the future and make plans, thereby operating most efficiently. (There is in fact evidence that even young children are capable of using representations to make predictions about the future; see Heller & Berndt, 1981.) The child is thought to rely on these models, for instance, when making decisions about which specific attachment behavior(s) to use in a specific situation with a specific person. Representational models are considered to work best when they are relatively accurate reflections of reality, and conscious processing is required to check and revise models in order to keep them up to date. Extensive discussion of these cognitive

models is provided by Bretherton (1990) and by Main, Kaplan, and Cassidy (1985); see also Baldwin (1992) for a review of similarities between these models and a variety of constructs within the literatures on developmental, social, clinical, and cognitive psychology. Bowlby (1969/1982, 1973, 1979, 1980a) also discussed the role within the attachment system of other cognitive processes, such as object permanence, discrimination learning, generalization, nonconscious processing, selective attention and memory, and interpretative biases.

Individual differences

In extending the biological emphasis of Bowlby's initial theorizing, Main (1990) proposed that the biologically based human tendency to become attached is paralleled by a biologically based ability to be flexible to the range of likely caregiving environments. This flexibility is thought to contribute to variations associated with quality of attachment. Whereas nearly all children become attached (even to mothers who abuse them; Bowlby, 1956), not all are securely attached. Striking individual differences exist. Secure attachment occurs when a child has a mental representation of the attachment figure as available and responsive when needed. Infants are considered to be insecurely attached when they lack such a representation. Bowlby's early clinical observations led him to predict that just as feeding does not cause attachment in infants, so individual differences in feeding (e.g., breast vs. bottle feeding) do not contribute to individual differences in attachment quality. In one of his earliest writings, Bowlby (1958) predicted that the important factor is "the extent to which the mother has permitted clinging and following, and all the behavior associated with them, or has refused them" (p. 370). This prediction has since gained empirical support (e.g., Ainsworth, Blehar, Waters, & Wall, 1978; see also De Wolff & van IJzendoorn, 1997).

Attachment in Relation to Other Behavioral Systems

The attachment behavioral system can be fully understood only in terms of its complex interplay with other biologically based behavioral systems. Bowlby highlighted two of these as being particularly related to the attachment system in young children: the exploratory behavioral system and the fear behavioral system. The activation of these other systems is related to activation of the attachment system. Activation of the fear system generally heightens activation of the attachment system. In contrast, activation of the exploratory system can, under certain circumstances, reduce activation of the attachment system. As any parent knows, providing a novel set of car keys can at least temporarily distract a baby who wants to be picked up, as long as the infant's attachment system is not intensely activated. These two behavioral systems are discussed in this section, as are the sociable and caregiving behavioral systems.

The exploratory system

The links between the exploratory behavioral system and the attachment behavioral system are thought to be particularly intricate. According to Bowlby, the exploratory system gives survival advantages to the child by providing important information about the workings of the environment: how to use tools, build structures, obtain food, and negotiate physical obstacles. Yet unbridled exploration with no attention to potential hazards can be dangerous. The complementary yet mutually inhibiting nature of the exploratory and attachment systems is thought to have evolved to ensure that while the child is protected by maintaining proximity to attachment figures, he or she nonetheless gradually learns about the environment through exploration. According to Ainsworth (1972), "the dynamic equilibrium between these two behavioral systems is even more significant for development (and for survival) than either in isolation" (p. 118).

The framework that best captures the links between the attachment and exploratory systems is that of an infant's use of an attachment figure as a "secure base from which to explore"—a concept first described by Ainsworth (1963) and central to attachment theory (Ainsworth et al., 1978; Bowlby, 1969/1982, 1988). On the basis of her observations during the infant's first year of life, Ainsworth referred to an "attachment–exploration balance" (Ainsworth, Bell, & Stayton, 1971). Most infants

balance these two behavioral systems, responding flexibly to a specific situation after assessing both the environment's characteristics and the caregiver's availability and likely behavior. For instance, when the infant experiences the environment as dangerous, exploration is unlikely. Furthermore, when the attachment system is activated (perhaps by separation from the attachment figure, illness, fatigue, or unfamiliar people and surroundings), infant exploration and play decline. Conversely, when the attachment system is not activated (e.g., when a healthy, well-rested infant is in a comfortable setting with an attachment figure nearby), exploration is enhanced. Thus attachment, far from interfering with exploration, is viewed as fostering exploration. Bowlby (1973) described as important not only the physical presence of an attachment figure, but also the infant's belief that the attachment figure will be available if needed. A converging body of empirical work, in which maternal physical or psychological presence was experimentally manipulated, has provided compelling evidence of the theoretically predicted associations between maternal availability and infant exploration (Ainsworth & Wittig, 1969; Carr, Dabbs, & Carr, 1975; Rheingold, 1969; Sorce & Emde, 1981).

The fear system

The fear behavioral system is also thought to be closely linked to the attachment system. For Bowlby, the biological function of the fear system, like that of the attachment system, is protection. It is biologically adaptive for children to be frightened of certain stimuli. Without such fear, survival and reproduction would be reduced. Bowlby (1973) described "natural clues to danger"—stimuli that are not inherently dangerous, but that increase the likelihood of danger. These include darkness, loud noises, aloneness, and sudden looming movements. Because the attachment and fear systems are intertwined, so that frightened infants increase their attachment behavior, infants who find these stimuli frightening are considered more likely to seek protection and thus to survive to pass on their genes. The presence or absence of the attachment figure is thought to play an important role in the activation of an infant's fear system, such that an available and accessible attachment figure makes the infant much less susceptible to fear, and there is evidence that this is so (Morgan & Ricciuti, 1969; Sorce & Emde, 1981). In fact, even photographs of the mother can calm a fearful infant, as can "security blankets" for children who are attached to such objects (Passman & Erck, 1977; Passman & Weisberg, 1975).

The sociable system

A complete understanding of the attachment behavioral system rests on an understanding of its distinction from the sociable (or "affiliative") behavioral system.[2] Although Bowlby did not discuss this behavioral system as extensively as he did some others, he did point out, as have other theorists, that the sociable system is distinct from the attachment behavioral system. Bowlby (1969/1982) wrote,

> "Affiliation" was introduced by Murray (1938): "Under this heading are classed all manifestations of friendliness and goodwill, of the desire to do things in company with others." As such it is a much broader concept than attachment and is not intended to cover behavior that is directed towards one or a few particular figures, which is the hallmark of attachment behavior. (p. 229)

According to Ainsworth (1989), it is "reasonable to believe that there is some basic behavioral system that has evolved in social species that leads individuals to seek to maintain proximity to conspecifics, even to those to whom they are not attached or otherwise bonded, and despite the fact that wariness is likely to be evoked by those who are unfamiliar" (p. 713). Harlow and Harlow (1965) described the "peer affectional system through which infants and children interrelate ... and develop persisting affection for each other" as an "affectional system" distinct from those involving infant and parents (p. 288). Bronson (1972) referred to affiliation as an "adaptive system" present in infancy and separate from attachment. Bretherton and Ainsworth (1974) examined the interplay among several behavioral systems in infants, including the sociable and the attachment systems, and Greenberg and Marvin (1982) examined this interplay in preschool children. Hinde (1974) described nonhuman primates'

play with peers, which he identified as different from mother–child interaction, as "consum[ing] so much time and energy that it must be of crucial adaptive importance" (p. 227).

The sociable system is thus defined as the organization of the biologically based, survival-promoting tendency to be sociable with others. An important predictable outcome of activation of this system is that individuals are likely to spend at least part of their time in the company of others. Given evidence from the primate literature that individuals in the company of others are much less likely to be killed by predators (Eisenberg, 1966), it seems reasonable to assume that humans too would derive the important survival advantage of protection from associating with others. The sociable system is likely to contribute to an individual's survival and reproductive fitness in other important ways: Primates biologically predisposed to be sociable with others increase their ability to gather food, build shelter, and create warmth; they learn about the environment more efficiently; and they gain access to a group of others with whom they may eventually mate (see Huntingford, 1984, for a review). Strong evidence of the importance of the sociable system for the development of young nonhuman primates comes from several studies, most notably those of Harlow and his associates (e.g., Harlow, 1969), in which monkeys reared with their mothers but without peers were seriously hindered in their social development and could not mate or parent effectively (see also Miller, Caul, & Mirsky, 1967).

Observations of both humans and other primates clearly show differences between the attachment and sociable systems in what activates behavior, in what terminates behavior, and in the way behaviors are organized (Bretherton & Ainsworth, 1974; Harlow, 1969; Vandell, 1980). The sociable system is most likely to be activated when the attachment system is not activated. According to Bowlby,

> A child seeks his attachment-figure when he is tired, hungry, ill, or alarmed and also when he is uncertain of that figure's whereabouts; when the attachment-figure is found he wants to remain in proximity to him or her and may want also to be held or cuddled. By contrast, a child seeks a playmate when he is in good spirits and confident of the whereabouts of his attachment-figure;

when the playmate is found, moreover, the child wants to engage in playful interaction with him or her. If this analysis is right, the roles of attachment-figure and playmate are distinct. (1969/1982, p. 307)

Lewis, Young, Brooks, and Michalson (1975) interpreted their observations of pairs of 1-year-olds and their mothers similarly: "Mothers are good for protection, peers for watching and playing with" (p. 56).

The caregiving system

In one of his earliest writings, Bowlby (1956) pointed out that further understanding of attachment could be gained from examination of the mother's tie to her infant. Bowlby later (1984) wrote briefly about "parenting behavior" from a biological perspective as "like attachment behavior, ... in some degree preprogrammed" (p. 271). He described the biologically based urge to care for and protect children, yet he simultaneously viewed individual differences in the nature of parenting as emerging largely through learning. Although Bowlby wrote little about this topic, his ethological perspective, his ideas about interrelated behavioral systems, and his interest in attachment-related processes across the lifespan lend themselves readily to an elaboration of the parental side of what he (Bowlby, 1969/1982) called the "attachment–caregiving social bond." Solomon and George (1996; George & Solomon, 1996) have filled this void, writing in detail about the "caregiving system." [...] it is difficult to delineate precisely which aspects of parenting behavior should be considered part of the caregiving system. I propose that the term "caregiving system" be used to describe a subset of parental behaviors—only those behaviors designed to promote proximity and comfort when the parent perceives that the child is in real or potential danger. The chief behavior within this system is retrieval (Bowlby, 1969/1982); others include calling, reaching, grasping, restraining, following, soothing, and rocking.[3]

Just as the child's interactions with the parent involve more than the attachment system (e.g., a child may approach the father not for comfort but for play), so other parental systems may be activated during interactions with the child (Bowlby, 1969/1982).

These various behavioral systems can all be viewed as enhancing the child's survival and reproductive fitness (e.g., teaching, feeding, playing). A parent may be differentially responsive to a child when each of these different parental behavioral systems is activated (e.g., sensitive when teaching or feeding, yet insensitive when the caregiving system is activated). The predominance of each of these parental behavioral systems varies considerably both across and within cultures. For instance, as Bretherton (1985) pointed out, among Mayan Indians in Mexico, mothers rarely serve as playmates for their infants but are quite available and responsive as caregivers (Brazelton, 1977). Similarly, Ainsworth (1990) noted that "the mothers of Ganda babies who were securely attached to them almost never played with them, even though they were highly sensitive caregivers" (p. 482). Within-culture variation exists as well: Within a particular culture, one mother may be a readily available attachment figure, yet stodgy and inept in the role of playmate; another mother may be comfortable in interaction with her children only in her roles as teacher or coach when attention is focused on a task or skill, and may be uncomfortable with attachment-related interactions. Main, Hesse, and Kaplan (2005) have proposed that such parental discomfort (anxiety) may emerge when infant behavior interferes with parents' ability to preserve "the state of mind that had seemed optimal for maintenance of the relationship to their own parents during childhood" (p. 292). (For additional discussion of the ways in which particular parents experience discomfort when faced with particular infant behavior, see Cassidy et al., 2005.)

As is the case with the child's attachment system, the predictable outcome of activation of the caregiving system is parent–child proximity, and the biological function is protection of the child. In most cases, both parent and child work together to maintain a comfortable degree of proximity. If the child moves away, the parent will retrieve him or her; if the parent moves away, the child will follow or signal for the parent to return. Following Bowlby's (1969/1982) thinking, it seems likely that when the caregiving system is relatively activated, the child's attachment system can be relatively deactivated; attachment behaviors are not needed, because the parent has assumed responsibility for maintaining proximity.

If the caregiving system is not relatively activated, then the child's attachment system becomes activated, should the context call for it. This is one reason why the mother's leaving is particularly disturbing to a child and particularly likely to activate attachment behavior. This "dynamic equilibrium" (Bowlby, 1969/1982, p. 236) contributes to understanding the notion of the mother's providing "a secure base from which to explore." The mother's monitoring of infant–mother proximity frees the infant from such monitoring and permits greater attention to exploring. For instance, if, when visiting a new park, a mother actively follows the infant in his or her explorations, the infant is much more likely to cover a wide area than if the mother sits on a bench talking with friends. Empirical support for this proposition comes from a study in which the simple act of a mother's diverting her attention away from the infant to a magazine in a brief laboratory procedure reduced the quality of infant exploration (Sorce & Emde, 1981).

Yet parent and child do not always agree on what distance between them is acceptable. For example, a mother's fear system may be activated and prompt her to retrieve an infant whose activated exploratory system leads him or her to prefer to move away. Parents and their children may also differ in terms of how their priorities guide activation of their behavioral systems. For instance, when an infant's attachment system is activated in the presence of the mother, the infant's sole wish is for her to respond. Although such infant behavior is usually a powerful activating stimulus for the mother's caregiving system, the mother may choose among several competing needs and may or may not provide care (Trivers, 1974). The child's concern is immediate and focused; the mother's concerns may be more diffuse and long-range. The mother may have to leave the infant to work to support the family (in which case activation of her food-getting behavioral system has taken precedence over her caregiving system). Or she may have several children to whose needs she must attend. Main (1990) has proposed that from an evolutionary perspective, maternal insensitivity to a particular child may be useful to the mother if it maximizes the total number of surviving off-spring.

As is true for many behavioral systems, activation of the caregiving system results from both internal and external cues. Internal cues include presence of hormones, cultural beliefs, parental state (e.g., whether the parent is tired or sick), and activation of other parental behavioral systems (e.g., exploratory, food-getting, fear). External cues include state of the environment (e.g., whether it is familiar, whether there is danger, whether others are present and who these others are), state of the infant (e.g., whether the infant is sick or tired), and behavior of the infant (e.g., whether he or she is exhibiting attachment behavior). Activation of the caregiving system has crucial implications for the infant, who cannot otherwise survive. Ethologists have suggested that infants therefore have evolved characteristics that serve to activate the caregiving system: their endearing "babyish" features (the large rounded head with the high forehead, the small nose) and their thrashing arm movements. Attachment behaviors, of course, motivate parents to respond; even aversive behaviors, such as crying, typically motivate parents to provide care in order to terminate them. Given that an infant's attachment system is activated by stimuli that indicate an increased risk of danger (e.g., loud noise, looming objects), a parent who increases proximity when a child's attachment behavior is activated increases the likelihood of being able to protect the child, should the danger prove real. Similarly, when the parent perceives or expects danger that the child does not, parental proximity also increases the likelihood of survival. Thus it is likely that the close link between the child's attachment and fear systems is paralleled by a close link between the parent's caregiving and fear systems, such that when a parent's fear system is activated, so too is his or her caregiving system.

Fear is only one of the powerful emotions likely to be linked to the caregiving system. Just as attachment is associated with powerful emotions (Bowlby, 1979), so is the caregiving system. These emotions may in fact be as strong as any an individual experiences in his or her lifetime. The birth of a first child (which establishes the adult as a parent) is often accompanied by feelings of great joy; threats to the child are accompanied by anxiety; the death of a child brings profound grief. This intertwining of the caregiving system with intense emotions may result from selective pressures during evolution: Enhanced reproductive fitness may result when, for instance, a parent's anxiety about threats to a child prompts the parent to seek effective interventions.

The role of parental soothing as a component of the caregiving system merits consideration. Why would a parent who safely holds a crying child out of reach of a large barking dog continue to comfort the child? Why would a parent pick up a distressed child whom the parent perceives to be in no danger? What could be the role of such soothing behaviors? I propose that soothing behaviors serve indirectly to facilitate the parent's monitoring of potential or real dangers to the child. Parental provision of contact usually comforts a distressed child. If the child continues to be distressed for a substantial time following contact, there may be another threat of which the parent is unaware. Through continuing attempts to soothe the child, the parent gains information about threat to the child. The parent may not realize, for instance, that the child has a painful splinter in his or her foot. Furthermore, there are many ways in which inconsolable crying (beyond early infancy) can signal serious health problems. And a parent will not know whether crying is inconsolable unless the parent attempts to console.

Further research is needed to illuminate additional aspects of the caregiving system. First, given that there are times when the child's distress does not stem from activation of his or her attachment system, research could examine whether it is best to consider parental behavior in response to such distress as part of the caregiving system. For instance, it seems plausible that a child may get upset because his or her exploratory system is frustrated, and that the child's distress prompts the mother to pick the child up and comfort him or her. It may be that the mother's behavior then contributes to the child's attachment-related expectations about the mother's likely responses to his or her distress, and thus to the formation of the child's representational model of the mother. Second, research is needed to determine how separate the caregiving system is from other parental systems, and whether it is only the caregiving system that affects the child's attachment system. Third, it is unclear whether it is best to think of a single parental caregiving system in humans or of separate maternal and paternal caregiving systems. Harlow has proposed separate maternal and paternal systems in primates (Harlow, Harlow, & Hansen, 1963). If two separate systems exist in humans, there must be considerable overlap, even though genetic, hormonal, and cultural factors may contribute to differences in the specific characteristics of these systems.[4]

The Attachment Bond

Whereas "attachment behavior" is behavior that promotes proximity to the attachment figure, and the "attachment behavioral system" is the organization of attachment behaviors within the individual, an "attachment bond" refers to an affectional tie. Ainsworth (1989) described an attachment bond not as dyadic, but rather as characteristic of the individual, "entailing representation in the internal organization of the individual" (p. 711). Thus this bond is not one between two people; it is instead a bond that one individual has to another individual who is perceived as stronger and wiser (e.g., the bond of an infant to the mother). A person can be attached to a person who is not in turn attached to him or her; as described below, this is usually the case with infants and their parents.[5]

The attachment bond is a specific type of a larger class of bonds that Bowlby and Ainsworth referred to as "affectional bonds." Throughout the lifespan, individuals form a variety of important affectional bonds that are not attachments. To make it completely clear what an attachment bond is, one needs to delineate what it is not. Ainsworth (1989) described the criteria for affectional bonds, and then the additional criterion for attachment bonds. First, an affectional bond is persistent, not transitory. Second, an affectional bond involves a specific person—a figure who is not interchangeable with anyone else. This bond reflects "the attraction that one individual has for another *individual*" (Bowlby, 1979, p. 67, emphasis in original). For instance, the sadness associated with the loss of a close friend is not lessened by the fact that one has other close friends. Bowlby emphasized specificity when he stated: "To complain because a child does not welcome being comforted by a kind but strange woman is as foolish as to complain that a young man deeply in love is not enthusiastic about some other good-looking girl" (1956, p. 58). Third, the relationship is emotionally significant. Fourth, the individual wishes to maintain proximity to or contact with the person.

The nature and extent of the proximity/contact desired vary as a function of a variety of factors (e.g., age and state of the individual, environmental conditions). Fifth, the individual feels distress at involuntary separation from the person. Even though the individual may choose separation from the figure, the individual experiences distress when proximity is desired but prevented. In addition to these five criteria, an additional criterion exists for an attachment bond: The individual seeks security and comfort in the relationship with the person (Ainsworth, 1989). (The attachment is considered "secure" if one achieves security and "insecure" if one does not; it is the seeking of security that is the defining feature. See also Hinde, 1982; Weiss, 1982.) It is this final criterion that leads attachment researchers to refer to "parental bonds" to children and "child attachments" to parents: When the roles are reversed and a parent attempts to seek security from a young child, it is "almost always not only a sign of pathology in the parent but also a cause of it in the child" (Bowlby, 1969/1982, p. 377). (The situation is viewed differently later in life, when a middle-aged offspring takes care of an increasingly infirm and dependent parent.)

The existence of an attachment bond cannot be inferred from the presence or absence of attachment behavior. To begin with, it is important to remember that most behaviors can serve more than one behavioral system (Bretherton & Ainsworth, 1974; Sroufe & Waters, 1977). Thus, for instance, every approach does not serve the attachment system; even though approach can be an attachment behavior, it can also be an exploratory or sociable behavior. Yet it is also the case that distressed infants separated from their mothers may seek comfort from strangers (Ainsworth et al., 1978; Bretherton, 1978; Rheingold, 1969), and approach in that context is considered attachment behavior. Nonetheless, an enduring attachment bond of an infant to a stranger cannot be assumed to exist, and it is thus possible for an infant to direct attachment behavior to an individual to whom he or she is not attached. Some babies will stop crying when comforted by a stranger, but observations in the Strange Situation reveal that this comfort is generally not as satisfying as that provided by the mother (Ainsworth et al., 1978).

Similarly, even during a period when the child is directing no attachment behavior to the parent, the child is still attached. When, for instance, a contented child is in comfortable surroundings with the mother present, the attachment system is not likely to be activated to a level that triggers attachment behavior. Thus activation of attachment behavior is largely situational; it may or may not be present at any given time. The attachment bond, however, is considered to exist consistently over time, whether or not attachment behavior is present. Bowlby (1969/1982) pointed out that even the cessation of behavior during a long separation cannot be considered an indication that the attachment bond no longer exists.

The strength of attachment behaviors is sometimes mistakenly regarded as reflecting the "strength" of the attachment bond. There are striking variations in strength of activation of attachment behaviors across contexts and across children. Yet no evidence exists that these variations in themselves map onto variations in child–mother attachment in any meaningful way. According to Ainsworth (1972),

> to equate strength of attachment with strength of attachment behavior under ordinary nonstressful circumstances would lead to the conclusion that an infant who explores when his mother is present is necessarily less attached than one who constantly seeks proximity to his mother, whereas, in fact, his freedom to explore away from her may well reflect the healthy security provided by a harmonious attachment relationship. (p. 119)

Ainsworth characterized individual differences in relationships with an attachment figure as variations in quality rather than in strength. Similarly, it is a mistake to label as "very attached" a young child who clings fearfully to the mother; such attachment behavior may reflect insecure attachment or secure use of the mother as a safe haven, depending on the context.

Given that the strength of attachment behaviors should not be confused with the strength of an attachment bond, is strength nonetheless a useful dimension on which to consider an attachment bond? One might assume that Bowlby's proposition that children develop "attachment hierarchies" (discussed in the following section) implies that some attachments are stronger than others. Although Bowlby himself did occasionally use this terminology— for example, "How do we understand the origin and nature of this extraordinarily strong tie between child and mother?" (Bowlby, 1988, p. 161)—such usage was relatively rare, particularly when he was comparing one attachment with another (when doing so, he referred instead to "secure" and "insecure" attachments). Ainsworth (1982a) suggested that Hinde's (1979) notion of "penetration," as opposed to notions of either strength or intensity, may provide a more useful framework for characterizing an attachment bond. According to Hinde, penetration is a dimension of relationships that describes the centrality of one person to another's life—the extent to which a person penetrates a variety of aspects of the other person's life. Ainsworth pointed out that the concept of penetration is particularly useful when considering the changing nature of a child's attachment to the parent as the child grows older. She proposed that it may be more appropriate not to talk of the bond as becoming "weaker," but rather as characterizing a relationship that penetrates fewer aspects of the growing child's life as he or she comes to spend more time away from the parents and to develop new relationships.

For Bowlby (1969/1982), there are two important propositions about the nature of the attachment bond within the larger context of a relationship. First, the attachment bond reflects only one feature of the child's relationship with the mother: the component that deals with behavior related to the child's protection and security in time of stress. The mother not only serves as an attachment figure, but may also serve as playmate, teacher, or disciplinarian. These various roles are not incompatible, and it is possible that two or more may be filled by the same person. Thus, for example, a child may direct attachment behavior to the mother when he or she is frightened, and yet at other times may interact with her in ways relatively unrelated to attachment (e.g., play). Consequently, it would be a mistake to label as an attachment behavior a child's approach to the mother in order to engage in peekaboo. As Bretherton (1980) noted, a behavior may serve different behavioral systems at different times, even when it is directed to the same individual. Yet it is important to note that even though a mother may be a frequent playmate for her 5-year-old, it does not negate the fact that this relationship is essentially characterized as an attachment

relationship. Bowlby summarized his position on this issue as follows:

> A parent—child relationship is by no means exclusively that of attachment—caregiving. The only justification, therefore, for referring to the bond between a child and his mother in this way is that the shared dyadic programme given top priority is one of attachment—caregiver. (p. 378)

Second, an attachment bond cannot be presumed to exist even though a relationship may contain an attachment component. As noted earlier, the fact that a 1-year-old distressed about separation from the mother will direct his or her attachment behaviors to a friendly stranger does not mean that the relationship with the stranger involves an attachment bond. This is true even in more ongoing relationships, such as relationships with peers. A young child may routinely direct attachment behavior to a close friend and feel comfort in the friend's presence (particularly in a context such as school, when a parent is not present) without that relationship's involving an attachment bond. This is evident from the fact that the loss of such a friend usually does not have the devastating effects on the child that loss of a true attachment figure (e.g., a parent) has. Thus, even though children may at times turn to friends for comfort (Hazan & Zeifman, 1994), these friendships need not be attachment relationships.

Multiple Attachments

Bowlby stated three principal propositions about multiple attachments in infancy. First, most young infants are thought to form more than one attachment. According to Bowlby (1969/1982), "almost from the first, many children have more than one figure to whom they direct attachment behavior" (p. 304).[6] Indeed, empirical observations have revealed that the majority of children become attached to more than one familiar person during their first year (Ainsworth, 1967; Schaffer & Emerson, 1964). According to Bowlby, "responsiveness to crying and readiness to interact socially are amongst the most relevant variables" (p. 315) in determining who will serve as an attachment figure. In most cultures, this means that the biological parents, older siblings, grandparents, aunts, and uncles are most likely to serve as attachment figures. Generally, the mother's role as an attachment figure is clear. The father is also particularly likely to become an additional attachment figure early in the infant's life. Observational studies have revealed that fathers are competent caregivers (Belsky, Gilstrap, & Rovine, 1984), and that children use their fathers as attachment figures (Ainsworth, 1967). Ainsworth (1967) noted the special infant–father relationship that sometimes emerged in Uganda:

> It seemed to be especially to the father that these other attachments were formed, even in the cases of babies who saw their fathers relatively infrequently. One can only assume that there was some special quality in the father's interaction with his child—whether of tenderness or intense delight—which evoked in turn a strength of attachment disproportionate to the frequency of his interaction with the baby. (p. 352)

Furthermore, there is evidence that individual differences in quality of infant–father attachment are related to paternal behavior: Infants are more likely to be securely attached to fathers who have been sensitively responsive to them (see van IJzendoorn & De Wolff, 1997, for meta-analytic findings). Evidence has also emerged that siblings (Stewart & Marvin, 1984; Teti & Ablard, 1989) and day care providers (Ahnert, Pinquart, & Lamb, 2006) can serve as attachment figures. In unusual and stressful situations, infants can even become attached to other infants (see Freud & Dann's [1951] observations of child survivors of a concentration camp).

Second, although there is usually more than one attachment figure, the potential number of attachment figures is not limitless. Bretherton (1980, p. 195) has described the infant as having a "small hierarchy of major caregivers," which is in contrast to the larger group of individuals with whom the infant has other sorts of relationships (Weinraub, Brooks, & Lewis, 1977). Marvin, VanDevender, Iwanaga, LeVine, and LeVine (1977) reported that most Hausa infants observed in Nigeria were attached to no more than

three or four attachment figures; Grossmann and Grossmann (1991) reported similar observations for a sample of German infants.

Third, although most infants have multiple attachment figures, it is important not to assume that an infant treats all attachment figures as equivalent, or that they are interchangeable; rather, an "attachment hierarchy" is thought to exist. According to Bowlby (1969/1982), "it is a mistake to suppose that a young child diffuses his attachment over many figures in such a way that he gets along with no strong attachment to anyone, and consequently without missing any particular person when that person is away" (p. 308). Bowlby proposed that this strong tendency for infants to prefer a principal attachment figure for comfort and security be termed "monotropy" (see also Ainsworth, 1964, 1982b).[7] Bowlby cited as evidence of this phenomenon the tendency of children in institutions to select, if given the opportunity, one "special" caregiver as their own (see Burlingham & Freud, 1944). Ainsworth (1982b) described responses to major separations from and losses of attachment figures as further support for the idea that a hierarchy exists: "The child would tolerate major separations from subsidiary figures with less distress than comparable separations from the principal attachment figure. Nor could the presence of several attachment figures altogether compensate for the loss of the principal attachment figure" (p. 19).[8] (For similar findings, see Heinicke & Westheimer, 1966.)

Also consistent with this hierarchy notion are data from observational studies of both mothers and fathers, which show that most infants prefer to seek comfort from their mothers when distressed; in the mother's absence, however, an infant is likely to seek and derive comfort and security from other attachment figures as well (Kagan, Kearsley, & Zelazo, 1978; Lamb, 1976a, 1976b, 1978; Rutter, 1981; see also Ainsworth, 1967; Schaffer & Emerson, 1964). For a review of the relatively few experimental studies examining attachment hierarchies, and a discussion of the relevant methodological issues, see Colin (1996). See also Kobak, Rosenthal, and Serwik (2005) for data and a discussion of attachment hierarchies in middle childhood, and Kobak, Rosenthal, Zajac, and Madsen (2007) for a discussion of how attachment hierarchies are transformed during adolescence.

What determines the structure of an infant's attachment hierarchy? Colin (1996) listed a likely set of contributing factors: "(1) how much time the infant spends in each figure's care; (2) the quality of care each provides, (3) each adult's emotional investment in the child, and (4) social cues" (p. 194). To this list, I would add that the repeated presence across time of the figure in the infant's life, even if each encounter is relatively brief, is likely to be important.

Why would monotropy have evolved as a tendency of human infants? Neither Bowlby nor Ainsworth addressed this question. I propose three possibilities here, all of which may operate simultaneously. The fact that there may be multiple ways in which the tendency toward monotropy contributes to infant survival and reproductive fitness increases the likelihood of its emerging through genetic selection. First, the infant's tendency to prefer a principal attachment figure may contribute to the establishment of a relationship in which that one attachment figure assumes principal responsibility for the child. Such a relationship should increase the child's likelihood of survival by helping to ensure that care of the child is not overlooked. This system seems more practical than the alternative, wherein a large number of caregivers have equal responsibility for a large number of offspring; this latter system might leave any individual child "falling between the cracks."

Second, monotropy may be most efficient for the child. When faced with danger, the child does not have to make a series of assessments and judgments about who may be most readily available, most responsive, and best suited to help. Rather, the child has a quick, automatic response to seek his or her principal attachment figure.

Third, monotropy may be the child's contribution to a process I term "reciprocal hierarchical bonding," in which the child matches an attachment hierarchy to the hierarchy of the caregiving in his or her environment. Evolutionary biologists writing on parental investment (e.g., Trivers, 1972) have suggested that adults vary in their investment in offspring largely as a function of the extent to which this investment contributes to the transmission of the adults' genes (i.e., their reproductive fitness). Following this reasoning, it should be most adaptive for the child to use as a principal attachment figure the person who, correspondingly, is most strongly bonded to him or her (i.e., the person who provides the most parental investment and has the most to gain—in terms of reproductive fitness—from the baby's healthy development). In most cases, it is the biological mother who has the greatest biological investment in the child. With the exception of an identical twin, there is no one with whom the child shares more genes than the mother (50%). Although the biological father and siblings also share 50% of their genes with a child, their investments are nonetheless considered to be less, because (1) only the mother can be certain of a true biological connection; (2) the mother devotes her body and bodily resources to the infant for 9 months of pregnancy and often nurses the child for a considerable period thereafter; and (3) the mother has fewer opportunities to produce additional offspring than fathers and siblings do. If this process of reciprocal hierarchical bonding exists, it may help to explain not only monotropy, but also, in part, why the biological mother is generally the principal attachment figure.

The infant's selection of the principal attachment figure occurs over time, and it is important to consider why it takes a period of time for this centrally important attachment to crystalize rather than happening immediately, as it does in some other mammals. Jay Belsky (personal communication, October 2007) has proposed two possible explanations, in addition to the obvious fact that human newborns do not possess the skills needed to form attachments because of their immature status at birth. First, the mother may not survive childbirth; many surely did not do so during our ancestral past. Second, the infant needs to be able to discern which individual is making the intensive investment upon which he or she is so dependent—a judgment that is likely to take some time.

Given the existence of multiple attachments, what is the course of their development across the lifespan? As noted earlier, two or three attachments usually develop during the infant's first year. These are usually with other family members or other people closely involved in the child's care. By middle childhood, when the child is spending more time with people outside the family, opportunities for new attachments may arise. In adolescence and young adulthood, individuals usually begin to develop attachments to sexual partners. Although attachments to parents typically remain throughout life, the later attachments may become the most central ones in the individual's adult life.

When considering multiple attachments, theorists are faced with several sets of questions. One of these has to do with similarities versus differences in quality across different attachments (i.e., concordance rate). To what extent are a child's attachments to different caregivers similar? Studies examining concordance rate yield inconsistent results. Some studies reveal independence of attachment across caregivers (Belsky & Rovine, 1987; Grossmann, Grossmann, Huber, & Wartner, 1981; Main & Weston, 1981); some studies reveal similarity of attachment across caregivers (Goossens & van IJzendoorn, 1990; Steele, Steele, & Fonagy, 1996); and two meta-analytic studies have revealed significant but weak concordance between attachment to mother and attachment to father (Fox, Kimmerly, & Schafer, 1991; van IJzendoorn & De Wolff, 1997).

Another question relates to the integration of multiple attachments. If a child's attachments are similar, he or she may develop a consistent set of internal working models of attachment figures, him- or herself, and relationships. Yet what if the child is faced with attachments that contribute to conflicting models? What if the child's experiences with one parent contribute to a model of the attachment figure as sensitively responsive and of the self as worthy of such care, but negative experiences with the other parent contribute to very different models? If differing models of attachment figures eventually become integrated, how does this happen? In relation to models of the self, Bretherton (1985) asked over two decades ago: "Is an integrated internal working model of the self built from participation in a number of nonconcordant relationships? If so, how and when? Or are self models, developed in different relationships, only partially integrated or sometimes not at all?" (p. 30). Researchers have made little progress in answering these questions.

Still another question about multiple attachments relates to the issue of how these different attachments influence children's functioning. It could be that the attachment to the principal attachment figure, usually the mother, is most influential. On the other hand, it could be that one attachment is most influential in some areas and another is most influential in other areas. Or perhaps having at least one secure attachment, no matter who the attachment figure is, serves as a protective factor to facilitate the child's functioning across areas. Relatively little empirical work has addressed these possibilities, given that most research examining the sequelae of attachment focuses only on infant–mother attachment. The research that is available suggests that when a child is securely attached to one individual and insecurely attached to another, the child behaves more competently when the secure relationship is with the mother than when it is with the other attachment figure (Easterbrooks & Goldberg, 1987; Howes, Rodning, Galluzzo, & Myers, 1988; Main et al., 1985; Main & Weston, 1981; Sagi-Schwartz & Aviezer, 2005). These same studies indicate, however, that the best-functioning individuals have two secure relationships, while the least competent children have none.

Summary

This chapter has addressed the issues that Bowlby presented in his initial ethological approach to understanding the nature of a child's tie to the mother. Bowlby's observations led him to be dissatisfied with the explanations provided by existing theories and prompted him to consider alternative explanations. Drawing on the thinking of evolutionary biologists, cognitive scientists, control systems theorists, and developmental psychologists, he initiated what proved to be one of the earliest neo-Darwinian theories of evolutionary psychology, tackling the problem of the ways humans evolved to master the primary task of genetic transmission: survival through infancy and childhood to reproductive age. This chapter has begun with a description of the biological bases of attachment and of how attachment may have evolved. I have then described the connections between the attachment behavioral system and other behavioral systems. Finally, I have provided a description of attachment and other affectional bonds and discussed the issue of multiple attachments. In general, Bowlby and Ainsworth's original ideas have held up well, while providing a remarkably fruitful foundation for related ideas and studies. Those ideas have yielded [a] huge research literature [...] and the torrent of new ideas, studies, and research methods shows no sign of letting up.

Notes

1 As Bowlby (1988) noted in his final collection of lectures, later revisions to evolutionary theory contain the thinking that demarcation of a "principal" biological function (i.e., Bowlby's initial selection of protection) is unnecessary; the multiple benefits of attachment all contribute to its conveying an evolutionary advantage.

2 See Greenberg and Marvin (1982; see also Ainsworth, 1989) for discussion of the advantages of the term "sociable system" rather than "affiliative system." For data and more extensive discussion related to the interplay of the sociable system with other behavior systems, see discussions by Ainsworth et al. (1978), Bretherton (1978), Bretherton and Ainsworth (1974), Cassidy and Berlin (1999), and Greenberg and Marvin (1982).

3 This perspective differs somewhat from that of Bowlby. Bowlby (1969/1982, p. 240) described "maternal retrieval behavior" as distinct from other parenting behavior, with the former having the predictable outcome of proximity and the biological function of protection. It is unclear, however, what for Bowlby would constitute a behavioral system. The position taken here is that retrieval is the parental equivalent to child proximity seeking; it is a behavior, not a behavioral system. The relevant behavioral system would be what here is called the "caregiving system," which includes a variety of behaviors, one of which is parental retrieval of the child. This perspective, along with Solomon and George's perspective, also differs from that proposed by Bretherton and her colleagues (Bretherton, Biringen, & Ridgeway, 1991). Their view incorporates the notion of a "parental side of attachment," in which the parent's bond to the child is considered part of the attachment system, in part because of its great emotional power.

4 Within the modern evolutionary perspective, the existence of separate maternal and paternal caregiving systems is readily understood. Both mothers and fathers are concerned with their own reproductive fitness. Yet, because mothers and fathers may differ substantially in the extent to which the survival of any one child enhances this fitness, their parenting behavior may differ. Compared to fathers, mothers have more to gain in terms of reproductive fitness from each child, for several reasons (e.g., mothers' certainty about parental status, shorter reproductive lifespan, longer interchild intervals, and greater energy expenditure per child [during pregnancy and lactation]; see Trivers, 1972).

5 Consensus is lacking about terminology related to the attachment bond. The description provided here is Ainsworth's (1989) and reflects Bowlby's most common usage. Yet in the second edition of the first volume of his trilogy, *Attachment and Loss*, Bowlby (1969/1982) described a bond as "a property of two parties," and labeled the child–parent bond as the "attachment–caregiving" bond (p. 377). In contrast to the implied notion of an "attachment relationship," Ainsworth (1982b) stated:

> That there is a "relationship" between mother and child, in Hinde's (1979) sense, from the time of the infant's birth onward, and that the nature of this relationship stems from the interaction between them, is not to be gainsaid, but neither the mother-to-infant bond nor the emergent infant-to-mother attachment seems to me to comprehend all the important aspects of this relationship. (p. 24)

Bretherton (1985) also pointed out the limits of considering an attachment a "property of two parties": "A representational view of relationships ... underscores that the two partners have, in another sense, two relationships: the relationship as mentally represented by the attached person and by the attachment figure" (p. 34). Ainsworth (personal communication, 1986) suggested that the most appropriate way to consider an "attachment relationship" is as a "shorthand" designation for "a relationship in which the attachment component is central" (see also Ainsworth, 1990).

6 There has been some confusion over Bowlby's position on this issue. Lamb, Thompson, Gardner, and Charnov (1985), for instance, mistakenly stated, "Bowlby was firmly convinced that infants were initially capable of forming only one attachment bond" (p. 21). In fact, from his earliest writings on (1958, 1969/1982), Bowlby described the role of multiple attachment figures. Bowlby (1969/1982) noted that "it has sometimes been alleged that I have expressed the view ... that mothering 'cannot be safely distributed among several figures' (Mead, 1962). No such views have been expressed by me" (p. 303).

7 Starting with his earliest writings, Bowlby (e.g., 1958) used the term "principal attachment-figure" or "mother-figure" rather than the term "mother." This usage underscored Bowlby's belief that although this figure is usually the biological mother, it is by no means necessarily so.

From the beginning, Bowlby recognized that the figure's status (father, adoptive parent, grandmother, aunt, nanny) is less important than the nature of the figure's interactions with the infant.

8   One of the most moving passages of Bowlby's writing illustrates how one attachment figure can be more centrally important to a child's well-being than others:

> About four weeks after mother had died, [4-year-old] Wendy complained that no one loved her. In an attempt to reassure her, father named a long list of people who did (naming those who cared for her). On this Wendy commented aptly, "But when my mommy wasn't dead I didn't need so many people—I needed just one." (Bowlby, 1980a, p. 280)

References

Ahnert, L., Pinquart, M., & Lamb, M. E. (2006). Security of children's relationships with nonparental care providers: A meta-analysis. *Child Development, 74,* 664–679.

Ainsworth, M. D. S. (1963). The development of infant–mother interaction among the Ganda. In B. M. Foss (Ed.), *Determinants of infant behavior* (Vol. 2, pp. 67–112). New York: Wiley.

Ainsworth, M. D. S. (1964). Patterns of attachment behavior shown by the infant in interaction with his mother. *Merrill – Palmer Quarterly, 10,* 51–58.

Ainsworth, M. D. S. (1967). *Infancy in Uganda: Infant care and the growth of attachment.* Baltimore: Johns Hopkins University Press.

Ainsworth, M. D. S. (1972). Attachment and dependency: A comparison. In J. L. Gewirtz (Ed.), *Attachment and dependency* (pp. 97–137). Washington, DC: V.H. Winston.

Ainsworth, M. D. S. (1982a). *Attachment across the lifespan.* Unpublished lecture notes, University of Virginia.

Ainsworth, M. D. S. (1982b). Attachment: Retrospect and prospect. In C. M. Parkes & J. Stevenson-Hinde (Eds.), *The place of attachment in human behavior* (pp. 3–30). New York: Basic Books.

Ainsworth, M. D. S. (1989). Attachments beyond infancy. *American Psychologist, 44,* 709–716.

Ainsworth, M. D. S. (1990). Some considerations regarding theory and assessment relevant to attachments beyond infancy. In M. T. Greenberg, D. Cicchetti, & E. M. Cummings (Eds.), *Attachment in the preschool years: Theory, research, and intervention* (pp. 463–488). Chicago: University of Chicago Press.

Ainsworth, M. D. S., Bell, S. M., & Stayton, D. J. (1971). Individual differences in Strange-Situation behavior of one-year-olds. In H. R. Schaffer (Ed.), *The origins of human social relations* (pp. 17–52). New York: Academic Press.

Ainsworth, M. D. S., Blehar, M., Waters, E., & Wall, S. (1978). *Patterns of attachment: A psychological study of the Strange Situation.* Hillsdale, NJ: Erlbaum.

Ainsworth, M. D. S., & Wittig, B. A. (1969). Attachment and exploratory behaviour of one-year-olds in a strange situation. In B. M. Foss (Ed.), *Determinants of infant behaviour* (Vol. 4, pp. 111–136). London: Methuen.

Baldwin, M. W. (1992). Relational schemas and the processing of social information. *Psychological Bulletin, 112,* 461–484.

Belsky, J., Gilstrap, B., & Rovine, M. (1984). The Pennsylvania Infant and Family Development Project: I. Stability and change in mother–infant and father–infant interaction in a family setting at one, three, and nine months. *Child Development, 55,* 692–705.

Belsky, J., & Rovine, M. (1987). Temperament and attachment security within the Strange Situation: An empirical rapprochement. *Child Development, 58,* 787–795.

Bender, L., & Yarnell, H. (1941). An observation nursery. *American Journal of Psychiatry, 97,* 1158–1174.

Bowlby, J. (1944). Forty-four juvenile thieves: Their characters and home life. *International Journal of Psycho-Analysis, 25,* 19–52, 107–127.

Bowlby, J. (1956). The growth of independence in the young child. *Royal Society of Health Journal, 76,* 587–591.

Bowlby, J. (1958). The nature of the child's tie to his mother. *International Journal of Psycho-Analysis, 39,* 350–373.

Bowlby, J. (1960a). Grief and mourning in infancy. *Psychoanalytic Study of the Child, 15,* 3–39.

Bowlby, J. (1960b). Separation anxiety. *International Journal of Psycho-Analysis, 41,* 1–25.

Bowlby, J. (1969/1982). *Attachment and loss: Vol. 1. Attachment.* New York: Basic Books.

Bowlby, J. (1973). *Attachment and loss: Vol. 2. Separation: Anxiety and anger.* New York: Basic Books.

Bowlby, J. (1979). *The making and breaking of affectional bonds.* London: Tavistock.

Bowlby, J. (1980a). *Attachment and loss: Vol. 3. Loss: Sadness and depression.* New York: Basic Books.

Bowlby, J. (1980b). By ethology out of psycho-analysis: An experiment in interbreeding. *Animal Behavior, 28,* 649–656.

Bowlby, J. (1984). Caring for the young: Influences on development. In R. S. Cohen, B. J. Cohler, & S. H. Weissman (Eds.), *Parenthood: A psychodynamic perspective* (pp. 269–284). New York: Guilford Press.

Bowlby, J. (1988). *A secure base.* New York: Basic Books.

Brazelton, T. B. (1977). Implications of infant development among the Mayan Indians of Mexico. In P. H. Leiderman,

S. R. Tulkin, & A. Rosenfeld (Eds.), *Culture and infancy* (pp. 151–187). New York: Academic Press.

Bretherton, I. (1978). Making friends with one-year-olds: An experimental study of infant–stranger interaction. *Merrill–Palmer Quarterly, 24,* 29–52.

Bretherton, I. (1980). Young children in stressful situations: The supporting role of attachment figures and unfamiliar caregivers. In G. V. Coelho & P. I. Ahmed (Eds.), *Uprooting and development* (pp. 179–210). New York: Plenum Press.

Bretherton, I. (1985). Attachment theory: Retrospect and prospect. In I. Bretherton & E. Waters (Eds.), Growing points of attachment theory and research. *Monographs of the Society for Research in Child Development, 50*(1–2, Serial No. 209), 3–38.

Bretherton, I. (1990). Open communication and internal working models: Their role in the development of attachment relationships. In R. A. Thompson (Ed.), *Nebraska Symposium on Motivation: Vol. 36. Socioemotional development* (pp. 59–113). Lincoln: University of Nebraska Press.

Bretherton, I. (1991). Pouring new wine into old bottles: The social self as internal working model. In M. Gunnar & L. A. Sroufe (Eds.), *Minnesota Symposium on Child Psychology: Vol. 23. Self processes in development* (pp. 1–41). Hillsdale, NJ: Erlbaum.

Bretherton, I. (1992). The origins of attachment theory: John Bowlby and Mary Ainsworth. *Developmental Psychology, 28,* 759–775.

Bretherton, I., & Ainsworth, M. D. S. (1974). Responses of one-year-olds to a stranger in a strange situation. In M. Lewis & L. A. Rosenblum (Eds.), *The origins of fear* (pp. 131–164). New York: Wiley.

Bretherton, I., Biringen, Z., & Ridgeway, D. (1991). The parental side of attachment. In K. Pillemer & K. McCartney (Eds.), *Parent–child relations through life* (pp. 1–22). Hillsdale, NJ: Erlbaum.

Bronson, G. (1972). Infants' reactions to unfamiliar persons and novel objects. *Monographs of the Society for Research in Child Development, 37*(3, Serial No. 148).

Burlingham, D., & Freud, A. (1944). *Infants without families.* London: Allen & Unwin.

Carr, S., Dabbs, J., & Carr, T. (1975). Mother–infant attachment: The importance of the mother's visual field. *Child Development, 46,* 331–338.

Cassidy, J. (1994). Emotion regulation: Influences of attachment relationships. In N. Fox (Ed.), The development of emotion regulation. *Monographs of the Society for Research in Child Development, 59*(2–3, Serial No. 240), 228–249.

Cassidy, J., & Berlin, L. J. (1994). The insecure/ambivalent pattern of attachment: Theory and research. *Child Development, 65,* 971–991.

Cassidy, J., & Berlin, L. J. (1999). Understanding the origins of childhood loneliness: Contributions of attachment theory. In K. J. Rotenberg & S. Hymel (Eds.), *Loneliness in childhood and adolescence* (pp. 34–55). New York: Cambridge University Press.

Cassidy, J., & Kobak, R. (1988). Avoidance and its relation to other defensive processes. In J. Belsky & T. Nezworski (Eds.), *Clinical implications of attachment* (pp. 300–323). Hillsdale, NJ: Erlbaum.

Cassidy, J., Woodhouse, S., Cooper, G., Hoffman, K., Powell, B., & Rodenberg, M. S. (2005). Examination of the precursors of infant attachment security: Implications for early intervention and intervention research. In L. J. Berlin, Y. Ziv, L. M. Amaya-Jackson, & M. T. Greenberg (Eds.), *Enhancing early attachments: Theory, research, intervention, and policy* (pp. 34–60). New York: Guilford Press.

Colin, V. L. (1996). *Human attachment.* New York: McGraw-Hill.

De Wolff, M. S., & van IJzendoorn, M. H. (1997). Sensitivity and attachment: A meta-analysis on parental antecedents of infant attachment. *Child Development, 68,* 571–591.

Easterbrooks, A., & Goldberg, W. (1987). *Consequences of early family attachment patterns for later social–personality development.* Paper presented at the biennial meeting of the Society for Research in Child Development, Baltimore.

Eisenberg, J. F. (1966). The social organization of mammals. *Handbuch Zoologie, 8,* 1–92.

Fox, N. A., Kimmerly, N. L., & Schafer, W. D. (1991). Attachment to mother/attachment to father: A meta-analysis. *Child Development, 62,* 210–225.

Freud, A., & Dann, S. (1951). An experiment in group upbringing. *Psychoanalytic Study of the Child, 6,* 127–168.

Freud, S. (1957). Five lectures on psycho-analysis. In J. Strachey (Ed. & Trans.), *The standard edition of the complete psychological works of Sigmund Freud* (Vol. 11, pp. 3–56). London: Hogarth Press. (Original work published 1910)

Freud, S. (1964). An outline of psycho-analysis. In J. Strachey (Ed. & Trans.), *The standard edition of the complete psychological works of Sigmund Freud* (Vol. 23, pp. 139–207). London: Hogarth Press. (Original work published 1940)

George, C., & Solomon, J. (1996). Representational models of relationships: Links between caregiving and attachment. *Infant Mental Health Journal, 17,* 198–216.

Goldfarb, W. (1943). The effects of early institutional care on adolescent personality. *Journal of Experimental Education, 12,* 106–129.

Goossens, F. A., & van IJzendoorn, M. (1990). Quality of infants' attachments to professional caregivers: Relations to infant–parent attachment and daycare characteristics. *Child Development, 61,* 832–837.

Greenberg, M., & Marvin, R. S. (1982). Reactions of pre-school children to an adult stranger: A behavioral systems approach. *Child Development, 53*, 481–490.

Grossmann, K., & Grossmann, K. E. (1991). Newborn behavior, early parenting quality, and later toddler-parent relationships in a group of German infants. In J. K. Nugent, B. M. Lester, & T. B. Brazelton (Eds.), *The cultural context of infancy* (Vol. 2, pp. 3–38). Norwood, NJ: Ablex.

Grossmann, K. E., Grossmann, K., Huber, F., & Wartner, U. (1981). German children's behavior towards their mothers at 12 months and their fathers at 18 months in Ainsworth's Strange Situation. *International Journal of Behavioral Development, 4*, 157–181.

Harlow, H. F. (1958). The nature of love. *American Psychologist, 13*, 673.

Harlow, H. F. (1962). The development of affectional patterns in infant monkeys. In B. M. Foss (Ed.), *Determinants of infant behavior* (Vol. 1, pp. 75–88). New York: Wiley.

Harlow, H. F. (1969). Age-mate or affectional system. In D. S. Lehrman, R. A. Hinde, & E. Shaw (Eds.), *Advances in the study of behavior* (Vol. 2, pp. 334–383). New York: Academic Press.

Harlow, H. F., & Harlow, M. K. (1965). The affectional systems. In A. M. Schrier, H. F. Harlow, & F. Stollnitz (Eds.), *Behavior of non-human primates* (Vol. 2, pp. 287–334). New York: Academic Press.

Harlow, H. F., Harlow, M. K., & Hansen, E. W. (1963). The maternal affectional system of rhesus monkeys. In H. R. Rheingold (Ed.), *Maternal behavior in mammals* (pp. 254–281). New York: Wiley.

Hazan, C., & Zeifman, D. (1994). Sex and the psychological tether. In K. Bartholomew & D. Perlman (Eds.), *Advances in personal relationships: Vol. 5. Attachment processes in adulthood* (pp. 151–177). London: Jessica Kingsley.

Heinicke, C., & Westheimer, I. (1966). *Brief separations.* New York: International Universities Press.

Heller, K. A., & Berndt, T. J. (1981). Developmental changes in the formation and organization of personality attributions. *Child Development, 52*, 683–691.

Hinde, R. A. (1974). *Biological bases of human social behavior.* New York: McGraw-Hill.

Hinde, R. A. (1979). *Towards understanding relationships.* London: Academic Press.

Hinde, R. A. (1982). Attachment: Some conceptual and biological issues. In C. M. Parkes & J. Stevenson-Hinde (Eds.), *The place of attachment in human behavior* (pp. 60–70). New York: Basic Books.

Howes, C., Rodning, C., Galluzzo, D. C., & Myers, L. (1988). Attachment and child care: Relationships with mother and caregiver. *Early Childhood Research Quarterly, 3*, 703–715.

Huntingford, F. (1984). *The study of animal behavior.* London: Chapman & Hall.

Kagan, J., Kearsley, R., & Zelazo, P. (1978). *Infancy: Its place in human development.* Cambridge, MA: Harvard University Press.

Kobak, R. R., & Duemmler, S. (1994). Attachment and conversation: Toward a discourse analysis of adolescent and adult security. In K. Bartholomew & D. Perlman (Eds.), *Advances in personal relationships: Vol. 5. Attachment processes in adulthood* (pp. 121–149). London: Jessica Kingsley.

Kobak, R., Rosenthal, N., & Serwik, A. (2005). The attachment hierarchy in middle childhood: Conceptual and methodological issues. In K. A. Kerns & R. A. Richardson (Eds.), *Attachment in middle childhood* (pp. 71–88). New York: Guilford Press.

Kobak, R., Rosenthal, N., Zajac, K., & Madsen, S. (2007). Adolescent attachment hierarchies and the search for an adult pair bond. *New Directions in Child and Adolescent Development, 117*, 57–72.

Lamb, M. (1976a). Effects of stress and cohort on mother–infant and father–infant interaction. *Developmental Psychology, 12*, 435–443.

Lamb, M. (1976b). Interactions between two-year-olds and their mothers and fathers. *Psychological Reports, 38*, 447–450.

Lamb, M. (1978). Qualitative aspects of mother–and father–infant attachments. *Infant Behavior and Development, 1*, 265–275.

Lamb, M., Thompson, R. A., Gardner, W. P., & Charnov, E. L. (1985). *Infant–mother attachment.* Hillsdale, NJ: Erlbaum.

Lewis, M., Young, G., Brooks, J., & Michalson, L. (1975). The beginning of friendship. In M. Lewis & R. A. Rosenblum (Eds.), *Friendship and peer relations* (pp. 27–60). New York: Wiley.

Lorenz, K. E. (1935). Der Kumpan in der Umvelt des Vogels. *Journal of Omithology, 83*, 137–213, 289–413.

Main, M. (1990). Cross-cultural studies of attachment organization: Recent studies, changing methodologies, and the concept of conditional strategies. *Human Development, 33*, 48–61.

Main, M., Hesse, E., & Kaplan, N. (2005). Predictability of attachment behavior and representational processes at 1, 6, and 19 years of age. In K. E. Grossmann, K. Grossmann, & E. Waters (Eds.), *Attachment from infancy to adulthood: The major longitudinal studies* (pp. 245–304). New York: Guilford Press.

Main, M., Kaplan, N., & Cassidy, J. (1985). Security in infancy, childhood, and adulthood: A move to the level of representation. In I. Bretherton & E. Waters (Eds.), *Growing points of attachment theory and research. Monographs of the Society for Research in Child Development, 50*(1–2, Serial No. 209), 66–104.

Main, M., & Weston, D. (1981). The quality of the toddler's relationship to mother and to father: Related to conflict behavior and the readiness to establish new relationships. *Child Development, 52,* 932–940.

Marvin, R. S., VanDevender, T. L., Iwanaga, M. I., LeVine, S., & LeVine, R. A. (1977). Infant–caregiver attachment among the Hausa of Nigeria. In H. McGurk (Ed.), *Ecological factors in human development* (pp. 247–259). Amsterdam: North-Holland.

Mead, M. (1962). A cultural anthropologist's approach to maternal deprivation. In *Deprivation of maternal care: A reassessment of its effects* (Public Health Papers No. 14). Geneva: World Health Organization.

Miller, R., Caul, W., & Mirsky, I. (1967). Communication of affect between feral and socially isolated monkeys. *Journal of Personality and Social Psychology, 7,* 231–239.

Morgan, G. A., & Ricciuti, H. N. (1969). Infants' responses to strangers during the first year. In B. M. Foss (Ed.), *Determinants of infant behaviour* (Vol. 4, pp. 253–272). London: Methuen.

Murray, H. A. (1938). *Explorations in personality.* New York: Oxford University Press.

Passman, R. H., & Erck, T. W. (1977, March). *Visual presentation of mothers for facilitating play in childhood; The effects of silent films of mothers.* Paper presented at the biennial meeting of the Society for Research in Child Development, New Orleans, LA.

Passman, R. H., & Weisberg, P. (1975). Mothers and blankets as agents for promoting play and exploration by young children in a novel environment: The effects of social and nonsocial attachment objects. *Developmental Psychology, 11,* 170–177.

Piaget, J. (1954). *The construction of reality in the child.* New York: Basic Books.

Rheingold, H. (1969). The effect of a strange environment on the behaviour of infants. In B. M. Foss (Ed.), *Determinants of infant behaviour* (Vol. 4, pp. 137–166). London: Methuen.

Robertson, J., & Bowlby, J. (1952). Responses of young children to separation from their mothers. *Courrier du Centre International de l'Enfance, 2,* 131–142.

Rutter, M. (1981). *Maternal deprivation reassessed* (2nd ed.). New York: Penguin.

Sagi-Schwartz, A., & Aviezer, O. (2005). Correlates of attachment to multiple caregivers in kibbutz children from birth to emerging adulthood: The Haifa longitudinal study. In K. E. Grossmann, K. Grossmann, & E. Waters (Eds.), *Attachment from infancy to adulthood: The major longitudinal studies* (pp. 165–197). New York: Guilford Press.

Schaffer, H. R., & Emerson, P. E. (1964). The development of social attachments in infancy. *Monographs of the Society for Research in Child Development, 29*(3, Serial No. 94), 1–77.

Sears, R. R., Maccoby, E. E., & Levin, H. (1957). *Patterns of child rearing.* Evanston, IL: Row, Peterson.

Sorce, J., & Emde, R. (1981). Mother's presence is not enough: Effect of emotional availability on infant explorations. *Developmental Psychology, 17,* 737–745.

Solomon, J., & George, C. (1996). Defining the caregiving system: Toward a theory of caregiving. *Infant Mental Health Journal, 17,* 183–197.

Sroufe, L. A., & Waters, E. (1977). Attachment as an organizational construct. *Child Development, 48,* 1184–1199.

Steele, H., Steele, M., & Fonagy, P. (1996). Associations among attachment classifications of mothers, fathers, and their infants. *Child Development, 67,* 541–555.

Stewart, R., & Marvin, R. S. (1984). Sibling relations: The role of conceptual perspective-taking in the ontogeny of sibling caregiving. *Child Development, 55,* 1322–1332.

Teti, D., & Ablard, K. (1989). Security of attachment and infant–sibling relationships. *Child Development, 60,* 1519–1528.

Thompson, R. A., & Meyer, S. (2007). The socialization of emotion regulation in the family. In J. Gross (Ed.), *Handbook of emotion regulation* (pp. 249–268). New York: Guilford Press.

Trivers, R. L. (1972). Parental investment and sexual selection. In B. Campbell (Ed.), *Sexual selection and the descent of man, 1871–1971* (pp. 136–179). Chicago: Aldine-Atherton.

Trivers, R. L. (1974). Parent–offspring conflict. *American Zoologist, 14,* 249–264.

Vandell, D. L. (1980). Sociability with peer and mother during the first year. *Developmental Psychology, 16,* 355–361.

van Ijzendoorn, M., & De Wolff, M. S. (1997). In search of the absent father—meta-analyses of infant–father attachment: A rejoinder to our discussants. *Child Development, 68,* 604–609.

Vaughn, B. E., Waters, H. S., Coppola, G., Cassidy, J., Bost, K. K., & Verissimo, M. (2006). Script-like attachment representations and behavior in families and across cultures: Studies of parental secure base narratives. *Attachment and Human Development, 8,* 179–184.

Weinraub, M., Brooks, J., & Lewis, M. (1977). The social network: A reconsideration of the concept of attachment. *Human Development, 20,* 31–47.

Weiss, R. S. (1982). Attachment in adult life. In C. M. Parkes & J. Stevenson-Hinde (Eds.), *The place of attachment in human behavior* (pp. 171–184). New York: Basic Books.

Attachment Security in Infancy and Early Adulthood: A Twenty-Year Longitudinal Study

Everett Waters, Susan Merrick, Dominique Treboux, Judith Crowell, and Leah Albersheim

Introduction

One of Bowlby's primary goals in developing modern attachment theory was to preserve what he considered Freud's genuine insights about close relationships and development. These included insights about (1) the complexity of social, cognitive, and emotional life in infancy, (2) underlying similarities in the nature of close relationships in infancy and adulthood, and (3) the importance of early experience.

To preserve these insights, Bowlby recast Freud's insights in terms of control systems and ethological theories. He also placed his own imprint on them by replacing cathectic bonding with evolved secure base patterns as the common thread in infant and adult relationships. He also placed greater emphasis on the openness of early relationships to change, especially in light of real-life experiences.

Ainsworth's observational studies of secure base behavior at home and in the laboratory (Ainsworth, Blehar, Waters, & Wall, 1978, Ch. 4, 5, 13) initially focused on normative trends in infants' responses to novelty, separation, and reunion. Her goal was to test the appropriateness of Bowlby's control systems model of infant behavior toward a caregiver. Subsequently, individual differences designs proved useful for examining the determinants and developmental significance of secure base behavior (Ainsworth et al., 1978, Ch. 7, 8, 14; Colin, 1996).

Working within Mischel's (1968) critique of the individual differences paradigm, Masters and Wellman (1974) examined intercorrelations and stability in several studies of infant behavior in brief laboratory separations. They concluded that, consistent with Mischel's (1968) situationist critique of the individual differences paradigm, there was little evidence of consistency in correlations across discrete "attachment behaviors" or of stability over intervals of weeks, days, or minutes. These conclusions carried considerable weight.

The present study began (Waters, 1978) as an effort to clarify issues raised by the Masters and Wellman (1974) review. Strange Situation data were collected on a middle-class sample at 12 and 18 months of age. In each episode, we counted the frequency of discrete "attachment behaviors" and rated key interactive behaviors (proximity seeking, contact maintaining, proximity and interaction avoiding, and contact resisting). In addition, we classified each infant as secure, insecure-avoidant, and insecure-resistant at each age. Reliability analysis indicated that most of the discrete behaviors examined in the Masters and Wellman (1974) review were far too rare to enable us to obtain a reliable estimate of an infant's typical behavior from brief episodes. That is, measurement failure could explain much of the negative evidence compiled by Masters and Wellman (1974). This interpretation was strengthened by evidence that stability across episodes and across time was much higher with the broader (and thus more reliable) rating scales and classifications. These results addressed the Masters and Wellman critique in detail and, in doing so, buttressed an emerging methodological defense of individual differences research (e.g., Block, 1977; Epstein, 1978). As a result, they too carried considerable weight.

Lacking attachment security measures that could be applied beyond infancy, few if any researchers in the mid-1970s planned long-term follow-up assessments. This obstacle was overcome with the development and validation of the Berkeley Adult Attachment Interview (Main, Kaplan, & Cassidy, 1985; see Crowell & Treboux, 1995, for a review). As Vaughn, Egeland, Sroufe, and Waters (1979) note, Bowlby's theory predicts that secure base use and attachment representations are significantly stable across time and yet open to change in light of significant attachment-related experience. The goal of this follow-up study was to examine the extent of stability and change in attachment patterns from infancy to early adulthood and to stimulate research into the mechanisms underlying these developmental trajectories.

Method

Participants and procedure

Sixty 12-month-olds recruited from newspaper birth announcements in Minneapolis and St. Paul were seen in the Ainsworth and Wittig Strange Situation in 1975 and 1976. Most also participated in a 6-month follow-up at 18 months of age (see Waters, 1978). Fifty of these participants (21 males, 29 females) were relocated 20 years later and agreed to participate in the Berkeley Adult Attachment Interview (George, Kaplan, & Main, 1985). Their ages at the time of the AAI were from 20–22 years. As was true for their families in the original study, their socio-economic status spanned the lower- to upper-middle classes. Living arrangements were diverse: 45% lived at college, 24% at home, 24% independently, 6% in other arrangements (e.g., military). Seventy-two percent described their primary occupation as "student"; 18% had completed high-school and were now employed; 4% had completed college and were now employed; 6% did not mention employment. In most instances (78%) the participants' parents had remained married. Two participants lost a parent before age 6. Two participants had a child of their own.

INFANT ATTACHMENT ASSESSMENT

Each participant was seen in the Ainsworth Strange Situation at 1 year of age. They were classified as secure, insecure-avoidant, or insecure-resistant, as described in Ainsworth et al. (1978). The insecure disorganized classification (Main & Solomon, 1986) was not yet developed when we scored these tapes. Independent coders assigned infant attachment classifications at 12 and 18 months. Each participant was classified by two independent coders; eighteen-month data were scored without the knowledge of 12-month classifications. Raters agreed on major classifications in 45 out of 50 (90%) of the cases (see Waters, 1978). Disagreements were resolved by conference. The distribution of attachment classifications at 12 months was 29 (58%) secure, 12 (24%) insecure-avoidant, and 9 (18%) insecure-resistant.

ADULT ATTACHMENT ASSESSMENT

Adult attachment status was assessed by using the Berkeley Adult Attachment Interview (George et al., 1985) when each participant was from 20 to 21 years of age. Administration and scoring procedures are summarized in the General Introduction and detailed in Main and Goldwyn (1994). The interviews were conducted by three of the authors. Thirty-seven interviews were conducted in a private room provided by a community library; three participants were interviewed in their parents' homes. We interviewed 10 participants by telephone, nine who had moved away from the Minneapolis area and had no plans to visit and one who was at sea with the Navy. The interviewers were blind to participants' infant attachment classifications.

Before scoring, each interview was typed, compared with the audiotape, and if necessary corrected. Two of the authors who had completed AAI training seminars conducted by Dr Mary Main served as coders. Inter-rater agreement was assessed by using 25 of 50 transcripts. Agreement for this sample on the three major attachment classification was 84%, $\kappa = .72$, $p < .001$. The distribution of AAI classifications was 25 (50%) secure, 16 (32%) insecure dismissing, and 9 (18%) insecure preoccupied. One participant in each group was classified unresolved.

NEGATIVE LIFE EVENTS

One of the cornerstones of Bowlby's theory is that attachment-related expectations and working models remain open to revision in light of changes in the availability and responsiveness of secure base figures. That is, attachment theory predicts both stability under ordinary circumstances and change when negative life events alter caregiver behavior. To test the hypothesis that changes in attachment classification would be related to negative life events, we obtained a score on negative life events from each participant's AAI transcript. Negative life events were defined as (1) loss of a parent, (2) parental divorce, (3) life-threatening illness of parent or child (e.g., diabetes, cancer, heart attack), (4) parental psychiatric disorder, and (5) physical or sexual abuse by a family member. The coders who counted negative life events did so without knowledge of the participants' Strange Situation or

Table 3.1   Stability of attachment classifications from infancy to adulthood

Adult Attachment Classification (AAI)	Infant Attachment Classification (Strange Situation at 12 months)		
	Secure (B)	Avoidant (A)	Resistant (C)
Secure (F)	20	2	3
Dismissing (D)	6	8	2
Preoccupied (E)	3	2	4

Note. S/S = Strange Situation.
Stability:
64% (3 groups each age) $\kappa = .40, p < .005$
   τ (S/S dependent) $= .17, p \cong .002$
   τ (AAI dependent) $= .17, p \cong .002$
72% (secure versus insecure) $\kappa = .44, p < .001$
   τ (S/S dependent) $= .20, p \cong .002$
   τ (AAI dependent) $= .20, \cong .002$.

AAI classification and without training in the AAI scoring system. To allow time for the impact of such events to be reflected in the AAI, we limited the counts to events that had occurred before age 18. To determine whether results were specific to this method of ascertaining stressful life events, we examined events reported by checklist 1 year later. Forty-seven completed a checklist of life events that included all of the events identified in the AAIs. This method depends less on free-recall, the manner in which interview questions are posed, the participant's state of mind, and the amount of material produced in the AAI. These data are relevant to the present study and to the accompanying studies that obtained life events from the AAI. Participants were divided into those reporting none and those reporting one or more of the target experiences. The one or greater criterion was set a priori on the basis that all of the target experiences would be considered major life events in current research on stress and coping; each has the potential, on its own, to change expectations about caregiver availability and responsiveness.

Agreement on life events classification (none versus one or more) by AAI and checklist was 78.7%, $\kappa = .57$, $p < .002$. Twenty-two participants were classified "none" and 15 were classified "one or more" by both methods. Eight were classified "one or more" by the checklist but "none" by the AAI. Two were classified "one or more" by the AAI but "none" by the checklist.

Results

As hypothesized, early attachment security with mother was significantly related to AAI attachment security 20 years later (see Table 3.1). Using three classifications at each age, 32 out of 50 participants (64%) were assigned to corresponding classifications in infancy and early adulthood, $\kappa = .40, p < .005; \tau = .17, p \cong .002$ (AAI dependent).[1] Thirty-six out of 50 participants (72%) received the same classification using the secure-insecure dichotomy, $\kappa = .44., p < .001; \tau = .20, p \cong .002$.

Thirty-six percent of the participants changed classification from infancy to early adulthood. Reliability and validity problems with the attachment measures certainly account for some portion of the observed change. Nonetheless, the results also suggest that experiences beyond infancy also play a role in adult security. We examined this by counting the number of attachment-relevant negative life events mentioned in each participant's AAI transcript and relating this to whether the participant retained or changed attachment classification across age. These results are presented in Table 3.2. When mothers had reported no stressful life events, attachment stability (three groups each age) was 72%, $\kappa = .465, p < .009; \tau$ (AAI dependent) $= .23, p \cong .006$. For the secure versus insecure dichotomy, stability was 78%, $\kappa = .525, p \le .009$; τ (AAI dependent) $= .28, p \cong .003$.

Table 3.2 Relations of stressful life events to change in attachment classifications

Number of stressful life events reported	Stability and change from 12 months to 21 years	
	Retained security classification on AAI	Changed security classification on AAI
None		
Total S/S sample (n = 32)	25 (78%)	7 (22%)
Secure in S/S (n = 20)	17 (85%)	3 (15%)
Insecure in S/S (n = 12)	8 (75%)	4 (25%)
One or more		
Total S/S sample (n = 18)	10 (61%)	8 (39%)
Secure in S/S (n = 9)	3 (33%)	6 (66%)
Insecure in S/S (n = 9)	7 (89%)	2 (11%)

Note. S/S = Strange Situation.

Hierarchical multiple regression analyses were used to determine whether (1) secure and insecure infants were equally likely to change attachment classification, (2) mothers of secure and insecure infants were equally likely to report stressful life events, (3) infants whose mothers reported experiencing stressful life events were more likely to change attachment classification from the initial to the follow-up assessment, and (4) secure versus insecure infants whose mothers report stressful life events were equally likely to change classification. The analyses used stressful life events (presence versus absence), infant attachment classification (secure versus insecure), and their interaction to predict whether infants' attachment classifications (secure versus insecure) changed or remained the same over the course of the study.[2]

After first entering stressful life events, R^2 change for infant classification = .01, $F(2, 47)$ = .50, $p < .49$. Thus, there was no difference in the likelihood that secure infants (31%, 9 of 29) and insecure infants (28.6%, 6 of 21) would change classification from infancy to early adulthood. After first entering infant attachment classification, R^2 change for presence or absence of stressful life events = .09, $F(2, 47)$ = 4.64, $p < .037$. Thus, infants whose mothers reported one or more stressful life events were more likely to change attachment classification (44.4%, 8 of 18) than infants whose mothers reported none (21.9%, 7 of 32). Finally, after both attachment classification and stressful life events were included in the analysis, the interaction term in the analysis was also significant, R^2 change =

.14, $F(3, 46)$ = 8.48, $p < .006$. Stressful life events were significantly related to the likelihood of a secure infant becoming insecure in early adulthood (66.6% if mother reported one or more events versus 15% if she reported none, $p < .01$) in secure infants. Stressful life events were not significantly related to classification changes in insecure infants. Among insecure infants whose mothers reported one or more such events, 22% became secure as young adults versus 33.3% if mother reported none ($p < .59$).

Although attachment-related stressful life events were most often associated with changes from secure to insecure attachment, this was not always the case. One participant, whose parents responded with consistent sensitive care to the childhood onset of a life-long illness, changed from insecure to secure. The relationship between life events and attachment patterns across time was not perfect. Eight participants reported significant attachment-related stressful life events and yet retained their infant attachment status in early adulthood. Similarly, nine participants reported no such events and yet changed attachment classification.

Discussion

The present data provide strong evidence for the value of the secure base concept as a conceptualization of attachment relationships in infancy and adulthood. They also support Bowlby's expectation that individual differences can be stable across significant portions of the life span. Finally, they confirm the notion that, throughout childhood, attachment representations remain open to revision in light of real experience.

The success of the secure base concept as a conceptual foundation for both the Strange Situation and the AAI is important support for the notion that early and late relationships have something in common. Moreover, the present stability data support the notion that these relationships are not merely similar in kind but somehow developmentally related. Processes that may be contributing to stability include (1) consistency in caregiver behavior across time, (2) a tendency toward persistence in early cognitive structures, (3) the relatively moderate intensity and low frequency of attachment-related stressful events in this middle-class sample, (4) the effects of individuals on their environment, and (5) stabilizing effects of personality trait variables (Waters, Kondo-Ikemura, Posada, & Richters, 1991). This study was designed to stimulate interest and help in the design of research into the roles that such mechanisms play in the consistency of attachment stability over time.

A portion of the change noted in this study is attributable to measurement error. Imperfect scoring agreement introduces approximately 10% error at each age. In addition, a similar amount of error is attributable to the fact that neither the Strange Situation nor the AAI is perfectly reliable; behavior observed in a given assessment may not be entirely representative of the person's typical behavior (see Ainsworth et al., 1978, and Crowell & Treboux, 1995, for test–retest data). Correctly estimating these psychometric factors in change is important to understanding our results. Accurately assessing both stability and change is important; minimizing either would be a mistake. As Vaughn, Egeland, Sroufe, and Waters (1979) emphasized, Bowlby's attachment theory predicts both stability *and* change.

The portion of change in attachment classifications that proved correlated with attachment-related stressful life events provides important support for Bowlby's ideas about (1) the openness to change of attachment representations, and (2) the importance of real-world experiences in such change. Research on the mechanisms through which experience leads to change in attachment representations deserves high priority in current attachment research. An important conclusion

from this study is that the AAI is sensitive enough to experience to serve usefully in such work. The types of events associated with change in attachment security and the underlying mechanisms of change deserve careful analysis in shorter-term longitudinal designs.

Middle-class samples offer both advantages and disadvantages. They represent a large segment of the population and are ordinarily accessible, cooperative, and interested in research. This was evident in the fact that each of the participants we recontacted agreed to participate in the AAI. The educational level of middle-class participants is also an asset because the AAI makes heavy demands on a wide range of conceptual and verbal abilities. At the same time, stability in middle-class samples may reflect more than simply the inherent stability of attachment security. Both a relatively low rate of negative attachment-relevant experiences and social support structures that buffer secure base expectations against such experiences may also contribute to the stability of secure attachment in middle-class samples, just as consistent high levels of stressful events contributes to the stability of insecure attachment in disadvantaged samples.

Strong social support structures might reduce the number or impact of negative experiences and thus increase stability; they could also attenuate links between negative experiences that occurred and attachment stability. The best way to address these concerns is to examine both the stability of attachment in other populations and the mechanisms of change in close detail to understand why any participant would stay the same or change. The accompanying studies provide important information about stability and change in populations with very different patterns of caregiving and life events.

Notes

1 Cohen's κ is computed from (1) the maximum level of agreement possible (100%), (2) the proportion of concordant cases (in the diagonal cells) expected by chance (from cross-multiplying marginals), and (3) the observed proportion of agreements. κ is equal to the proportion of possible agreement over and above chance that is actually obtained. In addition to the significance test associated with κ, the statistic itself can be construed as

an indication of effect size. To determine whether any of the present results are specific to the statistic used, we also report, where appropriate, an alternative concordance index (Goodman & Kruskal's τ, by means of SPSS) based on a different model of chance agreement levels. When computed with AAI dependent, τ reflects the proportional reduction in error when the Strange Situation classification is used to predict AAI classification. Complete data from which other indices can be computed are included in tables.

2   The results in Table 3.2 also suggest hypotheses about changes from insecure to secure attachment in the absence of stressful life events. These deserve to be pursued with appropriate statistical power in a larger sample or meta-analysis of data from several studies. Independent assessment of stressful life events and caregiver—child interaction at several points between the initial and follow-up attachment assessments would also be useful.

References

Ainsworth, M., Blehar, M., Waters, E., & Wall, S. (1978). *Patterns of attachment*. Hillsdale, NJ: Erlbaum.

Block, J. (1977). Advancing the psychology of personality: Paradigm shift of improving the quality of research? In D. Magnusson & N. Endler (Eds.), *Personality at the crossroads: Current issues in interactional psychology*. Hillsdale, NJ: Erlbaum.

Colin, V. (1996). *Human attachment*. Philadelphia: Temple University Press.

Crowell, J., & Treboux, D. (1995). A review of adult attachment measures: Implications for theory and research. *Social Development, 4*, 294–327.

Epstein, S. (1978). The stability of behavior: I. On predicting most of the people much of the time. *Journal of Personality and Social Psychology, 37*, 1097–1126.

George, C., Kaplan, N., & Main, M. (1985). The adult attachment interview. Unpublished manuscript, University of California at Berkeley.

Main, M., & Goldwyn, R. (1994). Adult attachment rating and classification systems (version 6.0). Unpublished manuscript, University of California at Berkeley.

Main, M., Kaplan, N., & Cassidy, J. (1985). Security in infancy, childhood, and adulthood: A move to the level of representation. In I. Bretherton & E. Waters (Eds.), *Monographs of the Society for Research in Child Development, 50* (1–2, Serial No. 209, pp. 66–106).

Main, M., & Solomon, J. (1986). Discovery of a new, insecure-disorganized/disoriented attachment pattern. In M. Yogman & B. Brazelton (Eds.), *Affective development in infancy*. Norwood, NJ: Ablex.

Masters, J., & Wellman, H. (1974). Human infant attachment: A procedural critique. *Psychological Bulletin, 81*, 218–237.

Mischel, W. (1968). *Personality and assessment*. New York: Wiley.

Vaughn, B., Egeland, B., Sroufe, L., & Waters, E. (1979). Individual differences in infant–mother attachment Stability and change in families under stress. *Child Development, 50*, 971–975.

Waters, E. (1978). The reliability and stability of individual differences in infant–mother attachment *Child Development, 49*, 483–494.

Waters, E., Kondo-Ikemura, K., Posada, G., & Richters, J. (1991). Learning to love: Mechanisms and milestones. In M. Gunnar & L. A. Sroufe (Eds.), *Minnesota symposia on child psychology: Vol. 23. Self processes and development* (pp. 217–255). Hillsdale, NJ: Erlbaum.

··

The Effects of Infant Child Care on Infant–Mother Attachment Security: Results of the NICHD Study of Early Child Care

NICHD Early Child Care Research Network

Introduction

The prospect that routine nonmaternal care in the first year of life might adversely affect the security of the infant's attachment to mother has been a subject of much discussion and debate (Belsky & Steinberg, 1978; Fox & Fein, 1990; Karen, 1994; Rutter, 1981). Evidence linking institutional rearing in the early years of life with affective and cognitive deficits led to early concerns that the experience of maternal deprivation posed hazards for the emotional well-being of young children (Bowlby, 1973). Later, these same concerns were voiced about day-care. Indeed, Barglow, Vaughn, and Molitor (1987) interpreted findings linking child care with elevated rates of insecure attachment, especially insecure-avoidant relationships, as evidence that babies experience daily separations as maternal rejection. Others drew attention to the possibility that nonmaternal care might affect proximal processes of mother–infant interaction and thus interfere with the infant–mother attachment relationship (Jaeger & Weinraub, 1990; Owen & Cox, 1988). Time away from baby, Brazelton argued (1985), might undermine a mother's ability to respond sensitively to the child, which would itself reduce the probability that a secure relationship would develop, and Sroufe (1988, p. 286) suggested that daily separations might both cause the infant to lose confidence in the availability and responsiveness of the parent and reduce the opportunities for "ongoing tuning of the emerging infant-caregiver interactive system."

Irrespective of the mechanisms responsible, it is notable that several multistudy analyses have documented statistically significant associations between routine nonmaternal care in the first year and elevated rates of insecure attachment as measured in the Strange Situation (Ainsworth & Wittig, 1969). In one of the first multistudy analyses of published research linking infant child care and attachment classifications, Belsky and Rovine (1988) evaluated child-care effects in five homogeneous samples of maritally intact, middle- and working-class families ($N = 491$). They found that infants who experienced 20 or more hours per week of routine child care in the first year were significantly more likely to be classified as insecurely attached to their mothers between 12 and 18 months of age than were infants with more limited child-care experience. The difference was particularly marked for insecure avoidance. In a subsequent analysis of 1,247 infants from a more heterogeneous set of studies, some of them unpublished, Clarke-Stewart (1989) documented a similar significant association. This pattern was confirmed by Lamb and Sternberg (1990), who included 790 cases from a subset of the studies compiled by Clarke-Stewart. Quite consistent across these multistudy investigations was the extent to which early and extensive child care, defined as 20 or more hours per week of routine child care in the first year, increased the risk of insecure infant–mother attachment. In

Belsky and Rovine's (1988) analysis, 43% of the infants in early and extensive care were classified as insecurely attached; in the Clarke-Stewart (1989) analysis, the comparable figure was 36% and in the data compiled by Lamb and Sternberg (1990), it was 40%. For infants with more limited child-care experience, the percentages of insecure attachment were 26%, 29%, and 27%, respectively, in the three investigations.

Despite the relative consistency of findings across these three compilations of multiple data sets, a more recent investigation of 105 infants revealed no significant relation between child-care experience and attachment security (Roggman, Langlois, Hubbs-Tait, & Rieser-Danner, 1994). One interpretation of Roggman et al.'s failure to replicate is that the studies in the compilations of Belsky, Clarke-Stewart, and Lamb were all published in the 1980s, when it was less common for mothers of infants to work full time than it is today. Perhaps now that a majority of mothers in the United States are employed outside the home in the infant's first year, there is no longer a difference in the likelihood of attachment insecurity. This could certainly be the case if mothers employed today represent a population that is demographically different (e.g., older) or more inclusive than those similarly employed a decade or more ago. A second possibility is that mothers placing their infants in child care in the 1990s are better informed about child-care issues and controversies. These mothers may attempt to compensate for potential deleterious effects of child care discussed at length in scholarly journals and the popular media over the past decade by being (on average) more sensitive, responsive, and involved with their infants when they are not at work, which could increase the probability of secure attachment in this group. Also worth considering are the possibilities that child-care providers have been affected by the ongoing discussion about the effects of infant care and of the importance of high-quality care, that employed mothers receive more social support today than they did in the past, and that families now have more work options and child-care choices.

The NICHD Study of Early Child Care, which was conducted in the 1990s, can shed light on this cohort issue. The study is nearly as large in terms of sample size ($N = 1,153$) as the largest of the multistudy analyses. It has the additional advantage of being a prospective, longitudinal investigation, in which infants were identified at birth and followed through their first 3 years—thus reducing selection biases. The kinds and amount of child care the children experienced were determined solely by their parents and tracked and observed by the researchers over this time period. The design of the NICHD Study was also unique in the opportunity it provided to examine the effects of child care "in context."

Examining child care in context is important because even multistudy analyses documenting elevated rates of insecurity among groups of infants with early and extensive child-care experience do not suggest that insecurity is inevitable. Although infants with early and extensive child care were more likely to be insecure than other infants, the majority—about 60%—of the infants with early and extensive child-care experience developed secure attachments to their mothers. Whether infant child-care experience is associated with increased rates of insecurity (or security) may depend on the nature of the care received and the ecological context—broadly conceived—in which it is embedded. More specifically, characteristics of child care (type, quality, amount, age of entry, and stability), as well as characteristics of the child (especially sex and temperament) and characteristics of the family (including social, psychological and economic resources), may interact with one another when it comes to shaping developmental outcomes, including attachment security.

Two types of hypotheses were advanced in this investigation regarding how this myriad of potentially influential factors might operate. Main effects hypotheses stipulated that features of child care in and of themselves would affect attachment security. More specifically, main effects hypotheses predicted that children in (1) early, (2) extensive, (3) unstable, or (4) poor quality care would have an increased likelihood of insecure attachment independent of conditions at home or in the child. Interactive effect hypotheses stipulated that child-care features would exert their influence on attachment security principally in interaction with aspects of the family and/or the child. One set of interaction effect hypotheses predicted that large amounts of child care, poor quality of child care, or frequent changes in care arrangements over time would promote insecure

infant–mother attachment relationships principally when the child was otherwise at risk—by having a difficult temperament, being a male (Zaslow & Hayes, 1986), or residing in a home in which the mother had poor psychological adjustment or provided less sensitive and responsive care to the infant. Another set of interaction effect hypotheses predicted that when family or child risks were high (e.g., a poorly adjusted mother, a difficult infant, unresponsive caregiving), child care would serve a compensatory function in fostering the formation of a more secure infant–mother attachment bond, particularly when child care began early in life, and was stable, extensive, and of high quality.

To test these hypotheses and examine relations between the complex ecology of infant child care and infant–mother attachment security, the NICHD Study of Early Child Care analyzed measures of multiple features of the family, the child, and the child-care experience. Main effects and interaction effects involving child-care variables were tested over and above main effects of mother and child variables. Our goal was to determine the conditions (in the mother and the child) under which routine child-care experience in the first 15 months of life could lead to increased or decreased rates of infant–mother attachment insecurity, as well as avoidant insecurity in particular.

The data from previous studies of infant child-care experience and infant–mother attachment security have been subject to varied interpretations. One interpretation is that early and extensive child care as routinely experienced in the United States is a risk factor for the development of insecure infant–mother attachment relationships (e.g., Belsky, 1990). An alternative interpretation is that the results might be an artifact of the measurement strategy used for assessing attachment security (e.g., Clarke-Stewart, 1989). The latter interpretation suggests that the apparent elevated rates of insecurity, and especially of avoidant insecurity, might be a result of the fact that children who have experienced the multiple separations associated with child care are not especially stressed by the Strange Situation episodes designed to elicit attachment behavior. Thus, the Strange Situation may not be a valid measure of attachment for these children.

A meta-analysis and a review of attachment studies revealed no significant differences in distress or exploration for children with and without child-care experience (Clarke-Stewart & Fein, 1983; McCartney & Phillips, 1988), and two more recent attempts to investigate this issue did not find that avoidant behavior in the Strange Situation was an artifact of past experience with separations and reunions. Belsky and Braungart (1991) found that the infants with extensive child-care experience who were classified as insecure-avoidant were no less distressed or more exploratory in the reunion episodes than similarly classified infants with limited child-care experience, and Berger, Levy, and Compaan (1995) found that classifications of children's attachment security in a standard pediatric check-up were highly concordant with Strange Situation classifications whether the infants had extensive child-care experience in the first year or not. However, these studies were based on small samples, and the issue merits further investigation.

One purpose of the current inquiry was to explore further the validity of the Strange Situation for assessing the attachment security of infants with extensive experience in child care. A subsample of infants who experienced more than 30 hr per week of child care from 4 months to 15 months was compared with a sample of infants who had fewer than 10 hr per week of child care during this period, in terms of (1) their distress during separations in the Strange Situation, and (2) the confidence with which coders assigned them secure or insecure classifications.

In brief, then, the aims of this investigation were fourfold: (1) to determine if attachment classifications made on the basis of Strange Situation behavior were equally valid for infants with and without extensive child-care experience in the first year of life; (2) to identify differences in the probability of attachment security in infants with varying child-care experience (in terms of quality, amount, age of entry, stability, and type of care); (3) to identify the combination of factors (mother/child and child-care) under which child-care experience was associated with increased or decreased rates of attachment security; and (4) to determine whether early child-care experience was associated specifically with insecure-avoidant attachment.

Method

Participants

Participants in the NICHD Study of Early Child Care were recruited throughout 1991 from 31 hospitals near the following sites; Little Rock, AR; Orange County, CA; Lawrence and Topeka, KS; Boston, MA; Philadelphia, PA; Pittsburgh, PA; Charlottesville, VA; Morganton and Hickory, NC; Seattle, WA; and Madison, WI. Potential participants were selected from among 8,986 mothers giving birth during selected 24 hr sampling periods. Participants were selected in accordance with a conditionally random sampling plan that was designed to ensure that the recruited families reflected the demographic diversity (economic, educational, and ethnic) of the catchment area at each site. The recruited families included 24% ethnic-minority children, 10% low-education mothers, and 14% single mothers (note that these percentages are not mutually exclusive), and did not differ significantly from the families in the catchment areas on these variables. Participants were excluded from the sample if (1) the mother was under 18; (2) the mother did not speak English; (3) the family planned to move; (4) the child was hospitalized for more than 7 days following birth or had obvious disabilities; or (5) the mother had a known or acknowledged substance abuse problem. A total of 1,364 families with healthy newborns were enrolled; 58% of the families who were asked agreed to participate in the study. Of the mothers recruited, 53% planned to work full time, 23% part time, and 24% did not intend to be employed during the child's first year.

Strange Situation data for 1,153 infants (84.5% of those recruited) are included in the major analyses in this report. (The Strange Situation was administered to 1,201 dyads; six were uncodable due to technical errors; 42 cases were eventually excluded because they received an Unclassifiable "U" code.) Characteristics of these families are presented in Table 3.3. The 211 mother–infant dyads who did not

Table 3.3 Sample characteristics for families included in attachment analyses

Characteristics	%
Child ethnicity	
European American, non-Hispanic	81.5
African American, non-Hispanic	11.9
Hispanic	5.7
Other	.9
Child sex	
Girls	49.4
Boys	50.6
Maternal education	
<12 years	8.4
High school or GED	20.2
Some college	34.2
B.A.	21.9
Postgraduate	15.3
Husband/partner in the home	86.9
Child-care plans at birth	
Full-time	53
Part-time	23
None	24

contribute Strange Situation data were compared with the rest of the sample on seven variables measured when the infants were 1 month old. There were no differences between the two groups on income-to-needs ratio, maternal depression, and mother's or child's race (European American versus non-European American). However, those who did not contribute Strange Situation data, compared with those who did, were more likely to have boys (61.7% versus 50.6%, likelihood chi-square ratio = 5.74, $p < .02$), to be single mothers (22.9% versus 12.9%, likelihood chi-square = 14.45, $p < .001$), and to have more positive attitudes about the benefits of maternal employment for children (20.0% versus 19.1%), $F(1, 1279) = 10.19$, $p < .002$. (See below for description of these measures.)

Overview of data collection

Visits to the families occurred when the infants were 1, 6, and 15 months old. Observations in child-care arrangements were conducted when the infants were 6 and 15 months old. The Strange Situation assessment of infant attachment security (Ainsworth, Blehar, Waters, & Wall, 1978) was conducted in a

laboratory playroom visit when the infants were 15 months old (±1 month). Telephone interviews to update maternal employment and child-care information were conducted when the infants were 3, 9, and 12 months old, and phone calls to update information on child care and to schedule the 6 and 15 month observations occurred when the infants were 5 and 14 months old.

At all home visits, mothers reported on a variety of factors, including household composition and family income. In addition, at the 1 month visit, mothers completed a modified Attitude toward Maternal Employment Questionnaire (Greenberger, Goldberg, Crawford, & Granger, 1988). At 6 months, they completed a modified Infant Temperament Questionnaire (ITQ; Carey & McDevitt, 1978), and selected scales of the NEO Personality Inventory (Costa & McCrae, 1985), and at 1, 6, and 15 months, the Center for Epidemiologic Studies Depression Scale (CES-D; Radloff, 1977). At the 6 and 15 month home visits, mothers and infants were videotaped in a 15 min semistructured play interaction adapted from a procedure used by Vandell (1979), and the home visitor completed the Infant/Toddler HOME Scale (HOME; Caldwell & Bradley, 1984).

Infants in child care at 6 and 15 months were observed for 2 half-days in the child-care arrangement in which they spent the most time, using the Observational Record of the Caregiving Environment (ORCE) developed for this project (see NICHD Early Child Care Research Network, 1996).

Overview of measures

The presentation of measures is conceptually organized to reflect how variables functioned in the analyses. We first present measures used as control variables in the substantive analyses of the effects of child care, followed by mother and child measures that are employed as ecological parameters likely to interact with child-care variables, then child-care variables themselves, and, finally, the dependent construct of the study, attachment security.

CONTROL VARIABLES
To reduce the risk of generating spurious findings, a number of possible control variables tapping family

and mother characteristics were used in correlational analyses with the child-care parameters under study and with attachment security. These included family income and structure, and maternal child-rearing beliefs, locus of control, feelings about the pregnancy, separation anxiety, parenting stress, education, race, and beliefs about the benefits of maternal employment.[1] Two variables met our criteria for control variables in that they were related to both attachment security and child-care parameters: an income-to-needs ratio and a measure of the mother's beliefs about the benefits of maternal employment.

The income-to-needs ratio is an index of family economic resources, with higher scores indicating greater financial resources per person in the household. It was computed from maternal interview items collected at each home visit. Family income (exclusive of welfare payments) was divided by the poverty threshold, which was based on total family size. This variable was averaged across the three assessments at 1, 6, and 15 months to create an overall *average income to needs* ratio. Higher average income-to-needs ratios significantly predicted younger age of entry into care, $r(1,149) = -.16, p < .001$. They also predicted higher-quality care, $r(690) = .18, p < .001$, for positive caregiving frequency, and $r(688) = .16, p < .001$, for positive caregiving ratings, the two measures of child-care quality described below; more hours of care, $r(1,149) = .17, p < .001$; and more starts of different care arrangements, $r(1,149) = .07, p < .05$. Families of secure infants had higher average income-to-needs ratios than did families of insecure infants, $t(1,149) = 2.24, p < .05$.

The *beliefs about benefits of maternal employment* measure was created by summing five 6 point items from the Attitude toward Maternal Employment Questionnaire administered at the 1 month visit (Greenberger et al., 1988). Cronbach's alpha was .80. Higher scores reflected the belief that maternal employment was beneficial for children (e.g., "Children whose mothers work are more independent and able to do things for themselves"). Stronger beliefs in the benefits of maternal employment for children's development were associated with earlier entry into child care, $r(1,151) = -.26, p < .001$; more hours of care, $r(1,151) = .38, p < .001$; more care starts, $r(1,151) = .18, p < .001$; and lower-quality care,

$r(691) = -.12, p = .001$, for positive caregiving frequency and $r(689) = -.19, p < .001$ for positive caregiving ratings. Mothers of secure infants had weaker beliefs about the benefits of maternal employment for child development than did mothers of insecure infants, $t(1,151) = 2.68, p < .01$.

CHILD AND FAMILY MEASURES

To reduce the number of variables analyzed, increase measurement reliability, and increase sample size by including participants with some missing values, five composite variables were created from the mother and child measures.

A composite measure of the mother's *psychological adjustment* was created by summing the average of the three CES-D depression scores (reverse-scored) from the three ages plus scores on three scales of the NEO Personality Inventory: neuroticism, the extent to which the mother indicated she is anxious, hostile, and depressed (reverse-scored); extraversion, the extent to which she is sociable, fun-loving, and optimistic; and agreeableness, the extent to which she is trusting, helpful, and forgiving. Cronbach's alpha was .80.

Mothers' sensitivity is a central construct for the study of attachment. For this reason, two measures of sensitivity were included. The first was derived from observations of mother–child interaction in a play task, in which tapes were rated for qualities such as positive regard and intrusiveness. The second measure was derived from a home observation using the HOME. These approaches to the study of sensitivity are very different, and the correlation between the two sensitivity indexes (described below) was only moderate, $r(1,148) = .41$. To determine whether effects replicated across these measures, it was important to keep them separate.

One of the composite measures of the mothers' sensitivity and responsiveness was constructed on the basis of ratings of videotaped episodes of mother–child play. Tapes from all sites were shipped to a central location for coding. Mother's sensitivity to distress and nondistress, intrusiveness, detachment/disengagement, stimulation of cognitive development, positive and negative regard for the child, and flatness of affect were rated by a single team of coders using 4 point scales. A composite variable was created by summing the individual scales for sensitivity to nondistress, positive regard, and intrusiveness (reverse-scored). Sensitivity to distress, negative regard, and detachment/disengagement were not considered for this composite due to kurtosis problems. Intercoder reliability on the composite was .87 at 6 months and .83 at 15 months, based on 17% and 16% of the cases, respectively. Cronbach's alphas were .75 and .70 for the 6 and 15 month composites, respectively. These two scores were averaged to create the overall *sensitivity in play* composite used in these analyses.

The second composite measure representing the mothers' sensitivity and responsiveness was constructed on the basis of data obtained from the Infant/Toddler HOME. The HOME is a semistructured interview/observational procedure in which a home visitor answers a set of binary questions based on maternal response to specific queries and makes observations of materials in the home and the mother's behavior toward the child. This instrument was used by research assistants who had passed two certification procedures: (1) agreement with the scoring of a "gold-standard" videotape of a HOME administration on 41 of 45 items prior to the onset of data collection, and (2) agreement with a certified HOME trainer on 41 of 45 items for three videotaped home visits during the course of data collection. In addition, research assistants submitted a tape and score sheet from a HOME administration for evaluation every 4 months. A composite score was computed by summing the positive involvement factor score (Cronbach's alpha = .52 at 6 months and .56 at 15 months; e.g., "Parent's voice conveys positive feelings toward child," "Parent caresses or kisses child at least once," "Parent responds to child's vocalizations") and the lack of negativity factor score (Cronbach's alpha = .50 at 6 months and .54 at 15 months; e.g., "Parent does not shout at child," "Parent is not hostile"). The 6 and 15 month scores were averaged to create the *sensitivity in the HOME* score used in these analyses (Cronbach's alpha = .60 and .64).

A measure of infant temperament was based on 55 6-point items from the Infant Temperament Questionnaire, administered at 6 months. The items represented the following subscales: approach, activity, intensity, mood, and adaptability. The composite measure, *difficult temperament*, was created by calculating the mean of the nonmissing items with appropriate reflection of items, so that numerically large scores consistently reflected a more "difficult" temperament (e.g., "My baby is fussy or cries during the physical examination by the doctor"). Cronbach's alpha was .81.

CHILD-CARE VARIABLES

At 5 and 14 months, mothers were telephoned and asked about their current child-care arrangements, if any, and if changes were anticipated. If no changes were anticipated, information about the child-care setting was obtained. This information was used to classify the *type of care* of the arrangement observed at 6 and 15 months: mother (i.e., those children not in any regular child care), father, other relative, in-home nonrelative, child-care home, and child-care center. Information provided in the telephone calls and interviews was used to calculate the monthly average for number of hours in care per week. A composite measure of *amount of care* was created by computing the mean hours per week from the monthly care average from 4 through 15 months.[2] Children who received no regular nonmaternal care through 15 months received scores of "0." On the basis of maternal reports, two additional measures were generated. One was *age of entry* into routine child care (1 = entered care at 0–3 months, 2 = entered care at 4–6 months, 3 = entered care at 7–15 months, 4 = children who had not entered care by 15 months when the Strange Situation procedure was conducted). The second one was *frequency of care starts*, a measure of stability of care, which reflected the number of different arrangements the child experienced through 15 months.

Observations of the child-care settings were conducted on 2 half-days that were scheduled within a 2 week interval. During these sessions, observers scored child-care quality using the Observational Record of the Caregiving Environment (ORCE; see NICHD Early Child Care Research Network, 1996). Because the ORCE is used to assess the quality of caregiving for an individual child rather than what happens at the level of caregivers or classrooms, it is an instrument that can be used in home and center settings alike.

Data collection using the ORCE consisted of four 44 min cycles spread over 2 days. Each 44 min cycle was broken into four 10 min observation periods, plus a 4 min period for rating global quality. Observers recorded the occurrence of specific behaviors directed by the caregiver to the study infant for each minute during the first three 10 min cycles. These behaviors focused on positive caregiving and included the following: positive affect, positive physical contact, response to distress, response to vocalization, positive talk, asking questions, other talk, stimulation of cognitive or social development, facilitation of the infant's behavior. At each age a composite variable was created by summing standardized scores for these behavior scales. This composite was based on an a priori conceptualization of positive caregiving and was supported by the results of factor analysis. It had good internal consistency (alphas = .87 at 6 months and .79 at 15 months).

At the end of the fourth cycle, observers made qualitative ratings of the observed caregiving. A second composite was based on 4 point qualitative ratings of the same dimensions of caregiving behavior that were rated for the mothers in the structured play task with their infants. This qualitative rating composite was created by summing ratings for sensitivity to nondistress, stimulation of cognitive development, positive regard, and the reflection of detachment and flatness of affect. This composite also had good internal consistency (alphas = .89 at 6 months and .88 at 15 months).

Both positive frequency scores and qualitative ratings had adequate interobserver reliability with "gold standard" videotapes and with live reliability partners at 6 and 15 months (.86 to .98). At 6 and 15 months, each observer participated in three rounds of gold standard reliability tests, consisting of six tapes each, at regular intervals throughout the year of data collection. In addition, live reliability was conducted on 17% of the cases at 6 months and 11% of the cases at 15 months. Two overall composite measures of the quality of child care were created by computing the mean of the behavior composites at 6 and 15 months (*positive caregiving frequency*) and the mean of the qualitative composites at 6 and 15 months (*positive caregiving ratings*). Although these two composites were highly correlated, $r(689) = .73$, they were designed to tap somewhat different aspects of the caregiving environment, namely, the frequency of caregiving behaviors viewed as positive (e.g., response to vocalization, positive physical contact) and ratings of the quality of caregiving behavior. The decision to retain the separate composites reflects the design of the ORCE, as well as a concern that measures of amount and quality would be differentially related to attachment security.

ATTACHMENT SECURITY

The Strange Situation is a 25 min procedure containing brief episodes of increasing stress for the infant, including two mother–infant separations and reunions. It is designed to elicit and measure infants' attachment behavior. Attachment behaviors may be categorized as secure (B) or insecure (A, C, D, or U; Main & Solomon, 1990). When stressed, secure (B) infants seek comfort from their mothers, which is effective and permits the infant to return to play. Avoidant (A) infants tend to show little overt distress and turn away from or ignore the mother on reunion. Resistant (C) infants are distressed and angry, but ambivalent about contact, which does not effectively comfort and allow the children to return to play. Examples of disorganized/disoriented (D) behaviors are prolonged stilling, rapid vacillation between approach and avoidance, sudden unexplained changes in affect, severe distress followed by avoidance, and expressions of fear or disorientation at the entrance of the mother. A case that cannot be assigned an A, B, C, or D classification is given the unclassifiable (U) code. The U classifications (3.5% of the sample) have been eliminated from the major analyses in this report.

The Strange Situation was administered according to standard procedures (Ainsworth et al., 1978) by research assistants who had been trained and certified according to a priori criteria to assure that the assessments were of very high quality. These research assistants were trained so that the child's child-care status was not discussed during the Strange Situation (so as not to bias coders). Videotapes of the Strange Situation episodes from all sites were shipped to a central location (different from the one responsible for coding mother–child interaction) and rated by a team of three coders who were blind to child-care status, although not to the fact that this was a study of the effects of child care. The three workers, all with a minimum of 4 years previous experience coding Strange Situations from a variety of low- and high-risk samples, received additional training using master-coded tapes (including tapes coded by Mary Main), and intensive supervision continued during formal scoring to maintain expertise. Before beginning formal scoring coders also passed the University of Minnesota Attachment Test Tapes for ABC classifications.

Coders rated their *confidence* in each classification on a 5 point scale. A score of 5 reflected the view that the child was a "classic" exemplar of a particular sub-category (e.g., B3,A2). A rating of 1 reflected the view that the child's behavior was ambiguous or that the assessment was difficult to code for technical reasons. Distress during the three mother-absent episodes was rated with a 5 point scale for each episode. A rating of 1 reflected no overt distress and no attenuation of the child's exploration. A rating of 5 reflected immediate, high distress resulting in termination of the separation. These ratings were summed across episodes to create a total Distress score, which could range from 3 to 15. Cronbach's alpha was .84.

The three coders double-coded 1,201 Strange Situation assessments. Disagreements were viewed by the group and discussed until a code was assigned by consensus. Across all coder pairs, before conferencing, agreement for the five-category classification system (ABCDU) was 83% (kappa = .69) and agreement for the two-category classification system (secure/insecure) was 86% (kappa = .70). Distress was coded by a single worker based on the written notes by all coders. A second worker coded 47 cases from the notes for reliability. Pearson correlations between the two ratings ranged from .93 for Episode 6 to .96 for Episode 7.

The 5 point confidence rating was related to interrater agreement in expectable ways. When both coders' confidence ratings were 3 or higher, agreement on ABCDU was very good (94%, kappa = .86). When both coders had confidence ratings below 3 (13% of the cases), agreement was low (53%, kappa = .35). Overall, the correlation between the confidence ratings across coders was .53.

Results

Two sets of analyses were performed. The first set was designed to assess the internal validity of the Strange Situation, and the second set tested the effects of child care on attachment security.

Assessing the validity of the Strange Situation

The issue of the internal validity of the Strange Situation was addressed for children with routine separation experience by investigating the infant's distress during mother-absent episodes of the Strange Situation, and the confidence of coders assigning attachment classifications. Two extreme groups of children were selected for these analyses: those with less than 10 hr of child care per week every month from 0 to 15 months ("low-intensity" child-care group, $n = 251$) and those with 30 or more hr per week in every month from 3 to 15 months ("high-intensity" child-care group, $n = 263$). In these validity analyses, the five-category attachment classification (ABCDU) was used.

One theoretical challenge to the validity of the Strange Situation for children with extensive child care is that these children are not as distressed by their mother's absence as are children without routine, daily separation experience, and therefore the Strange Situation, designed as a mild stressor for children in maternal care, is not sufficiently stressful to activate the attachment system and tap secure-base behavior for these children. This hypothesis would be supported if it were found that children with extensive child care showed less distress in the mother-absent episodes of the Strange Situation than the children with no child care, or if, among children classified as avoidant (A), those with extensive child care showed less distress in the mother-absent episodes, compared with children with no child care.

Results of a 2 (high/low child-care intensity) × 5 (attachment classification) ANOVA for the distress rating provided no support for the hypothesis that the Strange Situation was a less valid measure of attachment for children with extensive child-care experience. As expected, children classified as Cs showed the most distress (13.6) and As the least (6.3), $F(4, 492) = 37.34$, $p < .001$. However, there was no significant main effect for child-care experience. The mean distress level of children in high-intensity child care was 6.5, and in low-intensity child care was 6.0. (See Appendix for cell means.)

The validity of the Strange Situation as a measure of attachment for children with extensive child-care experience would also be called into question if coders were less confident about the classification given these children. This was not the case. A 2×5 ANOVA for the confidence rating revealed that Bs were rated with higher confidence (3.9) than any other classification (3.1 to 3.3), $F(4, 510) = 18.64, p < .001$, but there was no significant main effect for child-care experience on rater confidence. Moreover, D and U infants in the high-intensity child-care group were coded with higher confidence (3.9, 3.3) than were D and U infants in the low-intensity child-care group (2.8, 2.6) rather than the reverse, $F(4, 510) = 2.94, p < .02$. Thus, there was no evidence in these analyses that the Strange Situation was less valid for children with extensive child-care experience than for those without.

Effects of child care on attachment security

ANALYSIS PLAN
A number of approaches to analyzing the effects of child care on Strange Situation classifications were considered. A primary issue was the selection/construction of dependent variables from the attachment classification categories that would provide the most direct test of our major hypotheses as well as address the results of previous studies. Two parameterizations of attachment categories were selected: secure (B) versus insecure (A, C, and D), and secure (B) versus insecure-avoidant (A). The secure/insecure dependent variable afforded the testing of child-care effects at the most global level of adaptive versus maladaptive child outcomes. The secure/avoidant dependent variable provided a means for testing the proposition that infant child-care experiences were specifically related to the incidence of insecure-avoidant attachment.

A second issue concerned the type of analyses to be performed. Due to the categorical, binary nature of the dependent variables, logistic regression analyses were employed (with secure = 1 and insecure = 0, or avoidant = 0). In a series of analyses, the dependent variable (secure/insecure or secure/avoidant) was predicted from (1) one of five characteristics of the mother (psychological adjustment, sensitivity in play, sensitivity in the HOME) or the child (difficult temperament, sex), (2) one of five characteristics of child care (positive caregiving frequency, positive caregiving ratings, amount of care, age of entry, and frequency of

care starts), and (3) the interaction between the two selected (mother/child and child care) variables.

This analysis plan was preferred to a single analysis that included all five mother/child variables, all five child-care variables, and all possible interactions among these variables because of multicollinearity among the measures. In addition, it was impossible to include all participants in a single analysis because some of the child-care variables (age of entry, amount of care, stability of care) involved the total sample, whereas others (positive caregiving frequency, positive caregiving ratings) were available only for those infants in child care. Alpha was set at .05 for all analyses, rather than adjusting alpha for the number of analyses, because of a concern regarding Type II errors.

In performing the logistic regression analyses, the order of entry of predictor variables was guided by our theoretical rationale and our major hypotheses. In each analysis, control variables reflective of selection effects (income-to-needs ratio, beliefs about the benefits of maternal employment) were entered into the regression equation first, and then the main effect of a mother or child characteristic was tested. The main effect of a child-care variable was tested next, and then the interaction between (i.e., the product of) the mother/child variable and the child-care variable. When these two-way interactions proved significant, subsequent analyses were undertaken to determine whether they could be clarified by considering selected additional child-care predictors within the context of the two-way interaction.

After analyses of continuous child-care variables were completed, attention was turned to the categorical variable of type of child care. Chi-square analyses were performed to determine whether attachment security was related to type of care at 5 and at 14 months, and additional logistic regression analyses were used to evaluate the effects of child-care variables on attachment outcomes within types of care.

DESCRIPTIVE STATISTICS
Descriptive statistics and intercorrelations among control and predictor variables appear in Table 3.4. Table 3.5 presents unadjusted descriptive statistics for predictor variables by attachment classification (ABCD).

Table 3.4 Intercorrelations among control and predictor variables, and descriptive statistics

						Intercorrelations						
	Inc.	Work	Psych. adj	Sens. play	Sens. HOME	Temp.	Sex	PCF	PCR	Amt.	Age	Starts
Controls												
Income-to-needs												
Benefits of work	.01											
Mother/child predictors												
Psychological adjustment	.30***											
Sensitivity—Play	.37***	-.09**	.28***									
Sensitivity—HOME	.31***	-.06*	.25***	.41***								
Temperament	-.16***	-.04	-.27***	-.14***	-.13***							
Sex[a]	.02	-.01	-.01	.04	.06*	.04						
Child-care predictors												
Positive caregiving frequency (PCF)	.18***	-.12***	.05	.10**	.10**	.01	.07					
Positive caregiving ratings (PCR)	.16***	-.19***	.05	.13***	.12***	.02	.09*	.73***				
Amount of care	.17***	.38***	.08**	.02	.05	-.09**	.02	-.14***	-.19***			
Age of entry[b]	-.16***	-.26***	-.11***	-.06*	-.03	.08**	.01	.04	.05	-.67***		
Frequency of care starts	.07*	.18***	.09**	.03	-.01	-.01	-.01	.01	-.02	.44***	-.57***	
						Descriptive statistics						
n	1,151	1,153	1,131	1,151	1,150	1,138	1,153	693	691	1,153	1,153	1,353
M	3.28	19.06	-.02	.01	.00	3.17	50.60c	.07	14.76	23.13	1.84b	2.54
SD	2.80	3.13	2.83	.82	.63	.40	***	2.59	2.67	18.19	1.13	2.00

[a]1 = boys, 2 = girls.
[b]1 = 0–3 months, 2 = 4–6 months, 3 = 7–15 months, 4 = not entered by 15 months.
c% boys.

*p < .05. **p < .01. ***p < .001.

Table 3.5 Descriptive statistics for mother, child, and child-care variables, by ABCD classification.

				Classification								
	A			B			C			D		
Predictors	n	M or %	(SD)	n	M or %	(SD)	n	M or %	(SD)	n	M or %	(SD)
Mother variables												
Psychological adjustment	156	-.44	(3.05)	700	.14	(2.76)	101	-.10	(3.05)	174	-.28	(2.86)
Sensitivity—Play	161	-.25	(.56)	711	.06	(.79)	102	.21	(.78)	177	-.08	(.88)
Sensitivity—HOME	161	-.22	(.87)	710	.05	(.58)	102	.03	(.56)	177	-.02	(.58)
Child variables												
Temperament	157	3.16	(.44)	705	3.18	(.40)	101	3.16	(.38)	175	3.19	(.37)
Sex (%)												
Boys	94	16.12		352	60.38		58	9.95		79	13.55	
Girls	68	11.93		360	63.16		44	7.72		98	17.19	
Child-care variables												
Positive caregiving frequency	111	-.20	(2.70)	422	-.01	(2.58)	53	.78	(2.43)	107	.30	(2.52)
Positive caregiving ratings	111	14.36	(2.84)	420	14.74	(2.59)	53	15.66	(2.70)	107	14.79	(2.67)
Amount of care (hr/week)	162	25.42	(18.06)	712	22.97	(18.33)	102	19.42	(17.27)	177	23.80	(18.02)
Age of entry[a]	162	1.84	(1.11)	712	1.85	(1.14)	102	1.80	(1.13)	177	1.83	(1.12)
Frequency of care starts	162	2.37	(1.91)	712	2.56	(2.01)	102	2.25	(1.82)	177	2.76	(2.13)
Type of care—5 months (%)												
Mother	47	11.24		259	61.96		40	9.57		72	17.22	
Father	20	15.04		79	59.40		17	12.78		17	12.78	
Other relative	38	21.23		106	59.22		11	6.15		24	13.41	
In-home nonrelative	9	10.00		56	62.22		8	8.89		17	18.89	
Child-care home	31	14.69		137	64.93		15	7.11		28	13.27	
Child-care center	11	10.78		67	65.69		9	8.82		15	14.71	
Type of care—14 months (%)												
Mother	44	13.10		204	60.71		36	10.71		52	15.48	
Father	27	16.17		103	61.68		10	5.99		27	16.17	
Other relative	28	17.61		89	55.97		14	8.81		28	17.61	
In-home nonrelative	14	13.86		60	59.41		12	11.88		15	14.85	
Child-care home	34	14.47		147	62.55		18	7.66		36	15.32	
Child-care center	11	7.97		97	70.29		11	7.97		19	13.77	

[a] 1 = 0–3 months, 2 = 4–6 months, 3 = 7–15 months, 4 = not entered in care by 15 months.

Table 3.6 Mother/Child and child-care predictors (main effects of secure (B) versus insecure (A, C, D) attachment

Predictors	n	Wald χ^2	Odds ratio
Mother/child variables			
Psychological adjustment	1,129	3.90★	1.05
Sensitivity—Play	1,149	2.82	1.14
Sensitivity—HOME	1,148	7.25★★	1.32
Temperament	1,136	.26	1.08
Sex	1,151	.77	1.11
Child-care variables			
Positive caregiving frequency	692	2.24	.96
Positive caregiving ratings	690	.64	.98
Amount of care	1,151	.06	1.00
Age of entry	1,151	.01	.99
Frequency of care starts	1,151	.82	1.03

Note. In all analyses, income-to-needs ratio and work beliefs were entered first as control variables. For ease of presentation, reported Wald chi-square values for child-care predictors reflect the main effect of each variable on attachment security, following entry of control variables. In fact, child-care variables were entered following control variables and mother/child variables, yielding nonsignificant results similar to those reported above.
★$p < .05$. ★★$p < .01$.

SECURE/INSECURE ANALYSES

Results of the secure/insecure analyses are presented in Tables 3.6 and 3.7. These tables show the association of attachment security with each mother and child predictor (top panel of Table 3.6), each child-care predictor (bottom panel of Table 3.6), and each interaction term (Table 3.7). The Wald chi-square for each variable indicates the effect of adding that variable following entry of prior variables; the odds ratio is the ratio of the probability that an event will occur to the probability that it will not (i.e., the closer to 1.00, the smaller the effect).

Among the five mother/child variables, two were significant predictors of attachment security: psychological adjustment and sensitivity in the HOME. As expected, mothers who exhibited greater sensitivity and responsiveness toward their infants and mothers who had better psychological adjustment were more likely to have securely attached infants. Child tem-

Table 3.7 Child-care × mother/child interactions predicting secure (B) versus insecure (A, C, D) attachment

Predictors	n	Wald χ^3	Odds ratio
Psychological adjustment × …:			
Positive caregiving frequency	683	1.10	1.01
Positive caregiving ratings	681	.05	1.00
Amount of care	1,129	.14	1.00
Age of entry	1,129	2.67	1.03
Frequency of care starts	1,129	.06	1.00
Sensitivity – play × …:			
Positive caregiving frequency	692	4.28★	.93
Positive caregiving ratings	690	3.92★	.93
Amount of care	1,149	.00	1.00
Age of entry	1,149	.05	.98
Frequency of care starts	1,149	3.88★	1.08
Sensitivity – HOME × …:			
Positive caregiving frequency	692	.84	.95
Positive caregiving ratings	690	4.09★	.89
Amount of care	1,148	4.52★	1.01
Age of entry	1,148	1.34	.91
Frequency of care starts	1,148	1.97	1.07
Temperament × …:			
Positive caregiving frequency	689	.12	1.03
Positive caregiving ratings	687	2.49	1.14
Amount of care	1,136	.36	1.00
Age of entry	1,136	.28	1.07
Frequency of care starts	1,136	.17	.97
Sex × …:			
Positive caregiving frequency	692	.20	1.03
Positive caregiving ratings	690	.01	1.00
Amount of care	1,151	4.19★	1.01
Age of entry	1,151	.07	.97
Frequency of care starts	1,151	.71	1.05

Note. In all analyses, income-to-needs ratio and benefits of work were entered first as control variables, followed by the mother/child variable, then the child-care variable, and then the interaction term. The main effects of the mother/child variables when all terms were included in the model were as follows: sensitivity—play, positive caregiving frequency analysis: Wald $\chi^2 = 2.97$, $p = .08$, odds ratio = 1.20; sensitivity—play, positive caregiving ratings analysis: Wald $\chi^2 = 5.12$, $p < .05$, odds ratio = 3.42; sensitivity—play, frequency of care starts analysis: Wald $\chi^2 = .24$, $p > .10$, odds ratio = .94; Sensitivity—HOME, positive caregiving ratings analysis: Wald $\chi^2 = 6.25$, $p = .01$, odds ratio = 7.67; Sensitivity—HOME, amount of care analysis: Wald $\chi^2 = .04$, $p > .10$ odds ratio = 1.03, sex amount of care analysis: Wald $\chi^2 = 1.16$, $p > .10$, odds ratio = .81.
★$p < .05$.

perament, sex, and sensitivity in play were not significantly related to attachment security in these analyses.

None of the five child-care variables, entered after the mother/child variables, significantly predicted attachment security. That is, variations in the observed quality of care, the amount of care, the age of entry, and the frequency of care starts did not increase or decrease a child's chances of being securely attached to mother.[3] Thus, the "main effects" hypotheses for child care received no support.[4]

Of the 25 interaction terms included in the logistic regression analyses (Table 3.7), six were significant predictors of attachment security: (1) maternal sensitivity in play × positive caregiving ratings, (2) maternal sensitivity in the HOME × positive caregiving ratings, (3) maternal sensitivity in play × positive caregiving frequency, (4) maternal sensitivity in the HOME × amount of care, (5) maternal sensitivity in play × care starts, and (6) child sex × amount of care. Although significant (see Wald chi-squares), these interaction effects were relatively small (see odds ratios).

To explore the nature of the significant interactions in as simple a way as possible, categorical groupings were formed from the variables involved. It should be understood, however, that the particular groupings are solely for the purpose of illuminating the nature of the already established interactions, and should not be reified. For maternal sensitivity and quality-of-care variables, the continuous variables were transformed into categories reflecting low, moderate, and high sensitivity or quality. Participants who were in the highest quartile on any variable were in the "high" group, and participants in the lowest quartile were in the "low" group. The "moderate" group comprised participants in the middle 50% of the distribution. For amount of care, three categories were formed: full-time care (>30 hr/week), part-time care (10–30 hr/week), and minimal or no care (<10 hr/week). For care starts, the categories were 0, 1, and more than 1 start.

The results of these categorical breakdowns are presented in Table 3.8a–f. The tabled entries are mean security proportions (adjusted for the effects of the control variables), standard errors, and the n in each cell. The three sections of the table displaying the significant maternal sensitivity × child-care quality

interactions (6a–c) indicate a consistent pattern related to low maternal sensitivity and low-quality child care. In each section, the lowest proportion of secure attachment was obtained when both maternal sensitivity and child-care quality were low (top left cell in each section). For these three interactions, the proportions of secure children among those receiving low scores on both maternal sensitivity and positive caregiving were .44, .45, and .51; the mean proportion of secure attachment for the rest of the children, collapsed across all the other cells, was .62 in each of the three sections. For purposes of this article, this and similar patterns will be referred to as "dual-risk" effects, in the sense that they involve both child-care and maternal conditions that might be expected to have a negative effect on the development of secure attachment.

In Table 3.8d–e, the dual-risk pattern was evident but less pronounced for the interactions between the mother's sensitivity in the HOME and the amount of care, and for the mother's sensitivity in play and the number of care starts. In these analyses, the rates of security in the dual-risk cells, when low maternal sensitivity was coupled with more than 10 hr/week of care or more than one care arrangement, were among the lowest in the table (.54/.52 in the dual-risk cells versus .62 for the rest of the cells in section 6d, and .56 in the dual-risk cell versus .63 for the rest of the cells in section 6e).

A different pattern was evident in section 6f, which shows the sex × amount of care interaction. This section reveals that the proportion of security was lowest among boys in more than 30 hr of care per week and girls in less than 10 hr of care per week.[5]

Inspection of Table 3.8a–c also reveals some evidence of a compensatory interaction pattern in relation to high-quality child care. The proportions of secure attachment in the top rows of the three sections show that for children with less sensitive and responsive mothers, security proportions were higher if the children were in high-quality child care (.53, .63, .58) than if they were in low-quality child care (.44, .45, and .51), and a linear increase in security as child-care quality increased was observed in two of the three analyses. However, a compensatory effect was not found for amount of child care. Section 3.8d shows that the less time children of less sensitive and

Table 3.8 Adjusted proportion of securely attached children by group for significant secure/insecure interactions

a. Sensitivity—Play × Positive Caregiving Ratings

	Positive Caregiving Ratings								
	Low			Mod.			High		
	p	SE	n	p	SE	n	p	SE	n
Sensitivity—play:									
Low	.44	.07	(48)	.62	.06	(80)	.53	.09	(30)
Mod.	.65	.06	(76)	.65	.04	(192)	.59	.06	(77)
High	.73	.08	(37)	.54	.05	(86)	.61	.06	(64)

b. Sensitivity—HOME × Positive Caregiving Ratings

	Positive Caregiving Ratings								
	Low			Mod.			High		
	p	SE	n	p	SE	n	p	SE	n
Sensitivity—HOME:									
Low	.45	.07	(44)	.57	.06	(78)	.63	.08	(35)
Mod.	.64	.05	(80)	.60	.03	(202)	.55	.05	(85)
High	.72	.08	(37)	.70	.06	(78)	.62	.07	(51)

c. Sensitivity—Play × Positive Caregiving Frequency

	Positive Caregiving Frequency								
	Low			Mod.			High		
	p	SE	n	p	SE	n	p	SE	n
Sensitivity—play:									
Low	.51	.07	(49)	.56	.06	(75)	.58	.08	(35)
Mod.	.73	.05	(83)	.62	.04	(184)	.58	.05	(79)
High	.69	.08	(36)	.61	.05	(89)	.53	.06	(62)

d. Sensitivity—HOME × Amount of Care

	Amount of Care (hr)								
	>30			10–30			<10		
	p	SE	n	p	SE	n	p	SE	n
Sensitivity—HOME:									
Low	.54	.05	(94)	.52	.05	(83)	.62	.05	(105)
Mod.	.63	.03	(264)	.64	.04	(141)	.59	.04	(198)
High	.66	.05	(113)	.73	.06	(63)	.66	.05	(87)

(continued)

Table 3.8 *(cont'd)*

e. Sensitivity—Play × Frequency of Care Starts

| | Frequency of Care Starts | | | | | | | | |
| | >1 | | | 1 | | | 0 | | |
	p	SE	n	p	SE	n	p	SE	n
Sensitivity—Play:									
Low	.56	.04	(182)	.60	.07	(53)	.60	.07	(44)
Mod.	.66	.02	(366)	.59	.04	(124)	.64	.05	(91)
High	.64	.04	(198)	.54	.07	(54)	.62	.08	(37)

f. Sex × Amount of Care

| | Amount of Care (hr) | | | | | | | | |
| | >30 | | | 10–30 | | | <10 | | |
	p	SE	n	p	SE	n	p	SE	n
Sex:									
Boys	.59	.03	(233)	.60	.04	(150)	.65	.04	(198)
Girls	.66	.03	(238)	.65	.04	(137)	.58	.04	(195)

responsive mothers spent in child care, the more likely they were to be securely attached. If amount of child care were compensating for low maternal sensitivity, we would expect security to be less probable in this group.

A final pattern, one that was unanticipated but was indicated in the three sections pertaining to maternal sensitivity and child-care quality (3.8a–c), is that the influence of the mother appears to vary as a function of quality of child care. Specifically, the proportions of secure attachment in the left columns of the three sections show that, for children in low-quality child care, security proportions were higher if the mother was highly sensitive (.73, .72, .69 in sections 3.8a, 3.8b, and 3.8c, respectively) than if she was insensitive (.44, .45, .51), whereas for children in high-quality child care, maternal sensitivity did not appear to be related to attachment security (proportions ranged from .53 to .63 regardless of maternal sensitivity). (To be noted, however, is the finding that maternal sensitivity remained a significant predictor of security even after accounting for the interaction term.)

SECURE/INSECURE—FOLLOW-UP ANALYSES

For the secure/insecure analyses yielding significant two-way interactions, we sought to determine whether consideration of additional child-care conditions would further illuminate the dual-risk pattern of results. For example, among children experiencing low maternal sensitivity and responsiveness and low-quality child care, could the increased risk of insecurity be explained by the number of hours in child care? For the subsample of participants experiencing a dual risk in any given analysis, attachment security was crossed with an additional child-care variable (quality, amount of care, age of entry, care starts, type of care at 5 months, type of care at 14 months) grouped into the discrete categories described above. For example, security (secure, insecure) was crossed with amount of care (<10 hr, 10–30 hr, >30 hr) within the group of children at dual risk due to low maternal sensitivity and poor-quality child care. Chi-square analyses provided no evidence that low quality of care at home and in child care was associated with increased rates of insecurity only, or principally, when children were in care for longer hours, were in less stable care, or were in a particular type of care. There was no evidence that boys with more hours in care were more likely to be insecure than boys with fewer hours of care because they received poorer quality or less stable care. There was no evidence that children who received extensive child care and insensitive maternal care were more likely to be insecure because the child care they received was of poorer quality, less stable, or of a certain type. In sum, although significant two-way interactions were obtained, we did not find evidence that these interactions were moderated by additional features of child care.

SECURE/AVOIDANT ANALYSES

The set of logistic regression analyses used to predict secure/insecure attachment was repeated for secure/avoidant attachment. Two of the five mother/child predictors were significant: sensitivity in play, Wald $\chi^2(1, N = 871) = 7.16, p < .01$, odds ratio = 1.36, and sensitivity in the HOME, Wald $\chi^2(1, N = 870) = 10.54, p < .01$, odds ratio = 1.51. Infants whose mothers were more sensitive and responsive toward them were more likely to be securely attached than insecure-avoidant. The main effects of psychological adjustment, temperament, and sex were not significant. Paralleling the results of the secure/insecure analyses, none of the five child-care variables was significant as a main-effect predictor of secure/avoidant attachment.[6] Only one of the 25 interaction terms was significant—sensitivity in play × care starts, Wald $\chi^2(1, N = 871) = 6.24, p < .05$, odds ratio = 1.17. Examination of the data indicated that the group with low maternal sensitivity and more than one care start (i.e., the dual-risk condition) had one of the lowest proportions of secure attachment (.76 versus .83).

TYPE-OF-CARE ANALYSES

Chi-square analyses were performed on attachment security × type of care at 5 months and at 14 months of age. The types of care used were mother, father, other relative, in-home nonrelative, child-care home, and child-care center. The results indicated that type of care was not significantly related to secure/insecure or secure/avoidant attachment at either age. Similar analyses grouping type of care into mother versus all

other types, and relative versus nonrelative care, yielded nonsignificant results. The proportion of secure attachment for children in mother care was identical to the proportion secure for the rest of the sample (.62).

Additional analyses were performed to determine whether various aspects of child care—quality, amount, age of entry, and care starts—were related to attachment security within types of care. Because of sample size limitations, only two types of care were used in these analyses—relative care (mother, father, other relative) and nonrelative care (in-home nonrelative, child-care home, and child-care center). These analyses were designed to determine whether child-care parameters would have different effects on attachment security depending on the caregiver's relationship with the child. A logistic regression procedure was employed in which each child-care variable was used to predict attachment security separately within the two types of care. None of the analyses yielded significant results.

Discussion

The NICHD Study of Early Child Care was undertaken to study associations between infant child care and developmental outcomes in a comprehensive and detailed way (see NICHD Early Child Care Network, 1994). One of its main goals was to illuminate the conditions under which infant child care increases or decreases rates of security of infant–mother attachment. Notable and unique design features of the study include its large sample size, the diversity of its participants (varying in SES, race, and family structure, and living in nine different states), the breadth of naturally occurring child-care types included (fathers, other relatives, in-home caregivers, child-care homes, and centers), the variety of child-care settings observed (from a single child with a formally trained nanny to a center with 30 children in the class), the extensiveness of the observational procedures used to assess both child-care contexts and maternal behavior, the prospective and longitudinal design, and the multivariate statistical analyses that allowed us to explore interactions between mother/

child and child-care factors as well as main effects. At the same time, it is important to note that one limitation of the present study is that the sample was not designed to be nationally representative. Nor did it include mothers under 18, infants with perinatal problems requiring extensive hospitalization, or mothers who declined to participate (42% of those invited). Of those in the study, 15.5% did not contribute Strange Situation data to this report (12% dropped out or did not have a 15 month laboratory assessment; 3% had "U" Strange Situation classifications; the remainder had assessments that were not coded due to technical problems). Families who did not contribute Strange Situation data were more likely to have boys, to have single mothers, and to have more positive attitudes about the benefits of maternal employment for children. All of these variables are related to either attachment security of child-care parameters in this study. Taken together, the factors described above may limit the generalizability of the results.

Validity of the Strange Situation

The first purpose of the present study was to evaluate the internal validity of the Strange Situation assessment procedure. This was necessary because concerns have been raised about the appropriateness of using the separation-based Strange Situation to assess the attachment of infants in child care, who presumably have had more experience with absences from their mothers. It was predicted that if the Strange Situation was invalid for children with routine separation experiences, these children would exhibit less distress during the mother's absence or be more difficult to classify than children without regular absences from mother. No significant differences in ratings of infants' distress during mothers' absence in the Strange Situation or in coders' ratings of their own confidence in assigning attachment classifications were observed between children with less than 10 hr of care per week versus children with more than 30 hr of care over the first year of life. Thus, these tests did not reveal any differential internal validity for the Strange Situation as a function of child-care experience.

Another issue pertaining to the validity of the Strange Situation in the present study is the extent to which the distribution of attachment classifications parallels distributions reported in previous research. However, a comparison of absolute levels of particular categories is problematic, because in earlier studies the A, B, C classification system was used rather than the A, B, C, D classifications used in the present study. When the four-category system is used, children who are given a D classification are recruited from any one of the other classifications—A, B, or C. The result is that the proportions of A, B, and C in the present study (14, 62, 9) are all lower than those reported for normative populations (21, 65, 14) (van IJzendoorn & Kroonenberg, 1988).

Selection effects

Before we could examine differences in the rates of attachment security and insecurity for infants with varying child-care experiences, it was necessary to control for selection effects—because child-care experience is not randomly assigned, and family factors affect whether children receive child care, when such care begins, the type of care, and its quality (Clarke-Stewart, Gruber, & Fitzgerald, 1994; Howes, 1990; McCartney, 1984; Melhuish, Moss, Mooney, & Martin, 1991; NICHD Early Child Care Research Network, 1997; Owen & Henderson, 1989). In examining these factors, we found that children reared in economically disadvantaged homes were more likely to be insecurely attached to their mothers. This finding is consistent with evidence indicating that poorer children are more likely to be classified as insecurely attached in the Strange Situation (Spieker & Booth, 1988), as well as with data showing that economic stress undermines the quality of care that parents provide their offspring (for review, see McLoyd, 1990).

We also discovered that when mothers more strongly endorsed statements supporting the possible benefits of maternal employment for children's development, their infants were more likely to be insecurely attached. These mothers were also observed to be less sensitive and responsive and to have their children in poorer quality care, at earlier ages, for more hours per week (see Table 3.4). One might speculate that maternal concern about the effects of child care fosters the mother's sensitive attentiveness to the infant at home and leads her to a more careful and cautious selection of care, thereby increasing the likelihood that the infant will experience security-promoting interactions and develop a secure attachment.

Main effects of mother and child characteristics

Results of the study indicated that children's attachment security was related to the mother's sensitivity and responsiveness, especially observed in the natural setting of the home, and to her overall positive psychological adjustment. These findings are consistent with a substantial theoretical and empirical literature linking infants' attachment security to their mothers' psychological adjustment (e.g., Spieker & Booth, 1988; for a review see Belsky, Rosenberger & Crnic, 1995) and sensitive and responsive caregiving (e.g., Ainsworth et al., 1978; for reviews, see Belsky & Cassidy, 1994; Clarke-Stewart, 1988). Also, security of attachment was not related to the child's sex or to the mother-rated index of difficult temperament, results which are consistent with theorizing about the relation between temperament and attachment (e.g., Sroufe, 1985).

Main effects of infant child care

After selection effects were taken into account, along with child effects (i.e., temperament, sex) and mother effects (i.e., psychological adjustment, sensitivity), results pertaining to main effects of child care were clear and consistent: There were no significant differences in attachment security related to child-care participation. Even in extensive, early, unstable, or poor-quality care, the likelihood of infants' insecure attachment to mother did not increase, nor did stable or high-quality care increase the likelihood of developing a secure attachment to mother.

It is unclear why the results of this inquiry are different from those of past studies, especially the multistudy analyses of Belsky and Rovine (1988) and Clarke-Stewart (1989) in which the Strange Situation classifications of hundreds of infants were

examined. Perhaps as Roggman et al. (1994) suggested, null findings that would have reduced the multistudy analyses to nonsignificance were relegated to the "file drawer" (i.e., not published). However, Clarke-Stewart's analysis did include available unpublished data. Alternatively, as mentioned in the Introduction, it may be that the population of families using infant child care today is different from those families of a decade or more ago, on whom the multistudy analyses were based. It may also be the case that the past decade's scholarly debate about adverse effects of child care, which has been discussed widely in the popular media, has sensitized parents using infant care. That is, these parents may make special efforts to provide "quality interaction" when they are with their infants, thereby increasing the likelihood that their infants will develop secure attachments. Another possible explanation is that in the present study, extensive statistical controls were employed to eliminate spurious effects. However, no main effects of child care emerged even without such controls.

Comparison of our results with those of earlier studies must give substantial weight to the present findings because of the advantages of this study—its methodological strengths, its control for family selection effects, its recency, and its "quality control" (in which, for example, Strange Situation coders were highly trained, reliable, and blind to the child's care arrangement). Nevertheless, it should be noted that the present study shares a limitation with previous studies, namely, that it was not possible to conduct observations in all eligible child-care arrangements. Approximately 16% of the care providers contacted at 6 and 15 months were unwilling, unable, or unavailable to be observed. These unobserved care arrangements may have been of lower quality than observed arrangements. In the unobserved settings, the average child-adult ratio—a predictor of higher levels of positive caregiving (see NICHD Early Child Care Research Network, 1996)—was 3.1 children per adult, compared with 2.5 for the observed arrangements. It is possible that with a wider range of care arrangements, an effect of child care on attachment security might have been obtained. Nevertheless, this seems quite unlikely, given the complete lack of association between attachment security and quality of care in this study. In the 1990s, it appears, child care in the first year of life does not have a direct, main effect on infants' attachment security.

Interaction effects with child and mother characteristics

Although analyses revealed no significant main effects of child care, it was not the case that child care was totally unrelated to attachment security. Consistent with Bronfenbrenner's (1979, p. 38) assertion that "in the ecology of human development the principal main effects are likely to be interactions," results revealed that six of the 25 two-way interactions tested (five child-care measures × five mother/child measures) achieved conventional levels of statistical significance, and yielded small but consistent effects.

A consistent pattern observed across five of the six significant interactions supported the proposition that children's attachment is affected by a combination of maternal and child-care factors. Children with the highest rates of insecurity with their mothers experienced conditions that could be considered to constitute a dual risk. This was most clearly demonstrated by children whose mothers and caregivers were least sensitive and responsive to their needs and behavior. Children who received less sensitive and responsive caregiving in child care (as measured by ratings and by frequencies of caregivers' positive behaviors) as well as less sensitive and responsive care from their mothers (as measured by less frequent and responsive positive behavior in a semistructured play session and at home) had the highest rates of insecurity (ranging from .49 to .56, depending on the analysis). Children in less risky conditions (better child care or better maternal care) had a rate of insecurity that averaged only .38. Parallel but less pronounced effects were observed for children who experienced the dual risks of less sensitive and responsive mothering combined with more time spent in child care (rate of insecurity of .47 compared with .38 in the other cells) or more care arrangements over time (rate of insecurity of .44, compared with .37). These results support a dual risk model of development (see Belsky & Rovine, 1988; Werner & Smith, 1992).

Beyond the dual-risk effects, other significant interactions were observed. One is that children in low-quality child care were more strongly affected by their mothers' behavior than were children in high-quality care. For children in low-quality child care, the probability of a secure attachment was low (.44–.51) if the mother was less sensitive and responsive and high (.69–.73) if she was highly sensitive and responsive. For children in high-quality care, the security proportions were moderate (.53–.63) regardless of the mothers' behavior. This pattern, suggesting that child care had a moderating effect on the link between maternal sensitivity and attachment security, was not predicted a priori. A tentative explanation might be that the mother's behavior is more salient and significant in the lives of children in low-quality child care, who would be less likely to form secure attachments to their alternative caregivers (Howes & Hamilton, 1992).

A second pattern pertains to the interaction between maternal sensitivity and amount of child care. Children whose mothers exhibited less sensitive and responsive behavior toward them in the HOME observation and interview were more likely to be securely attached if they spent more time with mother (and less time in child care). This finding may, at first, appear to be counterintuitive. Why should spending more time with a relatively insensitive and unresponsive mother increase the probability of establishing a secure relationship with her? Our tentative explanation is that there may be a "dosage effect" for maternal sensitivity and involvement: Children with less involved mothers may need more time with them in order to develop the internalized sense that the mother is responsive and available, whereas children with more sensitive and responsive mothers may require less time to develop confidence in the mother's availability.

A third interaction pattern suggested different developmental processes for boys and girls. Whereas more time in child care was associated with a somewhat higher rate of insecurity for boys, less time in care associated with a somewhat higher rate of insecurity for girls. These data bring to mind two sets of findings in the developmental literature. Relevant to the elevated rate of insecurity for boys in child care is evidence that boys tend to be more vulnerable than girls to psychosocial stress generally (Zaslow & Hayes, 1986). Perhaps, for the boys in this study, the experience of spending a lot of time in child care was stressful enough to tip the balance toward a lower likelihood of secure attachment. Consistent with the elevated rate of insecurity for girls not in child care is evidence that girls lacking child-care experience in infancy score lower on later intelligence tests (Desai, Chase-Lansdale, & Michael, 1989; Mott, 1991). The reasons why girls in child care would benefit in terms of their attachment security remain unclear. Further analyses of child outcome measures in the NICHD Study will shed light on these possible developmental differences.

The interaction analyses provided evidence that high-quality child care served a compensatory function for children whose maternal care was lacking: The proportion of attachment security among children with the least sensitive and responsive mothers was higher in high-quality child care than in low-quality care. However, there was no evidence that amount of time in child care compensated for the mother's lack of sensitivity and involvement, because the proportion of secure attachment among the children with the least sensitive and responsive mothers was higher in minimal hours of child care than in many hours of care.

Effect of child care on avoidance

Previous studies (compiled by Belsky & Rovine, 1988, and Clarke-Stewart, 1989) suggested that effects of child care were most likely to increase the rate of one particular form of insecurity—insecure avoidance. Indeed, Barglow et al. (1987) contended that this was the case because infants interpreted the routine separations associated with child care as maternal rejection, which is theorized to foster insecure-avoidant attachment. Analyses of secure versus insecure-avoidant children in the present study revealed no main effects of child care, and only one of the 25 interactions tested was significant. Thus, in contrast to the results of earlier research, there was no

evidence that child-care experience is associated with avoidance per se.

Conclusion

The results of this study clearly indicate that child care by itself constitutes neither a risk nor a benefit for the development of the infant–mother attachment relationship as measured in the Strange Situation. However, poor quality, unstable, or more than minimal amounts of child care apparently added to the risks already inherent in poor mothering, so that the combined effects were worse than those of low maternal sensitivity and responsiveness alone. Such results suggest that the effects of child care on attachment, as well as the nature of the attachment relationship itself, depend primarily on the nature of ongoing interactions between mother and child (Ainsworth, 1973; Sroufe, 1988). Another finding of the study was that the influence of amount of care on attachment security varied as a function of the child's sex.

Our continuing, longitudinal investigation of children's development in the NICHD Study of Early Child Care will determine the ultimate importance of these findings for developmentalists, policy-makers, and parents, as we consider the effects of early child care on longer-term outcomes and on the broader variety of social-emotional, cognitive, and health outcomes the study was designed to assess. To the extent that evidence emerges in future analyses that early child care is associated with problem behavior or developmental deficits at older ages, these infant–mother attachment findings will take on greater importance. To the extent, however, that evaluations of child-care effects in the longitudinal follow-up to this investigation provide no evidence of developmental disadvantages associated with early care, then even concerns raised in this inquiry about dual risks with respect to attachment security would be mitigated. In sum, the full meaning of the child-care findings reported here will not become clear until more is known about the development of the children participating in the NICHD Study of Early Child Care.

Notes

1 These measures are described in NICHD Early Child Care Research Network (1997).

2 The decision to begin counting hours of care at 4 months rather than 1 month was made because this was the age by which the majority of infants who were in care during the first year had started care, and we did not want to deflate our estimate of hours of care by the "zeros" infants received in months 1–3.

3 The same results were obtained when child-care variables were entered prior to mother/child variables or prior to control variables, and when the two measures of child-care quality were aggregated.

4 In a logistic regression predicting attachment security from income-to-needs ratio, beliefs about the benefits of maternal employment, sensitivity—HOME and cumulative child-care risk (low quality, high amount, and frequent starts), the Wald chi-square for the cumulative child-care risk variable was .49 (ns).

5 In a separate analysis, we tested whether children in dual-risk groups for one analysis were also members of the dual-risk groups in other analyses. The majority of these children (65%, or 289) were in only one of the six dual-risk groups, 19% (83) were in two, and 16% (73) were in three or more.

6 The same results were obtained when child-care variables were entered prior to mother/child variables or prior to control variables.

References

Ainsworth, M. D. S. (1973). The development of infant–mother attachment. In B. Caldwell & H. Ricciuti (Eds.), *Review of child development research* (Vol. 3, pp. 1–94). Chicago: University of Chicago Press.

Ainsworth, M. D., Blehar, M., Waters, E., & Wall, S. (1978). *Patterns of attachment: A psychological study of the Strange Situation.* Hillsdale, NJ: Erlbaum.

Ainsworth, M. D. S., & Wittig, B. (1969). Attachment and exploratory behavior of one-year-olds in a strange situation. In B. M. Foss (Ed.), *Determinants of infant behavior* (Vol. 4, pp. 129–173). London: Methuen.

Barglow, P., Vaughn, B., & Molitor, N. (1987). Effects of maternal absence due to employment on the quality of infant–mother attachment in a low-risk sample. *Child Development, 58,* 945–954.

Belsky, J. (1990). Developmental risks associated with infant day-care: Attachment insecurity, noncompliance, and aggression? In S. Chehrazi (Ed.), *Psychosocial issues in day-care* (pp. 37–68). New York: American Psychiatric Press.

Belsky, J., & Braungart, J. (1991). Are insecure-avoidant infants with extensive day-care experience less stressed by and more independent in the Strange Situation? *Child Development, 62,* 567–571.

Belsky, J., & Cassidy, J. (1994). Attachment: Theory and evidence. In M. Rutter, D. Hay, & S. Baron-Cohen (Eds.), *Developmental principles and clinical issues in psychology and psychiatry* (pp. 373–402). London: Blackwell.

Belsky, J., Rosenberger, K., & Crnic, K. (1995). The origins of attachment security: Classical and contextual determinants. In S. Goldberg, R. Muir, & J. Kerr (Eds.), *Attachment theory: Social, developmental and clinical perspectives* (pp. 153–184). Hillsdale, NJ: Analytic Press.

Belsky, J., & Rovine, M. (1988). Nonmaternal care in the first year of life and the security of infant-parent attachment. *Child Development, 59,* 157–167.

Belsky, J., & Steinberg, L. (1978). The effects of day-care: A critical review. *Child Development, 49,* 929–949.

Berger, S., Levy, A., & Compaan, K. (1995, March). *Infant attachment outside the laboratory. New evidence in support of the Strange Situation.* Paper presented at the biennial meetings of the Society for Research in Child Development, Indianapolis, IN.

Bowlby, J. (1973). *Attachment and loss: Vol. 3. Separation Anxiety and anger.* New York: Basic.

Brazelton, T. B. (1985). *Working and caring.* New York: Basic.

Bronfenbrenner, U. (1979). *The ecology of human development.* Cambridge. MA: Harvard University Press.

Caldwell, B. M., & Bradley, R. H. (1984). *Home Observation for Measurement of the Environment.* Little Rock: University of Arkansas.

Carey, W., & McDevitt, S. (1978). Revision of the Infant Temperament Questionnaire. *Pediatrics, 61,* 735–739.

Clarke-Stewart, K. A. (1988). Parents' effects on children's development: A decade of progress? *Journal of Applied Developmental Psychology, 9,* 41–84.

Clarke-Stewart, K. A. (1989). Infant day-care: Maligned or malignant? *American Psychologist, 44,* 266–273.

Clarke-Stewart, K. A., & Fein, G. G. (1983). Early childhood programs. In M. Haith & J. Campos (Eds.), P. H. Mussen (Series Ed.), *Handbook of child psychology: Vol. 2. Infancy and developmental psychobiology* (pp. 917–1000). New York: Wiley.

Clarke-Stewart, K. A., Gruber, C. P., & Fitzgerald, L. M. (1994). *Children at home and in day-care.* Hillsdale, NJ: Erlbaum.

Costa, P. T., & McCrae, R. R. (1985). *The NEO Personality Inventory manual*. Odessa, FL: Psychological Assessment Resources.

Desal, S., Chase-Lansdale, P. L., & Michael, R. (1989). Mother or market? Effects of maternal employment on the intellectual ability of four-year-old children. *Demography, 26*, 545–561.

Fox, N., & Fein, G. (1990). *Infant day-care: The current debate*. Norwood, NJ: Ablex.

Greenberger, E., Goldberg, W., Crawford, T. J., & Granger, J. (1988). Beliefs about the consequences of maternal employment for children. *Psychology of Women Quarterly, 12*, 35–59.

Howes, C. (1990). Current research on early day-care. In S. S. Chehrazi (Ed.), *Psychosocial issues in day-care* (pp. 21–53). Washington, DC: American Psychiatric Press.

Howes, C., & Hamilton, C. E. (1992). Children's relationships with caregivers: Mothers and child-care teachers. *Child Development, 63*, 859–866.

Jaeger, E., & Weinraub, M. (1990). Early maternal care and infant attachment: In search of process. In K. McCartney (Ed.), *Child care and maternal employment: A social ecologogy approach* (pp. 71–90). San Francisco: Jossey-Bass.

Karen, R. (1994). *Becoming attached*. New York: Warner.

Lamb, M., & Sternberg, K. (1990). Do we really know how day-care affects children? *Journal of Applied Developmental Psychology, 11*, 351–379.

Main, M., & Solomon, J. (1990). Procedures for identifying disorganized/disoriented infants in the Ainsworth Strange Situation. In M. Greenberg, D. Cicchetti, & M. Cummings (Eds.), *Attachment in the preschool years: Theory, research, and intervention* (pp. 121–160). Chicago: University of Chicago Press.

McCartney, K. (1984). The effect of quality of day-care environment upon children's language development. *Developmental Psychology, 20*, 244–260.

McCartney, K., & Phillips, D. (1988). Motherhood and child care. In B. Birns & D. Hay (Eds.), *The different faces of motherhood* (pp. 157–183). New York: Plenum.

McLoyd, V. C. (1990). The impact of economic hardship on black families and children: Psychological distress, parenting, and socioemotional development. *Child Development, 61*, 311–436.

Melhuish, E. C., Moss, P., Mooney, A., & Martin, S. (1991). How similar are day-care groups before the start of day-care? *Journal of Applied Developmental Psychology, 12*, 331–335.

Mott, F. L. (1991). Developmental effects of infant care: The mediating role of gender and health. *Journal of Social Issues, 47*, 139–158.

NICHD Early Child Care Network, (1994). Child care and child development: The NICHD Study of Early Child Care. In S. Friedman & H. C. Haywood (Eds.), *Develop-*

mental follow-up, Concepts, domains, and methods (pp. 377–396). New York: Academic Press.

NICHD Early Child Care Research Network (1996). Characteristics of infant child care: Factors contributing to positive caregiving. *Early Childhood Research Quarterly, 11*, 269–306.

NICHD Early Child Care Research Network. (1997). Familial factors associated with the characteristics of nonmaternal care for infants. *Journal of Marriage and Family, 59*, 389–408.

Owen, M. T., & Cox, M. J. (1988). Maternal employment and the transition to parenthood: Family functioning and child development. In A. E. Gottfried & A. W. Gottfried (Eds.), *Maternal employment and children's development: Longitudinal research* (pp. 85–119). New York: Plenum.

Owen, M. R., & Henderson, B. K. (1989, April). *Relations between child care qualities and child behavior at age 4: Do parent-child interactions play a role?* Paper presented at the biennial meetings of the Society for Research in Child Development, Kansas City, MO.

Radloff, L. (1977). The CES-D Scale: A self-report depression scale for research in the general population. *Applied Psychological Measurement, 1*, 385–410.

Roggman, L., Langtois, J., Hubbs-Tait, L., & Rieser-Danner, L. (1994). Infant day-care, attachment, and the "file drawer problem." *Child Development, 65*, 1429–1443.

Rutter, M. (1981). Socioemotional consequences of daycare for preschool children. *American Journal of Orthopsychiatry, 51*, 4–28.

Spieker, S. J., & Booth, C. L. (1988). Maternal antecedents of attachment quality. In J. Belsky & T. Nezworski (Eds.), *Clinical implications of attachment* (pp. 95–135). Hillsdale, NJ: Erlbaum.

Sroufe, L. A. (1985). Attachment classification from the perspective of infant–caregiver relationships and infant temperament. *Child Development, 56*, 1–14.

Sroufe, L. A. (1988). A developmental perspective on daycare. *Early Childhood. Research Quarterly, 3*, 283–291.

Vandell, D. L. (1979). The effects of playgroup experiences on mother-son and father-son interactions. *Developmental Psychology, 15*, 379–385.

van IJzendoorn, M. H., & Kroonenberg, P. M. (1988). Cross-cultural patterns of attachments: A meta-analysis of the Strange Situation. *Child Development, 59*, 147–156.

Werner, E. E., & Smith, R. S. (1992). *Overcoming the odds*. Ithaca, NY: Cornell University Press.

Zaslow, M. S., & Hayes, C. D. (1986). Sex differences in children's responses to psychosocial stress: Toward a cross-context analysis. In M. Lamb & B. Rogoff (Eds.), *Advances in developmental psychology* (Vol. 4, pp. 289–337). Hillsdale, NJ: Erlbaum.

Appendix

Mean distress ratings for low- and high-child-care intensity groups by five-category attachment classification

	A		B		C		D		U		Total	
	n	M	n	M	n	M	n	M	n	M	n	M
Low intensity	26	6.0	164	10.5	27	13.4	33	9.3	13	9.4	263	9.7
High intensity	42	6.5	153	10.4	15	13.7	38	11.8	9	8.8	257	10.3
Total	68	6.3	317	10.5	42	13.6	71	10.6	22	9.1	520	...

Note. The results for the two main effects tests and the interaction were as follows: intensity child-care group $F(1, 492) = .04, p > .1$; attachment group $F(4, 492) = 37.34, p < .001$; intensity child-care group × attachment group $F(4, 492) = 2.50, p < .05$. There was no main effect of intensity and no difference between the low-intensity and high-intensity As, the group for which a difference could theoretically be predicted. The interaction between intensity and attachment classification appeared to involve the D group: Low-intensity Ds showed less separation distress than high-intensity Ds. Because this difference was not theoretically predicted, we concluded that the Strange Situation was equally valid for children with and without early child-care experience.

A Closer Look 2 How Do I Love Thee? Attachment and Romantic Relationships

Beyond the realms of mother–infant relationships, attachment theory has been expanded greatly to help describe and understand many other types of relationships, including friendships, teacher–child relationships, workplace relationships, and even relationships with pets! Hazan and Shaver (1987) sought to characterize romantic relationships from an attachment perspective. They surveyed over 600 adults and had them indicate which series of statements most described their views and expectations about romantic relationships. Their results indicated that 56% of respondents described themselves as "secure" (e.g., I find it relatively easy to get close to others, I am comfortable depending on them and having them depend on me). The rest of the participants were characterized as "insecure,"

describing themselves as either "avoidant" (25%, e.g., I am uncomfortable being close to others, I find it difficult to trust others, I am nervous when anyone gets too close) or "ambivalent" (19%, e.g., I worry that my partner doesn't really love me or won't want to stay with me). Individuals with secure attachment views were happier, more trusting, and more likely to be in positive romantic relationships that lasted longer. In contrast, those with insecure views were less satisfied with their relationships, reported more fear of intimacy and jealousy, and were more likely to be divorced.

Hazen, C., & Shaver, P. (1987). Romantic love conceptualized as an attachment process. *Journal of Personality and Social Psychology, 52,* 511–524.

Classroom Exercises, Debates, and Discussion Questions

- *Observation.* Watch a young child and his or her parent(s) during pick-up or drop-off at daycare/school, meeting a new person, or other potentially "stressful" situations. List all of the child and parent behaviors that you observed that might be related to attachment.
- *Classroom debate.* Divide into two teams and debate the following statement: Children's behaviors in the Strange Situation only reflect their temperamental predispositions and are not a true measure of attachment.
- *Classroom exercise.* Attachment theory has been expanded to apply to many different types of relationships. For this activity, divide into small groups. Each group should use an attachment theory perspective to characterize a different type of relationship in childhood/adolescence (e.g., with friend, sibling, teacher, pet, etc.)
- *Classroom discussion.* Previous research (e.g., see reader article Waters et al., 2000) has shown some stability between infant–mother attachment classification and adult internal working models of attachment many years later. However, this stability does not appear to be present in "higher risk" samples (i.e., low SES). Why might attachment be less stable under these circumstances?

- *Classroom discussion.* Children in all cultures form attachment relationships with their parents. Some studies using the Strange Situation to assess attachment in young children suggest that there may be different distributions/patterns of attachment classifications in different parts of the world. Why might children from different cultures behave differently in the Strange Situation? What are some of the pitfalls in conducting this research in different parts of the world?

Additional Resources

For more about attachment, see:

Bowlby, J. (1988). *A secure base.* New York: Basic Books.

Bretherton, I. (2010). Fathers in attachment theory and research: A review. *Early Child Development and Care, 180,* 9–23.

Kochanska, G. (1998). Motherchild relationship, child fearfulness, and emerging attachment: A short-term longitudinal study. *Developmental Psychology, 34,* 480–490.

Fearon, R. P., Bakermans-Kranenburg, M. J., van IJzendoorn, M. H., Lapsley, A. M., & Roisman, G. (2010). The significance of insecure attachment and disorganization in the development of children's externalizing behavior: A meta-analytic study. *Child Development, 81,* 435–456.

Vaughn, B. E., Waters, H. S., Coppola, G., Cassidy, J., Bost, K. K., & Verissimo, M. (2006). Script-like attachment representations and behavior in families across cultures: Studies of parental secure base narratives. *Attachment and Human Development, 8,* 179–184.

4 MENTAL STATES AND THEORY OF MIND

Introduction   117

Mind-Reading, Emotion Understanding, and Relationships   118

Judy Dunn

Individual Differences   118

Differentiation of Understanding of Mind and Emotion   118

Links between Emotion, Relationships, and Social Understanding   119

Links between Understanding and Social Relations in Extreme Groups   120

Implications for Theory   121

Twelve-Month-Old Infants Interpret Action in Context   122

Amanda L. Woodward and Jessica A. Sommerville

Experiment 1   123

Experiment 2   126

General Discussion   126

Scaling of Theory-of-Mind Tasks   129

Henry M. Wellman and David Liu

Study 1   130

Study 2   136

General Discussion   143

A Closer Look 3   Autism and Theory of Mind: Understanding Others' Beliefs, Desires, and Emotions   149

Introduction

An explosion of research over the past few decades has identified a key aspect of social cognition, referred to as "theory of mind." Theory of mind is the ability to infer mental states (beliefs, desires, intentions, imagination) that are held by other individuals. Almost all forms of social interaction and cooperation require modifying one's actions based on the anticipation of what another person knows, or does not know. An individual who lacks a theory of mind will assume that their own desires, beliefs, and intentions are the same as what everyone else desires, believes, and intends. For example, without a theory of mind, a young child would have trouble distinguishing pretend and real events, understanding deception and lies, and differentiating between beliefs and desires. Thus, the ability to understand that others have potentially different mental states is a hallmark of early childhood, and changes substantially from infancy to adolescence.

Early research about children's "beliefs about beliefs" focused on the understanding of deception. Deception poses an interesting example of theory of mind because in order to deceive someone it is necessary to understand that you have information that the other person lacks. More recently, this research has expanded to examine the multitude of ways that theory of mind manifests in children's representation, symbolic play, imagination, and understanding of the psychological states of others. Additionally, researchers have examined theory of mind from infancy through adolescence, although the original research was focused on the preschool age. There has also been interest in the developmental changes that are associated with the acquisition of a theory of mind, as well as theory of mind capabilities in children with special needs (i.e., autism). For example, research has shown that autistic children often lack a theory of mind, and have trouble adjusting their behavior to take into account the viewpoints of others, especially peers (see A Closer Look 3).

Much of theory of mind research has its origins in Piaget's classic research on children's acquisition of perspective-taking (i.e., the ability to take the viewpoint of another). Piaget (1952) studied when children could mentally consider the vantage point of someone else, and argued that this was necessary for communication and the development of social relationships.

The three articles in this chapter cover different aspects of theory of mind research. Dunn (2000) introduces theory of mind competence in the child as "mind-reading" and describes how this ability arises in the context of social relationships and understanding of emotions. The second study explores the development of intentionality in infancy. Woodward and Sommerville (2000) examined 12-month-old infants' responses to ambiguous actions (e.g., touching the lid of a box) that were paired with goal-directed behaviors (e.g., reaching for a toy in the box) to test their understanding of others' intentional behaviors.

Finally, Wellman and Liu (2004) conducted a meta-analysis to summarize and differentiate between different aspects of theory of mind (e.g., belief, desire, knowledge, ignorance, and emotion) and delineate different measures for assessing this competency (e.g., diverse desires, diverse beliefs, knowledge access, contents false belief, belief emotions, and real-apparent beliefs). These studies provide a general introduction to the many facets of children's acquisition of a "theory of mind" emerging in infancy and connecting to aspects of social development, such as emotional understanding and social relationships. There are many new areas of research regarding how theory of mind is related to the emergence of moral judgment, emotion attributions, psychological understanding, and attachment.

Reference

Piaget, J. (1952). *The origins of intelligence in children*. New York: International Universities Press.

Mind-Reading, Emotion Understanding, and Relationships

Judy Dunn

Interest in children's understanding of mind has blossomed in an extraordinary way over the last decade (e.g., Carrothers & Smith, 1996; Zelazo, Astington, & Olson, 1999). The mapping of young children's growing grasp of the links between what people desire, think, or believe, and their actions has come to dominate much of cognitive developmental psychology. One key set of questions for the future, in this flourishing field, centres on the implications of understanding mind for children's social and emotional development.

Three issues stand out: first, the study of individual differences in mind-reading and understanding of emotions, and the broadening of the age range and cultural groups within which these are studied; second, the issue of how far the various aspects of cognitive development brought under the general label of "social understanding" should be differentiated; third, and most important, is the relation of such developments in cognition to children's social relationships and their emotional experiences—both as antecedents and as sequelae. Each of these issues represents a broadening of interest away from the focus on analysing the normative age changes in understanding of mind between the ages of two and five years, which has been dominant in the field.

Individual Differences

There is now an increasing recognition of the marked individual differences in young children's ability to understand mental states and the links between such understanding and human action, as assessed in standard theory of mind and emotion understanding tests—a new interest in pursuing the implications of these differences, and their origins (e.g., Astington, 1993). Equally striking and important is the evidence that individual differences are marked too in those aspects of real-life behaviour that reflect relatively sophisticated or mature understanding of inner states (e.g., deception, management of conflict, engagement in shared imaginative play), and that these relate to differences in test performance (Astington, 1993; Dunn, 1996; Newton, 1994).

This evidence on individual differences opens up a whole series of new directions for research on mind-reading—for instance, the links between such differences and social experiences (see later). But what about beyond the early years? It is likely that there will be increasing interest in studying such individual differences in children in the middle childhood years and adolescents. In common sense terms it seems obvious that understanding the subtleties of links between what people feel, intend, think, and believe and how they *behave* continues to develop and change as children grow from preschoolers to adolescence—and indeed adulthood. An example of how fruitful such research can be is described later, in considering links between understanding and relationships between adolescents and their teachers (O'Connor & Hirsch, 1999). The developmental issues raised will be of great interest: To what extent are there continuities in individual differences in these domains of understanding as people move from one developmental phase to another, from one social world and peer group to another? A start on such research has been made for the early years (Dunn, 1995; Hughes & Dunn, 1998), but it is only a first step. And studies that examine and incorporate *cultural* variation will be especially valuable and welcome (see Lillard, 1999).

Differentiation of Understanding of Mind and Emotion

A set of questions that are likely to feature increasingly in research on children's social understanding concerns differentiation of various aspects of social understanding. How is children's understanding of mental life related to other aspects of their cognitive development? How is children's growing grasp of other people's emotions, for example, linked to their understanding of mental life? Do individual differences in children's discovery of the mind in fact reflect differences and development in a more general domain of cognition? And how are these aspects of cognitive development related develop-mentally?

Tackling these questions means facing some central issues in psychology (including, for instance, a topic of much current controversy—the modularity of brain function, see Moore, 1996). Several lines of research are beginning to develop here. For example, in relation to the intriguing questions about the general pattern of developmental change, Bartsch and her colleagues have used evidence on children's talk about the mind (Bartsch & Wellman, 1995), and experimental studies to make a key developmental point. Very young children explain people's actions at first in terms of emotions and desires. Then through their social experiences, Bartsch and Wellman argue, they come to incorporate the notion of belief into their understanding of why people behave the way they do. An important implication of this is that an understanding of cognitive states *arises through an earlier understanding of emotional states* (Bartsch & Estes, 1996). This, they point out, has wide implications for our understanding of development—that accounts of metacognition will have to be anchored in a much broader understanding of development, and will require "a better understanding of the relationship between cognitive and noncognitive psychological phenomena" (Bartsch & Estes, 1996, p. 299).

Two promising lines of research concerning the issue of differentiation both link up with the new interest in individual differences. First, there are findings from longitudinal research that suggest that the sequelae of individual differences in success on mind-reading tasks may differ from those of early success on emotion understanding tasks (note that these are by no means always found to be strongly related—though the findings of different studies vary). Early mind-reading skills have been found to be related to a high degree of connected communication with peers, to sophisticated and frequent role play (Dunn, 1996), and in two separate studies, to increased sensitivity to criticism when first adjusting to the world of school

(Cutting, Dunn, & Davies, 2000; Donelan-McCall & Dunn, 1997). In contrast, early skills at understanding emotions have been reported to be associated with later peer popularity, sophisticated understanding of feelings, and aspects of moral sensibility (Dunn, 1995; Dunn, Cutting, & Demetriou, 2000).

Second, research into mind-reading within an attachment framework—which is likely to be a very active field over the next few years—suggests that differences in early attachment security may be associated with some aspects of later mind-reading skills, *but not others* (Meins, 1997). Clearly, the question of what processes might mediate such connections deserves research attention (intractable though it may be).

Links between Emotion, Relationships, and Social Understanding

The issue of links between attachment relations and later understanding brings us to a centrally important future topic of research. What children understand about the feelings and inner states of those with whom they have close relationships clearly carries great importance for those relationships; their grasp of how others' behaviour is linked to their feelings, beliefs, thoughts, and intentions is likely to be of major importance in their social lives. But the development of their understanding of others may also be influenced by their emotional and social experiences, as the attachment research indicates. Exciting new areas of research are opening up as investigators explore the links between children's social and emotional experiences, and their abilities to understand mind and emotion, both as antecedents and as sequelae. The results of the first studies have exciting implications for both domains.

Antecedents and sequelae

Naturalistic observational studies, combined with standard assessments of theory of mind and emotion understanding, have highlighted several kinds of interactive events that not only reveal children's social understanding but may be implicated in fostering its development: Shared imaginative play, discourse about inner states, collaborative narratives, arguments in disputes, exposure to and engagement in deception. What is needed now is more work to help us to clarify the direction of effects in such associations: Not only longitudinal studies but experimental studies too—to move beyond correlational studies. Further sensitive observational studies are also likely to prove very illuminating (Newton, 1994), particularly in the very early stages of children's discovery of the mind—studies of the second year, for instance, which include observations of teasing, deception, and joking are likely to pay dividends, if they are conducted in the real worlds of children's social relationships.

Studies of discourse about inner states are likely to be very fruitful. Such research has repeatedly shown associations between children's conversational experience and their success on mind-reading tasks (Dunn, 1996). We need more longitudinal studies to tease apart the direction of effects here (e.g., see Hughes & Dunn, 1998). A whole range of questions have been raised that merit study: Is it the "content" of such conversations that is all-important, or do the pragmatics also play a role? What precipitates these conversations in children's lives? Is it the case that the social partner matters? Do other children, for instance, play a special role (e.g., see Dunn, 1996; Piaget, 1932/1965)? Does the child's emotional state, while engaging in such discourse, play a role in what is learned, as has been suggested (but by no means established)?

Studies that investigate the issue of antecedents and sequelae of social understanding in terms of *relationships* (rather than solely interactive events) are likely to be important—as we noted earlier in considering attachment and differentiation of aspects of mind-reading (see also Fonagy, Redfern, & Charman, 1997). Not only is the research on attachment promising here: There is new interest in the friendships of very young children, shown to be associated with individual differences in understanding of inner states (Dunn & Cutting, 1999).

Differential use of understanding in different relationships

The issue of how children's mind-reading and emotion understanding are linked to differences in the quality of their relationships is highlighted in a new way by some intriguing findings that suggest another fruitful direction for research. In a study in which children were observed within their various different relationships—with their mothers, siblings, and friends—it was found that the children used their powers of understanding differently in these relationships (Dunn, 1996). In three different domains (engaging in discourse about mental states, sharing imaginative worlds, handling disputes) there were no significant correlations between the same child's behaviour with mother, sibling, and friend. The key point suggested by these findings is that whether children use their understanding of other people's inner states depends on the nature of their relationship with the other. Of course, what happens within real-life interactions will depend on both partners, and is unlikely to be simply linked to the socio-cognitive skills of either partner in the interaction. This implies that different kinds of social relationships will play different roles in influencing the development of social understanding—a proposal that certainly deserves further research.

The potential importance of such study is well illustrated by a recent study of adolescents by O'Connor and his colleagues (O'Connor & Hirsch, 1999), in which adolescents' relationships with their various teachers, and their understanding and attributions concerning these individuals were investigated. The "accuracy" with which the adolescents mentalised about their teachers was relationship-specific, and predicted from the affective quality of their relationship.

Links between Understanding and Social Relations in Extreme Groups

How far do the patterns of connections between social relationships and understanding of mind and emotion hold for children who have problems in relationships, or who suffer from cognitive difficulties? With the notable exception of studies of autism, until very recently most research on the links between understanding and social relationships was focused on normal children. However, an exciting new direction in such research is to ask whether the nature and patterns of early connections between understanding, emotional experience, and social relationships differs for children with problems such as hyperactivity, conduct problems, language delay, or anxiety. In all of these groups, we know that by middle childhood, children are at risk for problems in both close relationships and social understanding (e.g., Dodge, 1991). But how are these related in early childhood? Little is currently known, though a promising start has been made in the case of hyperactive children by Hughes and her colleagues (Hughes, Dunn, & White, 1998). In a longitudinal study of "hard-to-manage" children, the children's cognitive differences were associated with their observed antisocial behaviour; cognitive, emotion regulation, and social problems were closely related. To address these issues longitudinally, with children who have other problems in cognition and relationships will be to make a contribution that is both theoretically and socially valuable.

Implications for Theory

In summary, the current research on children's discovery of the mind presents us with both challenges and opportunities; to address the central theoretical issue of how children's emotional and social experiences are linked to their cognitive development will be of particular significance. The cognitive research that has clarified children's growing understanding of mental life has opened up a new range of issues, whereas the naturalistic research has highlighted the significance of the emotional settings in which children's understanding is fostered. We now must address the exciting developmental questions raised by the current work, focus not only on children in their preschool years, and include cultural variation in our studies, if we are to make progress in understanding the nature of the links between social and cognitive change in children.

References

Astington, J. W. (1993). *The child's discovery of the mind*. Cambridge, MA: Harvard University Press.

Bartsch, K., & Estes, D. (1996). Individual differences in children's developing theory of mind and implications for

metacognition. *Learning and Individual Differences*, 8, 281–304.

Bartsch, K., & Wellman, H. M. (1995). *Children talk about the mind*. Oxford, UK: Oxford University Press.

Carrothers, P., & Smith, P. K. (1996). *Theories of theories of mind*. Cambridge, UK: Cambridge University Press.

Cutting, A, Dunn, J., & Davies, L. (2000). Making the transition to school: Preschool predictors and personal perceptions. Manuscript submitted for publication.

Dodge, K. A. (1991). Emotion and social information processing. In J. Garber & K. Dodge (Eds.), *Emotional regulation* (pp. 159–181). Cambridge, UK: Cambridge University Press.

Donelan-McCall, N., & Dunn, J. (1997). School work, teachers, and peers: The world of first grade. *International Journal of Behavioral Development*, 21, 155–178.

Dunn, J. (1995). Children as psychologists: The later correlates of individual differences in understanding of emotions and other minds. *Cognition and Emotion*, 9, 187–201.

Dunn, J. (1996). The Emanuel Miller Memorial Lecture 1995: Children's relationships: Bridging the divide between cognitive and social development. *Journal of Child Psychology and Psychiatry and Allied Disciplines*, 37, 507–518.

Dunn, J., & Cutting, A. (1999). Understanding others, and individual differences in friendship interactions in young children. *Social Development*, 8, 201–219.

Dunn, J., Cutting, A, & Demetriou, H. (2000). Moral sensibility, understanding other, and children's friendship interactions in the preschool period. *British Journal of Developmental Psychology*, 18, 159–177.

Fonagy, P., Redfern, S., & Charman, A. (1997). The relationship between belief-desire reasoning and projective measure of attachment security. *British Journal of Developmental Psychology*, 15, 51–61.

Hughes, C., & Dunn, J. (1998). Understanding mind and emotion: Longitudinal associations with mental-state talk between young friends. *Developmental Psychology*, 34, 1026–1037.

Hughes, C., Dunn, J., & White, A. (1998). Trick or treat?: Uneven understanding of mind and emotion and executive function among "hard to manage" preschoolers. *Journal of Child Psychology and Psychiatry*, 39, 981–994.

Lillard, A. (1999). Developing a cultural theory of mind: The CIAO approach. *Current Directions in Psychological Science*, 8, 57–61.

Meins, E. (1997). *Security of attachment and the social development of cognition*. Hove, UK: Psychology Press.

Moore, C. (1996). Evolution and the modularity of mindreading. *Cognitive Development*, 11, 605–621.

Newton, P. (1994). *Preschool prevarication: An investigation of the cognitive prerequisites for deception*. Unpublished Ph.D. thesis, Portsmouth University.

O'Connor, T., & Hirsch, N. (1999). Intra-individual differences and relationship-specificity of mentalising in early adolescence. *Social Development, 8*, 256–274.

Piaget, J. (1965). *The moral judgement of the child* New York: Academic Press. (Original work published 1932)

Zelazo, P. D., Astington, J. W., & Olson, D. R. (1999). *Developing theories of intention: Social understanding and self control*. Mahwah, NJ: Erlbaum.

....

Twelve-Month-Old Infants Interpret Action in Context

Amanda L. Woodward and Jessica A. Sommerville

The propensity to see action as goal-directed is a powerful organizer in human cognition. Adults and children describe sequences of action in terms of the actor's goals (Heider, 1958; Lillard & Flavell, 1990; Trabasso, Stein, Rodkin, Munger, & Baugh, 1992), knowing the goal behind a series of events renders the series more easily remembered (Bransford & Johnson, 1972), and elements of a story that are relevant to the actor's goals are represented more strongly in memory than those that are not (Black & Bower, 1980). Underlying this organizational ability is the understanding that actions can often be interpreted as sequences deployed in service of an overarching goal (Schank & Abelson, 1977; Searle, 1983). For example, imagine a woman moving objects from one side of a crowded garage to the other. The goal behind her actions may not be obvious. Next, the woman wheels a lawn mower in from the driveway, fitting it into the newly cleared space. It now becomes apparent that the goal behind her earlier actions was to make a space for the lawn mower. As this example illustrates, the ability to relate actions to overarching goals is particularly useful when dealing with actions that are difficult to interpret on their own. In the current studies, we investigated the early development of the ability to relate actions in sequence and to use this relation to infer the goal of an ambiguous action.

Recently, researchers have begun to explore infants' understanding of action. Their findings indicate that infants can use certain perceptual cues to break a continuous stream of behavior into action-sized units (Baldwin & Baird, 1999; Sharon & Wynn, 1998; Wynn, 1996). Moreover, babies understand human actions not simply as a series of motions through space, but

rather, as directed toward goals. Fourteen- to 24-month-olds draw on behavioral cues such as jerkiness of motion and vocal expressions of dismay to determine whether a novel action is intentional (Carpenter, Akhtar, & Tomasello, 1998; Tomasello & Barton, 1994), and, given contextual and behavioral cues, 18-month-olds can infer the goal of a novel action that is not completed (Meltzoff, 1995).

The roots of this ability extend earlier into infancy. Before they are a year old, infants interpret one familiar action, grasping, as goal-directed. In a previous study (Woodward, 1998), we used the visual habituation paradigm to investigate 6- and 9-month-old infants' representations of an event in which an actor moved her arm through a distinctive path in order to grasp one of two toys that sat side by side on a small stage. This event could be described in at least two ways: in terms of the motion of the actor's arm through space or in terms of the relation between the actor and the object that was her goal. The question was which of these features infants would weight more heavily in their representations of the event. This question was addressed by switching the positions of the toys following habituation to one event and then showing infants test events in which either the path of motion taken by the actor's arm or the object that was grasped had changed. Infants showed a greater novelty response (as indicated by longer looking) to the change in goal object than to the change in path. That is, when babies saw a person grasp an object, they paid special attention to the relation between the actor and the object. Moreover, infants differentiated between people and inanimate objects on this dimension. Infants who saw inanimate objects such as rods and mechanical claws move toward and touch or grasp the toy did not show this pattern. If anything, infants in these conditions tended to look longer when the path of motion was new. Follow-up analyses revealed that these results were not a by-product of infants' interest in hands versus rods or claws. Infants in all conditions had their attention drawn to the toy that was grasped or touched, but infants who saw a person grasp the toy differed from those who saw an inanimate claw in the features they weighted most heavily in their representation of the event.

In sum, infants give special weight to goal-related information in their representations of events in which a person acts. When dealing with single actions, then, infants' understanding of human behavior shares a critical feature with mature understandings. If infants were limited to construing only single actions as goal-directed, however, their understanding of human behavior would be fragmentary at best. For example, watching someone go to the kitchen to get a glass of milk, an infant limited in this way might construe some of the subunits as goal-directed (grasping the refrigerator door handle, grasping the milk carton, grasping a glass, etc.), but miss the fact that these units are parts of a higher-order plan. Moreover, the goals behind many aspects of the event (e.g., opening the milk carton, sniffing its contents, and pouring the milk into the glass) would remain uninterpretable.

These considerations raise the question of whether infants can interpret longer sequences of actions in terms of overarching goals. The current studies investigated this question for 12-month-old infants. We adapted the methodology developed by Woodward (1998) to ask whether infants' construal of a particular action is influenced by the actions that accompany it. We began with an action that was not interpretable as goal-directed by 12-month-olds, and then introduced it in a sequence that culminated in an action that infants readily interpret as goal-directed, namely, grasping. The question was whether this embedding would lead babies to interpret the ambiguous action as being directed toward a particular goal.

Babies saw a toy that was inside a closed, clear plastic box. An actor reached in and laid her hand on top of the box, hooking her thumb under the edge of the lid. We reasoned that this action might be ambiguous to infants. It could be directed at the box or at the toy

inside the box. We tested this possibility in the *single-action condition* by habituating infants to the first event and then showing them test events in which the actor completed the same action on either a new box or the same box, which now contained a new toy. We reasoned that if infants construed the reach as directed toward the box, they would show a stronger novelty response (i.e., look longer) to the change in box. If they construed the reach as directed toward the toy, they would show a greater novelty response to the change in toy. In the *embedded-action condition*, the ambiguous action was followed by the actor opening the box and grasping the toy inside. After habituation, infants saw the same test events as in the single-action condition. The question was whether this embedding would lead infants to interpret the touch to the box lid as being directed toward the toy inside the box. If so, then infants in this condition would be predicted to look longer when the relation between the actor and the toy had changed than when the relation between the actor and the box had changed.

Experiment 1

Participants

Forty full-term infants participated in Experiment 1 (mean age = 11 months, 22 days; range: 10 months, 21 days to 12 months, 26 days). Ten additional infants began testing but were excluded from the final sample because of experimental error ($n = 8$) or failing to complete all of the test trials as a result of distress ($n = 2$). Twenty infants were tested in the single-action condition, and 20 were tested in the embedded-action condition. There were 12 boys and 8 girls in the single-action condition (mean age = 11 months, 21 days) and 10 boys and 10 girls in the embedded-action condition (mean age = 11 months, 23 days).

Procedure

Infants saw the experimental events presented on a small stage at a distance of 30 in. Sitting side by side on the stage were two tinted clear plastic boxes (one purple and one blue), each of which contained a small toy (a bear or a tiger). At the start of each trial, an actor

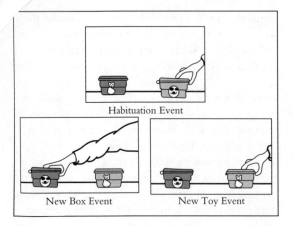

Figure 4.1   Sample events for the single-action condition.

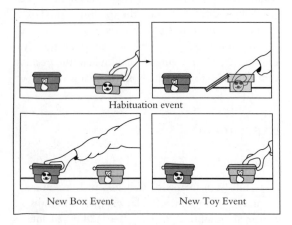

Figure 4.2   Sample events for the embedded-action condition.

reached in through a curtain at the side of the stage to lay her hand on top of one of the boxes, hooking her thumb under the edge of the lid. Only the actor's arm, clothed in a magenta sleeve, and her bare hand were visible to the infant. In the single-action condition, and during the test trials in both conditions, the event ended at this point (see Figure 4.1). In the habituation phase of the embedded-action condition, after the actor touched the lid, she opened the box, reached inside, and grasped the toy (see Figure 4.2). In each condition, the action was performed once per trial. The actor remained still, with her hand on the box or grasping the toy, until the trial ended. A screen was raised from below the stage to hide it from view

between trials. The actor retracted her hand (and closed the box if necessary) once the screen was in place. Then the screen was lowered and the next trial began. The infant's looking was timed beginning when the actor's hand had stopped moving and ending when the infant looked away for 2 s. Infants' looking was coded on-line over video by an observer who could not see the experimental events and was not informed of the condition to which the infant had been assigned.[1]

Infants were shown the same event on each trial during habituation. The habituation phase ended when the infant's looking had decreased by 50% over a 3-trial window, or when 14 trials had been completed. Following habituation, the positions of the toys were switched, and infants were given 1 trial in which the actor did not reach into the stage area to familiarize them with the new locations. Then, infants in both conditions saw the same two test events in alternation for a total of 6 trials: On *new-toy* trials, the actor reached in and touched the top of the box she had touched during habituation, which now contained a different toy; on *new-box* trials, the actor touched the top of the other box, which contained the same toy as the one contained in the box she had touched during habituation. This event also involved a new path of motion for the actor's arm. The side of the reach during habituation and the order of test trials were counterbalanced within each condition.

Results and discussion

Table 4.1 summarizes infants' looking times for the habituation and test trials in each condition. To reduce positive skew, we subjected the looking-time scores to a log transformation before parametric tests were conducted. Our first analyses confirmed that infants in the two conditions showed comparable levels of attention in the habituation phase. Looking times on the last three habituation trials did not differ as a function of condition ($t < 1$). Infants' rate of habituation did not differ as a function of condition. Infants in the single-action condition averaged 10.1 habituation trials, and infants in the embedded-action condition averaged 9.4 habituation trials ($t < 1$).[2]

Table 4.1 Median total looking time during the last three habituation trials and the three test trials of each type

		Test trials	
Condition	Last 3 habituation trials	New toy	New box
Experiment 1			
Single-action	7.7 (2.9)	13.9 (6.0)	15.1 (7.5)
Embedded-action	8.5 (3.8)	21.5 (6.6)★	15.5 (5.5)
Experiment 2			
Toy-out-of-box	9.4 (2.7)	14.5 (5.3)	20.0 (4.5)

Note. Median absolute deviations are given in parentheses.
★ Different from comparison test event, $p < .05$.

We next explored infants' responses to the two test events. Preliminary analyses revealed no reliable effects of the side of the habituation reach or the test trial given first. Therefore, subsequent analyses were collapsed across these dimensions. An analysis of variance (ANOVA) conducted on the looking times for each trial type with condition (single-action vs. embedded-action) as the between-subjects variable and trial type (new-box vs. new-toy events) as the within-subjects factor yielded a condition-by-trial-type interaction, $F(1, 38) = 4.79$, $p < .05$, and no other reliable effects. Planned comparisons revealed that infants in the single-action condition did not differ in their looking times on the two kinds of test trials, $t(19) = 0.78$, $p = .44$. Thus, infants in this condition did not clearly interpret the touch as directed at either the toy or the box. In contrast, infants in the embedded-action condition looked longer on new-toy trials than on new-box trials, $t(19) = 2.58$, $p < .05$. That is, infants looked longer when the actor's hand was in relation to a new toy, even though in this event the hand followed the same path of motion and rested on the same box as during the habituation trials. Thus, embedding the touch in a sequence culminating in a grasp of the toy within the box affected infants' interpretations of the touch.

In a follow-up analysis, we tested the possibility that infants in the single-action condition failed to differentiate between the new-toy and new-box events because of a lack of overall attention. One piece of evidence against this possibility is the absence of a main effect of condition during the test phase, which suggests that infants in the two conditions were equally attentive. We also approached this question by analyzing infants' recovery from habituation. Infants' total looking time on the last three habituation trials was compared with their total looking times on the three new-box events and the three new-toy events. These analyses revealed that infants in both conditions recovered attention on both types of test trials: single-action condition, new-toy trials, $t(19) = 3.53$, $p < .005$; single-action condition, new-box trials, $t(19) = 4.10$, $p < .001$; embedded-action condition, new-toy trials, $t(19) = 7.07$, $p < .0001$; embedded-action condition, new-box trials, $t(19) = 4.65$, $p < .001$. Thus, inattention does not account for the findings in the single-action condition.

The results of the first experiment indicate that infants attended to the sequence of actions, and used a familiar action in the sequence (grasping) to interpret a novel action (the touch to the box lid). This raises the question of how infants related the two actions. Recent evidence indicates that 8-month-old infants are adept at extracting the conditional probabilities of occurrence of sequential stimuli (Saffran, Aslin, & Newport, 1996). It is possible that infants use this ability when interpreting action, relating any two actions that occur in sequence. If so, infants would, of course, differ dramatically from mature reasoners. Adults do not assume that any two actions in sequence are in service of a single overarching goal. At a picnic, an adult who sees someone swat at a mosquito and then reach for another helping of potato salad would not assume that the swat and the reach were related to the same goal.

To inform inferences about how actions are related, adults draw on knowledge about the causal constraints in a situation (Schank & Abelson, 1977; Searle, 1983). The example we began with illustrates this process. If the woman working in her garage had cleared a space the size of a shoe box, an adult would not consider the possibility that her goal in doing so was to move the lawn mower inside. The physical constraints in the events in Experiment 1 could have led infants to relate the box touch to the grasp of the toy because in order to gain access to the toy, the actor had to first remove the box lid. Thus, touching the box lid was causally related to freeing access to the toy. Prior research indicates that infants under 1 year of age understand the physical constraints imposed by containment. Baillargeon, Graber, DeVos, and Black (1990) found that 5½-month-old infants did not expect a person to be able to retrieve a toy that was covered by a container if the container was not first removed. Did infants use this knowledge in interpreting the goals of the actor in Experiment 1? We conducted a second experiment to address this question. The procedure was identical to that of the embedded-action condition in Experiment 1 with one important difference: The toys sat outside and in front of the boxes. Thus, touching the lid and grasping the toy were no longer causally related, although they occurred in the same temporal sequence as in Experiment 1.

Experiment 2

Participants

Twenty full-term infants (8 boys and 12 girls) participated in Experiment 2 (mean age = 12 months, 0 days; range: 10 months, 24 days to 13 months, 12 days). Three additional infants began testing but were excluded from the final sample because of experimental error ($n = 1$) or because they moved off camera during test trials ($n = 2$).

Procedure

The design and procedure were the same as those in the embedded-action condition in Experiment 1 except that each toy sat outside and in front of one of the boxes.[3]

The toy was centered with respect to the front of the box, with its back surface 2 in. from the front of the box.

Results and discussion

Table 4.1 summarizes infants' looking times for the habituation and test trials. Infants in Experiment 2 averaged 8.9 habituation trials. To reduce positive skew, we subjected the looking-time scores to a log transformation before parametric tests were conducted. We first explored infants' responses to the two test events. Because preliminary analyses revealed no reliable effects of the side of the habituation reach or the test trial given first, subsequent analyses were collapsed across these dimensions. Planned comparisons revealed a nonsignificant trend for infants to look longer on new-box trials than on new-toy trials, $t(19) = 1.67, p = .11$.[4] Therefore, seeing the grasp and touch events in temporal sequence did not lead infants to interpret the touch as directed toward the toy.

In a second analysis, we compared the data from this study with the data from infants in the embedded-action condition in Experiment 1. An ANOVA conducted on the looking times for each trial type with condition (embedded-action vs. toy-out-of-box) as the between-subjects factor and trial type (new-box event vs. new-toy event) as the within-subjects factor revealed a trial-type-by-condition interaction, $F(1, 38) = 9.25, p < .005$, and no other reliable effects, confirming that infants responded differently to the sequence of events when the toy was inside the box as opposed to being outside of it.

Finally, we analyzed recovery from habituation to test the possibility that infants were inattentive on test trials. Comparisons between the final three habituation trials and the three test trials of each type revealed that infants recovered attention reliably for both new-toy and new-box trials, $t(19) = 2.39, p < .05$, and $t(19) = 3.28, p < .005$, respectively.

General Discussion

We began with an ambiguous action—when the actor touched the top of the box in the single-action condition in Experiment 1, 12-month-olds did not clearly interpret the touch as directed at either the box or the toy within it. After seeing the touch followed by the actor opening the box and grasping the toy, infants interpreted the touch as directed at the toy: During test trials, when the actor touched the box but did not open it, babies responded to a change in the relation between the actor and the toy. That is, 12-month-olds interpreted the first action, touching the box lid, on the basis of the action that occurred afterward, grasping the toy. The findings of Experiment 2 indicate that infants drew on the causal constraints in the situation in making the link between the two actions. When the two actions occurred in the same temporal sequence, but the causal relation between them was disrupted, infants did not link the two actions. These findings suggest that these 12-month-old infants interpreted action in context in two senses: They used both the other actions performed by the actor and the causal constraints in the situation to interpret an ambiguous action.

The ability to link actions that occur together provides infants with a powerful tool for making sense of human behavior. This ability would enable infants to form coherent representations of action sequences at the level of "getting a drink of milk" rather than at the level of "grasping the milk carton." In so doing, infants must represent goals as in some way separable from the particular actions that they drive. It is possible that younger infants initially conceive of goals as inherent in particular actions. Our findings indicate that by 12 months, infants are on the path to understanding a critical aspect of intentional action, namely, that goals exist independent of particular actions.

In addition, our findings suggest that the ability to relate actions in sequence enriches infants' understanding of particular actions. Through seeing actions such as touching the lid of a box, twisting the top to a jar, or pulling open the drawstrings of a bag in sequences that culminate in the actor obtaining the object within the container, infants may come to construe these actions as directed at particular kinds of goals.

Seeking connections between actions that co-occur is useful, but linking any two actions that occur in sequence would be a hazardous move, leading to potentially faulty inferences about goal structure. By using causal relations as a basis for linking actions in sequence, babies in the current studies avoided this error. More generally, seeking causal relations between

events has been argued to play a central role in conceptual development, leading to rich, theory-like knowledge structures (Carey, 1985; Gopnik & Meltzoff, 1997; Keil, 1992). Our findings indicate that by 12 months of age, infants construe goal-directed action in a causal framework. This early reasoning could contribute to the development of a theory of mind or theory of action.

One potential limit on infants' ability to relate actions in sequence is the complexity of causal relations they can consider. As part of reasoning that the actor did Y in order to get X, infants seem to have understood that in order for X to happen, Y had to happen first. Thus, one prerequisite for the ability to relate actions in sequence may be the attainment of means-end reasoning. There is debate in the literature about when this occurs. Some researchers place this achievement at around 12 months, based on infants' ability to solve problems such as removing a barrier to obtain a toy (Diamond, 1991; Piaget, 1952/1974). However, Baillargeon et al. (1990) reported that when infants observe actions rather than acting themselves, they understand means-end sequences well before this, at $5\frac{1}{2}$ months. Given this finding, and the fact that infants as young as 6 months construe grasping as goal-directed, infants under 12 months may be able to interpret the goal of an action on the basis of sequences like the ones used in the current studies. Further research is required to investigate this possibility.

In addition, infants' ability to relate actions in sequence would be limited by the kinds of causal constraints that they can consider. In understanding action, adults consider not only the physical constraints present in a situation, but also the psychological constraints (e.g., what a person knows) and social constraints (e.g., conventionally appropriate behaviors). To the extent that infants lack knowledge about these constraints, their ability to construe actions in context will be limited. In addition, it is not clear whether, like adults, infants can think ahead to possible actions. Seeing a lawn mower sitting in the driveway would suggest why someone would be clearing a space in the garage, just as seeing an actor with her hand on the lid of a box would suggest that she was interested in obtaining the toy inside. Twelve-month-old infants did not seem to make this inference in the current studies. When babies saw the actor repeatedly rest her hand on the box in the single-action condition in Experiment 1, they did not interpret this action as directed at the toy. It is possible that given additional behavioral cues (e.g., if the actor were shown to be looking into the box and smiling) or contextual information (e.g., if they were allowed to play with the boxes and toys before the study), babies might have made this inference. Nevertheless, in the absence of these potentially helpful cues, infants were able to interpret an ambiguous action on the basis of the behavioral and physical context.

Notes

1   To assess reliability, we asked a second observer to code each infant from videotape. The two observers were counted as agreeing if they identified the same endpoint for a trial. On this criterion, the coders agreed for 88% of test trials in the single-action condition and 84% in the embedded-action condition. Disagreements were categorized according to whether the video coder judged that the trial had ended too soon or too late. These disagreements were randomly distributed across trial types for each condition (Fisher's exact tests: $p > .99$ for the single-action condition, $p = .52$ for the embedded-action condition).

2   Seven infants in the single-action condition and 2 in the embedded-action condition completed 14 habituation trials without meeting the habituation criterion. When these infants were excluded from the analyses, the interpretation of the results was unchanged.

3   Reliability for this study, assessed as in Study 1, was 93%. The direction of disagreements was randomly distributed across trial types (Fisher's exact test: $p > .99$).

4   Three infants completed 14 habituation trials without meeting the habituation criterion. When these infants were excluded from the analysis, the preference for the new-box test event was somewhat stronger, $t(16) = 1.94$, $p = .07$.

References

Baillargeon, R., Graber, M., DeVos, J., & Black, J. C. (1990). Why do young infants fail to search for hidden objects? *Cognition, 36,* 255–284.

Baldwin, D. A., & Baird, J. A. (1999). Action analysis: A gateway to intentional inference. In P. Rochat (Ed.), *Early social cognition* (pp. 215–240). Hillsdale, NJ: Erlbaum.

Black, J. B., & Bower, G. H. (1980). Story understanding as problem-solving. *Poetics, 9,* 223–250.

Bransford, J., & Johnson, M. (1972). Contextual prerequisites for understanding. *Journal of Verbal Learning and Verbal Behavior, 11,* 717–726.

Carey, S. (1985). *Conceptual change in childhood.* Cambridge, MA: MIT Press.

Carpenter, M., Akhtar, N., & Tomasello, M. (1998). Fourteen through eighteen month old infants differentially imitate intentional and accidental actions. *Infant Behavior and Development, 21,* 315–330.

Diamond, A. (1991). Neuropsychological insights into the meaning of object concept development. In S. Carey & R. Gelman (Eds.), *The epigenesis of mind* (pp. 67–110). Hillsdale, NJ: Erlbaum.

Gopnik, A., & Meltzoff, A. (1997). *Words, thoughts, and theories.* Cambridge, MA: MIT Press.

Heider, F. (1958). *The psychology of interpersonal relations.* New York: John Wiley and Sons.

Keil, F. C. (1992). The origins of an autonomous biology. In M.R. Gunnar & M. Maratsos (Eds.), *Modularity and constraints in language and cognition* (pp. 103–138). Hillsdale, NJ: Erlbaum.

Lillard, A. S., & Flavell, J. H. (1990). Young children's preference for mental state versus behavioral descriptions of human action. *Child Development, 61,* 731–741.

Meltzoff, A. M. (1995). Understanding the intentions of others: Re-enactments of intended acts by 18-month-old children. *Developmental Psychology, 31,* 838–850.

Piaget, J. (1974). *The origins of intelligence in children* (M. Cook, Trans.). Madison, CT: International Universities Press. (Original work published 1952)

Saffran, J. R., Aslin, R. N., & Newport, E. L. (1996). Statistical learning by 8-month-old infants. *Science, 274,* 1926–1928.

Schank, R. C., & Abelson, R. P. (1977). *Scripts, plans, goals and understanding,* Hillsdale, NJ: Erlbaum.

Searle, J. R. (1983). *Intentionality: An essay in the philosophy of mind.* Cambridge, England: Cambridge University Press.

Sharon, T., & Wynn, K. (1998). Individuation of actions from continuous motion. *Psychological Science, 9,* 357–362.

Tomasello, M., & Barton, M. (1994). Learning words in non-ostensive contexts. *Developmental Psychology, 30,* 639–650.

Trabasso, T., Stein, N. L., Rodkin, P. C., Munger, M. P., & Baugh, C. R. (1992). Knowledge of goals and plans in the on-line narration of events. *Cognitive Development, 7,* 133–170.

Woodward, A. L. (1998). Infants selectively encode the goal object of an actor's reach. *Cognition, 69,* 1–34.

Wynn, K. (1996). Infants' individuation and enumeration of actions. *Psychological Science, 7,* 164–169.

Scaling of Theory-of-Mind Tasks

Henry M. Wellman and David Liu

Children's understanding of persons' mental states—their theory of mind—is a crucial cognitive development and has been intensely studied in the last 15 years (e.g., see Flavell & Miller, 1998). At times, theory of mind is discussed as a single cognitive process or achievement (especially in some areas of inquiry, such as primate cognition or research on autism). Relatedly, much theory-of-mind research has focused on a single task paradigm examining children's understanding of false belief. However, many researchers believe that developing a theory of mind includes understanding multiple concepts acquired in an extended series of developmental accomplishments (for a recent review, see Wellman, 2002). Consequently, investigations of young children's understandings of intentions, emotions, desires, knowledge, and other states have become prevalent. However, little research empirically establishes developmental progressions in children's various understandings. Support for one progression comes from studies showing that children's understanding of desires seems to precede their understanding of beliefs (e.g., Bartsch & Wellman, 1995; Flavell, Flavell, Green, & Moses, 1990; Gopnik & Slaughter, 1991; Wellman & Woolley, 1990). But other progressions are empirically unclear or contentious (e.g., Mitchell, 1996; Perner, 1995). More serious still, very little research has attempted to investigate comprehensively an extended series of theory-of-mind developments.

We assume that, for normally developing children, certain insights about the mind develop in a predictable sequence. We hypothesize that these insights index an underlying developmental progression that could be captured in a theory-of-mind scale. We provide two types of empirical support for this hypothesis. First, we report a preliminary meta-analysis of studies that have compared different types of mental state understandings (e.g., desires vs. beliefs or ignorance vs. false belief). A meta-analysis seems useful to integrate and clarify scattered individual

findings that are at times contradictory. Primarily, however, we report a study testing a theory-of-mind scale for preschool children—a set of methodologically comparable tasks that focus on differing conceptual constructs that may developmentally appear in sequence.

As background, our focus concerns preschool developments, a developmental period when there are many changes in mental sate understanding. We do not include second-order false-belief tasks (which regularly are acquired in the early school years, consistently after a first-order understanding of false belief; Perner & Wimmer, 1985), nor do we include tasks representing more mature (Wellman & Hickling, 1994) or advanced theory-of-mind understandings (Happé, 1994) thought to be acquired later in development and that focus largely on metaphor, irony, double deceptions, and complex narratives. Instead, we focus on younger children and consider tasks designed to assess children's understanding of desires, emotions, knowledge, and beliefs. These tasks are different in focusing on different states (e.g., wants vs. thoughts). Nonetheless, these states are all similarly mental. In particular, mental states such as desires, emotions, knowledge, and beliefs can be discrepant from reality (e.g., desires vs. outcomes, actuality vs. belief) and discrepant across individuals (e.g., when two persons have different desires for the same object or different beliefs about the same situation).

Potentially, a scaled set of tasks may have several advantages. It could more comprehensively capture children's developing understandings across a range of conceptions. A scale, based on sequences within children, provides stronger evidence for sequences than do inferences from group means. Establishing sequences of development would help constrain theorizing about theory-of-mind development. Moreover, a scaled set of tasks could provide a better measure to use in individual differences research examining the interplay between theory-of-mind understanding and other factors. This would include both the role of independent factors (e.g., family conversations, language, executive function) on theory of mind and the role of theory of mind as an independent factor contributing to other developments (e.g., social interactions, peer acceptance). Currently, research on these antecedents and consequents has been limited to simply using children's understanding of false belief as a marker of their theory-of-mind development (e.g., Astington & Jenkins, 1999; Dunn, Brown, Slomkowski, Tesla, & Youngblade, 1991; Lalonde & Chandler, 1995). However, if the intent of such studies is to index a broader construct of, and variation in, children's developing mental-state understanding, then a scale would capture such variation more informatively.

STUDY I

We conducted a simple meta-analysis to summarize prior research comparing one type of theory-of-mind reasoning with another to inform our selection of scale tasks for Study 2. Most studies comparing two different theory-of-mind tasks compare performance on one sort of false-belief task (e.g., a change-of-locations task) with performance on another sort of false-belief task (e.g., an unexpected-contents task), or compare performance on a standard false-belief task with a modified false-belief task. Such comparisons were reviewed by Wellman, Cross, and Watson (2001). In Study 1 we analyzed, instead, comparisons across different mental states, for example, between children's understanding of desires versus beliefs. We aimed for a general picture of which mental-state concepts were easier than others in the preschool-age period. We did not aim for a comprehensive meta-analysis, such as Wellman et al., that closely examined moderating effects (e.g., task type or nature of protagonist).

Obviously, a pair of tasks might yield different performances either because of conceptual differences between the tasks or because of less relevant differences between task demands or features (e.g., one requiring open-ended explanations vs. the other requiring yes-no judgments). We included only pairs of tasks where the formats and demands were similar and parallel.

Method

Sample of studies and conditions

We began by considering all the studies listed by Wellman et al. (2001), studies that typically included the key words *belief* or *false belief* in their titles. We supplemented those studies with a computerized search of the PsycINFO database (from 1987 through 2002). We searched for studies that included the key words *desire, belief, knowledge, ignorance*, and *emotion* in pairwise combinations (e.g., studies whose key words included both *desire* and *belief* or *belief* and *ignorance*, and so on). We also constrained this search to include only articles focusing on children and cognition. These two sources yielded a set of more than 600 research publications for initial consideration. In addition, we scanned, more haphazardly, conference abstracts from the Society for Research in Child Development and the Cognitive Development Society. By this process we gathered as many potentially relevant studies as we could find, but we did not comprehensively search through all published and unpublished research.

From the research we examined initially, to be included in our meta-analytic comparisons a study had to provide study details in English, had to report data for preschool children, and had to report comparable data for children's performance on tasks contrasting two constructs (e.g., desire vs. belief). Moreover, the contrasting tasks in any comparison had to be closely comparable in formats, materials, and questions. Many conceivable comparisons (e.g., between understandings of desire vs. knowledge) were not represented in the literature, were represented by only one or two comparisons in only one or two studies, or employed tasks with widely varying formats and demands. Because of these limitations, as shown in Table 4.2, we focused on three primary comparisons. Table 4.2 lists the studies and conditions we used for our quantitative comparisons. The names for different conditions as listed in that table adhere as closely as possible to the names used in the original

Table 4.2   Studies and conditions used for the meta-analysis in Study 1

Study	Condition	Mean age	Mean sample size	RD
Belief vs. false belief				
Bartsch (1996)	Study 1: Discrepant belief (XX) vs. false belief (XO)	3.50	20	.53
Bartsch (1996)	Study 2: Discrepant belief (XX) vs. false belief (XY)	3.42	24	.68
Gopnik & Slaughter (1991)	Experiment 2: Image (diverse thoughts) vs. belief	3.95	24	.29
Gopnik, Slaughter, & Meltzoff (1994)	Experiment 1: Diverse belief (Level 2 think) vs. false belief	3.58	14	.64
Gopnik et al. (1994)	Experiment 2: Diverse belief (Level 2 think) vs. false belief	3.67	12	.75
Gopnik et al. (1994)	Experiment 3: Diverse belief (Level 2 think) vs. false belief	3.58	18	.30
Harris, Johnson, Hutton, Andrews, & Cooke (1989)	Experiment 3 belief (nonpreferred) vs. Experiment 2 false belief	5.34	18	.42
Wellman & Bartsch (1988)	Study 3: Not-own belief vs. explicit false belief	4.13	40	.34
Wellman & Bartsch (1988)	Study 3: Discrepant belief vs. explicit false belief	3.67	16	.66
Wellman, Hollander, & Schult (1996)	Study 1 subjective thoughts vs. Study 4 false belief	4.08	31	.18
Desire vs. belief				
Flavell, Flavell, Green, & Moses (1990)	Study 1: Value belief vs. fact belief	3.25	32	.38
Flavell et al. (1990)	Study 2: Value belief vs. fact belief	3.08	16	.69
Flavell et al. (1990)	Study 3: Value belief vs. fact belief	3.17	20	.20
Flavell et al. (1990)	Study 4: Value belief vs. fact belief	3.25	32	.33
Gopnik & Slaughter (1991)	Experiment 1: Desire vs. belief	4.00	36	.17
Gopnik & Slaughter (1991)	Experiment 2: Desire vs. belief	3.95	24	.13
Gopnik & Slaughter (1991)	Experiment 1: Intentions vs. belief	4.00	36	.17
Ruffman, Slade, & Crowe (2002)	Time 1: Desire-emotion vs. transfer (false belief)	3.01	82	.27
Ruffman et al. (2002)	Time 2: Desire-emotion vs. transfer (false belief)	3.41	79	.21
Ruffman et al. (2002)	Time 2: Desire-action vs. contents (false belief)	3.41	79	.17
Ruffman et al. (2002)	Time 3: Desire-action vs. contents (false belief)	4.04	72	.24
Wellman & Woolley (1990)	Study 2: Not-own desire vs. not-own belief	3.00	20	.20
Wellman & Woolley (1990)	Study 2: Not-own desire vs. discrepant belief	3.00	20	.60
Knowledge vs. false belief				
Fabricius & Khalil (2003)	Study 1: Know (contents) vs. false belief (contents)	5.00	84	.21
Fabricius & Khalil (2003)	Study 1: Know (location) vs. false belief (location)	5.00	84	.08
Fabricius & Khalil (2003)	Study 2: Know (contents) vs. false belief (contents)	5.33	48	.07
Fabricius & Khalil (2003)	Study 2: Know (location) vs. false belief (location)	5.33	48	−.06
Fabricius & Khalil (2003)	Study 3: Know (contents) vs. false belief (contents)	5.58	32	−.19
Fabricius & Khalil (2003)	Study 3: Know (location) vs. false belief (location)	5.58	32	−.19
Flavell et al. (1990)	Study 1: Knowledge vs. fact belief	3.25	32	.05
Hogrefe, Wimmer, & Perner (1986)	Experiment 1: Ignorance vs. false belief	4.50	51	.36
Hogrefe et al. (1986)	Experiment 2: Ignorance vs. false belief	4.50	70	.14
Hogrefe et al. (1986)	Experiment 3: Ignorance vs. false belief	3.58	22	.25
Hogrefe et al. (1986)	Experiment 4: Ignorance vs. false belief	4.13	36	.27
Hogrefe et al. (1986)	Experiment 5: Ignorance vs. false belief	3.67	36	.44
Hogrefe et al. (1986)	Experiment 6: Ignorance vs. false belief	5.44	36	.35
Friedman, Griffin, Brownell, & Winner (2001)	Study 1: Ignorance (location) vs. belief (location)	4.50	54	.39

(continued)

Table 4.2   *(cont'd)*

Study	Condition	Mean age	Mean sample size	RD
Friedman et al. (2001)	Study 1: Ignorance (contents) vs. belief (contents)	4.50	49	.31
Friedman et al. (2001)	Study 2: Ignorance vs. belief	4.50	62	.13
Roth & Leslie (1998)	Study 1: Know (false-belief task) vs. predict (false-belief task; Figure 3)	3.50	47	.44
Sullivan & Winner (1991)	Ignorance (standard) vs. false belief	3.44	44	.03
Sullivan & Winner (1991)	Ignorance (trick) vs. false belief	3.44	71	.19
Sullivan & Winner (1993)	Ignorance (standard) vs. false belief	3.55	25	−.08
Sullivan & Winner (1993)	Ignorance (trick) vs. false belief	3.55	26	−.12
Surian & Leslie (1999)	Study 2: Know vs. think (false belief)	3.33	40	.23

Note. RD = risk difference.

articles (with additional brief description added by us in parentheses).

Study comparisons

Comparisons focusing on belief versus false belief in Table 4.2 essentially compared judgments of diverse belief versus false belief. In a diverse-belief task, truth is unknown to the child who judges that two people have differing beliefs about this (unknown) state of affairs. In false-belief tasks, in contrast, the child knows the truth. Thus, the two persons' beliefs not only differ, one person is correct and one person mistaken (i.e., has a false belief). A typical comparison is that between a not-own belief task and a false-belief task in Wellman and Bartsch (1988; see Table 4.2). In each task children saw a cardboard character (e.g., Bill) and a depiction of two locations (e.g., a classroom and a playground). In the not-own belief task the child was told Bill was looking for his bag, which might be in the classroom or on the playground. Then the child was asked where he or she thought the bag was likely to be. Whatever the child chose, he or she was told Bill had the opposite belief (e.g., on the playground not in the classroom) and he or she was then asked to predict what Bill would do (e.g., go to the classroom or go to the playground). Note that in such a task the child does not know where Bill's bag really is. In the comparable false-belief task (an explicit false-belief task) the child again saw a picture of Bill and of two locations (e.g., a classroom and playground). The child was told, "Bill's

bag is really on the playground," yet "Bill thinks his bag is in the classroom." The child was then asked to predict Bill's behavior (e.g., go to the classroom or go to the playground). To be correct, the child predicts Bill's behavior on the basis of Bill's false belief not his or her own true belief. The two tasks, belief and false belief, thus use comparable materials, formats, and questions. But one targets children's understanding that beliefs can diverge between people, thus affecting behavior, and the other targets children's understanding that someone can believe something directly counter to reality, thus affecting behavior.

Comparisons focusing on desires versus beliefs were more diverse, but again each comparison listed in Table 4.2 used comparable tasks for the judgments compared within a study. One sort of comparison between desires and beliefs was that between diverse beliefs and diverse desires. For example, the diverse-belief task for Wellman and Woolley (1990) was identical to the not-own belief task described earlier. Performance on that task was compared with a not-own desire task, which described two outcomes (e.g., Bill could play with puzzles in the classroom or play with sand on the playground), then asked the child's preference (e.g., play with sand), then attributed the opposite preference to the target character (e.g., Bill likes puzzles the best), and asked the child to predict Bill's action. Thus, using similar formats, one task asked the child to predict the action resulting from diverse beliefs and the other to predict the action resulting from diverse desires.

A second sort of comparison between desires and beliefs compared judgments of conflicting preferences versus conflicting beliefs, as in Flavell et al. (1990). For preferences (called *value beliefs* in that study) the child had to judge that a cookie that tastes yummy to him or her actually tastes yucky to someone else. For belief (called *fact beliefs*) the child had to judge that while he or she thinks a cup has X (which it does), someone else thinks it has Y instead.

A third sort of comparison between desire and belief concerned judgments of outdated (thus satiated) desires versus outdated (thus false) beliefs, as in Gopnik and Slaughter (1991). For desires, the child first chose one of two things (e.g., read Book A or Book B) as his or her preference, was satiated on that (e.g., read Book A), and then chose the second option as his or her current preference. The child was then asked to name his or her prior desire. For belief, the child was shown, for example, a crayon box, and then after saying he or she thought there were crayons inside, the child was shown that there really were candles inside. Then the child was asked to name his or her prior belief. Thus, the several comparisons between desires and beliefs used a variety of tasks, but in each case that we have included, the contrasting desire and belief tasks were made comparable in format and question structure.

Comparisons focusing on knowledge versus false belief in Table 4.2 compared judgments of ignorance versus false belief. For knowledge or ignorance judgments, the question is whether someone knows or does not know the true state of affairs. For false-belief judgments, the question is whether someone believes the true state of affairs or has a definite, alternative belief, one that contradicts reality. In a prototypical task, a character puts an object in Location A and does not see it moved to Location B. For a knowledge judgment, the child is asked if the character knows (or does not know) where the object is. For a false-belief judgment, the child is asked if the character thinks the object is in A or B. As this example shows, task materials and formats can be comparable.

Quantifying study comparisons

For each comparison in Table 4.2 we tabulated the proportion of correct responses to each contrasting task pair and the number of children (or sample size). Then, using procedures outlined in Deeks, Altman, and Bradburn (2001) and Rosenthal (1991), we calculated the risk difference (RD, or alternately d'), a measure of effect size indicating the size of the difference between contrasting conditions or judgments.

Results

Table 4.3 lists the combined results. For each set of comparisons (e.g., the 13 RD scores comparing desire vs. belief in Table 4.2) we list the range from highest to lowest and the mean RD. Note that RD, as calculated from these data, can be positive or negative. For example, a positive RD for desire versus belief would represent a study contrast showing desire judgments to be higher than belief judgments. A negative value would represent a contrast showing belief performance to be higher than desire.

Because diverse sets of studies (diverse in terms of the specific tasks used to measure concepts of desire, belief, or false belief across studies, and diverse in terms of the ages sampled) are grouped within each set of comparisons, the heterogeneity statistic is significant for belief versus false belief, $\chi^2(9) = 29.86$, $p < .01$; desire versus belief, $\chi^2(12) = 23.75$, $p < .05$; and knowledge versus false belief, $\chi^2(21) = 84.06$, $p < .01$. When heterogeneity is significant, a random-effects model, which incorporates both between- and within-study variance, is recommended for estimating combined effects (see Deeks et al., 2001). With a random-effects model, standard error for the combined effect increases with greater between-study variance and thus is more conservative (i.e., produces a wider confidence interval). We used the DerSimonian and Laird (1986) random-effects model to estimate combined effects, and Table 4.3 lists the random-effects-weighted mean RD, using the inverse variance method for combining conditions (see Deeks et al., 2001). This approach weighs each condition by the reciprocal of the within-study variance plus the between-study variance, thus taking into account sample size differences and heterogeneity and allowing for the estimation of the combined effect from a diverse set of studies.

Table 4.3   Meta-analytic comparisons and combined effects for Study 1

Comparison	No. of contrasts	Range	Mean RD	Random-effects-weighted mean RD	SE	95% CI lower bound	95% CI upper bound
Belief vs. false belief	10	.18–.75	.48	.47	.07	.33	.61
Desire vs. belief	13	.13–.69	.29	.29	.05	.20	.38
Knowledge vs. false belief	22	−.19–.44	.15	.15	.04	.07	.23

Note. RD = risk difference; CI = confidence interval.

Based on these procedures, Table 4.3 also shows the 95% confidence interval around each weighted mean RD. If studies show a random scatter of performance, sometimes favoring one concept but sometimes the other, the random-effects-weighted mean RD is expected to be zero. As shown in Table 4.3, the 95% confidence interval fails to include zero for all three contrasts. Therefore, each contrast significantly exceeds zero.

As a rule of thumb, mean RD is on the same scale as correlations and therefore can be considered small if it is in the .10 range, moderate in the .30 range, and large in the .50 range (Cohen, 1988). These data thus show moderate, but clearly significant, differences pooled across numerous studies for children's understanding of belief over false belief and desire over belief. Indeed, in these cases every RD from all studies is above zero. The results also show a smaller, yet significant, advantage for judging knowledge over false belief. In this case, although the data across studies are less consistent, with RD sometimes negative and sometimes positive, the average RD is reliably above zero.

A potential confound for estimating effect sizes might be ceiling effects that could decrease such estimates with increasing age. For example, if children typically develop concept X at 4 years of age and concept Y at 5 years of age, then examining the effect size between concepts X and Y in a sample of 6-year-olds (who would be largely at ceiling on both concepts) would underestimate any difference. However, within each of our three sets of comparisons, effect size does not correlate with mean age, all $ps > .05$. This result indicates that, given the range of ages sampled in the studies included here, potential ceiling effects do not significantly influence our estimates of effects size.

Discussion

Conceivably, all mental states might be equally hard for children to understand: All are nonobvious, internal states, and all are potentially at odds with overt behavior or external reality. Equally conceivable, children might understand some states before others, but early-understood versus late-understood states would not be consistent from one child to the next, depending on different individual experiences or family foci of conversations (e.g., emotions vs. wants vs. ignorance). In contrast to either of these alternatives, the meta-analytic data show distinct regularities in children's developing understanding of mind.

The meta-analytic contrast between desires and beliefs confirms a conclusion first advanced by Wellman and Woolley (1990) and now advocated more widely (e.g., Astington, 2001; Flavell & Miller, 1998; Repacholi & Gopnik, 1997) that, on comparable tasks, children correctly judge persons' desires before they correctly judge their beliefs. The meta-analysis provides quantitative support across studies for this claim.

The comparison between belief and false belief is equally consistent and empirically stronger in the meta-analysis. These data show that children can correctly judge persons' diverse beliefs before they can judge false beliefs, a claim that has been advanced in places (e.g., Wellman et al., 2001) but not previously tested systematically across studies. Specifically, in cases where the child does not know what is true, young children can first (a) correctly judge that two persons have different beliefs, and (b) correctly judge how a person's action follows from their beliefs (in contrast to the child's own opposite belief). Only later can children correctly make the same judgments when they do know what is true and hence can (c) correctly judge that one person's belief is true and the other person's belief is decidedly false, and (d) correctly judge how a person's actions mistakenly follow from a false belief.

The data also demonstrate that children understand ignorance (e.g., that Bill does not know what is in a container) before understanding false belief (e.g., that Bill falsely believes X is in a container). This possibility, first proposed by Hogrefe et al. (1986), has been controversial. For example, Perner (1995, 2000) has argued that ignorance judgments are, necessarily, methodologically easier than false-belief judgments. He contends that young children have a default theory of belief that people look for an object where it is and that people believe what is true. Thus, baseline performance on a false-belief task with two options is 0%. In contrast, young children have no such default expectation about knowing—sometimes people know; sometimes they do not know. Thus, baseline performance on a knowledge-ignorance task with two options is 50%. Therefore, from this perspective, performance above 50% means something different in the two tasks and is always easier to achieve for an ignorance judgment versus a false-belief judgment. This baseline difference alone could account for the meta-analytic difference we found.

We are not convinced that this is the proper perspective, however. First, young children often under-attribute ignorance, judging that both knowledgeable and ignorant protagonists are knowledgeable (e.g., young 3-year-olds in Woolley & Wellman, 1990, attributed ignorance 33% of the time to such protagonists rather than 50%). Yet, if Perner's (1995, 2000) argument is correct, even the youngest children's performance on ignorance judgments should average 50% correct. In the meta-analysis, the knowledge-ignorance condition with the youngest mean age was from Flavell et al. (1990). They found ignorance performance to be 36%, clearly below 50%. Thus, it is not clear empirically that young children's baseline for ignorance judgments is 50% whereas for false belief it is 0%. Second, note that some studies actually report false-belief judgments to be easier than ignorance judgments on comparable two-option tasks (i.e., studies with negative RDs in

Table 4.2, such as Sullivan & Winner, 1993). Such a finding is difficult to square with Perner's contention. Moreover, the meta-analytic results show that the knowledge versus false belief comparison, although significant, is smaller than some others, whereas Perner's argument suggests it should be especially, artifactually, large. Therefore, a baseline difference does not adequately account for the meta-analytic difference we have found. Instead, the meta-analysis indicates that understanding ignorance develops significantly earlier than understanding false belief.

Comparisons between beliefs versus emotions exemplify a contrast that we did not include in our analyses because in all the comparisons we found the tasks were very different. To illustrate, several studies have compared children's understanding of emotions as assessed by Denham's (1986) test versus assessments of the same children's understanding of false belief (Cutting & Dunn, 1999; Hughes & Dunn, 1998; Hughes, Dunn, & White, 1998; Olson, Liu, Kerr, & Wellman, 2003). The false-belief tasks were as described earlier. In contrast, the Denham's test summed up children's performance on emotion identification items (properly labeling various emotion expressions) and on emotion attribution scenarios (e.g., attributing happiness to a character who gets ice cream). Thus, the task formats, materials, and questions used in such an emotion versus false belief comparison would be different. If we ignore those task differences, the four studies just listed yield six contrasts between false belief and emotion. If we calculate RD for these comparisons we find a mean RD of 0.41 (*range* = 0.26 to 0.53) and a random effects weighted mean RD of 0.46 (*SE* = .004). The random-effects-weighted mean RD in this case is significantly greater than zero and is in the moderate to large range. Thus, understanding of emotion as measured by the Denham test consistently precedes understanding of false belief. But, given the great differences in task formats and question structures, it is unclear how to interpret this difference.

The meta-analytic findings we present are preliminary in several senses. The relevant studies are few (providing as few as 10 contrasts for a comparison) and we are not confident we have uncovered all of the relevant published and, especially, unpublished results. Fortunately, the results are only meant to be preliminary in the additional sense of informing the design of Study 2. For this purpose the meta-analysis does show reliable differences in children's understanding of different mental states as assessed in comparable task formats. Such findings suggest that it might be possible to construct a theory-of-mind scale such that as children get older they would pass a progressively greater number of items. We tackle this possibility in Study 2.

STUDY 2

Empirically, a scale can be formed from any collection of heterogeneous items as long as children only first pass some then successively pass some more. Theoretically, however, a scale would be more valid and useful to the extent that it reflects an underlying conceptual progression or trajectory (Guttman, 1944, 1950). We reasoned that mental states such as desires, knowledge, and beliefs, albeit different in many respects, are arguably similar in being subjective and thus contrasting across individuals and with objective events or behaviors. That is, two persons can have contrasting desires for the same object or situation; similarly, they can have contrasting beliefs, or one can be knowledgeable where the other is ignorant. Relatedly, a person's mental state can contrast with behavior or with reality, as when a person feels one thing but expresses something different, knows something but acts ignorant, or believes something not really true. Theoretically, these contrasts all reflect the fact that mental states can be said to be subjective rather than objective in varying ways. In these terms, our scale was aimed at addressing increasing steps in understanding mental subjectivity.

Based on the preliminary findings from Study 1, Study 2 includes tasks assessing diverse desires, diverse beliefs, knowledge and ignorance, and false belief. Furthermore, we reasoned that children's understanding of emotion, particularly how emotions connect with beliefs and desires, is also an important part of developing preschool theories of mind. Therefore, two other tasks involving emotion were included to capture a still broader developmental progression. One task (Belief–Emotion, as described in the Appendix) addresses how emotions connect to real situations ver-

sus to thoughts, and it is comparable in format to false-belief tasks. Another task we included (Real–Apparent Emotion, as described in the Appendix) addresses the distinction between felt versus displayed feelings.

As noted earlier, our goal was to assemble a set of tasks that are easier or harder because of conceptual differences among them (e.g., targeting desires vs. beliefs) not because of less relevant task–performance differences (e.g., one task requiring pointing, one requiring verbal judgments, one requiring written responses). Yet, strict task equivalence is often achievable only with pairs of tasks designed to compare a single conceptual contrast within a narrow age range. Thus, a consistent concern for developmental scale construction is devising tasks that span a range of ages and contents and yet are comparable or equivalent in formats and demands. We addressed this concern in several steps. We began with tasks representative of those used in the literature to connect our findings and our scale to existing studies and discussions. Each of the seven tasks included in this study was comparable to tasks in other published research, as detailed in the Appendix. However, we modified the tasks in several fashions to use more strictly comparable formats, materials, and questions across the tasks. These modifications were modest, however, to preserve the tasks' original structure and content. As a result, our tasks are not strictly comparable in all task features. Therefore, we analyzed the data in several fashions to address issues of task difficulty and comparability. One way, among others, that we addressed this issue was to include two false-belief tasks. The two false-belief tasks were not intended to yield sequentially different performance but to be roughly comparable. These two tasks could then be used to compare children's responding across different formats when the conceptual content is meant to be the same (i.e., false belief).

Method

Participants

Seventy-five 3-, 4-, and 5-year-olds (*range* = 2 years, 11 months to 6 years, 6 months) participated. Specifically, there were twenty-five 3-year-olds (*M* = 3,7; *range* = 2,11 to 3,11; 12 girls, 13 boys), twenty-five 4-year-olds

Table 4.4 Brief description of tasks in the scale

Task	Description
Diverse Desires (95%)	Child judges that two persons (the child vs. someone else) have different desires about the same objects.
Diverse Beliefs (84%)	Child judges that two persons (the child vs. someone else) have different beliefs about the same object, when the child does not know which belief is true or false.
Knowledge Access (73%)	Child sees what is in a box and judges (yes-no) the knowledge of another person who does not see what is in a box.
Contents False Belief (59%)	Child judges another person's false belief about what is in a distinctive container when child knows what it is in the container.
Explicit False Belief (57%)	Child judges how someone will search, given that person's mistaken belief.
Belief Emotion (52%)	Child judges how a person will feel, given a belief that is mistaken.
Real-Apparent Emotion (32%)	Child judges that a person can feel one thing but display a different emotion.

($M = 4,6$; *range* = 4,1 to 4,11; 10 girls, 15 boys), and twenty-five 5-year-olds ($M = 5,7$; *range* = 5,0 to 6,6; 11 girls, 14 boys). The children came from three preschools serving a population that was largely European American with approximately 25% Asian American, African American, and Hispanic American representation.

Tasks

Table 4.4 gives a brief description of the seven tasks, ordered in terms of their difficulty in our data (with children's percentage correct performance in parentheses). The Appendix provides a fuller description. For ease of presentation, all tasks used similar toy figurines for the target protagonists. Wellman et al. (2001) showed that, for false-belief tasks, children answer similarly when asked about real persons, videoed persons, dolls, toys, or story drawings.

Beyond using similar toy figurines, all tasks were similar in using picture props to show objects, situations, or facial expressions. These props helped present and remind children of the task contexts and response options. All tasks were also similar in being based on, and asking about, a target contrast, for example, between one person's desire and another's, one person's perception and another's, a mental state (e.g., emotion or desire) versus a related behavior (e.g., an emotional expression or a choice of action). As a result, in each task there were two important questions asked: a target question about the protagonist's mental state or behavior and a contrast or control question about reality or expression or someone else's state. These consistent features gave all tasks a similar two-part presentation and a similar two-part format.

However, to preserve the parallels between our tasks and those used in the literature certain differences remained across them. To account for these differences, in part, we chose subsets of the tasks that would be still more closely comparable in props, materials, and question formats. Specifically, Diverse Desires, Diverse Beliefs, and Explicit False Belief (Tasks 1, 2, and 5 in Table 4.4) formed one subset of tasks in which children saw a toy figure and a paper with two picture choices (e.g., cookie–carrot or bushes–garage). Their answer was always a verbal choice between one of these pictured choices, and the formats and questions asked were similar (as can be seen in the Appendix). Knowledge Access, Contents False Belief, and Belief–Emotion (Tasks 3, 4, and 6 in Table 4.4) formed a different subset in which children saw a container with a hidden item inside (e.g., a drawer with a toy dog inside, a Band-Aid box with a pig inside), and their answers were always verbal choices (e.g., "Does he think there are Band-Aids or a pig?"), although again their two response options were both embodied in the task materials. Across these three tasks, formats were similar (as can be seen in the Appendix). The Real–Apparent Emotion task, similar to other tasks, involved a toy figure, pictures (of three emotional expressions), and a short verbal story. The Real–Apparent Emotion task had a format different from any other task but was most similar to the Diverse-Desire, Diverse-Belief, and Explicit False-Belief tasks, where children made their judgment among pictured choices.

Note that each of the two primary subsets of tasks (Diverse Desires, Diverse Beliefs, and Explicit False Belief, which used toy figures and pictures, vs. Knowledge Access, Contents False Belief, and Belief–Emotion, which used toy figures and containers) included a false-belief task. As noted in our introduction, these two tasks were included, in part, to assess whether children's responding to these two different formats would be similar when conceptual content was meant to be the same. Appropriately, children performed similarly on these tasks, where 59% were correct on Contents False Belief and 57% were correct on Explicit False Belief, McNemar's $\chi^2(1) = 0$.

Procedures

Children were tested in a quiet room in their preschool by one of four adult experimenters. The seven tasks were presented in one of three orders. In all orders the Diverse-Desire task appeared early (as either the first or second task presented) to help children warm up to the process with a task hypothesized to be easier to understand. In all orders the Real–Apparent Emotion task appeared last or next to last. Otherwise, the three orders were composed by scrambling the tasks into three different sequences; 37 children received Order 1, 19 received Order 2, and 19 received Order 3.

Results and Discussion

Table 4.4 shows the proportion of children correct on the various tasks, ordered from the easiest to the hardest tasks in terms of children's performance. An initial 3 (age) × 3 (order) × 2 (gender) analysis of variance (ANOVA) was conducted by giving children a score of total number correct (out of seven possible tasks). This revealed a significant main effect only for age, $F(2, 57) = 25.45, p < .001$. With increasing age, children passed more tasks. There were no effects of task order or gender and no significant interactions. Additional analyses also confirmed that there was no significant difference in children's response to the Diverse-Desire

task if they received it first or second and no difference if children received the Real–Apparent Emotion task last or next to last.

As is clear in Table 4.4, performance on some pairs of items was essentially equivalent (e.g., Contents False Belief and Explicit False Belief, as just mentioned). Nonetheless, as shown in the table, the tasks form a general progression. Therefore, we next examined responses to the seven tasks to see whether a subset of items formed a strict Guttman scale. This was done by initially scrutinizing the data only from the first participants tested ($n = 37$). From this examination, we found that the five items listed in Table 4.5 formed a reproducible Guttman scale. We then confirmed this result on participants tested last ($n = 38$); the same five items again formed a reproducible Guttman scale. Based on these initial, confirmatory analyses, we analyzed the scale properties of these items for the entire sample ($N = 75$). Table 4.5 shows the resulting Guttman scalogram for these five tasks.

Five-item Guttman scale

Guttman (1944, 1950) argued for scales where items can be ranked in difficulty such that if a person responds positively to a given item, that person must respond positively to all easier items. Thus, theoretically, a given score on a Guttman scale can only be reached with one pattern of response, and if we know a person's score, we know how that person responded to all items in the scale. Guttman scaling, or scalogram analysis, then, is the estimation of reproducibility given knowledge of person scores, that is, the extent to which item responses fit the ideal patterns. As shown in Table 4.5, the responses of 80% of the children (60 of 75) fit this five-item Guttman scale exactly. The coefficient of reproducibility, using Green's (1956) method of estimation, from a scalogram analysis of these data was .96 (values greater than .90 indicate scalable items). Green's index of consistency, which tests whether the observed coefficient of reproducibility was greater than what could be achieved by chance alone, was .56 (values greater than .50 are significant). Thus, these five tasks form a highly scalable set. Moreover, as children get older they tend to pass more items in succession; the relationship between age (in months) and scale score (summing the items passed out of five) is high, $r(75) = 0.64, p < .001$.

Table 4.5   Guttman scalogam patterns for a five-item scale

Pattern	1	2	3	4	5	6	Other patterns	N
Diverse Desire	−	+	+	+	+	+		
Diverse Belief	−	−	+	+	+	+		
Knowledge Access	−	−	−	+	+	+		
Contents False Belief	−	−	−	−	+	+		
Real-Apparent Emotion	−	−	−	−	−	+		
Participant								
3-year-olds	1	2	8	4	1	0	9	25
4-year-olds	0	2	3	2	9	5	4	25
5-year-olds	0	0	0	2	9	12	2	25
Total	1	4	11	8	19	17	15	75
Average age	3–5	4–0	3–9	4–6	4–11	5–4	4–1	

Note. A minus sign means a child failed the task in question; a plus sign means the child passed. The 6 focal patterns represent 6 of the total possible 32 patterns of response encompassing the five dichotomous items. A child exhibiting any of the remaining 26 patterns was classified as other.

When children failed an item they tended to pass the relevant control questions, showing comprehension of the task formats and questions. Of course, the youngest children tended to fail both the control questions and the target questions for the very hardest items (e.g., Real–Apparent Emotion). The most relevant data, thus, concern the first task a child failed. That is, consider the tasks as ordered in Table 4.5. Children tended to pass the easier tasks, then reached a task where they failed, and then failed still harder tasks (a pattern that is significant in the scalogram analysis). On the first task children failed, in this order, they were 89% correct on the paired control question and 0% correct on the target question. Thus, children largely understood the task format for the first task they failed, yet nonetheless failed on the target question. To reiterate, however, to be scored as passing a task for Table 4.5, children had to be correct on both the target question and its control question.

Given that our tasks were not identical in materials and formats, we next considered whether differences in task difficulty due to differences in materials, questions, and test formats might account for the progression across tasks, rather than differences in conceptual content. First, recall that the two false-belief tasks differed in materials and formats as much as any other two tasks. In spite of these differences, performances were nearly identical, as predicted on the basis of their conceptual similarity. Second, pairs of tasks within the larger sequence were closely equivalent in form. For example, Diverse Desire and Diverse Belief were chosen and constructed to be nearly identical except for the focus on desires versus beliefs, respectively. Knowledge Access and Contents False Belief were also highly similar in form (see the Appendix). Thus, it is important that additional pairwise comparisons confirmed that Diverse Desire was significantly easier than Diverse Belief, McNemar's $\chi^2(1) = 4.08$, $p < .05$; Diverse Belief was significantly easier than Contents False Belief, McNemar's $\chi^2(1) = 12.00$, $p < .001$; Knowledge Access was significantly easier than Contents False Belief, McNemar's $\chi^2(1) = 5.89$, $p < .02$; and Contents False Belief was significantly easier than Real–Apparent Emotion, McNemar's $\chi^2(1) = 13.88$, $p < .001$. These comparisons show that the larger scale captures not only a general progression but also a series of significant paired-task sequences. Furthermore, paired tasks within the scale, those that are very similar in format and task structure, confirm the more general progression across all the tasks.

Finally, consider the following concern. Perhaps the progression in Table 4.5 reflects baseline probabilities of being correct on the tasks rather than a conceptual progression. For example, Diverse Desire and Diverse Belief (the easiest tasks in Table 4.5) have a 50% probability of being correct by chance alone (i.e., correct responding is based on a single two-choice target question). However, Knowledge Access and Contents False Belief have a 25% probability of being correct by chance alone (i.e., correct responding on a two-choice target question and a two-choice control question). Of course, the discussion of Study 1 outlines some of the ways it is difficult to know definitely what the baseline rates of performance are. Nonetheless, to address this sort of concern we reanalyzed the data with a different scoring. In this alternative scoring we considered only children's responses on the target questions (ignoring the control questions). Thus, for every task there was now a single two-option response measure, meaning there was a 50% chance of being correct by random guessing alone on every task. (Note that scoring for the Real–Apparent Emotion task is also dichotomous; children's responses are incorrect if apparent emotion is equal to or less happy than the real emotion, and correct if it is more happy.) With this alternative scoring, the sequence shown in Table 4.5 remains, and only one child goes from exhibiting the predicted patterns to exhibiting some other pattern (and none goes in the reverse direction). Thus, with this alternative scoring, the scale shown in Table 4.5 captures 59 of 75 children (79%), whereas before it was 60 of 75 (80%). With this alternative scoring, the scale remains highly reproducible and significantly consistent.

This alternative scoring and analysis provide an important control. But, for future research that might use the scale, we recommend the original scoring. Individual children's understanding is better assessed, we believe, by including their performance on the control tasks as well, not simply their responses to the target questions alone.

Rasch analyses

Guttman scales are stringent—items are scale appropriate only for fitting the exact step functions for increasing difficulty. Contemporary approaches to scale analysis have been developed, in part, to allow consideration of less strict scale progressions. Item-response theory (Bock, 1997; Embretson & Reise, 2000; Lord & Novick, 1968) consists of a family of mathematical measurement models for analyzing test or scale items. The most straightforward item-response-theory model, the Rasch measurement model, is a one-parameter logistic model for dichotomous items that estimates item difficulty and person ability levels (Rasch, 1960; Wright & Masters, 1982; Wright & Stone, 1979). The Rasch item-response-theory measurement model is often regarded as a probabilistic model for Guttman scaling (Andrich, 1985; Wilson, 1989). We analyzed our data with Rasch models to confirm and extend our Guttman scalogram analyses.

To preface the Rasch analyses, however, we believe that for cognitive development questions, Guttman scalogram analysis is an appropriate and useful analytical tool for establishing certain particularly informative developmental sequences. Although we are aware of criticisms of Guttman scaling for its stringency in creating measurement scales (e.g., Festinger, 1947; Guilford, 1954; Nunnally & Bernstein, 1994), it is nonetheless impressive that our data fit the stringent criteria of Guttman scaling so well. This speaks to the precise sequential nature of mental state concepts children come to understand.

Both the Guttman scale and the Rasch measurement model order dichotomous items and persons on a single continuum (Andrich, 1985). The shared notion is that a person with a given ability level on a continuum will (likely) respond positively to items with difficulty levels less than that person's ability level and will (likely) respond negatively to items with difficulty levels greater than that person's ability level. However, the item-response functions for a Guttman scale are deterministic (i.e., stepwise) whereas the item-response functions for a Rasch model are probabilistic. Thus, the Guttman scale embodies a stricter measurement model than the Rasch model. For the Guttman model, if a person answers item N correctly, that person *definitely* answers item N-1 correctly. On the other hand, for the Rasch model, if a person answers item N correctly, that person *probably* answers item N-1 correctly. Rasch measurement models aim for precise estimation of items and persons on a single, interval continuum. When item difficulty exceeds person ability, the probability of a positive response is less than 0.5, relative to the difference in levels. When person ability exceeds item difficulty, the probability of positive response is greater than 0.5, relative to the difference in levels. When item difficulty equals person ability, the probability of a positive response is 0.5.

Table 4.6 Item and person measure summary and fit statistics for the five-item Rasch model

	Measure	Error	Standardized infit	Standardized outfit
Item difficulty summary and fit statistics				
Real-Apparent Emotion	7.73	0.46	0.1	−0.1
Content False Belief	5.00	0.35	−1.9	−1.7
Knowledge Access	3.61	0.37	−0.1	0.7
Diverse Beliefs	2.43	0.42	0.2	0.9
Diverse Desires	0.48	0.69	0.3	0.2
M	3.85	0.46	−0.3	0.0
SD	2.44	0.12	0.8	0.9
Person ability summary and fit statistics				
M	4.66	1.65	−0.5	−0.2
SD	1.82	0.51	1.1	0.5

Note. Expected values for standardized infit and standardized outfit is a mean of 0 and standard deviation of 1.0; fit statistics > 2.0 indicate misfit.

FIVE-ITEM RASCH MODEL

Data for the five items in the Guttman scale were analyzed with a Rasch model using the WINSTEPS/ BIGSTEPS computer program (Linacre, 2003; Linacre & Wright, 1994). For numerical simplicity, the item difficulty and person ability measures on the linear logits scale were rescaled so that Contents False Belief (arbitrarily considered as the anchor task of the five tasks) had an item difficulty measure score of 5.0 on the linear scale. Table 4.6 shows the five items ordered from most difficult (highest measurement score) to least difficult (lowest measurement score). Not surprising, given the high coefficient of reproducibility of the five-item Guttman scale, the order of item difficulty is the same in the Rasch model as in the Guttman scale. However, the Rasch model allows for examination of relative distances between item difficulty scores. As shown in Table 4.6, although the five items are fairly evenly and widely spread, the differences (in score units) between successive items range from a low of about 1.2 to a high of more than 2.5. This is not a problem for the Rasch measurement model because it does not assume equal intervals between items; instead, it estimates the true interval between items.

Table 4.6 also shows summaries of item measurement scores, person measurement scores, and fit statistics. Rasch model fit statistics evaluate the notion that

a person with a given ability level will likely respond positively to less difficult items and will likely respond negatively to more difficult items. Two types of fit statistics are estimated for each item and each person: infit, which is more sensitive to unexpected responses near the item or person's measurement level, and outfit, which is more sensitive to unexpected responses far from the item or person's measurement level (Linacre & Wright, 1994; Wright & Masters, 1982). Standardized infit and outfit statistics for individual items have an expected value of 0. Positive values greater than 2.0 indicate greater unpredictable variation than expected. Negative values suggest the scale is more deterministic than expected because Rasch models are probabilistic. Therefore, negative values are acceptable for our comparison with the Guttman scale because they actually indicate overfit (Bond & Fox, 2001). Therefore, we consider standardized fit statistics for individual items greater than 2.0 as indicating misfit (Wright & Masters, 1982).

As shown in Table 4.6, all five items' standardized infit and outfit statistics fall well short of 2.0, and mean fit statistics are near the expected value of 0. Mean standardized infit and outfit statistics for person ability, which indicate overall fit of individual persons to the scale, also fall well short of 2.0 and are near their expected value of 0. Therefore, these five items fit the Rasch model well.

Table 4.7   Item and person measure summary and fit statistics for the seven-item Rasch model

	Measure	Error	Standardized infit	Standardized outfit
Item difficulty summary and fit statistics				
Real–Apparent Emotion	7.21	0.42	0.9	0.3
Belief Emotion	5.49	0.31	−1.0	−0.7
Explicit False Belief	5.10	0.36	1.9	2.6
Content False Belief	5.00	0.31	−1.9	−2.0
Knowledge Access	3.93	0.32	−1.7	−1.4
Diverse Beliefs	3.00	0.37	0.2	1.2
Diverse Desires	1.49	0.55	0.0	−0.1
M	4.46	0.38	−0.2	0.0
SD	1.71	0.08	1.3	1.5
Person ability summary and fit statistics				
M	4.96	1.15	−0.2	−0.1
SD	1.47	0.21	1.0	0.7

Note. Expected values for standardized infit and standardized outfit is a mean of 0 and standard deviation of 1.0; fit statistics > 2.0 indicate misfit.

SEVEN-ITEM RASCH MODEL

A problematic outcome of a Guttman scale's deterministic character is the fitting of items of similar difficulty levels on the same scale (Bond & Fox, 2001). For example, in Guttman scaling, if items J and K are very similar with item K only slightly more difficult, then permissible patterns of response are getting both items correct or getting both items wrong, and getting item J correct but item K wrong. However, the reverse pattern of getting item K correct but item J wrong (which is also likely when both items have similar difficulty levels) is not an acceptable pattern in Guttman scaling (and would greatly decrease reproducibility). As such, Guttman scales exclude items of highly similar difficulty even though those items represent similar constructs on the same scale. In our case, a five-item Guttman scale with two items excluded (Explicit False Belief and Belief–Emotion) has excellent model fit. Note that excluding two items does not mean they fail to represent the same theory-of-mind continuum as the five included items. Rather, it means that Contents False Belief, Explicit False Belief, and Belief–Emotion have similar difficulty levels and two are excluded because of the inability of

strict Guttman scales to accommodate items of similar difficulty. Rasch measurement models are less problematic in fitting items of similar difficulty on the same scale. Considering a seven-item Rasch model clarifies that our seven items fit a single scale construct, while further confirming that Contents False Belief, Explicit False Belief, and Belief–Emotion have similar difficulty levels.

For this Rasch analysis, the item difficulty and person ability measures on the linear logits scale were again rescaled so that Contents False Belief has an item difficulty measure score of 5.0 on the linear scale. Table 4.7 shows the seven items ordered from most difficult (highest measurement score) to least difficult (lowest measurement score). Content False Belief, Explicit False Belief, and Belief–Emotion have similar difficulty levels (5.00, 5.10, and 5.49, respectively). Overall item fit (standardized infit, $M = -0.2$, $SD = 1.3$; standardized outfit, $M = 0.0$, $SD = 1.5$) and overall person fit (standardized infit, $M = -0.2$, $SD = 1.0$; standardized outfit, $M = -0.1$, $SD = 0.7$) are excellent. One item among the seven, however, has poorer fit, although not extremely poor; Explicit False Belief has a standardized infit of 1.9 and a standardized outfit of 2.6. This does not indicate that the Explicit-False-Belief item assesses a different conceptual content from the other items. Rather, this finding again demonstrates how items with similar levels of difficulty can result in poor fit—slightly in Rasch models but drastically in Guttman scaling (Andrich, 1985).

Scoring individuals' performance

One potential advantage of Rasch measurement models over Guttman scaling is the precision with which individual person ability scores on an interval scale can be estimated. However, scoring of individual person ability with a Guttman scale is more practical because all it involves is simply adding up the number of items answered correctly. For our data, the five-item Rasch scores and the five-item Guttman scores are almost perfectly correlated, $r(75) = .998, p < .001$. Furthermore, the relation between the five-item Rasch scores and age, $r(75) = .645, p < .001$, and the relation between the five-item Guttman scores and age, $r(75) = .638, p < .001$, are almost identical. Therefore, for our five-item data, person ability scores estimated with both measurement models are so similar that any precision gained with the Rasch model is outweighed by the practicality of scoring the five-item Guttman scale.

GENERAL DISCUSSION

> The chronological order in which cognitive novelties emerge during childhood is a datum of central importance for the student of human cognitive growth. (Flavell 1972, p. 281)

The data from Study 2 demonstrate an extended series of conceptual insights that take place in the pre-school years as children acquire a theory of mind. In this regard they confirm but go beyond earlier studies, for example, those encompassed in the meta-analysis of Study 1.

Empirically, the findings demonstrate an understanding of desires that precedes an understanding of beliefs; in particular, children become aware that two persons can have different desires for the same object before they become aware that two persons can have different beliefs about the same object. They also demonstrate an understanding of diverse beliefs before false beliefs; that is, children can judge that they and someone else can have differing beliefs about the same situation (when the child does not know which belief is true and which is false) before they judge that someone else can have a false belief about a situation (where the child thus knows which belief is true and which is false). Finally, the results show that differentiating between real and apparent emotion is a late-developing understanding within the preschool years.

Using Flavell's (1972) taxonomy of developmental sequences, it is clear that the sequence charted in Study 2 is not one of addition (it is not the case that understandings tapped by later items are equal alternatives to those appearing earlier in this sequence) and not one of substitution (it is not the case that later understandings replace earlier understandings; earlier understandings in this sequence remain valid and older children pass later items and earlier items as well). Instead, the sequence represents one of modification or mediation. For modification, according to Flavell, earlier items represent initial insights that are broadened or generalized to encompass later insights. In this regard, our reasoning in choosing tasks was that the tasks similarly address issues of subjectivity but encompass subjective–objective distinctions of purposefully varying sorts. For example, some items focus on subjective–subjective individuation (where two persons could have contrasting mental states about the same situation), some items focus on sub-jective–objective contrasts (where some situation might be objectively true, but a person is ignorant of it or mistaken about it), and some items focus on internal–external contrasts (where an initial, subjective state might be of one sort but its external, overt expression is of a different sort). That the tasks scale into a single continuum is consistent with an inter-pretation that children's understanding of subjectiv-ity is progressively broadening and developing in the preschool years.

Mediation sequences go further in claiming that the earlier insights enable or aid in the attainment of later insights. In our case, it is possible to theorize that an initial understanding of the subjectivity of desires, once achieved, could mediate an understanding of the subjectivity of representational mental states such as belief. Furthermore, an understanding that two persons can have diverse beliefs in a situation where truth is not known (and so the contrast is only between two individuals' mental states), once achieved, could scaffold a later understanding of ignorance or false belief (and so the contrast is between individuals' mental states and reality). We favor this constructivist, theoretical interpretation, but data about sequences of acquisition alone do not provide definitive support for such a strong interpretation.

At the same time, taken together, the findings from Studies 1 and 2 shed light on some contrasting theoretical claims. In particular, the progression from desire to diverse belief to false belief is of interest. Both modular accounts (e.g., Leslie, 1994) and simulation accounts (e.g., Harris, 1992) claim that preschool children equally understand beliefs and desires; it is false belief that is peculiarly and distinctively difficult. In contrast, the data from Studies 1 and 2 show that understanding beliefs is more difficult than desires, even when understanding false belief is not at issue. In Study 2, for example, the Diverse-Belief task did not require understanding false belief but was nonetheless significantly more difficult than understanding Diverse Desires in spite of being almost identical in format, materials, and so on. Alternatively, executive function accounts (or more precisely what Carlson & Moses, 2001, called *executive function expression accounts*) suggest that children's difficulty with mental states in general, and false belief in particular, stem from difficulties in inhibiting a prepotent response to generate a different response. For example, responding correctly to a false-belief task requires not stating what one knows is true but stating instead what the other person thinks is true. However, both the Diverse-Desires and Diverse-Beliefs tasks in Study 2, and the Desire versus Belief comparisons in Study 1, are similar in requiring inhibition of one's own point of view to answer in terms of the other person's point of view. Performance in belief tasks is nonetheless still worse than performance in desire tasks.

The biggest contribution of our research, however, is more descriptive than explanatory. In particular, the studies confirm that theory-of-mind understandings represent an extended and progressive set of conceptual acquisitions. No single type of task—for example, false-belief tasks—can adequately capture this developmental progression. Similarly, no theory will be adequate that does not account for these various, developmentally sequenced acquisitions. Practically, this conclusion carries the implication that a theory-of-mind scale is needed to more adequately capture individual children's theory-of-mind developments.

In this vein, our findings in Study 2 provide a battery of items that constitutes a consistent scale that captures children's developmental progression. We believe this scale has several advantages for future research on theory of mind. For example, consider again research examining the interplay between theory-of-mind understanding and other factors. This includes both the role of independent factors (e.g., family conversations, language, executive function) on theory of mind and the role of theory of mind as a factor contributing to other developments (e.g., social interactions, peer acceptance). The burgeoning research on these issues faces measurement limitations by typically using single tasks, essentially false-belief tasks, to assess children's understanding (e.g., Astington & Jenkins, 1999; Dunn et al., 1991; Lalonde & Chandler, 1995). The current scale is usable with a wider range of ages, provides a more continuous variable for comparing individuals, and captures a greater variety of conceptual content. Wellman, Phillips, Dunphy-Lelii, and Lalonde (2004) provide an initial demonstration of the scale's utility in capturing individual differences.

As another example, consider research with individuals with autism, who are significantly impaired at theory-of-mind understandings (e.g., Baron-Cohen, 1995). Significantly, high-functioning individuals with autism typically fail false-belief tasks whereas comparable normal and mentally retarded individuals pass such tasks. Yet, about 20% to 25% of high-functioning individuals with autism pass false-belief tasks (Baron-Cohen, 1995; Happé, 1994). These data raise several questions. In particular: Are individuals with autism distinctively impaired in theory-of-mind understandings or only significantly delayed? More precisely, to the extent older children with autism achieve social cognitive understandings (e.g., understanding false beliefs), does this represent delay in a consistent developmental trajectory or an ad hoc or alternatively based understanding achieved via nonordinary strategies and mechanisms? Longitudinal data from individuals with autism on a variety of tasks could address such questions. But a theory-of-mind scale, such as the present one, could also provide critical data. It could disclose whether individuals with autism who pass (or fail) false-belief tasks do or do not exhibit the normally developing progression of related understandings evident in Table 4.5. A theory-of-mind scale could be used to address similar, comparative questions with other populations (e.g., deaf children; Peterson & Siegal, 1995).

The current scale also has several features that could prove useful in future research. The five-item version is highly scalable (approximating a strict Guttman scale), includes a false-belief task, yet spans a larger range of ages and tasks, yielding scale scores ranging from 0 to 5. The five task items can be administered in 15 to 20 min. Using six or seven items would include an increased array of task items, useful for more extended theoretical comparisons, but would still require only about 20 min to administer. Further information about materials and procedures are available on request from the authors.

In conclusion, the theory-of-mind scale validated in Study 2 establishes both (a) a progression of conceptual achievements that mark social cognitive understanding in normally developing preschool children and (b) a method for measuring that development accurately and informatively.

References

Andrich, D. (1985). An elaboration of Guttman scaling with Rasch models for measurement. *Sociological Methodology*, *15*, 33–80.

Astington, J. W. (2001). The future of theory-of-mind research: Understanding motivational states, the role of language, and real-world consequences. *Child Development*, *72*, 685–687.

Astington, J. W., & Jenkins, J. M. (1999). A longitudinal study of the relation between language and theory-of-mind development. *Developmental Psychology*, *35*, 1311–1320.

Baron-Cohen, S. (1995). *Mindblindness: An essay on autism and theory of mind*. Cambridge, MA: MIT Press.

Bartsch, K. (1996). Between desires and beliefs: Young children's action predictions. *Child Development*, *67*, 1671–1685.

Bartsch, K., & Wellman, H. M. (1995). *Children talk about the mind*. New York: Oxford University Press.

Bock, R. D. (1997). A brief history of item response theory. *Educational Measurement: Issues and Practice, 16*, 21–33.

Bond, T. G., & Fox, C. M. (2001). *Applying the Rasch model: Fundamental measurement in human sciences*. Mahwah, NJ: Erlbaum.

Carlson, S. M., & Moses, L. J. (2001). Individual differences in inhibitory control and children's theory of mind. *Child Development, 72*, 1032–1053.

Cohen, J. (1988). *Statistical power analysis for the behavioral sciences* (2nd ed.), Hillsdale, NJ: Erlbaum.

Cutting, A. L., & Dunn, J. (1999). Theory of mind, emotion understanding, language, and family background. *Child Development, 70*, 853–865.

Deeks, J. J., Altman, D. G., & Bradburn, M. J. (2001). Statistical methods for examining heterogeneity and combining results from several studies in meta-analysis. In M. Egger, D. G. Smith, & D. G. Altman (Eds.), *Systematic reviews in health care: Meta-analysis in context* (pp. 285–312). London: BMJ Books.

Denham, S. A. (1986). Social cognition, prosocial behavior and emotion in preschoolers. *Child Development, 57*, 194–201.

DerSimonian, R., & Laird, N. (1986). Meta-analysis in clinical trials. *Controlled Clinical Trials, 7*, 177–188.

Dunn, J., Brown, J., Slomkowski, C., Tesla, C., & Youngblade, L. (1991). Young children's understanding of other people's feelings and beliefs: Individual differences and their antecedents. *Child Development, 62*, 1352–1366.

Embretson, S. E., & Reise, S. P. (2000). *Item response theory for psychologists*. Mahwah, NJ: Erlbaum.

Fabricius, W. V., & Khalil, S. L. (2003). False beliefs or false positives? *Journal of Cognition and Development, 4*, 239–262.

Festinger, L. (1947). The treatment of qualitative data by scale analysis. *Psychological Bulletin, 44*, 149–161.

Flavell, J. H. (1972). An analysis of cognitive-developmental sequences. *Genetic Psychology Monographs, 86*, 279–350.

Flavell, J. H., Flavell, E. R., Green, F. L., & Moses, L. J. (1990). Young children's understanding of fact beliefs versus value beliefs. *Child Development, 61*, 915–928.

Flavell, J. H., & Miller, P. H. (1998). Social cognition. In D. Kuhn & R. Siegler (Eds.), *Handbook of child psychology: Vol. 2: Cognition, perception, and language* (pp. 851–898). New York: Wiley.

Friedman, O., Griffin, R., Brownell, H., & Winner, E. (2001). *Problems with the seeing = knowing rule*. Manuscript submitted for publication.

Gopnik, A., & Slaughter, V. (1991). Young children's understanding of changes in their mental states. *Child Development, 62*, 98–110.

Gopnik, A., Slaughter, V., & Meltzoff, A. (1994). Changing your views: How understanding visual perception can lead to a new theory of mind. In C. Lewis & P. Mitchell (Eds.), *Children's early understanding of mind: Origins and development* (pp. 157–181). Hove, England: Erlbaum.

Green, B. F. (1956). A method of scalogram analysis using summary statistics. *Psychometrica, 21,* 79–88.

Guilford, J. P. (1954). *Psychometric methods.* New York: McGraw-Hill.

Guttman, L. (1944). A basis of scaling quantitative data. *American Sociological Review, 9,* 139–150.

Guttman, L. (1950). The basis of scalogram analysis. In S. A. Stouffer, L. Guttman, E. A. Suchman, P. A. Lazarsfeld, S. A. Star, & J. A. Clausen (Eds.), *Measurement and prediction* (pp. 60–90). Princeton, NJ: Princeton University Press.

Happé, F. G. E. (1994). An advanced test of theory of mind: Understanding of story characters' thoughts and feelings by able autistic, mentally handicapped, and normal children and adults. *Journal of Autism & Developmental Disorders, 24,* 129–154.

Harris, P. L. (1992). From simulation to folk psychology: The case for development. *Mind & Language, 7,* 120–144.

Harris, P. L., Donnelly, K., Guz, G. R., & Pitt-Watson, R. (1986). Children's understanding of the distinction between real and apparent emotion. *Child Development, 57,* 895–909.

Harris, P. L., Johnson, C. N., Hutton, D., Andrews, G., & Cooke, T. (1989). Young children's theory of mind and emotion. *Cognition & Emotion, 3,* 379–400.

Hogrefe, G. J., Wimmer, H., & Perner, J. (1986). Ignorance versus false belief: A developmental lag in attribution of epistemic states. *Child Development, 57,* 567–582.

Hughes, C., & Dunn, J. (1998). Understanding and emotion: Longitudinal associations with mental-state talk between young friends. *Developmental Psychology, 34,* 1026–1037.

Hughes, C., Dunn, J., & White, A. (1998). Trick or treat? Uneven understanding of mind and emotion and executive dysfunction in "hard to manage" preschoolers. *Journal of Child Psychology & Psychiatry, 39,* 981–994.

Lalonde, C. E., & Chandler, M. J. (1995). False belief understanding goes to school: On the social-emotional consequences of coming early or late to a first theory of mind. *Cognition and Emotion, 9,* 167–185.

Leslie, A. M. (1994). ToMM, ToBy, and agency: Core architecture and domain specificity in cognition and culture. In L. Hirschfeld & S. Gelman (Eds.), *Mapping the mind: Domain specificity in cognition and culture* (pp. 119–148). New York: Cambridge University Press.

Linacre, J. M. (2003). *User's guide and program manual to WINSTEPS: Rasch model computer programs.* Chicago: MESA Press.

Linacre, J. M., & Wright, B. D. (1994). *A user's guide to BIGSTEPS: Rasch model computer programs.* Chicago: MESA Press.

Lord, F. N., & Novick, M. R. (1968). *Statistical theories of mental test scores.* Reading, MA: Addison-Wesley.

Mitchell, P. (1996). *Acquiring a conception of mind: A review of psychological research and theory.* Hove, England: Psychology Press.

Nunnally, J. C., & Bernstein, I. H. (1994). *Psychometric theory.* New York: McGraw-Hill.

Olson, S. L., Liu, D., Kerr, D. C., & Wellman, H. M. (2003). *Social and behavioral outcomes of children's theory of mind development.* Unpublished manuscript.

Perner, J. (1995). The many faces of belief. *Cognition, 57,* 241–269.

Perner, J. (2000). About + belief + counterfactual. In P. Mitchell & K. J. Riggs (Eds.), *Children's reasoning and the mind* (pp. 367–401). Hove, England: Taylor & Frances.

Perner, J., Leekam, S. R., & Wimmer, H. (1987). Three-year-olds' difficulty with false belief. *British Journal of Developmental Psychology, 5,* 125–137.

Perner, J., & Wimmer, H. (1985). "John thinks that Mary thinks that …": Attribution of second-order beliefs by 5- to 10-year-old children. *Journal of Experimental Child Psychology, 39,* 437–471.

Peterson, C. C., & Siegal, M. (1995). Deafness, conversation and theory of mind. *Journal of Child Psychology and Psychiatry, 36,* 459–474.

Pillow, B. H. (1989). Early understanding of perception as a source of knowledge. *Journal of Experimental Child Psychology, 47,* 116–129.

Pratt, C., & Bryant, P. E. (1990). Young children understand that looking leads to knowing (so long as they are looking into a single barrel). *Child Development, 61,* 973–982.

Rasch, G. (1960). *Probabilistic models for some intelligence and attainment tests.* Chicago: University of Chicago Press.

Repacholi, B. M., & Gopnik, A. (1997). Early reasoning about desires: Evidence from 14- and 18-month-olds. *Developmental Psychology, 33,* 12–21.

Rosenthal, R. (1991). *Meta-analytic procedures for social research.* Newbury Park, CA: Sage.

Roth, D., & Leslie, A. (1998). Solving belief problems: Toward a task analysis. *Cognition, 66,* 1–31.

Ruffman, T., Slade, L., & Crowe, E. (2002). The relation between children's and mothers' mental state language and theory-of-mind understanding. *Child Development, 73,* 734–751.

Siegal, M., & Beattie, K. (1991). Where to look first for children's understanding of false beliefs. *Cognition, 38,* 1–12.

Sullivan, K., & Winner, E. (1991). When 3-year-olds understand ignorance, false belief and representational change. *British Journal of Developmental Psychology, 9*, 159–171.

Sullivan, K., & Winner, E. (1993). Three-year-old's understanding of mental states: The influence of trickery. *Journal of Experimental Child Psychology, 56*, 135–148.

Surian, L., & Leslie, A. M. (1999). Competence and performance in false belief understanding. *British Journal of Developmental Psychology, 17*, 141–155.

Wellman, H. M. (2002). Understanding the psychological world: Developing a theory of mind. In U. Goswami (Ed.), *Handbook of childhood cognitive development* (pp. 167–187). Oxford, England: Blackwell.

Wellman, H. M., & Bartsch, K. (1988). Young children's reasoning about beliefs. *Cognition, 30*, 239–277.

Wellman, H. M., & Bartsch, K. (1989). 3-year-olds understand belief. *Cognition, 33*, 321–326.

Wellman, H. M., Cross, D., & Watson, J. (2001). Meta-analysis of theory of mind development: The truth about false belief. *Child Development, 72*, 655–684.

Wellman, H. M., & Hickling, A. K. (1994). The minds "I": Children's conception of the mind as an active agent. *Child Development, 65*, 1564–1580.

Wellman, H. M., Hollander, M., & Schult, C. A. (1996). Young children's understanding of thought-bubbles and of thoughts. *Child Development, 67*, 768–788.

Wellman, H. M., Phillips, A. T., Dunphy-Lelii, S., & Lalonde, N. (2004). Infant social attention predicts preschool social cognition. *Developmental Science, 7*, 283–288.

Wellman, H. M., & Woolley, J. D. (1990). From simple desires to ordinary beliefs: The early development of everyday psychology. *Cognition, 35*, 245–275.

Wilson, M. (1989). A comparison of deterministic and probabilistic approaches to measuring leaning structures. *Australian Journal of Education, 33*, 127–140.

Woolley, J., & Wellman, H. M. (1993). Origin and truth: Young children's understanding of imaginary mental representations. *Child Development, 64*, 1–17.

Wright, B. D., & Masters, G. N. (1982). *Rating scale analysis: Rasch measurement.* Chicago: MESA Press.

Wright, B. D., & Stone, M. H. (1979). *Best test design: Rasch measurement.* Chicago: MESA Press.

Appendix

Diverse Desires

Children see a toy figure of an adult and a sheet of paper with a carrot and a cookie drawn on it. "Here's Mr Jones. It's snack time, so, Mr Jones wants a snack to eat. Here are two different snacks: a carrot and a cookie. Which snack would you like best? Would you like a carrot or a cookie best?" This is the *own-desire* question.

If the child chooses the carrot: "Well, that's a good choice, but Mr Jones really likes cookies. He doesn't like carrots. What he likes best are cookies." (Or, if the child chooses the cookie, he or she is told Mr Jones likes carrots.) Then the child is asked the *target* question: "So, now it's time to eat. Mr Jones can only choose one snack, just one. Which snack will Mr Jones choose? A carrot or a cookie?"

To be scored as correct, or to pass this task, the child must answer the *target* question opposite from his or her answer to the *own-desire* question.

This task was derived from those used by Wellman and Woolley (1990) and Repacholi and Gopnik (1997).

Diverse Beliefs

Children see a toy figure of a girl and a sheet of paper with bushes and a garage drawn on it. "Here's Linda. Linda wants to find her cat. Her cat might be hiding in the bushes or it might be hiding in the garage. Where do you think the cat is? In the bushes or in the garage?" This is the *own-belief* question.

If the child chooses the bushes: "Well, that's a good idea, but Linda thinks her cat is in the garage. She thinks her cat is in the garage." (Or, if the child chooses the garage, he or she is told Linda thinks her cat is in the bushes.) Then the child is asked the *target* question: "So where will Linda look for her cat? In the bushes or in the garage?"

To be correct the child must answer the *target* question opposite from his or her answer to the *own-belief* question.

This task was derived from those used by Wellman and Bartsch (1989) and Wellman et al. (1996).

Knowledge Access

Children see a nondescript plastic box with a drawer containing a small plastic toy dog inside the closed drawer. "Here's a drawer. What do you think is inside the drawer?" (The child can give any answer he or she likes or indicate that he or she does not know). Next, the drawer is opened and the child is shown the content of the drawer. "Let's see … it's really a dog inside!" Close the drawer: "Okay, what is in the drawer?"

Then a toy figure of a girl is produced: "Polly has never ever seen inside this drawer. Now here comes Polly. So, does Polly know what is in the drawer? (the *target* question) "Did Polly see inside this drawer?" (the *memory* question).

To be correct the child must answer the *target* question "no" and answer the *memory* control question "no."

This task was derived from those used by Pratt and Bryant (1990) and Pillow (1989), although it was modified so that the format was more parallel to the contents False-Belief task.

Contents False Belief

The child sees a clearly identifiable Band-Aid box with a plastic toy pig inside the closed Band-Aid box. "Here's a Band-Aid box. What do you think is inside the Band-Aid box?" Next, the Band-Aid box is opened: "Let's see … it's really a pig inside!" The Band-Aid box is closed: "Okay, what is in the Band-Aid box?"

Then a toy figure of a boy is produced: "Peter has never ever seen inside this Band-Aid box. Now here comes Peter. So, what does Peter think is in the box? Band-Aids or a pig? (the *target* question) "Did Peter see inside this box?" (the *memory* question).

To be correct the child must answer the *target* question "Band-Aids" and answer the *memory* question "no."

This task was derived from one used initially by Perner, Leekam, and Wimmer (1987) and widely modified and used since then (see Wellman et al., 2001).

Explicit False Belief

Children see a toy figure of a boy and a sheet of paper with a backpack and a closet drawn on it. "Here's Scott. Scott wants to find his mittens. His mittens might be in his backpack or they might be in the closet. *Really*, Scott's mittens are in his backpack. But Scott *thinks* his mittens are in the closet."

"So, where will Scott look for his mittens? In his backpack or in the closet?" (the *target* question) "Where are Scott's mittens really? In his backpack or in the closet?" (the *reality* question).

To be correct the child must answer the *target* question "closet" and answer the *reality* question "backpack."

This task was derived from one used by Wellman and Bartsch (1989) and Siegal and Beattie (1991).

Belief–Emotion

Children see a toy figure of a boy and a clearly identifiable individual-size Cheerios box with rocks inside the closed box. "Here is a Cheerios box and here is Teddy. What do you think is inside the Cheerios box?" (Cheerios) Then the adult makes Teddy speak: "Teddy says, 'Oh good, because I love Cheerios. Cheerios are my favorite snack. Now I'll go play.'" Teddy is then put away and out of sight.

Next, the Cheerios box is opened and the contents are shown to the child: "Let's see … there are really rocks inside and no Cheerios! There's nothing but rocks." The Cheerios box is closed: "Okay, what is Teddy's favorite snack?" (Cheerios).

Then Teddy comes back: "Teddy has never ever seen inside this box. Now here comes Teddy. Teddy's back and it's snack time. Let's give Teddy this box. So, how does Teddy feel when he gets this box? Happy or sad?" (the *target* question) The adult opens the Cheerios box and lets the toy figure look inside: "How does Teddy feel after he looks inside the box? Happy or sad?" (the *emotion-control* question).

To be correct, the child must answer the *target* question "happy" and answer the *emotion-control* question "sad."

This task was derived from one used by Harris, Johnson, Hutton, Andrews, and Cooke (1989).

Real–Apparent Emotion

Initially, children see a sheet of paper with three faces drawn on it—a happy, a neutral, and a sad face—to check that the child knows these emotional expressions. Then that paper is put aside, and the task begins with the child being shown a cardboard cutout figure of a boy drawn from the back so that the boy's facial expression cannot be seen. "This story is about a boy. I'm going to ask you about how the boy really feels inside and how he looks on his face. He might really feel one way inside but look a different way on his face. Or, he might really feel the same way inside as he looks on his face. I want you to tell me how he really feels inside and how he looks on his face."

"This story is about Matt. Matt's friends were playing together and telling jokes. One of the older children, Rosie, told a mean joke about Matt and everyone laughed. Everyone thought it was very funny, but *not* Matt. But, Matt didn't want the other children to see how he felt about the joke, because they would call him a baby. So, Matt tried to *hide how he felt*." Then the child gets two memory checks: "What did the other children do when Rosie told a mean joke about Matt?" (Laughed or thought it was funny.) "In the story, what would the other children do if they knew how Matt felt?" (Call Matt a baby or tease him.)

Pointing to the three emotion pictures: "So, how did Matt really feel, when everyone laughed? Did he feel happy, sad, or okay?" (the *target-feel* question) "How did Matt try to look on his face, when everyone laughed? Did he look happy, sad, or okay? (the *target-look* question).

To be correct the child's answer to the *target-feel* question must be more negative than his or her answer to the *target-look* question (i.e., sad for target-feel and happy or okay for target-look, or okay for target-feel and happy for target-look).

This task was derived from one used by Harris, Donnelly, Guz, and Pitt-Watson (1986).

A Closer Look 3   Autism and Theory of Mind: Understanding Others' Beliefs, Desires, and Emotions

Autistic children have been known to have difficulty communicating with others and engaging in social collaboration and interaction. In this study (Perner, Frith, Leslie, & Leekam, 1989), 26 autistic children with mental ages of 3-13 years were tested on 3 tasks that are within the capability of 3- or 4-year-old normal children. The first task tested understanding of a mistaken belief. Children were shown a typical box of a certain brand of sweets, and they all thought that it contained that kind of sweet. To their surprise, however, the box contained something else. Yet, only 4 out of the 26 autistic children were able to anticipate that another child in the same situation would make the same mistake. In contrast, all but 1 of 12 children with specific language impairment, matched for mental age, understood that others would be as misled as they had been themselves. The autistic children were also tested for their ability to infer knowledge about the contents of a container from having or not having looked inside. All 4 children who had passed the belief task, and an additional 4 children, performed perfectly, but most failed. The third task assessed children's pragmatic ability to adjust their answers to provide new, rather than repeat old, information. Here, too, most autistic children seemed unable to reliably make the correct adjustment. This study was one of the first empirical demonstrations that autistic children have profound difficulty in taking account of mental states.

Perner, J., Frith, U., Leslie, A., & Leekam, S. R. (1989). Exploration of the autistic child's theory of mind: Knowledge, belief, and communication. *Child Development*, *60*, 688–700.

Classroom Exercises, Debates, and Discussion Questions

- *Classroom discussion.* Much of the research on theory of mind focuses on the "false belief" task which is typically difficult for 3-year-old children but is easy to solve by 5 years of age. This knowledge involves knowing that one person does not have access to the same information as another individual. In the false belief task the information has to do with the transfer of an object from one place in a room to another place. What other types of knowledge might be easy or difficult for children to think about as part of another person's mental state?

- *Classroom discussion.* What role do parents play in facilitating theory of mind competence? Can parent-child communication enhance theory of mind acquisition? If so, what type of discourse style would facilitate theory of mind? What type might hinder it?

- *Classroom discussion.* What are the early signs that a child might lack a theory of mind? What types of spontaneous behaviors might suggest a theory of mind deficit?

- *Classroom discussion.* What is the role of culture on theory of mind acquisition? Do you expect that there will be cultural differences in how early children acquire theory of mind, or in the way that theory of mind competence manifests?

- *Classroom discussion.* Recent studies have shown that infants have an early form of "theory of mind" in terms of intentional actions towards others with the aim of achieving a social goal. What would happen if infants did not have a theory of mind? What would make social life difficult if humans did not have an early theory of mind?

- *Classroom exercise.* Administer the "false belief task" to two children, ages 4 and 6 years of age.

False belief: Location change. Tell the children that:

> Sam leaves his colored pencils on the table and goes out to play. While Sam is outside, John moves the pencils into this closet. When Sam comes back inside, where will he look for his colored pencils? Why do you think this?

If children say "on the table" they have false belief theory of mind skill. If children say "in the closet" they do not yet have false belief knowledge because they are assuming that Sam has the same access to knowledge that they do.

Thus, children who have "false belief" knowledge will point to the table where the owner last left it, and children who do not have "false belief" knowledge will point to the closet, because this is where they know it is located.

Find out what reasons children provide for their decision. Do their reasons provide more information about their theory of mind knowledge?

Additional Resources

For more about theory of mind, see:

Flavell, J. H. (2000). Development of children's knowledge about the mental world. *International Journal of Behavioral Development, 24,* 15–23.

Leslie, A., German, T., & Polizzi, P. (2005). Belief-desire reasoning as a process of selection. *Cognitive Psychology, 50,* 45–85.

Repacholi, B. M., & Gopnik, A. (1997). Early reasoning about desires: Evidence from 14- and 18-month-olds. *Developmental Psychology, 33,* 12–21.

Wellman, H. M. (1990). *The child's theory of mind.* Cambridge, MA: MIT Press.

Wellman, H. M., & Liu, D. (2004). Scaling of theory-of-mind tasks. *Child Development, 75,* 502–517.

Part III

SELF, RELATIONSHIPS, AND SOCIAL GROUPS

5

CHILDREN'S PEER RELATIONSHIPS

Introduction   154

The Power of Friendship: Protection Against an Escalating Cycle of Peer Victimization   155

Ernest V. E. Hodges, Michel Boivin, Frank Vitaro, and William M. Bukowski

Method   157

Results   158

Discussion   161

Children's Social Constructions of Popularity   165

A. Michele Lease, Charlotte A. Kennedy, and Jennifer L. Axelrod

Method   169

Results   171

Discussion   179

Group Status, Group Bias, and Adolescents' Reasoning About the Treatment of Others in School Contexts   184

Stacey S. Horn

Social Stratification within the Peer System   184

Method   187

Results   189

Discussion   193

A Closer Look 4   Leaders and Followers: Peer Pressure in Adolescence   200

Social Development in Childhood and Adolescence: A Contemporary Reader, First Edition. Edited by Melanie Killen and Robert J. Coplan.

Introduction

Children spend almost half of their waking time in the company of peers. Thus, it should not be surprising that developmental psychologists have long considered the peer group to represent an important and unique context for children's social development. There is no denying the powerful influence of peers in children's lives. If you were laughed at or teased at school one day because your corduroy pants made "whiff-whiff" noises when you walked, would you ever want to wear those clothes to school again? Who did you share your "deepest darkest" secrets with? And what was more fun than hanging out with your friends during recess at school?

Parent–child relationships are typically defined as *vertical* in nature—with parents having most of the power and advantage. Consider a young child who wants to play games in the middle of the street. No matter the elegance or sophistication of this child's arguments, this is not a battle that he or she is going to win (even if the parent has to physically restrain him or her!). In contrast, peers are agemates who share similar levels of status. Accordingly, peer relationships are considered to be more *horizontal* in nature and are characterized as more balanced and egalitarian. In fact, many theories of social development have demonstrated how central peers are for children's developing sense of fairness and equality—because the relationships are "equal" and not necessarily "unilateral."

The peer group serves several critical functions for children. For example, peers are an important *source of information* for children, offering differential perspectives on such things as popular culture (music, movies), social norms (how to dress, how to act), and what makes a game rule fair or unfair. Peers also serve as a *comparison group* for children, providing both indirect and direct feedback that influences children's attitudes and behaviors. As well, peers afford children *support*, *intimacy*, and *companionship* outside of the familial environment. Finally, the horizontal nature of the peer group context promotes the development of important *social skills* (e.g., cooperation, negotiation, conflict resolution), *social-cognitive skills* (e.g., perspective-taking), and *group identity* (e.g., affiliation with an ingroup).

Children who experience poor quality peer relations (e.g., rejected/victimized) or do not frequently engage with peers over time may "miss out" on the benefits of peer interactions. Indeed, there is growing research indicating that poor peer relations in childhood are concurrently associated and predictive in the longer term of a host of negative outcomes, including internalizing problems (e.g., anxiety, depression, loneliness, low self-esteem), externalizing problems (aggression, conduct disorder, delinquency), and academic difficulties (e.g., poor achievement, school dropout). Moreover, group identity, which has positive aspects, such as affiliation and belongingness, also has negative aspects such as attitudes about the outgroup that can lead to stereotyping, bias, and prejudice.

The readings in this chapter address three different levels of children's peer relations. The first article focuses on the importance of children's *friendships*, which are defined as close, mutual, and dyadic relationships. Hodges et al. (1999) explored the role of friendship as a protective factor that might "buffer" children against the detrimental outcomes. The second article concerns the construct of *popularity*, which refers to the experience of being liked or accepted by the peer group (i.e., the group's view of an individual). Lease et al. (2002) examined the distinctions between and implications of being "liked" versus being "popular". The final article involves *crowds*, which are reputation-based social collectives that emerge in early adolescence. Horn (2006) investigated how adolescents' membership, group identity, and status in different peer groups was related to their judgments about the fair treatment and inclusion (or exclusion) of others.

The Power of Friendship: Protection Against an Escalating Cycle of Peer Victimization

Ernest V. E. Hodges, Michel Boivin, Frank Vitaro, and William M. Bukowski

Approximately 10% of elementary and middle-school children have been identified as being victimized by their peers on a regular basis (Kochenderfer & Ladd, 1996; Olweus, 1978; Perry, Kusel, & Perry, 1988). Moreover, victimization is highly stable, indicating that many of the same children experience verbal and physical attacks from peers over several years (Egan & Perry, 1998; Hodges, Malone, & Perry, 1995; Olweus, 1978). The experience of being victimized by one's classmates has been linked to several negative adjustment indexes, including anxiety, depression, loneliness, low self-esteem (Boivin & Hymel, 1997; Boivin, Hymel, & Bukowski, 1995; Egan & Perry, 1998; Olweus, 1978, 1992), school avoidance (Kochenderfer & Ladd, 1996), poor academic performance (Olweus, 1978), peer rejection (Hodges, Malone, & Perry, 1997; Perry et al., 1988), and a limited number of friends (Bukowski, Sippola, & Boivin, 1995; Hodges et al., 1995, 1997). Considering the wide range of negative adjustment indexes associated with peer victimization, it is important for researchers to understand the processes and conditions that are likely to put children at risk for peer victimization as well as factors that can temper the negative effects of victimization.

Several studies have sought to determine factors associated with risk for peer victimization. Much of this focus has been on proximal influences that operate within the peer group, especially forms of social impairment exhibited by children that might contribute to their victimization. The guiding assumption has been that victimized children behave in ways that invite and/or reinforce attacks against them. Many victimized children do exhibit behaviors that very probably signal that they will be unlikely to successfully defend themselves against attacks: They cry easily; are manifestly anxious and withdrawn; lack humor, self-confidence, and self-esteem; and use ineffectual persuasion tactics. Moreover, they reward their attackers by being submissive and by relinquishing resources

(Boivin & Hymel, 1997; Olweus, 1978; Patterson, Littman, & Bricker, 1967; Perry et al., 1988; Perry, Williard, & Perry, 1990; Schwartz, Dodge, & Coie, 1993). Many of the foregoing attributes are consistent with a picture of the victimized child as having *internalizing difficulties*. Some victimized children also display *externalizing problems*, such as disruptiveness, aggression, and argumentativeness (Boivin & Hymel, 1997; Olweus, 1978; Perry et al., 1988; Perry, Perry, & Kennedy, 1992). These behaviors have been hypothesized to irritate and provoke other children, especially bullies; victimized children with these attributes are sometimes called *provocative victims*.

Children's interpersonal relationships (e.g., friendships) have also been implicated as possible risk factors for peer victimization. Children's friendships serve many important developmental functions (Hartup, 1993). Friendships are contexts for learning social skills, are information sources for self-knowledge and self-esteem, and provide emotional and cognitive resources for support and coping, as well as practice for later relationships. One function, however, that has received relatively little attention is that of a protective function. Several investigators (Bukowski et al., 1995; Hodges et al., 1997; Kochenderfer & Ladd, 1997; Rizzo, 1989) have recently proposed that having one or more friends helps to protect children against victimization. Children are well aware of the social networks within the classroom (Cairns, Cairns, Neckerman, Gest, & Gariépy, 1988), and aggressive children probably prefer to target children who lack friends because they can do so without fear of retaliation or ostracism from the children's friends. Initial support for the hypothesis that friendship protects children at risk for victimization was offered by Bukowski et al. (1995) and Hodges et al. (1997), who found that friended children were less victimized.

In studying factors that may contribute to children's risk for being victimized by peers, Hodges et al. (1997)

found it useful to distinguish between the two sets of risk factors discussed above—behaviors relevant to the child (*individual risk factors*) and indexes relevant to the child's interpersonal relationships (*social risk factors*). Hodges et al. (1997) hypothesized that individual risk would be most strongly related to peer victimization when children were also at social risk. Indeed, having friends moderated the relation of several individual risk indexes to victimization. For example, the relations of internalizing (anxiety, depression, and withdrawal) and externalizing (aggression, dishonesty, and argumentativeness) problems to victimization were exacerbated when children had few friends but were minimized when children had many friends. However, interpretation of the Hodges et al. (1997) study was hampered by the concurrent design and by shared method variance. One purpose of the present study was to examine the Hodges et al. (1997) hypothesis within a developmentally (i.e., longitudinal) informative design and to use multiple sources of information. It was hypothesized, then, that having a best friend would minimize the relations of internalizing and externalizing behaviors to changes (i.e., increases) in victimization, whereas a lack of a best friend would maximize these relations.

Having a best friend may not be sufficient, however, in protecting children who are at risk for victimization. Variability exists in children's abilities to provide a protective function (Bukowski, Hoza, & Boivin, 1994; Hodges et al., 1997; Hodges & Perry, 1997). Hodges and Perry, for example, found that the relation of internalizing behaviors to victimization was attenuated when children's friends were known by the peer group to rescue children from bullies. In addition, Hodges et al. (1997) found that when children's friends exhibited behaviors that were thought to interfere with their ability to provide a protective function (i.e., friends who had internalizing problems or who lacked strength), the relation of individual risk to victimization was enhanced. The protective function of friendship, however, was inferred in the Hodges et al. (1997) study, whereas the Hodges and Perry study examined a general behavioral pattern of rescuing, aspecific to friendship. In the present study, children reported on the degree to which their best friend sticks up for them when they are attacked or threatened by other children. It was hypothesized

that under high levels of reported protection from a best friend, the relation of behavioral problems to increases in victimization would be minimized, but this relation would be maximized under low levels of protection.

Internalizing and externalizing behaviors are not likely to be related to peer abuse solely in a unidirectional manner. Indeed, recent longitudinal evidence indicates that increases in these behaviors also result from the experience of victimization (Boivin et al., 1995; Egan & Perry, 1998; Hodges et al., 1995; Olweus, 1992). Most of these longitudinal studies, however, are limited because of the use of common respondents (e.g., peers) for measures of victimization and behavioral problems, thus opening the door to alternative interpretations such as response biases and shared method variance. Stronger support for the hypothesis that behavioral problems and peer victimization reciprocally influence each other would be provided if independent sources of information were used within a longitudinal design. The present study used such a design, measuring behaviors with teacher reports and peer victimization with peer reports.

The hypothesis that friendship can buffer the negative effects of victimization discussed above was also examined. Sullivan (1953) suggested that during preadolescence, the establishment of a "chumship" becomes crucial in children's socioemotional development. Sullivan argued that children adjust their behaviors in this relationship to become increasingly similar to one another over time. The presence of a best friend, then, may serve to limit the effects of victimization on children's behavioral repertoire, such as internalizing and externalizing problems, because changes in these behaviors may threaten the child's relationship. Children who lack a best friendship are also less likely to have access to many of the benefits that friendships have to offer, such as companionship, intimacy, and emotional support (e.g., Bukowski et al., 1994). Thus, it was hypothesized that the experience of peer victimization would lead to increases in internalizing and externalizing behaviors primarily when children lacked a best friend. Finally, the possibility that individual differences in the quality of children's best friendship may buffer the negative effects of victimization was also examined.

Method

Participants

A total of 533 French-Canadian children (274 boys and 259 girls) in the fourth ($n = 259$) and fifth grades ($n = 274$) from seven elementary schools participated in the Time 1 data collection (mean age = 10 years 7 months). Participants were from diverse socioeconomic backgrounds. The participation rate for the Time 1 data collection exceeded 98%. Parents provided written consent for their children to participate.

Of the children who participated during the Time 1 data collection, 393 (188 boys and 205 girls) participated during the following school year (Time 2) when children were in the fifth and sixth grades. The 26% attrition rate was due primarily to missing data because of absenteeism and incomplete questionnaires as well as students moving to nonparticipating schools. Selective attrition was not evident in that participants who continued to participate in the second wave of data collection did not significantly differ from those who did not continue to participate on initial levels of the primary variable of interest (i.e., peer victimization).

Procedure

Measures were collected during the spring (April–May) within a 6-week time period. Children completed self-reports of loneliness and completed the victimization scale during separate group testing. Teachers completed a behavioral questionnaire. Each measure is described in detail below.

Measures

PEER VICTIMIZATION

The degree to which children were victimized by peers was assessed using the Perry et al. (1988) peer-report victimization scale. Children nominated two children on seven items describing victimization experiences such as getting hit, pushed, shoved, threatened, or called names. Victimization scores were computed for each child by summing the seven victimization items and standardizing the scores within class. This scale has been well validated by prior research (e.g., Boivin & Hymel, 1997; Hodges et al., 1997; Perry et al., 1988). Cronbach's alphas for Time 1 and Time 2 victimization were, respectively, .97 and .97.

BEHAVIORAL PROBLEMS

Teachers reported on children's behaviors using Rutter's (1967) Children's Behavioral Questionnaire (CBQ), a 26-item behavioral questionnaire using a 3-point scale ranging from 0 to 2. Four items were used to assess internalizing problems: (a) worried about many things; (b) tends to work alone, rather solitary; (c) looks sad, unfortunate, close to tears; and (d) tends to be fearful or afraid of novel things or situations. Five items were used to assess externalizing behaviors: (a) often destroys own or others' belongings, (b) frequently fights with other children, (c) often tells lies, (d) has stolen things on more than one occasion, and (e) bullies other children. These questions tap similar dimensions to those that have been used in prior research (e.g., Egan & Perry, 1998; Hodges et al., 1997) when studying the relation of internalizing and externalizing behaviors to victimization.[1]

Scores for each child were computed by summing across relevant items. High scores for the internalizing scale reflect greater internalizing difficulties, whereas high scores on the externalizing scale reflect greater externalizing behaviors. Cronbach's alphas for Time 1 and Time 2 internalizing behaviors were, respectively, .76 and .70. For Time 1 and Time 2 externalizing behaviors, Cronbach's alphas were, respectively, .83 and .80.

FRIENDSHIP

Children identified their three best friends. Children were considered to have a best friendship if their first choice reciprocally nominated them as one of their three best friends. Children were then asked to respond to the initial version of the Bukowski et al. (1994) Friendship Qualities Scale while thinking about their best friend. Four scales were computed from this questionnaire: (a) Protection, two items (e.g., My friend would stick up for me if another kid was causing me trouble; Cronbach's α = .78); (b) Companionship, seven items (e.g., My friend and I spend all our free time together; Cronbach's α = .79); (c) Security, five items (e.g., If my friend or I do something that the other doesn't like, we can make up easily; Cronbach's α = .72); and (d) Conflict, five items (e.g., My friend and I argue a lot; Cronbach's α = .67).

Table 5.1   Partial correlations among measures at each time of testing

Measure	1	2	3	4	5	6	7	8
1. Victimization	—	.29***	.33***					
2. Internalizing problems	.21***	—	.13 **					
3. Externalizing problems	.33***	.15**	—					
4. Mutual best friendship	−.28***	−.17***	−.19***	—				
5. Protection	−.02	−.11*	.01	—	—			
6. Companionship	−.15**	−.07	−.01	—	.42***	—		
7. Security	.01	.05	−.02	—	.37***	.53***	—	
8. Conflict	.00	.03	.18***	—	−.02	−.12*	−.15**	—

Note. Partial correlations were controlled for sex and age. Partial correlations among variables during Time 1 are presented below the diagonal, and for Time 2, above the diagonal. For Time 1, *ns* ranged from 479 to 529 for the first four measures. The *ns* for the friendship quality variables (Measures 5–8) ranged from 315 to 335 (these *ns* were restricted to those who had a reciprocated best friendship). For Time 2, *ns* ranged from 388 to 398.
*p < .05. **p < .01. ***p < .001.

Table 5.2   Partial correlations of Time 1 measures with Time 2 measures

Time 1 measure	Time 2 measure		
	1	2	3
1. Victimization	**.69***	.26***	.34***
2. Internalizing problems	.22***	**.23***	.04
3. Externalizing problems	.29***	.14***	**.63***
4. Mutual best friendship	−.28***	−.14**	−.16**
5. Protection	−.12*	.00	−.03
6. Companionship	−.09	.03	−.02
7. Security	.04	.02	−.04
8. Conflict	.04	.11	.18**

Note. Partial correlations were controlled for sex and age. The *ns* ranged from 377 to 393 for the first four measures. The *ns* for the friendship quality variables (Measures 5–8) ranged from 259 to 267 (these *ns* were restricted to those who had a reciprocated best friendship). Stability coefficients are in boldface.
*p < .05. **p < .01. ***p < .001.

Results

Results are divided into three major sections. First, intercorrelations among the measures are presented. Second, the hypotheses concerning the causes of victimization are tested. Third, the hypotheses regarding outcomes of victimization are examined.

Intercorrelations among variables

Table 5.1 presents partial correlations among all measures (controlling for age and sex) for each data collection (Times 1 and 2). Two aspects of Table 5.1 are noteworthy. First, both of the adjustment indexes (internalizing and externalizing problems) were significantly related (in expected directions) to peer victimization, replicating previous research (e.g., Boivin & Hymel, 1997; Egan & Perry, 1998; Hodges et al., 1997). In addition, the significant associations among teacher-reported behavior problems and peer-reported victimization eliminates the alternative explanation left open by prior research that these associations may be due to shared method variance. Second, in the bottom right-hand corner of Table 5.1, the usefulness of keeping the friendship variables as distinct dimensions is shown by the low-to-moderate relations among them.

Table 5.2 presents partial correlations of the measures across time. Three aspects of Table 5.2 deserve comment. First, all of the measures that were collected at both time points showed significant stability coefficients over the 1-year interval. However, the stability of internalizing problems was considerably lower than that of externalizing problems. The low stability of teacher-reported internalizing problems, however, is consistent with prior research (e.g., Vitaro, Gagnon, & Tremblay, 1991). Second, both types of behavioral problems significantly correlated with victimization 1 year later and both were significantly predicted by victimization the prior year. Third, two of the friendship variables also related to future victimization—the presence of a mutual friend and having a protective friend negatively related to future victimization. The hypotheses relating the adjustment indexes and friendship to victimization, however, were offered at the level of moderation and at the level of predicting change. These hypotheses are evaluated in the following sections.

Antecedents of victimization

Two regression analyses were performed to evaluate whether internalizing problems and externalizing problems predicted increases in victimization. For each analysis, Time 2 victimization was the criterion, victimization at Time 1 and age and sex were entered on the first step as control variables, and then one of the two Time 1 predictors was evaluated on the second step.

As predicted, internalizing behaviors, $\Delta F(1, 385) = 4.35$, $pr = .11$, $p < .05$, and externalizing behaviors, $\Delta F(1, 384) = 5.99$, $pr = .12$, $p < .05$, at Time 1 significantly accounted for increases in victimization over 1 year, over and above the control variables.

Does best friendship decrease risk for victimization? We first evaluated whether having a best friend would moderate the relation of behavioral problems to increases in victimization. To do so, one regression analysis was performed in which Time 2 victimization was the criterion. Time 1 victimization was entered on the first step. Age and sex were entered as controls on the second step. Time 1 internalizing problems and externalizing problems were entered on the third step. Reciprocated best friendship (coded 0 or 1) was entered on the fourth step, and the two internalizing and externalizing problems by reciprocated-friendship product terms were entered on the final step. The overall equation was significant, $F(8, 377) = 47.83$, $R^2 = 50.4\%$, $p < .001$. Victimization at Time 1 accounted for the majority of the variance, $F = 48.1\%$. On the second step, age and sex did not account for additional variance, $\Delta F = 1.90$, $\Delta R^2 = 0.5\%$. Internalizing problems ($pr = .09$, $p < .05$, one-tailed) and externalizing problems ($pr = .11$, $p < .05$) together accounted for an additional 1.2% of the variance at Step 3, $\Delta F =$

4.60, $p < .05$. The partial correlations for the behavioral problems on this step indicate that there was a small degree of overlap when predicting increases in victimization from internalizing and externalizing behaviors but that they were largely independent of one another. On the fourth step, having a best friend marginally added to the variance explained, $\Delta F = 3.27$, $pr = -.09$, $p < .05$, one-tailed, with the presence of a best friend predicting decreases in victimization. Internalizing and externalizing problems, however, did not differentially relate to increases in victimization depending on whether children had a mutual best friend, indicated by nonsignificant best friendship by internalizing-problems and friendship by externalizing-problems product terms.[2]

Behavioral problems were entered prior to friendship in the above analysis because internalizing and externalizing behaviors were considered to be more directly responsible for victimization than were children's interpersonal relationships. This equation was reanalyzed with the order of entry of behavioral problems and friendship reversed. Having a best friendship significantly predicted change in victimization when entered prior to behaviors, $\Delta F = 4.97$, $\Delta R^2 = 1.0\%$, $p < .05$. In addition, internalizing and externalizing problems together accounted for a significant increment in variance accounted for over and above that explained by Time 1 victimization, age, sex, and friendship, $\Delta F = 3.74$, $\Delta R^2 = 1.0\%$, $p < .01$. This pattern of results indicates that although the effect of friendship on victimization was partly explained by behavioral problems, behavioral problems predicted increases in victimization independent of having a friend.

Next, we evaluated whether the four friendship quality variables would moderate the relation of internalizing and externalizing problems to victimization. Because children reported on the friendship qualities of their best friend, it is only meaningful to discuss these qualities for children who had a best friend. Thus, the following analyses were restricted to children whose best friend reciprocally nominated the child as one of his or her three best friends. Initially, a regression analysis was performed with victimization at Time 2 as the criterion. Time 1 victimization, age, sex, and all six main effects (the two behavioral risk indexes and the four friendship quality measures) were entered on the first step. On the second step, the eight (4 friendship quality variables × 2 behavioral variables) product terms were tested. Because only one friendship quality (i.e., perceived protection) interacted with risk, the other three friendship quality variables and their respective interactions were dropped from the analysis.

As hypothesized, the friendship quality of protection interacted with internalizing problems to predict Time 2 victimization, $\Delta F(1, 247) = 4.96, \Delta R^2 = 1.3\%$, $p < .05$, after controlling for Time 1 victimization, age, sex, and the main effects of Time 1 externalizing behaviors, internalizing behaviors, and friendship protection. The nature of this significant interaction was examined using the appropriate standardized solution recommended by Aiken and West (1991). This procedure allows one to see how the relation of a predictor variable (e.g., Time 1 internalizing problems) to a criterion (e.g., Time 2 victimization) varies depending on the moderator variable (e.g., Time 1 friendship protection). Specifically, the relation of a predictor to the criterion is estimated in the form of a standardized regression coefficient (β) at each of three levels of the moderator variable ($-1, 0,$ and 1 SD; i.e., at low, medium, and high levels of the moderator). Comparing the βs across the three levels of the moderator variable allows one to see how the relation (i.e., slope) between the predictor and the criterion changes with level of the moderator.

The follow-up analysis confirmed that having a friend who served a protective function buffered the relation of internalizing problems to victimization. When children perceived decreasingly less protective friends from high (1 SD) to medium (0 SD) to low (-1 SD), the relation of internalizing problems to victimization increased (respective βs = .00, ns; .10, $p < .05$; .21, $p < .005$).[3] Note that children's internalizing problems no longer related to victimization if they had a friendship characterized by high protection, thus completely buffering children's risk at this level.

To summarize, internalizing and externalizing behaviors predicted increases in victimization over the 1-year interval of the study. In addition, having a best friend predicted decreases in victimization. Moreover, and as expected, having a friend characterized by high protection eliminated the relation of internalizing behaviors to changes in victimization,

whereas having a friend characterized by low protection exacerbated this relation.

Outcomes of victimization

To evaluate the hypothesis that the experience of victimization is likely to lead to increases in internalizing and externalizing problems, two multiple regression analyses were performed, one for each outcome. For each analysis, initial level (Time 1) of the outcome, age, and sex were entered on the first step, and victimization at Time 1 was entered on the second step.

Victimization at Time 1 significantly predicted both outcomes over and above initial levels and the control variables. Victimization predicted increases in internalizing problems, $\Delta F(1, 379) = 21.36, pr = .23$, $p < .001$, and increases in externalizing problems, $\Delta F(1, 378) = 13.83, pr = .19, p < .001$.

Does best friendship buffer the effects of victimization? First, we examined whether the sheer existence of a mutual best friendship would decrease the effects of peer victimization. Two regression equations were evaluated, one for each outcome. Initial levels of the criterion variable were entered on the first step. Age and sex were controlled on the second step. Time 1 victimization and best friendship were entered on the third step. And on the final step, the best friendship by victimization product term was evaluated.

When predicting Time 2 internalizing problems, the overall equation was significant, $F(6, 377) = 9.01$, $R^2 = 12.5\%, p < .001$. Time 1 internalizing problems accounted for 5.4% of the variance on the first step, $F = 21.67, p < .001$. On the second step, age and sex did not contribute additional variance, $\Delta F = .11, ns$. Together, victimization ($pr = .21, p < .001$) and having a best friend ($pr = -.05, ns$) accounted for an additional 5.3% of the variance on the third step, $\Delta F = 11.19, p < .001$. More important, and as expected, having a best friendship significantly interacted with victimization to predict change in internalizing problems, $\Delta F = 7.89, \Delta R^2 = 1.8\%, p < .005$.

To examine the nature of this interaction, separate regression analyses were performed for children who had a mutual best friendship and for children who did not. Victimization at Time 1 predicted increases in internalizing problems (after controlling for Time 1 internalizing problems, sex, and age), for children without a mutual best friend, $\Delta F(1, 110) = 15.30$, $pr = .35$, $p < .001$, but not for children with a best friend, $\Delta F(1, 264) = 0.42$, $pr = .04$, ns. Thus, having a best friend completely eliminated the effects of victimization to increases in internalizing problems.

When predicting externalizing problems, the overall equation was also significant, $F(6, 376) = 53.67$, $R^2 = 46.1\%$, $p < .001$. Initial levels of externalizing problems accounted for the majority of the variance explained, $\Delta F = 163.90$, $R^2 = 42.1\%$, $p < .001$. Sex and age did not explain additional variance on the second step, $\Delta F = 0.71$, ns. On the third step, victimization ($pr = .21$, $p < .001$) and having a best friend ($pr = -.01$, ns) together accounted for an additional 2.8% of the variance explained, $\Delta F = 9.54$, $p < .001$. More important, and as hypothesized, the presence of a mutual best friendship interacted with victimization to predict changes in externalizing problems, $\Delta F(1, 376) = 7.41$, $\Delta R^2 = 1.1\%$, $p < .01$.

Again, to examine the nature of this interaction, separate regression equations were analyzed for children with and without best friends. Time 1 victimization predicted increases in externalizing problems for children without a best friendship, $\Delta F(1, 259) = 0.79$, $pr = .06$, ns. Having a best friend, then, considerably reduced the relation of victimization to increases in externalization problems while enhancing this relation for children without a best friendship.

The two outcomes (internalizing and externalizing behaviors) were significantly associated with each other at Time 2. To ensure that the observed relations between victimization and increases in the two outcomes were not redundant (i.e., predicting a common latent construct), the analyses reported above were reanalyzed for each outcome while adding the other Time 2 outcome to the existing controls. Results were essentially the same.

To summarize, internalizing and externalizing behaviors were also a result of peer abuse. However, the experience of victimization did not affect changes in behaviors when children had a best friend.

Although victimization was not related to increases in internalizing and externalizing problems for children with a mutual best friend, it does not preclude the possibility that at different levels of friendship quality, victimization may still produce negative adjustment outcomes. To test this possibility, a series of

regression analyses were performed in which the product term of each friendship quality by victimization at Time 1 was evaluated when predicting the two adjustment indexes.

Only one of the eight interaction terms was significant. Companionship interacted with Time 1 victimization to predict Time 2 internalizing problems (after controlling for sex, age, Time 1 internalizing problems, and companionship), $\Delta F(1, 246) = 4.86$, $\Delta R^2 = 1.9\%$, $p < .05$. To examine the nature of this interaction, the Aiken and West (1991) procedure outlined previously was used. Unexpectedly, the relation of victimization to increases in internalizing problems was apparent when children reported high levels (1 SD) of companionship ($\beta = .26$, $p < .05$), but not at medium (0 SD; $\beta = .12$, ns), and low (-1 SD) levels of companionship ($\beta = -.02$, ns).[4]

Discussion

The list of concurrent adjustment correlates of victimization is long and growing, but longitudinal studies designed to shed light on antecedent–outcome relations are few and far between. The present study adds to the existing literature on peer victimization by shedding light on some of the processes that are responsible for victimization. In addition to answering questions about why children are victimized, the present study answers questions about when victimization is most likely to occur.

Hodges et al. (1997) postulated that peer victimization should be most likely to occur when children have behavioral problems that put them at individual risk and they have relational problems that put them at social risk. The results of the present study provide support for their conceptualization of children's interpersonal relationships as contexts that govern whether aggression is directed toward at-risk children. Moreover, the results of the present study indicate that friendship can be a powerful buffer against the negative adjustment often experienced by victimized children. We discuss, first, findings related to the children's risk for victimization and then turn to the consequences of victimization. Then, we note some strengths and limitations of the present study.

Both internalizing and externalizing behaviors predicted increases in peer victimization. These findings lend support to the conceptualization of behavioral problems as risk factors for peer abuse (Boivin & Hymel, 1997; Boivin et al., 1995; Egan & Perry, 1998; Hodges et al., 1997; Perry et al., 1992). Furthermore, that internalizing and externalizing behaviors were largely independent predictors of victimization indicates that behaviors that reinforce or provoke aggressors are likely to put children at risk for victimization.

Having a best friend did not interact with the individual risk variables to predict increases in victimization. However, having a best friend did predict decreases in victimization over the year, although marginally so after controlling for behavioral problems. Having a best friend, then, should still be considered important for warding off aggressive attacks. That is, having a best friend appears to decrease victimization for children, regardless of whether they have behavioral problems.

Moreover, the quality of friendship that was hypothesized to be the process by which friendship reduces children's risk for victimization was supported. Indeed, internalizing problems no longer predicted victimization for children who perceived a high (1 SD) level of protection from their friend. Having a friend characterized as providing little protection (−1 SD), however, exacerbated the relation of internalizing problems to victimization. These findings highlight the importance of assessing the quality of children's friendships in addition to the quantity of friendships and also show that friendships may not always be salutary for children's social experiences (Hartup & Stevens, 1997).

Friendship security, companionship, and conflict did not predict changes in victimization, alone or in combination with any risk factor. Other aspects of friendship, however, are likely to play a role in exacerbating or reducing children's risk for victimization. Hodges et al. (1997) pointed to characteristics (weakness and internalizing behaviors) of children's friends that exacerbate children's risk for victimization. In addition, friends' strategies for protecting their friend may also be important. As Kochenderfer and Ladd (1997) noted, children may attempt to protect their friends in a number of ways. For example, when a friend is being victimized, some friends may respond by telling the teacher, whereas others may respond by fighting back. Further research is needed to identify specific strategies that friends use to most effectively stop chronic victimization.

The results of the present study suggest an additional important role that friendship can play with regard to the behavioral consequences of peer victimization. As hypothesized, increases in behavioral problems were not apparent for children with a best friend—only children without a best friend showed increases in internalizing and externalizing behaviors. Children tend to befriend similar others on the basis of a number of salient behavioral dimensions such as externalizing and internalizing behaviors (e.g., Hodges et al., 1997; Hogue & Steinberg 1995). If behavioral similarity is important for the maintenance of friendships, changes in these observable behaviors may threaten children's relationships (Sullivan, 1953). Future research could examine the possibility by examining whether the maintenance of friendships is less likely when children's similarity on behavioral dimensions decreases over time.

Another possibility for the buffering role of friendship on the behavioral outcomes of victimization may be that victimization is not as chronic (i.e., stable) for children with a best friend. To test this possibility, a post hoc regression equation was analyzed, with Time 2 victimization as the criterion. The friendship by Time 1 victimization product term was evaluated after controlling for Time 1 victimization, sex, age, and best friendship. This interaction term was not significant, however, indicating that victimization is as chronic for children with a best friendship as it is for those without a best friend.

Unexpectedly, children who spent an above average (1 SD) amount of time with their friend evidenced increases in internalizing problems when they were victimized. Albeit speculative, a high degree of companionship may be reflective of an overly close and exclusive relationship, perhaps characteristic of children who use preoccupied coping strategies (which is also associated with internalizing behaviors) with their friend to deal with stressful situations at school (Hodges, Finnegan, & Perry, 1999).

A strength of the present study was the large number of participants and the strong methodological design. Much of the previous work on the relation of behavioral problems to peer victimization has been limited by shared method variance (Boivin & Hymel, 1997; Boivin et al., 1995; Egan & Perry, 1998; Hodges et al., 1997). The present study overcame this limitation by assessing behavioral problems through teachers, friendship qualities from children, and victimization by peer reports.

Another strength of the present study was the longitudinal design. Such designs are essential for evaluating causal models such as those tested in the present study. However, the high stability of the measures (except for internalizing problems) limited the amount of variance that could be explained by the predictors. When this occurs, even small percentages of variance accounted for become important, especially for making causal inferences. It is also important that the significant interactions indicate that the effects were much stronger at high levels of social risk. Moreover, the effects are likely to cumulate over several years in a compounding fashion, thereby adding up to be substantial. To optimize the amount of change that can be studied during middle childhood, researchers may wish to consider targeting transition periods (e.g., moving from elementary to middle school) or extended periods of time, in which there may be more opportunities for children to escape victimization (or to become victimized).

The present study focused on the friendship qualities of children's best friendships because Sullivan (1953) argued for the importance of this relationship over other friendships during pre-adolescence. However, children's larger social networks are clearly important as well (e.g., Harris, 1995). Research on friendship may benefit from what has occurred in the literature on attachment, which suggests that the quality of relationships may be quite different from one relationship partner to another (e.g., Cox, Owen, Henderson, & Margand, 1992; Hodges et al., 1999). Future research could examine, for example, whether some friends provide protection whereas other friends primarily provide intimacy exchange, self-validation, and so forth.

Victimization, in this study, was measured in terms of the receipt of direct physical and verbal aggression; other kinds of victimization, such as indirect or relational victimization (Crick & Grotpeter, 1995), may

operate according to different processes. Relational aggression refers to acts intended to harm a child's interpersonal relationships with peers (e.g., by encouraging one's friends to exclude someone from a social function or clique); girls are more likely than boys both to enact and to receive this form of aggression. It is important to keep in mind, however, that studies have shown that girls are just about as likely as boys to experience the kind of direct overt form of abuse investigated here (Egan & Perry, 1998; Hodges et al., 1997; Kochenderfer & Ladd, 1997; Perry et al., 1988). Moreover, the present results indicate that the antecedent–outcome relations of the type of victimization assessed here did not interact with sex, indicating that the results are equally applicable to boys and girls.

The overall pattern of results suggests an escalating cycle of peer abuse for children at risk who do not have a best friend. That is, because behavioral problems reciprocally influence victimization over time for children without a best friend, victimization may be especially difficult to escape. However, the findings also indicate that there is hope for intervention. Having a friend can help reduce the likelihood of being victimized in the first place, and having a friend can reduce the further exacerbation of behavioral problems due to being victimized. When designing interventions to ameliorate victimized children's plight, investigators should also keep in mind that children at risk for victimization need skills to establish friendships with those who can provide a protective function.

Notes

1   We also ran a factor analysis (with varimax rotation) on the nine items from the CBQ to ensure that the two expected factors would emerge. Two clear factors emerged, with eigenvalues greater than 1, with each item loading highly (range = .63 to .85) on the appropriate factor (i.e., Externalizing or Internalizing Dimensions) and low cross-factor loadings (less than .20).

2   These interaction terms were also tested using two other methods for determining friendship (number of reciprocated friendships, range = 0–3, and having any [second and third choices] reciprocated friend, range = 0 or 1).

Each interaction was nonsignificant. Furthermore, sex did not interact with any of the risk variables to predict change in victimization, nor were there any significant three-way interactions involving sex. Thus, all of the effects in this section are equally applicable to boys and girls.

3 All variables were standardized, thus effectively centering each variable (i.e., given a mean of zero). Centering of variables is necessary for the interpretation of interactions in multiple regression (Aiken & West, 1991).

4 Sex was also examined as a possible moderator of the main effects of victimization and as a moderator of all friendship by victimization product terms. No interaction term involving sex was significant, indicating that all observed findings reported here apply equally to both sexes.

References

Aiken, L. S., & West, S. G. (1991). *Multiple regression: Testing and interpreting interactions.* Newbury Park, CA: Sage.

Boivin, M., & Hymel, S. (1997). Peer expectations and social self-perceptions: A sequential model. *Developmental Psychology, 33,* 135–145.

Boivin, M., Hymel S., & Bukowski, W. M. (1995). The roles of social withdrawal, peer rejection, and victimization by peers in predicting loneliness and depressed mood in childhood. *Development and Psychopathology, 7,* 765–785.

Bukowski, W. M., Hoza, B., & Boivin, M. (1994). Measuring friendship quality during pre- and early adolescence: The development and psychometric properties of the Friendship Qualities scale. *Journal of Social and Personal Relationships, 11,* 471–484.

Bukowski, W. M., Sippola, L. K., & Boivin, M. (1995, March). Friendship protects "at risk" children from victimization by peers. In J. M. Price (Chair), *The role of friendship in children's developmental risk and resilience: A developmental psychopathology perspective.* Symposium conducted at the biennial meeting of the Society for Research in Child Development, Indianapolis, IN.

Cairns, R. B., Cairns, B. D., Neckerman, H. J., Gest, S. D., & Gariépy, J. (1988). Social networks and aggressive behavior: Peer support or peer rejection? *Developmental Psychology, 24,* 815–823.

Cox, M. J., Owen, M. T., Henderson, V. K., & Margand, N. A. (1992). Prediction of infant–father and infant–mother attachment. *Developmental Psychology, 28,* 474–483.

Crick, N. R., & Grotpeter, J. K. (1995). Relational aggression, gender and social–psychological adjustment. *Child Development, 66,* 710–722.

Egan, S. K., & Perry, D. G. (1998). Does low self-regard invite victimization? *Developmental Psychology, 34,* 299–309.

Harris, J. R. (1995). Where is the child's environment? A group socialization theory of development. *Psychological Review, 102,* 458–489.

Hartup, W. W. (1993). Adolescents and their friends. In B. Laursen (Ed.), *Close friendships in adolescence* (pp. 3–22). San Francisco: Jossey-Bass.

Hartup, W. W., & Stevens, N. (1997). Friendships and adaption in the life course. *Psychological Bulletin, 121,* 355–370.

Hodges, E. V. E., Finnegan, R. A., & Perry, D. G. (1999). Skewed autonomy-relatedness in preadolescents' conceptions of their relationships with mother, father, and best friend. *Developmental Psychology, 35,* 737–748.

Hodges, E. V. E., Malone, M. J., Jr., & Perry, D. G. (1995, March). Behavioral and social antecedents and consequences of victimization by peers. In N. R. Crick (Chair), *Recent trends in the study of peer victimization: Who is at risk and what are the consequences?* Symposium conducted at the biennial meeting of the Society for Research in Child Development, Indianapolis, IN.

Hodges, E. V. E., Malone, M. J., Jr., & Perry, D. G. (1997). Individual risk and social risk as interacting determinants of victimization in the peer group. *Developmental Psychology, 33,* 1032–1039.

Hodges, E. V. E., & Perry, D. G. (1997, April). Victimization by peers: The protective function of peer friendships. In B. J. Kochenderfer & G. W. Ladd (Chairs), *Research on bully/victim problems: Agendas from several cultures.* Poster symposium conducted at the biennial meeting of the Society for Research in Child Development. Washington, DC.

Hogue, A., & Steinberg, L. (1995). Homophily of internalized distress in adolescent peer groups. *Developmental Psychology, 31,* 897–906.

Kochenderfer, B. J., & Ladd, G. W. (1996). Peer victimization: Cause or consequence of school maladjustment? *Child Development, 67,* 1305–1317.

Kochenderfer, B. J., & Ladd, G. W. (1997). Victimized children's responses to peers' aggression: Behaviors associated with reduced versus continued victimization. *Development and Psychopathology, 9,* 59–73.

Olweus, D. (1978). *Aggression in the schools: Bullies and whipping boys.* Washington, DC: Hemisphere.

Olweus, D. (1992). Victimization by peers: Antecedents and long-term outcomes. In K. H. Rubin & J. B. Asendorpf (Eds.), *Social withdrawal, inhibition, and shyness in childhood* (pp. 315–341). Hillsdale, NJ: Erlbaum.

Patterson, G. R., Littman, R. A., & Bricker, W. (1967). Assertive behavior in children: A step toward a theory of aggression. *Monographs of the Society for Research in Child Development, 35* (Serial No. 113).

Perry, D. G., Kusel, S. J., & Perry, L. C. (1988). Victims of peer aggression. *Developmental Psychology, 24*, 807–814.

Perry, D. G., Perry, L. C., & Kennedy, E. (1992). Conflict and the development of antisocial behavior. In C. U. Shantz & W. W. Hartup (Eds.), *Conflict in child and adolescent development* (pp. 301–329). New York: Cambridge University Press.

Perry, D. G., Williard, J. C., & Perry, L. C. (1990). Peers' perceptions of the consequences that victimized children provide aggressors. *Child Development, 61*, 1310–1325.

Rizzo, T. A. (1989). *Friendship development among children in school.* Norwood, NJ: Ablex.

Rutter, M. (1967). Children's behavior questionnaire for completion by teachers: Preliminary findings. *Journal of Child Psychology and Psychiatry and Allied Disciplines, 8*, 1–11.

Schwartz, D., Dodge, K. A., & Coie, J. D. (1993). The emergence of chronic peer victimization in boys' play groups. *Child Development, 64*, 1755–1772.

Sullivan, H. S. (1953). *The interpersonal theory of psychiatry.* New York: Norton.

Vitaro, F., Gagnon, C., & Tremblay, R. E. (1991). Teachers' and mothers' assessment of children's behaviors from kindergarten to grade two: Stability and change within and across informants. *Journal of Psychopathology and Behavioral Assessment, 13*, 325–343.

Children's Social Constructions of Popularity

A. Michele Lease, Charlotte A. Kennedy, and Jennifer L. Axelrod

Based on the large amount of time children spend discussing who is popular and why, popularity and social position seem to be primary concerns for children and young adolescents (Adler & Adler, 1998; Parker & Gottman, 1989). Furthermore, many children expend a great deal of time and energy maneuvering for social position (Adler & Adler, 1998). Yet, the question arises: What does it mean to be 'popular'? Ultimately, the answer to that question depends on who is asked— e.g., researchers from various traditions, classroom teachers, or children—and on how the question is phrased.

Recently, a discussion has emerged about the meaning of popularity in childhood and early adolescence, in light of conflicting accounts of the defining characteristics of popular youth (Parkhurst & Hopmeyer, 1998; Rodkin, Farmer, Pearl, & Van Acker, 2000). That discussion provides the framework and starting point for the current study on popularity in the later elementary school years. Differing conclusions have been offered by investigators from two separate research traditions—psychology-based sociometric status and sociology of education (Rodkin et al., 2000). Specifically, sociometric research suggests that popular youth are prosocial and likeable (e.g., Newcomb, Bukowski, & Pattee, 1993), whereas sociological research suggests that popular youth are cool, socially dominant, and socially savvy yet not necessarily well-liked by the peer group as a whole (e.g., Adler & Adler, 1998).

Sociometric and sociological researchers might arrive at differing conclusions about popular youth because they make use of differing methodologies— methodologies that reflect differing assumptions about the meaning of popularity (Parkhurst & Hopmeyer, 1998). Building on prior research (Parkhurst & Hopmeyer, 1998; Rodkin et al., 2000), one goal of the current research was to directly compare the two conceptions of popularity in an elementary school sample by: (a) measuring both conceptions of popularity with the same method (i.e., peer nominations), (b) examining the meaning of popularity among elementary school children through a comparison of the correlates of each type of popularity, and (c) comparing the characteristics of the two types of popular children, including their social standing within the peer group. The ultimate goal of the current research was to shed light on elementary school children's understanding of popularity.

In the following sections, we (a) examine the differing assumptions of and methodological strategies employed in sociometric and sociological studies of popularity, and (b) provide an overview of sociometric and sociological conclusions about popularity, with specific attention given to points of convergence and divergence between the two disciplines.

Methodological distinctions and guiding assumptions

Sociologists and sociometric status researchers approach their studies of popularity with differing methodologies and assumptions (Parkhurst & Hopmeyer, 1998; Rodkin et al., 2000). Sociologists of education, who study a wide range of age groups (e.g., Adler & Adler, 1998; Corsaro, 1979; Eder, Evans, & Parker, 1995), tend to use qualitative, ethnographic methods in their research and rely on research participants' perceptions and social constructions of popularity (Parkhurst & Hopmeyer, 1998; Rodkin et al., 2000). However, researchers from that tradition also initiate studies of popularity with a priori assumptions, citing the definition advanced by Weber (1946) that popularity, or status, is comprised of 'honor, prestige, and power' (in Corsaro, 1979, p. 46; see also Adler & Adler, 1998). Thus, it is not surprising that, from preschool through high school, students identified as popular by sociologists have been socially prominent, prestigious, and dominant members of the peer group.

In contrast, sociometric status researchers primarily use quantitative methods, such as peer and teacher nominations/ratings. Sociometric research also is guided by theoretical assumptions about popularity, as reflected in the methods used to identify popular children. Specifically, popularity typically is assessed in sociometric classification systems (for a review of methods see Frederickson & Furnham, 1998; Newcomb et al., 1993; Terry & Coie, 1991) determined by the number of times a child is nominated as *like-most* and *like-least*, relative to peers. Consequently, sociometric popularity essentially is a summary measure of the degree to which a group member is liked or disliked by peers as a whole and, thus, is equated with likeability and social acceptance by peers (Newcomb et al., 1993).

Methodological factors are certain to have an impact on studies of popularity, given that ethnographic research methods are more likely to elicit children's constructions of popularity than are quantitative methods, with their fixed criteria for eliciting nominations of popular peers. However, the essential difference between sociometric and sociological studies of popularity might arguably be their implicit assumptions about the meaning of popularity. Those differences are likely the driving force behind the differing conclusions reached in their research.

Research conducted by Parkhurst and Hopmeyer (1998) with middle school students supports that contention. Specifically, participants were asked to nominate peers (a) who they liked the most and least, consistent with sociometric research, and (b) who they believed to be the most popular at school, which they termed '*perceived popularity*'. Perceived popularity is similar to sociological conceptions of popularity, given that 'popularity' was not defined for the participants, thus allowing participants' constructions of popularity to emerge. The behavioral description of children identified as sociometrically popular was consistent with sociometric literature, as expected, whereas the behavioral description of children identified as perceived popular was fairly consistent with sociological literature. Thus, it appears that guiding assumptions about the meaning of popularity, as opposed to methodological factors, drive the differing conclusions reached by sociometric and sociological researchers about popular children and their behavioral characteristics.

Sociometric and sociological conceptions of popularity

Popular children within the sociometric status literature have been characterized as prosocial and likeable, which is not surprising given the use of like-most and like-least nominations to identify sociometrically popular children. In a meta-analytic review, Newcomb and colleagues (1993) concluded that popular children, compared to peers, evidence higher levels of sociability, prosocial behavior, and cognitive abilities. They also evidence lower levels of aggressive, disruptive, and negative behaviors and social withdrawal. Narrative reviews have reached similar conclusions, with sociometrically popular children being rated as more friendly and socially sensitive by teachers, peers, and observers (Asher & Coie, 1990; Rubin, Bukowski, & Parker, 1998).

In general, sociometrically popular children exhibit what might be termed as politeness and good manners: they do not tend to draw attention to themselves when they enter a group, impose their social goals on others, or behave in disruptive ways that would interfere with others' social goals (Rubin et al., 1998). However, they also tend to be assertive children with strong leadership skills (Rubin et al., 1998). Although most sociometric status studies have been conducted with elementary school children, the few sociometric studies conducted with preschool and middle school students have produced comparable results (Coie, Dodge, & Kupersmidt, 1990; Denham & Holt, 1993; Parkhurst & Hopmeyer, 1998).

Within the sociology of education literature, popular status is marked by social prominence (Rodkin et al., 2000) and dominance (Parkhurst & Hopmeyer, 1998). Youth who belong to cliques at the top of the status hierarchy are considered to be the most popular, and students who engage in highly visible and prestigious activities (e.g., cheerleading, athletics) tend to be the ones who hold places at the top of that hierarchy (Adler & Adler, 1998; Eder, 1985; Eder, Evans, & Parker, 1995; Michell & Amos, 1997). Many of these studies have been conducted with adolescents (Parkhurst & Hopmeyer, 1998), although researchers have found similar results in elementary school populations (Adler & Adler, 1998; Michell, 1997; Michell & Amos, 1997).

In general, sociologically popular elementary school children in the Adler and Adler (1998) and Michell (1997; Michell & Amos, 1997) studies were observed to be dominant and to possess the 'expressive equipment' of social prestige (e.g., clothing, expensive hobbies). Furthermore, popular children were socially sophisticated, often using their socially savvy interpersonal skills to manipulate and control others, to enforce the social boundaries around their social groups by excluding others, and to maintain their position at the top of the social hierarchy (Adler & Adler, 1998).

However, some of the other characteristics associated with popularity noted in the Adler and Adler (1998) study differed for boys and girls. For instance,

the major factor affecting popularity for boys was athletic ability (see also Michell, 1997), which often was associated with physical displays of superiority, such as fighting and rough play. Being cool, tough, defiant of adult authority, and having sophisticated social skills made a large impact as well. In general, neither appearing to value academics nor being viewed as a 'dummy' was conducive to being popular, according to Adler and Adler (p. 45).

The major factor affecting sociological popularity for girls was family background (Adler & Adler, 1998). Not only were popular girls relatively more wealthy than peers, with expensive lifestyles and possessions, but they also were less monitored by their parents (Adler & Adler, 1998; Michell, 1997). Less parental monitoring allowed them the freedom to try out forbidden or risky activities (e.g., smoking; Michell, 1997) and spend time on activities (e.g., phone use, parties) designed to manipulate their social position and the positions of others (Adler & Adler, 1998). Furthermore, popularity for girls was heavily influenced by physical attractiveness, especially attractiveness to boys (Adler & Adler, 1998; Michell, 1997). Yet, unlike boys, cliques of popular girls who were academically inclined were identified, whereas non-academic popular girls tended to associate in their own cliques.

Points of convergence and divergence

Despite methodological and assumptive differences, points of convergence between sociological and sociometric studies of popularity in elementary school are evident. In both research traditions, immature behavior, passivity, and social withdrawal tend to be associated with lower levels of popularity, whereas self-confidence tends to be associated with popular status (Adler & Adler, 1998; Michell, 1997; Newcomb et al., 1993; Rubin et al., 1998). For example, children who are perceived by peers as 'acting like a baby' (Rubin et al., 1998, p. 654), to 'cry (or get flustered) easily' (Adler & Adler, 1998, p. 41), or being 'dead quiet' (Michell, 1997, p. 6) have a good chance of being classified as unpopular by either research tradition.

Convergences between the two literatures also are apparent for some types of aggression. On one hand, the use of aggression is viewed positively by peers when children are standing up for themselves in the face of provocation (Coie & Dodge, 1998). On the other hand, aggression that is emotionally charged, reactive, and undercontrolled (i.e., reactive aggression) appears to be related to unpopular status in both literatures (Coie & Dodge, 1998; Adler & Adler, 1998; Poulin & Boivin, 2000).

However, divergences between the two literatures also are evident. First, sociologically popular children often are not well-liked, given their elitist and exclusionary behavior (e.g., Adler & Adler, 1998), whereas sociometrically popular children are, by definition, well-liked by the peer group as a whole. Second, sociologically popular *boys* seem to feel that they should hide their interests in academic pursuits (Adler & Adler, 1998), whereas sociometrically popular children appear to value academic success (Rubin et al., 1998).

Lastly, proactive types of aggression and defiance typically have been predictive of sociometric peer rejection (Coie & Dodge, 1998; Rubin et al., 1998), unlike in sociological studies. In addition to the use of physical aggression to demonstrate physical prowess, sociologically popular boys in the Adler and Adler (1998) study challenged teachers' rules and had more disciplinary actions than peers (e.g., Rubin et al., 1998). Furthermore, sociologically popular children in the Adler and Adler study were observed to engage in relationally aggressive tactics (see Crick & Grotpeter, 1995)—for example, pitting friends against each other, using the fear of social exclusion to goad status-seeking peers into acting in undesirable ways, and using strategies such as gossiping, bossiness, and telling derisive rumors to maintain a position at the top of the social hierarchy (see Adler & Adler, 1998). Finally, Adler and Adler (1998) reported that bullying behaviors—for example, intimidation, coercion, ridicule, assault—were used by sociologically popular children for the express purpose of 'solidifying the group and asserting the power of the strong over the vulnerability of the weak,' (p. 65) but also 'because it's just fun to do' (p. 64). In contrast, bullying behaviors in the latter half of elementary school have been associated with sociometric unpopularity (Coie & Dodge, 1998), although some research questions that general conclusion (Poulin & Boivin, 2000).

Current study

What does it mean to be 'popular'? As noted above, researchers from sociometric and sociological traditions would answer that question differently. Yet when we posed that question in a meeting with a group of elementary school teachers, they suggested that two types of popular students exist in their classrooms—suggesting that both conceptions of popularity have merit. Furthermore, those teachers believed that each type was an influential force within the classroom environment and the social dynamics of the peer group, yet the specific type of influence each exerted was believed to be unique. Recent research would support those teachers' assessment that differing types of 'popular' students exist. Specifically, in research conducted by Rodkin and colleagues (2000) with 4th through 6th grade boys, two clusters of popular boys were identified based on a cluster analysis of teacher ratings: a 'model' type and a 'tough' type. Both clusters had high scores on the popularity subscale, which included items similar to Parkhurst and Hopmeyer's perceived popularity items (i.e., 'popular with boys', 'popular with girls') and items with a sociometric bent (i.e., 'has many friends'). Peers nominated both types as cool and athletic, and teachers rated both as physically competent. However, 'model' boys also were perceived to be prosocial, nonaggressive, and studious; in contrast, 'tough' boys were perceived to be aggressive, disruptive, not studious, and not friendly.

In the current study, we were interested in what elementary school children mean when they say that one of their classmates is 'popular.' If popular children are admired, revered, emulated by peers, or even feared—and thus play a large role in defining peer group dynamics—then children's implicit assumptions about popularity are important to understand. Thus, we assessed elementary school children's social constructions of popularity, or sociological popularity, through the use of *perceived popularity* nominations (Parkhurst & Hopmeyer, 1998). We compared children classified as popular using those nominations to children classified as popular using sociometric nominations.

The current research adds to the emerging research literature on the meaning of popularity (Parkhurst & Hopmeyer, 1998; Rodkin et al., 2000) by (a) assessing children's, rather than teachers', constructions of popularity within the same methodological framework as sociometric popularity and then comparing the two conceptions of popularity, (b) examining the meaning given to popularity by elementary school children by assessing a broader range of behavioral/personal characteristics than in previous studies, including characteristics reported to have a differing relation to sociometric and sociological popularity, and (c) examining the contention made by Parkhurst and Hopmeyer (1998) that socially constructed popularity essentially is nearly synonymous with social dominance.

Furthermore, the current study extends the research conducted by Parkhurst and Hopmeyer (1998) on middle school students' constructions of popularity by examining the meaning of popularity according to elementary school students. Constructions of popularity may differ between the two groups. For example, the much smaller, classroom-based peer groups in elementary school are likely to give rise to a differing set of social dynamics than the larger, grade-based peer groups of middle school. Thus, the relative importance of visibility for determining popularity may be reduced in the smaller peer groups of elementary school.

Method

Participants

Participants were 487 elementary school students from twenty-six 4th through 6th grade classrooms, located in three rural elementary schools in the southeastern region of the United States. Participants ranged from 9 through 13 years of age. Across the entire population of those three schools, 48% qualified for free lunch status and 9% qualified for reduced lunch status. According to school records, 56% of the sample were 'White' students, 42% were 'Black' students, and 2% were 'Asian', 'Hispanic', or 'Mixed' students. The ethnic compositions of the three schools were highly homogeneous: 91% of the participants were in classrooms/schools in which their ethnic group was the numerical majority. Fifty-one percent of the participants were girls. The classrooms in these three elementary schools were self-contained; class sizes ranged from eighteen to twenty-eight members.

Procedure

Parental consent forms that included a place for parents to sign if they were granting consent and a separate place to sign if denying consent were sent home with students in the spring of the school year. Parental consent and child assent were required for participation in the study. Consent/assent was obtained for 516 out of 606 (i.e., 85%) possible participants. However, only 487 children had complete data on the social status measures (e.g., like-most, most-popular), so only those 487 children were included in analyses.

Data collection took place during the late spring of the school year. Questionnaires were group administered and measures were read aloud in the classroom by one of the researchers. During data collection, nonparticipating classmates were asked to read or draw quietly at their desks. In addition, some classroom teachers permitted nonparticipating children to go to the library. Participants completed questionnaires in two one-hour sessions on consecutive days, to minimize fatigue. Participants were told that their responses to the questionnaire items would be confidential and were encouraged to cover their answers with a cover sheet. However, children were not repeatedly reminded to keep their responses a 'secret' as this directive may only draw attention to the nominations and make children uneasy about the task. To minimize discussion about the questionnaire, teachers were encouraged to schedule sessions so children would be engaged in a structured, academic activity immediately following the session. At the end of data collection each day, the researchers handed out a small gift to all children in the classroom, regardless of whether they participated.

Measures

(i) PERCEIVED POPULARITY

In a modification of Parkhurst and Hopmeyer (1998), participants viewed a roster with the names of their participating classmates and nominated three peers as (a) *most-popular* ('Who are the most popular students?')

and three peers as (b) *least-popular* ('Who are the least popular students?'). *Least-popular* nominations were added because sociometric research has demonstrated that positive and negative nominations tend to have a differing set of correlates (e.g., Newcomb et al., 1993). Numbers of most-popular and least-popular nominations received by each participant were each summed and standardized, within classroom and gender, to a mean of *0* and a standard deviation of *1*. In a modification of the Coie et al. (1982) procedure, *perceived preference* was calculated as most-popular scores minus least-popular scores; individuals were classified as *perceived popular* if they had a perceived preference score greater than *1*, a most-popular score greater than *0*, and a least-popular score less than *0*.

(II) SOCIOMETRIC POPULARITY

Participants nominated three peers as (a) *like-most* ('Who do you like to play with the most?') and three peers as (b) *like-least* ('Who do you like to play with the least?'). Numbers of like-most and like-least nominations received by each participant were each summed and standardized, within classroom and gender, to a mean of *0* and a standard deviation of *1*. *Social preference* was calculated as like-most scores minus like-least scores. Individuals were classified as *sociometrically popular*, or *liked*, if they had a social preference score greater than *1*, a like-most score greater than *0*, and a like-least score less than *0* (Coie et al., 1982).

(III) SOCIAL DOMINANCE

The procedure for assessing social dominance differed from the procedure reported in Parkhurst and Hopmeyer (1998). The definition of social dominance in the current study (i.e., power and influence) was congruent with the conceptualization that dominant individuals receive more attention, have greater influence over others within the group, and are able to control the outcomes of social interactions (Hawley, 1999). In addition, consistent with the suggestion by Hawley (1999) that dominance is manifested in dyadic interchanges, social dominance was assessed using a dyadic forced choice method (Axelrod, 2000). Dominance was assessed only with same-gender dyads, since cross-gender choices tend to favor boys and underestimate levels of social dominance observed within all-girl samples (Axelrod, 2000).

A list of all possible pairs of same-gender participants was created for each gender within each classroom. (However, dominance hierarchies were not assessed if a same-gender peer group in a classroom had fewer than five members [see Axelrod, 2000]; this affected 22 of the original 516 [contained in 5 classrooms] with consent to participate; 7 others were new to the classroom within the last month and so were not included on any of the social status measures). For each list of same-gender dyads (2 per classroom), the Ross order method (Ross, 1934) was used to ensure that each child's name appeared with the same frequency in the first half of the pair as in the second half and that each child's name was evenly spaced throughout the list of pairs. The Ross order procedure is recommended by Davison (1983) to balance potential 'time' and 'space' effects that can be associated with such lists (Lease & Axelrod, 2001). Participants were instructed to circle the child in each pair who has more influence and power over the other (i.e. 'Some kids have influence and power over other kids—they get others to do what they want'). A child's dominance score was created based on the number of times he/she was chosen as the dominant member of each pair. The number of choices that each child received was summed and standardized, within classroom and gender, to a mean of *0* and a standard deviation of *1*.

(IV) PERSONAL ATTRIBUTES AND BEHAVIORAL CHARACTERISTICS

Children were asked to nominate three participating classmates who best fit 37 personal and behavioral descriptors: 14 were chosen for use in the present research to represent a wide range of characteristics. Most items were based on previous research (e.g., Adler & Adler, 1998; Crick & Grotpeter, 1995; Masten, Morrison, & Pellegrini, 1985; Rodkin et al., 2000). The instructions given to the children were based on those used in the Revised Class Play (Masten et al., 1985): 'Pretend that you are assigning roles in the upcoming class play. We would like for you to nominate three children who fit each role as listed below. You can nominate a person for more than one role.' The number of nominations participants received for each descriptor was summed and then standardized by classroom to a mean of *0* and a standard deviation of *1*.

Peer nomination items included: (a) *helps others* ('helps others who are hurt, sick, or sad ... shows a lot of concern for others'), (b) *social skills* ('when kids are arguing and have trouble getting along, this person can help them solve the problem'), (c) *smart* ('makes good grades, is smart, and usually knows the right answer'), (d) *values school* ('tries hard to do good schoolwork'), (e) *athletic* ('very good at many outdoor sports and games'), (f) *snobby* ('looks down on others, is snobby, and acts like he or she is better than other'), (g) *cool* ('really cool—just about everybody in school knows this person'), (h) *defiant* ('doesn't follow the rules and talks back to the teacher'), (i) *bully* ('bullies and picks on other kids'), (j) *relationally aggressive* ('tells others they will stop liking them unless the friends do what they say, tries to keep certain people from being in their group during activities, and gets even by keeping people from being in their group of friends'), (k) *disruptive* ('interrupts others, can't wait his/her turn, and barges in when others are playing or talking'), (l) *reactive aggressive* ('even when others don't mean to make them mad, this person overreacts and is easily pushed to anger'); (m) *plays alone* ('would rather play alone'), (n) *shy/anxious* ('looks like they want to play with others or join in a game, but seems afraid or shy').

(v) TEACHER ASSESSED PERSONAL CHARACTERISTICS

Physical attractiveness and spending power were assessed, based on the report by Adler and Adler (1998) that these factors are important determinants of popularity for girls. Because school personnel deemed these too sensitive for peers to report on, classroom teachers rated children on a five-point scale (1 = not at all descriptive through 5 = very descriptive) for both items: (a) *spending power* ('compared to their classmates, some children have a lot of nice or expensive possessions—they wear expensive clothes, live in a very nice house, have a wide range of material possessions, and have money to spend'), and (b) *attractive* ('this student is physically attractive or good-looking'). One teacher found this task uncomfortable, thus ratings were completed for only 463 of the 487 participants. Scores for the two items were standardized, within class, to a mean of 0 and a standard deviation of 1.

(VI) PEER ASSESSED PREROGATIVES OF STATUS

Again using the instructions from the Revised Class Play (Masten et al., 1985), participants nominated peers for 4 descriptors that presumably signify the prerogatives of social position: (a) *influence* ('others listen to—this person has a lot of influence'), (b) *admiration* ('others in class admire this person—they want to be around this person and be like him/her'), (c) *leadership* ('gets chosen by the others as the leader—others like to have this person in charge'), and (d) *control* ('has a lot of control—they decide who gets to be in the popular group or "in crowd" '). The number of nominations participants received for each descriptor were summed and then standardized by classroom and gender to a mean of 0 and a standard deviation of 1, unlike the other peer-reported behavioral characteristics which were standardized by classroom but not gender. In the case of these four indicators of a child's influence and power among peers, we believed that children would be most likely to nominate same-gender peers—as is the case with like-most nominations—who presumably have the most impact on children's day-to-day social lives.

Results

Overview

The results are presented in three sections. In the first section, we report results of correlational and regression analyses designed to examine the relation between perceived popularity, sociometric popularity, and social dominance. In the second section, we report the outcomes of correlational analyses comparing the correlates of perceived popularity with those of sociometric popularity and social dominance. Finally, in the third section, groups of children identified as perceived popular, sociometrically popular, or both were compared on behavioral/personal characteristics and social prerogatives of status. Although gender differences in popularity were not the primary focus of the current research, most analyses were conducted separately for boys and girls, based on the research by Adler and Adler (1998) that the correlates of popularity differ for boys and girls.

Relation of perceived popularity to sociometric popularity and social dominance

In the first set of analyses, numbers of most-popular and least-popular nominations were correlated with numbers of like-most and like-least nominations and social dominance scores. The number of times children were nominated as most-popular was strongly and positively associated with the number of times children were nominated as like-most and chosen as socially dominant (Table 5.3). In addition, the number of times children were nominated as least-popular was strongly and positively associated with numbers of like-least nominations and negatively associated with social dominance scores. Overall, the perceived popularity indices—most-popular and least-popular—were strongly associated with sociometric popularity indices and social dominance scores, yet not so highly as to suggest that the measures are tapping identical constructs. Results were similar for boys and girls.

The next step was to examine the relative contributions of sociometric popularity nominations and social dominance scores to the prediction of perceived popularity nominations. Sociometric and social dominance indices were regressed onto most-popular nominations and then onto least-popular nominations. Predictor variables were entered simultaneously in these multiple regressions. The results of the first multiple regression, contained in Table 5.4, indicated that like-most nominations and social dominance scores contributed unique variance to the prediction of most-popular nominations; the contributions of each to the models were similar. Interestingly, the betaweight of the like-least nominations in the equation predicting most-popular nominations was positive and significant. In regard to least-popular nominations, the contribution of both like-least nominations and social dominance scores again was significant. Like-most nominations contributed a smaller amount of variance in the prediction as well and in the expected direction.

Overall, the results of the correlational and regression analyses suggested that perceived popularity is highly associated with both social dominance and sociometric popularity in elementary school. However, only half of the variability in numbers of most-popular nominations was accounted for by social dominance

Table 5.3   Intercorrelations between status indices for the total sample and separately by gender

| | Perceived popularity | | Sociometric popularity | | Social dominance |
	Most-pop	Least-pop	Like-most	Like-least	Dominance
TOTAL SAMPLE (n = 487)					
Most-popular	—	−.45	.62	−.14	.62
Least-popular		—	−.47	.59	−.57
Like-most			—	−.35	.57
Like-least				—	−.28
Dominance					—
BOYS (n = 237)					
Most-popular	—	−.46	.65	−.20[a]	.63
Least-popular		—	−.46	.66	−.56
Like-most			—	−.31	.57
Like-least				—	−.33
Dominance					—
GIRLS (n = 250)					
Most-popular	—	−.44	.59	−.09[b]	.61
Least-popular		—	−.49	.52	−.59
Like-most			—	−.40	.58
Like-least				—	−.22
Dominance					—

Note. Measures were standardized by classroom and gender; all measures are peer-report.
[a] $p = .002$; [b] $p > .05$; all other correlations, $p \leq .001$.

scores and numbers of sociometric nominations (i.e., like-most and like-least). The same was true for least-popular nominations. Thus, perceived popularity appears to be highly related to both constructs in this age group and yet not identical to either.

Table 5.4 Multiple regressions of sociometric popularity and social dominance indices onto perceived popularity indices (simultaneous entry of predictor variables)

	B	SE B	p	Total Model R^2
Most-popular nominations				.50
Like-most	.43	.04	.001	
Like-least	.12	.03	.001	
Social dominance	.41	.04	.001	
Least-popular nominations				.53
Like-most	−.08	.04	.030	
Like-least	.45	.03	.001	
Social dominance	−.40	.04	.001	

Note. Measures were standardized by classroom and gender; all measures are peer-report (*n* = 487).

Correlations of personal and behavioral characteristics with perceived popularity, sociometric popularity, and social dominance indices

Do the personal and behavioral characteristics associated with perceived popularity differ from those associated with sociometric popularity and social dominance? To answer that question, perceived popularity, sociometric popularity, and social dominance indices were correlated with indicators of personal attributes and behavioral characteristics. However, given the large number of behavioral/personal variables, a factor analysis with varimax rotation first was employed as a data reduction technique. The fourteen behavioral/personal variables were submitted to a principal components factor analysis (N = 487). Inspection of the eigenvalues, scree plot, and principal components suggested that five to six factors should be retained: the six-factor rotated solution was chosen based on interpretability of the factors and factor loadings. Results are presented in Table 5.5. Based on the results of the factor analysis, 8 factor scores were created: for conceptual reasons (e.g., Adler & Adler,

Table 5.5 Factor structure of behavioral/personal characteristics (N = 487)

	Bully/Disrupt	Prosocial/Bright	Social Withdrawal	Excluding	Socially Visible	Expressive Equipment
Defiant	.91	−.15	−.05	.06	.00	−.08
Disruptive	.83	−.17	−.09	.19	−.05	−.01
Bully	.82	−.09	−.16	.22	.15	−.04
Reactive agg.	.77	−.07	.07	.30	.12	.04
Social skills	−.13	.88	−.04	−.03	.10	.08
Smart	−.01	.85	−.06	.06	.02	.12
Helps others	−.16	.82	.03	.05	.09	.12
Values school	−.14	.81	.03	−.08	.13	.18
Plays alone	−.13	−.06	.86	−.09	−.14	−.06
Shy/anxious	−.04	.04	.86	−.05	−.17	−.11
Snobby	.29	.03	−.07	.87	.05	.03
Relational agg.	.39	−.02	−.10	.80	.07	.05
Athletic	.11	.06	−.18	−.05	.89	.12
Cool	.05	.26	−.20	.22	.80	.14
Spend. power	−.02	.23	−.24	.03	−.01	.82
Attractive	−.04	.21	.04	.05	.30	.80

Note. Values are factor loadings for each behavioral/personal characteristic following varimax rotation, n = 487. Italicized items were used to compute the factor score, except for Bully/Disruptive and Prosocial/Bright, each of which were split into two variables for conceptual reasons: (a) Bully, the mean of 'bully' and 'defiant', (b) Disrupt, the mean of 'disruptive' and 'reactive aggression', (c) Prosocial, the mean of 'helps others' and 'values school', and (d) Bright, the mean of 'smart' and 'social skills'.

Table 5.6   Correlations between status indices and behavioral/personal factors

	Perceived popularity		Sociometric popularity		Social dominance dominance rank
	Most-pop	Least-pop	Like-most	Like-least	
BOYS (n = 237)					
Prosocial	.33	−.20	.46$_b$	−.17$_a$	.17
Bright	.34	−.20	.37$_b$	−.17$_a$	.17
Socially visible	.86	−.49	.71$_{ab}$	−.24$_a$	.69$_{ab}$
Expressive equipment[1]	.34	−.33	.32$_b$	−.13$_a$	.28$_b$
Excluding	.30	.11	.09$_a$	.30	.25
Bully	.09	.23	−.05	.36	.16
Disruptive	.06	.31	−.10$_b$	.43$_a$	.06
Social withdrawal	−.33	.52	−.22$_b$	.41$_a$	−.51$_{ab}$
GIRLS (n = 250)					
Prosocial	.40	−.33	.54$_b$	−.33$_a$	.30$_b$
Bright	.50	−.32	.48$_b$	−.22$_a$	.34$_{ab}$
Socially visible	.69	−.41	.56$_{ab}$	−.15$_{ab}$	.56$_{ab}$
Expressive equipment[2]	.46	−.47	.39$_b$	−.19$_b$	.44$_b$
Excluding	.33	−.07	.07$_a$	.33$_b$	.37$_b$
Bully	.21	.05	.01$_a$	.22	.22
Disruptive	.26	.07	.02$_a$	.31$_b$	.26
Social withdrawal	−.37	.57	−.35$_b$	.26$_{ab}$	−.55$_{ab}$

Note. For boys, $p \leq .01$ for $r > \pm .19$; For girls, $p \leq .01$ for $r > \pm .15$.
[a] Magnitude of the correlation differed from the magnitude of the correlation between this same behavior and most-popular, $p \leq .001$;
[b] magnitude of the correlation differed from the magnitude of the correlation between this same behavior and least-popular, $p \leq .001$;
[1] $n = 226$; [2] $n = 238$.

1998), factors 1 and 2 were split to create two variables. Thus, eight factor scores were created: (a) *bully*, (b) *disrupt*, (c) *prosocial*, (d) *bright*, (e) *social withdrawal*, (f) *excluding*, (g) *socially visible*, (h) *expressive equipment*.

The correlations between social status indices and behavioral/personal factors are contained in Table 5.6. For each factor, the strength of its correlation with most-popular (or least-popular) nominations was compared to the strength of its correlation with the two sociometric indices and social dominance scores, using the method described by Weinburg and Goldberg (1979).

First, the number of most-popular nominations a child received from peers was highly and positively associated with being perceived as socially visible (i.e., athletic and cool) by peers for both boys and girls. Furthermore, most-popular nominations showed a positive association with being perceived as prosocial, bright, and in possession of the expressive equipment of popularity and a negative association with social withdrawal. However, a positive association also was observed for excluding types of behaviors and most-popular nominations. In regard to least-popular nominations received by a child, a strong positive association was found for social withdrawal and a moderate negative association was found for social visibility. Overall, gender differences were most notable for the bully and disruptive factors: whereas these two factors were positively associated with least-popular nominations for boys, these behavioral characteristics were positively associated with most-popular nominations for girls.

The strength of the association of behaviors with most-popular and least-popular nominations was compared to the strength of their association with sociometric and social dominance indices (see Table 5.6). Several of the findings were of particular interest. First, being perceived as socially visible was more highly associated with most-popular than like-most nominations and social dominance scores for both genders. However, the major distinction between perceived and sociometric popularity occurred with regard to aggressive and disruptive behaviors. Specifically, for both genders, excluding types of behaviors were more highly correlated with receiving most-popular nominations than like-most nominations. Furthermore, for girls, disruptive and bullying behaviors were more positively associated with most-popular than like-most nominations. Conversely, disruptive behaviors were more highly associated with like-least than least-popular nominations for girls.

The differences in correlation strength of the peer-nominated behaviors with perceived popularity and social dominance should be interpreted cautiously: the same method (i.e., peer nomination) was used to assess perceived popularity and behavior but a differing method (i.e., forced choice) was used to assess social dominance. However, comparing perceived popularity and social dominance, it appeared that the major differences occurred with regard to social withdrawal, which was more negatively associated with social dominance than perceived popularity, and social visibility, which was more highly associated with perceived popularity than social dominance scores.

Comparison of perceived popular and sociometrically popular children

Do children perceived to be popular by peers differ from sociometrically popular children? To answer this question, four types of children were identified (see Table 5.7): (a) children perceived to be *popular*, but not well-liked (i.e., sociometrically popular), (b) *liked* (i.e., sociometrically popular) children who were not perceived to be popular, (c) children perceived to be *both* popular and liked, and (d) an *average* group of children who were within the average range (+/−.5 SD) with regard to both social preference and perceived preference. Each group's mean and standard deviation on like-most, like-least, most-popular, and least-popular measures are listed in Table 5.7. Pairwise comparisons,

included in Table 5.7, were conducted to examine differences between groups on perceived and sociometric popularity indices. Duncan multiple range tests were used to control for the Type I comparison-wise error rate.

(I) BEHAVIORAL/PERSONAL CHARACTERISTICS

The goal of these analyses was to compare the behavioral and personal characteristics of the four types of children to investigate potentially significant differences. Multivariate analyses of variance (MANOVA) were conducted, separately by gender, with groupings of similar behavioral/personal factors as the dependent variables and group membership as the independent variable. Means and standard deviations on the eight behavioral/personal factor scores, by group and gender, are reported in Table 5.8. Significant results were followed by pairwise comparisons, again using Duncan multiple range tests.

In the first MANOVA, conducted separately by gender, *positive behavioral characteristics* (i.e., prosocial, bright) were the dependent variables. The results of this MANOVA revealed significant differences among the four groups of boys, $F(6, 210) = 3.45, p = .003$, and the four groups of girls, $F(6, 230) = 5.46, p = .0001$. In the second MANOVA, again conducted by gender, *personal characteristics* (i.e., social visibility, expressive equipment) were the dependent variables. The results of this MANOVA also revealed significant differences among the four groups of boys, $F(6, 198) = 14.93, p = .0001$, and the four groups of girls, $F(6, 220) = 6.81, p = .0001$. The third MANOVA, conducted to examine differences in *negative behavioral characteristics* (i.e., excluding, bully, disruptive), again revealed significant differences (for boys, $F(9, 253.3) = 3.28, p = .0008$; for girls, $F(9, 277.6) = 2.06, p = .03$). Finally, an analysis of variance (ANOVA) was conducted to examine group differences for *social withdrawal*. Results showed that the four groups did not differ with regard to socially withdrawn types of behavior (for boys, $F(3, 109) = 1.72, p = $ ns; for girls, $F(3, 119) = 1.17, p = $ ns).

A comparison of popular-only with liked-only boys showed that the two groups differed with regard to social visibility as well as excluding, bullying, and disruptive behaviors. Pairwise comparisons for girls also showed differences on those characteristics.

Table 5.7 Means and standard deviations on social characteristics for perceived popular, sociometrically popular, combined, and average groups

	Boys				Girls			
	Popular (n = 25)	Liked (n = 26)	Both (n = 32)	Average (n = 27)	Popular (n = 28)	Liked (n = 33)	Both (n = 33)	Average (n = 26)
Perceived Popularity								
Most-popular	1.44_a (0.53)	$-.28_b$ (0.35)	1.56_a (0.63)	$-.39_b$ (0.45)	1.54_w (0.83)	$-.28_x$ (0.51)	1.27_w (0.61)	$-.36_x$ (0.36)
Least-popular	$-.71_a$ (0.28)	$-.36_b$ (0.65)	$-.79_a$ (0.24)	$-.41_b$ (0.34)	$-.63_{xy}$ (0.34)	$-.32_w$ (0.74)	$-.85_y$ (0.36)	$-.39_{wx}$ (0.27)
Sociometric Popularity								
Like-most	$.53_b$ (1.02)	$.91_a$ (0.34)	1.25_a (.59)	$-.27_c$ (0.51)	$.33_y$ (0.80)	$.80_x$ (0.42)	1.40_w (0.59)	$-.26_z$ (0.50)
Like-least	$.14_a$ (0.62)	$-.80_c$ (0.47)	$-.67_c$ (.35)	$-.37_b$ (0.52)	$.32_w$ (0.72)	$-.75_y$ (0.33)	$-.80_y$ (0.48)	$-.34_x$ (0.48)
Social Dominance	$.75_{ab}$ (0.63)	$.47_b$ (0.50)	1.04_a (.49)	$-.18_c$ (0.81)	$.83_w$ (0.78)	$.40_x$ (0.64)	$.81_w$ (0.73)	$-.04_y$ (0.57)

Note. Measures were standardized by classroom and gender; all measures are peer-report. Within rows, means with the same subscript do not differ significantly; pairwise comparisons were computed within gender.

Table 5.8 Means and standard deviations on personal/behavioral factor scores for perceived popular, sociometrically popular, combined, and average groups

Factor scores	Boys				Girls			
	Popular (n = 25)	Liked (n = 26)	Both (n = 32)	Average (n = 27)	Popular (n = 28)	Liked (n = 33)	Both (n = 33)	Average (n = 26)
Prosocial	$.08_a$ (0.73)	$.12_a$ (0.82)	$.04_b$ (0.69)	$-.50_b$ (0.50)	$.57_{xy}$ (1.10)	$.75_{wx}$ (0.77)	1.14_w (0.86)	$.17_y$ (0.63)
Bright	$.27_a$ (0.88)	$.07_a$ (0.74)	$-.07_{ab}$ (0.61)	$-.40_b$ (0.44)	$.95_w$ (1.15)	$.53_w$ (1.15)	1.07_w (0.91)	$-.02_x$ (0.71)
Socially visible	1.41_a (0.99)	$.32_b$ (0.53)	1.82_a (0.66)	$-.10_c$ (0.64)	$.52_w$ (0.78)	$-.13_w$ (0.31)	$.36_w$ (0.85)	$-.32_x$ (0.36)
Expressive equip.	$.55_a$ (0.71)	$.18_{ab}$ (0.65)	$.19_{ab}$ (0.69)	$-.12_b$ (0.70)	$.66_w$ (0.77)	$.10_x$ (0.68)	$.62_w$ (0.70)	$.11_x$ (0.75)
Excluding	$.54_a$ (0.89)	$-.42_b$ (0.71)	$-.12_{ab}$ (0.61)	$-.35_b$ (0.77)	$.73_w$ (1.17)	$-.13_x$ (0.72)	$.24_w$ (1.04)	$-.13_x$ (0.67)
Bully	$.61_a$ (0.94)	$.04_b$ (0.89)	$.14_b$ (0.79)	$-.04_b$ (0.80)	$.00_w$ (0.84)	$-.37_x$ (0.55)	$-.29_{wx}$ (0.47)	$-.36_x$ (0.42)
Disruptive	$.47_a$ (0.89)	$-.13_b$ (0.62)	$.12_{ab}$ (0.71)	$-.23_b$ (0.72)	$.14_w$ (0.74)	$-.31_x$ (0.58)	$-.22_x$ (0.73)	$-.25_x$ (0.66)
Social withdrawal	$-.54$ (0.59)	$-.36$ (0.70)	$-.60$ (0.42)	$-.29$ (0.65)	$-.38$ (0.60)	$-.11$ (0.73)	$-.30$ (0.76)	$-.21$ (0.50)

Note. Factor scores are means of the original variables, which were standardized by classroom; all measures are based on peer-report except for the expressive equipment factor which is teacher-report. Within rows, means with the same subscript do not differ significantly; pairwise comparisons were computed within gender.

Table 5.9 Means and standard deviations on social prerogative variables for popular, liked, combined, and average groups

	Boys				Girls			
	Popular (n = 25)	*Liked* (n = 26)	*Both* (n = 32)	*Average* (n = 27)	*Popular* (n = 28)	*Liked* (n = 33)	*Both* (n = 33)	*Average* (n = 26)
Leadership	$.84_a$ (0.96)	$.34_b$ (0.81)	1.18_a (0.97)	$-.28_c$ (0.77)	$.81_w$ (1.17)	$.20_x$ (0.80)	1.05_w (0.90)	$-.21_x$ (0.74)
Admiration	$.92_b$ (1.02)	$.12_c$ (0.63)	1.50_a (0.74)	$-.29_d$ (0.53)	$.81_w$ (1.17)	$.19_x$ (0.69)	1.04_w (0.93)	$-.30_y$ (0.66)
Influence	$.78_{ab}$ (1.00)	$.41_b$ (0.79)	1.01_a (1.01)	$-.38_c$ (0.74)	$.73_{wx}$ (0.85)	$.43_x$ (0.86)	$.97_w$ (0.91)	$-.21_y$ (0.82)
Social control	1.02_a (0.84)	$.05_b$ (0.67)	1.18_a (0.83)	$-.29_b$ (0.58)	1.21_w (1.04)	$-.09_x$ (0.61)	$.97_w$ (0.84)	$-.41_x$ (0.51)

Note. Within rows, means with the same subscript do not differ significantly; pairwise comparisons were computed within gender.

Furthermore, popular-only girls also were rated higher by teachers than liked-only girls with regard to the expressive equipment of popularity. Contrary to expectations, popular-only children did not differ from liked-only children on the prosocial or bright factors. However, popular-only girls differed from the combined group of girls on the prosocial factor, but no differences were observed for boys. Popular-only children differed from the combined group primarily on aggressive types of behaviors: popular-only children were perceived to be more excluding, bullying, and disruptive (girls only) than children in the combined group. However, popular-only girls were perceived to be less prosocial than the combined group as well.

Overall, groups had their own distinct behavioral/personal profile; for descriptive purposes, +/−.50 SD was used as the cutoff to define above and below average mean scores. In general, popular-only boys were primarily socially visible, with moderate elevations on the expressive equipment of popularity, along with elevations on socially aggressive (i.e., bully, excluding) behaviors and low levels of social withdrawal. In contrast, the combined group of boys had the same high levels of social visibility as popular-only boys, but without the socially aggressive behaviors and expressive equipment of popularity.

Unlike popular-only boys, popular-only girls were above-average on the prosocial, bright, and expressive equipment factors, similar to the combined group of girls. However, popular-only girls also were above-average with regard to excluding behaviors and social visibility, which distinguished them from the combined group. In contrast to liked-only boys, girls in the liked-only group had scores outside of the average range with regard to two factors—prosocial and bright.

(II) PREROGATIVES OF SOCIAL STATUS

In the final set of analyses, the four types of children were compared in regard to the benefits and prerogatives that seem to accompany an elevated social position. A MANOVA was conducted, separately by gender, to examine whether differences exist between the four groups on four peer-reported measures: leadership, influence, admiration, and social control. The four measures of social prerogatives were the

dependent variables and group membership was the independent variable. Means and standard deviations of peer scores by group and gender are included in Table 5.9.

Overall, boys in the four groups differed with regard to the social prerogatives of social status ($F (4, 105) = 3.28, p = .01$), as did girls ($F (4, 115) = 5.13, p = .001$). Furthermore, follow-up pairwise comparisons, using Duncan's method, showed that popularity, either alone or in combination with likeability, comes with more social prerogatives than likeability alone. Specifically, popular-only children received more nominations from peers than liked-only children for all social prerogative variables except the measure of social influence. Furthermore, popular-only children did not differ from the combined group with regard to leadership, influence, social control, or admiration (girls only); in contrast, liked-only children differed from the combined group with regard to all social prerogative variables. Although liked-only children appeared to have fewer social prerogatives than children perceived to be popular, liked-only children also were perceived to have higher levels of leadership, admiration from peers (boys only), and influence than average children.

Discussion

The results from this study indicated that the social constructions of popularity (i.e., perceived popularity) held by children in later elementary school are related to sociometric popularity and social dominance. Furthermore, the correlations between perceived popularity and sociometric popularity nominations were higher than the correlations reported by Parkhurst and Hopmeyer (1998) with a middle school sample. Nevertheless, regression analyses demonstrated that sociometric popularity and dominance account for only half of the variability in popularity, thereby suggesting that older elementary school children perceive popularity to be more than the mere combination of likeability and dominance. Furthermore, Parkhurst and Hopmeyer (1998) noted that perceived popularity has been treated as nearly synonymous with social dominance with adolescent

180   PART III   SELF, RELATIONSHIPS, AND SOCIAL GROUPS

populations, but that did not appear to be the case for the current sample of older elementary school students.

A comparison of the correlates of perceived and sociometric popularity nominations and social dominance scores revealed substantive differences between the three constructs. For boys, social visibility was more highly related to being perceived as popular than it was to either sociometric popularity or dominance. However, excluding types of behaviors were related positively to perceived popularity but related negatively to sociometric popularity.

For girls, perceived popularity was more highly and positively associated with social visibility than sociometric popularity; whereas, the lack of attractiveness/ spending power and the presence of social withdrawal was more strongly associated with being nominated as least-popular than like-least. Interestingly, excluding and bullying behaviors, as well as disruptiveness, were positively associated with perceived popularity for girls but negatively associated with sociometric popularity. Social dominance and perceived popularity for girls were distinguished by the higher association of smartness/skillfulness and social visibility with perceived popularity than dominance.

An examination of the characteristics of children classified as perceived popular, sociometrically popular, or both further clarified the differences between being reported by peers as popular versus well-liked. Specifically, perceived popular-only boys were reported to be socially visible, attractive/ wealthy, socially aggressive, and not socially withdrawn. In contrast, boys who were both perceived popular and well-liked did not have above-average levels of either attractiveness/spending power or socially aggressive characteristics. The overall pattern of results underscores the importance of social visibility for popularity among boys. Furthermore, this pattern of results suggests that boys' displays of social aggression in the later grades of elementary school are incompatible with likeability but not socially constructed popularity, similar to the conclusions reached by sociological and sociometric researchers (e.g., Adler & Adler, 1998; Coie & Dodge, 1998). Perhaps increased levels of attractiveness/spending power gave the perceived popular group of boys their advantage in the peer group, even though they were somewhat antisocial relative to peers. It could

be that those types of boys believe that they can get away with acting aggressively, as a result of having such 'expressive equipment.'

Perceived popular-only girls were viewed by peers as bright, socially visible, socially aggressive, and with the expressive equipment of popularity, consistent with the portrayal of popular girls in sociological research (Adler & Adler, 1998). However, this group also was viewed as being fairly prosocial, which was not expected given the same sociological research. Interestingly, the group of perceived popular girls who were well-liked did not share above-average levels of social visibility with popular-only girls; popular/ well-liked girls also were not socially aggressive. The general pattern of results suggests that attractiveness/ spending power is a major requisite of girls being perceived as popular but not a requisite of being liked. However, it might be that the use of social aggression precludes perceived popular girls from being well-liked members of the peer group, even though they were perceived to have fairly high levels of prosocial characteristics. Alternatively, perceived popular girls might feel pressured to use socially aggressive strategies to establish and maintain a popular status, after more prosocial attempts have failed.

In general, social visibility seems to be an integral part of preadolescent boys' and girls' social constructions of popularity, although the method of attaining that visibility may differ between the genders. Specifically, boys may gain prominence and visibility primarily through physical prowess and athletic skills. In contrast, girls may gain visibility primarily by being physically attractive to boys and having access to material possessions, even as early as late elementary school (e.g., Adler & Adler, 1998), which may serve to enhance their attractiveness. Although speculative, it may be that the differing pathways to social prominence for boys and girls reflect well-entrenched societal patterns: brawny, athletic, dominant males and physically attractive, fashionable females tend to receive a great deal of positive attention across developmental periods.

In addition to differences in behavioral/personal characteristics, children perceived to be popular differed from their sociometrically popular peers with regard to the social prerogatives of an elevated social position. The participants in the current study told us, through their responses on the nomination measure, that they prefer to have perceived popular children be group leaders. Furthermore, children greatly admire children perceived to be popular and desire to be like them, suggesting that perceived popular children have a great deal of power in setting peer group norms and determining what behavior patterns are desirable, particularly for children who crave acceptance by the popular crowd. The power of perceived popular children to determine the membership of the 'in crowd' further underscores their influence over the dynamics and climate of the peer group. However, in line with our previously mentioned conversations with classroom teachers, perceived popular and well-liked children did not differ from each other in the amount of influence they have over peers. Yet both groups differed from the group who was average on both perceived popularity and like-ability, supporting the view that two types of influential, popular children exist. Tempering this conclusion is the finding that perceived popularity, either alone or in combination with sociometric popularity, is accompanied by more social prerogatives than likeability alone. Being perceived by peers as popular appears to be a key factor in the group dynamics underlying social power.

Speculations, limitations, and future directions

Perceived popular elementary school children in the current study seemed to have a great deal of political power and social advantage within the peer group. Thus, an understanding of these children—their motives, personalities, activities, aspirations, etc.—may be crucial for understanding the types of peer influences and pressures to which children are subjected. For example, Adler and Adler (1998) described scenarios in which sociologically popular boys were able to coerce lower status peers to engage in activities not of their choosing. Regardless of whether their influence is active (i.e., coercive) or passive (i.e., modeling), children perceived as popular seem to have a great deal of social power within the peer group. However, popularity is not without its disadvantages. For example, sociologically popular children seem to feel pressured to do things that are 'cool' and even risky, such as smoking (Michell, 1997) or behaving in a precocious manner for the purpose of attracting popular

boys (Adler & Adler, 1998). These findings are in line with the contention by Hollander (1958) that group leaders are pressured to be 'innovative' (p. 125) in order to maintain their status.

Unfortunately, the current study is limited in its ability to address such dynamic factors related to popularity. Longitudinal, process-oriented studies would provide much needed information concerning the impetus of popular students' behavior as well as their impact on group dynamics, which the current cross-sectional design was not designed to assess. For example, future research might examine what motivates some perceived popular girls, but not others (i.e., popular/well-liked), to behave in a socially aggressive manner. Do some girls feel that such tactics are the only means at their disposal to attaining and maintaining a popular status? Of course, the possibility exists that peers have a distorted perception of some popular girls as excessively exclusionary, when in fact they do not behave in such a manner. The latter scenario, however, still begs the question, 'Why misperceive some popular girls as socially aggressive/snobby but not others?' Unfortunately, the use of only peer-report as a source of behavioral information precludes our ability to answer these and similar questions. However, although observation or teacher-report might have been useful for addressing unanswered questions, such as the actual levels of aggression among perceived popular children, teachers and observers would not likely have had the same access as peers to socially aggressive behaviors, especially when they are performed by socially savvy children.

Even in light of its limitations, the results of the current research have highlighted the potential contribution of using perceived popularity nominations that presumably tap into children's constructions of popularity. If popularity is indeed a social construction, then no universal prescription for gaining and maintaining popular status is likely to exist. Rather, the behavioral and personal characteristics associated with popular status are likely to vary based on developmental and contextual factors, as was the case for gender. For example, the correlates of popularity might vary across ethnic groups, similar to the findings reported by Kistner and colleagues (Kistner, Metzler, Gatlin, & Risi, 1993) in regard to sociometric status.

Of course, the lack of an agreed-upon operational definition for popularity raises the conundrum that research findings across studies may not be comparable. However, if popularity is indeed a social construction, attempts to operationalize it for research purposes are likely to result in definitions that either are irrelevant or outmoded by the time the data are actually collected or definitions that do not quite capture the essence of the construct for children in that particular time and place. Allowing research participants to define 'popular' for themselves is likely to lead to more meaningful studies than when researchers impose their own meanings on these constructs. In addition, allowing children to identify popular peers, based on their own definitions, and their perceived characteristics, is important given the social power and influence popular children appear to hold within the peer group.

One distinct advantage of using perceived popularity nominations might be the identification of a group of children who have long been of interest to sociometric researchers—the sociometric controversial subtype. Unfortunately, the sociometric controversial subtype has poor psychometric characteristics and so has received little research attention (Frederickson & Furnham, 1998; Rubin et al., 1998). However, the behavioral profile of perceived popular children appears somewhat more similar—though not identical—to controversial children than to sociometrically popular children. That is, the sociometric controversial subtype has been described as having a combination of socially skilled, leadership, and aggressive characteristics (Coie & Dodge, 1988). Furthermore, controversial children are identified primarily by their large social impact scores (like-most + like-least), a score that often is compared with visibility (Terry, 2000). Similarly, in the current study social visibility was found to be a strong correlate of perceived popularity. In general, the behavioral profile and high visibility of popular-only students in the current research suggest that some controversial children might have been included in the popular-only group (to the extent that a controversial child was also perceived to be popular). The relation between controversial status and perceived popularity deserves exploration in future studies, an issue that we are currently examining (Lease, Musgrove, & Axelrod, 2001).

In sum, it has been argued in this research that the use of perceived popularity nominations may help researchers examine children's constructions of popularity and, thus, power dynamics within the peer group. However, many questions about the utility of perceived popularity nominations remain to be addressed in future studies. For instance, the utility of perceived popularity for predicting important developmental outcomes is untested, in contrast to the known predictive utility of sociometric status (e.g., Rubin et al., 1998). However, the studies reviewed by Rubin et al. (1998) seem to point out the developmental significance of being disliked by peers (i.e., sociometric rejection) rather than being liked by peers (i.e., sociometric popularity). In the future it is hoped that the current work, as well as the work of others (e.g., Adler & Adler, 1998; Parkhurst & Hopmeyer, 1998; Rodkin et al., 2000), can be used to further our understanding of the developmental significance of popularity and the impact of popular children on the social dynamics of the peer group.

References

Adler, P. A., & Adler, P. (1998). *Peer power: Preadolescent culture and identity.* New Brunswick, NJ: Rutgers University Press.

Asher, S. R. & Coie, J. D. (1990). *Peer rejection in childhood.* New York: Cambridge University Press.

Axelrod, J. L. (2000). *Behavioral and social correlates of social dominance.* Unpublished doctoral dissertation, University of Georgia, Athens.

Coie, J. D., & Dodge, K. A. (1998). Aggression and antisocial behavior. In W. Damon (Series Ed.) & N. Eisenberg (Vol. Ed.), *Handbook of child psychology: Vol. 3. Social, emotional, and personality development* (5th ed., pp. 779–862). New York: Wiley.

Coie, J. D., Dodge, K. A., & Coppotelli, H. (1982). Dimensions and types of social status: A cross-age perspective. *Developmental Psychology, 18,* 557–570.

Coie, J. D., Dodge, K. A., & Kupersmidt, J. B. (1990). Peer group behavior and social status. In S. A. Asher & J. D. Coie (Eds.), *Peer rejection in childhood* (pp. 17–59). New York: Cambridge University Press.

Corsaro, W.A. (1979). Young children's conception of status and role. *Sociology of Education, 52,* 46–59.

Crick, N. R., & Grotpeter, J. K. (1995). Relational aggression, gender, and social-psychological adjustment. *Child Development, 66,* 710–722.

Davison, M. L. (1983). *Multidimensional Scaling*. New York: John Wiley and Sons.

Denham, S. A., & Holt, R. W. (1993). Preschoolers' likability as cause or consequence of their social behavior. *Developmental Psychology, 29*, 271–275.

Eder, D. (1985). The cycle of popularity: Interpersonal relations among female adolescents. *Sociology of Education, 58*, 154–165.

Eder D., Evans, C. C., & Parker, S. (1995). *School talk: Gender and adolescent culture*. New Brunswick, NJ: Rutgers University of Press.

Frederickson, N. L., & Furnham, A. F. (1998). Sociometric classification methods in school peer groups: A comparative investigation. *Journal of Child Psychology and Psychiatry and Allied Disciplines, 39*, 921–933.

Hawley, P. H. (1999). The ontogenesis of social dominance: A strategy-based evolutionary perspective. *Developmental Review, 19*, 97–132.

Hollander, E. P. (1958). Conformity, status, and idiosyncrasy credit. *Psychological Review, 65*, 117–127.

Kistner, J., Metzler, A., Gatlin, D., & Risi, S. (1993). Classroom racial proportions and children's peer relations: Race and gender effects. *Journal of Educational Psychology, 85*, 446–452.

Lease, A. M., & Axelrod, J. L. (2001). Position in the peer group's perceived organizational structure: Relation to social status and friendship. *Journal of Early Adolescence, 21*, 376–403.

Lease, A. M., Musgrove, K. T., & Axelrod, J. L. (2001). Dimensions of social status in preadolescent peer groups: Likeability, popularity, and dominance. Unpublished manuscript.

Masten, A., Morison, P., & Pellegrini, D. (1985). A Revised Class Play method of peer assessment. *Developmental Psychology, 17*, 344–350.

Michell, L. (1997). Loud, sad, or bad: Young people's perceptions of peer groups and smoking. *Health Education Research, 12*, 1–14.

Michell, L., & Amos, A. (1997). Girls, pecking order and smoking. *Social Science and Medicine, 44*, 1861–1869.

Newcomb, A. F., Bukowski, W. M., & Pattee, L. (1993). Children's peer relations: A meta-analytic review of popular, rejected, neglected, controversial, and average sociometric status. *Psychological Bulletin, 113*, 99–128.

Parker, J. G., & Gottman, J. M. (1989). Social and emotional development in a relational context. In T. J. Berndt & G. W. Ladd (Eds.), *Peer relationships in child development* (pp. 95–131). New York: Wiley.

Parkhurst, J. T., & Hopmeyer, A. (1998). Sociometric popularity and peer-perceived popularity: Two distinct dimensions of peer status. *Journal of Early Adolescence, 18*, 125–144.

Poulin, F., & Boivin, M. (2000). Reactive and proactive aggression: Evidence of a two-factor model. *Psychological Assessment, 12*, 115–122.

Rodkin, P. C., Farmer, T. W., Pearl, R., & Van Acker, R. (2000). Heterogeneity of popular boys: Antisocial and prosocial configurations. *Developmental Psychology, 36*, 14–24.

Ross, R. T. (1934). Optimum orders for the presentation of pairs in the method of paired comparisons. *Journal of Educational Psychology, 25*, 375–382.

Rubin, K. H., Bukowski, W., & Parker, J. G. (1998). Peer interactions, relationships, and groups. In W. Damon & N. Eisenberg (Eds.) *Handbook of child psychology* (pp. 619–700), New York: Wiley.

Terry, R. (2000). Recent advances in measurement theory and the use of sociometric techniques. In W. Damon (Series Ed.) and A. N. Cillessen & W. M. Bukowski (Vol. Eds.) *New directions for child and adolescent development: No. 88. Recent advances in the measurement of acceptance and rejection in the peer system*, (pp. 27–54), San Francisco: Jossey-Bass.

Terry, R., & Coie, J. D. (1991). A comparison of methods for defining sociometric status among children. *Developmental Psychology, 27*, 867–880.

Weinburg, S. L., & Goldberg, K. P. (1979). The treatment of correlation and linear regression in inferential statistics. In *Basic statistics for education and the behavioral sciences* (pp. 400–415). Boston: Houghton Mifflin Company.

Group Status, Group Bias, and Adolescents' Reasoning About the Treatment of Others in School Contexts

Stacey S. Horn

Intergroup relationships in adolescence, and in particular issues of social acceptance based on adolescents' social reference groups (e.g., jocks, gothics), are complex, controversial, and multifaceted (Horn, 2003, 2005; Killen, Lee-Kim, McGlothlin, & Stangor, 2002; Killen, Margie, & Sinno, 2006). Recent work by Horn and her colleagues suggests that in some contexts, rather than viewing social exclusion as a matter of moral harm or injustice, adolescents view exclusion as a legitimate form of social regulation (Horn, 2003, 2005; Horn, Killen, & Stangor, 1999). This research is compelling in that it suggests that adolescents' knowledge of their social worlds and the norms, conventions, and stereotypes within the peer system are related to how adolescents construct an understanding of how to treat one another. Interestingly, even though the peer system in adolescence is highly stratified (Brown, Mory, & Kinney, 1994; Eckert, 1989; Youniss, McLellan, & Strouse, 1994), none of the research on adolescents' reasoning about social acceptance has investigated how social hierarchy within the peer system is related to adolescents' understanding of these issues. Research on individuals' social reasoning in hierarchical cultures, however, provides evidence that one's position within the social hierarchy is related to judgments about the legitimacy of cultural practices and customs and the type of reasoning that individuals bring to bear on these judgments (Turiel, 2002). Further, the social psychological literature provides evidence that issues of group status and group bias influence individuals' attitudes and beliefs about others (see Hagendoorn & Henke, 1991; Kirchler, Palmonari, & Pombeni, 1994; Otten, Mummendy, & Blanz, 1996; Sachdev & Bourhis, 1985, 1987; Turner, Hogg, Oakes, et al., 1987). The purpose of the present study was to explore the role that group status and group bias may play in adolescents' judgments and reasoning regarding the acceptance of others based on their peer group membership. Understanding how

peer social hierarchy and group bias are related to adolescents' reasoning about intergroup relationships can provide insight into the ways that intergroup relationships develop in adolescence and how they may lead to negative developmental outcomes for youth (i.e., extreme forms of retributive violence as happened at Columbine).

Social Stratification within the Peer System

Research on adolescents' peer groups in high school has shown that different peer groups (crowds) are afforded different levels of status within the adolescent social world (Brown & Lohr, 1987; Cusick, 1973; Deyhle, 1986; Eckert, 1989; Eder, 1985; Larkin, 1979; Schwartz & Merten, 1967; Schwedinger & Schwedinger, 1985) and that these status designations channel adolescents into certain relationships, thus impacting adolescents' intergroup relationships (Brown et al., 1994). With the transition to high school (particularly large comprehensive high schools typical within the United States), a peer system emerges that is based on abstract representations of groups determined by the normative understandings of the types of activities, attitudes, behaviors, and values that different groups have in common rather than on adolescents' specific social networks or personal relationships (McLellan & Youniss, 1999). These peer groups, then, get stratified within the social system and afforded status based on their position within that system. Typically, groups such as the jocks, the cheerleaders, and the populars or preppies hold high status positions within the social structure while groups such as druggies, punkers, and gothics hold low status positions within the social structure.

Research on adolescents' self-identification with a social reference group provides evidence that the status of adolescents' own groups are related to their descriptions and evaluations of other groups (Eckert, 1989; England & Petro, 1999; Kirchler et al., 1994; Schwartz & Merten, 1967) as well as their relationships with peers who are perceived to be members of groups whose status differs from their own (Eckert, 1989; Schwartz & Merten, 1967; Youniss et al., 1994). This research suggests that group status and group bias have an impact on adolescents' evaluative descriptions of their peers such that adolescents describe their own group more favorably and members of groups that are different from their own less favorably and more stereotypically (Kirchler et al., 1994; Stone & Brown, 1998, 1999). None of this work, however, investigated the types of reasoning adolescents brought to bear on their decisions. The present study attempted to expand on this research by investigating the way that group status and group bias were related to adolescents' judgments and reasoning about social acceptance of members of high status groups (jocks, cheerleaders, and preppies) versus members of low status groups (dirties, druggies, and gothics).

While evidence suggests that adolescent social reference groups are highly salient in high school and play a large role in determining the structure of the social context within a school, a number of adolescents within this structure do not identify themselves and are not identified by others with any of these groups (Brown et al., 1994; Youniss et al., 1994). Interestingly, even if they are not identified with a group, most adolescents within a school have knowledge of the social hierarchy within the peer group system and the norms, conventions, and stereotypes that go along with that system (McLellan & Youniss, 1999). Thus, to investigate the way in which adolescents' knowledge of the peer social structure was related to their reasoning about social acceptance independently of group bias, in addition to adolescents who identified with the high and low status groups, we also included students who did not identify with either the high status or the low status groups.

Social reasoning and intergroup relationships

As mentioned previously, a growing body of research suggests that during high school adolescents are applying their developing knowledge of societal conventions and norms to the social structure of the peer system within the school, as well as to their understanding of intergroup relationships (Horn, 2003; Horn, Killen, & Stangor, 2001). This research, as well as research by Killen and colleagues (Killen & Stangor, 2001; Killen, Lee-Kim, McGlothlin, & Stangor, 2002; Killen et al., 2006) investigating children's and adolescents' reasoning about exclusion based on gender and race, suggests that in ambiguous and complex situations children and adolescents are more likely to use their knowledge about group norms, group functioning and group stereotypes, as well as their expanded sense of their personal jurisdiction in making decisions about their peers, than in more straightforward situations. That is, in addition to focusing on issues of fairness, due process, and individual rights (as they do in evaluating issues of social acceptance in straightforward contexts), when evaluating exclusion in situations that are more complex, adolescents also focus on group functioning, group norms, stereotypes, and personal choice. For example, when asked who should be chosen to participate in a school activity, Killen and Stangor (2001) found that early adolescents focused more on group norms, group functioning, and stereotypes in justifying their choice (e.g., they should choose the girl to be in the ballet club because she is more likely to have the right outfit) than issues of fairness and equality.

Additionally, research by Horn (2003, Horn et al., 1999) provides evidence that middle adolescents (14- and 15-year-olds) are more likely to view exclusion as all right and to base their judgments on group conventions, norms, and stereotypes, as well as personal choice, than older adolescents (16-, 17- and 18-year-olds). Research on the development of social reasoning in children and adolescents suggests that while young children and adolescents make distinctions between moral issues (e.g., fairness, welfare, and individual rights) and societal issues (e.g. social conventions, dress norms, manners, social rules) (Nucci, 2001; Smetana & Turiel, 2003; Turiel, 1983, 1998), it is not until middle adolescence that individuals come to a full understanding that social norms and conventions serve a regulatory function in that they coordinate the social behavior of members within a social system (Turiel, 1983; Nucci, 2001; Nucci, Becker, &

Horn, 2004). During the middle adolescent period, however, social conventions are viewed and applied by adolescents in an extremely rigid manner (Turiel, 1983). In later adolescence and early adulthood individuals come to understand that social norms and conventions, while functional in coordinating social interactions, are also somewhat arbitrary and dependent upon the context and consensus of the social group (Turiel, 1983; Nucci, 2001). Additionally, research on the development of adolescents' social reasoning suggests that adolescents' knowledge about the kinds of issues that are under their legitimate jurisdiction is also developing and expanding (Nucci, 1996, 2001; Smetana & Turiel, 2003). As adolescents begin to form an identity separate from their parents, they begin to claim a greater number of issues as under their personal control (e.g., choice of friends, choice of leisure activities, choice of vocation), rather than as issues of legitimate parental or school regulation.

The growing body of research on adolescents' reasoning about intergroup relationships implies that judgments about social acceptance in ambiguous and complex contexts result from adolescents coordinating their knowledge of the potential harm inherent in systematically excluding someone simply because of their group membership with their developing knowledge of group norms, conventions, and stereotypes, as well as their expanding sense of autonomy and personal jurisdiction. None of this research, however, has investigated how group status or adolescents' positions within the peer social hierarchy are related to their social reasoning about issues of peer group acceptance. Therefore, the first goal of the present study was to investigate the role of group status and group bias on adolescents' judgments and reasoning about peer acceptance in a complex situation. The second goal was to investigate age-related differences in adolescents' reasoning about these issues.

Current study and hypotheses

In this study, adolescents were given five different hypothetical scenarios in which they were asked to evaluate who should be chosen to participate in a school activity: a high status or low status group member. For example, "Andy, who is a gothic, and Mike,

who is a jock, are both running for student council. They are both equally qualified. The students can only vote for one of them. Who should the students vote for?" Additionally, to investigate the type of reasoning adolescents brought to bear on the situation, as well as their use of group stereotypes in making their decisions, they were asked to provide a reason (justification) for why they chose the person they did.

Based on the research of Kirchler and colleagues (1994) described above, we expected that, overall, adolescents identified with both high and low status groups would exhibit bias in their judgments of who to include in a school activity. That is, adolescents identified with high status groups would be more likely to choose a high status group member, whereas adolescents identified with low status groups would be less likely to choose a high status group member to participate in the school activity.

While Kirchler and colleagues' research found that all adolescents exhibited some form of group bias in their judgments regarding others, they also found that adolescents who identified with being a member of a high status group were the most discriminatory in their attitudes in that they evaluated their own group the most positively and least stereotypically and members of low status groups the least positively and most stereotypically (Kirchler et al., 1994). Kirchler and his colleagues explain these results by suggesting that high status group members are the most invested in maintaining a social system that affords their group a positive/privileged position. Based on this evidence, we expected that adolescents identified with high status groups would exhibit more bias in the choice judgments regarding who to include in school activities than other adolescents (low status group members or those in no group). Further, research on social reasoning in hierarchical cultures suggests that individuals who hold high status positions within a culture are more likely to view cultural practices in which groups of individuals (e.g. women) are treated differently (and often unfairly) as legitimate and resulting from group norms, conventions, and customs rather than as moral issues involving individual rights, discrimination, or unfairness (Turiel, 2002; Wainryb & Turiel, 1994). Thus, we also expected, that in addition to exhibiting greater bias, adolescents in high status groups would be more likely than other adolescents to reason about issues of social acceptance in relation to the norms, conventions, and stereotypes embedded within the peer social system.

While adolescents who identify with high status groups have a lot to gain by maintaining a group structure that affords them status and privilege by virtue of their social reference group, adolescents who identify with low status groups gain seemingly little from a structure in which they are not involved and/or from which they may be marginalized. Further, research on low status or marginalized groups' reasoning about cultural practices within hierarchical cultures suggests that while these individuals understand and often adhere to the norms and customs of the culture, they also view them as unfair and harmful (Wainryb & Turiel, 1994). Therefore, it might be expected that adolescents who identify with low status groups would be more sensitive to the moral dimensions of situations involving social acceptance (e.g., fairness, distributive justice involving who gets access to various school resources). On the other hand, because low status groups are often described as being oppositional to or disinterested in school activities (Eckert, 1989; Kinney, 1999; MacLeod, 1987; Schwartz & Merten, 1967; Schwendinger & Schwendinger, 1985), as well as the value systems that define the adolescent peer world more generally, one could argue that some adolescents who identify with low status groups might also make appeals to the group norms and conventions inherent within the peer social structure in making decisions about who should be chosen to participate in school activities (e.g., preppies are always in student council, that's just how it is).

Similarly, because adolescents identifying with no peer group have knowledge of the social hierarchy of the peer system and its inherent conventions, norms, and stereotypes, they might be expected to rely on this knowledge in making their decisions. Because school activities are more frequently associated with high status peer groups (Brown et al., 1994; Stone & Brown, 1998, 1999), it might be the case, then, that adolescents not identifying with a group would also be more likely to choose a high status target than a low status target to participate in a school activity and would justify their choice using conventional reasoning (group norms) and stereotypes. Because these adolescents do not have a strong identification with a particular group, however, they may also be sensitive to the inherent unfairness of a stratified system that privileges individuals from some groups over individuals from other groups. Thus, adolescents identifying with no group might also be expected to choose low status group members to participate in school activities and to make appeals to moral issues such as fairness and equal access in justifying their judgments.

Finally, research on adolescent social references groups provides evidence that middle adolescents are more rigid in their stereotypes of these peer groups, perceive these groups as more cohesive and less permeable, and adhere more to group norms and conventions than younger or older adolescents (Brown et al., 1994; England & Petro, 1999). Evidence also suggests that middle adolescents are likely to utilize their group knowledge or stereotypes in making decisions about their peers (Horn et al., 1999). Additionally, research on the development of conventional knowledge and age-related differences in adolescents' reasoning about exclusion provides evidence that conventional knowledge changes during adolescence (Nucci, 2001; Turiel, 1983) and that middle adolescents are more likely than older adolescents to affirm conventions and to evaluate exclusion as a legitimate form of social regulation (Horn, 2003; Thorkildsen, Reese, & Corsino, 2002). Based on this evidence, it was expected that ninth-graders would exhibit more in-group bias in their choice judgments than eleventh-graders and that, overall, ninth-graders would use more stereotypes and conventional reasoning than eleventh-graders.

Method[1]

Participants

Participants in the study included 193 male and 186 female ninth- and eleventh-grade students attending a large high school in the Midwest (ninth: 114 male, 98 female [M = 14.9 years, SD = .46]; eleventh: 79 male, 88 female [M = 16.8 years, SD = .54]). The participants were primarily European American (89%). The remaining 11% of the students were from the following groups: Asian American (6%), Latino/a (2%), African American (2%) and Native American (1%).

The demographic distribution of the sample paralleled that of the school's population, which was 84% European American with 16% minority from the following ethnic groups: Asian American (8%), African and African American (7%) and Latino (2%). The school was located in a moderate-sized Midwestern city that is predominantly middle to upper middle class. Fourteen percent of the students attending the high school receive free or reduced price lunch. All students receiving parental permission (75%) enrolled in the required ninth-and eleventh-grade social studies courses participated in the survey.

Procedure

Participants were surveyed during their required social studies course. Participants were told that their responses to the survey items were completely confidential and anonymous, that their participation was voluntary, and that they could choose to stop at any time. Additionally, they were instructed to fill out the survey as completely as possible and that there were no right or wrong answers. The survey administration took approximately 45 minutes. Once all students had completed the survey, the researcher answered any questions they had regarding the study.

Measures

GROUP STATUS

A pilot study was conducted to determine the groups that would be used in the study as well as the status of these groups within the peer social system. The three high status groups were "cheerleaders", "jocks", and "preppies". The three low status groups were "dirties", "druggies", and "gothics". For a detailed description of the pilot study and the groups, see Horn (2003).

GROUP IDENTITY STATUS

To determine participants' *group identity status* participants were asked to check from a list of the six groups used in the study the group within which they identified themselves the most (cheerleaders, jocks, preppies, dirties, druggies, gothics). If they did not identify with any of the six groups they could also indicate this. Additionally, they could indicate if they identified with more than one group. Based on the status of the

specific group they chose, adolescents were coded as belonging to one of three group identity status categories: high status group identity, low status group identity, or none of the groups. Adolescents who identified with the cheerleading, jock, or preppie groups were coded as having a high status identity ($n = 128$; female, $n = 65$; male, $n = 56$). Adolescents who identified with the dirtie, druggie, or gothic groups were coded as having a low status identity ($n = 29$; female, $n = 14$; male, $n = 11$). Adolescents who identified with none of the six groups were coded as having not identifed with a group[2] ($n = 182$; female, $n = 68$; male, $n = 94$). If an adolescent identified with multiple groups that were of different statuses (e.g., jocks and dirties) they were excluded from the analyses ($n = 40$), thus, total $N = 339$.

SCENARIOS USED IN THE SURVEY

Using the groups identified in the pilot study, five different hypothetical scenarios involving the three high status and three low status groups were developed. The scenarios were pilot tested with a group of college undergraduates to ensure clarity. The scenarios involved having to choose between a high status or low status group member to participate in a school activity. The activities used in scenarios were student council, a school trip to a national convention, cheerleading, basketball, and a scholarship program. For example, "Andy, who is a gothic, and Mike, who is a jock, are both running for student council. They are both equally qualified. The students can only vote for one of them. Who should the students vote for?" (See Appendix A for a complete description of each scenario.)

DEPENDENT MEASURES

There were three dependent measures: (1) adolescents' choice *judgments* of either a high status or low status target; (2) adolescents' *domain justifications* (Why do you think they should choose_____?), and (3) adolescents' use of *stereotypes* in their justifications.

Design

All participants responded to all five of the scenarios. Scenarios were presented in counterbalanced order to control for order effects. The groups involved in the scenarios also were counter-balanced such that in each scenario the choice was between a high status and low status individual but the specific groups represented were varied within each scenario. Thus, all individuals responded to at least one scenario involving each of the six groups. Therefore, scenario and target group status were within-subject independent variables while specific group was a between-subjects variable. Gender, grade, and group identity status were also between-subjects variables.

Coding justification responses and reliability

Two separate systems were used to code participants' justifications. The first system coded for domain of social reasoning and the second for whether or not stereotypes were invoked.

DOMAIN DISTINCTIONS

For the domain of social reasoning system, codes were based on previous research (Horn et al., 1999; Killen & Stangor, 2001; Nucci, 1981, 1996; Smetana, 1995; Tisak, 1995; Turiel, 1983, 1998) and pilot data. Five coding categories were used to code adolescents' reasoning (justifications): "moral", "social-conventional", "personal", "undifferentiated" and "missing". (For definitions and examples of the coding categories, see Table 5.10.) Each statement could receive more than one code if it contained two or more distinct chunks of reasoning from different coding categories. There were, however, no instances of double coding for any of the participants. Two research assistants trained by the researcher independently coded justifications for 25% of the surveys. The coders were blind to the hypotheses of the study. Interrater reliability was 83% with Cohen's kappa = .77.

STEREOTYPE INVOKED

To determine the extent to which adolescents were using stereotypes in their reasoning, adolescents' justifications were also coded as "stereotype invoked" or "stereotype not invoked". Responses were coded as stereotype invoked if they included any reference to either positive or negative characteristics or traits about the individual or his/her group. For example, "All gothics are devil worshippers and wouldn't represent the school well", or "Preppies are smart and usually involved in activities so are more deserving of a

Table 5.10 Domain justification coding categories

Domain

Moral
Includes appeals to the individual's right to be included in the activity or given a chance at the opportunity; to the wrongfulness of judging or making a decision based solely on group membership, including statements denying group categorization or group stereotypes, as well as appeals to fairness or harm to the individual (e.g., "It isn't fair to exclude her just because she is a 'gothic'.").

Societal
Includes appeals to conventions, group norms, or group functioning such as an individual "fitting in" to a group, or the impact on school representation; appeals to positive or negative stereotypes based on group membership or group category without supporting information; and appeals to intergroup relationships (e.g., "Heather wouldn't fit in with the 'cheerleaders'.").

Personal
Includes appeals to the person's prerogative in making decisions or judgments, as well as appeals to the individual's skills or lack of skills necessary to be in the activity or receive the opportunity that do not contain a moral reference (e.g., "They can do whatever they want to.").

Undifferentiated
Justifications that were unreadable, didn't make sense, or were unrelated to the question asked.
Missing

scholarship". These codes were determined independently of the first coding system. Individuals' justifications within each condition could receive a code of 0 = stereotype not invoked or 1 = stereotype invoked. Two research assistants trained by the researcher independently coded stereotype invoked justifications for 25% of the surveys. The coders were blind to the hypotheses of the study. Interrater reliability was 94% total agreement with Cohen's kappa = .77.

Results

Data analysis plan

First, an ANOVA was conducted to determine whether there were differences in the level of importance of group membership amongst participants in the different group identity statuses. Then, an ANOVA was conducted to determine the relationship amongst target group status, participants' group identity status, and their choice judgments. Third, a repeated measures ANOVA was performed on adolescents' domain justifications to determine the relationship amongst target group status, participants' group identity status, and their reasoning regarding who to pick for the school activity. Fourth, an ANOVA was conducted on adolescents' stereotype invoked justifications to determine the relationship amongst target group status, participants' group identity status, and their use of stereotypes. Gender and grade level were included in each of the above analyses. Finally, to further explore the relationship between adolescents' judgments and their reasoning, repeated measures ANOVAs were performed for each scenario on adolescents' domain justifications and their use of stereotypes with choice judgment (high status or low status) as the between-subjects factor.

Follow-up tests of simple effects were conducted and Bonferroni adjustments to maintain a family-wise error rate of .05 were implemented. Arcsine transformations were conducted on the proportional data used in the justification analyses to correct for non-normality (see Winer, 1971; Winer, Brown, & Michels, 1991). Additionally, due to the low frequency of domain justifications in the "missing" and "undifferentiated" categories (<5% of all justifications), these categories were not included in analyses of adolescents' justifications.

Importance of group membership

In order to determine if importance of group membership was different based on adolescents' position within the peer system a 3 (group identity status: high, low, not listed) × 2 (grade: ninth, eleventh) × 2 (gender: male, female) univariate analysis of variance was performed on adolescents' importance of group membership scores. This analysis revealed a significant main effect for group identity status, $F(2, 296) = 29.67$, $p < .001$. Follow-up analyses of simple effects revealed that adolescents identifying with either a high status ($M = 2.94$) or low status ($M = 2.43$) group evaluated the importance of membership in that

group more highly than adolescents listing none of the six groups used in the study ($M = 1.49$), $p < .001$ and $p < .02$, respectively). Because of the difference in importance of group membership amongst the groups, in all subsequent analyses we controlled for importance of group membership by including it as a covariate.

Judgments

It was expected that if given a choice between a high and a low status target, adolescents, overall, would choose a high status target to participate in an activity more often than a low status target. Further, it was expected that, due to group bias, adolescents who had a high status group identity would choose high status targets significantly more than adolescents who had a low status group identity or those listing no group. Further, adolescents who had a low status group identity were expected to choose high status targets the least. Adolescents' choice scores were determined by calculating the proportion of times each participant chose a high status target across the five stories. Thirty-one of the participants did not answer this question on the survey for any of the scenarios and 12 did not rate the importance of group membership, thus, these participants were not included in the analyses regarding choice judgments (total: $N = 296$). To determine the relationship amongst target group status, participants' group identity status, and adolescents' choice of targets a 3 (group identity status: not listed, high status group identity, low status group identity) × 2 (grade: ninth, eleventh) × 2 (gender: male, female) univariate ANCOVA was performed on the proportion of high status targets chosen (controlling for importance of group membership). There was a significant main effect for group identity status, $F(2, 296) = 14.26$, $p < .001$. Follow-up tests of simple effects revealed that, as expected, adolescents with a high status group identity chose significantly more high status targets than adolescents with a low status group identity or those listing none of the groups. Adolescents listing none of the groups also chose significantly more high status targets than those with a low status group identity (see Table 5.11 for means and significance values). There were no interaction effects. These results suggest a slight in-group bias in that adolescents self-identified

Table 5.11 Means and SDs for proportion of high status targets chosen by group identity status

Group identity status	n	Choice of high status target
No group	150	.65★ (.31)
High status	121	.78★ (.31)
Low status	25	.45★ (.29)

Note. ★Means different at *p* < .01.

Table 5.12 Means and SDs for domain justifications by group identity status

Group identity status	n	Moral	Conventional	Personal
No group	150	.17ᵃ (.23)	.62ᵃ (.33)	.09ᵃ (.18)
High status group	121	.11ᵇ (.24)	.73ᵇ (.33)	.05ᵇ (.19)
Low status group	25	.26ᵃ (.22)	.55ᵃ (.32)	.07 (.18)

Note. ᵃᵇMeans with different superscripts different at *p* < .05.

into a high status social reference group were more likely to choose a high status target than other adolescents. The results that members listing none of the groups also chose high status targets more than low status targets suggest that group status may also contribute to adolescents' choice judgments through adolescents' conventional knowledge regarding group norms or stereotypes, independently of bias processes. The results that adolescents who identified with low status groups chose high status targets only 45% of the time suggest that low status targets were also somewhat likely to exhibit an in-group bias in their judgments, however, this bias was not very strong. The expected grade differences were not obtained, nor were any gender differences.

Domain justifications

It was expected that adolescents with a high status group identity would use more conventional reasoning in justifying their judgments than adolescents with a low status group identity or those listing none of the groups. Adolescents with a low status group identity were expected to use both conventional and moral reasoning in justifying their responses. It was also expected that adolescents listing none of the groups would likely use more moral reasons in their justifications than the adolescents with high status group identity, but might also be likely to use conventional reasoning in justifying their judgments. Grade differences in justifications were also expected. In order to determine the relationship amongst group identity status, grade, gender, and adolescents' domain justifications a 3 (justification type: moral, social-conventional, personal) × 3 (group identity status: not listed, high status group identity, low status group identity) × 2 (grade: ninth, eleventh) × 2

(gender: male, female) repeated measures ANCOVA with repeated measures on justification was performed on the proportion of adolescents' responses in each justification category (controlling for importance of group membership). This analysis revealed a significant main effect for justification type, $F(2, 566) = 47.45, p < .001$. Tests of simple effects reveal that, overall, adolescents used more social conventional ($M = .63$) than moral ($M = .18$) or personal justifications ($M = .07$), $t(596) = 14.61, p < .001$ and $t(596) = 19.56, p < .001$, respectively. Additionally, adolescents used more moral justifications (.18) than personal justifications (.07), $t(596) = 4.83, p < .001$.

This main effect was qualified by a significant two-way interaction between group identity status and justification, $F(4, 566) = 4.87, p < .001$. Overall, adolescents with a high status group identity used justifications less frequently than adolescents with a low status group identity or those listing none of the groups ($t(144) = 209.09, p < .001$ and $t(269) = 5.58, p < .001$, respectively). Additionally, adolescents with a high status group identity used conventional justifications more frequently than adolescents with a low status group identity or those listing none of the groups ($t(144) = 2.70, p < .01$ and $t(269) = 2.73, p < .01$, respectively). Further, adolescents not identified with any of the groups used personal justifications more frequently than adolescents identifying with a high status group (see Table 5.12 for means and standard deviations). There were no overall justification differences between adolescents with a low status group identity and those listing none of the groups. The expected grade differences were not obtained nor were any gender differences.

Table 5.13   Means and SDs for proportion of stereotypes invoked by group identity status

Group identity status	n	Stereotypes invoked
No group	150	.75[a] (.31)
High status	121	.82[b] (.31)
Low status	25	.62[ab] (.30)

Note. [a]Means different at $p < .05$; [b]means different at $p < .01$.

Use of stereotypes

It was also expected that adolescents with a high status group identity would invoke stereotypes more than adolescents with a low status group identity or those listing none of the groups. Additionally, it was expected that ninth graders would invoke more stereotypes than eleventh-graders. In order to test these hypotheses a 3 (group identity status: not listed, high status group identity, low status group identity) × 2 (grade: ninth, eleventh) × 2 (gender: male, female) repeated measures ANCOVA was preformed on the proportion of times adolescents invoked a stereotype across all three scenarios (controlling for importance of group membership). This analysis revealed a significant main effect for group identity status, $F(2, 296) = 4.93, p < .01$. Follow-up tests of simple effects revealed that adolescents with a low status group identity used stereotypes significantly less than either adolescents with a high status group identity or those listing none of the groups. Further, the difference in use of stereotypes between adolescents with a high status group identity and those listing none of the groups approached significance ($t(269) = 1.85, p < .07$) (See Table 5.13 for means and standard deviations.) The expected grade differences in use of stereotypes were not obtained, nor were any gender differences.

Relationships between choice judgments and adolescents' reasoning

To further explore the relationship between adolescents' choice judgments and their reasoning about social acceptance, a series of ANOVAs were conducted on adolescents' domain justifications with adolescents' choice judgments as the between–subjects factor. These analyses were conducted separately for

each scenario due to the fact that many adolescents' choice judgments varied by scenario. Further, because gender and grade were not significantly related to either judgments or justifications in previous analyses, these factors were dropped from the current analyses.

Five 3 (justification type: moral, social-conventional, personal) × 3 (group identity status: not listed, high status group identity, low status group identity) × 2 (choice judgment: low status, high status) repeated measures ANOVAs were conducted on the proportion of adolescents' responses in each justification category for each scenario. For all of the scenarios there was a main effect for justification type, $F(2, 572) = 67.52, p < .001; F(2, 566) = 62.44, p < .001; F(2, 574) = 116.26, p < .001; F(2, 564) = 32.17, p < .001$; and $F(2, 570) = 19.19, p < .001$, for the cheerleading, basketball, student council, national convention, and scholarship stories respectively. For all five scenarios, this main effect was qualified by a significant two–way interaction between justification type and choice judgment, $F(2, 572) = 87.79, p < .001; F(2, 566) = 58.65, p < .001; F(2, 574) = 18.69, p < .001; F(2, 564) = 35.81, p < .001$; and $F(2, 570) = 29.44, p < .001$ for the cheerleading, basketball, student council, national convention, and scholarship stories respectively. For all of the scenarios, adolescents who chose a high status target to participate in the activity were more likely to utilize conventional reasoning and less likely to utilize moral reasoning in justifying their choices (see Table 5.14 for means, standard deviations, and results of post hoc tests of significance). Conversely, adolescents who chose low status targets were more likely to use moral reasoning and less likely to use conventional reasoning to justify their choices. Additionally, for the cheerleading scenario only, adolescents who chose low status targets were more likely use personal reasoning than adolescents who chose high status targets.

Further, for the cheerleading scenario, there was a significant two–way interaction between justification category and group identity status, $F(4, 572) = 3.89, p < .01$. Follow-up tests of simple effects revealed that, for the cheerleading scenario, adolescents who were members of a high status group were more likely to use conventional reasoning and less likely to use moral reasoning than adolescents who were members of a low status group or no group, regardless of their choice judgment (see Table 5.15).

Table 5.14 Means and SDs for adolescents' domain justifications by their choice judgment for each scenario

Senario and choice judgment	n	Moral	Conventional	Personal
Cheerleading				
Low status	77	.48[a] (.50)	.24[a] (.38)	.14[a] (.37)
High status	215	.06[b] (.15)	.88[b] (.30)	.02[b] (.18)
Basketball				
Low status	72	.47[a] (.50)	.30[a] (.44)	.09 (.28)
High status	217	.03[b] (.18)	.84[b] (.33)	.06 (.21)
Student council				
Low status	101	.32[a] (.46)	.54[a] (.50)	.05 (.26)
High status	192	.04[b] (.13)	.79[b] (.39)	.03 (.20)
National convention				
Low status	96	.44[a] (.50)	.33[a] (.46)	.23 (.42)
High status	192	.02[b] (.16)	.84[b] (.38)	.13 (.35)
Scholarship				
Low status	121	.47[a] (.47)	.32[a] (.43)	.21 (.41)
High status	170	.01[b] (.13)	.76[b] (.42)	.22 (.40)

Note. [ab]Means with different superscripts within scenario and within column different at $p < .0001$.

Table 5.15 Means and SDs for adolescents' domain justifications by group identity status for the cheerleading scenario

Group identity status	n	Moral	Conventional	Personal
No group	152	.28[a] (.39)	.49[a] (.49)	.11 (.30)
High status group	116	.19[b] (.24)	.67[b] (.37)	.05 (.20)
Low status group	24	.35[a] (.48)	.51[a] (.51)	.09 (.33)

Note. [ab]Means with different superscripts within columns different at $p < .01$.

Overall, these results suggest that adolescents' choices of who should participate in school activities are related to the type of reasoning they bring to bear on the issue. That is, adolescents who chose a high status target (regardless of their own group membership) relied on their knowledge of group norms and conventions in justifying their choices, whereas adolescents who chose a low status target were more likely to view the issue in moral terms and to make appeals to issues of fairness and equal access in justifying their choices.

Discussion

This study provides evidence that group status was related to adolescents' judgments and reasoning about the treatment of others. Further, the results suggest that an adolescent's own position within the peer structure, as well as the group status of the targets being included in or excluded from the school activity, were both related to adolescents' judgments and reasoning about their peers. Adolescents who had a high status group identity, in comparison to adolescents with low status group identity or adolescents identifying with none of the groups, were more likely to choose another high status group member to participate in an activity, and were more likely to use conventional reasoning and less likely to use moral reasoning in justifying their choices. They were also more likely to use stereotypes than adolescents with a low status group identity in their reasoning. Adolescents who listed none of the groups, however, were also more likely to choose high status targets over low status targets to participate and were more likely to use stereotypes to justify their judgments than adolescents with a low status group identity. Adolescents with a low status group identity, on the other hand, chose high status targets almost as much as low status targets to participate in school activities, were the most likely to use moral reasoning and the least likely to use stereotypes in justifying their choices. These results provide some preliminary evidence that group bias and group status are related to adolescents' social judgments about who should participate in school activities, as well as the type of reasoning that adolescents bring to bear on these judgments.

The findings from this study contribute to our understanding of adolescents' reasoning about their peers and the treatment of others in three important ways. First, by providing evidence that adolescents' understanding of and reasoning about their peers is complex and is influenced by where adolescents perceive themselves and others to be situated within the peer structure of the school. Second, by providing evidence that in-group bias and group status not only influence adolescents' attitudes toward and descriptions of others but also their evaluations of how others are treated in a school context based on their peer group membership. Finally, this study extends previous work on adolescents' social reference groups by systematically investigating the reasoning processes underlying adolescents' decision-making involving their peers. Investigating the reasoning processes adolescents bring to bear on these issues helps us to further understand the mechanism through which group status is related to adolescents' attitudes about, evaluations of, and behavior toward their peers.

Relationships amongst adolescents' group membership, group status, and their choice judgments

As hypothesized, adolescents with high status group identities were more likely to choose high status group members and less likely to choose low status group members to participate in school activities. Similar to Kirchler and colleagues (1994) who suggested that high status adolescents overestimated the legitimacy of the social system that privileges certain groups over others, this study provides evidence that adolescents with a high status group identity extend this type of bias to who should and should not be chosen to participate in school activities. Adolescents identifying with a low status group identity expressed more variation in their choices with almost half choosing the high status group member. These results support research on the relationship of social identity to group bias in that they suggest that individuals (particularly those with a high status group identity) will promote their own group as a way to maintain or enhance their own sense of self-worth or self-esteem (Tajfel & Turner, 1979; Tarrant et al., 2001) or their own place at the top of the peer social structure.

Adolescents with high status group identities, who are themselves more likely to participate in school activities, may have more to gain by preserving the homogeneity of who gets chosen for these activities. That is, if membership in the activity is limited to high status group members, then the high status adolescents' position within those activities will not be

threatened. In fact, in a study on middle school girls and popularity, Eder (1985) found that when low status girls were given access to membership in the high status group, rather than encouraging the group to include other low status girls as members, they excluded and teased other girls from the lower status group who were previously their best friends. Eder hypothesized that these girls exhibited unfairness in their behaviors as a way to preserve the social structure and protect their new, yet vulnerable, membership in the high status group. Thus, in the current study for adolescents identifying with groups at the top of the social hierarchy, it could be the case that choosing other high status group members is a way to preserve the system that affords them greater access and privilege within the school system.

For adolescents at the bottom of the social hierarchy (those with a low status group identity), however, because they typically do not participate in school activities (such as those used in the study) as a result of not choosing to participate in them or not having access to them, they may have less invested in preserving the make-up of the group and, as such, some exhibit an in-group bias that gives access to more low status group members and use reasons such as equal access and fairness to justify their choice. Others, however, exhibit an out-group bias and use conventional reasoning (such as group norms) to justify their choice. This may be due to the fact that these adolescents view participation in school activities as conforming to a system that they see themselves in opposition to or as not belonging to. Thus, low status adolescents who want to participate in or belong to that system may view issues of inclusion in activities in terms of fairness and rights while individuals who are members of low status groups that define themselves in opposition to that system may be more likely to view these same issues in more conventional and stereotypical terms. The results illustrating the relationship between adolescents' choice judgments and their reasoning provide some support for this hypothesis. These results must be taken with caution, however, given the small number of participants who identified with the low status groups.

The results indicating that adolescents who did not identify with any of the groups used in the study also chose high status targets more than low status targets provides some preliminary (albeit tentative) evidence that group status may influence adolescents' judgments independently of in-group bias. The fact that adolescents' choice judgments were related to the type of reasoning they were using, independently of the adolescents' own group membership, provides further evidence for this idea. In the case of adolescent crowds, it is likely that all adolescents in the system have knowledge of these groups and the relative status of each group within the system. Thus, it is likely that adolescents' knowledge of the relative position of each group within the system will be related to their evaluations of who is more likely to conform to and fit in with the other students participating in those school activities. As such, for students not invested in promoting one group over another, evaluating who should be chosen to participate is likely to be influenced by their knowledge of the groups, the group structure of the social system, and the type of adolescent who typically participates in that specific activity, supporting McLellan's and Youniss' (1999) notion that crowds are delineated within a shared cognitive representational system. These interpretations must be taken with caution, however, because we did not know if adolescents who didn't identify with one of the six groups used in the study identified with another high or low status group in the school or simply did not identify with any group.

Further, it could also be the case that this shared cognitive representational understanding of the peer group structure was related to all adolescents' judgments and reasoning, even those who identified with high status or low status groups. That is, even adolescents who identify with high or low status groups could be basing their judgments about who to include in a school activity on the shared norms and conventions of those groups rather than solely group bias. To more accurately investigate the ways in which social identity and group status are related to adolescents' intergroup relationships, future research should more systematically investigate the evaluation and reasoning processes of adolescents who do not associate themselves with any group in the school, as well as the ways in which the shared understanding of the group structure is related to all adolescents' judgments and reasoning.

Relationships amongst adolescents' group membership, group status and domain related reasoning and use of stereotypes

The results regarding the underlying reasoning processes that adolescents bring to bear on their choice judgments help us to better understand the influence that group status has on these judgments. Overall, all adolescents used more conventional reasons to justify their choice judgments than either moral or personal reasons, suggesting that issues of who gets access to school activities draw upon adolescents' knowledge of groups, group norms, and group functioning similarly regardless of one's position within the peer social structure. That is, in situations in which one person must be chosen over another, necessitating excluding someone from the activity, adolescents were more likely to rely on group norms, conventions, and stereotypes in making their decisions than on issues of fairness. In fact, social and cultural groups often have associated with them prescribed norms for behavior, appearance, attitudes, and values that legitimately serve to regulate group membership and reduce the salience of the unfairness or harm that may result from denying an individual membership into a particular group. These results extend the work of Horn (2003) and Killen and colleagues (Killen, Lee-Kim, McGlothlin, & Stangor, 2002; Killen et al., 2006) by suggesting that in complex situations (having to choose one student over another) adolescents' understanding of group norms and group functioning is more salient than in more prototypic situations (involving straightforward exclusion or denial of resources to an individual) in which issues of fairness and individual rights take precedence.

The significant differences in the use of moral and conventional reasoning amongst adolescents with high status group identities and other adolescents provide evidence that group bias is related to adolescents' reasoning about their choices to some extent. These results support and extend the work of Kirchler and colleagues (1994) who found that adolescents in high status groups exhibited in-group bias more than other adolescents, thus seeming to overestimate the legitimacy of their own group and its position within the social hierarchy of the peer system. Similarly in this study, there is some preliminary evidence to suggest that adolescents at the top of the social hierarchy may be giving undue weight to the legitimacy of group norms and conventions in making decisions about their peers and in regulating their social worlds. On the other hand, both adolescents with high status group identities and those who listed none of the groups invoked stereotypes more than adolescents with low status group identities suggesting that group bias may not be the only factor related to adolescents' reasoning about their peers. As McClellan and Youniss (1999) suggest, crowds are delineated within a shared cognitive representational system that associates certain prototypes (or stereotypes) for behavior, dress, attitudes, and norms with particular groups and not others. The fact that adolescents who didn't list any of the six groups used in the study used stereotypes almost as much as adolescents identifying with high status groups provides some support for the notion that all adolescents, to some degree, apply their understanding of this system (and the stereotypes inherent in it) to the decisions they make about social relationships within this system. Further supporting this idea is the evidence that adolescents with low status group identities were also likely to use conventional reasoning and stereotypes in justifying their judgments. Moreover, all adolescents, regardless of their own group membership, used conventional reasoning significantly more when choosing a high status group member to participate in the school activity, whereas they used moral reasoning significantly more when they chose a low status group member to participate.

The fact that adolescents with low status group identities were more likely than other adolescents to use moral reasoning in justifying their judgments, however, suggests that even though there may be a shared understanding of the peer group system and norms, there may not be agreement regarding whether or not this system is just or fair. These results add to a growing body of work within social cognitive domain theory on the ways that cultural traditions influence individuals' social and moral reasoning (Turiel, 2002; Wainryb & Turiel, 1994). Turiel's and Wainryb's work suggests that there is great heterogeneity in individuals' reasoning regarding traditions and social practices that regulate individuals' access and behaviors within social systems. Members of the privileged group (e.g.,

men) view these cultural practices as legitimate and as providing benefit to the culture. Members of the non-privileged groups (e.g., women) express their adherence to the traditions, conventions, and rules but also express the unfairness and harm inherent within that system. Further, Turiel (2002) has documented the kinds of resistances that individuals who are not privileged (and often harmed) by the cultural traditions engage in in their everyday lives. Based on the results of the current study, it appears that similar processes may be happening within the peer system in that those who have status within it are more likely to justify the legitimacy of the system while those who do not have status within the system exhibit an understanding of the norms and conventions of the system while at the same time recognizing that those norms and conventions are often unfair or harmful to certain individuals or groups within the system. Future work in this area should investigate the ways in which adolescents from all positions within the peer social system reason about the social structure and practices within the system. In what ways do social identity and group status independently and interdependently influence adolescents' perceptions of the peer system, as well as their judgments and reasoning about social relationships and practices within that system? Further, research should investigate the kinds of resistance that adolescents who do not benefit from the system may engage in. Is it the case that some of these students resist by bringing guns and bombs to school and harming their classmates while others resist by rejecting the system all together? What factors are related to the different ways in which adolescents might deal with a system they deem oppressive and unfair?

Age-related differences

Surprisingly, none of the expected age-related differences were obtained. While these results seem to contradict Horn (2003), who found age-related differences in adolescents' use of conventional reasoning and stereotypes about straightforward exclusion, it could also be the case that in choice situations (such as those used in this study) knowledge about groups and group norms becomes so salient that all adolescents give priority to their conventional knowledge over moral knowledge despite developmental differences in their understanding of conventions. It could also be the case, however, that the age-related differences reported by Horn (2003) are not due to developmental differences in adolescents' conventional knowledge but, rather, are related to some other factor. Future research should more systematically investigate the relationships between adolescents' level of conventional reasoning (as proposed by Turiel, 1983 and Nucci, 2001), adolescents' understanding of peer "crowds", and their judgments and reasoning regarding including and excluding others based on their peer group membership.

Also surprising were the lack of gender differences in adolescents' judgments and reasoning in light of the fact that gender differences have been reported in most other studies investigating children and adolescents' reasoning about peer group exclusion and discrimination (Horn, 2003; Horn et al., 1999; Killen & Stangor, 2001; Theimer, Killen, & Stangor, 2001). In most of these studies, however, girls were more likely to use moral reasoning than boys. In the current study, the majority of adolescents used conventional rather than moral reasoning, suggesting that gender differences in children and adolescents' reasoning about exclusion may be due to differences in girls' and boys' moral knowledge rather than their conventional knowledge. In situations where adolescents have to choose one person over another, conventional knowledge may become so salient that all children and adolescents view the moral dimensions of the situation as less important. This could also explain why other researchers such as Crick (1997) and Eder (1985) have found that girls are much more likely to exclude others from their friendship groups than boys. That is, in those situations, it may be that the complexity of negotiating the size, membership, and identity of the group takes priority over the moral dimension of unfairness for girls. Thus, it will be important in future research on gender and peer relationships to include measures that investigate adolescents' underlying reasons for the decisions they make about their peers.

Conclusion

Negotiating high school is a very challenging task. Creating social categories and grouping people into these categories based on their appearance, activities, and attitudes is one way adolescents make sense of their complex social world and seems to be a natural part of what happens in high school. The results of this study, however, provide some preliminary evidence to suggest that it is important to understand how issues of power and privilege within this system are related to group membership, as well as intergroup attitudes, perceptions, and reasoning. Additionally, it is important to understand when this type of categorization may serve a useful function for adolescents and when it leads to subtle forms of exclusion and discrimination through legitimizing structures and practices that may be inherently unfair and that may have immediate or cumulative detrimental effects on adolescents' social lives through peer rejection, discrimination, or negative intergroup relationships.

Notes

1   The study described in this article was part of a larger study investigating adolescents' reasoning about issues of exclusion of or unfairness toward others based on social reference group membership. Other results from this project were presented in Horn (2003). The results presented in this study concern a question not analyzed in the Horn (2003) paper.

2   The no group listed category in this study refers to the fact that the students did not identify themselves with any of the six groups in the study. This does not mean, however, that they did not identify with any group given the fact that more than six groups were identified at this school. They are included in the analyses as "no group" to determine the impact that not identifying with one of the groups in the study has on adolescents' responses.

References

Brown, B. B., & Lohr, M. J. (1987). Peer-group affiliation and adolescent self-esteem: An integration of ego-identity and symbolic-interaction theories. *Journal of Personality and Social Psychology*, *52*, 47–55.

Brown, B. B., Mory, M., & Kinney, D. (1994). Casting adolescent crowds in a relational perspective: Caricature, channel, and context. In R. Montemayor, G.R. Adams, & T.P. Gullotta (Eds.), *Personal relationships during adolescence* (pp. 123–167). Thousand Oaks, CA: Sage.

Crick, N. (1997). Engagement in gender normative versus nonnormative forms of aggression: Links to social-psychological adjustment. *Developmental Psychology, 33,* 610–617.

Cusick, P. A. (1973). *Inside high school.* New York: Holt, Rinehart & Winston.

Deyhle, D. (1986). Break dancing and breaking out: Anglos, Utes, and Navajos in a border reservation high school. *Anthropology and Education Quarterly, 17,* 111–127.

Eckert, P. (1989). *Jocks and burnouts: Social categories and identity in the high school.* New York: Teachers' College Press.

Eder, D. (1985). The cycle of popularity: Interpersonal relations among female adolescents. *Sociology of Education, 58,* 154–165.

Eder, D., & Kinney, D. (1995). The effect of middle school extracurricular activities on adolescents' popularity and peer status. *Youth and Society, 26,* 298–324.

England, E. M., & Petro, K. D. (1999). Middle school students' perceptions of peer groups: Relative judgments about group characteristics. *Journal of Early Adolescence, 18,* 349–373.

Hagendoorn, L. H., & Henke, R. (1991). The effect of multiple category membership on intergroup evaluations in a north Indian context: Class, caste and religion. *British Journal of Social Psychology, 30,* 247–260.

Horn, S. S. (2003). Adolescents' reasoning about exclusion from social groups. *Developmental Psychology, 39,* 71–84.

Horn, S. S. (2005). Adolescents' peer interactions: Conflict and coordination among personal expression, social norms, and moral reasoning. In L. Nucci (Ed.), *Conflict, contradiction, and contrarian elements in moral development and education* (pp. 113–128). Mahwah, NJ: Erlbaum.

Horn, S. S., Killen, M., & Stangor, C. S. (1999). The influence of group stereotypes on adolescents' moral reasoning. *Journal of Early Adolescence, 19,* 98–113.

Killen, M., & Stangor, C. (2001). Social reasoning about group inclusion and exclusion. *Child Development, 72,* 174–186.

Killen, M., Lee-Kim, J., McGlothlin, H., & Stangor, C. (2002). How children and adolescents evaluate gender and racial exclusion. *Monograph of the Society for Research in Child Development, 67* (4, Serial No. 271).

Killen, M., McGlothlin, H., & Lee-Kim, J. (2002). Between individuals and culture: Individuals' evaluations of exclusion from social groups. In H. Keller, Y. Poortinga, & A. Schoelmerich (Eds.), *Between biology and culture: Perspectives on ontogenetic development.* Cambridge: Cambridge University Press.

Killen, M., Margie, N. G., & Sinno, S. (2006). Morality in the context of intergroup relations. In M. Killen & J.G. Smetana (Eds.), *Handbook of moral development* (pp. 155–184). Mahwah, NJ: Erlbaum.

Kinney, D. (1999). From "headbangers" to "hippies": Delineating adolescents' active attempts to form an alternative peer culture. In J. A. McLellan & M. J. Pugh (Eds.), *The role of peer groups in adolescent social identity: Exploring the importance of stability and change. (New Directions for Child and Adolescent Development)* (pp. 21–36). San Francisco: Jossey-Bass.

Kirchler, E., Palmonari, A., & Pombeni, M. L. (1994). Social categorization processes as dependent on status differences between groups: A step into adolescents' peer-groups. *European Journal of Social Psychology, 24,* 541–563.

Larkin, R. W. (1979). *Suburban youth in cultural crisis.* New York: Oxford University Press.

MacLeod, J. (1987). *Ain't no making it: Leveled aspirations in a low income neighborhood.* Boulder: Westview Press.

McLellan, J. A., & Youniss, J. (1999). A representational system for peer crowds. In I. E. Sigel (Ed.), *Development of mental representation: Theories and applications* (pp. 437–449). Mahwah, NJ: Erlbaum.

Nucci, L. P. (1981). The development of personal concepts: A domain distinct from moral and societal concepts. *Child Development, 52,* 114–121.

Nucci, L. P. (1996). Morality and the personal sphere of action. In E. Reed, E. Turiel, & T. Brown (Eds.), *Values and knowledge* (pp. 41–60). Hillsdale, NJ: Erlbaum.

Nucci, L. P. (2001). *Education in the moral domain.* Cambridge: Cambridge University Press.

Nucci, L., Becker, K., & Horn, S. (2004). Assessing the development of adolescent concepts of social convention. Paper presented at the annual meeting of the Jean Piaget Society, Toronto, Canada, June.

Otten, S., Mummendey, A., & Blanz, M. (1996). Intergroup discrimination in positive and negative outcome allocations: Impact of stimulus valence, relative group status, and relative group size. *Personality & Social Psychology Bulletin,* 568–581.

Sachdev, I. B., & Bourhis, R. Y. (1985). Social categorization and power differentials in group relations. *European Journal of Social Psychology, 15,* 415–434.

Sachdev, I. B., & Bourhis, R. Y. (1987). Status differentials and intergroup behaviour. *European Journal of Social Psychology, 17,* 277–293.

Schwartz, D., & Merten, D. (1967). The language of adolescence: An anthropological approach to the youth culture. *American Journal of Sociology, 72,* 453–468.

Schwendinger, H., & Schwendinger, J. (1985). *Adolescent subcultures and delinquency.* New York: Praeger.

Smetana, J. G. (1995). Morality in context: Abstractions, ambiguities and applications. *Annals of Child Development, 10,* 83–130.

Smetana, J. G., & Turiel, E. (2003). Morality during adolescence. In G. R. Adams & M. Berzonsky (Eds.), *The*

Blackwell handbook of adolescence (pp. 247–268). Oxford: Blackwell.

Stone, M., & Brown, B. B. (1998). In the eye of the beholder: Adolescents' perceptions of peer crowd stereotypes. In R. Muuss & D. Porton (Eds.), *Adolescent behavior and society: A book of readings* (5th edn, pp. 158–174). Boston: McGraw-Hill College.

Stone, M., & Brown, B. B. (1999). Identity claims and projections: Descriptions of self and crowds in secondary school. In J. A. McLellan & M. J. Pugh (Eds.), *The role of peer groups in adolescent social identity: Exploring the importance of stability and change. (New Directions for Child and Adolescent Development)* (pp. 7–20). San Francisco: Jossey-Bass.

Tajfel, H., & Turner, J. C. (1979). An integrative theory of social conflict. In W. G. Austin & S. Worchel (Eds.), *The social psychology of intergroup relations.* Monterey: Brooks & Cole.

Tarrant, M., North, A. C., Edridge, M. D., Kirk, L. E., Smith, E. A., & Turner, R. E. (2001). Social identity in adolescence. *Journal of Adolescence, 24,* 597–609.

Theimer, C. E., Killen, M., & Stangor, C. (2001). Preschool children's evaluations of exclusion in gender-stereotypic contexts. *Developmental Psychology, 37,* 1–10.

Thorkildsen, T. A., Reese, D., & Corsino, A. (2002). School ecologies and attitudes about exclusionary behavior among adolescents and young adults. *Merrill-Palmer Quarterly, 48,* 25–51.

Tisak, M. (1995). Domains of social reasoning and beyond. *Annals of Child Development, 11,* 95–130.

Turiel, E. (1983). *The development of social knowledge: Morality and convention.* Cambridge: Cambridge University Press.

Turiel, E. (1998). The development of morality. In W. Damon (Series Ed.) & N. Eisenberg (Vol. Ed.), *Handbook of child psychology: Vol. 3. Social, emotional, and personality development* (5th edn, pp. 863–932). New York: Wiley.

Turiel, E. (2002). *The culture of morality: Social development, context, and conflict.* Cambridge: Cambridge University Press.

Turner, J. C., Hogg, M. A., Oakes, P. J., Reicher, S. D., & Wetherell, M. (1987). *Rediscovering the social group: A self-categorization theory.* Oxford: Blackwell.

Wainryb, C., & Turiel, E. (1994). Dominance, subordination, and concepts of personal entitlements in cultural contexts. *Child Development, 65,* 1701–1722.

Winer, B. J. (1971). *Statistical principles in experimental design.* New York: McGraw-Hill.

Winer, B. J., Brown, D. R., & Michels, K. M. (1991). *Statistical principles in empirical design.* New York: McGraw-Hill.

Youniss, J., McLellan, J. A., & Strouse, D. (1994). We're popular, but we're not snobs: Adolescents describe their crowds. In R. Montemayor, G. R. Adams, & T. P. Gullotta (Eds.), *Personal relationships during adolescence* (pp. 101–122). Thousand Oaks, CA: Sage.

Appendix: Scenarios

Student council

Andy, who is a _____, and Mike, who is a _____, are both running for student council. They are both equally qualified. The students can only vote for one of them. Who should the students vote for?

Cheerleading

Allison, who is a _____, and Kylie, who is a _____, are both trying out for the cheerleading squad. They are both equally good at cheerleading at try-outs but there is only room for one more person on the squad. Who should the cheerleaders pick?

National leadership conference

Globe High School has received a grant to send some students to Washington, DC for a national convention on student leadership. The principal has asked the five students who attended the conference last year to select the students who will attend the conference this year. Shelly, who is a _____, and Renee, who is a _____, are both interested in attending the leadership conference. The committee can only nominate one more person to attend the conference. Shelly and Renee are equally qualified. Who should they choose?

Basketball

Brad, who is a _____, and Justin, who is a _____, are both trying out for the basketball team. They are both equally good at try-outs but there is only room for one more person on the team. Who should the jocks pick?

Scholarship

A former Globe High School student has set up a college scholarship fund for one Globe High School student who exhibits promising academic ability and a commitment of service to the community. The principal has put together a student committee to review the applications for the scholarship. Sean, who is a _____, and Tim, who is a _____, both applied for the scholarship. The committee can nominate only one more person for the scholarship. Sean and Tim are equally qualified. Who should they choose?

A Closer Look 4   Leaders and Followers: Peer Pressure in Adolescence

Peers are important contributors to children's social development. Although peers generally exert a positive influence (e.g., support, empathy, intimacy, cooperation), researchers have also explored some of the processes that peers employ that may influence children's behaviors in less positive ways. For example, *peer pressure* is a common experience in childhood and adolescence and refers to implicit or explicit demands to conform to peer requests. Among younger children, this pressure typically pertains to requests to socialize. In adolescence, however, peers often pressure others to engage in deviant activities. Peer pressure increases in later childhood and peaks around ages 13–15 years before decreasing in later adolescence. Allen, Porter, and Mcfarland (2006) explored adolescents' *susceptibility to peer pressure* as a predictor of later adjustment difficulties. Participants were 177 pairs of early adolescents and their nominated best friends. Susceptibility to peer pressure was assessed in terms of the proportion of time target adolescents "changed their mind" in a series of disagreements with their friends arranged during laboratory tasks. As compared to adolescents who were less susceptible to peer pressure, teens who more frequently "gave in" to peer influence had more negative outcomes one year later in terms of peer relationships (e.g., less stable friendships, lower peer acceptance) and socio-emotional functioning (e.g., increased depressive symptoms, externalizing problems, substance use, and likelihood of early sexual activity). The findings illustrate the importance of educating adolescents on the risks of always giving in to peer pressure and for promoting socially acceptable strategies for resisting inappropriate peer requests.

Allen, J. P., Porter, M. R., & Mcfarland, F. C. (2006). Leaders and followers in adolescent close friendships: Susceptibility to peer influence as a predictor of risky behavior, friendship instability, and depression. *Development and Psychopathology, 18,* 155–172.

Classroom Exercises, Debates, and Discussion Questions

- *Classroom discussion.* How might children of different ages answer the question "what is a friend?" What qualities characterize more positive vs. more negative relationships among friends? Does it matter whether friends stick up for you when others let you down? How central is the notion of mutual respect and fairness to being a good friend?
- *Classroom discussion.* What were the cliques and crowds in your high school? How did they differ in their appearance, behaviors, characteristics, and reputations? Why do many adolescents feel it is so important to belong to a crowd? What are the potential functions and benefits of crowd-membership during this age period?
- *Classroom discussion.* What do you think are some of the determinants of being "liked" and/or "disliked" by peers? Is it possible to be popular but have few friends? Are there any ethical issues in asking children to nominate others in their class whom they like or dislike?
- *Classroom debate.* When is it okay to exclude someone from a group? What does it mean to "not fit" the expectations of the group? Are there times when excluding someone from a peer group might be a form of prejudice or bias? What does it feel like to be excluded from a group, and what are the types of reasons that peers use for excluding others?
- *Classroom discussion.* What strategies would you promote among adolescents to resist peer pressure? Why do you think that peer pressure and crowd-membership both become reduced in later adolescence?

Additional Resources

For more about peer relations, see:

Brown, B., Eicher, S. A., & Petrie, S. (1986). The importance of peer group ('crowd') affiliation in adolescence. *Journal of Adolescence, 9*, 73–96.

Dodge, K. A. (1983). Behavioral antecedents of peer social status. *Child Development, 54*, 1386–1399.

Killen, M., Sinno, S., & Margie, N. G. (2007). Children's experiences and judgments about group exclusion and inclusion. In R. Kail (Ed.), *Advances in child psychology* (Vol. 35, pp. 173–218). New York: Elsevier.

Ladd, G. W., Herald-Brown, S. L., & Reiser, M. (2008). Does chronic classroom peer rejection predict the development of children's classroom participation during the grade school years? *Child Development, 79*, 1001–1015.

Rubin, K. H., Bukowski, W., & Parker, J. (2006). Peer interactions, relationships, and groups. In N. Eisenberg (Ed.), *Handbook of child psychology: Social, emotional, and personality development* (6th ed., pp. 571–645). New York: Wiley.

6

THE DEVELOPMENT OF MORALITY

Introduction   **203**

The Development of Children's Orientations toward Moral, Social, and Personal Orders: More than a Sequence in Development   **204**

Elliot Turiel

A New Vision of Moral Development: Epistemology in Psychology   204

Taking the Mind, the Person, and Morality Seriously   206

Progress and Regress in the Study of Morality   210

Conclusion   214

Consistency and Development of Prosocial Dispositions: A Longitudinal Study   **218**

Nancy Eisenberg, Ivanna K. Guthrie, Bridget C. Murphy, Stephanie A. Shepard, Amanda Cumberland, and Gustavo Carlo

Introduction   218

Method   221

Results   224

Discussion   229

Children's Thinking About Diversity of Belief in the Early School Years: Judgments of Relativism, Tolerance, and Disagreeing Persons   **233**

Cecilia Wainryb, Leigh A. Shaw, Marcie Langley, Kim Cottam, and Renee Lewis

Method   237

Results   239

Discussion   243

A Closer Look 5   Learning the Moral of the Story: Education in the Moral Domain   252

Social Development in Childhood and Adolescence: A Contemporary Reader, First Edition. Edited by Melanie Killen and Robert J. Coplan.

Introduction

What constitutes morality in the child? How early does it begin, and how do children acquire moral values? These questions have fascinated psychologists for almost a century. Freud theorized about the origins of morality based on the reflections of adult patients about their relationships with their parents in childhood. Even Darwin investigated the evolution of moral propensities in his diary studies. The contemporary study of morality has been heavily influenced by Piaget (1952) and Kohlberg (1971), who were the first to focus on children's reasoning and judgments about morality (and not just their behavior). This change in focus is significant because many behaviors may look moral or immoral, but without knowing an individual's intentions, the wrong inference can be made. For example, if a child pushes someone down to prevent him from being hit by a branch falling from a tree then this act has a different moral status than if the child pushes someone down because he has brown hair.

Initially, morality was defined as "rule-following behavior," and most research focused on when children complied with adult expectations and obeyed rules. It was postulated that children acquired morality by imitating and observing adults (particularly parents). This definition of morality, however, turned out to be too broad; many rules are not moral rules (e.g., rules concerning chewing gum and where to park your car are not about "morality"). Moreover, children do not passively imitate parents to acquire morality (and if they did, that might be pretty confusing, given that many adults do things that are not "morally" responsible). Subsequently, research focused on children's interpretation, evaluation, and understanding of rules rather than their strict compliance. In this regard, morality came to be seen as intentional behavior reflecting an understanding of the principles of how individuals ought to treat one another, particularly with respect to justice (fairness), others'

welfare (avoiding harm, acting from a prosocial position), and rights (basic rights).

As outlined in the papers in this section, morality is a complex construct and there are many different ways that it gets defined and assessed. For example, much of the research has focused on what criteria children use to distinguish "moral" rules (e.g., about harm and fairness) from "non-moral" (or social) rules (e.g., involving conventions and etiquette). In the first reading in this chapter, Turiel (2008) discusses research on children's moral understanding and theories about how it develops, with a particular focus on how actions, behaviors, and judgments are related. He compares stage theories to domain-specific models, such as the one that he proposes, and discusses current findings, drawing on observations and interviews with children. The second reading considers developmental changes in morality across different age periods. Eisenberg et al. (1999) explore the longitudinal links between prosocial dispositions (caring, sharing, offering comfort) in preschool and prosocial behavior in early adulthood. In the final paper, Wainryb and colleagues (2004) focus on the construct of "tolerance" and under what conditions tolerance might be considered a moral value.

There is a wealth of information about moral development, and research has expanded extensively over the past two decades. Other areas of interest could include how moral emotions are related to moral judgments, how stereotypes influence moral decision-making, how moral exclusion occurs (and why), moral identity, and moral neuroscience.

References

Kohlberg, L. (1971). From is to ought: How to commit the naturalistic fallacy and get away with it in the study of moral development. In T. Mischel (Ed.), *Psychology and genetic epistemology* (pp. 151–235). New York: Academic Press.

Piaget, J. (1952). *The origins of intelligence in children.* New York: International Universities Press.

The Development of Children's Orientations toward Moral, Social, and Personal Orders: More than a Sequence in Development

Elliot Turiel

In 1958, the same year as the first publication of what is now *Human Development* (then titled *Vita Humana: International Journal of Human Development*), Lawrence Kohlberg completed a lengthy, ambitious, and impressive doctoral dissertation at the University of Chicago. The title of the dissertation was *The development of modes of moral thinking and choice in the years 10 to 16*. The main component of the dissertation was Kohlberg's presentation of research he had conducted on the moral judgments of children and adolescents. The research itself was innovative and out of the mainstream of psychology in that it involved in-depth interviews and qualitative analyses of responses. The research and analyses of findings were, at the same time, mainstream in that Kohlberg took great care to account for scientific considerations. These included detailed analyses of the rationale for his samples of participants, for measurement issues, and the use of appropriate statistical analyses in a developmental study (including the use of the Guttman quasi-simplex correlation matrix and factor analyses). He combined the qualitative methods and analyses with quantitative analyses. He formulated a rigorous and complex system of coding in an attempt to account for 30 aspects or considerations that were used in the six 'types' of developmentally ordered structures of thought (in the dissertation these were types 0–5, which were subsequently changed to 1–6, and later to stages rather than types). The coding systematized the qualitative analyses in ways that could be put to quantitative analyses.

A New Vision of Moral Development: Epistemology in Psychology

In his dissertation, Kohlberg also extensively reviewed and critiqued other approaches to morality. He contrasted his approach with the then dominant behav-

iorist, socialization, and psychoanalytic approaches on several dimensions. One dimension of great significance that he emphasized was the need for inclusion of definitional-philosophical groundings for psychological analyses of morality. Kohlberg maintained that the failure of mainstream psychological research to attend to the definitional bases of morality was itself intellectually and scientifically unsound.

Within that context, Kohlberg had a big impact on the field within 10 years of the completion of his dissertation. Indeed, his first publications in the early 1960s were very influential. Book chapters published in 1963 ('Moral development and identification') and 1964 ('Development of moral character and ideology') were heavy in the presentation of theoretical arguments and data to refute the dominant approaches of the time. He later published very influential essays in which he linked his work on morality to general theory about social development and the child's interactions with the social environment (e.g., Kohlberg, 1969). In other essays (e.g., Kohlberg, 1971) he tackled in greater detail the problem of connecting social scientific research on morality with substantive philosophical-epistemological formulations about the moral realm. He argued that most of the social scientific research was inadequate because it identified variables of acquisition apart from considerations of the nature of that being acquired.

Although Kohlberg did present in those essays the findings of his research and the formulations of the six-type (stage) progression in the development of moral judgments, his article in *Vita Humana* was particularly important because it was the first report of his findings and theoretical formulations in a research article format. In my view, it is far from accidental that the research was published in *Vita Humana/Human Development*. It took a nontraditional and interdisciplinary journal (which was then only 5 years old) to publish the type of innovative research conducted by Kohlberg and presented in a somewhat unorthodox style. The article is not in the usual style of inclusion of delineated methods and results sections (but all of the procedures and findings are presented clearly) and includes, in the tradition of Piaget's book publications, the liberal use of participants' responses in order to illustrate the meaning of the findings (I venture to guess that Kohlberg would have encountered difficulties in getting the article published in standard journals).

In the intervening years much has occurred in theorizing and research on moral development, a good deal of which was influenced by Kohlberg. In my view, the most important consequence of Kohlberg's writings is that the psychological study of morality was taken out of the confines of narrow, strictly psychological analyses of biological determinism, learning, analyses of mechanisms of acquisition, and psychodynamic processes. Much of the extant psychological research had simply attempted to apply hypothesized psychological constructs regarding values or behavioral acquisition to explain some vaguely defined notions of morality. Accordingly, constructs like learning through stimulus-response reinforcement, imitation, modeling, internalization through identification, the effects of different child rearing practices, and learning of self-control—to name a few—were studied in relation to the child's acquisition of such features as social rules, values, norms, and sometimes arbitrarily defined restrictions established in laboratory or naturalistic settings. For the most part, the moral outcome variables, lacking theoretical formulations related to definitional criteria, were by-products stemming from the necessity for measures of moral acquisition to connect to the psychological constructs. In some of these formulations, especially psychoanalytic and behaviorist theories, there was a conscious intellectual effort to remove morality from its status as a unique realm of autonomous decision making through propositions that it is psychologically determined and that decisions reflect unconscious processes (lack of awareness or deeply unconscious in the Freudian sense). In conjunction with the epistemological considerations, Kohlberg (1963, 1964) reviewed evidence bearing on the prevalent ideas regarding the ways children acquired morality. He showed that the evidence did not lend support to the propositions that parental child rearing practices, positive and negative reinforcements, and processes of identification and imitation were associated with 'strength of conscience' or extent of feelings of guilt, adherence to societal rules or norms, or the acquisition of abilities to resist temptation.

It could be said that psychological and anthropological positions asserting that morality involves the incorporation of the values, standards, or norms of one's culture did include, at least implicitly, definitional criteria. This is because in some of these positions it was maintained that morality obtains its force by virtue of its place in the cultural context and, therefore, morality needs to be seen in relativistic terms. Norms are arbitrarily determined and comparisons of relative adequacy cannot be made between cultures. Kohlberg provided incisive critiques of this type of cultural relativism as well (see especially Kohlberg, 1971).

Kohlberg's critiques of the standard psychological explanations and of cultural relativism were not solely based on his formulations of the substance of morality. The critiques and assertions that substantive definitions of morality were not independent of psychological functioning were also based on theoretical propositions regarding thought and development in children, adolescents, and adults. He extended and developed theoretical propositions touched upon by others for the social and moral realms (e.g., Baldwin, 1906; Piaget, 1932) that had been applied more extensively to nonsocial cognitive development (especially by Piaget and his colleagues, and Werner, 1957 and his colleagues). To state it simply, humans are thinking beings and their mental development is a function of their interactions, starting in infancy, with complex and multifaceted environments. In these views, thought is not independent of emotions (Kohlberg, 1969; Piaget, 1981; Turiel, 2006). As stated by Kohlberg in the [2008] reprinted article, a goal of his research was to understand the relation of 'the development of moral thought to moral conduct and emotion' (p. 8). Two features are important to note in this regard. One is that the primary emotions associated with morality are positive ones like sympathy, empathy, and respect; they are not negative or aversive emotions like fear, anxiety, disgust, and guilt. The second is that emotions do not drive thought and behavior and individuals do not simply act nonrationally or irrationally because of unconscious or unreflective emotional reactions. Emotional appraisals are part of reasoning that involves taking into account the reactions of others and self (Nussbaum, 1999). The emotional reactions of people are a central part of moral judgments, and it is reciprocal interactions, along with reflections upon one's own judgments and cultural practices or societal arrangements, that influence development (Kohlberg, 1969; Turiel, 2002). Moral thinking is not a function of the internalization of social or cultural content. As put by Kohlberg (2008, p. 19), 'While these successive bases of moral order do spring from the child's awareness of the external world, they also represent active processes of organizing or ordering the world.'

Although many researchers were persuaded by Kohlberg's arguments and themselves applied his six-stage formulations to questions of their own interest, Kohlberg's influence was even wider and deeper. In my estimation, he at least indirectly influenced many researchers who took alternate theoretical perspectives. Researchers began to take the realm of morality seriously and did not view children as unwilling or reluctant recipients of coerced or imposed values, standards, or norms.

As an example, cultural psychologists like Shweder (Shweder, Mahapatra, & Miller, 1987; Shweder, Much, Mahapatra, & Park, 1997) took an epistemological standpoint in maintaining that there are alternative types of 'duty-based' and 'rights-based' moralities which stem from fundamentally different rationalities pertaining to conceptions of self and social relations that can differ by cultural frameworks. These analyses of the development of morality differ from prior culturally relativistic conceptions of morality as incorporation of standards, in that children are viewed as developing an organized moral system through participation in and communications about a system of cultural practices.

Another shift of some significance is that many researchers began to view children as possessing moral capacities, not imposed by adult authorities, at early ages. Researchers have attended to children's spontaneous reactions of a positive kind, as well as to their nonaversive emotional propensities. Observational studies were conducted to examine whether children engage in behaviors like helping others and sharing (Radke-Yarrow, Zahn-Waxler, & Chapman, 1983). It was well documented that children react to the needs and pain of others and act to further their welfare. Researchers also attended to emotions like sympathy and empathy, instead of solely or mainly looking to aversive emotions (Eisenberg & Fabes, 1991; Hoffman, 1984, 2000).

More generally, there was increased interest in placing the study of morality into the contexts of developmental transformations and judgments about issues of justice. Different aspects of justice, as guided by philosophical formulations, have been examined in younger and older children. This includes studies of concepts of distributive justice (Damon, 1977, 1980) and fairness in institutional contexts like schools (Thorkildsen, 1989). Another influence, I believe, is that the study of action is now usually connected to judgments (e.g., Blasi, 1993; Colby & Damon, 1992), as opposed to the earlier and common view that moral judgments are disembodied from individuals' actions (e.g., Aronfreed, 1968). Some have proposed that connections between moral judgments and actions are mediated by the strength of a sense of a moral self or a commitment to an identity strongly structured by morality (Blasi, 1993; Colby & Damon, 1992). By contrast, I have proposed that actions are closely tied to moral and other social judgments for most people because of the embodiment of reasoning in action, and that coming to decisions in thought and actions involves a coordination of different types of judgments (moral and otherwise) in particular contexts (Turiel, 2003, 2008a).

Taking the Mind, the Person, and Morality Seriously

My propositions regarding social actions as part of embodied human functioning that involves coordination of different types of judgments and their application in social contexts were put forth about 40 years after Kohlberg's publication in *Vita Humana*. Although aspects of these propositions diverge from some of Kohlberg's formulations, they are consistent with the general developmental, structural, and moral framework he pioneered. The idea that moral and social judgments are closely linked to actions is based on the assumptions that individuals are active in thinking about the social environment, that they have mental/emotional propensities to care about the welfare of others and fairness in their relationships, that they scrutinize their world and reflect upon their own and others' judgments and actions, and that in the process they are not driven solely by emotional or unconscious biological or psychological forces to act without choice. These are all assumptions embedded in Kohlberg's approach (as well as that of Piaget).

On a personal note, my work was directly influenced by Lawrence Kohlberg and his powerful theory, which was buttressed by sound empirical research (as embodied in the [2008] reprinted article). As a beginning graduate student in 1960 at Yale University I was able to study with Kohlberg (subsequently at longer distance as he moved to the University of Chicago). As a more advanced graduate student and later as a colleague, I collaborated with him on several projects (we also taught together).

I took up the important question emerging from Kohlberg's formulations as to how transformations occur from one stage to the next. One side of that question also entails specifying criteria to explain why one stage of thought represents an advance over previous stages. In recognizing the need to address the latter question directly in any developmental formulation, Kohlberg (and I for a time) worked with what seemed to be a promising model at the time. It was that development involves a process of differentiation and integration (Werner, 1957), and that any given stage of thought entails differentiations of moral value from nonmoral considerations. Each stage, therefore, would bring clarity (and increased equilibration) to matters that were previously confused (not differentiated from each other).

As Kohlberg discussed in the [2008] reprinted article, type (stage) 1 thinking entails recognition that the moral value of life is undifferentiated from material value. The thinking that characterizes this earliest developmental phase 'involves a failure to differentiate the self's point of view from that of others, or to differentiate what the community holds as a shared or moral value (the value of life) and what the individual holds as a private value (the desire for furniture)'

(p. 13). In the next type (2) of thinking there is a differentiation of the viewpoints of self and others so that there is 'an increase in the use of reciprocity' and in 'notions of relativism of value' (p. 14). However, a morality of need and reciprocity is not sufficiently advanced to account for a sense of obligation (p. 15). Kohlberg's analyses of the next four types are also based on specifications of increased differentiations with each developmental advance. In a later essay (Kohlberg, 1971), he summarized the differentiation process across stages as follows:

> The individual whose judgments are at stage 6 asks 'Is it morally right?' and means by morally right something different from punishment (stage 1), prudence (stage 2), conformity to authority (stages 3 and 4), etc. Thus, the responses of lower-stage subjects are not moral for the same reasons that responses of higher-stage subjects to aesthetic or other morally neutral matters fail to be moral. ... This is what we had in mind earlier when we spoke of our stages as representing an increased differentiation of moral values and judgments from other types of judgments and values. (p. 216)

This proposition about developmental progressions was not implausible and led to research on the processes of transition, in adolescence, from thought supposedly lacking a differentiation of morality and rules, authority and conventions (stage 4) to the next form of thinking (stage 5), in which a morality of justice and rights is differentiated from convention (Turiel, 1974). However, a series of studies (Nucci & Turiel, 1978; Turiel, 1975, 1978, 1979) showed that adolescents as well as younger children make judgments about the contingency of social conventions (i.e., they are contingent on rules, authority, and coordination in social systems) that differ from their judgments about the noncontingency and generalizability of moral issues based on furthering welfare, justice, and rights. It has now been very well documented (and widely reported) that judgments about the domain of morality differ in type from judgments about the conventions of social systems and about arenas of personal jurisdiction (for reviews, see Nucci, 2001; Smetana, 2006; Turiel, 1983, 1998, 2002, 2006). At early ages (4–6 years), children do not confuse morality with nonmoral issues like prudence, conformity to rules and authority, or personal choices. These constitute distinct social domains with separate developmental pathways.

Identifying judgments from different domains requires disentangling different components of social situations. Many social situations include moral and nonmoral components, perhaps posing people with conflicts, the need to coordinate the different domains of judgment, and to draw priorities among them (Turiel, 2008b). Many of the situations used by Kohlberg to elicit responses were multifaceted in these ways. An example is the story in which a doctor is deciding whether or not to adhere to the wishes of a dying woman in pain that he give her 'a good dose of painkiller like ether or morphine' to make her die sooner. Although this situation raises moral issues of the value of life, the responsibilities of doctors to patients, and legal issues, it also raises issues about the quality of life and personal choices in that regard and when it is legitimate for an individual to end her life in the context of a terminal illness and great pain. Recognizing that the doctor's decision has pragmatic consequences for him, the 10-year-old boy, Jimmy, said, 'From the doctor's point of view, it could be a murder charge.' Recognizing that the situation confronted the dying woman with personal choices regarding the quality of her life and the great pain she was experiencing, he said, 'It should be up to her; it's her life, not the law's life.' [quoted by Kohlberg, 2008, p. 14.]

Kohlberg interpreted these responses solely in terms of judgments of a moral kind: that morality for the 10-year-old is instrumental, hedonistic (pleasure and pain), and based on a person's ownership rights. An alternative interpretation is that the boy viewed the woman's wishes in terms of her legitimate realms of personal jurisdiction and the doctor's choices, which the boy assumed to be one of helping her or putting himself in legal jeopardy. Subsequent research showed that children of this age, as well as younger and older people, do form judgments in domains of personal choices, including pragmatics, that are different from moral considerations (Nucci, 1981, 1996). Therefore, it may well be that Jimmy was making judgments about what he saw as nonmoral features of the situation and that he was not defining morally right action instrumentally or in terms of hedonistic calculations.

We do not actually know whether Jimmy was making differentiations between the moral and personal

domains since his responses to those complex and domain-multifaceted situations were not analyzed for such a possibility. We do know, however, that children even younger than Jimmy make distinctly moral judgments when responding to straightforward (labeled prototypical) situations about issues of welfare, justice, and rights. Although the research on domains indicates that the six-stage sequence proposed by Kohlberg is inaccurate, it verifies several of his key propositions. In the first place, it was through attention to the definitional parameters of the moral realm and how it differs from other social realms that we were able to uncover the ways children make distinctions in social judgments. Moreover, the research shows that morality is a substantive and independent domain of thinking (but starting quite a bit earlier in age than thought by Kohlberg), that moral judgments are constructed through children's interactions with the social world, and not the incorporation of preexisting values (Nucci & Nucci, 1982a, 1982b; Nucci & Turiel, 1978; Nucci & Weber, 1995), that moral judgments are connected with early emerging positive emotions (Arsenio, 1988), and that moral judgments and emotions are associated with social actions (Turiel, 2003, 2008a). The identification of the domains of moral, social, and personal judgments has provided a better window into how individuals make decisions since in doing so they coordinate different considerations in social situations (Turiel, 2008b).

The issue of rights, an important aspect of morality, provides a clear example of how individuals coordinate different considerations in coming to decisions. In various disciplines, including philosophy, political science, and psychology, there has been a tendency to approach the concept of rights as either well understood and applied uniformly across situations or poorly understood and therefore subordinated to other moral or social considerations (e.g., Protho & Grigg, 1960; Sarat, 1975). For instance, findings from large-scale public opinion surveys that most people endorse rights in some situations but not in other situations have been interpreted to reflect inadequate understandings of rights. A psychological approach to rights as inadequately or adequately understood is evident in Kohlberg's six levels of conceptions of rights (2008, p. 10), as one of the cognitive aspects of morality, whereby it is not until levels 5 and 6 that there emerges a conception of universal rights having priority over other pragmatic, relativistic, and social considerations.

An alternative view taken by some philosophers (Dworkin, 1977; Gewirth, 1982) is that rights can be well understood and yet weighed against competing moral and social norms. Consistent with the domain approach and the proposition that decisions can involve coordination of different considerations, Helwig (1995, 1997) has shown that by early ages children do uphold and understand rights (e.g., freedom of speech and religion) in the abstract as obligatory norms that should apply to different groups or cultures. Across ages, including adulthood, rights are upheld in some situations and not in others. For example, in some contexts rights are given less priority than preventing psychological harm (e.g., a public speech with racial slurs), physical harm (a speech advocating violence), and inequalities (advocating exclusion). The research indicates that those who subordinate rights to other such considerations do not fail to understand concepts of rights.

A number of other studies point to the need to identify domains of judgment and coordination in social and moral decision making. In research on adolescents and parents it has been found that different domains are at play in both conflicted and harmonious relationships (Smetana, 2002). In turn, adolescents' social interactions differ in accord with the moral, conventional, and personal domains (Smetana, 1995). A series of studies with children and adolescents on social exclusion, as related to prejudice and discrimination, has used an analogous approach to the research on rights (Killen, Lee-Kim, McGlothlin, & Stagnor, 2002). Children do judge exclusion based on gender, race, or ethnicity to be morally wrong in the abstract and in particular situations. However, they also consider other group activities, such as goals in team competitions, in judging acts of exclusion. Group goals, as well as individual prerogatives, are coordinated with moral goals in coming to conclusions about the validity of excluding people from activities (see also Killen, Sinno, & Margie, 2007).

Honesty and deception are topics of recent research that exemplifies several of the principles of structure, thought, development, people's propensities to try to discriminate among different aspects of social relationships, as well as their continual scrutiny of justice in social relationships, systems of societal arrangements, and cultural practices. That honesty does all this work is somewhat ironic since the topic has so often been treated as a straightforward, quintessential moral good. Honesty is always at the forefront of lists of character traits and virtues given by those who regard morality to be the consistent application of one's acquired moral dispositions (Bennett, 1993; Ryan, 1989; Wynne, 1985). In many studies, children's internalization of morality was assessed by placing them into experimental and classroom situations where they would have the opportunity to cheat or lie (Aronfreed, 1968; Grinder, 1961, 1964; Hartshorne & May, 1928–1930; Parke & Walters, 1967). Children's acts of cheating or lying in these situations were regarded as indicators of a still insufficient incorporation of morality in their lives. Conceptions of trust and related honesty have also been regarded as central to the development of moral judgments (Colby & Kohlberg, 1987; Piaget, 1932).

Honesty is important in the realm of morality. It is not, however, a straightforward or simple indicator of more (acting honestly) or less (acting deceptively) adequate moral development or moral decisions. Two examples—one hypothetical, used in philosophical discourse, and the other from real-life events—can serve as a means to briefly illustrate that honesty is not the straightforward moral good it is often assumed to be. Philosophers arguing that acts of deception are not necessarily morally wrong have used the example of how one should respond to a murderer who asks where his intended victim has gone (Bok, 1978/1999). In this case, saving a life would take precedence over acting honestly. For those who hid Jews from Nazis and lied about it during World War II, deception at great risk to themselves was judged to be the morally right and courageous course of action. Research findings support the idea that people commonly weigh varying moral and social considerations in deciding whether to be honest. Although most people value honesty, research shows that deception is also judged to be necessary in some contexts. Deception is judged acceptable in order to spare the feelings of others, to protect people from physical harm and avoid injustices, and to promote perceived legitimate personal ends in the face of relationships of unequal power

(Abu-Lughod, 1993; Lewis, 1993; Perkins & Turiel, 2007; Turiel, 2002; Turiel & Perkins, 2004; Wikan, 1996).

As one example with adults, it was found that physicians judged deception of an insurance company acceptable if it was the only means of obtaining treatment for patients with serious medical conditions (Freeman, Rathore, Weinfurt, Schulman, & Sulmasy, 1999). Physicians (reluctantly) endorsing deception in such situations gave priority to protecting the welfare of their patients over honesty. Other research (Perkins & Turiel, 2007) similarly shows that adolescents judge it acceptable to lie to parents who attempt to get them to act in ways they consider morally wrong. The adolescents also judged deception acceptable as a way of circumventing perceived undue control by parents regarding issues considered to be legitimately part of the adolescents' personal jurisdiction. It is important to note, however, that the adolescents did judge deception wrong in contexts where parents exercise their legitimate authority or in relationships of greater equality (with peers). Corresponding results were obtained with adults regarding the acceptability of deception in the context of inequalities and power differences in marital relationships (Turiel & Perkins, 2004).

The uses of deception in relationships of inequality involve moral and social opposition and resistance to existing societal arrangements. It also involves resistance to cultural practices that foster inequalities in gender relationships within traditional, patriarchal contexts (Abu-Lughod, 1993; Wikan, 1996). Moral opposition and resistance occur in everyday life, at varying ages (at least by early adolescence) and in Western and non-Western cultures. The ubiquity of opposition and resistance shows, first of all, that scrutiny of existing norms and practices are not activities undertaken only by those at 'advanced' levels of moral development. Kohlberg did leave room in his theory for moral resistance, but he thought that it came only with advancement beyond a 'morality of conventional role-conformity' to a 'morality of self-accepted moral principles' (the two highest stages). He also implicitly assumed that it would not occur in all cultures since he thought that people in some cultures rarely advanced beyond the 'conventional' stages (Kohlberg, 1969, 1971). That morally motivated opposition and

resistance occurs at relatively young ages in a variety of social situations and various cultures provides additional support for the proposition that a differentiated domain of morality develops early.

The examples of resistance through acceptance and use of deception also point to the importance of reasoned choices in emotionally laden situations. Those decisions are by no means hard, cold calculations. As examples, Abu-Lughod (1993) and Wikan (1996) observed rural Bedouin and urban (in Cairo) women who engaged in acts of deliberate and planned deception in order to get around restrictions imposed by men on many of their activities, including work, education, and leisure. The restrictions evoked strong emotions of resentment and associated judgments of unfairness. The acts of resistance, in spite of fears of the risks involved, were motivated by emotional commitments to their justice. Part of the reasoned choices people make stem from their critical scrutiny of their social interactions.

Progress and Regress in the Study of Morality

Thus far, I have discussed what I consider to be social scientific advances in the study and explanations of moral development in the work of Lawrence Kohlberg and in subsequent work in a plurality of theoretical frameworks. Perhaps analogously to development, social scientific advances occur with starts and stops, progress and reversions to old ways. I believe we are experiencing reversions in some quarters in the study of moral development. We are witnessing a reversion to a reliance on psychological and biological variables to the exclusion of definitional-epistemological considerations and people's minds. Psychological and biological processes of emotional and thereby nonrational types are taken as given and seen as determining moral reactions.

The field of psychology always seems to be drawn to explaining people's decisions and actions as different from what they appear to be in laypersons' perceptions. Of course, the most visible and most popular theories during a good part of the twentieth century—psychoanalytic and behaviorist theories—took that approach. Psychoanalytic theory essentially transformed human beings into actors whose conscious thoughts, feelings, and actions for the most part disguised true but unknown, deep unconscious motivations. Equally radical behaviorist theories transformed humans into mechanistic responders whose actions were due to ways they had been shaped by environmental forces (reinforcement, conditioning). Behaviorism began with forceful denials of the existence of consciousness, which was treated as a secular version of the idea of a soul (Watson, 1924). B. F. Skinner (1971) famously proclaimed that just about all our mentalist terms, such as thinking, personality, autonomy, freedom, dignity, and choice, are illusions, with no psychological reality, that people maintain to elevate him or herself.

One does not have to be a Freudian or Skinnerian to provide psychological explanations based on the idea that people's decisions are not what they appear to be to laypersons or that many of their understandings are illusory. Two strands of this sort have been prominent. One is that the mind continually plays tricks on us (though 'us' does not usually include the theorists) and the other is that we are driven by our emotions, not our reasoning, and we are often fooled into believing that it is our reasoning and choices that produce decisions and actions. The field of social psychology, dating back at least to theories of cognitive dissonance (Festinger, 1957), is replete with experiments aimed at demonstrating the ways attitudes, thinking, and irrational processes most often override behaviors. Recently, there has been a focus in research on the use of 'heuristics' and biases, which presumably explain how people's use of cognitive short cuts results in nonrational economic decisions (e.g., that go against one's self-interest) and probabilistic choices (Kahneman, Slovic, & Tversky, 1982). Heuristics produce errors in judgment since they involve the application of rules of thumb instead of use of evidence and/or knowledge about probabilities (for a critique, see Turiel, 2008b).

Another current trend is to explain decisions in many realms as overdetermined by subconscious brain functions. Conscious, reasoned, or reflective decisions, as well as autonomy and choice, are seen to be as illusory as Skinner thought all mentalist explanations. One line of research has attempted to show that consciousness or awareness of decisions come after the decisions were already made. As an example, it has been found that in experimental situations actions like pressing a button or flicking a finger occurred slightly (½ s) after the occurrence of brain signals associated with the actions. These types of findings are interpreted to mean that conscious awareness of decisions comes after the decision has already been taken in a subconscious way. Therefore, our beliefs that we deliberately or consciously make decisions and choose from alternatives are merely illusions. They are after-the-fact explanations for what we have no alternative to doing[1]. Often there is little in the way of explanation of how it is that we act in these automatic ways—except that somehow, invoking material cause, the brain does it. Perhaps the most common explanation as to why the brain does it is that of genetic inheritance. The process of evolution has resulted in hard-wired, genetic makeup determining thoughts and actions.

Some of these propositions regarding moral evaluations are betwixt and between psychoanalytic and behaviorist theories in ways that render them with little explanatory power. Brain functioning, intuitions, or emotions that simply exist apart from awareness are said to result in (predetermined?) actions. By contrast, at the heart of psychoanalytic theory was an attempt to explain how and why conscious perceptions and awareness become deeply unconscious and placed out of awareness. The structure and functions of unconscious processes were described, which included explication of forces accounting for conscious unavailability. For strict behaviorists, the explanation of actions as independent of conscious awareness or reasoning was based on a duality between actions and mind, with actions following laws having nothing to do with cognitive activities.

Some speculate that individuals' moral positions are just there. They are just there as emotionally buttressed intuitions, which may be reinforced by cultural practices (Haidt, 2001). I label these speculations because of the lack of evidence to support the position and because of the minimal effort at explanation of their existence (that they are just there). The speculations go further with unsubstantiated and highly implausible, reductionist claims that reasoning is used only after decisions are reached as a means of either justifying the decision or, in a deprecation of human thinking, as lawyer-like ways of convincing others to agree with one's position. These claims rest on the idea, already discussed, that moral responses, which are emotionally based, occur automatically and rapidly, with no thought, reflection, or scrutiny (Haidt, 2001). Understandings of issues of welfare, justice, and rights are merely after-the-fact justifications and not the fundamental bases of morality that people are deluded to think they are. The layperson uses after-the-fact ideas instrumentally to justify predetermined decisions as would a lawyer (and not the psychologist putting forth these propositions) in attempts to convince a jury of a position on the case. The deprecation of layperson thinking (not to mention the implicit deprecation of lawyers) is based on a few dramatic examples taken as prototypical of morality and generalized to the many moral issues people confront. One is the issue of incest. Presumably, people react with intense negative emotions (perhaps disgust) in a rapid fashion in evaluating incest as wrong even when presented as occurring between consenting adults who take all the necessary precautions to avoid pregnancy. Another example is that people in some cultures respond in a similar way to eating dog meat (Haidt, Koller, & Dias, 1993). The line of reasoning is that since these types of issues evoke (supposedly) rapid emotional and unexplainable reactions, all of morality functions that way. These generalizations from the few examples to all the familiar moral issues and issues of social justice people deal with all the time are left untested. Moreover, the position by necessity must be absent of epistemological criteria for the moral realm since it is seen as a realm uninfluenced by analytic criteria. Moreover, it is the nature of behavioral reactions that renders an act moral. That is, the only available criterion for morality is the following: an issue that evokes an intense emotional evaluation or reaction of a rapid type would be moral by virtue of its reaction (for further discussion of these issues, see Turiel, 2006). In these formulations, the proposition central to Kohlberg that individuals engage in active processes of organizing the world is denied in favor of the proposition that morality is due to how individuals are buffeted by their own psyches. Morality is almost entirely taken out of the realm of philosophy and psychologized.

Recent neuroscience research on morality has also been insufficiently concerned with epistemological analyses and relies too much on a few dramatic examples (though different from incest and eating dog meat) involving tricky problems (the 'gotcha' kind too commonly used in psychological research). Neuroscience research on morality has failed to take into account established findings from developmental psychology, which might help guide the choices of tasks in neuroimaging studies. The result, I would argue, is a proliferation of mechanistic explanations in that the only features examined underlying moral decisions are brain functions and subconscious emotional reactions.

The lack of concern with epistemological issues in evolutionary and biological studies of morality goes back a number of years to when the sociobiologist, E.O. Wilson, proclaimed that 'Scientists and humanists should consider together the possibility that the time has come for ethics to be removed temporarily from the hands of the philosophers and biologicized' (Wilson, 1975, p. 562). At the time, Wilson's proclamation of independence from philosophy received a fair amount of criticism, not for the call for inclusion of biological analyses of morality, but for the call for exclusion of philosophy. Wilson's call went largely unheeded until recently when evolutionary psychologists and neuroscientists turned their attention to the biological side of morality without systematic or rigorous grounding in definitions of the moral realm.

Two prominent lines of research illustrate how this is the case. One line stems from researchers who study people with brain impairments (e.g., Damasio, 1994; Koenigs, Young, Adolphs, Tranel, Cushman, Hauser, & Damasio, 2007). Although these researchers have appropriately stated an interest in studying connections among biology, rationality, emotions, and feelings (Damasio, 1994), the analyses of morality leave much to be desired regarding the types of emotions involved and how morality is defined. As one example, Damasio lists a hodgepodge of emotions presumably associated with morality: sympathy, embarrassment, shame, guilt, pride, jealousy, envy, gratitude, admiration, indignation, contempt, and disgust. No effort is made to distinguish these very different types of emotions, some of which are positive and some aversive, or to specify which play what role in moral acquisition or moral decisions. Similarly, undifferentiated definitions are provided, which fail to account for the types of domain distinctions evident in the judgments of children and adults (Turiel, 2006; see also Killen & Smetana, 2007). Damasio reverts to vague notions, lumping together terms like social conventions, ethical rules, religious beliefs, law, and justice. No analyses are provided of these categories or how they are formed. Other references by Damasio (2003) to the moral realm include the idea that social conventions and ethical rules are manifestations of homeostatic and cooperative relationships regulated by culture. As we have seen, however, morality entails goals other than equilibrium and cooperation since it importantly involves struggle, opposition, and resistance to perceived unfair practices of inequality and hierarchy that are regulated by culture. By contrast, Damasio sees conventions and social rules as mechanisms for achieving homeostasis within social groups in the context of social hierarchies and inequalities: 'It is not difficult to imagine the emergence of justice and honor out of practices of cooperation. Yet another layer of social emotions, expressed in the form of dominant or submissive behaviors within the group, would have played an important role in the give and take that define cooperation' (Damasio, 2003, p. 163). The types of critical scrutiny of relationships of dominance and subordination documented in the research discussed above has little place in these formulations.

A second and related line of research has focused on neuroimaging studies of people making moral decisions. The apparent strategy is to use tasks or moral problems that clearly seem to have moral relevance and that can be approached from a utilitarian-philosophic perspective. The tasks have clear moral relevance because they pertain to the question of saving lives. However, the tasks are anything but straightforward regarding the issues of the value of life and decisions on acting to save lives. The way I would characterize it is that participants in these studies are essentially posed with the problem of whether it is permissible for them to act as executioners. In addition, the tasks are set up so as to maximize that people would make contradictory decisions (the gotcha part of proclivities in some psychological research). Participants are asked to 'act as executioners' by presenting them with what are referred to as

trolley-car-bystander and trolley-car-footbridge scenarios. The bystander scenario is as follows: 'A runaway trolley is about to run over and kill five people, but a bystander can throw a switch that will turn the trolley onto a side track, where it will kill only one person.' This scenario presents participants with the nightmarish problem, from a moral point of view, of whether it is alright to act as an executioner since the question posed is: 'Is it permissible to throw the switch?' The scenario involves a utilitarian calculation as to whether it is better to sacrifice one life to save more lives. The 'trick' part of the research comes in the even more nightmarish footbridge version: 'A runaway trolley is about to run over and kill five people, but a bystander who is standing on a footbridge can shove a man in front of the train, saving the five people but killing the man.' Still acting as utilitarian executioners, participants need to decide if it is permissible to save five lives by sacrificing one, but in this case by actually pushing a man to his death.

It has been found that people respond to the two scenarios differently. Most state that it is permissible to throw the switch in order to save five people, but most state as well that it is not permissible to push a man even though that act would save the same number of people. Since the utilitarian calculations are the same in the two scenarios, these findings are taken to mean that moral decisions are often non-rational, but instead intuitive, and emotionally determined. The argument is supposedly buttressed by findings that different parts of the brain are activated in the two scenarios.

There are several serious problems with these methods of study and interpretations of the findings that I briefly list here. First, the researchers treat the trolley car tasks as representative examples of moral problems involving utilitarian calculations. In real life, however, a decision as to whether to take a life in these ways is highly unusual for most people, poses complex considerations, and is particularly charged with emotion because of the very issues that make it moral: the perceived value and sacredness of life and prohibitions against taking a life. These scenarios are hard cases because meeting the value of life requires repudiating the value of life. Such situations pose very difficult decisions involving several considerations and requiring their coordination.

A second and related problem lies in the presumption that rationality entails utilitarian calculations only. It is this presumption that leads to the conclusion that as people judge the two trolley car problems differently they are acting out of emotion and intuitively. However, the trolley-car-footbridge scenario most likely constitutes a different situation from the trolley-car-bystander scenario. The former presents a compounded problem involving the saving of lives, taking a life, the natural course of events, the responsibility of individuals altering natural courses, and causing someone's death very directly. The emotions and coordination involved are more complex in one than the other. Another scenario that has been used in this line of research contains even more complex coordination. It is a scenario in which it is stated that a doctor can save five patients who are dying from organ failure by cutting up and killing a sixth healthy patient to use his organs for the others. In an even more complex way than the footbridge scenario, the 'transplant' scenario also raises issues about a doctor's duties and responsibilities, the power granted to individuals to make life-and-death decisions, the legal system, and societal roles and arrangements. Not very surprisingly, very few judged it permissible for the doctor to use a healthy patient's organs to save five others.

Therefore, these types of scenarios pose particular types of emotionally laden problems with multiple considerations that are difficult to reconcile without violating serious moral precepts in order to achieve serious moral goals. In this sense, the scenarios used in the neuroscience studies have affinities with the types of moral situations used by Kohlberg in his research. In both cases there has been a lack of attention to how individuals think and feel about the various components, and their coordination, in these types of situations. In the neuroscience research, gross generalizations are made from these unusual situations to moral functioning in general. The seeming inconsistencies in responses to the supposedly same situations (i.e., the utilitarian calculations) have been taken to mean that morality is due to evolutionarily determined, emotionally based intuitions and that reasoning is merely rationalization of and justification for subconscious decisions. These approaches to moral acquisition and functioning entail one-dimensional, causal explanations rather than ones that attempt to integrate biology, individual-environment interactions, thought, and emotions.

Conclusion

The commemoration of the 50th anniversary of *Human Development* provides a good opportunity to reflect upon progress and lack thereof in several areas of theory and research on human development. Reprinting a classic article by Lawrence Kohlberg helps bring to conscious awareness the role and influence he has had in promoting greater understandings of morality and its development, and has allowed me to reflect upon shifts that have occurred over the past 40 years and more. In the process, I have used the opportunity to point to what I view as lessons missed or ignored from Kohlberg's rich theoretical formulations, sound empirical work, and incisive reflections about and critiques of social scientific analyses of morality.

One lesson to be learned, in my view, is that we should not psychologize or biologicize morality and its development. By this I mean that morality, and much else in human functioning, should not be approached solely from the viewpoint of biological determinism or particular mechanisms that essentially serve to reduce moral functioning to processes that are strictly psychological mechanisms. The moral realm should not be rendered a one-dimensional, causal psychological phenomenon because much more is at work. Kohlberg pointed us in the right directions with a multifaceted conception of morality that included analyses of the integration of thought, emotions, actions, and development. In my view, he captured necessary aspects of morality through his emphasis on how, starting at an early age, individuals attempt to understand their social worlds, deal with how people should relate to one another, engage in reciprocal interactions, and in the process construct judgments about welfare, justice, and rights. Reciprocal interactions and moral concepts pertain to individuals' immediate relationships with others and their connections to cultural practices and systems of societal organization.

All this occurs because people are active in their concerns about their own plights in the world, the plights of others, and how to best establish personal, social, and moral orders. All this means that most of the time people are not prisoners of their genetic makeup, the effects of particular experiences, or tricks of their minds. Just as social scientific researchers and theorists engage in processes of thought to understand their disciplines of study, laypersons engage in thought to understand the multiple aspects of their worlds. As some philosophers have stressed, 'human beings are above all reasoning beings' (Nussbaum, 1999, p. 71), and as reasoning beings 'all, just by being human, are of equal dignity and worth, no matter where they are situated in society, and that the primary source of this worth is a power of moral choice within them, a power that consists in the ability to plan a life in accordance with one's own evaluation of ends' (Nussbaum, 1999, p. 57).

The philosophical tradition of which Nussbaum speaks presents a rather different picture (but one consistent with that of Kohlberg) of human functioning and capabilities from the deterministic view in some psychological traditions I have mentioned. Indeed, those psychological traditions have given little credence to reasoning, choice, and planning one's life. They have often led to one form or another of attempts at human engineering. For a time, behaviorist principles were used, not only in works of fiction (Skinner, 1948), but in real-life educational programs and enterprises of behavior modification, to attempt to shape people's actions in accord with someone else's conceptions and evaluations of ends. As is well known, psychological interpretations have been used to try to manipulate and control behavior through many means, including methods of advertising, presentation of subliminal messages, marketing techniques, and manipulation of strategies and messages in political campaigns. These efforts come and go with little success. I believe that the lack of success is because people reason about their experiences, and are in reciprocal interactions with others; attempts to manipulate them are met with efforts to understand and evaluate what is being done to them. As the philosopher Peter Singer put it: 'Reason is like an escalator—once we step on it, we cannot get off until we have gone where it takes us' (Wade, 2007, p. D3).

Morality is an area that defies efforts at human engineering and that has the property of the escalator.

Humans strive for social and moral harmony, but these qualities have proven difficult to achieve. Issues of fairness, justice, and rights permeate social relationships and result in constant struggle, conflicts, social opposition, and moral resistance. Conflicts are by no means restricted to group conflicts. Moral and social struggles are as evident within groups and even between people, such as males and females, in close units. Moral goals are often in conflict with personal and social goals. People's moral goals often clash with the social institutionalization of moral goals. Imperfect social institutions and cultural practices are challenged by reasoning individuals with their capacities to stand back and take a critical view from the perspective of their moral judgments.

Note

1 By necessity, experiments assessing actions and electroencephalograph brain wave activity have used simple motor actions like pressing a button. The implied generalization to more complex choices (say professional avenues to pursue, deciding where to live, or which restaurant or opera to go to) has little supportive evidence. Even with regard to seemingly straightforward decisions, the expectations that unconscious, unknown, and nonrational processes determine decisions and choices may not be warranted. For instance, it may well be that with regard to many arithmetical calculations (including ones as simple as $2 + 2 = 4$) some type of brain activity could be noticeable before conscious awareness of calculations. Most adults would automatically and immediately respond, perhaps with a lag in conscious awareness. Such findings would only show that well-developed and well-understood ideas are implicit and, after some point of acquisition, do not require much deliberation. A better way of examining conscious awareness of this type of knowledge and decision making would be to present people with an example of a different conclusion, such as $2 + 2 = 5$. Most likely, conscious activity would be involved.

References

Abu-Lughod, L. (1993). *Writing women's worlds: Bedouin stories*. Berkeley: University of California Press.

Aronfreed, J. (1968). *Conduct and conscience: The socialization of internalized control over behavior*. New York: Academic Press.

Arsenio, W. (1988). Children's conceptions of the situational affective consequences of sociomoral events. *Child Development, 59,* 1611–1622.

Baldwin, J. M. (1906). *Social and ethical interpretations in mental development.* New York: Macmillan.

Bennett, W. J. (1993). *The book of virtues.* New York: Simon & Schuster.

Blasi, A. (1993). The development of identity: Some implications for moral functioning. In G. Noam & T. Wren (Eds.), *The moral self* (pp. 99–122). Cambridge: MIT Press.

Bok, S. (1999). *Lying: Moral choice in public and private life.* New York: Vintage Books (original work published in 1978).

Colby, A., & Damon, W. (1992). *Some do care: Contemporary lives of moral commitment.* New York: Free Press.

Colby, A., & Kohlberg, L. (1987). *The measurement of moral judgment. Vol. 1: Theoretical foundations and research validation.* Cambridge: Cambridge University Press.

Damasio, A. R. (1994). *Descartes' error: Emotion, reason, and the human brain.* New York: Harper Collins.

Damasio, A. R. (2003). *Looking for Spinoza: Joy, sorrow, and the feeling brain.* New York: Harcourt, Inc.

Damon, W. (1977). *The social world of the child.* San Francisco: Jossey-Bass.

Damon, W. (1980). Patterns of change in children's social reasoning: A 2-year longitudinal study. *Child Development, 51,* 1010–1017.

Dworkin, R. (1977). *Taking rights seriously.* Cambridge: Harvard University Press.

Eisenberg, N., & Fabes, R. A. (1991). Prosocial behavior and empathy: A multimethod, developmental perspective. In P. Clark (Ed.), *Review of personality and social psychology. Vol. 12* (pp. 34–61). Newbury Park: Sage.

Festinger, L. (1957). *A theory of cognitive dissonance.* Stanford: Stanford University Press.

Freeman, V. G., Rathore, S. S., Weinfurt, K. P., Schulman, K. A., & Sulmasy, D. P. (1999). Lying for patients: Physician deception of third-party payers. *Archives of Internal Medicine, 159,* 2263–2270.

Gewirth, A. (1982). *Human rights: Essays on justification and applications.* Chicago: The University of Chicago Press.

Grinder, R. E. (1961). New techniques for research in children's temptation behavior. *Child Development, 32,* 679–688.

Grinder, R. E. (1964). Relations between behavioral and cognitive dimensions of conscience in middle childhood. *Child Development, 35,* 881–891.

Haidt, J. (2001). The emotional dog and its rational tail: A social intuitionist approach to moral judgment. *Psychological Review, 108,* 814–834.

Haidt, J., Koller, S. H., & Dias, M. G. (1993). Affect, culture, and morality, or is it wrong to eat your dog? *Journal of Personality and Social Psychology, 65,* 613–628.

Hartshorne, H., & May, M. A. (1928–1930). *Studies in the nature of character. Vol. 1: Studies in deceit. Vol. 2: Studies in self-control. Vol. 3: Studies in the organization of character.* New York: McMillan.

Helwig, C. C. (1995). Adolescents' and young adults' conceptions of civil liberties: Freedom of speech and religion. *Child Development, 66,* 152–166.

Helwig, C. C. (1997). The role of agent and social context in judgments of freedom of speech and religion. *Child Development, 68,* 484–495.

Hoffman, M. L. (1984). Empathy, its limitations, and its role in a comprehensive moral theory. In J. L. Gewirtz & W. M. Kurtines (Eds.), *Morality, moral development, and moral behavior* (pp. 283–302). New York: Wiley.

Hoffman, M. L. (2000). *Empathy and moral development: Implications for caring and justice.* Cambridge: Cambridge University Press.

Kahneman, D., Slovic, P., & Tversky, A. (1982). *Judgment under uncertainty: Heuristics and biases.* Cambridge: Cambridge University Press.

Killen, M., Lee-Kim, J., McGlothlin, H., & Stagnor, C. (2002). *How children and adolescents evaluate gender and racial exclusion. Monographs of the Society for Research in Child Development. Vol. 67* (No. 4, Serial No. 271). Boston: Blackwell.

Killen, M., Sinno, S., & Margie, N. G. (2007). Children's experiences and judgments about group exclusion and inclusion. In R. V. Kail (Ed.), *Advances in child development and behavior. Vol. 35* (pp. 173–218). New York: Academic Press.

Killen, M., & Smetana, J. (2007). The biology of morality: Human development and moral neuroscience. *Human Development, 50,* 241–243.

Koenigs, M., Young, L., Adolphs, R., Tranel, D., Cushman, F., Hauser, M., Damasio, A. (2007). Damage to the prefrontal cortex increases utilitarian moral judgements. *Nature, 446,* 908–911.

Kohlberg, L. (1958). The development of modes of moral thinking and choice in the years 10 to 16. Unpublished doctoral dissertation, University of Chicago.

Kohlberg, L. (1963). Moral development and identification. In H. Stevenson (Ed.), *Child psychology: The sixty-second yearbook of the National Society for the Study of Education* (pp. 277–332). Chicago: The University of Chicago Press.

Kohlberg, L. (1964). Development of moral character and moral ideology. In M. L. Hoffman & L. W. Hoffman (Eds.), *Review of child development research. Vol. 1* (pp. 383–432). New York: Russell Sage Foundation.

Kohlberg, L. (1969). Stage and sequence: The cognitive-developmental approach to socialization. In D. Goslin (Ed.), *Handbook of socialization theory and research* (pp. 347–480). Chicago: Rand McNally.

Kohlberg, L. (1971). From is to ought: How to commit the naturalistic fallacy and get away with it in the study of moral development. In T. Mischel (Ed.), *Psychology and genetic epistemology* (pp. 151–235). New York: Academic Press.

Kohlberg, L. (2008). The development of children's orientations toward a moral order. *Human Development, 51*, 8–20.

Lewis, M. (1993). The development of deception. In M. Lewis & C. Saarni (Eds.), *Lying and deception in everyday life* (pp. 90–105). New York: The Guilford Press.

Nucci, L. (1981). Conceptions of personal issues: A domain distinct from moral or societal concepts. *Child Development, 52*, 114–121.

Nucci, L. (1996). Morality and the personal sphere of actions. In E. Reed, E. Turiel, & T. Brown (Eds.), *Values and knowledge* (pp. 41–60). Hillsdale: Erlbaum.

Nucci, L. P. (2001). *Education in the moral domain.* Cambridge: Cambridge University Press.

Nucci, L. P., & Nucci, M. S. (1982a). Children's responses to moral and social conventional transgressions in free-play settings. *Child Development, 53*, 1337–1342.

Nucci, L. P., & Nucci, M. S. (1982b). Children's social interactions in the context of moral and conventional transgressions. *Child Development, 53*, 403–412.

Nucci, L. P., & Turiel, E. (1978). Social interactions and the development of social concepts in preschool children. *Child Development, 49*, 400–407.

Nucci, L. P., & Weber, E. (1995). Social interactions in the home and the development of young children's conceptions of the personal. *Child Development, 66*, 1438–1452.

Nussbaum, M. C. (1999). *Sex and social justice.* New York: Oxford University Press.

Parke, R. D., & Walters, R. (1967). *Some factors influencing the efficacy of punishment training for inducing response inhibition. Monographs of the Society for Research in Child Development. Vol. 32* (No. 1, Serial No. 109). Chicago: The University of Chicago Press.

Perkins, S. A., & Turiel, E. (2007). To lie or not to lie: To whom and under what circumstances. *Child Development, 78*, 609–621.

Piaget, J. (1932). *The moral judgment of the child.* London: Routledge & Kegan Paul.

Piaget, J. (1981). *Intelligence and affectivity: Their relationships during child development.* Palo Alto: Annual Reviews, Inc.

Protho, J. W., & Grigg, C. M. (1960). Fundamental principles of democracy: Bases of agreement and disagreement. *Journal of Politics, 22*, 276–294.

Radke-Yarrow, M., Zahn-Waxler, C., & Chapman, M. (1983). Children's prosocial dispositions and behavior. In P. Mussen (Ed.), *Handbook of child psychology. Vol. 4: Socialization, personality, and social development* (4th ed., pp. 469–545). New York: Wiley.

Ryan, K. (1989). In defense of character education. In L. P. Nucci (Ed.), *Moral development and character education: A dialogue* (pp. 3–18). Berkeley: McCutchan Publishing Corporation.

Sarat, A. (1975). Reasoning in politics: The social, political, and psychological bases of principled thought. *American Journal of Political Science, 19*, 247–261.

Shweder, R. A., Mahapatra, M., & Miller, J. G. (1987). Culture and moral development. In J. Kagan & S. Lamb (Eds.), *The emergence of morality in young children* (pp. 1–83). Chicago: The University of Chicago Press.

Shweder, R. A., Much, N. C., Mahapatra, M., & Park, L. (1997). The 'big three' of morality (autonomy, community, and divinity) and the 'big three' explanations of suffering. In A. Brandt & P. Rozin (Eds.), *Morality and health* (pp. 119–169). New York: Routledge.

Skinner, B. F. (1948). *Walden two.* Indianapolis: Hackett Publishing.

Skinner, B. F. (1971). *Beyond freedom and dignity.* New York: Knopf.

Smetana, J. G. (1995). Context, conflict, and constraint in adolescent parent authority relationships. In M. Killen & D. Hart (Eds.), *Morality in everyday life: Development perspectives* (pp. 225–256). Cambridge: Cambridge University Press.

Smetana, J. G. (2002). Culture, autonomy, and personal jurisdiction in adolescent-parent relationships. In H. W. Reese & R. Kail (Eds.), *Advances in child development and behavior. Vol. 29* (pp. 51–87). New York: Academic Press.

Smetana, J. G. (2006). Social domain theory: Consistencies and variations in children's moral and social judgments. In M. Killen & J. G. Smetana (Eds.), *Handbook of moral development* (pp. 119–153). Mahwah: Erlbaum.

Thorkildsen, T. A. (1989). Justice in the classroom: The student's view. *Child Development, 60*, 323–334.

Turiel, E. (1974). Conflict and transition in adolescent moral development. *Child Development, 45*, 14–29.

Turiel, E. (1975). The development of social concepts: Mores, customs, and conventions. In J. M. Foley & D. J. DePalma (Eds.), *Moral development: Current theory and research* (pp. 7–38). Hillsdale: Erlbaum.

Turiel, E. (1978). The development of concepts of social structure: Social-convention. In J. Click & A. Clarke-Stewart

(Eds.), *The development of social understanding* (pp. 25–107). New York: Gardner Press.

Turiel, E. (1979). Distinct conceptual and developmental domains: Social-convention and morality. In H. E. Howe & C. B. Keasey (Eds.), *Social cognitive development. Nebraska Symposium on Motivation, 1977. Vol. 25: Social cognitive development* (pp. 77–116). Lincoln: University of Nebraska Press.

Turiel, E. (1983). *The development of social knowledge: Morality and convention*. Cambridge: Cambridge University Press.

Turiel, E. (1998). The development of morality. In W. Damon (Ed.), *Handbook of child psychology. Vol. 3: Social, emotional, and personality development* (5th ed., pp. 863–932). New York: Wiley.

Turiel, E. (2002). *The culture of morality: Social development, context, and conflict*. Cambridge: Cambridge University Press.

Turiel, E. (2003). Morals, motives, and actions. In L. Smith, C. Rogers, & P. Tomlinson (Eds.), *Development and motivation: Joint perspectives* (Series II, Serial No. 2, pp. 29–40). Leicester: British Journal of Educational Psychology.

Turiel, E. (2006). Thought, emotions, and social interactional processes in moral development. In M. Killen & J. G. Smetana (Eds.), *Handbook of moral development* (pp. 7–35). Mahwah: Erlbaum.

Turiel, E. (2008a). Thought about actions in social domains: Morality, social conventions, and social interactions. *Cognitive Development, 23*, 136–154.

Turiel, E. (2008b). Social decisions, social interactions, and the coordination of diverse judgments. In U. Mueller, J. I. Carpendale, N. Budwig, & B. Sokol (Eds.), *Social life, social knowledge: Toward a process account of development* (pp. 255–276). Mahwah: Erlbaum.

Turiel, E., & Perkins, S. A. (2004). Flexibilities of mind: Conflict and Culture. *Human Development, 47*, 158–178.

Wade, N. (2007, March). Scientists find the beginnings of morality in primate behavior. *The New York Times*, p. D3.

Watson, J. B. (1924). *Behaviorism*. New York: The People's Institute.

Werner, H. (1957). *Comparative psychology of mental development*. New York: International Universities Press.

Wikan, U. (1996). *Tomorrow, God willing: Self-made destinies in Cairo*. Chicago: The University of Chicago Press.

Wilson, E. O. (1975). *Sociobiology: The new synthesis*. Cambridge: Harvard University Press.

Wynne, E. A. (1985). The great tradition in education: Transmitting moral values. *Educational Leadership, 43*, 4–9.

....

Consistency and Development of Prosocial Dispositions: A Longitudinal Study

Nancy Eisenberg, Ivanna K. Guthrie, Bridget C. Murphy, Stephanie A. Shepard, Amanda Cumberland, and Gustavo Carlo

Introduction

For decades, psychologists have discussed and debated whether there is such a thing as an altruistic or prosocial personality which is enduring over time and situations (Gergen, Gergen, & Meter, 1972; Rushton, 1980; Staub, 1974). Piliavin, Dovidio, Gaertner, and Clark (1981) asserted that the search for an altruistic personality was futile. More recently, Batson (1991) expressed doubts that an altruistic personality exists.

Penner and Finkelstein (1998) defined the prosocial personality as "an *enduring* tendency to think about the welfare and rights of other people, to feel concern and empathy for them, and to act in a way that benefits them" (italics are ours). Thus, the prosocial personality may include other-oriented cognitions and prosocial actions, as well as sympathy. Prosocial behavior generally is defined as voluntary behavior intended to benefit another (Eisenberg, 1986). One type of prosocial behavior is altruism. Altruism commonly is viewed as intrinsically motivated, voluntary behavior intended to benefit another—that is, behavior motivated by concern for others (sympathy) or by internalized values, goals, and self-rewards rather than by the expectation of concrete or social rewards, or the desire to avoid punishment or sanctions (Eisenberg & Fabes, 1998). Altruism, rather than other sorts of prosocial behaviors, is the essence of the prosocial personality. Unfortunately, it usually is impossible to unequivocally differentiate between altruistic and less lofty modes of prosocial behavior, so measures of prosocial behavior generally are considered indicative of an altruistic personality (Penner, Fritzsche, Craiger, & Freifeld, 1995; Rushton, Chrisjohn, & Fekken, 1981).

Empathy often is defined as an emotional reaction elicited by and congruent with another's emotional state or condition (Eisenberg & Fabes, 1998; Hoffman, 1982). It has been argued that empathic responding can result in either sympathy (concern for another based on the apprehension or comprehension of the other's emotional state or condition), personal distress (an aversive, self-focused emotional reaction to the apprehension or comprehension of another's emotional state or condition), or both (Eisenberg, Shea, Carlo, & Knight, 1991). It is hypothesized that sympathy involves other-oriented motivation whereas personal distress involves the egoistic motive of alleviating one's own aversive negative state (Batson, 1991).

Today there is a body of research indicating that there are individual differences in prosocial behavior in specific settings or at particular points in time (e.g., see Davis, 1994; Graziano & Eisenberg, 1997; Penner et al., 1995). Evidence for the premise that there are *stable* individual differences in the tendency to assist and care about others is still limited however. Two types of data are pertinent: data on the consistency of prosocial behaviors and dispositions across contexts or reporters, and data on stability of prosocial tendencies over time.

Evidence of consistency in prosocial behavior across specific helping opportunities is mixed. Findings of cross-situational consistency are weakest in studies of infants and preschoolers, but are modest for children, adolescents, and adults (Eisenberg & Fabes, 1998; Graziano & Eisenberg, 1997). The modest consistency findings noted in studies of this type are not surprising given the diversity of measures of prosocial behavior typically used. In many cases, some measures of prosocial behavior used in research are likely to be motivated by other-oriented motives whereas others are not and consistency would be expected only if comparable measures are used at different times.

Research examining consistency of prosocial tendencies across time is rare. Several researchers have reported modest correlations for raters' perceptions of children's prosocial behavior over a year or a few years (e.g., Bar-Tal & Raviv, 1979; Block & Block, 1973).

Eisenberg et al. (1987) found consistency in elementary schoolchildren's actual donating or helping behavior over 2 years; self- and other-reports of prosocial behavior were correlated over 4 years into adolescence (Eisenberg, Carlo, Murphy, & Van Court, 1995). Moreover, Davis and Franzoi (1991) obtained a relatively high correlation for high school students' self-reported sympathetic concern over 2 or 3 years, whereas Eisenberg et al. (1995) found evidence of consistency in empathy and sympathy in childhood and adolescence for up to 8 years. In many of these cases, the follow-up information was obtained primarily or solely from self-reports.

There are several reasons to expect consistency in prosocial responding across time. First, theorists have suggested that prosocial behavior and empathy-related responding have a genetic basis (e.g., Wilson, 1975). For example, Hoffman (1981) argued that empathy is the biological substrate for human altruism. Thus, biological factors could account for interspecies and intraspecies variation in prosocial responding. Consistent with this reasoning, evidence of heritability has been obtained in twin studies of empathy-related responding and prosocial behavior (Emde et al., 1992; Loehlin & Nichols, 1976; Matthews, Batson, Horn, & Rosenman, 1981; Rushton, Fulker, Neale, Nias, & Eysenck, 1986; Zahn-Waxler, Robinson, & Emde, 1992).

Second, there is evidence that both prosocial behavior and empathy are linked to temperamental predispositions such as regulation (e.g., Eisenberg, Fabes, Karbon, et al., 1996; Eisenberg, Fabes, Murphy, et al., 1996; Rothbart, Ahadi, & Hershey, 1994) that likely have a constitutional basis (albeit influenced by the environment; Rothbart & Bates, 1998). Prosocial behavior and empathy also may be part of an enduring personality trait (agreeableness; Graziano & Eisenberg, 1997). If prosocial tendencies are linked to early emerging temperament or personality, one would expect some consistency over time in prosocial behavior because temperament and personality are, by definition, relatively consistent over time.

It also is highly likely that environmental factors contribute to the development of a prosocial disposition. Bergeman et al. (1993) found that agreeableness, which can be viewed as including prosocial tendencies to some degree (Graziano, 1994), was influenced by shared environmental influences. Moreover, numerous parental childrearing practices appear to be associated with the development of prosocial behavior and sympathy (Eisenberg & Fabes, 1998); thus, continuity in the childrearing environment likely contributes to consistency in prosocial responding over time. Indeed, there is some evidence that parental child-rearing practices at age 5 years predict empathy at age 31 (Koestner, Franz, & Weinberger, 1990) and that a secure attachment in infancy (likely partly reflecting environmental factors) predicts empathy and prosocial behavior in preschool (Kestenbaum, Farber, & Sroufe, 1989). In brief, although it is unclear to what degree constitutional and environmental factors contribute to consistency in prosocial tendencies, the combination of these factors may be expected to result in some interindividual consistency in prosocial behavior from childhood to adulthood.

Empathy-related responding has been intimately linked to prosocial behavior, both conceptually and empirically. For many years, philosophers and psychologists have argued that people who experience another's emotional distress or need are likely to be motivated to assist the other person(s) (e.g., Hoffman, 1982; Hume, 1777/1966; Staub, 1979). This link between empathy-related responding and prosocial behavior has been supported empirically; the relation is much clearer, however, when various empathy-related reactions are differentiated (Eisenberg & Fabes, 1998). In general, sympathy has been positively related to prosocial behavior—especially behavior likely to be based on other-oriented emotions and values—whereas personal distress has been unrelated or negatively related to prosocial behavior (Batson, 1991; Eisenberg & Fabes, 1991). Moreover, cognitive perspective taking—cognitively taking the role of the other or accessing information from memory to assist in understanding another's situation—has been hypothesized to promote sympathy (Batson, 1991; Eisenberg, Shea, et al., 1991; Hoffman, 1982), and has been linked to prosocial behavior (e.g., Underwood & Moore, 1982; see also Eisenberg & Fabes, 1998). Thus, sympathy and perspective taking, and, to a limited degree, empathy, can be considered measures of a prosocial disposition which are expected to motivate altruistic behavior.

The goal of the present study was to examine the degree to which prosocial behavior that is likely to be motivated by other-oriented concern predicts prosocial behavior and attitudes and empathy-related responding over 19 years, and whether sympathetic responding mediated the relation between early prosocial behavior and prosocial behavior at an older age. Observational data were obtained for 32 children on naturally occurring prosocial behavior when they were in preschool. In elementary school and high school, participants' prosocial behaviors were assessed using a variety of tasks. In addition, mothers' and self-reports of prosocial behavior were obtained in a number of assessments, and self-reported empathy or sympathy, perspective taking, and personal distress were measured numerous times. In late adolescence and early adulthood, self-reports of empathy-related responding, prosocial behavior, and prosocial-relevant cognitions were obtained, and friends also reported on some of the same aspects of participants' prosocial functioning.

Eisenberg-Berg and Hand (1979) suggested that preschoolers' spontaneous sharing behaviors, which often involve a cost to the child, are more other-oriented than are everyday helping behaviors which generally entail little cost or are performed merely to comply with peers' requests. Consistent with these assertions, they found that spontaneous sharing, but not spontaneous helping or compliant sharing or helping, was associated with higher-level prosocial moral reasoning (Eisenberg-Berg & Hand, 1979; also see Eisenberg, Pasternack, Cameron, & Tryon, 1984). Moreover, spontaneous prosocial behavior, but not compliant prosocial behavior, has been correlated with sympathy in young children (Eisenberg, McCreath, & Ahn, 1988). In other studies, Eisenberg and colleagues have found that preschoolers who have a relatively high rate of responding to peers' requests appear to be those who are nonassertive and, consequently, were targets for peers' requests (Eisenberg, Cameron, Tryon, & Dodez, 1981; Eisenberg et al., 1990, 1984). Larrieu and Mussen (1986) obtained similar findings with elementary schoolchildren. In contrast, preschool children who have a high frequency of compliant prosocial behavior (and are asked to help or share frequently) seem to be prone to experience personal distress when exposed to another's negative emotion (Eisenberg et al., 1988, 1990).

Moreover, in laboratory studies involving pre-school, elementary, or high school students, higher-level (i.e., other-oriented and not hedonistic) prosocial moral reasoning has been associated more frequently with prosocial actions that incur a cost (e.g., donating or volunteering time after school) than with behaviors low in cost (e.g., helping pick up dropped paper clips; Eisenberg, Boehnke, Schuhler, & Silbereisen, 1985; Eisenberg & Shell, 1986; Eisenberg et al., 1987). Eisenberg and Shell hypothesized that low-cost behaviors are performed rather automatically, without much cognitive reflection—moral or otherwise. Because sharing usually involves a cost (giving up an object) whereas helping often does not, young children's spontaneous sharing behaviors, but not their compliant sharing or helping or spontaneous helping, were expected to predict prosocial behaviors (especially those involving a cost) and empathy-related responding over time.

Method

Participants

The longitudinal cohort consisted of 16 females and 16 males (30 White and 2 of Hispanic origin) who had been interviewed nine times previously, at ages 4–5, 5.5–6.5, 7–8, 9–10, 11–12, 13–14, 15–16, 17–18, and 19–20 years (see Eisenberg et al., 1995; Eisenberg, Miller, Shell, McNally, & Shea, 1991; Eisenberg et al., 1987). Two additional follow-up studies are discussed in this paper; the 11 testing sessions are hereafter referred to as T1 to T11. The mean ages of the participants at T10 and T11 were 258 months (range = 247–267 months, or approximately 21–22 years) and 281 months (approximately 23–24 years). The original sample (T1) was 37 children. At that time, this was not intended to be a longitudinal study; thus, families who were initially involved had not committed to a longi-tudinal study. Four children were lost at T2 (most had moved away), and one child was lost at T3. No par-ticipants were lost from T3 to T10; one woman refused any participation at T11 (n = 31 at T11). Mean years of maternal and paternal education for this sample (as reported at T8 for the 32 participants) were 16.0 and 17.0, respectively (range = 12–20 years for both). At

age 23–24, 2 participants had junior college degrees, 14 had graduated college (four of these were in grad-uate school), 1 had some college but did not seem to be in school, 10 were still in college, and 4 were high school graduates with very little or no college educa-tion. One woman was a homemaker, 1 participant was in the Peace Corps, 1 was on a religious mission, and 22 reported having jobs outside the home (two man-ual laborers, one chef, one waitress, two in sales; one in forestry; one chemist; one flight attendant; one hotel auditor; one health care administrator; one police dispatch operator; five low-level employees in business; five middle-level management personnel in industry or small businesses).

Measures

The measures over the many assessments included observational or experimental assessments of prosocial behavior; self-reports of prosocial behavior, empathy-related responding, perspective taking, and prosocial attitudes/values; mothers' reports of prosocial behav-ior; and friends' reports of participants' prosocial-relevant behavior/attitudes/values, sympathy, and perspective taking. Because all the measures except those obtained at T10 and T11 have been described in previous publications (Eisenberg et al., 1995; Eisenberg, Lennon, & Roth, 1983; Eisenberg, Miller, et al., 1991; Eisenberg et al., 1987; Eisenberg-Berg & Hand, 1979), T10 and T11 measures are presented in detail, whereas measures from earlier periods are briefly summarized.

PROSOCIAL BEHAVIOR IN PRESCHOOL

Children were observed by at least two observers in the preschool in random order for a minimum of 70 (a maximum of 113) 2-min timings over 6 to 11 weeks. Six observers coded each instance of three prosocial behaviors:

1. *Sharing.* The child gives away or allows another temporary use of a material object previously in the child's possession (but not as part of a game, e.g., sharing of tea cups when playing tea was not coded as sharing).
2. *Helping.* The child attempts to alleviate another's nonemotional needs. For example, the child assists

another by giving information, helps another with a task, or offers an object not previously in the giver's possession. (These behaviors were not coded as helping if they occurred as part of cooperative play *and* involved the completion of a mutual goal.)

3. *Offers comfort.* The child attempts to alleviate the emotional needs of another, for example, tries to make another feel better when in distress.

Each behavior was coded as having occurred spontaneously, as occurring in response to a verbal or nonverbal request from a peer ("asked for" or compliant prosocial behavior), or as not determined to be spontaneous or not spontaneous. Comforting was very infrequent and was combined with helping (see Eisenberg-Berg & Hand, 1979). Thus, the final categories of prosocial behavior were spontaneous sharing, compliant sharing, spontaneous helping, and compliant helping.

Each of the six observers coded with a reliability coder for a minimum of sixty 2-min timings. Percentages of exact agreement for each behavioral category were computed only for 2-min periods in which at least one coder observed prosocial behavior (there were many periods when neither coder observed any prosocial behavior). Mean interrater reliabilities ranged from 75% to 86% exact agreement.

ACTUAL PROSOCIAL BEHAVIOR IN ELEMENTARY SCHOOL

Donating. At T4 and T5, children had an opportunity to anonymously donate their earnings (eight nickels) to a charity for needy children. At the end of some tasks, children were paid the eight nickels, shown a poster of poor children, and left alone to donate money into a can (containing other money) if they desired (Eisenberg et al., 1987). The number of nickels donated (out of eight) was the index of donating.

Helping. At T6, T7, and T8, when the participants were leaving the laboratory and had been paid, they were given some extra questionnaires and asked to assist the experimenter by filling them out and returning them in a stamped envelope. Children were told that they need not help, but that the help would be appreciated. Two indexes of helping were computed: whether the students returned the questionnaires, and

whether all parts were completed. These measures were standardized and combined at each time period.

At T4 and T5, children also had an opportunity to assist an adult with low-cost helping tasks such as picking up dropped paper clips. These behaviors were not related to moral judgment in past research, and we have argued that they do not reflect moral behavior. Thus, they were not expected to relate to our target measures of prosocial responding. At T4, the helping measures were how much children helped an adult pick up 75 dropped paper clips for 60 s, and helping an adult pick up toys for 90 s so other children would not trip and hurt themselves. Latency to helping (of both types) and number of clips or duration of picking up toys were measured. Reliabilities between two observers' timings of seconds for 20–25% of the sample were .85 or higher (the observer was behind a mirror). At T5, children had an opportunity to help pick up fallen papers for 60 s; again, latency to helping (interrater reliability = .91) and number picked up were measured. At both time periods, latency scores were reversed and scores for latency and time helping were standardized and combined.

SELF-REPORTED PROSOCIAL-RELEVANT BEHAVIOR AND COGNITIONS

At T6, T7, and T8, children filled out a 23-item adapted version of Rushton, Chrisjohn, and Fekken's (1981) self-report altruism scale. On a scale ranging from 1 (never) to 5 (very often), children indicated how frequently they engaged in 23 behaviors such as giving money to charity or volunteer work (a = 36, .90, and .87 at T6, T7, and T8, respectively; Eisenberg et al., 1995; Eisenberg, Miller, et al., 1991). At T10 and T11, participants filled out a 14-item adapted version of Rushton et al.'s (1981) self-report altruism scale (a = .85 and .67 at T10 and T11, respectively; taken from Penner et al., 1995) using the same response scale. This measure overlaps in items with the longer 23-item version of the measure completed at T6 to T8.

At T9, T10, and T11, self-reported moral behavior was assessed with portions of Weinberger's Adjustment Inventory (WAI; Weinberger, 1991, 1997). Seven-item versions of the restraint subscales that concerned moral behavior were used and were rated 1 (false) to 5 (true). For T9, consideration for others was used (see Eisenberg et al., 1995, for T9 reliability). Sample items and as for

T10 and T11 were as follows: consideration for others ("I often go out of my way to do things for other people," a = .78 and 34, respectively), and suppression of aggression ("I lose my temper and 'let people have it' when I'm angry," a = .76 and 34, respectively). Items within each subscale were averaged.

At T10 and T11, several additional measures of prosocial behaviors/cognitions were taken from Penner's instrument (Penner & Finkelstein, 1998; Penner et al., 1995). These included social responsibility and a care orientation. The subset of 15 items from Schwartz's (1968) social responsibility scale used in the Penner et al. (1995) measure was included, rated 1 (strongly disagree) to 5 (strongly agree) (e.g., "If a good friend of mine wanted to injure an enemy of his/hers, it would be my duty to try to stop him/her; a = .81 and .70 at T10 and T11, respectively). In addition, four items reflecting a care orientation (e.g., "I chose alternatives that minimize the negative consequences to other people"; a = .81 at both T10 and T11) were rated on the same scale as that used for social responsibility (Penner et al., 1995).

MOTHERS' REPORTS OF PROSOCIAL BEHAVIOR
Mothers rated children's prosocial behavior using a slightly adapted 23-item version of the Rushton et al. (1981) scale at T6, T7, and T8, and the same response scale (Eisenberg et al., 1995; Eisenberg, Miller, et al., 1991). It was very similar to that filled out by the child participants. Alphas could not be computed because mothers frequently used the additional option of "don't know" (Eisenberg et al., 1995; Eisenberg, Miller, et al., 1991).

FRIENDS' REPORTS OF PROSOCIAL BEHAVIOR
At T9, T10, and T11, participants were asked to provide the names of friends who might be willing to fill out short questionnaires about the participants. At T9, friends of 25 participants filled out short questionnaires. At T10, reports from at least one friend were obtained for 28 participants; reports from two and three friends were obtained for 20 and 11 participants, respectively (for a total of 59 friends). At T11, analogous numbers were 24, 18, and 6 (total = 48). Only nine friends were the same individuals at T10 and T11. Mean lengths of the friendships at T10 and T11 (as reported by friends) were 68 and 86 months,

respectively. If reports from more than one friend were obtained, they were averaged across each item on each questionnaire.

At T10 and T11, friends responded to items from the short form of WAI, which contains three items per scale. Items on these subscales were similar to those used in the participant report measures. Alphas at T10 and T11 for the three-item scales were both .88 for consideration of others and .85 and .69, respectively, for suppression of aggression. Data at T9 on consideration for others were obtained with the same scale (a = .77). At T10 and T11, friends also reported on participants' social responsibility using 10 of the same items filled out by participants, with slight modifications (a = .72 and .85 at T10 and T11, respectively).

SELF-REPORTED EMPATHY-RELATED RESPONDING
Children completed Bryant's (1982) 22-item empathy scale for children at T4, T5, and T6 (Eisenberg, Miller, et al., 1991; Eisenberg et al., 1987; as = .60–.78). This scale likely taps a mix of empathy, sympathy, and personal distress. At T7, T8, T9, T10, and T11, participants responded to the empathic concern (sympathy), perspective taking, and personal distress scales from Davis's (1983, 1994) Interpersonal Reactivity Index (see Eisenberg et al., 1995; Eisenberg, Miller, et al., 1991). In addition, 19 children completed and returned these scales as part of the helping task at T6 (the Davis subscales are not appropriate for elementary schoolchildren). Definitions and as for the seven-item scales at T10 and T11 are as follows: sympathy (the tendency to experience feelings of warmth and concern for others; a = .81 and .83, respectively), perspective taking (the tendency to adopt the point of view of others; a = .82 and 30, respectively), and personal distress (the tendency to feel unease and discomfort in tense interpersonal settings involving others' needs or emotions; a = .76 and .66, respectively). Alphas for earlier periods ranged from .73 to .91 (with as for personal distress being the lowest, always in the .70–.79 range). Items were rated from 1 (strongly disagree) to 5 (strongly agree). Items on each scale were averaged (after reversing items if appropriate).

FRIENDS' REPORTS OF EMPATHY-RELATED RESPONDING
At T9, friends responded to the same seven-item sympathy and perspective taking scales as did participants

(with slight modifications in wording; a = .80–35; Eisenberg et al., 1995). The friends' questionnaire packet at T10 and T11 included the seven sympathy items from the Davis (1983) empathic concern scale plus one additional item ("My friend has a tendency to feel concern for others' misfortunes even when he/she doesn't know those people personally"; a = .89 and 38, respectively) and six of the seven perspective taking items (modified slightly from the original Davis, 1983, items for an other-report format; a = .84 and .92, respectively). The item dropped from the perspective taking scale seemed particularly difficult for friends to answer ("My friend sometimes tries to understand his/her friends better by imagining how things look from their perspective").

DATA REDUCTION OF MEASURES OF PROSOCIAL
AND EMPATHY-RELATED RESPONDING
AT T10 AND T11
Self-report data.   At T10 and T11, there were multiple measures of prosocial behavior and attitudes (besides empathy-related responding): self-reported helping behavior, social responsibility, consideration for others, suppression of aggression, and care orientation. All these measures grouped on the same factor in a principal components factor analysis with a varimax rotation at T10 (absolute value of loadings ranged from .57 to 38) and T11 (loadings from .57 to 87). Thus, scores on these measures were standardized and averaged (after reversing when appropriate) to form a composite prosocial index at each follow-up. Sympathy, perspective taking, and personal distress—all considered to be related to empathy (Davis, 1983)—were kept separate in the analyses. Although this aggregate score contains prosocial behaviors and cognitions, as well as low aggression toward others, it is labeled as self-reported prosocial behavior henceforth.

Friends' reports.   The friend measures of a prosocial orientation at T10 (consideration of others, suppression of aggression, and social responsibility) also grouped on a single factor in a principle components factor analysis with a varimax rotation at both T10 (loadings ranged from .66 to 37) and T11 (loading ranged from .85 to .92). Therefore, the various measures were standardized and averaged at both T10 and T11 to form composite measures of friends' reports of

participants' prosocial dispositions (henceforth labeled T10 and T11 friend prosocial measures). Empathy-related variables again were kept separate.

Procedures

At T1, children were observed for a semester at the preschool. At T2 through T8, mothers and children came to the laboratory together to participate. At T9, participants usually came to the laboratory by themselves.

At both T10 and T11, participants initially were contacted by phone, if possible; then a packet of questionnaires was sent for the participants to fill out and return (order of questionnaires was randomized). Participants were asked to supply names and addresses of friends, if they were willing to do so, when they returned the questionnaires. Participants were paid for their participation. Friends were sent packets of friend questionnaires and were also paid for their participation.

Results

Means and standard deviations for the major variables at T10 and T11 are presented in Table 6.1 (most means for variables from earlier periods are in Eisenberg et al., 1995; Eisenberg, Miller, et al., 1991; Eisenberg et al., 1987).

Prediction of later measures from preschool prosocial behavior

To examine the prediction of later prosocial characteristics and behavior from preschool prosocial behavior, spontaneous sharing, spontaneous helping, compliant sharing, and compliant helping were correlated with the various measures of prosocial behavior and empathy-relevant responding obtained in subsequent years. It was clear that most of the significant correlations between preschool prosocial behavior and later measures of a prosocial disposition were for spontaneous sharing. For spontaneous helping and compliant sharing (M = .03 and .01, SD = .03 and .01, respectively), there were no more significant

Table 6.1 Means and standard deviations for measures of T10 and T11 prosocial and empathy-related characteristics

Measure	T10 M	T10 SD	T11 M	T11 SD
Self-reported				
Self-reported helping	2.93	.59	2.92	.44
Consideration for others	4.29	.39	4.04	.60
Suppression of aggression[a]	2.32	.76	2.41	.66
Care orientation	3.59	.69	3.63	.72
Social responsibility	3.29	.61	3.64	.44
Sympathy	3.88	.67	4.06	.57
Perspective taking	3.62	.69	3.69	.64
Personal distress	2.33	.62	2.28	.51
Friend-reported				
Consideration for others	4.22	.79	4.26	.63
Suppression of aggression[a]	1.84	.63	1.84	.70
Social responsibility	3.36	.57	3.41	.57
Sympathy	3.60	.65	3.09	.72
Perspective taking	3.35	.72	3.69	.64

Note. For most measures, n = 32 and 31 at T10 and T11, respectively. Scores could range from 1 to 5 on all measures.
[a] High scores indicate more aggression.

correlations than would be expected by chance. In contrast, for spontaneous sharing (for the sample of 32, M = .023 per 2-min observation, SD = .02, range = 0–.08), there were many significant and marginally significant correlations. No significant sex differences were found in any type of preschool prosocial behavior.

The correlations are presented in Table 6.2. Note that two-tailed tests of significance were used, although specific hypotheses usually were formulated (e.g., that spontaneous sharing was hypothesized to predict later prosocial tendencies). Thus, the significance levels in the correlational analyses tend to be conservative. Spontaneous sharing was at least marginally correlated with costly donating at T4 and T5; self-reported helping at T7; self-reported consideration for others at T9; the prosocial aggregate self-report scores at T10 and T11; mothers' reports of helpfulness at T7 and T8; costly helping at T8; sympathy at T6, T7, T8, T9, and T10; perspective taking at T8, T9, and T10; and friends' reports of sympathy at T9, T10, and T11. Thus, spontaneous sharing in preschool was fairly consistently related to self-reports of prosocial responding

and sympathy in late childhood, adolescence, and early adulthood, and sometimes predicted actual prosocial behavior and mothers' reports thereof. Spontaneous sharing was unrelated to self-reported empathy (rather than sympathy) at younger ages, or to self-reported personal distress at any age; and it usually was not related to friends' reports of consideration for others or a prosocial disposition in adulthood (although it was related to friends' reports of sympathy). Although preschool spontaneous sharing was significantly related to high needs-oriented prosocial moral reasoning and negatively related to hedonistic reasoning at T1 (Eisenberg-Berg & Hand, 1979), it generally was unrelated to level of prosocial moral reasoning in later years.

There were fewer findings for compliant helping (M = .01, SD = .01) but they formed an interesting pattern. Unexpectedly, children rated high in compliant helping reported at T6, T7, T9, T10, and T11 that they were low in personal distress. Moreover, participants rated high for this type of prosocial behavior were viewed by friends at T9 as low in perspective taking, sympathy, and consideration for others. However, given that the latter findings were all marginally significant, and that these friend reports were from only one time period (indeed, friend-reported perspective taking was positively related to compliant helping at T11), they may not be statistically reliable.

Mediational analyses

In a series of analyses, we examined whether individual differences in sympathy mediate the relation of early spontaneous prosocial behavior to later prosocial tendencies. Sympathy was not assessed with the total sample before T7; thus, we examined whether sympathy at T7 and T8 mediated the relation of T1 spontaneous sharing to T9, T10, and T11 prosocial tendencies. Because spontaneous sharing was at least marginally related to self-reported prosocial behavior at T9, T10, and T11 (and not to friend-reported prosocial behavior), we used these indexes of prosocial behavior as the criterion variables in the mediational analyses.

For sympathy to mediate the relation of spontaneous sharing to prosocial tendencies, spontaneous sharing (variable A) should predict both the mediator, T7

Table 6.2   Correlations of preschool spontaneous sharing with prosocial-related measures from other assessments

Testing session	Other measures of prosocial or empathy-related responding	Measure of prosocial behavior in preschool and adulthood			
		Spontaneous		Compliant	
		Sharing	Helping	Sharing	Helping
T4	Costly donating	.35★	−.32†	−.12	−.07
	Low cost helping	.40★	−.16	.07	.13
	Empathy[a]	.09	−.07	.14	−.05
T5	Costly donating	.34†	−.46★	−.22	.07
	Low cost helping	.00	.17	−.02	.30†
	Empathy[a]	.15	.07	−.08	.10
T6	Self-reported helping[b]	.24	.21	.40★	.14
	Costly helping	.0?	.17	.03	.19
	Mother-reported helpfulness[b]	.19	.07	.13	.19
	Empathy[a]	.17	.18	.15	−.13
	Sympathy[c]	.55★	−.36	.26	−.04
	Perspective taking[c]	.33	.18	.16	.41★
	Personal distress[c]	.22	−.28	.01	−.58★★
T7	Self-reported helping[b]	.38★	−.10	.49★★	.08
	Mother-reported helpfulness[b]	.46★	−.08	.01	.12
	Costly helping	.09	−.10	.15	−.30
	Sympathy[d]	.36★	−.12	.29	−.03
	Perspective taking[d]	.22	−.05	.27	.03
	Personal distress[d]	.01	.31†	−.13	−.33†
T8	Self-reported helping[b]	.18	.07	.49★★	.21
	Costly helping	.38★	−.10	−.27	−.13
	Mother-reported helpfulness[b]	.35†	−.27	.07	.23
	Sympathy[d]	.39★★	−.13	.18	−.04
	Perspective taking[d]	.48★★	.00	.21	.15
T9	Self-reported consideration[c]	.41★	.00	.12	−.08
	Friend-reported consideration[e]	.15	.04	−.10	−.37†
	Sympathy[d]	.41★	−.05	.16	.11
	Friend-reported sympathy[f]	.36†	−.19	−.04	−.35†
	Perspective taking[d]	.39★	.01	.36★	.17
	Friend-reported perspective taking[f]	−.08	−.02	−.13	−.35†
	Personal distress[d]	.08	.00	−.16	−.48★★
T10	Self-reported prosocial behavior[g]	.45★★	−.02	.06	.09
	Friend-reported prosocial behavior[h]	.18	−.17	−.02	.01
	Sympathy[d]	.49★★	.05	−.01	.10
	Perspective taking	.41★	.08	.13	.23
	Friend-reported sympathy[f]	.39★	−.30	.05	−.08
	Friend-reported perspective taking	.19	−.31	.17	.18
	Personal distress[d]	.06	.15	−.06	−.39★
T11	Self-reported prosocial behavior	.32†	.09	.23	.17
	Friend-reported prosocial behavior	.15	−.13	.07	.29
	Sympathy	.23	.04	.14	.04
	Perspective taking	.19	.29	−.01	.29

Table 6.2 *(cont'd)*

| | | Measure of prosocial behavior in preschool and adulthood | | | |
| | | Spontaneous | | Compliant | |
Testing session	Other measures of prosocial or empathy-related responding	Sharing	Helping	Sharing	Helping
	Friend-reported sympathy	.36†	−.31	.19	.20
	Friend-reported perspective taking	.01	−.20	−.02	.46*
	Personal distress	.17	−.02	−.11	−.49**

[a]Using the Bryant (1982) empathy scale.
[b]Using the adapted Rushton et al. (1981) measure.
[c]Using Davis's (1983) Interpersonal Reactivity Index for a subsample of 19 children.
[d]Using Davis's (1983) empathic concern (for sympathy), perspective taking, or personal distress subscales.
[e]Using the Weinberger's Adjustment Inventory (Weinberger, 1991, 1997) subscale at T9.
[f]Adapted from Davis's (1983) empathic concern (for sympathy) or perspective taking subscales.
[g]At T10 and T11, this was an aggregate score of self-reported helping, consideration of others, social responsibility, suppression of aggression, and care orientation.
[h]This was an aggregate score of friends' reports of participants' consideration of others, suppression of aggression, and social responsibility.
$\star p < .05. \star\star p < .01. \star\star\star p < .001. ^†p < .10.$

or T8 sympathy (B, so A + B), and the criterion, T9, T10, or T11 prosocial behavior (C, so A + C). In addition, sympathy (B) should predict prosocial behavior (C, B + C), and the prediction of prosocial behavior (C) from spontaneous sharing (A) should drop to nonsignificance when both A and B are used as predictors of prosocial behavior simultaneously in a regression equation (whereas B should still be a significant predictor; Baron & Kenny, 1986). Using regression analyses, we computed the aforementioned equations. Six sets of regression equations were computed: T7 or T8 sympathy was used as a mediator when predicting T9, T10, or T11 prosocial behavior.

As can be seen in Table 6.3, the aforementioned pattern generally held. Spontaneous prosocial behavior always predicted T9, T10, or T11 measures of prosocial behavior at $p < .08$ (for T7 sympathy and T11 prosocial behavior) or better (A + C). In addition, spontaneous sharing always significantly predicted T7 or T8 sympathy (A + B) and T7 or T8 sympathy always predicted subsequent prosocial behavior (B + C). Moreover, when spontaneous sharing and sympathy were entered together to predict T9, T10, or T11 prosocial behavior (A & B + C), in all cases sympathy, but not spontaneous sharing, was a significant predictor

(although it was a marginally significant predictor for T7 sympathy predicting T10 prosocial behavior).

In five of the six cases in Table 6.3, the data fully met Baron and Kenny's (1986) criteria for mediation. We also computed MacKinnon and Dwyer's (1994) test of whether the mediation was significant. Using two-tailed tests, mediation was marginally significant for T7 sympathy predicting T9 and T11 prosocial behavior, $z = 1.65$ and 1.81, $p < .10$ and $.07$, respectively, as well as T8 sympathy predicting T9 and T10 prosocial behavior, $z = 1.91$ and 1.92, $p < .057$ and $.055$, respectively. Mediation was significant for T8 sympathy predicting T11 prosocial behavior, $z = 2.07$, $p < .05$. Thus, using this stringent test, there was evidence for some mediation of the effects of early spontaneous sharing on later prosocial behavior.

To test the alternative hypothesis that prosocial behavior in elementary school mediates the relation between early prosocial behavior and later sympathy, similar analyses were conducted to test whether children's reports of helping at T7 or T8, mothers' reports of helping at T7 or T8, or costly helping at T8 mediated the relation between spontaneous sharing and sympathy at T9, T10, or T11. Mediation was not found in any of these cases.

Table 6.3 Tests of children's T7 and T8 sympathy as a mediator between spontaneous sharing and adults' self-reported prosocial behavior at T9, T10, and T11

	T9			T10			T11		
Regressions	R^2	Beta spontaneous sharing	Beta mediator	R^2	Beta spontaneous sharing	Beta mediator	R^2	Beta spontaneous sharing	Beta mediator
T1 spontaneous sharing → T7 sympathy → prosocial behavior									
IV → DV (A → C)	.17*	.41*		.21**	.45**		.10†	.32†	
IV → mediator (A → B)	.13*	.36*		.13*	.36*		.13*	.37*	
Mediator → DV (B → C)ᵃ	.27**	.52**		.24**	.49**		.36***	.60***	
Mediator, IV → DVᵃ (A & B → C)	.33*	.28	.43*	.33*	.32†	.38*	.37**	.12	.56**
Number of study participants in analysis	32			32			31		
T1 spontaneous sharing → T8 sympathy → prosocial behavior									
IV → DV (A → C)	.15*	.38*		.17*	.42*		.13*	.36*	
IV → mediator (A → B)	.15*	.39*		.15*	.39*		.16*	.39*	
Mediator → DV (B → C)ᵃ	.40***	.63***		.39***	.62***		.53***	.73***	
Mediator, IV → DVᵃ (A & B → C)	.42***	.16	.57***	.43***	.20	.55**	.54***	.09	.69***
Number of study participants in analysis	31			30			31		

Note. IV = independent variable or predictor (A); DV (or C) = criterion; mediator = B.

ᵃThe first beta presented is for the IV (spontaneous sharing); the second is for the mediator (sympathy).

$*p < .05$. $**p < .01$. $***p < .001$. $†p < .10$.

Discussion

The results of this study support the view that there is a prosocial personality disposition that emerges early and is somewhat consistent over time. Spontaneous sharing in the preschool classroom, the type of preschoolers' prosocial behavior viewed as involving other-oriented motivation (Eisenberg et al., 1984; Eisenberg-Berg & Hand, 1979), predicted prosocial behavior/cognitions and empathy-related responding up to 17 years later. Sympathy, including friends' reports of sympathy, was especially linked to early spontaneous sharing and appeared to partially mediate the relation of spontaneous sharing to later prosocial behavior. The mediational effects were likely due to the fact that preschoolers who shared spontaneously were prone to sympathy. Such an assumption is consistent with the fact that preschoolers' spontaneous prosocial behavior was significantly related to their moral judgments involving references to others' needs at that early age.

It is likely that the stability in markers of a prosocial disposition is due to a number of factors. These include temperamental and/or genetic contributions to empathy-related responding (Eisenberg, Fabes, Karbon, et al., 1996; Eisenberg, Fabes, Murphy, et al., 1996; Rothbart et al., 1994), as well as continuity of socialization influences that affect prosocial behavior. Although it is difficult to discern the degree of biological and environmental contributions to the pattern of findings, it is likely that dispositional differences in sympathy, inhibitory control, and a more general other-orientation underlie the variation among people in their prosocial responding from childhood to adulthood. Even among two- and three-year-olds, prosocial behavior often seems to be motivated by empathy or sympathy (Zahn-Waxler et al., 1992; see Radke-Yarrow, Zahn-Waxler, & Chapman, 1983). As early as 4 to 6 years of age, children differ considerably in their reasoning about prosocial and related moral conflicts, and these differences are linked to prosocial behavior (Eisenberg & Shell, 1986; Eisenberg-Berg & Hand, 1979) and to the ability to inhibit behavior in the toddler and preschool years (Kochanska, Murray, & Coy, 1997). Preschoolers' moral cognitions also have been linked to behaviors reflecting individual

differences in conscience (Kochanska, Padavich, & Koenig, 1996). Thus, even by preschool, there seem to be emotional, cognitive, and regulatory underpinnings to individual differences in prosocial responding. Because moral and prosocial behaviors often require self-control and self-denial, it is logical that the ability to regulate one's own behavior is intimately involved in the development of prosocial behavior. Inhibitory control is viewed as an aspect of temperament with some constitutional basis (Rothbart & Bates, 1998); yet it is likely that socialization also affects children's early regulation of behavior, especially moral behavior, (see Eisenberg & Fabes, 1998; Kochanska et al., 1996).[1]

Individual differences in children's prosocial behavior may be based, in part, on differences among children in the relative or combined contributions of emotion, cognition, and regulation to children's responding to others' distress or need (as well as on individual differences in each of these factors). Children seem to have a fairly stable mode of dealing with others' negative emotions by 2 years of age, a style that is still evident for many children by age 7. Some children's prosocial behavior has a large component of emotional arousal; some approach others' distress with careful cognitive processing; others shut out signals of distress and turn or run away; and still other young children have an aggressive component in their prosocial interactions (e.g., hit the person who made the baby cry; Radke-Yarrow & Zahn-Waxler, 1984). The combination of dispositional emotionality and regulation has been found to predict both sympathy (Eisenberg, Fabes, Murphy, et al., 1996) and prosocial behavior (Eisenberg, Fabes, Karbon, et al., 1996). For example, children who are emotionally reactive and also are emotionally regulated may be especially prone to spontaneous sharing; children who are emotionally reactive and under-regulated may find exposure to others' distress so aversive that they try to shut out the information or leave the situation. Thus, the pattern of individual differences in empathy-related reactions, other-oriented and moral cognitions, and regulation likely contributes to stable patterns of prosocial responding.

The lack of relation between dispositional personal distress and spontaneous sharing is evidence of the importance of distinguishing between sympathy and dispositional personal distress, both of which may stem from empathy. Personal distress, however, was at least marginally negatively related to preschoolers' compliant helping at five points in time. This finding was unexpected because compliant prosocial behavior (helping and sharing combined) generally has been positively related to young children's personal distress reactions to films (Eisenberg et al., 1990; Eisenberg, McCreath, & Ahn, 1988). Perhaps the difference in findings across studies is due to the use of observed facial personal distress in studies with young children and self-reported dispositional personal distress in this study. Children who experience personal distress may not be aware of their feelings or may wish to deny such feelings. In addition, the relation between compliant prosocial behavior and personal distress found in studies of preschoolers may be due primarily to findings for compliant sharing, not helping (e.g., sharing was much more common than helping in Eisenberg et al., 1988). Thus, preschool children prone to personal distress in laboratory studies may not be those who were high in compliant helping. Indeed, compliant helpers in preschool may have been children requested to help due to their instrumental skills, and individuals with instrumental skills are likely to score low on personal distress as adults due to the nature of the questions on Davis's personal distress scale (e.g., "I sometimes feel helpless when I am in the middle of a very emotional situation").

The fact that preschool spontaneous sharing was positively related to sympathy but not empathy scores is of particular interest. It is possible that the difference in findings was due to empathy being assessed in childhood, whereas sympathy was assessed in adolescence and adulthood. When this study began, there was, to our knowledge, no self-report measure of sympathy for younger children; consequently, only empathy was assessed. Thus, the difference in findings for empathy and sympathy could be due to validity of self-reports of empathy at a younger age versus sympathy at older ages. Nonetheless, both empathy and sympathy (for a subsample) were assessed at T6 (age 11–12 years), and at that age, spontaneous sharing was substantially correlated with sympathy and not empathy. Moreover, Eisenberg, Shea, et al. (1991) argued that empathy can evoke either sympathy or personal distress, and that only sympathy is reliably associated with prosocial behavior. Our data provide some support for the argument that sympathy, but not empathy, elicits prosocial motivation and action and serves as a mediator between early and later prosocial tendencies.

In summary, the results of this study support the conclusions that there are individual differences in prosocial dispositions, and that these differences emerge by adolescence and are somewhat stable into adulthood. However, although there are consistencies in prosocial responding over time, it is quite possible that prosocial tendencies become more consolidated, and individual differences become more evident, as children grow into adults. As individuals become capable of understanding higher level moral principles and develop sophisticated perspective-taking abilities and a coherent set of values and goals, it is reasonable to expect greater consistency in prosocial responding. This developmental hypothesis merits further attention.

There are several limitations of the present study. The sample in this study was rather small and homogeneous in its composition. Thus, the results may not be generalizable to different socioeconomic or racial/ethnic groups. Moreover, it is possible that the families who participated were especially helpful or compliant families. In addition, the children in the original study were in only three classes, so their data may not have been entirely independent. Nonetheless, given that many of the findings were obtained despite limited statistical power, it is likely that a number of the correlational findings will be found in larger samples.

Note

1   At T9 only, we used the WAI scale (eight items, $\text{ct} = .77$) to assess impulsivity. Self-reported impulsivity was significantly negatively related to children's spontaneous prosocial behavior, $r(30)= -.40, p < .024$.

References

Baron, R. M., & Kenny, D. A. (1986). The moderator-mediator variable distinction in social psychological research: Conceptual, strategic, and statistical considerations. *Journal of Personality and Social Psychology*, *51*, 1173–1182.

Bar-Tal, D., & Raviv, A. (1979). Consistency in helping-behavior measures. *Child Development*, *50*, 1235–1238.

Batson, C. D. (1991). *The altruism question*. Hillsdale, NJ: Erlbaum.

Bergeman, C. S., Chipuer, H., Plomin, R., Pedersen, N. L., Mc-Clearn, G. E., Nesselroade, J. R., Costa, P. T., & McCrae, R. R. (1993). Genetic and environmental effects on openness to experience, agreeableness, and conscientiousness: An adoption/twin study. *Journal of Personality, 61*, 159–180.

Block, J., & Block, J. H. (1973, January). *Ego development and the provenance of thought: A longitudinal study of ego and cognitive development in young children*. Progress report for the National Institute of Mental Health (Grant No. MH16080). Berkeley, CA: University of California.

Bryant, B. K. (1982). An index of empathy for children and adolescents. *Child Development, 53*, 413–425.

Davis, M. H. (1983). Measuring individual differences in empathy: Evidence for a multidimensional approach. *Journal of Personality and Social Psychology, 44*, 113–126.

Davis, M. H. (1994). *Empathy: A social psychological approach*. Madison, WI: Brown & Benchmark.

Davis, M. H., & Franzoi, S. (1991). Stability and change in adolescent self-consciousness and empathy. *Journal of Research in Personality, 25*, 70–87.

Eisenberg, N. (1986). *Altruistic emotion, cognition and behavior*. Hillsdale, NJ: Erlbaum.

Eisenberg, N., Boehnke, K., Schuhler, P., & Silbereisen, R. K. (1985). The development of prosocial behavior and cognitions in German children. *Journal of Cross-Cultural Psychology, 16*, 69–82.

Eisenberg, N., Cameron, E., Tryon, K., & Dodez, R. (1981). Socialization of prosocial behavior in the preschool classroom. *Developmental Psychology, 17*, 773–782.

Eisenberg, N., Carlo, G., Murphy, B., & Van Court, P. (1995). Prosocial development in late adolescence: A longitudinal study. *Child Development, 66*, 911–936.

Eisenberg, N., & Fabes, R. A. (1991). Prosocial behavior and empathy: A multi-method, developmental perspective. In P. Clark (Ed.), *Review of personality and social psychology* (Vol. 12, pp. 34–61). Newbury Park, CA: Sage.

Eisenberg, N., & Fabes, R. A. (1998). Prosocial development. In N. Eisenberg (Ed.), W. Damon (Series Ed.), *Handbook of child psychology: Vol. 3. Social, emotional, and personality development* (5th ed., pp. 701–778). New York: Wiley.

Eisenberg, N., Fabes, R. A., Karbon, M., Murphy, B. C., Wosinski, M., Polazzi, L., Carlo, G., & Juhnke, C. (1996). The relations of children's dispositional prosocial behavior to emotionality, regulation, and social functioning. *Child Development, 67*, 974–992.

Eisenberg, N., Fabes, R. A., Miller, P. A., Shell, C., Shea, R., & May-Plumlee, T. (1990). Preschoolers' vicarious emotional responding and their situational and dispositional prosocial behavior. *Merrill-Palmer Quarterly, 36*, 507–529.

Eisenberg, N., Fabes, R. A., Murphy, B., Karbon, M., Smith, M., & Maszk, P. (1996). The relations of children's dispositional empathy-related responding to their emotionality, regulation, and social functioning. *Developmental Psychology, 32*, 195–209.

Eisenberg, N., Lennon, R., & Roth, K. (1983). Prosocial development: A longitudinal study. *Developmental Psychology, 19*, 846–855.

Eisenberg, N., McCreath, H., & Ahn, R. (1988). Vicarious emotional responsiveness and prosocial behavior: Their interrelations in young children. *Personality and Social Psychology Bulletin, 14*, 298–311.

Eisenberg, N., Miller, P. A., Shell, R., McNalley, S., & Shea, C. (1991). Prosocial development in adolescence: A longitudinal study. *Developmental Psychology, 27*, 849–857.

Eisenberg, N., Pasternack, J. F., Cameron, E., & Tryon, K. (1984). The relation of quality and mode of prosocial behavior to moral cognitions and social style. *Child Development, 155*, 1479–1485.

Eisenberg, N., Shea, C. L., Carlo, G., & Knight, G. (1991). Empathy-related responding and cognition: A "chicken and the egg" dilemma. In W. Kurtines & J. Gewirtz (Eds.), *Handbook of moral behavior and development: Vol. 2. Research* (pp. 63–88). Hillsdale, NJ: Erlbaum.

Eisenberg, N., & Shell, R. (1986). The relation of prosocial moral judgment and behavior in children: The mediating role of cost. *Personality and Social Psychology Bulletin, 12*, 426–433.

Eisenberg, N., Shell, R., Pasternack, J., Lennon, R., Beller, R., & Mathy, R. M. (1987). Prosocial development in middle childhood: A longitudinal study. *Developmental Psychology, 23*, 712–718.

Eisenberg-Berg, N., & Hand, M. (1979). The relationship of preschoolers' reasoning about prosocial moral conflicts to prosocial behavior. *Child Development, 50*, 356–363.

Emde, R. N., Plomin, R., Robinson, J., Corley, R., DeFries, J., Fulker, D. W., Reznick, J. S., Campos, J., Kagan, J., & Zahn-Waxler, C. (1992). Temperament, emotion, and cognition at fourteen months: The MacArthur Longitudinal Twin Study. *Child Development, 63*, 1437–1455.

Gergen, K. J., Gergen, M. M., & Meter, K. (1972). Individual orientations to prosocial behavior. *Journal of Social Issues, 28*, 105–130.

Graziano, W. G. (1994). The development of agreeableness as a dimension of personality. In C. F. Halverson, Jr., G. A. Kohnstamm, & R. P. Martin (Eds.), *The developing structure of temperament and personality from infancy to adulthood* (pp. 339–354). Hillsdale, NJ: Erlbaum.

Graziano, W. G., & Eisenberg, N. H. (1997). Agreeableness: A dimension of personality. In R. Hogan, J. Johnson, &

S. Briggs (Eds.), *Handbook of personality psychology* (pp. 795–824). San Diego, CA: Academic Press.

Hoffman, M. L. (1981). Is altruism part of human nature? *Journal of Personality and Social Psychology, 40*, 121–137.

Hoffman, M. L. (1982). Development of prosocial motivation: Empathy and guilt. In N. Eisenberg (Ed.), *The development of prosocial behavior* (pp. 281–313). New York: Academic Press.

Hume, D. (1966). *Enquiries concerning the human understanding and concerning the principles of morals* (2nd ed.). Oxford, UK: Clarendon Press. (Original work published 1777)

Kestenbaum, R., Farber, E. A., & Sroufe, L. A. (1989). Individual differences in empathy among preschoolers: Relation to attachment history. In N. Eisenberg (Ed.), *New directions for child development: Vol. 44. Empathy and related emotional responses* (pp. 51–64). San Francisco: Jossey-Bass.

Kochanska, G., Murray, K., & Coy, K. C. (1997). Inhibitory control as a contributor to conscience in childhood: From toddler to early school age. *Child Development, 68*, 263–277.

Kochanska, G., Padavich, D. L., & Koenig, A. L. (1996). Children's narratives about hypothetical moral dilemmas and objective measures of their conscience: Mutual relations and socialization antecedents. *Child Development, 67*, 1420–1436.

Koestner, R., Franz, C., & Weinberger, J. (1990). The family origins of empathic concern: A 26-year longitudinal study. *Journal of Personality and Social Psychology, 58*, 709–717.

Larrieu, J., & Mussen, P. (1986). Some personality and motivational correlates of children's prosocial behavior. *Journal of Genetic Psychology, 147*, 529–542.

Loehlin, J. C., & Nichols, R. C. (1976). *Heredity, environment, and personality.* Austin: University Of Texas Press.

MacKinnon, D. P., & Dwyer, J. H. (1994). Estimating mediated effects in prevention studies. *Evaluation Review, 17*, 144–158.

Matthews, K. A., Batson, C. D., Horn, J., & Rosenman, R. H. (1981). Principles in his nature which interest him in the fortune of others: The heritability of empathic concern for others. *Journal of Personality, 49*, 237–247.

Penner, L. A., & Finkelstein, M. A. (1998). Dispositional and structural determinants of volunteerism. *Journal of Personality and Social Psychology, 74*, 525–537.

Penner, L. A., Fritzsche, B. A., Craiger, J. P., & Freifeld, T. S. (1995). Measuring the prosocial personality. In J. Butcher & C. D. Spielberger (Eds.), *Advances in personality assessment* (Vol. 10, pp. 147–163). Hillsdale, NJ: Erlbaum.

Piliavin, J. A., Dovidio, J. F., Gaertner, S. L., & Clark, R. D., 111. (1981). *Emergency intervention.* New York: Academic Press.

Radke-Yarrow, M., & Zahn-Waxler, C. (1984). Roots, motives, and patterns in children's prosocial behavior. In E. Staub, D. Bar-Tal, J. Karylowski, & J. Reykowski (Eds.), *Development and maintenance of prosocial behavior: International perspectives on positive behavior* (pp. 81–99). New York: Plenum.

Radke-Yarrow, M., Zahn-Waxler, C., & Chapman, M. (1983). Children's prosocial dispositions and behaviors. In P. H. Mussen (Ed.), *Handbook of child psychology: Vol. 4. Socialization, personality, and social development* (pp. 469–545). New York: John Wiley & Sons.

Rothbart, M. K., Ahadi, S. A., & Hershey, K. L. (1994). Temperament and social behavior in childhood. *Merrill-Palmer Quarterly, 40*, 21–39.

Rothbart, M. K., & Bates, J. E. (1998). Temperament. In N. Eisenberg (Ed.), W. Damon (Series Ed.), *Handbook of Child Psychology: Vol. 3. Social, emotional, and personality development* (5th ed., pp. 105–176). New York: Wiley.

Rushton, J. P. (1980). *Altruism, socialization, and society.* Englewood Cliffs, NJ: Prentice-Hall.

Rushton, J. P., Chrisjohn, R. D., & Fekken, G. C. (1981). The altruistic personality and the self-report altruism scale. *Personality and Individual Differences, 2*, 1–11.

Rushton, J. P., Fulker, D. W., Neale, M. C., Nias, D. K. B., & Eysenck, H. J. (1986). Altruism and aggression: The heritability of individual differences. *Journal of Personality and Social Psychology, 50*, 1192–1198.

Schwartz, S. H. (1968). Words, deeds, and the perception of consequences and responsibility in social situations. *Journal of Personality and Social Psychology, 10*, 232–242.

Staub, E. (1974). Helping a distressed person: Social, personality, and stimulus determinants. In L. Berkowitz (Ed.), *Advances in experimental social psychology* (Vol. 7, pp. 293–341). New York: Academic Press.

Staub, E. (1979). *Positive social behavior and morality: Vol 2. Socialization and development.* New York: Academic Press.

Underwood, B., & Moore, B. (1982). Perspective-taking and altruism. *Psychological Bulletin, 91*, 143–173.

Weinberger, D. A. (1991). Social-emotional adjustment in older children and adults: I. Psychometric properties of the Weinberger Adjustment Inventory. Unpublished manuscript, Case Western Reserve University, Cleveland, OH.

Weinberger, D. A. (1997). Distress and self-restraint as measures of adjustment across the life span: Confirmatory factor analyses in clinical and nonclinical samples. *Psychological Assessment, 9*, 132–135.

Wilson, E. O. (1975). *Sociobiology: The new synthesis.* Cambridge, MA: Harvard University Press.

Zahn-Waxler, C., Robinson, J., & Emde, R. N. (1992). The development of empathy in twins. *Developmental Psychology, 28*, 1038–1047.

Children's Thinking About Diversity of Belief in the Early School Years: Judgments of Relativism, Tolerance, and Disagreeing Persons

Cecilia Wainryb, Leigh A. Shaw, Marcie Langley, Kim Cottam, and Renee Lewis

Young children, like their older peers, grow up and function in a world where diversity of belief and opinion is ubiquitous. In their conversations and arguments with friends and parents, children as young as 4 or 5 use expressions bearing on knowing and believing, and on truth and falsehood (Hugues & Dunn, 1998; Sabbagh & Callanan, 1998; Walton, 2000). Teachers and parents, furthermore, can attest to how seriously children take some of their differences in belief and opinion. Whereas research has documented how adolescents and young adults think about diversity of belief (e.g., Chandler, 1987; King & Kitchener, 1994; Kuhn, Amsel, & O'Loughlin, 1988; Perry 1970) and how they judge the acceptability of divergent beliefs in different contexts (e.g., Wainryb, Shaw, Laupa & Smith, 2001), little such research has been conducted with children in their early school years. Nonetheless, there is evidence that between the ages of 3 and 9 children go from viewing the mind as a passive recipient of information to understanding that the mind can influence the contents of beliefs. Theory-of-mind research has shown that children progress from a primitive assumption that beliefs are copies of reality at age 3 to an elementary understanding, at the age of 4 or 5, that beliefs are representations of reality and can therefore be mistaken (Astington, Harris, & Olson, 1988). At around the age of 7 or 8, children begin recognizing that differences in belief may also reflect different interpretations of reality (Carpendale & Chandler, 1996; Chandler & Lalonde, 1996). Given children's developing understandings of the mind, and the inescapable existence of divergent beliefs and opinions in their lives, it is reasonable to ask how young children think about diversity of belief.

The assessment of children's thinking about diversity of belief may be approached in more than one way. Given a particular disagreement, one possibility is to examine whether children think that multiple beliefs may be right or that only one belief is right; another possibility is to examine whether children think it acceptable or unacceptable for persons to endorse beliefs different from their own. The first approach suggests the notion of relativism; the second approach suggests the notion of tolerance. Relativism and tolerance are often used interchangeably in discussions bearing on issues related to diversity. This confusion found its way into psychological research, where relativism and tolerance are rarely recognized as separate dimensions and where data concerning children's tolerant or intolerant attitudes toward diverse beliefs or toward the proponents of diverse beliefs are used to infer their conceptions of knowledge as relative or nonrelative, and vice versa (e.g., Enright & Lapsley, 1981; Mansfield & Clinchy, 1997).

The muddling of relativism and tolerance is unfortunate, however, because assuming a tolerant attitude toward diversity does not require one to judge that all ideas are equally right and does not presume that beliefs cannot be evaluated against nonrelativistic criteria. Moreover, it is possible that relativism and tolerance follow different developmental paths. To obtain a comprehensive picture of young children's thinking about diversity of belief, it becomes necessary to assess each dimension separately. In the present study we asked participants to consider a series of disagreements between pairs of characters who expressed opposite beliefs, and elicited their judgments of relativism (i.e., whether only one or both beliefs are right) and their judgments of tolerance (i.e., whether it is acceptable or unacceptable for a character to believe a divergent belief). Because previous research has equated tolerance to a positive evaluation of the proponents of divergent beliefs (Enright & Lapsley, 1981; Sigelman & Toebben, 1992), participants' judgments about the disagreeing persons were also elicited.

The assessment of children's thinking about diversity of belief also draws attention to the realms of diversity. Diversity of belief is not limited to a particular realm of thought; people endorse divergent beliefs about, among others, what is morally right, what is true, and what is valuable or aesthetic. Moreover, children as young as 4 or 5 have been shown to recognize that people may hold diverse ("false") beliefs in different realms of thought (Flavell, Flavell, Green, & Moses, 1990; Flavell, Mumme, Green, & Flavell, 1992). Typically, however, researchers investigating how children think about beliefs and belief diversity have focused on how children's thinking changes with age rather than on how it varies with the realm of belief.

Enright and Lapsley (1981), for example, asked children and adolescents to state their opinion about a broadly diverse set of issues, such as whether it is best to obey a teacher or help a friend, to keep a date with a friend or accept a more alluring invitation, or to allow the American Nazi party to stage a march or protect the community from offense. Subsequently, they were asked to judge hypothetical individuals who allegedly took the opposite stand. Regardless of whether the dissenting opinions expressed just positions, unjust positions, personal preferences, or a combination of all, all dissenting positions, because they were dissenting, were implicitly considered to be conceptually equivalent and were combined into a single score. Based on age differences in modal responses across issues, Enright and Lapsley depicted a developmental progression from a generalized intolerant attitude during the childhood years through a tolerant evaluation of disagreement during adolescence.

A similar emphasis on the sequence of development has characterized research on epistemological thinking. Although this research has been typically conducted with adolescents and adults (e.g., Chandler, 1987; King & Kitchener, 1994; Kuhn et al., 1988; Perry, 1970), research conducted with children suggests that before the age of 4 or 5, children assume that knowledge mirrors objective reality—an epistemological position known as naive realism or "egocentric subjectivity" (Burr & Hofer, 2002, p. 220). Next, children progress to a position of absolutism or objectivism; although they recognize the distinction between knowledge and reality, they still judge beliefs against standards of truth dictated by objective reality and "postulat(e) a single right answer even to questions of value and interpretation" (Mansfield & Clinchy, 1993, p. 7). School-age children acknowledge that exposure to different information may lead to differences in knowledge but still believe that the source of these differences lies in the external world and that there is only one valid belief for any given issue. Researchers have proposed that only in middle to late childhood do children develop a relativist or multiplist level of epistemological understanding, "leading eventually to the idea that knowing can never be more than subjective opinion" (Kuhn & Weinstock, 2002, p. 126). Although researchers of epistemological development have not stated in any explicit way that epistemological positions are stages, recent comprehensive reviews of this research (Hofer & Pintrich, 1997; Kitchener, 2002; Pillow, 1999) have concurred that most major attempts at characterizing epistemic thinking have endorsed, at least implicitly, the notion of a sequence of stages that transcends domain boundaries.

Research on other aspects of development, by contrast, suggests that domain specificity merits attention even in early childhood. Beginning in the 1980s, a growing body of research on cognitive development has demonstrated that children's thinking includes separate systems of thought, and that children as young as 4 or 5 draw distinctions among different types of categories (e.g., Carey, 1984; Gelman, 1988; Keil, 1986). Similarly, a large body of research on sociomoral development has shown that children's judgments of right and wrong are organized according to specific systems of knowledge, and that by the age of 4 or 5 children make different types of judgments depending on whether they evaluate wrongs in the realm of morality, social convention, or personal preference (e.g., Damon, 1983; Turiel, 1983). In general, this research suggests the possibility that children might think differently about divergent beliefs bearing on different realms of thought.

Further support for this proposition comes from recent studies conducted, from different traditions, with participants in their teens, 20s, and adult years. In one study, participants were asked about instances of conflicting beliefs that varied, among other dimensions, in terms of the realm of thought. Participants did not think that all divergent beliefs were equally acceptable; rather, they drew distinctions according to the realm of conflict. Most participants, regardless of age, thought it was acceptable, and in some cases desirable, to hold divergent metaphysical, conventional, and psychological beliefs but also thought that divergent moral beliefs were wrong and unacceptable (Wainryb et al., 2001). In another study investigating developing conceptions of knowledge, participants were shown to adhere to different epistemological positions with regard to different realms of knowledge. For example, they expressed objectivist views about matters of fact and moral values, and relativistic views about matters of personal preference and aesthetics (Kuhn, Cheney, & Weinstock, 2000; see also Mansfield & Clinchy, 2002). Although these studies did not include children younger than 10, the previously mentioned findings from cognitive and sociomoral development research led us to expect that even young children will draw such domain-specific distinctions in their thinking.

To examine this hypothesis, it is necessary to define the domains of interest and their boundaries; the task is not straightforward. One possibility is to rely on the distinction between values and facts and to think of domains of knowledge as representing "different points along a rough continuum from highly subjective matters of personal preference to highly objective matters of fact" (Mansfield & Clinchy, 2002, p. 230). The approach taken in this study relies on a different conceptual framework (Turiel & Davidson, 1986). In this framework, the strategy for domain identification involves considerations concerning both the substance of epistemological categories and the type of subject–object interaction. This strategy yields several domains that, rather than representing points along a subjectivity–objectivity continuum, constitute qualitatively different systems of thought that can be distinguished in terms of specific criteria. Research proceeding from this conceptual framework, dealing largely with the social realm of thought, has shown that even young children recognize that not all value judgments are subjective and distinguish among qualitatively different realms of values. Value judgments made about matters of taste and personal preference are, indeed, recognized as subjective, relative, arbitrary, and nonprescriptive, as well as within the realm of personal jurisdiction. By contrast, value judgments bearing on matters of morality and justice are understood to be nonsubjective, nonrelative, and nonarbitrary, as well as prescriptive across social contexts and independent of personal considerations. Finally,

value judgments bearing on matters of convention and social organization, though also nonsubjective, prescriptive within social contexts, and independent of personal considerations, are nonetheless arbitrary and relative (for a comprehensive review of this research, see Turiel, 1998).

Although children's thinking about facts and truths has not been as extensively investigated from a domain-specific perspective as their thinking about values, recent research suggests that children also draw distinctions among different types of facts. As examples, in studies comparing children's thinking about facts bearing on easily perceptible and unequivocal features in the external world and their thinking about facts that refer to ambiguous features of reality (e.g., Carpendale & Chandler, 1996; Chandler & Lalonde, 1996) or facts that are the product of societal construction (e.g., Kalish, 1998), young children recognize that some fact beliefs are true or false regardless of personal considerations, others are open to subjective interpretation and support more than a single reasonable interpretation, and still others are subjective and relative inasmuch as they reflect societal processes and consensus.

Findings supportive of the domain-specific nature of children's thinking about both value beliefs and fact beliefs led us to expect that, when thinking about beliefs different from their own, young children would not make the same types of judgments about all beliefs. Instead, we expected that their judgments about diversity of belief (i.e., their judgments concerning relativism, tolerance, and disagreeing others) would vary systematically according to the realm of diversity. To investigate these issues, we contrasted children's thinking about diversity in four realms of belief: (a) beliefs about morals are value statements that refer to nonsubjective and nonrelative principles of fairness and welfare, (b) beliefs about matters of taste are value statements that refer to subjective matters of preference and choice, (c) beliefs about matters of fact are truth statements about matters that are easily perceptible and verifiable, and (d) beliefs about ambiguous facts are also truth statements that concern matters about which it is impossible to determine what is true given the available information. The beliefs bearing on morality and taste were chosen to represent value beliefs corresponding, respectively, to the moral and personal domains (Turiel, 1983); the beliefs bearing on facts and ambiguous facts were chosen to represent fact beliefs. (Beliefs bearing on conventions, though distinct and important, were not included in this study. Because conventions are prescriptive within context and relative across contexts, to study appropriately children's understanding of conventionality it would have been necessary to also include context as a variable. This would have resulted in a design far too complicated for this very young sample, but see Wainryb et al., 2001.)

The notion of domain specificity does not preclude development but rather posits that developmental changes take place within domains. Indeed, outlines for within-domain conceptual development have been proposed for the moral (Davidson, Turiel, & Black, 1983), conventional (Turiel, 1983), and personal (Nucci & Lee, 1993) domains. A relatively well-documented manifestation of domain-specific conceptual development concerns the changes in children's understandings of the defining criteria of each domain. As an example, research has shown that by the age of 4 or 5, children understand criteria such as seriousness, permissibility, or rule contingency, and recognize how these criteria distinguish among realms of thought; by contrast, children's understanding of the criterion of relativity lags by several years. Data from several studies, for example, indicate that before the ages of 7 or 8, children tend to judge concerns in the conventional realm in nonrelative terms (Smetana, 1981; Smetana & Braeges, 1990; Smetana, Schlagman, & Adams, 1993).

Based on these findings, we thought it likely that children's judgments about the relativism of beliefs (i.e., whether only one or more than one belief are right) might undergo changes between the ages of 5 and 9, but only with respect to those realms of belief whose features include relativity. (Children younger than 5 were not included in this study, as they are unlikely to consider beliefs different from their own in meaningful ways; Astington et al., 1988). Accordingly, with regard to the realms of taste and ambiguous facts, we expected 9-year-olds, but not yet 5-year-olds, to reason that multiple beliefs can be right because they refer to subjective matters (as in the case of taste) or to matters of fact that cannot be known with certainty (as in the case of ambiguous

facts). Because of their difficulty grasping the notion of relativism, we expected 5-year-olds (more so than their older peers) to reason that multiple beliefs cannot be right even in the realms of taste and ambiguous facts. With regard to the realms of morality and fact, which do not comprise relativism, we expected children, regardless of age, to make nonrelative judgments based on concerns with fairness (morality) or truth (fact).

Recent research suggests that young children's judgments of tolerance also are likely to be informed by both age and the realm of diversity. Like previous research (Enright & Lapsely, 1981), our research with children in their teens and 20s has indicated that, with age, children become more tolerant of divergent beliefs (Wainryb et al., 2001; Wainryb, Shaw, & Maianu, 1998). However, our data also showed that even adolescents and young adults make less tolerant judgments of divergent beliefs bearing on morality and justice than of other divergent beliefs; they also judge more negatively persons who endorse divergent moral beliefs. On the basis of these findings we expected that, when compared with their older peers, 5-year-olds might make fewer tolerant judgments of divergent beliefs and of the characters who endorse them. We also expected that children of all ages would make less tolerant judgments of divergent moral beliefs than of other divergent beliefs and would evaluate less positively proponents of divergent moral beliefs than proponents of other divergent beliefs.

A secondary question of the study was whether children's thinking about diversity varies with the status of the person endorsing the divergent belief. The notion of status (in terms of age, expertise, or power) has figured prominently in stage-related explanations of the development of epistemological (Perry, 1970) and moral (Kohlberg, 1969) concepts. Research conducted from a domain-specific perspective, however, has indicated that the effect of status on children's thinking is not uniform across domains. As examples, it has been found that even young children are not blindly obedient or uncritical of adults and judge that adults cannot legitimately change moral, logical, or physical rules or issue orders to violate those rules (e.g., Komatsu & Galotti, 1986; Laupa & Turiel, 1986; Nicholls & Thorkildsen, 1988). It bears asking, therefore, how children judge divergent beliefs that are endorsed by persons with more and less status. To examine this question, we contrasted participants' judgments (i.e., relativism, tolerance, and disagreeing person) about divergent beliefs endorsed by an adult character and by a child character. Although a character's age is only a proxy for status, it is common for adults to directly and indirectly instruct children about what is true and right, and for children to turn to adults when they want to know what is true and right. Therefore, children (especially young children) are likely to perceive an adult character as having more status than a child character. Although findings from previous research do not bear directly on children's thinking about diversity of belief, they do suggest that the status of the character endorsing the divergent belief might inform participants' judgments about diversity (especially their judgments of tolerance) in some realms (e.g., beliefs about taste or ambiguous facts) but not—or less—in others (e.g., moral or fact beliefs).

Method

Participants

The sample included 96 participants, 16 males and 16 females in each of three age levels: 5-year-olds ($M = 4$ years, 11 months; range = 4,6 to 5,6), 7-year-olds ($M = 6,11$; range = 6,6 to 7,5), and 9-year-olds ($M = 9,1$; range = 8,7 to 9,9). Participants were of middle class and were primarily (72%) Caucasian (the proportion of Hispanic (16%), African American (7%), Asian (4%), and American Indian (1%) participants is representative of the population from which the sample was recruited). Participants attended a local preschool and a public school in a mid-size Western city. Parental consent and participant assent were obtained for all participants.

Design and assessments

The overall purpose of this study was to examine whether young children's thinking about beliefs different from their own varies with age, realm of disagreement, and status of the disagreeing character. For this purpose, participants in three age groups were told about a series of two characters that express conflicting beliefs.

The status of the disagreeing character (child or adult) was varied between participants. Half of the participants in each age group were told that the characters expressing conflicting beliefs were two children of the participant's age (e.g., "Sarah and Sophie are first graders, just like you"). The other half were told that the characters were a child of the participant's age and an adult (e.g., "Sarah is a first grader, just like you; Mrs. Davidson is a grown-up"); in this condition, the adult character was always the one who expressed the belief with which participants disagreed. To facilitate comprehension and retention, participants were shown 8.5 in. × 11 in. colorful drawings depicting either two same-age children or a child and an adult, and interviewers pointed to the characters and named them as they presented the characters' beliefs.

The realm of disagreement was manipulated within participants. All participants were told about four disagreements each bearing on a different realm, as follows:

1. moral disagreements, bearing on matters of fairness and welfare (e.g., "Sarah believes that it's okay to hit and kick other children, and Sophie believes that it's wrong to hit and kick other children");
2. taste disagreements, bearing on matters of taste and preference (e.g., "Daniel believes that chocolate ice cream tastes yucky, and David believes that chocolate ice cream tastes yummy");
3. fact disagreements, bearing on perceptible and easily verifiable physical facts (e.g., "Paula believes that when you let go of pencils the pencils go up, and Leah believes that they fall down");
4. ambiguous fact disagreements, bearing on ambiguous matters that support more than one interpretation (e.g., "Ben believes that the dog is not eating because it doesn't like the food, and Lucas believes that the dog is not eating because it's not hungry").

Before the presentation of each set of two characters and their conflicting beliefs, a baseline assessment was included to ascertain participants' own belief (e.g., "Do you think it is okay or not okay to hit and kick other children?" "If you let go of a pencil, do you think it will go up or fall down?") and thereby ensure that, for each disagreement, one of the characters endorsed a belief consistent with the participant's belief and the other endorsed a belief not shared by the participant. After answering the baseline question and hearing the description of the disagreement, participants were asked recall questions (e.g., "What does Sarah believe?" "And what does Sophie believe?"); all participants were able to recall accurately and attribute accurately the beliefs to the characters in each of the four scenarios. Subsequently, the following assessments were obtained for each disagreement.

Relativism judgment. "Do you think that only one belief [what Sophie believes] is right, or do you think that both beliefs [what both Sophie and Sarah believe] are right?" (Participants who stated that only one belief is right were also asked, "Which one is right?") "Why [is only one belief right/are both beliefs right]?"

Tolerance judgment. "Do you think that it is okay for [disagreeing character] to believe [divergent belief] or do you think that it is not okay for him/her to believe that? Why is it okay/not okay for him/her to believe that?"

Judgment of disagreeing person. "What do you think about [disagreeing character], the [child/grown-up] who believes [divergent belief]? What kind of person do you think he/she is?"

To allow for generalizability across content areas and to reduce the effects of a monomethod bias, two comparable versions of each disagreement were designed. One version included disagreements over whether it is okay for a child to hit other children (morality), whether chocolate ice cream tastes yummy or yucky (taste), whether pencils fall up or down (fact), and whether a dog refuses to eat because it does not like the food or because it is not hungry (ambiguous fact). The other version included disagreements over whether it is okay for a child to break other children's toys (morality), whether red flowers are pretty or ugly (taste), whether rain is dry or wet (fact), and whether a dog refuses to play because it does not like the ball or because it is tired (ambiguous fact). Half of the participants in each age group heard one of the versions of each realm of disagreement. Each pair of characters expressing conflicting beliefs was always of the same gender (i.e., either both male or both female); the characters' gender was counterbalanced within each age and gender group and status condition, using a Latin square design. The presentation order of the four disagreements was also counterbalanced with a Latin square design within each age and gender group and status condition. Participants were individually interviewed; interviews were tape recorded and subsequently transcribed for analysis.

Scoring and reliability

Scoring categories were formulated on the basis of scoring systems developed in previous related studies (Davidson et al., 1983; Wainryb et al., 2001; Wainryb et al., 1998) and elaborated by scoring 20% of this study's protocols. Relativism judgments were scored dichotomously, with a score of 1 indicating nonrelativism (i.e., only one belief is right) and a score of 2 indicating relativism (i.e., both beliefs are right). Tolerance judgments were also scored dichotomously, with scores of 1 and 2 indicating, respectively, nontolerance and tolerance (i.e., that it is unacceptable or acceptable for the character to believe the divergent belief). In addition to scoring the judgments, the justifications given for relativism judgments (i.e., the reasons for judging that beliefs are relative or nonrelative) and for tolerance judgments (i.e., the reasons for judging it acceptable or unacceptable to hold the divergent belief) were also scored. Multiple justifications were allowed in each case, but participants gave only one response per question, which is not unusual in research with young children. Justifications were thus scored dichotomously, with scores of 1 and 0 indicating, respectively, that each relevant category was used or not used.

Justification categories for relativism included references to subjectivity (e.g., "What she thinks is right and what she thinks is also right because ice cream can taste good to her and gross to her"), uncertainty (e.g., "They can both be right because there's no way to know for sure, maybe the dog is hungry and maybe he doesn't like the food"), truth (e.g., "What that girl says is wrong and what this one says is right because pencils fall down, for sure, they never fall up"), and fairness (e.g., "What this one says is very wrong because it's mean and it's unfair to break other people's toys").

Justification categories for tolerance included references to personal choice (e.g., "It's okay for her to believe that, it's the way she thinks and it's her choice"), uncertainty (e.g., "It's okay that he believes that because no one can tell what's really true"), diverse experience (e.g., "It's okay for her to think that because maybe she saw something fall and then bounce, and so she thought that things fall up"), truth (e.g., "It's not okay for him to believe that because it's not true; rain is always wet"), and consequences (e.g., "She shouldn't believe that because then she's gonna start hurting little kids").

Categories for scoring judgments of disagreeing persons included the following person descriptors: bad (e.g., "He's a bad person, really mean"), not smart (e.g., "He's not very smart if he thinks that there's no gravity on earth"), weird (e.g., "She's really weird if she doesn't like chocolate"), and nice/normal (e.g., "She just thinks bad things but she's nice"; "He doesn't like ice cream but he can still be normal"). Statements that persons cannot be judged based only on their beliefs were coded as judgment withheld (e.g., "You don't know a person just from what they say; she could be anything"). Although multiple person descriptors were allowed, participants gave a single descriptor per disagreement. Person descriptors were thus scored dichotomously, with scores of 1 and 0 indicating, respectively, that each relevant descriptor was used or not used.

Scoring reliability was assessed through recoding of 20% of the protocols. Interjudge agreement was 100% for the scoring of relativism judgments, 100% for tolerance judgments, 99% for relativism justifications (Cohen's kappa = .981), 97% for tolerance justifications (Cohen's kappa = .958), and 93% for person descriptors (Cohen's kappa = .939).

Results

Preliminary analyses of all assessments by sex and version were conducted. Only 1% of the main effects and interactions involving sex or version was significant; both variables were dropped from subsequent analyses. Judgments about whether only one or both beliefs are right (relativism judgments) and whether it is acceptable or unacceptable to believe the divergent belief (tolerance judgments) were analyzed using analyses of variance[1] (ANOVAs) by realm of disagreement, status of disagreeing character, and age, with realm as a repeated measure. Multivariate analyses of variance (MANOVAs) by realm, status, and age, with realm as a repeated measure, were performed on the proportional use of relativism justifications, tolerance justifications, and judgments of disagreeing persons (unelaborated responses were not included in the analyses). Sphericity checks were conducted and, where appropriate, the Huynh-Feldt adjustment was used; analyses with and without the adjustments yielded identical results. For all analyses, post hoc comparisons using Duncan multiple-range tests and Bonferroni t tests were performed to test significant between-subjects and within-subjects effects, respectively.

Relativism

JUDGMENTS
Relativism judgments, by realm of disagreement and age, are presented in the upper half of Table 6.4. The ANOVA yielded the predicted Realm × Age interaction, $F(6, 258) = 4.07, p < .001, \eta^2 = .08$. As expected, regardless of age, nearly all participants made the nonrelative judgment that moral and factual disagreements support a single right belief. By contrast, significant age differences were found in participants' judgments about the realms of ambiguous facts and taste. Only about one third of 5-year-olds but most of the 7- and 9-year-olds judged that disagreements bearing on ambiguous facts and on taste support multiple right beliefs. No significant effects or interactions were found for the status of the disagreeing character.

JUSTIFICATIONS
The distribution of justifications given for relativism judgments, by realm and age, is presented in Table 6.5. The MANOVA on the justifications yielded significant effects for realm, $p < .001$, and age, $p < .001$, and a significant Realm × Age interaction, $p < .01$; no significant effects were found for status. Follow-up ANOVAs by realm and age were subsequently performed. As expected, participants gave two types of

Table 6.4 Judgments about the relativism and tolerance of divergent beliefs, by realm of disagreement and age (means and percentages)

Judgment	Morality			Facts			Ambiguous facts			Taste		
	5	7	9	5	7	9	5	7	9	5	7	9
Relativism												
M^a	1.0	1.0	1.1	1.0	1.0	1.1	1.4	1.5	1.7	1.4	1.7	1.9
SD	(.0)	(.0)	(.2)	(.0)	(.2)	(.2)	(.5)	(.5)	(.5)	(.5)	(.5)	(.2)
% relative	0	0	6	0	3	6	37	48	69	35	66	94
Tolerance												
M^b	1.1	1.2	1.2	1.6	1.8	1.8	1.7	1.8	1.9	1.6	1.8	2.0
SD	(.3)	(.4)	(.4)	(.5)	(.4)	(.4)	(.5)	(.4)	(.2)	(.5)	(.4)	(.2)
% tolerant	6	16	22	55	81	78	73	84	94	56	81	97

[a] 1 = nonrelative (only one belief is right); 2 = relative (both beliefs are right). [b] 1 = nontolerant (it is not okay to believe); 2 = tolerant (it is okay to believe).

Table 6.5 Justifications for relativism judgments, by realm of disagreement and age (percentages)

Justification	Morality			Facts			Ambiguous facts			Taste		
	5	7	9	5	7	9	5	7	9	5	7	9
Fairness	100	100	94	0	0	0	3	0	0	16	6	0
Truth	0	0	0	97	97	94	56	50	34	47	28	6
Subjectivity	0	0	6	0	3	6	6	6	0	34	66	94
Uncertainty	0	0	0	0	0	0	28	41	66	0	0	0
Unelaborated	0	0	0	3	0	0	6	3	0	3	0	0

Note. Percentages may not add up to 100 because of rounding.

justifications for their nonrelativistic judgments: They referred exclusively to moral criteria (fairness) to justify why moral beliefs are nonrelative, and they referred to the beliefs' correspondence with reality (truth) to justify the nonrelative judgments about all other beliefs. Whereas nearly all participants referred to the notion of truth to justify the nonrelative nature of fact beliefs, fewer did so in regard to beliefs about ambiguous facts, and still fewer in regard to taste, $F(3, 279) = 146.47, p < .001, \eta^2 = .61$. As expected, however, 5-year-olds referred to the notion of truth in regard to beliefs about taste more often than did older participants, $F(6, 279) = 2.68, p < .05, \eta^2 = .05$. Two types of justifications were also commonly given for relativistic judgments. References to the subjective

nature of reality (subjectivity) were more common for justifying the relativism of beliefs bearing on taste, $F(3, 279) = 141.54, p < .001, \eta^2 = .60$, and references to the inscrutable nature of reality (uncertainty) were made exclusively in regard to beliefs that concern ambiguous facts. As expected, older participants appealed to each of these justifications more than did younger participants, $Fs(6, 279) > 5.07, ps < .001, \eta^2s > .10$.

Tolerance

JUDGMENTS

Tolerance judgments, by realm of disagreement and age, are presented in the lower half of Table 6.4. As expected, 7- and 9-year-olds made more positive

Table 6.6 Justifications for tolerance judgments, by realm of disagreement and age (percentages)

Justification	Morality			Facts			Ambiguous facts			Taste		
	5	7	9	5	7	9	5	7	9	5	7	9
Consequences	94	84	78	0	0	0	3	0	0	16	6	0
Truth	0	0	0	44	19	22	22	16	6	25	13	3
Personal choice	6	13	22	34	38	34	50	53	44	56	78	97
Diverse experience	0	3	0	19	44	44	3	6	13	0	0	0
Uncertainty	0	0	0	0	0	0	13	25	38	0	0	0
Unelaborated	0	0	0	3	0	0	9	0	0	3	3	0

Note. Percentages may not add up to 100 because of rounding.

judgments of divergent beliefs than did 5-year-olds, $F(2, 87) = 6.62$, $p < .001$, $\eta^2 = .13$, and, regardless of age, participants made more positive judgments of divergent beliefs about facts, ambiguous facts, and taste than about morality, $F(3, 261) = 94.15$, $p < .001$, $\eta^2 = .52$. As also expected (though the effect only approached significance), participants' judgments of the acceptability of divergent beliefs varied with the status of the character proposing them, and the effect was not uniform across realms, $F(3, 261) = 2.18$, $p < .05$, $\eta^2 = .02$. Participants were more tolerant of divergent moral beliefs proposed by child characters (19%) than by adult characters (10%). Conversely, they were more tolerant of divergent taste and fact beliefs proposed by adult characters (83% and 79%, respectively) than by child characters (73% and 64%, respectively).

JUSTIFICATIONS

The distribution of justifications for why divergent beliefs are acceptable or unacceptable, by realm and age, is presented in Table 6.6. The MANOVA on the justifications for tolerance judgments yielded significant effects for realm, $p < .001$, and age, $p < .05$, and a marginally significant Realm × Age interaction, $p < .10$; no significant effects for status were found. Follow-up ANOVAs by realm and age were subsequently performed. In justifying their judgment that diversity in moral beliefs was unacceptable, most participants referred, as expected, to the harm that might ensue from those beliefs (consequences). Concerns with harmful consequences were rarely raised in

regard to other types of divergent beliefs; instead, participants reasoned that it was unacceptable to hold divergent factual beliefs, and to a lesser extent divergent beliefs about taste and ambiguous facts, because those beliefs fail to accurately represent reality (truth). Also as expected, the most common justification for judging that diversity of belief was acceptable was that the content of one's beliefs is a matter of personal choice. This reason was used to justify the acceptability of divergent beliefs bearing on taste more than the acceptability of divergent beliefs bearing on facts or ambiguous facts, and was used rarely in reference to divergent moral beliefs. In addition, participants stated that it is acceptable to endorse divergent beliefs about facts (more than other beliefs) because such beliefs ensue from a person's unique experiences (diverse experience), and divergent beliefs about ambiguous facts (but not other beliefs) because of the uncertain nature of reality, $Fs(3, 279) > 15.47$, $ps < .001$, $\eta^2s > .14$. Several significant effects involving age were also found. Regardless of the realm of disagreement, 5-year-olds referred more frequently than did older participants to the harmful consequences ensuing from divergent beliefs and to the inaccuracy of these beliefs, $Fs(2, 93) > 4.05$, $ps < .05$, $\eta^2s > .08$. Older participants also referred to certain justifications with greater frequency than did their younger peers, but did so only in the context of specific realms of disagreement. Older participants, more often than younger participants, referred to personal choice to justify the acceptability of divergent beliefs bearing on

Table 6.7   Relativism and tolerance judgments, by realm of disagreement and age (percentages)

Judgment	Morality			Facts			Ambiguous facts			Taste		
	5	7	9	5	7	9	5	7	9	5	7	9
Nonrelative–nontolerant (NR–NT)	94	84	77	45	19	22	24	16	3	42	19	3
Nonrelative–tolerant (NR–T)	6	16	19	55	78	72	41	35	29	23	16	3
Relative–tolerant (R–T)	0	0	3	0	3	6	34	48	68	34	66	94
n	32	32	31	31	32	32	29	31	31	31	32	32

Note. Percentages may not add up to 100 because of rounding.

taste, to the uncertain nature of reality to justify the acceptability of divergent beliefs bearing on ambiguous facts, and to the diversity of persons' experiences to justify the acceptability of divergent beliefs bearing on facts, $Fs(6, 279) > 2.19, ps < .05, \eta^2s > .05$.

Relativism and tolerance

Collectively, the findings reported in the previous sections indicate that, in regard to whether multiple beliefs can be right, participants made both relativistic and nonrelativistic judgments. Similarly, in judging the acceptability of diversity of belief, they made both tolerant and nontolerant judgments. In this section we examine the various combinations of judgments about relativism and tolerance. Children might assume a nonrelativistic and nontolerant stance or a relativistic and tolerant stance, or they might make nonrelativistic judgments (e.g., that beliefs can be evaluated according to nonsubjective criteria) while assuming a tolerant position (e.g., that it is acceptable for persons to hold to the "wrong" or "mistaken" beliefs). Our hypothesis was that specific combinations of judgments bearing on the acceptability and relativity of beliefs are systematically associated with specific realms of disagreement, and that age-related shifts occur within realms of disagreement. To examine this question, participants' judgments of relativism and tolerance (for each realm of disagreement) were sorted into three combinations, or profiles, as follows: nonrelativistic–nontolerant (NR–NT), nonrelativistic–tolerant (NR–T), and relativistic–tolerant (R–T). Virtually all judgments could be sorted into one of the three profiles. (A fourth relativistic–nontolerant combination, though empirically possible, makes no

conceptual sense. This fourth combination was observed in 3 of 384 cases; those responses were excluded from the subsequent analyses.) Participants were thus assigned four profile scores, one for each realm of disagreement. The distribution of the proportional use of each profile, by realm and age, is presented in Table 6.7. Perusal of these data indicates that participants were not constrained to an NR–NT profile. Furthermore, statistical analyses (the proportional use of each profile was subjected to a repeated-measures ANOVA by realm and age, with realm as a repeated measure) indicated that each profile was associated with a particular realm (or realms) of diversity. Although 5-year-olds resorted to the NR–NT profile more often than did 7- or 9-year-olds, $F(2, 93) = 6.74, p < .01, \eta^2 = .13$, participants in all age groups resorted to this profile more often for judging moral diversity than all other realms of diversity, $F(3, 279) = 100.25, p < .001, \eta^2 = .52$. Similarly, although 7- and 9-year-olds resorted to the R–T profile more often than did 5-year-olds, $F(2, 93) = 14.57, p < .001, \eta^2 = .24$, participants in all age groups resorted to this profile almost exclusively for judging diversity about matters of taste and ambiguous facts, $F(3, 279) = 95.96, p < .001, \eta^2 = .51$. Regardless of their age, participants resorted to the NR–T profile for judging diversity bearing on facts more than any other realm of diversity, $F(3, 279) = 42.47, p < .001, \eta^2 = .31$.

Disagreeing persons

The distribution of person descriptors, by realm and age, is presented in Table 6.8. The MANOVA on the person descriptors yielded significant effects for realm and age, $ps < .001$, and a significant Realm × Age

Table 6.8 Person descriptors, by realm of disagreement and age (percentages)

Person descriptor	Morality			Facts			Ambiguous facts			Taste		
	5	7	9	5	7	9	5	7	9	5	7	9
Nice/normal	6	16	6	22	53	34	50	72	69	37	66	69
Bad	63	66	78	16	3	3	16	6	0	41	22	6
Not smart	25	13	9	50	28	41	19	9	0	9	0	3
Judgment withheld	3	3	0	0	3	13	3	3	28	3	0	19
Weird	0	3	6	6	13	9	6	6	3	3	9	3
Unelaborated	3	0	0	6	0	0	6	3	0	6	3	0

Note. Percentages may not add up to 100 because of rounding.

interaction, $p < .05$; no significant effects involving status were observed. Follow-up ANOVAs by realm and age were subsequently performed. As expected, participants used positive descriptors (nice/normal) to describe characters who expressed divergent beliefs bearing on taste, ambiguous facts, and (to a lesser extent) facts, but rarely for characters who expressed divergent moral beliefs, $F(3, 279) = 40.9, p < .001, \eta^2 = .31$. Conversely, participants described characters as bad who expressed divergent moral beliefs more often than those who expressed divergent taste beliefs, and they rarely described characters as bad who expressed divergent beliefs bearing on facts or ambiguous facts, $F(3, 279) = 85.2, p < .001, \eta^2 = .48$. Participants described characters as not smart who expressed divergent fact beliefs more often than other beliefs, $F(3, 279) = 24.3, p < .001, \eta^2 = .21$, and described characters as weird only infrequently. Several significant findings involving age were observed. Regardless of the realm of disagreement, 7- and 9-year-olds described disagreeing characters as nice/normal more often than did 5-year-olds, $F(2, 93) = 4.9, p < .001, \eta^2 = .10$. Nine-year-olds, more often than 5- and 7-year-olds, withheld judgment about characters who expressed divergent beliefs bearing on the realms of taste and ambiguous facts but not other realms, $F(6, 279) = 3.5, p < .001, \eta^2 = .07$. Five-year-olds, more often than 9-year-olds, described characters as bad who expressed divergent beliefs about taste, but there were no age differences in the frequency of negative descriptions of characters who expressed other divergent beliefs, $F(6, 279) = 3.6, p < .001, \eta^2 = .07$.

Discussion

This research bears on how children in their early school years think about diversity of belief. Recall—for this is an important feature of this study's design—that participants were asked to judge beliefs that were different from those they had endorsed in a baseline assessment. In their judgments, children distinguished between divergent beliefs that in their view were wrong and those that, though different from their own, could nevertheless be right; they also judged that it was unacceptable for people to endorse certain divergent beliefs but acceptable for them to endorse others (including some that participants themselves considered to be wrong). The realm of diversity stood out as a central feature according to which these young children distinguished between relative and nonrelative beliefs and between acceptable and unacceptable diversity; age-related effects were also embedded in the matrix of this realm-specific organization. Because children's judgments of relativity and tolerance displayed distinct realm-related patterns we, first, recapitulate the main results for each type of judgment.

Consider children's judgments concerning the relativity (or nonrelativity) of beliefs. Only a minority of children in this study (22%) judged that the divergent beliefs in all four realms of disagreement were wrong. For the most part, children judged that divergent beliefs bearing on morality (e.g., "It is okay to hit and kick others") and fact (e.g., "Rain is dry") were wrong but also judged that more than one belief may be right in the context of disagreements bearing on taste (e.g., "Chocolate ice cream tastes yucky") and ambiguous facts (e.g., "The dog isn't eating because it isn't hungry"). In justifying their judgments, children referred to concerns that were consistent with the epistemological features of each realm. The majority referred to concerns with others' welfare and with fairness as the grounds for judging that moral beliefs are not relative (e.g., "Kicking other kids is mean because it hurts them, so what that kid said is just wrong, very wrong"), and to concerns with truth as the grounds for judging that fact beliefs are not relative (e.g., "If she goed outside she'd see that rain is always wet, so her belief is all wrong"). In justifying the relativity of beliefs bearing on taste and ambiguous facts, children referred to the subjective nature of reality (e.g., "People have their own tastes, so both beliefs are right actually") or the uncertain nature of reality (e.g., "It's not like we can ask the dog if he's hungry, so maybe this kid is right and the other kid is right too").

Children's judgments of tolerance were also differentiated by realm, but in a different manner. In this case, children distinguished systematically between the realm of morality, in which diversity is not (or is less) acceptable, and all other realms, in which diversity is relatively more acceptable. Most children made nontolerant judgments of divergent moral beliefs, reasoned that divergent moral beliefs (but rarely other divergent beliefs) result in harm or unfairness to others, and described characters who endorsed divergent moral beliefs (but rarely those endorsing other divergent beliefs) as bad. By contrast, children reasoned that it is acceptable (or at least more acceptable) for persons to endorse divergent beliefs bearing on realms other than morality, mostly because the content of those beliefs is a matter of personal choice.

When considered jointly, children's judgments of relativism and tolerance provide further evidence to the differentiations that young children make when they think about diversity. Children displayed three distinct views of diversity of belief. One view, that divergent beliefs are wrong or mistaken (i.e., not relative) and diversity of belief is unacceptable (NR–NT), was primarily associated with the moral realm of belief. The opposite view, that beliefs are relative and diversity of belief is acceptable (R–T), was held mostly in regard to beliefs bearing on taste and ambiguous

facts. A third view, that divergent beliefs are wrong or mistaken (not relative) but it is nonetheless acceptable for persons to endorse them (NR–T), was in the main associated with fact beliefs. Although it is interesting enough that children between the ages of 5 and 9 have three distinct views of diversity, the truly noteworthy findings were that only a minority (29%, 13%, and 3%, respectively, for 5-, 7-, and 9-year-olds) endorsed only one view of diversity across all realms of belief, and more than half (50%, 52%, and 63%, respectively, for 5-, 7-, and 9-year-olds) endorsed each of the three views.

Collectively, these findings indicate that children between the ages of 5 and 9 have multiple and well-differentiated perspectives on the relativity and acceptability of diverse beliefs—perspectives that are systematically associated with specific realms of thought. This pattern of results is consistent with the body of research indicating that children's thinking is organized in a domain-specific fashion (Carey, 1984; Damon, 1983; Gelman, 1988; Keil, 1986; Turiel, 1983). It does, indeed, make sense that young children who draw distinctions among different types of rights and wrongs and different types of categories when they make judgments about the world would also draw distinctions among different types of divergent beliefs about the world. This is not to say that the two tasks, making judgments about the world and making judgments about beliefs about the world, are identical. Conceptually, the latter (but not the former) requires that children understand that beliefs are representations of the world and, as such, can be accurate or inaccurate. As abundantly demonstrated by theory-of-mind research, 3-year-olds do not yet have such an understanding (which, incidentally, is why we did not include children younger than 5 in this study). Although it is unclear whether children acquire this understanding earlier for some domains than for others (Flavell et al., 1990) or simultaneously across domains (Flavell et al., 1992; Kalish, Weissman, & Bernstein, 2000), by the age of 5 children understand that persons form representations of all kinds of aspects of reality—representations that might or might not match reality. The findings from the present study suggest, furthermore, that those children think differently (and in a systematic way) about different kinds of divergent representations of reality.

The findings of the present study, on the other hand, are not consistent with depictions of young children as intolerant and rejecting of people with whom they disagree (Enright & Lapsley, 1981) or as espousing the objectivist view that there can be only one valid belief about any issue (Clinchy & Mansfield, 1985; Mansfield & Clinchy, 1993). We suggest (as have others; Hofer & Pintrich, 1997; Kitchener, 2002; Pillow, 1999) that propositions that cast development in terms of a sequence of stages tend to disregard tacitly domain specificity. We propose, furthermore, that in overlooking the domain-specific differentiations made by young children, stage-related propositions end up underestimating children's abilities to appreciate diversity in belief.

Further support for this proposition comes from recent research on epistemological thinking that, by directly examining domain-specific differences, yielded findings that were remarkably consistent with our own. Kuhn et al. (2000), for example, found that epistemic thinking varies by domain. More specifically, absolutism (only one view can be right) was prevalent both in the realm of truths and in the realm of moral values, and these objectivist views lingered even as individuals expressed multiplist (both views could have some rightness) or evaluativist (one view can be more right than the other) positions in regards to the realms of personal preference and aesthetics. Furthermore, participants did not express objectivist views in regards to the realm of personal preference, and only 2 of 107 participants expressed objectivist views in reference to the four other realms tested (aesthetics, values, social truth, and physical truth). In spite of the different methods used, these findings were consistent with our own in that they, too, indicated that individuals make non-relative judgments about matters of fact and morality, and relative judgments about matters of personal preference and aesthetics. Similar domain-specific findings were reported by Mansfield and Clinchy (2002). Although neither Kuhn et al. nor Mansfield and Clinchy examined the thinking of children younger than 10, our data suggest that a generalized objectivist position across domains of knowledge would also be highly unlikely even among 5-year-olds. (In a second study, Kuhn et al., 2000, tested a small group of 21 children aged 7 to 8 for the sole purpose of examining the transition from absolutism to multiplism.)

The proposition of domain differences and the findings of domain differences can be couched within different interpretive frameworks. One possible conceptualization of domain specificity is that development across domains proceeds through the same sequence of stages (e.g., from objectivism to evaluativism), but the rate of development is specific to each domain. Kuhn et al. (2000), for example, set out to examine the hypotheses that absolutism declines with age in a systematic order across domains of judgment (beginning at the subjective end, with judgments of taste, and moving across the continuum, with judgments of aesthetics, judgments of moral values, and judgments of fact), and that the transition from multiplism to evaluativism proceeds in the reversed order. This framework, though attentive to domain differences, preserves the tacit endorsement of a stage model and, more important, the presumption that, across realms of thought, absolutism is less adequate than multiplism, which in turn is less adequate than evaluativism. In this framework, the earliest developmental phase is likely to be common to all domains (hence, perhaps, the expectation that young children would be objectivists across the board), and the developmental endpoint is likely to be the same across domains of knowledge (except for development in the realm of personal preference; see Kuhn et al., 2000, p. 314).

We have put forth a different view, namely, that children develop qualitatively different types of thinking about qualitatively different realms of knowledge. In our framework, relative judgments are neither more nor less developmentally advanced or desirable than nonrelative judgments in any general sense. Rather, their adequacy can be ascertained only within the context of the epistemological attributes of the specific system (or realm) of knowledge to which the judgment refers. Thus, for example, the judgment that only one view is right may be inadequate when made in reference to conflicts over matters of taste (e.g., whether chocolate is delicious or unpalatable) but adequate when made in reference to conflicts over moral principles (e.g., whether causing harm to people is right or wrong). Altogether, then, there is an appreciable and meaningful difference between the two frameworks. Whereas the concurrent expression of different types of judgments or positions is likely to be interpreted in the former framework as indicative of protracted development in some realms of thought, in our framework such a combination of judgments is expected, even among adults.

Even as we conclude that the evidence of this and other studies furnishes support for the proposition that children assume a domain-specific perspective with regard to belief diversity, we reiterate what we have stated at the outset, namely, that the domain-specific proposition does not preclude development. Indeed, several significant age differences emerged in our study. Recall that when compared with their slightly older peers, 5-year-olds in this study made fewer relative judgments, more nontolerant judgments, and more negative descriptions of disagreeing characters, and they resorted more often to an NR–NT view of diversity. Given these findings, one might ask whether the conclusion that children make differentiated judgments about diversity might apply only to the 7- and 9-year-olds. Are these findings not indicative of a generalized negative view of diversity among the 5-year-olds—one that might be consistent with the depictions of young children as objectivists and generally intolerant? We suggest they are not. For although there were substantial differences between the thinking of the 5-year-olds and the thinking of the 7- and 9-year-olds, there are several ways in which the thinking of the 5-year-olds is nonetheless not uniformly negative or intolerant. Consider the following.

Although, when compared with their older peers, 5-year-olds made fewer relative judgments about beliefs bearing on taste and ambiguous facts, their judgments about those realms of belief differed significantly from their judgments about beliefs in the realms of morality and fact. Whereas their thinking about morality and facts was characterized by seamless uniformity (100% made nonrelative judgments about both moral and fact beliefs), their thinking about taste and ambiguous facts comprised substantial variability (42% of 5-year-olds made relative judgments about either taste or ambiguous facts, and 17% made relative judgments about both taste and ambiguous facts). Furthermore, although 5-year-olds made more negative judgments than their older peers about divergent beliefs and disagreeing characters, most 5-year-olds nevertheless judged that it was acceptable for persons

to endorse beliefs bearing on facts (55%), taste (56%), and ambiguous facts (73%) that they themselves did not endorse. The justifications they offered also reflected systematic differentiations in their thinking. When reasoning about moral beliefs, 5-year-olds raised concerns with fairness and with the consequences to the welfare of others; when reasoning about fact beliefs, they were concerned with truth. Although 5-year-olds referred to concerns with personal choice and with the uncertain or subjective nature of reality less frequently than did their older peers, their references to those concerns were nonetheless systematically associated with beliefs bearing on ambiguous facts and taste. Finally, consider that, though less frequently than 7- and 9-year-olds, 5-year-olds did express an NR–T view of diversity in regard to certain realms of belief, thereby asserting that it is acceptable for others to endorse beliefs that they themselves judge to be wrong according to nonrelative criteria. Also indicative of the systematic differentiations in 5-year-olds' thinking was that they did not endorse the NR–T view indiscriminately. Indeed, many 5-year-olds endorsed this view in regard to beliefs bearing on matters of taste (23%), ambiguous fact (41%), and fact (55%), but only a small number (6%) endorsed it in regard to moral diversity. Instead, the large majority of 5-year-olds (94%) held the view that moral beliefs are nonrelative and that divergent moral beliefs should not be tolerated—the same view upheld by a large majority of their older peers. We concluded, therefore, that the overall pattern of findings (as opposed to any one finding) bearing on the judgments made by 5-year-old participants is markedly inconsistent with the depiction of 5-year-olds as uniformly incapable of appreciating diversity of belief.

This is not to say that the differences between the views held by 5-year-olds and those held by 7- and 9-year-olds are not meaningful or do not bear explanation. Although the present study was not designed to answer questions about the sources of such differences (as in "why are they different?"), the data support some speculations better than others. One possibility is that children's understandings of belief diversity hinge on their developing understandings of the workings of the mind. One might expect that 5-year-olds, who are constrained by a false-belief understanding of the mind that renders divergent beliefs as mistaken or wrong, think of diversity in more negative terms. One might also expect that between the ages of 7 and 9, when children begin grasping the role of interpretation and conceiving of beliefs different from their own as alternative interpretations, they are more likely to have a relatively more positive view of diversity. This proposition, we underscore, is merely speculative as the relation between children's understandings of the mind and their judgments of relativism and tolerance cannot be inferred from perceived parallelisms or even from correlational data, and research that directly investigates the nature of this relation has not yet been attempted. The results of the present study—bearing on the lack of uniformity in children's thinking about different realms of diversity—suggest fairly conclusively that the relation between children's understandings of the mind and their judgments of diversity is not likely to take the form of one-to-one correspondence. Although we do think it likely that children's developing understandings of the mind inform their judgments about diversity (Wainryb, 2000; Wainryb & Ford, 1998), and we have underscored the need for more research at the juncture of theory of mind and moral development (Chandler, Sokol, & Wainryb, 2000; Wainryb, 2000), we also think that it is unlikely that any one theory or conception of mind (whether it is a false-belief theory of mind or an interpretive theory of mind) translates directly into a particular (positive or negative, realist or relativist, tolerant or intolerant) view of diversity, given that 5- and 9-year-olds endorsed simultaneously all of those views.

Another, not mutually exclusive, possibility (also requiring further study) is that the differences between the views of 5-year-olds and those of 7- and 9-year-olds can be understood in terms of the conceptual development that takes place within realms of thought. Notably, 5-year-olds' thinking about divergent beliefs bearing on matters of taste and ambiguous facts is reminiscent of 5-year-olds' primitive understandings of conventionality. Before age 5, children tend to think of conventions not as arbitrary systems for coordinating social interactions but, rather, as descriptive uniformities in behavior (Turiel, 1983). The difficulties of young children in understanding the relativity

of conventions has been amply documented (Smetana, 1981; Smetana & Braeges, 1990; Smetana et al., 1993). In young children's view, the very existence of conventions makes them binding. Therefore, they tend to judge that it is wrong to call teachers by their first name because "I've never seen kids call teachers by their names," or that it is wrong to change an established seating arrangement in the classroom because "we always sit in the same place when it's sharing time." Similarly, in the present study, 5-year-olds judged that only the belief that ice cream is yummy is right because "it's really true, everyone loves ice cream," and that it would be wrong to endorse the opposite belief because "what she says is not true, ice cream *is* yummy." Along with Turiel (1983), we suggest that the inconsistencies and contradictions in the thinking of 5-year-olds about social conventions or personal taste both foreshadow and constitute the basis of future conceptual development in each of these realms.

In discussing the developments between the ages of 5 and 9, we implicitly emphasized the accomplished understandings of 9-year-olds. This in turn raises questions about development beyond age 9. Previous research suggests that the pattern of findings in this study—where the realm of diversity dictates both whether beliefs are relative or non-relative and whether belief diversity is more or less acceptable—is not confined to the thinking of young children. Research in sociocognitive development indicates that the distinction between relative and nonrelative realms of thought remains stable with age (e.g., Kalish, 1998; Turiel, 1998). Research also suggests that tolerance of moral diversity continues to lag significantly behind tolerance of diversity in other realms, even among adolescents and young adults (Wainryb et al., 2001; Wainryb et al., 1998). We therefore suggest that the thinking of individuals beyond age 9 is likely to retain a domain-specific organization. This is not to say that 9-year-olds are fully competent adult thinkers or that there is no development beyond age 9.

Development might take two forms. One, alluded to briefly earlier, entails conceptual development that takes place within domains. Findings of this study suggest that conceptual development in the understanding of relativism is likely to underlie the age differences observed in children's views of diversity in the realms of personal taste and ambiguous facts. Conceptual development does not end at age 9; although the notion of relativism seems to be in place by then, so that 9-year-olds distinguish between beliefs that are relative and those that are not, further conceptual development within realms of thought might be associated with age-related changes in other aspects of older children's thinking about belief diversity.

Development might also be manifested in children's thinking about divergent beliefs bearing on multifaceted issues. Multifaceted issues pertain to more than one realm; examples are disagreements about whether it is right or wrong for a gay person to adopt (an issue combining conventional expectations and moral concerns with welfare and rights), for a parent to refuse medical treatment for her children on religious grounds (metaphysical and moral considerations), or for a coach to exclude certain children to increase the team's chances to win (moral and conventional considerations). We think it is likely that children of different ages make different judgments about the relativity and acceptability of multifaceted divergent beliefs. This is not merely because these issues are more difficult but, rather, because thinking about these issues involves patterns of interdomain correspondences and coordinations. To understand fully (or even predict) age-related differences in children's thinking about such issues, it is first necessary to ascertain how children think about diversity within each realm and how their thinking changes with age within each realm. Hence, in the present study we focused on children's thinking about divergent beliefs that were prototypical of each realm. Knowledge derived from the present study can inform the interpretation of any age-related differences that may arise in children's thinking about divergent multifaceted beliefs. Regardless of the forms that thinking about diversity might take beyond age 9, the findings of this study strongly indicate that the investigation of the development of children's and adolescents' thinking about belief diversity must be grounded on a thorough consideration of the distinctive epistemological features of each realm of thought.

Before drawing final conclusions, we turn briefly to the question of the role of status in children's thinking about diversity of belief. Whereas, in this study the realm of belief was a central feature in children's organization of their thinking about diversity, the status of the character endorsing the divergent beliefs had a more limited role. Children's judgments concerning the relativity of beliefs did not vary with the status of the character endorsing the beliefs. Their judgments of the acceptability of divergent beliefs did vary (slightly, $p < .09$) but not across the board (i.e., children did not merely judge, for example, that all divergent beliefs are more acceptable when endorsed by an adult). Whereas children judged that divergent taste and fact beliefs were more acceptable when endorsed by an adult (83% and 79%, respectively) rather than by a child (73% and 64%, respectively), they judged that divergent moral beliefs were more acceptable when endorsed by a child (19%) rather than by an adult (10%). We did not make specific predictions regarding the direction of these differences, and it is difficult to make sense, in a post hoc fashion, of differences of such small magnitude. Instead, it seems more important to underscore that the differences in the acceptability of divergent beliefs that were due to the character's status are minor when compared with those that were associated with the realm of diversity. Indeed, divergent beliefs bearing on taste, facts, and ambiguous facts were generally viewed as acceptable regardless of who endorsed them, and divergent moral beliefs were generally viewed as unacceptable regardless of who endorsed them. It is also noteworthy that participants never referred to the characters' greater or lesser status when justifying their judgments, even though they had the opportunity to do so. Instead, their justifications referred exclusively to the nature of the beliefs (i.e., whether the beliefs were true, harmful, and so on).

These findings do not imply that the status of the person endorsing divergent beliefs is irrelevant to young children's thinking about diversity of belief. A character's status might be more relevant to children's thinking about diversity if the notion of status were couched in terms of specific roles and were given more or less institutional legitimacy. As an example, young children are likely to judge divergent beliefs as more acceptable (and perhaps even as right) if the beliefs were endorsed by a status-bearing teacher during a lecture rather than (or more than) by a statusless student. As suggested by previous research (e.g., Laupa & Turiel, 1986; Tisak, 1986), however, even in that case children's judgments are likely to be informed also by the realm of the belief endorsed (e.g., divergent moral beliefs are likely to be judged as wrong and unacceptable even if endorsed by status-bearing teachers). We therefore conclude not that the status of the proponent of divergent beliefs should be dismissed as irrelevant to children's thinking about diversity of belief but that the role of status in children's thinking about diversity of belief is likely to intersect with the realm of diversity.

Multiple findings, then, jointly bespeak of the realm of diversity as being central to the organization of children's thinking about diversity. Although one does not expect young children to articulate epistemological or ethical theories, the present findings have demonstrated that their thinking about diversity is organized according to distinctions dictated by the realm of diversity. We have furthermore shown that this is true even in the case of the more rudimentary understandings displayed by 5-year-olds. In underscoring the importance of the realm of diversity, the present findings dispute the soundness of the dichotomy of values and facts; even young children understood that not all beliefs concerning values are relative and not all beliefs concerning facts are not relative, and they recognized that divergent beliefs may be acceptable even when they concern facts and unacceptable even when they concern values.

The present findings also challenge the practice of inferring children's tolerance from their judgments of relativity (or vice versa), as participants' judgments of tolerance and judgments of relativity did not mirror one another. In discussing the findings of their study, Kuhn et al. (2000) voiced the concern that Western societies' emphasis on tolerance might lead individuals to treat all contrasting views as matters of personal taste or opinion. In their words, "It is a deceptively simple step, down a slippery slope, from the belief that everyone has a right to their opinion to the belief that all opinions are equally right. Tolerance of multiple positions, in other words, becomes confused with discriminability among them" (pp. 325–326). Relying on separate assessments of children's

thinking about the relative nature of beliefs and about the acceptability of divergent beliefs, the findings of the present study indicated that even young children distinguished between the notions of tolerance and relativism. Indeed, even 5-year-olds endorsed the position that some beliefs are wrong according to nonrelative criteria but should be, nonetheless, tolerated. These findings, we argue, suggest that the concern expressed by Kuhn et al. might not be entirely justified; they also demonstrate that to understand adequately children's developing thinking about diversity it is necessary to assess concurrently their judgments of relativity and tolerance.

It is not uncommon for children in their early school years to witness and participate in disagreements of many kinds. During such episodes of disagreement and conflict, children are called on to articulate their own beliefs and to consider those of others, to determine the truth and validity of their own and others' beliefs, and to negotiate the differences among them. The ways children do that are likely to be associated in complex ways with the quality of their social interactions and relationships. Unquestionably, diversity of belief is ubiquitous in children's lives and has potentially significant consequences for their social and emotional development. Understanding diversity, however, does not appear to be a simple task. A premise of our study is that diversity of belief is not all of one kind; therefore, there is not one type of thinking or one type of judgment that is well suited to address all diversity of belief. Rather than learning to process all instances of diversity through a particular mode of thinking (such as a tolerant attitude), the developmental task faced by children is to learn to recognize the features that distinguish among different types of differences. Our findings suggest that children are already engaged in this task by age 5, long before their high school or college years. Our data also suggest that rather than attempting to teach children one attitude toward diversity of belief (the "right" attitude, the tolerant attitude, etc.), it might be more appropriate to encourage them to attend to the distinct features of different types of beliefs and to facilitate their attempts at endorsing different, seemingly conflicting, views with respect to different instances of diversity.

Note

1   An extensive empirical investigation using the Monte Carlo technique demonstrated that ANOVA-based procedures are robust when used with dichotomous data (Lunney, 1970; see also D'Agostino, 1971; Gaito, 1980). The alternative analytic strategy based on log-linear models is likely to run into a distinct estimation problem when applied to designs in which a powerful experimental manipulation yields a fair number of empty cells. Empty cells represent a fundamental constraint for log-linear models as the log of zero is undefined. The standard strategy of deleting empty cells by excluding levels of the dependent or independent variables compromises the integrity of the data. The other standard strategy, of adding a small constant to empty cells, does not work well with repeated-measures designs. ANOVA models, by contrast, can get around this estimation problem as even minimal variance makes it possible to calculate means and generate estimates (Wainryb et al., 2001).

References

Astington, J. W., Harris, P. L., & Olson, D. R. (1988). *Developing theories of mind*. New York: Cambridge University Press.

Burr, J. E., & Hofer, B. K. (2002). Personal epistemology and theory of mind: Deciphering young children's beliefs about knowledge and knowing. *New Ideas in Psychology*, *20*, 199–224.

Carey, S. (1984). Are children fundamentally different kinds of thinkers and learners than adults? In S. Chipman, J. Segal, & R. Glaser (Eds.), *Thinking and learning skills* (Vol. 2, pp. 485–517). Hillsdale, NJ: Erlbaum.

Carpendale, J. I., & Chandler, M. J. (1996). On the distinction between false-belief understanding and subscribing to an interpretive theory of mind. *Child Development*, *67*, 1686–1706.

Chandler, M. J. (1987). The Othello effect: Essay on the emergence and eclipse of skeptical doubt. *Human Development*, *30*, 137–159.

Chandler, M. J., & Lalonde, C. (1996). Shifting to an interpretive theory of mind. In A. Sameroff & M. Haith (Eds.), *Reason and responsibility: The passage through childhood* (pp. 111–139). Chicago: University of Chicago Press.

Chandler, M. J., Sokol, B. W., & Wainryb, C. (2000). Beliefs about truth and beliefs about rightness. *Child Development*, *71*, 91–97.

Clinchy, B., & Mansfield, A. (1985, March). *Justifications offered by children to support positions on issues of "fact" and "opinion."* Paper presented at the meeting of the Eastern Psychological Association, Boston.

D'Agostino, R. B. (1971). A second look at analysis of variance on dichotomous data. *Journal of Educational Measurement*, *8*, 327–333.

Damon, W. (1983). The nature of social-cognitive changes in the developing child. In W. Overton (Ed.), *The relationship between social and cognitive development* (pp. 103–141). Hillsdale, NJ: Erlbaum.

Davidson, P., Turiel, E., & Black, A. (1983). The effect of stimulus familiarity on the use of criteria and justifications in children's social reasoning. *British Journal of Developmental Psychology*, *1*, 49–65.

Enright, R. D., & Lapsley, D. K. (1981). Judging others who hold opposite beliefs: The development of belief-discrepancy reasoning. *Child Development*, *52*, 1053–1063.

Flavell, J. H., Flavell, E. R., Green, F. L., & Moses, L. J. (1990). Young children's understanding of fact beliefs versus value beliefs. *Child Development*, *61*, 915–928.

Flavell, J. H., Mumme, D. L., Green, F. L., & Flavell, E. R. (1992). Young children's understanding of different types of beliefs. *Child Development*, *63*, 960–977.

Gaito, J. (1980). Measurement scales and statistics: Resurgence of an old misconception. *Psychological Bulletin*, *87*, 564–567.

Gelman, S. A. (1988). The development of inductions within natural kinds and artifact categories. *Cognitive Psychology*, *20*, 65–95.

Hofer, B. K., & Pintrich, P. R. (1997). The development of epistemological theories: Beliefs about knowledge and knowing and their relation to learning. *Review of Educational Research*, *67*, 88–140.

Hugues, C., & Dunn, J. (1998). Understanding mind and emotion: Longitudinal associations with mental-state talk between young friends. *Developmental Psychology*, *34*, 1026–1037.

Kalish, C. W. (1998). Natural and artifactual kinds: Are children realists or relativists about categories. *Developmental Psychology*, *34*, 376–391.

Kalish, C. W., Weissman, M., & Bernstein, D. (2000). Taking decisions seriously: Young children's understanding of conventional truth. *Child Development*, *71*, 1289–1308.

Keil, F. C. (1986). On the structure-dependent nature of stages of cognitive development. In I. Levin (Ed.), *Stage and structure: Reopening the debate* (pp. 144–163). Norwood, NJ: Ablex.

King, P., & Kitchener, K. S. (1994). *Developing reflective judgment: Understanding and promoting intellectual growth and critical thinking in adolescents and adults.* San Francisco: Jossey-Bass.

Kitchener, R. F. (2002). Folk epistemology: An introduction. *New Ideas in Psychology, 20,* 89–105.

Kohlberg, L. (1969). Stage and sequence: The cognitive-developmental approach to socialization. In D. A. Goslin (Ed.), *Handbook of socialization* (pp. 347–480). Chicago: Rand McNally.

Komatsu, L. K., & Galotti, K. M. (1986). Children's reasoning about social, physical, and logical regularities: A look at two worlds. *Child Development, 57,* 413–420.

Kuhn, D., Amsel, E., & O'Loughlin, M. (1988). *The development of scientific thinking skills.* Orlando, FL: Academic Press.

Kuhn, D., Cheney, R., & Weinstock, M. (2000). The development of epistemological understanding. *Cognitive Development, 15,* 309–328.

Kuhn, D., & Weinstock, M. (2002). What is epistemological thinking and why does it matter? In B. K. Hofer & P. R. Pintrich (Eds.), *The psychology of beliefs about knowledge and knowing* (pp. 121–144). Mahwah, NJ: Erlbaum.

Laupa, M., & Turiel, E. (1986). Children's conceptions of adult and non-hierarchical authority. *Child Development, 57,* 405–412.

Lunney, G. H. (1970). Using analysis of variance with a dichotomous dependent variable: An empirical study. *Journal of Educational Measurement, 7,* 263–269.

Mansfield, A. F., & Clinchy, B. M. (1993, April). *Continuity and change in children's epistemologies from ages 4 to 10.* Poster presented at the biennial meeting of the Society for Research in Child Development, New Orleans, LA.

Mansfield, A. F., & Clinchy, B. M. (1997, April). *Toward the integration of objectivity and subjectivity: A longitudinal study of epistemological development between the ages of 9 and 13.* Poster presented at the biennial meeting of the Society for Research in Child Development, Washington, DC.

Mansfield, A. F., & Clinchy, B. M. (2002). Toward the integration of objectivity and subjectivity: Epistemological development from 10 to 16. *New Ideas in Psychology, 20,* 225–262.

Nicholls, J. G., & Thorkildsen, T. A. (1988). Children's distinctions among matters of intellectual convention, logic, fact, and personal preference. *Child Development, 59,* 939–949.

Nucci, L., & Lee, J. Y. (1993). Morality and personal autonomy. In G. Noam & T. Wren (Eds.), *The moral self* (pp. 123–148). Cambridge, MA: MIT Press.

Perry, W. G. (1970). *Forms of intellectual and ethical development in the college years: A scheme.* New York: Holt, Rinehart, & Winston.

Pillow, B. H. (1999). Epistemological development in adolescence and adulthood: A multidimensional framework. *Genetic, Social, and General Psychology Monographs, 125,* 413–432.

Sabbagh, M. A., & Callanan, M. A. (1998). Metarepresentation in action: 3-, 4-, and 5-year-olds' developing theories of mind in parent—child conversations. *Developmental Psychology, 34,* 491–502.

Sigelman, C. K., & Toebben, J. L. (1992). Tolerant reactions to advocates of disagreeable ideas in childhood and adolescence. *Merrill-Palmer Quarterly, 38,* 542–557.

Smetana, J. G. (1981). Preschool conceptions of moral and social rules. *Child Development, 52,* 1333–1336.

Smetana, J. G., & Braeges, J. L. (1990). The development of toddler's moral and conventional judgments. *Merrill-Palmer Quarterly, 36,* 329–346.

Smetana, J. G., Schlagman, N., & Adams, P. W. (1993). Preschool children's judgments about hypothetical and actual transgressions. *Child Development, 64,* 202–214.

Tisak, M. S. (1986). Children's conceptions of parental authority. *Child Development, 57,* 166–176.

Turiel, E. (1983). *The development of social knowledge: Morality and convention.* Cambridge, England: Cambridge University Press.

Turiel, E. (1998). The development of morality. In W. Damon, (Series Ed.) & N. Eisenberg (Vol. Ed.), *Handbook of child psychology, Vol. 3: Social, emotional, and personality development* (5th ed., pp. 863–932). New York: Wiley.

Turiel, E., & Davidson, P. (1986). Heterogeneity, inconsistency, and asynchrony in the development of cognitive structures. In I. Levin (Ed.), *Stage and structure: Reopening the debate* (pp. 106–143). Norwood, NJ: Ablex.

Wainryb, C. (2000). Values and truths: The making and judging of moral decisions. In M. Laupa (Ed.), *New directions for child development: Rights and wrongs: How children evaluate the world* (pp. 33–46). San Francisco: Jossey-Bass.

Wainryb, C., & Ford, S. (1998). Young children's evaluations of acts based on beliefs different from their own. *Merrill-Palmer Quarterly, 44,* 484–503.

Wainryb, C., Shaw, L. A., Laupa, M., & Smith, K. (2001). Children's, adolescents', and young adults' thinking about different types of disagreements. *Developmental Psychology, 37,* 373–386.

Wainryb, C., Shaw, L. A., & Maianu, C. (1998). Tolerance and intolerance: Children's and adolescents' judgments of dissenting beliefs, speech, persons, and conduct. *Child Development, 69,* 1541–1555.

Walton, M. D. (2000). Say it's a lie or I'll punch you: Naive epistemology in classroom conflict episodes. *Discourse Processes, 29,* 113–136.

A Closer Look 5   Learning the Moral of the Story: Education in the Moral Domain

The expectation for new teachers is that their major concern in the classroom will have to do with establishing control over the students. In this article by Nucci (2006), the author, a moral developmental researcher and teacher educator, provides new perspectives on the connection between classroom management and facilitating children's social and moral development. Although no one would dispute the need for classroom order as an essential component of effective teaching, the emphasis on teacher control obscures the role that effective classroom management can have in contributing to students' moral and social development. All classrooms, no matter how they are run, constitute social environments that influence students' construction of morality and social values. The issue, then, is not whether classroom management affects

social development, but rather how classroom management may contribute positively to students' moral and social growth. This requires teachers to engage in the same kind of critical analysis of practice as would be directed to the teaching of subject matter. Not only is it important to have an awareness of available options or strategies for how to handle classroom situations, but it is also important to be knowledgeable about the "subject matter" of social and moral development and how it relates to a given set of practices. This article provides strategies for achieving this goal in school contexts.

Nucci, L. (2006). Classroom management for moral and social development. In C. Evertson & C. Weinstein (Eds.), *Handbook of classroom management: Research, practice, and contemporary issues* (pp. 711–731). Mahwah, NJ: Laurence Erlbaum Associates.

Classroom Exercises, Debates, and Discussion Questions

- *Classroom discussion.* Lawrence Kohlberg (1971) used a complex hypothetical dilemma, referred to as the Heinz dilemma, to measure moral judgment in adolescence and adulthood, and formulate stages of moral judgment. This dilemma provides a source for discussing moral issues: "A man [Heinz] has a wife who has cancer. A druggist created a drug that could save her life. He charges 10 times what it cost him to make it. Heinz decides to break into the druggist store to steal the drug to save his wife's life. Is that all right or not all right?" (Kohlberg, 1971). Discuss different reasons for why or why not. What priority do individuals place on the value of human life, the role of property rights, laws about stealing, the importance of spousal obligations, and the profit motive regarding the creation of a drug to save lives?
- *Observation.* Elliot Turiel (1983, 1998) proposed and demonstrated that young children evaluate

social rules in school differently, and that their conflicts reflect these differences. Whereas some rules pertain to "moral" issues, such as hitting someone, other rules pertain to "conventions," such as wearing a smock to paint a picture. In this observation, you will record children's conflicts and determine whether conflicts about moral issues are resolved differently from conflicts about conventional issues. Observe preschool children's interactions at a preschool during free-play. Record all conflicts that occur (defined as any "protest, resistance, or retaliation" or "No!"). Code conflicts for the "Type of conflict," such as about moral issues (involving a victim, such as harm, not sharing, not taking turns) or conventional issues (not following a game rule, not cleaning up, not structuring activities, being loud indoors). Then record the "Type of Conflict Resolution," such as child-generated (children work it out through negotiation, bargaining), teacher-generated (teacher intervenes), or topic dropped. What types of conflicts do children resolve on their own? What types of conflicts do teachers intervene in the most?

- *Focused debate.* Judith Smetana (2006) studied parent–adolescent discourse about conflicts and found that some issues that are viewed as conventional by parents are viewed as personal by adolescents. Divide the class up into three groups: "Mothers," "Fathers," and "Adolescents." Then distribute slips of paper with typical "conflicts" on each paper: Cleaning one's room, Staying out late, Not taking out the garbage, Not cleaning up after a party, Stealing, Drinking while driving, Wearing a tattoo, Calling a teacher by his or her first name. Ask each group to categorize the "conflict" as one of three options: "Wrong, even if there is no house rule about it," "Wrong, only if there is a house rule about it," or "Not a matter of right or wrong; personal choice." Then, find out whether the "mothers," "fathers," and "adolescents" agree or disagree about the categorization of each conflict and why.
- *Focused debate.* Divide up into two groups. Debate the issue "What is morality?" with one group making the case for a universal perspective, and one group making the case for culturally specific perspectives.
- *Classroom discussion.* What experiences lead some children to be more prosocial than other children, and some children to be more aggressive? Discuss the role of personality differences, peer relationships, and authority influences.

References

Kohlberg, L. (1971). From is to ought: How to commit the naturalistic fallacy and get away with it in the study of moral development. In T. Mischel (Ed.), *Psychology and genetic epistemology* (pp. 151–235). New York: Academic Press.

Smetana, J. G. (2006). Social-cognitive domain theory: Consistencies and variations in children's moral and social judgments. In M. Killen & J. G. Smetana (Eds.), *Handbook of moral development* (pp. 119–154). Mahwah, NJ: Lawrence Erlbaum Associates.

Turiel, E. (1983). *The development of social knowledge: Morality and convention.* Cambridge: Cambridge University Press.

Turiel, E. (1998). The development of morality. In W. Damon (Ed.), *Handbook of child psychology: Vol. 3. Social, emotional, and personality development* (5th ed., pp. 863–932). New York: Wiley.

Additional Resources

For more about moral development, see:

Carlo, G., Mestre, M. V., Samper, P., Tur, A., & Armenta, B. (2010). Feelings or emotions? Moral cognitions and emotions as longitudinal predictors of prosocial and aggressive behaviors. *Personality and Individual Differences, 48,* 872–877.

de Waal, F. B. M. (1996). *Good natured: The origins of right and wrong in humans and other animals.* Cambridge, MA: Harvard University Press.

Dunn, J., Brown, J. R., & Maguire, M. (1995). The development of children's moral sensibility: Individual differences and emotion understanding. *Developmental Psychology, 31*(4), 649–659.

Killen, M., & Smetana, J. G. (Eds.). (2006). *Handbook of moral development.* Mahwah, NJ: Lawrence Erlbaum Associates.

Malti, T., Gummerum, M., Keller, M., & Buchmann, M. (2009). Children's moral motivation, sympathy, and prosocial behavior. *Child Development, 80,* 442–460.

Nucci, L. P. (2001). *Education in the moral domain.* Cambridge: Cambridge University Press.

Turiel, E. (2006). The development of morality. In W. Damon & R. M. Lerner (Eds.), *Handbook of child psychology: Social, emotional, and personality development* (pp. 789–857). New York: Wiley-Blackwell.

7

SELF IDENTITY AND GROUP IDENTITY

Introduction　255

**Changes in Children's
Self-Competence and Values: Gender
and Domain Differences Across Grades
One through Twelve**　256

*Janis E. Jacobs, Stephanie Lanza, D. Wayne Osgood,
Jacquelynne S. Eccles, and Allan Wigfield*

　Introduction　256

　Method　260

　Results　264

　Discussion　271

**Ethnic Identity and the Daily
Psychological Well-Being of
Adolescents From Mexican
and Chinese Backgrounds**　278

*Lisa Kiang, Tiffany Yip, Melinda Gonzales-Backen,
Melissa Witkow, and Andrew J. Fuligni*

　Method　281

　Results　283

　Discussion　288

**The Development of Subjective Group
Dynamics: Children's Judgments of
Normative and Deviant In-Group
and Out-Group Individuals**　292

*Dominic Abrams, Adam Rutland,
and Lindsey Cameron*

　Method　296

　Results　299

　Discussion　305

**A Closer Look 6　Who Am I and
What Group Do I Belong to?
Self Identity in the Context
of Social Interactions**　311

Introduction

A fundamental question in children's social development is "Who am I?" Identity can be defined as knowledge of the self and includes self-concept, self-esteem, and self-efficacy. Each of these terms describes different aspects of self-identity. Self-concept refers to the categories that you associate with your identity, your estimates of competence, and how you expect others to think about you. Self-esteem refers to the opinion and the value that you hold of yourself. Self-efficacy pertains to how accomplished and effective you view yourself in terms of accomplishing goals and fulfilling tasks. The development of the self-system in childhood progresses from the most rudimentary sense of self (i.e., the ability to recognize oneself in a mirror) in toddlerhood, to concrete conceptions in early childhood (e.g., "I am a boy"; "I am 4 years old"), to a more abstractly defined and differentiated self in later childhood and adolescence (e.g., "I am a caring person"; "I am good at math but not so good at baseball").

Erikson (1968) was the first psychologist to chart age-related changes regarding conceptions of identity throughout the life span. From a neo-Freudian perspective, Erickson characterized identity at different life periods as the outcome of a series of eight different psychosocial conflicts, each with the potential to create an "identity crisis." These conflicts reflect a series of tensions that have to be resolved, from "basic trust vs. basic mistrust" in infancy through to "ego integrity vs. despair" in old age. For example, when the infant begins to trust the world, he or she can move on to the next phase of identity development. The major contribution of Erikson's work was to bring a strong focus to identity, or self-understanding, throughout development, and his theories provided the foundations for contemporary theoretical models of identity development (e.g., Damon & Hart, 1988; Phinney, 2003).

Identity can reflect a range of categories, including gender, race/ethnicity, and nationality. Some categories of identity are relatively fixed in life, such as gender and ethnicity; and other categories are relatively changeable (such as religion, nationality, and political party affiliation). Group identity is how you define yourself in relation to groups that you identify with, who constitutes your "ingroup" and your "outgroup," and the associated beliefs, judgments, and values that result from affiliation with a group. Stemming from Social Identity Theory (Tajfel & Turner, 1979), research on group identity demonstrates how children's identity with groups is related to their self-esteem and self-concept. Self-identity and group identity are both part of how an individual relates to the social world and are core parts of social development.

In this section, we feature three articles on very different aspects of identity, which each reflect important and timely areas of research. The article by Jacobs et al. (2002) describes a longitudinal investigation of children's identity regarding perceptions of self-competence. These authors explored whether children's beliefs about their own "talents" in given academic areas (e.g., math, language, arts, sports) might be related to how much "value" they placed on these different tasks. The second article focuses on the links between ethnic identity and psychological well-being. Kiang et al. (2006) asked adolescents (living in California) from Mexican or Chinese family backgrounds to keep a "daily diary" tracking their feelings and assessed ethnic identity by adolescents' responses to statements about how they felt about their own ethnic identity. The third article focused on *group* identity. Abrams, Rutland, and Cameron (2003) examined how 5–11-year-old English children evaluated English and German soccer teams, and whether they were supportive or critical of a soccer fan who cheered for the other team. The goals of the study were to determine how children would evaluate: (1) someone who deviates from the ingroup norm; (2) someone who supports the outgroup; and (3) someone who expresses a deviant view from the group. Determining the processes that underlie exclusion and deviance in social groups is relevant for understanding many social outcomes in childhood and adolescence. Thus, these three lines of research, self-identity, ethnic identity, and group identity, are related to many areas of social development, including academic success, life satisfaction, and experiences of inclusion.

References

Damon, W., & Hart, D. (1988). *Self-understanding in childhood and adolescence*. New York: Cambridge University Press.

Erikson, E. H. (1968). *Identity: Youth and crisis*. Oxford: Norton & Co.

Phinney, J. (2003). Ethnic identity and acculturation. In K. Chun, P. Ball, & G. Marin (Eds.), *Acculturation:*

Advances in theory, measurement, and applied research (pp. 63–81). Washington, DC: American Psychological Association.

Tajfel, H., & Turner, J. C. (1979). An integrative theory of intergroup conflict. In W. G. Austin & S. Worchel (Eds.), *The social psychology of intergroup relations* (pp. 33–47). Monterey, CA: Brooks-Cole.

··

Changes in Children's Self-Competence and Values: Gender and Domain Differences Across Grades One through Twelve

Janis E. Jacobs, Stephanie Lanza, D. Wayne Osgood, Jacquelynne S. Eccles, and Allan Wigfield

Introduction

The development of children's beliefs about self-competence has been of great interest to researchers because such beliefs are related to both achievement motivation and self-esteem. Research on achievement motivation has documented the role of self-competence beliefs as mediators of actual achievement in various domains (for a review, see Eccles, Wigfield, & Schiefele, 1998). According to numerous theories (e.g., attribution theory, self-efficacy theory, self-worth theory) children perform better and are more motivated to select increasingly challenging tasks when they believe that they have the ability to accomplish a particular task (e.g., Bandura, 1994; Covington, 1984; Weiner, 1985). Although early work (e.g., Shavelson, Hubner, & Stanton, 1976) emphasized the relations between global beliefs about the self and achievement, most current research and theory (e.g., Byrne, 1996; Eccles et al., 1998; Harter, 1998; Marsh, 1993a for review) focuses on the links between domain-specific self-competence beliefs and domain-specific motivation and performance.

In addition to competence-related beliefs, motivation researchers have assessed other constructs that may be crucial to children's achievement choices (see Eccles et al., 1998). One such construct is children's valuing of particular tasks or activities. Although less empirical work has focused on the role of task-specific values, related constructs (e.g., importance, intrinsic motivation) have been emphasized in the theoretical models of Harter (1986) and Deci and Ryan (1985). Larson (2000) also highlighted the role of intrinsic motivation in maintaining involvement in extracurricular activities, such as sports. Eccles' and colleagues (Eccles et al., 1983) have developed an expectancy-value theory of task choice in which children's competence beliefs and subjective task values within a specific domain are crucial to motivation and to future achievement choices within that domain. They have emphasized the distinctive contributions made by competence beliefs, expectations for success, and task values to achievement and choice in different domains (e.g., math, English, sports), and have provided support for the expectancy-value model by showing that self-competence beliefs are related to achievement, even after controlling for previous achievement or ability in a variety of domains (Eccles, 1987; Eccles, Adler, & Meece, 1984; Eccles, Wigfield, Harold, & Blumenfeld, 1993; Meece, Parsons, Kaczala, Goff, & Futterman, 1982; Wigfield, Eccles, Mac Iver, Reuman, & Midgley, 1991). In addition, they have found that domain-specific values predict current and future activity choices (Eccles & Harold, 1991; Eccles & Wigfield, 1995; Feather, 1988; Meece, Wigfield, & Eccles, 1990; Wigfield, 1994). Research in the area of sports participation supports the link between values and activity choices by showing that interest is highly related to involvement in sports (Garton & Pratt, 1987), fun or enjoyment is the most often reported reason for continued involvement in sports (Wankel & Berger, 1990), and adolescents choose leisure activities that they consider intrinsically motivating and challenging (Larson, 2000; Larson & Verma, 1999).

Given the predictive role of children's competence-related beliefs and values, a major emphasis in research on motivation has been an assessment of how these constructs change as children develop (for reviews, see Eccles et al., 1998; Stipek & Mac Iver, 1989). Extant studies have relied primarily on cross-sectional or short-term longitudinal data. In these studies (e.g., Alexander & Entwisle, 1988; Eccles, Wigfield, et al., 1993; Marsh, 1989; Nicholls, 1978; Nicholls & Miller, 1984; Wigfield et al., 1997), researchers report that self-competence beliefs decline across middle childhood and early adolescence. Decreases in perceptions of academic self-competence have sometimes been linked with the transition into junior high (e.g., Eccles et al., 1989; Eccles, Midgley, et al., 1993), leading to suggestions about the "goodness of fit" between the adolescent's developmental stage and the junior high or middle school environment (Eccles & Midgley, 1989; Eccles, Midgley, et al., 1993). Others (Skinner, Zimmer-Gembeck, & Connell, 1998) have suggested that a developmental trend toward viewing self-competence, rather than effort, as a cause of school performance may be linked to beliefs about perceived control and the decline in school engagement for some children during the transition to middle school. Although no prior studies have tracked the developmental trajectories of self-beliefs from early elementary school through high school, evidence from studies of adolescents (e.g., Eccles et al., 1983; Eccles et al., 1989; Wigfield et al., 1991) suggest that declines in perceptions of self-competence may continue through secondary school, particularly for math.

Age differences in perceptions of competence also appear to differ by domain. For example, some studies (Eccles et al., 1983; Eccles et al., 1989; Marsh, 1989; Wigfield et al., 1991) have found that adolescents have more positive competence beliefs than do elementary children in English, but that the pattern is reversed in math. In some less studied domains (e.g., sports), conflicting results have been reported. Some researchers (Eccles & Harold, 1991; Wigfield et al.,

1997) have found no age differences in self-competence perceptions across middle childhood. Others (e.g., Marsh, 1989; Marsh, Barnes, Cairns, & Tidman, 1984) have reported age-related declines in self-concept of physical abilities during middle childhood, a decline and then increase during early adolescence, and an increase during later adolescence. These discrepancies may have been due to the cross-sectional nature of these studies or to the fact that sports participation has more options than involvement in academics. Individuals may select types of sports (e.g., football versus badminton) and competition levels (e.g., varsity teams versus intramurals) that maintain positive self-perceptions of competence. Participation in sports clearly becomes increasingly diverse with age (Flammer, Alsaker, & Noack, 1999; Snyder & Spreitzer, 1992; Wankel & Berger, 1990), and this may be due to the optional nature of involvement.

Fewer studies on developmental trends in task values have been performed, especially during the elementary school years. The one longitudinal study of changes in elementary school-aged children's values (Wigfield et al., 1997) showed sharp declines across the elementary school years for their valuing of music and sports, and more gradual declines for their valuing of math and reading. Studies of adolescents also show domain-specific changes in subjective task values that vary by domain. Early adolescents' values for math and sports decrease, but their values for English remain stable and then increase (Eccles et al., 1984; Eccles et al., 1983; Eccles et al., 1989; Wigfield et al., 1991). Similar to the patterns for competence beliefs, decreases in values for math and English have been linked to the transition to junior high (Eccles et al., 1989; Wigfield et al., 1991). No research examining longitudinal change in task values spanning middle childhood and adolescence has been reported for any of these domains.

Although task values and perceptions of competence have each been linked to achievement outcomes, few studies have examined the relation between the two sets of beliefs over time. Harter's research (1986, 1990) has shown that even when children perform similarly in a domain, their self-esteem varies depending on how much they value the domain. Poor performance is related to lower self-esteem only for those who value the domain, suggesting that the relation between competence and values is important for self-esteem within a particular domain. Eccles' model (Eccles et al., 1983) suggests that perceptions of self-competence impact subjective task values for a domain, which, in turn, contribute to achievement outcomes. If children feel competent at a task, they are more likely to value it over time. Some evidence for this can be found in earlier research (Eccles & Wigfield, 1995) showing that self-competence and task values are positively related to each other and that the relation between competence beliefs and utility value increases as children get older. Both Harter's and Eccles' models and the earlier research suggest that perceptions of competence are likely to be related to increased interest and value for an activity; this may lead children to spend more time on the task, improve their skills, and result in greater long-term engagement over time (Jacobs & Eccles, 2000; Wigfield, 1994). Many others (e.g., Deci & Ryan, 1985; Jacobs, Finken, Griffin, & Wright, 1998; Sansone & Harackiewicz, 1996) have suggested that self-competence is related to intrinsic value for a task and other self-beliefs for children, adolescents, and adults; however, the effects of changes in self-competence beliefs on changes in values have not previously been studied longitudinally. The current study presents the trajectories for longitudinal changes in task values, before and after controlling for self-competence beliefs, to document the effect of one set of beliefs on the other.

An important emphasis of much of the research using the Eccles et al. model has been the role of gender differences in self-perceptions and values as potential mediators of gender differences in achievement choices (e.g., Eccles, Wigfield, et al., 1993; Jacobs & Eccles, 1992; Wigfield et al., 1997). Although gender differences in actual achievement in some academic domains have declined (e.g., math and biology), gender differences in domain-specific self-beliefs continue to be reported (e.g., Crain, 1996; Eccles, Wigfield, et al., 1993; Jacobs et al., 1998; Marsh, 1993a; Marsh & Yeung, 1998; Wigfield et al., 1997). In these studies, boys systematically rated their expectations for success and abilities in male-typed domains (e.g., math, sports) higher than did girls, and girls rated their expectations and abilities in female-typed domains

(e.g., English) higher than did boys. In addition, gender differences in participation in sports and other discretionary leisure activities continue to be reported; girls play fewer sports than boys and the differences increase with age (Archer & McDonald, 1990; Larson & Verma, 1999; Shaw, Kleiber, & Caldwell, 1995).

In previous research (Eccles, 1987; Eccles et al., 1984), domain-stereotyped gender differences in self-beliefs appear to emerge during early adolescence and grow larger during the adolescent years. These developmental changes were attributed to differential socialization processes (Eccles, 1987; Maccoby, 1966) and to "gender-role intensification" (Hill & Lynch, 1983). More recently, however, researchers have found that gender differences in competence beliefs and values emerge quite early during the elementary school years (Eccles, Wigfield, et al., 1993; Marsh, 1989; Wigfield et al., 1997), and that the gender differences remain in place through the school years. Interactions of gender and age generally have not been found, providing little evidence for age-related changes in the magnitude of gender differences (Marsh, 1993b; Marsh & Yeung, 1998; Wigfield et al., 1997). No previous studies have traced gender differences in children's competence beliefs and values across the elementary school, middle school, and high school years. The present study did so.

The evidence just reviewed suggests that critical theoretical and empirical links have already been established between self-beliefs and achievement motivation and that gender differences in self-beliefs may mediate gender differences in selected achievement behaviors. Much less is known about the long-term changes in self-competence beliefs and values during childhood and adolescence, and what is already known is based primarily on cross-sectional or short-term longitudinal data. The goal of this study was to extend previous research by documenting age-related trends across grades 1 through 12 in perceptions of self-competence and activity values across the mathematics, language arts, and sports domains. Although previous studies have investigated changes in children's perceptions of competence and values, few have used longitudinal data and none have spanned such a large age range. Small perturbations may be magnified and subtle trends may go unnoticed in cross-sectional and short-term longitudinal studies; thus, it is critical to begin to chart changes across longer time periods to create a comprehensive picture of the development of children's self-beliefs. To accomplish this, we used a cohort-sequential longitudinal design to span a larger age range than has been possible in earlier studies. This design allows for an examination of both longitudinal change and cohort differences, resulting in the strongest test of developmental shifts (see Baltes & Nesselroade, 1979; Menard, 1991); it is rarely used in the field, however, due to the high expense and time demands.

In addition, no previous studies have attempted to examine the impact of changes in competence beliefs on changes in values over time. Changes in the trajectories of subjective task values may be explained, in part, by changes in competence beliefs; but previous studies have been unable to adequately describe the potential impact of changes in self-competence on changes in values over a long period of time, because the appropriate longitudinal data and statistical techniques have not previously been available.

The current study is also unique in that it compared children's self-beliefs and subjective task values in the three domains of mathematics, language arts, and sports. As suggested earlier, previous studies (Eccles, Wigfield, et al., 1993; Harter, 1982; Marsh, 1989; Wigfield et al., 1997) have shown that children have clearly differentiated task-specific self-beliefs as early as first grade; therefore, it is important to examine self-beliefs in specific activity domains. Based on the previous literature and our own work, we expected competence beliefs and subjective task values to be highest in the first grade, with decreases across grades 1 through 12 in all domains. In addition, we expected the shape of growth (decline) over time to be generally linear or to be quadratic with a steeper decline during early adolescence, reflecting either gender-role intensification or middle school transition (e.g., Eccles et al., 1989; Nottelmann, 1987; Wigfield et al., 1991). Finally, we expected declining competence beliefs to explain some of the decline in values, resulting in flatter trajectories for subjective task values after controlling for competence beliefs. This prediction was based on the expected similarity between the growth curves and the strong relation between changes in competence beliefs and changes in subjective task values.

Due to our interest in gender (e.g., Eccles et al., 1983; Jacobs, 1991; Jacobs & Eccles, 1992; Wigfield et al., 1991),

we also examined gender differences in trajectories for these domains. We specifically chose one clearly male-typed domain (sports) and one clearly female-typed domain (language arts). Math was chosen as the third domain, an area that recent research (Campbell, Hombo, & Mazzeo, 2000) suggests is either similar for males and females or only slightly male typed. Based on earlier work (Marsh, 1989; Wigfield et al., 1997) that reported gender differences in both values and competence beliefs exist as early as first grade, we expected to find gender-role stereotypic differences even in the youngest children. In addition, previous reports (Eccles, Midgley, et al., 1993; Huston, 1983; Ruble & Martin, 1998) of increases in gender differences in self-beliefs in middle childhood and adolescence led us to expect longitudinal changes in gender differences that would vary by domain. If gender socialization actually increases differences between males and females over time, we would expect the gaps to increase in line with gender stereotyping, favoring males in the domains of math and sports and favoring females in the domain of language arts.

An important advance in the present study was the use of Hierarchical Linear Modeling (HLM; Bryk & Raudenbush, 1987, 1992) to implement a growth curve analysis to test our hypotheses. This is a particularly good technique for examining the gender differences in developmental trajectories that have been suggested by cross-sectional and short-term longitudinal analyses, because it provides a flexible framework for parsimoniously capturing patterns of linear or nonlinear change over time. Thus, because HLM is not limited to linear change, it allows us to examine patterns that include both increases and declines in gender differences over the course of development. Using HLM, we were able to implement an analysis that was strictly limited to within-individual change, controlling for all stable individual differences, while addressing the possible nonindependence of measurement due to repeated measures. This approach also allowed us to take full advantage of our cohort-sequential design by testing for and modeling cohort effects.

The use of growth modeling in the present study contrasts with the many studies of the development of self-beliefs that have relied on path analyses or structural equation models, in which explanatory variables on one occasion influence later perceptions of self-competence or values (e.g., Marsh & Yeung, 1998). Such analyses did not suit our purposes because they do not address changes in mean levels over time, which is our focus. Although changes in mean levels of self-beliefs have been tested in short-term longitudinal studies (e.g., Wigfield et al., 1997) by using repeated-measures MANOVA, such an approach becomes quite unwieldy for six waves of data covering a span of 12 grade levels. The HLM growth model used in this research was an improvement over that approach because it efficiently captured developmental trajectories with only a few parameters and allowed us to include all respondents, even when they did not provide data for the full set of six observations. A similar strategy was used by Skinner and colleagues (Skinner, Zimmer-Gembeck, & Connell, 1998) to examine longitudinal changes in perceived self-control during middle childhood and early adolescence.

Method

Participants

The present study is part of the Childhood and Beyond longitudinal project (Eccles et al., 1983) investigating the development of children's self-perceptions, task values, and activity choices. Children, parents, and teachers were recruited through the children's schools; all children in each classroom were asked to participate. Seventy-five percent of the children both agreed to participate and obtained parental permission. Data were collected between 1989 and 1999 from children who were attending 10 elementary schools in four middle-class, primarily European American school districts in the suburbs of a large midwestern city. The schools were all public schools with varied curricula. Due to the longitudinal nature of the study, as students moved through middle and high school, they experienced a wide variety of teachers and courses. No attempt was made to limit the sample by ability, course selection, or school context, although performance was controlled in the analyses.

A cross-sequential design was employed, in which three cohorts of children were followed longitudi-

Table 7.1 Sample size for each cohort, grade of subjects at each year of data collection

Cohort	Year					
	1	2	3	4	5	6
1 ($n = 250$)	1	2	3	7	8	9
2 ($n = 278$)	2	3	4	8	9	10
3 ($n = 233$)	4	5	6	10	11	12

nally across the elementary, middle, and high school years. Children were in the first, second, and fourth grades during Year 1. The results reported here are based on 761 students who were present at the first wave and who provided data for both gender and grade. Additionally, for each outcome measure, participants were excluded if they were missing the relevant objective indicator of performance. The grade at each wave and sample size for each cohort appear in Table 7.1. Due to a 3-year gap in the data collection, these children were in grades 9, 10, and 12 at Year 6; thus, the combined cross-sequential sample provides information on children from grade 1 through grade 12. In addition, the design yielded data for more than one cohort of children at the same grade level at various time points in the study, which provided replication of grade-level effects across cohorts.

The original sample consisted of 53% girls and 47% boys, and these proportions remained the same throughout the waves of data collection. Information about income provided by the school districts indicated that the children were from middle-class backgrounds; average family income in the districts in 1990 was $50,000. Over 95% of the children were European American. Attrition in the sample was due mostly to children moving far away from the school districts sampled. Every effort was made to locate the participants each year, and the longitudinal sample included children who continued to live in the same general area, even if they no longer attended the participating schools. Analyses reported elsewhere (see Wigfield et al., 1997) indicated that for each of the variables of interest, the mean scores for the full cross-sectional sample and the longitudinal sample were not significantly different.

Table 7.2 Reliabilities of seven outcome measures

	Wave 2	Wave 3	Wave 4	Wave 5	Wave 6	Wave 7
Math ability (5 items)	.76 (855)	.79 (992)	.84 (910)	.90 (706)	.92 (488)	.92 (545)
Math value (4 items)	N.A.	.61 (995)	.71 (917)	.79 (708)	.84 (491)	.84 (551)
Reading ability (5 items)	.82 (862)	.84 (986)	.86 (910)	.93 (708)	N.A.	.93 (545)
Reading value (4 items)	N.A.	.73 (992)	.73 (906)	.84 (709)	N.A.	.86 (547)
Sports ability (5 items)	.84 (850)	.84 (982)	.89 (906)	.93 (707)	.93 (480)	.94 (525)
Sports value (4 items)	N.A.	.85 (987)	.89 (881)	.92 (711)	.93 (491)	.92 (548)
Social ability (2 items)	N.A.	.84 (998)	.79 (910)	.88 (711)	.89 (487)	.90 (548)

Note. Values represent Cronbach's α (*n*). Alphas are based on complete sample, not restricted sample used in analyses. N.A. = not available.

Procedure and measures

Each spring, the children completed questionnaires measuring their competence beliefs and subjective task values about the math, language arts, and sports, as well as many other constructs. Children completed the questionnaires in their classrooms in the participating schools. Most items were answered using 1 to 7 Likert-style response scales, and the items were modified from earlier questionnaire items developed by Eccles and colleagues to assess children's and adolescents' beliefs about the same domains. The items have good psychometric properties (see Eccles et al., 1983; Eccles et al., 1984; Eccles & Wigfield, 1995; Eccles, Wigfield, et al., 1993; Parsons, Adler, & Kaczala, 1982). Because the current study included children younger than those in previous studies using these measures, great care was taken to ensure that the children understood the constructs being assessed. The items were pilot tested on 100 children to check for comprehension, and illustrations were added to the answer scales to foster children's understanding of how to use them (for a more detailed discussion, see Eccles, Wigfield, et al., 1993). All questions were read aloud to all the children in Years 1 and 2 and to the youngest cohort in Year 3; after that, all children read the questionnaires on their own. The questionnaires were administered in three sessions lasting 20 min each.

Competence belief items

For math, language arts, and sports, five competence belief items were asked to assess children's self-perceptions of their abilities in each domain.

Comparable wording was used in each domain. Alphas are presented in Table 7.2.

Subjective task value items

For math, language, and sports, the subjective task value items asked children how interesting/fun each activity was, how important they thought being good at the activity was, and how useful they thought each activity was. Four items were used at each year and comparable wording was used in each domain, except for the name of the domain. Alphas are presented in Table 7.2.

Scale construction

Based on factor analyses and theoretical considerations (for more details about the factor analyses, see Eccles, Wigfield, et al., 1993), scales were developed for the competence belief and subjective value constructs. Internal consistency reliabilities for the various competence belief scales ranged from .73 to .92 across domains and times of measurement (see Table 7.2). Thus, overall the internal consistency of the competence beliefs and interest measures ranged from good to excellent.

Performance measures

Indicators of performance in each domain were collected for all children. The Slossen Intelligence Test–Revised (1991 edition) was given to all children when they joined the study. This measure, which yields a total score only, is designed for use as a "quick estimate of general cognitive ability" (Slosson, Nicholson, & Hibpshman, 1991, p. 1). The Bruininks–Osertsky Test of Motor Proficiency (Bruininks, 1977) also was given to all children when they joined the study. This measure includes the performance of gross motor tasks, such as running, ball throwing, and jumping, as well as fine motor tasks, such as tracing and joining dots (Bruininks & Bruininks, 1977).

Description of analyses

The central goal of the present study was to describe the changes in children's ability perceptions and task values in three domains from first through twelfth grade. Hierarchical Linear Modeling (HLM; Bryk & Raudenbush, 1987, 1992) was used for the analyses. HLM extends multiple regression to nested or repeated-measures data. Because there are several observations for each person, waves of data are nested within persons. In the terminology of HLM, the Level 1 units of analysis are waves or occasions of measurement, and the Level 2 units of analysis are persons.

When applied to the cohort sequential research design, HLM provides a powerful and flexible framework for analyzing individual change over time; determining whether individual characteristics, such as gender, are related to initial status or to change; and analyzing time-varying factors that might explain change over time in the outcome. The HLM framework was especially useful for our purposes because there is no assumption that the number and spacing of observations will be consistent across individuals or across time. Thus, HLM was quite compatible with the complexities of this study's research design (which are apparent in Table 7.1), including multiple cohorts sampled in different years of school, a 3-year gap in data collection, and sample attrition.

THE LEVEL I MODEL

A two-level HLM model such as ours is defined by two types of regression equations. The first is the Level 1 or within-person model, which expresses the outcome variable in relation to explanatory variables that vary across time. This study used a growth curve model, which means that the pattern of change for each person was modeled by a polynomial function of time (Bryk & Raudenbush, 1987, 1992):

$$Y_{it} = \beta_{0i} + \beta_{1i}(\text{Grade}_{it} - 6)$$
$$+ \beta_{2i}(\text{Grade}_{it} - 6)^2 + e_{it} \qquad (1)$$

In this equation, person i's score on the outcome variable Y at time t equals a quadratic function of current grade, plus the residual term e_{it}. Three β parameters capture the quadratic growth function, and each carries the subscript i to indicate that it is specific to this individual. β_{0i} is a constant term, indicating the expected value of Y for this person when other variables in this equation equal 0. Notice that the value of 6 has been subtracted from grade, so this constant characterizes the sixth grade (when β_{1i} and β_{2i} will be multiplied by 0). By "centering" the equation in this way, parameters that would otherwise be meaningless can be interpreted in relation to the age in the middle of the span being studied (Bryk & Raudenbush, 1992, pp. 25–29). The coefficients β_{1i} and β_{2i} summarize change over time, with β_{1i} equal to the rate of change at grade 6, and β_{2i} expressing change in slope over time. The three parameters of the growth curve provide an efficient summary of patterns of change across the 12 grades spanned by this study.

THE LEVEL 2 MODEL

The Level 1 model defines the meaning of the Level 2 model because the coefficients of the Level 1 equation serve as the outcome variables for the Level 2 equations. The explanatory variables for the Level 2 equations are variables that do not change over time, either because they are inherently stable characteristics or because they were measured on only one occasion. The individual level constant, β_{0i}, serves as the outcome measure in the first Level 2 equation:

$$\beta_{0i} = \gamma_{00} + \gamma_{01}\text{Gender}_i + \gamma_{02}\text{Ability}_i + \gamma_{03}$$
$$Mean(\text{Grade} - 6)_i + \gamma_{04}Mean(\text{Grade} - 6)^2_i \quad (2)$$
$$+ u_{0i}$$

This equation indicates that person i's level on the outcome variable in the sixth grade, β_{0i}, is equal to a constant, γ_{00}, plus the products of several regression coefficients, γ_{0j}, times explanatory variables, plus a residual term, u_{0i}. The individual slope and "acceleration" terms from Equation 1 serve as the outcome variables in the remaining Level 2 equations:

$$\beta_{1i} = \gamma_{10} + \gamma_{11}\text{Gender}_i + \gamma_{12}\text{Ability}_i + \gamma_{13}$$
$$\text{Grade2}_i + \gamma_{14}\text{Grade4}_i + u_{1i} \qquad (3)$$

$$\beta_{2i} = \gamma_{20} + \gamma_{21}\text{Gender}_i + \gamma_{22}\text{Ability}_i + \gamma_{23}$$
$$\text{Grade4}_i + \gamma_{24}\text{Grade4}_i + u_{2i} \qquad (4)$$

The set of constant terms for the Level-2 equations defines the growth curve when all of the explanatory variables in those equations equal 0. In the present study, all of those explanatory variables were centered at their sample means (i.e., the mean was subtracted from the original scores) so that these constant terms characterized the average growth curves for the entire sample. Thus, γ_{00} was the sample mean in grade 6, γ_{10} was the average rate of change in the outcome variable at that grade, and γ_{20} reflected the degree of curvature averaged across the sample (Bryk & Raudenbush, 1992, pp. 25–29).

The coefficients for gender, γ_{01}, γ_{11}, and γ_{21}, indicate the difference in the growth curves for males and females, with γ_{01} reflecting the mean gender difference in the sixth grade; γ_{11} the difference in slope in the sixth grade; and γ_{21} the difference in curvature. Because gender is a dummy variable with 0 assigned to males and 1 to females, positive values indicate higher means, slopes, and more convex curvature for females than for males. The coefficients γ_{02}, γ_{12}, and γ_{22} play the corresponding role for the relation of growth curves to the measure of ability for each domain. We include this element in our analysis as a statistical control to ensure that the findings for gender differences in patterns of change were not attributable to initial differences in ability. Thus, although we present these coefficients in tables, they are not discussed in the presentation of results.

Individuals' means for grade and grade-squared appear in the equation for the Level 1 constant (Equation 2). These terms serve the important function of ensuring that the equations for linear and quadratic change (Equations 3 and 4) reflect only within-individual change, and not stable individual differences that are confounded with the timing of data collection. Growth curve models are not inherently analyses of within-individual change. Random coefficient statistical models such as HLM use all of the available variance of a Level 1 variable to estimate the relations in the corresponding Level 2 equation. Consider a single cohort panel study with no attrition, in which every person contributes data on the same set of occasions. In that case, there is no between-person variance on the Level 1 explanatory variables for time, which define the growth curve, so the growth curves can only reflect within-individual change. In our analysis, however, age differences

between cohorts and attrition create differences between people in average grade. As a result, growth curve estimates would be influenced not only by within-individual change over time, but also by any stable individual differences between cohorts or between respondents who stayed in the study and those who were lost. Fortunately, Bryk and Raudenbush (1992, pp. 121–123) showed that adding the means of the Level 1 variables to Equation 2 solves this problem by separating within-individual relations from between-individual relations. As with the coefficients for ability, these elements of the model are of no substantive interest in their own right, but serve as a control for extraneous individual differences.

Two dummy variables representing cohort membership are the final explanatory variables in the Level 2 model. Including these terms in Equations 3 and 4 allows for the possibility that the pattern of within-individual change differs across cohorts by allowing each cohort to have different average values for β_1 and β_2. Intercepts will also differ across cohorts due to γ_{03} and γ_{04}. Students who were in the first grade at the beginning of the study serve as the reference group for the comparisons between cohorts. The variable *Grade2* identifies students who were in the second grade during the first year of data collection, whereas the variable *Grade4* identifies students who were in the fourth grade.

The last element in each of the Level 2 models is the residual term u_{ki}. For each equation containing this residual, HLM estimates a variance component that reflects unexplained individual differences in the corresponding growth curve coefficient, β_{ki}. Under the HLM model, it is assumed that these residual terms have a multivariate normal distribution.

SIMPLIFYING THE MODEL

Equations 1 through 4 present the most complex version of our model. We began our analysis by determining whether it was appropriate to simplify this model in two ways that would aid in the interpretation of results. Although this full model allowed the pattern of change over time to vary across cohorts, our interest was in consistencies that generalized across them. Thus, the first step was to test whether cohorts differed in their growth curves, which was accomplished with a multiple-parameter significance test of whether the four coefficients for the cohort variables differed from 0. For all but one of the outcome measures, this test failed to reach significance, indicating that a single growth curve could be generalized to all three cohorts and that these terms could be eliminated from the model.

Significant cohort differences in patterns of change emerged only for the value respondents placed on math. Comparison of fitted values to actual means suggested that this result might really be due to a period effect. All cohorts placed exceptionally high value on math in the first wave included in this analysis, even though that wave occurred at different grades for the different cohorts. We therefore expanded Equation 1 by adding a dummy variable for the period-specific effect (coded 1 for that wave and 0 for all others), and this eliminated the significant cohort differences. Therefore, the final model for this outcome included the dummy variable for the period specific effect, but not the cohort differences. It is important to note that the source of this single period effect could not be identified; however, we were confident that it was not an artifact created by changes in the wording of the items or response categories, because no changes occurred.

Significance tests were also conducted to determine whether a linear, rather than quadratic, growth curve model was adequate to characterize patterns of change, using a multiple-parameter significance test for the regression coefficients of Equation 4 (γ_{2j}). This test proved significant for all but one of the outcome measures, indicating that the changes in those variables were curvilinear. For the single exception, the quadratic elements were dropped from the model. Finally, the quadratic element of change did not vary significantly across individuals for any of the variables, so we eliminated this variance component from the model.

Results

In this section the results of three sets of HLM analyses are presented. The first set examined gender differences in the trajectories for competence beliefs in the domains of mathematics, language arts, and sports.

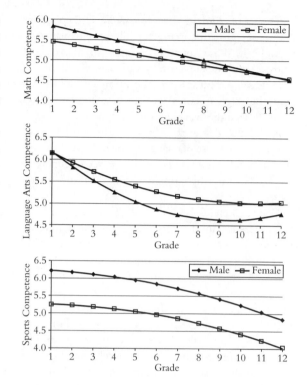

Figure 7.1   Growth curves for competence beliefs.

This was followed by a set of analyses that examined gender differences in the trajectories for subjective task values in each of the same domains. The final set of analyses examined the potential of self-competence beliefs to account for gender differences and trajectories of change in task values. This final set of analyses required some elaboration of our HLM model, which is described below.

Competence beliefs

Competence beliefs were examined in three domains: math, language arts, and sports ability. On the basis of previous research, competence beliefs were expected to be highest in first grade with declines across the school years; in other words, the fitted values for the earliest grade would be near the top of the possible range and the slopes would be significant and negative. As shown in Figure 7.1, competence beliefs were highest in first grade in all three domains, at least 5.8 for boys and 5.2 for girls out of a possible score of 7.0.

Table 7.3 Coefficients for competence beliefs

	Math		Language arts		Sports	
	Coefficient	SE	Coefficient	SE	Coefficient	SE
For intercept						
Intercept	5.142★	.033	5.055★	.042	5.378★	.044
Gender	−.202★	.065	.406★	.079	−.868★	.087
Ability test	.011★	.002	.17★	.003	.008★	.002
Average T	.002	.017	.028	.022	.018	.020
Average T^2			.005	.008	−.011	.008
Average value						
For linear change						
Intercept	−.100★	.008	−.131★	.008	−.107★	.008
Gender	.038★	.015	.037★	.016	.016	.015
Ability test	.002★	.000	.001★	.001	.001	.000
For quadratic change						
Intercept			.017★	.002	−.008★	.002
Gender			−.010★	.005	−.001	.004
Ability test			.000★	.000	.000	.000
Residual variance						
For intercept	.501		.472		.815	
For linear change	.017		.012		.017	
For value	.576		.746		.541	
Within individual						

★$p < .05$.

Figure 7.1 reveals that decline was clearly the dominant trend for competence beliefs in all three domains, and tests indicate that the rate of decline was highly significant (see Table 7.3).[1]

The quadratic aspects of the growth curves were significant for competence beliefs about language arts and sports, but the curves were in opposite directions. For language arts, the intercept term for grade-squared was positive, so the rate of decline slowed over time. As can be seen in Figure 7.1, average beliefs in ability for language arts declined more rapidly during the elementary years, but changed very little after the seventh or eighth grade, perhaps even increasing for males during the final years of high school. In contrast, the rate of decline in competence beliefs for sports accelerated over this age span (see Figure 7.1). Although there was minimal change during the first years of elementary school, the average student's sense of competence in sports fell faster and faster as the end of high school approached.

Prior research led us to expect that males would have much higher competence beliefs in sports, females would have much higher competence beliefs in language arts, and males would have slightly higher competence beliefs in math. As can be seen in Table 7.3, tests of gender differences in the Level 1 intercept indicated that, at grade 6, males and females held significantly different competence beliefs in math, language arts, and sports. Males believed that they were more competent, on average, in the domains of sports and math; whereas females believed that they were more competent, on average, in the domain of language arts. This upheld our expectations for all domains.

Although gender differences in the Level 1 intercept were found in all achievement areas, gender differences in the rate of change varied by domain. As can be seen in Figure 7.1, males and females began with significantly different perceptions of their math competence, and significant gender effects for slope

Table 7.4 Growth models for values in three domains, with and without controlling for competence beliefs

	Math values				Reading values				Sports values			
	Model 1		Model 2		Model 1		Model 2		Model 1		Model 2	
	Coef.	SE	Coef.	SE	Coef.	SE	Coef.	SE	Coef.	SE	Coef.	SE
For Intercept												
Intercept	5.084★	.043	5.091★	.039	5.008★	.042	5.095★	.036	4.659★	.060	4.539★	.043
Gender	.025	.085	.058	.074	.189★	.080	-.011	.068	-1.005★	.118	-.237★	.086
Ability test	-.008★	.003	-.012★	.002	-.002	.003	-.008★	.002	-.046	.031	.012	.023
Average T	.005	.025	-.018	.023	-.066★	.022	-.040★	.019	-.037★	.014	-.019★	.010
Average T²	-.021★	.010	-.013	.009	-.008	.010	-.008	.008	.005★	.002	-.002	.002
Average competence beliefs			-.020	.043			.068	.039			.159★	.044
For linear change												
Intercept	-.120★	.014	-.068★	.013	-.122★	.010	-.060★	.009	-.170★	.013	-.092★	.011
Gender	-.016	.021	-.047★	.019	.002	.018	-.013	.016	.027	.025	-.015	.019
Ability test	-.0006	.0006	-.0015★	.0006	-.0002	.0006	-.0006	.0005	.0005	.0005	.0001	.0004
For quadratic change												
Intercept	-.007	.004	-.008★	.004	.017★	.003	.009★	.003	.003	.004	.012★	.003
Gender	.007	.007	.011	.006	.009	.006	.012★	.005	.020★	.008	.029★	.006
Ability test	.0008★	.0002	.0008★	.0002	.0003	.0002	.0004★	.0002	-.0001	.0002	.0001	.0001
For period												
Intercept	.605★	.063	.626★	.060								
For competence beliefs												
Intercept			.428★	.029			.433★	.029			.780★	.032
Residual variance	Variance		Variance		Variance		Variance		Variance		Variance	
For intercept	.358★		.223★		.320★		.155★		1.142★		.325★	
For linear change	.029★		.020★		.011★		.006★		.030★		.013★	
For competence beliefs			.067★				.083★					
Within individual	.714		.603		.802		.594		1.209		.963	

Note. Coef. = coefficient.

★ *p* < .05.

and acceleration emerged by grade 6. Boys had higher perceptions of their competence in math at first grade, but their competence beliefs decreased at a faster rate than did those of girls, as evidenced by the significant and positive coefficient for gender in relation to linear change. As a result of differential rates of decline, boys and girls had similar beliefs about their math abilities by high school.

The picture was very different in the language arts domain (see Figure 7.1). Although males and females had the same level of competence beliefs in first grade, their growth curves differed considerably in slope and acceleration, so that there was a dramatic gender difference by grade 6. Boys' competence beliefs decreased rapidly until they reached a plateau during middle school. Girls' beliefs dropped more slowly and more steadily over time, reaching a plateau during middle school that remained higher than the boys' level during both middle school and high school. It appears that the gender difference in language arts shrank somewhat during high school. Finally, a third pattern emerged for the sports domain, with no effects of gender on the slope or acceleration for sports (see Figure 7.1). Boys had significantly higher competence beliefs in sports at grade 1, and both boys and girls declined in competence beliefs at similar rates. Thus, boys consistently perceived themselves as markedly better at sports than did girls across all grades of school.

In summary, our predictions about gender differences across the three domains were generally supported; however, the gaps between males and females decreased or remained the same, rather than increasing. Although boys began elementary school with slightly higher math competence beliefs than girls, these gender differences disappeared by high school because boys' math beliefs decreased more rapidly than girls' beliefs. In contrast, girls and boys had similar competence beliefs for language arts in the first grade, but their beliefs diverged in elementary school, with girls maintaining higher self-perceptions over time because their beliefs again decreased at a slower rate than boys' beliefs. The only domain in which there was no effect of gender on the rate of change was sports: boys had higher competence beliefs in sports ability initially and these gender differences were maintained over time.

Subjective task value

Subjective task values were expected to follow patterns similar to those found for competence beliefs, with students' values declining across grades in all domains. This expectation was upheld: the fitted values were highest in the early grades and the slopes were significant and negative (see Table 7.4). As can be seen in Figure 7.2, initial subjective task values were high in all domains; above 5.4 for boys and above 5.3 for girls out of a possible score of 7.0, and the slopes at grade 6 ranged from $-.11$ to $-.20$ for both boys and girls. Although the growth curves are all curvilinear, the figures suggest that decline was the dominant trend for task value beliefs in all three domains. In Table 7.4, tests of the intercept term for linear change in all models indicated that the overall rate of decline was highly significant.

The curvilinear aspects of the task value growth curves take different forms for math and language arts. In language arts, the intercept term for grade-squared was positive, so the rate of decline slowed over time; in math, the intercept was negative, indicating a slight increase in the rate of decline over time. Average values for language arts declined most rapidly during the elementary years, whereas average values for math declined most sharply during high school. For sports values, the curvilinear component was not significant on average, but as we shall see, this average masked opposite patterns for boys and girls.

Prior research led us to expect that males would have higher values for sports and math and that females would have higher values for language arts. These differences were expected to grow larger over time due to gender role socialization. As can be seen in Table 7.4, tests of the Level 1 intercept for gender indicate that males and females held significantly different task values in language arts and sports at grade 6, but not in math. Males placed higher value on sports than did females, on average; females held higher values for language arts than did males, on average; and no gender differences in the intercept were found in the domain of math.

Although gender differences in the Level 1 intercept were found in language arts and sports, significant gender differences were found in the rate of change only in sports. In that domain, boys and girls

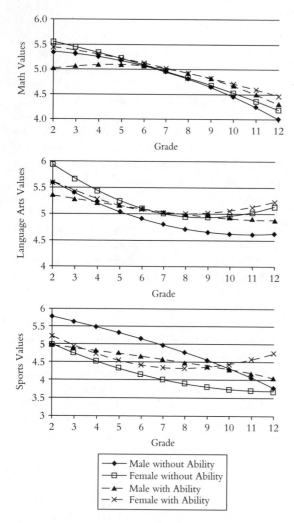

Figure 7.2 Growth curves for values, with and without controlling for competence beliefs.

statistical trend, $p = .12$, girls began higher than boys in first grade; but because girls' values declined more rapidly than did boys, the gap narrowed by late elementary school, and then increased again during high school as girls' values for language arts increased and boys' values leveled off (see Figure 7.2).

In summary, the dominant pattern was once again one of declining values across all domains. Significant gender differences in the average values were found only for language arts and sports, but no gender differences for average math values were found. A significant gender difference in the rate of change was found only for sports, with the greatest similarity between boys and girls found at the end of high school, because boys' values for sports declined more rapidly than girls' values. Nonetheless, the trend for differences in slope for language arts suggested that girls' valuing of language arts may increase during the high school years whereas boys' valuing does not rebound during high school.

The contribution of competence beliefs to subjective task values

This final set of analyses examined the potential of competence beliefs to account for gender differences and trajectories of change in subjective task values. Theoretical links between those constructs have been suggested (Eccles et al., 1983; Harter, 1983, 1992, 1998) and prior cross-sectional research has demonstrated relations between them (Deci & Ryan, 1985; Eccles & Wigfield, 1995; Sansone & Harackiewicz, 1996); however, longitudinal analyses demonstrating how increases or decreases in perceived competence are associated with shifts in values have not been conducted. It is possible to determine this by adding competence beliefs as an explanatory variable in the HLM model for task values. To the extent that competence beliefs are related to trajectories of change in subjective task values, introducing that variable to the model would reduce coefficients for change over time and the trajectories would become more flat, showing less change. To the extent that competence beliefs are related to gender differences, the coefficients for gender would be reduced, the trajectories for males and females would be more similar in slope and shape, and their trajectories would lie closer together.

differed in the quadratic component of the growth curve, with a convex curve for females and a concave curve for males (see solid lines in Figure 7.2). The large gender difference favoring males in the first grade increased until grade 6, because females' values for sports fell more rapidly than males' values. After grade 6, however, the gap gradually shrank because females' values reached a plateau, whereas males' values for sports continued to fall at an accelerating rate. By grade 12, the gender difference was negligible. Although the pattern in language arts was only a

These analyses are more illustrative than definitive for two reasons. First, based on prior research (e.g., Wigfield & Eccles, 1992) and theoretical models (e.g., Eccles et al., 1983; Harter, 1986), the direction of influence specified in these analyses is from competence beliefs to subjective task values, but it is also possible that there is influence in the opposite direction as well. If so, then our analyses will tend to overestimate the influence of competence beliefs. Second, like most other multiple regression models, HLM assumes that all explanatory variables are measured without error, and the presence of error would reduce the weight placed on a variable. There was a moderate amount of error variance in our measures of competence beliefs (see Table 7.2), which resulted in a slight underestimation of the influence of competence beliefs. These two limitations of the analysis tend to cancel one another out.

MODIFYING THE HLM MODEL

For these analyses, our original HLM model was modified by adding the time-specific measure of competence beliefs to the Level 1 equation of the model (Equation 1) and the individual mean for competence beliefs to the Level 2 equation for the Level 1 intercept (Equation 2). Including both ensured that the Level 1 relation was restricted to within-individual change. Both measures of subjective task value were grand mean centered, which ensured that adding these variables did not change the meaning of other coefficients and variance components in the model. Also, in the domains of math and language arts, the Level 1 relation of subjective task values to competence beliefs varied significantly across individuals, so this variance component was added to the HLM model.

THE RELATION OF COMPETENCE BELIEFS
TO SUBJECTIVE TASK VALUES

Table 7.4 shows that respondents were much more likely to value math, language arts, and sports when they felt competent in the domain. All three coefficients for competence beliefs were large (at least .43) and highly significant, t values above 14. The strength of the relation was also reflected in the variance explained by competence beliefs. Perceptions of competence explained between 38% and 71% of the

previously unexplained variance in stable individual differences in subjective task values (i.e., residual variance for intercept) for each domain. Competence beliefs also explained substantial portions of variance in change over time, in the form of both individual differences in slope (31% for math, 46% for language arts, and 57% for sports) and within-individual variation around the growth curves (16% for math, 26% for language arts, and 20% for sports). In sum, individuals' competence beliefs were strongly associated with their entire pattern of task values over time.

TRAJECTORIES OF SUBJECTIVE TASK VALUES

A time-varying explanatory variable like competence beliefs has the potential to explain not only between-individual variation in trajectories of task values, but also the amount and pattern of change in the average trajectory. For this to occur, competence beliefs must be strongly associated with subjective task values, and, as previously shown, this was the case. Furthermore, the pattern of change in competence beliefs must be similar to that of task values, and many similarities are apparent when Figures 7.1 and 7.2 are compared. The extent to which competence beliefs account for the overall trajectory will be reflected in the impact of controlling for competence beliefs on the intercept terms for linear and quadratic change in Table 7.4 and in the difference in trajectories before and after controlling for competence beliefs, as shown in Figure 7.2.

For the domain of math, controlling for competence beliefs reduced the linear trend at grade 6 by over 43%, γ from −.120 to −.068, but raised the curvilinear component of the trend to statistical significance, γ from −.007 to −.008. Figure 7.2 reveals that the curvilinearity arose because self-competence beliefs explained almost all of the decline in math values for grades 2 through 5 (i.e., the slope became much flatter), relatively little of the decline from grades 6 through 8, and some of the decline from grades 9 through 12. This effect was especially pronounced for boys in the early grades. This was consistent with the trajectories for math competence beliefs shown in Figure 7.1, which declined most dramatically during the elementary years. Osgood et al.'s (1996) index of the strength of a curvilinear relation was used to determine the change in the relation between the dependent variable and the explanatory variable. Competence beliefs accounted for 41% of the change over time for boys and 28% of the change for girls. It appears that self-perceptions of competence in math explained a substantial share of the changes in boys' and girls' math values over time.

Competence beliefs were also closely tied to the trajectory of values for language arts. Coefficients for both linear and quadratic change were reduced over 40% by controlling competence beliefs, and competence accounted for 54% of age-related change for boys and 44% for girls. Our earlier analyses found that self-competence in language arts declined rapidly during the elementary school years. Accordingly, Figure 7.2 shows that competence beliefs accounted for much of the decline in language arts values during that period for both boys and girls.

Competence beliefs played a somewhat smaller, although still substantial, role for trajectories of task values for sports. In this case, controlling for competence beliefs reduced the intercept coefficient for linear change by 46%, although the originally small coefficient for quadratic change increased significantly. Our analysis of competence beliefs for sports (see Figure 7.1) showed that the trajectory of change for boys' competence beliefs matched that of values (see Figure 7.2), with a gradual rate of decline in the elementary years accelerating to faster decline through high school. As a result, competence beliefs accounted for 55% of age-related change in boys' competence beliefs about sports, leaving an essentially linear trend. For girls, the timing of decline in competence beliefs differed from that of task values, with the decline in self-competence concentrated in the high school years and the decline in values concentrated in the elementary school years. Therefore, competence beliefs did not explain much of the change in girls' values for sports during the early years, but the inclusion of competence beliefs resulted in a reversal of the trend in the later years. Overall, competence beliefs explained 36% of the change in girls' values for sports and altered the shape of the trajectory considerably.

GENDER DIFFERENCES IN SUBJECTIVE TASK VALUES
The pattern of gender differences in subjective values was quite different for the three domains. As a result, the degree to which competence beliefs accounted

for gender differences in subjective task values varied as well. Competence beliefs in math differed for boys and girls, both in mean level over time and in trajectory over time, although boys and girls were nearly identical in math values. Accordingly, controlling for those competence beliefs raised the coefficients for gender in the model for math values, and the corresponding change in trajectories can be seen in Figure 7.2. Controlling for competence beliefs raised the modest average gender difference across waves by 52%, from .08 to .13.

Our earlier analyses indicated that girls consistently felt more competent in language arts than did boys after first grade, and boys' competence beliefs declined at a faster rate than did those of girls. Figure 7.2 shows that competence beliefs explained much of the gender difference during the middle grades, whereas a moderate difference remained during the earlier and later grades. Averaging across grades, controlling for competence beliefs reduced the gender difference in values by 62%, from .28 to .11. Thus, the higher sense of self-competence that girls experienced in language arts may have been an important source of the higher value they placed in this domain.

The connection of competence beliefs to gender differences in values was strongest and most complex for the domain of sports. Boys had higher competence beliefs in sports than did girls at all ages, as can be seen in Figure 7.2. When competence beliefs were not taken into account, boys typically placed more value on sports than did girls, but the gender difference varied widely over time, growing until grade 6, and then shrinking to near equality at grade 12. The consequence of this combination was apparent in the second set of lines in Figure 7.2, demonstrating that competence beliefs in sports accounted for a substantial portion of the gender difference in values at all ages, causing mirror-image curves for girls and boys that came together and crossed at third and ninth grades. This unusual pattern showed that when competence beliefs were controlled, girls and boys had a similar value for sports in the early years, and girls had lower values for sports in the middle school years and finished high school with higher values for sports. Controlling for competence beliefs reduced the average gender difference in values from .76 to −.06, a decline of 108%.

Discussion

The purpose of this study was threefold: (1) to describe changes in self-competence beliefs and values across childhood and adolescence within the domains of mathematics, language arts, and sports; (2) to examine the impact of changes in competence beliefs on changes in values over time in the same domains; and (3) to describe gender differences in mean levels and trajectories of change in each. The domains were selected to represent one strongly male-typed area of achievement (sports), one strongly female-typed area (language arts), and one achievement arena that has been male-typed in the past, but has become more gender neutral in recent years (math).

The most striking finding across all domains was that self-perceptions of competence and subjective task values declined as children got older. This pattern was expected for competence beliefs during the early elementary school years, because previous research has shown that before the age of 7 or 8, children's perceptions may be unrealistically high (Nicholls & Miller, 1984; Stipek, 1984), they may not make use of social comparison (Marsh et al., 1984; Stipek & Mac Iver, 1989), and they may have limited opportunities for comparison (Wigfield et al., 1997). The downward trajectory found in these data, however clearly continued beyond the early elementary school years. Although previous short-term longitudinal studies have reported sharp drops in academic self-perceptions at about the point of transition into junior high or middle school (e.g., Eccles, Midgley, et al., 1993; Marsh, 1989; Nottelmann, 1987), the value of having a longer time perspective is that it is clear that the declines at that period are part of a larger and consistent downward trend rather than a qualitative leap in self-perceptions (a similar continuous decline in perceived control beliefs between grades 3–7 was reported by Skinner et al., 1998). It should be noted, however, that a downside to a longitudinal study that follows groups of children as they make two school transitions is that the researcher has limited control over the kinds of teachers, teaching methods, and courses that the children will experience over the course of the study. Thus, the downward trajectories documented in this sample and in other studies could

have been due to common factors experienced in the classroom or elsewhere, but the causal factors cannot be pinpointed.

Declines in academic self-beliefs have been found in other studies, albeit not over such long periods; however, the decline in sports self-perceptions has not been documented previously. One explanation for such declines in self-beliefs is that they are reality based and inevitable in any skill-based domain as children become aware of others' levels of competence and where they fall in the "pecking order" (Jacobs & Eccles, 2000; Nicholls & Miller, 1984). This may continue throughout the years of formal schooling, because children move into situations in which there are larger pools of potential competitors and the number of "slots" on sports teams or in advanced-placement classes is limited. During the elementary school years children play a variety of and are greatly interested in sports (Wigfield et al., 1997). As children get older, sport activities become more selective and comparative, and fewer children are selected to be on competitive teams. The child who was the best basketball player in his or her elementary school may feel less skilled after playing with others on the basketball team in middle school, and, after sitting on the bench some of the time in middle school, may decide not to try out in high school. A similar phenomenon occurs for the child who is a star academically in the lower grades, but encounters higher standards (e.g., Eccles & Midgley, 1989) and others who are equally talented in advanced grades. However, children and adolescents cannot select themselves out of academic courses in quite the same way as they do with sports activities (e.g., Flammer et al., 1992; Snyder & Spreitzer, 1992; Wankel & Berger, 1990) if they find that they are not succeeding as well as they did at younger ages.

It is not surprising that the same downward trend was seen for subjective task values. Most theories that relate values to achievement suggest that values and perceptions of competence should be linked (e.g., Deci & Ryan, 1985; Eccles et al., 1983; Harter, 1983; Renninger, 1990; Schiefele, 1991). The analyses of subjective task values alone indicated that growth trajectories were similar, although not identical, to those found for competence beliefs in each domain. Once again, these data showed a consistent downward trend over most years of schooling that has not been clear in short-term studies.

Although the relation between task values and perceptions of competence has been highlighted in research and theory (e.g., Eccles et al., 1983; Harter, 1986, 1990; Wigfield & Eccles, 1992; Wigfield et al., 1997), other studies have not examined the way in which changes in one set of beliefs might impact changes in the other. The earlier work suggested that children's beliefs about their competence in a given domain should influence their subjective valuing of tasks in the same domain; thus, the second goal of the present study was to examine the impact of changes in competence beliefs on changes in values over time for mathematics, language arts, and sports. We found that perceptions of ability accounted for much of the decline in each case, explaining over 40% of the decrease in values in every domain and flattening the downward trajectories. This finding supports both Harter's and Eccles' models (e.g., Eccles et al., 1983; Harter, 1986) and is consistent with previous research suggesting that self-perceptions of competence are related to changes in value for an activity over time (e.g., Wigfield & Eccles, 1992; Wigfield et al., 1997). These data make it clear that children's and adolescents' changes in self-perceptions of competence explain a large percentage of their changing values for particular domains.

The third major goal in this study was to document gender differences in the developmental trajectories of self-competence and subjective task values. Previous studies have documented gender differences in sports beliefs, favoring boys (Eccles & Harold, 1991; Hyde, Fenema, & Lamon, 1990; Jacobs & Eccles, 1992; Wigfield et al., 1997) and differences in English beliefs, favoring girls (Eccles et al., 1984; Hyde & Linn, 1988; Jacobs & Eccles, 1992). In addition, earlier studies typically found differences in math beliefs favoring boys (Eccles et al., 1983; Linn & Hyde, 1989), although more recent investigations have reported only small gender differences in math self-beliefs and no differences in math achievement, at least during adolescence (e.g., Hyde et al., 1990; Marsh, 1989; Marsh & Yeung, 1998). Explanations for such gender differences have focused on gender role socialization by parents, peers, media, and schools (e.g., Eccles, 1987; Maccoby, 1966) and on gender intensification at puberty that may heighten boys' and girls' interest in doing gender-appropriate activities (e.g., Hill &

Lynch, 1983). Both gender intensification and gender socialization hypotheses are predicated on the idea that the gender gap increases with age; however, the longitudinal data presented here does not suggest a consistent increase in the differences between boys and girls with age. Indeed, the gender gap is not generally widening, but decreasing (math competence, sports values) or not changing (sports competence, math values). Language arts is the only domain in which any increase in the gender gap was found across time, and even in that domain, the gender difference in slope was significant only for perceptions of competence. Interestingly, the gender differences in subjective task values for language arts and sports were even smaller after controlling for competence beliefs. In the math domain, in which little gender difference was found for values, girls valued math more than did boys by the end of high school, after controlling for their perceptions of competence in the area.

These results showed no dramatic shift in trajectories during early adolescence that would be consistent with a gender intensification hypothesis. Instead, gender differences in perceptions were largest at the youngest ages and the rates of change in perceptions for both boys and girls were most dramatic during elementary school, typically leveling off during middle school and into high school. The gender intensification issue, although intuitively appealing, has not been systematically assessed in long-term longitudinal studies. The results of the present study, which indicated that gender differences decline with age, complement and extend earlier shorter term longitudinal studies (e.g., Eccles et al., 1989; Wigfield et al., 1991, 1997). The findings also are consistent with those reported by Marsh that showed no age-related changes in gender differences for self-concept (Marsh, 1993b) and no gender differences in developmental models (Marsh & Yeung, 1997, 1998). All of this work leads to the conclusion that at least in the domains considered here, most gender differences in beliefs decrease or remain stable over time. If any gender difference gets magnified during adolescence, it is in language arts, with boys' feelings of competence and values decreasing more rapidly than girls during the middle school or junior high years.

Boys and girls in the present study apparently entered school with different competence beliefs and values. Others have suggested that such differences may be due to socialization experiences in the home and in the larger society, such as the portrayals of males and females in the media and role models they see around them (e.g., Lytton & Romney, 1991; Signorella, 1990). The experiences that these children had both in and out of the classroom during the school years appeared to lessen these differences. Thus, rather than gender intensification, these data from the present research suggest a growing similarity in the competence beliefs and values of the participating boys and girls in the study who were attending school between 1989 and 1999. It should be noted, however, that the sample used in this study was not representative of the general population. The children came from predominantly European American middle-class and upper middle-class homes, and they attended public schools within four districts surrounding a large midwestern city. The trends toward decreasing differences between boys' and girls' academic self-competence beliefs, however, parallel recent reports of diminishing differences in actual achievement with much more representative samples of high school students, such as the National Assessment of Educational Progress (NAEP) and National Educational Longitudinal Study (NELS) data sets (see Marsh & Yeung, 1998 for the NELS88 data; and Campbell et al., 2000 for the NAEP data, 13-year-olds and 17-year-olds in 1999).

Unfortunately, the large, representative data sets that are currently available do not have longitudinal data on the broad span of ages found in the present study's data set. This necessitates relying on less representative data sets and existing theoretical frameworks to begin to examine longitudinal changes in self-beliefs, while remaining mindful of the fact that the same pattern may not be found in more diverse populations or in different educational contexts. Before drawing any definitive conclusions, it will be important to document trends in more diverse samples and contexts. It also would be worthwhile to extend this work to other domains or to specific activities within domains to assess the prevalence of this phenomenon.

With those caveats in mind, the findings from this study lead us to four general conclusions about the population studied here. First, the gender differences in growth trajectories appear to be domain specific rather than global. This suggests that explanations for gender differences also may have to be domain specific rather than general. Factors such as changing cultural stereotypes about an area of achievement (e.g., math) and local school expectations and opportunities for each gender may need to be considered for the particular achievement arena. Theoretical achievement models, such as the one proposed by Eccles and colleagues (Eccles et al., 1983), that incorporate information about the task are more likely to be successful than global models for explaining gender differences.

A second important point that comes out of these findings is that language arts is clearly gender typed. This domain has not been the focus of attention as frequently as math or science, but the fact that self-competence beliefs in this domain become increasingly differentiated by gender with age suggests that the skills emphasized in language arts may be one factor to consider in future research. According to a recent report, most children master decoding and comprehension skills during the early grades, but by middle school they are typically interpreting what they read, making inferences, analyzing literature, and writing (National Center for Education Statistics, 1999). At least one author (Brush, 1980) has suggested that girls prefer language arts because of the emphasis on interpretation and opinions that allows them to use their verbal skills. It is possible that girls' feelings of competence in language arts are related to other factors, however, such as reading more books (Hedges & Nowell, 1995), early gender differences in language development (Hyde & Linn, 1988), or general stereotypes about reading being a feminine activity (Eccles, Jacobs, & Harold, 1990; Stein, 1971).

The third point that we would like to raise is that boys' self-perceptions were declining more rapidly than girls' perceptions in both of the academic domains of the present study. The gender gap in math decreased because the self-competence beliefs of boys declined at a faster rate than those of girls. In fact, in the twelfth grade, there was some indication that girls' self-perceptions were higher than boys' self-perceptions in math. In the area of language arts, boys and girls started similarly, but the boys' perceptions of competence again declined more rapidly than the girls' perceptions—in this case, leaving girls with much higher self-perceptions. Although no significant gender differences in math values were found, boys' values for language arts continued to decline whereas girls' values appeared to level off. These trends may reflect patterns of actual achievement because research over the past decade has shown a consistent pattern of diminishing gender differences in math and no differences in language arts or differences favoring girls. Although girls' self-perceptions have often been a cause for concern, these trends for boys are troubling. If boys do not feel successful in school or value academics, they are more likely to drop out or turn to other achievement domains. Recent data suggest that this may be happening already—boys comprise only 43% of the college population at this point (compared with 48% in 1985), and that percentage is expected to decrease (Gerald & Hussar, 2000). The fact that boys have not kept pace with the educational gains made by girls has been noted by other researchers (e.g., Marsh & Yeung, 1998), as well as in the popular press (e.g., Sommers, 2000). Research efforts may need to focus on boys' declining self-beliefs as they move through school, as well as on continuing to monitor girls' self-perceptions.

The final general observation that can be made based on these results is that competence beliefs and task values need to be studied together, rather than separately. We found that changes in competence beliefs had a dramatic impact on changes in values, explaining most of the gender differences and much of the change over time. The implication of this finding is that beliefs within the self-system are closely linked and the importance of changes in one versus another may be overestimated if they are studied in isolation. It should be noted that based on earlier research (e.g., Wigfield & Eccles, 1992) and theoretical models (e.g., Eccles et al., 1983; Harter, 1986), the direction of influence in these analyses was specified to be from competence beliefs to subjective task values. As mentioned earlier, however, it is also possible that the influence is bidirectional. Therefore, the critical point for future research is that the changes in beliefs are highly related and need to be studied within the same longitudinal models.

In conclusion, we found that the competence beliefs and subjective task values of boys and girls in this study generally declined across the entire elementary and secondary school period. These results complement and extend earlier studies that used cross-sectional and short-term longitudinal designs by examining within-individual change between first and twelfth grades and by showing that changes in competence beliefs explain most of the changes in task values over time. Our data also provide new information suggesting that gender differences in children's and adolescents' competence beliefs and values in this sample decreased rather than increased with age. Despite these contributions to the understanding of age-related changes in self-beliefs, generalizations from this study are limited due to the homogeneity of the sample. Future research should examine patterns of change for more diverse groups of children and adolescents and in different educational contexts. It would also be worthwhile to extend this work to other domains or to specific activities within domains to assess the prevalence of the patterns of growth trajectories and gender differences in trajectories described here.

Note

1   For both linear and quadratic models, the intercept term for linear change (γ_{10} from Equation 3) provides a useful index of the average rate of change over the period of study. The model for beliefs about math ability is linear, so in this case this term is the constant rate of change for the entire period. In the quadratic models, the rate of change at any grade equals $\gamma_{10} + 2\gamma_{20}$ (Grade − 6), that is, the derivative with respect to grade, which means that the rate of change grows by $2\gamma_{20}$ (or shrinks if γ_{20} is negative) for each unit of increase in grade level. Thus, the average rate of change would fall at the middle of the range of grades under study, which is roughly grade 6. γ_{10} is the rate of change at that grade.

References

Alexander, K., & Entwisle, D. (1988). Achievement in the first two years of school: Patterns and processes. *Monographs of the Society for Research in Child Development, 53* (2, Serial No. 218).

Archer, J., & McDonald, M. (1990). Gender roles and sports in adolescent girls. *Leisure Studies, 9*, 225–240.

Baltes, P. B., & Nesselroade, J. R. (Eds.). (1979). *Longitudinal research in the study of behavior and development*. New York: Academic Press.

Bandura, A. (1994). *Self-efficacy: The exercise of control.* New York: Freeman.

Bruininks, R. H. (1977). *Bruininks–Osertesky Test of Motor Proficiency.* Circle Pines, MN: American Guidance Service.

Bruininks, V. L., & Bruininks, R. H. (1977). Motor proficiency of learning disabled and nondisabled students. *Perceptual and Motor Skills, 44,* 1131–1137.

Brush, L. R. (1980). *Encouraging girls in mathematics: The problem and the solution.* Boston: Abt Associates.

Bryk, A. S., & Raudenbush, S. W. (1987). Application of hierarchical linear models to assessing change. *Psychological Bulletin, 101,* 147–158.

Bryk, A. S., & Raudenbush, S. W. (1992). *Hierarchical linear models.* Newbury Park, CA: Sage.

Byrne, B. M. (1996). Academic self-concept: Its structure, measurement, and relation to academic achievement. In B. A. Bracken (Ed.), *Handbook of self-concept* (pp. 287–316). New York: Wiley.

Campbell, J. R., Hombo, C. M., & Mazzeo, J. (2000). *NAEP 1999 trends in academic progress: Three decades of student performance.* Washington DC: Department of Education, National Center for Education Statistics.

Covington, M. V. (1984). The motive for self-worth. In R. Ames & C. Ames (Eds.), *Research on motivation in education* (Vol. 1, pp. 77–113). New York: Academic Press.

Crain, R. M. (1996). The influence of age, race, and gender on child and adolescent multidimensional self-concept. In B. A. Bracken (Ed.), *Handbook of self-concept: Developmental, social and clinical considerations* (pp. 240–280). New York: Oxford University Press.

Deci, E. L., & Ryan, R. M. (1985). *Intrinsic motivation and self-determination in human behavior.* New York: Plenum Press.

Eccles, J. S. (1987). Gender roles and achievement patterns: An expectancy value perspective. In J. M. Reinisch, L. A. Rosenblum, & S. A. Sanders (Eds.), *Masculinity/femininity: Basic perspectives* (pp. 240–280). New York: Oxford University Press.

Eccles, J. S., Adler, T. F., Futterman, R., Goff, S. B., Kaczala, C. M., Meece, J., & Midgley, C. (1983). Expectancies, values and academic behaviors. In J. T. Spence (Ed.), *Achievement and achievement motives* (pp. 75–146). San Francisco: Freeman.

Eccles, J. S., Adler, T. F., & Meece, J. L. (1984). Sex differences in achievement: A test of alternative theories. *Journal of Personality and Social Psychology, 46,* 26–43.

Eccles, J. S., & Harold, R. D. (1991). Gender differences in sport involvement: Applying the Eccles' expectancy-value model. *Journal of Applied Sport Psychology, 3,* 7–35.

Eccles, J. S., Jacobs, J. E., & Harold, R. D. (1990). Gender-role stereotypes, expectancy effects, and parents' role in the socialization of gender differences in self-perceptions and skill acquisition. *Journal of Social Issues, 46,* 183–201.

Eccles, J. S., & Midgley, C. (1989). Stage/environment fit: Developmentally appropriate classrooms for early adolescents. In R. Ames & C. Ames (Eds.), *Research on motivation in education* (Vol. 3, pp. 139–181). New York: Academic Press.

Eccles, J. S., Midgley, C., Wigfield, A., Buchanan, C. M., Reuman, D., Flanagan, C., & Mac Iver, D. (1993). Development during adolescence: The impact of stage environment fit on young adolescents' experiences in schools and families. *American Psychologist, 48,* 90–101.

Eccles, J. S., & Wigfield, A. (1995). In the mind of the actor: The structure of adolescents' achievement tasks values and expectancy-related beliefs. *Personality and Social Psychology Bulletin, 21,* 215–225.

Eccles, J. S., Wigfield, A., Flanagan, C., Miller, C., Reuman, D., & Yee, D. (1989). Self-concepts, domain values, and self-esteem: Relations and changes at early adolescence. *Journal of Personality, 57,* 283–310.

Eccles, J. S., Wigfield, A., Harold, R., & Blumenfeld, P. (1993). Age and gender differences in children's achievement self-perceptions during the elementary school years. *Child Development, 64,* 830–847.

Eccles, J. S., Wigfield, A., & Schiefele, U. (1998). Motivation to succeed. In N. Eisenberg (Ed.), W. Damon (Series Ed.), *Handbook of child psychology: Vol. 3. Social, emotional, and personality development* (5th ed., pp. 1051–1071). New York: Wiley.

Feather, N. T. (1988). Values, valences, and course enrollment: Testing the role of personal values within an expectancy-value framework. *Journal of Educational Psychology, 80,* 381–391.

Flammer, A., Alsaker, F. D., & Noack, P. (1999). Time use by adolescents in an international perspective. In F. D. Alsaker & A. Flammer (Eds.), *The adolescent experience: European and American adolescents in the 1990s* (pp. 33–60). Mahwah, NJ: Erlbaum.

Garton, A. F., & Pratt, C. (1987). Participation and interest in leisure activities by adolescent school children. *Journal of Adolescence, 10,* 341–351.

Gerald, D. E., & Hussar, W. J. (2000). *Projections of education statistics to 2010.* Washington, DC: Department of Education, National Center for Education Statistics.

Harter, S. (1982). The perceived competence scale for children. *Child Development, 53,* 87–97.

Harter, S. (1983). Development perspectives on the self-system. In E. M. Hetherington (Ed.), P. H. Mussen (Series Ed.), *Handbook of child psychology: Vol. 4. Socialization, personality, and social development* (pp. 275–386). New York: Wiley.

Harter, S. (1986). Processes underlying the construction, maintenance, and enhancement of the self-concept in children. In J. Suls & A. G. Greenwald (Eds.), *Psychological perspectives on the self* (Vol. 3, pp. 137–181). Hillsdale, NJ: Erlbaum.

Harter, S. (1990). Causes, correlates, and the functional role of global self-worth: A life-span perspective. In J. Kolligan & R. Sternberg (Eds.), *Perceptions of competence and incompetence across the life span* (pp. 43–70). New York: Springer-Verlag.

Harter, S. (1992). Visions of self: Beyond the me in the mirror. In J. E. Jacobs (Ed.), *Developmental perspectives on motivation, Vol. 40, Nebraska Symposium on Motivation, 1992* (pp. 99–144). Lincoln: University of Nebraska Press.

Harter, S. (1998). The development of self-representations. In N. Eisenberg (Ed.), W. Damon (Series Ed.), *Handbook of child psychology: Vol. 3. Social, emotional, and personality development* (5th ed., pp. 553–617). New York: Wiley.

Hedges, L.V., & Nowell, A. (1995). Sex differences in mental test scores: Variability and numbers of high-scoring individuals. *Science, 269*, 41–45.

Hill, J. P., & Lynch, M. E. (1983). The intensification of gender-related role expectations during early adolescence. In J. Brooks-Gunn & A. C. Peterson (Eds.), *Girls at puberty* (pp. 201–228). New York: Plenum Press.

Huston, A. (1983). Sex typing. In E. M. Hetherington (Ed.), P. H. Mussen (Series Ed.), *Handbook of child psychology: Vol. 4. Socialization, personality, and social development* (pp. 387–467). New York: Wiley.

Hyde, J. S., Fenema, E., & Lamon, S. J. (1990). Gender differences in mathematics performance: A meta-analysis. *Psychological Bulletin, 107*, 139–155.

Hyde, J. S., & Linn, M. C. (1988). Gender differences in verbal ability: A meta-analysis. *Psychological Bulletin, 104*, 533–569.

Jacobs, J. E. (1991). The influence of gender stereotypes on parent and child math attitudes: Differences across grade-levels. *Journal of Educational Psychology, 83*, 518–527.

Jacobs, J. E., & Eccles, J. S. (1992). The impact of mothers' gender-role stereotypic beliefs on mothers' and children's ability perceptions. *Journal of Personality and Social Psychology, 63*, 932–944.

Jacobs, J. E., & Eccles, J. S. (2000). Parents, task values, and real-life achievement related choices. In C. Sansone & J. M. Harackiewicz (Eds.), *Intrinsic motivation* (pp. 405–439). San Diego, CA: Academic Press.

Jacobs, J. E., Finken, L. L., Griffin, N. L., & Wright, J. D. (1998). The career plans of science-talented rural adolescent girls. *American Educational Research Journal, 35*, 681–704.

Larson, R. (2000). Toward a psychology of positive youth development. *American Psychologist, 55*(1), 170–183.

Larson, R. W., & Verma, S. (1999). How children and adolescents spend time across the world: Work, play, and developmental opportunities. *Psychological Bulletin, 125*, 701–736.

Linn, M. C., & Hyde, J. S. (1989). Gender, mathematics, and science. *Educational Researcher, 18*, 17–27.

Lytton, H., & Romney, D. M. (1991). Parents' sex-related differential socialization of boys and girls: A meta-analysis. *Psychological Bulletin, 109*, 267–296.

Maccoby, E. E. (1966). *The development of sex differences.* Stanford, CA: Stanford University Press.

Marsh, H. W. (1989). Age and sex effects in multiple dimensions of self-concept: Preadolescence to early adulthood. *Journal of Educational Psychology, 81*, 417–430.

Marsh, H. W. (1993a). Academic self-concept: Theory, measurement, and research. In J. Suls (Ed.), *Psychological perspectives on the self* (Vol. 4, pp. 59–98). Hillsdale, NJ: Erlbaum.

Marsh, H. W. (1993b). The multidimensional structure of academic self-concept: Invariance over gender and age. *American Educational Research Journal, 30*, 341–360.

Marsh, H. W., Barnes, J., Cairns, L., & Tidman, M. (1984). Self-description questionnaire: Age and sex effects in the structure and level of self-concept for preadolescent children. *Journal of Educational Psychology, 83*, 377–392.

Marsh, H. W., & Yeung, A. S. (1997). Causal effects of academic self-concept on academic achievement. *American Educational Research Journal, 34*, 691–720.

Marsh, H. W., & Yeung, A. S. (1998). Longitudinal structural equation models of academic self-concept and achievement: Gender differences in the development of math and English constructs. *American Educational Research Journal, 35*, 705–738.

Meece, J. L., Parsons, J. E., Kaczala, C. M., Goff, S. B., & Futterman, R. (1982). Sex differences in math achievement: Toward a model of academic choice. *Psychological Bulletin, 91*, 324–348.

Meece, J. L., Wigfield, A., & Eccles, J. S. (1990). Predictors of math anxiety and its consequences for young adolescents' course enrollment intentions and performance in mathematics. *Journal of Educational Psychology, 82*, 60–70.

Menard, S. (1991). *Longitudinal research.* Newbury Park, CA: Sage.

National Center for Education Statistics. (1999). *National assessment of educational progress: The nation's report card, focus on reading.* Washington, DC: National Center for Education Statistics.

Nicholls, J. G. (1978). The development of the concepts of effort and ability, perceptions of academic attainment, and the understanding that difficult tasks require more ability. *Child Development, 49*, 800–814.

Nicholls, J. G., & Miller, A. T. (1984). Development and its discontents: The differentiation of the concept of ability. In J. G. Nicholls (Ed.), *Advances in motivation and achievement: Vol. 3. The development of achievement motivation*. Greenwich, CT: JAI.

Nottelmann, E. D. (1987). Competence and self-esteem during transition from childhood to adolescence. *Developmental Psychology, 23*, 441–450.

Osgood, D. W., Wilson, J. K., Bachman, J. G., O'Malley, P. M., & Johnston, L. D. (1996). Routine activities and individual deviant behavior. *American Sociological Review, 61*, 635–655.

Parsons, J. E., Adler, T., & Kaczala, C. (1982). Socialization of achievement attitudes and beliefs: Parental influences. *Child Development, 53*, 310–321.

Renninger, K. A. (1990). Children's play interests, representation, and activity. In R. Fivush & J. Hudson (Eds.), *Knowing and remembering in young children* (pp. 127–165). Cambridge, MA: Cambridge University Press.

Ruble, D., & Martin, C. L. (1998). Gender. In N. Eisenberg (Ed.), W. Damon (Series Ed.), *Handbook of child psychology: Vol. 3. Social, emotional, and personality development* (5th ed., pp. 993–1016). New York: Wiley.

Sansone, C., & Harackiewicz, J. M. (1996). "I don't feel like it": The function of interest in self-regulation. In L. Martin & A. Tesser (Eds.), *Striving and feeling: Interactions between goals, affect, and self-regulation* (pp. 203–228). Hillsdale, NJ: Erlbaum.

Schiefele, U. (1991). Interest, learning, and motivation. *Educational Psychologist, 26*, 299–323.

Shavelson, R. J., Hubner, J. J., & Stanton, G. C. (1976). Self-concept: Validation of construct interpretations. *Review of Educational Research, 46*, 407–441.

Shaw, S. M., Kleiber, D. A., & Caldwell, L. L. (1995). Leisure and identity information in male and female adolescents: A preliminary examination. *Journal of Leisure Research, 27*, 245–263.

Signorella, N. (1990). Children, television, and gender roles. *Journal of Adolescent Health Care, 11*, 50–58.

Skinner, E. A., Zimmer-Gembeck, M. J., & Connell, J. P. (1998). Individual differences and the development of perceived control. *Monographs of the Society for Research in Child Development, 63*(2–3, Serial No. 254).

Slosson, R. L., Nicholson, C. L., & Hibpshman, T. H. (1991). *Slosson Intelligence Test–Revised*. East Amora, NY: Slosson Educational Publications.

Snyder, E. E., & Spreitzer, E. (1992). Social psychological concomitants of adolescents' role identities as scholars and athletes: A longitudinal analysis. *Youth and Society, 23*, 507–522.

Sommers, C. H. (2000). The war against boys. *The Atlantic Monthly, 285*, 59–74.

Stein, A. H. (1971). The effects of sex-role standards for achievement and sex-role preference on three determinants of achievement motivation. *Developmental Psychology, 4*, 219–231.

Stipek, D. J. (1984). The development of achievement motivation. In C. Ames & R. Ames (Eds.), *Research on motivation and education: Student motivation* (Vol. 1, pp. 145–174). San Diego, CA: Academic.

Stipek, D. J., & Mac Iver, D. (1989). Developmental changes in children's assessment of intellectual competence. *Child Development, 60*, 531–538.

Wankel, L. M., & Berger, B. G. (1990). The psychological and social benefits of sport and physical activity. *Journal of Leisure Research, 22*, 167–182.

Weiner, B. (1985). An attributional theory of achievement motivation and emotion. *Psychological Review, 92*, 548–573.

Wigfield, A. (1994). Expectancy-value theory of achievement motivation: A developmental perspective. *Educational Psychology Review, 6*, 49–78.

Wigfield, A., & Eccles, J. S. (1992). The development of achievement task values: A theoretical analysis. *Developmental Review, 12*, 265–310.

Wigfield, A., Eccles, J. S., Mac Iver, D., Reuman, D. A., & Midgley, C. (1991). Transitions during early adolescence: Changes in children's domain specific self-perceptions and general self-esteem across the transition to junior high school. *Developmental Psychology, 27*, 552–565.

Wigfield, A., Eccles, J. S., Yoon, K. S., Harold, R. D., Arbreton, A. J. A., & Blumenfeld, P. C. (1997). Changes in children's competence beliefs and subjective task values across the elementary school years: A three-year study. *Journal of Educational Psychology, 89*, 451–469.

Ethnic Identity and the Daily Psychological Well-Being of Adolescents From Mexican and Chinese Backgrounds

Lisa Kiang, Tiffany Yip, Melinda Gonzales-Backen, Melissa Witkow, and Andrew J. Fuligni

A major task during adolescence is to ascertain a sense of identity, theorized to play a vital role in development (Erikson, 1968). Fundamentally relevant to adolescents from ethnic minority backgrounds, *ethnic* identity may have a similarly critical influence, directly and indirectly affecting well-being by providing a buffer against stressful experiences.

Ethnic identity and psychological well-being

Across a variety of ethnically diverse samples, contemporary research has documented positive links between ethnic identity and well-being (Gray-Little & Hafdahl, 2000; Ryff, Keyes, & Hughes, 2003; Tsai, Ying, & Lee, 2001; Umaña-Taylor, 2004; Umaña-Taylor, Diversi, & Fine, 2002). Individuals with high levels of ethnic identity have also been found to exhibit a high quality of life, a common indicator of well-being (Utsey, Chae, Brown, & Kelly, 2002). Research involving stage models has found similar associations such that individuals with achieved or integrated statuses, or those with a more advanced sense of ethnic identity, exhibit better adjustment than those in earlier stages of development (see Phinney, 1990). One caveat is that some studies have found weak or nonsignificant associations (Cross, 1991). Indeed, alternative perspectives caution against routinely expecting ethnic identity and well-being to be related (e.g., Cross & Fhagen-Smith, 2001; Yip & Cross, 2004). Such cautionary approaches are due to the multitude of identity patterns or configurations available to individuals and to the variation in personality characteristics, including well-being, which are thought to be randomly distributed within and across these patterns. Although it may be imperfect to predict reflexive or automatic links, ethnic identity clearly remains a pervasive influence in development, albeit as one of a variety of social identities that adolescents may acquire.

Ethnic identity as a moderator of stressful demands

Theoretically, a social identity framework supports linkages between ethnic identity, race, or ethnic-related stress, and well-being. According to social identity theorists (e.g. Tajfel, 1981), several strategies may be enlisted to deal with such stress. Although some may disidentify or distance themselves from their ethnic group, others may choose to assert or strengthen their ethnic or group identity, which, in turn, can create a sense of affiliation that provides protection against negative effects of race-related stress on well-being (Phinney, 2003; Sellers, Caldwell, Schmeelk-Cone, & Zimmerman, 2003; Tajfel & Forgas, 2000). In fact, one of the very functions of ethnic identity may be to shield against negative or stressful experiences (Cross, Parham, & Helms, 1998; Mossakowski, 2003).

Protective stress buffering effects of ethnic identity have recently been found across several programs of research (Shelton et al., 2005). For example, Sellers and colleagues found that African Americans who indicated race to be central to their self-concept were buffered from the negative impact of race-related hassles and discrimination (Shelton et al., in press). Protective effects were also found using other dimensions of identity (e.g., regard). In another program of research, adolescents from African American backgrounds who experienced racial discrimination at school exhibited subsequent declines in mental health and academic achievement. However, those with positive connections to their ethnic group were protected from deleterious effects (Wong, Eccles, & Sameroff, 2003).

Existing research has tended to highlight the African American struggle to negotiate race-related stress and perceived discrimination (e.g., Branscombe, Schmitt, & Harvey, 1999; Sellers et al., 2003). Although discrimination is salient in the lives of ethnic minorities, the impact of more *normative* stressors, which also play an important role in development, has been largely overlooked. Furthermore, this line of research needs to be extended to the experiences of other, often understudied minority groups. The current venture focuses on normative stressful demands as experienced by Chinese and Mexican youth in a daily diary study that captures stress and well-being encounters on an everyday basis, and potentially protective effects of ethnic identity.

General, everyday stress is a pervasive risk factor for poor psychological adjustment (Gonzales, Tein, Sandler, & Friedman, 2001), yet surprisingly little research has examined the impact of normative stressful demands in adolescents' development. Typical adolescent stressors include pressure to balance demands and responsibilities related to maturation, and can stem from several domains including the school environment and family and peer relationships (Compas, 1987; Lohman & Jarvis, 2000). For example, stressful increases in schoolwork may occur due to more demanding classes or in preparation of a college placement test (Eccles et al., 1993). Socially, adolescents may experience a stressful shift in peer groups upon entering high school, and stress associated with developing more intimate peer relationships while maintaining family relationships and establishing autonomy (Eccles et al., 1993; Lohman & Jarvis, 2000).

Although normative stressful demands affect all youth regardless of ethnicity, effectively coping with demands can be exacerbated or at least present a distinctive conflict in those from Mexican and Chinese backgrounds. Youth from these families, often socialized by collectivistic values (Corsaro & Fingerson, 2003), may be particularly vulnerable due to a high importance placed on family obligation (Fuligni, Tseng, & Lam, 1999). For example, although balancing homework with family chores can be stressful for anyone, these demands may be more salient for an adolescent with a stronger sense of obligation to meet them. Furthermore, these adolescents may not have the benefit of parents who are familiar with the U.S. school system and curriculum (Cooper, Cooper, Azmitia, Chavira, & Gullatt, 2002), and thus face challenges in completing schoolwork. An additional obstacle involves socioeconomic status. In particular,

parents of Mexican immigrant families often earn low incomes and have limited English fluency; thus, adolescents' school demands may face stiff competition with family demands such as helping earn additional income after school or helping around the house while parents work long hours (Fuligni & Witkow, 2004).

Notably, the focus of this paper was not to compare average levels of stress experienced by ethnic minority versus European adolescents. Rather, we examined unique cultural resources from which ethnic minority youth can draw when coping with normative stressful demands. Indeed, in spite of potential obstacles associated with immigrant status, youth from immigrant families actually fare quite well in terms of adjustment and academic achievement, often matching American-born peers from similar ethnic backgrounds (Fuligni & Witkow, 2004). One resource from which adolescents can draw to help deal with these obstacles is their cultural orientation. For instance, individuals from collectivistic backgrounds typically exhibit strong levels of interdependence and communal and interpersonal connectedness with others (Greenfield, Keller, Fuligni, & Maynard, 2003). Such feelings of connectedness could, in turn, serve a variety of protective functions, especially in light of coping with difficult situations (e.g., stress). Similarly, the role of ethnic identity, the major focus of this study, could offer an additional source of strength or protection.

Similar to research on ethnic-related stress, we expected ethnic identity to protect against the negative effect of normative stressful demands, but what theoretical orientation supports this prediction? Above and beyond applying social identity principles to normative stress research, we expected ethnic identity to serve a positive function in adolescents' lives because cultural identification involves some element of social integration. Feeling socially integrated (e.g., having social ties and a sense of connectedness), in turn, has a wide range of benefits in terms of health and development (Seeman, 1996). Thus, the extent to which one holds positive perceptions about one's ethnic group (private regard) and the degree to which ethnicity is core to one's self-concept (centrality) could relate to a more general sense of social integration, and thus moderate the negative impact of normative stressful demands.

Recent research by Yip and Fuligni (see Shelton et al., 2005) provided initial support for the role of ethnic identity as a normative stress buffer. In a daily diary study, adolescents from Chinese backgrounds experienced greater anxiety on days in which they also experienced a greater number of demands, but those with a strong ethnic identity (assessed via the identity achievement subscale of Phinney's, 1992, Multigroup Ethnic Identity Measure) were protected. For these individuals, stressful demands did not negatively impact daily anxiety. Consequently, continuing this preliminary line of research could aid in a better understanding of the many ways in which ethnic identity can serve a protective function in individuals' lives.

A daily diary approach

A unique strength of the daily diary method is that the intense, repeated measures design provides more reliable and valid data for multilevel modeling than traditionally used single surveyed accounts. Successful in the stress and coping literature, this method has determined how individual differences in, for instance, personality or demographic traits predict daily stress reactivity (e.g., Almeida & Kessler, 1998; Bolger & Zuckerman, 1995). For example, Mroczek and Almeida (2004) found daily levels of stress to predict negative affect, but this daily association was significantly stronger in older adults and in those with high neuroticism. In another study using a multilevel design with ethnic minority youth, Yip and Fuligni (2002) found Chinese Americans to report more positive affect on days in which they felt more "Chinese," but this association was found only in those who reported ethnic identity as central in their lives.

In search of new insight into the role that ethnic identity plays in the rhythm of individuals' lives, we used a daily diary approach and explicitly asked adolescents to report the number of stressful demands they experienced each day and how happy and anxious they felt each day over a 14-day period. This methodology allowed us to determine daily level associations between normative stressful demands and well-being, and whether ethnic identity moderated this daily level association. Did adolescents from Mexican and Chinese backgrounds feel less happy and more anxious on days in which they experienced a greater number of stressful demands? Did ethnic identity have a protective effect on well-being by predicting how happy or anxious individuals felt on a daily basis, despite the daily stressors they experienced? We expected more stressful demands to predict less happiness and more anxiety, but that individuals with a strong ethnic identity would be buffered from deleterious effects.

Recent research has argued that a multidimensional conceptualization provides the most accurate assessment of how ethnic identity influences psychological outcomes (Sellers, Smith, Shelton, Rowley, & Chavous, 1998). Hence, we focused on two dimensions of identity, namely, ethnic regard, an affective evaluation of one's ethnicity, and ethnic centrality, the extent to which ethnicity plays a central role in one's self-concept. Regard and centrality are thought to capture different aspects of identity and, interestingly, may have differential associations with outcomes (Sellers et al., 1998; Yip, 2005). Consideration of both subscales also allows for the analysis of important interaction effects. For instance, in a sample of African Americans, Rowley, Sellers, Chavous, and Smith (1998) found racial regard to predict self-esteem positively, but only for those who considered race as central in their lives. To examine both differential and interactive effects, we analyzed models with (1) ethnic regard, (2) ethnic centrality, and (3) the interaction between these two dimensions as individual level predictors of daily well-being.

Two additional issues were also addressed. Daily assessments of well-being allowed us to determine whether ethnic identity had a more enduring role in stress reactivity by moderating the effect of stressful demands on well-being assessed 1 day after original stressors occurred. We also considered potential confounds that could obscure the link between identity and well-being. Given long-established links between self-esteem and well-being (see Harter, 1999) and between self-esteem and ethnic identity (e.g., Gray-Little & Hafdahl, 2000), we included self-esteem as an important control. To the extent that ethnic identity moderated the impact of stressful demands, we attempted to isolate the effect by examining whether moderation existed even after controlling for self-esteem. Ethnicity and gender were also considered.

Method

Participants

Ninth graders from the Los Angeles metropolitan area were invited to participate in a study about their daily lives. Students were recruited from three high schools varying in ethnic composition, socioeconomic status, and academic achievement. One school was predominantly populated by Latino and Asian American students with families from lower-middle to middle-class backgrounds. A second consisted of students with mostly Latino and European American families from lower-middle to middle-class backgrounds. The third school included mostly Asian and European American students with families that tended to be middle to upper-middle class. No single ethnicity dominated any of these schools; rather, the two largest ethnic groups each comprised 30–50% of the total population in each school. All ninth graders in two of the three schools and approximately half of the ninth graders in the third school were invited to participate. Of those invited, 65% participated, resulting in a total sample of 783 ninth-grade students with a wide range of ethnic, socioeconomic, and immigrant backgrounds.

The current study focused on the potential strengths that ethnic identity can provide for individuals who are in the ethnic minority; thus, a subsample of adolescents from Latino and Asian American backgrounds was selected from our larger, full sample. Within these broader categories, 86% of Latino Americans had Mexican ancestry, and 67% of Asian Americans had Chinese ancestry. As these larger subgroups could be used to provide meaningful group comparisons, our final sample used for this paper consisted of the 415 participants from Mexican (52%) and Chinese (48%) backgrounds. Adolescents from European backgrounds and from ethnic minority groups who comprised too small a number for meaningful comparisons (e.g., Middle Eastern, Guatemalan) were not included in analyses. Participants in our final sample were predominantly from immigrant families: Mexican: 75%; Chinese: 95%. Most students were of the second generation, that is, born in the United States but had at least one parent who was foreign-born: Mexican: 76%; Chinese: 67%. Approximately 24% and 33% of adolescents from Mexican and Chinese backgrounds, respectively, were of the first generation, that is, foreign-born. The average age was 14.83 years (SD = .38), with an even split between males (49%) and females (51%). In terms of demographic differences between youth from Mexican and Chinese families, parents in Mexican families had lower levels of education: mothers, $t(370) = 3.20, p < .01$; fathers, $t(352) = 2.43, p < .05$. Ethnic differences in occupation followed a similar pattern such that parents of students from Mexican backgrounds worked in lower status occupations than Chinese parents: mothers; $t(229) = 3.17, p < .01$; fathers, $t(255) = 4.05, p < .001$. Effect sizes for all of these differences ranged from small to moderate, Cohen's d = .26–.51.

Procedure

Students who returned assent and parent consent forms were given a series of self-report questionnaires to complete in small-group settings during school time. Questionnaires included ethnic identity and self-esteem measures and took approximately 30 min to complete. Students were then given a 14-day supply of daily diary checklists and told to complete one checklist each night before going to bed. Daily assessments of stressful demands and well-being were collected via these checklists, each of which took about 5–10 min to complete. Participants sealed each day's responses in a manila envelope and stamped the seal with a hand-held electronic time stamper provided by the researchers. The stamper imprinted the current date and time and was programmed such that the date and time could not be altered. At the end of the study period, research assistants entered schools to collect completed checklists. Consent forms and study materials were available in English, Spanish, and Chinese. Spanish and Chinese versions were developed through a series of translations and back-translations conducted by bilingual speakers. Eight participants chose to complete measures in Spanish (n = 4) and Chinese (n = 4). Adolescents received $30 for participating and were told they would also receive two movie passes if inspection of the data indicated that they completed diaries correctly and on time (e.g., diaries completed on consecutive days with correct date stamped on seal). The time stamper method of monitoring diary completion, cash, and movie pass incentives resulted in a very high rate of compliance that did not differ by gender or ethnicity. Approximately 95% of the diaries were completed and, of these, 86% were completed on time, either on the correct night or before noon the following day. Analyses examining only diaries completed on time revealed no significant effect of lateness. All final analyses, therefore, were conducted with all diary days, regardless of lateness.

Measures

ETHNIC IDENTITY

Two subscales were adapted from the Multi-dimensional Inventory of Black Identity (MIBI; Sellers, Rowley, Chavous, Shelton, & Smith, 1997) to measure ethnic identity. Scales were shortened and items modified so that they could be relevant to and completed by members of any ethnic group. All items were scored on a 5-point scale ranging from *strongly disagree* to *strongly agree*, with higher scores reflecting higher levels of regard and centrality. The Regard subscale, consisting of eight items, measured the extent to which students had positive feelings toward their ethnic group. Sample items read, "I feel good about the people in my ethnic group," "I believe that I have many strengths because I am a member of my ethnic group," and, "I often regret that I am a member of my ethnic group" (reverse scored). Internal consistencies were acceptable across both ethnic groups: Mexican, α = .72; Chinese, α = .65. The Centrality subscale, consisting of five items, assessed the extent to which individuals felt their ethnicity to be central to their self-concept. Sample items read, "In general, being a member of my ethnic group is an important part of my self-image," "Being a part of my ethnic group is an important reflection of who I am," and, "Being a part of my ethnic group is unimportant to my sense of what kind of person I am" (reverse scored). This subscale was also fairly reliable across both ethnic groups; Mexican, α = .64; Chinese, α = .76.

SELF-ESTEEM

The 10-item Rosenberg Self-Esteem Scale (Rosenberg, 1965) measured individuals' global self-esteem. Sample items read, "I feel that I have a number of good qualities," "I take a positive attitude toward myself," and, "I certainly feel useless at times" (reverse scored). Items were scored on a 5-point Likert-type scale rather than the originally conceived 4-point scale in order to remain consistent with other study measures. Responses ranged from *strongly disagree* to *strongly agree*, with higher scores reflecting higher self-esteem. Internal consistencies were good (Mexican: α = .82; Chinese: α = .85).

STRESSFUL DEMANDS

A checklist of daily stressors was adapted from items used successfully in previous research (e.g., Bolger & Zuckerman, 1995). For each day of the 14-day study period, participants indicated whether the following four stressful events or situations were experienced that day: (1) had a lot of work at home, (2) had a lot of work at school, (3) had a lot of demands made by family, and (4) had a lot of demands made by friends. These items are classic indices often used in daily diary studies of stress, but were adapted to be more developmentally appropriate for adolescents. They represent normative stressors that may be particularly salient to adolescents who, with increased autonomy and maturity, need to learn how to manage their demands effectively. Total demands experienced each day (range = 0–4) were summed to represent daily indicators of stressful demands.

DAILY WELL-BEING

Daily well-being was assessed using (1) a newly created Happiness scale modeled after the Profile of Moods States (POMS; Lorr & McNair, 1971) and (2) the Anxiety subscale of the POMS, used successfully in previous diary studies. For each day during the study period, participants reported on a 5-point Likert-type scale (range = 0–4) the extent to which they felt each of three items for each subscale (Happiness: happy, joy, calm; Anxiety: on edge, nervous, uneasy). Responses ranged from *not at all* to *extremely*, with higher scores reflecting greater happiness and anxiety. Across Mexican and Chinese adolescents, respectively, internal consistencies were averaged across each daily assessment and were acceptable: Happiness, α = .80, .83; Anxiety, α = .64, .73.

Table 7.5 Correlations and means of study variables

	(1)	(2)	(3)	(4)	(5)	(6)	Mean	SD
(1) Ethnic regard							4.08	.66
(2) Ethnic centrality	.44***						3.25	.84
(3) Self-esteem	.35***	.17***					3.80	.73
(4) Average stressful demands	.09†	.10*	−.03				0.67	.63
(5) Average happiness	.22***	.12**	.31***	.04			3.32	.78
(6) Average anxiety	−.05	.04	−.19***	.30***	−.18***		1.55	.58

Note. †p < .10. *p < .05. **p < .01. ***p < .001.

Results

Means and correlational analyses

As shown in Table 7.5, adolescents scored above the midpoint for regard, centrality, and self-esteem. No significant ethnic or gender mean differences were found. In terms of daily demands, adolescents experienced, on average, less than one stressful demand each day. No significant differences in average stressful demands were found across ethnicity, but females reported experiencing more demands than males, females: $M = .73, SD = .64$; males: $M = .61, SD = .62$; $t(402) = 2.11, p < .05$, Cohen's $d = .21$. Adolescents were relatively happy and not very anxious, scoring above and below the midpoints of each scale, respectively. Group differences in average well-being were found such that adolescents from Chinese backgrounds exhibited higher levels of anxiety than those from Mexican backgrounds, Chinese: $M = 1.62$, $SD = .64$; Mexican: $M = 1.50, SD = .52$; $t(406) = 1.99$, $p < .05$, and females were significantly more anxious than males, females: $M = 1.61$, $SD = .56$; males: $M = 1.48, SD = .59$; $t(402) = 2.40, p < .05$. However, effect sizes for these differences were small, Cohen's $d = .21 - .24$.

As expected and also shown in Table 7.5, ethnic regard, centrality, and self-esteem were significantly and positively correlated. Regard and centrality were positively associated with average happiness, but were not significantly related to average anxiety. Self-esteem was significantly associated with both indices of well-being, and in expected directions. Interestingly, ethnic identity was positively associated with stressful demands, averaged across the study period. Stressful demands were positively associated with anxiety, but were not significantly related to happiness. Not surprisingly, a negative association was found between happiness and anxiety. Although these basic associations shed some light on how these variables are related, our major research questions pertained to important daily level associations.

Daily and individual level predictors of daily well-being

Hierarchical Linear Modeling (HLM; Bryk & Raudenbush, 1992), a statistical procedure used to analyze nested models, determined whether ethnic identity directly predicted average daily well-being and moderated daily level associations between stressful demands and well-being. Happiness and anxiety were separately analyzed in two identical models consisting of two-levels of analyses: (1) a daily level reflecting daily variation in well-being within individuals over the study period, and (2) an individual level reflecting variation in daily level processes (e.g., the daily association between stressful demands and well-being) attributable to individual differences in ethnic identity and other characteristics.

Same-day stressful demands predicting well-being

STATISTICAL MODEL

Daily levels of well-being were predicted from same-day stressful demands and important control variables typically used in diary methods (e.g., Bolger & Zuckerman, 1995; Yip & Fuligni, 2002), resulting in the following daily level modeling equation:

Well-being$_{ij}$ = b_{0j} + b_{1j}(same-day stressful

demands)

+b_{2j}(prior-day well-being)

+b_{3j}(day of week)   (1)

+b_{4j}(week of study)+e_{ij}.

Well-being on a given day (i) for a particular adolescent (j) was modeled as a function of each person's intercept, namely, their average well-being across days (b_{0j}) and daily experience of stressful demands (b_{1j}). Prior-day well-being (b_{2j}) was included to control for any prior-day effects and to better isolate the daily level association between same-day stressful demands and well-being. In doing so, we could only analyze the association between stressful demands and well-being for days 2–14 of the study as we did not have data for adolescents' well-being before day 1. Additional control variables included the day of the week (weekdays coded −1 and weekends coded 1) (b_{3j}) and the week of the study period (days 2–7 coded −1 and days 8–14 coded 1) (b_{4j}) in which the diary was completed. The error term in the equation contributing to variance unexplained by other predictors was represented by e_{ij}.

For the individual level component of our multilevel analyses, daily level estimates in question (i.e., b_{0j}, b_{1j}) were modeled as a function of individual level factors:

(Intercept)b_{0j} = c_{00} + c_{01}(ethnic identity)

+ c_{02}(ethnicity)

+ c_{03}(gender)+ u_{0j},   (2)

(Slope)b_{1j} = c_{10} + c_{11}(ethnic identity)

+ c_{12}(ethnicity)

+ c_{13}(Gender)+ u_{1j}.   (3)

Individuals' average daily well-being (b_{0j}) and the daily association between stressful demands and well-being (b_{1j}) were predicted from averages of these estimates across the sample (c_{00}, c_{10}), ethnic identity (c_{01}, c_{11}), ethnicity (c_{02}, c_{12}), and gender (c_{03}, c_{13}). Error terms contributing to variance unexplained by other predictors were represented by u_{0j} and u_{1j}. Ethnic identity and self-esteem were centered at the midpoint of each scale and ethnicity and gender were effect coded (−1 = *Mexican*, 1 = *Chinese*; −1 = *Males*, 1 = *Females*).

Table 7.6   HLM estimates of ethnic regard moderating same-day stressful demands

Daily level (individual level)	Happiness		Anxiety	
	b	SE	b	SE
Intercept (average daily well-being)	1.67	.08★★★	.43	.05★★★
Ethnic regard	0.16	.05★★	−.06	.04†
Ethnicity	−0.05	.03	.04	.02†
Gender	−0.01	.03	.06	.02★★
Daily stress	−0.06	.04	.09	.03★★
Ethnic regard	0.06	.03★	−.01	.03
Ethnicity	0.00	.02	.01	.01
Gender	−0.06	.02★★	.01	.02
Daily level controls				
Prior-day well-being	0.21	.02★★★	.17	.03★★★
Day of week	0.05	.01★★★	−.03	.01★★★
Week of study	0.01	.01	−.04	.01★★★

Note. For HLM analyses, ethnicity, gender, day of week, and week of study were effect coded (Mexican, Male, Weekday, Week 1 of study = −1; Chinese, Female, Weekend, Week 2 of study = 1), and Regard, Centrality, and Self-Esteem were centered at the midpoint of each scale. HLM = hierarchical linear modeling. †p<.10. ★p<.05. ★★p<.01. ★★★p<.001.

For each outcome of well-being (happiness, anxiety), three models were analyzed that focused on individual level predictors of ethnic identity defined by (1) ethnic regard, (2) ethnic centrality, and (3) main effects of regard and centrality and their interaction.

Results: Daily happiness

As shown in Table 7.6, individuals with higher levels of ethnic regard were happier on average, b = .16, p<.01. Ethnicity and gender did not significantly predict average daily happiness. Although the experience of more daily stressful demands was not significantly related to less daily happiness, the overall association was moderated by ethnic regard, b = .06, p<.05. As depicted in Figure 7.3, for those with low and moderate levels of ethnic regard, daily levels of happiness decreased as daily stressful demands increased; however, individuals with high levels of ethnic regard were protected from this negative effect. Gender also appeared to have a moderating effect such that females exhibited greater stress reactivity compared with males (see Figure 7.4). In terms of daily level control variables, prior-day

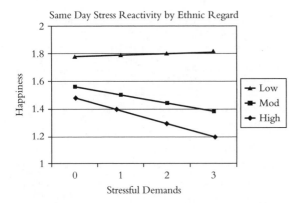

Figure 7.3 Same-day stress reactivity by ethnic regard. Associations between daily stressful demands and daily levels of happiness plotted by ethnic regard. Individuals "Mod" in regard were adolescents who scored at the midpoint of the ethnic regard scale. Individuals "Low" in regard were those who scored below the midpoint of the scale, whereas those "High" in regard scored above the midpoint.

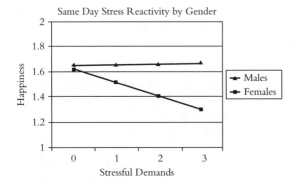

Figure 7.4 Same-day stress reactivity by gender. Associations between daily stressful demands and daily levels of happiness plotted according to gender.

Table 7.7 HLM estimates of ethnic centrality moderating same-day stressful demands

	Happiness		Anxiety	
Daily level (individual level)	b	SE	b	SE
Intercept (average daily well-being)	1.81	.05***	.36	.03***
Ethnic centrality	.07	.04	.00	.03
Ethnicity	−.06	.03†	.04	.02†
Gender	.00	.03	.06	.02**
Daily stress	.00	.02	.08	.02***
Ethnic centrality	.03	.02	.01	.02
Ethnicity	.00	.02	.01	.01
Gender	−.05	.02**	.01	.01
Daily level controls				
Prior-day well-being	.21	.02***	.17	.03***
Day of week	.04	.01***	−.03	.01***
Week of study	.01	.01	−.04	.01***

Note. HLM = hierarchical linear modeling.
†$p < .10$. **$p < .01$. ***$p < .001$.

happiness significantly predicted current-day happiness and day of the week was also significant such that people tended to be happier on weekends.

In the model with ethnic centrality as an individual level predictor, no significant effects on daily happiness were found, either directly or indirectly as a moderator of daily demands (see Table 7.7). However, coefficients were in expected directions, implicating protective effects. Similarly, an additional model with individual level predictors including the interaction between regard and centrality revealed nonsignificant

direct, $b = .02$, *ns*, and indirect effects, $b = .02$, *ns*, of the interaction term. It thus appears that, contrary to Rowley et al.'s (1998) findings concerning the importance of considering both regard and centrality as dual predictors of self-esteem, only ethnic regard played a significant role in individuals' daily happiness.

RESULTS: DAILY ANXIETY

As shown in Table 7.6, individuals with a higher ethnic regard exhibited less daily anxiety, but this direct effect was only marginally significant, $b = −.06, p < .10$. The direct effect of ethnicity also approached significance such that adolescents with Chinese backgrounds exhibited higher levels of anxiety compared with those with Mexican backgrounds. A significant effect of gender was found such that females exhibited higher levels of anxiety than males. Although individuals experienced greater anxiety on days in which they also experienced more stressful demands, $b = .09$, $p < .01$, no moderating effects were found. Prior-day anxiety, day of week, and day of study were significant control variables such that participants were less anxious on weekends and on later days of measurement.

Results from an additional model including ethnic centrality as an individual level predictor revealed no significant direct or moderating effects of centrality (see Table 7.7). A third model including the interaction term between regard and centrality as an individual level predictor was similar to previous findings predicting happiness in that no significant direct, $b = .03$, ns, or indirect, $b = .03$, ns, effects of the interaction term were found.

Prior-day stressful demands predicting well-being

STATISTICAL MODEL

Additional HLM models determined whether ethnic identity moderated the effect of prior-day stressful demands $(d - 1)$ on current day well-being (d). Daily level equations were estimated as shown:

$$\text{Well-being}_{ij}(d) = b_{0j} + b_{1j}(\text{prior-day stressful}$$
$$\text{demands}, d - 1)$$
$$+ b_{2j}(\text{current-day stressful}$$
$$\text{demands}, d) \qquad (4)$$
$$+ b_{3j}(\text{prior-day well-being},$$
$$d - 1)$$
$$+ b_{4j}(\text{day of week}, d)$$
$$+ b_{5j}(\text{week of study}, d) + e_{ij}.$$

Well-being on a particular day (i) for a particular adolescent (j) was modeled as a function of his or her average well-being across days (b_{0j}), prior-day stressful demands (b_{1j}), current-day stressful demands (b_{2j}), prior-day well-being (b_{3j}), day of the week (b_{4j}), and week of the study (b_{5j}) in which the current day diary was completed. The error term in the equation contributing to variance unexplained by other predictors was represented by e_{ij}.

As presented earlier in Equations 2 and 3, daily level estimates (i.e., b_{0j}, b_{1j}) were modeled as a function of individual level factors:

$$(\text{Intercept})b_{0j} = c_{00} + c_{01}(\text{ethnic identity})$$
$$+ c_{02}(\text{ethnicity}) + c_{03}(\text{gender}) \qquad (5)$$
$$+ u_{0j},$$

$$(\text{Slope})b_{1j} = c_{10} + c_{11}(\text{ethnic identity})$$
$$+ c_{12}(\text{ethnicity}) + c_{13}(\text{gender}) \qquad (6)$$
$$+ u_{1j}.$$

Table 7.8 HLM estimates of ethnic regard moderating prior-day stressful demands

Daily level (individual level)	Happiness (d)		Anxiety (d)	
	b	SE	b	SE
Intercept (average daily well-being)	1.65	.08***	.42	.05***
Ethnic regard	0.15	.05**	−.06	.04†
Ethnicity	−0.07	.03*	.04	.02†
Gender	−0.04	.03	.06	.02*
Prior-day stress $(d - 1)$	−0.02	.04	.03	.03
Ethnic regard	0.05	.03*	−.01	.02
Ethnicity	0.03	.02	.01	.01
Gender	−0.00	.02	.02	.01
Daily level controls				
Same-day stress (d)	0.00	.02	.08	.01***
Prior-day well-being (d)	0.22	.02***	.17	.03***
Day of week	0.05	.01***	−.03	.01***
Week of study	0.02	.01	−.04	.01***

Note. HLM = hierarchical linear modeling.
†$p < .10$. *$p < .05$. **$p < .01$. ***$p < .001$.

Individuals' average daily well-being (b_{0j}) and the association between prior-day stressful demands and current day well-being (b_{1j}) were estimated using averages of these estimates across the sample (c_{00}, c_{10}), as well as the effect of ethnic identity (c_{01}, c_{11}), ethnicity (c_{02}, c_{12}), and gender (c_{03}, c_{13}). Error terms contributing to variance unexplained by other predictors were represented by u_{0j} and u_{1j}. Again, for each outcome (happiness, anxiety), three models were analyzed that focused on individual level predictors including (1) ethnic regard, (2) ethnic centrality, and (3) the interaction between regard and centrality.

RESULTS: PRIOR-DAY STRESSFUL DEMANDS AND DAILY HAPPINESS

Similar to previous results, ethnic regard significantly and positively predicted average daily levels of happiness (see Table 7.8). Ethnicity emerged as significant such that individuals from Chinese backgrounds were significantly less happy than individuals from Mexican backgrounds. In terms of indirect effects, individuals with a high ethnic regard were again protected from

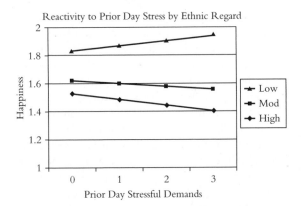

Figure 7.5 Reactivity to prior-day stress by ethnic regard. Associations between daily stressful demands and daily levels of happiness 1 day later plotted by ethnic regard. Individuals "Mod" in regard refer to those who scored at the midpoint of the ethnic regard scale. Individuals "Low" in regard refer to those who scored below midpoint of the scale, whereas those "High" in regard scored above the midpoint.

the negative effects of stress (see Figure 7.5). Ethnic regard moderated the association between prior-day stressful demands and current day-happiness, even after controlling for prior-day happiness and current-day stress, $b = .05$, $p < .05$. These results implicate the strength of ethnic regard as an ongoing buffer of stress reactivity. Unlike previous results, gender was not a significant moderator of the daily level association between prior-day stressful demands and current-day happiness. Prior-day happiness and day of the week remained significant control variables.

Models including ethnic centrality and the interaction between regard and centrality again revealed largely nonsignificant findings. The direct effect of centrality was marginally significant, $b = .07$, $p < .10$, but the moderating effect was not, $b = .02$, *ns*. Both direct, $b = .03$, *ns*, and indirect, $b = -.02$, *ns*, effects of the interaction term were nonsignificant.

RESULTS: PRIOR-DAY STRESSFUL DEMANDS
AND DAILY ANXIETY
Models predicting current-day anxiety from prior-day stress revealed results similar to those presented in Table 7.6. Ethnic regard, ethnicity, and gender predicted average daily anxiety, but did not moderate the daily level association between prior-day stress and current-

day anxiety. All daily level controls were also significant. Neither ethnic centrality nor the interaction between regard and centrality exerted significant direct, centrality: $b = .01$, *ns*; interaction: $b = .03$, *ns*, or indirect, centrality: $b = -.01$, *ns*; interaction: $b = .04$, *ns*, effects.

MODELS CONTROLLING FOR SELF-ESTEEM
As self-esteem has been consistently shown to affect both psychological well-being and reactivity to stress (see Harter, 1999), we sought to determine whether the protective effects of ethnic regard emerged above and beyond the confounding effect of self-esteem. As moderation was found only with ethnic regard and happiness (predicted by both current-day and prior-day stress), we reanalyzed these two models after controlling for self-esteem.

STATISTICAL MODEL
Daily level equations were identical to those presented earlier (see Equations 1 and 4, but self-esteem was included as an additional individual level predictor. Hence, daily level estimates (i.e., b_{0j}, b_{1j}) were modeled as follows:

$$
\begin{aligned}
\text{(Intercept)}\, b_{0j} &= c_{00} + c_{01}(\text{ethnic regard}) \\
&\quad + c_{02}(\text{self-esteem}) + c_{03}(\text{ethnicity}) \\
&\quad + c_{04}(\text{gender}) + u_{0j},
\end{aligned} \tag{7}
$$

$$
\begin{aligned}
\text{(Slope)}\, b_{1j} &= c_{10} + c_{11}(\text{ethnic regard}) \\
&\quad + c_{12}(\text{self-esteem}) + c_{13}(\text{ethnicity}) \\
&\quad + c_{14}(\text{gender}) + u_{1j}.
\end{aligned} \tag{8}
$$

Average daily well-being (b_{0j}) and the associations between current-day and prior-day stressful demands and current-day well-being (b_{1j}) were estimated using averages of these estimates across the sample (c_{00}, c_{10}), as well as the effect of ethnic regard (c_{01}, c_{11}), self-esteem (c_{02}, c_{12}), ethnicity (c_{03}, c_{13}), and gender (c_{04}, c_{14}). Error terms contributing to variance unexplained by other predictors were represented by u_{0j} and u_{1j}.

RESULTS: DAILY HAPPINESS CONTROLLING
FOR SELF-ESTEEM
As shown in Table 7.9, the direct effect of ethnic regard predicting average daily happiness no longer emerged as significant after controlling for self-esteem. However, for both same-day and prior-day stressful

Table 7.9   HLM estimates of ethnic regard predicting happiness after controlling for self-esteem

Daily level (individual level)	Same day happiness (d)		Next day happiness (d=1)	
	b	SE	b	SE
Intercept (average daily well-being)	1.59	.08***	1.56	.07***
Ethnic regard	.06	.06	.05	.05
Self-esteem	.24	.05***	.24	.05***
Ethnicity	−.04	.03	−.06	.03*
Gender	.01	.03	−.02	.03
Daily stress (d)	−.04	.04	−.01	.04
Ethnic regard	.07	.03*	.07	.03*
Self-esteem	−.04	.03	−.04	.02†
Ethnicity	.00	.02	.02	.02
Gender	−.06	.02**	−.01	.02
Daily level controls				
Prior-day stress			.00	.02
Prior-day well-being	.21	.02***	.22	.02***
Day of week	.05	.01***	.05	.01***
Week of study	.01	.01	.02	.01

Note. HLM = hierarchical linear modeling.
†$p < .10$. *$p < .05$. **$p < .01$. ***$p < .001$.

demands predicting happiness, the buffering effect of ethnic regard remained significant, suggesting that ethnic regard had a protective role above and beyond the effect of self-esteem.

Discussion

In the current study, we used a daily diary approach to extend the empirical literature and examine the protective effects of ethnic regard and ethnic centrality on the daily well-being of adolescents from Mexican and Chinese backgrounds. The uniqueness of utilizing an intensive daily diary approach was that it provided a window into important developmental processes that occur on a daily level and that are often overlooked by traditional, single surveyed accounts. A more precise influence on well-being was thus investigated by using two components of ethnic identity to predict how individuals feel on a day-to-day basis. We found that adolescents with a higher regard for their ethnic

group were happier and generally less anxious when daily assessments were averaged over the 14-day study period, suggesting that individuals derived direct psychological benefits from holding positive perceptions about their ethnic group.

From a social identity perspective, holding positive perceptions about and identifying with one's ethnic group can theoretically provide a foundation from which individuals can draw in the face of stress (Tajfel, 1981). In the current study, ethnic regard and not centrality proved to be the more important identity component with regard to stress reactivity. Ethnic regard indirectly influenced daily well-being by serving as a buffer against normative stressful demands. Although the experience of more daily stressors predicted less daily happiness in individuals with a low to moderate ethnic regard, individuals with a high ethnic regard were protected from these negative effects. What was particularly striking was that the moderating effect of ethnic regard was based on fairly conservative estimates even after controlling for influential variables such as prior-day well-being.

Another important finding was that the enhancement in happiness or positivity that ethnic regard provided not only influenced the same-day association between stressful demands and well-being but also had a longer-lasting influence in the association between daily stressors on a given day and happiness reported 1 day later. Again, these lingering effects were noteworthy considering our statistical control of both prior-day well-being and current-day stressors. An additional variable that we controlled for was self-esteem, a construct known to impact a host of psychological outcomes including well-being (Harter, 1999) and that may also act as a buffer in the face of stress (Mossakowski, 2003). We found ethnic regard to play an independent role as a moderator between stressful demands and daily levels of happiness above and beyond the influence of self-esteem, thereby emphasizing and isolating its protective effects.

New insight into the stress and coping of adolescents from ethnic minority backgrounds can be obtained from the current study. Although some have examined the stress-buffering role of different components of ethnic identity, research has been limited in its focus on perceived discrimination and other race-related hassles as sources of stress. Virtually no work has examined the impact of the normative stressful demands that are particularly salient during adolescence due to increased autonomy and a greater responsibility to manage stress from multiple domains (e.g., school, peers, and family). Our focus on normative stressors built upon existing research and acknowledged an important developmental influence that has been largely understudied. Furthermore, our successful use of the daily diary method suggests that it may be worthwhile to utilize this multilevel approach in future research on adolescent stress processes. For instance, it may be particularly interesting to revisit ethnic identity, ethnic discrimination, and well-being, but with a focus on daily level associations.

Interestingly, ethnic regard did not moderate the effect of stressful demands on daily anxiety. That is, daily demands had a powerful impact on anxiety despite how highly one perceived one's ethnic group. As might be expected, individuals are vulnerable and not immune to the negative impact of stress. What was highly notable, however, was that adolescents with a high ethnic regard maintained a generally positive and happy attitude in the face of daily stressors and despite their anxious feelings. Thus, having positive feelings about one's ethnic group appeared to provide an extra boost of positivity in individuals' daily lives. A sense of positivity could then translate into a protective resource that individuals can use to cope with their stressful demands and feelings of anxiety that can stem from such stressors.

Still, one explanation for our weaker predictions of daily anxiety could involve potential developmental differences related to the meaning placed on one's ethnic identity. Much of the ethnic identity research demonstrating stress-buffering effects has focused on older adolescents and adults (e.g., Mossakowski, 2003; Sellers et al., 2003). During adolescence, identities may still be in the process of being established; thus, obtaining a high score on a measure of ethnic regard may have a fundamentally different meaning for an individual who may not yet have a full grasp of what their identity means compared with an older individual for whom identity may be more established. Thus, the full potential for ethnic identity to serve a protective function in individuals' lives may not be completely realized for many individuals until later in adult years.

Similarly, developmental differences could account for the lack of effects found with ethnic centrality. Indeed, it is interesting that significant moderating effects centered on ethnic regard, not centrality. Perhaps the concept of ethnic importance or centrality does not play as powerful a role in early adolescent development, as it does in later adolescence or adulthood. Indeed, previous self-esteem research documenting significant regard by centrality interactions has been conducted using adults and older adolescents ranging from 16 to 18 years of age (Rowley et al., 1998). Perhaps our lack of interaction effects and of centrality main effects was due to our use of ninth graders in early adolescence who, again, may have yet to fully establish what their ethnic identity is and what it means to them.

On the other hand, our findings are consistent with those of Vandiver, Cross, Worrell, and Fhagen-Smith (2002), which showed that while the meaning (e.g., centrality) attributed to one's race or ethnicity did not predict mental health and well-being, holding negative attitudes about one's group decreased well-being. Thus, the degree to which ethnicity or race is central to one's self may not be as critical to well-being or development, but what is critical is the actual valence of one's perceptions about one's group. Nevertheless, in light of possible developmental differences, it would be important to replicate results in older samples; consequently, stronger buffering effects or significant interaction effects could be found in older individuals who may have a more developed sense of both ethnic regard and centrality. It would also be worthwhile to examine stress reactivity at younger ages to determine how early a protective effect exists.

To further explicate protective functions of ethnic identity, in particular, ethnic regard, future work might examine, more specifically, the mechanisms by which identity translates into positive developmental outcomes. For instance, it is possible that a strong ethnic regard relates to a solid network of social support or more proactive coping strategies. These support and coping factors could then positively influence well-being. Or, it is possible that the well-being arising out of ethnic regard somehow evolves into a broader sense of eudaimonic well-being or purpose in life (Ryff et al., 2003) that then pervades other areas of development.

Although the focus of this study was on ethnic regard and centrality, representing core features of ethnic identity and important resources in adolescents' lives, ethnic identity is only one of many group identities (Cross & Fhagen-Smith, 2001). Thus, from a true social identity perspective, feeling affiliated with and having *any* group identity (e.g., ethnic, mainstream, gender) could have equally important effects. For example, Yip and Cross (2004) found that well-being did not differentiate Chinese Americans who strongly identified with being either Chinese or American. That is, having some form of positive group identity seemed more important than whether that group identity was grounded in one's ethnicity. Hence, future research might be worthwhile in examining different configurations of group identity and whether different identities do indeed carry similar weight in terms of psychological outcomes.

Several limitations should be noted. First, although the results point to ethnic regard as an important predictor of daily well-being, it is possible that additional factors, beyond what we controlled for, may be involved. As suggested above, perhaps ethnic identity relates to other influential variables that could also provide protective effects on development, for instance, having a sense of social support. Second, although one of the strengths of this study was its focus on traditionally understudied groups, additional research is needed before generalizing to other groups. Moderating effects of ethnic identity could vary across ethnic groups with different immigration histories, for instance, Vietnamese refugees seeking asylum in the United States, or within broader group contexts, for instance, Latino adolescents with Mexican versus Central American backgrounds. Similarly, it would be interesting to determine whether these processes differ in the more often studied adolescents from African American backgrounds, whose experiences may differ significantly from those of other minority groups (Sellers et al., 1998).

Despite these limitations, the current study provided evidence for the protective role that ethnic regard plays in the daily psychological well-being of adolescents from Mexican and Chinese backgrounds. In line with the current movement in positive psychology (Seligman & Csikszentmihalyi, 2000) and much of the recent research emphasizing positive

developmental outcomes and cultural resources, we adopted a strength-based approach in examining the influence of ethnic identity in individuals' daily lives. Although this approach is critical in advancing our understanding, it is also important not to neglect those who exhibit low levels of ethnic identity. Indeed, in achieving a better understanding of the role that ethnic identity plays in development, the next logical step is to use this information effectively to benefit and improve individuals' daily lives and functioning more directly.

References

Almeida, D. M., & Kessler, R. C. (1998). Everyday stressors and gender differences in daily distress. *Journal of Personality and Social Psychology, 75*, 670–680.

Bolger, N., & Zuckerman, A. (1995). A framework for studying personality in the stress process. *Journal of Personality & Social Psychology, 69*, 890–902.

Branscombe, N. R., Schmitt, M. T., & Harvey, R. D. (1999). Perceiving pervasive discrimination among African Americans: Implications for group identification and well-being. *Journal of Personality and Social Psychology, 77*, 135–149.

Bryk, A. S., & Raudenbush, S. W. (1992). *Hierarchical linear models: Applications and data analysis methods.* Newbury Park, CA: Sage.

Compas, B. (1987). Coping with stress during childhood and adolescence. *Psychological Bulletin, 101*, 393–403.

Cooper, C. R., Cooper, R. G., Azmitia, M., Chavira, G., & Gullatt, Y. (2002). Bridging multiple worlds: How African American and Latino youth in academic outreach programs navigate math pathways to college. *Applied Developmental Science, 6*, 73–87.

Corsaro, W. A., & Fingerson, L. (2003). Development and socialization in childhood. In J. Delamater (Ed.), *Handbook of social psychology: Handbooks of sociology and social research* (pp. 125–155). New York: Kluwer/Plenum.

Cross, J. E. Jr. (1991). *Shades of black: Diversity in African-American identity.* Philadelphia: Temple University Press.

Cross, W. E., & Fhagen-Smith, P. (2001). Patterns of African American identity development: A life span perspective. In C. L. Wijeyesinghe & B. W. Jackson III (Eds.), *New perspectives on racial identity development: A theoretical and practical anthology* (pp. 243–270). New York: New York University Press.

Cross, W. E., Parham, T. A., & Helms, J. E. (1998). Nigrescence revisited: Theory and research. In R. L. Jones (Ed.), *African*

American identity development: Theory, research, and intervention. Hampton, VA: Cobb and Henry.

Eccles, J. S., Midgley, C., Wigfield, A., Buchanan, C. M., Reuman, D., Flanagan, C., et al. (1993). Development during adolescence: The impact of stage-environment fit on young adolescents' experiences in schools and in families. *American Psychologist, 48,* 90–101.

Erikson, E. H. (1968). *Identity: Youth and crisis.* New York: Norton.

Fuligni, A. J., Tseng, V., & Lam, M. (1999). Attitudes toward family obligations among American adolescents from Asian, Latin American, and European backgrounds. *Child Development, 70,* 1030–1044.

Fuligni, A. J., & Witkow, M. (2004). The postsecondary educational progress of youth from immigrant families. *Journal of Research on Adolescence, 14,* 159–183.

Gonzales, N. A., Tein, J., Sandler, I. N., & Friedman, R. J. (2001). On the limits of coping: Interaction between stress and coping for inner-city adolescents. *Journal of Adolescent Research, 16,* 372–395.

Gray-Little, B., & Hafdahl, A. R. (2000). Factors influencing racial comparisons of self-esteem: A quantitative review. *Psychological Bulletin, 126,* 26–54.

Greenfield, P. M., Keller, H., Fuligni, A. J., & Maynard, A. (2003). Cultural pathways through universal development. *Annual Review of Psychology, 54,* 461–490.

Harter, S. (1999). *The construction of the self: A developmental perspective.* New York: Guilford.

Lohman, B. J., & Jarvis, P. A. (2000). Adolescent stressors, coping strategies, and psychological health studied in the family context. *Journal of Youth and Adolescence, 29,* 15–43.

Lorr, M., & McNair, D. M. (1971). *The profile of mood states manual.* San Francisco, CA: Educational and Industrial Testing Service.

Mossakowski, K. N. (2003). Coping with perceived discrimination: Does ethnic identity protect mental health? *Journal of Health and Social Behavior, 44,* 318–331.

Mroczek, D. K., & Almeida, D. M. (2004). The effect of daily stress, personality, and age on daily negative affect. *Journal of Personality, 72,* 355–378.

Phinney, J. S. (1990). Ethnic identity in adolescence and adults: A review of research. *Psychological Bulletin, 108,* 499–514.

Phinney, J. S. (1992). The Multigroup Ethnic Identity Measure: A new scale for use with diverse groups. *Journal of Adolescent Research, 7,* 156–176.

Phinney, J. S. (2003). Ethnic identity and acculturation. In K. M. Chun, P. B. Organista, & G. Marin (Eds.), *Acculturation: Advances in theory, measurement, and applied research* (pp. 63–81). Washington, DC: American Psychological Association.

Rosenberg, M. (1965). *Society and the adolescent self-image.* Princeton, NJ: Princeton University Press.

Rowley, S. J., Sellers, R. M., Chavous, T. M., & Smith, M. A. (1998). The relationship between racial identity and self-esteem in African American college and high school students. *Journal of Personality and Social Psychology, 74,* 715–724.

Ryff, C. D., Keyes, C. L. M., & Hughes, D. L. (2003). Status inequalities, perceived discrimination, and eudaimonic well-being: Do the challenges of minority life hone purpose and growth? *Journal of Health and Social Behavior, 44,* 275–290.

Seeman, T. E. (1996). Social ties and health: The benefits of social integration. *Annals of Epidemiology, 6,* 442–451.

Seligman, M. E. P., & Csikszentmihalyi, M. (2000). Positive psychology: An introduction. *American Psychologist, 55,* 5–14.

Sellers, R. M., Caldwell, C. H., Schmeelk-Cone, K. H., & Zimmerman, M. A. (2003). Racial identity, racial discrimination, perceived stress, and psychological distress among African American young adults. *Journal of Health and Social Behavior, 44,* 302–317.

Sellers, R. M., Rowley, S. J., Chavous, T. M., Shelton, J. N., & Smith, M. A. (1997). Multidimensional inventory of black identity: A preliminary investigation of reliability and construct validity. *Journal of Personality and Social Psychology, 73,* 805–815.

Sellers, R. M., Smith, M. A., Shelton, J. N., Rowley, S. A. J., & Chavous, T. M. (1998). Multidimensional model of racial identity: A reconceptualization of African American racial identity. *Personality and Social Psychology Review, 2,* 18–39.

Shelton, J. N., Yip, T., Eccles, J. S., Chatman, C., Fuligni, A. J., & Wong, C. (2005). Ethnic identity as a buffer in psychological adjustment. In G. Downey, J. Eccles, & C. Chatman (Eds.), *Navigating the future: Social identity, coping and life tasks.* New York: The Russell Sage Foundation.

Tajfel, H. (1981). *Human groups and social categories.* New York: Cambridge University Press.

Tajfel, H., & Forgas, J. P. (2000). Social categorization: Cognitions, values, and groups. In C. Stangor (Ed.), *Stereotypes and prejudice: Essential readings* (pp. 49–63). New York: Psychology Press.

Tsai, J. L., Ying, Y., & Lee, P. A. (2001). Cultural predictors of self-esteem: A study of Chinese American female and male young adults. *Cultural Diversity & Ethnic Minority Psychology, 7,* 284–297.

Umaña-Taylor, A. J. (2004). Ethnic identity and self-esteem: Examining the role of social context. *Journal of Adolescence, 27,* 139–146.

Umaña-Taylor, A. J., Diversi, M., & Fine, M. A. (2002). Ethnic identity and self-esteem among Latino adolescents: Making distinctions among the Latino populations. *Journal of Adolescent Research, 17,* 303–327.

Utsey, S. O., Chae, M. H., Brown, C. F., & Kelly, D. (2002). Effect of ethnic group membership on ethnic identity, race-related stress and quality of life. *Cultural Diversity & Ethnic Minority Psychology, 8*, 367–378.

Vandiver, B. J., Cross, W. E., Worrell, F. C., & Fhagen-Smith, P. E. (2002). Validating the Cross Racial Identity Scale. *Journal of Counseling Psychology, 49*, 71–85.

Wong, C. A., Eccles, J. S., & Sameroff, A. (2003). The influence of ethnic discrimination and ethnic identification on African American adolescents' school and socio-emotional adjustment. *Journal of Personality, 71*, 1197–1232.

Yip, T. (2005). Sources of situational variation in ethnic identity and psychological well-being: A palm pilot study of Chinese American students. *Personality and Social Psychology Bulletin, 31*, 1603–1616.

Yip, T., & Cross, W. E. (2004). A daily diary study of mental health and community involvement outcomes for three Chinese American social identities. *Cultural Diversity and Mental Health, 10*, 394–408.

Yip, T., & Fuligni, A. J. (2002). Daily variation in ethnic identity, ethnic behaviors, and psychological well-being among American adolescents of Chinese descent. *Child Development, 73*, 1557–1572.

....

The Development of Subjective Group Dynamics: Children's Judgments of Normative and Deviant In-Group and Out-Group Individuals

Dominic Abrams, Adam Rutland, and Lindsey Cameron

The present research investigated developmental changes in children's intergroup bias and judgments of in-group and out-group members who conform to or deviate from the norms of those groups. Intergroup biases are known to emerge relatively early in childhood (see Aboud, 1988; Bigler, 1995; Bigler & Liben, 1992; Nesdale, 2001; Powlishta, Serbin, Doyle, & White, 1994; Yee & Brown, 1994). Research into children's intergroup attitudes has frequently employed measures of group preference, whereby children are required to evaluate targets that represent the whole social group (e.g., a boy vs. a girl; see reviews by Aboud, 1988; Aboud & Amato, 2001; Katz, 1976; Nesdale, 2001). This methodology does not distinguish between evaluations of individual in-group and out-group members and evaluations of the groups as a whole. Developmental research suggests that in addition to understanding group membership, children begin to attend to what is normative and deviant in their group during social reasoning about inclusion and exclusion (Killen, Crystal, & Watanabe, 2002; Killen & Stangor, 2001). However, relatively little is known about the development of children's direct judgments of specific normative and deviant members of social groups (Ruble et al., 2004). The aim of the present research

was to investigate children's intergroup judgments and differentiated evaluations of individual group members in terms of their adherence to group norms.

Our research was set in the highly competitive and involving intergroup context of the 2002 World Cup Soccer Finals. In particular, our focus was on an explicit in-group versus out-group comparison known to be salient among English schoolchildren (i.e., England vs. Germany; see Barrett & Short, 1992; Rutland, 1999). English children evaluated the English and German soccer teams, and judged a normative and deviant soccer fan from either the in-group or out-group. The normative target expressed normative attitudes by favoring their own group. The attitudes of the deviant target were counternormative (i.e., disloyal) because they evaluated both the in-group and out-group positively. To examine whether there are developmental changes in reactions to normative and deviant group members, we examined responses from children 5 to 11 years old. This age range was chosen because evidence suggests that between these ages children develop the ability to attend to individuating information and multiple classifications (e.g., Bigler, 1995; Doyle & Aboud, 1995), a necessary requirement for intragroup differentiation.

Cognitive-developmental theory (cf. Aboud, 1988; Katz, 1976; Lambert & Klineberg, 1967) was developed to explain children's group attitudes in contexts less explicitly competitive than the one used within this study. Nevertheless, relevant to our concerns, cognitive-developmental theory suggests a given relationship between intragroup and intergroup judgments. This theory holds that with age children cease to focus only on group differences, and they become capable of making social judgments also on the basis of unique characteristics of an individual. Consequently with age, the availability of information about individuals' characteristics should help reduce intergroup biases. Specifically, Aboud's (1988) theory of social-cognitive development holds that there is a developmental sequence in which the child's focus of attention shifts from self to group (i.e., intergroup) and finally to individual (i.e., intragroup) characteristics. At this final stage, children may still express more positive evaluations of some individuals over others, but the criterion for judgment will not be solely that of group membership (see Aboud, 1988, pp. 23–25).

A significant body of research on adults has examined how deviant members of in-groups and out-groups are evaluated (e.g., Abrams, Marques, Bown, & Henson, 2000; Marques, Abrams, Pàez, & Martinez-Taboada, 1998; Marques, Abrams, & Serôdio, 2001). The findings of this adult research suggest a less sequential and more dynamic relationship between intragroup and intergroup judgments. Adults commonly express bias in favor of their in-groups and in favor of typical or normative in-group members over out-group members. However in-group bias appears to be eliminated or even reversed when deviant group members are judged (Abrams, Marques, Randsley de Moura, Hutchinson, & Bown, 2004; Marques & Pàez, 1994). For example, Marques, Yzerbyt, and Leyens (1988) found that likable in-group members were favored over likable out-group members, but unlikable out-group members were favored over unlikable in-group members, a phenomenon they labeled the *black sheep effect*.

The black sheep effect and related findings have been explained using the subjective group dynamics (SGD) model (Abrams et al., 2000; Marques et al., 1998). The term *subjective group dynamics* describes the psychological dynamics that affect judgments of groups and their members when social identity is relevant (see Marques, Abrams, Pàez, & Hogg, 2001; Abrams et al., 2004, for details). Group dynamics of small face-to-face groups include efforts to constrain and control deviants to maintain consensus surrounding group norms (e.g., Schachter, 1951; see also Levine, 1989). The SGD model assumes that an analogous process occurs subjectively even when the groups are social categories and when the individuals do not have interpersonal contact. The model adds a further level to these dynamics, namely, the intergroup context, and the premise from social identity theory (SIT; e.g., Tajfel, 1981; Tajfel & Turner, 1986) that people are motivated to sustain a positive social identity (i.e., identification with self-inclusive social categories).

Based on group dynamics research and SIT, the SGD model holds that group members strive to attain both positive in-group distinctiveness and support for in-group norms within groups. The former process implies a general preference for the in-group over the out-group, and the latter process involves vigilant attention to individual group members, both to detect possible dissent from norms and to respond in a way that upholds the in-group's norms. The crucial comparison within groups is between individuals who appear to uphold the group's norms and those who do not. In an intergroup context, the relevant norms to be upheld and rejected are those of the in-group and out-group, respectively. Therefore, the process of intragroup differentiation responds dynamically to the comparison groups that are relevant within a social context. Consequently, the same deviant behavior may be evaluated differently depending on whether it is exhibited by an in-group or an out-group member and depending on whether it implies support or rejection of the norms for each group. Because group members must attain both intergroup and intragroup differentiation to achieve subjectively valid intergroup differences, the SGD model holds that the two processes should be positively related. The consequence is that people who show the greatest biases in favor of their own group are also likely to differentiate most strongly between normative and deviant members within groups, for example, showing a stronger black sheep effect (e.g., Abrams et al., 2000; Abrams, Marques, Bown, & Dougill, 2002).

Based on cognitive-developmental theory and research it is reasonable to expect that, as they get older, children attend more closely to individuating characteristics of group members (Bigler, 1995; Black-Gutman & Hickson, 1996; Doyle & Aboud, 1995; Katz, Sohn, & Zalk, 1975, Martin, 1989). However, bearing in mind the SGD model, we believe this may not always be at the expense of, or detriment to, category-based judgment. Instead, children's developing ability to engage in multiple classifications and perceive within-group differences may augment, rather than inhibit, their use of social category memberships for making judgments about individuals.

Some existing evidence (e.g., Bigler, 1995; Doyle & Aboud, 1995) leads us to expect that SGD will operate increasingly with age. The use of intragroup differentiation to sustain the subjective validity and legitimacy of in-group norms requires the ability to attend to individuating information and multiple classifications. These social cognitive skills are known to develop in middle childhood. From the ages of approximately 7 to 8 years, children have made important social cognitive transitions from judgments based on a few primarily physical categories (e.g., sex, hair color) to judgments formulated using a multitude of psychological categories (e.g., intelligent, altruistic, friendly). This shift with age from physical to psychological descriptors is evident within the developmental literatures on person perception (e.g., Barenboim, 1978, 1981; Livesley & Bromley, 1973; Peevers & Secord, 1973), social perspective taking (Selman, 1971, 1980), and ethnic perspective taking (Quintana, 1998, 1999). Other studies suggest that around 9 years children no longer perceive people primarily through global descriptors (i.e., boy or girl) but also begin to acknowledge individual differences in dispositional characteristics (Alvarez, Ruble, & Bolger, 2001; Ruble & Dweck, 1995).

In line with the preceding evidence, our developmental SGD model holds that, as children get older they become more able to recognize that deviance constitutes a departure from norms that other group members would want to preserve (i.e., that it is a variation between individuals that is relevant to their group membership). Once children are able to recognize these potential group dynamics they can engage in evaluative intragroup differentiation. They will then also be able subjectively to sustain valued differences between in-groups and out-groups by expressing positive evaluations of individuals from both the in-group and the out-group who provide relative support for in-group categories.

A limited number of studies have asked children to evaluate or make judgments relating to individual members of social groups (Abrams, Rutland, Cameron, & Marques, 2003; Berndt & Heller, 1986; Biernat, 1991; Martin, 1989; Serbin & Sprafkin, 1986). These studies indicate an increasing use of individuated information with age, but they also suggest that older children continue to consider intergroup characteristics when forming social judgments about group members. However, previous developmental research on children's judgments of individual social group members has not focused specifically on the linkage between intergroup and intragroup judgments.

One study (Abrams et al., 2003) examined the relationship between intergroup and intragroup evaluations directly. Six- to 7-year-olds and 10- to 11-year-olds evaluated normative and deviant targets from the in-group or out-group summer play scheme. As expected, all ages expressed general intergroup bias. In line with the idea that SGD emerge later than general intergroup bias, the older children differentiated more strongly between the two targets in terms of how acceptable each target would be to other members of each group (a measure we label *differential inclusion*). Differential inclusion is similar to the concept of perspective taking that has been researched previously in the social (Selman, 1971, 1980) and ethnic domains (Quintana, 1998, 1999). That research shows that from approximately 10 years of age children are able to understand how social groups will view the actions of other individuals. It may follow that older children also become more sensitive to the evaluative implications for other members of the group when a group member undermines group norms (cf. Quintana, 1994, 1998; Ruble et al., 2004). In line with this idea, Abrams et al. (2003) found only the older children evaluated the normative in-group and deviant out-group member more positively than the deviant in-group member and normative out-group member. That is, they favored the target from either group who showed relatively greater support for the in-group (differential evaluation measure).

Moreover, the effects of age and intergroup bias on differential evaluation were mediated by differential inclusion.

The Abrams et al. (2003) study has several limitations and leaves important questions unanswered. First, Abrams et al. only compared two age groups (6- to 7-year-olds and 10- to 11-year-olds) and for practical reasons had only small numbers of participants ($N = 64$), and one age group was sampled only from one play scheme. The present study includes 476 children whose ages ranged from 5 to more than 11 years and who were drawn randomly from different schools within each condition. This allowed us to investigate evidence for SGD among slightly younger children than before and to use age as a continuous variable. This larger sample and better control allows us to investigate potentially important but small effects, and to examine effects of moderating variables, including identification with the in-group. Second, a methodological limitation in the Abrams et al. study was that the deviant target, but not the normative target, was given a gender-ambiguous name (i.e., Jo). This confound between target gender ambiguity and the normative or deviant factor meant it was possible that evaluation of the deviant target was somehow affected by gender ambiguity. Thus, we removed the confound from the present study by using only male targets.

A central variable in the SGD model is identification with the group. The motivation to upgrade individuals who provide validation for in-group norms arises because that group is important to the self-concept. Abrams et al. (2003) aimed only to determine whether there was an age difference in evaluations of deviant group members but did not investigate the role of social identification. Therefore, in the present study, we included measures of children's identification with the in-group. Identification is an important moderating cognitive-motivational variable in the SGD model. Research with adults shows that SGD operate more strongly when group membership is more salient (Marques et al., 1998) and when people identify more with the group (Abrams et al., 2000, Experiment 2; Abrams et al., 2002, Study 1; Coull, Yzerbyt, Castano, Paladino, & Leemans, 2001; Hutchison & Abrams, 2003). It seems reasonable to expect that high-identifying children should also be more concerned than low-identifying children to

express different evaluations of people who are more and less acceptable to in-group members.

With age, children develop a more sophisticated understanding of how group members' behavior reflects on their own and others' social identity (Quintana, 1994, 1998; Ruble et al., 2004). Consequently, we might expect older children to use their identity-based concerns more systematically when making a connection between differential inclusion and differential evaluation. Thus, as children get older we expect the high identifiers' evaluations of group members to be based more strongly on their perceptions of differential inclusion, but low identifiers to be less likely to use that criterion when evaluating group members.

We expected children of all ages to show significant in-group preference on measures of general support for each soccer team (general intergroup bias hypothesis).

The remaining measures focused on intragroup judgments. First, as a manipulation check, we measured children's perceptual accuracy in reporting the behavior of normative and deviant individuals. We also measured how typical they judged normative and deviant targets to be of the member's group. On the basis of previous work, we expected children of all ages to be able to detect that normative and deviant targets differed in typicality.

The general SGD hypothesis is that intergroup and intragroup differentiation should be positively related. Therefore, intergroup bias should be related positively to measures of intragroup differentiation among group members (described later) in terms of their acceptability within the groups and evaluations of the members.

SGD involve a subjective sense of how other group members would feel about deviants within the group context, that is, how the group dynamics might affect the way the group responds to deviant members. To tap this type of understanding, we measured judgments of how acceptable normative and deviant members would be to other members of each group (group inclusion measures). We expected that normative members would be perceived as being more acceptable to their own group than to the opposite group, and more acceptable to their own group than to deviant members. We also expected that deviant members would be perceived as more acceptable to opposing groups than to their own groups.

The SGD model proposes that evaluations of members within either group (target evaluations) will be differentiated such that most positive evaluations will be toward those who provide relatively greater support for in-group norms. We expect that normative in-group members will be favored over deviant in-group members, and deviant out-group members will be favored over normative out-group members. When this effect becomes strong, deviant out-group members will be evaluated more positively than deviant in-group members, similar to the black sheep effect.

Our developmental SGD hypothesis was that older children should differentiate more strongly than younger children on both group inclusion and target evaluations. Specifically, older children should be able to distinguish more clearly between the acceptability of normative and deviant targets to each group (on an overall index of differential inclusion), and they should show stronger differential evaluation between normative and deviant group members (on an overall index of differential evaluation).

Differential evaluations (such as the black sheep effect) that are associated with the operation of SGD should reflect in part an understanding how acceptable a particular behavior is to members of different groups. This understanding should increase with age. We therefore predicted that differential inclusion would mediate the effects of age on differential evaluation (mediation hypothesis). We also considered the possibility that age might augment the effects of differential inclusion on differential evaluation because older children would be better able to understand the implications of differential inclusion for the way group members should be evaluated. This would be reflected in a significant Age × Differential Inclusion interaction that affects differential evaluations (developmental moderation hypothesis).

Finally, the SGD model holds that stronger identification with the in-group is associated with increased differential evaluations of among-group members because of heightened desire to sustain in-group norms (SGD identification hypothesis). It also follows that the effect of differential inclusion on differential evaluation will also be larger among people who identify more strongly (identity moderation hypoth-

esis). Given our expectations that age and social identification could increase the effect of differential inclusion on differential evaluation for different reasons, we also predicted a significant three-way interaction such that support for the identity moderation hypothesis should be manifested more strongly among older children (developmental identity moderation hypothesis).

Method

A preliminary study was conducted 8 weeks before the start of the June 2002 World Cup Soccer Finals in Japan and South Korea. The main study was conducted 4 weeks later during a 2-week period in May 2002.

Preliminary study of normative expectations

DESIGN AND METHOD
The preliminary study was conducted to ensure that children could distinguish between the typicality of statements designed to be normative and deviant in the main study. We also wanted to ensure that these statements would be viewed as normative or deviant regardless of whether they were made by in-group and out-group members. The design of the main study required it to be clear that even the deviant target was a supporter of his or her own team. For this reason, the deviant group member (target) would make one normative statement and one deviant statement. We also decided the main study should include two statements for each target, to ensure the amount of content was equivalent for the two targets. Therefore, in the preliminary study, we aimed to find three equally normative statements (two to be made by normative targets and one to be made by deviant targets) and one statement that would be considered deviant (to be made by deviant targets).

Twenty-seven male children (fifteen 6- to 7-year-olds and twelve 10- to 11-year-olds) from a school in the southeast of England were tested individually by a female experimenter. Children were asked to estimate the proportion of England and Germany soccer supporters who would agree with a series of statements.

First, the response format was explained. A picture of 12 stick people was presented and described as a group of children. Then, it was explained how to answer the question, "How many of these children do you think would say 'I love eating sweets'?" A series of response scales was presented, showing proportionate numbers of stick people with labels representing all the children, most of the children, about half of the children, a few of the children, and none of the children. This was later scored as a scale from 1 (*none*) to 5 (*all*). Once the child's responses indicated that he or she understood how to use the response format, the main questionnaire was presented.

Children were asked to, "Think about England soccer supporters. Here is a group of 15 supporters of the England soccer team talking about the England soccer team and the World Cup. This group of England soccer fans was asked to imagine that England have to play Germany in the World Cup final this summer. Think about what the fans might say about the England soccer team. How many of the England soccer supporters in this group would say each of these statements?" There followed a series of normative and deviant statements for potential inclusion in the main study. For economy of space we report analyses only for the items that were retained for use in the main study. The normative statements were positive statements about the team. In the main study in the in-group condition, two of these were attributed to the normative target: "I think England is the best team" and "Even if we lost the game to Germany I'd still say that England are the better team." Another was attributed to the deviant target, "It's great when England play well. They are a fantastic team." The deviant target also uttered a deviant statement, "When Germany play well, I always clap and cheer" (when targets were German the referent in-group was Germany rather than England).

RESULTS

The average of the two normative target statements were judged to be equally typical when attributed to in-group targets ($M = 4.61$, $SD = .51$) and out-group targets ($M = 4.40$, $SD = 0.74$), $t(24) = 1.04$, $p < .31$. The single normative statement attributed to deviant in-group ($M = 4.74$, $SD = 0.66$) and out-group target ($M = 4.60$, $SD = 0.91$) was also equivalent,

$t(24) = 0.35$, $p < .73$. Comparison of the average of the two normative statements attributed to the normative target and the single normative statement attributed to the deviant target in the main study revealed that they were judged to be equally typical, both when uttered by in-group targets, $t(26) = 1.02$, $p < .32$, and by out-group targets, $t(24) = 1.73$, $p < .10$.

Next, we checked that the deviant statements were judged to be less typical than the normative statements. This was confirmed both when the statements were attributed to the in-group targets ($M = 2.59$, $SD = 1.31$ and $M = 4.74$, $SD = 0.66$, respectively), $t(26) = 7.94$, $p < 001$, and to the out-group targets ($M = 2.88$, $SD = 1.42$ and $M = 4.64$, $SD = 0.91$, respectively), $t(24) = 5.06$, $p < .001$. The pairs of statements made by in-group and out-group deviant targets were judged as similarly atypical, $t(24) = 0.30$, $p = 0.77$. Finally, the mean typicality of the two statements to be made by normative targets was significantly greater than the mean typicality of the two statements uttered by deviant targets, either when the statements were attributed to in-group targets, $t(26) = 6.43$, $p < .001$, or to out-group targets, $t(24) = 2.92$, $p < .007$. Based on these data we felt confident that the normative and deviant statements differed in terms of their perceived typicality, and that the degree of typicality of each type of statement did not vary as a function of the group membership of the speaker. These results confirmed that both younger and older children expected that soccer fans will normally only express attitudes that support fans' own team. Expressing a positive evaluation of the opposing team is judged to be deviant.

Finally, we checked for age differences in judgments of typicality and found that older children rated normative statements to be more typical ($M = 4.73$, $SD = 0.39$) than did younger children ($M = 4.37$, $SD = 0.47$), $F(1, 23) = 7.86$, $p < .01$. However, age did not interact with any of the differences between typicality ratings mentioned earlier, all $Fs < 1.07$, all $ps > .30$. Therefore, we decided to use these statements as stimuli in the main study.

Main study design and participants

Age was a continuous independent variable ($M = 104.63$ months, $SD = 21.91$; *range* = 62 months to 143 months), crossed with a between-participants variable (group: in-group vs. out-group) and a within-participants variable (target: normative vs. deviant).

Participants were 519 children, and data were treated as valid for 476. A criterion for participation was that the child was self-defined as English. The children were predominantly of Caucasian origin (86%), and all were English by nationality. Assignment to condition was random within each school. Forty seven percent of the participants were female, and gender was evenly distributed between conditions, $\chi^2(1) = 0.32, p = .57$.

PROCEDURE

All children participated individually under the supervision of a female experimenter. The experimenter interviewed the younger children with the questionnaire in front of them. The older children, given their more advanced reading ability, were allowed to self-complete the questionnaire in the presence of the experimenter who sat directly next to each child. The experimenter monitored all children's progress through each question ensuring and checking with them whether they understood the questions. This procedure was used to ensure that the accountability cues were similar for children in all age groups because previous research with adults suggested that variations in accountability (to other group members) may increase SGD effects (Marques et al., 1998).

STIMULUS MATERIALS AND MEASURES

The first page of the questionnaire was used to introduce the study and to ensure that children understood how to use the response scales. It included a series of statements about the weather that day, accompanied by an explanation of which face to tick to describe it. A circular feeling face was used to represent each point on the 5-point scale. The scale had the mouth in a downward position (1) through horizontal (3) to a large smile position (5). After the child had correctly identified the relevant response for each type of weather the experimenter proceeded with the experiment.

The questionnaire had two sections: team identification, and intergroup and target judgments. The sequence of the sections was counterbalanced. The team identification measures determined children's

identification with the England soccer team. Responses were made on the feeling faces scale anchored with *not at all* (1) and *very much* (5). There were four items: "How much do you like the England soccer team?" "Do you like it when England win soccer matches?" "Do you like to watch England games on TV?" "Do you cheer for England in soccer?"

The intergroup and target judgments section of the questionnaire began with two items to measure general intergroup bias: "How do you feel about supporting the England soccer team?" "How do you feel about supporting the German soccer team?"

Next, children were presented with statements made by two male target characters, Alex and Mark, who were introduced as real fans of either the England or German soccer team, who had supported their teams since they were children and went to all the games and watched them on TV. In the in-group condition Alex and Mark were described as England soccer supporters and in the out-group condition they were described as German soccer supporters. Children were told that "Alex and Mark were asked to imagine that England have to play Germany in the World Cup final next month. Here are some of the things Alex and Mark said." Across conditions, Alex was presented as a normative target and Mark was presented as a deviant target. The statements made by the normative and deviant targets are described in our preliminary study of normative expectations.

There followed a series of nine questions about Alex and Mark. These were designed to assess whether children correctly perceived that the deviant was deviant, how typical the targets were of their groups, how likely they were to be accepted by other members of each group, and how the child evaluated the target. The order in which targets were judged was counterbalanced so that half the children judged the normative target first, and the rest judged the deviant target first. Before answering the questions, children were reminded of what the target had said.

The first two questions provided a perceptual accuracy check to see whether children understood which preferences the member had expressed: "What does [target] feel about being an [in-group team] supporter?" "What do you think [target] would feel about being an [out-group team] supporter instead?"

The next item tapped target typicality to check that the normative targets were viewed as more typical (i.e., normative) of their groups than were the deviant targets. The item asked, "How many other [same team] supporters would think the same as [target]?" The response options (scored from 1 to 5) were: none, hardly any, quite a few, a lot, and almost all. Above each label was a schematic picture that depicted 0, 4, 10, 18, or 40 people, respectively.

Two questions used the face scales to measure perceived same-group inclusion and other-group inclusion. These were designed to reveal whether children understood the implications of the targets' attitudes for the acceptability of the target to members of each group. The questions were: "How do you think other [same team] supporters would feel towards [target]?" "How do you think [opposing team] supporters would feel toward [target]?"

Four items tapped target evaluations. These asked, "How do you feel towards [target]?" "How do you feel about what [target] said?" "How much would you like to be [target's] friend?" "In a game, how much would you want [target] to be on your team?" Responses were made using the feeling face scales.

Results

We first analyzed the data to investigate possible effects of school and gender. Previous research has revealed pronounced in-group gender bias among children (e.g., Bigler, 1995; Martin, 1989; Powlishta, 1995; Yee & Brown, 1994). Gender is not strictly relevant to the present hypotheses, or to the comparison between the soccer teams, and we had no a priori reason to expect gender to affect responses (cf. Abrams et al., 2003). To minimize the complexity of the design, we had elected to use only male targets and to check if gender bias was manifested. This could happen if male participants favored all targets more than female participants or if males would differentiate more between normative and deviant targets than females. In fact, there were no significant multivariate main effects or interactions involving either gender or school, $Fs < 1.17$, $ps > .20$. Therefore, these variables were not included in the analyses reported.

Table 7.10   Means (standard deviations) for measures of typicality, group inclusion, and evaluation as a function of group membership and target type

	In-group		Out-group	
Group target	Normative	Deviant	Normative	Deviant
Typicality	4.60$_a$	2.64	4.31$_a$	3.00
	(0.67)	(1.29)	(0.97)	(1.22)
Inclusion by	4.60$_b$	2.65$_c$	4.43$_b$	2.92$_c$
target's group	(0.79)	(1.43)	(1.04)	(1.39)
Inclusion by	1.72$_*$	4.20$_c$	1.70$_*$	3.87$_c$
other group	(1.21)	(1.08)	(1.15)	(1.22)
Evaluation	4.35	3.08	2.49	3.69
	(0.72)	(1.29)	(1.23)	(1.05)

Note. Scores on each variable may range from 1 to 5. Within rows all means differ significantly ($p < .001$) with the exception of those sharing subscripts a ($p < .01$), b or c ($p < .05$), or * (ns). For each target, inclusion by target's group differs significantly from inclusion by other group ($p < .001$).

To ascertain whether the basic pattern of findings fits the SGD model, we conducted mixed analyses of variance (ANOVAs) with target (normative vs. deviant) as a within-participants variable and group (in-group vs. out-group) as a between-participants variable. The means for simple measures of typicality, inclusion, and evaluation as a function of group and target type are shown in Table 7.10, and correlations among variables within levels of group are presented for information in Table 7.11. Our developmental and identity hypotheses were tested using multiple regression analyses with age (in months) or identification as continuous independent variables. We were primarily interested in differences in judgments of normative and deviant targets; therefore, these analyses focus on the magnitude of these differences (cf. Judd, Kenny, & McClelland, 2001). A summary of the way these difference scores were derived is provided in Table 7.12. We also conducted regression analyses of judgments of each target separately. These analyses are not reported here for reasons of space and clarity, and because they do not substantively alter the findings or conclusions. Details of these analyses are available from the first author.

Table 7.11 Zero-order correlations among variables within in-group and out-group conditions

	1	2	3	4	5	6	7	8	9
1. Age	—	.00	.23***	.07	-.22***	-.30***	.16**	-.24***	-.37***
2. Identification	-.05	—	.51***	.06	-.04	.14*	.07	.33***	.06
3. Intergroup bias	.18**	.59***	—	.15*	-.14*	-.11	.12	.26***	-.23***
4. Normative target same-group inclusion	.12	.04	.14*	—	-.21***	-.08	.03	.24***	-.05
5. Normative target opposite-group inclusion	-.22***	.00	-.19**	-.08	—	.21***	-.09	-.14*	.19**
6. Deviant target same-group inclusion	-.23***	-.03	-.09	-.06	.21**	—	-.30***	.09	.61***
7. Deviant target opposite-group inclusion	.03	.13*	.21**	.25***	-.03	-.03	—	-.07	-.18**
8. Evaluation of normative	-.22***	-.24***	-.40***	-.03	.32***	.18**	.00	—	.03
9. Evaluation of deviant	-.08	.27***	.13*	.06	-.03	.08	.45***	-.09	—

Note. In-group and out-group condition correlations are above and below the diagonal, respectively. Intergroup bias is the difference between general in-group evaluation and general out-group evaluation.

*p<.05. **p<.01. ***p<.001.

Table 7.12 Summary of computation and interpretation of differentiation scores

Variable	Computation and constituent variables	Interpretation
General intergroup bias	Support for England minus support for Germany.	Higher score = more bias in favor of England.
Group inclusion	Rating of target's acceptability to target's group minus rating of target's acceptability to opposing group.	More positive score = more inclusion in same group relative to opposing group.
Differential inclusion	Group-inclusion score for normative target minus group-inclusion score for deviant target.	Higher score = judging larger differences in the acceptability of normative and deviant members to same and opposing groups.
Target bias	Evaluation of normative target minus evaluation of deviant target.	Positive score = normative target is favored; negative score = deviant target is favored.
Differential evaluation	In the in-group condition the score is derived from evaluation of normative target minus evaluation of deviant target. In the out-group condition the score is derived from evaluation of deviant target minus normative target.	Across the in-group and out-group conditions, positive score = greater favorability toward target that shows most support for the in group.

Manipulation checks

PERCEPTUAL ACCURACY

Data from 8 children were excluded because it was evident during testing that they were not paying attention to the task. We screened the perceptual accuracy measure data from the remaining children and excluded 35 (7%) participants who had inaccurately judged the deviant targets to be more favorable to the target's group than the normative target was (although all significant effects were unaffected by this). Younger children were slightly more likely to have failed the manipulation check, $r(519) = -.15, p < .001$. Data for the remaining 476 children were used for subsequent analyses. The initial and final numbers included for analysis reflected the availability of children at the time of the study. When classified in 12-month age bands, the initial (final) numbers were 38 (31) aged 5, 75 (59) aged 6, 88 (83) aged 7, 76 (72) aged 8, 80 (79) aged 9, 85 (80) aged 10, and 77 (72) aged 11. Random assignment to condition was successful within all age levels, maximum difference between cell sizes in the in-group and out-group condition = 4, modal difference = 1, $\chi^2(6) = 0.32, p = .99$.

ORDER EFFECTS

We examined all the main dependent variables described next to see whether there were any effects of order of presentation of the team identification section, and order of presentation of the normative and deviant targets. Across all the measures none of the differences was significant, smallest $t(474) = 0.54, p < .39$, largest $t(474) = 1.77, p = .077$. Therefore, we collapsed across these factors for subsequent analyses.

General intergroup bias

The two measures of support for the in-group and out-group teams were answered before children received information about the target individuals. Consistent with the general intergroup bias hypothesis, children supported England ($M = 4.31, SD = 1.17$) significantly more than Germany ($M = 1.88, SD = 1.30$), $t(473) = 38.5, p < .001$.

We computed a measure of general intergroup bias by subtracting support for the out-group from support for the in-group. Regression analysis revealed a highly significant effect of age, $\beta = 0.20, t(471) = 4.45, p < .001$. Children expressed stronger intergroup bias with age. As expected, there was no effect of group on intergroup bias, $\beta = .03, t(471) = 0.70$, and no interaction between age and group, $\beta = -0.16, t(471) = 0.37$. When we examined bias within each 12-month age category we found it to be significantly different from zero in all ages (all $ps < .05$).

Target typicality

Normative targets were viewed as more typical ($M = 4.46$) than deviant targets ($M = 2.82$), $F(1, 459) = 432.7$, $p < .001$. The normative target was rated significantly lower in the in-group condition than in the out-group condition, $\beta = 0.20, t(471) = 3.66, p < .001$. Ratings of deviant typicality were lower in the in-group condition, $\beta = 0.14, t(471) = 3.12, p < .01$, and reduced significantly with age, $\beta = -.22, t(471) = 4.89, p < .001$. We computed a score to reflect the difference in perceived typicality of the two targets (normative minus deviant). The regression analysis revealed significant effects of group, $\beta = -.20, t = 4.50, p < .001$, and age, $\beta = 0.17, t = 3.79, p < .001$, but no interaction between them, $\beta = .08, t = 1.72, p = .09$. Normative and deviant in-group targets were judged to differ more in typicality than normative and deviant out-group targets regardless of children's age. Children also distinguished the typicality of normative and deviant targets more as they got older.

Group inclusion

The measures of group inclusion were intended to capture children's interpretation of the meaning of deviance for dynamics within the target's group. Same-group inclusion was perceived to be higher for the normative than deviant target, whereas opposite-group inclusion was perceived to be lower for the normative than deviant target, $F(1, 460) = 389.9$, $p < .001; F(1, 460) = 768.5, p < .001$, respectively. We reduced the measures of group inclusion for the two targets to a single index. For each target we subtracted the other-group inclusion rating from the same-group inclusion rating (the score would typically be positive for a normative target and negative for a deviant target). We then subtracted the score for the deviant from the score for the normative target. This provided an overall measure of differential inclusion. The higher the score, the more the children expected normative targets to be accepted by the target's group and rejected by the opposing group, and the more they expected deviant targets to be accepted by the opposing group but rejected by the target's group.

Regression analysis on this score revealed a significant effect of group, $\beta = -.15, t = 3.46, p < .001$, and

a significant effect of age, $\beta = .20, t(473) = 4.56$, $p < .001$, but no interaction between them, $\delta = -.02$, $t = 0.54$. Thus, children expected in-group members to distinguish more strongly than out-group members between the acceptability of normative and deviant targets. With increasing age children developed stronger expectations that normative members would be accepted and deviant targets rejected by their respective groups relative to their treatment by opposing groups (see also Table 7.11). This is consistent with our developmental SGD hypothesis that older children would be more sensitive to the intergroup implications of deviance.

Target evaluations

The four items used to evaluate normative members and the four used to evaluate deviant members were factor analyzed. This revealed two distinct factors, eigenvalues = 3.54 and 2.42, accounting for 44.2% and 30.2% of the variance, respectively. The significant items in each factor correspond to the two different targets. We therefore averaged the responses to the four items for each target to produce measures of normative target evaluation and deviant target evaluation (Cronbach's alpha = 0.90 and 0.86, respectively). The ANOVA revealed no significant effect of target, $F(1, 474) = 0.24$, but highly significant effects of group, $F(1, 474) = 81.03, p < .001$, and Group × Target interaction, $F(1, 474) = 292.74, p < .001$.

Simple effects analyses revealed that within the in-group condition the normative target ($M = 4.35$, $SD = 0.72$) was favored over the deviant target, ($M = 3.08, SD = 1.29$), $F(1, 474) = 156.85, p < .001$. Within the out-group condition the reverse was true ($M = 2.49, SD = 1.23$ and $M = 3.69, SD = 1.05$, respectively), $F(1, 474) = 136.39, p < .001$. Moreover, the in-group normative target was favored over the out-group normative target, $F(1, 474) = 408.16$, $p < .001$, whereas the out-group deviant was favored over the in-group deviant, $F(1, 474) = 32.01, p < .001$, consistent with the operation of SGD and a pattern comparable to the black sheep effect.

Next, we subtracted the rating of the deviant target from the rating of the normative target (target bias). A positive target bias score represents preference of

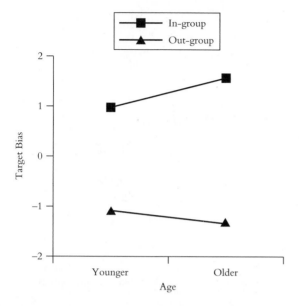

Figure 7.6 Evaluation of normative group members minus evaluation of deviant group members (target bias) in the in-group condition and out-group condition, as a function of age. Values of target bias are derived from a regression equation in which target bias is the dependent variable and age, group (in-group vs. out-group), and their interaction, are independent variables. Effects of age are represented by values ±1 *SD* from the mean age.

the normative over the deviant target, and a negative score represents preference of the deviant over the normative target. We used multiple regression to analyze the effects of group and age on this measure. There was a significant effect of group, corresponding to the Group × Target interaction on target evaluations reported earlier, $\beta = -.62$, $t(470) = 17.02$, $p < .001$. There was no significant effect of age, $\beta = .03$, but there was a significant Age × Group interaction, $\beta = -.12$, $t(470) = 3.39$, $p < .001$, indicating that the effect of group increases with age. Figure 7.6 illustrates this interaction by plotting the slopes for children 1 *SD* below and above the mean age for the sample, derived from the regression equation. Compared with younger children, older children show a relatively stronger target bias in favor of the in-group normative versus the in-group deviant target, and in favor of the out-group deviant versus the out-group normative target. This is in line with the developmental SGD hypothesis.

Intergroup and intragroup differentiation

The general SGD hypothesis is that differentiation among group members occurs in concert with general intergroup bias. The previous analyses demonstrated that general intergroup bias, differential inclusion, and target bias in support of the in-group all increase with age. To test the general SGD hypothesis we used differential inclusion as a dependent measure and general intergroup bias and age as predictors in a regression analysis. Consistent with the hypothesis, independent of the significant effects of age, $\beta = .18$, $t(471) = 3.89$, $p < .001$, there was a significant effect of intergroup bias, $\beta = .13$, $t = 2.76$, $p < .006$. The Age × Bias interaction was not significant, $\beta = -.05$, $t = .99$. To conduct a comparable analysis for target bias that could be used with the same conceptual status across the in-group and out-group conditions, we followed previous research (Abrams et al., 2002; Abrams et al., 2003) to derive an index of differential evaluation. Specifically, we used the target bias score in the in-group condition (evaluation of normative minus evaluation of deviant) and the reversed target bias score in the out-group condition (evaluation of the deviant target minus evaluation of the normative target). Higher differential evaluation scores represent a stronger preference for the target that provides most support for the in-group.

When we used differential evaluation as the dependent variable the pattern was similar to that for differential inclusion. Independent of the significant effect of age, $\beta = .15$, $t(471) = 3.33$, $p < .001$, there was a significant effect of general intergroup bias, $\beta = .34$, $t = 7.65$, $p < .001$, but no significant interaction, $\beta = .07$, $t = 1.47$, $p < .14$. Thus, for both differential inclusion and differential evaluation, children who expressed more intergroup bias also expressed greater differentiation between targets, in line with the general SGD hypothesis.

Mediation and developmental moderation

Our mediation hypothesis was that the effect of age on differential evaluation should be mediated by differential inclusiveness. To test this hypothesis we used differential evaluation as a dependent variable and then entered differential inclusiveness before testing the

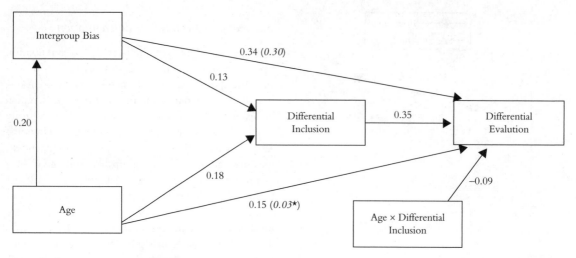

Figure 7.7 Path diagram of the effects of intergroup bias and age on differential inclusion and differential evaluation. Path weights are standardized regression coefficients. Italicized coefficients are the effects when differential inclusion is partialed out. All paths are significant except $\star p > .05$.

remaining variance attributable to age and intergroup bias. The relationship between differential evaluation and differential inclusiveness was significant, $\beta = .35$, $t(471) = 8.11$, $p < .001$. Moreover, the effect of age on differential evaluation was nonsignificant once differential inclusiveness was included in the regression, $\beta = .03$, $t = .75$, $p < .45$, and the effect of intergroup bias remained significant, $\beta = .30$, $t = 7.08$, $p < .001$.

A formal test of the significance of mediation is provided by the Goodman (I) version of the Sobel test (Goodman, 1960), as specified in Baron and Kenny (1986; see also MacKinnon, Warsi, & Dwyer, 1995). This showed that the effect of intergroup bias on differential evaluation is partly, and significantly, mediated by differential inclusion, $Z = 2.76$, $p < .01$. Moreover, the effect of age on differential evaluation is entirely and significantly mediated by differential inclusion, $Z = 3.41$, $p < .001$, as predicted by our developmental model. At the suggestion of a reviewer, we also checked for reverse mediation, that is, that the effects of age on differential inclusion may be mediated by differential evaluation. When differential evaluation was included as a mediator, the effect of age on differential inclusion remained significant, $\beta = .15$, $t = 3.44$, $p < .001$. The Sobel test revealed only marginally significant evidence of partial mediation by differen-

tial evaluation, $Z = 1.92$, $p = .054$. In summary, the age-related increase in differential evaluation depends on age-related increases in differential inclusion.

Finally, we investigated whether age and differential inclusiveness interacted to predict differential evaluation. Consistent with the developmental moderation hypothesis, the Age × Differential Inclusiveness interaction was significant, $\beta = -.09$, $t = 2.11$, $p < .035$, showing that the impact of differential inclusiveness on differential evaluation increased with age.

These analyses are consistent with the following conclusions. Age affects intergroup bias, and both variables affect differential inclusion. Intergroup bias and differential inclusion both affect differential evaluation. Finally, the impact of differential inclusiveness on differential evaluation increases slightly with age. These findings are summarized in the path model in Figure 7.7, and zero-order correlations among variables are shown in Table 7.11.

Group identification

The four team-identification items were averaged to form a measure of group identification. This was reliable (Cronbach's alpha = 0.80). Levels of identification did not differ as a function of group, $F(1, 474) = .08$.

To test the SGD identification hypothesis, we used multiple regression to examine whether age, identification, and their interaction affected intergroup bias, differential inclusion, and differential evaluation. For intergroup bias there were highly significant effects of age, $\beta = .21$, $t = 5.77$, $p < .001$, and identification, $\beta = .56$, $t = 15.98$, $p < .001$, but no interaction between these variables, $\beta = .01$, $t = 0.39$. For differential inclusion there was only a significant effect of age, $\beta = .20$, $t = 4.50$, $p < .001$, and no effect of identification or interaction between these variables, $\beta s = .02$ and $-.02$, $t s = .40$ and $.38$, respectively. For differential evaluation there was a significant effect of both age, $\beta = .16$, $t = 3.56$, $p < .001$, and identification, $\beta = .24$, $t = 5.44$, $p < .001$, but no significant interaction, $\beta = .05$, $t = 1.03$, $p < .30$. Therefore, independent of the effects of age described earlier and consistent with the hypothesis, identification significantly affected intergroup bias and differential evaluation. However, identification did not affect differential inclusion.

Identity moderation analyses

From SIT and research on SGD in adults, we hypothesized that the impact of differential inclusiveness on differential evaluation should be moderated by the strength of identification with the in-group (identity moderation hypothesis). Therefore, we conducted a regression analysis using differential evaluation as the dependent variable, and identification, differential inclusion, and their interaction as predictor variables. There were significant effects of differential inclusion, $\beta = .34$, $t = 8.24$, $p < .001$, and identification, $\beta = .23$, $t = 5.55$, $p < .001$. Increases in differential inclusion and identification both related to increased differential evaluation. Moreover, the interaction between these variables was significant, $\beta = .10$, $t = 2.31$, $p < .021$. We examined the simple regression slopes of differential inclusion on evaluative differentiation within high identifiers and low identifiers (defined by scores 1 SD above and below the mean identification score), following the procedures outlined by Aiken and West (1991). In line with the identity moderation hypothesis, the relationship was larger among high identifiers, $\beta = .45$, $t = 7.71$, $p < .001$, than among low identifiers, $\beta = .24$, $t = 4.22$, $p < .001$.

The developmental identity moderation hypothesis was that as children get older the moderating effect of identification on the relationship between differential inclusion and differential evaluation should increase. Consistent with this expectation, when age was included in the regression analysis, the main effect of differential inclusion, $\beta = .33$, $t = 7.80$, $p < .001$, and the Differential Inclusion $\times$ Age interaction, $\beta = -.09$, $t = 2.14$, $p < .04$, remained significant. The effects of identification, $\beta = .19$, $t = 4.39$, $p < .001$, and the Identification $\times$ Differential Inclusion interaction remained significant, $\beta = .09$, $t = 2.06$, $p < .04$. Moreover, the Age $\times$ Identification $\times$ Differential Inclusion interaction was also significant, $\beta = .11$, $t = 2.53$, $p < .012$. We decomposed the significant three-way interaction to examine the simple two-way interactions within levels of age, using values ± 1 SD above and below the mean. The Differential Inclusion $\times$ Identification interaction was significant among older children, $\beta = .22$, $t = 3.43$, $p < .001$, but not among younger children, $\beta = -.04$, $t = 0.57$. Further analysis of the simple effect of differential inclusion on differential evaluation within high and low identifiers among older children revealed that differential inclusion was significantly related to differential evaluation among high identifiers, $\beta = .44$, $t = 5.40$, $p < .001$, but not among low identifiers, $\beta = .03$, $t = 0.36$. The pattern is consistent with the developmental identity moderation hypothesis. Whereas identification does not affect the relationship between differential inclusion and differential evaluation among younger children, it has a significant impact among older children. Only among those who identify highly with the group does a perception of differential inclusion relate to their own evaluations of normative and deviant group members. The pattern for this interaction is displayed in Figure 7.8, which presents the separate figures for older and younger age groups, and depicts predicted levels of differential evaluation when identification and differential inclusion are ± 1 SD from the mean.

Discussion

Several findings emerge from this study to show that, as children get older, their judgments of deviants reflect their increasing understanding of the relationship between the individual's behavior and their group membership. We discuss each finding separately and then consider the relationship among them.

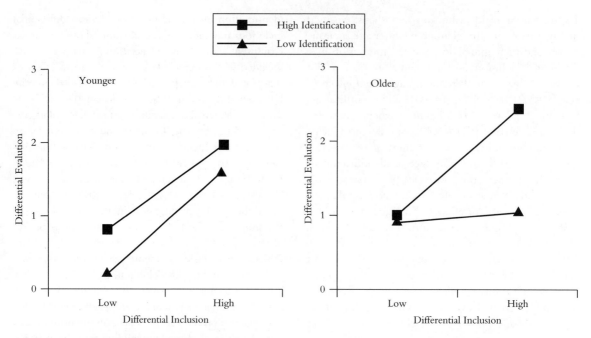

Figure 7.8   Effects of age, differential inclusion, and social identity on differential evaluation. Values for differential evaluation are derived from the regression analysis within which identification, differential inclusion, age, and their two-way and three-way interactions were used as predictors. In the figures, to represent younger and older age groups, higher and lower identifiers, and high- and low-differential inclusion, we substituted values 1 *SD* above and below the means for those variables.

Intergroup bias

Children of all ages showed significant bias in favor of the English soccer team versus the German soccer team. This effect was also significantly stronger as a function of age, consistent with our general intergroup bias hypothesis.

Perceptions of target typicality

The perceptual accuracy check showed that 93% of children correctly understood that normative targets were more favorable than deviants to the target's team. Moreover, the typicality measure showed that children in all age groups recognized that deviant targets were less typical than normative targets. As expected, this suggests that children as young as 5 years of age are familiar with the idea of loyalty norms, at least in the area of sports team support. This is consistent with theorizing that loyalty norms are basic and pervasive in society, perhaps for evolu-

tionary as well as social reasons (cf. Kurzban & Leary, 2001; Zdaniuk & Levine, 2001). The preliminary study and main study both showed that children distinguished the typicality of normative and deviant targets more as they got older.

Differential inclusion

In line with our developmental SGD hypothesis, older children were more sensitive to the group-related implications of deviance. As predicted, when asked to rate how acceptable the normative and deviant targets would be from the perspective of other members of each group (differential inclusion), differentiation between these targets was significantly greater among older children. This is important for our developmental SGD model because understanding of the intergroup and intragroup implications of deviance is assumed to be a precursor to identity-serving evaluations of group members.

Target evaluation

The classic finding in SGD research is that in an inter-group context in which deviants imply support for opposing group norms, normative in-group members are preferred over deviant in-group members, whereas deviant out-group members are preferred over normative out-group members. The so-called black sheep effect (Marques et al., 1988) occurs when deviant out-group members are evaluated more highly than similar deviant in-group members. The results for target evaluations showed that both of these patterns were obtained in the present study. These findings verify a similar but marginally significant pattern in our previous study (Abrams et al., 2003).

Cognitive-developmental theory holds that older children should engage in more individuated judgments and therefore could be expected to base evaluations less on the group membership of the targets. Thus, we might have expected older children to evaluate in-group and out-group deviant targets more similarly to one another because both targets expressed positive sentiments toward both teams. Conversely, evaluations of normative targets would become more divergent with age because normative targets favored different teams. This did not occur. Instead, consistent with our developmental SGD hypothesis, in-group-serving differential evaluation among targets increased with age.

The relationship among general intergroup bias, intragroup differentiation, and age

In line with the general SGD hypothesis, general intergroup bias and differential evaluation were positively related, and this finding is the background against which age differences emerged. In particular, our mediation hypothesis was that age differences in evaluative biases toward individual targets would be dependent on children's comprehension of how the social group would perceive the normative and deviant targets (i.e., differential inclusion). Consistent with this idea we found that, independent of the relationship between age and intergroup bias, both age and intergroup bias were associated with a stronger awareness of differential inclusion. As predicted by our developmental moderation hypothesis, the effect of

age on differential evaluation was fully mediated by (and augmented the effects of) differential inclusion. Moreover, there was little evidence that differential evaluation mediated effects of age on differential inclusion. This suggests that age-related effects on differential evaluation reflect children's developing social-cognitive capacity to make sense of normative and deviant behavior in an intergroup context. In contrast, the effects of intergroup bias on differential evaluation were only partially mediated by differential inclusion.

Group identification

The SGD model holds that evaluations of groups and their members serve an identity-maintenance function. As expected, we found that identification was strongly related to intergroup bias, independent of age-related changes. In line with our SGD identification hypothesis, identification also affected differential evaluation. It is interesting that identification had no effect on differential inclusion. Thus, identification affected only the measures that related theoretically to positive social identity. Although it is always difficult to separate cognitive and motivational processes, this pattern of findings suggests that the measure of differential inclusion may tap a relatively cognitive process that is independent of identity-relevant goals, whereas the measure of differential evaluation may tap relatively more identity-serving processes.

Based on the SGD model, we predicted that those who identify more strongly should be more motivated to express evaluative biases to the extent that they perceive targets to be deviant in an intergroup context. This identity moderation hypothesis was upheld. The relationship between differential inclusion and differential evaluation was stronger among children who identified more with their group (see also Abrams et al., 2000; Abrams et al., 2002). Finally, consistent with our developmental identity moderation hypothesis, this interaction effect was strongest among the oldest children. Among older children, only when identity concerns are strong are perceptions of differential inclusion related to differential evaluations. Lower identifiers engage in less evaluative differentiation between normative and deviant members, and they do not relate their evaluations to perceptions of group inclusion. Thus, the present findings show that, for the groups used in this research, older children's evaluations of group members are related to perceptions of differential inclusion more systematically as their own level of identification with the group increases.

Limitations

There exist some limitations in the present research. For example, we deliberately used only male targets. We employed an intergroup context that was highly competitive and salient—an international sports competition. This could be viewed as a male-relevant intergroup situation with strong norms. It turned out that there were no sex differences in evaluations of these targets, but it remains conceivable that girls and boys might react differently to female targets in the same situation.

It is also noteworthy that cognitive-developmental theory was not specifically developed to understand children's group attitudes in such explicitly competitive intergroup contexts. Some intergroup relationships may be sufficiently competitive that even the most despicable in-group member would be preferred over any out-group member. Given the competitive intergroup context of the present study we might have expected some inhibition of positive evaluations of deviant out-group members or negative evaluations of deviant in-group members, or both. However, despite the strong intergroup differentiation that results from competition, out-group deviants were favored significantly over in-group deviants. This effect is more substantial than that in our previous study that involved a relatively noncompetitive context (Abrams et al., 2003), in which older children showed a significant preference for an in-group normative over an in-group deviant, and an out-group deviant over an out-group normative, but only a nonsignificant preference for an out-group deviant over an in-group deviant. This difference between the Abrams et al. (2003) and the present research is consistent with evidence in the adult literature that intergroup competition results in larger SGD effects (e.g., Marques, Abrams, & Serôdio, 2001).

We are also aware that there may be particular types of group membership (e.g., religious denomination) or cultural factors that could encourage or inhibit differential evaluations of members within groups. The present study was conducted in the relatively individualistic context of England. It may be that children in more collectivist cultures are encouraged to treat in-group and out-group deviants differently (see Abrams, Ando, & Hinkle, 1998; Smith & Bond, 1994; Triandis, 1995). A further issue is what form we would expect SGD to take with pervasive group memberships such as gender or ethnicity. Most previous research has concentrated on in-group biases in judgments of typical members of these groups rather than on comparative judgments of normative and deviant members. We would expect that when these naturally occurring groups are in direct comparison, older children are likely to be more attentive to intragroup differences that are relevant to the distinct norms of each group. This is a potentially useful avenue for future research.

A further limitation is that the measures used in this study were necessarily simpler than those used in research with adults. However, we are reassured that the question-and-response formats were easily understood by the youngest children and were sufficiently sensitive to detect differences in judgments even among those children (e.g., general intergroup biases). In addition, no attempt was made to measure motivational processes or perceptions of subjective validity of the group norms. Future research is needed to examine these variables and more subtle implications of the SGD model, such as reactions to different types of deviant (Abrams et al., 2000) and different types of norm violation (Marques, Abrams & Serôdio, 2001). These issues may require different or more complex measurement techniques to be devised.

Conclusions

The present findings support the idea that SGD emerge in children later than basic in-group preferences. Children of all ages showed evidence of significant in-group bias, whereas only the older children showed bias in both intergroup and intragroup judgments. There is a developmental strengthening of the relationship between in-group bias and intragroup differential evaluation, both of which may enhance in-group social identity. Taken together, these results are consistent with our developmental model of SGD. As children begin to attend to multiple categories and individuating information they also show evidence of combining the processes of intragroup and intergroup comparison.

We found children's evaluations of individual targets were not just influenced by what was said but also by the group membership of the target person. That is, when children pay closer attention to detailed information about individual others, they also integrate such information with their knowledge of a person's group membership and their own social identity. In addition, we found when children understand the implications of deviant behavior within the group and they demonstrate strong identification, SGD emerge most clearly.

There are interesting implications of this research for the way children understand, and respond to, a range of potentially deviant behaviors. In a school a child may be viewed as deviant as a result of bullying, physical differences, overworking, selection of out-group friends, and expression of attitudes that implies movement toward or away from the perceiver's group. Children's understanding of, and reactions to, deviance in an intergroup context appears to change substantially between the ages of 5 and 11. This suggests that strategies for adult intervention (e.g., to prevent victimization) may need to be different for children of different ages.

Our findings show that, by the age of 11, some of the psychological processes that underpin social regulation of the behavior of members of adult groups may be well established. Future research is needed to investigate whether these developmental changes occur in other intergroup contexts (e.g. ethnic, gender, and minimal groups) and to see how intergroup biases may combine with other aspects of social and moral development to affect children's judgments of individuals within groups.

References

Aboud, F. E. (1988). *Children and prejudice*. Oxford, England: Blackwell.

Aboud, F. E., & Amato, M. (2001). Developmental and socialization influences on intergroup bias. In R. Brown & S. L. Gaertner (Eds.), *Blackwell handbook of social psychology: Intergroup processes* (pp. 65–85). Oxford, England: Blackwell.

Abrams, D., Ando, K., & Hinkle, S. (1998). Psychological attachment to the group: Cross-cultural differences in organizational identification and subjective norms as predictors or workers' turnover intentions. *Personality and Social Psychology Bulletin, 24*, 1027–1039.

Abrams, D., Marques, J. M., Bown, N., & Dougill, M. (2002). Anti-norm and pro-norm deviance in the bank and on the campus: Two experiments on subjective group dynamics. *Group Processes and Intergroup Relations, 5*, 163–182.

Abrams, D., Marques, J. M., Bown, N. J., & Henson, M. (2000). Pro-norm and anti-norm deviance within in-groups and out-groups. *Journal of Personality and Social Psychology, 78*, 906–912.

Abrams, D., Marques, J. M., Randsley de Moura, G., Hutchison, P., & Bown, N. J. (2004). The maintenance of entitativity: A subjective group dynamics approach. In V. Y. Yzerbyt, C. M. Judd, & O. Corneille (Eds.), *The psychology of group perception: Contribution to the study of homogeneity, entitativity, and essentialism* (pp. 361–380) Philadelphia: Psychology Press.

Abrams, D., Rutland, A., Cameron, L., & Marques, J. M. (2003). The development of subjective group dynamics: When in-group bias gets specific. *British Journal of Developmental Psychology, 21*, 155–176.

Aiken, L. S., & West, S. G. (1991). *Multiple regression: Testing and interpreting interactions*. Thousand Oaks, CA: Sage.

Alvarez, J. M, Ruble, D. N., & Bolger, N. (2001). Trait understanding or evaluative reasoning? An analysis of children's behavioral predictions. *Child Development, 72*, 1409–1425.

Barenboim, C. (1978). The development of recursive and non-recursive thinking about persons. *Developmental Psychology, 52*, 129–144.

Barenboim, C. (1981). The development of person perception in childhood adolescence: From behavioral comparisons to psychological constructs to psychological comparisons. *Child Development, 52*, 129–144.

Baron, R. M., & Kenny, D. A. (1986). The moderator-mediator variable distinction in social psychological research: Conceptual, strategic, and statistical considerations. *Journal of Personality and Social Psychology, 51*, 1173–1182.

Barrett, M., & Short, J. (1992). Images of European people in a group of 5–10 year old English schoolchildren. *British Journal of Developmental Psychology, 10*, 339–363.

Berndt, T. J., & Heller, K. A. (1986). Gender stereotypes and social inferences: A developmental study. *Journal of Personality and Social Psychology, 50*, 889–898.

Biernat, M. (1991). Gender stereotypes and the relationship between masculinity and femininity: A developmental analysis. *Journal of Personality and Social Psychology, 61*, 351–365.

Bigler, R. S. (1995). The role of classification skill in moderating environmental influences on children's gender stereotyping: A study of the functional use of gender in the classroom. *Child Development, 66*, 1072–1087.

Bigler, R. S., & Liben, L. S. (1992). Cognitive mechanisms in children's gender stereotyping: Theoretical and educational implications of a cognitive-based intervention. *Child Development, 63*, 1351–1363.

Black-Gutman, D., & Hickson, F. (1996). The relationship between racial attitudes and social-cognitive development in children: An Australian study. *Developmental Psychology, 32*, 448–456.

Coull, A., Yzerbyt, V. Y., Castano, E., Paladino, M. P., & Leemans, V. (2001). Protecting the ingroup: Motivated allocation of cognitive resources in the presence of threatening ingroup members. *Group Processes and Intergroup Relations, 4*, 327–339.

Doyle, A., & Aboud, F. (1995). A longitudinal study of white children's racial prejudice as a social-cognitive development. *Merrill-Palmer Quarterly, 41*, 2, 209–228.

Durkin, K., & Judge, J. (2001). Effects of language and social behavior on children's reactions to foreign people in television. *British Journal of Developmental Psychology, 19*, 597–612.

Goodman, L. A. (1960). On the exact variance of products. *Journal of the American Statistical Association, 55*, 708–71.

Hutchison, P., & Abrams, D. (2003). Ingroup identification moderates stereotype change in reaction to ingroup deviance. *European Journal of Social Psychology, 33*, 497–506.

Judd, C. M., Kenny, D. A., & McClelland, G. H. (2001). Estimating and testing mediation and moderation in within subjects designs. *Psychological Methods, 6*, 115–134.

Katz, P. A. (1976). The acquisition of racial attitudes in children. In P. A. Katz (Ed.), *Towards the elimination of racism* (pp. 125–154). New York: Pergamon.

Katz, P. A., Sohn, M., & Zalk, S. R. (1975). Perceptual concomitants of racial attitudes in urban grade-school children. *Developmental Psychology, 11*, 135–144.

Killen, M., Crystal, D. S., & Watanabe, H. (2002). Japanese and American children's evaluations of peer exclusion, tolerance of differences, and prescriptions for conformity. *Child Development, 73*, 1788–1802.

Killen, M., & Stangor, C. (2001). Children's social reasoning about inclusion and exclusion in gender and race peer groups contexts. *Child Development, 72*, 174–186.

Kurzban, R., & Leary, M. R. (2001). Evolutionary origins or stigmatization: The functions of social exclusion. *Psychological Bulletin, 127*, 187–208.

Lambert, W. E., & Klineberg, O. (1967). *Children's views of foreign peoples: A cross-national study.* New York: Appleton-Century-Crofts.

Levine, J. M. (1989). Reaction to opinion deviance in small groups. In P. B. Paulus (Ed.), *Psychology of group influence* (2nd ed., pp. 187–231). Hillsdale, NJ: Erlbaum.

Livesley, W. J., & Bromley, D. B. (1973). *Person perception in childhood & adolescence.* Oxford, England: Wiley.

MacKinnon, D. P., Warsi, G., & Dwyer, J. H. (1995). A simulation study of mediated effect measures. *Multi-variate Behavioral Research, 30*, 41–62.

Marques, J. M., Abrams, D., Pàez, D., & Hogg, M. A. (2001). Social categorization, social identification, and rejection of deviant group members. In M. A. Hogg & R. S. Tindale (Eds.), *Blackwell handbook of social psychology (Vol. 3): Group processes* (pp. 400–424). Oxford, England: Blackwell.

Marques, J. M., Abrams, D., Pàez, D., & Martinez-Taboada, C. (1998). The role of categorization and in-group norms in judgments of groups and their members. *Journal of Personality and Social Psychology, 75*, 976–988.

Marques, J. M., Abrams, D., & Serôdio, R. G. (2001). Being better by being right: Subjective group dynamics and derogation of in-group deviants when generic norms are undermined. *Journal of Personality and Social Psychology, 81*, 436–447.

Marques, J. M., & Pàez, D. (1994). The "black sheep effect": Social categorization, rejection of in-group deviates, and perception of group variability. In W. Stroebe & M. Hewstone (Eds.), *European review of social psychology* (*Vol. 5*, pp. 38–68). Chichester, England: Wiley.

Marques, J. M., Yzerbyt, V. Y., & Leyens, J. -P. (1988). The black sheep effect: Judgmental extremity towards ingroup members as a function of ingroup identification. *European Journal of Social Psychology, 18*, 1–16.

Martin, C. L. (1989). Children's use of gender-related information in making social judgments. *Developmental Psychology, 25*, 80–88.

Nesdale, D. (2001). Development of prejudice in children. In M. Augoustinos & K. J. Reynolds (Eds.), *Understanding prejudice, racism and social conflict.* London: Sage.

Peevers, B. H., & Secord, P. F. (1973). Developmental changes in attribution of descriptive concepts to persons. *Journal of Personality and Social Psychology, 27*, 120–128.

Piaget, J., & Weil, A. (1951). The development in children of the idea of the homeland and of relations with other countries. *International Social Science Bulletin, 3*, 561–578.

Powlishta, K. K. (1995). Intergroup processes in childhood: Social categorization and sex role development. *Developmental Psychology, 31*, 781–788.

Powlishta, K., Serbin, L. A., Doyle, A., & White, D. R. (1994). Gender, ethnic, and body type biases: The generality of prejudice in childhood. *Developmental Psychology, 30*, 526–536.

Quintana, S. M. (1994). A model of ethnic perspective-taking ability applied to Mexican-American children and youth. *International Journal of Intercultural Relations, 18*, 419–448.

Quintana, S. M. (1998). Children's developmental understanding of ethnicity and race. *Applied and Preventative Psychology, 7*, 27–45.

Quintana, S. M. (1999). Role of perspective-taking abilities and ethnic socialization in development of adolescent ethnic identity. *Journal of Research on Adolescence, 19*, 161–184.

Ruble, D. N., Alvarez, J. M., Bachman, M., Cameron, J. A., Fuligni, A. J., Garcia-Coll, C., & Rhee, E. (2004). The development of a sense of "we": The emergence and implications of children's collective identity. In M. Bennett & F. Sani (Eds.), *The development of the social self*. East Sussex, England: Psychology Press.

Ruble, D. N., & Dweck, C. S. (1995). Self-conceptions, person conceptions, and their development. In N. Eisenberg (Ed.), *Review of personality and social psychology: Social development* (Vol. 15, pp. 109–139). Thousand Oaks, CA: Sage.

Rutland, A. (1999). The development of national prejudice, in-group favoritism and self stereotypes in British children. *British Journal of Social Psychology, 38*, 55–70.

Schachter, S. (1951). Deviation, rejection and communication. *Journal of Abnormal and Social Psychology, 46*, 190–207.

Selman, R. L. (1971). Taking another's perspective: Role-taking development in early childhood. *Child Development, 42*, 1721–1734.

Selman, R. L. (1980). *The growth of interpersonal understanding: Development and clinical analyses*. San Diego, CA: Academic Press.

Serbin, L. A., & Sprafkin, C. (1986). The salience of gender and the process of sex typing in three- to seven-year-old children. *Child Development, 57*, 1188–1199.

Smith, P. B., & Bond, M. H. (1994). *Social psychology across cultures: Analysis and perspectives*. Boston: Allyn & Bacon.

Tajfel, H. (1981). *Human groups and social categories: Studies in social psychology*. Cambridge, England: Cambridge University Press.

Tajfel, H., & Turner, J. C. (1986). The social identity theory of intergroup behavior. In S. Worchel & W. G. Austin (Eds.), *The psychology of intergroup relations* (pp. 7–24). Chicago: Nelson-Hall.

Triandis, H. C. (1995). A theoretical framework for the study of diversity. In H. M. Chemers & S. Oskamp (Eds.), *Diversity in organizations: New perspectives for a changing workplace. Claremont Symposium on Applied Social Psychology 8*, 11–36.

Yee, M. D., & Brown, R. (1994). The development of gender differentiation in young children. *British Journal of Social Psychology, 33*, 183–196.

Zdaniuk, B., & Levine, J. M. (2001). Group loyalty: Impact of members' identification and contributions. *Journal of Experimental Social Psychology, 37*, 502–509.

A Closer Look 6   Who Am I and What Group Do I Belong to? Self Identity in the Context of Social Interactions

Commonly, the self is equated with one's sense of personal identity, defined by idiosyncratic characteristics (e.g., kind, outgoing, daughter of X, etc.). However, a central insight of Social Identity Theory is that groups, too (such as national, gender, religious, and political groups), can become part of the self-concept. Within this approach, the self is taken to comprise both personal and social identity, and neither is seen as more fundamental or authentic than the other. Developmental psychologists have shown that children's social identities are often about gender, ethnicity, and nationality. The assessments of social identity have not been adequately aligned with the important theoretical assumption that the group can become part of the self. Usually assessment is "Who are you?" which is too global and too general to be of much meaning for children. Three studies are reported that assess 5-, 7- and 10-year-old children's cognitive group identity (Sani & Bennett, 2009). Each study investigated a different ingroup: gender, family, and age group. Children were shown sets of cards identifying particular trait adjectives and were asked to rate the extent to which the traits applied to the self, the ingroup, and the outgroup. After a distraction task, they were asked to remember for whom (self, ingroup, or outgroup) each trait had been rated. In all studies and for all age groups, traits rated for the self were confused more frequently with traits rated for the ingroup than with traits rated for the outgroup. It is concluded that, at least from the age of 5 years, psychologically relevant ingroups have become integral parts of the self-system.

Sani, F., & Bennett, M. (2009). Children's inclusion of the group in the self: Evidence from a self-ingroup confusion paradigm. *Developmental Psychology, 45*, 503–510.

Classroom Exercises, Debates, and Discussion Questions

- *Classroom discussion: Multiplicity of selves.* Research points to a multiplicity of selves: the psychological, social, and familial. What are valid and reliable measures of the self? For a class debate, students can debate the importance of a group identity for the self. Does a sense of self depend on the groups that one identifies with or is self-identity an independent definition of the self? Which of the following groups are essential aspects for the self: gender, ethnicity, nationality, age, culture, religion? What groups are missing from this list? Which represents the most frequent categories focused on in research studies?

- *Classroom discussion: Ethnic identity.* Ethnic identity is about belonging to and identifying with an ethnic group. This type of identity often involves being part of a minority or a majority in a culture, with different status. Researchers have pointed to different types of experiences with ethnic identity in cultures which often involve either *assimilation* (identification with the majority group, rejecting the minority identity) or maintaining *dual-identity* (identification with both cultures). Discuss the advantages and disadvantages of these forms of cultural identity.

- *Classroom discussion: Cultural assimilation and multiculturalism.* Researchers have written about the "cafeteria phenomenon" in which adolescents sit in the cafeteria at lunchtime in segregated social groups, often defined by ethnicity, gender, and race. What factors contribute to this phenomenon? Do parents, schools, and the larger society send messages about cross-group friendships (and dating)? What types of implicit and explicit messages are communicated to adolescents?

Additional Resources

For more about self-identity and group identity, see:

Bennett, M., & Sani, F. (Eds.). (2004). *The development of the social self.* Hove, England: Psychology Press.

Cameron, L., Rutland, A., Brown, R., & Douch, R. (2006). Changing children's intergroup attitudes toward refugees: Testing different models of extended contact. *Child Development, 77,* 1208–1219.

Erikson, E. (1960). *Childhood and society.* New York: Norton.

Harter, S. (2006). The self. In W. Damon, R. Lerner, & N. Eisenberg (Eds.), *Handbook of child psychology: Vol. 3. Social, emotional and personality development* (6th ed., pp. 505–570). Hoboken, NJ: John Wiley & Sons.

Phinney, J. S. (2003). Ethnic identity and acculturation. In K. M. Chun, P. B. Organista, & G. Marin (Eds.), *Acculturation: Advances in theory, measurement, and applied research* (pp. 63–81). Washington, DC: American Psychological Association.

Ruble, D., Alvarez, J., Bachman, M., Cameron, J., Fuligni, A., Garcia Coll, C., & Rhee, E. (2004). The development of a sense of "we": The emergence and implications of children's collective identity. In M. Bennett & F. Sani (Eds.), *The development of the social self* (pp. 29–76). Hove, England: Psychology Press.

Part IV

PEER REJECTION
AND EXCLUSION

8 SHYNESS AND SOCIAL WITHDRAWAL

Introduction 316

**Don't Fret, Be Supportive! Maternal
Characteristics Linking Child Shyness
to Psychosocial and School
Adjustment in Kindergarten 317**

*Robert J. Coplan, Kimberley A. Arbeau,
and Mandana Armer*

  Shyness in Early Childhood 317

  The Role of Maternal Characteristics in the

  Development of Child Shyness 318

  The Current Study 319

  Methods 320

  Results 322

  Discussion 326

**Trajectories of Social Withdrawal
from Middle Childhood to Early
Adolescence 332**

*Wonjung Oh, Kenneth H. Rubin, Julie C. Bowker,
Cathryn Booth-LaForce, Linda Rose-Krasnor,
and Brett Laursen*

Social Withdrawal, and Individual

Characteristics, Friendship, and Peer

Exclusion/Victimization 333

Overview of the Present Study 334

Method 335

Results 338

Discussion 343

**Social Functioning and Adjustment
in Chinese Children: The Imprint
of Historical Time 348**

Xinyin Chen, Guozhen Cen, Dan Li, and Yunfeng He

Method 352

Results 355

Discussion 358

**A Closer Look 7 But I Like to Be
Alone! Unsociability and the Benefits
of Solitude 363**

Social Development in Childhood and Adolescence: A Contemporary Reader, First Edition. Edited by Melanie Killen
and Robert J. Coplan.

Introduction

Feeling somewhat wary or nervous when meeting new people is a common experience for many children. About 15% of children are considered extremely shy, routinely experiencing fear and anxiety in social contexts to a degree that hinders their abilities to interact with other children. In early childhood, shyness is manifested primarily when children are in novel situations. With age, shyness also comes to include feelings of self-consciousness and embarrassment that children experience when they are being evaluated by their peers or they find themselves the "center of attention."

Extremely shy children are often observed hovering on the edges of social interactions, watching but not joining in. This behavior is thought to reflect a motivational "approach-avoidance" conflict in shy children. That is, although shy children might *want* to play with others (high social-approach motivation), this desire for social interaction is simultaneously inhibited by social fears and anxiety (high social-avoidance motivation). There is evidence to suggest that this type of feeling of avoidance from social interaction has strong biological underpinnings. As compared to their non-shy counterparts, shy children display heightened psychophysiological reactivity (e.g., faster heart-rates, a distinct pattern of right-frontal asymmetrical electroencephalogram (EEG) responses, higher levels of the hormone cortisol) when confronted with the "stress" of a social situation. This lower threshold for arousal in response to such "threats" has important implications for how shy children come to perceive and respond to their social worlds.

Because shy children tend to withdraw from opportunities for social interaction, they may miss out on the important and unique opportunities for learning afforded by the peer group context (see Chapter 5). Even when they do engage with others, shy children tend to have difficulties in their peer relationships, and are prone to peer rejection and victimization. Over time, extremely shy children are also at increased risk for internalizing problems, including anxiety, loneliness, depressive symptoms, and low self-esteem. It is certainly not the case, however, that all shy children experience problems or become anxious over time. In fact, as described in the readings in this chapter, there are a number of protective factors that help shy children feel more comfortable in social interactions, less anxious, and more confident overall.

The readings in this chapter describe the developmental models that link shyness and socio-emotional functioning in childhood and adolescence. The first article considers the role of the family environment. Coplan et al. (2008) explored how different parenting characteristics and socialization practices might serve as "protective" or "exacerbating" factors in the school adjustment of young shy children. The second study pertains to what happens to shy children in peer group encounters. Oh and colleagues (2008) examined the impact of friendships and victimization on the stability and change in shyness from late childhood to early adolescence. The article by Chen et al. (2005) reflects the growing cross-cultural interest in shyness research and the view that the expression and interpretation of shyness may have different implications for children's development in different parts of the world. These authors explored the changing views of shyness in the People's Republic of China.

Don't Fret, Be Supportive! Maternal Characteristics Linking Child Shyness to Psychosocial and School Adjustment in Kindergarten

Robert J. Coplan, Kimberley A. Arbeau, and Mandana Armer

Shyness refers to wariness and anxiety in the face of social novelty and perceived social-evaluation and is characterized by an approach–avoidance conflict in such situations (Coplan et al. 2004). Thus, although shy children may desire social interaction, this social approach motivation is simultaneously inhibited by social fear and anxiety. There is growing evidence to suggest an underlying biological component related to shyness. For example, as compared to their nonshy peers, extremely shy children are thought to have a lower threshold for arousal in the central nucleus of the amygdala, and demonstrate increased heart rate acceleration to mild stress, higher early morning levels of salivary cortisol, and patterns of EEG responses characterized by greater right frontal activation (e.g., Henderson et al. 2004; Kagan 1997; Schmidt and Tasker 2000).

Shy children appear to be at increased risk for a host of social, emotional, and adjustment difficulties, particularly along the internalizing dimension (Rubin et al. 2002a). For example, from middle childhood through to adolescence, shyness becomes increasingly related to internalizing problems such as loneliness, depression, and social anxiety, as well as deficits in social competence, lower self-esteem, and peer rejection (e.g., Fordham and Stevenson-Hinde 1999; Prior et al. 2000). Moreover, shyness in early childhood appears to be a risk factor for the later development of anxiety disorders (e.g., Schwartz et al. 1999; Van Ameringen et al. 1998). Remarkably, Rapee and colleagues (Rapee et al. 2005) recently reported that 90% of an "extremely shy" (i.e., top 15% of the sample on scores of behavioral inhibition) group of preschool-aged children also met criteria for an existing anxiety disorder.

Researchers have postulated a number of risk and protective factors that may influence the life pathways of shy children (Rubin and Coplan 2004). In the cur-rent study, we focus specifically on maternal factors. Within the conceptual framework of "goodness-of-fit" theory (Thomas and Chess 1977), the goal of the present study was to explore the *moderating* role of maternal personality characteristics and parenting in the links between shyness and adjustment in kindergarten.

Shyness in Early Childhood

Young shy children appear to be at risk for adjustment difficulties when starting school (Coplan et al. 2001). It has been suggested that the increased demands of the early school environment may be particularly stressful for shy children and serve to exacerbate their feelings of social fear and self-consciousness (Evans 2001). For example, shy children speak less frequently than their peers at school and this quietness may be perceived by teachers as a lack of interest or understanding of the topic (Crozier and Perkins 2002). Moreover, even when given the opportunity to demonstrate their academic competence, shy children may evidence performance deficits because of stresses associated with test performance (Crozier and Hostettler 2003). Thus, it is not surprising that shyness in childhood has been associated with a lack of displayed academic competence (Coplan et al. 2001; Nelson et al. 2005).

Shyness in early education settings appears to be manifested behaviorally through the display of *reticent* behavior. Reticent behavior is considered a behavioral expression of a social approach–avoidance conflict, and includes the prolonged watching of other children without accompanying play (onlooking) and being unoccupied (Coplan et al. 1994). There is strong empirical support linking shyness with the display of reticent behavior in the classroom, both on the first day of school (Coplan 2000), as well as several months into the school year (Coplan et al. 2004). Perhaps as a result, shy children are also not considered attractive playmates by peers (Coplan et al. 2007). Even in early childhood, shyness and reticent behavior have been associated with peer rejection, exclusion, and victimization in preschool and kindergarten (Coplan et al. 2004; Gazelle and Ladd 2003; Hart et al. 2000; Perren and Alsaker 2006).

In and of themselves, poor quality relationships with peers are a significant risk factor for a host of negative outcomes in childhood (see Rubin et al. 2006, for a recent review). It seems likely that these difficulties with peers serve to exacerbate shy children's already existing tendency towards negative moods, worries, and fears (Stevenson-Hinde and Glover 1996). Results from several studies have subsequently linked shyness and reticent behavior with the overt display of anxious behaviors during play, parent/teacher ratings of anxiety and internalizing problems, as well as self-reported lower self-esteem (e.g., Coplan and Armer 2005; Coplan et al. 2004; Henderson et al. 2004; Spinrad et al. 2004).

Finally, the adjustment difficulties experienced by shy children do not go unnoticed by teachers. Shy young children require more attention from teachers (Coplan and Prakash 2003) and their behaviors are considered to be problematic and worthy of teacher intervention (Arbeau and Coplan 2007). These factors likely account for the finding that shy–withdrawn young children tend to form less close relationships with teachers (Rydell et al. 2005). This also does not bode well for shy children, as student–teacher relationships have important and unique implications for children's academic development, social development, and developmental psychopathology (Pianta 2006).

The Role of Maternal Characteristics in the Development of Child Shyness

Notwithstanding the growing empirical literature linking shyness in early childhood with adjustment difficulties, not all young children who are shy develop problems later on (e.g., Arcus 2001). In the present

study we explored the *moderating* effect of mothers on the outcomes of shy children, which can be construed as a child temperament × family environment interaction (Rothbart and Bates 2006).

The role of parental socialization practices in the development of shyness has received increased research attention in recent years (Burgess et al. 2005), including a few studies related to interaction effects between child shyness and family environment variables (e.g., Crockenberg and Leerkes 2006; Early et al. 2002; Leve et al. 2005). We propose that a child shyness × maternal characteristics interaction can best be elucidated within the rubric of *goodness-of-fit* theory. The principle of goodness-of-fit (Thomas and Chess 1977) holds that socialization effects depend upon child temperamental characteristics (e.g., Rothbart and Ahadi 1994). In the current study, we speculated that there are certain maternal parenting styles and personality traits that would represent a particularly "good fit" or "bad fit" for temperamentally shy children. In this regard, we identified constellations of maternal characteristics that we predicted would act as either negative moderators (i.e., *exacerbating* process) or positive moderators (i.e., *buffering* process) of the "risk factor" of shyness for socio-emotional and school adjustment difficulties.

Parenting styles Most of the recent research related to parenting styles and child shyness has focused on overprotective parenting (Rubin and Burgess 2002). Parents who are *overprotective* tend to overmanage situations for their child, restrict child behaviors, discourage child independence, and direct child activities. Overprotective parenting is believed to undermine the development of necessary coping strategies in shy children and thus maintain or exacerbate social wariness (Rubin and Burgess 2002). Results from several recent studies have documented a relation between overprotective parenting and social wariness in early childhood (e.g., Lieb et al. 2000; Rubin et al. 2001). Moreover, Rubin et al. (2002b) reported that shyness at age 2-years was predictive of anxiety during free play with peers at age 4-years only for children with more overprotective (and intrusive) parents.

In contrast, parents who engage in *authoritative* parenting exercise control in combination with warmth, nurturance, democracy, and open parent–child communication (Baumrind 1971). An authoritative parenting style is generally considered advantageous to many aspects of child development (e.g., Lamborn et al. 1991), and may be particularly beneficial in the socialization of emotion regulation (Sheffield Morris et al. 2007). Moreover, Coplan et al. (2004) reported a negative association between shyness and maternal authoritative parenting among preschool children. Thus, it was speculated that for shy children, authoritative parenting would be particularly helpful whereas overprotective parenting would be particularly problematic.

Maternal personality We also postulated that certain maternal personality characteristics would serve to create a particularly adaptive or maladaptive family environment for shy children (Rapee 1997; Wood et al. 2003). For example, a person high in *neuroticism* is characterized as emotionally unstable, nervous, self-conscious, insecure, and prone to psychological distress such as anxiety and excessive worry (e.g., Jorm et al. 2000; Weinstock and Whisman 2006). Neurotic individuals also tend to employ maladaptive parenting behaviors (e.g., Metsäpelto and Pulkkinen 2003), including being overprotective (Kendler et al. 1997). Thus, it can be speculated that neurotic mothers of shy children might be more likely to model and reinforce anxious behaviors.

Agreeableness concerns the ability to control emotions and avoid emotional outbursts. Agreeable individuals tend to be trusting, altruistic, modest, and have more warm, sensitive and responsive interactions (i.e., more authoritative) with their children (Metsäpelto and Pulkkinen 2003). It can be speculated that the warm and responsive interactive nature of agreeable parents, accompanied by the modeling and socialization of positive emotion regulation skills, would create a particularly positive environment for shy children.

Shy children might also benefit from having mothers high in *extraversion*. Extraverts tend to be more talkative, outgoing, adventurous, and assertive than their peers. Moreover, extraverted parents are more likely to encourage independence in their children (Losoya et al. 1997). Thus, an extraverted mother may be particularly helpful to shy children by providing a strong model of outgoing social behaviors.

Finally, we further speculated that maternal approach and avoidance tendencies would influence outcomes associated with young children's shyness. Such feelings are believed to be regulated by the *behavioral inhibition system* and *behavioral activation system* (BIS/BAS; Gray 1987). Individuals with higher BIS sensitivity tend to become emotionally distressed in highly threatening situations, and higher BIS has been related to neuroticism, anxiety, depression and negative affect. In contrast, higher BAS sensitivity contributes towards impulsiveness, approach behaviors and goal-directed activity, and is related to extraversion and positive affect (e.g., Carver 2004; Jorm et al. 2000; Meyer et al. 2005).

It has been speculated that parental BIS sensitivity may influence the degree to which children focus on threats and perceived dangers in their own environment (Carver 2004). This may promote child withdrawal and avoidance of negative outcomes, particularly during emotionally challenging situations. In contrast, as with extraversion, mothers high in BAS may model risk-taking and approach behaviors that may be particularly important for shy children to acquire.

The Current Study

The goal of the present study was to explore the moderating role of clusters of maternal personality and parenting characteristics in the associations between shyness and indices of adjustment in kindergarten. In order to accomplish this goal, we followed a sample of children over the course of a kindergarten school year. Mothers provided assessments of their personality characteristics and parenting styles. For this reason, we felt it was particularly important to have multisource assessments of shy–reticence (i.e., maternal ratings, behavioral observations, teacher ratings) and outcome indices of psychosocial and school adjustment (i.e., maternal ratings, child self-reports, teacher ratings).

To begin with, we hypothesized that shy–reticence would be associated with multiple indices of maladjustment in kindergarten. Drawing upon previous research in this area, we expected shy–reticence to be associated with greater internalizing problems (e.g., anxiety, emotion symptoms), social dissatisfaction (e.g., loneliness, lower perceived peer acceptance), and difficulties with peers (e.g., peer exclusion), and poorer school adjustment (e.g., academic deficits, low perceived academic competence, lower school liking, less positive relationships with teachers).

We further speculated that the combination of maternal neuroticism, BIS sensitivity, and overprotective parenting would represent a particularly maladaptive family environment for shy children. We labeled this cluster of maternal characteristics as *fretful* parenting. We also proposed that certain maternal characteristics would serve to "buffer" shy children from negative adjustment outcomes. In this regard, we explored the combination of maternal agreeableness and authoritative parenting style, labeled *warm/supportive* parenting, as well as the aggregate of maternal extraversion and BAS sensitivity, labeled *uninhibited* parenting. It was hypothesized that relations between shy–reticence and indices of maladjustment would be stronger among children with mothers who reported higher levels of fretful parenting (i.e., exacerbating process), and weaker among children with mothers who reported higher levels of warm/supportive and uninhibited parenting (i.e., buffering process).

Methods

Participants

The participants in this study were 197 children (103 boys, 94 girls, $M_{age} = 64.13$ months, $SD = 4.85$ months). Children were enrolled in kindergarten programs in 15 public schools located in a mid-sized city in southeastern Ontario, Canada. Parental consent was sought through sending home information letters with children from school. Parents and children were not compensated for their participation. The overall consent rate was estimated at about 65%.

The sample was 70% Caucasian, with a variety of other ethnicities also represented (e.g., 17% Asian, 5% Black). The public school board from which the sample was drawn did not permit the collection of information regarding parental employment status and income. However, approximately 17% of mothers and 19% of fathers had completed high school, 69% of

mothers and 61% of fathers had a college/university degree, and 11% of mothers and 16% of fathers had a graduate level degree. Thus, participants appeared to be of varied socioeconomic status.

Procedure

This was a short-term longitudinal study, with data collected at three time periods over the course of a single kindergarten school year. Multisource assessment was employed, including maternal ratings, behavioral observations, teacher ratings, and individual child interviews. At Time 1 (October/November), mothers rated their personality and parenting styles and their child's shyness. At Time 2 (January), observations of children's reticent behavior at school were collected and teachers rated children's shy–reticent behaviors at school. At Time 3 (May/June), children's socio-emotional and school adjustment were assessed using parent-ratings, teacher-ratings, and child interviews.

Measures

TIME 1

At the start of the school year, mothers completed the *Child Social Preference Scale* (CSPS; Coplan et al. 2004) to assess child *shyness* (7 items, $\alpha = 0.88$, e.g., "My child seems to want to play with others, but is sometimes nervous to"). Coplan and colleagues (2004) reported good psychometric properties and validity for the CSPS.

Mothers also rated their own personality using the *BIS/BAS Scales* (Carver and White 1994). The BAS subscale items (13 items, $\alpha = 0.77$) assess orientation towards drive, reward, and fun, and the BIS subscale items (7 items, $\alpha = 0.74$) assess orientation towards punishment. An additional measure of maternal personality was provided by the *Ten Item Personality Inventory* (TIPI; Gosling et al. 2003), a brief but psychometrically sound assessment of the Big Five personality characteristics. Of interest for the present study were the subscales of *neuroticism* (two items, $r = 0.48$), *agreeableness* (two items, $r = 0.40$), and *extraversion* (two items, $r = 0.49$).

Finally, mothers rated their parenting styles with the *Parenting Styles and Dimensions Questionnaire*

(Robinson et al. 2001). Of particular interest for the present study was the subscale of *authoritative* parenting with items pertaining to warmth, reasoning, and democratic participation (15 items, $\alpha = 0.81$). *Overprotective* parenting was assessed by having parents respond to five items originally developed by Nelson and colleagues (Nelson et al. 2006; see also Coplan et al. 2004). These five items (e.g., "I get anxious when my child tries to do something new or difficult"; "I readily intervene if there is a chance my child will fail at something") loaded onto a single factor (with loadings ranging from 0.70 to 0.74) and were subsequently tallied to yield a summary score of maternal *overprotective parenting* ($\alpha = 0.73$).

Time 2

A few months into the school year, children's behaviors during indoor free play were observed and coded over a 3- to 4-week period using an adapted version of the *Play Observation Scale* (POS; Rubin 2001). Observational data were collected by six trained research assistants. Each child was observed (in random order) for a series of 10-s intervals on at least three separate days until a total of 15 min (90 coding intervals) were collected per child. For each coding interval, the child's predominant free-play behavior was recorded (for a more detailed description, see Coplan 2000). Of particular interest for the present study was the behavioral code of *reticent* behavior, which consisted of onlooking (e.g., watching other children without accompanying play) and remaining unoccupied (e.g., wandering aimlessly, staring off into space). Before the start of data collection, inter-rater reliability was computed for pairs of researchers based on 540 codes of data (90 min) coded live at a separate facility from children not involved in the study. For observed reticent behavior, Cohen's kappa between pairs of observers were all above 0.85. Observers met regularly during data collection to discuss any issues arising and to reduce rater drift.

During this same time period, teachers rated children's shy–reticent behavior in class using the *Social Competence Inventory* (Rydell et al. 1997). This rating scale was originally designed to assess the broader constructs of prosocial orientation and social initiative. However, five items from the social initiative subscale were selected on a conceptual basis because of

their more specific assessment of shy (e.g., "hesitant with peers") and reticent behaviors ("is more often a spectator than a participant while others play"). Results from factor analyses indicated that these 5 items loaded on a single factor (factor loadings ranged from 0.78 to 0.90). These items were subsequently tallied to yield a summary score of teacher-rated *shy–reticent* behaviors ($\alpha = 0.89$).

Time 3

Near the end of the school year, assessments of children's socio-emotional and school adjustment were collected. Mothers completed the *Strengths and Difficulties Questionnaire* (Goodman 2001). For the current study, we were particularly interested in the subscales assessing child *emotion symptoms* (5 items, $\alpha = 0.74$, e.g., "Many worries, often seems worried") and *peer problems* (5 items, $\alpha = 0.69$, e.g., "Picked on or bullied by other children"). Concurrently, teachers completed the *Child Behavior Scale* (Ladd and Profilet 1996), designed to assess young children's social adjustment and behavior problems. Of particular interest for the present study were the subscales of *excluded by peers* (seven items, $\alpha = 0.90$, e.g., "peers refuse to let this child play with them"), and *anxious with peers* (four items, $\alpha = 0.84$, e.g., "Cries easily").

Teachers also completed the *Student–Teacher Relationship Scale* (Pianta 2001), a norm-referenced and widely used measure of teacher–child relationships with excellent psychometric properties (e.g., Hamre and Pianta 2001). For the purposes of the present study, we were primarily interested in the subscale assessing *close teacher–child relationships* designed to measure the degree of warmth and affection as well as open communication between teachers and children (11 items, $\alpha = 0.84$). Finally, teachers provided a rating scale assessment of child early academic skills (Coplan et al. 2001), including language, reading/writing, math, science, motor skills, and reasoning (9 items $\alpha = 0.94$).

Finally, trained female research assistants interviewed children individually. Measures included: (1) the *Loneliness and Social Dissatisfaction Questionnaire for Young Children* (Cassidy and Asher 1992) to assess child loneliness (16 items, $\alpha = 0.76$); (2) the *Pictorial Scale of Perceived Competence and Social Acceptance for Young Children* (Harter and Pike 1984) to assess *perceived cognitive competence* (6 items, $\alpha = 0.74$), and *perceived peer acceptance* (6 items, $\alpha = 0.72$); and (3) the *School Liking and Avoidance Scale* (Ladd et al. 2000) to assess *school liking* (9 items, $\alpha = 0.83$).

Creation of aggregate variables

CHILD SHYNESS/RETICENCE

Conceptually, we were interested in creating a multi-source assessment aggregate of shyness and social reticence. Results from factor analysis indicated that maternal-rated shyness, observed reticent behavior, and teacher-rated shy–reticent behavior all loaded on a single factor (with factor loadings ranging from 0.65 to 0.76). Factor scores were saved to create a composite score representing child *shyness/reticence*.

MATERNAL CHARACTERISTICS

Results from factor analyses of maternal personality and parenting variables provided empirical support for our three conceptually derived "clusters" of parenting characteristics. The first factor, labeled *fretful* parenting, consisted of maternal neuroticism, BIS, and overprotective parenting (factor loadings from 0.66 to 0.85). The second factor, *warm–supportive* parenting, included maternal agreeableness and authoritative parenting (factor loadings of 0.79 and 0.73, respectively). The final factor, *uninhibited* parenting, consisted of maternal BAS and extroversion (factor loadings of 0.75 and 0.89, respectively).

CHILD PSYCHOSOCIAL AND SCHOOL ADJUSTMENT

Several additional aggregate variables were created to allow for multisource assessment of indices of child psychosocial and school adjustment. To begin with, maternal-rated child emotion symptoms and teacher-rated child anxiety ($r = 0.37$, $p < 0.001$) were combined to create an aggregate variable of child *internalizing problems*. Results from factor analysis indicated that parent-rated child problems with peers and teacher-rated child peer exclusion loaded on one factor (factor loadings of 0.75 and 0.79) whereas child-reported loneliness and perceived peer acceptance (reverse scored) loaded on a separate factor (with factor loadings of 0.76 and 0.81). As such, two separate summary scores were computed, representing *peer difficulties* and *social dissatisfaction*, respectively. Finally, we also sought to create a more global multisource index

of school adjustment that did not include variables related to social interaction with peers. Indices of school adjustment included close teacher–child relationships, child academic skills, child perceived academic competence, and child school liking. Results from factor analysis indicated that these four variables loaded on a single factor (factor loadings from 0.58 to 0.67), and a composite score was created representing child *school adjustment*. Summaries of the aggregate variables are provided in Table 8.1.

Results

Preliminary analyses

There were no significant correlations between parental education and child shy–reticence or either of the maternal parenting aggregates (fretful, warm/supportive, uninhibited). As such, parental education was not controlled for statistically in subsequent analyses. As well, results from a series of t-tests indicated that there were no significant differences for any of these variables as a function of child gender.

Inter-associations between variables

The correlations between all study variables are displayed in Table 8.2. Child shyness/reticence was significantly and positively associated with internalizing problems and peer difficulties, and significantly and negatively related to school adjustment. Overall, the three maternal parenting factors were not associated with child shyness or child outcome variables, with the exception of a significant (albeit modest) and negative correlation between warm–supportive parenting and peer difficulties. Finally, results also indicated moderate but statistically significant inter-associations between the various indices of adjustment (in theoretically expected directions).

Hierarchical regression analyses

OVERVIEW

The primary goal of the present study was to explore the interactive relations between child shyness/reticence and maternal parenting in the prediction of

Table 8.1 Summary of aggregate variables and descriptive statistics

Aggregate	Variables included	Source of assessment
Child shyness/reticence	Shyness ($M = 2.27$, $SD = 0.83$)	CSPS-Mother
	Reticent behavior ($M = .11$, $SD = .12$)	POS-Observed
	Shy–reticent behavior ($M = 2.37$, $SD = .95$)	SCI-Teacher
Maternal characteristics		
Fretful	Maternal neuroticism ($M = 3.09$, $SD = 1.31$)	TIPI-Mother
	Maternal BIS ($M = 2.95$, $SD = 0.49$)	BIS/BAS-Mother
	Overprotective parenting ($M = 2.27$, $SD = 0.68$)	PSDQ-Mother
Warm/supportive	Maternal agreeableness ($M = 2.27$, $SD = 0.83$)	TIPI-Mother
	Authoritative parenting ($M = 4.03$, $SD = 0.43$)	PSDQ-Mother
Uninhibited	Maternal extraversion ($M = 4.47$, $SD = 1.57$)	TIPI-Mother
	Maternal BAS ($M = 3.03$, $SD = 0.42$)	TIPI-Mother
Child outcomes		
Internalizing	Anxiety ($M = 1.27$, $SD = 0.43$)	CBS-Teacher
	Emotion symptoms ($M = 1.54$, $SD = 1.67$)	SDQ-Mother
Peer difficulties	Peer exclusion ($M = 1.25$, $SD = 0.27$)	CBS-Teacher
	Problems with peers ($M = 1.46$, $SD = 1.69$)	SDQ-Mother
Social dissatisfaction	Loneliness ($M = 1.36$, $SD = 0.31$)	LSDQ-Child
	(*reversed*) Perceived peer-acceptance ($M = 2.44$, $SD = 0.62$)	PSPCSA-Child
School adjustment	Close teacher relationship ($M = 4.11$, $SD = 0.60$)	STRS-Teacher
	Academic skills ($M = 3.31$, $SD = 0.79$)	ASC-Teacher
	Perceived academics ($M = 3.50$, $SD = 0.42$)	PSPCSA-Child
	School liking ($M = 2.78$, $SD = 0.36$)	SLAS-Child

CSPS Child Social Preference Scale, 5-point scale, *POS* Play Observation Scale, proportion of observed intervals, *SCI* Social Competence Inventory, 5-point scale, *TIPI* Ten Item Personality Scale, 7-point scale, *BIS/BAS* BIS/BAS Scales, 5-point scale; *PSDQ* Parenting Styles and Dimensions Questionnaire, 5-point scale, *CBS* Child Behavior Scale, 5-point scale, *SDQ* Strengths & Difficulties Questionnaire, 3-point scale, *LSDQ* Loneliness and Social Dissatisfaction Questionnaire, 3-point scale, *PSPCSA* Pictorial Scale of Perceived Competence and Social Acceptance for Young Children, 4-point scale, *STRS* Student–Teacher Relationship Scale, 5-point scale, *ASC* Academic Skills Checklist, 5-point scale, *SLAS* School Liking and Avoidance Scale, 3-point scale.

Table 8.2 Correlations between variables

Variables	2	3	4	5	6	7	8
1. Shyness/reticence	0.04	−0.06	0.04	0.34★★★	0.32★★★	0.06	−0.26★★★
2. Fretful parenting		−0.21★★	0.10	0.04	0.04	0.02	−0.02
3. Warm/supportive parenting			0.05	−0.10	−0.15★	−0.12	0.04
4. Uninhibited parenting				−0.02	−0.04	0.01	−0.13
5. Internalizing					0.36★★★	0.18★	−0.25★★★
6. Peer difficulties						0.19★	−0.24★★★
7. Social dissatisfaction							−0.38★★★
8. School adjustment							

★★★$p < 0.001$. ★★$p < 0.01$. ★$p < 0.05$.

Table 8.3 Results of regression analyses predicting indices of adjustment from interactions between child shyness/reticence and parenting (fretful, warm/supportive, uninhibited)

Dependent variable	Interaction terms (sr^2)		
	Shy × fretful	Shy × supportive	Shyness × uninhibited
Internalizing	0.023★	0.038★★	0.002
Peer difficulties	0.010	0.050★★★	0.001
Social dissatisfaction	0.030★	0.001	0.001
School adjustment	0.001	0.022★	0.006

Internalizing: overall $R^2 = 0.181$, $F(7,189) = 5.97$, $p < 0.001$; peer difficulties: overall $R^2 = 0.161$, $F(7,189) = 5.17$, $p < 0.001$; social dissatisfaction: overall $R^2 = .045$, $F(7,189) = 1.82$, $p < .05$; school adjustment: overall $R^2 = .113$, $F(7,189) = 3.46$, $p < .01$
★★★$p < 0.001$. ★★$p < 0.01$. ★$p < 0.05$.

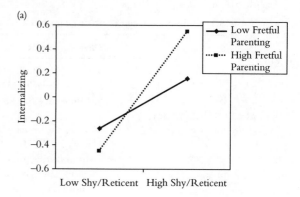

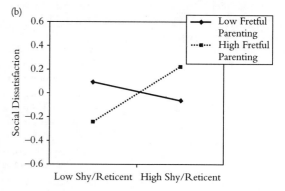

Figure 8.1 Interactions between shyness/reticence and maternal fretful parenting in the prediction of child (a) internalizing problems; and (b) social dissatisfaction.

indices of adjustment. To accomplish this goal, a series of hierarchical regression analyses was computed following procedures outlined by Aiken and West (1991). Separate equations were computed to predict each of the four indices of adjustment (i.e., internalizing problems, peer difficulties, social dissatisfaction, and school adjustment). The "main effects" variables (standardized) of child shyness/reticence, fretful parenting, warm–supportive parenting, and uninhibited parenting were entered together in Step 1. At Step 2, the two-way interaction terms (shyness by parenting–multiplicative products) were entered (shyness × fretful, shyness × warm/supportive, shyness × uninhibited). The "main effect" associations between shyness and child outcomes as well as parenting factors and child outcomes are already displayed in Table 8.2. As such, and to ease presentation, only results pertaining to interaction effects are presented in Table 8.3 and described below. Significant interactions were explored statistically using simple slope analyses (Aiken and West 1991).

SHYNESS × FRETFUL PARENTING
Significant interaction effects between shyness and maternal fretful parenting were observed in the prediction of child internalizing problems and social

dissatisfaction (see Table 8.3). Results from follow up simple slopes analyses illustrated a pattern consistent with an *exacerbating* process. Shyness was *more* strongly associated with both internalizing problems and social dissatisfaction at *higher* levels of fretful parenting scores (see Figure 8.1).

SHYNESS × SUPPORTIVE PARENTING
Significant interaction effects between shyness and maternal warm/supportive parenting were observed in the prediction of child internalizing problems, peer difficulties, and school adjustment (see Table 8.3). Results from follow up simple slopes analyses illustrated a pattern consistent with a *buffering* process. Shyness was *more* strongly associated with internalizing problems, peer difficulties, and school adjustment (negative association) at *lower* levels of warm/supportive parenting scores (see Figure 8.2).

(a)

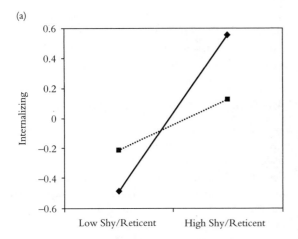

(b)

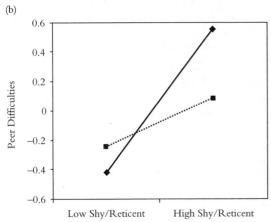

(c)

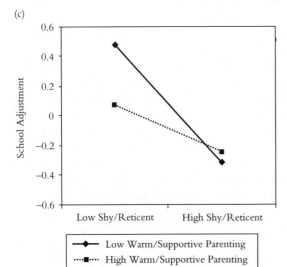

Low Warm/Supportive Parenting
High Warm/Supportive Parenting

SHYNESS × UNINHIBITED PARENTING

As indicated in Table 8.3, there were no significant interactions between shy and maternal uninhibited parenting in the prediction of child adjustment outcome variables.

SHYNESS AS MODERATOR?

When evaluating a significant interaction between two continuous variables, the decision as to which one is treated as the *moderator* for simple slopes analyses should be made on a theoretical basis (Aiken and West 1991). For this reason, we elected to explore the moderating role of parenting in the relation between shyness and indices of adjustment. However, from a statistical standpoint, it must be acknowledged that either variable can serve as the potential moderator. In this regard, we re-computed simple slopes analyses for statistically significant interactions treating *shyness* as the moderating variable in the relations between parenting and adjustment outcomes. We describe these results only briefly.

For interactions involving shyness and *fretful* parenting, results appeared to be consistent with the notion that the *combination* of shyness and fretful parenting is particularly problematic. At lower levels of child shyness, fretful parenting was not significantly associated with child internalizing problems or social dissatisfaction. However, with increasing child shyness scores, fretful parenting became increasingly associated with these negative outcomes.

For interactions involving shyness and *supportive* parenting, results predicting internalizing problems and peer difficulties were also as expected. At lower levels of child shyness, supportive parenting was not significantly associated with child internalizing problems or peer difficulties. However, with increasing child shyness scores, supportive parenting became increasingly *negatively* associated with these problematic outcomes. However, results predicting school adjustment were less clear. In this case, at *lower* levels of child shyness, supportive parenting was actually

Figure 8.2 Interactions between shyness/reticence and maternal warm/supportive parenting in the prediction of child (a) internalizing problems; (b) peer difficulties; and (c) school adjustment.

significantly and *negatively* related to school adjustment. With increasing child shyness scores, this association decreased and became nonsignificant.

Discussion

The primary goal of this study was to explore the moderating role of maternal characteristics in the relations between shyness and adjustment in early childhood. Overall, a multisource assessed composite of shyness–reticence predicted a range of social, emotional, and school adjustment difficulties in kindergarten.

Consistent with previous research in early childhood settings (e.g., Coplan et al. 2004), shy–reticence was associated with internalizing problems, difficulties with peers and teachers, as well as lower perceived and demonstrated academic competence, and lower school liking. Although the magnitude of these associations was moderate (i.e., correlations in the 0.30 range), shyness does appear to place children at least at some increased risk for experiencing difficulties across several domains of adaptation in kindergarten. Moreover, the nature of these specific difficulties may also pose additional risk for shy children in the longer term.

For example, "subclinical" levels of anxiety in early childhood are considered a risk factor for the later development of internalizing disorders (e.g., Goodwin et al. 2004). As well, shy and anxious children may be particularly vulnerable to the negative effects of peer exclusion (Gazelle and Ladd 2003). Finally, problems with teacher–child relationships, poorer academic performance, and school disliking are by themselves important indicators of concurrent and future school adjustment (Hamre and Pianta 2001).

Notwithstanding these linear associations, a number of significant child temperament by parenting interactions were also observed. The pattern of these results indicated that the relations between shyness and psychosocial *difficulties* in kindergarten (i.e., internalizing problems, social dissatisfaction, peer difficulties) were particularly pronounced among children with mothers higher in *fretful* parenting (neurotic, high BIS, overprotective) and lower in *warm/supportive* (i.e., agreeable, authoritative style) parenting. However, results predicting school *adjustment* (e.g., positive

teacher–child relationships, academic skills) were less clear, with the combination of warm–supportive parenting and *low*–shyness apparently associated with a *lack* of school adjustment.

Moderating role of maternal characteristics

We explored the moderating role of three conceptually identified and empirically verified clusters of maternal characteristics in the relations between shyness and adjustment in kindergarten. We must begin by acknowledging that underlying causal mechanisms cannot be ascertained from our results. For example, our decision to treat "parenting variables" as the *moderators* in our analyses was based on our theoretical approach. However, many other conceptual interpretations of these findings are possible. For example, it may be that child temperament characteristics (i.e., shyness) serve to moderate the relation between parenting characteristics and child outcomes. Moreover, parents might even play more of a reactive role, responding differently to shy children who are experiencing more/less difficulties at school. Within these constraints, we consider each of our shyness by parenting interactions in turn.

FRETFUL PARENTING

We speculated that the combination of maternal neuroticism, BIS sensitivity, and overprotective parenting style (fretful parenting) would create a particularly maladaptive family environment for shy children. Findings with regard to this particular parenting cluster appeared to be the most consistent. Among children with more fretful mothers, shyness was more strongly associated with internalizing problems and social dissatisfaction. The strength of these associations was significantly reduced among children with less fretful mothers. This pattern of results suggests that maternal fretful parenting has an *exacerbating* effect on the relations between shyness and adjustment to kindergarten. Overall, shy children were more likely to experience difficulties with peers, teachers, and academics in kindergarten. However, the composite measure of fretful parenting did not demonstrate any significant linear associations with any of the outcome variables explored in this study. Moreover, fretful parenting itself was only associated with certain negative outcomes (i.e., internalizing problems, social dissatisfaction) at higher levels of child shyness. As well, among less fretful mothers, shy children were not more likely to also feel anxious and lonely. Taken together, these results are certainly consistent with the notion that fretful parenting creates a family environment that is a particularly "bad fit" for shy children.

Mothers high in neuroticism and BIS sensitivity might be more likely to model anxious behaviors and highlight risks and dangers in the environment to their shy child (Carver 2004; Jorm et al. 2000). Moreover, the tendency to overprotect children, perhaps by intervening too early and too often, or simply removing the child from socially challenging and stressful environments, may inhibit the shy children's development of appropriate coping strategies (Rubin and Burgess 2002).

We speculate that the family environment created by fretful mothers exacerbates shy children's responses to the stresses of the school environment. Shy children with more fretful mothers may not develop appropriate coping strategies, which may serve to compound the difficulties that shy children already experience when starting kindergarten. This appears to increase the risk of shy children to experience anxiety and other internalizing problems, as well as feeling worse about their peer relationships at school.

WARM/SUPPORTIVE PARENTING

We also postulated that maternal agreeableness and an authoritative parenting style (i.e., warm/supportive parenting) might buffer shy children from negative adjustment outcomes. Results indicated several significant interactions between shyness and warm/supportive parenting. However, the pattern of these results provided somewhat mixed empirical support for our hypothesized conceptual model.

Among mothers who were more warm/supportive parents, relations between shyness and internalizing problems and peer difficulties were significantly less pronounced. That is, having a warm/supportive mother appears to reduce the risk for certain indices of psychosocial maladjustment associated with being shy in kindergarten. Alternatively, it can also be speculated that shy children were particularly susceptible to the negative adjustment outcomes associated with having a mother low in warmth and support.

More agreeable mothers may promote positive emotion regulation in shy children (Sheffield Morris et al. 2007). Moreover, a supportive and authoritative parenting style promotes the development of social skills (Metsäpelto and Pulkkinen 2003) which would serve shy children particularly well. In concert, the improved emotional and social skills might serve to ameliorate the quality and quantity of shy children's social interactions with peers. These positive relationships at school might in turn serve to "protect" against the negative emotions and poorer self-perceptions that may accompany shyness.

However, results regarding the prediction of overall positive school adjustment were less clear. On the one hand, a similar argument can be postulated in terms of the potential "protective role" of supportive parenting for shy children. That is, across the entire sample, shyness was negatively related to the composite measure of school adjustment. However, although this significant association remains at lower levels of supportive parenting, with increasing supportive parenting the negative relation between shyness and adjustment diminishes.

In contrast, results from simple slopes analyses where *shyness* was considered the moderating variable suggested a somewhat different interpretation. That is, among non-shy children, supportive parenting actually predicted *lower* school adjustment; whereas among more shy children, this association was attenuated and no longer statistically significant. Thus, in this case, it appeared that the effects of this parenting cluster were more pronounced at *lower* levels of child shyness. These findings could be interpreted to suggest that the combination of low shyness and highly supportive parenting may actually have *negative* implications for children's overall school adjustment.

It has been previously postulated that some highly sociable children are at risk for *externalizing* difficulties (e.g., Rubin et al. 1995). Less positive relationships with teachers and poorer academic performance are outcomes typically related to children with tendencies towards externalizing problems (Dodge et al. 2006). In the present sample, extremely "non-shy" children may have been more likely to experience poorer school adjustment if they also had parents who focused more on warmth and support as opposed to, for example, stricter discipline. These issues clearly warrant future investigation.

UNINHIBITED PARENTING

Finally, contrary to initial expectations, maternal uninhibited parenting (i.e., extraverted and high BAS) was *not* found to moderate (i.e., buffering effect) the associations between shyness and indices of adjustment in kindergarten. It had been speculated that extraverted and high BAS mothers might be particularly helpful to shy children as models of sociable and risk-taking behaviors (e.g., Carver 2004). However, it has also been suggested that extraverted parents may create an environment that is overly stimulating for their children (Kochanska et al. 1997). This might be particularly true for shy children. Moreover, extraverted parents may also have tendencies to be permissive (Metsäpelto and Pulkkinen 2003), which may not provide enough structure to support shy children's social needs. Thus, maternal modeling of non-shy behaviors in and of itself may not be enough to assist shy children, who may benefit more from the emotional and social support inherent in an authoritative parenting style. Clearly, further research is required to explore these possibilities in more detail.

Limitations and future directions

There are some limitations that need to be considered in the interpretation of our results, which are suggestive of areas of future research attention. To begin with, these findings need to be replicated in samples reflecting greater socio-economic and ethnic diversity, as shy and anxious behaviors may be responded to quite differently and have different implications in different cultural contexts (Chen et al. 1995). Moreover, despite statistically significant findings, the overall small effect sizes observed in the current study suggest that there are other important constructs to be considered in the developmental pathways of shy children.

For example, noticeably lacking in the current study was information regarding the personality characteristics and parenting styles of *fathers*. There have only been a handful of studies exploring the role of fathers in the development of children's shyness and social anxiety (e.g., Greco and Morris 2002). Thus, it will be important for future researchers to explicitly explore how fathers' personality and parenting characteristics (both alone and in combination with mothers) influence the development and outcomes of shyness in their sons and daughters.

In addition, although we identified and explored three specific clusters of maternal characteristics in the current study, there are likely other personality and parenting styles that also impact upon the development of shy children. Moreover, other characteristic parenting behaviors (e.g., sensitivity; Early et al. 2002), parental beliefs (Rubin and Mills 1990) and qualities of the parent–child relationship (e.g., mother–child attachment quality; Calkins and Fox 1992) have also been linked to the developmental course of shyness and social withdrawal.

It was also somewhat surprising to note a lack of significant *linear* associations between maternal characteristics and child shyness. Future research should consider having parents complete a measure of adult shyness themselves, in order to explore the direct associations between parental and child personality traits. In this vein, it is possible that there was some bias in our sample selection. For example, the most overprotective and anxious parents of the most shy children may not have opted to participate in the study. However, it should be noted that the means of all variables in the present study were consistent with previous assessments in other unselected samples.

It will also be important to consider the longer term outcomes associated with shyness and fretful parenting in early childhood. In particular, multiple assessments of parenting, shyness, and adjustment outcomes should be undertaken in order to assess the dynamic and transactional interplay between parenting beliefs and behaviors, child temperament, and child adjustment outcomes.

Finally, given the potentially large number of extremely shy young children that may also suffer from concurrent anxiety disorders (Rapee et al. 2005), it is important to consider the implications of the results of the current study for early intervention and prevention. Our results provide some preliminary evidence to suggest that intervening directly with parents may be an effective strategy in improving outcomes for shy/anxious young children (see also Lafreniere and Capuano 1997). In support of this notion, Rapee et al. (2005) recently reported that compared to a monitoring group, extremely shy preschoolers whose parents participated in a parenting education and training intervention had a significantly greater reduction in clinically diagnosed anxiety disorders at one year post intervention. Taken together, these findings suggest that parents should be additionally included in ameliorative intervention and prevention programs designed to improve the developmental trajectories of shy and anxious young children.

References

Aiken, L. S., & West, S. G. (1991). *Multiple regression: Testing and interpreting interactions.* Thousand Oaks, CA, US: Sage Publications, Inc.

Arbeau, K. A., & Coplan, R. J. (2007). Kindergarten teachers' beliefs and responses to hypothetical prosocial, asocial, and antisocial children. *Merrill-Palmer Quarterly, 53,* 291–318.

Arcus, D. (2001). Inhibited and uninhibited children: Biology in the social context. In T. D. Wachs & G. A. Kohnstamm (Eds.), *Temperament in context* (pp. 43–60). Mahwah, NJ, US: Lawrence Erlbaum Associates, Publishers.

Baumrind, D. (1971). Current patterns of parental authority. *Developmental Psychology Monographs, 4,* 1–103.

Burgess, K. B., Rubin, K. H., Cheah, C. S. L., & Nelson, L. J. (2005). Behavioral inhibition, social withdrawal, and parenting. In W. R. Crozier & L. E. Alden (Eds.), *The essential handbook of social anxiety for clinicians* (pp. 99–120). New York, NY. US: John Wiley & Sons Ltd.

Calkins, S. D., & Fox, N. A. (1992). The relations among infant temperament, security of attachment, and behavioral inhibition at twenty-four months. *Child Development, 63,* 1456–1472.

Carver, C. S. (2004). Negative affects deriving from the behavioral approach system. *Emotion, 4,* 3–22.

Carver, C. S., & White, T. L. (1994). Behavioral inhibition, behavioral activation, and the affective responses to impending reward and punishment: The BIS/BAS scale. *Journal of Personality and Social Psychology, 69,* 319–333.

Cassidy, J., & Asher, S. R. (1992). Loneliness and peer relations in young children. *Child Development, 63,* 350–365.

Chen, X., Rubin, K. H., & Li, B. (1995). Social and school adjustment of shy and aggressive children in China. *Development and Psychopathology, 7,* 337–349.

Coplan, R. J. (2000). Assessing nonsocial play in early childhood: Conceptual and methodological approaches. In K. Gitlin-Weiner, A. Sandgrund, & C. Schaefer (Eds.), *Play diagnosis and assessment, 2nd edition* (pp. 563–598). New York: Wiley.

Coplan, R. J., & Armer, M. (2005). 'Talking yourself out of being shy': Shyness, expressive vocabulary, and adjustment in preschool. *Merrill-Palmer Quarterly, 51,* 20–41.

Coplan, R. J., Gavinsky-Molina, M. H., Lagace-Seguin, D., & Wichmann, C. (2001). When girls versus boys play alone: Gender differences in the associates of nonsocial play in kindergarten. *Developmental Psychology, 37,* 464–474.

Coplan, R. J., Girardi, A., Findlay, L. C., & Frohlick, S. L. (2007). Understanding solitude: Young children's attitudes and responses towards hypothetical socially-withdrawn peers. *Social Development, 16,* 390–409.

Coplan, R. J., & Prakash, K. (2003). Spending time with teacher: Characteristics of preschoolers who frequently elicit versus initiate interactions with teachers. *Early Childhood Research Quarterly, 18,* 143–158.

Coplan, R. J., Prakash, K., O'Neil, K., & Armer, M. (2004). Do you 'want' to play? Distinguishing between conflicted-shyness and social disinterest in early childhood. *Developmental Psychology, 40,* 244–258.

Coplan, R. J., Rubin, K. H., Fox, N. A., Calkins, S. D., & Stewart, S. L. (1994). Being alone, playing alone, and acting alone: Distinguishing among reticence, and passive- and active-solitude in young children. *Child Development, 65,* 129–138.

Crockenberg, S. C., & Leerkes, E. M. (2006). Infant and maternal behavior moderate reactivity to novelty to predict anxious behavior at 2.5 years. *Development and Psychopathology, 18,* 17–34.

Crozier, W. R., & Hostettler, K. (2003). The influence of shyness on children's test performance. *British Journal of Educational Psychology, 73,* 317–328.

Crozier, W. R., & Perkins, P. (2002). Shyness as a factor when assessing children. *Educational Psychology in Practice, 18,* 239–244.

Dodge, K. A., Coie, J. D., & Lynam, D. (2006). Aggression and antisocial behavior in youth. In N. Eisenberg (Ed.), *Handbook of Child Psychology: Social, emotional, and personality development* (6th edn., pp. 719–788). New York: Wiley.

Early, D. M., Rimm-Kaufman, S. E., Cox, M. J., Saluja, G., Pianta, R. C., Bradley, R. H., et al. (2002). Maternal sensitivity and child wariness in the transition to kindergarten. *Parenting: Science & Practice, 2,* 355–377.

Evans, M. A. (2001). Shyness in the classroom and home. In W. R. Crozier & L. E. Alden (Eds.), *International handbook of social anxiety: Concepts, research and interventions relating to the self and shyness* (pp. 159–183). Westport, CT: John Wiley & Sons Ltd.

Fordham, K., & Stevenson-Hinde, J. (1999). Shyness, friendship quality, and adjustment during middle childhood.

Journal of Child Psychology and Psychiatry and Allied Disciplines, 40, 757–768.

Gazelle, H., & Ladd, G. W. (2003). Anxious solitude and peer exclusion: A diathesis-stress model of internalizing trajectories in childhood. *Child Development, 74,* 257–278.

Goodman, R. (2001). Psychometric properties of the strengths and difficulties questionnaire. *Journal of the American Academy of Child and Adolescent Psychiatry, 40,* 1337–1345.

Goodwin, R. D., Fergusson, D. M., & Horwood, J. (2004). Early anxious/withdrawn behaviors predict later internalizing disorders. *Journal of Child Psychology and Psychiatry, 45,* 874–883.

Gosling, S. D., Rentfrow, P. J., & Swann, W. B. J. (2003). A very brief measure of the Big-Five personality domains. *Journal of Research in Personality, 37,* 504–528.

Gray, J. A. (1987). *The psychology of fear and stress* (2nd ed.). Cambridge, England: Cambridge University Press.

Greco, L. A., & Morris, T. L. (2002). Paternal child-rearing style and child social anxiety: Investigation of child perceptions and actual father behavior. *Journal of Psychopathology and Behavioral Assessment, 24,* 259–267.

Hamre, B. K., & Pianta, R. C. (2001). Early teacher–child relationships and the trajectory of children's school outcomes through eighth grade. *Child Development, 72,* 625–638.

Hart, C. H., Yang, C., Nelson, L. J., Robinson, C. C., Olsen, J. A., Nelson, D. A., et al. (2000). Peer acceptance in early childhood and subtypes of socially withdrawn behavior in China, Russia, and the United States. *International Journal of Behavioural Development, 24,* 73–81.

Harter, S., & Pike, R. (1984). The pictorial scale of perceived competence and social acceptance for young children. *Child Development, 55,* 1969–1982.

Henderson, H. A., Marshall, P. J., Fox, N. A., & Rubin, K. H. (2004). Psychophysiological and behavioral evidence for varying forms and functions of nonsocial behavior in preschoolers. *Child Development, 75,* 236–250.

Jorm, A. F., Christensen, H., Henderson, A. S., Jacomb, P. A., Korten, A. E., & Rodgers, B. (2000). Predicting anxiety and depression from personality: Is there a synergistic effect of neuroticism and extraversion? *Journal of Abnormal Psychology, 109,* 145–149.

Kagan, J. (1997). Temperament and the reactions to the unfamiliarity. *Child Development, 68,* 139–143.

Kendler, K. S., Sham, P. C., & MacLean, C. J. (1997). The determinants of parenting: An epidemiological, multi-informant, retrospective study. *Psychological Medicine, 27,* 549–563.

Kochanska, G., Clark, L., & Goldman, M. (1997). Implications of mother's personality for their parenting and their young children's developmental outcomes. *Journal of Personality, 65,* 387–420.

Ladd, G. W., Buhs, E. S., & Seid, M. (2000). Children's initial sentiments about kindergarten: Is school liking an antecedent of early classroom participation and achievement? *Merrill-Palmer Quarterly, 46,* 255–279.

Ladd, G. W., & Profilet, S. M. (1996). The Child Behavior Scale: A teacher-report measure of young children's aggressive, withdrawn, and prosocial behaviors. *Developmental Psychology, 32,* 1008–1024.

LaFreniere, P. J., & Capuano, F. (1997). Preventive intervention as means of clarifying direction of effects in socialization: Anxious withdrawn preschoolers case. *Development and Psychopathology, 9,* 551–564.

Lamborn, S., Mounts, N., Steinberg, L., & Dornbusch, S. (1991). Patterns of competence and adjustment among adolescents from authoritative, authoritarian, indulgent, and neglectful families. *Child Development, 62,* 1149–1065.

Leve, L. D., Kim, H. K., & Pears, K. C. (2005). Childhood temperament and family environment as predictors of internalizing and externalizing trajectories from ages 5 to 17. *Journal of Abnormal Child Psychology, 33,* 505–520.

Lieb, R., Wittchen, H. U., Hofler, M., Fuetsch, M., Stein, M. B., & Merikangas, K. R. (2000). Parental psychopathology, parenting styles, and the risk of social phobia in offspring: A prospective-longitudinal community study. *Archives of General Psychiatry, 57,* 859–866.

Losoya, S., Callor, S., Rowe, D., & Goldsmith, H. (1997). Origins of familial similarity in parenting. *Developmental Psychology, 33,* 1012–1023.

Metsäpelto, R. L., & Pulkkinen, L. (2003). Personality traits and parenting: Neuroticism, extraversion, and openness to experience as discriminative factors. *European Journal of Personality, 17,* 59–78.

Meyer, B., Olivier, L., & Roth, D. A. (2005). Please don't leave me! BIS/BAS, attachment styles, and responses to a relationship threat. *Personality and Individual Differences, 38,* 151–162.

Nelson, D. A., Hart, C. H., Yang, C., Olsen, J. A., & Jin, S. (2006). Aversive parenting in China: Associations with child physical and relational aggression. *Child Development, 77,* 554–572.

Nelson, L. J., Rubin, K. H., & Fox, N. A. (2005). Social withdrawal, observed peer acceptance, and the development of self-perceptions in children ages 4 to 7 years. *Early Childhood Research Quarterly, 20,* 185–200.

Perren, S., & Alsaker, F. D. (2006). Social behavior and peer relationships of victims, bully-victims, and bullies in kindergarten. *Journal of Child Psychology and Psychiatry, 47*, 45–57.

Pianta, R. C. (2001). *Student–Teacher Relationship Scale: Professional manual*. Odessa, FL: Psychological Assessment Resources.

Pianta, R. C. (2006). Schools, schooling, and developmental psychopathology. In D. Cicchetti (Ed.), *Handbook of Developmental Psychopathology, Vol. 2*. New York: John Wiley & Sons.

Prior, M., Smart, D., Sanson, A., & Oberklaid, F. (2000). Does shy-inhibited temperament in childhood lead to anxiety problems in adolescence? *Journal of the American Academy of Child and Adolescent Psychiatry, 39*, 461–468.

Rapee, R. M. (1997). Potential role of child rearing practices in the development of anxiety and depression. *Clinical Psychology Review, 17*, 47–67.

Rapee, R. M., Kennedy, S., Ingram, M., Edwards, S., & Sweeney, L. (2005). Prevention and early intervention of anxiety disorders in inhibited preschool children. *Journal of Consulting and Clinical Psychology, 73*, 488–497.

Robinson, C. C., Mandleco, B., Olsen, S. F., & Hart, C. H. (2001). The parenting styles and dimensions questionnaire. In B. F. Perlmutter, J. Touliatos, & G. W. Holden (Eds.), *Handbook of family measurement techniques: Vol. 3. Instruments & index* (pp. 319–321). Thousand Oaks: Sage.

Rothbart, M. K., & Ahadi, S. A. (1994). Temperament and the development of personality. *Journal of Abnormal Psychology, 103*, 55–66.

Rothbart, M. K., & Bates, J. E. (2006). Temperament. In N. Eisenberg (Ed.), *Handbook of Child Psychology: Social, emotional, and personality development* (6th edn., pp. 99–166). New York: Wiley.

Rubin, K. H. (2001). *The Play Observation Scale (POS)*. University of Maryland.

Rubin, K. H., Bukowski, W., & Parker, J. (2006). Peer interactions, relationships, and groups. In N. Eisenberg (Ed.), *Handbook of Child Psychology: Social, emotional, and personality development* (6th edn., pp. 571–645). New York: Wiley.

Rubin, K. H., & Burgess, K. (2002). Parents of aggressive and withdrawn children. In M. Bornstein (Ed.), *Handbook of Parenting*, Volume 1 (2nd Edn., pp. 383–418). Hillsdale, N.J.: Lawrence Erlbaum Associates.

Rubin, K. H., Burgess, K. B., & Coplan, R. J. (2002a). Social withdrawal and shyness. In P. K. Smith & C. H. Hart (Eds.), *Blackwell handbook of childhood social development. Blackwell handbooks of developmental psychology* (pp. 330–352). Malden, MA: Blackwell Publishers.

Rubin, K. H., Burgess, K. B., & Hastings, P. D. (2002b). Stability and social-behavioral consequences of toddlers' inhibited temperament and parenting behaviors. *Child Development, 73*, 483–495.

Rubin, K. H., Cheah, C. S. L., & Fox, N. (2001). Emotion regulation, parenting, and display of social reticence in preschoolers. *Early Education and Development, 1*, 97–115.

Rubin, K. H., & Coplan, R. J. (2004). Paying attention to and not neglecting social withdrawal and social isolation. *Merrill-Palmer Quarterly, 50*, 506–534.

Rubin, K. H., Coplan, R. J., Fox, N. A., & Calkins, S. D. (1995). Emotionality, emotion regulation, and preschoolers' social adaptation. *Development and Psychopathology, 7*, 49–62.

Rubin, K., & Mills, R. S. L. (1990). Maternal beliefs about adaptive and maladaptive social behavior in aggressive, normal, and withdrawn preschoolers. *Journal of Abnormal Psychology, 18*, 419–435.

Rydell, A. M., Bohlin, G., & Thorell, L. B. (2005). Representations of attachment to parents and shyness as predictors of children's relationships with teachers and peer competence in preschool. *Attachment and Human Development, 7*, 187–204.

Rydell, A. M., Hagekull, B., & Bohlin, G. (1997). Measurement of two social competence aspects in middle childhood. *Developmental Psychology, 33*, 824–833.

Schmidt, L. A., & Tasker, S. L. (2000). Childhood shyness: Determinants, development and 'depathology'. In W. R. Crozier (Ed.), *Shyness: Development, consolidation and change* (pp. 30–46). New York, NY, US: Routledge.

Schwartz, C. E., Snidman, N., & Kagan, J. (1999). Adolescent social anxiety as an outcome of inhibited temperament in childhood. *Journal of the American Academy of Child & Adolescent Psychiatry, 38*, 1008–1015.

Sheffield Morris, A., Silk, J. S., Steinberg, L., Myers, S. S., & Robinson, L. (2007). The role of family context in the development of emotion regulation. *Social Development, 16*, 361–388.

Spinrad, T. L., Eisenberg, N., Harris, E., Hanish. L., Fabes, R. A., Kupanoff, K., et al. (2004). The relation of children's everyday nonsocial peer play behavior to their emotionality, regulation, and social functioning. *Developmental Psychology, 40*, 67–80.

Stevenson-Hinde, J., & Glover, A. (1996). Shy girls and boys: A new look. *Journal of Child Psychology and Psychiatry and Allied Disciplines, 37*, 181–187.

Thomas, A., & Chess, S. (1977). *Temperament and development*. New York: Bruner/Mazel.

Van Ameringen, M., Mancini, C., & Oakman, J. M. (1998). The relationship of behavioral inhibition and shyness to anxiety disorder. *Journal of Nervous and Mental Disease, 186*, 425–431.

Weinstock, L. M., & Whisman, M. A. (2006). Neuroticism as a common feature of the depressive and anxiety disorders: A test of the revised integrative hierarchical model in a national sample. *Journal of Abnormal Psychology, 115,* 68–74.

Wood, J. J., McLeod, B. D., Sigman, M., Hwang, W. C., & Chu, B. C. (2003). Parenting and childhood anxiety: Theory, empirical findings, and future directions. *Journal of Child Psychology and Psychiatry, 44,* 134–151.

Trajectories of Social Withdrawal from Middle Childhood to Early Adolescence

Wonjung Oh, Kenneth H. Rubin, Julie C. Bowker, Cathryn Booth-LaForce, Linda Rose-Krasnor, and Brett Laursen

The study of developmental psychopathology has characterized maladjustment as comprising two broad forms of difficulties—undercontrol (e.g., aggression) and overcontrol (e.g., social withdrawal; Mash and Barkley 2003). And yet, it remains the case that the developmental course of psychological overcontrol problems has received relatively less conceptual and empirical attention than that of psychological under-control problems. One example of such understudied psychological overcontrol difficulties is social withdrawal.

Social withdrawal may be defined as the consistent display of all forms of solitary behavior when encountering familiar and/or unfamiliar peers across situations and over time (Rubin and Asendorpf 1993; Rubin and Coplan 2004). Children characterized as socially withdrawn spend most of their time playing alone and on the periphery of the social scene, often due to shyness or social anxiety. Importantly, social withdrawal has been shown to be moderately stable from early through middle childhood (Hymel et al. 1990; Rubin et al. 1989, 1995) and from late childhood through early adolescence (e.g., Schneider et al. 1998). For example, in the *Waterloo Longitudinal Project*, Rubin and colleagues reported that *observed* social withdrawal (the aggregate of [unoccupied onlooker solitary play] among familiar peers) was stable from ages 5 to 9 years and that peer perceptions of social withdrawal (peer nominations for such items as *Someone who is shy* and *Someone who likes to play alone*) were stable between ages 7 years and 10 years (e.g., Hymel et al. 1990; Rubin et al. 1995). Data also revealed that approximately two-thirds of extremely socially withdrawn children maintained their status from ages 5 to 11 years across every 2-year period (Rubin 1993).

Beyond stability, social withdrawal has been identified as a risk factor for psychosocial maladjustment (for a recent review, see Rubin et al. 2003). To begin with, observed and peer- and teacher-reports of social withdrawal are contemporaneously associated with such negative, intrapersonal difficulties as low self-esteem, negative self-perceptions of social competence, and anxiety during middle and late childhood (e.g., Hymel et al. 1993; Rubin et al. 1993). Moreover, researchers have shown that social withdrawal during childhood predicts such internalizing problems in early adolescence as depression and loneliness (e.g., Boivin et al. 1995; Gazelle and Rudolph 2004; Gazelle and Ladd 2003; Rubin et al. 1995). Furthermore, social withdrawal is associated with, and predictive of, such interpersonal difficulties as peer rejection (e.g., Bowker et al. 1998), and victimization (Boivin and Hymel 1997).

Despite these well-documented psychological and peer difficulty correlates and consequences of social withdrawal, researchers have recently demonstrated that not all socially withdrawn children experience psychosocial and emotional difficulties or continue to remain highly socially withdrawn over time. Gazelle and Rudolph (2004), for example, reported that anxious-solitary youth displayed *increased* social approach in the context of *low* peer exclusion, suggesting that peer difficulty or the lack thereof may alter longitudinal trajectories of social withdrawal. Beyond this work, however, few longitudinal studies exist that chart the pathways of social withdrawal in childhood or that address developmental heterogeneity among individuals. Furthermore, most of the studies that do exist are largely focused on the early years (e.g., Gazelle and Ladd 2003) or involve, at best, only two or three assessments during childhood, and use variable-oriented rather than person-oriented approaches (Gazelle and Rudolph 2004; Rubin et al. 1995). The one exception is a recent study by Booth-LaForce and Oxford (2006, submitted), in which distinct trajectory patterns of social withdrawal from early childhood (first grade) to early adolescence (sixth grade) were identified, predicted by early temperament, insensitive parenting styles, and attachment, and related to varying psychosocial and emotional outcomes. Specifically, children whose social withdrawal increased over time (compared with those whose withdrawal decreased or who were never withdrawn) were more lonely, depressed, victimized, and excluded by peers. Because this aforementioned study focused on younger children, it is important to examine the issue of developmental heterogeneity among older children and adolescents, particularly since the strength of associations between social withdrawal and indices of psychosocial maladjustment increase with age (Rubin et al. 2003).

Hinde (1987) has argued that social development is best considered from a multi-level perspective that includes individual characteristics, social interactions, relationships, and groups. Although it is clear that peer acceptance or rejection at the group level of social complexity can ameliorate or exacerbate difficulties associated with social withdrawal during mid-to-late childhood (e.g., Gazelle and Rudolph 2004; Hymel et al. 1990), few researchers, if any, have targeted the friends of withdrawn children at the relationship-level as a potentially significant developmental force. To address this research gap and to examine the significance of Hinde's (1987) multi-levels of influence on the development of social withdrawal, in the present study we examined distinct pathways of social withdrawal during the transition from elementary-to-middle school and then through the years of middle school; we further investigated the extent to which multi-level covariates of individual, interactional (prosocial behavior), relationship- (friendship), and group-level (peer exclusion/victimization) factors

ameliorated or exacerbated the course of social withdrawal. To this end, this set of interactional, friendship and group-level covariates was explored in relation to both the levels of social withdrawal in middle childhood (i.e., the intercept) and the rates of change over time across early adolescence (i.e., the slope).

Social Withdrawal, and Individual Characteristics, Friendship, and Peer Exclusion/Victimization

From a social motivation viewpoint (e.g., Asendorpf 1993), individuals' tendencies to engage in social interaction may be constrained by such internal mechanisms as anxiety, fear or social disinterest. Growing evidence suggests that these social orientations may result in diverging pathways depending on the peer environments that each individual experiences. As noted previously, Gazelle and Rudolph (2004) found that children who were socially anxious and withdrawn developed distinct trajectories of social approach and social avoidance depending on the degree to which they experienced peer exclusion. Specifically, anxious-solitary youth increased social approach, demonstrating more prosocial behavior when they experienced less peer exclusion; when they encountered considerable peer exclusion, social avoidance and the display of helpless behavior resulted. It is also the case that children who display prosocial behavior are regarded by peers, parents, and teachers as more popular, socially competent, and well-adjusted than those who are aggressive and disruptive (see Rubin et al. 2006a for a recent review). As such, the display of prosocial behaviors may play an important role in determining longitudinal trajectories of social withdrawal. In contrast to the effects of peer exclusion, one might expect *decreasing* withdrawal for those children who exhibit prosocial behavior.

Moving to the relationship level, friendships have long been viewed as significant sources of social support in individual growth and development (e.g., Sullivan 1953). Much of the research supporting this view emanates from studies of friendless children. For instance, friendless children are more likely to be lonely and victimized by peers than those children who have friends (Brendgen et al. 2000; Kochenderfer and Ladd 1996). And Hodges et al. (1999) reported that victimization by peers predicted increases in internalizing and externalizing problems across the school year *only* for those children who lacked a mutual best friendship. Despite the reported relations between friendlessness and peer rejection and victimization, it is certainly the case that not all friendless children experience peer exclusion or victimization (Ladd and Troop-Gordon 2003). Accordingly, it could be that friendlessness and peer rejection or exclusion have markedly different effects on adjustment trajectories.

Approximately 60-to-65% of socially withdrawn 8-to-11 year olds are known to have a mutual best friend (Schneider 1999; Rubin et al. 2006b); this is similar to the prevalence of friendship among non-withdrawn children and young adolescents (Rubin et al. 2006b). Moreover, the social support of a high-quality *stable* friendship has been shown to be helpful for children during times of school transition (e.g., Berndt et al. 1999). Yet, the extent to which the presence of a mutual stable friendship is helpful for withdrawn children is unknown. Thus, in the present study, we examined the significance of friendship involvement and stability as it may affect trajectories of social withdrawal.

When considering the possible influence of friendship on adjustment, it is important to consider the characteristics of friends and similarities between friends (e.g., Haselager et al. 1998). Researchers have shown that there are greater similarities between friends than non-friends in terms of social withdrawal (Rubin et al. 2006b), shyness (Haselager et al. 1998), and shared internalized distress (Hogue and Steinberg 1995). Yet, whether having a friend who shares behavioral characteristics known to be associated with maladaptation serves an ameliorative or exacerbating function is heretofore largely unknown. Drawing from the literature on deviancy training among aggressive youth (e.g., Dishion et al. 1996), keeping company with maladjusted friends may augment rather than ameliorate maladjustment. Withdrawn children and their best friends have been found to be more victimized than non-withdrawn children and their best friends, suggesting that friendships may not be protective when best friends share maladaptive

behavioral similarity (Rubin et al. 2006b). In the present study, the characteristics of the child's best friend were examined with reference to the role of friendship on developmental *trajectories* of social withdrawal for those who had identifiable mutual friendship.

Lastly, it has been suggested that friendships of high quality can buffer, or protect children from negative outcomes (e.g., Parker and Asher 1993). There is evidence, however, indicating that the friendships of socially withdrawn children are lower in relationship quality than those of non-withdrawn children. For example, Rubin et al. (2006b) found that withdrawn 10-year-old children reported their best friendships as significantly less fun, helpful and intimate than non-withdrawn children; their friendships were perceived as being less likely to lead to the resolution of conflict than those of their non-withdrawn age-mates. Both withdrawn children and their best friends rated their friendships to be lower in overall quality than their non-withdrawn counterparts and the best friends of non-withdrawn children. In light of these findings, it is reasonable to query whether friendship quality can influence or modify individual trajectories of social withdrawal over time. The present study is the first to consider this possibility. It is also the first to examine whether individual variations of social orientation, the demonstration of socially competent behavior, and the experience of peer exclusion and victimization individually and collectively predicted varying developmental trajectories of social withdrawal.

Overview of the Present Study

In summary, the purposes of the present study were threefold. First, we sought to identify trajectories of social withdrawal from elementary school to middle school in a large community sample. Specifically, we followed children as they made a transition from the familiar milieu of their elementary schools into larger, unfamiliar middle schools. Given that accompanying (and defining) characteristics of social withdrawal in mid-to-late childhood are shyness and social anxiety (Rubin et al. 2003), a school transition was posited to be especially stressful for those children who were socially withdrawn as elementary schoolers (Barber and Olsen 2004). We employed General Growth Mixture Modeling (*GGMM*) to examine whether there are distinct trajectory patterns of social withdrawal across this school transition and thereafter, through the middle school years.

Second, we examined a set of covariates to determine whether distinct factors are predictive of class membership and to evaluate the class-specific associations among interactional, relationship, and group-level factors and the development of social withdrawal for different classes. Thus, our goals were to (a) identify those factors that predict distinct trajectory class membership, and (b) examine factors that buffer or exacerbate developmental pathways of social withdrawal (i.e., intercept and slope) *within* class across the transition from elementary-to-middle school.

Third, in a final set of analyses, we focused specifically on children who had a mutual best friendship after the transition from elementary-to-middle school (i.e., fall semester of grade 6). We did so to investigate the extent to which specific individual characteristics of the best friend (the best friend's social withdrawal, peer exclusion and victimization), and the quality of the friendship affected trajectories of social withdrawal.

Given the general lack of research on the developmental trajectories of social withdrawal, we relied on the extant literature to derive our hypotheses. Despite evidence that extremely withdrawn children are likely to remain withdrawn throughout childhood (e.g., Rubin et al. 1995; Schneider et al. 1998), we posited that considerable heterogeneity in the developmental pathways of social withdrawal would be evinced in analyses of intrapersonal change. Booth-LaForce and Oxford (2006, submitted) found three distinct trajectories of social withdrawal (characterized by increasing, decreasing, and low-stable patterns) from first-to-sixth grades in the only other study investigating heterogeneity in developmental patterns of social withdrawal; consequently, we anticipated that we might discover similar patterns in the present study.

Additionally, we predicted that, in general, the presence of a mutual friendship would ameliorate social withdrawal over time. Specifically, the existence of a reciprocal best friendship in sixth grade, the year during which the transition from elementary school occurred, was posited to have a significant impact on

the rate of change in social withdrawal over time. Also, it was predicted that for those children whose best friends were also socially withdrawn, their own development of social withdrawal would be exacerbated over time. Moreover, we posited that a supportive friendship would ameliorate social withdrawal during the transition from elementary-to-middle school. Lastly, we hypothesized that if children were viewed by their peers as helpful and prosocial, they would evidence a decrease in social withdrawal; alternately, if the peer group excluded and victimized the child, we hypothesized that there would be an increase in social withdrawal over time. Given evidence that the consequences of social withdrawal are greater for boys than girls (Rubin and Coplan 2004), sex was included as a control variable in each set of analyses.

Method

Participants

Participants were drawn from a larger longitudinal sample of fifth-grade students ($N = 556$ children, 271 girls) from 26 classrooms in eight public elementary schools in the Washington DC Metropolitan Area, for whom written parental permission was received (consent rate = 84%). The mean age of the sample at the start of the study (fall, fifth grade) was 10.23 years ($SD = 0.48$); males, $M = 10.23$ years ($SD = 0.45$) and females, $M = 10.21$ years ($SD = 0.51$). As they moved to middle school (sixth grade), we followed the participants longitudinally and administered the questionnaires described below. Available demographic school information indicated similar county-wide ethnic and racial compositions of the elementary (40% Caucasian, 22% Hispanic/Latino, 22% African American, 15% Asian American) and middle schools (43% Caucasian, 19% Hispanic/Latino, 23% African American, 15% Asian American). Based on mutuality of friendship nominations, pairs of friends in the sixth grade were invited to visit a laboratory at a large public university to complete an additional battery of questionnaires, including those pertaining to friendship quality and support. Of the original 556 participants, 446 children remained in the longitudinal study, participating in at least three waves of in-school assessment (attrition rate: 19%). The final sample for this study comprised 392 children (202 girls) who contributed data for variables after handling missing data with General Growth Mixture Modeling (*GGMM*) which allows partial participation in trajectory variables (i.e., social withdrawal), but not predictor variables. To examine the possibility of attrition biases, the final sample of 392 participants was compared with those who participated in fewer than three time points. Logit analysis, a common method of detecting attrition bias (Miller and Wright 1995), was performed to estimate the probability that the first wave respondents would participate in later waves and remain in the study. Results revealed no significant differences between longitudinal participants and those who dropped out of the study in terms of sex of participant, friendship involvement, friendship stability, prosocial behavior, peer exclusion and victimization in the fall of fifth grade. Additional details with reference to the sample size for each variable are presented below in the "*Statistical Methodology and Data Analytic Plan*" section. A follow-up analysis of the Latent Growth Curve Modeling (LGCM) was conducted for the subgroup of participants (i.e., *friended* group) who had an identifiable mutual friend after the school transition as well as friendship predictor covariate data ($n = 262$).

Procedure

During the fall (November or December) and spring (April or May) semesters of the fifth and sixth grades and during the spring of eight grade (April or May), participants completed a battery of group-administered questionnaires in their classrooms. The questionnaires identified the children's best friends in the school, and the behavioral characteristics of each participant. In addition, data on perceived friendship support were obtained from the sixth grade participants with mutual best friends during laboratory visits, which typically occurred between the fall and spring school assessments.

School measures

FRIENDSHIP NOMINATIONS
Participants were asked to write the names of their "very best friend" and their "second best friend" at

their school (Bukowski et al. 1994). Children could only name same-sex friends in their grade, and only *mutual* (reciprocated) *best* friendships were subsequently considered. Children were considered "best friends" if they were each other's very best or second best friend choice. This procedure was identical to that used in many other studies of best friendship (e.g., Parker and Asher 1993; Rubin et al. 2006b). Although children could nominate any same-sex child in their grade as a best friend, only participating children completed the friendship nominations; it was impossible to determine whether a friendship was reciprocated when a nonparticipating child was identified as a best friend. Therefore, only identifiable mutual friendships were considered herein; the consideration of the "very best" *and* "second best" friendship choices was necessary to ensure sufficient power for the data analyses. Friendship involvement data (the presence or absence of a mutual best friendship) in the fall of the fifth and sixth grades (after the school transition) were of particular interest. We also examined friendship involvement data in the spring of the fifth grade to determine friendship stability during the fifth grade.

EXTENDED CLASS PLAY (ECP)
Following completion of the friendship nomination questionnaire, participants completed an extended version of the Revised Class Play (*RCP*; Masten et al. 1985; Wojslawowicz Bowker et al. 2006). The children were instructed to pretend to be the directors of an imaginary class play and to nominate their classmates for various roles. Similar to the original *RCP* procedure, grade 5 children were instructed to nominate one boy and one girl within their classroom for each role. To adjust for an increased number of peers and changes in classroom that occur throughout the day, grade 6 and 8 children could nominate up to three same-sex and three opposite-sex peers across the entire grade for each role. In all grades, only nominations for participating children were considered, and to eliminate possible sex-stereotyping, only same-sex nominations were utilized (Zeller et al. 2003). All item scores were standardized within sex and within classroom (fifth grade) or within grade (sixth, eighth) in order to adjust for the number of nominations received and also the number of nominators.

Items were added to the original *RCP* to more fully capture different types of aggression (e.g., *Someone who spreads rumors*), assess peer victimization (e.g., *Someone who is hit/kicked*), and better distinguish between active isolation (e.g., *Someone who is often left out*) and social withdrawal (e.g., *Someone who prefers to be alone*). An exploratory principal components factor analysis with varimax rotation yielded *five* orthogonal factors (in contrast to the RCP's three broad factors of Aggressive/Disruptive, Sensitive/Isolated, and Sociability/Leadership): Aggression, Withdrawal/Shyness, Exclusion/Victimization, Prosocial Behaviors, and Popularity/Sociability. The standardized item scores were summed to yield five different total factor scores for each participant. Only the subscale scores for the constructs of withdrawal (items "*A person who hardly ever starts up a conversation*", "*Someone who talks quietly or rarely*", "*Someone who is very shy*", and "*Someone who gets nervous about group discussion*") at all five data points, and exclusion/victimization and prosocial behavior in the fall of fifth and sixth grades were used herein. Internal consistency (Cronbach's alphas) for these factors were as follows: Withdrawal/Shyness (4-items): grade 5 fall: .83; grade 5 spring: .87; grade 6 fall: .85; grade 6 spring: .91; grade 8 spring: .90; Exclusion/Victimization (8-items): grade 5 fall: .88, grade 6 fall: .94; and Prosocial Behaviors (6-items): grade 5 fall: .82, grade 6 fall: .88. Detailed psychometric and factor analytic information has been reported elsewhere (Rubin et al. 2006b), along with results from confirmatory factor analyses that supported the five-factor model in the fifth and sixth grades (Wojslawowicz Bowker et al. 2006). For example, teacher-reports of shy and anxious behaviors distinguish between withdrawn and non-withdrawn children who were identified by the *ECP* measure (Rubin et al. 2006b).

Laboratory measures (sixth grade only)

NETWORK OF RELATIONSHIP INVENTORY (NRI)

The *NRI* was used to assess adolescents' perceptions of friendship support (Furman and Buhrmester 1985). The 30-item Likert-type questionnaire yields 11 subscales that load on four factors: (1) *social support* (companionship, instrumental help, intimacy, nurturance of the other, affection, reliable alliance, enhancement of worth), (2) *satisfaction*, (3) *negativity* (punishment, conflict,

relative power), and (4) *relative power* (Furman 1996). Only the social support subscale was used in this study (alpha = 0.88). Reliability and validity of this measure has been previously established (see Furman 1996).

FRIENDSHIP QUALITY
QUESTIONNAIRE-REVISED (FQQ)

The *FQQ* was used to assess the young adolescents' perception of the quality of their dyadic-relationship with their best friend (Parker and Asher 1993). The 40-item Likert-type questionnaire yields six subscales in the areas of companionship and recreation, validation and caring, help and guidance, intimate disclosure, conflict and betrayal, and conflict resolution (alphas = 0.73–0.90); higher scores indicated greater perceived friendship quality or higher levels of conflict. The positive *FQQ* sub-scales were highly correlated (range: $r = 0.36$ to $r = 0.74$). Thus, in keeping with the procedures recommended by Parker and colleagues (e.g. Parker and Asher 1989), only the total positive *FQQ* score (the total of companionship and recreation, validation and caring, help and guidance, intimate disclosure) was used in this study.

The correlation between the two indices of perceived friendship quality (*NRI* friendship support score and the *FQQ* total positive score) was $r = 0.62, p < 0.001$. Thus, a composite friendship quality score was created to prevent a statistical violation of independence assumptions using the positive *FQQ* and *NRI* social support scores; this centered composite score was included in the *GGMM* model as a covariate.

Statistical methodology and data analytic plan

A person-oriented approach to data analysis was used in the present study to examine individual differences as well as heterogeneity in development. This approach is useful with longitudinal research designs where data often include heterogeneous subgroups of individuals. A General Growth Mixture Model (*GGMM*) approach was employed to examine the pathways of individual social withdrawal trajectories with the goal of determining optimal class membership and intrapersonal growth for each individual by estimating latent variables (i.e., the intercept and slope) based on multiple repeated indicators. *GGMM* also allows investigation of the possibility of heterogeneity; in this case, testing whether the population was constructed of two or more distinct subgroups that follow similar longitudinal mean pathways of social withdrawal. Data analysis was conducted using *Mplus Version 3.12 and 4.0* (Muthén and Muthén 2004, 2006).

MISSING DATA

In this study, models were estimated using the *Mplus* statistical program which uses a full-information maximum-likelihood (FIML) estimation. This procedure allows partial data on the trajectory variables (i.e., social withdrawal), but not missing data on predictor variables (Muthén and Shedden 1999). Of 446 participants with partial data, complete data on predictor variables were available for 392 children: 17 children (3%), 9 children (2%), and 37 children (8%) were missing data for fifth grade friendship involvement, fifth grade friendship stability, and sixth grade friendship involvement after the school transition, respectively. The *Mplus* software program uses a FIML estimation operating under the assumption that data are missing at random (*MAR*). *MAR* assumes that the reason for missing data is either random or random after incorporating other variables measured in the study (Arbuckle 1996; Little 1995).

Results

The results are presented in two parts. First, we describe varying developmental trajectories of social withdrawal and the predictors of varying class membership. We also describe factors that predicted initial status as well as growth within class (i.e., the predictors of the intercept and slope within each class); specifically, we describe interactive, relationship, and group-level factors. Second, for those participants who had a mutual best friendship when they made the transition from elementary-to-middle school (fall semester, grade 6), we examined the relations between a variety of friendship constructs and the developmental pathways of social withdrawal.

Model testing was used to determine growth patterns of social withdrawal, the number of distinct class trajectories, and the relations with covariates from the fall of fifth grade *for the initial level* and from the fall of sixth grade for the *rate of growth*. To evaluate which model best fit the growth pattern for the whole sample, intercept-only, intercept+linear, and intercept+linear+nonlinear (quadratic) growth models were fit to the data. The intercept+linear growth model was selected as the baseline model given that it appeared to provide the most parsimonious fit to the data. During the estimation of mixture models, 500 different random start values were initiated to ensure that maximum likelihood (ML) estimation searches for a global maximum solution and prevent local maximized solutions that ML estimation may have when the estimation algorithm searches for an optimum solution.

Based on the intercept+linear growth model, GGMM tested whether the entire sample consisted of two or more distinct subgroups that have different patterns of social withdrawal trajectories. We estimated fit indices for one-to-four classes (see Table 8.4). Models with different numbers of latent classes were compared to evaluate which model provided the best fit to the data. Because models with different numbers of classes are not nested, a model comparison was conducted using a series of fit indices such as the Bayesian Information Criterion (*BIC*; Schwarz 1978), the sample size adjusted *BIC* (*SSA BIC*; Sclove 1987), and the Akaike Information Criterion (*AIC*; Akaike 1987). Lower scores represent better fitting models. Entropy refers to the average classification accuracy in assigning individuals to classes; values range from 0 to 1, with higher scores reflecting a better accuracy in classification of class membership. As shown in Table 8.4, the model fit improved when more latent classes were included. However, the Lo-Mendell-Rubin (*LMR*) likelihood ratio test of model fit indicated that the increment of estimate from a model with three classes to a model with four classes was not significant ($p = 0.1905$). Thus, the three-class model was chosen as optimal in that it best balanced goodness-of-fit and parsimony.

Heterogeniety of trajectory patterns and latent class membership

Growth patterns of developmental trajectories, characteristics of class membership, and associations between a set of covariates and class trajectories are described in this section. Three distinct trajectory classes of social withdrawal were identified: (1) A *low-stable* social withdrawal trajectory, consisting of 333 children (84.9% of the sample) whose social withdrawal scores started low in the fall of grade 5

Table 8.4 Model comparison

Class	Loglikelihood	# of parameter	BIC	SSA BIC	AIC	Entropy	LRT p-value for k^{-1}
1 (growth model)	−7,861.350	19	15,838.521	15,778.223	15,760.700	−	−
2	−1,657.426	38	3,541.761	3,421.188	3,390.853	0.921	0.0986
3	−1,562.072	57	3,464.507	3,283.648	3,238.145	0.935	0.1291
4	−1,490.388	69	3,392.794	3,173.859	3,118.777	0.974	0.1905

BIC Bayesian information criterion; *SSABIC* sample-size adjusted BIC; *AIC* Akaike information criterion; *LRT* Loglikelihood ratio test; *Entropy* classification accuracy in assigning participants to classes.

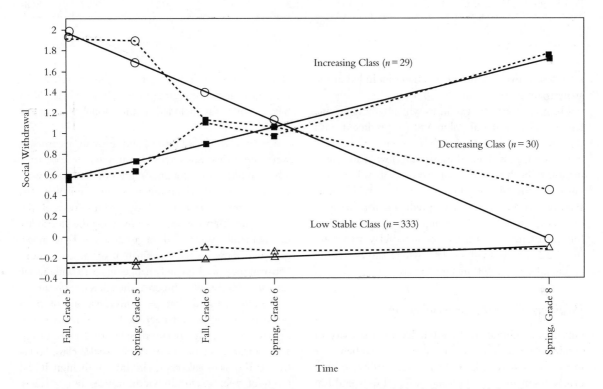

Figure 8.3 Mean class trajectories (*dashed lines*) and fitted mean trajectories (*solid lines*) for social withdrawal.

and remained low throughout elementary (grade 5 fall and spring) and middle school (grade 6 fall and spring; grade 8 spring); (2) a *decreasing* social withdrawal trajectory, comprising 30 participants (7.7% of the sample) who exhibited the highest level of social withdrawal in the fall of grade 5 and decreased thereafter through to the eight grade; and (3) an *increasing* trajectory, comprising 29 participants (7.3% of the sample) whose social withdrawal scores were rela-

tively high in the fall of grade 5 (i.e., higher than the low-stable class and lower than the decreasing class), became increasingly withdrawn through to the eighth grade, and eventually displayed the highest level of social withdrawal in that latter grade. Model-estimated means and mean trajectories for the three-class general growth mixture solution are presented in Figure 8.3. The estimated linear mean trajectories fitted mean class trajectories reasonably well. Latent

Table 8.5 Descriptive statistics for covariates across three trajectory classes

Covariates	Increasing		Decreasing		Low stable	
	Mean/%	SD	Mean/%	SD	Mean/%	SD
Sex (Female)	62.1%		46.7%		51.1%	
Prosocial Behavior (fall, G5)	0.56	1.04	0.38	0.90	−0.03	0.69
Friendship Involvement (fall, G5)	75.9%		63.3%		65.2%	
Peer Exclusion/Vic (fall, G5)	0.26	0.91	0.44	0.91	−0.13	0.59
Prosocial Behavior (fall, G6)	0.26	0.77	−0.02	0.62	0.11	0.84
Friendship Involvement (fall, G6)	89.7%		66.7%		62.2%	
Friendship Stability (fall to spring, G5)	41.4%		53.3%		39.0%	
Peer Exclusion/Vic (fall, G6)	0.49	1.31	0.13	0.71	0.02	0.84

class descriptive statistics of covariates included in the analysis are presented in Table 8.5.

Of interest was the extent to which factors (a) differentiated class membership and (b) predicted both the initial status and growth of social withdrawal within each class. Thus, the analyses allowed an examination of both ameliorating and exacerbating factors vis-à-vis the development of social withdrawal. Results revealed class-specific predictors for the three distinct patterns of developmental trajectory. We found that some constructs predicted class membership and growth within class, whereas others only predicted growth within a given class.

Predictors of latent class membership

Given our interests in the multi-level complexity of children's social world, interactive (prosocial behavior in the fall of grades 5 and 6), relationship (friendship involvement in the fall of grades 5 and 6; friendship stability during grade 5) and group-level (peer exclusion/victimization in the fall of grades 5 and 6) factors were included in model-building as a means of improving model fit and accuracy of assignments of individuals to valid classes (Muthén 2003). Because a major goal of the study was to identify factors that related to a transition period wherein children moved from elementary to middle school, we defined the growth function (i.e., slope) with middle school entry (sixth grade, fall semester) covariates including prosocial behavior, friendship involvement (presence or

absence), peer exclusion/victimization as well as the previous school year's (fifth grade) stability of friendship. Sex of child was included in the model as a control variable.

Latent class membership and growth parameters were simultaneously regressed on a set of covariates. Then, multinomial logistic regression analyses were conducted to test which predictors discriminated class membership. This required designating one of the classes as a reference group and predicting the probability of class membership in a given group versus the reference group. To allow for the examination of the associations between the covariates and changes in social withdrawal, the *low-stable* class was chosen as the reference group.

Results revealed that peer nominations of both prosocial behavior and peer exclusion/victimization in grade 5 uniquely discriminated both the decreasing and increasing classes from the *low-stable* class. Relative to the *low-stable* class, children with high initial levels of peer exclusion/victimization (est. = 1.260, $SE = 0.294$) and prosocial behavior (est. = 1.061, $SE = 0.289$) in the fall of fifth grade had a greater probability of being in the *decreasing* class, in which the trajectory started out at the highest level of social withdrawal in the fall of grade 5 and gradually decreased over time. These same constructs (exclusion/victimization and prosocial behavior), as assessed in the fall of fifth grade, also predicted a greater likelihood of being in the *increasing* class, relative to the *low-stable* class (est. = 1.203, $SE = 0.344$; est = 0.875, $SE = 0.341$, respectively).

Table 8.6 Parameter estimates for three-class GGMM model with covariates

Parameter	Increasing class		Decreasing class		Low stable class	
	Estimate	SE	Estimate	SE	Estimate	SE
Intercept						
Sex	0.829	0.264	0.709	0.382	−0.071	0.044
Prosocial behavior (G5 fall)	0.208	0.143	0.077	0.124	0.117★★★	0.031
Friendship involvement (G5 fall)	0.010	0.214	−0.264	0.337	0.004	0.041
Peer exclusion/Vic (G5 fall)	0.371★★	0.138	−0.116	0.133	0.163★★★	0.037
Slope						
Sex	−0.368★★★	0.058	−0.015	0.088	0.009	0.010
Prosocial behavior (G6 fall)	0.043★	0.022	0.094	0.050	0.002	0.005
Friendship involvement (G6 fall)	−0.621★★★	0.134	−0.075	0.105	−0.012	0.010
Friendship stability (G5)	−0.247★★★	0.053	−0.079	0.095	0.006	0.010
Peer exclusion/Vic (G6 fall)	−0.003	0.014	0.292★★★	0.066	0.009	0.007

★$p = 0.05$. ★★$p < 0.01$. ★★★$p < 0.001$.

Exclusion/victimization after the transition from elementary-to-middle school (i.e., fall, grade 6) marginally differentiated the *increasing* trajectory pattern from that of the *low-stable* reference group, suggesting that peer exclusion and victimization *after* the school transition may be a unique risk factor for being in the *increasing* class membership, relative to the low-stable class (est. = 0.333, $SE = 0.207$). Friendship involvement in the fall of sixth grade (after the middle school transition) differentiated the *increasing* class from both the *low-stable* and *decreasing* classes when the decreasing class was designated as a reference group (est = 2.000, $SE = 0.790$; est = 1.827, $SE = 0.868$, respectively), indicating that having a reciprocal friend after the school transition predicted a *greater* likelihood of being in the *increasing* class, relative to the low-stable or decreasing classes. This particular finding was further investigated below with regard to the friendship factors.

Predictors of initial status and growth within class

All of the predictors, with the exception of friendship involvement in the fifth grade, were significantly associated with within-class growth (Table 8.6).

THE INCREASING TRAJECTORY CLASS

For children in the *increasing* group, exclusion/victimization predicted the initial level of social withdrawal in the fifth grade (this class trajectory started at a moderately high initial level of social withdrawal relative to the other two groups). An unstable friendship in the fifth grade and the absence of a mutual best friendship in the sixth grade were found to exacerbate this group's social withdrawal over time. Greater prosocial behavior after the school transition in the fall of grade 6 also predicted increased growth of withdrawal over time.

THE DECREASING TRAJECTORY CLASS

Children in the *decreasing* trajectory of social withdrawal actually entered the study at the highest level of withdrawal relative to the children in the other two trajectories. Significantly, if the children in this group experienced less exclusion and victimization *after* the school transition, they were more likely to show a decrease in social withdrawal over time. There was no significant predictor of initial status for this class.

THE LOW-STABLE TRAJECTORY CLASS

As expected, a substantial proportion of the participants (85%) displayed a consistently low level of social withdrawal over time without any notable growth. Yet, in terms of within-class initial status for the *low-stable* class, those who experienced greater peer exclusion/victimization and exhibited more prosocial behavior were more likely to evidence higher initial social withdrawal in the fifth grade. There was no significant predictor for within-class growth for this class.

Friendship factors as buffers or exacerbators of social withdrawal

As noted previously, results from analyses predicting latent class membership indicated that children who had a mutual friendship after the transition from elementary-to-middle school were more likely to be in the *increasing* trajectory class, relative to the *low stable* and *decreasing* classes, suggesting that friendship involvement may have a different impact on children's behavior depending on class membership. To better understand this unexpected finding, we attempted to distinguish between friendships that may serve as buffers and those that serve as exacerbators of maladjustment after the participants made the transition from elementary-to-middle school. To do so, we performed follow-up analyses (Latent Growth Curve Modeling) to examine the trajectory of social withdrawal with an expanded set of relationship-level friendship variables as covariates. The friendship covariates were included to examine the influence of friendship factors on both the initial level of social withdrawal and on changes over time. These analyses focused on those children who had a mutual best friendship after the transition from elementary-to-middle school (65% of the sample).

The expanded set of friendship covariates included the reciprocal best friend's own initial level of social withdrawal at the outset of the study (fall, grade 5), the best friend's own level of exclusion/victimization and withdrawal at middle school entry (fall, grade 6), and the target child's perception of friendship quality in the sixth grade. It is important to note that the best friend at middle school entry was not necessarily the focal child's best friend during the fifth grade. Because the index of friendship quality was available for only a subset of the total sample, only those participants who

had an identifiable mutual friend and relevant data for the friendship covariates were included in the further analysis; the listwise deletion method was used ($n = 262$).

THE FRIENDED GROUP: PREDICTORS OF INITIAL STATUS AND GROWTH OVER TIME

To examine why some children start at a higher initial level of social withdrawal (i.e., intercept) and change (i.e., slope) more or less than others, the LGCM was performed. The variances of the intercept and slope were 0.704 ($z = 10.209$) and 0.065 ($z = 9.414$), respectively; both are significantly different from zero, showing that there were significant individual variations of initial status and growth on social withdrawal. The overall fit indices for the latent growth curve model with the friendship covariates indicated that this model did fit the data relatively well, $\chi^2 (29) = 95.76$, $p < 0.001$; comparative fit index (CFI) = 0.909, Tucker-Lewis Index (TLI) = 0.891, root mean square error of approximation (RMSEA) = 0.094 (with 90% confidence interval of 0.073, 0.115); Akaike (AIC) = 5,724.52. This model had a better fit than the interaction model that included the identical friendship covariates *plus* an interaction variable between friend's social withdrawal and perceived friend's support examining the potential interactive effect of friendship quality and the degree of social withdrawal, $\chi^2 (33) = 106.97$, $p < 0.001$; CFI = 0.901, TLI = 0.880, RMSEA = 0.092 (with 90% CI of 0.073, 0.112); AIC = 55,872.29.

Although friendship quality and the best friends' level of exclusion/victimization were not significant predictors of growth, the reciprocal friends' levels of social withdrawal both in grades 5 and 6 were significantly and positively related to the intercept (grade 5; est = 0.222, $SE = 0.072$) and to the slope (grade 6; est = 0.073, $SE = 0.026$), respectively. Results indicated that the greater the best friend's social withdrawal, the more likely it was that the target child would be highly withdrawn in the fifth grade. It was also revealed that children whose best friends were socially withdrawn in the sixth grade (after the school transition), were more likely to evidence a pattern of increasing growth in social withdrawal over time.

Discussion

Few researchers have examined long-term developmental trajectories of social withdrawal. Those that have typically report that social withdrawal is relatively stable and that the late childhood and early adolescent outcomes of the phenomenon are by-and-large, negative (see Rubin et al. 2003 for a relevant review). Notably, with the development of complex statistical procedures that allow examination of intraindividual change, there is growing evidence of heterogeneity in behavioral and developmental psychopathology growth trajectories. Significantly, in this study, we discovered three different developmental pathways of social withdrawal from the period beginning with the fall of the "senior" year of elementary school (fifth grade), across the transition into the "freshman" year of middle school (sixth grade), and into early adolescence and the "senior" year of middle school (eighth grade). Using General Growth Mixture Modeling, three latent growth trajectory classes of social withdrawal identified: (a) *increasing*; (b) *decreasing*; and (c) *low-stable* classes.

Given that the participants were drawn from a community sample, as we anticipated, a substantial proportion of the participants (85%) could best be described as maintaining a *low-stable* trajectory of social withdrawal. However, approximately 8% of the sample exhibited a *decreasing* trajectory of social withdrawal from middle childhood through early adolescence, suggesting that not all withdrawn children maintain their risk status. In contrast, approximately 7% of the sample demonstrated an *increasing* pattern of social withdrawal over time. Although small in size, the identification of these two sub-samples is particularly notable because the only other study of trajectories of social withdrawal (from grades 1 to 6) similarly identified these same three patterns—a low-stable (*normative*) group (86% of the sample), a *decreasing* group (5%), and an *increasing* (9%) group (Booth-LaForce and Oxford 2006, submitted).

Predictors of initial status, growth within class, and latent class membership

Drawing from conceptual models developed by Hinde (1987) and Rubin et al. (2006a), we examined a set of covariates as predictors of initial status, within-class growth, and class membership that characterized *individual* characteristics of the target children and their best friends, the extent to which individuals *interacted* with others in a prosocial manner, the quality of the target children's best *friendships*, and the *group* status that the target children had achieved within their respective schools (in this case, the extent to which they were excluded [rejected] and victimized by the peer group). Significantly, important class-specific predictors were revealed for the three distinct withdrawal trajectories. Some factors predicted initial class membership and growth within each class; others only predicted growth within each class.

THE DECREASING TRAJECTORY

Children in the *decreasing* trajectory entered the fall of grade 5 with the highest level of withdrawal relative to the children in the other two trajectories. Despite their initially high levels of withdrawal, however, if these children experienced less exclusion and victimization after the transition to middle school, they were more likely to show a decrease in social withdrawal over time. This finding is consistent with those of Gazelle and Rudolph (2004) who reported that when anxious-solitary youth experienced less peer exclusion they displayed an *increase* in social approach. Importantly, our findings along with those of Gazelle and Rudolph (2004) and Salmivalli and Isaacs (2005) suggest that withdrawn children may experience increased motivation to engage others in interaction when the social landscape becomes "kinder" and "gentler." Although bullying and victimization increases in frequency and intensity during the middle school years (Juvonen et al. 2004), perhaps those withdrawn children who experience less peer exclusion and victimization than their classmates gain greater confidence in social interactions, thereby becoming increasingly sociable.

THE INCREASING TRAJECTORY

For the *increasing* class, peer exclusion in the fifth grade predicted initial status, a finding that was not surprising because it is well known that negative peer relationships (exclusion and victimization) place *all* children at risk for social and emotional difficulties (Rubin et al. 2006a). However, the finding that peer

exclusion and victimization were significant predictors for both the increasing and decreasing classes is
notable because it clearly highlights the central role of
peer group adversity (or lack thereof) in the development course of social withdrawal during late childhood and early adolescence. Also newsworthy were
the findings that the absence of a mutual friendship
and the presence of unstable best friendships further
exacerbated social withdrawal for children in the
increasing class. Thus, significant risk factors for these
children included both the lack of a friendship as they
made the transition into middle school and unstable
best friendship involvement during their last year of
elementary school. When faced with a series of
"unsuccessful," unstable close dyadic relationships,
withdrawn children may increasingly remove themselves from social encounters. In this regard, withdrawal may be viewed as a defensive or protective
coping strategy. Indeed, there is some evidence to
indicate that withdrawn children without mutual best
friendships are viewed by their peers as less sociable
and popular than withdrawn children with mutual
best friendships (Rubin et al. 2006b). Taken together,
the findings of the present study strongly suggest that
difficulties at the group and relationship levels of social
complexity may collide for some withdrawn children,
thereby making the transition from elementary to
middle school all the more difficult, as was evidenced
by increased growth of social withdrawal.

PREDICTORS OF CLASS MEMBERSHIP
Exclusion and victimization in the fifth grade uniquely
distinguished both the *increasing* and *decreasing* classes
from the *low-stable* class. Note that both the increasing
and decreasing classes demonstrated a higher initial
level of social withdrawal than did the low-stable class.
Thus, our results fit nicely with previous research
findings demonstrating strong associations between
problematic peer relations and social withdrawal
during late childhood and early adolescence (e.g.,
Ollendick et al. 1990).

Interestingly, however, peers' perceptions of the
extent to which children were altruistic and prosocial
also discriminated the increasing and decreasing trajectory groups from the low-stable class. The extant
literature suggests that socially withdrawn children

are compliant to the requests of others, unassertive and
non-managerial when they approach peers, and generally well-behaved (e.g., Stewart and Rubin 1995).
The prosocial behavior construct in the present study
comprised such items as *Someone who is polite*, and
Someone who waits his or her turn. In the social worlds of
late-elementary school and middle-school children,
within which dominance appears to be associated with
perceived popularity (e.g., Rose et al. 2004), it may be
that the quiet, unassertive, well-behaved, and submissive child is not viewed as preferable company by peers,
thereby leaving her or him disengaged from peer
group. Within-class analyses also revealed that greater
prosocial behavior after the middle school transition
predicted increased growth of withdrawal over time
for the *increasing-class*. Thus, despite best efforts to
behave in a kind and prosocial fashion (perhaps in an
attempt to protect against bullying and peer manipulation), such behaviors may, ironically, work *against* the
better interests of the socially withdrawn child.

A somewhat unexpected finding was that friendship involvement in the fall of grade 6, immediately
after the school transition, distinguished the *increasing*
class from both the *low-stable* and *decreasing* classes.
This finding led us to examine whether the characteristics of the target children's best friend and the
quality of the friendship served as buffers or exacerbators of the developmental course of social withdrawal
for particular subgroups.

Friended children: Predictors of initial status and growth

It is well-known that friends are likely to share similar characteristics (Rubin et al. 2006a). And when
friends share similarities in maladaptation, friendship
appears to be a risk rather than a protective factor
(e.g., Dishion et al. 1996; Haselager et al. 1998;
Rubin et al. 2006b). Results from the present study
certainly support this supposition. In follow-up
analyses focused on all children with mutual best
friends at the start of middle school, children who
had a socially withdrawn friend were more likely to
show an initially high level of social withdrawal at
the outset of the study (fall, grade 5). More importantly, having a socially withdrawn friend after the

school transition (fall, grade 6) appeared to increase children's social withdrawal over time.

What might account for this negative friendship influence? Perhaps when withdrawn children interact with their best friends, they engage in co-ruminative exchanges (Rose 2002). Given that the best friends of many withdrawn children are similarly withdrawn and excluded/victimized, discussions between friends may focus on negative thoughts and feelings about themselves and about the negative aspects of their social experiences in school. In this way, co-ruminative activity may lead to increased withdrawal from the peer group for these children and their friends.

Importantly, the index of friendship quality used in this study did not predict growth in social withdrawal and our hypothesized model had a better model fit than the alternative model that included an interaction effect between the best friend's level of social withdrawal and the quality of the best friendship. Perhaps because socially withdrawn children view their friendships as less helpful and fun than those of non-withdrawn children (see Rubin et al. 2006b), quality may be less influential on their level of social withdrawal than their best friends' behavioral characteristics. Additional research is clearly required to better understand the influence of having a close and positive friendship in the lives of socially withdrawn children.

Nonetheless, the findings highlight the significance of friendship in predicting developmental trajectories of social withdrawal in terms of the characteristics that their friends bring to the relationship. That is, if a child's mutual friend is less socially withdrawn, he or she is less likely to become withdrawn over time; alternatively, if a child's friend is socially withdrawn, he or she is more likely to show an increase in social withdrawal. These findings add to the growing literature on the protective and risk factors associated with peer exclusion and homophilous relationships (e.g., Gazelle and Rudolph 2004; Salmivalli and Isaacs 2005).

The present study did have a number of limitations. First, friendships were only studied within the school context. It may well be that friendships outside of school affect growth trajectories of social withdrawal. Indeed, outside-of-school friends are generally neglected in the child and adolescent development literatures. The foci of the study included such facets of friendship as reciprocal friendship involvement, stability of friendship, friendship quality and friends' level of social withdrawal. However, we only examined the target child's perceptions of friendship quality; it may be that the friend's perceptions of quality were unlike those of the target. Thus, in subsequent research, researchers might do well to consider the dyadic perspective on the quality of friendship. Furthermore, whilst our focus on friendships in relation to trajectories of social withdrawal was unique, friendships often exist within a larger peer group network, which may also impact socially withdrawn behavior over time. Researchers would do well to consider the importance of these other types of peer relationships in future work to further elucidate the complex linkages between the individual, relationship and group levels of social complexity. Beyond peer relationships, it is important to acknowledge the potential significance of other close relationships in children's lives (e.g., parent–child and sibling relationships). In fact, very little is known of the parenting experiences and parent–child relationships of socially withdrawn middle schoolers and adolescents. Even less is known of the effects of these relationships on the developmental course of withdrawal. This latter emphasis on parenting and family relationships would be a significant avenue of future research.

It is also important to note that the sizes of our *increasing* and *decreasing* trajectory classes were small; this may reflect the characteristics of a community sample. Clearly additional research is needed to replicate our findings and to better understand differences between the *increasing* and *decreasing* trajectory groups. Figure 8.3 clearly demonstrates that while these two groups did not differ in social withdrawal throughout the sixth grade, differences became striking by the end of middle school (eight grade). It may be the case that certain aspects of the sixth grade masked possible underlying differences in these trajectories. For example, upon entry into middle school, children are faced with both familiar *and* unfamiliar peers. It is possible, therefore, that despite some changes in behavior, some elementary-school "reputations" persist throughout the first-year of middle school because they are perpetuated by "old" or familiar elementary school classmates. Researchers could consider teacher- and also self-reports of withdrawn behavior to further explore possible differences in behavior among *increasing* and *decreasing* class children in the sixth grade.

Peer exclusion, victimization, and friendlessness have been previously identified as major risk factors for internalizing and externalizing difficulties (see Rubin et al. 2006a); current findings strongly suggest that these factors also exacerbate socially withdrawn trajectories. Given the strong associations between social withdrawal, peer difficulties, and also internalizing difficulties (e.g., Gazelle and Ladd 2003), the next step for researchers is to examine the influence of internalizing difficulties on the developmental course of social withdrawal from childhood to early adolescence.

Despite these limitations, a primary strength of this study of social withdrawal was its use of five waves and four years of longitudinal data for a large community sample of children/young adolescents experiencing the transition from elementary-to-middle school. Additionally, the use of peer assessments derived from multiple "observers" was a clear strength of the study. Using a person-oriented approach, we discovered heterogeneous developmental trajectories of social withdrawal. These trajectories were predicted by multi-level social complexities such as individual characteristics, friendship constructs and characteristics, and peer-group experiences to better understand the nature of developmental pathways of social withdrawal.

References

Akaike, H. (1987). Factor analysis and AIC. *Psychometrika*, *52*, 317–332.

Arbuckle, J. (1996). Full information estimation in the presence of incomplete data. In G. A. Marcoulides, & R. E. Schumacker (Eds.) *Advanced structural equation modeling*. Mahwah, New Jersey: Lawrence Erlbaum Associates.

Asendorpf, J. (1993). Abnormal shyness in children. *Journal of Child Psychology and Psychiatry*, *34*, 1069–1081.

Barber, B., & Olsen, J. (2004). Assessing the transitions to middle and high school. *Journal of Adolescent Research*, *19*, 3–30.

Berndt, T., Hawkins, J., & Jiao, Z. (1999). Influences of friends and friendship on adjustment to junior high school. *Merrill Palmer Quarterly*, *45*, 13–41.

Boivin, M., & Hymel, S. (1997). Peer experiences and social self-perceptions: a sequential model. *Developmental Psychology*, *33*, 135–145.

Boivin, M., Hymel, S., & Bukowski, W. (1995). The roles of social withdrawal, peer rejection, and victimization by peers in predicting loneliness and depressed mood in childhood. *Development and Psychopathology*, *7*, 765–785.

Bowker, A., Bukowski, W., Zargarpour, S., & Hoza, B. (1998). A structural and functional analysis of a two-dimensional model of withdrawal. *Merrill-Palmer Quarterly*, *44*, 447–463.

Brendgen, M., Vitaro, F., & Bukowski, W. (2000). Deviant friends and early adolescents' emotional and behavioral adjustment. *Journal of Research on Adolescence*, *10*, 173–189.

Bukowski, W., Hoza, B., & Boivin, M. (1994). Measuring friendship quality during pre- and early adolescence: The development and psychometric properties of the Friendship Qualities Scale. *Journal of Social and Personal Relationships*, *11*(3), 472–484.

Dishion, T., Spracklen, K., Andrews, D., & Patterson, G. (1996). Deviancy training in male adolescents friendships. *Behavior Therapy*, *27*(3), 373–390.

Furman, W. (1996). The measurement of friendship perceptions: Conceptual and methodological issues. In W. M. Bukowski, A. F. Newcomb, & W. W. Hartup (Eds.) *The company they keep: Friendship in childhood and adolescence* (pp. 41–65). New York: Cambridge University Press.

Furman, W., & Buhrmester, D. (1985). Children's perceptions of the personal relationships in their social networks. *Developmental Psychology*, *21*, 1016–1024.

Gazelle, H., & Ladd, G. (2003). Anxious solitude and peer exclusion: A diathesis-stress model of internalizing trajectories in childhood. *Child Development*, *74*, 257–278.

Gazelle, H., & Rudolph, K. (2004). Moving toward and away from the world: Social approach and avoidance trajectories in anxious solitary youth. *Child Development*, *75*, 829–849.

Haselager, G., Hartup, W., van Lieshout, C., & Riksen-Walraven, J. (1998). Similarities between friends and non-friends in middle childhood. *Child Development*, *69*(4), 1198–1208.

Hinde, R. (1987). *Individuals, relationships and culture: Links between ethology and the social sciences*. NY: Cambridge University Press.

Hodges, E., Boivin, M., Vitaro, F., & Bukowski, W. (1999). The power of friendship: Protection against an escalating cycle of peer victimization. *Developmental Psychology*, *35*, 94–101.

Hogue, A., & Steinberg, L. (1995). Homophily of internalized distress in adolescent peer groups. *Developmental Psychology*, *31*, 897–906.

Hymel, S., Rubin, K., Rowden, L., & LeMare, L. (1990). Children's peer relationships: Longitudinal prediction of internalizing and externalizing problems from middle to late childhood. *Child Development*, *61*(6), 2004–2021.

Hymel, S., Woody, E., & Bowker, A. (1993). Social withdrawal in childhood: Considering the child's perspective. In K. H. Rubin, & J. B. Asendorpf (Eds.) *Social withdrawal, inhibition, & shyness in childhood* (pp. 237–262). Hillsdale, NJ: Erlbaum.

Juvonen, J., Le, V, Kaganoff, T., Augustine, C., & Constant, L. (2004). *Focus on the wonder years: Challenges facing the American middle school*. Santa Monica, CA: RAND.

Kochenderfer, B., & Ladd, G. (1996). Peer victimization: Cause or consequence of school maladjustment? *Child Development*, *67*, 1305–1317.

Ladd, G., & Troop-Gordon, W. (2003). The role of chronic peer difficulties in the development of children's psychological adjustment problems. *Child Development*, *74*, 1344–1367.

Little, R. J. A. (1995). Modeling the drop-out mechanism in longitudinal studies. *Journal of the American Statistical Association*, *90*, 1112–1121.

Mash, E. & Barkley, R. (Eds.) (2003). *Child Psychopathology* (2nd ed). New York: Guilford.

Masten, A., Morison, P., & Pellegrini, D. (1985). A revised class play method of peer assessment. *Developmental Psychology*, *21*(3), 523–533.

Miller, R., & Wright, D. W. (1995). Detecting and correcting attrition bias in longitudinal family research. *Journal of Marriage and Family*, *57*, 921–929.

Muthén, B. (2003). Statistical and substantive checking in growth mixture modeling: Comment on Bauer and Curran (2003). *Psychological Methods*, *8*, 369–377.

Muthén, B., & Muthén, L. (2004). *Mplus user's guide* (3rd ed.). Los Angeles, CA: Muthén & Muthén.

Muthén, B., & Muthén, L. (2006). *Mplus user's guide* (4th ed.). Los Angeles, CA: Muthén & Muthén.

Muthén, B., & Shedden, K. (1999). Finite mixture modeling with mixture, outcomes using the EM algorithm. *Biometrics*, *55*, 463–469.

Ollendick, T., Greene, R., Weist, M., & Oswald, D. (1990). The predictive validity of teacher nominations: A five-year follow-up of at risk youth. *Journal of Abnormal Child Psychology*, *18*, 699–713.

Parker, J., & Asher, S. (1989). *Friendship quality questionnaire-revised: instrument and administrative manual*. Available from the author, Department of Psychology, Penn State University.

Parker, J., & Asher, S. (1993). Friendship and friendship quality in middle childhood: Links with peer group acceptance and feelings of loneliness and social dissatisfaction. *Developmental Psychology*, *29*, 611–621.

Rose, A. (2002). Co-rumination in the friendships of girls and boys. *Child Development*, *73*, 1830–1843.

Rose, A., Swenson, L., & Waller, E. (2004). Overt and relational aggression and perceived popularity: Developmental differences in concurrent and prospective relations. *Developmental Psychology*, *40*, 378–387.

Rubin, K. (1993). The waterloo longitudinal project: Correlates and consequences of social withdrawal from childhood to adolescence. In K. H. Rubin, & J. B. Asendorpf (Eds.) *Social withdrawal, inhibition, & shyness in childhood* (pp. 291–314). Hillsdale, NJ: Erlbaum.

Rubin, K., & Asendorpf, J. (1993). *Social withdrawal, inhibition, and shyness in childhood*. Hillsdale, NJ: Erlbaum.

Rubin, K., Bukowski, W., & Parker, J. (2006a). Peer interactions, relationships, and groups. In W. Damon, & N. Eisenberg (Eds.) *Handbook of child psychology: Social, Emotional, and Personality Development* (Vol. 3, 6th ed.). New York: Wiley.

Rubin, K., Burgess, K., Kennedy, A., & Stewart, S. (2003). Social withdrawal in childhood. In E. Mash, & R. Barkley (Eds.) *Child psychopathology* (pp. 372–406, 2nd ed.). New York: Guilford Press.

Rubin, K., Chen, X., & Hymel, S. (1993). The socio-emotional characteristics of extremely aggressive and extremely withdrawn children. *Merrill-Palmer Quarterly*, *39*, 518–534.

Rubin, K., Chen, X., McDougall, P., Bowker, A., & McKinnon, J. (1995). The waterloo longitudinal project: Predicting adolescent internalizing and externalizing problems from early and mid-childhood. *Development and Psychopathology*, *7*, 751–764.

Rubin, K. H., & Coplan, R. J. (2004). Paying attention to and not neglecting social withdrawal and social isolation. *Merrill-Palmer Quarterly*, *50*, 506–534.

Rubin, K., Hymel, S., & Mills, R. (1989). Sociability and social withdrawal in childhood: Stability and outcomes. *Journal of Personality*, *57*, 237–255.

Rubin, K., Wojslawowicz, J., Burgess, K., Rose-Krasnor, L., & Booth-LaForce, C. (2006b). The friendships of socially withdrawn and competent young adolescents. *Journal of Abnormal Child Psychology*, *34*, 139–153.

Salmivalli, C., & Isaacs, J. (2005). Prospective relations among victimization, rejection, friendlessness, and children's self- and peer-perceptions. *Child Development*, *76*, 1161–1171.

Schneider, B. (1999). A multi-method exploration of the friendships of children considered socially withdrawn by their peers. *Journal of Abnormal Psychology*, *27*, 115–123.

Schneider, B., Younger, A., Smith, T., & Freeman, P. (1998). A longitudinal exploration of the cross-context stability of social withdrawal in early adolescence. *Journal of Early Adolescence, 18,* 734–396.

Schwarz, G. (1978). Estimating the dimension of a model. *Annals of Statistics, 6,* 461–464.

Sclove, S. (1987). Application of model-selection criteria to some problems in multivariate analysis. *Psychometrika, 52,* 333–343.

Stewart, S. L., & Rubin, K. H. (1995). The social problem solving skills of anxious-withdrawn children. *Development and Psychopathology, 7,* 323–336.

Sullivan, H. S. (1953). *The interpersonal theory of psychiatry.* New York: Norton.

Wojslawowicz Bowker, J. C., Rubin, K. H., Burgess, K. B., Rose-Krasnor, L., & Booth-LaForce, C. L. (2006). Behavioral characteristics associated with stable and fluid best friendship patterns in middle childhood. *Merrill-Palmer Quarterly, 52,* 671–693.

Zeller, M., Vannatta, K., Schafer, J., & Noll, R. B. (2003). Behavioral reputation: A cross-age perspective. *Developmental Psychology, 39*(1), 129–139.

Social Functioning and Adjustment in Chinese Children: The Imprint of Historical Time

Xinyin Chen, Guozhen Cen, Dan Li, and Yunfeng He

Developmental research has indicated that how children behave in social situations is important for their social and psychological adjustment. According to studies conducted in the United States and Canada, sociable-prosocial behavior is associated with peer acceptance, teacher-rated competence, and academic achievement (e.g., Morison & Masten, 1991). In contrast, aggression-disruption is associated with poor quality of social relationships and learning problems (e.g., Coie, Terry, Lenox, Lochman, & Hyman, 1995). In addition, shy-anxious behavior may contribute to difficulties in peer interactions and socioemotional adjustment (e.g., Coplan, Prakash, O'Neil, & Armer, 2004; Rubin, Chen, McDougall, Bowker, & McKinnon, 1995). Therefore, it has been argued that whereas sociable-prosocial behavior is adaptive and indicative of social competence, aggression and shyness-anxiety reflect externalizing and internalizing problems, respectively (Achenbach & Edelbrock, 1981; Rubin, Burgess, & Coplan, 2002).

Nevertheless, the significance of social functioning may be moderated by cultural context. As a result, adaptive and maladaptive behaviors may be defined similarly or differently across cultures (Benedict, 1934; Bornstein, 1995; Chen, 2000). Support for this argument comes from a series of cross-cultural studies (e.g., Casiglia, Lo Coco, & Zappulla, 1998; Chen, Rubin, & Sun, 1992). For example, researchers have

found that, consistent with the literature from the United States and Canada, sociable-prosocial behavior is associated with peer acceptance, leadership, and academic achievement, whereas aggression-disruption is associated with social and school problems in Chinese children (Chen, Rubin, & Li, 1995b; Chen et al., 1992). Unlike aggressive children in the United States and Canada who display mainly externalizing problems (e.g., Coie & Dodge, 1998), however, aggressive children in China experience pervasive difficulties including both externalizing and internalizing problems such as feelings of loneliness and depression (Chen, Rubin, & Li, 1995a). This may be because aggressive and disruptive behaviors are strictly prohibited in Chinese society and children who display deviant behaviors are often publicly criticized and even humiliated by teachers and peers in Chinese schools (Chen, 2000).

Furthermore, inconsistent with the findings based on U.S. and Canadian children (e.g., Rubin & Asendorpf, 1993), shy, anxious, and sensitive behavior has been found to be associated with positive peer relationships, school competence, and psychological well-being in China (e.g., Chen, Dong, & Zhou, 1997; Chen et al., 1995b; Chen et al., 1992). Shy Chinese children are accepted by peers and are well adjusted to the social environment. The social and psychological adjustment of shy children in China may be due to the cultural endorsement of wary, sensitive, and socially restrained behaviors and specific social-ecological conditions.

In the literature (Asendorpf, 1990; Stevenson-Hinde & Shouldice, 1993), shy, wary, and sensitive behavior, derived from conflictual approach–avoidance motives, is taken to reflect internal anxiety and fearfulness and a lack of self-confidence in social-evaluative situations. Because of the cultural values on assertiveness, expressiveness, and competitiveness (Larson, 1999), individuals in the United States and Canada may regard children who display shy behavior as socially incompetent and immature (Rubin & Asendorpf, 1993). When shy children recognize their social difficulties, they tend to develop negative self-perceptions and self-feelings such as depression (e.g., Boivin, Hymel, & Bukowski, 1995). In traditional Chinese culture, however, shy, sensitive, and restrained behaviors are often considered an indication of social accomplishment and maturity; shy-sensitive children are perceived as well behaved and understanding (King & Bond, 1985; Yang, 1986). The cultural endorsement is likely to help shy children obtain social support in peer interactions and develop confidence in social and school performance. In addition, the stable social environment and extensive peer contacts that Chinese children have in school and in the neighborhood may reduce the stress of interpersonal interactions and provide a variety of opportunities for children to establish intimate social relationships and support systems. These social conditions may be particularly beneficial for shy children who tend to experience difficulties in stressful and challenging situations (Chen, 2000).

It should be noted that the construct of shyness-sensitivity in Chen and colleagues' (e.g., Chen et al., 1992) studies may be different from those assessed in studies of social withdrawal in Chinese children (e.g., Chang, 2003; Cheah & Rubin, 2004; Hart et al., 2000). Whereas shyness-sensitivity represents wariness and anxious social reactivity, studies conducted by Chang (2003) and Cheah and Rubin (2004) focused on aspects of social withdrawal such as social solitude, social disinterest, or unsociability (e.g., "kids who are often alone" or "would rather be alone") that are driven by the low approach motivation (Asendorpf, 1990). In Hart et al.'s (2000) study, teachers rated

children's behavior labeled as *reticence* using items such as "wanders aimlessly during free play" and "watches other children playing without joining in." These items, however, appear primarily to assess social solitude because they focus on observable behaviors without tapping internal anxious feelings. As a result, the reticence items may be viewed as similar to the items on passive solitary behavior from the teachers' perspective (e.g., $r = .76$ in the Chinese sample in Hart et al.'s, 2000, study), even though only reticence was related to peer rejection. In this regard, the measure labeled *conflicted shyness* (e.g., "The child seems to want to play with others, but is nervous to"), developed recently by Coplan et al. (2004), may be more comparable with the assessment of shyness-sensitivity in Chen and colleagues' studies.

Social and cultural changes in china

Cross-cultural research has indicated the importance of social and cultural background for children's socio-emotional functioning and adjustment (e.g., Chen et al., 1992). However, social and cultural conditions for individual development are not static but rather constantly changing (Silbereisen, 2000). Indeed, Chinese society has been changing dramatically since the early 1980s, particularly in the last decade. During this period, China has carried out a full-scale reform toward a market economy that allows for the adoption of many aspects of capitalism. The rapid expansion of the market systems to different sectors has led to major changes in economic and social structures. Consequently, there are increased variations in individual and family income, massive movement of the population, decline in the government control of social welfare and protection, and rapid rise in the unemployment rate and competition (e.g., Zhang, 2000). The social and economic changes correspond to the introduction of individualistic values and ideologies such as liberty, individual freedom, and independence, along with advanced technologies from nations in North America and Western Europe. These values and ideologies have been gradually accepted by many Chinese people, especially in the younger generation (e.g., Cai & Wu, 1999; Huang, 1999).

The comprehensive social, economic, and cultural changes have inevitably affected other aspects of the society. Of particular relevance to child development are the significant changes in educational policies and practices in Chinese schools. In the "Outline of the Educational Reform," the Ministry of Education of China has called for modifications of educational goals, models, and methods to accommodate the demands of the market-oriented economy (Yu, 2002). As a result, many schools have expanded the goals of education to include helping children develop social and behavioral qualities that are required for adaptation in the competitive society. Whereas academic achievement continues to be emphasized, children are encouraged to develop social skills such as expression of personal opinions, self-direction, and self-confidence, which have traditionally been neglected in Chinese culture (Xu & Peng, 2001; Yu, 2002).

Children's social functioning and adjustment in the changing society

The linkage between social circumstances and individual behaviors is an important issue in the study of human development. According to the ecological and life-course perspectives (e.g., Bronfenbrenner & Morris, 1998; Elder, 1998), human lives carry the imprint of their particular social worlds that are subject to historical change. Consequently, the development of individual social and psychological functioning cannot be understood without considering "historical structures in which the milieux of their everyday life are organized" (Mills, 1959, p. 157). These arguments have been supported by the results of Elder's studies of the Great Depression in the 1930s (Elder, 1974) and the Iowa farm crisis in the 1980s and 1990s (Elder & Conger, 2000) concerning the effects of economic hardship during stressful times on family organization and child behaviors. The impact of historical conditions has also been demonstrated in recent studies in Eastern European nations (Flanagan, 2000; Silbereisen, Reitzle, & Juang, 2002). The results of these studies indicate that the dramatic transformation in social institutions, such as parliamentary democracy and the capitalistic economy, may affect individual behaviors including financial independence, civic responsibilities, and relationship patterns.

The social structure and cultural context may not only affect the display of a specific behavior in children and adolescents, but more important, impart meanings to the behavior (Chen, 2000). Specifically, macro-level social and cultural conditions are likely to influence group and individual beliefs, attitudes, and value systems, which may serve as guidance for social judgments and evaluations of behaviors (Bornstein, 1995; Kleinman, 1988). These social judgments and evaluations may in turn determine, to a large extent, how others interpret and react to one's behaviors in social interactions, and thus define the functional meanings of the behaviors. Moreover, the feedback from others may affect children's perceptions and feelings about their own competencies and eventually contribute to their adjustment in broad areas (Cole, 1991). Therefore, historical transitions in the society may influence the nature of relations between individual behaviors and social and psychological adjustment. In the present study, we focused on relations between children's social functioning, particularly shyness-sensitivity, and peer acceptance and rejection and school competence at three different time points during the transition of Chinese society over the last decade. We were also interested in how social behaviors were associated with self-reported depression at each time.

The present study

We collected data on children's social functioning and social, school, and psychological adjustment from three cohorts of elementary school children in China. The data were collected in 1990, 1998, and 2002. These three time points represent different phases of social and economic reform in Chinese society. China implemented an internal vitalization policy in rural areas and an open-door policy in some Southern regions in the early 1980s. The full-scale social and economic reform was expanded to cities and other parts of the country in the early 1990s. Since then, the impact of the reform has rapidly spread to various aspects of the society and individual daily lives (Zhang, 2000).

The influence of the social and historical transition on individual attitudes and behaviors and social relationships may be an ongoing process that may occur gradually and cumulatively through a variety of means (Silbereisen, 2000). Whereas children in our 1990 cohort experienced relatively limited influence of the comprehensive reform, children in the 2002 cohort might be socialized in a context in which increased self-oriented cultural values played an important role in social and individual lives. Compared with these two cohorts, the 1998 cohort represented an intermediate phase; children in this cohort might be exposed to different views in the mass media and social settings, and have different socialization experiences in the family and peer group. If this is the case, we would expect that a mixture of traditional values such as self-restraint and new values such as independence and assertiveness might be reflected in social interactions and relationships among children in the 1998 cohort.

In the present study, we were interested in how children's social functioning was related to peer relationships, school achievement, and psychological adjustment at each time and whether the patterns of the relations were different across the cohorts. Researchers who study children's social functioning have focused on sociability-cooperation, aggression-disruption, and shyness-sensitivity (e.g., Morison & Masten, 1991). Although our primary interest was in shyness, examining relations between other aspects of social functioning and adjustment in the three cohorts might help us understand the domain-general or—specific nature of the contextual influence on children's behaviors. We expected that sociability-cooperation would be associated with peer acceptance and school achievement in all three cohorts because socially competent children may be capable of developing effective strategies to cope with stress and adapting to different circumstances (e.g., Chen et al., 1995a; Masten & Coatsworth, 1995). In contrast, because aggressive-disruptive behavior may threaten group harmony and the well-being of others and disrupt the processes of learning, it seems reasonable to expect that aggression would be associated with peer rejection and school adjustment problems. Given that aggressive children are often criticized in public situations in Chinese schools, which may result in negative self-regards (e.g., Cole, 1991), in keeping with previous findings (e.g., Chen et al., 1995a) we also hypothesized that aggression would be associated with psychological difficulties such as depression in Chinese children.

Shyness-sensitivity might be associated with social, school, and psychological adjustment differently in the three cohorts. As social assertiveness and competitiveness are increasingly required in contemporary Chinese society (Xu & Peng, 2001; Yu, 2002), shy-sensitive behavior may be less adaptive and beneficial for social interactions and achievement. Wary, anxious, and restrained reactions that shy children display in stressful and challenging social situations may be considered incompetent or abnormal because they are incompatible with behavioral qualities such as independence, exploration, and self-confidence that are important in the new environment (e.g., Huang, 1999; Xu & Peng, 2001). Thus, shy-sensitive behavior may not be as valued in the society as before. In other words, shy-sensitive behavior may become increasingly unsuitable for the demands of the changing society. Some researchers may argue that the recent findings concerning negative adult and peer attitudes toward social withdrawal in China (e.g., Chang, 2003; Cheah & Rubin, 2004) may indicate the cultural changes on shyness-sensitivity, although we are hesitant to endorse this argument because of the differences in the constructs.

The increase of self-direction and the decline of perceived adult authority in children's social interactions may also undermine the adaptive value of shy-sensitive behavior. Chinese parents and teachers traditionally tend to be highly involved in children's social activities and exert control over children's behaviors (Ho, 1986). Thus, children's social judgments and attitudes are likely to be affected by adults' social standards. The social and school adjustment of shy children found in previous studies (e.g., Chen et al., 1992) may be due in part to the influence of adult norms and standards that support shy-sensitive behavior. As a result of the encouragement of autonomous and assertive behaviors in Chinese schools in recent years (e.g., Yu, 2002), adult influence may become less significant and children may be more independent in making their own judgments in social interactions. Consequently, shy-sensitive children may have difficulties in obtaining social recognition and support from peers. The frustration shy children experience may lead to their increasingly negative attitudes toward others and the school environment, which may in turn exacerbate their social and psychological difficulties. These speculations led us to predict that whereas shyness-sensitivity was associated with peer acceptance, school competence, and academic achievement in the early cohort, the associations would be increasingly weaker in the 1998 and 2002 cohorts. Indeed, we expected that shyness-sensitivity would be associated with social, school, and emotional difficulties in the 2002 cohort.

Gender differences have been found in the prevalence of social functioning in U.S., Canadian, and Chinese children (e.g., Rubin et al., 2002). Girls are generally more shy, anxious, and sensitive than boys (Chen et al., 1995b; Rubin et al., 1995). Concerning gender differences in the relations between shyness and adjustment, findings are mixed in the literature. Whereas some researchers have reported that shy boys display more problems than shy girls in social and psychological areas (e.g., Caspi, Elder, & Bern, 1988; Morison & Masten, 1991), others have found that shy girls have more problems than shy boys (e.g., French, 1990) or have failed to find significant gender differences in shy children's adjustment status (e.g., Bukowski, Gauze, Hoza, & Newcomb, 1993). Shy-sensitive behavior may be perceived as more acceptable for girls than for boys in traditional Chinese culture (Ho, 1986). If the traditional norms are less emphasized in recent years, we would expect that shy girls might receive greater pressure and attempt to regulate their shy and wary behavior in social situations. Nevertheless, as social assertiveness is more required in the competitive environment, girls and boys who maintain their shy-sensitive behavior may both experience more difficulties in social and psychological adjustment.

In short, the systematic historical changes in Chinese society offer a unique opportunity for a quasi-experimental study of era effects on social functioning and adjustment in Chinese children. We sought to examine relations between social functioning, particularly shyness-sensitivity, and social, school, and psychological adjustment in Chinese children at different times of the societal transition. We believe the study provides valuable information about the nature of social functioning in Chinese context and the implications of social context for individual development.

Method

Participants

Three cohorts of children in Shanghai, P. R. China, participated in the study. The data were collected in 1990, 1998, and 2002. There were 429 (226 boys, 203 girls), 390 (181 boys, 209 girls), and 266 (136 boys, 130 girls) third- and fourth-grade children in the three cohorts, respectively. The data for the 1990 cohort were drawn from a larger longitudinal project concerning social competence and peer relationships (e.g., Chen et al., 1995a; Chen et al., 1992). The data for the other two cohorts were collected for the present study. The children in the three cohorts were from ordinary elementary schools. Unlike a small number of key schools in the city in which students were often selected from different areas based on their school performance, students in the ordinary schools came from the area where the school was located. The mean age of the children was 10 years 1 months ($SD = 8$ months), 10 years 3 months ($SD = 7$ months), and 10 years 5 months ($SD = 9$ months).

In the 1990, 1998, and 2002 cohorts, 70%, 63%, and 60% of the children, respectively, were from families in which parents were nonprofessional workers; most of them had an educational level of high school or below high school. And 30%, 37%, and 40% of the children were from scholastic families in which one or both of the parents were teachers, doctors, engineers, or civil officials; their educational levels ranged mainly from college to university graduate. Concerning the family structure, 96%, 98%, and 98% of the children were from intact families, and others were living with one parent because of parental divorce, death, or other reasons. Among the families, 64%, 69%, and 69% consisted of two generations (parents and the child), and 36%, 31%, and 31% consisted of three generations (grandparents, parents, and the child). Of the children, 86%, 93%, and 91% were only children in the family and the others had one or more siblings; the only-child phenomenon has been an integral part of the family and sociocultural background for child development in contemporary China because of the one-child-per-family policy that was implemented in the late 1970s. The average monthly family income (per person) was 161 ($SD = 243$), 816 ($SD = 587$), and

1431 (SD = 1836) *yuan* in 1990, 1998, and 2002, respectively ($1 US = approximately 5.2 *yuan* in 1990 and 8.3 *yuan* in 1998 and 2002). Nonsignificant differences were found among children from the different types of families on the variables and relations of interest in the study. The demographic data for these samples were similar to those reported by the China State Statistics Bureau concerning urban population in China in the past 12 years (e.g., *Bulletin*, 1991, 2003). The samples were representative of elementary school children in urban China at the time.

Procedure

We group administered to the children a peer assessment measure of social functioning, a sociometric nomination measure, and a depression measure. Teachers were asked to complete a rating scale for each participant concerning his or her school-related competence. In addition, data concerning children's leadership and academic achievement were obtained from school records. The same procedure was used in the three cohorts.

The members of our research team carefully examined the items in the measures that were initially developed in the United States, using a variety of formal and informal strategies (e.g., repeated discussion in the research group, interviews with children and teachers, psychometric analysis). We translated and then back-translated the measures to ensure comparability with the English versions. The measures have proved valid and appropriate in Chinese as well as some other cultures (e.g., Casiglia et al., 1998; Chen et al., 1995b). Extensive explanations of the procedure were provided during administration. No evidence was found that Chinese children had difficulties understanding the procedure or the items in the measures.

Measures

PEER ASSESSMENTS OF SOCIAL FUNCTIONING

We conducted peer assessments of social functioning using a Chinese version of the Revised Class Play (RCP; Masten, Morison, & Pelligrini, 1985). The RCP is widely used in the United States and other countries. This technique has been found particularly useful in assessing children's social functioning in different contexts because it taps insiders' perspectives. Consistent with the procedure outlined by Masten et al. (1985), during administration, each child was provided a booklet in which each of 30 behavioral descriptors and the names of all students in the class were printed on each page. After the administrator read one behavioral descriptor, children were requested to nominate up to three classmates who could best play the role if they were to direct a class play. When all children in the class completed their nominations, they turned to the next item, until nominations for all 30 items were obtained. Subsequently, nominations received from all classmates were used to compute each item score for each child. The item scores were standardized within the class to adjust for differences in the number of nominators.

The RCP measure consists of items in broad areas of sociability, aggression, and shyness. Factor analysis of the data in the Chinese samples indicated that the factor structure was similar to that in Masten et al.'s (1985) study except for the isolation items ("often left out," "has trouble making friends," "rather play alone than with others"). These items did not load on the original shyness factor in the Chinese samples and thus were not included in the calculation of the final variables in the present study. Consequently, three variables formed by the items were sociability-cooperation, aggression-disruption, and shyness-sensitivity. Sociability-cooperation included items tapping several aspects of social competence (e.g., "makes new friends easily," "helps others when they need it"). Items in aggression-disruption were concerned with physical and verbal aggressive behaviors (e.g., "gets into a lot of fights," "picks on other kids"). Shyness-sensitivity consisted of items assessing shy-anxious behavior in social context (e.g., "very shy," "feelings get hurt easily"); the constellation of the items indicates social wariness and sensitivity from the peers' perspective (Masten et al., 1985; see Chen et al., 1992, for further details about the measure in Chinese children). Internal reliabilities were .97, .90, and .94 for sociability; .92, .93, and .90 for aggression; and .78, .74, and .73 for shyness in the 1990, 1998, and 2002 cohorts, respectively. Test–retest reliabilities (interval of 2 weeks) based on a sample of Chinese children (N = 132) were .85, .97, and .84 for sociability, aggression, and shyness, respectively.

SOCIOMETRIC NOMINATIONS

Children were asked to nominate up to three classmates whom they most liked to be with and three classmates whom they least liked to be with (positive and negative nominations). The nominations received from all classmates were totaled and then standardized within each class to permit appropriate comparisons. As suggested by other researchers (e.g., Coie et al., 1995), cross-gender nominations were allowed. The positive and negative nominations received from peers provided indexes of peer acceptance and peer rejection, respectively. Test–retest reliabilities were .77 and .93 for positive and negative sociometric nominations, respectively.

TEACHER RATINGS

In Chinese schools, one teacher is usually in charge of a class. This head instructor often teaches a major course and takes care of various social and daily activities of the class. The head teacher usually instructs the same group of children over several years and is very familiar with the students. Following procedures outlined by Hightower et al. (1986), the head teacher was asked to rate each child in his or her class on the 20 items of school-related social competence in the Teacher–Child Rating Scale (T–CRS; Hightower et al., 1986). Teachers rated on a 5-point scale how well each of these items described each child, ranging from 1 (not at all) to 5 (very well).

The items in the measure (e.g., "participates in class discussion," "copes well with failure") involved various aspects of school-related competence such as frustration tolerance, task orientation, and social skills. Consistent with the procedure used in previous studies (e.g., Chen et al., 1995b), a global score of school competence was calculated in this study. The teacher rating scores were standardized within the class to control for the teacher's response style and to allow for appropriate comparisons. The internal reliability of this score was .96, .92, and .94 in the 1990, 1998, and 2002 cohorts, respectively. Test–retest reliability was .86 for teacher-rated school competence in Chinese children.

LEADERSHIP

There are various formal student organizations, which are often hierarchical in nature, in Chinese schools. Leaders of these organizations, elected by peers and teachers, are usually believed to be good students in social and school performance. Leadership at a higher level, such as school or municipal level, is considered as indicating greater competence than that at a lower level, such as the class or within-class group level. Leadership status is moderately associated with other measures of social and school achievement (rs range from .40s to .60s; Chen et al., 1995b). Data on student leadership were collected from school records. Leadership was coded as follows: Students who were group leaders within the class received a score of 1; students who held leadership positions at the class level and at the school or municipal level, or both, received scores of 2 and 3, respectively; and students who did not hold leadership positions were given a score of 0. This information has proved to be a useful and reliable indicator of school competence in Chinese children (e.g., 2-year stability was .72; Chen et al., 1995b). The validity of the measure has also been demonstrated in several studies in predicting Chinese children's social and psychological adjustment (e.g., Chen & Li, 2000; Chen, Rubin, & Li, 1997).

ACADEMIC ACHIEVEMENT

Information concerning academic achievement in Chinese and mathematics was obtained for all participants from the school records. The scores of academic achievement were based on objective examinations conducted by the school. Grades in Chinese and mathematics, reported in the form of a percentage, have been found to be a valid measure of school academic achievement in Chinese children (e.g., Chen et al., 1995b). In the present study, scores on Chinese and mathematics were significantly correlated (rs = .67, .61, and .65, ps < .001, in the three cohorts, respectively) and thus were summed and standardized within the class to form a single index of academic achievement.

DEPRESSION

Children's depression was measured by administering a Chinese version of the Childhood Depression Inventory (CDI; Kovacs, 1992). Each of the 27 items provides three alternative responses from which the participant must choose the one that best describes him or her in the past 2 weeks. The items center on a given thought, feeling, or behavior associated with depression, including self-deprecation, loneliness, reduced social interest, anhedonia, self-hate, self-blame, sleep disturbance, fatigue, somatic concerns, and reduced appetite. The items were scored 0, 1, or 2, with a higher score indicative of greater depression. The measure has proved reliable and valid in Chinese children (e.g., Chen & Li, 2000; Dong Yang & Ollendick, 1994). Internal reliabilities were .84, .84, and .87 in the 1990, 1998, and 2002 cohorts, respectively, in the present study. Following the procedure outlined by Kovacs (1992), a total score of depression was computed by summing all item scores, with higher scores indicative of greater depression.

Results

Descriptive data

Means and standard deviations of the variables for boys and girls in each cohort are presented in Table 8.7. A multivariate analysis of variance (MANOVA) was conducted to examine the overall effects of gender, cohort, and their interactions on all variables. Significant effects of gender, $F(9, 1071) = 29.56$, Wilks = .81, $p < .001$, a Gender × Cohort interaction, $F(9, 1071) = 2.13$, Wilks = .97, $p < .01$, were found. Follow-up univariate analyses indicated that boys had higher scores on negative sociometric nominations, depression, and aggression, and lower scores on positive sociometric nominations, teacher-rated competence, leadership, academic achievement, sociability-cooperation, and shyness-sensitivity than did girls. In addition, the analysis revealed a Gender × Cohort interaction on shyness-sensitivity; boys had significantly lower scores on shyness than did girls in the 1990 and 1998 cohorts, but the difference was nonsignificant in the 2002 cohort. There were no significant grade effects on the variables. Intercorrelations among the variables are presented in Table 8.8. The magnitudes of the correlations were generally moderate, suggesting that these measures tapped different, overlapping aspects of social, school, and psychological adjustment.

Table 8.7 Means and standard deviations of the variables for boys and girls in three cohorts

Variable	1990 cohort Boys	1990 cohort Girls	1998 cohort Boys	1998 cohort Girls	2002 cohort Boys	2002 cohort Girls	F value Gender	F value Cohort	F value Gender × Cohort
Pos. socio. nom.	−0.06	0.11	−0.18	0.17	−0.09	0.11	13.57***	ns	ns
	(0.98)	(1.04)	(1.00)	(0.99)	(1.08)	(0.90)			
Neg. socio. nom.	0.13	−0.22	0.10	−0.14	0.19	−0.20	27.79***	ns	ns
	(1.21)	(0.52)	(1.17)	(0.72)	(1.21)	(0.67)			
TR competence	−0.31	0.37	−0.37	0.35	−0.26	0.27	114.89***	ns	ns
	(0.85)	(1.02)	(0.93)	(0.93)	(0.98)	(0.95)			
Leadership	−0.22	0.35	−0.31	0.12	−0.13	0.15	49.20***	ns	ns
	(0.82)	(1.14)	(0.68)	(1.02)	(0.95)	(1.02)			
Academic ach.	−0.14	0.10	−0.25	0.22	−0.14	0.16	21.92***	ns	ns
	(0.87)	(1.08)	(0.84)	(1.09)	(1.08)	(0.89)			
Depression	10.28	8.51	11.16	8.35	10.48	8.93	18.22***	ns	ns
	(7.01)	(6.39)	(6.62)	(5.46)	(7.42)	(6.36)			
Sociability	−0.17	0.26	−0.26	0.20	−0.14	0.15	40.18***	ns	ns
	(0.74)	(1.26)	(0.47)	(1.19)	(0.74)	(1.21)			
Aggression	0.28	−0.31	0.25	−0.27	0.26	−0.24	76.13***	ns	ns
	(1.26)	(0.28)	(1.33)	(0.32)	(1.19)	(0.62)			
Shyness	−0.32	0.38	−0.25	0.18	−0.09	0.11	53.44***	ns	5.40**
	(0.60)	(1.18)	(0.69)	(1.11)	(0.96)	(1.04)			

Note. Standard deviations are in parentheses under *M* scores. Pos. socio. nom. = positive sociometric nomination; Neg. socio. nom. = negative sociometric nomination; TR = teacher rated; Academic ach. = academic achievement.
**$p < .01$. ***$p < .001$.

Table 8.8   Intercorrelations among variables

	1	2	3	4	5	6	7	8
				1990 cohort				
1. Pos. socio. nom.								
2. Neg. socio. nom.	−.22***							
3. Teacher-rated competence	.43***	−.37***						
4. Leadership	.42***	−.14**	.65***					
5. Academic achievement	.40***	−.27***	.63***	.47***				
6. Depression	−.28***	.37***	−.45***	−.36***	−.32***			
7. Sociability-cooperation	.52***	−.11**	.60***	.66***	.48***	−.28***		
8. Aggression-disruption	−.09	.73***	−.29***	−.16***	−.09	.28***	−.06	
9. Shyness-sensitivity	.16***	.00	.26***	.27***	.17***	−.08	.36***	.03
				1998 cohort				
1. Pos. socio. nom.								
2. Neg. socio. nom.	−.12**							
3. Teacher-rated competence	.33***	−.24***						
4. Leadership	.27***	−.04	.45***					
5. Academic achievement	.22**	−.14***	.43***	.35***				
6. Depression	−.20***	.19***	−.29***	−.27***	−.30***			
7. Sociability-cooperation	.47***	−.03	.43***	.51***	.43***	−.27***		
8. Aggression-disruption	−.08	.75***	−.29***	−.10	−.10	.17***	−.02	
9. Shyness-sensitivity	.15***	.24***	.04	.16***	.14**	−.04	.15***	.08
				2002 cohort				
1. Pos. socio. nom.								
2. Neg. socio. nom.	−.22***							
3. Teacher-rated competence	.37***	−.37***						
4. Leadership	.40***	−.22**	.55***					
5. Academic achievement	.34***	−.34***	.40***	.52***				
6. Depression	−.17***	.22***	−.30***	−.26***	−.27***			
7. Sociability-cooperation	.54***	−.07	.47***	.60***	.37***	−.24***		
8. Aggression-disruption	−.08	.68***	−.31***	−.11	−.18***	.15**	.13	
9. Shyness-sensitivity	−.12	.24***	−.17**	−.08	−.06	.18**	−.07	.17**

Note. Pos. socio. nom. = positive sociometric nomination; Neg. socio. nom. = negative sociometric nomination.
**$p < .01$. ***$p < .001$.

Relations between social functioning and adjustment variables, and tests for cross-cohort differences

Cross-cohort differences in the relations between social behaviors and adjustment variables were examined through the multigroup invariance test using LISREL 8.54. The analysis involved comparing nested models with and without specific relations constrained to be equal across the cohorts (e.g., Jöreskog, 1971). A significant chi-square value resulting from the constraint indicates that the relation is different across the cohorts. An invariance test was first conducted to examine the overall model in which the three social behavior variables were associated with all adjustment variables. A significant difference was found between the original unconstrained model and the constrained model with all of the relations set equal

Table 8.9 Effects of social functioning in predicting adjustment variables

Adjustment variable / Social variable	1990 cohort		1998 cohort		2002 cohort		$\chi^2(df=2)$
	B (SE)	t value	B (SE)	t value	B (SE)	t value	
Positive sociometric nomination							
Sociability-cooperation	.52 (.04)	12.93***	.47 (.05)	10.09***	.55 (.05)	9.98***	1.84
Aggression-disruption	−.08 (.05)	−1.70	−.03 (.05)	−0.52	−.05 (.07)	−0.82	0.50
Shyness-sensitivity	.17 (.05)	3.28**	.14 (.06)	2.35*	−.15 (.07)	−2.18*	13.56***
Negative sociometric nomination							
Sociability-cooperation	−.09 (.05)	−1.89	.01 (.06)	0.18	−.04 (.07)	−0.65	1.66
Aggression-disruption	.74 (.04)	22.45***	.78 (.04)	22.40***	.70 (.05)	14.76***	1.50
Shyness-sensitivity	.05 (.06)	0.93	.35 (.06)	5.73***	.34 (.07)	4.50***	14.34***
Teacher-rated competence							
Sociability-cooperation	.61 (.04)	15.18***	.42 (.05)	8.86***	.48 (.06)	8.21***	8.80**
Aggression-disruption	−.25 (.05)	−4.90***	−.22 (.05)	−4.34***	−.29 (.06)	−4.52***	0.70
Shyness-sensitivity	.20 (.05)	4.14***	−.05 (.05)	−1.01	−.22 (.06)	−3.36***	25.88***
Leadership							
Sociability-cooperation	.71 (.04)	17.58***	.61 (.05)	13.12***	.66 (.05)	11.70***	2.65
Aggression-disruption	−.12 (.05)	−2.27*	−.03 (.05)	−0.62	−.10 (.07)	−1.43	1.33
Shyness-sensitivity	.23 (.05)	4.68***	.11 (.05)	2.15*	−.11 (.07)	−1.57	14.76***
Academic achievement							
Sociability-cooperation	.50 (.04)	11.82***	.35 (.04)	8.84***	.36 (.06)	6.15***	5.78
Aggression-disruption	−.09 (.05)	−1.76	−.05 (.04)	−1.11	−.17 (.06)	−2.63*	2.10
Shyness-sensitivity	.18 (.05)	3.67***	.07 (.04)	1.59	−.08 (.06)	−1.27	9.52**
Depression							
Sociability-cooperation	−.28 (.04)	−7.43***	−.24 (.05)	−4.58***	−.26 (.07)	−3.85***	0.56
Aggression-disruption	.27 (.04)	3.48***	.13 (.05)	2.40*	.16 (.07)	2.27*	4.00
Shyness-sensitivity	−.06 (.08)	−1.48	.01 (.05)	0.24	.22 (.07)	3.21**	11.38**

Note. The effect of sex was controlled in the analyses.
*p < .05. **p < .01. ***p < .001.

across the cohorts, $\chi^2(36) = 84.26$, $p < .001$, indicating that there were overall significant cross-cohort differences in the relations between social behaviors and adjustment variables. Next, multigroup invariance tests were conducted separately for the relations between each of the social behaviors and the entire set of adjustment variables. The analyses revealed significant differences across the cohorts in the relations between sociability and adjustment variables, $\chi^2(12) = 38.12$, $p < .01$, and between shyness and adjustment variables, $\chi^2(12) = 489.71$, $p < .001$, but not in the relations between aggression and adjustment variables.

Follow-up analyses, separate for each adjustment variable, were conducted to detect sources of cross-cohort differences in the relations between sociability and shyness and the adjustment variables. The results of the cross-cohort tests and the effects of social behaviors in predicting specific adjustment variables are presented in Table 8.9. The results indicated that the relations between shyness and all adjustment variables were different between the 1990 cohort and the 2002 cohort, $\chi^2 s = 7.31$ to 27.67, $ps < .01$. The results also indicated that the relations between shyness and negative sociometric nominations and teacher-rated competence were significantly different between the 1990 cohort and the 1998 cohort, χ^2s = 12.51 and 11.67, $p < .001$. Finally, the relations between shyness and all adjustment variables were different between the 1998 cohort and the 2002 cohort, χ^2s = 4.10 to 9.41, ps $< .05$, except for negative sociometric nominations. In general, shyness was positively associated with indexes of social and school adjustment in the 1990 cohort. However, shyness was negatively associated with social and school adjustment and positively associated with social and psychological problems in the 2002 cohort. The patterns of the relations between shyness and adjustment variables were mixed in the 1998 cohort.

The results indicated that sociability was positively associated with positive sociometric nominations, teacher-rated competence, leadership, and academic achievement, and negatively associated with depression in all three cohorts. The cross-cohort difference was found in the relation between sociability and teacher-rated competence; the magnitude of the association was greater in the 1990 cohort than in the 1998 cohort, $\chi^2 = 11.12$, $p < .01$. Aggression was positively associated with negative sociometric nominations and depression, and negatively associated with teacher-rated competence in all three cohorts.

Significant gender differences were found in the relations between aggression, on the one hand, and negative sociometric nominations, teacher-rated competence, leadership, academic achievement, and depression, on the other: $\chi^2(18) = 104.09$, $p < .001$, for the overall model, and $\chi^2(6) = 70.81$, $p < .001$, for the relations between aggression and all adjustment variables. The effects of aggression in the prediction of the adjustment variables were stronger for boys than for girls: χ^2s(1) = 19.87 to 51.56, ps $< .001$, for specific relations, indicating that aggressive boys had more adjustment problems than did aggressive girls. No significant Gender × Cohort interactions were found on the relations in the study.

Discussion

According to the ecological perspective (e.g., Bronfenbrenner & Morris, 1998; Elder, 1998), individual socioemotional and cognitive functioning develops in social context that is subject to histori-

cal change. The contextual influence may occur through a variety of processes involving socialization forces; social interactions and relationships; and group and individual beliefs, attitudes, and value systems (Silbereisen, 2000). Whereas findings from previous studies (e.g., Elder, 1998; Flanagan, 2000) have demonstrated the impact of drastic social circumstances on the display of specific behaviors in children and adolescents, researchers have paid little attention to how the social structure and cultural norms may affect the significance of behaviors. The results of the present study concerning the different relations between social functioning, particularly shyness-sensitivity, and peer relationships, teacher-rated competence, and psychological well-being in different phases of the transformation of Chinese society clearly indicated the role of social context in defining the adaptive value of social behaviors in children's adjustment in various areas.

Gender differences in social functioning and adjustment

The results first indicated that there were gender differences in social functioning and adjustment. Boys were more aggressive and had more difficulties in social and school performance. These results are consistent with what has been found in previous studies (e.g., Chen & Li, 2000; Coie & Dodge, 1998). In the literature from the United States and Canada (e.g., Achenbach, 1991; Kovacs, 1992), boys often report fewer internalizing symptoms such as depression than do girls. This may be because boys who display externalizing social and behavioral problems tend to overestimate their competencies and develop biased or inflated self-images (Asher, Parkhurst, Hymel, & Williams, 1990). However, we found in the present study that Chinese boys had higher scores on depression than did Chinese girls. The results are not surprising given that boys had more adjustment problems than did girls in social and academic areas, and that these problems were associated with depression in Chinese children (e.g., Chen et al., 1995a).

A more interesting finding is the significant Gender × Cohort interaction on shyness-sensitivity. Girls were more shy-sensitive than boys in the 1990 and 1998 cohorts, but not in the 2002 cohort. The gender difference in the earlier cohorts may be related to gender-stereotypical ideologies in socialization. Girls have traditionally been expected to be obedient, passive, and behaviorally restrained in Chinese culture. These traditional expectations and beliefs may be less emphasized in recent years because they are in conflict with the requirements of self-direction and assertiveness in the new environment. As the influence of the stereotypical norms and values are gradually weakened and assertiveness is encouraged, Chinese girls may adjust their behaviors accordingly and regulate their shy and wary reactions in social interactions, which may attenuate gender differences in shyness-sensitivity. We elaborate further on this issue later when we discuss relations between shyness and peer relationships and school adjustment.

Relations between social functioning and adjustment

The primary purpose of the study was to examine relations between social functioning and adjustment variables in the three cohorts. Our results indicated that sociability-cooperation was positively associated with indexes of social and school adjustment and negatively associated with depression across the cohorts. The association between sociability-cooperation and teacher-rated competence declined in magnitude in the later cohorts, which seems to suggest that some aspects of prosocial-cooperative behavior such as politeness might have become less valuable for school adjustment. In general, however, despite the dramatic changes in Chinese society, sociability-cooperation remains an important behavioral characteristic that is conducive to the establishment and maintenance of social status and school achievement. In contrast to sociability-cooperation, aggression was generally associated with peer rejection and adjustment problems. Aggressive-disruptive children are likely to express their anger and frustration in an explosive manner and cause damage and harm on others and the group. Although competitiveness and self-oriented values may be relatively more appreciated and endorsed in a market-oriented society, our results suggest that aggressive children, particularly boys, who have difficulty controlling their behaviors in social situations may continue to be rejected in the peer group. The findings that the negative effects of aggression on

adjustment were more evident for boys than for girls were largely consistent with the literature (e.g., Casiglia et al., 1998; Coie et al., 1995), suggesting that aggressive girls might be more likely to maintain a balance between pursuing their own ends and establishing group harmony (e.g., Maccoby, 1998) and thus adjust better than aggressive boys.

The effect of different social contexts was reflected mainly in the relations between shyness-sensitivity and social, emotional, and school adjustment in the present study. Whereas shyness was positively associated with peer acceptance, teacher-rated competence, leadership, and academic achievement in the 1990 cohort, the associations became weaker or nonsignificant in the 1998 cohort. Furthermore, shyness-sensitivity was positively associated with peer rejection and self-reported depression, and negatively associated with teacher-rated school competence in the 2002 cohort. The different patterns of the relations across the cohorts suggest that the functional meaning of shy-sensitive behavior might have changed in social, school, and psychological adjustment in Chinese children over the last decade.

As indicated earlier, shy, wary, and sensitive behavior has been traditionally valued and encouraged in Chinese children (Feng, 1962; Ho, 1986; Yang, 1986). Shy-sensitive children are often regarded as well behaved and socially mature. However, the extensive changes toward the capitalistic system in the social and economic reforms may have led to a decline in the adaptive value of shy-sensitive behavior. In the new, competitive environment, behavioral characteristics that facilitate the achievement of personal goals such as social assertiveness and initiative may be highly appreciated and encouraged. In contrast, shy, anxious, and restrained behavior that may impede self-expression, active social communication, and exploration, particularly in stressful situations, may no longer be regarded as adaptive and competent. As a result, shy-sensitive children may be at a disadvantage in obtaining social acceptance and approval and maintaining social status. Moreover, like their counterparts in the United States and Canada (e.g., Rubin et al., 2002), when they realize their social difficulties, they may develop negative attitudes toward others and themselves. Thus, shyness-sensitivity becomes an undesirable behavioral characteristic in social and psychological adjustment.

As indicated by Asendorpf (1990) and Coplan et al. (2004), the construct of shyness-sensitivity differs from that of unsociability or social solitude. Whether and how they are associated with each other may depend on the social and cultural context (e.g., Asendorpf, 1993; Chen, 2000). When shyness-sensitivity is culturally endorsed and shy-sensitive children receive social approval and support, shy-sensitive children are not withdrawn or isolated from the peer group; they may be socially competent and liked by peers and even obtain leadership status in the school. In this article we argued that this occurred in China in the early 1990s. With the changes in social and cultural norms in recent years, however, shyness-sensitivity has become associated with social and psychological difficulties in Chinese children.

Compared with the results in the 1990 and 2002 cohorts, the relations between shyness and adjustment variables in the 1998 cohort were less straightforward. Shyness was positively associated with positive sociometric nominations and leadership, as well as negative sociometric nominations. Nevertheless, the results in the 1998 cohort are important when they are considered in the larger historical context because they might represent a transition in Chinese society from a system with hierarchical social structure to a system that allows for diverse social and cultural values. The positive associations between shyness-sensitivity and both peer acceptance and peer rejection indicate mixed attitudes of peers toward shy-sensitive children, which to some extent may reflect the cultural conflict between imported values on social initiative and individual autonomy and traditional Chinese values on self-restraint.

It is interesting to note that significant differences in the relations between shyness and adjustment emerged mainly between 1998 and 2002. Whereas the results seemed to correspond to the accelerated social and economic changes in Chinese society in recent years, it is possible that the extensive differences between the latter cohorts may reflect the lagged and cumulative effects of the macro-level context on individual attitudes and behaviors. As indicated by Silbereisen (2000), social factors may influence individual attitudes and behaviors gradually and progressively. Whereas there were uncertainties and different reactions among Chinese people with regard to the social and economic reform in its early stage, the consensus has grown steadily in the society that massive change is unavoidable and irreversible. Parents, educators, and professionals have eventually realized that it is necessary to modify their childrearing and educational goals, styles, and strategies so children can be adequately prepared for the challenges (Cheah & Rubin, 2004; Huang, 1999). The different relations between shyness and peer rejection and teacher-rated competence in the 1990 and 1998 cohorts seem to suggest that social evaluations and relationships might be more sensitive than other aspects of adjustment to the change in social and cultural norms. The influence of contextual forces on children's school performance and psychopathological feelings may occur through relatively complicated interpersonal and intrapersonal processes.

Conclusions, limitations, and future directions

The results of the present study suggest that the dramatic changes in China in the last decade might have considerable implications for children's social and psychological functioning. The different patterns of relations between shyness-sensitivity and peer relationships, school performance, and emotional adjustment across the cohorts indicate the imprint of historical time on children's social behavior. Our results support the argument that historical time is an important aspect of social-ecological context for human development, which should be considered seriously in the study of individual behaviors and social relationships.

Our results also indicate that whereas social context may have significant effects on children's behaviors, the effects may be domain specific. As indicated earlier, a salient aspect of the social and economic reforms in China is the increased requirement of assertiveness, self-direction, and exploration in the challenging market-oriented society (e.g., Cai & Wu, 1999; Yu, 2002). Children's shy and wary behaviors are clearly incompatible with this requirement and thus may be particularly vulnerable to the influence of the new social norms and expectations. The changing social context appears to have less evident effects on sociable-cooperative and aggressive behaviors, which may be because the significance of these behaviors is relatively robust and stable for group harmony, interpersonal relationships, and individual adjustment in diverse settings (e.g., Coie & Dodge, 1998; Eisenberg & Fabes, 1998). The domain-specific nature of contextual influence on children's behaviors is another important message from the present study.

As indicated earlier, researchers have been interested in the phenomenon of social withdrawal in Chinese children, and different results have been reported (e.g., Chang, 2003; Cheah & Rubin, 2004; Hart et al., 2000). Whereas the mixed findings have been explained by the researchers mainly in terms of differences in constructs and research methods, historical changes in the society should be considered as well. The similar results of our and others' studies that were conducted in late 1990s or in recent years suggest that different aspects of social withdrawal and shyness-sensitivity in Chinese children may merge to form a broad band of maladaptive behavioral characteristics of an internalizing nature in a context in which assertiveness and competitiveness are increasingly encouraged in social interactions.

Like China, many other countries have been undergoing major social, economic, and cultural changes. Given the traditions and conditions of each nation, however, social and cultural changes may affect individual behaviors differently across societies. Thus, it remains to be examined whether the results of the present study can be generalized to children in other societies. Even within China, there are regional differences in the pace and magnitude of the social and economic reforms. One should be careful in generalizing the results of the present study, which were based on a major city in China, to other areas of the country.

As the first systematic study tapping the implications of different social-historical contexts for individual adjustment in China, we focused on the relations between children's social functioning and peer relationships, school competence, and depressed feelings. It is important to investigate in the future the processes by which the social and economic transformation affects the significance of children's social functioning. The processes likely involve various situational and personal factors at multiple levels, including policy and social institutions, cultural conventions, school context and practices, family organization such as parental socialization expectations and strategies, peer group activities, and individual lifestyles and goals (e.g., Kleinman, 1988; Silbereisen et al., 2002). Therefore, it is necessary to examine children's social functioning, relationships, and adjustment from a broader perspective. Despite the limitations and weaknesses, the present study constitutes a significant contribution to our understanding of children's social functioning in the changing Chinese society and the role of the macro-level context in human development.

References

Achenbach, T. M. (1991). *Manual for the Child Behavior Checklist /4–18 and 1991 Profile*. Burlington, VT: University of Vermont.

Achenbach, T. M., & Edelbrock, C. (1981). Behavioural problems and competencies reported by parents of normal and disturbed children aged four through sixteen. *Monographs of the Society for Research in Child Development*, *46*, (Serial No. 188).

Asendorpf, J. (1990). Beyond social withdrawal: Shyness, unsociability and peer avoidance. *Human Development, 33*, 250–259.

Asendorpf, J. (1993). Abnormal shyness in children. *Journal of Child Psychology & Psychiatry & Allied Disciplines, 34*, 1069–1081.

Asher, S., Parkhurst, J. T., Hymel, S., & Williams, G. A. (1990). Peer rejection and loneliness in childhood. In S. R. Asher & J. D. Coie (Eds.), *Peer rejection in childhood* (pp. 253–273). New York: Cambridge University Press.

Benedict, R. F. (1934). Anthropology and the abnormal. *Journal of General Psychology, 10*, 59–80.

Boivin, M., Hymel, S., & Bukowski, W. M. (1995). The roles of social withdrawal, peer rejection, and victimization by peers in predicting loneliness and depressed mood in childhood. *Development and Psychopathology, 7*, 765–785.

Bornstein, M. H. (1995). Form and function: Implications for studies of culture and human development. *Culture and Psychology, 1*, 123–138.

Bronfenbrenner, U., & Morris, P. A. (1998). The ecology of developmental processes. In W. Damon (Series Ed.) R. M. Lerner (Vol. Ed.), *Handbook of child psychology: Vol. 1. Theoretical models of human development* (pp. 993–1028). New York: Wiley.

Bukowski, W. M., Gauze, C., Hoza, B., & Newcomb, A. F. (1993). Differences and consistency in relations with same-sex and other-sex peers during early adolescence. *Developmental Psychology, 29*, 255–263.

Bulletin of China's Economic and Social Development in 1990 (1991, February 28). Beijing: Xin Hua She. (in Chinese)

Bulletin of China's Economic and Social Development in 2002 (2003, October 2). Beijing: Xin Hua She. (in Chinese)

Cai, X., & Wu, P. (1999). A study of the modernity of social concept of younger students in China. *Psychological Science (China), 22*, 148–152.

Casiglia, A. C., Lo Coco, A., & Zappulla, C. (1998). Aspects of social reputation and peer relationships in

Italian children: A cross-cultural perspective. *Developmental Psychology, 34,* 723–730.

Caspi, A., Elder, G. H., Jr., & Bem, D. J. (1988). Moving away from the world: Life-course patterns of shy children. *Developmental Psychology, 24,* 824–831.

Chang, L. (2003). Variable effects of children's aggression, social withdrawal, and prosocial leadership as functions of teacher beliefs and behaviors. *Child Development, 74,* 538–548.

Cheah, C. L., & Rubin, K. H. (2004). European American and Mainland Chinese mothers' responses to aggression and social withdrawal in preschoolers. *International Journal of Behavioral Development, 28,* 83–94.

Chen, X. (2000). Social and emotional development in Chinese children and adolescents: A contextual cross-cultural perspective. In F. Columbus (Ed.), *Advances in psychology research, Vol. I* (pp. 229–251). Huntington, NY: Nova Science.

Chen, X., Dong, Q., & Zhou, H. (1997). Authoritative and authoritarian parenting practices and social and school adjustment. *International Journal of Behavioral Development, 20,* 855–873.

Chen, X., & Li, B. (2000). Depressed mood in Chinese children: Developmental significance for social and school adjustment. *International Journal of Behavioral Development, 24,* 472–479.

Chen, X., Rubin, K. H., & Li, B. (1995a). Depressed mood in Chinese children: Relations with school performance and family environment. *Journal of Consulting and Clinical Psychology, 63,* 938–947.

Chen, X., Rubin, K. H., & Li, D. (1995b). Social functioning and adjustment in Chinese children: A longitudinal study. *Developmental Psychology, 31,* 531–539.

Chen, X., Rubin, K. H., & Li, D. (1997). Relation between academic achievement and social adjustment: Evidence from Chinese children. *Developmental Psychology, 33,* 518–525.

Chen, X., Rubin, K. H., & Sun, Y. (1992). Social reputation and peer relationships in Chinese and Canadian children: A cross-cultural study. *Child Development, 63,* 1336–1343.

Coie, J. D., & Dodge, K. A. (1998). Aggression and antisocial behavior. In N. Eisenberg (Ed.), *Handbook of child psychology: Vol. 3. Social, emotional, and personality development* (pp. 779–862). New York: Wiley.

Coie, J. D., Terry, R., Lenox, K., Lochman, J., & Hyman, C. (1995). Childhood peer rejection and aggression as predictors of stable patterns of adolescent disorder. *Development and Psychopathology, 7,* 697–713.

Cole, D. A. (1991). Preliminary support for a competency-based model of depression in children. *Journal of Abnormal Psychology, 100,* 181–190.

Coplan, R. J., Prakash, K., O'Neil, K., & Armer, M. (2004). Do you "want" to play?: Distinguishing between conflicted shyness and social disinterest in early childhood. *Developmental Psychology, 40,* 244–258.

Dong, Q., Yang, B., & Ollendick, T. H. (1994). Fears in Chinese children and adolescents and their relations to anxiety and depression. *Journal of Child Psychology and Psychiatry, 35,* 351–363.

Eisenberg, N., & Fabes, R. A. (1998). Prosocial development. In N. Eisenberg (Ed.), *Handbook of child psychology: Vol. 3. Social, emotional, and personality development* (pp. 701–778). New York: Wiley.

Elder, G. H., Jr. (1974). *Children of the Great Depression.* Chicago: University of Chicago Press.

Elder, G. H., Jr. (1998). The life course and human development. In W. Damon (Series Ed.) R. M. Lerner (Vol. Ed.), *Handbook of child psychology: Vol. 1. Theoretical models of human development* (pp. 939–991). New York: Wiley.

Elder, G. H., Jr., & Conger, R. D. (2000). *Children of the land: Adversity and success in rural America.* Chicago: University of Chicago Press.

Feng, Y. L. (1962). *The spirit of Chinese philosophy.* London: Routledge & Kegan Paul.

Flanagan, C. A. (2000). Social change and the "social contract" in adolescent development. In L. J. Crockett & R. K. Silbereisen (Eds.), *Negotiating adolescence in times of social change* (pp. 191–198). New York: Cambridge University Press.

French, D. C. (1990). Heterogeneity of peer rejected girls. *Child Development, 61,* 2028–2031.

Hart, C. H., Yang, C., Nelson, L. J., Robinson, C. C., Olson, J. A., Nelson, D. A., et al. (2000). Peer acceptance in early childhood and subtypes of socially withdrawn behaviour in China, Russia and the United States. *International Journal of Behavioral Development, 24,* 73–81.

Hightower, A. D., Work, W. C., Cohen, E. L., Lotyczewski, B. S., Spinell, A. P., Guare, J. C., et al. (1986). The Teacher–Child Rating Scale: A brief objective measure of elementary children's school problem behaviours and competences. *School Psychology Review, 15,* 393–409.

Ho, D.Y. F. (1986). Chinese pattern of socialization: A critical review. In M. H. Bond (Ed.), *The psychology of the Chinese people* (pp. 1–37). New York: Oxford University Press.

Huang, M. (1999). A comparative study of the value outlook of Chinese adolescent students. *Journal of Southwest China Normal University (Philosophy and Social Sciences), 25,* 83–88.

Jöreskog, K. (1971). Simultaneous factor analysis in several populations. *Psychometrika, 36,* 409–426.

King, A. Y. C., & Bond, M. H. (1985). The Confucian paradigm of man: A sociological view. In W. S. Tseng &

D. Y. H. Wu (Eds.), *Chinese culture and mental health* (pp. 29–45). San Diego, CA: Academic Press.

Kleinman, A. (1988). *Rethinking psychiatry: From cultural category to personal experience.* New York: Free Press.

Kovacs, M. (1992). *The Children's Depression Inventory manual.* Toronto: Multi-Health Systems.

Larson, R. W. (1999). The uses of loneliness in adolescence. In K. J. Rotenberg & S. Hymel (Eds.), *Loneliness in childhood and adolescence* (pp. 244–262). New York: Cambridge University Press.

Maccoby, E. E. (1998). *The two sexes: Growing up apart, coming together.* Cambridge, MA: Harvard University Press.

Masten, A. S., & Coatsworth, J. D. (1995). Competence, resilience, and psychopathology. In D. Cicchetti & D. J. Cohen (Eds.), *Developmental psychopathology: Vol. 2. Risk, disorder, and adaptation* (pp. 715–752). New York: Wiley.

Masten, A., Morison, P., & Pellegrini, D. (1985). A revised class play method of peer assessment. *Developmental Psychology, 21,* 523–533.

Mills, C. W. (1959). *The sociological imagination.* New York: Oxford University Press.

Morison, P., & Masten, A. (1991). Peer reputation in middle childhood as a predictor of adaptation in adolescence: A seven-year follow-up. *Child Development, 62,* 991–1007.

Rubin, K. H., & Asendorpf, J. (1993). *Social withdrawal, inhibition, and shyness in childhood.* Hillsdale, NJ: Erlbaum.

Rubin, K. H., Burgess, K. B., & Coplan, R. J. (2002). Social withdrawal and shyness. In P. K. Smith & C. H. Hart (Eds.), *Blackwell handbook of childhood social development* (pp. 330–352). Malden, MA: Blackwell.

Rubin, K. H., Chen, X., McDougall, P., Bowker, A., & McKinnon, J. (1995). The Waterloo Longitudinal Project: Predicting internalizing and externalizing problems in adolescence. *Development and Psychopathology, 7,* 751–764.

Silbereisen, R. K. (2000). German unification and adolescents' developmental timetables: Continuities and discontinuities. In L. A. Crockett & R. K. Silbereisen (Eds.), *Negotiating adolescence in times of social change.* Cambridge, England: Cambridge University Press.

Silbereisen, R. K., Reitzle, M., & Juang, L. (2002). Time and change: Psychosocial transitions in German young adults 1991 and 1996. In L. Pulkkinen & A. Caspi (Eds.), *Paths to successful development: Personality in the life course* (pp. 227–256). New York: Cambridge University Press.

Stevenson-Hinde, J., & Shouldice, A. (1993). Wariness to strangers: A behavior systems perspective revisited. In K. H. Rubin & J. Asendorpf (Eds.), *Social withdrawal, inhibition, and shyness in childhood* (pp. 101–116). Hillsdale, NJ: Erlbaum.

Xu, X., & Peng, L. (2001). Reflection on parents' educational beliefs in the new century. *Theory and Practice of Education, 21,* 62–63.

Yang, K. S. (1986). Chinese personality and its change. In M. H. Bond (Ed.), *The psychology of the Chinese people* (pp. 106–170). New York: Oxford University Press.

Yu, R. (2002). On the reform of elementary school education in China. *Educational Exploration, 129,* 56–57.

Zhang, W. W. (2000). *Transforming China: Economic reform and its political implications.* New York: St. Martin's Press.

A Closer Look 7 But I Like to Be Alone! Unsociability and the Benefits of Solitude

Most previous research on social withdrawal has focused on shy children, who refrain from social interaction because of social fear and anxiety. Some children are quite content to play alone, however, and although they may not actively avoid social interactions, they also do not display a high motivation to seek out social contacts. Unsociability (or social disinterest) refers to the non-fearful preference for solitude. Although philosophers and social psychologists have long extolled the benefits of solitude in adulthood, unsociability has only recently begun to receive attention from developmental psychology researchers.

Asendorpf and Meier (1993) were among the first to specifically explore distinctions between shyness and unsociability in childhood. Groups of unsociable and shy children were indentified. From an original sample of over 140 children, distinct groups of unsociable, shy, and sociable children were identified based on parental ratings. Children's speech patterns were monitored continuously from morning to evening over a 7-day period. Results indicated that shy children tended to speak less than sociable children during unfamiliar situations but spoke as much as more sociable children when in more familiar social environments. In contrast, although unsociable children spent less overall time engaged in conversation with their peers than their sociable agemates, the two groups did not differ in terms of their verbal participation within the conversations. Thus, aside from a lower rate of social interaction with peers, unsociable children did not tend to differ from more gregarious children. However, despite the relatively "benign nature" of unsociability in childhood, Asendorpf and Meier speculate that this form of

social withdrawal may become increasingly problematic in later childhood and adolescence because older peers may perceive spending time alone as an increasingly "non-normative" behavior.

Asendorpf, J., & Meier, G. H. (1993). Personality effects on children's speech in everyday life: Sociability-mediated exposure and shyness-mediated reactivity to social situations. *Journal of Personality and Social Psychology, 64,* 1072–1083.

Classroom Exercises, Debates, and Discussion Questions

- *Observations.* Watch a group of young children on the playground or in the schoolyard. How might you identify the shy children? Do you think all children who are "off by themselves" are shy? What other reasons might some children end up playing alone?
- *Classroom debate.* Many shy children grow up to be happy and well adjusted. Divide into smaller groups and debate the following questions: (1) Are there positive aspects of shyness? (2) From an evolutionary perspective, under what circumstances might shyness be an adaptive trait?
- *Exercise.* There are no overall differences in the "amount" or "frequency" of shyness between boys and girls. However, there is growing research evidence to suggest that across the lifespan, shyness is associated with more negative outcomes for boys vs. girls. Why do you think shyness seems to be more of a problem for boys than for girls? Do you think it is more socially acceptable to be a shy girl than a shy boy?
- *Exercise.* How might parents inadvertently exacerbate feelings of anxiety and social unease among shy children? What advice would you give to parents of young shy children?
- *Exercise.* Shyness becomes increasingly problematic in later childhood and adolescence. What aspects of adolescent peer relations might be particularly challenging for shy individuals?

- *Exercise.* Given cross-cultural differences in the meanings and implications of shyness, what challenges might shy children face when immigrating to North America? How might the acculturation process of shy children differ for first- vs. second-generation immigrants?
- *Exercise.* If a child is content to play alone most of the time, should parents or teachers intervene to promote increased social interaction? How might peer responses to unsociable children change at different age periods? What are some of the "benefits" of solitude in adulthood?

Additional Resources

For more about shyness and social withdrawal, see:

Degnan, K. A., & Fox, N. A. (2007). Behavioral inhibition and anxiety disorders: Multiple levels of a resilience process. *Development and Psychopathology, 19,* 729–746.

Gazelle, H. (2008). Behavioral profiles of anxious solitary children and heterogeneity in peer relations. *Developmental Psychology, 44,* 1604–1624.

Kagan, J., Snidman, N., Kahn, V., & Towsley, S. (2007). The preservation of two infant temperaments into adolescence. *Monographs of the Society for Research in Child Development,* Serial No. 287, 72.

Rubin, K. H., Coplan, R. J., & Bowker, J. (2009). Social withdrawal in childhood. *Annual Review of Psychology, 60,* 11.1–11.31.

Schmidt, L. A. (1999). Frontal brain electrical activity in shyness and sociability. *Psychological Science, 10,* 316–320.

9

AGGRESSION AND BULLYING

Introduction   366

An Integrated Model of Emotion Processes and Cognition in Social Information Processing   367

Elizabeth A. Lemerise and William F. Arsenio

Introduction   367

Historical Background and Overview   367

Social Information Processing   368

Emotion Processes   368

Integrating Emotion Processes and Social Information Processing   372

Future Directions for Research   376

A Short-Term Longitudinal Study of Growth of Relational Aggression during Middle Childhood: Associations with Gender, Friendship Intimacy, and Internalizing Problems   379

Dianna Murray-Close, Jamie M. Ostrov, and Nicki R. Crick

Methods   383

Results   385

Discussion   389

Conclusion   392

A Peek Behind the Fence: Naturalistic Observations of Aggressive Children with Remote Audiovisual Recording   395

Debra J. Pepler and Wendy M. Craig

Laboratory Observational Studies   396

Naturalistic Observations   396

Remote Audiovisual Observations   398

A Peek Behind the Fence   401

A Closer Look 8   A Slap in the "Facebook": The Study of Cyber-Bullying   403

Introduction

Aggression is a widely studied phenomenon in the area of children's social development. This is perhaps not surprising given the "costs" of aggression to the perpetrator, victim, and larger community. Across the lifespan, aggression is concurrently associated with a host of negative outcomes, including externalizing problems (antisocial behaviors, delinquency, substance use) and academic problems (truancy, school dropout, poor school achievement). Aggression is also one of the strongest predictors of being disliked, excluded, and rejected by peers, and in later childhood and adolescence also comes to be associated with depression.

In its most general form, aggression is defined as behavior aimed at intentionally harming another person. In early childhood, aggression is most often *physical* (i.e., hitting, kicking, biting) and *instrumental* (i.e., centered around conflicts over objects and possessions), where the aggressive act is a means to achieve a non-interpersonal goal (i.e., "I want that toy right now!").

Aggressive behaviors among younger children can be difficult to alter, because in many ways aggression "works" in terms of achieving short-term goals. What happens during the preschool years is that children receive extensive feedback from their peers, which helps them to better understand the relationship between short-term goals and long-term goals. For example, a preschooler at daycare who wants to play with a toy dog currently being used by another child might walk over to the other child and obtain the toy through the use of physical force; this achieves the short-term goal of getting the toy dog quickly. However, as recipients of aggressive acts, peers often provide negative feedback ("that's not fair!") and children begin to acquire non-aggressive means of conflict resolution, such as socially skilled strategies (e.g., asking the other child if they can have a turn, waiting until the child is finished, asking the teacher for help).

Overall levels of aggression decline from early childhood to later childhood. However, with increasing age, aggression also becomes less physical and more *verbal* (i.e., teasing, threats, name-calling) and *relational* (i.e., spreading rumors, getting others to exclude someone, manipulating or damaging someone's social relationships). This may be related to the development of theory of mind, social information processing skills, and moral judgments, as children better understand the motives and intentions of others, and respond in ways consistent with their emerging concepts about fairness and reciprocity. Yet, a small group of children (10–15%) become increasingly involved in bullying ("harm-doing" that is carried out repeatedly in an interpersonal relationship characterized by an imbalance in power), often as both bullies and victims.

The first reading in this chapter presents a conceptual model of the social-cognitive and emotional processes that are thought to underlie children's display of aggressive behaviors. In their influential theoretical paper, Lemerise and Arsenio (2000) provided step-by-step depictions of the patterns of thoughts and feelings that children may experience when encountering social situations. The second study concerns the development of relational aggression. Murray-Close and colleagues (2007) tracked changes in relational aggression over time and explored the implications of this form of aggression for children's social relationships and interpersonal functioning. The final paper is a significant study of bullying and victimization. Pepler and Craig (1995) were among the first to systematically observe bullying and victimization on the playground. Their results greatly promoted increased awareness in this area and were instrumental in the development and implementation of anti-bullying programs in many schools.

An Integrated Model of Emotion Processes and Cognition in Social Information Processing

Elizabeth A. Lemerise and William F. Arsenio

Introduction

The last two decades have witnessed rapid progress in research and theory regarding the contributions of social information processing (e.g., Crick & Dodge, 1994; Dodge, 1986) and emotionality and regulation (e.g., Eisenberg & Fabes, 1992; Eisenberg et al., 1997; Hubbard & Coie, 1994; Saarni, 1999) to children's social competence. Although both research traditions share a focus on social competence, integration across the domains of social information processing and emotionality and regulation has been minimal. We argue here that (1) it is vitally important for developmental psychologists to take a broader view of children's social and cognitive development, and (2) an essential aspect of this broader view involves considering, both theoretically and empirically, how emotional and cognitive processes can be integrated in models of social competence.

Historical Background and Overview

There is a long-standing theoretical interest in understanding the multiple ways affect and cognition interact. Cognitive psychologists have been interested in the critical role of emotions in prioritizing and weighting multiple goals and objectives in real-time human information processing (e.g., Simon, 1967). Attachment and emotion researchers have been interested in working models (e.g., Bowlby, 1988; Bretherton, Ridgeway, & Cassidy, 1990) and emotion–event representations (e.g., Arsenio & Lover, 1995) of affectively charged relationships and events. Despite this interest, and a journal devoted to the topic (*Cognition and Emotion*), progress has been slower than expected.

An early reflection of the interest and difficulties in integrating emotion and cognition was Piaget's (1981)

Intelligence and Affectivity. Piaget described affect and cognition as being indissociably linked ("two sides of the same coin," Cowan, 1981, p. xiv), where affect plays a role "... like gasoline, which activates the motor of an automobile but does not modify its structure" (Piaget, 1981, p. 5). Although this book sparked considerable interest (Bearison & Zimiles, 1986; Brown, 1996; Cowan, 1981), the analogy of affect as gasoline and intelligence as the motor of human functioning reflects a key limitation found in various attempts to include emotion within cognitive models of development. For example, both Piaget (1981) and Crick and Dodge (1994) acknowledge the central importance of emotion, but provide a detailed and elaborated description of cognition without providing a comparably differentiated account of emotions.

In this paper, we define the domain of emotion broadly to include processes that vary in duration from briefly experienced feelings resulting from conscious or unconscious appraisal to more enduring affective styles (see, e.g., Ekman & Davidson, 1994; Oatley & Jenkins, 1996). Therefore, we deliberately use the term *emotion processes*. Delineating the difference between emotion and cognition is a difficult task for which there is little consensus. To some extent, whether one sees emotion and cognition as separate or as one process depends on how broadly cognition is defined (Dodge, 1991; Ekman & Davidson, 1994). Moreover, both emotion and cognitive processes develop, and the nature of their relations changes (e.g., Denham, 1998; Saarni, 1999).

At a very general level, both emotion and cognition are types of information processing, but the functions they serve are distinct. Izard (1994, p. 204) stated "Emotion is about motivation, cognition about knowledge." This view is shared by functionalist theorists, neurophysiologists, and some cognitive theorists who see the function of emotion as alerting individuals to important features of the environment and providing direction for cognitive processes and behavior in ways that are mostly adaptive (e.g., Campos, Mumme, Kermoian, & Campos, 1994; Damasio, 1994; Oatley & Jenkins, 1996). Recent neurophysiological evidence (e.g., LeDoux, 1995) suggests that emotion processes and cognitive processes influence one another, making it difficult to isolate cases of pure emotion or pure cognition, *except* where brain damage has severed this connection (e.g., Damasio, 1994, and see below). We argue that emotion processes serve motivational, communicative, and regulatory functions within and between individuals that are distinct from the contributions of cognitive processes (attention, learning, memory, logic) to social competence. Regardless of how broadly or narrowly cognition is defined, in our view the inclusion of emotion processes in models of personal–social decision making will expand their explanatory power.

Our primary goal is to offer a model of social information processing that (1) brings together affective and cognitive contributions without distorting or minimizing the literatures from which these contributions are drawn, and (2) is theoretically coherent enough to spur empirical examination of many of these proposed connections. To accomplish this goal, three basic topics will be covered. First, a brief overview is presented of Crick and Dodge's (1994) information processing model of social competence. The model was chosen both because it is well articulated and has received considerable empirical support, and because Crick and Dodge themselves acknowledge the need to consider emotion-related processes more fully. Next, there is a brief summary of the types of emotion processes that are relevant to social competence and are likely to be influential in social information processing. The final section illustrates the specific ways emotion processes can be integrated into a social information processing model.

Social Information Processing

A basic premise of social information processing (and of other social cognitive models, e.g., Piaget 1932/1965; Turiel, 1998) is that children's understanding and interpretation of situations influences their related behaviors. Social information processing theory offers a detailed model of how children process and interpret cues in a social situation and arrive at a decision that is more or less competent (Crick & Dodge, 1994; Dodge, 1986). Crick and Dodge assume children enter a social situation with past experiences and biologically determined capabilities which they may access during the encounter. The processing steps they describe are hypothesized to occur relatively rapidly and in parallel, with numerous feedback loops (see Figure 9.1), but for clarity, we describe them sequentially (see Crick & Dodge, 1994; Dodge, 1986, 1991, for more details).

Briefly, social information processing begins when the child attends to, encodes, and interprets social cues (steps one and two in the model). Imagine a child who gets hit by a ball while walking across the playground. The child must figure out what happened (attention, encoding) and why it happened (interpretation: an accident or on purpose?). In the third step of the model, the child's goals for the situation are clarified. Possible goals might be to maintain friendly relations with classmates, or to show others you won't tolerate this intrusion of your personal space. In steps four and five of the model, possible responses to the situation are generated and evaluated in terms of anticipated outcomes, relations to goal(s), and self-efficacy for performing the response. The child may consider retaliating in kind, but rejects that alternative because of a fear the conflict will escalate or a recognition that he/she can't throw the ball hard enough. Finally, the most positively evaluated response with respect to goals, anticipated outcomes, and self-efficacy is selected and behaviorally enacted (Crick & Dodge, 1994).

Although Crick and Dodge explicitly assert that emotion is an important component of social information processing, they also acknowledge that emotion's role is not well articulated in their model. In what follows, we describe the kinds of emotion processes that need to be integrated into cognitive models of behavior. Finally, we illustrate how emotion processes can be integrated into Crick and Dodge's (1994) model.

Emotion Processes

Some aspects of emotional functioning apply more generally, whereas others vary across individuals. Accordingly, we begin by describing normative emotion processes and then consider individual variations.

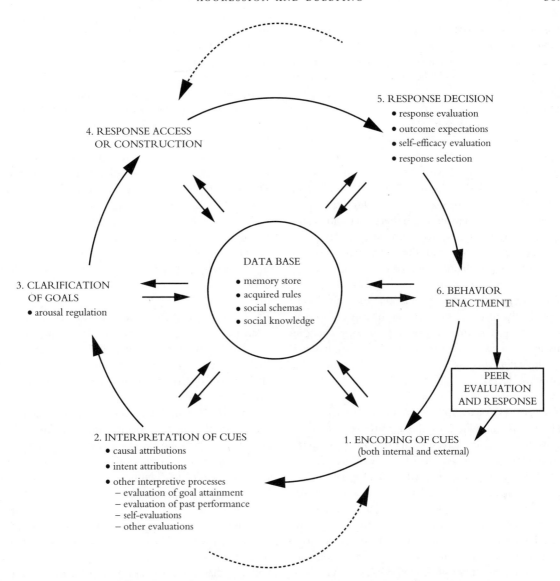

Figure 9.1 Crick and Dodge's social information processing model of children's social adjustment.
Note. From "A review and reformulation of social-information-processing mechanisms of children's social adjustment," by
N. R. Crick & K. A. Dodge (1994), *Psychological Bulletin, 115*, p. 74. Copyright 1994 by the American Psychological Association.
Reprinted with permission.

Normative aspects of emotions

FUNCTIONALIST THEORIES

Functionalist theories of emotion emphasize the biologically adaptive role of emotions in person/environment transactions (Lazarus, 1991; Malatesta, 1990). Although there are important differences in various versions of these theories (Saarni, Mumme, & Campos, 1998), many emphasize both the innate communicative and motivational aspects of emotion. Some theories (Ekman 1984, 1993; Izard, 1977, 1991; Plutchik, 1980) propose a limited number of discrete emotions that are associated with more or less universal emotion expressions and related recognition abilities.

These emotions are seen as serving a vital interpsychological function by providing information about intended or likely behaviors and underlying mental states of others, although the emergence of emotion display rules (Saarni, 1999) makes these links less transparent.

Emotions also are seen as having an intrapsychological function of organizing and motivating behaviors and cognition to facilitate adaptive goal-directed behaviors. Given the numerous reviews available on such theories (e.g., Magai & McFadden, 1995; Malatesta, 1990; Saarni et al., 1998), little more will be said other than although there is a biologically based substrate of adaptive emotional functioning, learning, experience, and the active socialization of emotions (Denham, 1998) all significantly influence this biological substrate (Malatesta, 1990). Similarly, emotions may be adaptive in general, but biological and social stressors can distort emotional functioning, resulting in psychopathology and the disruptive picture of emotions typically emphasized in clinical psychology (Malatesta & Wilson, 1988; Plutchik, 1993).

Neurophysiology and functionalist theories

The functionalist focus on the adaptive role of emotions is receiving increasing attention and support from neurophysiologists. Work by LeDoux (1993, 1995) and others (e.g., Kandel & Kupferman, 1995) has documented the complex interconnections between parts of the brain that address emotional responsiveness and a variety of cognitive functions. The Damasios, in particular, have documented how disruptions in the connections between emotional and rational substrates of the brain can disrupt competent human functioning (Damasio, 1994; Damasio, Grabowski, Frank, Galaburda, & Damasio, 1994). They acknowledge that emotions can sometimes disrupt reason but also note that "Reduction in emotion may constitute an equally important source of irrational behavior" (Damasio, 1994, p. 53).

The Damasios have examined the consequences for decision making of damage to ventromedial prefrontal cortex that leaves patients with motor and cognitive functions intact but with impaired emotional functioning. Unlike participants with no brain damage and those with other kinds of brain damage, when patients with prefrontal lesions were shown disturbing images, they showed no skin conductance response. These patients could report the content of the slides and were aware of the emotional significance of the images, but they did not *feel* the emotions they *knew* they should (Damasio, 1994; Damasio, Tranel, & Damasio, 1991). The practical effects of this deficit are seen most clearly for decision making where outcomes are uncertain or for which there is no clear correct answer (Bechara, Damasio, Damasio, & Anderson, 1994; Bechara, Tranel, Damasio, & Damasio, 1993). In one telling example, a patient who was asked to choose between two dates for his next appointment spent over thirty minutes calmly listing pros and cons for each date until it was suggested that he come on the second date (Damasio, 1994).

Emotional prioritizing and somatic markers

A critical issue in the interaction of affect and cognition involves how the nearly unlimited considerations that enter into any choice are reduced to a manageable number. Extrapolating from Simon's (1967) discussion, Damasio (1994), Brown (1996), Oatley and Jenkins (1996), and others have argued that emotions not only help to prioritize among different plans and options; they also help to narrow the search space during "on-line" information processing. In a summary of Pugh's (1977) influential book, Brown (1996, p. 154) noted that "rigorously logical decisions are impossible in most of the situations adapting organisms face.... affectivity provides a method for inventing provisional or 'good enough' knowledge structures."

A mechanism for emotional prioritizing is the formation of somatic markers (Damasio, 1994). Briefly, when a negative outcome becomes linked with a specific behavior or cognition, a negative somatic or gut feeling is experienced which "... protects you against future losses, ... and then allows you *to choose from fewer alternatives*" (Damasio, 1994, p. 173). Once the field of alternatives has been narrowed, the individual can still use higher-level cognitive processes, but with greater efficiency. Damasio acknowledges that somatic markers are a form of bias that can contribute to maladaptive behavior (see below), but for the most part, somatic markers support adaptive behavior.

Secondary emotions/affect–event links

Damasio (1994) made an important distinction between primary and secondary emotions. Primary emotions are innate, preorganized, and relatively inflexible responses to certain combinations of stimuli. They are the sorts of emotions described by functionalists where certain classes of events (e.g., loss of a loved one, being attacked by a wild animal) are likely to be linked with specific emotions and their associated motivational tendencies. Although these primary emotions provide a quick and efficient set of responses, "the next step is the *feeling of emotion* in connection to the object that excited it" (i.e., secondary emotion, Damasio, 1994, p. 132; see also Piaget, 1981).

Awareness of the connections between object X and certain emotions serves several adaptive purposes (Damasio, 1994). For example, knowing about the connection between seeing a large animal running nearby and fear allows one to plan ahead ("Where and when did I see it?"), and to make more fine-tuned discriminations ("Does it run toward me or away?"). Thus, the more automatic event–emotion connections can be loosened somewhat, and conscious understanding of event–emotion links provides adaptive behavioral flexibility. Damasio sees experience as important in fine-tuning secondary emotions, with adaptive functioning the product of a normal brain and a normal set of experiences. Brain damage and/or experience that influences secondary emotions, however, can produce maladaptive functioning.

Individual variations in emotional functioning

Although functionalists stress the normative, adaptive role emotions serve, there is a growing interest in individual variations in affective systems (Thompson, 1994). Just as psychologists have realized that basic similarities and constraints on human cognition do not preclude meaningful individual differences in cognitive functioning, emotion theorists have begun to expand their understanding of emotions to include individual differences. Two somewhat separable lines of research focus on temperament/emotionality and the regulation of emotions.

Temperament/emotionality

Rothbart and Bates (1998, p. 109) define temperament as "constitutionally based individual differences in emotional, motor, and attentional reactivity and self-regulation. ... Reactive parameters of temperament can be measured in terms of the onset, duration, and intensity of expression of affective reaction.... variability in arousability, and distress to overstimulation, activity and attention." Although temperament includes more than emotions, variations in emotionality, which are at least partially biologically based, are central to modern conceptualizations of temperament.

Eisenberg and colleagues have conducted a systematic program of research focusing on the contributions of emotionality and emotion regulation to social competence. They define emotionality as "stable individual differences in the typical intensity with which individuals experience their emotions ... and in threshold to relatively intense levels of emotional responding" (Eisenberg & Fabes, 1992, p. 122) and include both positive and negative emotionality in this temperament-based definition. Eisenberg and colleagues developed methods to measure emotionality and found individual differences to be reasonably stable from preschool to elementary school (Eisenberg et al., 1997). Emotionality's impact on social functioning, however, depends on skill at regulating emotion.

Emotion regulation

Along with the focus on temperamental aspects of emotionality, there has been much interest in children's abilities to regulate emotions, that is, to control, modify, and manage aspects of their emotional reactivity and expressivity (e.g., Eisenberg & Fabes, 1992; Thompson, 1990, 1994). It should be noted that children who vary in temperament face quite different tasks in regulating their emotions (Thompson, 1990, 1994). A child with a positive, even-tempered disposition has a very different set of regulatory tasks than one prone to intense, long-lasting negative emotions.

Although the more innate aspects of emotionality clearly interact with socialization patterns in ways that may even alter the underlying physiology of emotional reactivity (Gottman, Katz, &

Hooven, 1997), it seems important to distinguish between the more innate aspects of emotionality and attempts to manage/regulate whatever those biological substrates provide. For example, in their extensive, ongoing research on children's social and emotional competence, Eisenberg and colleagues include separate assessments of emotionality and emotion regulation. Emotions may be regulated with attentional mechanisms, through approach or avoidance, or by cognitive or behavioral coping (Eisenberg & Fabes, 1992). Eisenberg and colleagues found that a combination of regulatory abilities and low emotionality predicted social competence concurrently and longitudinally (e.g., Eisenberg, Fabes, Nyman, Bernzweig, & Pinuelas, 1994; Eisenberg et al., 1997). High emotionality combined with poor regulation skills predicted poorer social functioning and problem behaviors, whereas children with high emotionality and good regulation skills were *not* at risk for behavior problems (Eisenberg et al., 1996).

MOOD STATE/BACKGROUND EMOTIONS

Mood states (Clark & Isen, 1981) or background emotions (Damasio, 1994) also are likely to influence social information processing. There is an extensive social psychology literature on how experimentally induced moods influence a wide variety of behaviors and cognitions (e.g., Berkowitz, 1990; Isen, Shalker, Clark, & Karp, 1978; Moore, Underwood, & Rosenhan, 1984). More recently, Lemerise, Harper, Caverly, and Hobgood (1998) found that induced moods influence children's goals for hypothetical provocation situations.

Little is known about how or whether ongoing emotions or moods serve an adaptive role or whether they are "unintended" consequences of the larger functional organization of human emotions. Another unresolved issue is whether ongoing emotions act as short-term influences or in more long-term, trait-like ways (e.g., Arsenio, Cooperman, & Lover, 2000; Arsenio & Lover, 1997; Denham, 1986; Denham, McKinley, Couchoud, & Holt, 1990). Regardless of their presumed functions or duration, it is clear that more empirical attention should be directed to the influence of ongoing emotions on social information processing.

Integrating Emotion Processes and Social Information Processing

An important way in which thinking about people is different from thinking about things is that social interaction is likely to be associated with a variety of strong emotions (Hoffman, 1981). The peer entry and provocation situations examined by social information processing theory (e.g., being excluded from play or teased in front of others) are especially likely to be emotionally arousing for children. Moreover, in these situations, children are unlikely to know all relevant information which would assist problem solving, and the outcomes of these situations are uncertain. Despite these limitations, the child still needs to do something.

Emotion theorists have argued that conditions of uncertainty and incomplete knowledge are the very contexts in which emotion processes can play an adaptive (or maladaptive) role by reducing information processing demands so the individual can arrive at some course of action (e.g., Damasio, 1994; Oatley & Jenkins, 1996). Crick and Dodge (1994) also acknowledge that emotion processes play important roles in social information processing, but suggest that the cognitive nature of their model may prevent a full examination of the contribution of emotion. We argue that it is possible to integrate emotion processes into Crick and Dodge's model (see Figure 9.2), and the integration of emotion and social information processing expands the model's explanatory power.

We agree that the child enters a given social situation with a combination of "biologically limited capabilities and a database of memories of past experiences" (Crick & Dodge, 1994, p.76), and that selective attention, perception, memory, and processing speed set limits on what children notice and process about a situation. In addition, we suggest that emotion processes are part of these givens. An important component of the child's biological predispositions is his/her emotion style or emotionality (Eisenberg & Fabes, 1992; Rothbart & Derryberry, 1981). Children vary in the intensity with which they experience and express emotions and in their skills for regulating emotions. These individual differences in emotionality and regulatory

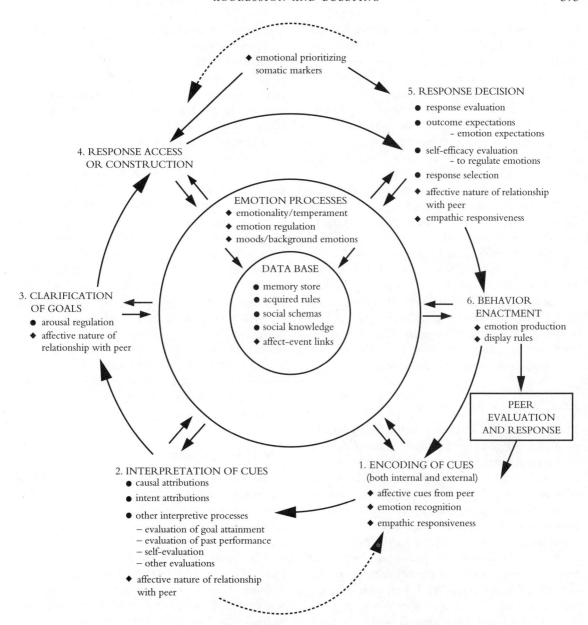

◆ emotional prioritizing
  somatic markers

5. RESPONSE DECISION
- response evaluation
- outcome expectations
  - emotion expectations
- self-efficacy evaluation
  - to regulate emotions
- response selection
- affective nature of relationship
  with peer
- empathic responsiveness

**4. RESPONSE ACCESS
OR CONSTRUCTION**

EMOTION PROCESSES
◆ emotionality/temperament
◆ emotion regulation
◆ moods/background emotions

DATA BASE
- memory store
- acquired rules
- social schemas
- social knowledge
◆ affect-event links

**3. CLARIFICATION
OF GOALS**
- arousal regulation
◆ affective nature of
  relationship with peer

**6. BEHAVIOR
ENACTMENT**
◆ emotion production
◆ display rules

PEER
EVALUATION
AND RESPONSE

2. INTERPRETATION OF CUES
- causal attributions
- intent attributions
- other interpretive processes
  - evaluation of goal attainment
  - evaluation of past performance
  - self-evaluation
  - other evaluations
◆ affective nature of relationship
  with peer

1. ENCODING OF CUES
(both internal and external)
◆ affective cues from peer
◆ emotion recognition
◆ empathic responsiveness

Figure 9.2 An integrated model of emotion processes and cognition in social information processing. Items marked with filled circles are from Crick and Dodge's model; those marked with filled diamonds represent emotion processes added to the model. *Note.* From "A review and reformulation of social-information-processing mechanisms of children's social adjustment," N. R. Crick & K. A. Dodge, *Psychological Bulletin, 115*, p. 74. Copyright 1994 by the American Psychological Association. Adapted with permission.

abilities are related to social competence (e.g., Eisenberg et al., 1997). We hypothesize that emotionality and regulatory ability will affect both processing of social (and emotional) information

and decision making in challenging social situations (see Figure 9.2).

In Crick and Dodge's (1994) model of social information processing, children's database includes a memory store of acquired rules, social knowledge, and social schemas. Based on current models of the neurophysiology of emotion and cognition (Damasio, 1994; LeDoux, 1995), we argue that the child's representations of past experience include affective as well as cognitive components, similar to what Arsenio and Lover (1995, p.90) termed "affect–event links" (see Figure 9.2). Thus, children's social knowledge can be cued by events and/or by emotion cues, and events may cue emotions.

Finally, children enter a social situation with a general level of physiological arousal and/or mood (see Figure 9.2) which may not necessarily be related to that situation. For example, feelings of anxiety in a peer entry situation may be related to the terrible fight your parents had this morning *or* to past experiences of rebuff by peers. Children also differ in their skill at regulating arousal or mood (Eisenberg et al., 1997). Because children who are poor regulators have a higher risk for maladjustment (Eisenberg et al., 1996), we hypothesize that poor regulators also will show social information processing deficits.

Encoding and interpreting cues

The first two steps of the Crick and Dodge (1994) model involve encoding and interpreting social cues. Crick and Dodge point out that one's own internal emotion cues must be encoded and interpreted along with other situational cues. They also suggest that the process of encoding and interpreting cues can result in a change in the discrete emotion experienced or in the intensity of a pre-existing emotion (see Crick & Ladd, 1993).

We would add that others' affective cues are an important source of information and must be encoded and interpreted (Saarni, 1999). For example, provocateurs' anger cues in the context of ambiguous provocation facilitate hostile attributions (Lemerise, Gregory, Leitner, & Hobgood, 1999; see also Dodge & Somberg, 1987). Functionalist theories of emotion stress the mutual regulatory function of affective signals (Magai & McFadden, 1995). One's own and others' affective signals provide ongoing information about how the encounter is proceeding, allowing for sensitive adjustments to behavior. The mutual regulatory function of affective signals may work especially well with familiar, well-liked interaction partners (at first parents, and later friends) whose signals may be easier to read and interpret and with whom the child is more likely to feel empathy (Hoffman, 1981; Parker & Gottman, 1989). The nature of emotional ties with an interaction partner also may influence encoding and interpretation. Being teased by a friend is quite different from being teased by the class bully. Children with conduct disorder have difficulty reading their own and others' affective signals and have deficits in their expressive behavior (Casey, 1996; Casey & Schlosser, 1994) and in empathy (Cohen & Strayer, 1996). These deficits are thought to contribute to behavior problems.

Finally, encoding and interpretation can be influenced by mood, level of arousal, or by discrete emotions (whether pre-existing or the result of appraisal). Mood, emotions, and/or arousal can affect what is noticed about a social encounter and make the recollection of mood-congruent information more likely, thus influencing interpretation of social cues. Moreover, the effects of a happy mood may be quite distinct from those of a sad or angry mood (Oatley & Jenkins, 1996). The intensity with which children experience emotions and their skill at regulating emotion also will influence what is noticed and the meaning attributed to the situation.

Clarification of goals

Crick and Dodge (1994) consider the role of emotion processes in a more explicit fashion for step 3 of their model, clarification of goals. They define goals as "focused arousal states that function toward producing (or wanting to produce) particular outcomes" (p. 87). Goals are conceptualized as either internal (maintaining or regulating emotion) or external (e.g., instrumental goals, such as getting the swing, or social relational goals, like getting another to play with you). According to Crick and Dodge, emotions can act to energize particular goals. For example, being in an angry mood makes it more likely that a child will focus on instrumental goals (Lemerise et al., 1998), whereas children in positive moods may choose goals that maintain their pleasant moods. Finally, Crick and Dodge assert that goal selection and/or attainment may modify mood or emotion.

We suggest that peers' affective cues also can influence children's goals. Positive affective signals may promote affiliative goals, whereas negative cues may discourage affiliation (Sroufe, Schork, Motti, Lawroski, & LaFreniere, 1984). Moreover, the intensity with which children experience emotions and their efficacy for regulating emotions will influence the types of goals pursued in social encounters (Eisenberg & Fabes, 1992; Eisenberg et al., 1994; Saarni, 1999). Children who are overwhelmed by their own and/or others' emotions may choose avoidant or hostile goals to reduce their own arousal. Children with deficits in affective cue detection and empathy may find it easier to pursue goals that are destructive to relationships because they literally do not "feel other children's pain" (Cohen & Strayer, 1996). Poor regulatory abilities may interfere with assessing the situation from different cognitive and affective perspectives and prevent a flexible approach to goal selection which takes into account contextual factors (Saarni, 1999). Instead, children's goals may be rigid because they result from "preemptive processing" (Costanzo & Dix, 1983; Crick & Dodge, 1994).

Finally, the nature of the emotional ties between a child and others involved in an encounter may bias goal selection. Social relational goals may be facilitated by friendship ties, whereas less positive relationships elicit quite different goals (e.g., avoidance, revenge). Social relational goals are both cognitively and emotionally more complex because they require consideration and coordination of multiple cognitive and affective perspectives. Friendship ties may motivate children to engage in this more effortful processing, partly because of the negative emotional consequences associated with hurting a friend and partly because of the desire to maintain enjoyable play activities (Arsenio & Lover, 1995; Parker & Gottman, 1989).

Response generation, evaluation, and decision

In steps 4 and 5 of the Crick and Dodge model, children access possible responses to the situation and evaluate these in terms of likely outcomes, goals, and self-efficacy for performing the response; the most positively evaluated response with respect to the child's goals is selected. They also suggest that children's accessing of responses could be influenced by an emotion they are experiencing, and that accessing particular responses may modify an emotion. Both of these possibilities are consistent with the idea that representations of past experiences include an affective component (e.g., Damasio, 1994). Thus, feeling angry, frightened, or happy may cue different response types. Given that representations of these responses include an affective component, retrieval of particular strategies should cue certain emotions. For example, if experiences of avoidance are associated with a reduction in anxiety, accessing avoidant responses may moderate feelings of fear.

Other emotion processes that can influence accessing and evaluation of responses are the intensity with which emotions are experienced and the capacity to regulate emotion. Children who experience strong emotions may be too overwhelmed and self-focused to generate a variety of responses and evaluate them from all parties' perspectives. Such children may be likely to engage in "preemptive processing" (Crick & Dodge, 1994) which can result in a response that is unlikely to further social interaction (e.g., running away, angrily retaliating, or venting; see Eisenberg et al., 1994). Skill at regulating emotions in challenging situations makes possible the more effortful processing involved in accessing and evaluating several responses. Good regulators may be more likely to consider the situation from multiple cognitive and affective perspectives which should facilitate selecting a more competent response (Saarni, 1999).

We agree with Crick and Dodge (1994) that children's expectations about the emotional consequences of various responses constitute an important component of the response evaluation process, and have argued elsewhere that emotion expectations contribute importantly to socio-moral reasoning and behavior (Arsenio, 1988; Arsenio & Lover, 1995). Finally, we add that children's emotional ties (or lack thereof) to others involved in the encounter and/or the reputations of the other children (Perry, Willard, & Perry, 1990) may motivate the child to engage in the effortful processing involved in considering various perspectives and response options. In other words, a child may be more likely to consider another's reaction if he/she cares about and wants that person to like him/her.

Response enactment

In the final step of Crick and Dodge's (1994) model, the child enacts the chosen response. Several emotion-related processes can influence response enactment. The intensity with which emotions are experienced and the child's regulatory capacities can influence response enactment. For example, under calm conditions, even maladjusted children are well aware of display rules for challenging situations (Underwood, 1997), but under highly arousing conditions, this knowledge may not be put into practice (Parker & Hubbard, 1998). The ability to flexibly display emotions appropriate to the situation requires both control over one's expressivity and sensitivity to the situation from multiple perspectives (Saarni, 1999). Moreover, the child's and others' emotion cues provide an ongoing source of information concerning how the encounter is proceeding, allowing the child to make adjustments to his/her response enactment. Children with deficits in reading and sending emotion cues may resort to relatively rigid approaches to situations (Casey, 1996; Casey & Schlosser, 1994; Saarni, 1999). Emotion cues also can inform the child about the ultimate success or failure of his/her response enactment. Finally, emotion cues are part of the representation of the encounter stored in the child's database of social knowledge. Consider a situation in which a child wants to play with a peer's toy. An affectively positive offer to trade toys may be successful in that the child not only gets the desired toy but both children feel positive about the encounter and may even play together. An angry demand that the peer hand over the toy, however, may elicit anger and resistance, with the result that the child has neither the toy nor a playmate. In these examples, the affective cues that were part of the child's enactment influenced the peer's reaction and ultimately the outcome of the encounter, including associated emotions.

Future Directions for Research

A number of hypotheses can be derived from the proposed model. At a general level, we hypothesize that individual differences in emotionality and emotion regulation can influence each step of social informa-tion processing. Specifically, children who are high in emotionality and poor at regulating emotion will show deficits in social information processing (e.g., Murphy & Eisenberg, 1997). Also, because emotions within the person and in others function to mutually regulate encounters, we hypothesize that manipulating these cues can affect each social information processing step and that the effects of different discrete emotions may be distinct. Specifically, manipulation of emotion or mood in the child via mood induction or situational manipulations (see Lemerise & Dodge, 2000, for a review) will influence social information processing. Also, manipulation of emotion cues or the nature of emotional ties to targets (peers about whom judgments are made) will influence social information processing. Research on target effects on social information processing has been especially rare (Crick & Dodge, 1994). Given our hypothesis that emotionality and emotion regulation skills influence social information processing, we hypothesize that the above described emotion manipulations will have a greater effect on children who are high in emotionality and poor in regulatory abilities. In addition, we suggest that there is a need to explore the emotion content of children's database of knowledge about social situations (e.g., Arsenio, 1988). Recent research has shown that children's knowledge structures predict aggressive behavior (Burks, Laird, Dodge, Pettit, & Bates, 1999), but the emotion content of children's knowledge structures has received little empirical attention.

Beyond these specific hypotheses, we hope the present model will encourage other systematic attempts to integrate affect and cognition. These efforts should prove fruitful for a fuller understanding not only of children's social competence, but also of other areas in which motivation and reasoning combine in essential ways, including socio-moral development, academic achievement, and developmental psychopathology.

References

Arsenio, W. (1988). Children's conceptions of the affective consequences of socio-moral events. *Child Development, 59*, 1611–1622.

Arsenio, W., Cooperman, S., & Lover, A. (2000). Affective predictors of preschoolers' aggression: and peer acceptance: Direct and indirect effects. *Developmental Psychology*, *36*, 438–448.

Arsenio, W., & Lover, A. (1995). Children's conceptions of sociomoral affect: Happy victimizers, mixed emotions, and other expectancies. In M. Killen & D. Hart (Eds.), *Morality in everyday life: Developmental perspectives* (pp. 87–128). New York: Cambridge University Press.

Arsenio, W., & Lover, A. (1997). Emotions, conflicts and aggression during preschoolers' freeplay. *British Journal of Developmental Psychology*, *15*, 531–542.

Bearison, D., & Zimiles H. (Eds.). (1986). *Thought and emotion: Developmental perspectives*. Hillsdale, NJ: Erlbaum.

Bechara, A., Damasio, A. R., Damasio, H., & Anderson, S. (1994). Insensitivity to future consequences following damage to human prefrontal cortex. *Cognition, 50*, 7–12.

Bechara, A., Tranel, D., Damasio, H., & Damasio, A. R. (1993). Failure to respond autonomically in anticipation of future outcomes following damage to prefrontal cortex. *Society for Neuroscience, 19*, 791.

Berkowitz, J. (1990). On the formation and regulation of anger and aggression: A cognitive-neoassociationistic analysis. *American Psychologist, 45*, 494–503.

Bowlby, J. (1988). *A secure base: Parent-child attachment and healthy human development*. New York: Basic Books.

Bretherton, I., Ridgeway, D., & Cassidy, J. (1990). Assessing internal working models of the attachment relationship. In M. Greenberg, D. Cicchetti, & M. Greenberg (Eds.), *Attachment in the preschool years: Theory, research, and intervention* (pp. 273–310). Chicago: University of Chicago Press.

Brown, T. (1996). Values, knowledge, and Piaget. In E. Reed, E. Turiel, & T. Brown (Eds.), *Values and knowledge* (pp. 137–170). Mahwah, NJ: Erlbaum.

Burks, V. S., Laird, R. D., Dodge, K. A., Pettit, G. S., & Bates, J. E. (1999). Knowledge structures, social information processing and children's aggressive behavior. *Social Development, 8*(2), 220–236.

Campos, J. J., Mumme, D. L., Kermoian, R., & Campos, R. G. (1994). A functionalist perspective on the nature of emotion. *Monographs of the Society for Research in Child Development, 59*(2–3, Serial No. 240), 284–303.

Casey, R. J. (1996). Emotional competence in children with externalizing and internalizing disorders. In M. Lewis & M. W. Sullivan (Eds.), *Emotional development in atypical children* (pp. 161–183). Mahwah, NJ: Erlbaum.

Casey, R. J., & Schlosser, S. (1994). Emotional responses to peer praise in children with and without a diagnosed externalizing disorder. *Merrill-Palmer Quarterly, 40*, 60–81.

Clark, M. S., & Isen, A. M. (1981). Toward understanding the relationship between feeling states and social behavior. In A. Hastorf & A. M. Isen (Eds.), *Cognitive social psychology* (pp. 73–108). New York: Elsevier.

Cohen, D., & Strayer, J. (1996). Empathy in conduct-disordered and comparison youth. *Developmental Psychology, 32*, 988–998.

Costanzo, P. R., & Dix, T. H. (1983). Beyond the information processed: Socialization in the development of attributional processes. In E. T. Higgins, D. N. Ruble, & W. W. Hartup (Eds.), *Social cognition and social development: A sociocultural perspective* (pp. 63–81). Cambridge, UK: Cambridge University Press.

Cowan, P. (1981). Preface. In J. Piaget, *Intelligence and affectivity: Their relationship during child development* (pp. ix–xiv). Palo Alto, CA: Annual Reviews.

Crick, N. R., & Dodge, K. A. (1994). A review and reformulation of social-information-processing mechanisms in children's social adjustment. *Psychological Bulletin, 115*, 74–101.

Crick, N. R., & Ladd, G. W. (1993). Children's perceptions of their peer experiences: Attributions, loneliness, social anxiety, and social avoidance. *Developmental Psychology, 29*, 244–254.

Damasio, A. R. (1994). *Descartes' error: Emotion, reason, and the human brain*. New York: Avon Books.

Damasio, A. R., Tranel, D., & Damasio, H. (1991). Somatic markers and the guidance of behavior: Theory and preliminary testing. In H. S. Levin, H. M. Eisenberg, & A. L. Benton (Eds.), *Frontal lobe function and dysfunction* (pp. 217–229). New York: Oxford University Press.

Damasio, H., Grabowski, T., Frank, R., Galaburda, A. M., & Damasio, A. R. (1994). The return of Phineas Gage: Clues about the brain from the skull of a famous patient. *Science, 264*, 1102–1105.

Denham, S. A. (1986). Social cognition, prosocial behavior and emotion in preschoolers: Contextual validation. *Child Development, 57*, 194–201.

Denham, S. A. (1998). *Emotional development in young children*. New York: Guilford.

Denham, S. A., McKinley, M., Couchoud, E. A., & Holt, R. (1990). Emotional and behavioral predictors of preschool peer ratings. *Child Development, 61*, 1145–1152.

Dodge, K. A. (1986). A social information processing model of social competence in children. In M. Perlmutter (Ed.), *Minnesota Symposium in Child Psychology* (Vol. 18, pp. 77–125). Hillsdale, NJ: Erlbaum.

Dodge, K. A. (1991). Emotion and social information processing. In J. Garber & K. Dodge (Eds.), *The development of emotion regulation and dysregulation* (pp. 159–181). New York: Cambridge University Press.

Dodge, K. A., & Somberg, D. (1987). Hostile attributional biases are exacerbated under conditions of threat to the self. *Child Development, 58,* 213–224.

Eisenberg, N., & Fabes, R. A. (1992). Emotion regulation and the development of social competence. In M. S. Clark (Ed.), *Emotion and social behavior: Vol. 14. Review of personality and social psychology* (pp. 119–150). Newbury Park, CA: Sage.

Eisenberg, N., Fabes, R. A., Guthrie, I. K., Murphy, B. C., Maszk, P., Holmgren, R., & Suh, K. (1996). The relations of regulation and emotionality to problem behavior in elementary school children. *Development and Psychopathology, 8,* 141–162.

Eisenberg, N., Fabes, R. A., Nyman, M., Bernzweig, J., & Pinuelas, A. (1994). The relations of emotionality and regulation to children's anger-related reactions. *Child Development, 65,* 109–128.

Eisenberg, N., Fabes, R. A., Shepard, S. A., Murphy, B. C., Guthrie, I. K., Jones, S., Friedman, J., Poulin, R., & Maszk, P. (1997). Contemporaneous and longitudinal prediction of children's social functioning from regulation and emotionality. *Child Development, 68,* 642–664.

Ekman, P. (1984). Expression and the nature of emotions. In K. Sherer & P. Ekman (Eds.), *Approaches to emotion* (pp. 329–343). New York: Prentice Hall.

Ekman, P. (1993). Facial expression and emotion. *American Psychologist, 48,* 384–392.

Ekman, P., & Davidson, R. J. (Eds.). (1994). *The nature of emotion: Fundamental questions.* New York: Oxford University Press.

Gottman, J., Katz, L., & Hooven, C. (1997). *Meta-emotion: How families communicate emotionally.* Mahwah, NJ: Erlbaum.

Hoffman, M. L. (1981). Perspectives on the difference between understanding people and understanding things: The role of affect. In J. H. Flavell & L. Ross (Eds.), *Social cognitive development: Frontiers and possible futures* (pp. 67–81). Cambridge: Cambridge University Press.

Hubbard, J. A., & Coie, J. D. (1994). Emotional correlates of social competence in children's peer relationships. *Merrill-Palmer Quarterly, 40,* 1–20.

Isen, A., Shalker, T., Clark, M., & Karp, L. (1978). Affect, accessibility of material in memory, and behavior: A cognitive loop. *Journal of Personality and Social Psychology, 35,* 1–12.

Izard, C. E. (1977). *Human emotions.* New York: Plenum.

Izard, C. E. (1991). *The psychology of emotions.* New York: Plenum.

Izard, C. E. (1994). Cognition is one of four types of emotion-activating systems. In P. Ekman & R. J. Davidson (Eds.), *The nature of emotion: Fundamental questions* (pp. 203–207). New York: Oxford University Press.

Kandel, E. R., & Kupferman, I. (1995). Emotional states. In E. R. Kandel, J. H. Schwartz, & T. M. Jessell (Eds.), *Essentials of neural science and behavior* (pp. 595–612). Norwalk, CT: Appleton & Lange.

Lazarus, R. S. (1991). *Emotion and adaptation.* New York: Oxford University Press.

LeDoux, J. E. (1993). Emotional networks in the brain. In M. Lewis & J. M. Haviland (Eds.), *Handbook of emotions* (pp. 109–118). New York: Guilford.

LeDoux, J. E. (1995). Emotion: Clues from the brain. *Annual Review of Psychology, 46,* 209–235.

Lemerise, E. A., & Dodge, K. A. (2000). The development of anger and hostile interactions. In M. Lewis & J. M. Haviland-Jones (Eds.), *Handbook of emotions* (2nd ed, pp. 594–606). New York: Guilford.

Lemerise, E. A., Gregory, D., Leitner, K., & Hobgood, C. (1999, April). *The effect of affective cues on children's social information processing.* Poster session presented at the biennial meeting of the Society for Research in Child Development, Albuquerque, NM.

Lemerise, E. A., Harper, B. D., Caverly, S., & Hobgood, C. (1998, March). *Mood, social goals, and children's outcome expectations.* Poster session presented at the biennial Conference on Human Development, Mobile, AL.

Magai, C., & McFadden, S. (1995). *The role of emotions in social and personality development.* New York: Plenum Press.

Malatesta, C. (1990). The role of emotions in the development and organization of personality. In R. Thompson (Ed.), *Nebraska Symposium on Motivation, Vol. 36: Socioemotional development* (pp. 1–56). Lincoln: University of Nebraska Press.

Malatesta, C., & Wilson, A. (1988). Emotion/cognition interaction in personality development: A discrete emotion, functionalist analysis. *British Journal of Social Psychology, 27,* 91–112.

Moore, B., Underwood, B., & Rosenhan, D. L. (1984). Emotion, self, and others. In C. Izard, J. Kagan, & R. Zajonc (Eds.), *Emotions, cognition, and behavior* (pp. 464–483). New York: Cambridge University Press.

Murphy, B. C., & Eisenberg, N. (1997). Young children's emotionality: Regulation and social functioning and their responses when they are targets of a peer's anger. *Social Development, 6,* 18–36.

Oatley, K., & Jenkins, J. M. (1996). *Understanding emotions.* Cambridge, MA: Blackwell.

Parker, E. H., & Hubbard, J. A. (1998, March). *Children's understanding of emotion following hypothetical vignettes versus real-life peer interaction.* Paper presented at the biennial Conference on Human Development, Mobile, AL.

Parker, J. G., & Gottman, J. M. (1989). Social and emotional development in a relational context: Friendship interaction from early childhood to adolescence. In T. J. Berndt & G. W. Ladd (Eds.), *Peer relationships in child development* (pp. 95–131). New York: Wiley.

Perry, D. G., Willard, J. C., & Perry, L. C. (1990). Peers' perceptions of the consequences that victimized children provide aggressors. *Child Development, 61,* 1310–1325.

Piaget, J. (1965). *The moral judgement of the child* (M. Gabain, Trans.). New York: Free Press. (Original work published 1932)

Piaget, J. (1981). *Intelligence and affectivity: Their relationship during child development* (T. A. Brown & C. E. Kaegi, Trans. & Eds.). Palo Alto, CA: Annual Reviews.

Plutchik, R (1980). *Emotions: A psychoevolutionary synthesis.* New York: Harper & Row.

Plutchik, R. (1993). Emotions and their vicissitudes: Emotions and psychopathology. In M. Lewis & J. Haviland (Eds.), *Handbook of emotions* (pp. 53–66). New York: Guilford.

Pugh, G. (1977). *The biological origins of human values.* New York: Basic Books.

Rothbart, M., & Bates, J. E. (1998). Temperament. In N. Eisenberg (Ed.), W. Damon (Series Ed.), *Handbook of child psychology: Vol. 3. Social, emotional, and personality development* (5th ed., pp. 105–176). New York: Wiley.

Rothbart, M. K., & Derryberry, D. (1981). Development of individual differences in temperament. In M. E. Lamb & A. L. Brown (Eds.), *Advances in developmental psychology* (Vol. 1, pp. 37–86). Hillsdale, NJ: Erlbaum.

Saarni, C. (1999). *The development of emotional competence.* New York: Guilford.

Saarni, C., Mumme, D. L., & Campos, J. (1998). Emotional development: Action, communication, and understanding. In N. Eisenberg (Ed.), W. Damon (Series Ed.), *Handbook of child psychology: Vol. 3. Social, emotional, and personality development* (5th ed., pp. 237–309). New York: Wiley.

Simon, H. A. (1967). Motivational and emotional controls of cognition. *Psychological Review, 74,* 29–39.

Sroufe, L. A., Schork, E., Motti, F., Lawroski, N., & LaFreniere, P. (1984). The role of affect in social competence. In C. E. Izard, J. Kagan, & R. B. Zajonc (Eds.), *Emotions, cognition, and behavior* (pp. 289–319). New York: Cambridge University Press.

Thompson, R. (1990). Emotion and self-regulation. In R. Thompson (Ed.), R. Dienstbier (Series Ed.), *Nebraska Symposium on Motivation: Vol. 36. Socioemotional development* (pp. 367–467). Lincoln: University of Nebraska Press.

Thompson, R. (1994). Emotion regulation: A theme in search of definition. *Monographs of the Society for Research in Child Development, 59*(2–3, Serial No. 240), 25–52.

Turiel, E. (1998). The development of morality. In N. Eisenberg (Ed.), W. Damon (Series Ed.), *Handbook of child psychology: Vol. 3. Social, emotional, and personality development* (5th ed., pp. 863–932). New York: Wiley.

Underwood, M. K. (1997). Peer social status and children's understanding of the expression and control of positive and negative emotions. *Merrill-Palmer Quarterly, 43,* 610–634.

....

A Short-Term Longitudinal Study of Growth of Relational Aggression during Middle Childhood: Associations with Gender, Friendship Intimacy, and Internalizing Problems

Dianna Murray-Close, Jamie M. Ostrov, and Nicki R. Crick

The study of relational aggression in middle childhood has burgeoned in recent years (e.g., Crick & Grotpeter, 1995; Crick, Grotpeter, & Bigbee, 2002; Crick & Werner, 1998; French, Jansen, & Pidada, 2002; Rys & Bear, 1997; Werner & Crick, 2004; Zalecki & Hinshaw, 2004). Relational aggression, defined as using the removal or threat of removal of relationships as the vehicle of harm, includes behaviors such as spreading malicious lies, gossip or secrets, ignoring or

giving the silent treatment, and directly or covertly excluding a peer from an activity (see Crick et al., 1999). Despite clear advances in the study of the causes and correlates of relational aggression, the field is lacking a clear understanding of change in relational aggression during middle childhood. In particular, we do not know if relational aggression use increases in frequency over time or whether short-term relational aggression trajectories are similar for girls and boys. In addition, it is unclear whether changes in relationship factors such as intimate exchange with friends is associated with increases in relational aggression. Finally, researchers have not yet examined whether growth in relational aggression over time is dynamically associated with maladaptive problems such as internalizing symptoms. The present study was designed to address mean change in relational aggression over the course of 1 year in middle childhood and to explore potential gender differences in relational aggression growth using a large, multimethod longitudinal sample.

Although some mixed findings have been reported (Henington, Hughes, Cavell, & Thompson, 1998), researchers have generally found that girls are more relationally aggressive than boys in middle childhood (for reviews see Crick et al., 1999; Tomada & Schneider, 1997; for discussion regarding related constructs such as indirect or social aggression, see Bjorkqvist, Lagerspetz, & Kaukianen, 1992; Galen & Underwood, 1997). Contrary to the common belief that boys are more aggressive than girls, studies that include measures of both physical and relational aggression report almost equal proportions of aggressive boys and girls (Crick & Grotpeter, 1995; Rys & Bear, 1997). For example, Crick and Grotpeter (1995) found that although children identified more physically aggressive boys than girls in their classroom (16% of boys but only 0.4% of girls), relationally aggressive girls outnumbered relationally aggressive boys (17% of girls but only 2% of boys). Overall, then, evidence suggests that relational aggression is more common among girls during elementary school. Given these gender differences in use of relational aggression, it is important to explore the trajectories of relational aggression in middle childhood so that social experiences particularly salient among females of this age may be examined.

In recent years, developmental scholars have begun to address fundamental questions related to the growth trajectories of both boys' and girls' aggressive behavior (e.g., Pellegrini & Long, 2002). Evidence suggests that the frequency of physical aggression use changes during middle childhood. For example, longitudinal studies indicate a steady decline in physical aggression during the first decade of life, with the largest drop occurring during the transition from the early to middle childhood periods (Tremblay et al., 1996).

Examining trajectories of aggressive behavior is particularly important given the theorized association between chronic externalizing problem pathways and psychopathology (Moffitt, 1993; Patterson, 1982).

Given the developmental changes in physical aggression use and the association of such trajectories with psychopathology, it is important to consider how the frequency of relational aggression may change over time. Previous research has documented moderate to high levels of individual stability for relational aggression during a 6-month period among elementary school children; thus, there is some evidence that relationally aggressive behaviors may continue over time during this developmental period (Crick, 1996). However, it is unclear whether use of relational aggression increases or decreases during late middle childhood. To date, little work has explored the developmental trajectories of relational aggression. In the one prior study to investigate growth in relational aggression, the authors revealed that relationally aggressive behaviors among adolescents decreased over time (sixth to eighth grade; Pellegrini & Long, 2003). However, little research has examined whether elementary school children exhibit increases or decreases in their relationally aggressive behavior.

Given the many cognitive and social changes occurring during late elementary school (i.e., fourth and fifth grade), we hypothesized that relational aggression may actually become *more* common during this developmental period. Indeed, as children acquire language skills (Bonica, Yeshova, Arnold, Fisher, & Zeljo, 2003) and other social-cognitive capacities (e.g., perspective taking, emotion regulation, memory) during early childhood and into middle childhood, they may be more able to learn and effectively use sophisticated and in some cases covert relationally aggressive behaviors (Bjorkqvist, 1994; Crick et al., 1999). In particular, increased cognitive capacities allow children to recall specific relationship history information and to retaliate in response to behaviors that were conducted in the past (Crick et al., 1999).

In addition, social changes emerging in middle childhood may provide fertile ground for relational aggression use. Indeed, given the definition of relational aggression as intentionally harmful behaviors that use the manipulation of *relationships* as the vehicle of harm, it is likely that relational aggression use will change depending on children's relationship context. For instance, the emerging importance of intimacy among friends during late middle childhood may make this developmental period a salient time for investigating growth in relational aggression (Berndt, 1996; Bukowski & Kramer, 1988). Indeed, researchers have found that children tend to use relationally aggressive behaviors against their close friends and high levels of intimacy and exclusivity within the friendship dyad are associated with relational aggression use (Grotpeter & Crick, 1996). As such, as close, intimate friendships with others emerge and as children spend more time with their friends in middle childhood (Higgins & Parsons, 1983), relational aggression use may correspondingly increase.

Moreover, trajectories of relational aggression may differ for boys and girls. Given the gender differences typically observed in cross-sectional studies of relational aggression, it is possible that, by the fourth grade, girls are already exhibiting higher levels of relational aggression than boys. In addition to intercept differences, it is possible that boys and girls exhibit different growth patterns in relational aggression. In the context of gender-segregated peer interactions typical among elementary school children (Maccoby, 1990), boys' and girls' growth in relational aggression may look quite different. Research has established that the relationship contexts of boys and girls are rather distinct at this age; girls tend to be involved in intimate friendships with a few close peers whereas boys tend to participate in larger friendship groups (Degirmencioglu et al., 1998; Maccoby, 1990). In addition, there is evidence that girls and boys differ in the quality of their friendships; for instance, girls' friendships are characterized by greater levels of intimate exchange than boys' (Parker & Asher, 1993), which in turn, has been associated with increased involvement in relational aggression (Grotpeter & Crick, 1996). Finally, girls are more likely to adopt a relational orientation (Crick & Zahn-Waxler, 2003; Cross & Madsen, 1997) and to report distress when involved in relational conflicts with peers (Crick, 1995). Given that relational aggression is often used in the context of close relationships (Grotpeter & Crick, 1996), girls' friendship structure may provide a developmental context for emerging relationally aggressive behaviors. As a result, girls' use of relationally aggres-

sive strategies may increase at faster rates than boys' over this developmental period.

Thus, the first goal of the present study was to investigate whether there were increases in relational aggression over time, and whether such change differed for elementary school girls and boys. In particular, we examined whether relational aggression exhibited linear growth over the course of 1 calendar year, whether girls started at a higher initial level than boys (i.e., an intercept difference), and whether this growth during middle childhood was moderated by gender (i.e., gender differences in linear change).

Given our hypothesis that changing relationship contexts (e.g., increasing importance of intimate friendships) may set the stage for increases in relational aggression over time, the second goal of this study was to empirically investigate whether growth in intimacy within the context of close friendships was associated with increases in relational aggression. Grotpeter and Crick (1996) propose that high levels of disclosure by friends may provide relationally aggressive children with ammunition for aggressing. Indeed, it is intimate sharing by friends that is associated with children's relational aggression rather than the children's own self-disclosure to their friends (Grotpeter & Crick, 1996). Having intimate knowledge of others may increase relationally aggressive children's opportunities to manipulate others with relationship-damaging tactics such as gossip (e.g., "I'll tell Ryan that you like him if you don't do what I say").

Intimate exchange with friends may be especially predictive of relational aggression among girls. Girls tend to report greater emotional distress when facing relational provocation by peers (Crick, 1995), suggesting that experiences such as having personal secrets shared with others is more threatening for girls than for boys. Moreover, the relatively high levels of intimacy in girls' friendships may make intimate exchange with friends an especially salient factor in girls' use of relational aggression. In addition, it has been proposed that girls' attempts to inflict interpersonal harm focus predominantly on manipulating dyadic relationships, whereas boys' attempts instead focus on harm to membership and status within the larger peer group (Rudolph, 2002). Thus, the knowledge gained through friend intimate exchange may be more closely aligned with the relational aggression goals of girls than those of boys. The second goal of the present study was to investigate whether friend intimate exchange was associated with relational aggression use over time, particularly among girls.

In addition to its relation to high levels of friend intimacy, relational aggression has been shown to be associated with various forms of maladaptive functioning, including an increased prevalence of psychopathology (e.g., depressive symptoms, borderline personality disorder features, attention-deficit/hyperactivity disorder, problematic eating patterns, etc.; see Crick et al., 1999; Crick & Zahn-Waxler, 2003) and social–psychological adjustment problems (e.g., asocial behavior, loneliness, hostile attribution bias, peer exclusion, peer rejection, and a lack of prosocial behavior; see Crick, 1996; Crick et al., 1999; Ostrov, Woods, Jansen, Casas, & Crick, 2004). Some findings suggest that relationally aggressive behaviors are more salient and associated with more adjustment problems for girls (Blachman & Hinshaw, 2002; Leff, Costigan, Eiraldi, & Power, 2001; Ostrov et al., 2004; Sebanc, 2003; Zalecki & Hinshaw, 2004), although relationally aggressive boys may also exhibit social–psychological problems (e.g., peer rejection, loneliness, depressed affect), especially when they are frequent aggressors (Crick, 1997). Thus, growth in relational aggression may be associated with gender differences in trajectories of psychopathology, a topic that has increasingly captured the attention of researchers in the field of developmental psychopathology (Cicchetti & Sroufe, 2000).

Relational aggression has been particularly associated with an increased incidence of internalizing problems (e.g., depressive and anxious symptoms) during middle childhood for both boys and girls (Crick, 1997; Crick & Grotpeter, 1995). Previous longitudinal research has found that externalizing behaviors can predict internalizing problems (Capaldi, 1992; Kiesner, 2002), perhaps due to failing social relationships and school problems resulting from aggressive and delinquent conduct (Kiesner, 2002; Masten et al., 2005). Although externalizing problems include a variety of difficulties such as attention problems, hyperactivity, and impulsivity (Keenan & Shaw, 1997), the conduct problems typical of externalizing problems may include both physical and relational

aggression. For example, Crick and Zahn-Waxler (2003) propose that relational aggression may be a more typical manifestation of conduct problems for girls. Like other aspects of externalizing problems, childhood relational aggression may be related to internalizing symptoms over time.

Moreover, longitudinal work may indicate that relational aggression is more strongly associated with internalizing problems for girls than for boys. Interpersonal stressors have often been identified as important in the development of internalizing problems (such as depression) among children and adolescents (e.g., Garber & Flynn, 2001; Panak & Garber, 1992). For instance, children diagnosed with depression are more likely than their peers to be rejected, to report a negative self-appraisal of their social competency, and to exhibit a diminished social problem-solving capacity (see Hammen & Rudolph, 1996). Moreover, it has been suggested that, based on their strong interpersonal orientation (e.g., Cross & Madsen, 1997) and ruminative style, girls may experience increased vulnerability to internalizing symptoms in the context of interpersonal stress and conflictual peer relationships (e.g., Crick & Zahn-Waxler, 2003; Nolen-Hoeksema & Girgus, 1994). Thus, the strained peer interactions associated with relational aggression may be particularly problematic for girls; that is, relationally aggressive girls may be more likely to exhibit internalizing symptoms than their male counterparts. To date, few longitudinal studies have examined the association of relationally aggressive behavior with internalizing symptoms. Therefore, the third goal of the present study was to explore whether internalizing problems would be dynamically associated with relational aggression over time and to examine whether this association was stronger for girls than for boys.

To address the three goals of the present study, we used hierarchical linear models (HLM). The use of HLM has numerous advantages over traditional methods (repeated measures analysis of variance [ANOVA]) when analyzing longitudinal data (see Bryk & Raudenbush, 1992; Long & Pellegrini, 2003; Verbeke & Molenberghs, 2000). For example, HLM procedures are more robust to violations of the assumptions of repeated-measures ANOVA and permit more parsimonious models than traditional methods, which in turn, yield higher power in the testing of effects (Long & Pellegrini, 2003; Verbeke & Molenberghs, 2000). In addition, these techniques are capable of modeling dynamic (time-varying) longitudinal predictors (see Long & Pellegrini, 2003; Pellegrini & Long, 2002). Thus, in the present study, HLM techniques were used to estimate the growth in relational aggression over time for a relatively large sample of girls and boys (for a detailed explanation of this procedure, see Long & Pellegrini, 2003) and to test the dynamic association of friend intimate exchange and internalizing problems with relational aggression.

In the first study of the growth of relational aggression during middle childhood, we made several predictions based on prior theory and research. First, we believed that there would be significant change in relational aggression over time, and that relational aggression trajectories would differ for boys and girls. Specifically, we hypothesized that there would be significant linear growth in relational aggression based on past work demonstrating the increased salience and sophistication of relational aggression during middle childhood (see Crick, 1996; Crick et al., 1999). Moreover, based on findings that suggest that levels of relational aggression are higher for females than males in middle childhood (e.g., Crick & Grotpeter, 1995; French et al., 2002), we hypothesized that a significant intercept difference would emerge, with girls starting at higher levels of relational aggression than boys. Finally, we hypothesized that relational aggression growth would be conditional on (i.e., moderated by) gender; in particular, given that these behaviors tend to be more common among girls during this period, and given that girls' social contexts may promote relational aggression use, we expected that girls would increase at a faster rate than boys (Crick, 1996; Crick & Grotpeter, 1995; Grotpeter & Crick, 1996).

Second, based on the contention that friend intimate disclosure provides children with ammunition for relationally aggressive behaviors (Grotpeter & Crick, 1996), we expected that changes in relational aggression would be dynamically associated with friend intimate exchange such that increases in friend intimacy would be associated with time-dependent increases in relational aggression. In addition, given girls' relatively high levels of intimate exchange and interpersonal orientation, we predicted that the dynamic association between relational aggression and friend intimate exchange would be especially strong among girls. Third, we hypothesized that relational aggression would be a significant dynamic covariate of internalizing symptoms. That is, as relational aggression increases, we predicted that internalizing problems would significantly increase as well. In keeping with past findings suggesting that interpersonal stress may be a particularly salient predictor of depressive symptoms among females, we expected that internalizing symptoms and relational aggression would be associated more strongly for girls than for boys.

Methods

Participants

Participants were part of a short-term longitudinal study examining the relation between aggression and adjustment. A total of 604 fourth graders were recruited from 41 public elementary school classrooms (in 16 schools) in a large midwestern city. In the present sample, there was a relatively high attrition rate (the relational aggression scores of only 64% of the original sample was assessed at all three time points). The vast majority of children who were not assessed at Time 2 or Time 3 were not included because they had moved out of participating elementary schools or the participating school districts. Only participants with complete relational aggression data were included in the present analyses ($N = 385$; 48% female). Thus, the sample in the present study included a total of 385 participants. Of these 385 participants, approximately 35% of the sample was European American, 27% was African American, 15% was Asian American, 13% was Latino, 4% was Native American, and 6% represented other ethnic groups.

Analyses indicated that individuals who participated in the study at all three assessment periods did not differ from their peers who dropped out in their initial relational aggression scores, $F(1, 603) = 1.75$, ns, initial internalizing symptoms, $F(1, 603) = .14$, ns, initial friend intimate exchange scores, $F(1, 569) = .32$, ns, or gender, $\chi^2 = 1.50$, ns. However, analyses revealed that attrition did differ based on race, $\chi^2 = 24.99$, $p < .001$, with African American, Latino, and Asian American participants dropping out at greater rates than expected. HLM techniques can accommodate missing data (see Long & Pellegrini, 2003), and analyses were run with both the full sample and including only those participants with complete data. The significant findings from the subsample of participants presented here were confirmed with the entire sample.

The socioeconomic status of the sample was estimated to be lower class to middle class based on school demographic information. Each participant had parental consent to participate; the average consent rate at the first assessment period was 73% of all students in participating classrooms.

Procedure

Participants' aggressive behavior, friendship intimacy, and internalizing symptoms were assessed at three times: Time 1 (the fall of Grade 4), Time 2 (the spring of Grade 4), and Time 3 (the fall of Grade 5). Measures were completed near the end of each semester so that children and teachers would be familiar with one another and thus able to rate each other's behavior. The spacing between assessment periods was approximately 4–6 months. A widely used peer nomination instrument was used to identify children's use of relational aggression, participants' internalizing symptoms were assessed using standard teacher reports, and friend intimate exchange was assessed with a self-report measure. Thus, the analyses from the present study relied on different informants regarding children's behavior, friendship experiences, and adjustment.

Peer assessments

Children's relational aggression levels and best friend relationships were identified by a traditional peer nomination task (Crick & Grotpeter, 1995). Peer reports of relational aggression were chosen for the analyses for three reasons. First, the only study to date exploring growth in relational aggression using HLM procedures used limited nomination peer reports of children's aggressive behavior (Pellegrini & Long, 2003). Thus, peer reports were selected in an effort to

make the results of the present study comparable to this prior research. In addition, the majority of relational aggression research during middle childhood and adolescence has employed these reliable peer report measures because it has been suggested that occurrences of relational aggression may be more apparent or visible to peers than to other informants (e.g., relational aggression on the school bus; Crick et al., 1999; Leff, Kupersmidt, Patterson, & Power, 1999). Finally, with relatively large samples, these techniques are more efficient and cost effective than observational or individual interview methodologies.

All participating children with informed parental consent and who provided assent participated in a classroom-administered assessment period. In the assessment session, peer nomination procedures were used to assess children's relational aggression use. Participating children were provided with a class roster and a trained research assistant read aloud five items describing relationally aggressive behaviors (e.g., "people who let their friends know that they will stop liking them unless the friends do what they want them to do"), which was part of a larger battery of instruments for purposes of a different study. Participants were asked to select up to three male or female students in the class who fit the description of each item (Crick et al., 1999; Leff et al., 1999; Terry & Coie, 1991). The number of nominations each participant received for the relational aggression items was summed and divided by the number of participating students in the classroom to yield a relational aggression score for each student.[1] In addition, participants were asked to identify up to five best friends in their classroom, which were then used to assign a best friend at each time period for the self-report of friend intimacy. Children were provided with a small gift (e.g., pencil, toy) for their participation.

Self-reports

A self-report measure was used to assess friend intimate exchange. Specifically, participants completed the intimate exchange II—friend toward subject subscale of the Friendship Quality Measure (Grotpeter & Crick, 1996) as a part of a number of self-report instruments used for a different study. Participants were assigned a best friend to report on during the self-report session and asked to rate how true items describing friend intimate disclosure (e.g., "She can tell me her secrets"; three items) were of their friend on a scale of 1 (*not at all true*) to 5 (*almost always true*). Participant's responses were summed to yield a total friend intimate exchange score. Best friend assignments were made based on information gathered during the peer report session; in particular, efforts were made to have participants report on reciprocated best friends (i.e., best friends who had nominated the child as one of their best friends; Parker & Asher, 1993). The majority of children (>78% at each assessment period) were assigned a reciprocated best friend. Analyses including only children with reciprocated best friends did not differ from those reported here; thus, we included all participating children in the present analyses. The internal reliability of the friend intimate exchange measure at all three time points was acceptable (all Cronbach αs > .76).

Teacher assessments

Teacher reports of participants' internalizing symptoms were assessed using the Teacher Report Form of the Child Behavior Checklist (TRF; Achenbach & Edelbrock, 1991). Teacher reports were selected because they avoid self-serving biases found with self-reports of such experiences during this developmental period (Crick, 1997). As part of the larger teacher report battery, at each assessment period, teachers were presented with items describing symptoms of anxiety, depression, withdrawal, and somatic complaints (e.g., "Unhappy, sad, or depressed"). Teachers rated how true each item was of participants on a scale from 0 (*not true*) to 2 (*very true or often true*). Students' scores were summed across three subscales (anxious/depressed, withdrawn, and somatic complaints) including a total of 36 items (the item assessing suicidal ideation was dropped for ethical reasons). The internalizing scale of TRF exhibited acceptable internal consistency at all three time points in the present sample (all Cronbach αs > .85). Teachers were provided with a payment in the amount of $150 for their extensive time in completing study packets for the children in their classrooms.

Results

Modeling growth in relational aggression over time

The first goal of this study was to model the mean trajectory of relational aggression over time and to explore whether these trajectories differed for boys and girls. Examination of the mean relational aggression scores across the three assessment periods (see Table 9.1) suggested potential change in relational aggression over time.

Analyses exploring potential quadratic change in relational aggression (not shown) indicated that there was not significant quadratic change in relational aggression. As such, a linear model was adopted.[2]

HLMs can be conceptualized and presented as multilevel models exploring individual and group-level change over time. In the first analysis, the individual-level model explores within-person growth in relational aggression. The equation expressing this individual change is

$$y_{ij} = \beta_{0i} + \beta_{1i}l_j + e_{ij},\qquad(1)$$

where y_{ij} is the *i*th person's relational aggression score at the *j*th time point and l_j is the term used to model the linear trend across time. In this analysis, $l_j = 0$, 1, and 2 for Time 1, Time 2, and Time 3, respectively, so that the intercept value in the analyses would reflect children's relational aggression at the first assessment period (see Bryk & Raudenbush, 1992). In addition, β_{0i} is the person-specific intercept, β_{1i} is the person-specific slope, and e_{ij} are the residuals.

The equations for group-level change incorporated gender parameters so that gender differences in children's relational aggression at Time 1 (i.e., intercept) and growth in relational aggression (i.e., slope) could be explored. To explore group-level change in relational aggression over time, the following set of equations were used:

$$\beta_{0i} = \gamma_{00} + \gamma_{01}g_i + u_{0i},\qquad(2)$$

$$\beta_{1i} = \gamma_{10} + \gamma_{11}g_i + u_{1i},\qquad(3)$$

Table 9.1 Descriptive information regarding relational aggression, internalizing, and friend intimate exchange across time

Variable	Time 1		Time 2		Time 3	
	Mean	SD	Mean	SD	Mean	SD
Entire sample						
Relational aggression	0.51	0.41	0.57	0.57	0.56	0.61
Internalizing symptoms	5.73	7.00	5.49	6.67	5.94	6.25
Friend intimate exchange	10.35	3.71	10.37	3.71	10.69	3.82
Male						
Relational aggression	0.48	0.39	0.49	0.47	0.48	0.47
Internalizing symptoms	5.55	6.94	5.28	6.51	6.03	6.71
Friend intimate exchange	9.93	3.64	9.86	3.66	10.32	3.78
Female						
Relational aggression	0.55	0.44	0.66	0.65	0.65	0.72
Internalizing symptoms	5.92	7.07	5.72	6.84	5.85	5.82
Friend intimate exchange	10.78	3.75	10.92	3.70	11.01	3.83

where γ_{00} is the group intercept, γ_{01} is the index of the gender effect on intercept, g_i is the participant's gender (-1 = male, 1 = female), and u_{0i} is the residual indicating deviations from the group intercept. In addition, γ_{10} is the group slope, γ_{11} is the index of the gender effect on slope, and u_{1i} is the residual indicating individual deviations from the group slope. Combining the individual and group-level equations, the HLM used to estimate the conditional HLM analysis was

$$y_{ij} = (\gamma_{00} + \gamma_{01}g_i + u_{0i}) + (\gamma_{10} + \gamma_{11}g_i + u_{1i})l_{ij} + e_{ij}. \quad (4)$$

This equation demonstrates that the model of growth in relational aggression includes group-level change (i.e., average change in relational aggression over time, captured by γ_{00} and γ_{10}, and individual deviations from those trajectories, captured by u_{0i}, u_{1i}, and e_{ij}). In addition, this analysis allowed us to explore whether males and females differed in their relational aggression intercepts (as indexed by γ_{01}) and linear trajectories (as indexed by γ_{11}) over time. The SAS Proc Mixed syntax used to test all models are included in Appendix A. The results of the analysis are presented in Table 9.2.

Results indicated that the linear increase in relational aggression over time approached statistical significance. In addition, the gender difference in relational aggression at the first assessment period approached statistical significance, with girls exhibiting greater relational aggression than their male peers. Finally, the interaction between gender and linear growth was significant, suggesting that increases in relational aggression were exhibited among girls only. The actual relational aggression scores at each time point and the predicted relational aggression trajectories of males and females are presented in Figure 9.3.

Friendship intimacy and growth in relational aggression

To address the second goal of this study, analyses were conducted to explore whether change in friendship intimacy was associated with time-dependent growth in relational aggression. We expected that children who had friends that increasingly disclosed personal information to them would exhibit increases in relational aggression over time. Consistent with previous work, girls in the present study reported greater intimate exchange in the friendship context than did boys. Specifically, a one-way ANOVA examining gender differences in friend intimate exchange at Time 1 indicated that girls reported more intimate exchange than boys, $F(1, 366) = 4.92$, $p < .05$ (see Table 9.1). Given the relatively high levels of intimacy in girls'

Table 9.2 Parameter estimates in hierarchical linear modeling analyses

Model	Parameter	Estimate	df	F Value
1. Relational aggression trajectories	γ_{00}: Intercept[a]	0.53★★★	1,383	522.48
	γ_{01}: Gender × Intercept	0.04†	1,385	2.88
	γ_{10}: Linear growth	0.03†	1,383	3.79
	γ_{11}: Gender × Linear Growth	0.03★	1,385	4.21
2. Friend intimate exchange and relational aggression	γ_{00}: Intercept[a]	0.50★★★	1,663	165.38
	γ_{10}: Dynamic covariation	0.00	1,377	0.66
	γ_{11}: Gender × Dynamic Covariation	0.01★	1,657	6.14
3. Relational aggression and internalizing symptoms	γ_{00}: Intercept[a]	4.89★★★	1,614	211.74
	γ_{10}: Dynamic covariation	1.49★★★	1,614	11.70
	γ_{11}: Gender × Dynamic Covariation	0.19	1,614	0.35

[a]Although not pertinent to the hypotheses of the present study, group intercept estimates are reported for completeness.
†$p < .10$. ★$p < .05$. ★★$p < .01$. ★★★$p < .001$.

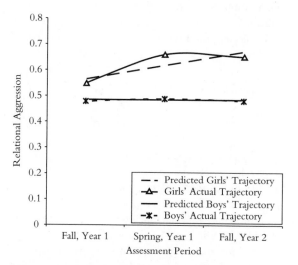

Figure 9.3 Predicted relational aggression trajectories and actual relational aggression scores for males and females.

friendships, we examined whether the association between friendship intimacy and relational aggression was particularly strong for girls.

For this analysis, relational aggression served as the dependent variable and intimate disclosure by a friend toward the participant served as the independent variable. The equation for individual-level change in this analysis was

$$y_{ij} = \beta_{0i} + \beta_{1i} ie_{ij} + e_{ij}, \tag{5}$$

where y_{ij} is the ith person's relational aggression score at the jth time point, ie_{ij} is the participant's level of intimate exchange from a friend at the jth time point, β_{0i} is the predicted relational aggression score if the participant's friendship intimacy score is 0, β_{1i} is the strength of the longitudinal relationship between relational aggression and friendship intimacy, and e_{ij} are the residuals.

To model group-level change, the following equations were used:

$$\beta_{0i} = \gamma_{00} + u_{0i}, \tag{6}$$

$$\beta_{1i} = \gamma_{10} + \gamma_{11} g_i + u_{1i}, \tag{7}$$

where γ_{00} is the group intercept of relational aggression when friendship intimacy scores are 0, u_{0i} is the residual indicating deviations from the group intercept, γ_{10} is the average covariation between relational aggression and friendship intimacy across subjects, γ_{11} is the gender difference in the covariation of relational aggression and friendship intimacy, g_i is the participant's gender (-1 = male, 1 = female), and u_{1i} is the residual indicating individual deviations from the group covariation.

Combining the multilevel equations yields the equation used to estimate the parameters:

$$y_{ij} = (\gamma_{00} + u_{0i}) \\ + (\gamma_{10} + \gamma_{11}g_i + u_{1i})ie_{ij} + e_{ij}. \tag{8}$$

We expected that relational aggression and friendship intimacy would be related such that increases in self-disclosure of a close friend over time would predict increases in children's relational aggression use. The results of this analysis are presented in Table 9.2. Results indicated that, overall, children's relational aggression trajectories were not associated with growth in friend intimate exchange. However, the interaction between gender and friend intimate exchange was significant, indicating that increases in intimate disclosure by a close friend were associated with increases in relational aggression use for girls only.

One concern that arises when using friendship quality measures is that there may be dependence in that data. In particular, when each member of a dyad reports on their friendship experiences, the data will not be independent. For the present study, some participants reported on a friend who reported on them as well (i.e., reciprocal reporting), and others reported on a friend who did not report on them in return. We reran this analysis excluding dyads who reported on one another at any of the three time points. Results indicated that the estimate for the interaction between gender and the dynamic association between friend intimate exchange and relational aggression did not change. In addition, this interaction approached statistical significance ($p < .08$) even though the sample size was reduced to 104. Thus, we believe that dependence in the data does not account for the present findings.

Relational aggression and growth in internalizing symptoms

To address the third goal of this study, a dynamic covariate analysis exploring the covariation of relational aggression and internalizing symptoms across time was conducted. In this model, relational aggression served as the dynamic predictor of change in internalizing symptoms. In other words, this analysis allowed us to explore whether children whose involvement in relational aggression increased over time exhibited time-dependent increases in internalizing symptoms. In this model, internalizing symptoms were conceptualized as the dependent variable, with relational aggression use serving as the dynamic predictor of growth in internalizing symptoms over time. The equation for individual-level change in this analysis was

$$y_{ij} = \beta_{0i} + \beta_{1i}r_{ij} + e_{ij}, \tag{9}$$

where y_{ij} is the ith person's internalizing score at the jth time point, r_{ij} is the participant's relational aggression score at the jth time point, β_{0i} is the predicted internalizing score if the participant's relational aggression score is 0, β_{1i} is the strength of the longitudinal relationship between relational aggression and internalizing symptoms, and e_{ij} are the residuals.

To model group-level change, the following equations were used:

$$\beta_{0i} = \gamma_{00} + u_{0i}, \tag{10}$$

$$\beta_{1i} = \gamma_{10} + \gamma_{11}g_i + u_{1i}, \tag{11}$$

where γ_{00} is the group intercept of internalizing symptoms when relational aggression scores are 0, u_{0i} is the residual indicating deviation from the group intercept, γ_{10} is the average covariation between relational aggression and internalizing across time, γ_{11} is the gender difference in the covariation of relational aggression and internalizing symptoms, g_i is the participant's gender (-1 = male, 1 = female), and u_{1i} is the residual indicating individual deviations from the group covariation.

Thus, the HLM equation used to estimate the parameters for this analysis was

$$y_{ij} = (\gamma_{00} + u_{0i}) \\ + (\gamma_{10} + \gamma_{11}g_i + u_{1i})r_j + e_{ij}. \tag{12}$$

We expected that relational aggression and internalizing symptoms would be related such that increases in children's relational aggression over time would predict increases in their internalizing symptoms. The results of this analysis, presented in Table 9.2, indicated that children's relational aggression trajectories were positively associated with growth in internalizing symptoms. In other words, an increase over time of relational aggression was positively associated with an increase in internalizing symptoms. However, the results of this analysis indicated that this association was equally strong for males and females (i.e., gender did not moderate this relation).

Discussion

The present study was designed to advance the extant peer relations literature in several ways. This large and diverse longitudinal sample was used to assess hypotheses related to growth of relational aggression: specifically, we examined mean-level change in relational aggression occurring over time and the moderating role of gender concerning children's aggression trajectories over the course of 1 year. In addition, using sophisticated statistical procedures, we tested for the time-dependent associations between friend intimate exchange and relational aggression. Finally, we examined the dynamic association between relationally aggressive behavior and internalizing problems.

The present findings suggest that, consistent with our first hypothesis, relational aggression appeared to increase over the course of the study. This finding is consistent with past theory suggesting that as children acquire more social–cognitive capacities and spend more time with close, intimate friends, we would predict more sophisticated and frequent displays of relational aggression (see Bjorkqvist, 1994; Crick et al., 1999; Pellegrini & Archer, 2005). However, increases in relational aggression over time were exhibited by girls only. This finding supports the idea that the social contexts of girls (e.g., intimate friendships) during this developmental period may facilitate the use of relationally aggressive strategies over time. In addition, a gender difference in boys' and girls' relational aggression at the first assessment period (i.e., intercept difference) approached statistical significance, with girls exhibiting greater involvement in relational aggression than boys. This finding is consistent with research

reporting gender differences in relationally aggressive behaviors among young children (Crick et al., 1999; Ostrov & Keating, 2004; Ostrov et al., 2004). Overall, the results of the present study suggest that relational aggression becomes an increasingly common behavior during late elementary school for girls.

Of interest, the findings of the present study differ from those reported by Pellegrini and Long (2003). In particular, these researchers found a negative linear trend for relational aggression growth. It is important to note that Pellegrini and Long (2003) were exploring growth in relational aggression among adolescents. One possible explanation of these different findings is that relational aggression may peak in the late elementary school years and then become less and less common. Alternatively, perhaps adolescents' use of relational aggression is less evident to the peer group as a whole than relational aggression among elementary school children. As children become involved in romantic relationships, relational aggression may be often used in the context of these close, exclusive relationships (Linder, Crick, & Collins, 2002). Moreover, as children spend increasing amounts of time alone with romantic partners during adolescence, peer observation of relational aggression against romantic partners may become more difficult. As such, peers may be less likely to observe relational aggression during this developmental period. We believe that longer term longitudinal studies are warranted to replicate this decrease in growth as children transition into adolescence, and propose that such studies would benefit from multiple informants of relational aggression, including romantic relationship partners.

In support of our second hypothesis, increases in friend intimate exchange were associated with time-dependent increases in relational aggression for girls. This finding is consistent with the proposition that increasing knowledge of close others may provide ammunition for relationally aggressive conduct. Of interest, growth in friend intimate exchange predicted increases in relational aggression among girls only. This finding is provocative, and may reflect differences in the friendship structure of boys and girls in middle childhood. For example, girls tend to report high levels of intimacy within their friendships and to place a greater emphasis on close relationships (Maccoby, 1990; Parker & Asher, 1993). Moreover, the relational aggression goals of girls may be more likely to involve disruption of dyadic relationships (Rudolph, 2002), perhaps making intimate exchange an especially salient factor in relationally aggressive conduct among girls.

Consistent with our third hypothesis, relational aggression significantly tracked with internalizing symptoms over time. That is, children's relational aggression trajectories were positively associated with growth in internalizing problems. These findings bolster the existing literature, suggesting that interpersonal stress is associated with depressive disorders (Garber & Flynn, 2001; Hammen & Rudolph, 1996; Nolen-Hoeksema & Girgus, 1994). However, contrary to our predictions, the relation between internalizing symptoms and relational aggression was not moderated by gender, and instead was of equal strength for girls and boys. Thus, relational aggression appears to be dynamically associated with harmful problems for both girls and boys (for a review, see Crick & Zahn-Waxler, 2003).

The findings of the present study have a number of important implications regarding relational aggression research and applications. First, the finding that relational aggression increases in frequency over the late elementary school years among girls suggests that relationally aggressive behaviors may be particularly salient experiences among girls of this age. Indeed, despite the abundance of research examining physical aggression and its correlates during the late elementary school years (for a review, see Coie & Dodge, 1998), physical aggression is actually decreasing in frequency during this time (Tremblay et al., 1996). In contrast, the present work indicates that relational aggression is becoming increasingly common for girls. Thus, when attempting to understand the use of harmful behaviors during this developmental period, especially among girls, our findings suggest that relational aggression is an essential piece of the puzzle.

Second, the present findings have important implications regarding interventions aimed at reducing relationally aggressive behavior. In particular, interventions may benefit from targeting girls in the late elementary school years given the increasing emergence of such behaviors across this developmental period (in contrast to, e.g., adolescence, when relational aggression may be less frequent; Pellegrini

& Long, 2003). In addition, efforts to reduce relationally aggressive behavior should be sensitive to the possibility that intimate knowledge of friends may be used in a maladaptive manner. For example, relationally aggressive children may benefit from training regarding the appropriate use of intimate knowledge of friends.

Third, the findings of the present study indicate that children's relational aggression trajectories were dynamically associated with internalizing problems for both girls and boys. This suggests that research and interventions should explore the negative correlates of relational aggression in children of both genders. Moreover, this work does not support the contention that, during the elementary school years, girls are relatively problem free (Keenan & Shaw, 1997). Instead, girls do exhibit problem behaviors such as relational aggression at this age, and these behaviors are, in turn, dynamically associated with maladaptive problems such as internalizing symptoms.

The results of the present study offer a number of avenues concerning future work exploring growth in relational aggression over time. First, the use of HLM statistical procedures permitted an investigation of both growth in relational aggression and associations with both static (i.e., gender) and dynamic covariates (e.g., friend intimate exchange) over time. The successful use of these methods during both middle childhood and adolescence suggests that future research should continue to use these techniques across developmental periods. For example, it would be beneficial to explore relational aggression trajectories over middle childhood and into adolescence and adulthood.

Second, although this study used peer reports of relational aggression, future work should include relational aggression from other informants, such as teachers, parents, siblings, self-reports, and observations. Indeed, relational aggression can occur in many relationship contexts, including sibling–sibling, parent–teacher, teacher–child, coach–athlete, friendships, and mutual antipathies. Because the present study used peer reports of relational aggression, it likely captured the frequency of such behaviors in the school context in general and within peer relationships in particular. As a result, future work would benefit from the inclusion of relational aggression from multiple sources, as these informants may be privy to behaviors unique to particular contexts or relationships. Indeed, it is possible that the developmental trajectories of relational aggression differ depending on the context in which they are examined (e.g., relational aggression at school and between peers could be increasing at the same time that relational aggression among siblings and within the home is decreasing).

Additional measures of relational aggression may be particularly useful in exploring changes in relational aggression because such instruments often directly assess the frequency of aggressive behavior. In contrast, peer nominations assess the number of peers who consider each participant to be aggressive (i.e., participants with more nominations are considered more aggressive than their peers). In the present study, participants who are increasingly nominated as aggressive by increasing numbers of peers over time are considered to exhibit increases in aggressive conduct. However, it is possible that such increases reflect, for instance, increases in the diversity of contexts in which individuals exhibit relationally aggressive behavior or increases in children's ability to discern aggression in their peers, perhaps due to increasing familiarity. Thus, future work including more direct tests of frequency of aggression (e.g., teacher ratings using a scale to explicitly rate the frequency of aggressive conduct) use over time is warranted. Third, the results of the present study support the hypothesis that relational aggression increases during late elementary school for girls and these girls also experience time-dependent increases in friend intimate exchange. Future work would benefit from directly assessing additional social and cognitive changes (e.g., perspective taking abilities) and to explore their dynamic association with relational aggression use.

An important extension of the present study would be research that addresses causal relations between friend intimate exchange, growth in relational aggression, and internalizing trajectories. Indeed, one limitation of the present research is that causal conclusions are not possible. For example, we demonstrated that increases in relational aggression were dynamically associated with growth in internalizing symptoms. We proposed that relational aggression may serve as an interpersonal stressor, which in turn, increases children's likelihood of exhibiting internalizing problems.

However, an alternative interpretation is that children exhibiting symptoms of anxiety and depression may engage in relational aggression as a result. Consistent with this idea, Devine, Kempton, and Forehand (1995) found evidence indicating that depressive symptoms in adolescence predicted externalizing problems in early adulthood. Similar tests with relational aggression outcomes are warranted. In addition, it is possible that another factor, such as strained parent–child relationships, may place children at risk for the development of both internalizing symptoms and relationally aggressive conduct. Thus, future research would benefit from examining the association between early relational aggression trajectories and future internalizing problems to address causal, prospective relations between these variables.

Fifth, future studies should include additional measures of adjustment found to be relevant in past concurrent studies of relational aggression. It is possible that children's relational aggression trajectories track with a number of important developmental indices of adjustment in addition to internalizing symptoms. Cross-sectional studies have revealed that relational aggression is associated with problems such as problematic eating patterns, self-harm, and attention problems (see Blachman & Hinshaw, 2002; Crick et al., 1999; Zalecki & Hinshaw, 2004). An important extension of this cross-sectional research is the examination of whether these experiences track dynamically with relational aggression over time.

Sixth, in the present study, teachers rated children's internalizing symptoms. There is evidence suggesting that teachers are reliable informants of depressive and anxious problems during middle childhood (Achenbach & Edelbrock, 1991; Briggs-Gowan, Carter, & Schwab-Stone, 1996; Crick, 1997), but there is a substantial body of research that relies on self-reported measures of depressive symptoms (e.g., Kovacs, 1985; Nolen-Hoeksema & Girgus, 1994). It is possible that the teachers' responses were based on gender biases (Condry & Ross, 1985; Leff et al., 1999; Ostrov, Crick, & Keating, 2005), and thus our findings must be replicated using multiple informants. In a similar vein, friendship intimate exchange was assessed with self-reports in the present study. This method was chosen because self-reports were used in previous work with this age group examining the quality of relationally aggressive children's friendships (i.e., Crick & Grotepeter, 1995). However, additional studies replicating our findings using alternative measures (e.g., friends' reports of intimate exchange in the friendship context) would bolster the findings of this study.

It would also be important for future research to include multiple years and seasons (Fall to Spring) to model expected changes across the school year. In addition, replicating these findings in other cultures (e.g., Japan, Indonesia) that are more collectivistic and display interdependent self-views (see French et al., 2002) would be helpful to begin to explicate the role of context and self-construal (Cross & Madsen, 1997) in the development of relational aggression. For example, interpersonal stress resulting from relational aggression may be more strongly related to adjustment problems in collectivistic cultures where social harmony and relationships are emphasized.

Conclusion

In conclusion, the present study advances in the field in several ways. This short-term longitudinal study reveals that relationally aggressive behavior increases over time, but only for girls during middle childhood. In addition, increases in friendship intimacy were associated with a time-dependent increase in relational aggression, which supports the hypothesis that close voluntary dyadic relationships may fuel relationally aggressive behavior in some contexts. Finally, relationally aggressive behavior tracked over time with symptoms of anxiety and depression during middle childhood. Collectively, these findings indicate that we must continue to explore how relational aggression is impacted by and affects change in both typical (i.e., friendship formation) and atypical (i.e., internalizing problems) developmental processes.

Notes

1   Researchers generally standardize children's number of nominations within classroom to yield relational aggression scores (e.g., Grotpeter & Crick, 1995). However, given that the goal of the present study was to explore mean change over time, standardized scores could not be used (i.e., because standardized scores have, by definition,

a mean of 0). Thus, in the present study, the number of nominations a child received was divided by the number of participating students in his or her classroom in order to yield relational aggression scores. This method allowed exploration of mean changes over time while still controlling for varying class sizes. Given the possibility that class size may be a biasing factor in our analyses, we reran all analyses with class size entered as a covariate. All findings were replicated with this control. Thus, we believe that our results are not an artifact of changing class size.

2   When analyses included individuals without complete data, the quadratic term did reach statistical significance, $\hat{\gamma}_2 = -.05$, $F(1, 408) = 6.11$, $p < .05$. Given the high level of attrition in the present study, the integrity of these findings is questionable. However, it is possible that relational aggression may depend in part on the social context of the school given that relational aggression is often used in the context of close relationships (Grotpeter & Crick, 1996). For instance, when a new school year begins, children must once again form social relationships with their peers; thus, a drop in relational aggression may occur. Additional research is necessary to examine whether quadratic change is present in relational aggression over time, and, if so, whether such contextual effects are a contributing factor.

References

Achenbach, T. M., & Edelbrock, C. S. (1991). *Manual for the Teacher's Report Form and 1991 Profile*. Burlington, VT: University of Vermont, Department of Psychiatry.

Berndt, T. J. (1996). Transitions in friendship and friends' influence. In J. A. Graber & J. Brooks-Gunn (Eds.), *Transitions through adolescence: Interpersonal domains and contexts* (pp. 57–84). Hillsdale, NJ: Erlbaum.

Bjorkqvist, K. (1994). Sex differences in physical, verbal, and indirect aggression: A review of recent research. *Sex Roles*, 30, 177–187.

Bjorkqvist, K., Lagerspetz, K., & Kaukianen, A. (1992). Do girls manipulate and boys fight? Developmental trends in regard to direct and indirect aggression. *Aggressive Behavior*, 18, 117–127.

Blachman, D. R., & Hinshaw, S. P. (2002). Patterns of friendship among girls with and without attention-deficit/ hyperactivity disorder. *Journal of Abnormal Child Psychology*, 30, 625–640.

Bonica, C., Yeshova, K., Arnold, D. H., Fisher, P. H., & Zeljo, A. (2003). Relational aggression and language development in preschoolers. *Social Development*, 12, 551–562.

Briggs-Gowan, M. J., Carter, A. S., & Schwab-Stone, M. (1996). Discrepancies among mother, child, and teacher reports: Examining the contributions of maternal depression and anxiety. *Journal of Abnormal Child Psychology, 24,* 749–765.

Bukowski, W. M., & Kramer, T. L. (1988). Judgments of the features of friendships among early adolescent girls and boys. *Journal of Early Adolescence, 6,* 331–338.

Bryk, A. S., & Raudenbush, S. W. (1992). *Hierarchical linear models.* Newbury Park, CA: Sage.

Capaldi, D. M. (1992). Co-occurrence of conduct problems and depressive symptoms in early adolescent boys II: A 2-year follow-up at grade 8. *Development and Psychopathology, 4,* 125–144.

Cicchetti, D., & Sroufe, L. A. (2000). The past as prologue to the future: The times, they've been a'changin'. [Editorial]. *Development and Psychopathology, 12,* 255–264.

Coie, J. D., & Dodge, K. A. (1998). The development of aggression and antisocial behavior. In W. Damon (Ed.) and N. Eisenberg (Vol. Ed.), *Handbook of child psychology: Vol. 3. Social, emotional, and personality development* (5th ed., pp. 779–861). New York: Wiley.

Condry, J. C., & Ross, D. F. (1985). Sex and aggression: The influence of gender label on the perception of aggression in children. *Child Development, 56,* 225–233.

Crick, N. R. (1995). Relational aggression: The role of intent attributions, feelings of distress, and provocation type. *Development and Psychopathology, 7,* 313–322.

Crick, N. R. (1996). The role of overt aggression, relational aggression, and prosocial behavior in the prediction of children's future social adjustment. *Child Development, 67,* 2317–2327.

Crick, N. R. (1997). Engagement in gender normative versus non-normative forms of aggression: Links to social–psychological adjustment. *Developmental Psychology, 33,* 610–617.

Crick, N. R., & Grotpeter, J. K. (1995). Relational aggression, gender, and social–psychological adjustment. *Child Development, 66,* 710–722.

Crick, N. R., Grotpeter, J. K., & Bigbee, M. A. (2002). Relationally and physically aggressive children's intent attributions and feelings of distress for relational and instrumental peer provocations. *Child Development, 73,* 1134–1142.

Crick, N. R., & Werner, N. E. (1998). Response decision processes in relational and overt aggression. *Child Development, 69,* 1630–1639.

Crick, N. R., Werner, N. E., Casas, J. F., O'Brien, K. M., Nelson, D. A., Grotpeter, J. K., & Markon, K. (1999). Childhood aggression and gender: A new look at an old problem. In D. Bernstein (Ed.). *Nebraska Symposium on Motivation.* Lincoln, NE: University of Nebraska Press.

Crick, N. R., & Zahn-Waxler, C. (2003). The development of psychopathology in females and males: Current progress and future challenges. *Development and Psychopathology, 15,* 719–742.

Cross, S. E., & Madsen, L. (1997). Models of the self: Self-construals and gender. *Psychological Bulletin, 122,* 5–37.

Degirmencioglu, S. M., Urberg, K. A., Tolson, J. M., & Richard, P. (1998). Adolescent friendship networks: Continuity and change over the school year. *Merrill-Palmer Quarterly, 44,* 313–337.

Devine, D., Kempton, T., & Forehand, R. (1995). Adolescent mood and young adult functioning: A longitudinal study. *Journal of Abnormal Child Psychology, 22,* 629–640.

French, D. C., Jansen, E. A., & Pidada, S. (2002). United States and Indonesian children's and adolescents' reports of relational aggression by disliked peers. *Child Development, 73,* 1143–1150.

Galen, B. R., & Underwood, M. (1997). A developmental investigation of social aggression among girls. *Developmental Psychology, 33,* 589–599.

Garber, J., & Flynn, C. (2001). Vulnerability to depression in childhood and adolescence. In R. E. Ingram & J. M. Price (Eds.), *Vulnerability to psychopathology: Risk across the lifespan.* New York: Guilford Press.

Grotpeter, J. K., & Crick, N. R. (1996). Relational aggression, overt aggression, and friendship. *Child Development, 67,* 2328–2338

Hammen, C., & Rudolph, K. D. (1996). Childhood depression. In E. J. Mash & R. A. Barkley (Eds.), *Child psychopathology* (pp. 153–195). New York: Guilford Press.

Henington, C., Hughes, J. N., Cavell, T. A., & Thompson, B. (1998). The role of relational aggression in identifying aggressive boys and girls. *Journal of School Psychology, 36,* 457–477.

Higgins, E. T., & Parsons, J. E. (1983). Stages as subcultures: Social–cognitive development and the social life of the child. In E. T. Higgins, W. W. Hartup, & D. N. Ruble (Eds.), *Social cognition and social development: A sociocultural perspective.* New York: Cambridge University Press.

Keenan, K., & Shaw, D. (1997). Developmental and social influences on young girls' early problem behavior. *Psychological Bulletin, 121,* 95–113.

Kiesner, J. (2002). Depressive symptoms in early adolescence: Their relations with classroom problem behavior and peer status. *Journal of Research on Adolescence, 12,* 463–478.

Kovacs, M. (1985). The Children's Depression Inventory. *Psychopharmacology Bulletin, 21,* 995–998.

Leff, S. S., Costigan, T. E., Eiraldi, R., & Power, T. J. (2001, April). *An examination of children's aggressive behaviors and social skills as a function of ADHD subtype and gender.* Poster presented at the Biennial Meeting of the Society for Research in Child Development, Minneapolis, MN.

Leff, S. S., Kupersmidt, J. B., Patterson, C. J., & Power, T. J. (1999). Factors influencing teacher identification of peer bullies and victims. *School Psychology Review, 28*, 505–517.

Linder, J. R., Crick, N. R., & Collins, W. A. (2002). Relational aggression and victimization in young adults' romantic relationships: Associations with perceptions of parent, peer, and romantic relationship quality. *Social Development, 11*, 69–86.

Long, J. D., & Pellegrini, A. D. (2003). Studying change in dominance and bullying with Hierarchical Linear Models. *School Psychology Review, 32*, 401–417.

Maccoby, E. E. (1990). Gender and relationships: A developmental account. *American Psychologist, 45*, 513–520.

Masten, A. S., Roisman, G. I., Long, J. D., Burt, K. B., Obradović, J., Riley, J. R., et al. (2005). Developmental cascades: Linking academic achievement, externalizing, and internalizing symptoms over 20 years. *Developmental Psychology, 41*, 733–746.

Moffitt, T. E. (1993). Adolescent-limited and life-course persistent antisocial behavior: A developmental taxonomy. *Psychological Review, 100*, 674–701.

Nolen-Hoeksema, S., & Girgus, J. S. (1994). The emergence of gender differences in depression during adolescence. *Psychological Bulletin, 115*, 424–443.

Ostrov, J. M., Crick, N. R., & Keating, C. F. (2005). Gender biased perceptions of preschoolers' behavior: How much is aggression and prosocial behavior in the eye of the beholder? *Sex Roles: A Journal of Research, 52*, 393–398.

Ostrov, J. M., & Keating, C. F. (2004). Gender differences in preschool aggression during free play and structured interactions: An observational study. *Social Development, 13*, 255–277.

Ostrov, J. M., Woods, K. E., Jansen, E. A., Casas, J. F., & Crick, N. R. (2004). An observational study of delivered and received aggression and social psychological adjustment in preschool: "This white crayon doesn't work." *Early Childhood Research Quarterly, 19*, 355–371.

Panak, W. F., & Garber, J. (1992). Role of aggression, rejection, and attributions in the prediction of depression in children. *Development and Psychopathology, 4*, 145–165.

Parker, J. G., & Asher, S. R. (1993). Friendship and friendship quality in middle childhood: Links with peer group acceptance and feelings of loneliness and social dissatisfaction. *Developmental Psychology, 29*, 611–621.

Patterson, G. R. (1982). *Coercive family processes: A social learning approach* (Vol. 3). Eugene, OR: Castalia Publishing Co.

Pellegrini, A. D., & Archer, J. (2005). Sex differences in competitive and aggressive behavior: A view from sexual selection theory. In B. J. Ellis & D. J. Bjorklund (Eds.), *Origins of the social mind: Evolutionary psychology and child development* (pp. 219–244). New York: Guilford Press.

Pellegrini, A. D., & Long, J. D. (2002). A longitudinal study of bullying, dominance, and victimization during the transition from primary school through secondary school. *British Journal of Developmental Psychology, 20*, 259–280.

Pellegrini, A. D., & Long, J. D. (2003). A sexual selection theory longitudinal analysis of sexual segregation and integration in early adolescence. *Journal of Experimental Child Psychology, 85*, 257–278.

Rudolph, K. D. (2002). Gender differences in emotional responses to interpersonal stress during adolescence. *Journal of Adolescent Health, 30*, 3–13.

Rys, G. S., & Bear, G. G. (1997). Relational aggression and peer relations: Gender and developmental issues. *Merrill–Palmer Quarterly, 43*, 87–106.

Sebanc, A. M. (2003). The friendship features of preschool children: Links with prosocial behavior and aggression. *Social Development, 12*, 249–268.

Terry, R., & Coie, J. D. (1991). A comparison of methods for defining sociometric status among children. *Developmental Psychology, 27*, 867–880.

Tomada, G., & Schneider, B. H. (1997). Relational aggression, gender, and peer acceptance: Invariance across culture, stability over time, and concordance among informants. *Developmental Psychology, 33*, 601–609.

Tremblay, R. E., Boulerice, B., Harden, P. W., McDuff, P., Pérusse, D., Pihl, R. O., & Zoccolillo, M. (1996). Do children in Canada become more aggressive as they approach adolescence? In Human Resources Development Canada & Statistics Canada (Eds.). *Growing up in Canada: National Longitudinal Survey of Children and Youth* (pp. 127–137). Ottawa: Statistics Canada.

Werner, N. E., & Crick, N. R. (2004). Maladaptive peer relationships and the development of relational and physical aggression during middle childhood. *Social Development, 13*, 495–514.

Verbeke, G., & Molenberghs, G. (2000). *Hierarchical linear models for longitudinal data*. New York: Springer.

Zalecki, C. A., & Hinshaw, S. P. (2004). Overt and relational aggression in girls with attention deficit hyperactivity disorder. *Journal of Clinical Child and Adolescent Psychology, 33*, 125–137.

Appendix A

SAS PROC MIXED Syntax for Models

TRAJECTORIES OF RELATIONAL AGGRESSION FOR BOYS AND GIRLS

```
proc mixed data = work.file method = reml ic covtest;
class id wave;
model ragg = linear gender linear * gender/intercept solution;
random intercept linear/type = un subject = id g gcorr v vcorr;
repeated wave/type = simple subject = id r;
title "linear growth in relational aggression conditional on gender";
run;
```

DYNAMIC ASSOCIATION BETWEEN FRIEND INTIMATE EXCHANGE AND RELATIONAL AGGRESSION

```
proc mixed data = work.file method = reml ic covtest;
class id wave;
model ragg = ie ie * gender/intercept solution;
random ie/type = un subject = id g gcorr v vcorr;
repeated wave/type = simple subject = id r;
title "friend intimate exchange and relational aggression";
run;
```

DYNAMIC ASSOCIATION BETWEEN RELATIONAL AGGRESSION AND INTERNALIZING SYMPTOMS

```
proc mixed data = work.file method = reml ic covtest;
class id wave;
model int = ragg gender * ragg/intercept solution;
random ragg/type = un subject = id g gcorr v vcorr;
repeated wave/type = simple subject = id r;
title "relational aggression and internalizing";
run;
```

Key: id, child identification number; wave 1, 2, and 3 for T1, T2, and T3, respectively; ragg, relational aggression; linear 0, 1, and 2 for T1, T2, and T3, respectively; ie, friend intimate exchange; int, internalizing symptoms.

....

A Peek Behind the Fence: Naturalistic Observations of Aggressive Children with Remote Audiovisual Recording

Debra J. Pepler and Wendy M. Craig

Researchers have identified peer relations as an important mechanism in the development of adaptive and maladaptive behaviors (e.g., Hartup, 1983; Parker & Asher, 1987). In the case of aggressive children, peer interactions are presumed to exacerbate behavior problems and propel these children along the trajectory to an antisocial lifestyle (Cairns, Cairns, Neckerman, Gest, & Gariepy, 1988; Patterson, DeBaryshe, & Ramsey, 1989). The study of aggressive children's peer relations has taken many forms: self-reports, peer reports, and adult reports; laboratory paradigms; and naturalistic observations. At present, there are gaps and inconsistencies in our understanding of the peer relations of aggressive children because of methodological issues such as the lack of agreement between raters (Loeber, Green, Lahey, & Stouthamer-Loeber, 1989), the constraints of laboratory situations, and the difficulty of naturalistic observations with school-age children (Asher & Hymel, 1981). To overcome some of these methodological difficulties, we used video cameras and remote microphones to observe peer interactions of aggressive and nonaggressive children on the school playground. In this article, we discuss observational methodologies commonly used in the study of children's aggressive behavior, review the strengths and weaknesses of each methodology, describe our alternative observational strategy, and illustrate its effectiveness in addressing the challenge of naturalistic observations of aggressive children on the school playground. Even though the present discussion focuses on our use of the methodology to study aggression, it would lend itself to the study of many other aspects of peer interaction (e.g., friendship patterns, social support, prosocial behavior, victimization, and discourse analysis).

The paucity of research on the unstructured free play of school-age children may be attributable, in part, to the difficulty of obtaining observations. Whereas younger children can be observed during extended periods of free play with peers in a preschool setting, elementary school children seldom have unstructured play periods in class. On the school playground, children's free play tends to be diverse and wide-ranging. It varies from overt physical activity to subtle and private interactions and may occur anywhere on large school playgrounds. Nevertheless, the school playground is an ideal venue for studying naturalistic peer interactions and processes. Children spend a substantial portion of their school day on the playground, during which time they are free to choose their play partners and activities. Children's playground behaviors are markedly understudied even though they have important implications for development (Pellegrini, 1993).

Researchers have overcome the difficulties of observing school-age children's social interactions in a variety of ways, both in controlled laboratory and in unstructured free-play settings. The advantages and limitations of several observational strategies are briefly delineated below with reference to the study of children's aggressive interactions.

Laboratory Observational Studies

Observational studies in laboratory or contrived play group situations have substantially augmented our understanding of aggressive children's peer interactions (e.g., Dodge, Coie, Pettit, & Price, 1990). There are several advantages to this methodology. In the laboratory, the experimenter has control over the chil-

dren involved, the materials, the space for play, and the duration of the play period. Interactions can be easily heard and seen, thus providing high internal validity.

The primary limitations of laboratory methodologies relate to external validity: Interactions in contrived play groups may not be representative of children's everyday peer interactions. The presence of an adult and controls in the physical setting may constrain children's behavior and compromise external validity. The number and characteristics of peer partners may also influence aggression observed in a laboratory setting. In natural settings, aggressive children tend to affiliate with groups of similarly deviant peers; these peer groups may be breeding grounds for subsequent antisocial behaviors (Cairns et al., 1988; Patterson et al., 1989). Peer processes such as social contagion, modeling, and reinforcement likely influence the frequency and nature of children's aggression (Coie & Jacobs, 1993; Olweus, 1987). In summary, laboratory settings offer unique opportunities for controlling and assessing developing peer relations; however, the potential contextual effects of laboratory play groups raise concerns for their generalizability.

Naturalistic Observations

With minimal constraints on children's interactions, the results of naturalistic studies can be generalized to real-life situations more confidently than those of laboratory studies (Attili, 1985). Furthermore, it would not be ethically possible to recreate some everyday interactions in the laboratory. For example, staging intense and prolonged bullying episodes such as those observed on our playground tapes (Craig & Pepler, 1994) would be unethical because of the stresses that children would experience. Consequently, naturalistic observations may be the only ethical means to study certain aggressive behaviors. Before describing our observational strategy, we consider the strengths and limitations of two other techniques that have been used to study children's aggressive interactions on the school playground: proximal observations and observations conducted with video or audio recordings.

Proximal observations

Researchers have typically used live observational coding systems to study children's playground behaviors (Asher & Gabriel, 1993). Coders follow children on the playground to record their interactions with checklists, written or dictated running descriptions, or handheld computers (e.g., Coie & Dodge, 1988; Sluckin, 1981). Within preschool settings, proximal observations of peer groups are more reliable than observations coded from videotape, because coders can make discriminations on the basis of the full context of the behavioral interactions (Fagot & Hagan, 1988). On the school playground, however, the wide-ranging and subtle nature of children's play poses difficulties for proximal observations and limits the detail within coding systems (Asher & Hymel, 1981; Putallaz & Wasserman, 1989).

Reactivity to the observer's presence is a concern with proximal observations, with the corresponding dilemma of choosing the optimal distance from which to observe. If observers are too close, children may be reactive and restrict their interactions. If observers maintain distance to minimize reactivity, they may not detect verbal behaviors of interest, such as threats or insults, which are often brief and covert. Our observations of school-age children suggest that verbal behaviors comprise the majority of aggressive initiations on the school playground (Pepler, Craig, & Roberts, 1993). The ability to detect verbalizations may be particularly critical for investigations of aggression by girls, who are more likely than boys to engage in verbal as compared with physical aggression (Lagerspetz, Bjorkqvist, & Peltonen, 1988). Hence, the distance an observer maintains from the interaction may compromise the validity or quality of data.

There may be a limited age range for the use of proximal observations of naturalistic interactions. With age, children's aggression develops from physical to direct verbal aggression to indirect aggression (Bjorkqvist, Osterman, & Kaukiainen, 1992). The latter forms of verbal and indirect aggression are subtle and may be difficult to detect with proximal observations. Furthermore, as children become more cognitively and socially mature, they may restrict their aggressive interactions when being observed (Lagerspetz et al., 1988). Similarly, as children become increasingly aware of the expectations and rules regarding aggression, they may be more likely to hide or avoid aggressive interactions when under scrutiny. On the basis of his observations on the school playground, Sluckin (1981) noted that older children were more aware of his interests and more protective of their privacy than younger children. The external validity of proximal observations, therefore, may be inversely related to the age of the children being observed.

In summary, the external validity of naturalistic proximal observations is generally stronger than that of laboratory studies. On the other hand, proximal observations raise concerns for reactivity to the observer, the quality of obtainable data, and the age appropriateness of the observational strategy. Some of these concerns are minimized with video or audio recordings.

Video or audio recordings of social interactions

Reactivity can be minimized by videotaping children on the playground from an unobtrusive position in the school (Serbin, Marchessault, McAffer, Peters, & Schwartzman, 1993). Children take little notice of the observers and are not aware of the individual targets of filming. The drawback of this video-only methodology is that children's conversations cannot be recorded. The lack of information on the verbal interactions seems particularly problematic for research on aggressive behavior, which is often preceded by a verbal instigation (Coie, Dodge, & Kupersmidt, 1990). Video-only recordings, therefore, may provide an incomplete account of the complex nature of aggressive interactions among school-age peers.

An alternative observational strategy is to use audio recordings accompanied by a predetermined coding scheme, narrative, or video recordings (e.g., Abramovitch, Corter, Pepler, & Stanhope, 1986; McCabe & Lipscomb, 1988). Audiotapes are transcribed and merged with behavioral records for interactional coding. Audiotaping has several advantages over live observations when the research interests comprise verbal interactions (Asher & Gabriel, 1993), and audio recorders are less expensive than video equipment.

Limitations in the use of an audio record arise in the accuracy of the accompanying behavioral record.

Narrative or pen-and-paper behavioral records may not be adequate to capture the subtle and rapidly occurring behaviors of interactions among school-age children. For example, the use of knives on our school playground tapes was so covert that it often took several passes through the audiovisual tapes to discern their presence. Although aggressive behaviors such as these may be low base rate events and very covert, they are nevertheless important in understanding the complexities of life on school playgrounds in the 1990s.

Remote Audiovisual Observations

To observe naturalistic peer interactions of aggressive children in an unobtrusive yet externally valid manner, we developed a methodology using wireless microphones and video cameras. With this equipment, we were able to see and hear all aspects of children's interactions on the school playground. This methodology offers a unique opportunity for researchers interested in children's social interaction to gain access to a world not normally privy to adults. The target child wears a wireless microphone and a lightweight transmitter, which detect the speech of the target child and the speech of children with whom the target child is interacting, despite their distance from the camera. With a zoom lens on the camera, the researcher can remain remote from the target child while recording the child's behaviors at close range. This technology offers all the benefits of videotaping, including the ability to code in fine detail, code interactive behavior, review repeatedly, and train extensively for observer reliability (Coie et al., 1990). A significant benefit of the remote technology is that target children are free to roam on the playground, far from the camera, thereby decreasing reactivity.

Equipment

In developing this methodology for our observational study of aggressive and nonaggressive children on the playground (Pepler, Craig, & Roberts, 1995), we experimented with three generations of microphones before achieving reliable recordings. When children played near metal fences, near the playground equip-

ment, or at the outer edges of the school yard, the metal interfered with the FM transmission. We overcame these difficulties with a true diversity, dipolar remote microphone system. The system operates on dual FM radio frequencies so that when one signal fails, the other signal is automatically transmitted.

The TELEX true diversity systems, which we purchased for approximately $700 per unit, comprise a small microphone, a transmitter, and a receiver. The microphone is approximately 2 cm long and is connected with a thin wire to a transmitter that measures $7 \times 10 \times 2$ cm and weighs approximately 150 g. We made pouches for the transmitters that hung around the children's necks or fastened around their waists. The microphone attached to the children's clothing with a clip. The equipment was relatively unobtrusive during the fall and winter when the transmitters were placed inside the target children's coats. In the late spring, however, the transmitters were visible, making it evident which children were being observed. The challenge of unobtrusive observations is addressed later.

The receiver, with two antennae to receive both channel transmissions, was located beside the video camera. We videotaped the target children's playground interactions with an 8-mm SONY Camcorder fitted with a telephoto lens and mounted on a tripod. The audio signal was fed directly into the camera for a simultaneously recorded video and audio record. Although a light on the receiver indicated whether the sound was being received, we found it essential to monitor the sound transmission with earphones plugged directly into the receiver. The advertised range for this system is 300 m in open field conditions or 80 m in adverse conditions. With the critical feature of dual audio transmission channels, this system worked reliably and provided complete remote audiovisual recordings of children's naturalistic interactions on the playground.

Procedure

We conducted observations at two schools with playgrounds that measured approximately 70×100 m. The camera was set up in classrooms overlooking the playground. Two observers were required at all times: One researcher operated the camera, and the other researcher remained on the playground to place the microphones on the target children and assist in tracking them. The researcher on the playground carried a list of names of children to be observed. On locating a target child, the researcher approached the child and asked whether he or she would be willing to wear the microphone for a period of 10 min. The researcher then switched on the transmitter, placed it on the child, and clipped the microphone to the child's clothing. Children were instructed to play as they normally would. All children knew they were being filmed. In the course of conversation with the child, the researcher mentioned the child's name and identified the color of the child's clothes. This identifying information was essential to track target children among the approximately 250 children on the playground.

Equipment and procedural considerations

In addition to reliability of the audio transmission, we had several other concerns in selecting equipment for the playground observations. First, we were concerned that the children, especially the aggressive boys involved in rough-and-tumble play and skirmishes, might be too rough with the equipment. In spite of highly active and aggressive play, the transmitters were not damaged during 72 hr of playground observations.

Given that the microphones and transmitters identified the focal children in any observation period, we were concerned about children's reactivity to being filmed. Similar to Asher and Gabriel (1993), we observed only occasional and brief reactivity to the remote audiovisual system, such as a comment about the observer, microphone, or camera, or a brief glance in the direction of the camera. In a subsequent study of bullying, we assessed the extent of the reactivity problem. Observers rated the children's reactivity on a scale from 1 (*not at all reactive*) to 5 (*highly reactive*). These global ratings indicated that children were reactive to the camera and microphone in fewer than 10% of the episodes (Craig & Pepler, 1994). A possible explanation for the low levels of reactivity is that elementary-age children are not capable of sustained self-monitoring, particularly when the camera is operated from a remote location.

In subsequent research, we have addressed concerns regarding reactivity and identification of the children being observed. Borrowing from the methodology of Hinde and his colleagues (R. Hinde, personal communication, July 6, 1991), we now place live microphones on the target children being observed and dummy microphones on all other children in their classes. For the 120 dummy sets, we used a wooden block to simulate the transmitter and a small metal plug to simulate the microphone. The transmitters are placed in commercially available waist pouches that are sewn closed. The microphone is sewn into a pocket that attaches to the child's clothing with an alligator clip. The dummy sets were virtually indistinguishable in appearance from the actual transmitters and microphones.

Another procedural consideration of filming is the camera placement to maximize the field of view and minimize reactivity. During unstructured play times, children move freely around the school yard and occasionally move out of the camera's field of view (e.g., close to the wall, around a corner). As a consequence of not controlling children's movements, we lost approximately 4% of our observations because of children moving out of the field of view. In some schools, it is not possible to view the entire school playground from a second-floor classroom location. Under these circumstances, it is necessary to film from a position on the playground.

Finally, tracking the target child continuously among 250 other children on the playground is difficult given the limited view through the camera lens. One solution to this problem is to attach a small colored television monitor for additional clarity. We chose less expensive walkie-talkies for communication between the camera person and the researcher on the playground. An advantage of this communication link is that the researcher on the playground can provide information on the whereabouts of target children without having to approach and signal which child is wearing the live microphone.

Reliability and validity

To date, our playground tapes have been analyzed with two coding schemes adapted from the Playground Code of Rusby and Dishion (1991). The first microsocial coding scheme comprised two stages: coding of play states and a fine-grained coding of behaviors with affective valence (Pepler et al., 1995). The social overtures and responses of peers to the target children were also coded. Kappa coefficients were calculated for the frequencies, durations, and sequences of states and events with a 5-s tolerance interval. Kappas were .76 for state coding and .69 for event coding. The second coding scheme was used in an analysis of bullying on the school yard. Bullying episodes were identified with 93% interobserver agreement. The average agreement for coding contextual variables (e.g., peer roles, type of aggression, and gender of bully) was 93%. Two variables, height and weight, could not be coded reliably from the tapes.

Validity of the observations is supported by their ability to differentiate the playground interactions of aggressive and non-aggressive children (Pepler et al., 1993) and their relation to other measures of aggression. There was a significant correlation between children's verbal aggression and teacher ratings of externalizing behavior problems, $r(39) = .41, p < .01$, and a trend for the relation with peer ratings of aggression, $r(39) = .24, p < .15$. Global ratings of physical aggression observed on the tapes correlated with rates of verbal and physical aggression, $r(39) = .31, p < .05$ and $r(39) = .34, p < .04$, respectively.

Ethical issues

We encountered several ethical concerns in developing the remote observational methodology: obtaining consent, duty to report, and limits of communication. The advantage of remote naturalistic observations is that children's behaviors are not constrained. At the same time, children other than those targeted for the research may enter the camera frame. Their presence poses a problem with respect to obtaining informed consent. One solution is to obtain consent for all the children in the school. If some parents do not consent to their child's participation, the researcher is obliged to avoid gathering data on these children. It may be possible to discard film segments with children for whom there is no consent or to prevent these children from going onto the playground during filming. The former strategy requires the costly and difficult task of identifying all children. The latter strategy places artificial constraints on children's interactions: Friends of the target may not be present on the play-

ground. Under these circumstances, the disadvantages are similar to those for contrived play-group situations in which the external validity of the observations is jeopardized. Because the research projects in which we have used this methodology have all been integral to intervention and prevention programs being offered within the school, we have been able to obtain *in loco parentis* consent from the school principal for those children not directly involved in the observational research. Within pure research studies, however, the task of obtaining consent for all children may be too formidable to make this methodology viable.

Teachers and supervising adults must also be informed about the nature of the research. If some of these adults do not consent, the aforementioned strategies may be used. For example, teachers who do not consent might be removed from yard duty during filming.

A second ethical issue concerns duty to warn (for fuller discussion, see Fisher, 1993). In conducting observations of aggressive children's playground interactions, one may observe interactions in which children's safety is a concern (e.g., extreme aggression or weapons). Coie and his colleagues (Coie et al., 1990) acknowledged a similar concern within a laboratory situation. Researchers, in conjunction with the school staff, can develop definitions of situations that merit duty to warn and procedures to be followed. These procedures should address the ethical responsibility of duty to warn, while at the same time maintaining the integrity of the research. We developed procedures to inform the supervising adults on the playground concerning harmful and dangerous behaviors. This strategy protected the children, while at the same time alleviating direct involvement by the researchers.

A final ethical concern is clarifying the limits of communication (Fisher, 1993). To ensure confidentiality for the children and teachers filmed, we did not show our tapes to the school staff, children, or parents involved in the study. Hence, the schools were not able to use the tapes as a form of surveillance to assess, diagnose, or determine treatment plans for individual children. The consent form specified that the tapes would be used for research and educational purposes only.

A Peek Behind the Fence

Remote audiovisual observations provide a unique opportunity to observe children's interactions that generally occur beyond our view. The primary strength of this observational methodology is its external validity. Children being observed are completely mobile on the school playground and are able to choose the activities and partners for their play. Aggression is thought to occur relatively infrequently on school playgrounds (Hartup & Laursen, 1993). With the ability to "peek" into the playground, we were able to observe the full range of aggressive behaviors and to determine that aggression is not a rare event. Aggressive children were observed to be verbally and physically aggressive once every 3 and 8 min, respectively. Nonaggressive children were observed to be verbally and physically aggressive once every 5 and 11 min, respectively (Pepler et al., 1993). The remote audiovisual observations allowed fine-grained analyses of affect associated with each behavior, which further differentiated the aggressive and nonaggressive children (Pepler et al., 1993). This observational methodology provides a complete record of the behaviors and verbalizations of both the target children and those around them. With this rich, naturalistic view, we were able to observe some subtle forms of aggression, typically associated with girls' aggression. The efficacy of this methodology was apparent in our study of bullying on the playground. Although significantly fewer girls than boys admit to bullying on surveys (Pepler, Ziegler, & Charach, 1994), we observed girls bullying at the same rate as boys (Craig & Pepler, 1994). Studies of girls' aggressive behaviors are notably scant, perhaps because we lack the appropriate tools for detecting and understanding girls' aggression. This methodology, which captures the subtle forms of verbal and indirect aggression, may prove particularly effective in our attempts to understand the complexities of girls' aggression.

There are several limitations associated with this methodology. First, as in any naturalistic study, experimental control is sacrificed to observe behavioral interactions as they unfold in everyday life. Second, the equipment cannot be easily switched from one child to another for frequent time sampling. On the other hand, with remote observations, we have observed occasional long episodes of aggressive interactions, such as bullying. Finally, there appears to be a ceiling for the age at which this is a suitable methodology. The oldest children in our studies (11 and 12 years of age) appeared to be more aware of the equipment and more self-conscious than younger children, and a few of the older children were reticent to be observed. The various validity and ethical elements of this methodology must be considered within the specific contexts of a given research program.

In summary, the remote audiovisual observational methodology provided continuous event sampling that could be analyzed according to the frequency, sequence, and affective intensity of behaviors initiated and received by the target children. This methodology may be uniquely suited for the naturalistic study of aggressive and other interactions among school children. While laboratory studies have added substantially to our understanding of aggressive children's interactions, we need to move into children's natural environments and groups to validate and extend the conclusions drawn about the peer relations of aggressive children. With this methodology, we can observe without being present, thereby maximizing the potential to learn about children's everyday interactions.

References

Abramovitch, R., Corter, C., Pepler, D., & Stanhope, L. (1986). Sibling and peer interactions: A final follow-up and a comparison. *Child Development, 57,* 217–229.

Asher, S. R., & Gabriel, S. W. (1993). Using a wireless transmission system to observe conversation and social interaction on the playground. In C. H. Hart (Ed.), *Children on playgrounds* (pp. 184–209). Albany: State University of New York Press.

Asher, S. R., & Hymel, S. (1981). Children's social competence in peer relations: Sociometric and behavioral assessment. In J. K. Wine & M. D. Smye (Eds.), *Social competence* (pp. 125–157). New York: Guilford Press.

Attili, G. (1985). Aggression in young children—Introduction: Some methodological issues related to the nature of aggression. *Aggressive Behavior, 11,* 279–281.

Bjorkqvist, K., Osterman, K., & Kaukiainen, A. (1992). The development of direct and indirect aggressive strategies in males and females. In K. Bjorkqvist & P. Niemela (Eds.),

Of mice and women: Aspects of female aggression (pp. 51–64). San Diego, CA: Academic Press.

Cairns, R. B., Cairns, B. D., Neckerman, H. J., Gest, S. D., & Gariepy, J. L. (1988). Social networks and aggressive behavior: Peer support or peer rejection. *Developmental Psychology, 24*, 815–826.

Coie, J. D., & Dodge, K. A. (1988). Multiple sources of data on social behavior and social status in the school: A cross-age comparison. *Child Development, 59*, 815–829.

Coie, J. D., Dodge, K. A., & Kupersmidt, J. B. (1990). Peer group behavior and social status. In S. R. Asher & J. D. Coie (Eds.), *Peer rejection in childhood* (pp. 17–59). New York: Cambridge University Press.

Coie, J. D., & Jacobs, M. R. (1993). The role of social context in the preventions of conduct disorder. *Development and Psychopathology, 5*, 263–275.

Craig, W. M., & Pepler, D. J. (1994). *Naturalistic observations of bullying and victimization in the school-yard*. Manuscript submitted for publication.

Dodge, K., Coie, J. D., Pettit, G. S., & Price, J. M. (1990). Peer status and aggression in boys' groups: Developmental and contextual analyses. *Child Development, 61*, 1289–1309.

Fagot, B., & Hagan, R. (1988). Is what we see what we get? Comparisons of taped and live observations. *Behavioral Assessment, 10*, 367–374.

Fisher, C. B. (1993). Integrating science and ethics in research with highrisk children and youth. *SRCD Social Policy Report, 7*, 1–27.

Hartup, W. W. (1983). Peer relations. In M. Hetherington (Ed.), *Handbook of child psychology: Vol IV. Socialization, personality, and social development* (pp. 103–196). New York: Wiley.

Hartup, W. W., & Laursen, B. (1993). Conflict and context in peer relations. In C. Hart (Ed.), *Children on playgrounds* (pp. 44–84). Albany: State University of New York Press.

Lagerspetz, K., Bjorkqvist, K., & Peltonen, T. (1988). Is indirect aggression typical of females? Gender differences in aggressiveness in 11- to 12-year-old children. *Aggressive Behavior, 14*, 403–404.

Loeber, R., Green, S., Lahey, B., & Stouthamer-Loeber, M. (1989). Optimal informant on childhood disruptive behaviors. *Development and Psychopathology, 1*, 317–337.

McCabe, A., & Lipscomb, T. J. (1988). Sex differences in children's verbal aggression. *Merrill-Palmer Quarterly, 34*, 389–401.

Olweus, D. (1987). School-yard bullying: Grounds for intervention. *School Safety, 6*, 4–11.

Parker, J. G., & Asher, S. R. (1987). Peer relations and later personal adjustment: Are low-accepted children at risk? *Psychological Bulletin, 102*, 357–389.

Patterson, G. R., DeBaryshe, B. D., & Ramsey, E. (1989). A developmental perspective on antisocial behavior. *American Psychologist, 44*, 329–335.

Pellegrini, A. D. (1993). An inside look at the outside. In C. H. Hart (Ed.), *Children on playgrounds* (pp. xi–xii). Albany: State University of New York Press.

Pepler, D. J., Craig, W. M., & Roberts, W. R. (1993, March). *Aggression on the playground: A normative behavior?* Paper presented at the biennial meetings of the Society for Research in Child Development, New Orleans, LA.

Pepler, D. J., Craig, W. M., & Roberts, W. R. (1995). Social skills training and aggression in the peer group. In J. McCord (Ed.), *Coercion and punishment in long-term perspectives* (pp. 213–228). New York: Cambridge University Press.

Pepler, D., Ziegler, S., & Charach, A. (1994). *Bullying in school*. Manuscript submitted for publication.

Putallaz, M., & Wasserman, A. (1989). Children's naturalistic entry behavior and sociometric status: A developmental perspective. *Developmental Psychology, 25*, 297–305.

Rusby, J. C., & Dishion, T. J. (1991). [The Playground Code (PGC): Observing school children at play]. Unpublished training manual, Oregon Social Learning Center, Eugene, OR.

Serbin, L. A., Marchessault, K., McAffer, V., Peters, P., & Schwartzman, A. E. (1993). Patterns of social behavior on the playground in 9- to 11-year-old girls and boys: Relation to teacher perceptions and to peer ratings of aggression, withdrawal and likability. In C. H. Hart (Ed.), *Children on playgrounds* (pp. 162–183). Albany: State University of New York Press.

Sluckin, A. (1981). *Growing up in the playground*. London: Routledge.

A Closer Look 8   A Slap in the "Facebook": The Study of Cyber-Bullying

Rapid advances in technology over the past 20 years have led to new contexts for the study of children's aggression and bullying. Indeed, the study of "online aggression" has emerged as a recent "hot topic" for social development researchers. So-called *cyber-bullying* has been defined as aggressive and intentional acts carried out repeatedly and over time by a group or individual using electronic forms of contact (e.g., e-mail, text/video-messaging, websites, etc.).

Smith and colleagues (2008) explored the prevalence and consequences of cyber-bullying in two studies of over 600 adolescents. In a series of focus groups and surveys, the authors also sought to examine links between cyber-bullying, traditional bullying, and typical internet use. Among their results, although cyber-bullying was reported to occur less frequently than traditional bullying overall, cyber-bullying was more common outside of school. Notwithstanding, cyber-bullying was perceived to have a similar negative impact as traditional bullying. Moreover, similar to victims of traditional bullying, cyber-bullying victims often told no one about their victimization experiences. These findings speak to the growing emergence of the internet as a new "context" for bullying and victimization and have critically important implications for the development and implementation of anti-bullying programs.

Smith, P. K., Mahdavi, J., Carvalho, M., Fisher, S., Russell, S., & Tippett, N. (2008). Cyberbullying: Its nature and impact in secondary school pupils. *Journal of Child Psychology and Psychiatry*, *49*, 376–385.

Classroom Exercises, Debates, and Discussion Questions

- *Classroom debate*. Divide up into teams and formulate arguments "for" vs. "against" this resolution: Aggression is more socially acceptable in boys vs. girls. As a follow-up for discussion and debate, are different *types* of aggression (e.g., physical vs. relational) more or less socially acceptable for boys vs. girls?
- *Observation*. Watch a group of children at play (schoolyard, playground, etc.). List all of the aggressive behaviors you observe. What different behaviors might represent different types of aggression (i.e., physical, verbal, relational, instrumental, hostile)?
- *Classroom discussion*. Many episodes of bullying are witnessed by peers. How might these peers implicitly or explicitly encourage or discourage bullies?

How would you suggest that peers be involved to reduce bullying at school?
- *Classroom discussion*. Based on a social-cognitive/emotional processes model of aggression, how should we intervene to reduce children's aggressive behaviors?
- *Classroom discussion*. Researchers continue to debate the "distinctiveness" of different forms of aggression and bullying. Is it important to distinguish between physical, verbal, relational, and cyber-aggression/bullying? Do you think that these different forms of aggression and bullying have the same implications for bullies and/or victims?
- *Classroom discussion*. Bullying can take place in many environments and in many different ways. Taking into account the definition and theories of bullying discussed in this chapter, describe what form bullying might take: (1) among toddlers vs. preschoolers vs. older children vs. adolescents; and (2) at school vs. on a sports team vs. in the workplace.

Additional Resources

For more about aggression, see:

Card, N. A., Stucky, B. D., Sawalani, G. M., & Little, T. D. (2008). Direct and indirect aggression during childhood and adolescence: A meta-analytic review of gender differences, intercorrelations, and relations to maladjustment. *Child Development, 79*, 185–1229.

Côté, S. M., Vaillancourt, T., Barker, E. D., Nagin, D., & Tremblay, R. (2007). The joint development of physical and indirect aggression: Predictors of continuity and change during childhood. *Development and Psychopathology, 19*, 37–55.

Dodge, K., Coie, J., & Lynam, D. (2006). Aggression and antisocial behavior in youth. In W. Damon & R. M. Lerner (Series Eds.) & N. Eisenberg (Vol. Ed.), *Handbook of child psychology: Vol. 3. Social, emotional, and personality development* (6th ed., pp. 719–788). New York: Wiley.

Lacourse, É., Côté, S., Nagin, D. S., Vitaro, F., Brendgen, M., & Tremblay, R. E. (2002). A longitudinal-experimental approach to testing theories of antisocial behavior development. *Development and Psychopathology, 14*(4), 909–924.

Olweus, D. (1991). Bully/victim problems among school-children: Basic facts and effects of a school based intervention program. In D. J Pepler & K. H. Rubin (Eds.), *The development and treatment of childhood aggression* (pp. 411–448). Hillsdale, NJ: Lawrence Erlbaum Associates.

10

STEREOTYPING, PREJUDICE, AND EXCLUSION

Introduction   406

Children's Social Reasoning About Inclusion and Exclusion in Gender and Race Peer Group Contexts   407

Melanie Killen and Charles Stangor

Introduction   407

Method   410

Results   413

Discussion   417

The Development and Consequences of Stereotype Consciousness in Middle Childhood   421

Clark McKown and Rhona S. Weinstein

Study 1   426

Study 2   430

General Discussion   436

In-group and Out-group Attitudes of Ethnic Majority and Minority Children   441

Judith A. Griffiths and Drew Nesdale

Introduction   441

Method   444

Results   446

Discussion   448

Conclusions   450

A Closer Look 9   Stereotyping and Discrimination: What Factors Help to Reduce Prejudice?   451

Social Development in Childhood and Adolescence: A Contemporary Reader, First Edition. Edited by Melanie Killen and Robert J. Coplan.
Editorial material and organization © 2011 Blackwell Publishing Ltd. Published 2011 by Blackwell Publishing Ltd.

Introduction

Do children exclude others based on gender, race, and ethnicity? Are young children prejudiced? When do stereotypes emerge? What are the factors that contribute to the emergence of stereotyping, prejudice, and exclusion? These questions are central to fostering civil societies and are of utmost importance in understanding social development. There is a continuing trend for most societies and cultures to become increasingly diverse and heterogeneous. Increased diversity can have positive consequences for children's social development, such as the possibility for increased empathy, tolerance, perspective-taking, and the celebration of various cultural traditions and values. At the same time, increased diversity may also result in increased prejudice, bias, and discrimination.

In this chapter, three articles address different aspects of the larger complex phenomenon referred to as prejudice. Prejudice refers to negative attitudes towards others that are often based on group membership and without sufficient knowledge or information. Whereas prejudice was initially studied as a part of psychopathology (a personality disorder), following World War II, research in the past 50 years has documented the normative ways in which individuals in societies perpetuate stereotypic expectations about others, often to enhance group identity (such as has been described in Social Identity Theory), and to maintain hierarchies, status, and privileges. Studies of prejudice with adults typically involve direct measures of prejudiced behaviors towards others in a controlled laboratory setting. Researchers exploring this phenomenon in children have relied on a wider range of methodologies. These methods include explicit measures focusing on judgments, evaluations, and interpretations of social interactions, as well as implicit and indirect methods, which tap biases, attributions of intentions, and perceptions.

Overall, these studies have shown that children form biases about others very early in life, and that stereotypes about one another emerge as early as 4–5 years of age. Notwithstanding, research has also demonstrated that in childhood stereotypes are not yet deeply entrenched and that interventions can modify and change stereotyping and prejudice. Further, research has shown that children's early fairness judgments reflect an underlying conceptual framework that enables them to reject stereotypic attitudes and prejudicial messages from the culture, and from the adult world.

The first article in this chapter considers how children weigh fairness judgments in the context of gender and racial exclusion in peer groups. Killen and Stangor (2001) investigated whether children and early adolescents view it as legitimate for a group to exclude someone from joining when that person does not "fit" the stereotypic expectations of the group (such as excluding a boy from a ballet club, or a girl from a baseball club). In the second article, McKown and Weinstein (2003) explored factors that might contribute to children's awareness of stereotyping, and how stereotyping is related to stereotype threat. Stereotype threat refers to the phenomenon in which students who are exposed to negative stereotypic expectations about their own group membership are likely to do more poorly on academic tests than students who are not exposed to such messages. Finally, the third article is about group identity and how ingroup and outgroup attitudes in children's peer groups have different implications for ethnic minority and majority children. Griffiths and Nesdale (2006) focused on Australian children, including children from Anglo-Australian and Pacific Islander backgrounds. Given the multicultural world, and the fact that many more individuals will work in a diverse workforce today than ever before, understanding the origins and emergence of intergroup attitudes is crucial, and a few of the new lines of developmental research are featured in this chapter.

Children's Social Reasoning About Inclusion and Exclusion in Gender and Race Peer Group Contexts

Melanie Killen and Charles Stangor

Introduction

Many studies have shown that children, as early as the preschool years, are well aware that it is wrong to harm and to act in ways that are unfair to others (for reviews, see Killen, 1991; Smetana, 1995; Tisak, 1995; Turiel, Killen, & Helwig, 1987). These studies, however, have primarily focused upon direct physical harm (such as hitting) or denial of access to resources (such as unfair distribution; see Turiel, 1983, 1998). Much less is known about whether children view other types of potentially harmful activities, such as excluding children from peer group activities on the basis of group memberships, as unfair (but see Short, 1993; Theimer, Killen, & Stangor, 2001). Although the literature on peer exclusion (in general) is quite extensive, most of this work has concentrated on the traits of the individual child being excluded and how this accounts for peer rejection (Asher & Coie, 1990). Recently, one study has examined the behavioral patterns of exclusion by groups (see Zarbatany, Van Brun-schot, Meadows, & Pepper, 1996), but no work, to the authors' knowledge, has examined how children evaluate peer exclusion from the viewpoint of the group and intergroup relationships (an exception is Theimer et al., 2001). Understanding how children reason about such decisions, however, is important because decisions about the appropriateness of inclusion or exclusion represent an integral part of reasoning about intergroup relationships in adults (such as including or excluding women from the military services or minorities from job opportunities; e.g., Macrae, Stangor, & Hewstone, 1996).

One study that has investigated this issue has shown that young children judge it as wrong to exclude someone from a play activity solely on the basis of their gender. Theimer et al. (2001) found that preschool children thought it was wrong for a group of girls to exclude a boy from playing with dolls, even

though these same children saw doll-playing as an activity that was primarily performed by girls (likewise, it was viewed as wrong for a group of boys to exclude a girl from playing with trucks, even though truck-playing was seen as an activity more appropriate for boys). The goal of the present research was to study the developmental trajectory of decisions about inclusion and exclusion in gender and race peer contexts into adolescence.

On the basis of social-cognitive development theory, it was hypothesized that decisions about the appropriateness of excluding children from social groups (particularly, gender and race) involve two forms of social reasoning—moral beliefs about the wrongfulness of exclusion, and social-conventional beliefs about social group processes and group functioning. Moral beliefs include concepts about fairness and rights, equal treatment, and equal access (Damon, 1983; Turiel, 1998). Social-conventional beliefs entail several forms of reasoning, including those that concern group functioning (Turiel, 1978, 1983, 1998), group identity (Brown, 1989), and stereotypes about others based on their group membership (Carter & Patterson, 1982; Liben & Signorella, 1993; Stangor & Ruble, 1989; Stoddart & Turiel, 1985).

Research on children's reasoning about social conventions has shown that social-conventional concepts change with age, and particularly so in terms of taking social group roles and expectations into account (Helwig, 1995, 1997; Killen, 1991; Turiel, 1978, 1983, 1998). Whereas young children reason about social conventions in terms of social uniformity and rule systems (e.g., "It's wrong to call a teacher by her first name because there is a rule about it"), older children reason about social group customs in terms of societal standards and social coordination (e.g., "It's wrong to call a teacher by her first name because maybe the other students would think of her as a peer instead of someone with authority and a higher status"; see Turiel, 1983, p. 103). With age, children become increasingly concerned about the nature of social groups, the norms and expectations that go along with the structure of the group, and effective group functioning.

Theoretically, then, decisions about potential exclusion from social groups involve the coordination of moral judgments about the wrongfulness of exclusion with a range of social-conventional judgments about social group functioning, group identity, and group stereotypes. Evaluating acts of exclusion from groups involves weighing these competing moral and social-conventional considerations. Given that research has shown that children are sensitive to context issues (Helwig, 1995) and that, with age, children increasingly use more complex social group reasoning processes (Tisak, 1995; Turiel, 1983), it was predicted that children's judgments about exclusion from peer groups would be sensitive to the context in which the exclusion occurred and that sensitivity to the impact of exclusion on effective group functioning would increase with age.

To test these hypotheses, children were asked to make judgments about the appropriateness of exclusion in gender and racial peer group contexts. Gender and race were selected for several reasons. First, gender and race are two of the most salient social group membership categories to emerge in development (see Aboud, 1992). Second, gender and racial stereotypes are a common source of prejudice and contribute to intergroup tensions and conflicts. In addition, children's and adolescents' exclusion in peer group contexts is most frequently about gender (Maccoby, 1988) and race (Aboud, 1992). No studies of which the authors are aware have compared children's judgments about gender and racial exclusion in peer group contexts, but research on stereotypes indicates that both gender and racial stereotypes emerge during the preschool period (Aboud, 1992).

Three exclusion contexts were designed for children's evaluation. In the first context, called the *straightforward exclusion context*, a group of peers is considering excluding a child from the group for solely stereotypic reasons, without any other justification except that the children might feel "uncomfortable" having the child who was not stereotypical for the activity (e.g., a boy in a ballet class) in the group. It was expected that despite the possibility of using the stereotype to justify exclusion, moral reasons would prevail for all children in this context. Straightforward exclusion contexts are similar to straightforward moral transgressions in which one person inflicts harm on another for no reason and there are few competing considerations.

Two *multifaceted* contexts were also created. In these, the cost to group functioning was increased and the morally relevant salience of the exclusion decision was decreased. In each of these contexts, the participant was asked to pick one of two children to join the group—one who fit the stereotype of the peer group activity and one who did not fit the stereotype. This resulted in the inclusion of one child and the exclusion of another, which made the decision to exclude a child who did not fit the stereotype less morally difficult because one was including someone else at the same time.

The cost to group functioning was manipulated by providing information about the child's qualifications to join the group between the two multifaceted contexts. In the first context, called *equal qualifications*, two children were said to be equally qualified to join the group (e.g., "A boy and a girl are equally good at ballet"). In the second context, called *unequal qualifications*, the child who did not fit the stereotype was said to be less qualified than the child who fit the stereotype (e.g., "The girl is better at ballet than is the boy"). The child who did not fit the stereotype was made less qualified to test the extent to which children would continue to apply their judgment about not excluding others on the basis of gender and race (as measured in the straightforward context) in different contexts with competing considerations. Would children who judged it wrong to exclude solely on the basis of gender or race (straightforward context) be willing to exclude a child when that child was less qualified than another child who fit the stereotype of the activity?

It was expected that both moral and social-conventional reasoning would be relevant to decisions in multifaceted contexts. In these contexts, it was expected that decisions to include the child who did not fit the stereotype would be justified in terms of moral reasons of fairness and equity, whereas decisions to exclude the child who did fit the stereotype would be justified in terms of social conventional reasons regarding effective group functioning. On the one hand, moral reasoning would be reflected when it was judged as wrong to exclude someone who did not have an equal opportunity to join (e.g., fair and equal treatment). On the other hand, social conventional reasoning would be reflected in children's reasoning when it was judged as all right to exclude a child on the basis of social-conventions, such as stereotypes (e.g., "Ballet is for girls"; see Carter & Patterson, 1982; Stoddart & Turiel, 1985), group functioning (e.g., "The group will work better with someone who knows how to do the activity"), or group identity (e.g., "The club needs to feel like a group"). It was expected that, with age, children would increasingly focus on group functioning and view it as wrong to include someone who did not have familiarity with the activity and thus could not contribute to the group identity or the effective functioning of the group.

Further, it was expected that, with age, children would be increasingly able to differentiate between different contexts of exclusion. The difference between the equal and the unequal qualifications contexts is that in the unequal qualifications context (in which the girl is better at ballet, for example), the cost of including the child for whom the activity is not stereotypical (such as a boy for ballet) is higher than in the equal qualifications context. In the equal qualifications context both children are equally qualified at the activity (even though one child is more typically associated with the activity). It was expected that children would be more likely to choose to include the nonstereotypical child in the equal qualifications context than in the unequal qualifications context. The reasons for picking the nonstereotypical child in the equal qualifications context could be due to either judgments about equal access or to judgments about group functioning. It was predicted that it would be more likely for equal access justifications to emerge in the equal qualifications context than in the unequal qualifications context given the higher cost to group functioning in the unequal qualifications context (when one child is less qualified to participate in the peer group activity). It was also expected that older children would be more likely than younger children to differentiate their judgments by context because older children would be more sensitive to the potential influence upon effective group functioning in the unequal qualifications context.

To test these hypotheses, European American children, equally divided between boys and girls, between the ages of 7 and 13 were interviewed regarding their beliefs about the appropriateness of excluding children from stereotypical peer group activities on the basis of their gender and race.[1]

Four different peer group activities, stereotypical of girls, of boys, of White children, and of Black children, were used. These activities were ballet club, baseball card club, math club, and basketball club, respectively. Although three peer group activities associated with gender or race categories (e.g., ballet for girls, baseball card clubs for boys, basketball for Black children) were identified, finding a peer group activity associated with White children was more difficult. A math club was found to be somewhat associated with White children, particularly for older children. Thus, the math club was used even though it was somewhat different from the other three clubs because of the academic content. It was emphasized that the clubs were voluntary and not associated with school work After-school peer group activities were chosen so that children's evaluations of authority would not enter into their decision making. To avoid introducing racial stereotypes to younger children, the words "Black" and "White" were not mentioned to children in the race stories. Instead, the picture cards were simply shown and the child was asked whether it would be all right or not all right to exclude the child "standing at the door?" The children rated the appropriateness of excluding children from these peer group activities for each of the three separate exclusion contexts. In addition, a group activity knowledge assessment was administered to ensure that the participants viewed the peer group activities as associated with gender and race group membership.

The research design also allowed us to test two subsidiary hypotheses. In the Theimer et al. (2001) study on preschool-aged children's evaluations, it was found that girls were more likely to evaluate exclusion negatively than were boys. In general, several studies have indicated that girls are more sensitive to prosocial issues and to exclusion than are boys (Killen & Turiel, 1998; Wentzel & Erdley, 1993; Zahn-Waxler, Cole, Welsh, & Fox, 1995; Zarbatany et al., 1996). On the basis of these findings it was predicted that girls would rate exclusion more harshly across all contexts. Second, research with children and adults has indicated that individuals often display an ingroup bias or *ingroup favoritism* (Bennett, Barrett, Lyons, & Sani, 1998; Brewer, 1979; Damon, 1977, chapter 3; Mackie, Hamilton, Susskind, & Rosselli, 1996; Tajfel, Billig, Bundy, & Flament, 1971; Van Avermaet & McClin-tock, 1988; Yee & Brown, 1992), in which they make more positive judgments or assign more positive rewards to other members of their own group. No research, however, has been conducted to determine whether children display an ingroup bias in their social judgments about exclusion. In this study, whether girls and boys were more willing to condone exclusion of opposite-sex than same-sex children from group activities was tested. Finally, to provide breadth for the types of social group categories children think about, exclusion scenarios were included for both gender and race. No hypotheses were formulated to distinguish these types of exclusion, however, because of a lack of prior findings directly bearing on this comparison.

Method

Participants

Participants were 65 girls and 65 boys from three grades. There were 19 female and 20 male first graders, $M = 6.6$, $SD = .4$, *range* = 5.11–7.4, 25 female and 23 male fourth graders, $M = 9.6$, $SD = .5$, *range* = 8.11–10.9, and 21 female and 22 male seventh graders, $M = 12.6$, $SD = .4$, *range* = 12.0–13.5. All students were European American. The children were enrolled in mixed-ethnicity, middle-class public schools in a suburban area of Maryland, outside of Washington, DC. All students were informed that the interviews were confidential, voluntary, and anonymous. Parental consent was obtained for all participants.

Procedure and design

All students were individually interviewed for about 35 min by a graduate research assistant in a quiet room at school. The three parts of the interview, a warm-up task, a group activity knowledge assessment, and a group exclusion evaluation, were administered to all children.

WARM-UP TASK

The purpose of the warm-up task was to familiarize students with the use of the 7-point Likert response format that was to be used in the group exclusion evaluations and to validate that the students could use the scale. Three transgressions were described, accompanied by picture cards, and participants were asked to rate the "badness" of each of three acts by using a scale (0 = not at all bad; 6 = very, very bad). The three acts were hitting someone for no reason, calling a principal by her first name, and sleeping late. Confirming that the children understood the task and were able to use the Likert scale measure, the three acts were rated significantly differently, $Ms = 5.5$, 2.5, and 2.14, respectively, in a manner that accurately reflects the severity of the transgressions (there were no significant age or gender differences).

GROUP ACTIVITY KNOWLEDGE ASSESSMENT

In the knowledge assessment task, children were asked to decide who liked to do particular activities by pointing to a laminated 8½" × 11" card that had a row of five sets of very simple "smiley" faces. To depict girl as opposed to boy faces, a bow was drawn on the head of the girls; to depict White versus Black faces, the Black faces were shaded. To assess knowledge of gender-related activities, children were asked "Who likes to do X?" and were asked to point to one of five sets of faces: (1) only girls: four girl faces; (2) mostly girls: one boy and three girl faces; (3) same: two boy and two girl faces; (4) mostly boys: three boy faces and one girl face: (5) only boys: four boy faces. The questions were ballet (girl activity), baseball cards (boy activity), tennis (neutral activity), and reading books (neutral activity). Responses were coded on a 5-point scale corresponding to each choice (1 = only girls to 5 = only boys). For the race measure, children were asked "Who likes to do X?" and were asked to point to one of five sets of faces: (1) only Black children: four Black child faces; (2) mostly Black children: one White child face and three Black child faces; (3) same: two Black and two White child faces; (4) mostly White children: three White child faces and one Black child face; and (5) only White children: four White child faces. The questions were math (White activity), basketball (Black activity), art (neutral activity), and singing (neutral activity). Responses were coded on a 5-point scale corresponding to each choice (1 = only Black children to 5 = only White children). The order in which the gender and race items were presented was counterbalanced.

GROUP EXCLUSION EVALUATION

The group exclusion evaluation comprised four descriptions of children in different after school peer clubs in which the group was considering excluding a child from participating in the group. The exclusions involved ballet (girls exclude a boy), baseball cards (boys exclude a girl), math (White children exclude a Black child), and basketball (Black children exclude a White child). Each exclusion event was described by using 8½" × 11" picture cards that illustrated the scene (e.g., for the ballet scenario, there was a picture of girls in a room with a ballet bar and a mirror and a boy at the door looking in the room). For the race contexts, the gender of the children described in the event matched the gender of the participant. The interviewer began the interview by saying, "I am going to tell you about a number of different afterschool clubs and some of the things that happened to the kids in the clubs. These clubs are for kids and there are no teachers or adults in the clubs. These kids are about your age. There are no right or wrong answers. I'm just interested in whatever you think about these stories."

For each of the four exclusion events, three different judgmental contexts were presented to the child—straightforward exclusion, equal qualifications, and unequal qualifications. Furthermore, in describing each of the contexts, the children were told that some children were of one opinion about the appropriateness of exclusion, whereas other children had the opposite opinion. This was done to suggest that either of the two decisions would be appropriate because some children already favored it. These competing suggestions were made to avoid problems related to social desirability (see Harter, 1998).

In the straightforward exclusion contexts, participants were told that a child wanted to join an activity and it was said that some of the children in the group would be uncomfortable if the child joined and that they might quit if the child was included—that is, that some children would like the (peer) to be included and some would not like the (peer) to be included. In

the equal qualifications context, participants were told that two children wanted to join the club (one child fit the stereotype and one child did not), that the two children were known to be equally good at the activity, and that the club members were divided about who to include—some of the children want to give the (nonstereotypical peer) a chance because (he or she) does not usually do the activity, whereas the others think that it would be good to have another (peer) join who was like the others. Finally, in the unequal qualifications context, the children were again told that two children wanted to join the club—one child fit the stereotype and one child did not, that one child was better at the activity (than the one who fit the stereotype), and (again) that the children were divided about which child to include.

As an example, in the ballet scenario, for the straightforward exclusion context, participants were told that some of the girls in the ballet club did not want a boy to join because they would be uncomfortable. Children were asked whether it was alright or not alright to let the boy into the ballet club. In the equal qualifications context, participants were told that both a boy and a girl wanted to join the club but there was room for only one more person to join and the boy and girl were equally good at ballet. In the unequal qualifications context, participants were told that two children, a boy and a girl, both wanted to join the ballet club but that there was only room for one more person and that the girl was better at ballet.

Five assessments were made of participants' responses. First, participants were asked for their *judgment* about the exclusion in the straightforward context: "Is it alright or not alright for the group to exclude the [nonstereotypical] child from the activity?" Then they were asked for their *choice* of who to pick (in both the equal qualifications and in the unequal qualifications scenarios, e.g., "Who should the club pick?"). Children were asked for their *justifications* about their judgments (straightforward context) and choices (multifaceted contexts). Children were also asked how bad it would be for the club members to exclude the child who was not stereotypical for the activity and to make a *rating* of how bad excluding this child would be on a scale from 0 (Not at all bad) to 6 (Very, very bad). Because it had been found in pilot testing that questions about race were

Table 10.1   Justification coding categories

Moral

    Fairness and rights.   Appeals to the maintenance of fairness in the treatment of persons (e.g., "It wouldn't be fair to exclude him"), to the rights of individuals (e.g., "She has a right to join the club if she wants to"), and to the wrongfulness of discrimination based on race or gender or both (e.g., "You shouldn't discriminate against someone just because of their color or gender").

    Equal treatment.   Appeals to the equal treatment of individuals (e.g., "Everyone should be treated the same").

    Equal access.   Appeals to the learning opportunities of those, as members of discriminated groups, who have not previously had the chance (e.g., "Boys should have a chance to do ballet because they usually don't get to do it"; "Teach her about baseball cards because girls don't often get a chance and they should have the same opportunity").

Social Conventional

    Social conventions.   Appeals to the expectations of the group (e.g., "The other kids would think that John is strange if he takes ballet"; "The boy would feel strange if he was in a group with all girls"), traditions, customs, and norms of a society (e.g., "Girls are not supposed to play with baseball cards"; "Girls usually like to play jumprope and games like that").

    Group functioning.   Appeals to making the group function well. This includes statements about admitting someone who will make the club more enjoyable or more interesting to its members (e.g., "Admit the one who is more qualified because then the club will know more and work much better as a group together"; "Choose her because she's better at ballet and that's what their club's about, and so you want to have the better person, because they'll probably enjoy it more"; "Since he knows a lot more he can be more useful in the club"; "Because they don't want someone in there who doesn't know the same as them. They might get bored of… like when they say something she might not understand and they have to explain it."

    Group identity.   Appeals to the identity of the group (e.g., "The black kids on the basketball team need to have their own team"; "The girls will feel uncomfortable if a boy is in the club") and group decision making ("The group can decide whatever they want").

more socially sensitive than questions about gender, the gender scenarios were always described first, followed by the race scenarios; and girls heard the girl-excluded scenario first whereas boys heard the boy-excluded scenario first. In addition, a separate analysis was conducted on the number of times that children invoked explicit *stereotypes* about the group activity when providing a justification for their judgments and choices (for instance, "Boys aren't good at ballet"). Because this analysis revealed that very few of the children (less than 8%) used explicit stereotypes to justify exclusion, no further analyses were conducted for this assessment.

Coding and reliability

Judgments and choices were coded dichotomously. Justifications were coded by using a coding system based both on previous categories used in the literature (Smetana, 1995; Tisak 1995) and on the results of pilot data. The coding category system comprised three moral (fairness, equal treatment, equal access)

and three social-conventional (social conventions, group functioning, and group identity) codes (see Table 10.1). For the primary analyses, the three moral categories were collapsed as "moral" and the three social-conventional were collapsed as "social-conventional." Three subcategories, included in the pilot system, were deleted in the final version of the coding system because of low frequency (less than 6%). Two moral subcategories were deleted: prosocial ("You should include someone in order to be nice"), from research by Eisenberg and Miller (1987); and individual merit ("A person who is good at something deserves to be in the club"), from research by Damon (1977); and a third social-conventional subcategory was deleted: stereotypic beliefs ("Boys are not good at ballet"), from research by Carter and Patterson (1982).

Responses that used more than one type of justification were coded for each applicable justification, although less than 5% of the participants used more than one justification per response. Reliability was conducted on 25% of the protocols (390 data points) by two trained coders. For justifications in the straightforward context, Cohen's κ = .88, for the equal qualifications context, κ = .80, and for the unequal qualifications context, κ = .88.

Results

The report of the analyses begins with the findings for the Group Activity Knowledge measure to demonstrate that children were aware of the normatively appropriate activities for the target groups that we were using. Next, the analyses for judgments, ratings and justifications within the straightforward exclusion context is described to affirm that all children at all ages saw such unjustified exclusion as wrong. Then the two multifaceted contexts (equal qualifications and unequal qualifications) are compared. Analyses were conducted on three separate measures—judgments, ratings, and justifications. Judgments were coded dichotomously (0 and 1), ratings were on a 7-point scale, and justifications were the proportion of moral and social conventional justifications. The findings for our expectations that inclusion would be justified on moral grounds, whereas exclusion would be based on social conventional reasoning, are also described. In all subsequent analyses, post hoc comparisons were performed by using Bonferroni corrections to correct for Type I error. In cases where proportions were used, arcsine transformations were conducted to normalize the distributions (Winer, 1971).

Group activity knowledge assessment

To investigate whether children held the appropriate beliefs about the gender activities, 2 (gender of child) × 3 (grade) × 3 (type of activity; baseball, ballet, gender-neutral) ANOVAs were conducted, with repeated measures on the last factor on the 5-point scale responses (1 = "only girls," 5 = "only boys"). Because they did not differ, analysis of the two gender-neutral activities (books and tennis) were combined. The analysis revealed a significant main effect of type of activity, $F(2, 248) = 652.77$, $p < .001$, $\eta^2 = .84$. Follow-up comparisons showed that the children evaluated ballet, $M = 1.57$, as significantly more likely to be performed by girls than the neutral activities,

$M = 3.10$, $F(1, 248) = 473.69$, $p < .001$, $\eta^2 = .66$, and also rated baseball, $M = 4.42$, as significantly more likely to be performed by boys than the neutral activities, $F(1, 248) = 319.46$, $p < .001$, $\eta^2 = .56$. There was also a Gender × Activity interaction, $F(4, 248) = 3.47$, $p < .01$, $\eta^2 = .05$, which indicated that first graders, $M = 1.30$, saw ballet as more likely to be performed by girls than did fourth, $M = 1.73$, or seventh graders, $M = 1.63$ and that first graders, $M = 3.25$, also rated the neutral activities (books and tennis) as more likely to be performed by boys than did fourth, $M = 3.00$, or seventh graders, $M = 2.97$.

To investigate whether children held the appropriate beliefs about the race activities, 2 (gender of child) × 3 (grade) × 3 (type of activity; math, basketball, race-neutral) ANOVAs were conducted, with repeated measures on the last factor on the 5-point scale responses (1 = "only Black children," 5 = "only White children"). Because they did not differ, analysis of the two race-neutral activities (art and singing) were combined. The analysis revealed only a main effect of activity, $F(2, 248) = 42.75$, $p < .001$, $\eta^2 = .26$. (There were no significant findings for grade level or gender of the child.) Follow-up analyses showed that ratings for basketball, $M = 2.52$, were significantly lower than the neutral items, $M = 3.19$, $F(1, 248) = 47.25$, $p < .001$, $\eta^2 = .16$, although the math rating, $M = 3.43$, was not significantly higher than the rating of the neutral items, $F(1, 248) < 1.00$. Taken together, then, these analyses indicate that children were aware of three out of the four stereotypes (only math was not significantly different from the neutral ratings).

Straightforward exclusion

It was expected that exclusion in the straightforward context would be seen as unwarranted by all children and that the inappropriateness would be justified by using moral reasons because the social-conventional aspect (some children would feel uncomfortable having the stereotyped child in the group) was not very strong. This hypothesis was tested by using 2 (gender of child) × 3 (grade) × 2 (group excluded: gender, race) ANOVAs with repeated measures on the last factor. There were no significant differences for these judgments across either gender of child or grade level.

Table 10.2 Judgments, justifications, and ratings by excluded group and grade:
Straightforward context

Excluded group	Grade		
	1st	4th	7th
Gender exclusion			
Judgments	.94 (.17)	.94 (.19)	.93 (.20)
Ratings	4.86 (1.47)	4.24 (1.30)	4.17 (1.25)
Justifications			
Moral	.89 (.23)	.91 (.25)	.88 (.25)
Social-conventional	.09 (.20)	.08 (.24)	.11 (.25)
Race exclusion			
Judgments	.95 (.19)	.97 (.12)	(.13)
Ratings	4.94 (1.40)	4.49 (1.19)	4.97 (1.02)
Justifications			
Moral	.90 (.23)	.92 (.21)	.99 (.08)
Social-conventional	.05 (.19)	.04 (.13)	.01 (.08)

Note. Judgments are mean proportions of children stating "Not alright to exclude" (0 = alright;
1 = not alright). Ratings: 0 (not at all bad) to 6 (very, very bad) for excluding someone. Justifications
are mean proportions of children using moral and social-conventional reasons for their judgment.
Standard deviations are in parentheses.

As expected, even though children possessed the appropriate knowledge about the activities, they did not use this knowledge to justify the exclusion as legitimate in the straightforward context. Rather, the vast majority of children, $M = .96$, judged that it was wrong for the peer groups to exclude a child from the activity acros all contexts (see Table 10.2). In addition, children justified their decisions by using moral criteria. All children gave primarily moral, $M = .92$, rather than social-conventional, $M = .06$, justifications (see Table 10.2), and this tendency did not differ across either gender of child or grade level. There was also a main effect of type of exclusion, $F(1, 124) = 5.48$, $p < .05$, $\eta^2 = .04$, which indicates that children judged exclusion as more wrong in the race, $M = .98$, than the gender, $M = .94$, stories. This result appeared in every other analysis of both judgments and ratings, across each of the three contexts. This finding is hard to interpret, however, because the activities from which the children were excluded also varied between gender and race groups. Therefore, it is not reported again.

The ratings of how bad it would be to exclude a child reflected a pattern similar to the judgment data. All children judged such exclusion to be wrong, $M = 4.59$ out of 6.00 overall, and there were no grade differences on these ratings. There was a main effect, however, of gender of child, $F(1, 124) = 9.28$, $p < .001$, $\eta^2 = .07$, which showed that girls, $M = 4.89$, rated exclusion as more bad than boys, $M = 4.29$, $p < .001$. There was also an unexpected grade × type of exclusion interaction, $F(2,124) = 7.76$, $p < .001$, $\eta^2 = .11$. As revealed in Table 10.2, this interaction showed that children's negative ratings of exclusion in the gender scenarios decreased with age, $Ms = 4.86, 4.24, 4.17$ for first, fourth, and seventh grades, $p < .001$, whereas there was no corresponding pattern for the ratings about race.

In sum, strong support was found for the expectation that all children would see straightforward exclusion as wrong and that they would justify these decisions with moral reasoning. Even the youngest children were quite aware of the inappropriateness of exclusion, despite the fact that they judged the activities as stereotypically inappropriate for the child. Also, as expected, girls saw this exclusion as more wrong overall than did boys. A separate analysis was conducted for the two gender-related stories but no evidence was found for ingroup favoritism; that is, girls and boys did not judge that it was more all right for a group to exclude someone from the opposite sex than from one's own sex.

Table 10.3 Choices and ratings by children who chose the child who did not fit the stereotype in the multifaceted contexts

Excluded group by context	Grade		
	1st	4th	7th
Gender exclusion			
Choices			
Equal qualifications	.71 (.39)	.67 (.40)	.60 (.46)
Unequal qualifications	.41 (.46)	.55 (.46)	.22 (.40)
Ratings			
Equal qualifications	2.88 (1.90)	2.49 (1.64)	2.94 (1.40)
Unequal qualifications	2.83 (1.90)	2.35 (1.65)	2.05 (1.60)
Racial exclusion			
Choices			
Equal qualifications	.79 (.32)	.88 (.28)	.77 (.37)
Unequal qualifications	.51 (.46)	.74 (.40)	.29 (.43)
Ratings			
Equal qualifications	3.49 (1.83)	3.79 (1.58)	3.51 (1.75)
Unequal qualifications	3.40 (1.91)	3.56 (1.73)	2.44 (1.70)

Note. Judgments are mean proportions of children who chose the child who did not fit the stereotype (0 = child who fit the stereotype; 1 = child who did not fit the stereotype). Ratings: 0 (not bad) to 6 (very, very bad) for not picking the child who did not fit the stereotype. Standard deviations are in parentheses.

Multifaceted contexts

Children's choices in the multifaceted contexts involved choosing which of two children should join the club when only one place was left and when there were competing reasons for the decision. Thus, in these contexts children needed to weigh both moral and social conventional considerations to make their decisions. In the equal qualifications context, both children were said to have equal skills at the activity. In the unequal qualifications context, the child who fit the activity was also said to be better at it, thus making salient the potential cost to effective functioning of the group if the nonstereotypical child was included. The hypotheses were tested by using 2 (gender of child) × 3 (grade) × 2 (group excluded; gender, race) × 2 (context: equal qualifications, unequal qualifications) ANOVAs, with repeated measures on the last two factors. Because it was found that the patterns of the dependent variables did not differ for race versus gender exclusion, this factor was collapsed across for the remaining analyses. Thus, 2 (gender of child) × 3 (grade level) × 2 (context: equal qualifications,

unequal qualifications) ANOVAs with repeated measures were conducted on the last factor.

Choices

Across all of the multifaceted contexts (equal and unequal qualifications), the majority of the children, $M = .60$, favored including the nonstereotypical child (that is, the boy for ballet, the girl for baseball cards, the Black child for math, and the White child for basketball) as shown in Table 10.3. Demonstrating, however, that the manipulation of the salience of social conventional factors was successful, this tendency was significantly greater in the equal, $M = .74$, than in the unequal qualifications context, $M = .52$, $F(1, 124) = 61.33, p < .001, \eta^2 = .33$. There was also a main effect of gender of child, $F(1, 124) = 6.15, p < .001, \eta^2 = .05$, which indicates that, across both contexts, girls, $M = .67$, were more likely to choose the nonstereotypical child than were boys, $M = .52, p < .001$.

More importantly, the expected Grade Level × Context (equal or unequal qualifications) interaction emerged, $F(2, 124) = 6.15, p < .01, \eta^2 = .09$, on the choices. Suggesting that they were not sensitive to the potential negative effects of including an unskilled child in the group, the fourth-grade children did not significantly differentiate between the unequal, $M = .77$, and equal, $M = .74$, contexts, $p > 1.00$. The seventh-grade children, however, did rate exclusion less negatively in the unequal qualifications context in which the unskilled child might have influenced effective group functioning, $F(1, 42) = 33.1, p < .001, \eta^2 = .44$, $Ms = .69$ and $.29$, respectively. Unexpectedly, the first-grade children were also more likely to choose the nonstereotypical child in the equal, $M = .75$, than the unequal, $M = .50$, contexts, $F(1, 38) = 10.35, p < .01, \eta^2 = .21$. There were no main effects for either grade or gender on this measure. Moreover, there was no evidence for an ingroup bias (girls did not choose girls in girl-typed contexts more than did boys; nor did boys choose boys in boy-typed contexts more than did girls).

JUSTIFICATIONS

The justification measure provided the most important test of the expectation that social-conventional reasoning about group functioning varied across age. Overall, it was found that children used more moral, $M = .67$, than social-conventional, $M = .29$, justifications, $F(1, 124) = 46.02, p < .001, \eta^2 = .27$; however, children used more moral than social-conventional justifications in the equal, $Ms = .67$ and $.35$, respectively, than in the unequal contexts, $Ms = .50$ and $.41$, $F(1, 124) = 22.78, p < .001, \eta^2 = .26$. Furthermore, although the proportion of social conventional versus moral justifications increased across grade, $F(2,124) = 5.92, p < .05, \eta^2 = .09$ in both contexts, this tendency was significantly greater in the unequal than the equal context contexts; the expected Grade × Context × Type of Justification interaction was significant, $F(2,124) = 4.08, p < .05, \eta^2 = .06$. The results of this analysis are shown in Table 10.4. This interaction is also charted in Figure 10.1, which represents a difference score between moral and social conventional reasoning at each age level and for each context such that higher numbers indicate a greater proportion of moral (versus social-conventional) reasoning. The first and fourth graders were not as sensitive to context as were the seventh graders and gave more moral than social conventional justifications for

Table 10.4 Children's justification for their choice in the multifaceted contexts

Excluded group by context	Grade		
	1st	4th	7th
Gender exclusion			
Equal qualifications			
Moral	.64 (.41)	.59 (.41)	.51 (.40)
SC	.31 (.31)	.39 (.41)	.49 (.40)
Unequal qualifications			
Moral	.55 (.40)	.54 (.43)	.37 (.37)
SC	.30 (.36)	.41 (.41)	.62 (.38)
Racial exclusion			
Equal qualifications			
Moral	.69 (.37)	.81 (.34)	.77 (.37)
SC	.19 (.32)	.13 (.30)	.22 (.37)
Unequal qualifications			
Moral	.55 (.40)	.65 (.41)	.35 (.43)
SC	.26 (.33)	.27 (.39)	.64 (.44)

Note. Justifications are proportions of children using moral and social-conventional reasons for their choices. Moral = moral justifications; SC = social-conventional justifications. Standard deviations are in parentheses.

both the equal and unequal contexts. The seventh graders, on the other hand, viewed the equal context in moral terms and the unequal context in social-conventional terms.

To determine the nature of the justifications, the use of the three subcategories of social-conventional justifications was examined. In the unequal contexts, the vast majority of justifications, $M = .83$, were about group functioning (with the remaining justifications being about conventions, $M = .08$, and group identity, $M = .09$). In fact, for the seventh-grade children, the vast majority, $M = .92$, of the social-conventional justifications in the unequal context were about group functioning. When the nonstereotypical child threatened group functioning, the older children were less willing to choose this child to participate. In the equal qualifications contexts, however, in which "all things were equal," most participants used moral justifications (and chose someone who did not fit the stereotype of the activity). Of those participants who used social-conventional justifications in the equal

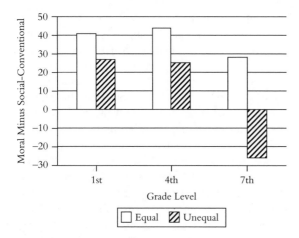

Figure 10.1 The proportion of moral minus the proportion of social-conventional justifications given by children at each grade for equal and unequal contexts.

qualifications contexts, only a minority used ones based on group functioning, M = .11; most participants gave justifications based on conventions, M = .51, and group identity, M = .38.

RATINGS

Across all of the multifaceted contexts, the mean rating (how bad would it be to exclude the nonstereotypical child?), on a 0 (not at all bad) to 6 (very, very bad) scale, was M = 2.98. These data are depicted in Table 10.3. Excluding the nonstereotypical child, however, was seen as less bad in the unequal, M = 3.18, than in the equal qualifications context, M = 2.77, $F(1, 124)$ = 23.24, p < .001, η^2 = .16. Again, the expected Grade × Context interaction emerged, $F(2,124)$ = 11.07, p < .01, η^2 = .15, on the ratings. Neither the first- nor the fourth-grade children significantly differentiated between the unequal and equal contexts, Ms = 3.18 and 3.11 for the first graders and 3.14 and 2.95 for the fourth graders, both ps > .16. The seventh-grade children, however, did differentiate between the two contexts, $F(1, 42)$ = 40.19, p < .001, η^2 = .49, Ms = 3.22 and 2.24, respectively, rating it as more bad to exclude the stereotypical child in the equal than the unequal contexts. Again there were no main effects for either grade or gender on this measure.

Relation between judgments and justifications

The analyses are based on the theory that children are more likely to allow exclusion on the basis of gender or race when they perceive the issue to be one involving social-conventional rather than moral considerations. To examine the hypothesis that decisions to exclude individuals from activities would be justified primarily by using social-conventional justifications, whereas decisions of inclusion would be justified primarily by using moral reasoning, the proportion of moral and social-conventional justifications given by children who picked the stereotypical or nonstereotypical child were calculated (the straightforward context was not included in this analysis because the vast majority of all participants stated that it was wrong to exclude and gave moral justifications).

Confirming the expected relation between judgment and justification, across both equal and unequal contexts, children who picked the stereotypical child used a greater proportion of moral, M = .87, than social-conventional, M = .17, reasoning, p < .001. Children who picked the nonstereotypical child, however, used a greater proportion of social-conventional, M = .85, than moral, M = .04, reasoning, p < .001.

Discussion

Overwhelmingly, children and adolescents rejected straightforward exclusion on the basis of gender or race, even in contexts in which gender or racial stereotypic expectations could provide a basis for condoning exclusion (such as excluding a boy from ballet because ballet is an activity primarily performed by girls). The reasons given for rejecting exclusion were primarily fairness and rights, equal treatment, and equal access. Thus, children interpreted straightforward exclusion, even in stereotypic contexts, as wrong from a moral viewpoint, which supports other findings regarding children's judgments of straightforward violations of rights and equality (Helwig, 1995, 1997; Killen, 1991; Smetana, 1995; Tisak, 1995).

Also supporting predictions derived from social-cognitive developmental theories, in multifaceted situations in which participants were asked to pick one of two children to join a peer group club, children weighed a variety of issues to make their decisions of whom to pick. The children were influenced by considerations of the qualifications of the children (how good they were at the club's activity) as well as issues of fairness and equal opportunity. When a choice had to be made between two equally qualified children, most of the participants stated that the child who did not fit the stereotype should be picked and gave reasons based on equal treatment and equal access. Justifications such as "Boys don't get a chance to take ballet" and "A girl could learn how to play baseball cards and then she could teach other girls how to play" were used in the gender contexts. Similarly, for the race stories, children who picked the child who did not fit the stereotype used reasons such as "It's good for Black and White children to play together and learn about each other so they'll get along well and not be prejudiced."

These results are different than those from previous research that used a similar methodology in preschool-aged children (Theimer et al., 2001) and in which a majority of young children chose a child who fit the stereotype (e.g., a girl for ballet) in contexts in which the qualifications were equal. Perhaps older children are more sensitive to considerations involving prior history of opportunity, whereas young children may rely more upon their beliefs about group-appropriate activities to make a decision about whom to pick (influencing them, for instance, to pick a girl instead of a boy for ballet). Supporting this interpretation was the finding that first graders were more likely to identify ballet as a girls' activity than were fourth and seventh graders. However, the contexts used in our study and the preschool study just cited were somewhat different, so further research will be needed to substantiate this interpretation.

Although the activity knowledge measure confirmed that the children were well aware of differences in the appropriateness of the activities across racial and gender groups, it was found that only a very few children (less than 8% overall) used stereotypes to justify their answers (and these justifications were found only in the equal opportunity gender contexts). These few responses included statements such as "It's okay to pick the girl for ballet because boys aren't

good at ballet." In short, moral and other types of social-conventional reasons appear to have been more important to these children than stereotypes about appropriate peer group activities as judged by their use of justifications. Unexpectedly, first-grade children were more likely to pick the nonstereotypic child in the equal qualifications context than were older children even though they were also more likely to identify ballet as a "girls' activity" in the group activity knowledge assessment. Thus, the younger children did not focus on the group-functioning dimension of the multifaceted contexts to the extent that older children did despite their stronger associations of gender with the types of group activities being discussed. This could be a lack of coordination of different aspects of social knowledge or it could pertain to their concepts of group functioning. Further research is needed to fully interpret this pattern of results.

The seventh graders were most sensitive to context in that they differentiated between the equal and unequal qualifications contexts. For the dimension of a child's qualifications to join a group, the older children seemed to be more aware of the potential cost to group functioning of including a child who was not qualified than were the younger children. Although issues of fairness prevailed overall, older children qualified these judgments in cases where there was a potential threat to group functioning. In the unequal qualifications contexts, the seventh graders were more likely to choose the more qualified child to join the club and to use social-conventional reasons (particularly those relating to group functioning) to justify these choices. An exception to this pattern occurred on the choice measures, in which the first graders also differentiated between the equal opportunity and the unequal opportunity contexts (although it did not occur on ratings or justifications). Although there is no clear explanation for this pattern, it is similar to previously documented u-shaped developmental curves for children's social-conventional knowledge about gender roles (see Carter & Patterson, 1982; Stoddart & Turiel, 1985). Turiel's (1983) findings on children's social-conventional knowledge has revealed an affirmation-negation fluctuation, in which children affirm and then negate conventions throughout development so that curvilinear patterns result. No curvilinear pattern was found for our group activity knowledge, however, and so more work on this finding is warranted.

Prior research by Damon (1977, 1983) found that children used justifications based on individual merit (such as "He deserves to be in the club because he is good at it") and that older children take merit and effort into consideration more than younger children when deciding how to divide resources. In this study, children who picked a child who was better at the activity than another child took the group-functioning considerations into account more than they did the individual merit of the child (less than 6% of the justifications were individual merit). Apparently, group functioning (making the club better) was a more salient feature of this type of decision making than was individual merit. Reasoning about individual merit may be more prominent for decisions involving the distribution of resources or rewards than for decisions about inclusion and exclusion. A child's qualifications, however, is only one consideration that bears on children's judgments about group functioning and social group processes. Further research is needed to examine the many other relevant dimensions that bear on judgments about exclusion. In addition, it would be important to examine children's developmental knowledge about stereotypes in a more detailed way than was done in the present study to analyze direct relationships between children's developmental knowledge about stereotypes and their judgments about exclusion.

In general, it was found that children viewed exclusion by race to be more inappropriate than exclusion by gender. Although this could indicate a greater concern with racial exclusion, the activities that were used in the race and gender contexts were not the same (math and basketball for the race activities, ballet and baseball for the gender activities), so it is difficult to draw firm conclusions about this. Other than this, however, little evidence was found that children's judgments about inclusion and exclusion were influenced either by the race or gender of the child being excluded or by the relation between one's own category membership and that of the child being excluded (girls did not rate girl-excluded contexts as more wrong than boy-excluded contexts nor did boys rate boy-excluded contexts as more wrong than girl-excluded contexts). Thus, the children did not see it as differentially wrong to exclude White children versus Black children from activities or to exclude girls versus boys from activities. In short, children did not display ingroup favoritism (consistent with previous research on the decline of prejudice during the middle-school years; see Aboud, 1988). Further research is needed to determine whether children show a concern with the potential for "affirmative action" type decisions, in which groups that have traditionally been excluded might be given more access.

Overall, and as expected, girls were more concerned with fairness and equal access than were boys. In the straightforward scenarios, they rated exclusion as more wrong, and in the multifaceted contexts they were more likely to want to include the child who was nonstereotypical for the activity (that is, the child who had less experience). These findings support previous research indicating that girls rate helping and caring as more obligatory than do boys in certain contexts (Killen & Turiel, 1998; Wentzel & Erdley, 1993; Zarbatany et al., 1996). Girls may be more sensitive to exclusion than boys on the basis of their own experience of being excluded from gender-specific activities such as sports. Children and adolescents who are members of groups that have been historically excluded from participating in group activities may be more sensitive to issues of inclusion. This hypothesis, however, remains to be tested in future work.

The sample of children in this study were from a mixed-ethnicity, middle-class, suburban city outside of Washington, DC. It is feasible that this environment would facilitate an awareness of the wrongfulness of holding and using prejudice and stereotypes. To test this hypothesis, further research in other communities, and in more homogeneous regions, needs to be conducted to fully understand how children evaluate group inclusion and exclusion, particularly on the basis of gender or race. Preliminary analyses with a small sample of African American children indicated that African American children were more likely to pick a child (boy or girl; Black or White child) who did not fit the stereotype than were the children reported in this paper. This also suggests that children who experience exclusion and who may be targets of discrimination may be more sensitive to decision making involving inclusion and exclusion, consistent with the finding that girls were more concerned with fairness and equal access than were boys. To systematically test this hypothesis, research has to be conducted with children who are from different ethnic backgrounds and who have interacted with others who differ from members of their own group. To adequately examine the role of experience, however, comprehensive measures of personal experience of exclusion, discrimination, and contact with others have to be developed and employed. In the authors' view, inferences about children's experience with exclusion cannot be made solely on the basis of their gender or racial group membership but, rather, should be made as a function of self-perception and of actual recorded experience. Further, a child's degree of experience of interacting with others from different social groups may or may not contribute to a sensitivity about exclusion. Again, detailed measures of this type of experience have to be documented and analyzed in relation to children's social judgments and evaluations of inclusion and exclusion.

In sum, the children in this study judged that it was wrong to exclude someone from a peer group activity on the basis of gender or race. In multifaceted contexts, however, other considerations, such as group functioning, entered into children's judgments, and particularly so with age. In this sense, it appears that judgments about the appropriateness of exclusion on the basis of gender or race in peer group activities may not be based so much upon direct prejudice or stereotypes about those groups or group members but rather more indirectly in terms of the perceived costs of excluding individuals from group activities. Other contexts, such as the family, school, and workplace, may be very different and require further investigation. Future work involving a wider range of contexts, observational data, and reports from teachers and parents is needed to provide more insight into why social group functioning becomes important with age, and how it affects reasoning about intergroup relationships.

Note

1   All children whose parents gave consent were interviewed. In addition to the 130 European American students, 31 African American students were also interviewed. Originally, the study was designed to include an equal number of European American and African American students to include race as a participant variable. Because an equal race sample size was not obtained, only the

findings for the European American sample are reported in this paper. Results from the sample of African American children do, however, provide some information about how the findings might generalize to other groups, and this is mentioned briefly in the Discussion section. A larger African American sample is currently being collected.

References

Aboud, F. E. (1988). *Children and prejudice*. New York: Basil Blackwell.

Aboud, F. E. (1992). Conflict and group relations. In C. U. Shantz & W. W. Hartup (Eds.), *Conflict in child and adolescent development* (pp. 356–379). Cambridge, U.K.: Cambridge University Press.

Asher, S., & Coie, J. (1990). *Peer rejection in childhood*. Cambridge, U.K.: Cambridge University Press.

Bennett, M., Barrett, M., Lyons, E., & Sani, F. (1998). Children's subjective identification with the group and ingroup favoritism. *Developmental Psychology, 34*, 902–909.

Brewer, M. B. (1979). In-group bias in the minimal intergroup situation: A cognitive-motivational hypothesis. *Psychological Bulletin, 86*, 307–324.

Brown, B. (1989). The role of peer groups in adolescent's adjustment to secondary school. In T. Berndt & G. Ladd (Eds.), *Peer relationships in child development* (pp. 188–215). New York: Wiley.

Carter, D. B., & Patterson, C. J. (1982). Sex roles as social conventions: The development of children's conceptions of sex-role stereotypes. *Developmental Psychology, 18*, 812–824.

Damon, W. (1977). *The social world of the child*. San Francisco: Jossey-Bass.

Damon, W. (1983). *Social and personality development*. New York: Norton.

Eisenberg, N., & Miller, P. (1987). The relation of empathy to prosocial and related behaviors. *Psychological Bulletin, 101*, 91–119.

Harter, S. (1998). The development of self-representations. In N. Eisenberg (Ed.), W. Damon (Series Ed.), *Handbook of child psychology: Vol. 3. Social, emotional, and personality development* (5th ed., pp. 553–617). New York: Wiley.

Helwig, C. C. (1995). Adolescents' and young adults' conceptions of civil liberties: Freedom of speech and religion. *Child Development, 66*, 152–166.

Helwig, C. C. (1997). The role of agent and social context in judgments of freedom of speech and religion. *Child Development, 68*, 484–495.

Killen, M. (1991). Social and moral development in early childhood. In W. M. Kurtines & J. L. Gewirtz (Eds.), *Handbook of moral behavior and development* (Vol. 2, pp. 115–138). Hillsdale, NJ: Erlbaum.

Killen, M., & Turiel, E. (1998). Adolescents' and young adults' evaluations of helping and sacrificing for others. *Journal of Research on Adolescence, 8*, 355–375.

Liben, L. S., & Signorella, M. L. (1993). Gender-schematic processing in children: The role of initial interpretations of stimuli. *Developmental Psychology, 29*, 141–149.

Maccoby, E. (1988). Gender as a social category. *Developmental Psychology, 24*, 765–775.

Mackie, D. M., Hamilton, D. L., Susskind, J., & Rosselli, F. (1996). Social psychological foundations of stereotype formation. In C. Macrae, C Stangor, & M. Hewstone (Eds.), *Stereotypes and stereotyping* (pp. 41–77). New York: Guilford Press.

Macrae, C., Stangor, C., & Hewstone, M. (Eds.). (1996). *Stereotypes and stereotyping.* New York: Guilford Press.

Short, G. (1993). Sex-typed behavior in the primary school: The significance of contrasting explanations. *Educational Research, 35*, 77–87.

Smetana, J. G. (1995). Morality in context: Abstractions, ambiguities, and applications. In R. Vasta (Ed.), *Annals of child development* (Vol. 10, pp. 83–130). London: Jessica Kingsley.

Stangor, C., & Ruble, D. N. (1989). Differential influences of gender schemata and gender constancy on children's information processing behavior. *Social Cognition, 7*, 353–372.

Stoddart, T., & Turiel, E. (1985). Children's concepts of cross-gender activities. *Child Development, 56*, 1241–1252.

Tajfel, H., Billig, M., Bundy, R. P., & Flament, C. (1971). Social categorization and intergroup behavior. *European Journal of Social Psychology, 1*, 149–177.

Theimer, C. E., Killen, M., & Stangor, C. (2001). Preschool children's evaluations of exclusion in gender-stereotypic contexts. *Developmental Psychology, 37*, 1–10.

Tisak, M. (1995). Domains of social reasoning and beyond. In R. Vasta (Ed.), *Annals of child development* (Vol 11, pp. 95–130). London: Jessica Kingsley.

Turiel, E. (1978). The development of concepts of social structure: Social convention. In J. Glick & K. A. Clarke-Stewart (Eds.), *The development of social understanding* (pp. 25–107). New York: Gardner Press.

Turiel, E. (1983). *The development of social knowledge: Morality and convention.* Cambridge, U.K.: Cambridge University Press.

Turiel, E. (1998). The development of morality. In N. Eisenberg (Ed.), W. Damon (Series Ed.), *Handbook of child psychology: Vol. 3. Social, emotional, and personality development* (5th ed., pp. 863–932). New York: Wiley.

Turiel, E., Killen, M., & Helwig, C. C. (1987). Morality: Its structure, functions, and vagaries. In J. Kagan & S. Lamb (Eds.), *The emergence of morality in young children* (pp. 155–244). Chicago: University of Chicago Press.

Van Avermaet, E., & McClintock, L. G. (1988). Intergroup fairness and bias in children. *European Journal of Social Psychology, 18*, 407–427.

Winer, B. J. (1971). *Statistical principles in experimental design.* New York: McGraw-Hill.

Wentzel, K., & Erdley, C. (1993). Strategies for making friends: Relations to social behavior and peer acceptance in early adolescence. *Developmental Psychology, 29*, 819–826.

Yee, M. D., & Brown, R. J. (1992). Self evaluations and intergroup attitudes in children aged three to nine. *Child Development, 63*, 619–629.

Zahn-Waxler, C., Cole, P. M., Welsh, J. D., & Fox, N. (1995). Psychophysiological correlates of empathy and prosocial behavior in preschool children with behavior problems. *Development and Psychopathology, 1*, 27–48.

Zarbatany, L., Van Brunschot, M., Meadows, K., & Pepper, S. (1996). Effects of friendship and gender on peer group entry. *Child Development, 67*, 2287–2300.

The Development and Consequences of Stereotype Consciousness in Middle Childhood

Clark McKown and Rhona S. Weinstein

When children come to understand that others endorse stereotypic beliefs, they gain an insight into others' social motives that profoundly affects their relationship to other individuals, social settings, and society. Awareness that others endorse stereotypes—herein referred to as stereotype consciousness—represents a radical change in children's understanding of the social world, and its consequences are not hard to imagine, especially in the arena of schooling. For example, a child taking a standardized test may become concerned that his performance will be judged through the lenses of an ethnic stereotype about intellectual ability. Under this pressure, the child's performance may be hampered. Another child may infer that her teacher expects less of children from her ethnic group; this observation may in turn affect how the child responds to the teacher's instructional strategies. As these examples illustrate, a range of social processes including stereotype threat (Steele & Aronson, 1995) and interpersonal expectancy effects (Rosenthal & Jacobsen, 1968) may recapitulate social divisions, including the ethnic achievement gap (Jencks & Phillips, 1998).

Children's stereotype consciousness may play an important role in how children appraise and respond to being stereotyped. However, we know little about children's awareness of others' stereotypes, children's response to stereotype-laden situations, and the relationship between children's awareness of others' stereotypes and their response to stereotype-laden situations. The main aims of this study were: (a) to examine age-related changes in children's stereotype consciousness, (b) to evaluate children's response to stereotype threat conditions, and (c) to specify what type of stereotype consciousness is necessary for stereotype-laden situations to affect children's cognitive performance. We also explored mechanisms through which those situations affect children's cognitive performance.

The development of stereotype consciousness

The first aim of this study was to evaluate the age at which children develop stereotype consciousness. In this article, we distinguish clearly between personal stereotypes, or children's own stereotypic beliefs, and stereotype consciousness, or children's awareness of stereotypes held by others but not necessarily personally endorsed (Stangor & Schaller, 1996). Children who themselves believe that Whites are smarter than Blacks endorse a personal stereotype. Previous research has established that between the ages of 3 and 4, children become aware of ethnicity and gender (Aboud, 1988, 2001; Hirschfeld, 1996; Holmes, 1995; Katz & Kofkin, 1997; Quintana, 1998), begin to sort themselves and others by ethnicity (Aboud, 1988; Holmes, 1995; Quintana, 1998), and develop personal

stereotypes (Aboud, 1988; Aboud & Skerry, 1984; Doyle & Aboud, 1995; Doyle, Beaudet, & Aboud, 1988). Other research has examined social cognitive (Averhart & Bigler, 1997; Bigler, 1995; Levy & Dweck, 1999; Levy, Stroessner, & Dweck, 1998) and social-contextual (Bigler, Jones, & Lobliner, 1997) factors that promote or impede children's personal stereotypes.

This study focused on children's awareness of others' stereotypes, not children's personal stereotypes, and not the expectation of being stereotyped, which in the adult literature is called stigma consciousness (Pinel, 1999, 2002) or metastereotype awareness (Vorauer, Hunter, Main, & Roy, 2000; Vorauer & Kumhyr, 2002; Vorauer, Main, & O'Connell, 1998). Little is known about the age of onset and age-related changes in children's awareness of others' stereotypes. One important unexamined aspect of children's stereotype consciousness is children's ability to infer a specific individual's stereotypes. For example, a child who observes an interracial exchange and infers from a White person's behavior toward a Black person that the White person endorses a stereotype about Blacks is able to infer an individual's stereotype. Although no research has explored the age at which children become able to infer an individual's stereotype, several bodies of research suggest that only after age 6 do children become skilled at inferring others' specific social beliefs, including their psychological perspectives (Selman, 1980), psychological traits (Peevers & Secord, 1973; Rholes & Ruble, 1984), interpretation of social events (Carpendale & Chandler, 1996; Chandler & Carpendale, 1998; Pillow, 1991; Pillow & Henrichon, 1996; Pillow & Weed, 1995), and beliefs about the beliefs of a third party (Flavell, 1999, 2000; Gopnik & Meltzoff, 1997; Happe, 1994; Perner & Wimmer, 1985). To the extent that being able to infer an individual's stereotype presupposes being able to infer others' social beliefs, we estimate that children will be able to infer an individual's stereotypes after age 6.

It is important that a child might be able to infer an individual's stereotype, but still not be aware that the stereotype is broadly held by many people. In the earlier example, the child who inferred the particular White actor's belief about Blacks might not yet be aware that many White people endorse that belief. Being aware of broadly held stereotypes is important because this awareness raises the possibility in a range of situations that a child will be judged stereotypically. Quintana and colleagues assessed children's awareness of broadly held stereotypes, asking school-aged children why someone might not like a member of their own ethnic group (Quintana, 1994, 1998; Quintana & Baessa, 1996; Quintana & Vera, 1999). They found that children ages 6 to 8 years old refer to the superficial characteristics of ethnicity, saying, for example, that someone might not like Mexican Americans because they do not like Mexican food. Only after the age of 10 did children consistently refer to stereotyping and prejudice as a reason why someone might not like a member of their ethnic group. Children in these studies were scored as reporting knowledge of broadly held stereotypes when they used words such as *stereotype, prejudice,* and *racism.* However, it is possible that some children are aware of broadly held stereotypes before they are fluent in the vocabulary of intergroup relations. We evaluate the hypothesis that even some young children are aware of broadly held stereotypes by employing measures that depend less on children's knowledge of the vocabulary of intergroup relations.

How are these two capacities—the ability to infer an individual's stereotype and awareness of broadly held stereotypes—related? Social perspective-taking theory (Selman, 1980) and ethnic perspective-taking theory (Quintana, 1998) emphasize that children develop the ability to take another individual's perspective before they develop awareness of societal or institutional or (by implication) intergroup perspectives. These theories would thus predict that children will first develop the ability to infer an individual's stereotype and then become aware of broadly held stereotypes. Other research suggests that social context affects children's developing beliefs about themselves (Stipek & Daniels, 1988) and others (Weinstein, Marshall, Sharp, & Botkin, 1987). With regard to children's beliefs about others' stereotypes, research on ethnic minority children's developmental competence (Garcia Coll et al., 1996), ethnic identity development (Phinney & Chavira, 1995; Phinney & Cobb, 1996; Tatum, 1997), and racial socialization (Bowman & Howard, 1985; Miller & MacIntosh, 1999; Sanders, 1997) suggests that for children from stigmatized groups, the social context of stereotyping, prejudice, and discrimination may cause earlier awareness of broadly held stereotypes, perhaps through direct teaching, without any requirement that the child be able to infer an individual's stereotype. These theories thus predict that at least some children will become aware of broadly held stereotypes before they become able to infer an individual's stereotype. This study examined the developmental sequence of stereotype consciousness.

Because of differences in the lived experiences of children from different ethnic groups, we anticipated that overall, children who have been targets of stereotypes would be more likely to be aware of broadly held stereotypes. Negative stereotypes persist about the academic ability of African Americans, Latinos, and Native Americans (Bobo, 2001; Eberhardt & Fiske, 1998; Fisher et al., 1996; Steele, 1997; Steele & Aronson, 1995; Swim & Stangor, 1998). Simons et al. (2002) found that 67% of a diverse sample of 867 African American 10- to 12-year-olds reported that someone had insulted them because they were African American and 47% had been the targets of racial slurs. We thus anticipated that children from these academically stigmatized ethnic groups would come into awareness of broadly held stereotypes at a younger age than children from academically nonstigmatized ethnic groups, specifically White and Asian American children.

In sum, this study sought to add to what is known about children's stereotype consciousness by examining early manifestations of stereotype consciousness (children's ability to infer an individual's stereotypes), by measuring conceptually distinct aspects of children's stereotype consciousness (children's ability to infer an individual's stereotype and children's awareness of broadly held stereotypes), and by explicitly examining ethnic differences in the age of onset of children's stereotype consciousness.

The consequences of stereotype consciousness

A second aim of this study was to evaluate the relationship between children's stereotype consciousness and their response to stereotype-laden testing conditions. What follows is a review of social processes through which stereotypes may affect children's achievement and a discussion of the relationship between those processes and children's stereotype consciousness.

TEACHER EXPECTANCY EFFECTS AND CHILD STEREOTYPE CONSCIOUSNESS

Teacher expectancy effects are one route through which stereotypes about intellectual ability can be expressed in the daily routine of the classroom (Wolfe & Spencer, 1996). Both experimental and correlational studies in which student prior performance is controlled show that teachers' expectations can affect teacher behavior toward children, in turn affecting children's achievement (Braun, 1976; Darley & Fazio, 1980; Raudenbush, 1984; Rosenthal & Rubin, 1978). Children's perceptions of teacher expectancy behavior play an important role in the unfolding of expectancy effects. As early as first grade, children are aware of teacher expectations (Babad, 1998; Weinstein et al., 1987), and the magnitude of teacher expectancy effects is higher in classrooms in which children perceive high degrees of differential teacher treatment (Brattesani, Weinstein, & Marshall, 1984; Kuklinski & Weinstein, 2001). Furthermore, children from stigmatized groups are often faced with low expectations (Rist, 1973), even when accounting for prior achievement (Baron, Tom, & Cooper, 1985; Dusek & Joseph, 1983; Hall, Merkel, Howe, & Naderman, 1986; Moore & Johnson, 1983). Children from stigmatized groups may be particularly susceptible to expectancy effects (Ferguson, 1998; Jussim, Eccles, & Madon, 1996; Taylor, 1993; Weinstein & McKown, 1998), especially negative teacher expectancy effects (McKown & Weinstein, 2002). Stereotype consciousness may affect how children from stigmatized groups appraise the causes of teacher expectations. For example, a child who is aware that others endorse stereotypes may infer that a teacher expects less of some children because of their ethnicity; this attribution may in turn affect the child's response to school.

STEREOTYPE THREAT AND CHILD STEREOTYPE CONSCIOUSNESS

Other aspects of schooling's shared institutional regularities may also embody ethnic stereotypes about academic ability and lead to self-fulfilling prophecies. For example, although all students face regular performance evaluations, the meaning and consequences of those evaluations may depend on child ethnicity, stereotypes about a child's ethnic group, and child stereotype consciousness. In particular, when taking a test, children from stigmatized groups who are aware of a broadly held stereotype about their group's intellectual ability may become concerned that their test performance will be judged on the basis of the stereotype, and this concern may negatively affect performance (Steele & Aronson, 1995). Steele and colleagues have called this variant on Merton's (1948, 1957) self-fulfilling prophecy "stereotype threat."

Stereotype threat assumes that something in the social environment activates a relevant stereotype. In this case, the testing situation activates a stereotype about intellectual ability (Wheeler & Petty, 2001), making salient that the stereotype might be used to judge target test performance (Steele, 1997). Stereotypes may be activated directly when ethnicity is made explicitly salient before a performance task by having participants report their own ethnicity (Shih, Pittinsky, & Ambady, 1999; Steele & Aronson, 1995), by having participants do a task that makes ethnicity salient (Ambady, Shih, Kim, & Pittinsky, 2001), or by telling participants that their group typically performs poorly on the performance task (Spencer, Steele, & Quinn, 1999). In contrast, stereotypes may be activated indirectly when the social context invokes stereotypes without explicitly priming a stereotyped identity. For example, Steele and Aronson (1995) activated stereotypes indirectly by telling students before a performance task that the task was diagnostic of intellectual ability; in the nonthreat condition, students were told that the task was not diagnostic of intellectual ability. Note that race was not made salient directly, but diagnostic testing conditions raised the prospect of being judged according to a negative stereotype about ability. Across several studies, Steele and Aronson found that under diagnostic conditions only African American students showed evidence of stereotype activation and reduced cognitive performance.

In one study with children, direct ethnic or gender primes affected math test performance in a stereotype-consistent direction (Ambady et al., 2001). Specifically, Ambady et al. (2001) found that among Asian American female elementary and middle school students, priming gender identity reduced math performance and priming Asian ethnic identity increased performance, although this effect was not found among late elementary school students. Ambady et al.

activated stereotypes directly by having children do tasks that made child ethnicity or gender salient. Thus, it remains to be seen whether and at what age the conditions of testing might indirectly activate stereotypes and adversely affect achievement among children from stigmatized groups. It also remains to be seen what children must understand about others' stereotypes for indirectly activated stereotypes to be threatening when activated indirectly.

Indirectly activated stereotypes are particularly important because in the natural context of school, stereotypes are often likely to be activated indirectly. We were particularly interested in examining the possibility that just as in adulthood (Steele & Aronson, 1995), in childhood, stereotypes and their threat might be activated indirectly in a situation resembling standardized testing conditions. To mirror more closely the natural conditions of testing, we adapted the Steele and Aronson (1995) procedures, manipulating threat conditions indirectly by characterizing a challenging task as either diagnostic of ability (threat) or nondiagnostic of ability (nonthreat). As in previous research, stereotype threat is inferred when the effects of threat conditions on cognitive performance are different between children from stigmatized and nonstigmatized groups, and children from stigmatized groups perform more poorly under diagnostic than nondiagnostic testing conditions.

We were also interested in evaluating a central tenet of stereotype-threat theory—that concern about others' stereotypes causes members of stigmatized groups to perform poorly under diagnostic testing conditions. Stereotype-threat theory implies that for indirectly activated stereotypes to affect performance, the test taker must be aware: (a) that the test is diagnostic of his or her ability, (b) that others endorse broadly held stereotypes about his or her ethnic group, and (c) that performance on the test may be judged on the basis of the stereotype. Children provide a perfect test of this assumption. If concern about others' stereotypes is a key mechanism driving stereotype threat, then only when children from stigmatized groups have developed salient mental representations of others' broadly held stereotypes can those stereotypes, activated under testing conditions, pose a threat to children and affect cognitive performance.

The evidence regarding what factors mediate the effects of stereotype activation on performance is mixed. In a comprehensive review of research on mediating pathways of stereotype activation. Wheeler and Petty (2001) argued that a large number of hypothesized mediators, including various forms of cognitive interference, affective arousal, self-efficacy, and self-expectations, have yielded little or no effect. Some studies show evidence that anxiety mediates the effects of threat conditions on performance (see Wheeler & Petty, 2001, p. 806). Because evidence for mediation in adults is mixed, and no tests of mediation have been attempted with children, this study investigated three potential mediators—anxiety, effort, and self-appraised performance—and explored the contribution of each of these variables in mediating the effects of stereotype threat conditions on cognitive performance.

Overview of methods

Two linked studies constitute the research reported here. Study 1 is a cross-sectional developmental study of children's stereotype consciousness. Study 2 is an experimental study testing the effects of stereotype threat conditions on cognitive task performance. Children who participated in Study 2 also participated in Study 1, permitting an examination of the relationship between children's stereotype consciousness and their response to stereotype threat conditions. Study 1 and Study 2 were completed in a quiet location at the child's school site 1 to 3 weeks apart (mean number of days between interviews was 6.5; maximum was 20). After each interview, children were given the opportunity to ask questions or to comment on the experience.

Participants were recruited from one summer enrichment program for gifted and talented students, a summer school program for Latino elementary school students, a public elementary school's gifted and talented education program, and the general student body at three public elementary schools and one private elementary school in the San Francisco Bay area. At each participating program, consent forms were given to children in first through fourth grades. A total of 202 eligible children between the ages of 6 and 10 submitted consent forms signed by their parents. Children who participated in the study were not significantly different from nonparticipants in terms of ethnicity. At the four sites where general data on parent level of education were available, average parent level of education was higher among study participants than among nonparticipants, $\chi^2(3) = 156.37, p < .05$.

STUDY 1

Study 1 tested the following hypotheses regarding age and ethnic differences in children's stereotype consciousness: (a) with age, the proportion of children who can infer an individual's stereotype will increase; (b) with age, the proportion of children aware of broadly held stereotypes will increase; (c) at each age, children from stigmatized groups will be more likely than children from nonstigmatized groups to be aware of broadly held stereotypes; and (d) being able to infer an individual's stereotype will precede being aware of broadly held stereotypes.

Methods

Measures

AGE
Child birth date was obtained from record review and was used to calculate chronological age at the time of interview.

ETHNICITY AND CHILD STIGMA STATUS
Child ethnicity was obtained from records. African American and Latino children were designated as coming from academically stigmatized groups; White and Asian American children were designated as coming from academically nonstigmatized groups. The 1 Native American child in the sample was designated as coming from a stigmatized group. In the American context, people from mixed ethnic backgrounds are often judged based on the more stigmatized ethnic identity (Myrdal, 1944). As a result, children of mixed ethnic heritage were designated as coming from a stigmatized group if they reported that either parent was from a stigmatized ethnic group. Demographic and other sample characteristics are summarized in Table 10.5.

Table 10.5   Demographic characteristics of participants and descriptive statistics

Panel A. Demographic characteristics

Characteristic	n	%
Gender		
Boy	101	(50.0)
Girl	101	(50.0)
Ethnicity[a]		
White	84	(41.6)
African American	48	(23.8)
Latino	36	(17.8)
Asian	32	(15.8)
Native American	1	(.5)
Other	1	(.5)
Age		
<7	24	(11.9)
7–8	32	(15.8)
8–9	41	(20.3)
9–10	67	(33.2)
>10	38	(18.8)
Highest parent education		
Graduate degree	73	(36.1)
College degree	52	(25.7)
High school degree	70	(34.7)
Primary education	7	(3.5)

[a]At only one of seven sites did records permit the designation of mixed ethnicity. At this site, 18 of 79 children were biracial. Of those 18, 10 had 1 White parent and 1 Asian American parent, 5 had 1 Latino parent and 1 White parent, 2 had 1 African American parent and 1 Asian American parent, and 1 had 1 Latino parent and 1 Asian American parent.

Panel B. Descriptive statistics

Measure	M	SD	n
Vocabulary raw score	26.2	(8.6)	202
Vocabulary scaled score	12.5	(4.0)	202
Ranked alphabet score	83.0	(47.6)	165
Word puzzle score	43.9	(14.2)	160
Anxiety	1.6	(.6)	175
Effort withdrawn	2.1	(1.0)	175
Self-appraisal	1.7	(.6)	175

SOCIOECONOMIC STATUS
Highest parent educational attainment was obtained from records.

VOCABULARY

Each child was administered the Vocabulary subtest of the Wechsler Intelligence Scale for Children-III (WISC-III). Vocabulary scaled score was used as a covariate in various analyses that follow.

Stimulus materials and scoring

We created and administered a two-part measure of children's stereotype consciousness. The first part, which measured children's ability to infer a specific individual's stereotype, involved a vignette-based experimental task. The second part, which measured children's awareness of broadly held stereotypes, involved an open-ended task.

With regard to measuring children's ability to infer a specific individual's stereotype, children were told two vignettes about an imaginary land called Kidland populated by two groups of people—the Greens and the Blues. In each vignette, a Green protagonist must pick either a Green or a Blue child to do something for which academic ability is important. The vignettes were identical except for the task for which the protagonist chooses a Green or Blue child. In one story, the protagonist picks a study partner, and in the other the protagonist picks someone to be on the spelling team. These two vignettes were presented in counterbalanced order to rule out any idiosyncratic effects of the vignette content on children's responses. After each vignette, children were asked comprehension questions to ensure that they understood the story. Children were also asked to say whom the protagonist will pick and why, and who the protagonist thinks is smarter and why.

For the first vignette, children were given no specific information about the protagonist's beliefs or broadly held beliefs in Kidland. Before the second vignette, an experimental manipulation was introduced that provided information to the children that in Kidland, Greens think Blues are not smart. Our main goal here was to ascertain whether children can use information about the broadly held stereotype in Kidland to infer that an individual Green protagonist endorses a stereotype. Children who reasoned that the protagonist thinks the Blues are not smart were scored as able to infer an individual's stereotype. For example, a child would be scored as able to infer an individual's

stereotypes if he or she said, "The Green [protagonist] picks the Green child because she thinks Blues are not smart." Children who reported other reasons (e.g., "The Green picks the Green because ... green is his favorite color [or] ... because they are both Green") were scored as not able to infer an individual's stereotype. Throughout, we used standard prompts to elicit children's responses.

Following the vignette-based task, to measure children's awareness of broadly held stereotypes, we asked children to describe any ways in which the real world is like the imaginary land. Their free-response answers were elicited using standard prompts. Children were scored as being aware of broadly held stereotypes if they reported ethnic stereotypes ("White people think Black people are not smart"), ethnic prejudice ("White people don't like Black people"), ethnic discrimination ("Sometimes police pull over Black people just because they are Black"), or ethnic conflict ("People from different races fight a lot"). A team of five raters coded transcripts of the stereotype consciousness interviews. Raters were blind to child age and ethnicity. Raters coded whether children were able to infer the protagonist's stereotype in the vignette and whether children reported awareness of broadly held stereotypes about race or ethnicity. After two coding trials using sample transcripts, pairs of raters independently coded all transcripts. Final kappas ranged between .67 and .94.

Procedures

DATA COLLECTION AND ORDER OF MEASURES

Trained interviewers completed the stereotype consciousness interviews. The interviewer first reminded children of the purpose of the study. In addition, each child was reminded that participation was voluntary and that all the information gathered was confidential. All stereotype consciousness interviews were audio recorded and transcribed verbatim. Following completion of the stereotype consciousness interview, the interviewer administered the Vocabulary subtest of the WISC-III.

MISSING DATA

Sixteen children (8%) who completed the first interview did not complete the Vocabulary measure. For

Table 10.6 Logistical model predicting stereotype consciousness

Predictor	B	SE	Wald statistic	Odds ratio
Logistic model predicting ability to infer an individual's stereotype				
Constant	−11.17	1.83	37.17★	
Vocabulary	.28	.06	24.79★	1.32
Age	1.03	.17	35.06★	2.81
Logistic model predicting awareness of broadly held stereotypes				
Constant	.42	5.21	.01	
Vocabulary	−.55	.40	1.86	.58
Age	−.37	.59	.39	.69
Stigmatized ethnicity	.86	.39	4.74★	2.36
Vocabulary × Age	.09	.05	3.93★	1.10

★$p < .05$.

Results

Preliminary analyses

COMPREHENSION QUESTIONS

We first tested children's understanding of the vignettes. Logistic regression with age as the independent variable, failing one or more comprehension questions as the dependent variable, and Vocabulary scaled score as the covariate suggested that the younger the child, the more likely the child was to fail one or more comprehension questions (Wald statistic for age = 15.53, $p < .05$, odds ratio = .49). Overall, 86% of the sample ($n = 174$) got all nine comprehension questions correct, 11% ($n = 22$) answered one question incorrectly, and 3% ($n = 6$) answered two or more questions incorrectly. Thus, most of the children understood all or most of the key facts in the vignettes.

EFFECTS OF VIGNETTE ORDER

There was no effect of vignette order on the likelihood of inferring an individual's stereotype either in the first vignette, $\chi^2(1) = 1.52$, $p = .22$, or in the second vignette, $\chi^2(1) = .00$, $p = .99$.

these 16 children, regression substitution was employed with age, site, and ethnicity used to estimate raw scores for Vocabulary.

Stereotype consciousness analyses

Next, we evaluated the relationship between the independent variables of age and child stigma status and the dependent variable of children's stereotype consciousness. The WISC-III Vocabulary scaled score was used as a covariate. Analyses were performed separately using ability to infer an individual's stereotype and awareness of broadly held stereotypes as the dependent variables. Both dependent measures were conceptualized as binary variables—a child either could or could not infer an individual's stereotype and a child either was or was not aware of broadly held stereotypes. Because the predictors included continuous (age and Vocabulary scaled scores) and categorical (child stigma status) variables and the criterion was binary, logistic regression was employed to evaluate hypotheses.

INFERRING AN INDIVIDUAL'S STEREOTYPE

A first analysis evaluated the relationship among age, child stigma status, and ability to infer an individual's stereotype. Greater age but not child stigma status predicted greater likelihood of inferring an individual's stereotype. Because child stigma status did not predict the ability to infer an individual's stereotype, a final logistic model excluded stigma status as an independent variable. In the final model, higher age predicted increased likelihood of being able to infer an individual's stereotype (Wald statistic for age = 35.06, $p < .05$, odds ratio = 2.81, see Table 10.6 and Figure 10.2).

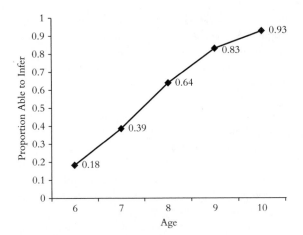

Figure 10.2   Proportion of children able to infer an individual's stereotype, by age.

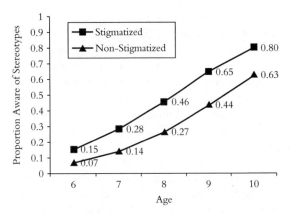

Figure 10.3   Proportion of children aware of broadly held stereotypes, by age and child stigma status.

Adjusting for differences in Vocabulary scaled score, at ages 6, 7, 8, 9, and 10, respectively, 18%, 39%, 64%, 83%, and 93% of children were able to infer an individual's stereotype.

AWARENESS OF BROADLY HELD STEREOTYPES

A second analysis evaluated the relationship among age, child stigma status, and the likelihood of being aware of broadly held stereotypes. With increasing age, children were more likely to report being aware of broadly held stereotypes. This finding was qualified by a significant Age × Vocabulary Scaled Score interaction, suggesting that although increasing age predicted increased likelihood of reporting broadly held stereotypes, the slope of that curve was greater when children's Vocabulary scaled score was higher (see Table 10.6). In addition, at each age and level of Vocabulary scaled score, children from stigmatized groups were more likely than children from non-stigmatized groups to be aware of broadly held stereotypes (at age 6, 15% vs. 7%; at age 7, 28% vs. 14%; at age 8, 46% vs. 27%; at age 9, 65% vs. 44%; and at age 10, 80% vs. 63%—see Figure 10.3).

RELATIONSHIP BETWEEN ABILITY TO INFER
AN INDIVIDUAL'S STEREOTYPE AND AWARENESS
OF BROADLY HELD STEREOTYPES

We hypothesized that being able to infer an individual's stereotype precedes awareness of broadly held stereotypes. If this were true, all children aware of broadly held stereotypes would be able to infer an individual's stereotype (Dixon & Moore, 2000). To test this hypothesis, we cross-tabulated the ability to infer an individual's stereotype with awareness of broadly held stereotypes. In this sample, 85% of children who were aware of broadly held stereotypes could infer an individual's stereotype.

Discussion

This study portrays changes in children's stereotype consciousness during the elementary school years, supporting the first three of our four hypotheses. First, with regard to children's ability to infer an individual's stereotype, at age 6, a very small proportion of children (18%) were able to infer an individual's stereotype. After age 6, the proportion of children able to infer an individual's stereotype increased linearly with age, peaking at 93% at age 10. This finding is consistent with and extends developmental research suggesting that children become better at inferring others' specific social beliefs after age 6 (Carpendale & Chandler, 1996; Chandler & Carpendale, 1998; Flavell, 1999, 2000; Gopnik & Meltzoff, 1997; Happe, 1994; Peevers & Secord, 1973; Perner & Wimmer, 1985; Pillow, 1991; Pillow & Henrichon, 1996; Pillow & Weed, 1995; Rholes & Ruble, 1984; Selman, 1980). Indeed, the developmental curve of children's ability to infer an individual's stereotype closely mirrors the developmental curve of children's second order theory of mind understanding (Perner & Wimmer, 1985). We found that age-related changes in children's ability to infer an individual's stereotype were equivalent for children from all ethnic groups and both genders, suggesting that the timing of onset of children's ability to infer an individual's stereotype is similar across groups.

Next, with regard to awareness of broadly held stereotypes, results support our second and third hypotheses. Consistent with Quintana's work on ethnic perspective-taking (Quintana, 1994, 1998; Quintana & Baessa, 1995; Quintana & Vera, 1999), we found that by age 10, most children were aware of broadly held stereotypes. Extending that work, we found that as early as age 6, some children were aware of broadly held stereotypes, and that higher age, especially in the context of higher verbal ability, was related to increased likelihood of awareness of broadly held stereotypes. Our finding that some children are aware of broadly held stereotypes before age 10 may be a consequence of our measurement strategy. With our measure, to be credited with awareness of broadly held stereotypes, children did not have to articulate the word *prejudice* or related constructs; rather, they had to describe at least one example of stereotyping, prejudice, discrimination, or ethnic conflict.

This is the first study we are aware of that shows that a greater proportion of children from stigmatized groups are aware of broadly held stereotypes. That children from stigmatized groups were more likely to be aware of broadly held stereotypes probably reflects the greater salience of stereotypes in the daily life of children from stigmatized groups. This is consistent with research showing that ethnic minority children's development is partly shaped by the experience of minority status (Bowman & Howard, 1985; Garcia Coll et al., 1996; Miller & MacIntosh, 1999; Phinney & Chavira, 1995; Phinney & Cobb, 1996; Sanders, 1997; Tatum, 1997).

Our fourth hypothesis, that the ability to infer an individual's stereotype is necessary for awareness of broadly held stereotypes, received partial support. Consistent with our hypothesis, most children (85%) who were aware of broadly held stereotypes inferred an individual's stereotype. However, 15% of children who were aware of broadly held stereotypes did not

infer an individual's stereotype. These exceptions might have resulted from measurement error alone. Alternatively, some children might not have articulated their inference about the story character's stereotype because of concerns about social desirability. It is conceivable, however, that some children who did not yet infer others' stereotypes might have been taught directly about stereotyping and prejudice, and so may have been aware of broadly held stereotypes with no inference required. That a comparatively small proportion of children who did not infer others' stereotypes were aware of broadly held stereotypes suggests that the ability to infer others' stereotypes most often precedes awareness of broadly held stereotypes. When a child has developed the ability to infer an individual's stereotype, indirect evidence of others' stereotypic beliefs—inferred from others' behavior—becomes available to the child. With a broader range of available evidence about others' stereotypes, the likelihood that children will learn about broadly held stereotypes increases.

STUDY 2

The central hypothesis of Study 2 was that stereotype threat conditions will negatively affect cognitive task performance among children from stigmatized groups, but only if they are aware of broadly held stereotypes. A secondary hypothesis tested in Study 2 was that the effect of stereotype threat conditions on cognitive performance is mediated by increased anxiety, withdrawn effort, and decreased self-appraised performance (Wheeler & Petty, 2001).

Methods

Measures

PERFORMANCE TASKS

The first performance task for the stereotype threat experiment consisted of writing as many letters of the alphabet as possible in 45 s, starting with the letter Z and going backward one letter at a time. Two consecutive letters incorrectly sequenced were scored as an error. Final score on the alphabet task was the number of letters completed in the allotted time minus the number of errors. We selected this task because it depends heavily on concentration and working memory, which are sensitive to anxiety (Dutke & Stroebber, 2001; Hyun, 1999). The second performance task involved selecting from groups of four similar words one word that does not belong. Children were instructed to indicate when they had guessed on a given item. Skipped items preceding the terminal item were counted as incorrect. The word search task final score was the percentage of items correct. We selected this task because it more closely resembled a school task.

MEDIATORS

Hypothesized mediators were measured with a 25-item self-report questionnaire containing items adapted from Sarason's (1973) scale of the cognitive, physiological, and affective dimensions of anxiety. Children were specifically asked how they felt while completing the performance tasks. Additional items were created and included to measure children's effort withdrawal and their self-appraised performance. Because we modified Sarason's measure, we could not use the Sarason scoring system. Principal components analysis with varimax rotation suggested a four-factor solution accounting for 44% of the total scale variance. Three of the four scales had good face validity and adequate internal consistency reliability. We defined these factors as affective and physiological arousal (e.g., "I felt nervous," 7 items, α = .80), effort withdrawal (e.g., "I could have tried harder," 2 items, α = .83), and self-appraised performance (e.g., "I got a lot of the problems right," 3 items, α = .69). Items were scored such that a high score represented a more negative outcome. Scale items were summed to yield scores for each of the hypothesized mediators. Because scale totals were not highly correlated (*range r* = .01 to *r* = .26), a composite score was not created.

Procedures

The first author of this article (a White man) conducted the stereotype threat experiment. Block randomization to instructional set was employed to ensure roughly equal cell sizes. Blocks included age (older or younger than 7.5 years) and child stigma status (from a stigmatized group or not). Children were randomly assigned to instructional set with order of recruitment as an additional blocking factor to minimize any biasing effect of order of recruitment. The experiment was completed in unused rooms in small groups ranging from 3 to 5 similar-aged children.

The experimenter first reminded children of the purpose of the study, that participation was voluntary, and that the all information gathered was confidential. Children were then given a test booklet and told not to open the booklet until instructed to do so. The experimenter then oriented children to the next part of the experiment by saying, "Now we are going to do something different. I am going to ask you to do some word problems and puzzles. Some of the problems are easy and some are hard. You probably will not get all of the questions correct. Let me tell you why I am having you do these problems."

EXPERIMENTAL MANIPULATION

The experimental manipulation consisted of task instructions that either characterized challenging cognitive tasks as diagnostic of ability (threat) or nondiagnostic of ability (nonthreat). Children in the diagnostic testing condition were told: "The problems you are about to do are a very, very good way of testing how good you are at different kinds of school problems. The test is difficult so that we can really learn how good you are at these kinds of problems. How well you do on this test will show what kinds of school problems you are good at and what kinds of school problems you are not so good at. Please do the best you can so that we can learn about your strengths and weaknesses." In both conditions, children were told that some of the problems would be easy and some would be hard, and that it was important that they try to do their best.

In the nondiagnostic testing condition, children were told: "The problems you are about to do will help us understand how children learn different kinds of things. These problems are not a test. The problems are difficult so that we can really learn how children solve problems when they have to think hard about their work. By doing this task, you will help us learn how children remember things and solve different kinds of problems. Please try the best you can so we can understand how children learn and solve problems." To ensure adequate comprehension of instructions, children in both conditions were asked to repeat why they were doing the problems and misconceptions were corrected as needed.

MANIPULATION CHECK

To check children's understanding of the task instructions, children were asked to circle whether they thought the purpose of doing the problems was "A. To test how good you are at different kinds of school problems"; or "B. To help us understand how children learn different kinds of things."

ORDER OF MEASURES

Following instructions, the backward alphabet task, word search, and mediator measures were administered in that order. The manipulation check followed administration of the mediator measure.

ATTRITION

Not all children who completed the stereotype consciousness interview participated in the stereotype threat experiment, although all children who participated in the stereotype threat experiment completed the stereotype consciousness interview. Children were assigned to experimental condition only when it was clear that their schedule permitted participation. As a result, only children who participated in the experiment were assigned to experimental condition, and 95% of children who were assigned to condition completed the experiment, representing very small attrition.

MISSING DATA

Ninety-seven percent of children completed the alphabet task correctly; the rest wrote the alphabet forward. Data from children who did the alphabet task forward were discarded. Ninety-two percent of children were able to do the word search task; the remainder were unable to do the task because they had not yet learned to read or write sufficiently well. Children with missing data on either measure were equally likely to have been assigned to the threat and nonthreat conditions. With regard to the mediation questionnaire, 95% of children missed fewer than six items. If a child missed fewer than six items across the questionnaire, the child's scale average was used as the

final measure for each scale. Among children who missed more than five items on the questionnaire, regression substitution was used, with each subscale total as the criterion and Vocabulary raw score and child stigma status as the predictors.

Results

Study 2 comprised a 2 (stigmatized versus non-stigmatized child ethnicity) × 2 (diagnostic vs. non-diagnostic testing conditions) × 2 (awareness of broadly held stereotypes) experimental design. Multiple regression was used to estimate model parameters. This strategy is equivalent to using ANOVA with weighted means to eliminate statistical bias from unequal cell sizes (see Keppel & Zedeck, 1989). For all analyses, age and Vocabulary scaled score were entered as covariates.

Preliminary analyses

TREATMENT OF OUTLIERS

Studentized residuals of the alphabet task score using the full model suggested that there were eight outliers greater than 2 SDs above the predicted value. Four of those outliers lay greater than 3 SDs above the predicted value. No observations were greater than 2 SDs below the predicted value. We were concerned that these few extremely high observations would unduly bias the statistical model. To reduce the biasing effects of extreme outliers, we ranked the alphabet task score and used the rank score as the dependent variable for the following analyses. This transformation reduced the distance between extreme observations, decreasing the biasing effect of outliers while avoiding the pitfalls of discarding extreme observations (see Judd & McClelland, 1989).

MANIPULATION CHECK

Analysis of children's response to the question about the purpose of the study revealed a significant relationship between instructional set and child-reported purpose of the study, $\chi^2(1) = 46.5, p < .05$, suggesting that overall, children understood the instructional set. When asked to choose a statement that best represents the purpose of the study, participants were more likely to select the statement "to help us understand how children learn different kinds of things" in the nondiagnostic testing condition (95%) and "to test how good you are at different kinds of school problems" in the diagnostic testing condition (52%).

Stereotype threat analyses

PLANNED COMPARISONS

We hypothesized that stereotype threat, induced indirectly under diagnostic testing conditions, only affects the cognitive performance of children from stigmatized groups after they become aware of broadly held stereotypes. To test this hypothesis, a series of single-degree-of-freedom planned comparisons were undertaken (Judd & McClelland, 1989). In all tests, we controlled for age and Vocabulary scaled score. We performed separate tests for the two components of stereotype consciousness—ability to infer an individual's stereotype and awareness of broadly held stereotypes. First, we estimated a three-factor (Testing Conditions × Child Stigma Status × Stereotype Consciousness) regression to evaluate whether testing conditions differentially affected the cognitive performance of children from stigmatized and non-stigmatized groups only among children who had attained stereotype consciousness. If the three-way interaction was significant, we performed further tests to see whether the direction of interaction was consistent with a stereotype threat interpretation. Specifically, we estimated a two-factor (Testing Conditions × Child Stigma Status) regression model, focusing only on children who had attained stereotype consciousness, to evaluate whether testing conditions had a differential impact on the cognitive performance of children from stigmatized and nonstigmatized groups. If the two-way interaction was significant, we estimated a single factor (testing conditions) regression model, focusing only on children from stigmatized groups who had attained stereotype consciousness, to evaluate whether diagnostic testing conditions had a negative impact on the cognitive performance specifically of children from stigmatized groups. If all three conditions were met, we interpreted this as evidence that stereotype consciousness is a necessary condition for indirectly activated stereotype threat to affect cognitive performance.

Table 10.7 Alphabet task means and standard errors

Source	n	M	SE
Aware of broadly held stereotypes			
Diagnostic testing condition			
Stigmatized	19	63.6	9.2
Nonstigmatized	22	92.1	8.7
Nondiagnostic testing condition			
Stigmatized	16	99.7	10.0
Nonstigmatized	29	90.7	7.9
Not aware of broadly held stereotypes			
Diagnostic testing condition			
Stigmatized	18	55.6	9.8
Nonstigmatized	27	81.6	7.8
Nondiagnostic testing condition			
Stigmatized	13	66.3	11.1
Nonstigmatized	21	103.3	8.7

Note. Means are adjusted for age and Vocabulary standard score.

RELATIONSHIP BETWEEN ABILITY TO INFER AN INDIVIDUAL'S STEREOTYPE AND RESPONSE TO DIAGNOSTIC TESTING CONDITIONS

With the alphabet task as the dependent variable, the three-way 2 (child stigma status) × 2 (testing conditions) × 2 (ability to infer an individual's stereotype) interaction was not significant, $F(1, 155) = .75, p = .39, R^2 = .00$, suggesting that the effect of stereotype threat conditions on children's cognitive performance does not depend on children's ability to infer an individual's stereotype. No further analyses were conducted.

RELATIONSHIP BETWEEN AWARENESS OF BROADLY HELD STEREOTYPES AND RESPONSE TO DIAGNOSTIC TESTING CONDITIONS

With the alphabet task as the dependent variable, the single-degree-of-freedom 2 (child stigma status) × 2 (testing conditions) × 2 (awareness of broadly held stereotypes) regression revealed a marginally significant three-way interaction, $F(1, 155) = 3.69, p = .056, R^2 = .02$ (see Table 10.7). Means were in the predicted direction and the interaction effect size of $R^2 = .02$ was substantial for a three-way interaction with naturalistic data (McClelland & Judd, 1993). Moreover,

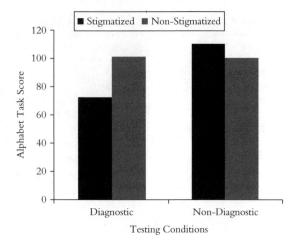

Figure 10.4   Mean alphabet task score among children aware of broadly held stereotypes.

with extreme outliers excluded from the model, the interaction was statistically significant, $F(1, 146) = 5.23$, $p < .05$, $R^2 = .02$. Therefore, the next planned comparison, examining only children who were aware of broadly held stereotypes, was undertaken. This comparison revealed a significant 2 (child stigma status) × 2 (testing condition) interaction with mean alphabet task scores in the predicted direction, $F(1, 80) = 4.02, p < .05, R^2 = .04$. The next planned comparison, testing only children from stigmatized groups who were aware of broadly held stereotypes, revealed a simple main effect of testing condition on performance, $F(1, 31) = 6.65, p < .05, R^2 = .15$), with children from stigmatized groups performing significantly worse under diagnostic testing conditions than under nondiagnostic testing conditions (see Figure 10.4).

Analyses were performed with percent correct on the word puzzle task as the dependent variable. The three-way interactions were not significant, $F(1, 146) = .23, p = .63, R^2 = .00$ with ability to infer an individual's stereotype as the third factor, and $F(1, 146) = .81, p = .37, R^2 = .00$ with awareness of broadly held stereotypes as the third factor; therefore, no further analyses using the word puzzle were conducted.

ALTERNATIVE PREDICTOR OF RESPONSE
TO THREAT CONDITIONS
To rule out the possibility that awareness of broadly held stereotypes was serving as a proxy for age, we

evaluated whether children's response to stereotype threat conditions depended on age. Age did not predict different response of children from stigmatized and nonstigmatized groups to the different testing conditions for the alphabet task, $F(1, 156) = 1.12$, $p = .29, R^2 = .00$, or for the word puzzle, $F(1, 147) = .19, p = .66, R^2 = .00$.

MEDIATION ANALYSIS
Evidence that a variable mediates the effect of an independent variable on a dependent variable is provided when, in separately estimated regression equations: (a) the independent variable affects the dependent variable, (b) the independent variable affects the mediator, and (c) the mediator affects the dependent variable when the independent variable is included in the equation. A final condition of mediation is met when in the latter statistical model, including the mediator in the equation reduces the magnitude of the relationship between the independent variable and the dependent variable (Baron & Kenny, 1986). In the present case, the independent variable was the testing condition. The dependent variable was the alphabet task score. The hypothesized mediators were anxiety, self-appraised performance, and effort withdrawal. Mediator analyses included only those children affected by stereotype threat— specifically, children from stigmatized groups who were aware of broadly held stereotypes.

The results reported earlier support the first proposition, that the independent variable affects the dependent variable: When controlling for age and Vocabulary standard score, the diagnostic testing condition was associated with poorer performance on the alphabet task, $F(1, 31) = 6.65, \beta = -.39, p < .05$, $R^2 = .15$. To test the second proposition, that the independent variable affects the mediator, we estimated a separate regression for each hypothesized mediator variable. In each model, testing condition was entered as the independent variable, the mediator was entered as the dependent variable, and child age and Vocabulary standard score were entered as control variables. In these analyses, testing condition had no effect on anxiety, $F(1, 34) = 1.55, \beta = .20, p = .22$, $R^2 = .04$, or self-appraised performance, $F(1, 34) = .01$, $\beta = -.02, p = .90, R^2 = .00$. However, diagnostic testing conditions were associated with greater self-reported effort withdrawal, $F(1, 34) = 10.81$, $\beta = .43, p < .05, R^2 = .19$.

Because effort withdrawal was the only mediator affected by testing condition, we performed the final test of mediation only on effort withdrawal. To test the third proposition, that the mediator affects the dependent variable when the independent variable is included in the equation, we estimated a regression model with alphabet task score as the dependent variable, testing condition as the independent variable, and effort withdrawal as an additional predictor, and controlling for child age and Vocabulary standard score. In this equation, effort withdrawal did not affect alphabet task performance, $F(1, 30) = .00$, $\beta = .01$, $p = .95$, $R^2 = .00$. Including effort withdrawal in the equation did not reduce the effect of testing condition on alphabet task performance, $F(1, 30) = 4.90$, $\beta = -.40, p < .05, R^2 = .12$.

Discussion

Results of this study support our main hypothesis, suggesting that when children from stigmatized groups become aware of broadly held stereotypes, indirectly activated stereotype threat can significantly hamper cognitive performance. Stereotype-threat theory posits that others' stereotypes are threatening and hamper performance when situations induce targets to become concerned that others will judge their performance stereotypically (Spencer et al., 1999; Steele, 1997; Steele & Aronson, 1995). This implies that awareness of others' stereotypes is necessary for indirectly activated stereotypes to be threatening and affect performance. Supporting this central proposition, we found that indirectly activated stereotypes only adversely affect the performance of children from stigmatized ethnic groups who are aware of others' broadly held stereotypes. It is important that this awareness is a specific requirement of stereotype threat effects—neither age nor the ability to infer an individual's stereotype predicts response to stereotype threat conditions. Thus, knowing about broadly held stereotypes opens the possibility that children from stigmatized groups will be concerned about being judged on the basis of those stereotypes, a possibility that can lead to a self-fulfilling prophecy.

Together, findings from Study 1 and Study 2 provide evidence about the age at which indirectly activated stereotype threat conditions might reasonably be expected to affect children's academic performance. In Study 1, we found that 46% of children from stigmatized groups report broadly held stereotypes by age 8. By age 9, that proportion increases to 65%. Based on these findings, we infer that stereotype threat effects induced by performance conditions become salient for a large number of children by third grade. Note, however, that some children from stigmatized groups report broadly held stereotypes as young as age 6. At a time in which high-stakes standardized testing is a central component of school reform, these findings raise the worrisome possibility that from elementary school on, the conditions of testing in their own right may differentially affect the performance of children from different ethnic groups.

It is interesting that a substantial minority (48%) of children who were assigned to the threat condition identified the purpose of the study consistent with nonthreat instructions. This finding is similar to previous stereotype threat research with adults in which a substantial minority of research participants in the threat condition (35%) reported that the purpose of the research was something other than threat (Steele & Aronson, 1995). These findings suggest that stereotype threat primes may be subtle, acting out of target awareness. Given that a large number of children did not retain the instructions, it also suggests that the current findings may underestimate the magnitude of stereotype threat conditions when they are created clearly enough to lead to greater retention of the instructional set.

Although we did not find support for mediation effects, mediation analyses did suggest that among children from stigmatized groups who are aware of broadly held stereotypes, stereotype threat conditions lead to greater levels of self-reported effort withdrawal. Measuring mediators through retrospective self-report represented a major shortcoming of the mediator analyses. It is possible that some children did not accurately remember or report their levels of anxiety or self-appraised performance after the performance task. Thus, our lack of findings leaves open the possibility that anxiety does mediate stereotype threat effects in childhood, but that our methods were not sensitive enough to detect those effects. Future work should measure hypothesized mediators immediately following threat induction and throughout the performance tasks.

GENERAL DISCUSSION

These two studies describe important and dramatic changes in children's stereotype consciousness in middle childhood. Between the ages of 6 and 10, most children move from virtually no awareness of others' stereotypes, to being able to infer an individual's stereotype, to awareness of broadly held stereotypes. Furthermore, although age-related changes in children's ability to infer an individual's stereotype are similar for children from all ethnic groups and for boys and girls, children from academically stigmatized ethnic groups show earlier and greater awareness of broadly held stereotypes. We also found that awareness of broadly held stereotypes is highly consequential to children's response to a stereotype-laden situation resembling standardized testing conditions. Under diagnostic testing conditions, children from stigmatized groups who are aware of broadly held stereotypes withdraw more effort and perform worse on one of two performance tasks. Children who are not aware of broadly held stereotypes do not show this pattern of performance. These findings raise important questions about the impact high-stakes testing might have on educational equity.

Future Directions

The observed ethnic difference in awareness of broadly held stereotypes raises two important questions. First, what are the origins of children's awareness of broadly held stereotypes? Parental socialization, media representations, direct experience with discrimination, and observation of intergroup relations are all potential sources of learning about broadly held stereotypes. Ethnic differences in rates of awareness of broadly held stereotypes suggest different pathways to awareness. Future work should examine pathways to awareness of broadly held stereotypes. Second, are

there ethnic differences in what children believe constitutes stereotyping, prejudice, and discrimination? Ethnic differences in children's lay theories of prejudice could mark the beginning of a difference in worldview that affects how people interpret and respond to social phenomena ranging from interpersonal interaction to government social policy.

Important questions also remain regarding the consequences of stereotype consciousness. This study found evidence of stereotype threat in the experimental context. In weighing the implications of these findings for educational practice, it will be important to evaluate in the natural context of schooling whether the conditions of testing activate stereotypes among members of stigmatized groups and cause differential performance. In addition, it seems likely that when children become aware of broadly held stereotypes, this newfound awareness may affect their response to a range of situations beyond the standardized test. For example, to a child who is aware of broadly held stereotypes, the meaning of a teacher's negative evaluation or a peer's cross-ethnic friendship is likely to include inferences about the teacher's and the peer's intergroup beliefs and attitudes. These inferences may in turn affect the child's behavior toward that teacher and that peer, and toward school and friends in general. Future work should examine the consequences of stereotype consciousness outside the context of standardized testing.

Limitations

The stereotype consciousness measure was both reliable and valid. The codes exhibited excellent interrater reliability and predictive validity, with age predicting both types of stereotype consciousness as anticipated, and awareness of broadly held stereotypes predicting response to stereotype threat conditions. In addition, there was no effect of vignette order, suggesting that children's ability to infer stereotypes generalizes across situations. However, younger children were more likely to fail one or more comprehension questions. Future work, using a simpler measurement strategy, would likely remedy this shortcoming.

Children's response to stereotype threat was detected with the alphabet task and with the effort withdrawal measure, but not with the word search task as the dependent variable. Is the backward alphabet task sufficiently analogous to a standardized test to infer that threat effects might affect children's performance in naturally occurring evaluative situations? The backward alphabet task requires intense concentration, and concentration is an important component of academic performance, especially when time pressure is involved. In the daily context of schooling, and particularly under testing conditions, stereotype threat conditions may hamper concentration, in turn affecting children's ability to perform academically. The word search task may not have been sufficiently sensitive across a wide age range to detect effects. A natural future remedy to these problems would be to use actual standardized tests as the dependent variable, as Ambady et al. (2001) did.

Although the sample was not randomly selected, participants were recruited from sites that differed widely in terms of demographic characteristics, socioeconomic status, and achievement, which resulted in an ethnically and academically heterogeneous sample. This lends confidence that the developmental and stereotype threat processes identified herein are robust across a range of populations. Steele (1997) has argued that only people who are personally identified with the stereotyped domain can be affected by stereotype threat. This raises interesting questions about children and stereotype threat. One possibility is that highly academically identified children—children in gifted and talented education programs, for example—are at greater risk from stereotype threat. Another possibility is that in elementary school, all children are still sufficiently identified with school to be adversely affected by stereotype threat conditions. Although our findings that stereotype threat affected an academically diverse sample support the latter proposition, future research should directly test these competing hypotheses.

The inference should not be drawn from this study that children who are not yet aware of broadly held stereotypes cannot be harmed by others' stereotypes. In this study, stereotype threat was invoked indirectly by varying whether the performance task was characterized as diagnostic of ability. In the daily life of children, stereotypes may be expressed in a way that would not require that a child be aware of others'

stereotypes to be harmed by them. For example, if a teacher who endorses an ethnic stereotype about intellectual ability teaches children from different ethnic different groups differently, children's academic performance might be affected without any requirement of the child's stereotype consciousness.

This study examined the risks associated with stereotype consciousness. There are likely to be benefits as well. Awareness of others' stereotypes may be necessary for members of stigmatized groups to recognize, negotiate, and cope with others' stereotypes effectively (Branscombe & Ellemers, 1998; Foster, 2000; Freire, 1970; Gaines, 2001; Miller & Kaiser, 2001; Miller & Major, 2000; Phinney & Chavira, 1995; Schmader, Major, & Gramzow, 2001; Utsey, Ponterotto, Reynolds, & Cancelli, 2000). In addition, stereotype consciousness might be necessary for children from nonstigmatized groups to develop a personal commitment to racial tolerance. What kind of stereotype consciousness is protective in what developmental contexts for which children is ultimately a question for future research.

References

Aboud, F. E. (1988). *Children and prejudice*. New York: Blackwell.

Aboud, F. E. (2001). Developmental and socialization influences on intergroup bias. In R. Brown & S. Gaertner (Eds.), *Blackwell handbook in social Psychology: Vol. 4: Intergroup processes* (pp. 65–85). New York: Blackwell.

Aboud, F. E., & Skerry, S. A. (1984). The development of ethnic attitudes: A critical review. *Journal of Cross-Cultural Psychology, 15*, 3–34.

Ambady, N., Shih, M., Kim, A., & Pittinsky, T. L. (2001). Stereotype susceptibility in children: Effects of identity activation on quantitative performance. *Psychological Science, 12*, 385–390.

Averhart, C. J., & Bigler, R. S. (1997). Shades of meaning: Skin tone, racial attitudes, and constructive memory in African American children. *Journal of Experimental Child Psychology, 67*, 363–388.

Babad, E. (1998). Preferential affect: The crux of the teacher expectancy issue. In J. Brophy (Ed.), *Advances in research on teaching (Vol. 7): Expectations in the classroom* (pp. 183–214). Greenwich, CT: JAI Press.

Baron, R. M., & Kenny, D. A. (1986). The moderator/mediator distinction in social psychological research:

Conceptual, strategic, and statistical considerations. *Journal of Personality and Social Psychology, 51*, 1173–1182.

Baron, R. M., Tom, D. Y., & Cooper, H. M. (1985). Social class, race, and teacher expectations. In J. B. Dusek (Ed.), *Teacher expectancies* (pp. 251–270). Hillsdale, NJ: Erl-baum.

Bigler, R. S. (1995). The role of classification skill in moderating environmental influences on children's gender stereotyping: A study of the functional use of gender in the classroom. *Child Development, 66*, 1072–1087.

Bigler, R. S., Jones, L. C, & Lobliner, D. B. (1997). Social categorization and the formation of intergroup attitudes in children. *Child Development, 68*, 530–543.

Bobo, L. (2001). Racial attitudes and relations at the close of the twentieth century. In N. J. Smelser, W. J. Wilson, and F. Mitchell (Eds.), *America becoming: Racial trends and their consequences* (pp. 264–301). Washington, DC: National Academy Press.

Bowman, P. J., & Howard, C. (1985). Race-related socialization, motivation, and academic achievement: A study of black youths in three-generation families. *Journal of the American Academy of Child Psychiatry, 24*, 134–141.

Branscombe, N. R., & Ellemers, N. (1998). Coping with group-based discrimination: Individualistic versus group-level strategies. In J. K. Swim & C. Stangor (Eds.), *Prejudice: The target's perspective* (pp. 242–266). San Diego, CA: Academic Press.

Brattesani, K. A., Weinstein, R. S., Marshall, H. H. (1984). Student perceptions of differential teacher treatment as moderators of teacher expectation effects. *Journal of Educational Psychology, 76*, 236–247.

Braun, C. (1976). Teacher expectations, sociopsychological dynamics. *Review of Educational Research, 46*, 236–247.

Carpendale, J. I., & Chandler, M. J. (1996). On the distinction between false belief understanding and subscribing to an interpretive theory of mind. *Child Development, 67*, 1686–1706.

Chandler, M. J., & Carpendale, J. I. (1998). Inching toward a mature theory of mind. In M. Ferrari & R. J. Sternberg (Eds.), *Self-awareness: Its nature and development* (pp. 148–190). New York: Guilford.

Darley, J., & Fazio, R. (1980). Expectancy confirmation processes arising in the interaction sequence. *American Psychologist, 35*, 867–881.

Dixon, J. A., & Moore, C. F. (2000). The logic of interpreting evidence of developmental ordering Strong inference and categorical measures. *Developmental Psychology, 36*, 826–834.

Doyle, A. B., & Aboud, F. E. (1995). A longitudinal study of white children's racial prejudice as a social-cognitive development. *Merrill-Palmer Quarterly, 41*, 209–228.

Doyle, A. B., Beaudet, J., & Aboud, F. E. (1988). Developmental patterns in the flexibility of children's ethnic attitudes. *Journal of Cross-Cultural Psychology, 19*, 3–18.

Dusek, J. B., & Joseph, G. (1983). The bases of teacher expectancies: A meta-analysis. *Journal of Educational Psychology, 75*, 327–346.

Dutke, S., & Stoeber, J. (2001). Test anxiety, working memory, and cognitive performance: Supportive effects of sequential demands. *Cognition and Emotion, 15*, 381–389.

Eberhardt, J. L., & Fiske, S. T. (1998). *Confronting racism: The problem and the response.* London: Sage.

Ferguson, R. F. (1998). Teachers' perceptions and expectations and the black-white test score gap. In C. Jencks & M. Phillips (Eds.), *The black-white test score gap* (pp. 273–317). Washington, DC: Brookings Institution Press.

Fischer, C. S., Hout, M., Jankowski, M. S., Lucas, S. R., Sanchez, M., Swidler, A., & Voss, K. (1996). *Inequality by design: Cracking the bell curve myth.* Princeton, NJ: Princeton University Press.

Flavell, J. H. (1999). Cognitive development Children's knowledge about the mind. *Annual Review of Psychology, 50*, 21–45.

Flavell, J. H. (2000). Development of children's knowledge about the mental world. *International Journal of Behavioral Development, 24*, 15–23.

Foster, M. D. (2000). Positive and negative responses to personal discrimination: Does coping make a difference? *Journal of Social Psychology, 140*, 93–106.

Freire, P. (1970). *Pedagogy of the oppressed.* New York: Continuum.

Gaines, S. O. (2001). Coping with prejudice: Personal relationship partners as sources of socioemotional support for stigmatized individuals. *Journal of Social Issues, 57*, 113–128.

Garcia Coll., C., Crnic, K., Lamberty, G., Wasik, B. H., Jenkins, R., Garcia, H. V., et al. (1996). An integrative model for the study of developmental competencies in minority children. *Child Development, 67*, 1891–1914.

Gopnik, A., & Meltzoff, A. N. (1997). *Words, thoughts, and theories.* Cambridge, MA: MIT Press.

Hall, V. C., Merkel, S., Howe, A., & Nederman, N. (1986). Behavior, motivation, and achievement in desegregated junior high school science classes. *Journal of Educational Psychology, 78*, 108–115.

Happe, F. (1994). An advanced test of theory of mind: Understanding of story characters' thoughts and feeling by able autistic, mentally handicapped, and normal children and adults. *Journal of Autism and Developmental Disorders, 24*, 129–154.

Hirschfeld, L. (1996). *Race in the making: Cognition, culture, and the child's construction of human kind.* Cambridge, MA: MIT Press.

Holmes, R. (1995). *How young children perceive race.* Thousand Oaks, CA: Sage.

Hyun, J. H. (1999). Test anxiety and working memory. *Journal of Experimental Education, 67,* 218–240.

Jencks, C., & Phillips, M. (Eds.). (1998). *The black-white test score gap.* Washington, DC: Brookings Institution Press.

Judd, C. M., & McClelland, G. H. (1989). *Data analysis: A model comparison approach.* New York: Harcourt Brace Jovanovich.

Jussim, L., Eccles, J. S., & Madon, S. (1996). Social perception, social stereotypes, and teacher expectations: Accuracy and the quest for the powerful self-fulfilling prophecy. *Advances in Experimental Social Psychology, 28,* 281–388.

Katz, P. A., & Kofkin, J. A. (1997). Race, gender, and young children. In S. S. Luthar, J. A. Burack, D. Cicchetti, & J. Weisz (Eds.), *Developmental psychopathology: Perspectives on adjustment, risk, and disorder* (pp. 51–74). New York: Cambridge University Press.

Keppel, G., & Zedeck, S. (1989). *Data analysis for research designs.* New York: Freeman.

Kuklinski, M., & Weinstein, R. S. (2001). Classroom and developmental differences in a path model of teacher expectancy effects. *Child Development, 72,* 1554–1578.

Levy, S. R., & Dweck, C. S. (1999). The impact of children's static versus dynamic conceptions of people on stereotype formation. *Child Development, 70,* 1163–1180.

Levy, S. R., Stroessner, S. J., & Dweck, C. S. (1998). Stereotype formation and endorsement: The role of implicit theories. *Journal of Personality and Social Psychology, 74,* 1421–1436.

McClelland, G. H., & Judd, C. M. (1993). Statistical difficulties of detecting interactions and moderator effects. *Psychological Bulletin, 114,* 376–390.

McKown, C., & Weinstein, R. S. (2002). Modeling the role of child ethnicity and gender in children's differential response to teacher expectations. *Journal of Applied Social Psychology, 32,* 159–184.

Merton, R. K. (1948). The self-fulfilling prophecy. *Antioch Review, 8,* 193–210.

Merton, R. K. (1957). *Social theory and social structure.* Toronto, Canada: Free Press.

Miller, C. T., & Kaiser, C. R. (2001). A theoretical perspective on coping with stigma. *Journal of Social Issues, 57,* 73–92.

Miller, D. B., & Macintosh, R. (1999). Promoting resilience in urban African American adolescents: Racial socialization and identity as protective factors. *Social Work Research, 23,* 159–169.

Miller, C. T., & Major, B. (2000). Coping with stigma and prejudice. In T. E. Heatherton, & E. Kleck (Ed.), *The social psychology of stigma* (pp. 243–272). New York: Guilford.

Moore, H. A., & Johnson, D. R. (1983). A re-examination of elementary school teachers' expectations: Evidence of sex and ethnic segmentation. *Social Science Quarterly, 63,* 460–475.

Myrdal, G. (1944). *An American dilemma: The Negro problem and modern democracy.* New York: Harper.

Peevers, B. H., & Secord, P. F. (1973). Developmental changes in attribution of descriptive concepts to persons. *Journal of Personality and Social Psychology, 27,* 120–128.

Perner, J., & Wimmer, H. (1985). "John *thinks* that Mary *thinks* that…": Attribution of second-order beliefs by 5- to 10-year-old children. *Journal of Experimental Child Psychology, 39,* 437–471.

Phinney, J. S., & Chavira, V. (1995). Parental ethnic socialization and adolescent coping with problems related to ethnicity. *Journal of Research on Adolescence, 5,* 31–53.

Phinney, J. S., & Cobb, N. J. (1996. Reasoning about intergroup relations among Hispanic and European-American adolescents. *Journal of Adolescent Research, 11,* 306–324.

Pillow, B. H. (1991). Children's understanding of biased social cognition. *Developmental Psychology, 27,* 539–551.

Pillow, B. H., & Henrichon, A. J. (1996). There's more to the picture than meets the eye: Young children's difficulty understanding biased interpretation. *Child Development, 67,* 803–819.

Pillow, B. H., & Weed, S. T. (1995). Children's understanding of biased interpretation: Generality and limitation. *British Journal of Developmental Psychology, 13,* 347–366.

Pinel, E. (1999). Stigma-consciousness: The psychological legacy of stereotypes. *Journal of Personality and Social Psychology, 76,* 114–128.

Pinel, E. (2002). Stigma-consciousness in intergroup contexts: The power of conviction. *Journal of Experimental Social Psychology, 38,* 178–185.

Quintana, S. M. (1994). A model of ethnic perspective taking ability applied to Mexican-American children and youth *International Journal of Intercultural Relations, 18,* 419–448.

Quintana, S. M. (1998). Children's developmental understanding of ethnicity and race. *Applied and Preventive Psychology, 7,* 27–45.

Quintana, S. M., & Baessa, Y. (1996). *Autoestima, preferencia y conocimiento etnico en ninos quiches.* UNESCO. New York: UNICEF.

Quintana, S. M., & Vera, E. M. (1999). Mexican American children's ethnic identity, understanding of ethnic prejudice, and parental ethnic socialization. *Hispanic Journal of Behavioral Sciences, 21,* 387–404.

Raudenbush, S. W. (1984). Magnitude of teacher expectancy effects on pupil IQ as a function of the credibility of expectancy induction: A synthesis of findings from 18 experiments. *Journal of Educational Psychology*, *76*, 85–97.

Rholes, W. S., & Ruble, D. N. (1984). Children's understanding of dispositional characteristics of others. *Child Development*, *55*, 550–560.

Rist R. C. (1973). *The urban school: A factory for failure: A study of education in American society*. Cambridge, MA: MIT Press.

Rosenthal, R., & Jacobsen, L. (1968). *Pygmalion in the classroom: Teacher expectations and student intellectual development*. New York: Holt, Rinehart & Winston.

Rosenthal, R., & Rubin, D. B. (1978). Interpersonal expectancy effects: The first 345 studies. *Behavioral & Brain Sciences*, *1*, 377–415.

Sanders, M. G. (1997). Overcoming obstacles: Academic achievement as a response to racism and discrimination. *Journal of Negro Education*, *66*, 83–93.

Sarason, I. G. (1973). Test anxiety and cognitive modeling. *Journal of Personality and Social Psychology*, *28*, 58–61.

Schmader, T., Major, B., & Gramzow, R. H. (2001). Coping with ethnic stereotypes in the academic domain: Perceived injustice and psychological disengagement. *Journal of Social Issues*, *57*, 93–112.

Selman, R. (1980). *The growth of interpersonal understanding: Developmental and clinical analysis*. New York: Academic Press.

Shih, M., Pittinsky, T. L., & Ambady, N. (1999). Stereotype susceptibility: Identity salience and shifts in quantitative performance. *Psychological Science*, *10*, 80–83.

Simons, R. L., Murry, V., McLoyd, V., Lin, K., Cutrona, C, & Conger, R. D. (2002). Discrimination, crime, ethnic identity, and parenting as correlates of depressive symptoms among African American children: A multilevel analysis. *Development and Psychopathology*, *14*, 371–393.

Spencer, S. J., Steele, C. M., & Quinn, D. M. (1999). Stereotype threat and women's math performance. *Journal of Experimental Social Psychology*, *35*, 4–28.

Stangor, C., & Schaller, M. (1996). Stereotypes as individual and collective representations. In C. N. Macrae, C. Stangor, & M. Hewstone (Eds.), *Stereotypes and stereotyping* (pp. 3–37). New York: Guilford Press.

Steele, C. M. (1997). A threat in the air: How stereotypes shape intellectual identity and performance. *American Psychologist*, *52*, 613–629.

Steele, C. M., & Aronson, J. (1995). Stereotype threat and the intellectual test performance of African Americans. *Journal of Personality and Social Psychology*, *69*, 797–811.

Stipek, D. J., & Daniels, D. H. (1988). Declining perceptions of competence: A consequence of changes in the child or in the educational environment? *Journal of Educational Psychology*, *80*, 352–356.

Swim, J. K., & Stangor, C. (1998). *Prejudice: The target's perspective*. New York- Academic Press.

Tatum, B. D. (1997). *Why are all the black kids sitting together in the cafeteria*. New York: Basic Books.

Taylor, M. C. (1993). Expectancies and the perpetuation of racial inequality. In P. D. Blanck (Ed.), *Interpersonal expectations: Theory, research, and applications* (pp. 88–124). Paris: Cambridge University Press.

Utsey, S. O., Ponterotto, J. G., Reynolds, A. L., & Cancelli, A. A. (2000). Racial discrimination, coping, life satisfaction, and self-esteem among African Americans. *Journal of Counseling & Development*, *78*, 72–80.

Vorauer, J. D., Hunter, A. J., Main, K. J., & Roy, S. A. (2000). Meta-stereotype activation: Evidence from indirect measures for specific evaluative concerns experienced by members of dominant groups in intergroup interaction. *Journal of Personality and Social Psychology*, *78*, 690–707.

Vorauer, J. D., & Kuhmyr, S. M. (2002). Is this about you or me? Self- versus other-directed judgments and feelings in response to intergroup interactions. *Personality and Social Psychology Bulletin*, *27*, 706–719.

Vorauer, J. D., Main, K. J., & O'Connell, G. B. (1998). How do individuals expect to be viewed by members of lower status groups? Content and implications of meta-stereotypes. *Journal of Personality and Social Psychology*, *75*, 917–937.

Weinstein, R., Marshall, H., Sharp, L., & Botkin, M. (1987). Pygmalion and the student: Age and classroom differences in children's awareness of teacher expectations. *Child Development*, *58*, 1079–1093.

Weinstein, R. S., & McKown, C. (1998). Expectancy effects in context: Listening to the voices of students and teachers. In J. Brophy (Ed.), *Advances in research on teaching, Vol. 7* (pp. 215–242). Greenwich, CT: JAI Press.

Wheeler, C. S., & Petty, R. E. (2001). The effects of stereotype activation on behavior: A review of possible mechanisms. *Psychological Bulletin*, *127*, 797–826.

Wolfe, C. T., & Spencer, S. J. (1996). Stereotypes and prejudice: Their overt and subtle influence in the classroom. *American Behavioral Scientist*, *40*, 176–185.

In-group and Out-group Attitudes of Ethnic Majority and Minority Children

Judith A. Griffiths and Drew Nesdale

1. Introduction

The focus of this research was on childeren's ethnic attitudes. In particular, it was concerned with the implicit and explicit attitudes of children from a majority/dominant (Anglo-Australian) ethnic group compared with those from an ethnic minority/migrant (Pacific Island) group, towards their ethnic in-group, as well as towards the ethnic out-group. In addition, the research examined the attitudes of both of these groups to a third (Indigenous Australian) out-group.

The migration of people from one country or region to another is not a new phenomenon, but rather dates back thousands of years. Migration occurs for a number of reasons but regardless of the underlying motivation to migrate, one of the consequences of migration for immigrants is that they face the task of adapting to living in a new (host) culture (Nesdale, Rooney, & Smith, 1997). An important component of this is the increased contact between immigrants and members of the host country. As members of the host and immigrant groups come in contact with each other, attitudes are formed by both groups toward the other, and these attitudes are played out daily in a multicultural community.

Australia has experienced several phases of migration. The outcome of the first phase resulted in Anglo-Australian immigrants establishing themselves as the dominant group displacing the indigenous (Aboriginal) peoples. Subsequently, there have been significant increases of European groups (e.g., Greeks and Italians) during the 1950s and 1960s. More recently, there has been significant migration by Middle-Eastern, Asian, and Pacific Islander ethnic groups (Nesdale et al., 1997).

The acculturation strategies and the related ethnic attitudes and preferences of migrant adults, especially those from Asia and Europe have been documented in Australia (e.g., Mak & Nesdale, 2001). However, little research has focused on immigration and its effects in relation to young children, especially those from the Pacific Islands. Consequently, the present research focused on the ethnic attitudes of two groups, the dominant Anglo-Australian group and more recent migrants from the Pacific Islands.

Research investigating ethnic attitudes of children in Australia to date has tended to focus on the attitudes of Anglo-Australian children toward ethnic out-groups. For example Augoustinos and Rosewarne (2001) measured Anglo-Australian children's stereotype knowledge as it related to indigenous (Aboriginal) Australians, whereas Black-Gutman and Hickson (1996) and Nesdale and colleagues (Nesdale, Durkin, Maass, & Griffiths, 2004; Nesdale, Griffiths, Durkin, & Maass, 2005; Nesdale, Maass, Griffiths, & Durkin, 2003) were interested in Anglo-Australian attitudes toward the ethnic in-group and an ethnic out-group. There has been little or no research on the attitudes of an ethnic minority group toward either their in-group, the dominant group, nor toward the Aboriginal out-group. By investigating only one ethnic group, it is difficult to establish the current state of ethnic relations both within and between groups in Australia. The present study sought to address this research imbalance by examining the attitudes of dominant and ethnic minority children in order to allow direct comparison to be drawn.

1.1. Ethnic attitudes

In general, research on adults, adolescents, and children has revealed a strong preference towards the ethnic in-group (Brown, 1995; Doyle & Aboud, 1995). Although initial explanations of such findings focused on the possibility of groups attitudes being influenced by the competition for scarce resources (Campbell, 1965), a more widely accepted explanation has been provided by social identity theory (SIT) (Tajfel & Turner, 1979). SIT argues that in-group preference is the outcome of the process of self-categorization into, and subjective identification with, the in-group by its members, and results in the perceptual creation of groups comprised of 'us' and 'them'. According to SIT, these distinctions are applied to a range of social groups, including gender, religion, and ethnicity. SIT argues that, group members are motivated to make favourable in-group comparisons that will protect or enhance their social identity by imbuing the group and, by extension, themselves with positive qualities. Consistent with this approach, in-group preference has been demonstrated when group members rate the in-group more favourably, show a preference for other in-group members and reward the in-group more than the out-group (see Hogg & Abrams, 1998). This in-group preference is also enhanced as the status of the in-group increases and there is greater identification with the in-group by its members (see Brown, 1995; Hogg & Abrams, 1998).

Although much of the preceding research has been carried out using artificial and short-lived groups in laboratory settings, research into the ethnic preferences of adults and adolescents has also reported in-group preference across a number of dimensions including choice of friends (Lenin, van Laar, & Sidanius, 2003; Shams, 2001), preferred neighbours (Valk & Karu, 2001), and the allocation of traits (Rustemli, Mertan, & Ciftci, 2000).

Importantly, although there is clear research support for in-group preference, research has shown that this does not necessarily equate to hatred for the out-group. A number of studies with adults have indicated low correlations between in-group positivity and the expression of negativity toward the out-group (Brewer, 1979).

I.I.I.   CHILDREN'S ETHNIC ATTITUDES

Researchers have also been interested in the ethnic attitudes and preferences of children. Early research (Horowitz & Horowitz, 1938) was primarily interested in the attitudes and preferences of white American children. The results of this research showed that these children had an overwhelming and consistent preference for their ethnic in-group. In contrast, the seminal work of Clark and Clark (1947) using the doll paradigm investigated Black American children's ethnic awareness and attitudes towards the ethnic in-group and the dominant white ethnic out-group. They reported that the majority of the Black American participants exhibited out-group preference and described the white doll as being better, being a nicer colour, and having more favourable attributes. Clark and Clark interpreted these results as indicating that the Black children's preference for the white group reflected a rejection of their own ethnic group.

Although the validity of the doll paradigm, and the findings relation to ethnic minority children, have been questioned by some authors (e.g., Foster, 1994; Vaughan, 1986), the methodology of Clark and Clark (1947) and Horowitz and Horowitz (1938) was subsequently embraced by many researchers and applied to different populations of children. To investigate the ethnic attitudes and preferences for their own and other ethnic groups and, in some cases, national groups, researchers have presented children with a range of stimuli representing different ethnic groups, including dolls (Hraba & Grant, 1970) and photographs (Nesdale et al., 2003, 2004, 2005). Children from different ethnic groups have then been asked to indicate which doll or photograph they would prefer to have as a friend, which has the more positive qualities, and which they liked more. The use of interviews (Loomis, 1943), naturalistic observation (McCandless & Hoyt, 1961) and less overt measures such as attribution tasks (Williams, Best, Boswell, Mattson, & Graves, 1975) have also been employed.

The results of these studies indicated that children from majority or dominant groups in different countries display ethnic in-group preference (e.g., Genesee, Tucker, & Lambert, 1978; Nesdale et al., 2003; Vaughan, 1964, 1978). In contrast to the findings of Clark and Clark (1947), the responses of ethnic minority children have been less consistent than those from the dominant group children. In a review of the American literature from the 1930s until the 1970s, Banks (1976) indicated that unlike white Americans, Black American children showed no clear pattern of responses. The lack of consistency shown by the Black Americans has also been revealed in research focussing on other ethnic minority children (see Vaughan, 1964, 1978).

In an effort to overcome the limitations of the doll technique, in particular the forced-choice response options, multiple-item tests, including the Preschool Racial Attitude Measure II (PRAM II) (Williams et al., 1975), and, more recently, the Multi-response Racial Attitude Measure (MRA) (Doyle, Beaudet, & Aboud, 1988) have been developed. While the PRAM II was limited by its forced choice methodology, the MRA gave children the opportunity to rate each of the groups independently, as they were able to separately allocate the positive and negative attributes to both groups. Doyle and Aboud (1995) reported that when given the opportunity to rate ethnic groups independently, ethnic majority children rated both the ethnic in-group and out-groups equally positively with increasing age. In contrast, the ratings were significantly less positive for the ethnic out-group than the ethnic in-group using the PRAM II. In a further comparative study, between the PRAM II and an independent rating measure (where the dolls are presented individually and the participants rate each doll independently of the other), Kowalski (2003) reported that using independent measures resulted in more favourable ratings of the out-groups by both dominant and minority group children than when using a forced choice methodology. In addition, although the children differentiated between the ethnic in-group and out-groups, out-groups were still rated favourably. Kowalski concluded that children do not hold strong negative out-group attitudes; instead, they simply hold less positive attitudes.

This result is interesting as it indicates that children as young as 3 years are capable of holding attitudes similar to those reported in older children (Nesdale et al., 2003, 2004) and adults (Brewer, 1979). For example, in a study using the minimal group paradigm, Nesdale et al. (2003) reported that the participants indicated greater liking for the in-group than for the out-group. Importantly, however, while the children indicated greater liking for the ingroup, they did not report dislike or hatred for the out-group, only that they liked them less.

1.2. Rationale for the present study

Although much has been learnt about the ethnic attitudes of children from the dominant ethnic group, a number of issues remain to be addressed. First, conclusions concerning children's ethnic attitudes have primarily been based on research assessing children's ethnic preferences or choices rather than on a direct assessment of their attitudes toward different ethnic groups. When assessing children's ethnic preferences the questions have frequently been comparative, that is, participants have typically been asked to name which group (out of two or more) they prefer. The conclusion often drawn from this type of assessment is that preference of one group indicates rejection of the other group (Aboud, 1988). In contrast, the use of independent measures allows researchers to investigate attitudes towards both groups separately rather than assuming that a positive attitude toward one group represents a rejection of the other group. For example, participants might prefer one group to the other, but may dislike both, or conversely, they might indicate a preference for one group while indicating liking for both groups. One aim of the present research was to give participants the opportunity to indicate their ethnic attitudes to one group without reference to the other ethnic groups.

Second, much of the research into children's ethnic preferences has focused on children from the dominant ethnic group. As noted earlier, there has been less research examining these issues with ethnic minority children. Accordingly, the second aim of the present study was to compare the attitudes of both the ethnic majority and minority groups. Specifically, we were interested in investigating whether ethnic majority (Anglo-Australian) and ethnic minority (Pacific Island) children hold more favourable attitudes toward their own ethnic in-group than ethnic out-groups. Based on the earlier findings, it was predicted that the ethnic in-group would be rated more favourably than ethnic out-groups by the ethnic majority group. However, although there is some ambiguity about how ethnic minority children would respond, based on earlier research by Kowalski (2003) it was expected that ethnic minority group children would express less positive, attitudes toward ethnic out-groups. In addition, it was expected that both majority and minority group children would express less positive, rather than negative, attitudes towards ethnic out-groups.

Third, the majority of the research to date has compared children's attitudes towards their ethnic in-group and one other ethnic out-group, for example, white vs. African Americans (Epstein, Krupat, & Obudho, 1976), Anglo–New Zealanders vs. Maori (Vaughan, 1963, 1964), and Anglo–Australian vs. Pacific Islanders (Nesdale et al., 2003). In order to extend our understanding of children's ethnic attitudes, the participants' attitudes toward a third group, were also assessed. The Aboriginal group was included because it was an ethnic out-group of which none of the participants was a member. In addition, it holds a special status as the original group of inhabitants of Australia. Further, comparatively little research has addressed children's attitudes toward Aboriginal children (see Augoustinos & Rosewarne, 2001; Black-Gutman & Hickson, 1996) hence it comprised an important comparison group. In the present study, the participants (Anglo-Australian and Pacific Islander) were familiar with, and knowledgeable of, Aborigines through contact at the school and in the local community. The inclusion of the Aboriginal people as a target group meant that each participant group (i.e., Anglo-Australian and Pacific Islander) were asked to rate two out-groups, one of which was Aboriginal. It was not immediately clear how the participants would rate the two out-groups. One possibility was that they would simply be rated equally positively. However, another possibility was that the two groups were be rated differently with, perhaps the Aboriginal group rated least positively, to reflect their lower status in Australian society.

Fourth, researchers have typically assessed children's ethnic attitudes using a variety of explicit measures. For example, as noted previously, children have been presented with a representative of an ethnic group (usually via a doll or picture) and have been asked to choose a friend or the person that they thought was 'nice'. One problem with such measures is that their focus (i.e., children's ethnic group attitudes) is quite explicit thus raising the possibility of constructed responses. Accordingly, the present study employed both an explicit and an implicit measure of children's ethnic attitudes. To assess children's explicit ethnic attitudes, a modification of the MRA (Doyle et al., 1988) was developed. This measure allowed participants to rate the three ethnic groups independently of each other on a common series of traits, with each trait being rated on a bi-polar scale, which allowed for the intensity of the children's attribution on each trait

to be measured. In addition, a more implicit measure of ethnic attitudes was employed via a modification of Valk and Karu's (2001) street exercise. Specifically, children in the present study were asked to allocate families from the ethnic in-group and out-groups to one of a set of houses in a hypothetical street. Arguably, this exercise is more realistic and possibly more implicit than trait ratings and conceivably reflects more closely the attitudes of the community in which the child lives. Extrapolating from Valk and Karu's results with young adults, it was expected that the children would allocate a house to the ethnic in-group family significantly closer to their own house than they would to families from the ethnic out-groups. Also of interest, however, was whether the children would differentiate between the ethnic out-groups, perhaps choosing to locate one ethnic out-group closer than the other.

Finally, we examined the participants' ethnic attitudes as a function of their age. Socio-cognitive theory (ST) (Aboud, 1988) predicts that, beyond 7 years of age, children's attitudes towards ethnic out-groups become more positive whereas their attitudes towards the in-group become less positive, as the members of the two groups are viewed in an increasingly similar way (Doyle et al., 1988). Aboud suggests that these attitudinal changes are a consequence of children's ability to differentiate individuals instead of responding to them simply as category members. Accordingly, to enable a test of this view, the present study included samples of 6-, 8- and 10-year-old children.

2. Method

2.1. Participants

The sample consisted of 119 children; 59 Anglo-Australian and 60 Pacific Islanders. Of these 40 were from Grades 1 and 2 (age $M = 6.5$, $SD = .6$); 41 from Grades 3 and 4 (age $M = 8.4$, $SD = .5$), and 38 from Grades 5 and 6 (age $M = 10.7$, $SD = .6$). There were approximately equal numbers of males and females at each age level in the sample. Participants attended two primary schools in South-East Queensland, servicing a lower-middle class community. Only those children who had been granted parental permission were included in the sample.

2.2. Materials

2.2.1. PHOTOGRAPHS

The procedure for producing the pool of photos used in the present study has been detailed in an earlier report (Nesdale et al., 2003). Briefly, following parental permission, a head-and-shoulders photo was taken of individual children between the ages of 5 and 13 years. The children were from Anglo-Australian, Pacific Islander and Aboriginal ethnic groups. From the pool of photos, 36 were randomly selected to form three groups corresponding to each age × gender × ethnic group combination. For each age, gender, and ethnic group, six photographs, each measuring 75 × 98 mm, depicting two Anglo-v Australian, Pacific Island, and Aboriginal children were used. The six photographs were displayed on a single landscaped A4 page. Each group was separated by a 5 mm vertical red line.

2.2.2. RESPONSE BOOKLET

A response booklet was produced containing two sections, relating to the different measures of interest.

2.2.2.1. Explicit attitudes. Seven adjective pairs were adapted from the Preschool Racial Attitude Measure II (Williams et al., 1975) and included (*bad–good; friendly–unfriendly; unhelpful–helpful; smart–stupid; clean–dirty*). Each pair was presented on a 5-point bi-polar response scale. Participants indicated the extent to which each adjective best described the children from the three ethnic groups. The bi-polar scales were anchored by 1 (*very negative rating—e.g., very unfriendly*) and 5 (*very positive rating—e.g., very friendly*), with 3 indicating a neutral point. A total score was calculated for each participant in relation to each of the ethnic groups that ranged from 7 (very negative) to 35 (very positive). This scale had a Cronbach reliability of .87.

Implicit attitudes. The street exercise (Valk & Karu, 2001) was modified for use with young children. A diagram of nine 'houses' (represented as boxes, each with a gabled roof) was used. The middle house was shaded blue and labelled 'your house'; the other eight houses were not shaded. Participants were required to indicate which house they would allocate to an Anglo-Australian, a Pacific Islander, and an Aboriginal family. A distance score was calculated with a range of 1 (*immediately next door*)–4 (*furthest house from the child's house*).

2.3. Procedure

Participants were tested individually in a quiet location near to their classroom during scheduled school hours by the first author. After some initial conversation designed to make the participant feel relaxed and comfortable, the participants were directed to the response booklet. They were told that they would be shown some photographs of other children and that they would be asked some questions about them. To ensure that the participants were comfortable with using the bi-polar scales they completed several practise questions. The procedure for each of the measures is presented separately for ease of comprehension.

2.3.1. EXPLICIT ATTITUDES

Participants were shown the photographs of the representatives of the three ethnic groups (Anglo-Australian, Pacific Island, Aboriginal) in turn, and were asked to rate the groups on the adjective pairs using the scale. To control for order effects, the order of presentation of each group was randomized. The questions and the response options were read aloud to accommodate the limited reading ability of the youngest participants.

2.3.2. IMPLICIT ATTITUDES

Participants were directed to the diagram in their response booklet displaying a row of nine 'houses'. The participants were told, "Let's pretend that an Anglo-Australian, a Pacific Island, and an Aboriginal family is going to move into your street. You do not know anything about these families except which group they come from. Because it is your street you are allowed to choose who lives in which house. This is your house here (the experimenter pointed to the blue house). Where in relation to your house would you like these families to live? You can put the different families on any side of your house, but you can only put each family into one house". Once participants had completed the two measures, they were thanked for their participation, and returned to their classroom.

3.   Results

Exploratory data analyses were conducted to ensure that the data met the assumptions of normality and homogeneity of variance for ANOVA. An alpha level of .05 was used as the significance level for all the analyses and Duncan's multiple range test (α = .05) was used to assess the significance of differences between cell means. Partial η^2 is reported as an estimate of effect size.

3.1.   Explicit attitudes

The participants' summed scores on the trait rating scales data were subjected to a 3 (age: 6- vs. 8- vs. 10-years) × 2 (gender: male vs. female) × 2 (participant ethnicity: Anglo-Australian vs. Pacific Island) × 3 (target ethnic group: Anglo-Australian vs. Pacific Island vs. Aboriginal) ANOVA, with the last factor within subjects.

The results revealed one significant main effect and two interactions. There was a significant main effect for target ethnic group $F(2, 214) = 33.31, p = .0005$, partial $\eta^2 = .24$, which was qualified by two significant interactions. First, the analysis revealed a significant target ethnic group × participant ethnic group interaction $F(2, 214) = 7.254, p = .001$, partial $\eta^2 = .06$ (Figure 10.5). The Anglo-Australian participants rated their ethnic in-group as possessing more positive attributes ($M = 28.88, SD = 4.63$), than the Pacific Island group ($M = 26.22, SD = 4.71$) who were rated more positively than the Aboriginal group ($M = 23.78, SD = 6.51$). In comparison, the Pacific Island participants rated the ethnic in-group and the Anglo-Australian out-group equally positively ($M = 28.25, 27.03, SD = 4.98, 4.14$, respectively), and significantly more positively than the Aboriginal out-group ($M = 24.03, SD = 5.66$). From another perspective, both the Anglo-Australian and Pacific Island participants rated the Aboriginal group significantly less positively than the other two groups.

The analysis also revealed a significant target ethnic group × age group interaction $F(4, 214) = 3.99$,

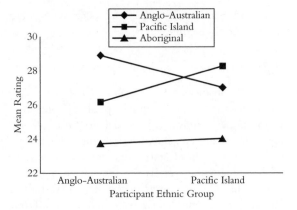

Figure 10.5   Target ethnic group × participant ethnic group interaction on mean trait rating (summed scale range 7–35).

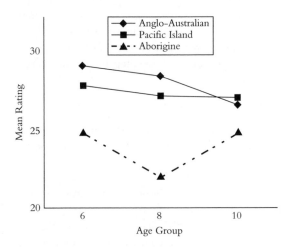

Figure 10.6   Target × age interaction on mean trait attribute rating (summed scale range 7–35).

$p = .004$, partial $\eta^2 = .07$, which is illustrated in Figure 10.6.

The 6-year-old rated the Aboriginal group less positively ($M = 24.87, SD = 6.40$) than either the Anglo-Australian ($M = 29.00, SD = 4.40$) and Pacific Island groups ($M = 27.73, SD = 4.43$), whose ratings did not differ significantly. There was no significant difference in the ratings of the Anglo-Australian and Pacific Island groups ($M = 28.32, 27.10$ and $SD = 4.639, 6.37$ respectively) by the 8-year-old. In addition, these groups were rated significantly more positively than the Aboriginal group ($M = 22.10, SD = 6.79$).

In contrast, at 10 years of age, there were no significant differences in the ratings of the three ethnic groups (Anglo-Australian, $M = 26.45$, $SD = 4.04$; Pacific Island $M = 26.89$, $SD = 3,55$; Aboriginal group $M = 24.84$, $SD = 4.04$). The results also revealed that while there were no age differences in the ratings of the Anglo-Australian and Pacific Island ethnic groups by the participants, the 8-year-old rated the Aboriginal ethnic group significantly less positively than the 6- and 10-year-old.

In addition, related samples t-tests comparing each cell mean with the neutral mid-point of the scale were conducted to investigate whether the attitudes toward the ethnic out-groups were negative, or simply less positive. The findings revealed that the trait ratings for the each of the groups was located in the positive half of the scale and were all significantly different from the neutral scale point ($t = 5.22–16.98$, $p < .05$). These results indicated that the ethnic out-groups were not hated; they were simply liked less than the ethnic in-group.

3.2. Implicit attitudes

Participants' housing allocation scores for each of the ethnic group 'families' were analysed in a 3 (age: 6- vs. 8- vs. 10-years) × 2 (gender: male vs. female) × 2 (participant ethnic group: Anglo-Australian vs. Pacific Island) × 3 (target ethnic group: Anglo-Australian vs. Pacific Island vs. Aboriginal) ANOVA, with the last factor within subjects. The analysis yielded two main effects and two interactions.

Main effects were revealed for target ethnic group $F(2, 214) = 27.74$, $p = .0005$, partial $\eta^2 = .21$ and age, $F(2, 107) = 4.91$, $p = .009$, partial $\eta^2 = .10$. These effects were qualified by a significant target ethnic group × participant ethnic group interaction $F(2, 214) = 11.71$, $p = .0005$, partial $\eta^2 = .10$ and, in turn, by a significant target ethnic group × age group × participant ethnic group interaction, $F(4, 214) = 2.65$, $p = .034$, partial $\eta^2 = .047$. This interaction is shown in Figure 10.7.

The results for the Anglo-Australian participants indicated that at each age the children displayed a preference for ethnic in-group (Anglo-Australian) neighbours rather than families from either of the ethnic out-groups. A comparison of the cell means

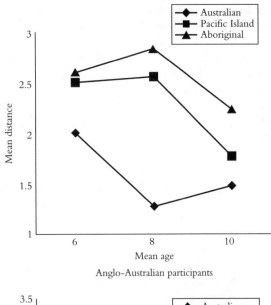

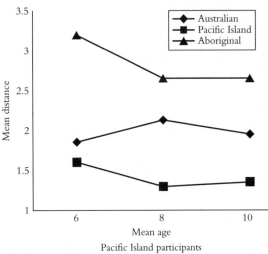

Figure 10.7 Target × age × participant ethnic group interaction on proximity of housing (scale range 1–4).

also revealed that the children's attitudes towards all three ethnic groups underwent change as a function of increasing age, with attitudes becoming more positive. The attitude towards the ethnic in-group became more positive between 6 years ($M = 2.00$, $SD = 1.34$) and 8 years ($M = 1.28$, $SD = .83$), while their attitude remained unchanged at 10 years ($M = 1.48$, $SD = .93$). Attitudes towards the ethnic out-groups also underwent changes with increasing age. There was no difference in the preference ratings for either the 6-year-old or 8-year-old towards the Pacific Island (M = 2.50, 2.56; SD = 1.25, 1.34, respectively) or the Aboriginal (M = 2.60, 2.83; SD = 1.00, 1.04, respectively) ethnic minority families. However, the attitude of the 10-year-old became significantly more positive toward the Pacific Island ethnic out-group (M = 1.76, SD = .77) and the Aboriginal out-group (M = 2.24, SD = .94) families.

The 6-year-olds did not significantly differentiate between either an in-group family or an Anglo-Australian family (M = 1.60, 1.85, SD = .88, 1.23, respectively) when allocating these families a 'house'. Both groups were preferred as neighbours significantly more than the Aboriginal family (M = 3.20, SD = .89). By 8 years, these children exhibited a clear in-group preference, locating the in-group family (M = 1.30, SD = .82) significantly closer than the Anglo-Australian family (M = 2.13, SD = .1.06) and the Aboriginal family (M = 2.65, SD = 1.06). This in-group preference continued in the allocations of the 10-year-old. Again, the ethnic in-group family (M = 1.30, SD = .82) was located closer than the Anglo-Australian out-group (M = 1.94, SD = .83) and the Aboriginal out-group (M = 2.65, SD = 1.06). Like the Anglo-Australian participants, the Pacific Island participants discriminated between the ethnic out-groups, demonstrating the least preference for the Aboriginal out-group.

4.   Discussion

The aim of the present study was to compare the attitudes of ethnic majority and minority group children toward ethnic in-groups and out-groups, using both explicit and implicit measures. Consistent with previous findings, it was predicted that the ethnic majority (Anglo-Australian) participants would rate their in-group more favourably than both the ethnic out-groups (i.e. Pacific Islander and Aboriginal). This prediction received clear support, confirming the findings of other studies which have also shown that ethnic majority children hold more favourable attitudes towards their ethnic in-group than they hold for ethnic out-groups (Doyle & Aboud, 1995; Kowalski, 2003; Nesdale et al., 2003).

However, the findings for the ethnic minority (Pacific Islander) participants contrasted with those of the ethnic majority participants. The former group indicated equally positive attitudes toward their ethnic in-group and the ethnic majority group, while a less positive attitude was displayed toward the Aboriginal ethnic group. Thus, both the ethnic majority and ethnic minority children differentiated between the respective ethnic out-groups in their ethnic attitudes but in different ways. Although both groups rated the Aboriginal group significantly less favourably than the other ethnic out-group, the ethnic majority groups participants rated both out-groups less favourably than the in-group, whereas, the ethnic minority group participants rated their own group and the ethnic majority groups equally favourably.

The present study also measured the participants' in-group and out-group attitudes by having them respond to an implicit attitude measure. The results indicated that the ethnic majority participants expressed a preference for the ethnic in-group family to live closest to themselves. In contrast, the youngest aged minority children failed to differentiate their preferences for neighbours between the in-group and the ethnic majority group, rating them equally positively. However, by 8 years, their in-group preference was evident in their responses. The results also indicated that the children differentiated between the ethnic out-groups. Both the ethnic majority and the ethnic minority allocated the least favourable location to the Aboriginal out-group.

The preceding results are noteworthy for several reasons. First, they indicated a certain consistency in the participants' responses on the explicit and implicit measures by the ethnic majority and minority children. This is noteworthy because the implicit measure used in the present study was actually a social distance measure, which may be viewed as a more realistic measure of attitudes than the explicit measure that was used. Indeed, whereas research has frequently revealed differences between the results obtained on explicit versus implicit measures (see Maass, Castelli, & Arcuri, 2000), the present findings suggest that children's ethnic attitudes are consolidated at an early age and/or that they are sufficiently comfortable to express them overtly. Second, the results indicate that ethnic majority children display clear and consistently favourable in-group attitudes, further supporting previous results. This was demonstrated by the more favourable in-group rating and was reinforced by their preference for ethnic in-group neighbours. In contrast, the responses of the ethnic minority children revealed a different pattern of results to the ethnic majority children. In the explicit measure, these children indicated equally favourable attitudes toward the ethnic in-group and the ethnic majority group. However, their responses to the implicit measure showed a clear in-group preference by 8- and 10-year-old.

In accounting for these results, it might be argued that the different responses are a by-product of how these children differentially perceive the status of ethnic groups in their community. Thus, the more favourable ratings given to the ethnic in-group by the ethnic majority children may reflect their perception of the different social status achieved by the ethnic majority and minority groups in the community. That is to say, the attitudes of these majority children may simply be a reflection of the ethnic status quo and they are reporting community reality. In contrast, the responses of the ethnic minority participants may be a reflection of how they would *like* the ethnic status quo to be. That is, they are reporting how they would like things to be rather than how they actually are.

While these groups indicated different patterns of attitudes toward the ethnic majority and minority groups, they were nevertheless in agreement in revealing the least positive attitudes towards one of the ethnic out-groups, the Aboriginal group. Again, it may be that these children are simply responding on the basis of established community status and ethnic status quo. Children do not live in a vacuum, but rather they live and operate in societies where the social structure and status of ethnic groups are established. In Australia, the Aboriginal group is generally acknowledged as holding the lowest social status in the eyes of the community (Griffiths, 2006). However, it is clear that the underlying motivations for the children's responses require further investigation.

Interestingly, independent of the above findings, age effects were also revealed on both the measures used in this study. Unlike previous studies (e.g., Nesdale et al., 2003) that reported no effects of age, the present study revealed changes in attitude as a function of the participant's age toward the Aboriginal

ethnic out-group. The participants' attitudes toward the Aboriginal group decreased from 6- to 8-years and then increased to 10 years of age. The basis of the differences between the ages is not immediately clear. One possibility is that the more extreme attitudes of the 8-year-old compared with the 6- and 10-year-old may be accounted for by the particular 8-year-old age cohort that participated in this study. Specifically, this particular group might have had bad experiences with Aboriginal children in their community.

Alternatively, ST (Aboud, 1988) hypothesizes that with increasing age, children's attitudes toward out-groups should become more positive as they are increasingly able to differentiate and respond to people as individuals rather than as category members. This hypothesis was supported in relation to attitudes toward the Aboriginal ethnic out-group on both measures in that, compared with the 8-year-old, the 10-year old (both ethnic majority and ethnic minority children) indicated more positive ratings and expressed greater preference to live closer to this ethnic out-group. Additionally, the ethnic majority participants also expressed greater preference for the ethnic minority (Pacific Island) as neighbours. In addition, according to ST, it should also be the case that attitudes toward the ethnic in-group should become less positive with increasing age, as children are increasingly able to differentiate members of the in-group. This hypothesis was not supported for either the ethnic majority or the ethnic minority groups. There was no decline in in-group ratings by either the ethnic majority or the ethnic minority (Pacific Island) participants.

Another possible explanation is that the change in attitudes with increasing age may lie in the 10-year-old being more image conscious than the younger children and hence the results might reflect their increasing ability to self-regulate the expression of less positive out-group responses in accordance with their beliefs of what constitutes socially accepted behaviour (Rutland, Cameron, Milne, & McGeorge, 2003). However, whereas this interpretation accounts for the increase from 8- to 10-years, it does not account for the decrease from 6- to 8-years, nor can it account for the parity between the responses of the 6- and 10-year-old. Clearly, the issue of changes in children's ethnic attitudes as a function of their age also needs further investigation.

5. Conclusions

In conclusion, the present findings highlight a number of points. First, attitudes towards the ethnic in-group and out-groups by ethnic majority and minority children are expressed in different ways. While the ethnic majority group expressed consistent in-group attitude bias, there was no similar in-group bias in the explicit attitudes of ethnic minority children. However, both the ethnic majority and the ethnic minority children displayed less favourable attitudes toward the Aboriginal ethnic out-group. These findings are important as they suggest that children's ethnic attitudes are not applied uniformly across ethnic out-groups, but rather are influenced by the particular target out-group. They further raise the possibility that social factors including social knowledge contribute to children's ethnic attitudes.

These results are also interesting in the context of intercultural relations. On the one hand, whereas succeeding generations of immigrant groups tend to enhance their relative societal position as a result of education and career progression (Nesdale, 1987), the present results suggested that such was not the case for indigenous Australians. On the other hand, it also appears likely that, although the efforts of the schools from which the samples were drawn in promoting multiculturalism have contributed to positive attitudes towards the immigrant ethnic group members, they have not influenced their attitudes toward the indigenous ethnic group. That is, whereas the multicultural policies may have been successful in relation to immigrant groups, the less positive attitude toward the indigenous group should be of concern and their basis should be a focus in future research.

References

Aboud, F. (1988). *Children and prejudice*. Oxford: Blackwell.

Augoustinos, M., & Rosewarne, D. L. (2001). Stereotype knowledge and prejudice in children. *British Journal of Developmental Psychology*, *19*(1), 143–156.

Banks, W. C. (1976). White preference in Blacks: A paradigm in search of a phenomenon. *Psychological Bulletin*, *83*, 1179–1186.

Black-Gutman, D., & Hickson, F. (1996). The relationship between racial attitudes and social-cognitive develop-ment in children: An Australian study. *Developmental Psychology*, *32*(3), 448–456.

Brewer, M. B. (1979). In-group bias in the minimal intergroup situation: A cognitive motivational analysis. *Psychological Bulletin*, *86*, 307–324.

Brown, R. (1995). *Prejudice: Its social psychology*. Oxford: Blackwell.

Campbell, D. T. (1965). Ethnocentric and other altruistic motives. In D. Levine (Ed.), *Nebraska symposium on motivation* (pp. 283–311). Lincoln: University of Nebraska Press.

Clark, K. B., & Clark, M. P. (1947). Racial identification and preference in Negro children. In T. M. Newcomb, & E. L. Hartley (Eds.), *Readings in social psychology* (pp. 169–178). New York: Holt.

Doyle, A-B., & Aboud, F. E. (1995). A longitudinal study of white children's racial prejudice as a social-cognitivedevelopment. *Merrill-Palmer Quarterly*, *41*(2), 209–228.

Doyle, A-B., Beaudet, J., & Aboud, F. (1988). Developmental patterns in the flexibility of children's ethnic attitudes. *Journal of Cross-Cultural psychology*, *19*, 3–18.

Epstein, Y. M., Krupat, E., & Obudho, C. (1976). Clean is beautiful: Identification and preference as a function of race and cleanliness. *Journal of Social Issues*, *32*(2), 109–118.

Foster, D. (1994). Racism and children's intergroup orienta-tions: Their development and the question of psychologi-cal effects in minority-group children. In A. Dawes, & D. Donald (Eds.), *Childhood and adversity: Psychological perspectives from South African research*. Claremont, South Africa: David Philip Publishers.

Genesee, F., Tucker, G. R., & Lambert, W. E. (1978). The development of ethnic identity and ethnic role-takingskills in children from difference school settings. *International Journal of Psychology*, *13*, 39–57.

Griffiths, J. A. (2006). *Children's understanding of, and attitudes toward, ethnic in-groups and out-groups*. Griffith University, Australia, Unpublished manuscript.

Hogg, M. A., & Abrams, D. (1998). *Social identifications: A social psychology of intergroup relations and group processes*. London: Routledge.

Horowitz, E. L., & Horowitz, R. E. (1938). Development of social attitudes in children. *Sociometry*, *1*, 301–338.

Hraba, J., & Grant, G. (1970). Black is beautiful: A re-examination of racial preference and identification. *Journal of Personality and Social Psychology*, *16*, 389–402.

Kowalski, K. (2003). The emergence of ethnic and racial attitudes in preschool-aged children. *Journal of Social Psychology*, *143*(6), 677–690.

Lenin, S., van Laar, C, & Sidanius, J. (2003). The effects of ingroup and outgroup friendship in ethnic attitudes in college: A longitudinal study. *Group Processes and Intergroup Relations, 6*(1), 76–92.

Loomis, C. P. (1943). Ethnic cleavages in the Southwest as reflected in two high schools. *Sociometry, 6,* 7–26.

Maass, A., Castelli, L., & Arcuri, L. (2000). Measuring prejudice: Implicit versus explicit techniques. In D. Capozza, & R. Brown (Eds.), *Social identity processes: Trends in theory and research* (pp. 96–116). Thousands Oaks, CA: Sage.

McCandless, B., & Hoyt, J. (1961). Sex, ethnicity and play preference of preschool children. *Journal of Abnormal and Social Psychology, 62*(3), 683–685.

Mak, A., & Nesdale, D. (2001). Migrant distress: The role of perceived racial discrimination and coping resources. *Journal of Applied Social Psychology, 31*(12), 2632–2647.

Nesdale, A. R. (1987). Ethnic stereotypes and children. *Multicultural Australia Papers,* Whole no. 57.

Nesdale, D., Durkin, K., Maass, A., & Griffiths, J. (2004). Group status, out-group ethnicity, and children's ethnic attitudes. *Journal of Applied Developmental Psychology, 25,* 237–251.

Nesdale, D., Griffiths, J., Durkin, K., & Maass, A. (2005). Empathy, group norms, and children's ethnic attitudes. *Journal of Applied Developmental Psychology, 26*(6), 623–637.

Nesdale, D., Maass, A., Griffiths, J., & Durkin, K. (2003). Effects of in-group and out-group ethnicity on children's attitudes towards members of the in-group and out-group. *British Journal of Developmental Psychology, 21,* 177–192.

Nesdale, D., Rooney, R., & Smith, L. (1997). Migrant ethnic identity and psychological distress. *Journal of Cross-Cultural Psychology, 28*(5), 569–588.

Rustemli, A., Mertan, B., & Ciftci, O. (2000). In-group favoritism among native and immigrant Turkish Cypriots:

Trait evaluations of in-group and out-group targets. *Journal of Social Psychology, 140*(1), 26–34.

Rutland, A., Cameron, L., Milne, A., & McGeorge, P. (2003). Self-presentation and intergroup attitudes in children. In *Paper presented at the XIth European conference on developmental psychology,* Catholic University of Milan, August.

Shams, M. (2001). Social support, loneliness and friendship preference among British Asian and non-Asian adolescents. *Social Behavior and Personality, 29*(4), 399–404.

Tajfel, H., & Turner, J. C. (1979). An integrative theory of intergroup conflict. In W. G. Austin, & S. Worchel (Eds.), *The social psychology of intergroup relations* (pp. 33–47). Monterey: Brooks/Cole.

Valk, A., & Karu, K. (2001). Ethnic attitudes in relation to ethnic pride and ethnic differentiation. *Journal of Social Psychology, 141*(5), 583–601.

Vaughan, G. M. (1963). Concept formation and the development of ethnic awareness. *Journal of Genetic Psychology, 103,* 93–103.

Vaughan, G. M. (1964). The development of ethnic attitudes in New Zealand school children. *Genetic Psychology Monographs, 70*(1), 135–175.

Vaughan, G. M. (1978). Social change and intergroup preferences in New Zealand. *European Journal of Social Psychology, 8,* 297–314.

Vaughan, G. M. (1986). Social change and racial identity: Issues in the use of picture and doll measures. *Australian Journal of Psychology, 38*(3), 359–370.

Williams, J. E., Best, D. L., Boswell, D. A., Mattson, L. A., & Graves, D. J. (1975). Preschool racial attitude measure II. *Educational and Psychological Measurement, 35,* 3–18.

A Closer Look 9   Stereotyping and Discrimination: What Factors Help to Reduce Prejudice?

Given the prevalence of prejudice attitudes, it is not surprising that there have been a variety of attempts to develop intervention programs that serve to reduce prejudicial attitudes in children and adults. Interventions in childhood are particularly important given that stereotypes and prejudice are emerging, and thus tend to be more malleable. In contrast, by adulthood, stereotypes tend to be more deeply entrenched and are more difficult to change.

Aboud and Levy (2000) identified five types of interventions that are organized according to the theoretical rationales underlying development. The first two intervention programs are integrated schooling and bilingual education, which are based on intergroup contact theory. The goal is to encourage contact with members of outgroups under a set of positive conditions, which include equal status, common goals, cooperation, cross-group friendships, and support from authorities.

When these conditions are met, diverse school environments can encourage acceptance of members of outgroups. The third type is multicultural and anti-racist education, which involves teaching children positive values about the importance of integration and equality. The fourth type is social-cognitive skills training, which typically consists of emphasizing perspective-taking and moral judgment. Finally, empathy and role-playing-based interventions include an emphasis on caring and understanding. The review covers how each type of intervention has been designed, the types of data that support the effectiveness of these programs, and avenues for further research and intervention curricula.

Aboud, F. E., & Levy, S. R. (2000). Interventions to reduce prejudice and discrimination in children and adolescents. In S. Oskamp (Ed.), *Reducing prejudice and discrimination* (pp. 269–293). Mahwah, NJ: Lawrence Erlbaum Associates.

Classroom Exercises, Debates, and Discussion Questions

- *Classroom exercise.* Break up into groups of four students and pick one of the following scenarios to discuss. Use the questions below as guides. Return to the entire group to discuss the issues.
  A. *Friendship Context.* Sally, who is from France, says that she doesn't want to invite Diane, who is from Germany, to have lunch with her because she thinks that they won't have much in common.
  B. *Sleepover Context.* Joe, who is European-American, will have a sleepover birthday party with a bunch of friends but does not want to invite Jordan, who is Arab, because his parents might be uncomfortable.
  C. *School Dance Context.* George is close friends with Sally and wants to invite her to the school dance but, because she is from Brazil, he thinks his friends, who are not from Brazil, will make fun of her and so he does not invite her to the school dance.
  [These scenarios were adapted from: Crystal, D., Killen, M., & Ruck, M. (2008). It's who you know that counts: Intergroup contact and judgments about race-based exclusion. *British Journal of Developmental Psychology, 26,* 51–70.]

  How often do you think individuals might not invite someone to lunch/a sleepover/date because a peer is from a different background? Why?

  Is it all right to not invite someone to join your own group if it is because of a lack of shared interests?
  What about not inviting someone because parents or peers would be uncomfortable?
  When is it okay to not invite someone over because of their "group membership"?
  What factors contribute to these decisions?
  What is the role of parents in these types of decisions?
  What is the role of peers and friends?

- *Classroom discussion.* What types of stereotypes exist regarding groups based on gender, race, and ethnicity? Where do stereotypes come from? How do stereotypes get perpetuated in cultures, and what role do media outlets play in this process?
- *Classroom discussion.* Some forms of exclusion are legitimate, such as excluding a slow runner from a track team. Other forms of exclusion are viewed as wrong, such as excluding someone from a sports team based on religious affiliation. How do children learn to distinguish these different types of exclusion?
- *Classroom discussion.* What types of stereotypic expectations exist in the classroom? How can teachers suppress biases and what factors motivate individuals to suppress biases about others?
- *Classroom discussion.* Intergroup contact, that is, contact with members of outgroups, has been

shown to reduce prejudice. Why is contact with others, such as through cross-group friendships, effective in reducing prejudice? What role do parents play in facilitating or hindering prejudice and contact with outgroups?

- *Classroom discussion.* Implicit forms of bias emerge early in development. How is implicit bias related to behavior towards others, and what factors reduce implicit bias?

Additional Resources

For more information about stereotypes, prejudice, and exclusion, see:

Ambady, N., Shih, M., Kim, A., & Pittinsky, T. (2001). Stereotype suceptability in children. *Psychological Science*, *12*, 385–390.

Brown, C. B., & Bigler, R. S. (2005). Children's perceptions of discrimination: A developmental model. *Child Development*, *76*, 533–553.

Dunham, Y., Baron, A. S., & Banaji, M. R. (2008). The development of implicit intergroup cognition. *Trends in Cognitive Sciences*, *12*, 248–253.

Levy, S. R., & Killen, M. (2008). *Intergroup attitudes and relations in childhood through adulthood*. Oxford: Oxford University Press.

Monteiro, M. B., de Franca, X. D., & Rodriques, R. (2009). The development of intergroup bias in childhood: How social norms can shape children's racial behaviors. *International Journal of Psychology*, *44*, 29–39.

Rowley, S., Kurtz-Costes, B., Mistry, R., & Leagans, L. (2007). Social status as a predictor of race and gender stereotypes in childhood and early adolescence. *Social Development*, *16*, 151–168.

Part V

FAMILY, COMMUNITY, AND CULTURE

11

PARENTING ATTITUDES AND BELIEFS

Introduction   458

The Company They Keep: Relation of Adolescents' Adjustment and Behavior to Their Friends' Perceptions of Authoritative Parenting in the Social Network   459

Anne C. Fletcher, Nancy E. Darling, Laurence Steinberg, and Sanford M. Dornbusch

  Method   460

  Results   466

  Discussion   471

Individual Differences in Adolescents' Beliefs About the Legitimacy of Parental Authority and Their Own Obligation to Obey: A Longitudinal Investigation   476

Nancy Darling, Patricio Cumsille, and M. Loreto Martínez

  Method   480

  Results   482

  Discussion   487

Domain-Specific Antecedents of Parental Psychological Control and Monitoring: The Role of Parenting Beliefs and Practices   493

Judith G. Smetana and Christopher Daddis

  Introduction   493

  Method   498

  Results   500

  Discussion   506

A Closer Look 10   Bridging the Generation Gap: Promoting Healthy Parent–Adolescent Relationships   513

Introduction

Parent–child relationships are central to social development across the lifespan. In the present chapter, the focus is on how parental attitudes and beliefs are related to aspects of older children's and adolescents' social adjustment and development. This age period poses unique challenges to the parent–child relationship because of the increased emergence issues surrounding adolescents' autonomy, independence, and the influence of peers. Baumrind (1971) proposed three parenting styles that were thought to reflect most parents' global socialization practices. *Authoritarian* parents are high in control (i.e., "power" resides solely with the parent) and low on warmth and tend to employ harsh and coercive discipline. *Permissive* parents do not consistently enforce rules and grant the child a high degree of "power" in the relationship. Finally, *authoritative* parents are warm and supportive, consistently enforce rules, and "share power" with the child where appropriate (e.g., use reason and induction to explain rules, allow the child to have some input into the decision-making process).

Research over the past few decades has shown that most parents use a mixture of styles across different contexts and situations. As an example, parents are often more permissive regarding issues about dress and choice of friends, and more authoritative about acts involving harm to others or safety concerns. Parents may start off with one style of parenting and then this style changes as a function of the child's personality, autonomy, and social orientation.

Previously, it was also suggested that parental influence was strongest in infancy and early childhood and that it waned during the adolescent years (in the face of the increasing importance of peers). As demonstrated in the three articles in this chapter, however, parents play a critical role in the social development of adolescents. In the first article, Fletcher et al. (1995) explored how adolescents' perceptions of their parents' parenting were related to aspects of their social adjustment, including levels of delinquency and substance use. This study was among the first to investigate how parent–adolescent interactions and relationships might extend beyond the home context and impact upon adolescents' peer relations. In the second article, Darling et al. (2008) examined individual differences and normative change in Chilean adolescents' beliefs about the legitimacy of parental authority and the obligation to obey parents. In particular, they were interested in understanding how adolescents' perspectives about parental authority and monitoring is related to positive parent–adolescent relationships. The final study in this section examined the consequences of different ways that parents might monitor the activities of their adolescents across different social domains of interactions. Smetana and Daddis (2002) were particularly interested in the construct of *psychological control*, which refers to parents' attempts to control children's activities in ways that negatively affect children's psychological development. Over-controlling parents can interfere with children's ability to become independent and develop a strong sense of personal identity.

Overall, parents who believe that adolescence is a time to "pull away" from their children may end up paying a high cost. Results from a growing number of studies make it clear that adolescents learn and benefit from parent–child interactions and discussions that involve not only the details of social life but also the range of psychologically important issues that may arise. Such interactions benefit both parents and adolescents and provide opportunities to learn about oneself and to understand different perspectives about complex issues in social development.

Reference

Baumrind, D. (1971). Current patterns of parental authority. *Developmental Psychology Monograph, 1* (1, Part 1).

The Company They Keep: Relation of Adolescents' Adjustment and Behavior to Their Friends' Perceptions of Authoritative Parenting in the Social Network

Anne C. Fletcher, Nancy E. Darling, Laurence Steinberg, and Sanford M. Dornbusch

Ecologically oriented developmentalists influenced by Bronfenbrenner (1979, 1986) during the past two decades have emphasized the importance of considering the various levels of environment that influence individual growth and behavior. Originally, most research attention heeding Bronfenbrenner's advice focused attention on the level of the environment he termed the *microsystem*. Specifically, these studies have focused on the influence on children of their immediate surroundings, such as the family or the peer group. It is only more recently that researchers have begun to branch out in their consideration of context, extending the map of children's social worlds to include the larger and more distal influences in their lives, including their social networks outside the family.

Although many developmentals believe that social networks are an important influence on the development of children, little theoretical work exists that might explain how these networks actually exert their influence. One exception is a model proposed by Coleman and Hoffer (1987), who suggested that community norms are maintained and enforced when unrelated adults within the community communicate with one another, and that children's socialization is facilitated when closure exists within the social network that encompasses the child and his or her parents. Contact among parents in a community, and between adolescents and nonfamilial adults, is presumed to benefit children through the increased prevalence of norm consensus within the community (Coleman, 1988).

Blyth and his colleagues (Blyth, Hill, & Thiel, 1982) have shown that when given opportunity to record all individuals who have an influence on their lives, early adolescents mention a large number of unrelated adults. In their study, approximately 10% of significant others named were nonrelated adults, most of whom resided within the same neighborhoods as the participants. It is likely that many of these adults were parents of adolescents' friends, because unrelated adults who do not have adolescent children of their own would have little interest in, or opportunity for, developing relationships with unrelated adolescents in their neighborhoods. Cochran (1990) suggested that the importance of nonrelated adults as influences in children's lives may also increase as children grow older, with such individuals becoming especially influential during adolescence. It is likely that the increased freedom from parental supervision that occurs with age may result in adolescents having more opportunities to interact with adults in the community, and especially with the parents of their friends.

We found only one study of the actual influence of relationships with nonrelated adults on adolescent functioning, however. Cochran and Bo (1989) reported that having larger numbers of nonrelated adults within social networks is associated with better school performance and attendance and more positive social behavior among adolescent boys. It is interesting to note that these researchers did not find significant effects of nonkin adult relationships on antisocial outcomes such as alcohol use and delinquency.

The purpose of this article is to investigate whether adolescents are influenced by one particular set of nonrelated adults: their friends' parents. Specifically, we hypothesized that an adolescent will benefit from having friends who characterize their own parents as authoritative, over and above the benefits of having authoritative parents of his or her own. Authoritativeness, a style of parenting identified in the seminal studies of Baumrind (1967, 1971), combines high levels of parental warmth with high levels of firm control. Baumrind's original work on the dimensions of parenting style investigated the effects of her classification scheme on the adjustment of preschool children. She found that authoritative parenting was strongly associated with child competence, although its positive effects varied somewhat as a function of child gender. More recently, authoritative parenting has been shown to have beneficial effects on adolescent competence and adjustment across a wide array of domains, including academic achievement, mental health, behavior problems, and psychosocial competence (see Maccoby & Martin, 1983; Steinberg, 1990, for reviews).

In testing the hypothesis that authoritativeness in the adolescent's peer network will have beneficial effects on the child's development, we also ask whether any effect of authoritativeness in the social network is predominantly proximal or distal. Proximal influences occur through face-to-face contact between a nonkin adult and a child. In such instances, adults influence adolescents by acting as models, norm reinforcers, or sources of information (Case & Katz, 1992; Cochran, 1990).

Nonrelated adults also may influence adolescents distally; two mechanisms have been posited to explain this distal influence. First, nonrelated adults may affect adolescents through the adolescents' own parents, by providing emotional and instrumental support, by encouraging or discouraging specific parenting behaviors, or by providing models of various parenting practices (Case & Katz, 1992). Adolescents are then influenced by these network effects through the changed behavior of their own parents (for a review, see Cochran, 1990). Second, nonrelated adults may influence adolescents through the actions of the nonrelated adults' children. For example, a parent may inculcate a set of values or standards for behavior among his or her own children, who may then influence their peers to behave in a similar manner (Case & Katz, 1992). This second mechanism is considered within this article.

In addition to examining whether the parenting practices of one's friends' parents influence adolescents, whether proximally or distally, we also asked whether such an effect differs according to the home environment of the target adolescent. According to Coleman and Hoffer (1987), the positive outcomes of strong community ties may differentially affect children whose own families differ in their internal strength. Coleman and Hoffer offered two alternative scenarios for how the presence of a functional community may

influence children: what we term *amplification* and *countermanding*. In the case of amplification, children who are already advantaged by the human and social capital within their own families are hypothesized to benefit most from residence in a functional community. In contrast, in the case of countermanding influence, the advantage conferred by the social structures of a functional community may benefit more those individuals who have fewer advantages within their own families. In the present study, we ask whether the parenting practices used in the adolescent's peer network amplify or countermand the practices that the youngsters experience at home.

Method

Participants

Our sample is drawn from students at nine high schools in Wisconsin and northern California. The schools were selected to yield a sample of students from different socioeconomic brackets, a variety of ethnic backgrounds (African American, Asian American, European American, and Hispanic American), different family structures (e.g., first-time two-parent, divorced, and remarried), and different types of communities (urban, suburban, and rural). Data for the present analyses were collected during the 1987–1988 school year by means of self-report surveys filled out by the students on 2 days of survey administration. (Because of its length, the survey was divided into two parts.)

Analyses conducted in our sample schools 1 year subsequent to the analyses presented in this article indicated that 60% of participants at that time reported knowing personally the parents of at least half of their school friends, and 91% reported knowing the parents of at least some of their school friends. This suggested to us that it was not inappropriate to conclude that our participants, for the most part, spent some time with their friends' parents.

Procedure

Recent reports suggest that the use of active-consent procedures in research on adolescents and their families (i.e., procedures requiring active parental written consent in order for their adolescents to participate in the research) may result in sampling biases that over-represent well-functioning teenagers and families (e.g., Weinberger, Tublin, Ford, & Feldman, 1990). Although groups of participants and nonparticipants generated through such consent procedures may be comparable demographically (the dimension along which investigators typically look for evidence of selective participation), the procedure screens out a disproportionate number of adolescents who have adjustment problems or family difficulties. Because we were interested in studying adolescents with dis-engaged or hostile parents, as well as those with involved and warm parents, we were concerned that using the standard active-consent procedure (in which both parents and adolescents are asked to return signed consent forms to their child's school) would bias our sample toward families who were more authoritative. In addition, studies that consider outcome measures of deviant behaviors, such as substance abuse and delinquency, are virtually required to make use of self-report data, as more "objective" measures of such behaviors (such as official police reports) themselves suffer from biases and omissions (McCord, 1990).

After considering the age of our respondents and their ability to provide informed consent, and with the support of the administrators of our participating schools, the school districts' research review commit-tees, representatives of the U.S. Department of Education (our chief funding agent), and our own institutions' human subjects committees, we decided to use a consent procedure that required "active" informed consent from the adolescents but "passive" informed consent from their parents. All parents in the participating schools were informed, by first-class mail, of the date and nature of our study well in advance of the scheduled questionnaire administra-tion. (We provided schools with letters in stamped, unaddressed envelopes to be mailed by school officials to protect the privacy of the families.) Parents were asked to call or write to their child's school or our research office if they did not want their child to par-ticipate in the study. Fewer than 1% of the adolescents in each of the target schools had their participation withheld by their parents.

All of the students in attendance on each day of testing were advised of the purposes of the study and

were asked to complete the questionnaires. Informed consent was obtained from all participating students. For each questionnaire administration, out of the total school populations, approximately 5% of the students chose not to participate (or had their participation withheld by parents), approximately 15% were absent from school on the day of questionnaire administra-tion (this figure is comparable with national figures on daily school attendance), and approximately 80% provided completed questionnaires.

The use of this consent procedure had both costs and benefits. On the positive side, we had responses from a more representative sample of adolescents, including adolescents whose parents were not involved in school, than one would otherwise have. On the negative side, however, our consent procedure did not permit us to obtain information from an equally rep-resentative set of parents. Rather than limit our study to the well-functioning parents who volunteered to participate in research of this sort, we chose to collect information on parenting practices from the adoles-cents themselves. We recognize that youngsters' reports of their parents' behavior maybe colored by a variety of factors and should not be taken as objective assess-ments of parents' practices. Our use of adolescents' reports, however, permitted us to study a larger and more representative sample of young people than would have been the case if parents' participation in the study were required. Nevertheless, we recognize that it also is necessary to investigate the relation between parenting and adolescent adjustment using multiple methods and different sources of informa-tion. It is important to note, however, that informa-tion on the behavior of each adolescent's friends' parents was provided by the friends themselves and not by the target adolescent. Thus, any observed cor-relation between adolescent outcomes and the prac-tices of their friends' parents cannot be an artifact of shared source variance.

Although over 11,000 adolescents participated in the survey, the number of participants used in the present analyses was reduced considerably by constraints imposed by the nature of the analyses. Only those stu-dents providing full answers to questions on parenting dimensions and demographics and who reported three or more identifiable friends who had provided infor-mation on their parents' behavior were retained in the analyses. This resulted in a sample of 4,431 students. Of this sample, 43% of participants were male, and 57% female. The sample was 19% seniors, 23% juniors, 28% sophomores, and 30% freshmen. Ethnic representation was as follows: 65% non-Hispanic White, 14% Asian American, 9% African American, 10% Hispanic American, and less than 1% each Native American, Middle Eastern, and Pacific Islander.

Despite this ethnic diversity, the sample was pre-dominantly middleclass and professional (as indexed by parental education), with only about 8% of respondents from lower- or working-class origins, a homogeneity that is due, we believe, to the fact that less economically advantaged youths were less willing to provide the names of their friends on the question-naire.[1] It is also important to bear in mind that partici-pants in the study were students who attended school on the days of testing. Therefore, despite its ethnic heterogeneity, the sample on whom the analyses were performed is in all likelihood relatively more advan-taged and more academically engaged than were nonparticipants.

Our requirement that participants included in the analyses provide the names of three or more friends who attended the same school and also provided questionnaire data resulted in the elimination from our sample of over half of all possible participants. We were concerned that this selective attrition would result in a sample of adolescents who were dispropor-tionately well-adjusted. To test this possibility, we conducted a series of t tests comparing mean scores on all dependent variables for our retained partici-pants versus those who did not report three or more identifiable friends. The results of the t tests indicated that, on all variables except school misconduct, psychological symptoms, and somatic symptoms, the retained participants were significantly more well-adjusted. More important than these mean differ-ences, however, are differences in the variability in our outcome measures between the two samples of youngsters: Virtually without exception, there was significantly less variance in outcome scores among the students who participated fully in the study than among the students who did not. One important ramification of this is that our estimates of the effects of network authoritativeness are likely to be on the conservative side: Because variability in our outcome

measures is constrained, it is more difficult to find sig-nificant relations between these measures and our independent variables.

Measures

DEMOGRAPHICS
Students reported their sex, ethnicity, and the highest level of education completed by their parents.

AUTHORITATIVENESS OF RESPONDENT'S PARENTS
The questionnaire contained many items on parent-ing practices that were taken or adapted from existing measures (e.g., Dornbusch et al., 1985; Patterson & Stouthamer-Loeber, 1984; Rodgers, 1966) or devel-oped for this program of work. On the basis of the previous work of Steinberg, Elmen, and Mounts (1989), a number of items were selected to correspond with the three dimensions of authoritative parenting identified earlier, and these were subjected to explora-tory factor analyses by using an oblique rotation. Three factors emerged, corresponding to the dimensions of Acceptance–Involvement, Behavioral Supervision and Strictness, and Psychological Autonomy Granting.[2] These factors are similar to those suggested in the earlier work of Schaefer (1965) and the recent work of Baumrind (1991a, 1991b). We labeled these scales in ways that both capture the item content of each and emphasize parallels between our measures and those used by other researchers.

The Acceptance–Involvement scale measures the extent to which the adolescent perceives his or her parents as loving, responsive, and involved (sample items: "I can count on her to help me out if I have some kind of problem" or "How often does your family do something fun together?"; 15 items, $\alpha = .72$). The Strictness–Supervision scale assesses adolescents' experience of parental monitoring and limit-setting (sample items: "How much do your par-ents try to know where you go at night?"; "In a typical week, what is the latest you can stay out on school nights [Monday–Thursday]?"; or "How much do your parents really know what you do with your free time?": 9 items, $\alpha = .76$). The Psychological Auton-omy Granting scale assesses the extent to which ado-lescents feel their parents use noncoercive, democratic discipline and encourage their offspring to express individuality within the family (sample items, reverse scored: "How often do your parents tell you that their ideas are correct and that you should not question them?" or "How often do your parents answer your arguments by saying something like 'You'll know better when you grow up'?"; 12 items, α = .82). The items comprising these three dimensions cover a wide variety of topics and index the child's perception of the parent's overall behavior, rather than the parent's specific socialization practices.

Composite scores were calculated on each of the three parenting dimensions. For most of the items, students were asked to describe the parent or parents with whom they lived. On those items for which students in two-parent homes were asked to answer separately for their mother and father, scores were averaged before forming composites. (Baumrind [1991b] reported that there is considerable convergence between mothers' and fathers' ratings.) On the basis of previous work and the theoretical model of authoritative parenting tested in this study, we constructed an ordinal measure of authoritativeness as follows: families scoring above the sample median on Acceptance–Involvement, Strictness–Supervision, and Psychological Autonomy (*authoritative*) were assigned an authoritativeness score of 3. Families scoring below the sample median on all three of the dimensions (*nonauthoritative*) were assigned an authoritativeness score of 0. Families scoring above the sample median on one (*somewhat nonauthoritative*) or two (*somewhat authoritative*) of the perceived parenting dimensions were assigned scores of 1 or 2, respectively. Previous work using these instruments and this operationalizalion (Steinberg, Lamborn, Darling, Mounts, & Dornbusch, 1994; Steinberg, Lamborn, Dornbusch, & Darling, 1992; Steinberg, Mounts, Lamborn, & Dornbusch, 1991) has demonstrated that adolescents from authoritative families, so defined, score more positively than their peers and those from nonauthoritative families score lower than their peers on a wide range of outcome variables, including those tapping school performance and engagement, psychosocial competence, internalized distress, and behavior problems.

AUTHORITATIVENESS IN THE PEER NETWORK

Participants provided the names of up to five of their closest friends. Only those target participants who provided names of at least three friends who had also answered questions about their own parents' perceived parenting dimensions were retained in the present analyses. We calculated the authoritativeness of each friend's parents according to the procedure described earlier (i.e., each friend's parents received a score ranging from 0 to 3).

Target participants were then classified into one of five levels reflecting the prevalence of authoritativeness among their friends' parents:

Level 1, mostly nonauthoritative: At least half of the reported friends had nonauthoritative parents, and no friends had authoritative parents.

Level 2, some nonauthoritative: At least one of the reported friends had nonauthoritative parents, and no friends had authoritative parents.

Level 3, neither authoritative nor nonauthoritative: No reported friends had authoritative or nonauthoritative parents.

Level 4, some authoritative: At least one of the reported friends had authoritative parents.

Level 5, mostly authoritative: At least half of the reported friends had authoritative parents.

The degree of authoritativeness in the adolescent's home was only modestly correlated with the prevalence of authoritativeness in his or her peer network (r = .14).

ACADEMIC ACHIEVEMENT

The questionnaire battery contained five measures of academic achievement. Students provided a self-report of their grade point average (GPA) scored on a conventional 4-point scale. Previous work has indicated that self-reported grades and actual grades taken from official school records are highly correlated (r = .80; Donovan & Jessor, 1985; Dornbusch, Ritter, Leiderman, Roberts, & Fraleigh, 1987).[3] Students also reported on the amount of time spent on homework each week, averaged across their four major classes (mathematics, English, social studies, and science). Time spent on homework responses were on a 6-point scale for each participant with responses ranging from *none* (1) to *about 4 hours or more* (6). Bonding to teachers and school orientation are two scales that were derived by factor analyzing a set of items that assesses the students' feelings of attachment to school (Wehlage, Rutter, Smith, Lesko, & Fernandez, 1989). Responses to these items were on a 4-point scale, from *strongly agree* (1) to *strongly disagree* (4). Bonding to teachers (five items; $\alpha = .75$) assesses the student's attachment to his or her teachers. A sample item is, "I care what most of my teachers think of me." School orientation (six items; $\alpha = .69$) measures students' valuing of and commitment to school. A sample item is, "I feel satisfied with school because I'm learning a lot." Finally, the academic competence subscale of the Youth Self-Perception Profile (Harter, 1982) includes five items asking about the student's perceptions of his or her intelligence in relation to classmates, ability to complete homework quickly, and capability in classwork ($\alpha = .73$).

BEHAVIOR PROBLEMS

Four measures were used to assess behavior problems. First, respondents provided information on their frequency of cigarette, alcohol, marijuana, and other drug use since the beginning of the school year, which was used to form an index of drug and alcohol use ($\alpha = .86$; Greenberger, Steinberg, & Vaux, 1981). Second, respondents reported on their frequency of involvement in such delinquent activities as theft, carrying a weapon, vandalism, and using a phony I.D. since the beginning of the school year, used to form an index of delinquent activity ($\alpha = .82$; Gold, 1970). Third, information was gathered on respondents' school misconduct since the beginning of the school year (cheating, copying homework, etc.; $\alpha = .68$; Ruggiero, 1984). All three of these measures incorporated items measured on a 4-point scale with responses ranging from *never* (1) to *often* (4). Finally, a measure of susceptibility to antisocial peer pressure presented five hypothetical situations in which peers urge the target to participate in misconduct ($\alpha = .75$; adapted from Berndt, 1979). Responses to these items were measured on a 4-point scale assessing whether an adolescent *definitely would* (1) to *definitely would not* (4) engage in the misconduct urged by peers.

PSYCHOSOCIAL COMPETENCE

The four indexes of psychosocial competence include a measure of Global Self-Esteem (Rosenberg, 1965), the Social Competence subscale of the Adolescent Self-Perception Profile (Harter, 1982), and two subscales from the Psychosocial Maturity Inventory,

Work Orientation and Self-Reliance (Form D; Greenberger, Josselson, Knerr, & Knerr, 1974). The Self-Esteem scale is a 10-item measure ($\alpha = .87$) of global self-worth adapted from Rosenberg (1965; sample item: "On the whole, I am satisfied with myself"). The measure contained items for which responses were scored on a 4-point scale ranging from *strongly agree* (1) to *strongly disagree* (4). The Social Competence measure ($\alpha = .78$) includes five items that ask students whether they perceive themselves as popular, as having many friends, and as making friends easily. The participants are asked to read two alternatives (e.g., "Some teenagers feel that they are socially accepted, but other teenagers wish that more people their age would accept them") and choose the one that is more like themselves. The Work Orientation ($\alpha = .73$) and Self-Reliance ($\alpha = .81$) subscales are each composed of 10 items. The Work Orientation scale measures the adolescent's pride in the successful completion of tasks. A sample item, reverse coded, is "I find it hard to stick to anything that takes a long time." The Self-Reliance scale measures the adolescent's feelings of internal control and ability to make decisions without extreme reliance on others. A sample item, reverse coded, is "Luck decides most things that happen to me." Both subscales contained measures for which responses were scored on a 4-point scale ranging from *strongly agree* (1) to *strongly disagree* (4).

INTERNALIZED DISTRESS

Two indexes of internalized distress were adapted from the Center for Epidemiologic Studies Depression Scale (CES-D; Radloff, 1977): Psychological Symptoms (anxiety, depression, tension, fatigue, insomnia, etc.; $\alpha = .88$) and Somatic Symptoms (headaches, stomach aches, colds, etc.; $\alpha = .67$). For each scale, participants were asked how often during the past month they had experienced the symptoms. They responded on a 4-point scale ranging from *never* (1) to *3 times or more* (4).

Means and standard deviations of the independent and dependent variables are presented in Table 11.1.

Plan of analysis

In light of prior research indicating that the impact of authoritative parenting on some aspects of adolescent

Table 11.1 Means and standard deviations of variables

Variable	Boys (n = 1,905)		Girls (n = 2,526)	
	M	SD	M	SD
Home authoritativeness[a]	1.57	0.95	1.70	0.95
Network authoritativeness[a]	3.36	1.05	3.54	1.06
Grade point average[a]	2.95	0.77	3.03	0.74
Homework[a]	3.81	1.26	4.00	1.16
Bonding to teachers[a]	2.99	0.60	3.09	0.57
School orientation[a]	2.78	0.56	2.84	0.55
Academic competence[a]	3.01	0.58	2.89	0.64
Delinquency[a]	1.21	0.35	1.09	0.21
Drug and alcohol use	1.58	0.72	1.54	0.70
School misconduct[b]	2.38	0.70	2.34	0.63
Peer susceptibility[a]	2.10	0.63	1.92	0.57
Work orientation[a]	2.79	0.48	2.86	0.48
Self-reliance[a]	3.03	0.50	3.16	0.47
Self-esteem[a]	3.11	0.50	2.93	0.52
Social competence[c]	3.03	0.60	3.08	0.60
Psychological symptoms[a]	2.25	0.75	2.73	0.75
Somatic symptoms[a]	1.99	0.60	2.28	0.58

[a]$p < .001$ for contrast between boys and girls. [b]$p < .05$ for contrast between boys and girls. [c]$p < .01$ for contrast between boys and girls.

adjustment may vary as a function of ethnicity or family structure (see Steinberg et al., 1991) and that the impact of social networks on individual behavior may vary as a function of gender (Blyth et al., 1982; Cochran, 1990), all analyses were first conducted separately within groups defined by adolescent ethnicity and gender (e.g., African American boys, African American girls, Asian American boys, Asian American girls, etc.) and family structure and gender. Because results indicated no significant ethnic or family structure differences in patterns of relations between perceived parenting practices and adolescent outcomes, analyses were conducted with the sample split by sex only.

The analysis proceeded in two steps. First, we wished to examine the association between the parenting practices of each adolescent's close friends (as reported by those friends) and the adolescent's own behavior, after taking into account the perceived parenting practices of the adolescent's own parents. To do this, we conducted a series of hierarchical regression analyses in which we first entered a score reflecting the level of perceived authoritativeness in the respondent's home, next entered a score reflecting the prevalence of authoritativeness in the respondent's peer group, and finally entered a term reflecting the interaction between the two parenting measures. The interaction term was tested to examine whether the impact of perceived authoritative parenting in the adolescent's social network is differentially predictive of adjustment among adolescents whose own parents are described as relatively high versus relatively low in authoritativeness themselves (i.e., whether authoritativeness in the peer network amplifies authoritativeness at home, countermands nonauthoritativeness at home, or neither).

The second series of analyses were conducted to determine whether any observed association between authoritative parenting in the adolescent's peer network and adolescent adjustment was mediated proximally by the behavior of the adolescent's peers themselves. In these analyses, hierarchical regressions were conducted in which we first entered a score reflecting the level of perceived authoritativeness in the respondent's home, next entered a score reflecting the prevalence of authoritativeness in the respondent's peer group, and finally entered a term reflecting the behavior of the adolescent's peers on the outcome in question. These analyses were conducted only for those outcomes that had been significantly predicted by the network parenting measure in the first series of regressions. Peer behavior was presumed to mediate the connection between network parenting and adolescent adjustment if a significant association between network parenting and adolescent adjustment diminished to nonsignificance once peer behavior was taken into account.

Our decision to enter network authoritativeness into the regression before entering peer behavior was based on our interest in testing a particular model examining the proximal (i.e., direct) and distal (i.e., indirect) influence of friends' parents on adolescent behavior. The moderate correlations ($-.23$ to $.31$) between network authoritativeness and our indexes of peer behavior suggest that their potentially differing roles in the socialization of adolescents can to some extent be disentangled.

Table 11.2   Correlations of all variables by sex

Variable	1	2	3	4	5	6	7
1. Home authoritativeness	—	.15***	.20***	.18***	.23***	.24***	.27***
2. Network authoritativeness	.12***	—	.14***	.09***	.06***	.04**	.15***
3. Grade point average	.19***	.14***	—	.41***	.19***	.27***	.54***
4. Homework	.12***	.08***	.35***	—	.14***	.21***	.26***
5. Bonding to teachers	.23***	.03	.16***	.15***	—	.46***	.23***
6. School orientation	.24***	.07***	.25***	.25***	.45***	—	.26***
7. Academic competence	.25***	.10***	.52***	.23***	.15***	.22***	—
8. Delinquency	−.17***	−.12***	−.19***	−.14***	−.24***	−.25***	−.15***
9. Drug and alcohol use	−.16***	−.15***	−.24***	−.09***	−.21***	−.28***	−.13***
10. School misconduct	−.17***	−.07***	−.17***	−.13***	−.23***	−.34***	−.15***
11. Peer susceptibility	−.22***	−.08***	−.21***	−.18***	−.27***	−.41***	−.12***
12. Word orientation	.25***	.07***	.26***	.23***	.20***	.47***	.34***
13. Self-reliance	.19***	.01	.20***	.16***	.13***	.25***	.32***
14. Self-esteem	.25***	.06***	.16***	.10***	.24***	.26***	.35***
15. Social competence	.15***	.00	.00	.09***	.18***	.08***	.22***
16. Psychological symptoms	−.18***	−.05	−.02	.03	−.11***	−.18***	−.12***
17. Somatic symptoms	−.09***	−.03	−.10***	.00	−.08***	−.15***	−.11***

Note. Correlations for girls are above the diagonal; correlations for boys are below the diagonal.
**p < .05. ***p < .01.

Results

Correlations between independent and dependent variables

Table 11.2 presents the intercorrelations among all independent and dependent variables for male and female participants. As these matrices indicate, there are significant correlations between parental authoritativeness and all outcome variables for both boys and girls. There are also significant correlations between parental authoritativeness in the peer network and most outcome variables for both boys and girls. In addition, patterns of significant correlations among variables within each domain for both sexes indicate coherent groupings of outcome measures.

Relation between authoritative perceived parenting at home and adolescent adjustment

As Tables 11.3 through 11.6 indicate, and consistent with much previous research, across all outcomes and among both sexes, adolescents' reports of their parents'

behavior are significantly related to their scores on measures of adjustment. Specifically, higher levels of perceived authoritativeness are associated with lower levels of misconduct and internalized distress and higher levels of academic achievement and psychosocial adjustment.

Relation between authoritative parenting in the peer network and adolescent adjustment

ACADEMIC ACHIEVEMENT
Table 11.3 indicates that the level of authoritative parenting in the adolescent's peer network is positively related to his or her performance in school, even after taking into account adolescents' reports of the degree of authoritativeness in their own household. Among both male and female participants, there is a significant positive relation between network authoritativeness and GPA, time spent on homework, and academic competence. In addition to these main effects of network parenting, inspection of the interaction terms indicates that for GPA, bonding to teacher, and academic competence,

8	9	10	11	12	13	14	15	16	17
-.20***	-.19***	-.15***	-.23***	.28***	.21***	.26***	.16***	-.24***	-.14***
-.13***	-.12***	-.05**	-.08***	.09***	.08***	.09***	.06***	-.09***	-.02
-.21***	-.22***	-.17***	-.17***	.33***	.18***	.20***	.02	-.04	-.07***
-.14***	-.09***	-.07***	-.12***	.26***	.18***	.12***	.06**	.04***	-.01
-.19***	-.22***	-.19***	-.27***	.29***	.15***	.28***	.18***	-.14***	-.09
-.25***	-.31***	-.33***	-.38***	.45***	.24***	.27***	.12***	.22***	-.17***
-.12***	-.15***	-.11***	-.16***	.39***	.34***	.39***	.30***	-.15***	-.11***
—	.43***	.26***	.36***	-.20***	-.12***	-.11***	-.01	.19***	.19***
.47***	—	.45***	.52***	-.19***	.01	-.10***	.12***	.26***	.21***
.36***	.44***	—	.49***	-.30***	-.00	-.09***	.09***	.24***	.22***
.40***	.50***	.48***	—	-.33***	-.15***	-.18***	.07***	.21***	.15***
-.20***	.17***	-.28***	-.35***	—	.49***	.42***	.20***	-.19***	-.17***
-.17***	-.04	-.01	-.24***	.56***	—	.43***	.30***	-.07***	-.07***
-.12***	-.04	-.08***	-.12***	.39***	.41***	—	.34***	-.32***	-.21***
-.00	.13***	.08***	.05	.17***	.22***	.36***	—	-.12***	-.08***
.07**	.18***	.21***	.09***	-.15***	-.02	-.30***	-.16***	—	.54***
.10***	.20***	.18***	.16***	-.16***	-.08***	-.15***	-.02	.51**	—

among girls, the positive relation between network parenting and adolescent adjustment varies as a function of the level of perceived authoritativeness in the adolescent's own home. The negative interaction term for bonding to teacher suggests that the positive effects of network authoritativeness are strongest for those adolescents who characterize their own parents as relatively less authoritative (a countermanding effect). The positive interaction terms for academic competence and GPA, however, suggest that the beneficial effects of network authoritativeness on these variables are strongest for girls whose own parents are themselves characterized as relatively more authoritative (an amplification effect).

BEHAVIOR PROBLEMS

Among both boys and girls, authoritativeness in the peer network is associated with lower rates of delinquency and substance use, above and beyond the effects of perceived authoritativeness at home (see Table 11.4). Among boys, network authoritativeness is also negatively related to school misconduct and susceptibility to antisocial peer pressure. The interaction terms indicate that, among girls, the relation between network authoritativeness and minor delinquency and substance use is strongest for adolescents whose parents are described as relatively more authoritative (an amplification effect).

PSYCHOSOCIAL COMPETENCE

Regression analyses examining the relation between network authoritativeness and adolescent psychosocial competence indicate significant main effects only among girls. Among girls, network authoritativeness is positively related to work orientation, self-reliance, and self-esteem, even after the effects of perceived authoritativeness at home are taken into account (Table 11.5). Among boys, the main effect of network authoritativeness is not significant, but the significant positive interaction term indicates that the beneficial impact of network authoritativeness on work orientation is strongest among boys who describe their parents as relatively more authoritative (an amplification effect).

INTERNALIZED DISTRESS

Among girls, parental authoritativeness in the peer network is associated with less psychological

Table 11.3   Unstandardized (*B*) and standardized (*β*) regression coefficients for relations between authoritativeness in the adolescent's home, prevalence of parental authoritativeness in the peer network, and indicators of academic achievement

	Boys		Girls	
Variable	B	β	B	β
Grade point average				
1. Home authoritativeness	.15	.19★★★	.15	.20★★★
2. Home authoritativeness	.14	.17★★★	.14	.18★★★
Network authoritativeness	.08	.11★★★	.08	.11★★★
3. Home authoritativeness	.08	.10	.04	.05
Network authoritativeness	.06	.08★	.03	.05
Interaction	.02	.08	.03	.16★
Time on homework				
1. Home authoritativeness	.16	.12★★★	.23	.18★★★
2. Home authoritativeness	.15	.11★★★	.21	.17★★★
Network authoritativeness	.08	.06★★★	.08	.07★★★
3. Home authoritativeness	.12	.09	.21	.17★
Network authoritativeness	.06	.05	.08	.07★
Interaction	.01	.03	.00	.00
Bonding to teachers				
1. Home authoritativeness	.14	.23★★★	.14	.23★★★
2. Home authoritativeness	.14	.23★★★	.14	.23★★★
Network authoritativeness	−.00	−.01	.02	.03
3. Home authoritativeness	.09	.14★	.23	.38★★★
Network authoritativeness	−.03	−.05	.06	.11★★★
Interaction	.02	.11	−.03	−.19★★
School orientation				
1. Home authoritativeness	.14	.24★★★	.14	.24★★★
2. Home authoritativeness	.14	.24★★★	.14	.24★★★
Network authoritativeness	.02	.04	.00	.01
3. Home authoritativeness	.09	.16★★	.15	.25★★★
Network authoritativeness	−.00	−.00	.01	.02
Interaction	.01	.10	.00	−.02
Academic competence				
1. Home authoritativeness	.15	.25★★★	.18	.27★★★
2. Home authoritativeness	.15	.24★★★	.17	.25★★★
Network authoritativeness	.04	.07★★★	.06	.11★★★
3. Home authoritativeness	.06	.10	.07	.10
Network authoritativeness	.00	.00	.02	.03
Interaction	.03	.16	.03	.19★★

★*p* < .10. ★★*p* < .05. ★*p* < .01.

distress, even after taking into account the beneficial effects of having authoritative parents at home (see Table 11.6). Among boys, the main effect of network authoritativeness is not significant, but the positive interaction between psychological symptoms and network authoritativeness indicates that the beneficial influence of network authoritativeness is stronger among adolescents whose parents are described as relatively more authoritative (an amplification effect).

Table 11.4 Unstandardized (B) and standardized (β) regression coefficients for relations between authoritativeness in the adolescent's home, prevalence of parental authoritativeness in the peer network, and indicators of behavior problems

Variable	Boys		Girls	
	B	β	B	β
Delinquency				
1. Home authoritativeness	−.06	−.17***	−.04	−.20***
2. Home authoritativeness	−.06	−.16***	.04	−.18***
Network authoritativeness	−.03	−.09***	−.02	−.11***
3. Home authoritativeness	−.09	−.25***	−.08	−.38***
Network authoritativeness	−.05	−.14***	−.04	−.21***
Interaction	.01	.10	.01	.25***
Drug and alcohol use				
1. Home authoritativeness	−.12	−.16***	−.14	−.20***
2. Home authoritativeness	−.11	−.14***	−.13	−.18***
Network authoritativeness	−.08	−.12***	−.07	−.10***
3. Home authoritativeness	−.15	−.21***	.23	−.32***
Network authoritativeness	−.10	−.15***	−.11	−.18***
Interaction	.01	.08	.03	.17**
School misconduct				
1. Home authoritativeness	−.12	−.17***	−.10	−.15***
2. Home authoritativeness	−.12	−.16***	−.10	−.15***
Network authoritativeness	−.03	−.05**	−.02	−.03
3. Home authoritativeness	−.10	−.13	−.09	−.14*
Network authoritativeness	−.02	−.03	−.02	−.13
Interaction	−.01	−.04	.00	−.01
Susceptibility to antisocial peer pressure				
1. Home authoritativeness	−.15	−.22***	−.14	−.23***
2. Home authoritativeness	−.14	−.21***	−.13	−.23***
Network authoritativeness	−.03	−.05**	−.02	−.03
3. Home authoritativeness	−.08	−.12	−.08	−.30***
Network authoritativeness	−.00	−.01	−.04	−.08*
Interaction	−.02	−.12	.01	.10

*$p < .10$. **$p < .05$. ***$p < .01$.

Mediating role of friends' behavior

The results described thus far indicate that having friends who describe their parents as authoritative is associated with greater academic competence and less problem behavior among adolescent boys and girls and, among girls, with greater psychosocial competence and less psychological distress. These apparent benefits are over and above the advantages associated with describing one's own parents as authoritative. In the next series of analyses, we ask whether the positive impact of parental authoritativeness in the peer network is proximal (i.e., a direct influence of the friends' parents on the target adolescent) or distal (i.e., transmitted indirectly, through the behavior of the peers). Recall that this question was examined by reconsidering the relation between perceived network authoritativeness and adolescent adjustment while controlling not only for authoritativeness in the adolescent's home but also for the adolescent's peers' behavior.

Table 11.5 Unstandardized (*B*) and standardized (*β*) regression coefficients for relations between authoritativeness in the adolescent's home, prevalence of parental authoritativeness in the peer network, and indicators of psychosocial competence

Variable	Boys		Girls	
	B	β	B	β
Work orientation				
1. Home authoritativeness	.13	.25★★★	.14	.28★★★
2. Home authoritativeness	.12	.24★★★	.14	.27★★★
Network authoritativeness	.02	.04	.02	.05★★
3. Home authoritativeness	.03	.06	.15	.30★★★
Network authoritativeness	−.03	−.06	.03	.07★
Interaction	.03	.22★	−.01	−.04
Self-reliance				
1. Home authoritativeness	.10	.19★★★	.10	.21★★★
2. Home authoritativeness	.10	.19★★★	.10	.20★★★
Network authoritativeness	−.01	−.01	.02	.05★★
3. Home authoritativeness	.05	.09	.10	.21★★★
Network authoritativeness	−.03	−.06	.02	.06
Interaction	.02	.12	.00	−.01
Self-esteem				
1. Home authoritativeness	.13	.25★★★	.14	.26★★★
2. Home authoritativeness	.13	.25★★★	.14	.25★★★
Network authoritativeness	.01	.03	.03	.05★★
3. Home authoritativeness	.12	.24★★★	.11	.21★★★
Network authoritativeness	.01	.02	.01	.03
Interaction	.00	.02	.01	.06
Social competence				
1. Home authoritativeness	.10	.15★★★	.10	.16★★★
2. Home authoritativeness	.10	.16★★★	.10	.15★★★
Network authoritativeness	−.01	−.02	.02	.04
3. Home authoritativeness	.08	.13	.11	.18★★
Network authoritativeness	−.02	−.03	.03	.05
Interaction	.01	.03	.00	−.03

★*p* <.10. ★★*p* < .05. ★★*p* < .01.

ACADEMIC ACHIEVEMENT

The relations between parenting in the peer network and adolescent academic competence are indeed mediated by the behavior of the adolescent's peers. Specifically, the previously significant relations between network authoritativeness and school performance, time spent on homework, and academic self-conceptions are each diminished to nonsignificance once the parallel characteristic of the adolescent's peers is taken into account. Among girls only,

there remains a trend (*B* =.03, *β* = .05), *t*(3, 1460) = 1.79, *p* = .07, in the relation between network authoritativeness and academic competence after controlling for the average academic competence of their peers.

BEHAVIOR PROBLEMS

Most of the relations between perceived network authoritativeness and adolescent problem behavior also are mediated by the behavior of the adolescent's peers. Among boys, the previously observed significant

Table 11.6 Unstandardized (B) and standardized (β) regression coefficients for relations between authoritativeness in the adolescent's home, prevalence of parental authoritativeness in the peer network, and indicators of internalized distress

Variable	Boys		Girls	
	B	β	B	β
Psychological symptoms				
1. Home authoritativeness	−.14	−.18★★★	−.19	−.24★★★
2. Home authoritativeness	−.14	−.18★★★	−.18	−.23★★★
Network authoritativeness	−.02	−.02	−.04	−.06★★★
3. Home authoritativeness	−.28	−.36★★★	−.13	−.16★★
Network authoritativeness	−.08	−.16★★	−.02	−.02
Interaction	.04	.22★★	−.01	−.08
Somatic symptoms				
1. Home authoritativeness	−.06	−.09★★★	−.09	−.14★★★
2. Home authoritativeness	−.06	−.09★★★	−.09	−.14★★★
Network authoritativeness	−.01	−.02	.00	.00
3. Home authoritativeness	−.12	−.19★★	−.10	−.16★★
Network authoritativeness	−.04	−.07	−.00	−.01
Interaction	.02	.12	.00	.02

★★$p < .05$. ★★★$p < .01$.

relations between network authoritativeness and substance use, school misconduct, and susceptibility to antisocial peer pressure all become nonsignificant once friends' scores on the same outcome variables are taken into account. Among girls, this is also the case with respect to substance use. It is interesting to note, however, that the negative relation between perceived network authoritativeness and delinquency remains significant for both boys ($B = -.02$, $\beta = -.06$), $t(3, 1379) = -2.35$, $p < .05$, and girls ($B = -.01$, $\beta = -.07$), $t(3, 1894) = -3.07$, $p < .01$, after controlling for peer delinquency, suggesting that an adolescent's friends' parents may have a proximal effect on his or her behavior in this specific domain. That is, the deterrent effect of network authoritativeness on adolescent delinquency is not mediated solely through the proximal influence of peers.

PSYCHOSOCIAL ADJUSTMENT

The relation between perceived network authoritativeness and psychosocial adjustment for girls is also mediated by the adjustment of peers, as the previously significant coefficients for work orientation, self-reliance, and self-esteem are diminished to nonsignificance by controlling for peer scores on these variables.

INTERNALIZED DISTRESS

The significant relation between perceived network authoritativeness and psychological symptoms among girls is reduced to nonsignificance by the addition of peer psychological symptoms to the regression equation, indicating that the relation between parental authoritativeness among one's peers and internalized distress is mediated through the psychological state of the peers themselves.

Discussion

The link between parental authoritativeness and adolescent adjustment is well established in the literature on the socialization of young people (Maccoby & Martin, 1983). The present investigation extends this connection between authoritative parenting and adolescent competence to yet a more distal context, by demonstrating that the prevalence of parental authoritativeness in an adolescent's network of peers is also associated with a variety of indicators of healthy adjustment, above and beyond the contribution of perceived authoritativeness in the adolescent's family of origin. Specifically, adolescents whose friends describe their parents as authoritative earn higher grades in school, spend more time on homework, have more positive perceptions of their academic competence, and report lower levels of delinquency and substance use. In addition, boys whose friends describe their parents as authoritative report lower levels of peer conformity and are less likely to engage in school misconduct. Among girls, higher levels of network authoritativeness are associated with better psychological functioning (as indexed by higher scores on our measures of work orientation, self-reliance, and self-esteem) and lower levels of psychological distress, such as depressed affect or anxiety.

The results presented here also suggest a mechanism through which authoritative parenting in the adolescent's peer network may operate. The influence of authoritativeness among the adolescent's friends' parents is not, for the most part, direct but is indirect, with the proximal influence being the friends' behavior. Our interpretation of the results is that authoritative parenting is associated with adolescent competence, and competent youngsters are attracted to, and influence, each other. We recognize, however, that this research effort has tested only one of several possible models to account for these findings, and that longitudinal and experimental data are needed to further understand the causal and temporal relations among these variables. The preliminary results reported here nevertheless should encourage other investigators to examine further the direct and indirect roles of nonfamilial adults in adolescents' socialization.

Although the design of this study does not allow us to disentangle the contributions of peer socialization versus peer selection, prior research has shown that both processes operate in domains such as problem behavior (e.g., Kandel, 1978) and academic achievement (Epstein, 1983). In all likelihood, therefore, well-adjusted adolescents from authoritative homes select (and are selected by) similarly competent—and to a certain extent, similarly raised—peers, and experiences within their peer group serve to amplify and

maintain their higher level of adjustment. In contrast, less competent adolescents from nonauthoritative homes are more likely to select comparably less competent peers—from comparably nonauthoritative homes—and their peer group amplifies and maintains their disadvantage (see also Brown, Mounts, Lamborn, & Steinberg, 1993).

A different mechanism must be proposed to account for the link between network authoritativeness and delinquency, however. Among both boys and girls, the relation between network authoritativeness and involvement in delinquent activities remains significant even after controlling for the level of delinquency among the adolescents' peers. The possibility cannot be dismissed that these relations remained significant only by chance, although the fact that the same finding emerged independently among both boys and girls argues against this. We think it plausible that the prevalence of authoritativeness among one's friends' parents may proximally diminish the likelihood of an adolescent engaging in delinquent activities, perhaps because of the higher level of shared social control provided by a network of authoritative parents—an interpretation consistent with research on the impact of parental vigilance on communitywide delinquency (see also Sampson & Groves, 1989). By definition, authoritative parents are careful monitors of their children's behavior; intentionally or inadvertently, they may monitor their children's associates as well.

As one of the first studies to date to examine the potential impact of friends' parents on adolescent behavior, the results presented here are in need of replication and should be viewed with caution. Because of the reluctance of less economically advantaged adolescents to provide the names of their friends, the sample within which these analyses have been performed, while ethnically diverse, is predominantly a sample of adolescents from middle-class and professional families. We do not know whether the effects of authoritativeness in the peer network vary at different levels of family socioeconomic status, nor do we know if the results reported here would be comparable in a sample of less well-adjusted teens. Within this socioeconomically and psychologically advantaged group, however, we do find that the observed effects of network authoritativeness are comparable across ethnic groups. Researchers involved in similar research efforts in the future should be aware that poorer and less well-adjusted adolescents may be less likely to provide the information necessary for conducting network analyses, and they should take special measures to overcome this restriction.

It is also important to bear in mind that the reports of parenting practices and outcome variables in this study were obtained from adolescents themselves. As has been argued elsewhere, there is an extensive literature documenting that adolescents can accurately and reliably report on their parents' practices (see Golden, 1969; Moscowitz & Schwarz, 1982) and on their own academic achievement (Dornbusch et al., 1987), problem behavior (McCord, 1990), psychological distress (Roberts, Andrews, Lewinson, & Hops, 1990), and psychosocial competence (Greenberger & Bond, 1976). Moreover, longitudinal analyses of this same data set have shown that the predictive validity of our self-report measures of parenting cannot be explained by common source or method variance (Steinberg et al., 1994). Most important, our measures of authoritativeness among peers' parents, as well as our measures of peer behavior, are obtained from peers themselves and are not based on target adolescents' perceptions. Nevertheless, we recognize that future studies of adolescent socialization by peers and nonfamilial adults would be strengthened by the use of data from multiple methods and sources.

In the present study, the influence of network authoritativeness is more consistently observed among girls than boys, and, more important, this influence is observed in different domains for the two sexes. Only among girls are effects of network authoritativeness observed in the areas of psychosocial adjustment and internalized distress. In contrast, misconduct is more consistently related to network authoritativeness among boys than girls. One reason for this sex difference may inhere in Cochran and Bo's (1989) suggestion that boys are mainly influenced by extensive casual involvement with nonrelated adults, whereas girls are influenced by intimate involvement. That network authoritativeness among girls is associated with such outcomes as work orientation, self-reliance, self-esteem, and psychological distress may reflect the fact that girls' relationships with significant others are more intimate, and thus more likely to influence internal psychological states. Behavioral outcomes, such as misconduct, may be more influenced by the casual interactions with network adults experienced by boys.

Theorists have disagreed over whether the potential beneficial impact of membership in a network high in social capital is likely to be strongest among those who are already advantaged (what Coleman and Hotter [1987] referred to as *amplification*) or, in contrast, among those with limited resources of their own (i.e., *countermanding*). Consideration of the interaction effects found in the present study suggest that, where network authoritativeness differentially influences adolescents whose parents vary in their own levels of authoritativeness, the effect is more often than not one of amplification. In other words, adolescents who characterize their own parents as relatively more authoritative appear to benefit more from membership in a peer network with other authoritatively reared youngsters than do adolescents in similar networks but who are from less authoritative homes. It may be the case that adolescents may need certain "home advantages" to be able to take advantage of the social capital in their networks.

On the basis of the work presented here, it appears that Coleman's (1988) ideas concerning the importance of social capital within a network are important notions that can assist researchers interested in extending the current understanding of influences on child adjustment beyond those of parents and peers separately. This research indicates that membership in a community of peers and adults who encourage adjustment and good behavior on the parts of other adolescents within the community is beneficial above and beyond the presence of such positive influences within the immediate family. It is expected that future research efforts that focus even more clearly on the influence of time spent with community adults will find even stronger effects of functional communities and the social capital within them.

Notes

1 Researchers interested in collecting similar data should bear this in mind. We did not find that less-advantaged students were reluctant to complete the questionnaires in general, but they specifically balked at providing the names of their friends.

2   As we report elsewhere in detail (Steinberg, Mounts, Lamborn, & Dornbusch, 1991), this factor structure is virtually identical across ethnic, social class, and family structure groups.

3   The use of our particular consent procedure prohibited our obtaining grades from official school records in many of our schools. In Wisconsin, for example, active parental consent is required to gain access to school records. Given the advantages of the passive consent procedure we used, and in light of the high correlation between actual grades and high school students' reports, we believe that using self-reports of school performance was justified.

References

Baumrind, D. (1967). Child care practices anteceding three patterns of preschool behavior. *Genetic Psychology Monographs, 75,* 43–88.

Baumrind, D. (1971). Current patterns of parental authority *Developmental Psychology Monograph, 4* (1, Pt. 2).

Baumrind, D. (1991a). Effective parenting during the early adolescent transition. In P. A. Cowan & E. M. Hetherington (Eds.), *Advances in family research* (Vol. 2, pp. 111–163). Hillsdale, NJ: Erlbaum.

Baumrind, D. (199lb). The influence of parenting style on adolescent competence and substance use. *Journal of Early Adolescence. 11,* 56–95.

Berndt, T. (1979). Developmental changes in conformity to peers and parents. *Developmental Psychology, 15,* 608–616.

Blyth, D., Hill, J., & Thiel, K. (1982). Early adolescents' significant others: Grade and gender differences in perceived relationships with familial and nonfamilial adults and young people. *Journal of Youth and Adolescence, 11,* 425–450.

Bronfenbrenner, U. (1979). *The ecology of human development: Experiments by nature and design.* Cambridge, MA: Harvard University Press.

Bronfenbrenner, U. (1986). Ecology of the family as a context for human development: Research perspectives. *Developmental Psychology, 22,* 723–742.

Brawn, B., Mounts, N., Lamborn, S., & Steinberg, L. (1993). Parenting practices and peer group affiliation in adolescence. *Child Development, 64,* 467–482.

Case, A., & Katz, L. (1992). *The company you keep: The effects of family and neighborhood on disadvantaged youths.* Unpublished manuscript, Princeton University, Department of Economics.

Cochran, M. (1990). Personal networks in the ecology of human development. In M. Cochran, M. Larner, D. Riley, L. Gunnarsson, & C. Henderson, Jr. (Eds.), *Extending families: The social networks of parents and their children* (pp. 3–33). New York: Cambridge University Press.

Cochran, M., & Bo, I. (1989). The social networks, family involvement, and pro- and antisocial behavior of adolescent males in Norway. *Journal of youth and Adolescence, 18,* 377–398.

Coleman. J. (1988). Social capital in the creation of human capital. *American Journal of Sociology, 94,* s95–s120.

Coleman, J., & Hoffer, T. (1987). *Public and private high schools: The impact of communities.* New York: Basic Books.

Donovan, J., & Jessor, R. (1985). Structure of problem behavior in adolescence and young adulthood. *Journal of Consulting and Clinical Psychology, 53,* 890–904.

Dornbusch, S., Carlsmith, J., Bushwall, S., Ritter, P., Leiderman, H., Hastorf, A., & Gross, R. (1985). Single parents, extended households and the control of adolescents. *Child Development, 56,* 326–341.

Dornbusch, S. M., Ritter, P. L., Liederman, P., Roberts, D., & Fraleigh, M. (1987). The relation of parenting style to adolescent school performance. *Child Development, 58,* 1244–1257.

Epstein, J. (1983). The influence of friends on achievement and affective outcomes. In J. Epstein & N. Karweit (Eds.), *Friends in school* (pp. 177–200). New York: Academic Press.

Gold, M. (1970). *Delinquent behavior in an American city.* Belmont, CA: Brooks/Cole.

Golden, P. (1969). A review of children's reports of parental behaviors. *Psychological Bulletin, 71,* 222–235.

Greenberger, E., & Bond, L. (1976). *Technical manual for the Psychosocial Maturity Inventory.* Unpublished manuscript, University of California, Irvine, Program in Social Ecology.

Greenberger, E., Josselson, R., Knerr, C., & Knerr, B. (1974). The measurement and structure of psychosocial maturity. *Journal of Mouth and Adolescence, 4,* 127–143.

Greenberger, E., Steinberg, L., & Vaux, A. (1981). Adolescents who work: Health and behavioral consequences of job stress. *Developmental Psychology, 17,* 691–703.

Harter, S. (1982). The perceived competence scale for children. *Child Development, 53,* 87–97.

Hetherington, E. M., Clingempeel, W., Anderson, E., Deal, J., Hagan, M., Hollier, E., & Lindner, M. (1992). Coping with marital transitions. *Monographs of the Society for Research in Child Development, 57* (2–3, Serial No. 227).

Ianni, F. (1983). *Home, school, and community in adolescent education.* New York: Eric Clearinghouse on Urban Education.

Kandel, D. (1978). Homophify, selection, and socialization in adolescent friendships. *American Journal of Sociology, 84,* 427–436.

Kurdek, L., & Sinclair, R. (1988). Adjustment of young adolescents in two-parent nuclear, stepfather, and mother-custody families. *Journal of Consulting and Clinical Psychology, 56,* 91–96.

Lamborn, S., Mounts, N., Steinberg, L., & Dornbusch, S. (1991). Patterns of competence and adjustment among adolescents from authoritative, authoritarian, indulgent, and neglectful homes. *Child Development, 62,* 1049–1065.

Maccoby, E., & Martin, J. (1983). Socialization in the context of the family: Parent-child interaction. In E. M. Hetherington (Ed.), *Handbook of child psychology: Vol. 4. Socialization, personality, and social development* (pp. 1–101). New York: Wiley.

McCord, J. (1990). Problem behaviors. In S. Feldman & G. Elliott (Eds.), *At the threshold: The developing adolescent* (pp. 414–430). Cambridge, MA: Harvard University Press.

Moscowitz, D., & Schwarz, J. (1982). A validity comparison of behavior counts and ratings by knowledgeable informants. *Journal of Personality and Social Psychology, 42,* 518–528.

Mounts, N., & Steinberg, L. (1992). *Peer influences on adolescent achievement and deviance: An ecological approach.* Manuscript submitted for publication, University of Illinois at Urbana-Champaign, Department of Educational Psychology.

Patterson, G., & Stouthamer-Loeber, M. (1984). The correlation of family management practices and delinquency. *Child Development, 55,* 1299–1307.

Radloff, L. S. (1977). The CES-D scale: A self-report depression scale for research in the general population. *Applied Psychological Measurement, 1,* 385–401.

Roberts, R., Andrews, J., Lewinson, P., & Hops, H. (1990). Assessment of depression in adolescents using the Center for Epidemiological Depression Scale. *Psychological Assessment, 2,* 122–128.

Rodgers, R. R. (1966). *Cornell parent behavior description—an interim report.* Unpublished manuscript, Department of Human Development and Family Studies, Cornell University.

Rosenberg, M. (1965). *Society and the adolescent self-image.* Princeton, NJ: Princeton University Press.

Ruggiero, M. (1984). *Work as an impetus to delinquency: An examination of theoretical and empirical connections.* Unpublished doctoral dissertation, University of California, Irvine.

Sampson, R., & Groves, W. (1989). Community structure and crime: Testing social-disorganization theory. *American Journal of Sociology, 94,* 774–802.

Schaefer, E. (1965). Children's reports of parental behavior An inventory. *Child Development, 36,* 413–424.

Schwartz, J., Barton-Henry, M., & Pruzinsky, T. (1985). Assessing child-rearing behaviors: A comparison of ratings made by mother, father, child, and sibling on the CRPBI. *Child Development, 56,* 462–479.

Shaw, C., Zorbaugh, F., McKay, H., & Cottrell, L. (1929). *Delinquency areas.* Chicago: University of Chicago Press.

Steinberg, L. (1990). Interdependency in the family: Autonomy, conflict, and harmony. In S. Feldman & G. Elliot (Eds.), *At the threshold: the developing adolescent* (pp. 255–276). Cambridge, MA: Harvard University Press.

Steinberg, L., Elmen, J., & Mounts, N. (1989). Authoritative parenting, psychosocial maturity, and academic success among adolescents. *Child Development, 60,* 1424–1436.

Steinberg, L., Lamborn, S. D., Darling, N., Mounts, N. S., & Dornbusch, S. M. (1994). Over-time changes in adjustment and competence among adolescents from authoritative, authoritarian, indulgent, and neglectful families. *Child Development, 65,* 754–770.

Steinberg, L., Lamborn, S., Dornbusch, S., & Darling, N. (1992). Impact of parenting practices on adolescent achievement: Authoritative parenting, school involvement, and encouragement to succeed. *Child Development, 63,* 1266–1281.

Steinberg, L., Mounts, N., Lamborn, S., & Dornbusch, S. (1991). Authoritative parenting and adolescent adjustment across varied ecological niches. *Journal of Research on Adolescence, 1,* 19–36.

Wehlage, G., Rutter, R., Smith, G., Lesko, N., & Fernandez, R. (1989). *Reducing the risk: Schools as communities of support.* London: Falmer Press.

Weinberger, D., Tublin, S., Ford, M., & Feldman, S. (1990). Preadolescents' social–emotional adjustment and selective attrition in family research. *Child Development, 61,* 1374–1386.

Individual Differences in Adolescents' Beliefs About the Legitimacy of Parental Authority and Their Own Obligation to Obey: A Longitudinal Investigation

Nancy Darling, Patricio Cumsille, and M. Loreto Martínez

When parents set rules that adolescents disagree with, adolescents usually obey (Darling, Cumsille, & Martínez, 2007; Darling, Cumsille, & Peña-Alampay, 2005). Why? Most research on adolescent socialization has focused on what parents do to facilitate positive adolescent development (Parke & Buriel, 1998), with extensive literatures concerning both stylistic differences in parents' characteristics, such as support, and behavioral and psychological control (e.g., Barber, Stolz, & Olsen, 2005; Pettit, Laird, Dodge, Bates, & Criss, 2001), and on specific parenting practices such as monitoring (e.g., Crouter & Head, 2002). Although developmental researchers have long recognized that effective parenting is made easier with a cooperative child (Thomas & Chess, 1968), relatively less attention has been given to the processes underlying differences in adolescents' willingness to be socialized (although see Kerr, Stattin, & Trost, 1999; Moffitt, 1993; Patterson, DeBaryshe, & Ramsey, 1989, for important exceptions). Understanding these processes is particularly important during adolescence, when normative increases in adolescents' desire for psychological and behavioral autonomy are likely to conflict with continued parental efforts to protect, socialize, and regulate their children (Smetana, 2002). This article examines normative change and individual differences in adolescents' beliefs that parents have the right to set rules about particular areas of their lives (the legitimacy of parental authority) and their beliefs that they must obey parental rules they disagree with (obligation to obey). Both characteristics of adolescents and of their parents are examined as predictors of individual differences in adolescents' beliefs and as moderators of normative change.

Parents' knowledge of their adolescent children's lives, adolescents' decisions to share information about their lives, and adolescents' decisions to obey parents when they disagree with them depend in part upon adolescents' beliefs about the legitimacy of parental authority and their own obligation to obey. Legitimacy of parental authority refers to the extent to which parents' assertion of control over an area is believed to be a natural or an appropriate extension of their role as parents (e.g., Smetana, 1988). Obligation to obey is a related construct, referring to the belief that children are obliged to obey parents, even when they and their parents disagree. Darling and Steinberg (1993) hypothesized that one reason that the adolescents of authoritative parents (i.e., those who are warm and high in behavioral control but low in psychological control) evince positive developmental outcomes is that they (a) are more likely to see their parents as legitimate authorities and believe themselves obliged to obey them, (b) are more likely to internalize their values, and (c) are thus both more open to parental socialization and more likely to make autonomous decisions consonant with parental values. Research on the association of legitimacy beliefs and parenting has been consistent with this prediction. Early adolescents who believe that their parents have legitimate authority to regulate personal issues, such as who their friends are or how they dress, also report that their parents have more knowledge of their lives (Smetana & Daddis, 2002). Adolescents' beliefs about their obligation to disclose information to parents, as well as greater trust, and in the case of personal issues, more parental acceptance, predicts more disclosure and less secrecy (Smetana, Metzger, Gettman, & Campione-Barr, 2006). Parents whose knowledge of their adolescents' lives stems from voluntary disclosure are most likely to have adolescents with lower levels of problem behavior (Crouter, Bumpus, Davis, & McHale, 2005; Kerr & Stattin, 2000). Further, adolescents' decisions to disclose information to parents depends upon both the adolescents' perception that parents are supportive

(Crouter et al., 2005; Darling, Cumsille, Caldwell, & Dowdy, 2006) and, in case of disagreement, adolescents' beliefs that they are obliged to obey parents in spite of disagreement (Darling et al., 2006). Adolescents who express general agreement with parents and who feel obliged to obey parents across a range of issues are more likely to obey parents than are their peers, controlling for parental support and monitoring. Examining variability within adolescents across different issues and controlling for both the presence of rules and the parents' reports of rule enforcement, adolescents are most likely to obey parents in situations where they agree with parents, believe that parents have legitimate authority, and believe that they are obliged to obey parents in spite of disagreement (Darling et al., 2007).

Research on adolescents' and parents' beliefs about the legitimacy of parental authority and the obligation to obey emerged from research on social cognition and moral development (e.g., Turiel, 1983) and has primarily focused on (a) differences in legitimacy beliefs depending upon the domain of the issue in question; (b) normative, age-related differences in adolescents' and parents' legitimacy beliefs; and (c) differences in the legitimacy beliefs of adolescents and parents. Research in the United States in samples of African-, Cuban-, Chinese-, European-, Filipino-, and Mexican-American backgrounds (e.g., Darling et al., 2005; Fuligni, 1998; Smetana, 2000) and in samples from Brazil, Chile, China, Japan, and the Philippines (e.g., Darling et al., 2005; Hasebe, Nucci, & Nucci, 2004; Nucci, Camino, & Sapiro, 1996; Yau & Smetana, 2003) has yielded strikingly consistent results. Adolescents and their parents are more likely to judge issues that are defined as moral (e.g., hitting or stealing), prudential (e.g., drinking, using drugs), and conventional (e.g., talking back to parents, cursing) as legitimately within the domain of parental authority, and to judge issues defined as personal (e.g., choice of friends or extracurricular activities) as outside legitimate parental control (see Smetana, 1997, for a detailed review of this perspective). As adolescents become older, both they and their parents define more issues as falling outside the legitimate domain of parental authority, although parents lag behind adolescents in the speed of this transition (Smetana, 2000). Much of this normative contraction in the legitimate domain

of parental authority occurs in the personal domain and in multidomain issues that have personal aspects.

Differences between adolescents' and parents' beliefs about the legitimacy of parental authority have been hypothesized to cause conflict within the family, especially in early and middle adolescence (Smetana, 1996). Parental assertion of control over personal issues is also associated with adolescents' perceptions that parents are exerting inappropriate psychological control (Smetana & Daddis, 2002) and with more internalizing symptoms (Hasebe et al., 2004). Nucci and Smetana have argued that adolescents' assertion of control over personal issues is a fundamental part of the development of healthy autonomy (Nucci, Killen, & Smetana, 1996; Smetana, Crean, & Campione-Barr, 2005). Moderate amounts of resistance to parental authority, or even subversion, may be a sign of healthy development (Smetana et al., 2005). However, premature assertion of personal control (or, conversely, premature rejection of parental legitimacy) over areas normatively defined as legitimately within parental control may be both symptomatic of poor parent–adolescent relationships (Darling et al., 2005) and indicative of problematic developmental pathways (Steinberg & Silverberg, 1986).

Although there is a clear, age-related decline in the range of issues that adolescents and parents believe to be within the legitimate sphere of parental authority, there is considerable within-age variability in adolescents' endorsement of parental authority (Darling et al., 2005). In a recent article in which latent class analyses were used to examine the patterning of adolescents' legitimacy beliefs (Cumsille, Darling, Flaherty, & Martínez, 2006), three distinct patterns emerged. In the first pattern (parent centered), adolescents were likely to grant parents legitimacy over both multidomain and prudential issues and were more likely than their peers to grant parents authority over personal issues. In the second pattern (adolescent centered), adolescents were unlikely to grant parents legitimacy over personal, prudential, or multidomain issues. In the third pattern (shared), adolescents clearly differentiated parental legitimacy across domains and were likely to grant parents authority over prudential issues but unlikely to grant them authority over personal issues. Analogous patterns emerged among early, middle, and late adolescents, with the parent-centered pattern most common at each age (ranging between 49% and 58% of each age group). Although cross-sectional, the proportion of adolescents evincing each pattern was relatively stable across age groups, suggesting that youth showing different patterns may be following different trajectories in the development of legitimacy beliefs.

Individual differences in adolescents' beliefs are associated with differences in adolescents' behavior in ways that may undermine or facilitate parenting. For example, adolescents who are heavy drug users tend to see substance use as a personal rather than prudential issue and thus outside the legitimate sphere of parental authority (Nucci, Guerra, & Lee, 1991). In case of disagreement, adolescents who believe that parents have legitimate authority with regard to specific issues and feel obliged to obey are (a) more likely to disclose information to parents about that issue rather than lie (Darling et al., 2006), (b) more likely to argue about the issue with parents (Cumsille, Darling, & Peña-Alampay, 2002), and (c) more likely to obey (Darling et al., 2007). Further, adolescents who believe that they are obliged to disclose to parents both disclose more to parents and are less likely to keep secrets from them (Smetana et al., 2006). We know little about where these differences in adolescents' beliefs about parental legitimacy and obligation to obey come from or how they may unfold over time. In addition, research on normative changes in adolescents' beliefs has focused on adolescents' beliefs in the legitimacy of parental authority. Much less is known about children's beliefs about their obligation to obey parents when they disagree with them. These beliefs may be particularly important in understanding decision making in situations where direct parental supervision or distal monitoring is difficult or dependent on children's willingness to disclose.

The goals of the present article were (a) to examine longitudinal change in Chilean adolescents' beliefs about the legitimacy of parental authority and their own obligation to obey parents in case of disagreement and (b) to predict individual differences in adolescents' beliefs and changes in those beliefs as a function of their own and their parents' characteristics. Adolescents were in early to middle adolescence at Wave 1 of the study (11–14 years old) and were followed once a year for 4 years. Five specific issues were addressed:

1. Do adolescents become less likely to endorse the legitimacy of parental authority and their own obligation to obey with age?

2. Is the decline in adolescents' endorsement of parental legitimacy and their own obligation to obey uniform across adolescence, or does it decline more rapidly in early adolescence than in middle or later adolescence?

3. Is the decline in endorsement of parental legitimacy and obligation to obey parallel in all domains, or does it decline more quickly in some domains than in others?

4. Are adolescents who perceive their parents to be supportive and high in monitoring more likely to endorse the legitimacy of parental authority and their own obligation to obey than those whose parents do not? Are adolescents who were relatively more involved in problem behavior less likely to endorse parental authority and their own obligation to obey?

5. Do adolescents' beliefs in the legitimacy of parental authority and their own obligation to obey decline less rapidly when they see their parents as supportive and high in monitoring? Do the beliefs of adolescents who are relatively more involved in problem behavior decline more rapidly?

Questions 1–3 provide a partial replication and extension of longitudinal research by Smetana (2000), in which changes from ages 13 to 15 in a sample of 82 African American adolescents' beliefs about parental authority, were documented. In the present study, the sample included 568 Chilean adolescents. Because adolescents ranged in age from early to middle adolescence at Wave 1 of this study, differences in belief trajectories from early to middle and from middle to late adolescence could be compared. Based on prior research, it was hypothesized that normative declines would be most rapid in the personal and multidimensional domains. Because previous research has suggested that a normative shift in parental authority occurs during the pubertal transition, it was further hypothesized that the decline in endorsement of parental authority would be more marked in the transition from early to middle adolescence than during later periods (Smetana, 1996).

Questions 4 and 5 focus on individual differences and changes in adolescents' beliefs about the legitimacy of parental authority and their own obligation to obey as a function of initial parental support and monitoring and initial adolescent problem behavior. The former question focuses on overall differences in adolescents' beliefs across ages (Which adolescents are most likely to believe that parents have legitimate authority and that they are obliged to obey?). Although research has consistently shown that monitoring and support are associated with more positive development outcomes (Steinberg & Silk, 2002), the underlying processes linking parent attributes and adolescent outcomes have been studied less frequently, and until recently, the empirical literature has neglected the adolescent as an active participant in the processes. It was hypothesized that adolescents who see their parents as supportive and expressing interest in their adolescents' lives through monitoring will be more likely to believe that parents have legitimate authority and themselves as obliged to obey (Darling & Steinberg, 1993) and that adolescents who are relatively more involved in problem behavior will be less likely to do so (Jessor & Jessor, 1977; Kerr et al., 1999; Moffitt, 1993; Nucci et al., 1991).

Question 5 focuses on individual differences in the trajectories of adolescents' beliefs over time. It is possible that children come into adolescence with different beliefs about parental authority and that these relative differences remain stable over time. For example, adolescents who see their parents as supportive may also see them as more legitimate, but the decline in legitimacy endorsement over time may be parallel for adolescents with supportive and less supportive parents. Alternatively, seeing parents as supportive may slow the rate at which adolescents' belief in the legitimacy of parental authority declines. These two models of change have very different implications for understanding the association of parenting and adolescents' characteristics with individual differences in adolescents' legitimacy beliefs.

The Chilean family context

Chilean adolescents' relations with their parents have not been studied extensively. Chilean culture has been changing rapidly due to urbanization and outside-media influences from Europe, the United States, and other Latin American countries (Instituto Nacional de la Juventud, 1999). In addition, Chile is in the midst of a profound cultural shift resulting from the fall of the military dictatorship and the reinstitution of democracy in 1990. Political changes, combined with rapid economic development, have resulted in a sharp rejection of authoritarian values and liberalization of social and sexual norms (Martínez, Cumsille, & Thibaut, 2006). Reflecting these changes, contemporary Chilean parents appear to be relatively uncomfortable with direct assertion of control and rule enforcement and report that they are less authoritarian and less likely to use power-assertive parenting techniques than did their own parents (Martínez et al., 2006). For example, parents reported discussing areas of parent–adolescent disagreement but leaving the decision to adolescents 78% of the time, letting the adolescent do as they wanted 11% of the time, and enforcing rules only 11% of the time (Darling et al., 2007). Chilean youth appear to share this discomfort with parental control. Chilean youth are less likely than Filipino or U.S. youth to (a) believe that their parents have the right to govern their behavior (particularly with regard to prudential areas, such as alcohol use or curfew), (b) believe that they are obliged to obey parents when they disagree, or (c) agree with parents (Darling et al., 2005). More than 85% of Chilean youth think of themselves as different from the adult generation both in how they think and in how they act (Martínez et al., 2006). Across all social classes, younger Chileans espouse more individualistic values than older cohorts, although the society remains highly family oriented (Programa de Naciones Unidas para el Desarollo, 2002). Taken together, these findings suggest that family relations in contemporary Chile are typically close but that both parents and adolescents tend to expect less direct assertion of parental control and less strict adolescent obedience than might be typical in the contemporary United States.

Although Chile remains a socially conservative country in many ways (e.g., divorce was only legalized in the country in 2005), political and social changes in Chile have been accompanied by problems usually associated with urban youth in Western countries, including relatively high rates of alcohol use (the legal drinking age is 18), substance use, vandalism, and petty theft (Darling et al., 2007; Martínez et al., 2006). In a nationally representative sample, 83% of Chilean youth reported onset of sexual intercourse prior to age 20, 15% reporting onset prior to age 15, and 24% of 15- to 19-year-olds reported that their last sexual encounter was in a casual relationship rather than with a boyfriend, girlfriend, or fiancé (Instituto Nacional de la Juventud, 1999). Despite these changes, adolescents tend to hold fairly traditional ideas about gender roles within the family. These beliefs about the division of parental responsibilities may reflect the fact that fewer Chilean women participate in the paid labor force than in any other South American country (39%; Martínez et al., 2006).

Method

Participants and procedure

The sample included 568 sixth to ninth graders recruited to participate in a longitudinal study of parenting, adolescent risk, and resilience (mean Wave 1 age = 12.95 years, SD = 0.99, range = 11–14 years), each of whom had participated in at least two waves of the 4-year study. Participants were recruited from seven schools from two counties in Santiago, Chile (92% of 14- to 17-year-old Chileans are enrolled in school; Martínez et al., 2006). Schools are typically organized from Grades 1 to 8 and from Grades 9 to 12; therefore, sixth and seventh graders experienced a transition from primary to secondary school during the study's duration. Schools were selected to represent the diversity of socioeconomic status (SES) observed in the Chilean educational system and included two private, one subsidized private, and four public schools, thus oversampling for lower SES students. Fifty-six percent of the sample were female. Seventy-four percent of the adolescents lived with both biological parents at the time of the first assessment.

Public schools were contacted through the board of education of each county. Private schools were contacted directly. Consistent with Chilean regulations and research practices, active adolescent assent and passive parental consent were used. After mailing descriptions of the study home to parents, students were given oral and written information about the study's purpose and procedure, invited to sign written consent forms, and completed questionnaires within their classrooms. Consent procedures and survey administration were carried out by upper-level psychology students trained by the researchers. Participants received a candy bar as a thank you for their participation. During each wave of the study, fewer than 2% of students declined to participate or had permission withheld by parents. Subsequent survey administrations took place approximately 1 year apart. Because of budgetary limitations, follow-up data collection for each wave was limited to only a randomly selected subset of the original sample. During follow-up, classrooms within schools and then individuals within classrooms were selected at random. In addition, because student contact and data collection were entirely school based, somewhat less than 5% of total data loss occurred due to absences or because students changed or left school during the course of the study. For these analyses, data are included for all individuals who participated in at least two waves of data collection, including both Wave 1 and Wave 2, when predictor variables (parental monitoring and support and substance use) were measured. Thirty-three percent of students provided data for 2 years of the study, 44% for 3 years, and 23% for 4 years. Years of participation did not vary by age, family type, adolescent problem behavior, or parental support or monitoring (p > .05).

Adolescents provided information on demographic background, attitudes toward school and civic involvement, activities, self-esteem, problem behavior, parenting practices, and risk and protective factors. In addition, adolescents each completed a Strategic Disclosure Questionnaire (Darling et al., 2007), with adolescents answering six questions about each of 20 different issues. Issues were selected to represent areas that are frequent sources of parent–adolescent disagreement and were identified through review of the extant literature and focus groups. Questionnaires were developed jointly by native American English and Chilean speakers, with the translation of individual items discussed and reviewed by bilingual, native Chilean speakers. Cultural appropriateness of stems and questions were validated in a separate pilot study involving more than 200 Chilean adolescents. Measures are described here in English.

Measures

LEGITIMACY OF PARENTAL AUTHORITY AND OBLIGATION TO OBEY

To assess adolescents' legitimacy beliefs, adolescents were asked, "Is it okay for your parents to set rules about this issue?" for each of the 20 issues on the Strategic Disclosure Questionnaire ($0 = no$, $1 = yes$). Obligation to obey was assessed by asking adolescents "If you disagree with your parents, do you have to obey?" ($0 = no$, $1 = yes$). Across issues and wave of data collection, adolescents reported that they believed that parents had the right to set rules for 57.7% of issues and that they were obliged to obey for 59.9% of issues. As expected, adolescents' beliefs about legitimacy and obligation to obey were related, although not identical. If an adolescent endorsed parental legitimacy for a given issue, they also endorsed their own obligation to obey 83.7% of the time. If adolescents did not endorse legitimacy for an issue, they reported that they were obliged to obey only 27.7% of the time.

Between-person predictors

PARENTAL MONITORING

At Wave 1, adolescents reported on the extent to which their mothers and fathers tried to know (a) who their friends were, (b) what they did after school, (c) what they did in the evenings, (d) what they did with their free time, (e) how they spent their money, and (f) how they were doing in school. Adolescents responded on a 1–3 scale, with 3 indicating *parents tried a lot* and 1 indicating *parents did not try*. A mean score was calculated (mother $\alpha = .80$, father $\alpha = .86$), and the maximum of either mother or father monitoring was used as an indicator of parental monitoring ($M = 2.47$, $SD = 0.49$). The decision to use the maximum of mother or father score rather than a mean was made because the normative difference in ratings of maternal and paternal monitoring and the amount of missing father data resulted in an artificial inflation of monitoring scores for those who reported on only one parent.

PARENTAL SUPPORT

Because parental support was not measured at Wave 1, a Wave 2 assessment was used. Using a 5-point scale, adolescents reported on the extent to which they agreed with four items describing each of their parents (sample items: "My mother/father likes to spend time just talking with me" and "I can count on my mother/father to help me with my problems"; mother $\alpha = .80$, father $\alpha = .83$). Items were recoded such that high scores indicated high support. Mean scores were calculated for each parent. The maximum of mother or father score was used as an indicator of parental support ($M = 4.36$, $SD = 0.79$) to reduce artificial bias favoring adolescents who reported on only one parent.

PROBLEM BEHAVIOR

At Wave 1, adolescents reported on how frequently they had engaged in five problem behaviors from *never in my life* (1) to *more than once in the last month* (5). Sample items included damaged public or private property, taken something from a store without paying for it, been in a fist fight, brought a weapon to school, or been in a fight that resulted in an injury in which someone needed to be seen by a doctor or nurse ($M = 1.31$, $SD = 0.59$). (Substance use was excluded because of normative age differences in use.)

Within-person predictors

TIME

Time was coded from 0 to 3, with 0 indicating *baseline assessment* and 3 indicating *Wave 4 of the study*.

DOMAIN

Because issues in this study were chosen to reflect common sources of parent–adolescent disagreement, rather than a specific theoretical model, issue domain membership was empirically derived from factor analysis of adolescents' ratings of parental legitimacy using a separate sample (Darling et al., 2005). Each issue was classified into one of five domains: personal (choice of friends, what you wear, use of free time, extracurricular activities, use of money), prudential (smoking, alcohol, and drug use), parent expectations (time on the telephone, homework, school performance), opposite-sex relations ("Your relationships with the opposite sex [phone calls, going to dances or out with mixed sex groups, dating]" and "Your relationship with your boyfriend or girlfriend [time you spend together, privacy you are allowed, how serious you are, your sexual relationship]"), and multidomain (type of video viewed, spending time with people parents do not like, unsupervised time with friends, where you go with friends, hanging out after school and after dinner, curfew). Empirical classification differs from prior theoretical research on domains primarily in the separation of the opposite-sex relations and personal domains. Issues classified here in the opposite-sex relations domain are quite similar to those classified as multifaceted in stimulus material currently used by Smetana (e.g., Smetana et al., 2006).

Analytic strategy

A series of analyses was undertaken predicting (a) change in adolescents' beliefs as a function of age and time, (b) change in adolescents' beliefs as a function of age and time run separately by domain, and (c) individual differences in adolescents' beliefs as a function of age, time, parenting, and adolescent problem behavior. Analysis of these data was complicated by the nonindependence of each participant's assessment of 20 issues for up to four waves of data collection, which violates the assumptions of techniques such as multiple regression, and thus artificially inflates error terms. In this study, data were available from 568 adolescents reporting on 22,589 issues over the four waves. Hierarchical general linear modeling (HGLM) was specifically designed to adjust the degrees of freedom in the model to compensate for nonindependence of observations (Raudenbush & Bryk, 2002). In these analyses, HGLM was used to parse variance in adolescents' beliefs into a participant component (differences between different adolescents' beliefs predicted from adolescents' age and gender, parental monitoring, parental support, and adolescent problem behaviors) and a within-adolescent issues component (differences in beliefs with regard to specific issues predicted from domain membership and time). Because of its structure, all within-person HGLM analyses effectively control for between-person differences. In these analyses, therefore, analyses predicting within-person differences in legitimacy beliefs and obligation to obey from time and domain controlled for between-person differences in gender, age, and initial perceived parental support and monitoring and adolescent problem behavior. All HGLM

analyses were performed using the Bernoulli procedure with logit link for dichotomous outcomes, such that predictors discriminate between two dichotomous choices. Because Level 1 variance is heterogeneous in Bernoulli logit-link analyses (Snijders & Bosker, 1999), the percentage of variance attributed to each level and explained by each model was not calculated. Unit-specific models are reported.

Results

Legitimacy of parental authority and obligation to obey as a function of age, time, and domain

A series of two-level (issue within adolescent) HGLM Bernoulli logit-link analyses were used to test the hypotheses that (a) older adolescents would be less likely to endorse the legitimacy of parental authority and (b) belief in the legitimacy of parental authority would decrease over time. In these analyses, Wave 1 age was used to predict between-adolescent differences in adolescents' beliefs about legitimacy. Time (Years 0, 1, 2, 3) was used to predict within-adolescent differences in beliefs. The interaction between Wave 1 age and time tested the hypothesis that the time-related decline in likelihood is steeper for younger adolescents than for older adolescents. Analyses were first run for all issues and then run separately by domain. A series of three-level HGLM models (issue within domain within person) were used to test for domain difference in the intercepts, age, and time model coefficients (Level 1 $df = 22589$, Level 2 $df = 2752$, Level 3 $df = 550$). In preliminary analyses, a curvilinear time function (time^2) was also added to the models, with mixed results. Based on the recommendations of Raudenbush and Bryk (2002) regarding the fitting of longitudinal models with a small number of measurement points and the significant interaction of initial age and time of measurement, the decision was made to use the more parsimonious linear model for the final analyses. Curvilinear results are very similar to those presented here and are available from the first author.

The predicted probabilities of endorsing parental legitimacy and obligation to obey for all items are graphed in Figure 11.1. In this figure, separate cohorts are indicated by different lines (i.e., adolescents in the

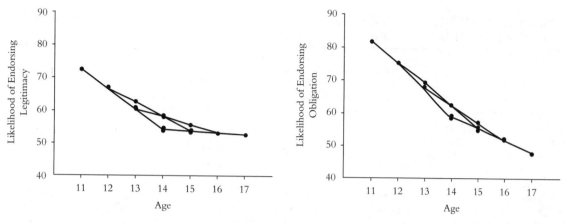

Figure 11.1 Predicted likelihood of endorsing parental legitimacy and obligation to obey by age. *Note.* Separate lines indicate adolescents who began the study at different ages.

study from ages 11 to 14, 12 to 15, 13 to 16, and 14 to 17). The likelihood of endorsing parental legitimacy and the obligation to obey decreased with both initial age and time ($ps \leq .000$). Adolescents who entered the study at an older age were less likely to endorse parental legitimacy or their own obligation to obey. Predicting within-person change, endorsement decreased with time. The interactions between both legitimacy and obligation to obey with Wave 1 age were significant ($ps \leq .000$), such that the within-person decrease in legitimacy over time was greater for those adolescents who had started the study at a younger age.

Results of both the two- and three-level HGLM models calculated separately by domain are reported in Table 11.7. The likelihood that adolescents would endorse parental authority varied by domain ($p \leq .01$), with adolescents most likely to endorse parental authority in the prudential domain and least likely to endorse parental authority in the personal domain. In all domains, adolescents who were youngest at Wave 1 were most likely to endorse parental authority ($p \leq .05$). Within adolescents, the likelihood of endorsing parental authority declined with time ($p \leq .05$). The difference in endorsement of legitimacy between older and younger adolescents was largest in the prudential domain and smallest for multidomain issues. The within-adolescent decline in legitimacy with time was also steepest in the prudential domain and shallowest for multidomain issues. In the personal

domain only, the decline in endorsement of legitimacy was steeper for younger adolescents than for older adolescents ($p \leq .01$).

Identical analyses were carried out predicting between- and within-adolescent differences in the likelihood that adolescents believed that they were obliged to obey parents in case of disagreement. Results of the analyses predicting obligation to obey paralleled those predicting legitimacy of parental authority (Table 11.7, bottom). Adolescents were most likely to endorse their own obligation to obey for issues in the prudential domain and least likely to endorse these beliefs in the personal domain ($p \leq .001$). In all domains, younger adolescents were more likely to believe that they were obliged to obey parents than were older adolescents ($p \leq .05$), although the age-related differences varied by domain. Interestingly, although adolescents were least likely to feel obliged to obey in the personal domain, this domain also showed a relatively large age-related difference in endorsement of parental legitimacy. Predicting within-adolescent change, the likelihood that adolescents believed that they were obliged to obey declined with time in all domains ($p \leq .001$). For personal and multidomain issues, endorsement of obligation to obey declined more steeply for younger adolescents than for older adolescents ($p \leq .01$).

Together, these analyses confirm previously reported differences in adolescents' beliefs about the legitimacy

Table 11.7   Results of HGLM analyses predicting adolescents' beliefs that issues are within the legitimate domain of parental authority and that they are obliged to obey from age, time, and domain

		Domain			
	Personal	Opposite-sex relations	Prudential	Expectations	Multidomain
		Legitimacy			
Between person					
Intercept	−0.42***$_a$	0.24**$_b$	2.06***$_c$	1.26***$_d$	0.59***$_e$
Wave 1 Age	−0.32***$_{ac}$	−0.21*$_{ab}$	−0.43***$_c$	−0.33***$_{ac}$	−0.22***$_b$
Within person					
Time	−0.16***$_{ac}$	−0.19***$_{ac}$	−0.27***$_c$	−0.11*$_{ab}$	−0.06*$_b$
Time × Wave 1 Age	0.09**	0.09	0.10	0.09	0.10
		Obligation to obey			
Between person					
Intercept	0.15*$_a$	0.49***$_b$	1.93***$_c$	1.35***$_d$	0.89***$_e$
Wave 1 Age	−0.51***$_{ac}$	−0.34***$_b$	−0.54***$_a$	−0.19*$_{bc}$	−0.32**$_b$
Within person					
Time	−0.37***$_a$	−0.26***$_{bd}$	−0.40***$_{ab}$	−0.17***$_{cd}$	−0.15***$_c$
Time × Wave 1 Age	0.13***	0.08	0.05	−0.06	0.08**
		Two-level model approximate df			
Between person	559	558	557	559	559
Within person	7217	2844	2844	2887	7175

Note. Positive coefficients indicate greater likelihood of endorsing legitimacy and obligation to obey. Results of the three-level HGLM analyses comparing the coefficients of models of different domains are summarized in the subscript. Within rows, coefficients that share lowercase subscripts are not significantly different from one another ($p > .05$). HGLM = hierarchical general linear modeling. *$p \leq .05$. **$p \leq .01$. ***$p < .001$.

of parental authority and their own obligation to obey. Cross-sectional age differences were replicated by within-person declines in endorsements with time. Overall, the decline in the likelihood that adolescents would endorse the legitimacy of parental authority and their own obligation to obey was steeper for younger adolescents than for older adolescents. However, this interaction was only statistically significant in the personal domain and, for obligation to obey, for multidomain issues.

Individual differences in adolescents' beliefs as a function of parents' and adolescents' characteristics

A series of two-level (issue within adolescent) HGLM Bernoulli logit-link analyses were conducted to examine the hypotheses that (a) adolescents who initially described their parents as relatively supportive and high in monitoring would be more likely to grant parents legitimacy and feel that they were obliged to obey over the course of the study and (b) adolescents who were involved in relatively high initial rates of problem behaviors would be less likely to do so. As in the previous analyses, analyses were first conducted for all items and then run separately by domain. Between-adolescent differences in adolescents' beliefs were predicted from parental support, parental monitoring, and problem behavior, controlling for initial age and gender. As in the previous analyses, within-adolescent differences were predicted by time. We also tested hypotheses that the decline in endorsement over time would be smaller for older adolescents and for adolescents whose parents were relatively

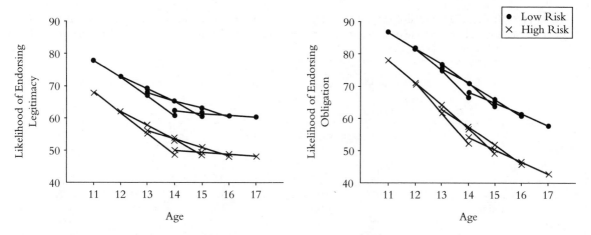

Figure 11.2   Predicted likelihood of endorsing parental legitimacy and obligation to obey by age. Trajectories of adolescents who are low in parental monitoring and warmth and high in problem behavior (high risk) and adolescents who are high in monitoring and warmth and low in problem behavior (low risk).
Note. Separate lines indicate adolescents who began the study at different ages.

supportive and high in monitoring, and steeper for adolescents who were initially more involved in problem behavior. In these analyses, variables predicting between-adolescent differences in legitimacy beliefs were centered around the grand mean. Time was entered uncentered, with 0 representing the first wave of data collection. Because previous research indicated that beliefs about parental legitimacy varied by parents' marital status and SES (i.e., Nucci, Camino, et al., 1996; Smetana, 2000; Smetana, Yau, Restrepo, & Braeges, 1991), preliminary analyses were undertaken in which parents' marital status and education were used as predictors. The variables neither predicted adolescents' beliefs nor moderated the association of age or time with beliefs in this sample, and these variables were dropped from subsequent analyses.

Results of the combined model are illustrated in Figure 11.2. Differences in the predicted likelihood of endorsing legitimacy and obligation are plotted for adolescents who were high in problem behavior and whose parents were low in perceived warmth and monitoring (high risk) and for a comparison group of adolescents who were low in problem behavior and whose parents were high in perceived warmth and monitoring (low risk). High and low problem behavior, warmth, and monitoring were defined by the 25th and 75th percentile. In this figure, separate cohorts are

indicated by different lines. In the combined model, younger adolescents were more likely to grant parents legitimate authority than were older adolescents and, looking within adolescents, grew less likely to do so with time ($ps \leq .001$). As in the previous analyses, the decline in endorsement of parental authority was steeper for younger adolescents than for older adolescents ($ps \leq .001$). Both higher initial monitoring and support were associated with greater likelihood of endorsing parental legitimacy ($p \leq .005$) and obligation to obey ($p \leq .05$) over the course of the study. Adolescents who initially reported higher rates of problem behavior were less likely to endorse parental legitimacy or obligation to obey ($p \leq .001$). The decline in endorsement with time did not vary by initial perceived monitoring or warmth ($p > .09$). The decline in adolescents' endorsement of the legitimacy of parental authority (but not obligation to obey) was less steep for those initially high in problem behavior ($p = .005$).

Results of the two-level HGLM models calculated separately by domain are reported in Table 11.8. In all domains, younger adolescents were more likely to grant parents legitimate authority than were older adolescents and, looking within adolescents, grew less likely to do so with time ($p \leq .01$). For personal and multidomain issues, the decline in likelihood of

Table 11.8   Results of HGLM analyses predicting adolescents' beliefs that issues are within the legitimate domain of parental authority and that they are obligated to obey parents from sex, and Wave 1 age, parental monitoring, parental support, and adolescent problem behavior

			Domain		
	Personal	Opposite-sex relations	Prudential	Expectations	Multidomain
Legitimacy of parental authority					
Between person					
Intercept	−0.42	0.25	2.10	1.29	0.62
Sex	0.23★	−0.70★★	0.24	0.37★★	−0.18
Wave 1 Age	−0.30★★	−0.21★★	−0.42★★	−0.33★★	−0.22★★
Parental Monitoring	0.25	0.15	0.16	0.48★★	0.36★★
Support	0.18★	0.18	0.24★	0.10	0.30★★
Problem Behavior	−0.37★★	−0.34★	−0.47★★	−0.17	−0.47★★
Within person					
Time	−0.16★★	−0.19★★	−0.28★★	−0.12★★	−0.07★★
Time × Wave 1 Age	0.09★★	0.09	0.10	0.09	0.10★★
Time × Monitoring	0.03	0.03	0.06	−0.27★★	−0.06
Time × Support	0.00	−0.05	−0.01	0.04	−0.06
Time × Problem Behavior	0.02	0.03	0.04	0.14	0.15★★
Obligation to obey					
Between person					
Intercept	0.15	0.52	1.99	1.37	0.90
Sex	0.20	−0.68★★★	0.33★	0.41★★	−0.25★
Wave 1 Age	−0.49★★★	−0.35★★★	−0.54★★★	−0.18★	−0.32★★★
Parental Monitoring	0.22	0.25	0.45★	0.41★	0.29★
Support	0.13	0.26★	0.20	0.07	0.16★
Problem Behavior	−0.45★★★	−0.63★★★	−0.83★★★	−0.33★	−0.61★★★
Within person					
Time	−0.37★★★	−0.28★	−0.42★	−0.19★★★	−0.16★★★
Time × Wave 1 Age	0.13★★★	0.09	0.06	−0.06	0.09★★
Time × Monitoring	−0.02	−0.07	−0.08	−0.19	−0.06
Time × Support	−0.02	−0.06	−0.06	0.07	−0.01
Time × Problem Behavior	−0.03	0.02	0.06	0.10	0.02

Note. Positive coefficients indicate greater likelihood of endorsing legitimacy. HGLM = hierarchical general linear modeling.
★$p \le .05$. ★★$p \le .01$. ★★★$p \le .001$.

endorsement with time was steeper among the younger adolescents than among the older adolescents ($p \le .01$). A similar trend was found for opposite-sex relations issues ($p = .055$). Boys were more likely to grant parents authority over issues in the personal and expectations domains but less likely than girls to grant parents authority over issues in the opposite-sex relations domain.

Although parenting predicted legitimacy beliefs in all domains except for opposite-sex relations, there was little evidence that perceived parents' characteristics moderated the decline in adolescents' legitimacy beliefs with time. Adolescents who described their parents as relatively supportive were more likely than their peers to believe that parents had legitimate authority over personal, prudential, and multidomain issues ($p \leq .05$). Adolescents who described their parents as relatively high in monitoring were more likely to believe that parents had legitimate authority over issues in the expectations domain and over multidomain issues ($p \leq .01$). Of the 10 interactions between parenting and time, only 1 was statistically significant. In the parent expectations domain only, the decline in the likelihood of endorsing parental legitimacy with time was steeper for adolescents who described their parents as high in monitoring than for their peers ($p \leq .01$). As hypothesized, adolescents who were initially more involved in problem behavior were less likely to endorse parental legitimacy for personal, opposite-sex relations, prudential, and multidomain issues ($p \leq .05$). For multidomain issues only, adolescents who were involved in problem behavior were less likely to endorse parental authority, but their beliefs declined less over time as well ($p \leq .01$), indicating a potential floor effect.

Results of the domain-specific analyses predicting adolescents' obligation to obey are reported in the bottom of Table 11.8. In all domains, younger adolescents were more likely to believe that they were obliged to obey parents in case of disagreement than were their older peers ($p \leq .001$). Within persons, adolescents grew less likely to feel obliged to obey with time ($p \leq .001$). For both personal and multidomain issues, the decline over time in likelihood of believing one was obliged to obey was steeper for younger adolescents than for older adolescents ($p \leq .001$). As hypothesized, in the opposite-sex relations, prudential, and expectations domains and for multidomain issues, adolescents who reported positive parenting were relatively more likely to feel obliged to obey than their peers. Greater likelihood of endorsing their own obligation to obey was predicted by higher parental monitoring for prudential, expectations, and multidomain issues ($p \leq .05$). Higher parental support was associated with greater likelihood of believing one was obliged to obey for opposite-sex relations and multidomain issues ($p \leq .05$). Adolescents' beliefs about personal issues were not predicted by perceived parenting. Contrary to our hypothesis, parenting did not moderate changes in adolescents' beliefs about their own obligation to obey over time. As hypothesized, adolescents who were initially more involved in problem behavior were less likely to believe that they

were obliged to obey parents in case of disagreement ($p \leq .05$). Contrary to our hypothesis, when examined by domain, initial problem behavior did not moderate change in beliefs over time.

Discussion

The purpose of this article was to examine normative change and individual differences in adolescents' beliefs about the legitimacy of parental authority and obligation to obey. These findings replicate and confirm prior cross-sectional (e.g., Darling et al., 2005; Nucci, Camino et al., 1996; Smetana, 1988; Yau & Smetana, 2003) and longitudinal (Smetana, 2000) research showing that as adolescents grow older, they are less likely to believe that issues are within the legitimate domain of parental authority and that they are obliged to obey parents in case of disagreement. This consistency with prior research reinforces interpretation of the contraction of adolescents' understandings of the legitimate domain of parental authority as a reflection of the development of adolescent autonomy, effectance, and agency that is consistent across cultures (e.g., Nucci, Killen, et al., 1996; Smetana et al., 2005). It is notable that these findings have now been replicated in cultures that are strict and parent centered (e.g., China; Yau & Smetana, 2003) as well as those that are relatively low in adolescents' endorsement of parental legitimacy and obligation to obey and in which parents are reluctant to exert control (e.g., Chile; Darling et al., 2005, 2007).

Overall, the sharpest decline in adolescents' endorsement of parental legitimacy and obligation to obey occurs during early adolescence in our sample, growing less steep as adolescents move from middle into later adolescence. Early adolescence is the period during which the gap between adolescents' and their parents' beliefs about legitimacy is largest (Smetana, Yau, & Hanson, 1991). Rapid change in adolescents' beliefs during this period may be one of many factors contributing to the realignment of power relations during the pubertal transition (Collins, 1992). Although adolescents' endorsement of parental legitimacy and their own obligation to obey declines for issues in all domains, the relatively steep decline during early adolescence is seen most clearly in the personal domain for parental legitimacy and for personal and multidomain issues with regard to obligation to obey. Six of the seven multidomain issues combine elements of the personal and prudential domains (e.g., "spending time with people your parents don't like" and "spending time with friends when no adults are around"). Prior work has shown that early adolescents broaden the number of issues they consider to be within the personal domain and that this change is largely responsible for the difference between the boundaries adolescents and parents set for legitimate authority (e.g., Smetana, Daddis, & Chuang, 2003). In particular, adolescents reason about issues that are conceptually defined as multidomain as if they were personal.

In addition to the biological and cognitive changes associated with the transition from early to middle adolescence, it is important to note that social transitions are also likely to contribute to changes in beliefs during this period. In Chile, the transition from early to middle adolescence is marked by a transition from primary to secondary school. Chilean youth also begin spending considerable time socializing with friends on weekends during early adolescence, particularly during the late evening and early morning hours. Although most socializing occurs in family homes (Martínez et al., 2006), adolescent gatherings become both less family centered and less supervised at this age. Spending times in these settings may thus provide an impetus for changing adolescents' beliefs about parental legitimacy and their own obligation to obey, particularly with regard to issues that have elements that are both personal and prudential. More detailed longitudinal analyses that focus on specific contextual and behavioral changes and their temporal relationship to changing legitimacy beliefs would shed additional light on the processes underlying normative change.

The present article extends previous research by focusing on how characteristics of both parents and adolescents predict individual differences in the trajectory of normative change in adolescents' beliefs over time. Adolescents who perceived their parents to be supportive and high in monitoring at the beginning of the study were more likely to endorse parental legitimacy and their own obligation to obey both

contemporaneously and in subsequent years. Specifically, adolescents who perceived their parents to be supportive were more likely to believe that parents had legitimate authority over personal, prudential, and multidomain issues. They were more likely to feel obliged to obey with regard to issues in the opposite-sex relations and multidomain domains. Adolescents who perceived their parents to be high in monitoring were more likely to endorse legitimacy and obligation to obey for issues in the parental expectations and multidomain domains and more likely to feel obliged to obey in the prudential domain as well.

The finding that good parenting predicts adolescents' beliefs about parental legitimacy highlights the interrelationship of parent and adolescent attributes that have been prominent in recent developmental research (Crouter & Head, 2002). Support and monitoring are two components of the constellation of parent attributes associated with the authoritative parenting style. The present findings and those linking adolescents' beliefs with adolescents' disclosure and obedience (Darling et al., 2007) are consistent with the hypothesis that adolescents' legitimacy beliefs are a central link between authoritative parenting and positive adolescent outcomes (Darling & Steinberg, 1993). Further, authoritative parents differ from their authoritarian and permissive peers in making clearer distinctions between personal issues and other domains when regulating adolescent behavior (Smetana, 1995). Parents who are authoritarian (high in behavioral control and intrusive psychological control but relatively low in support) are more likely to set rules in the personal domain, tending to reason about them in either moral or conventional terms. Recent research suggests that adolescents whose parents attempt to regulate issues adolescents define as personal report more internalizing symptoms (Hasebe et al., 2004) and see their parents as more psychologically controlling (Smetana & Daddis, 2002). Thus, adolescents who perceive their parents to be supportive and high in monitoring are more likely to believe parents to be legitimate authorities and to believe that they are obliged to obey them. Adolescents' beliefs predict self-reported adolescent obedience (Darling et al., 2007), voluntary disclosure of information, and perceived parental knowledge (Darling et al., 2006; Smetana et al., 2006). The latter two processes are associated with positive outcomes during adolescence (Crouter & Head, 2002). In addition, because adolescents who perceive their parents to be supportive or high in monitoring are also more likely to believe that parents are legitimate authorities, they are less likely to perceive parents as intruding into their personal jurisdiction.

Adolescent attributes are also important predictors of beliefs. Adolescents who were initially more involved in problem behavior were less likely to believe that parents had legitimate authority over issues in all domains and were less likely to believe that they were obliged to obey parents when they disagreed. These individual differences in problem behavior at the beginning of the study predicted differences in the endorsement of parental legitimacy and obligation to obey both contemporaneously and at each subsequent wave of data collection. Previous research had revealed a relatively small number of adolescents (16% during early and middle adolescence, 9% during late adolescence) who were unlikely to endorse parental authority over issues in the personal, prudential, or multidomain domains (Cumsille et al., 2006). The present findings suggest that relatively high involvement in problem behavior may be one correlate of rejection of parental authority—both as legitimate and as requiring obedience. This co-occurrence of involvement in problem behavior and rejection of authority is consistent with much of what is known of the etiology of chronic adolescent delinquency (e.g., Jessor & Jessor, 1977; Moffitt, 1993; Patterson et al., 1989) and research on adolescent substance users' belief that substance use is a matter of personal discretion (Nucci et al., 1991). It should be noted, however, that prior research on adolescents' attitudes toward authority and delinquency has focused on rebelliousness or rejection of authority as a global or personality characteristic. When examined at the issue level, however, there is evidence that the voluntary disclosure of adolescents who are involved in disapproved activities is more sensitive to their own beliefs about their obligation to obey and to parental rules than is that of their peers (Darling et al., 2007). Thus, although adolescents who are relatively more involved in problem behavior are less likely to endorse parental authority or obligation to obey, they may

nonetheless believe that parents are legitimate authorities in some areas and these beliefs have consequences. The direction of the causal relationship between involvement in problem behavior and adolescents' beliefs remains unclear.

This research is also unique in examining longitudinal changes in both legitimacy beliefs and beliefs in adolescents' obligation to obey. Research on normative change in adolescents' and parents' beliefs has primarily focused on beliefs about the legitimacy of parental authority. This is a natural extension of the theoretical underpinnings of social-cognitive domain theory and the processes leading to developmental change in parent–adolescent conflict (e.g., Smetana, 1999). More recently, however, researchers have begun to focus on individual differences in adolescents' beliefs and the consequences of individual differences for adolescent disclosure (Darling et al., 2006; Smetana et al., 2006) and obedience (Darling et al., 2007). Although legitimacy beliefs and beliefs in the obligation to obey are interrelated, they are not identical either conceptually or empirically. For example, U.S. adolescents who were interviewed about their reasoning about disobedience often described areas that parents can (or even should) try to control but which they do not feel obliged to obey (data available upon request). Romantic relations, where they go with friends, substance use, and other issues that combine facets of the prudential and the personal are often cited as examples of issues where adolescents acknowledge their parents' concerns but believe that their own judgment supersedes their obligation to obey. As researchers begin to try to understand the active role that adolescents play in their own development, in shaping parent–adolescent relationships, and in the socialization process, adolescents' beliefs and reasoning about their obligation to obey parents may emerge as a key concept.

Although adolescents whose perceptions of parents and problem behavior differ at the start of the study also differ in beliefs about legitimacy and obligation to obey, the developmental trajectories of their beliefs do not appear to. There is very limited evidence that change in beliefs over time varies with either initial perceptions of parenting or problem behavior. This suggests a model of normative change in adolescents' beliefs such that children enter adolescence differing in their likelihood of endorsing parental authority and obligation to obey and become decreasingly likely to do so as they move toward adulthood. In other words, all adolescents grow less likely to endorse parental authority as they get older, but some adolescents begin that decline believing that parents have the right to set rules about many areas of their lives, and others enter adolescence believing that their parents have a right to set rules about few. For example, the predicted likelihood of endorsing legitimacy by a 12-year-old adolescent who experiences low support and monitoring and is involved in problem behavior is roughly equivalent to the predicted likelihood of a 17-year-old adolescent uninvolved in problem behavior who experiences high support and monitoring. Investigation of the consequences of the premature assertion of personal jurisdiction over areas normatively defined as legitimately within parental control may offer a promising avenue for distinguishing between pseudo- and mature autonomy.

Should this work be replicated and extended, lack of variation in the decline in adolescents' beliefs in the legitimacy of parental authority and obligation to obey would be important in what it tells us about the developmental course of individual differences in adolescents' beliefs. In particular, a limited body of cross-sectional research has documented the association of family climate with individual differences in legitimacy beliefs during adolescence (e.g., Smetana et al., 2006). Cross-sectional research does not, however, allow insight into whether these differences reflect differences that existed in childhood and remained stable throughout adolescence, differences from childhood that grew larger or smaller over time, or differences that emerged only during adolescence. The present research suggests that differences in adolescents' beliefs about legitimacy and obligation to obey have already emerged prior to adolescence and remain stable, despite a normative decline. If so, the focus of future research into the sources of these differences should be on middle childhood and early adolescence rather than on the middle or the late adolescent periods.

The setting for this study, Chile, is somewhat atypical for a study of normative change and individual differences in adolescents' beliefs about parental legitimacy and their own obligation to obey. Because contemporary Chile is in the midst of a societal change perhaps analogous to that of the 1960s in the United States and Western Europe, the extent to which these findings will generalize to other social contexts or historical periods is unclear. For this reason, the consistency of these findings and previous research on normative changes in adolescents' legitimacy beliefs is reassuring. It should be noted that these findings differ from those previously reported in two ways, however. First, prior interview research conducted in Brazil (Nucci, Camino, et al., 1996) revealed social class differences in adolescents' reasoning about parental legitimacy that were not found in this Chilean sample. Although it is possible that this reflects a difference between Chilean and Brazilian society, it is perhaps more likely that these findings reflect methodological differences in how the focal constructs of the studies were assessed. In addition, the antiauthoritarian social climate of contemporary Chile may flatten social differences in adolescents' beliefs, making them more difficult to detect using survey methodology. This study also failed to replicate previously reported differences in adolescents' legitimacy beliefs as a function of family structure (e.g., Smetana, Yau, Restrepo, et al., 1991). It is important to note in this regard that recent changes in the divorce laws make marital status somewhat difficult to assess in Chile. Until 2005, legal divorce could only be obtained through the Catholic Church. It was thus very common for couples to separate and establish long-term relationships and households with new partners while remaining legally married to their first spouse. These cultural practices may muddy the distinction between marital statuses both in terms of measurement and in the way that adolescents think about marital status, thus contributing to our null findings.

The present study is limited in several respects, most importantly in that it relies solely on adolescents' self-reports, limiting causal inference. Although self-report may be the most accurate way to measure adolescents' beliefs and perceptions of parents, objective measures of parent behavior and adolescents' involvement in problem behavior would allow us to make clearer inferences. The scarcity of significant interactions between time and either perceived parenting or problem behavior, however, suggests that bias associated with concurrent reports of predictors and outcomes are minimized in these data. In addition, because HGLM controls for between-adolescent differences when modeling within-adolescent differences, reporter biases are also minimized at this level. These data are also limited by the dichotomous measurement of adolescents' beliefs about the legitimacy of parental authority and obligation to obey. Although this was a necessary compromise to facilitate gathering data in a large and varied sample, it might not fully reflect the complex beliefs that adolescents are likely to hold about parental authority. The consistency of these results with prior findings using in-depth interviews (e.g., Smetana, 1988) and surveys that allowed for multicategorical responses (e.g., Smetana & Chuang, 2001) are thus particularly reassuring. Finally, as is true of most longitudinal studies, self-selection bias is likely to have made this sample better functioning than the population of adolescents as a whole. However, this bias will tend to reduce variability in the measures, thus making our tests more conservative than they would be in a more representative sample.

Adolescence is a liminal period when youth are in the process of establishing autonomous self-regulation at the same time that many parents are still actively trying to regulate their behavior. During this period, parents may continue to monitor their adolescents and set rules for them, but the extent to which those efforts are successful depends upon the adolescents themselves. It is unlikely, for example, for adolescents to be offered drinks when their parents are standing next to them. Although adolescents' beliefs that parents can legitimately regulate their behavior and that they are obliged to obey parents' rules decline as they move toward adulthood, the starting point of that downward trajectory may partly depend upon their perception of parents and the success of socialization during childhood and early adolescence. The extent to which adolescents' beliefs about parental legitimacy and obligation to obey can be reestablished, once lost, is unclear. Individual differences in adolescents' beliefs about parental legitimacy and obligation to obey highlight the difference between rejection of parental oversight and the development of mature autonomy (Darling et al., 2005). Recent work on the central role adolescents play in the ability of parents to monitor effectively (Crouter & Head, 2002) has focused attention on the systemic nature of what have been called "parenting" processes and the active

role that adolescents play in them. These results suggest that adolescents' beliefs may be an important part of that system.

References

Barber, B. K., Stolz, H. E., & Olsen, J. A. (2005). Parental support, psychological control, and behavioral control: Assessing relevance across time, culture, and method. *Monographs of the Society for Research in Child Development*, 70(4).

Collins, W. A. (1992). Parents' cognitions and developmental changes in relationships during adolescence. In I. E. Sigel & A. V. McGillicuddy-DeLisi (Eds.), *Parental belief systems: The psychological consequences for children* (2nd ed., pp. 175–197). Hillsdale, NJ: Lawrence Erlbaum.

Crouter, A. C., Bumpus, M. F., Davis, K. D., & McHale, S. M. (2005). How do parents learn about adolescents' experiences? Implications for parental knowledge and adolescent risky behavior. *Child Development*, 76, 869–882.

Crouter, A. C., & Head, M. R. (2002). Parental monitoring and knowledge of children. In M. H. Bornstein (Ed.), *Handbook of parenting* (Vol. 3, pp. 461–484). Mahwah, NJ: Lawrence Erlbaum.

Cumsille, P., Darling, N., Flaherty, B. P., & Martínez, M. L. (2006). Chilean adolescents' beliefs about the legitimacy of parental authority: Individual and age-related differences. *International Journal of Behavioral Development*, 30, 97–106.

Cumsille, P., Darling, N., & Peña-Alampay, L. (2002, April). *Legitimacy beliefs and parent-adolescent conflict and adjustment in adolescence: A Chilean and Filipino comparison.* Poster session presented at the biennial meeting Society for Research on Adolescent Development, New Orleans, LA.

Darling, N., Cumsille, P., Caldwell, L. L., & Dowdy, B. (2006). Predictors of adolescents' disclosure strategies and perceptions of parental knowledge. *Journal of Youth and Adolescence*, 35, 667–678.

Darling, N., Cumsille, P., & Martínez, M. L. (2007). Adolescents as active agents in the socialization process: Legitimacy of parental authority and obligation to obey as predictors of obedience. *Journal of Adolescence*, 30, 297–311.

Darling, N., Cumsille, P., & Peña-Alampay, L. (2005, Summer). Rules, legitimacy of parental authority, and obligation to obey in Chile, the Philippines, and the United States. *New Directions for Child and Adolescent Development*, 108, 47–60.

Darling, N., & Steinberg, L. (1993). Parenting style as context An integrative model. *Psychological Bulletin, 113,* 487–496.

Fuligni, A. J. (1998). Authority, autonomy, and parent–adolescent conflict and cohesion: A study of adolescents from Mexican, Chinese, Filipino, and European backgrounds. *Developmental Psychology, 34,* 782–792.

Hasebe, Y., Nucci, L., & Nucci, M. S. (2004). Parental control of the personal domain and adolescent symptoms of psychopathology: A cross-national study in the United States and Japan. *Child Development, 75,* 815–828.

Instituto Nacional de la Juventud. (1999). *Familia y vida privada de los jóvenes (No. Análisis y difusión de la segunda encuesta nacional de juventud: Cuadernillo Tematico 4).* Santiago de Chile: Instituto Nacional de la Juventud.

Jessor, R., & Jessor, S. (1977). *Problem behavior and psychosocial development: A longitudinal study of youth.* New York: Academic Press.

Kerr, M., & Stattin, H. (2000). What parents know, how they know it, and several forms of adolescent adjustment: Further support for a reinterpretation of monitoring. *Developmental Psychology, 36,* 366–380.

Kerr, M., Stattin, H., & Trost, K. (1999). To know you is to trust you: Parents' trust is rooted in child disclosure of information. *Journal of Adolescence, 22,* 737–752.

Martínez, M. L., Cumsille, P., & Thibaut, C. (2006). Chile. In J. J. Arnett (Ed.), *International encyclopedia of adolescence* (Vol. 2, pp. 167–178). Oxford, England: Routledge.

Moffitt, T. E. (1993). Adolescent-limited and life-course-persistent antisocial behavior: A developmental taxonomy. *Psychological Review, 100,* 674–701.

Nucci, L. P., Camino, C., & Sapiro, C. M. (1996). Social class effects on northeastern Brazilian children's conceptions of areas of personal choice and social regulation. *Child Development, 67,* 1223–1242.

Nucci, L. P., Guerra, N., & Lee, J. (1991). Adolescent judgments of the personal, prudential, and normative aspects of drug usage. *Developmental Psychology, 27,* 841–848.

Nucci, L. P., Killen, M., & Smetana, J. G. (1996). Autonomy and the personal: Negotiation and social reciprocity in adult-child social exchanges. *New Directions for Child Development, 73,* 7–24.

Parke, R. D., & Buriel, R. (1998). Socialization in the family: Ethnic and ecological perspectives. In N. Eisenberg (Ed.), *Handbook of child psychology* (Vol. 3, pp. 463–546). New York: Wiley.

Patterson, G. R., DeBaryshe, B. D., & Ramsey, E. (1989). A developmental perspective on antisocial behavior. *American Psychologist, 44,* 329–335.

Pettit, G. S., Laird, R. D., Dodge, K A., Bates, J. E., & Criss, M. M. (2001). Antecedents and behavior-problem outcomes of parental monitoring and psychological control in early adolescence. *Child Development, 72,* 583–598.

Programa de Naciones Urtidas para el Desarollo. (2002). *Desarrollo humano en Chile: Nosotros los Chilenos: Un desafio cultural.* Retrieved May 17, 2006, from http://www.desarollohtmiano.cl/eleccion2002.htm

Raudenbush, S. W., & Bryk, A. S. (2002). *Hierarchical linear models: Applications and data analysis methods* (2nd ed.). Newbury Park, CA: Sage.

Smetana, J. G. (1988). Adolescents' and parents' conceptions of parental authority. *Child Development, 59,* 321–335.

Smetana, J. G. (1995). Parenting styles and conceptions of parental authority during adolescence. *Child Development, 66,* 299–316.

Smetana, J. G. (1996). Adolescent-parent conflict: Implications for adaptive and maladaptive development. In D. Cicchetti & S. L. Toth (Eds.), *Adolescence: Opportunities and challenges. Rochester symposium on developmental psychopathology* (Vol. 7, pp. 1–46). Rochester, NY: University of Rochester Press.

Smetana, J. G. (1997). Parenting and the development of social knowledge reconceptualized: A social domain analysis. In J. E. Grusec & L. Kuczynski (Eds.), *Parenting and children's internalization of values: A handbook of contemporary theory* (pp. 162–192). New York: Wiley.

Smetana, J. G. (1999). Context, conflict, and constraint in adolescent-parent authority relationships. In M. Killen & D. Hart (Eds.), *Morality in everyday life: Developmental perspectives* (pp. 225–255). New York: Cambridge University Press.

Smetana, J. G. (2000). Middle-class African American adolescents' and parents' conceptions of parental authority and parenting practices: A longitudinal investigation. *Child Development, 71,* 1672–1686.

Smetana, J. G. (2002). Culture, autonomy, and personal jurisdiction in adolescent-parent relationships. In R. V. R. Kail & Hayne W. (Eds.), *Advances in child development and behavior* (Vol. 29, pp. 51–87). San Diego, CA: Academic Press.

Smetana, J. G., & Chuang, S. (2001). Middle-class African American parents' conceptions of parenting in early adolescence. *Journal of Research on Adolescence, 11,* 177–198.

Smetana, J. G., Crean, H. F., & Campione-Barr, N. (2005, Summer). Adolescents' and parents changing conceptions of parental authority. *New Directions for Child and Adolescent Development, 108,* 31–46.

Smetana, J. G., & Daddis, C. (2002). Domain-specific antecedents of parental psychological control and monitoring: The role of parenting beliefs and practices. *Child Development, 73,* 563–580.

Smetana, J. G., Daddis, C., & Chuang, S. S. (2003). "Cleans your room!" A longitudinal investigation of adolescent–parent conflict and conflict resolution in middle-class African American families. *Journal of Adolescent Research, 18,* 631–650.

Smetana, J. G., Metzger, A., Gettman, D. C., & Campione-Barr, N. (2006). Disclosure and secrecy in adolescent-parent relationships. *Child Development,* 77, 201–217.

Smetana, J. G., Yau, J., & Hanson, S. (1991). Conflict resolution in families with adolescents. *Journal of Research on Adolescence,* 1, 189–206.

Smetana, J. G., Yau, J., Restrepo, A., & Braeges, J. L. (1991). Adolescent-parent conflict in married and divorced families. *Developmental Psychology,* 27, 1000–1010.

Snijders, T., & Bosker, R. (1999). *Multilevel analysis.* Thousand Oaks, CA: Sage.

Steinberg, L., & Silk, J. S. (2002). Parenting adolescents. In M. H. Bornstein (Ed.), *The handbook of parenting* (Vol. 1, pp. 133–134). Mahwah, NJ: Lawrence Erlbaum.

Steinberg, L., & Silverberg, S. (1986). The vicissitudes of autonomy in early adolescence. *Child Development,* 57, 841–851.

Thomas, A., & Chess, S. (1968). *Temperament and behavior disorders in children.* New York: New York University Press.

Turiel, E. (1983). *The development of social knowledge: Morality and convention.* Cambridge, England: Cambridge University Press.

Yau, J., & Smetana, J. (2003). Adolescent-parent conflict in Hong Kong and Shenzhen: A comparison of youth in two cultural contexts. *International Journal of Behavioral Development,* 27, 201–211.

Domain-Specific Antecedents of Parental Psychological Control and Monitoring: The Role of Parenting Beliefs and Practices

Judith G. Smetana and Christopher Daddis

Introduction

Increasingly, researchers have argued for the importance of disaggregating parenting typologies to better understand contextual variations in the effectiveness of different parenting attributes and the component processes that affect child and adolescent development (Barber, Bean, & Erickson, 2002; Barber & Harmon, 2002; Collins, Maccoby, Steinberg, Hetherington, & Bornstein, 2000; Darling & Steinberg, 1993; Grusec & Goodnow, 1994). For instance, based on early work by Schaefer (1965), recent research has demonstrated the importance of distinguishing between parental psychological and behavioral control (Barber, 1996; Barber & Harmon, 2002; Barber, Olsen, & Shagle, 1994; Steinberg, 1990). As described by Steinberg (1990) and more recently elaborated by Barber and colleagues (Barber, 1996; Barber & Harmon, 2002), psychological control refers to parents' attempts to control the child's activities in ways that negatively affect the child's psychological world and thereby undermine the child's psychological development. Psychological control, including parental intrusiveness, guilt induction, and love withdrawal, interferes with the child's ability to become independent and to develop a healthy sense of self and personal identity (Barber, 1996; Barber & Harmon, 2002). In contrast, behavioral control refers to the rules, regulations, and restrictions that parents have for their adolescent and their awareness of their adolescent's activities. Whereas psychological control is seen as inhibiting development through an excessive use of control, behavioral control is thought to facilitate development by providing the adolescent with necessary supervision and guidance.

Psychological control and monitoring

Psychological control and monitoring are seen as differing conceptually rather than as opposite ends of a single continuum ranging from excessive to insufficient control. In support of this proposition, research has demonstrated that high levels of psychological control predict internalizing problems, such as anxiety, depression, loneliness, and confusion, as well as externalizing problems (Barber, 1996; Pettit, Laird, Dodge, Bates, & Criss, 2001). In contrast, inadequate behavioral control has been found to predict externalizing problems such as drug use, truancy, and antisocial behavior (for a review of studies, see Barber & Harmon, 2002). Barber et al. (1994, p. 1122) have asserted that behavioral and psychological control differ in terms of "the domain over which control is exercised." This proposition has been examined primarily in terms of whether the two forms of control differentially predict child outcomes. As has been noted (Barber et al., 2002), there has been little research examining the parenting antecedents of psychological control and monitoring.

One notable exception is a longitudinal study by Pettit and colleagues (Pettit & Laird, 2002; Pettit et al., 2001) which extended from prekindergarten to early adolescence. They found that proactive parenting in early childhood predicted both mother- and adolescent-reported parental monitoring in early adolescence. In addition, child gender (being female), higher socioeconomic status (SES), and intact marital status significantly influenced mother-reported monitoring. Proactive parenting, as well as earlier reports of children's externalizing problems, predicted mother-reported psychological control in early adolescence, whereas early childhood reports of harsh parental discipline predicted early adolescents' ratings of parental psychological control. Subsequent analyses revealed that the effects of proactive parenting were moderated by childhood adjustment problems. Early proactive involvement predicted later psychological control only among children perceived to have low levels of childhood externalizing difficulties. In contrast, proactive parenting predicted greater monitoring only for children rated as higher in externalizing problems. Thus, monitoring was linked to a more anticipatory, proactive parenting style. Pettit and Laird (2002) speculated that mothers who are overly attentive in early childhood may have difficulty with the autonomy issues of early adolescence, which may lead them to use more psychological control.

This research provides methodologically rigorous and theoretically grounded evidence for different developmental pathways leading to parental monitoring and psychological control (as well as different antecedents for mothers and adolescents). The research, however, has not specifically examined associations between different conceptual domains of parenting beliefs and practices and behavioral and psychological control. In the present study, the influence of domain-specific beliefs about parental authority and parenting on psychological and behavioral control were examined in a sample of middle-class African American families. Domain-specific antecedents of monitoring and psychological control were examined for both mothers' and adolescents' reports.

Domain differences in psychological and behavioral control

Barber et al. (1994) have asserted that a fundamental principle of development is that children must acquire an understanding that social interactions are governed by rules and structures that must be recognized and followed to be competent members of society. Although these rules and structures have not been further defined, research from a domain model of social–cognitive development (Nucci, 2001; Smetana, 1995a; Tisak, 1995; Turiel, 1983, 1998) has defined two distinct types of social rules and behaviors. Morality pertains to acts that are prescriptively wrong because they have consequences for the rights or welfare of others. In contrast, social conventions are arbitrary, agreed-on behavioral norms that structure social interactions in different social settings (Turiel, 1983, 1998). Research has indicated that morality and social convention differ both conceptually and empirically (for reviews, see Smetana, 1995a; Tisak, 1995; Turiel, 1983, 1998), but both pertain to socially regulated acts that are proscribed for children and adults alike. Moreover, parents' early socialization attempts and rules pertain primarily to these issues (e.g., Gralinski & Kopp, 1993; Smetana, Kochanska, & Chuang, 2000). Consistent with this assertion, research has examined adolescents' and parents' judgments of legitimate parental authority, and has demonstrated that across ages, adolescents and their parents agree that parents should retain the legitimate authority to regulate family moral and conventional issues (Smetana, 1988, 2000; Smetana & Asquith, 1994) and that teachers and school principals should have the legitimate authority to regulate moral and conventional issues in school (Smetana & Bitz, 1996).

Barber et al. (1994) also have asserted that all children require an adequate degree of psychological autonomy for healthy psychosocial development and that through their social interactions, children must develop an understanding that they are effective, competent individuals with a clear sense of personal identity. Barber and colleagues (Barber, 1996; Barber & Harmon, 2002; Barber et al., 1994) have focused primarily on the style of social interactions that may undermine the healthy development of self, identity, and autonomy. They have not specified whether certain types of social interactions may lead children and adolescents to feel more psychologically controlled by their parents. In a theoretically complementary fashion, however, Nucci and colleagues (Nucci, 1996; Nucci & Lee, 1993; Nucci & Smetana, 1996) have asserted that the psychological need for autonomy, personal agency, and effectance may be satisfied when individuals define an arena of control over personal issues. Personal issues have been defined as comprising the private aspects of one's life and entailing issues of preference and choice pertaining to friends or activities, the state of one's body, and privacy. Asserting control over personal issues and making autonomous decisions is seen as an aspect of the self that forms the boundary between the self and the social world (Nucci, 2001; Nucci & Lee, 1993). Furthermore, it has been proposed that although the content and boundaries of the personal domain may be canalized by culture, all societies treat some issues as personal and up to the individual to decide (Nucci, 1996, 2001).

Research has indicated that adolescents and parents disagree over where to draw the boundaries of legitimate parental authority for adolescents, and has found that adolescents of varying ethnicities consistently define a broader range of issues as beyond the confines of legitimate parental authority and under adolescents' personal jurisdiction than do parents (Smetana, 1988, 2000; Smetana & Asquith, 1994). As demonstrated in both cross-sectional (Fuligni, 1998; Smetana, 1988; Smetana & Asquith, 1994; Smetana & Bitz, 1996) and longitudinal studies (Smetana, 2000), the boundaries of what adolescents consider to be within their personal domain increase as they get older. Parents' judgments of their legitimate authority likewise decrease as they grant adolescents more autonomy to decide personal issues, but parents' judgments consistently lag behind adolescents' views.

The findings from the research on parental authority (Smetana, 1988, 2000; Smetana & Asquith, 1994)

suggest that parents need to balance appropriate control over and regulation of their adolescents' behavior with developmentally appropriate attempts to grant them more autonomy over personal issues, particularly as they get older. Furthermore, research (Fuligni, 1998; Smetana, 1989; Smetana & Asquith, 1994) indicates that parents' attempts to control or infringe on what adolescents perceive as their personal domain lead to conflict in adolescent–parent relationships, thus suggesting that parents' control over personal issues and the extent to which adolescents view that control as legitimate may influence adolescents' feelings of psychological control. Adolescents may be less likely to perceive parents as being psychologically controlling when parents exert control over moral and conventional issues, because adolescents typically view these issues as legitimately regulated by parents throughout adolescence. Perceptions of psychological control may be heightened, however, when parents exercise control over personal issues, because adolescents may disagree with both the types of behaviors that are being controlled (and the resulting infringement on what is perceived as an arena of personal freedom) as well as the style in which control is exercised. In this regard, separate lines of investigation have revealed that overcontrol of the personal domain (Nucci, 1996, 2001), as well as excessive psychological control (Barber & Harmon, 2002; Barber et al., 1994), lead to disorders of the self.

This speculation about the domain-specific developmental origins of psychological control focuses on the stage-salient tasks of adolescence. Therefore, it seems unlikely that greater parental control and restriction of adolescents' personal domain would be associated with parent-reported psychological control. The hypothesis that adolescent- and parent-reported psychological control may have different antecedents is in line with findings from previous research (Pettit et al., 2001). Support of this hypothesis would partially explain the generally low to moderate associations that have been found between parents' and adolescents' reports of parenting (Cook & Goldstein, 1993; Gonzales, Cauce, & Mason, 1996), and, in particular, the very modest associations found between parent- and adolescent-reported psychological control (Pettit et al., 2001). Parent-reported psychological control may have its antecedents in social-ecological variables such as family background. For instance, after reviewing the available evidence, Hoff-Ginsberg and Tardif (1995) advocated disaggregating SES to better determine the components that influence different parenting beliefs and behaviors. They concluded that maternal education may be the most salient sociodemographic variable in determining mothers' parenting beliefs and practices.

Parents clearly monitor a wide range of behaviors, including interpersonal relationships, cultural norms and standards, whether adolescents do their homework, and where they go after school. It is unclear whether adolescents are more attuned to their parents' supervision when parents monitor some types of acts rather than others. Because adolescents may see issues such as doing homework and choosing friends as personal issues, parents' attempts to monitor these aspects of adolescents' behavior may be interpreted as psychologically intrusive and controlling, especially during adolescence (Pettit & Laird, 2002). Previous research, however, has shown that interpersonal (moral) violations—such as aggression and status offenses—and inappropriate (conventional) behaviors—such as acting out—when enacted in the extreme, are defined as externalizing behaviors, and externalizing behaviors have been associated with (lack of) behavioral control. In turn, this suggests that adolescents may perceive that they are monitored more when parents exert control over moral and conventional acts than when they monitor issues that adolescents may view as within their personal domain. Whereas domain-specific parenting beliefs and practices may influence adolescents' reports of parental monitoring, previous research (Pettit et al., 2001) indicates that monitoring is greater among families with females, intact families, and families higher in SES, perhaps because they have more psychological and other resources to monitor their children's behavior. These may be better predictors of parent-reported monitoring than domain-specific parenting beliefs and practices.

The present study

To test these hypotheses in the present study, we distinguished between issues that should be socially regulated, including moral and conventional issues, and a category that we referred to as ambiguously personal issues. These included issues that adolescents

and their parents agree are personal issues, as found in previous research (Smetana, 2000; Smetana & Asquith, 1994), as well as issues that are seen as personal by adolescents, but not necessarily by parents. The latter included multifaceted issues, which contain both conventional and personal components (e.g., keeping the bedroom clean or neat may be seen as a conventional issue of maintaining parental standards when the adolescent's bedroom is seen as part of the parents' house; whereas when the room is treated as part of the adolescent's territory, it may be viewed as an issue of personal choice, identity, or style). The category also included friendship issues, which contain overlapping personal, conventional, and psychological components (Smetana, 2000; Smetana & Asquith, 1994).

Socially regulated and ambiguously personal issues each were examined in terms of two dimensions: parenting beliefs and parenting practices. Parenting beliefs pertained to domain-specific beliefs (socially regulated and personal) regarding the legitimacy of parental authority. Parenting practices, which we referred to as ratings of restrictive parental control, were operationalized in terms of the extent to which parents have firm rules about social and personal acts (Smetana, 2000; Smetana & Asquith, 1994) and are parental unilateral in their family decision making about these issues (Lamborn, Dornbusch, & Steinberg, 1996). The present study examined whether adolescents' and mothers' domain-differentiated beliefs regarding legitimate parental authority and ratings of restrictive parental control differentially influenced psychological and behavioral control. Psychological control was assessed primarily in terms of the authoritarian, intrusive dimension and focused on a global assessment of this construct, as has been done by others (Barber & Harmon, 2002). Behavioral control was assessed in terms of parental monitoring. Recent research has indicated that parental monitoring is a multidimensional construct and that parental knowledge of adolescents' activities (primarily through child disclosure) is most closely associated with lower levels of problem behavior (Kerr & Stattin, 2000; Stattin & Kerr, 2000). In the present study, parental monitoring was assessed in terms of parents' knowledge of children's activities.

This study investigated whether psychological control and monitoring have different antecedents and whether these antecedents differ for adolescents and mothers. The distinctiveness of psychological and behavioral control was also tested by including ratings of parental monitoring in the analyses of psychological control and ratings of psychological control in the analyses of parental monitoring, as has been done by others (Barber et al., 1994; Pettit et al., 2001). Recently, Darling and Steinberg (1993) have proposed that global parenting styles influence domain-specific parenting practices, and psychological control has been treated as a proxy for authoritarian parenting (e.g., see Barber et al., 2002). Our model suggests, in contrast, that adolescents' perceptions of domain-specific parenting practices influence their more globally assessed perceptions of parenting (psychological control and monitoring).

It was expected that only perceptions of parenting in the hypothesized domain would significantly predict each form of control. More specifically, we hypothesized that controlling for adolescents' age, parents' (intact) marital status, and maternal education, adolescents who endorsed less legitimate parental authority over ambiguously personal acts and rated parents as more restrictive in their control of these acts would report higher levels of maternal psychological control. Adolescents' authority beliefs and ratings of restrictive parental control regarding socially regulated acts were not expected to significantly influence these ratings. The opposite predictions were made with regard to adolescents' perceptions of parental monitoring. Controlling for background variables, we hypothesized that adolescents who believed that parents have less legitimate authority over social acts and rated their parents as more restrictively controlling these acts would report more parental monitoring. In keeping with previous research (Pettit et al., 2001), parents' marital status or family sociodemographic background (assessed here in terms of maternal education) were not expected to affect adolescents' perceptions of either psychological control or monitoring. Previous research has indicated that parental psychological control is higher among boys than girls (Barber et al., 2002), whereas monitoring is greater among girls than boys (Barnes & Farrell, 1992); similar effects were expected in the present study. In addition, we examined whether child gender moderated the effects of domain-specific parenting beliefs and practices on monitoring and psychological control.

Consistent with Pettit et al. (2001), higher SES, intact family status, and child gender (being female) were expected to be associated with more mother-reported monitoring. In contrast, mothers' ratings of psychological control were expected to be associated with lower SES, as suggested by Hoff-Ginsberg and Tardif (1995). Mother-rated psychological control was also expected to be greater among families with males than with females, as has been found by others (Barber et al., 2002). Domain-differentiated beliefs about parental authority or ratings of restrictive parenting were not expected to be associated with either mother-rated monitoring or psychological control. As in the analyses for adolescents, we examined whether adolescents' gender moderated the effects of domain-specific beliefs and parenting practices on mother-reported monitoring and psychological control.

Data for this study came from a longitudinal study of adolescent-parent relationships in middle-income African American families, and these hypotheses were tested in both concurrent and longitudinal analyses. Although much of the previous research on psychological control has been conducted on European American families, there were several compelling reasons to examine these questions in a relatively homogeneous sample of African American families. First, numerous commentators have noted the need for more research on normative developmental processes among well-functioning minority families (Graham, 1992; McLoyd, 1998; Spencer & Dornbusch, 1990) and for more studies that focus specifically on within-group variation rather than cross-ethnic comparisons (Garcia Coll, Meyer, & Brillon, 1995; McLoyd, 1998). Much of the previous research on African American families has focused on families living in poverty (Garcia Coll et al., 1995; Hoff-Ginsberg & Tardif, 1995; Parke & Buriel, 1998), yet the findings typically have been compared with research employing more middle-class European American families. Therefore, the present study's focus on middle-income African American families addressed a lacunae in previous research, reduced the potential confounding of ethnicity and SES in studies of African American families, and enhanced the likelihood that the findings might be comparable with other samples typically used in this line of investigation. Moreover, psychological control has been reported to be greater among ethnic minority than among European American families (Barber et al., 2002), but the potentially confounding effects of SES have not been controlled.

Method

Participants

The original sample consisted of 95 African American families with early adolescents. The present analyses focused only on mothers and adolescents, and, therefore, 2 families were dropped because they were father headed; this resulted in a Time 1 sample of 93 families. Adolescents were, on average, 13.11 years old (SD = 1.29) and were nearly evenly divided by gender (46 males, 47 females). Attrition was 10% over the 2 years, resulting in a Time 2 sample of 85 families with middle adolescents (M = 15.05 years, SD = 1.28). Analyses indicated that the families who were lost to attrition did not differ significantly in sociodemographic background from participating families. At Time 2, the same 2 father-headed families were dropped, and 1 family was omitted due to incomplete data. Therefore, the longitudinal analyses were performed on 82 mother–adolescent pairs.

In all of the participating families, both parents were Black and nearly all (over 95%) were African American, with the remaining parents identifying themselves as of Caribbean, African, or Black and Hispanic origin. At Time 1, 66% (n = 61) of the mothers were married, with 54% in intact marriages (n = 50) and 12% (n = 11) in stepparent families. Three percent (n = 4) were cohabiting. Twenty-nine percent (n = 25) were single-parent families, with 20% (n = 19) divorced and 9% (n = 8) never married (data on marital status were missing for 1 family). Although fathers were included in the larger study, the number of single-parent, mother-headed households resulted in too small a sample of fathers to include in the present analyses.

Four percent of the families (all single parent) lived in multigenerational households. Mothers were, on average, 40.63 years of age (SD = 6.33 years) and had 14.86 years of formal education (SD = 2.27). Reported family income at Time 1 indicated that 29%

of the families had incomes between \$25,000 and \$40,000 a year, 31% had incomes between \$40,000 and \$70,000 a year, and 37% had incomes over \$70,000 a year. Family income was highly stable over time, $r(80)$ = .86, p < .001. The families resided in and around an upstate New York city.

Measures of behavioral and psychological control

PSYCHOLOGICAL CONTROL
Seven items employed by Dornbusch, Steinberg, and colleagues (Dornbusch et al., 1985; Steinberg, 1987), drawn from the Children's Report of Parents' Behavior Inventory (CRPBI; Schaefer, 1965), were administered to mothers and adolescents to assess psychological control. Responses were scored on a 3-point scale ranging from 1 (not like the parent) to 3 (a lot like the parent). Based on Knight and Hill's (1998) recommendations regarding the equivalence of scales for minority samples, the items were factor analyzed and all of these hypothesized items were found to load highly on this scale. Adolescents separately rated mothers and fathers for psychological control, but only adolescents' ratings of mothers were used in the present study. Adolescents' ratings of mothers and fathers were highly related, $r(82)$ = .66, p < .001, as were mothers' and fathers' ratings of their own psychological control in the subset of families with fathers present, $r(60)$ = .43, p < .001. Cronbach's αs were .76 for mothers' reports and .72 for adolescents' reports.

PARENTAL MONITORING
Parental monitoring was assessed using Dornbusch et al.'s (1985) and Steinberg, Mounts, Lamborn, and Dornbusch's (1991) 10-item Monitoring Scale. Again, based on Knight and Hill's recommendations (1998), a principal components analysis of the 10-item Monitoring Scale was conducted to determine whether the items represented a unidimensional construct. For both mother and adolescent reports, three different factors assessing communication, family rules, and monitoring/awareness emerged. Therefore, only the four items that loaded highly (.50 or greater) on the monitoring and awareness factor were selected for use in this study. These items assessed adolescents' and mothers' perceptions of

how well the parents were aware of the adolescent's activities and whereabouts. Responses were scored on a 5-point Likert scale, with higher scores indicating greater parental monitoring. Mean responses were obtained. Although only mothers' reports of monitoring were used here, mother- and father-rated monitoring were found to be highly related, $r(60) = .46, p < .001$, and did not differ significantly. Internal consistencies (Cronbach's αs) were .74 for mothers and .67 for adolescents.

Assessments of beliefs about parental authority and ratings of restrictive parenting

STIMULI FOR ASSESSMENTS

The same 19 stimulus items were used in the assessment of parental beliefs about authority and restrictive parenting. As reported in more detail elsewhere (Smetana, 2000), the definitions of the domains and the selection of items were based on previous theorizing and research (Nucci, 1996; Smetana, 1988, 1995a; Smetana & Asquith, 1994), as well as a focus group with a separate group of African American parents. The socially regulated items included a mix of moral (hitting [not getting along with] brothers and sisters, lying to parents, breaking a promise to parents) and conventional items (not doing assigned chores, talking back to parents, using bad manners, and cursing). The ambiguously personal items included personal items (sleeping late on weekends, choice of music, choosing own clothes, choosing own hairstyles, and choosing how to spend allowance money), multifaceted items (getting ears pierced with multiple holes, not cleaning bedroom, watching cable TV, and staying out late), and friendship items (staying over at a friend's house, seeing friends that parents do not like, seeing friends rather than going out with family, and when to start dating).

DOMAIN-SPECIFIC BELIEFS ABOUT PARENTAL AUTHORITY

Based on previous research (Smetana, 1995b, 2000; Smetana & Asquith, 1994), two questions were used to assess beliefs about parental authority. For each of the 19 stimulus items just described, respondents were asked "whether it is OK or not OK for parents to make a rule about_____" to assess the legitimacy of

parental authority, and "Do children have a duty or obligation to follow the rule about _____ if parents make a rule and the child doesn't agree with it?" to assess adolescents' rule obligation. Responses that indicated nonlegitimacy and rule nonobligation were each scored as 0, and responses that indicated legitimacy and rule obligation were scored as 1. For each act, responses to the two questions were summed, resulting in a 3-point scale ranging from 0 to 2, with higher scores indicating more legitimate authority.

To determine whether the conceptual separation between socially regulated and ambiguously personal issues was empirically warranted, principal components analyses with varimax rotation were run on adolescents' Time 1 (combined) legitimacy and obligation judgments for moral, conventional, personal, multifaceted, and friendship items. As expected, two factors with eigenvalues greater than 1.00 emerged. The first factor (eigenvalue = 2.30, 46% of the variance) included the two hypothesized socially regulated sets of issues: moral items (factor loading = .93) and conventional items (.94). As expected, the second factor (eigenvalue = 1.61, 32% of the variance) included personal (.86), multifaceted (.79), and friendship items (.76).

Similar analyses were performed on mothers' legitimacy and obligation judgments. Again, the results confirmed the hypothesized two-factor structure. The first factor (eigenvalue = 2.44, 49% of the variance) included personal (factor loading = .89), multifaceted (.70), and friendship items (.78); and the second factor (eigenvalue = 1.22, 24% of the variance) included moral (.82) and conventional items (.92).

Based on these analyses, responses regarding personal, multifaceted, and friendship items were summed to obtain a score for beliefs about parental authority over ambiguously personal issues. Likewise, responses regarding moral and conventional items were summed to obtain a score for socially regulated issues. Alphas for socially regulated and ambiguously personal acts were .90 and .86, respectively, for adolescents and .80 and .88 for mothers.

DOMAIN-SPECIFIC RATINGS OF RESTRICTIVE PARENTAL CONTROL

Based on previous research (Smetana & Asquith, 1994), and as described in more detail elsewhere (Smetana, 2000), participants rated the extent to which each of the

19 issues described previously was governed by rules in their family. Ratings were made on a 5-point scale ranging from 1 (no rules or expectations) to 5 (firm rules or explicit expectations). Then, using procedures developed by Dornbusch et al. (1985), adolescents and mothers rated the extent of parent-unilateral decision making for each issue on a 5-point scale ranging from 1 (child decides) to 5 (parent decides). For each issue, responses to the two questions were summed; scores could range from 2 to 10 for each item. Higher scores indicated more restrictive parenting practices (e.g., more rules and more parent-unilateral decision making).

Again, principal components analyses with varimax rotation were run on adolescents' (combined) judgments of rules and parent-unilateral decision making for moral, conventional personal, multifaceted, and friendship items. These analyses were run to examine whether the hypothesized socially regulated and ambiguously personal issues were empirically distinct. A two-factor solution was obtained. As expected, moral (.88) and conventional items (.79) loaded highly on the first factor (eigenvalue = 3.28, 55% of the variance); and personal (.85), multifaceted (.84), and friendship (.73) items loaded highly on the second factor (eigenvalue = 1.33, 19% of the variance).

In contrast to expectations, however, the principal components analysis of mothers' ratings of rules and parent-unilateral decision making for moral, conventional, personal, multifaceted, and friendship items revealed a single-factor solution (eigenvalue = 3.22, 64% of the variance), with all five sets of items loading on a single factor of restrictive parenting (moral = .75, conventional = .72, personal = .82, multifaceted = .88, and friendship = .83).

To obtain restrictive parenting scores for the two types of acts, adolescents' responses were summed separately for socially regulated and ambiguously personal acts; Cronbach's αs were .82 and .90, respectively. Based on the results of the principal component analysis, mothers' responses were treated as a single composite scale, which had an α of .89.

Procedures

Families were initially recruited through African American churches and African American social and professional organizations as part of a larger project on adolescent–parent relationships (for more detail, see Smetana & Gaines, 1999). Prospective families were identified through these settings, and their participation was solicited. Churches, as well as most of the other groups, did not keep detailed membership information; therefore, estimates of participation rates could not be obtained. Because the present study focused on middle-class families, family income (minimum of $25,000 a year as assessed in 1995) was employed as a criterion for participation.

At Time 1, all questionnaires were completed during a home visit (or in a smaller number of cases, a visit to the university) conducted by two African American interviewers. The research was briefly explained to the participants, and informed consent was obtained from adolescents and parents. Mothers and adolescents were administered the questionnaires in separate rooms. To ensure full comprehension, the interviewers read all questionnaire instructions to adolescents and were available to answer their questions.

Families were recontacted 2 years later and invited to participate again in the project. At Time 2, families were sent the same set of measures as part of a larger packet of questionnaires to complete; they were collected during a home (or university) visit. Incomplete questionnaires were finished at that time.

Results

First, bivariate correlations between adolescents' and mothers' ratings of psychological control and monitoring were examined. As shown in Table 11.9, adolescents' and mothers' reports of parental monitoring were significantly but moderately associated at Time 1, but not at Time 2. In contrast, adolescents' and mothers' ratings of mothers' psychological control were not significantly related at Time 1 and moderately and positively associated at Time 2. Mothers' ratings of monitoring and psychological control were moderately associated at Time 2, $r(81) = .26$, $p < .05$, but none of the other correlations between monitoring and psychological control were significant for either mothers or adolescents at Time 1 or Time 2. Finally, both adolescents' and mothers' ratings of parental monitoring and psychological control showed strong

Table 11.9 Correlations among adolescents' and mothers' ratings of psychological and behavioral control at Times 1 (T1) and 2 (T2)

	2	3	4	5	6	7	8
1. T1 adolescent monitoring	−.17	.32★★★	−.06	.44★★★	−.17	.45★	−.02
2. T1 adolescent psychological control		−.08	.27★	.16	.51★★★	.03	.32★★
3. T1 mother monitoring			−.12	.24★	−.12	.42★★★	−.01
4. T1 mother psychological control				−.07	.19⁺	−.19⁺	.63★★★
5. T2 adolescent monitoring					.06	.17	.02
6. T2 adolescent psychological control						−.05	.26★
7. T2 mother monitoring							.06
8. T2 mother psychological control							

Note. Ns = 93 at Time 1 and 82 at Time 2.
★$p < .05$. ★★$p < .01$. ★★★$p < .001$. ⁺$p < .10$.

and significant stability over time, with correlations ranging from .42 to .63.

Means, standard deviations, and bivariate correlations among the independent and dependent variables are shown in Table 11.10. Mothers' education was significantly and negatively associated with their ratings of psychological control at Time 1, but not at Time 2. At both Time 1 and Time 2, mothers' (but not adolescents') reports of parental monitoring were significantly and positively associated with intact family status and significantly and negatively associated with adolescents' age. There also was a significant, negative correlation between adolescents' age and their beliefs that parents have legitimate authority over ambiguously personal acts. Beliefs about parental authority over socially regulated and ambiguously personal acts were uncorrelated for adolescents, but were significantly associated for mothers, as were adolescents' ratings of restrictive parental control over social and personal acts.

Adolescents' perceptions of psychological control and monitoring

Hierarchical regressions were used to test the hypotheses with regard to the effects of domain-differentiated beliefs about parental authority and ratings of restrictive parenting on adolescents' perceptions of mothers' psychological control and monitoring. Adolescents' age (in years), gender (with boys coded as −1 and girls coded as 1), and parental marital status (with families with both natural parents coded as 1 and other families coded as −1) were entered in a block to control for their effects. Based on Hoff-Ginsberg and Tardif's (1995) conclusion that maternal education is the SES variable most closely associated with parenting, mothers' educational background (coded in number of years of formal education attained) was included in this block as a proxy for SES. Yearly family income was strongly and positively associated with mothers' education and intact family status, $rs(82) = .52, .40, ps < .001$.

Adolescents' Time 1 beliefs about legitimate parental authority of socially regulated and ambiguously personal acts and their ratings of restrictive control for the two types of acts were entered as a block in the second step of the analyses. Adolescents' Time 1 ratings of parental monitoring (in the analyses of psychological control) or psychological control (in the analyses of parental monitoring) were also entered in this step of the analyses to test for their distinctiveness in this sample. All variables were centered prior to analyses to reduce problems with multicollinearity (Aiken & West, 1991), and analyses were performed separately on adolescents' ratings of psychological control and monitoring at Time 1 and Time 2.

In addition, four variables that reflected the interaction terms for adolescents' gender and perceptions of domain-differentiated parenting beliefs and practices (e.g., the product of child gender and each parenting variable) were created and entered as a block in the third step to test for moderating effects. Across the four analyses, only 1 of the 16 possible interaction

Table 11.10 Correlations among independent and dependent variables

	M	SD	1	2	3	4	5	6	7	8	9	10	11	12	13
1. Teen gender (Female)	.51	.50	—	.02	.05	.10	.03	.09	-.05	-.01	—	.34**	.31**	-.05	-.17
2. Teen age	13.11	1.29	.02	—	-.11	-.08	.09	-.44***	.01	-.20+	—	-.19+	-.09	.13	.11
3. Intact marital status	.55	.50	.05	-.11	—	.27**	.07	.05	-.03	.08	—	.12	-.15	-.11	-.21+
4. Mother's education (yr)	14.86	2.27	.10	-.08	.27**	—	-.03	-.01	-.09	-.12	—	-.05	-.01	-.01	-.07
5. Beliefs—social	13.05/14.55	4.07/2.83	-.14	.10	.10	.18+	—	.20+	.10	-.04	—	.04	.02	-.12	-.07
6. Beliefs—personal	13.74/18.98	5.36/4.76	.07	-.02	.17	.07	.48***	—	.14	.40***	—	.50***	.16	-.24*	-.11
7. Adolescent control—social	53.46	8.55	—	—	—	—	—	—	—	.51***	—	.20+	.18	.13	.04
8. Adolescent control—personal	65.56	14.93	—	—	—	—	—	—	—	—	—	.31**	.17	.22*	.19+
9. Mother restrictive control	59.33	6.67	.00	.03	.00	-.10	.04	.23*	—	—	—	—	—	—	—
10. T1 monitoring	16.97/18.55	2.29/1.67	.05	-.29**	.27*	.18+	-.07	.11	—	—	.18+	—	.44***	-.17	-.17
11. T2 monitoring	16.73/18.06	1.14/1.41	.19+	-.28*	.23*	.13	.07	.14	—	—	.00	.42***	—	-.19+	-.09
12. T1 psychological control	14.03/13.16	3.13/2.68	.02	-.12	-.12	-.22*	.03	.12	—	—	.15	-.12	.16	—	.51***
13. T2 psychological control	13.72/13.00	2.88/2.62	.00	-.01	-.01	-.19	-.07	—	—	—	.31**	-.01	-.09	.65***	—

Note. Correlations above the diagonal are for adolescents; correlations below the diagonal are for mothers. Means and standard deviations for beliefs, monitoring, and psychological control are provided for adolescents/mothers, respectively. T1 = Time 1; T2 = Time 2.

*p < .05. **p < .01. ***p < .001. +p < .10.

Table 11.11 Regressions on adolescents' ratings of maternal psychological control and parental monitoring

	Maternal psychological control						Parental monitoring					
	Time 1			Time 2			Time 1			Time 2		
	FΔ	R^2	β	FΔ	R^2	β	FΔ	R^2	β	FΔ	R^2	β
Step 1 (background variables)	.65	.03		1.85	.09		4.24**	.17		2.54*	.12	
Teen gender (female)			.07			−.14			.33***			.30**
Teen age			.05			.06			.03			−.16
Mother's education			.03			.03			−.10			.05
Intact marital status			−.13			−.28*			.06			.16
Step 2 (domain-specific parenting)	3.64**	.21		1.64	.19		5.73***	.39		1.64	.22	
Parental monitoring			−.15			−.08			—			—
Psychological control			—			—			−.11			.19+
Authority beliefs—social			−.08			−.03			−.11			.10
Authority beliefs—personal			−.28*			−.12			.43***			.15
Restrictive control—social			.05			−.09			.16			.17
Restrictive control—personal			.38**			.36**			.07			.03

Note. Parental monitoring was included only in the analyses of psychological control; psychological control was included only in the analyses of parental monitoring. These values represent final βs.
*p < .05. **p < .01. ***p < .001. +p < .10.

terms was found to be significant. Because there were no specific hypotheses about these interactions, these findings are not discussed further.

CONCURRENT (TIME 1) ANALYSES OF PSYCHOLOGICAL CONTROL

The results of the Time 1 analyses of psychological control are shown in Table 11.11. As can be seen, none of the background variables (adolescents' age, gender, mothers' education, and family marital status) had a significant effect on adolescents' perceptions of maternal psychological control. With the effects of these variables controlled, both adolescents' beliefs about legitimate parental authority over ambiguously personal acts and their ratings of parents' restrictive control over ambiguously personal acts contributed significantly to the prediction of psychological control, as hypothesized.

Adolescents who rated their parents as having less legitimate control over ambiguously personal issues and viewed their parents as being more restrictive in controlling those acts rated their mothers as higher in psychological control. As expected, adolescents' beliefs about and ratings of parents' restrictive control over socially regulated acts and their ratings of parental monitoring were not significant in this analysis.

PREDICTIVE (TIME 2) ANALYSES OF PSYCHOLOGICAL CONTROL

Parents' marital status at Time 1 had a significant effect on adolescents' Time 2 ratings of maternal psychological control. Early adolescents who lived with both biological parents rated their mothers as lower in psychological control in middle adolescence (see Table 11.11) than did adolescents who lived in nonintact families. With the effects of background variables controlled, the analyses revealed that adolescents who rated their parents as more restrictively controlling ambiguously personal acts at Time 1 rated their mothers as higher in psychological control at Time 2. None of the other variables were significant in the analysis.

CONCURRENT (TIME 1) ANALYSES OF MONITORING
The results of the Time 1 analyses of monitoring are also shown in Table 11.11. As can be seen, adolescent gender was significant in the regression equation. Girls reported being monitored more than did boys. Adolescent age entered the equation significantly at Step 1, $\beta = -.20$, $p < .05$, indicating that younger adolescents reported being monitored more than did older adolescents. Age was not significant when all the variables were entered in the model, however. The results indicated that adolescents who believed that parents should have more control over ambiguously personal acts reported more monitoring. The findings for restrictive control over social acts were in the expected direction, but did not achieve statistical significance, $p < .14$. As expected, adolescent-rated psychological control was not significant in the analysis.

PREDICTIVE (TIME 2) ANALYSES OF MONITORING
Adolescents' gender contributed significantly to adolescents' Time 2 ratings of parental monitoring. As was found at Time 1, girls reported being monitored more than did boys. In addition, there was a trend toward higher ratings of parental monitoring at Time 2 among adolescents who rated their mothers as more psychologically controlling at Time 1.

Mother-rated psychological control and monitoring

As in the previous analyses, regressions were run to examine the influence of mothers' sociodemographic background and domain-differentiated beliefs and parenting practices on mother-rated psychological control and monitoring. Adolescents' age, gender, maternal education (coded in years), and intact marital status were entered as a block in the first step of the analysis. The second step included mothers' Time 1 ratings of monitoring (in the analyses of psychological

control) or psychological control (in the analyses of monitoring), their Time 1 beliefs about legitimate control over socially regulated and ambiguously personal acts, and their (combined) ratings of restrictive control. As was done in the analyses for adolescents, interaction terms (the product of adolescents' gender and mothers' domain-specific authority beliefs and ratings of restrictive parental control) were created to test their moderating effects. These were entered as a block in the third step. All variables were centered prior to analyses. Analyses were performed separately on psychological control and monitoring at Time 1 and Time 2.

CONCURRENT (TIME 1) ANALYSES
OF PSYCHOLOGICAL CONTROL
As shown in Table 11.12, mothers' education approached significance in the regression equation, $p < .09$, with mothers reporting less psychological control as their educational level increased. Neither mothers' reports of monitoring nor their domain-specific beliefs regarding the legitimacy of parental authority predicted their ratings of psychological control, as expected. There was a significant moderation effect for child gender and restrictive control, however. Significant interactions were interpreted by plotting the regression lines for the predicted high (+1 SD) versus low (−1 SD) values of the moderator (Aiken & West, 1991). These are depicted in Figure 11.3. The statistical significance of the regression slopes was then examined to determine whether each slope differed significantly from zero. Psychological control increased as restrictive control increased, but only among mothers of girls.

PREDICTIVE (TIME 2) ANALYSES OF
PSYCHOLOGICAL CONTROL
Contrary to expectations, the background variables were not significant in the longitudinal analyses. Mothers' ratings of more restrictive control at Time 1 entered the equation significantly at Step 2, $\beta = .27$, $p < .05$, indicating that mothers who reported more restrictive control at Time 1 rated themselves higher in psychological control at Time 2. The effects of restrictive control were only marginally significant, however, when all the variables were entered in the model, $p < .07$. As expected, domain-specific beliefs were not significant in the analysis.

Table 11.12 Regressions on mothers' ratings of psychological control and monitoring

	Psychological control Time 1			Psychological control Time 2			Monitoring Time 1			Monitoring Time 2		
	FΔ	R²	β	FΔ	R²	β	FΔ	R²	β	FΔ	R²	β
Step 1 (background variable)	1.11	.05		.56	.03		3.87**	.15		3.78**	.17	
Teen gender (female)			.06			−.04			.01			.23+
Teen age			−.06			.04			−.21*			−.32**
Mother's education			−19+			−.13			.09			−.04
Intact marital status			−.07			−.05			.14			.12
Step 2 (domain-specific parenting)	.97	.09		2.11+	.14		1.80	.22		.86	.21	
Monitoring			−.15			−.06			—			—
Psychological control			—			—			−.13			−.19
Authority beliefs—social			−.12			−.05			−.18			−.04
Authority beliefs—personal			.08			.19			.12			.10
Restrictive control (combined)			.12			.24+			.19+			−.00
Step 3 (gender interactions)	2.50+	.17		.82	.17		2.26+	.29		.08	.21	
Gender × Authority beliefs—social			.01			−.18			.08			.02
Gender × Authority beliefs—personal			−.05			.12			−.05			.04
Gender × Restrictive control			.32**			.11			.27*			.02

Note. Parental monitoring was included only in the analyses of psychological control and vice versa. These values represent final βs.
*$p < .05$. **$p < .01$. +$p < .10$.

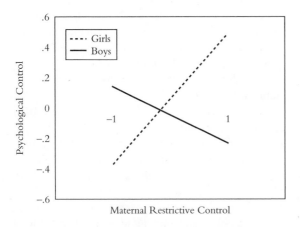

Figure 11.3 Adolescent Gender × Parental Restrictive Control interaction for adolescent-rated maternal psychological control at Time 1.

CONCURRENT (TIME 1) ANALYSES OF MONITORING
As shown in Table 11.12, adolescents' age was significant in the analysis of Time 1 monitoring. Mother-reported monitoring decreased as adolescent age increased. Contrary to hypotheses, family background (marital status or mothers' education) did not contribute significantly to mother-reported monitoring. With the effects of background variables controlled, there was a trend toward greater monitoring among mothers who rated themselves as higher in restrictive control, $p < .06$. In addition, the Child Gender × Restrictive Control interaction was significant. Again, the regression lines for the predicted high (+1 SD) versus low (−1 SD) values of the moderator were plotted, and the regression slopes were examined to determine whether each slope differed significantly

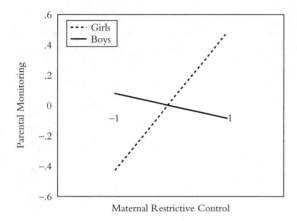

Figure 11.4 Adolescent Gender × Parental Restrictive Control interaction for adolescent-rated parental monitoring at Time 1.

from 0 (see Figure 11.4). As found in the analysis of psychological control, restrictive control increased as monitoring increased, but only for mothers of girls.

PREDICTIVE (TIME 2) ANALYSES OF MONITORING.
As found in the concurrent analysis, mother-reported monitoring decreased as age increased. Furthermore, mothers monitored girls more than boys, $p < .055$. None of the other variables were significant in this analysis.

Discussion

The present study examined the domain-differentiated antecedents of psychological and behavioral control in a sample of middle-income African American families. Specificity was examined in terms of the domains of parenting beliefs and practices associated with psychological and behavioral control, the different antecedents of mothers' and adolescents' reports, and the distinctiveness of monitoring and psychological control. The results demonstrated that monitoring and psychological control were distinct along all three of the dimensions examined. Different domain-specific beliefs about the legitimacy of parental authority and ratings of restrictive control were found to influence adolescents' perceptions of maternal psychological control and parental monitoring. In contrast, mothers'

ratings of psychological control and parental monitoring were associated with adolescents' age and gender, and the effects of adolescents' gender were found to be significantly moderated by mothers' ratings of restrictive control.

Finally, a relatively consistent finding from the present study was that monitoring did not predict psychological control and vice versa. These findings further validate the theoretical distinction between behavioral and psychological control, because they demonstrated that behavioral and psychological control are not simply two ends of a single continuum of control (Barber & Harmon, 2002; Barber et al., 1994; Steinberg, 1990).

Domain specificity in adolescents' ratings of psychological and behavioral control

Based on previous research describing conceptual and developmental differences in social knowledge (Nucci, 2001; Smetana, 1995a; Tisak, 1995; Turiel, 1983, 1998), parenting beliefs and practices were examined with regard to two different realms of adolescent behavior: socially regulated acts (including moral and conventional issues), and ambiguously personal issues. The latter included a range of issues that previous research has indicated are regarded as personal by adolescents, but whose status as personal issues may be contested by parents. The distinction between social and personal issues was theoretically derived, but was empirically validated in the present study. Social and personal factors were found to be distinct and internally consistent in mothers' and adolescents' beliefs about parental authority and in adolescents' ratings of restrictive control.

As hypothesized, adolescents who believed that parents should have less legitimate control over ambiguously personal acts and rated their parents as higher in restrictive control over these issues viewed their mothers as more psychologically controlling, as assessed both concurrently and longitudinally over the 2 years of the study. As a further test of our hypotheses, we also examined whether adolescents' beliefs and parenting ratings regarding socially regulated acts influenced their ratings of mothers' psychological control in early and middle adolescence and found that they did not. Previous research (Pettit et al., 2001) has found that hostile, coercive parenting in early childhood predicts early adolescents' reports of psychological control. The results of the present study suggest further that at least in adolescence, perceived psychological control is influenced by adolescents' perceptions of the particular behaviors that are controlled, as well as the style in which that control is exercised.

Previous research has indicated that the boundaries of adolescents' personal domain are continually renegotiated during adolescence and that adolescents' claims to an arena of personal discretion reflect a normative developmental process (Smetana, 1995a, 1995b; Smetana & Asquith, 1994). The present analyses focused primarily on the boundaries between what adolescents perceive to be legitimately regulated and subject to parents' authority (i.e., moral and conventional issues) and issues that adolescents consider to be outside of those boundaries and legitimately under their personal jurisdiction. The results of the present study showed that adolescents who believed that they should have more control over personal issues and also viewed their parents as especially restrictive of their personal freedom rated their mothers as higher in psychological control. These findings highlight the importance of considering parental psychological control in a developmental framework, because they suggest that shifts in the boundaries of personal jurisdiction lead to corresponding changes between what is perceived by adolescents to be appropriate control and what is seen as overcontrol. Thus, the definition of what is seen as psychologically controlling behaviors appears to shift during adolescence, as the boundaries of adolescents' personal domain increase. These findings highlight the challenges of parenting an early adolescent. They demonstrate the delicate balance that parents must strike between providing sufficient control to keep their adolescents safe and providing too much control over personal issues, which may be perceived as psychologically intrusive and coercive. Mason, Cauce, Gonzales, and Hiraga (1996) have referred to this balance as "precision parenting"; the present findings clarify that discretion must be granted primarily over personal issues.

In turn, these findings have implications for research and theorizing regarding psychological control.

A growing body of literature has described the correlates of psychological control and the effects of psychological control on different developmental outcomes (for a comprehensive review, see Barber & Harmon, 2002). Although various measures of psychological control have been employed, most measures include global descriptions of the parenting behaviors that may be seen as psychologically intrusive or guilt inducing. The results of the present study suggest that better prediction might be achieved if these more global measures were combined with more domain-specific and developmentally sensitive assessments that reflected changes in the boundaries of the personal domain.

Only a modest association was obtained in the present research between adolescent- and mother-rated psychological control, and then only at Time 2 (in middle adolescence). These findings suggest that psychological control may have a psychological reality that is, as others (Barber & Harmon, 2002; Pettit et al., 2001) have asserted, partially "in the eye of the beholder." The present results provide empirical support for the claim that adolescents' perceptions of parental psychological control are related to how they view their parents as responding to the autonomy-related developmental tasks of adolescence (Barber & Harmon, 2002; Steinberg, 1990). The finding that mother-rated restrictive control at Time 1 contributed significantly to mother-reported psychological control at Time 2, however, suggests that adolescents' perceptions may have some basis in reality.

The findings for adolescents' perceptions of monitoring also revealed domain-specific associations that were partially, but not entirely, in the direction hypothesized. As expected, adolescents' ratings of restrictive parental control over socially regulated acts were concurrently associated with adolescents' perceptions of greater parental monitoring. Longitudinal associations were in the expected direction, but did not achieve statistical significance. In contrast to predictions, however, adolescents' beliefs about the legitimacy of parental authority over ambiguously personal acts also contributed significantly to concurrent perceptions of parental monitoring. It is important to note that these associations were in the opposite direction from the findings obtained in the analysis of psychological control. That is, adolescents who believed that parents should have more legitimate control over personal issues also reported being monitored more. Because these findings were obtained concurrently, the causal direction of the findings is unclear. It is possible that adolescents who are monitored more come to believe that parents have more legitimate authority over their personal domain; this interpretation, however, needs to be examined in future research.

Adolescents' beliefs about parents' legitimate authority to regulate personal issues did not predict their perceptions of parental monitoring in the longitudinal analyses. Instead, a somewhat different pattern of associations was obtained. The trend was that adolescents who rated their mothers as more psychologically controlling in early adolescence rated their parents as monitoring them more in middle adolescence. These findings are in line with Pettit and Laird's (2002) speculation that mothers who are overly attentive to their child's behavior in earlier developmental periods may have difficulty with the autonomy issues of adolescence. The longitudinal findings suggest that adolescents may find parental monitoring and supervision psychologically intrusive as they get older.

Differences between adolescents' and mothers' reports

Our ability to test hypotheses about the role (or lack thereof) of domain-specific parenting beliefs and practices for mothers was weakened somewhat by the finding that social and personal factors were not distinct in mothers' ratings of restrictive control (although they were distinct in mothers' beliefs about their legitimate authority). As expected, however, mothers' domain-specific beliefs regarding legitimate parental authority did not contribute significantly to mother-rated psychological control or monitoring. Rather, the findings revealed a consistent gender-differentiated pattern of findings for mothers' ratings of restrictive control.

As others have found (Barnes & Farrell, 1992; Pettit et al., 2001), and as confirmed in the analyses for both mothers and adolescents, girls in the present study were monitored more than were boys. Furthermore,

the effects of gender on both monitoring and psychological control were moderated by mothers' ratings of restrictive control. More restrictive control (e.g., more rules and more parent-unilateral decision making) was associated with both greater monitoring and more psychological control, but only among mothers of early adolescent girls. Previous research has indicated that African American adolescent boys are granted independence earlier and face different perceived risks than do African American girls (Cauce et al., 1996; Smetana, 2000; Spencer & Dupree, 1996). Parents are particularly concerned with girls' friendships, dating, and interactions with the opposite sex (Cauce et al., 1996; Smetana, 2000). The present findings suggest that parents use a constellation of parenting techniques to control their early adolescent girls' behavior; parents who impose more rules and are more parent unilateral in their decision making also use more psychological control and monitor their daughters more in early adolescence. The fact that similar moderating effects were obtained for both psychological control and parental monitoring is especially striking, because these variables were not significantly related at Time 1. In contrast, mothers of early adolescent boys who exerted more restrictive control reported using less psychological control. The implications of these different patterns of control for African American adolescent boys' and girls' development and adjustment deserve more attention in future research.

Moreover, this gender-differentiated pattern was not evident 2 years later. Instead, the findings showed that mothers' ratings of restrictive control at Time 1 predicted their ratings of psychological control in middle adolescence. Inspection of the means suggests that there was little overall change in mothers' use of psychological control over time; rather, mothers' use of psychological control to manage their daughters' behavior declined over time.

Socioeconomic status, and particularly maternal education, consistently have been found to influence parenting beliefs and practices (Hoff-Ginsberg & Tardif, 1995), and both SES and intact family status in early childhood have been related to higher mother-reported monitoring in early adolescence (Pettit et al., 2001). Therefore, it was surprising that neither mothers' education nor intact family status significantly predicted mothers' ratings, although there was a trend in the expected direction for maternal education in the analysis of psychological control at Time 1. Preliminary analyses substituting family income for maternal education likewise did not yield significant effects. The lack of effects for SES may have been due to the present study's focus on middle-income families, and hence, the restricted range of the sample. Single-parent families are relatively common in the African American community (Billingsley, 1992), and extended families and the broader community have been found to provide families with additional sources of support (Hatchett & Jackson, 1993). Therefore, African American mothers in single-parent households may have had more resources than other families to help them effectively monitor their adolescents' behavior and keep track of their whereabouts. Interestingly, however, intact family status did influence adolescents' ratings of psychological control, and the findings were in line with previous research (Barber et al., 2002). That is, adolescents living in intact families at Time 1 reported that their mothers used less psychological control in middle adolescence. This suggests that parents in intact families may have less need to rely on psychological control as a way of controlling their adolescents' behavior.

Adolescent- and mother-rated parental monitoring were moderately associated, but only at Time 1. This may be because forms of monitoring and supervision change during adolescence, as adolescents spend less time with their parents and increasingly more time with peers (Steinberg, 1986). Thus, parents may have more direct sources of information about their early adolescents' activities and whereabouts, leading to greater convergence in their reports. Recent research has indicated that parental knowledge of children's activities is more important than parental control or supervision in avoiding negative adolescent outcomes (Kerr & Stattin, 2000; Stattin & Kerr, 2000). Although the measure of monitoring used in the present study focused on parental knowledge, information about the sources of that knowledge was not obtained. Kerr and Stattin also found that monitoring is most effective when it is obtained from child disclosure. Mothers in the present study reported more monitoring among younger

than older adolescents, but whether this was due to declines in adolescents' disclosure of their activities or reduced parental surveillance remains a question for future research.

Study limitations and future directions

Some limitations of the present study should be acknowledged. First, the assessment of adolescents' perceptions of psychological control was parent specific and focused on predicting perceptions of mothers' psychological control, whereas the other measures of parenting beliefs and practices were not parent specific. Therefore, in future research, measures of parenting should focus more consistently on either one or both parents. Discrepancies in the present assessment, however, may have increased the variability in the analyses and thus may have provided a conservative test of our hypotheses. Also, the same stimulus items were used in the assessment of adolescents' restrictive parental control and in beliefs about authority. This may have led to more convergence among these measures than would have been obtained if different items had been used, but it should be noted that the associations among the measures of parenting beliefs and restrictive control were low, leading us to have confidence in the results. Nevertheless, the present findings should be validated using different measures.

Furthermore, preliminary analyses suggested that there was a great deal of convergence between adolescents' reports of mothers' and fathers' psychological control and in mother- and father-reported monitoring and psychological control. Much of the previous research on the effects of parenting during adolescence has relied solely on adolescents' reports (i.e., Lamborn et al., 1996), and therefore, the use of multiple informants and the comparison of findings for adolescents and mothers were strengths of the present study. Studies of parenting, however, should be broadened still further to also include fathers (Parke & Buriel, 1998) and to compare mothers' and fathers' use of monitoring and psychological control.

Although moral and conventional issues were combined to form the socially regulated category, the present research should not be taken to imply that future research should ignore conceptual distinctions between morality and convention in favor of a more undifferentiated approach. As reviewed elsewhere (Smetana, 1995a; Tisak, 1995; Turiel, 1983, 1998), extensive evidence indicates that morality and social convention have different antecedents in children's social interactions, are distinct in children's social judgments, and follow different developmental pathways. The socially regulated category was useful here, however, in extending a line of investigation that has examined adolescents' and parents' judgments of the boundaries of legitimate parental authority during adolescence and adolescents' growing claims to an arena of personal freedom (Smetana, 1995b; Smetana & Asquith, 1994). Thus, our primary concern was with how adolescents and mothers draw boundaries between the self and the social world.

Finally, the present study examined relations among domain-specific and more general parenting orientations in a primarily middle-class African American sample. Studying middle-class African American families provides much-needed information on basic developmental processes in an understudied population (Garcia Coll et al., 1995; McLoyd, 1998; Spencer & Dornbusch, 1990). Because most of the measures used were derived from research on European American samples, preliminary analyses were run to examine whether the measures were acceptable for use in our sample. Given the ongoing debates about the application of parenting measures developed on majority families for use in African American families (Garcia Coll et al., 1995; Spencer & Dornbusch, 1990), the finding that these measures had acceptable reliabilities may provide useful information for future research.

More generally, previous research suggests that African American middle-class parents may be more restrictive of adolescents' personal arenas than are European American middle-class parents (Smetana, 1988, 2000). This may be due to African American parents' perceptions of the risks that their adolescents face in a cultural environment in which racism and prejudice remain pervasive (Spencer & Dupree, 1996). We assume that how adolescents and parents draw boundaries to adolescents' personal arenas may differ somewhat in different ecological niches and that the absolute levels of psychological control and monitoring

may vary in different ethnic groups, as has been reported elsewhere (e.g., Barber et al., 2002). We are in agreement with others (Steinberg & Fletcher, 1998), however, who have proposed that the processes described here (and thus, the relations among the variables) are more broadly generalizable. This assertion bears careful scrutiny in future research. The present findings should be replicated using families of other ethnicities and more varied SES.

It is also important to note that few significant associations were found between the domain-specific measures (e.g., restrictive parenting and beliefs about authority), and the measures of psychological control and monitoring. These findings lend support to our assertion that the constructs examined are independent. The model tested in the present study—that domain-differentiated beliefs and parenting practices influence adolescents' perceptions of psychological control and monitoring—is consistent with the recent call for more research that examines the influence of different parenting attributes on other parenting behaviors or styles (Collins et al., 2000), but different models of these interrelations have been proposed. For instance, Darling and Steinberg (1993) have proposed that parenting styles provide a context in which the meaning of particular parenting practices are interpreted. The present research suggests instead that domain-specific parenting practices lead to overall evaluations of parents as psychologically or behaviorally controlling. Further longitudinal research will be needed to test these different models and to determine the contexts and samples in which they best apply. Research should examine changes in domain-specific parenting in late adolescence and young adulthood, as well as whether the effects of psychological control and monitoring on adolescent adjustment are moderated by domain-specific parenting beliefs and practices.

References

Aiken, L. S., & West, S. G. (1991). *Multiple regression: Testing and interpreting interactions.* Newbury Park, CA: Sage.

Barber, B. K. (1996). Parental psychological control: Revisiting a neglected construct. *Child Development, 67,* 3296–3319.

Barber, B. K., Bean, R. L., & Erickson, L. D. (2002). Expanding the study and understanding of parental psychological control. In B. K. Barber (Ed.), *Intrusive parenting: How psychological control affects children and adolescents* (pp. 262–289). Washington, DC: American Psychological Association.

Barber, B. K., & Harmon, E. L. (2002). Violating the self: Parental psychological control of children and adolescents. In B. K. Barber (Ed.), *Intrusive parenting. How psychological control affects children and adolescents* (pp. 15–52). Washington, DC: American Psychological Association.

Barber, B. K., Olsen, J. E., & Shagle, S. C. (1994). Associations between parental psychological and behavioral control and youth internalized and externalized behaviors. *Child Development, 65*, 1120–1136.

Barnes, G. M., & Farrell, M. P. (1992). Parental support and control as predictors of adolescent drinking, delinquency, and related problem behaviors. *Journal of Marriage and the Family, 54*, 763–776.

Billingsley, A. (1992). *Climbing Jacob's ladder: The enduring legacy of African American families.* New York: Simon & Schuster.

Cauce, A. M., Hiraga, Y., Graves, D., Gonzales, N., Ryan-Finn, K., & Grove, K. (1996). African-American mothers and their adolescent daughters: Intimacy, autonomy, and conflict. In B. J. Leadbeater & N. Way (Eds.), *Urban girls: Resisting stereotypes, creating identities* (pp. 100–116). New York: New York University Press.

Collins, W. A., Maccoby, E., Steinberg, L., Hetherington, E. M., & Bomstein, M. (2000). Contemporary research on parenting: The case for nature and nurture. *American Psychologist, 55*, 218–232.

Cook, W. L., & Goldstein, M. J. (1993). Multiple perspectives on family relationships: A latent variables model. *Child Development, 64*, 1377–1388.

Darling, N., & Steinberg, L. (1993). Parenting style as context: An integrative model. *Psychological Bulletin, 113*, 486–496.

Dornbusch, S. M., Carlsmith, J. M., Bushwall, S. J., Ritter, P. L., Leiderman, H., Hastorf, A. H., & Gross, R. T. (1985). Single-parents, extended households, and control of adolescents. *Child Development, 56*, 326–341.

Fuligni, A. J. (1998). Authority, autonomy, and parent-adolescent conflict and cohesion: A study of adolescents from Mexican, Chinese, Filipino, and European backgrounds. *Developmental Psychology, 34*, 782–792.

Garcia Coll, C. G., Meyer, E. C., & Brillon, L. (1995). Ethnic and minority parenting. In M. H. Bomstein (Ed.), *Handbook of parenting: Vol. 2. Biology and ecology of parenting* (pp. 189–209). Mahwah, NJ: Erlbaum.

Gonzales, N. A., Cauce, A. M., & Mason, C. A. (1996). Interobserver agreement in the assessment of parental behavior and parent-adolescent conflict: African American mothers, daughters, and independent observers. *Child Development, 67*, 1483–1498.

Graham, S. (1992). Most of the subjects were white and middle class: Trends in published research on African-Americans in selected APA journals, 1970–1989. *American Psychologist, 47*, 629–639.

Gralinski, H. H., & Kopp, C. B. (1993). Everyday rules for behavior: Mothers' requests to young children. *Developmental Psychology, 29*, 573–584.

Grusec, J. E., & Goodnow, J. J. (1994). Impact of parental discipline methods on the child's internalization of values: A reconceptualization of current points of view. *Developmental Psychology, 30*, 4–19.

Hatchett, S. J., & Jackson, J. S. (1993). African American extended kin systems. In H. P. McAdoo (Ed.), *Family ethnicity: Strength in diversity* (pp. 90–108). Newbury Park, CA: Sage.

Hoff-Ginsberg, E., & Tardif, T. (1995). Socioeconomic status and parenting. In M. H. Bornstein (Ed.), *Handbook of parenting: Vol. 2. Biology and ecology of parenting* (pp. 161–188). Mahwah, NJ: Erlbaum.

Kerr, M., & Stattin, H. (2000). What parents know, how they know it, and several forms of adolescent adjustment: Further support for a reinterpretation of monitoring. *Developmental Psychology, 36*, 366–380.

Knight, G. P., & Hill, N. E. (1998). Measurement equivalence in research involving rninority adolescents. In V. C. McLoyd & L. Steinberg (Eds.), *Studying minority adolescents: Conceptual, methodological, and theoretical issues* (pp. 183–210). Mahwah, NJ: Erlbaum.

Lamborn, S. D., Dornbusch, S. M., & Steinberg, L. (1996). Ethnicity and community context as moderators of the relations between family decision making and adolescent adjustment. *Child Development, 67*, 283–301.

Mason, C. A., Cauce, A. N., Gonzales, N., & Hiraga, Y. (1996). Neither too sweet nor too sour: Problem peers, maternal control, and problem behavior in African American adolescents. *Child Development, 67*, 2115–2130.

McLoyd, V. (1998). Changing demographics in the American population: Implications for research on minority children and adolescents. In V. C. McLoyd & L. Steinberg (Eds.), *Studying minority adolescents: Conceptual, methodological, and theoretical issues* (pp. 3–28). Mahwah, NJ: Erlbaum.

Nucci, L. P. (1996). Morality and personal freedom. In E. S. Reed, E. Turiel, & T. Brown (Eds.), *Values and knowledge* (pp. 41–60). Mahwah, NJ: Erlbaum.

Nucci, L. P. (2001). *Education in the moral domain.* Cambridge, U.K.: Cambridge University Press.

Nucci, L. P., & Lee, J. (1993). Morality and personal auton-
omy. In G. G. Noam & T. Wren (Eds.), *The moral self:
Building a better paradigm* (pp. 123–148). Cambridge, MA:
MIT Press.

Nucci, L. P., & Smetana, J. G. (1996). Mothers' concepts of
young children's areas of personal freedom. *Child
Development, 67*, 1870–1886.

Parke, R D., & Buriel, R (1998). Socialization in the family:
Ethnic and ecological perspectives. In N. Eisenberg (Ed.),
(W. Damon, Series Ed.), *Handbook of child psychology:
Vol. 3. Social, emotional, and personality development* (5th ed.,
pp. 463–552). New York: Wiley.

Pettit, G. S., & Laird, R. D. (2002). Psychological control and monitoring in early adolescence: The role
of parental involvement and prior child adjustment
In B. K. Barber (Ed.), *Intrusive parenting: How
psychological control affects children and adolescents*
(pp. 97–123). Washington, DC: American Psychological
Association.

Pettit, G. S., Laird, R D., Dodge, K. A., Bates, J. E., & Criss,
M. M. (2001). Antecedents and behavior-problem
outcomes of parental monitoring and psychological
control in early adolescence. *Child Development, 72*,
583–599.

Schaefer, E. S. (1965). A configurational analysis of children's
reports of parental behaviors: An inventory. *Child
Development, 36*, 417–424.

Smetana, J. G. (1988). Adolescents' and parents' conceptions of parental authority. *Child Development, 59*,
321–335.

Smetana, J. G. (1989). Adolescents' and parents' reasoning
about actual family conflict. *Child Development, 60*,
1052–1067.

Smetana, J. G. (1995a). Morality in context Abstractions,
ambiguities, and applications. In R. Vasta (Ed.), *Annals of
child development. Vol. 10* (pp. 83–130). London: Jessica
Kingsley.

Smetana, J. G. (1995b). Parenting styles and conceptions of
parental authority during adolescence. *Child Development,
66*, 299–316.

Smetana, J. G. (2000). Middle-class African American adolescents' and parents' conceptions of parental authority
and parenting practices: A longimdinal investigation.
Child Development, 71, 1672–1686.

Smetana, J. G., & Asquith, P. (1994). Adolescents' and parents'
conceptions of parental authority and adolescent autonomy. *Child Development, 65*, 1147–1162.

Smetana, J. G., & Bitz, B. (1996) Adolescents' conceptions of
teachers' authority and their relations to rule violations in
school. *Child Development, 67*, 1153–1172.

Setana, J. G., & Gaines, C. (1999). Adolescent-parent conflict
in middle-class African American families. *Child
Development, 70*, 1447–1463.

Smetana, J. G., Kochanska, G., & Chuang, S. (2000). Mothers'
conceptions of everyday rules for young toddlers: A longitudinal investigation of the effects of maternal reasoning and child temperament. *Merrill-Palmer Quarterly, 3*,
391–416.

Spencer, M., & Dornbusch, S. M. (1990). Challenges in stud-
ying minority youth. In S. S. Feldman & G. R Elliot (Eds.),
At the threshold: The developing adolescent (pp. 123–146).
Cambridge, MA: Harvard University Presss.

Spencer, M., & Dupree, D. (1996). African American youths'
ecocultural challenges and psychosocial opportunities:
An alternative analysis of problem behavior outcomes.
In D. Cicchetti & S. L. Toth (Eds.), *Adolescence: Opportunities
and challenges* (pp. 259–282). Rochester, NY: University of
Rochester Press.

Stattin, H., & Kerr, M. (2000). Parental monitoring:
A reinterpretation. *Child Development, 71*, 1072–1085.

Steinberg, L. (1986). Latchkey children and susceptibility to
peer pressure: An ecological analysis. *Developmental
Psychology, 22*, 433–439.

Steinberg, L. (1987). Single-parents, stepparents, and the susceptibility of adolescents to antisocial peer pressure. *Child
Development, 58*, 269–275.

Steinberg, L. (1990). Interdependency in the family:
Autonomy, conflict, and harmony in the parent-adolescent
relationship. In S. S. Feldman & G. R. Elliot (Eds.), *At
the threshold: The developing adolescent* (pp. 255–276).
Cambridge, MA: Harvard University Press.

Steinberg, L., & Fletcher, A. C. (1998). Data analytic
strategies in research on ethnic minority youth. In V. C.
McLoyd & L. Steinberg (Eds.), *Studying minority adolescents: Conceptual, methodological, and theoretical issues*
(pp. 279–294). Mahwah, NJ: Erlbaum.

Steinberg, L., Mounts, N. S., Lamborn, S. D., & Dornbusch,
S. M. (1991). Authoritative parenting and adolescent
adjustment across varied ecological niches. *Journal of
Research on Adolescence, 1*, 19–36.

Tisak, M. (1995). Domains of social reasoning and beyond.
In R. Vasta (Ed.), *Annals of child development. Vol. 11*
(pp. 95–130). London: Jessica Kingsley.

Turiel, E. (1983). *The development of social knowledge: Morality
and convention*. Cambridge, U.K.: Cambridge University
Press.

Turiel, E. (1998). Moral development. In N. Eisenberg (Ed.),
William Damon (Series Ed.), *Handbook of child psychology:
Vol. 3. Social, emotional, and personality development* (5th ed.,
pp. 863–932). New York: Wiley.

A Closer Look 10   Bridging the Generation Gap: Promoting Healthy
Parent–Adolescent Relationships

The nature–nurture debate in social development has evolved historically from asking "which one?" to "how much of each?" to "how do these factors jointly contribute?" Accordingly, whereas traditional research has focused on parenting styles, current research also examines the role that children and adolescents bring to the parent–child relationship. This includes children's biological make-up and temperamental differences, as well as how children interpret everyday issues that matter to them.

In this review article, Collins and colleagues (2000) describe contemporary research approaches in this area, which include (a) behavior-genetic designs, augmented with direct measures of potential environmental influences; (b) studies distinguishing among children with different genetically influenced predispositions in terms of their responses to different environmental conditions; (c) experimental and quasi-experimental studies of change in children's behavior as a result of their exposure to parents' behavior, after controlling for children's initial characteristics; and (d) research on interactions between parenting and nonfamilial environmental influences and contexts, illustrating the important sources of influences beyond the parent–child dyad. It is important to focus on all of the factors that make parents and adolescents get along well and contribute to the development of autonomy and independence as adolescents transition to adulthood.

Collins, W. A., Maccoby, E., Steinberg, L., Hetherington, E. M., & Bornstein, M. (2000). Contemporary research on parenting: The case for nature and nurture. *American Psychologist, 55*, 218–232.

Classroom Exercises, Debates, and Discussion Questions

- *Classroom discussion: Disciplinary strategies with adolescents.* How should parents respond to transgressions by their adolescent children? What strategies work? What strategies backfire?
- *Classroom discussion.* What should adolescents do to maintain a positive relationship with their parents? What are the most important issues for parents and adolescents to discuss, and how often should parents and adolescents communicate? What contexts are most effective for parent–adolescent communication? What enables parents and adolescents to communicate in an open and direct manner as recommended by research studies?
- *Classroom discussion.* Research studies indicate that adolescents are selective about the information that they disclose to parents, keeping the personal domain private (such as choice of friends or decisions about decorating one's bedroom) but revealing issues pertaining to morality (such as issues about potential harm or unfairness) or conventional rules, such as mode of dress and manners. What issues should adolescents reveal and why?
- *Focused discussion: Poverty and parenting.* Research shows that poverty diminishes psychological well-being for both parents and children. Families that are well-off sometimes find their situations greatly change as a result of tough economic times. How should parents modify their behavior? What can adolescents do to help their parents and maintain positive family relationships through difficult economic times?
- *Focused debate: Authoritarian or authoritative?* What are examples of "authoritarian" parenting styles and "authoritative" parenting styles? What strategies work to help adolescents develop as autonomous and independent human beings?

Additional Resources

For more about parental attitudes and beliefs, see:

Barber, B. K., & Harmon, E. L. (2002). Violating the self: Parental psychological control of children and adolescents. In B. K. Barber (Ed.), *Intrusive parenting: How psychological control affects children and adolescents* (pp. 15–52). Washington, DC: American Psychological Association.

Coplan, R. J., Hastings, P., Lagacé-Séguin, D., & Moulton, C. E. (2002). Authoritative and authoritarian mothers' parenting goals, attributions, and emotions across different childrearing contexts. *Parenting: Science and Practice, 2,* 1–26.

Grusec, J. E., & Goodnow, J. J. (1994). Impact of parental discipline methods on the child's internalization of values: A reconceptualization of current points of view. *Developmental Psychology, 30,* 4–19.

Steinberg, L., & Silk, J. S. (2002). Parenting adolescents. In M. H. Bornstein (Ed.), *The handbook of parenting* (Vol. 1, pp. 133–134). Mahwah, NJ: Lawrence Erlbaum Associates.

12

CULTURE, ETHNICITY, AND RIGHTS

Introduction   516

Parents' Goals for Children: The Dynamic Coexistence of Individualism and Collectivism in Cultures and Individuals   517

Catherine S. Tamis-LeMonda, Niobe Way, Diane Hughes, Hirokazu Yoshikawa, Ronit Kahana Kalman, and Erika Y. Niwa

Introduction   517

Individualism and Collectivism   518

Forms of Coexistence of Individualism and Collectivism in Individuals and Societies   521

Dynamic and Changing Values   526

Conclusions   532

Muslim and Non-Muslim Adolescents' Reasoning About Freedom of Speech and Minority Rights   537

Maykel Verkuyten and Luuk Slooter

Method   542

Results   545

Discussion   549

Chinese Adolescents' Reasoning About Democratic and Authority-Based Decision Making in Peer, Family, and School Contexts   554

Charles C. Helwig, Mary Louise Arnold, Dingliang Tan, and Dwight Boyd

Method   557

Results   560

Discussion   566

A Closer Look 11   African-American Culture: Understanding the Past to Make Predictions About Development   574

Introduction

The exploration of cross-cultural similarities and differences in children's social development has emerged as a major area of research over the past 35 years. Anthropologists Whiting and Whiting (1979) provided a foundational study in this area with their "psycho-cultural" analysis of children from six diverse cross-cultural contexts (New England Baptist community; a Philippine barrio; an Okinawan village; an Indian village in Mexico; a northern Indian caste group; and a rural tribal group in Kenya). What has changed dramatically since this foundational research project is the growing *multicultural* nature of children's environments due to immigration and increased ease in the facility of mobility and communication around the globe.

In the 21st century, areas of the world that were once homogeneous (where most people shared the same background, grew up together and stayed in their own community) are now heterogeneous (where families from different backgrounds attend the same schools and work together). In order to understand how children adapt to cultural transformations it is important to have a theory of culture that also takes into account the child's perspective. In the past few decades, categories such as *individualism* and *collectivism* have been used to understand the role of traditions, customs, values, and beliefs in different areas of the world. Although there have been some attempts to broadly categorize different cultures as being more collectivistic or individualistic, growing research suggests that individuals everywhere have both individualistic (e.g., autonomy) and collectivistic goals (e.g., valuing community, interpersonal relationships). It is how these values and beliefs differentially emerge from culturally influenced social interactions that appears to vary in different cultural contexts.

In the three articles in this chapter, researchers have examined the role of culture on children's and adolescents' values, beliefs, rights, and development. In the first article, Tamis-LeMonda et al. (2008) propose a theoretical model which describes the dynamic coexistence of individualism and collectivism in cultures and individuals. Drawing on a large ethnically diverse sample collected in New York City, quotes from children, adolescents, and parents are presented to demonstrate how children and parents value both individualism and collectivism.

The second study is an example of an emerging research trend of studying a cultural group that was previously fairly homogeneous but more recently has experienced a transformation towards heterogeneity. Verkuyten and Slooter (2008) address how Muslim and non-Muslim majority adolescents in the Netherlands evaluate complex issues involving freedom of speech and minority rights, revealing a number of significant commonalities across these two groups regarding basic rights. The third paper focused on social development in China. Helwig and colleagues (2003) explored how Chinese adolescents evaluated decision-making in the peer, family, and school contexts. The study in China provided a number of surprising counter-intuitive findings such as the strong value placed on autonomy by adolescents as well as the view that democratic principles should be part of the government. Overall, the papers in this section examine the notion of rights and the types of decisions that emerge regarding individual and group rights. The topic of culture has fascinated developmental scientists studying social development for decades.

Reference

Whiting, B. H., & Whiting, J. W. M. (1979). *Children of six cultures: A psych-cultural analysis.* Cambridge, MA: Harvard University Press.

Parents' Goals for Children: The Dynamic Coexistence of Individualism and Collectivism in Cultures and Individuals

Catherine S. Tamis-LeMonda, Niobe Way, Diane Hughes, Hirokazu Yoshikawa, Ronit Kahana Kalman, and Erika Y. Niwa

Introduction

A universal task of parenting is to support children's acquisition of the skills necessary to function adaptively in their local communities. Parents transmit values, rules, and standards about ways of thinking and acting, and provide an interpretive lens through which children view social relationships and structures (McGillicuddy-De Lisi & Sigel, 1995; Ogbu, 1988; Super & Harkness, 2002). Parents' beliefs and practices reflect the norms and expectations of the cultures in which they are embedded and are core conduits for perpetuating 'systems of cultural priorities' (Kagitcibasi, 1996; Keller, 2003). Therefore, although transmission of beliefs and practices from parents to children is universal, the content of such beliefs and practices varies widely across cultures (Harwood, Miller, & Irizarry, 1995).

Perhaps the most influential framework for conceptualising cultural variation in parental beliefs and practices is the distinction scholars have made between 'collectivism' and 'individualism' (e.g., Hofstede, 1980; Triandis, 1988; see Oyserman, Coon, & Kemmelmeier, 2002 for review). The terms collectivism and individualism have been used to refer to value systems existing within and across large cultural groups as defined by nationality, race, or ethnicity (e.g., Asian) and small subcultural communities (e.g., Anglo, middle class, and American) (Rothbaum & Trommsdorff, 2007). The collectivism–individualism distinction has a long history that is rooted in western philosophy (see Triandis, 1995 for discussion) as well as in writings on collectivity vs. self-emphasis (Parsons & Shils, 1951), community vs. agency (Bakan, 1966), dependent vs. independent cognitive styles (Witken & Berry, 1975), and relationship-oriented vs. independent orientations (Markus & Kitayama, 1991). The developmental literature is also replete with theories and

research that draw on the constructs of individualism and collectivism, with most writings emphasizing the psychological and behavioral goals of autonomy and relatedness. Attachment theory, for example, highlights the parent's role as a 'secure base' (relatedness) from which infants venture out and 'explore' (autonomy); theories on social relationships point to the continual tensions that exist between 'co-operation' (relatedness) and 'competition' (autonomy) (Johnson & Johnson, 1989); and theories of moral development highlight the tension between the goals of autonomy and relatedness in the development of moral reasoning (e.g., Gilligan, 1982; Kohlberg, 1981).

At the most general level, social scientists have portrayed parents in 'western' cultures as promoting developmental goals that are autonomy-oriented or, at the more macro or community level, individualistic, and parents in most Asian, Latin, African, and rural, indigenous societies as promoting developmental goals that are relationship-oriented or, at the more macro level, collectivistic (e.g., Harwood, Schoelmerich, Schulze, & Gonzalez, 1999; Hofstede, 1980; Kohn, 1969; Lieber, Yang, & Lin, 2000; Triandis, 1995, 2000). Triandis' extensive empirical work with college students and adults from various countries, including the USA, Hong Kong, and China, identified 64 attributes that were hypothesized to contrast collectivistic vs. individualistic cultures (e.g., Triandis, 1994; Triandis, McCusker, & Hui, 1990).

There is growing recognition, however, that dichotomous depictions of value systems and developmental goals are theoretically and empirically limiting (e.g., Kagitcibasi, 1996; Rothbaum & Trommsdorff, 2007). A common critique has been that an individualist–collectivist framework is overly simplistic, especially during the current era of increased globalization and more complex conceptualizations of child development. Worldwide, macro-level changes in immigration, political and economic trends, and technological advances mean that cultures cannot be neatly classified as collectivist or individualist just as any given person cannot be described as valuing *either* relatedness *or* autonomy. Thus, a dichotomous framework that pits individualism against collectivism, or autonomy against relatedness, is neither accurate nor useful in understanding parents' socialization of their young (Keller, 2003; Shweder et al., 1998). Furthermore, different cultural environments can endorse similar developmental goals (e.g., Harkness, Super, & van Tijen, 2000; Killen, McGlothlin, & Lee-Kim, 2002) just as different developmental goals can be found in subgroups of a given culture (e.g., Bornstein, Venuti, & Hahn, 2002).

Although there has been widespread recognition of the limitations of this dichotomous framework, few scholars have proposed an alternative framework beyond stating that orientations toward individualism and collectivism (and associated developmental goals of autonomy and relatedness) exist to some degree in all communities and individuals. The aim of the present article is to propose a typology for understanding the ways in which communities maintain the values of individualism and collectivism, and likewise how individuals experience the developmental goals of autonomy and relatedness. In our discussion, we focus specifically on these issues as they are manifested in parents' socialization goals and practices. We use the terms individualism and collectivism to refer to macro-, overarching value systems, and the term developmental goals to refer to specific psychological and behavioral qualities that parents wish their children to develop (e.g., self-esteem and respect).

The article is divided into three main sections. The first section briefly describes components of individualism and collectivism, and highlights the specific developmental goals that have traditionally been classified under these two orientations, including personal choice, intrinsic motivation, self-esteem, and self-maximization as values associated with autonomy; and connection to family, group harmony, and respect and obedience as values associated with relatedness. In the second section, we propose a new typology for conceptualizing relations between group orientations toward individualism and collectivism, as well as parents' specific developmental goals of autonomy and relatedness. This typology is grounded in our

national and international research on hundreds of parents of infants, preschoolers, and adolescents from a variety of ethnic, racial, and economic backgrounds, including low-income African-American, Mexican-American, Puerto Rican, Dominican-American, and Chinese-American mothers (and sometimes fathers) living in New York City (NYC); middle-income, Anglo-American mothers from the USA (Boston and NYC), Greece (Athens) and Taiwan (Tainan), and Chinese mothers and fathers living in Nanjing, China. Over the past five years, these parents have spoken at length about the values they wish to instill in their children and the immediate and long-term goals they have for their children and themselves as parents.

In the third section, we address the dynamic nature of individualism and collectivism, and the developmental goals of autonomy and relatedness, by focusing on how forms of association change over time, at micro and macro levels. We move beyond static conceptualizations to show that parents shift in the goals they endorse for their children across situations (including immigration) and developmental periods. At the more macro level, economic and political changes in countries are reflected in shifting value systems of parents across generations. Once more, we draw upon parents' narratives to illustrate micro-level changes as well as evidence for the influence of macro-level contexts on micro-level processes.

Individualism and Collectivism

The concept of individualism can be traced to the Protestant work ethic first proposed by Max Weber (1904–1905/1958) as an economic theory to account for the evolution of capitalism (Jones, 1997). At its core, Weber's theory proposed that the seeds of capitalism lay in the Protestant ideals of personal responsibility, pushing aside distractions in order to achieve goals, hard work, and innovation. These values are assumed to undergird American ideals and are the foundations of an individualistic orientation.

In line with the Protestant work ethic, parents in individualistic cultures have been described as encouraging their children to develop into independent, autonomous individuals who have fragile social ties to the larger group. Four key values are associated with the overarching developmental goal of autonomy, as expressed by the parents in our studies: (1) personal choice ('That's why I'll let them decide what they want to do. If I like something but they don't, they won't have to do it'); (2) intrinsic forms of motivation and persistence ('You know, no matter what happens, just kind of have that positive, you know optimism'); (3) self-esteem ('That's the way you learn … Love what you are'); and (4) self-maximization ('I don't want him to think that he can't have or he can't do or he can't accomplish') (e.g., Bridges, 2003; Hofstede, 1980; Markus & Kitayama, 1991; Rothbaum & Trommsdorff, 2007; Ryan & Deci, 2000a, 2000b; Sampson, 1977; Smetana, 2002, Smith & Schwartz, 1997; Triandis, 1995).

The first value, *personal choice*, is common in many cultures that are considered to emphasize individualism, such as the USA (see Deci, Ryan, & Koestner, 1999 for review). Iyengar and Lepper (1999) note that for individuals in the USA, the act of making a personal choice provides opportunities to both assert personal preferences and establish a unique identity. These personal choices are associated with enhanced motivation and achievement.

A second common value in cultures thought to be individualistic is *intrinsic motivation*, that is, being internally driven to achieve one's goals. This value is often implicitly linked to other traits such as optimism about one's chances of success. In the USA, for example, optimism is viewed as a critical precursor to happiness, psychological well-being, health and longevity (e.g., Mesquita & Walker, 2003). Intrinsic motivation and personal choice are also thought to be intimately related, with personal choice facilitating motivation. Studies with primarily Anglo-American children have found that children's intrinsic motivation and interest in a task declines when they are externally rewarded for their task engagement or completion (Deci et al., 1999). A primary goal for families and schools in many cultures that are considered to be individualistically oriented is to raise children who are intrinsically motivated to learn (Iyengar & Lepper, 1999).

A third value common in cultures considered Individualistic is *self-esteem*, which arises out of the belief that feeling good about oneself is the key to successful outcomes. Self-esteem is considered to be fundamental to happiness and the achievement of personal goals. Numerous studies have highlighted the greater value that European-American parents, typically described as emphasizing individualistism or autonomy, place on self-esteem compared to their Japanese, Chinese, and Puerto Rican counterparts, who have often been described as more collectivistic (Harwood et al., 1995; Stevenson et al., 1990). European-American mothers uniformly note the importance of self-esteem in children's healthy development and feel responsible for inculcating it in their children (Miller, Wang, Sandel, & Cho, 2002).

Finally, *self-maximization*, another common value in cultures considered to be more individualistic refers to achieving one's full potential as an individual, a term introduced in Harwood's highly influential study of parental socialization goals (Harwood et al., 1995). In this study, Anglo-American mothers were more likely than Puerto Rican mothers to mention the importance of their children reaching their full potential. The emphasis in cultures considered to be individualistic is on reaching one's full potential, which is also evident in the clinical (e.g., Maslow, 1943, 1948) and developmental (e.g., Vygotsky, 1978) literatures and is, perhaps, the most important component of an individualistic orientation.

Together, these four values reflect parents' beliefs about the fundamental requirements for children's successful achievement of autonomy: children who make their own choices, are intrinsically motivated, feel good about themselves, and realize their full potential will ultimately develop into unique, autonomous beings.

In contrast to the emphasis on the autonomous self in cultures that are characterized as more individualistic, parents in cultures considered to be more collectivistic are thought to promote relatedness and interdependence in their children (Grotevant, 1998). The values implicit in the developmental goals of relatedness are: (1) connection to the family and other close relationships ('I want him to be an active person who loves his family very much and does not forget about his mother'); (2) orientation to the larger group ('And just be able to get along with kids, and be able to share, to socialize … Help each other'); and (3) respect and obedience ('If there's no respect, that's a bad thing, you know? Listening, and obeying, that's important'). Together, this constellation of developmental goals highlights both 'horizontal' collectivism, in which the self is part of a collective group that is characterized by equality, as well as 'vertical' collectivism, in which there exist inequalities in power within the collective that require obedience and respect (Triandis, 1995).

Connection to the family is frequently described as a distinguishing characteristic of rural, indigenous, and East Asian cultures, as well as of various ethnic minority groups in the USA who are considered to be more collectivistic, including East Asian, Hispanic, and African/African-American communities (Cortes, 1995; Fuligni, Tseng, & Lam, 1999; Spencer & Dornsbusch, 1990). Constructs such as 'familism' among Latino families, 'family obligation' and 'filial piety' among Asian families, and 'extended kin' for African-American families each encompass feelings of closeness, allegiance, and mutuality with family members, as well as notions of the self as an extension of the family (e.g., Cortes, 1995; Gonzalez-Ramos, Zayas, & Cohen, 1998; Sabogal, Marin, Otero-Sabogal, & Marin, 1987). A strong family orientation is believed to be linked to preindustrial agrarian societies in combination with influences from religion and Confucianism in the case of East Asian families. In its broader application, connection to the family also extends to other people with whom an individual shares close relationships. This aspect of collectivism has been referred to as 'relational collectivism' and is distinguished from 'group collectivism' in which the group is a depersonalized social category (Brewer & Chen, 2007).

Orientation to the larger group, also considered a key socialization goal among parents in cultures considered to have a collectivist orientation, has been the focus of much research (e.g., Chen, Cen, Li, & He, 2005). Whereas individualistic-oriented communities are thought to emphasize self-growth and individual well-being, collectivistic-oriented communities are thought to emphasize the good of the larger community of which one is a member. Thus, researchers contend that individuals in collectivist cultures such as China, conscious that their actions reflect upon the larger group, consider the repercussions of their actions for the family or larger community before acting. In contrast, those in more invididualistic communities primarily consider the consequences of their actions for the self.

Respect and obedience are considered central to many collectivist-oriented communities. To achieve harmony within the group—whether it be with other children, parents, or relatives—children must learn to be respectful of others as well as obedient to authority. The emphasis on obedience is the outgrowth of a hierarchical or vertical social structure, in which parents and elders of the community make decisions for the young (Kagitcibasi, 1996; Keller, 2003; Triandis, 1995). Such hierarchical social structures present clear boundaries of authority that function to prevent dissent in the group, which in turn facilitates harmony among group participants. In Latino families, the construct of 'respeto' and the associated importance of raising a child who is 'bien educate' (Gonzalez-Ramos et al., 1998; Harwood et al., 1995) are examples of the emphasis on respect and obedience for the purposes of group harmony. In Harwood and colleagues' (1995) study, Puerto Rican mothers described ideal children as those who were obedient to elders, calm in order to attend to the needs of others, and polite and kind. In contrast, Anglo-American mothers emphasized qualities that highlighted self-maximization. A comprehensive review of over 20 studies indicates greater parental control and exercise of authority, and less encouragement of autonomy and personal choice, in Asian families (Indians, Filipinos, Japanese and Vietnamese, as well as Chinese) as compared to White families (Chao & Tseng, 2002).

Summary

According to current scholarship, personal choice, intrinsic motivation, self-esteem, and self-maximization have been described as laying the foundation for children's development of autonomy. In contrast, connection to the family, orientation to the group, and respect and obedience are thought to promote a strong sense of relatedness or interdependence. Although autonomy and relatedness are often contrasted in the literature, current research suggests that these value systems and developmental goals coexist in most cultures and within most parents. In the next section, we present a typology of how these value systems and developmental goals may coexist, followed by discussion of how forms of coexistence may change over time.

Forms of Coexistence of Individualism and Collectivism in Individuals and Societies

Despite a plethora of studies on the contrasting developmental goals of parents from different cultural communities, many scholars note that the boundaries between collectivistic and individualistic orientations are blurred. For example, Triandis (1995) asserts that collectivistic vs. individualistic value systems are probabilistic rather than deterministic, and recommends that these values be viewed as central tendencies in which it is *more likely* that an individual of a certain culture will subordinate personal goals to the group's goals, or the group's goals to personal goals, rather than be guided by a single orientation. Moreover, he describes a number of variables that increase the probability of collectivism or individualism, including an individual's affluence and educational level. Similarly, Smetana (2002) notes that although European-American children expect and assert earlier autonomy than Mexican, Asian-American and African-American children, *children in all cultures* value autonomy. Kagitcibasi (1996, 2005) observes that developmental goals such as emotional interdependence can coexist with developmental goals such as economic independence within a given family system, which led her to propose the construct of an 'autonomous relational self'. Weisner (2002) points to US parents' simultaneous socialization of dependence and independence in their young, referring to these seeming contradictions as the 'US dependency conflict'. Others point to the pervasiveness of sports teams and school clubs that emphasize goals of relatedness as being inconsistent with the overarching orientations of cultures that are considered to be individualistic, such as the United States (Bugental & Goodnow, 1998). Finally, Confucianism, which is typically described as a set of principles that advance collectivist goals, emphasizes hard work and achievement in order to uncover one's innate nature. This more individualistic side of Confucian principles is often excluded from descriptions of East Asian cultures, thereby resulting in selective treatment of value systems that serve to reify the collectivistic–individualistic dichotomy.

Together, these ideas challenge the bifurcation of value systems and associated goals, and instead highlight their coexistence both within individuals and societies. The next step is to identify the ways in which developmental goals of autonomy and relatedness, and the superordinate value systems of individualism and collectivism relate to one another at micro and macro levels. In this section, we present a typology of these relations that is grounded in the ongoing research at our center (http://steinhardt.nyu.edu/crcde/). We distinguish among three forms of association: (1) *conflicting*, in which collectivistic value systems and associated developmental goals are seen as interfering with individualistic value systems and goals, and/or the reverse (2) *additive*, in which both collectivistic and individualistic value systems and developmental goals are endorsed in the absence of an explicit connection between the two, and (3) *functional dependence*, in which the value system of collectivism and associated developmental goal of relatedness are thought to be a path to individualism and autonomy, and/or vice versa.

Conflicting associations

At a societal and individual level, collectivism or individualism or autonomy and relatedness may be viewed as conflicting; that is, the characteristics or developmental goals of one orientation are constructed as inhibiting or interfering with the characteristics or developmental goals associated with the other. Conflicting associations most closely align with the dichotomous conceptualization of individualistic and collectivistic communities as anchored at opposite poles. There is evidence that individualism and collectivism may at times be inversely related, such that societies high in one tend to be low in the other (Triandis, 1995). To date, however, little research has explored the ways in which parents view goals of relatedness as potentially interfering with goals of autonomy and vice versa.

In terms of *relatedness interfering with autonomy*, parents may view children's close relationships with others as detrimental to children's personal success. In our research,[1] this wariness of relatedness often took the form of concerns that children would 'follow' their friends, and therefore, compromise children's chances of attaining autonomy-oriented goals such as leadership and personal choice. One Puerto Rican mother of a two-year-old girl was fearful that her daughter would copy other children rather than be herself:

> That's what I want Cora to be. Herself. Without having to look at another person, another kid, and say, 'I wanna be like that'. You know? 'I wanna do that' ... You do what's natural, you know, what comes natural. Because I know when she does it naturally, that's being herself ... But when she starts observing, you know ... I know she's doing it, you know, because she saw it from another kid, you know? I just want her to be herself.

Similarly, an African-American mother of a 12-year-old girl spoke with pride about her child's *lack* of sociability and friends. This mother was pleased with her daughter's ability to think for herself and to be independent, and perceived close friendships as threats to her daughter's individuality:

> So that is why I'm proud of her too ... She's not a, um, follower. She don't care about, she's could come home and don't talk to nobody, she don't beg-friend. Like, she don't care you could be her friend today, tomorrow. She's not like, she's not, um, sociable a lot. She's not highly sociable.

Similarly, immigrant Chinese mothers revealed concerns about friends interfering with their children's self-maximization, and ultimately autonomy. One mother of a two-year-old boy spoke about what it meant to be 'rebellious'. To her, being rebellious meant spending time with friends rather than doing homework or following rules—activities thought to promote individual achievement:

> For example [being rebellious means], the child doesn't do the homework assigned by the teacher. He/she doesn't go home by the time he/she should, instead, he hangs out with friends.

Youth in our studies were aware of their parents' views that relationships with others might interfere with individual achievement. In interviews with Chinese-American youth (Way, Becker, & Greene, 2005; Way, Greene, & Pandey, 2007), adolescents noted that their parents believed that relationships would get in the way of individual achievement or self-maximization:

> My mom thinks that friendships are not that important. Yeah, because she said that being yourself is important not that you have friends.
>
> My dad thinks that friendships are not important because all he thinks about is school. He said a book is better than a friend.

It is also possible for parents to view *autonomy as interfering with relatedness*, as illustrated in Miller and colleagues' (2002) research on Taiwanese and US parents' views about self-esteem. In contrast to the individualistic emphasis on the importance of self-esteem. Miller notes that the term 'self-esteem' does not exist in the Chinese language. When probing Taiwanese mothers about this construct, she relied on the closest translation—'self-respect in heart and mind'. She found that although US mothers spoke at length about the importance of self-esteem when asked about their child-rearing views, Taiwanese mothers rarely spoke of self-esteem, and when they did they spoke of it as an undesired quality that would interfere with their children's social adjustment.

Parents' fears about the adverse consequences of children's personal success for family relations presents another way in which individualistic goals might be viewed as interfering with relatedness. Parents may feel that children who attain high levels of success might ultimately reject their family background as they move on to live at a new tier of society. Such concerns might be especially salient in immigrant families who are wary of US American ideologies. In our work, immigrant parents from the Dominican Republic, Mexico, and China often expressed concerns that the individualistic orientation of the USA would result in high success for their children, but would also lead to increased selfishness and decreased care for parents. These parents expressed clear sentiments that the goals of autonomy would create barriers to relatedness. As noted by one Chinese mother of an adolescent male:

> When you were born in the US, educated in the US, you would become independent when you are 18, and don't like to talk to your parents, and don't want to live with your parents, just like this.

This same mother spoke of the different expectations she had for her younger children who were born in the USA vs. her older child who was born in China. She described a conversation she had with her husband in which they spoke of the future trajectories of their children. They believed their children's outcomes would depend on how much exposure they had to the individualistic culture of the USA:

> [He told me], you see how you spoiled the younger ones? They will become even worse than I am, and they won't give you the money, even if they are making money in the future. He said the older one [who was not raised in the US] will be the one who treats us nice, and the younger ones who were born in the US will run away in the future.

Additive relations

In contrast to conflicting patterns of association, *both* collectivism and individualism at the cultural level and autonomy and relatedness at the individual level might be viewed as fundamental, yet independent, aspects of successful child development. This view builds on the notion that individuals must both assimilate to and distinguish themselves from the larger communities of which they are members (Brewer, 1991; Brewer & Chen, 2007). Parents' role, therefore, is to simultaneously socialize children to integrate themselves with others and differentiate themselves from others (Dennis, Cole, Zahn-Waxier, & Mizuta, 2002; Kagitcibasi, 1996, 2005).

The additive coexistence of individualistic and collectivistic goals has a longstanding history dating back to John and Beatrice Whiting's (1974, 1978) seminal cross-cultural research, which emphasized the seemingly contrasting goals that parents endorse for their children. Their work in Kenya, for example, indicated that mothers simultaneously wished their children to be obedient, generous, respectful, and connected to the family as well as capable of developing skills such as independence, so as to better function in a market economy. In their observations of American family life, they noted that middle-income European-American parents stressed independence and self-reliance in interactions with their infants, while fostering strong affective bonds and dependencies. Two decades later, Kagitcibasi (1996) pointed to problems with the assumption that the development of

autonomy necessarily requires separation from others, especially the family. As a result, she suggested two orthogonal dimensions to capture family socialization of children: autonomy vs. heteronomy and relatedness vs. separation. From these dimensions, Kagitcibasi identified three patterns of socialization: (1) traditional, characterized by high material and emotional interdependence, (2) independent, characterized by high autonomy and individualism, and (3) a synergy of the two. Others have also observed that although autonomy is a fundamental attribute of individualism, it does not necessarily involve separation or detachment (Smith & Schwartz, 1997).

Recent empirical work demonstrates that both parents and youth emphasize the dual goals of autonomy and relatedness. For example, studies of Korean parents indicate that although Koreans have historically placed greater emphasis on collectivist values such as in-group obligations, parents stress individualism when their children's personal improvement or pleasure is compromised (Cha, 1994). In another study, Chinese and Chinese-American parents placed more emphasis on obedience to authority than did their Anglo-American counterparts (Lin & Fu, 1990). However, they *also* rated encouragement of independence higher than Anglo-American parents, a seeming contradiction if obedience and independence are viewed as opposing developmental goals. The findings on Korean and Chinese-American parents suggest that hierarchical relationships, including respect and obligation, can harmoniously coexist with individualistic goals such as self-maximization and independence.

The additive coexistence of the value systems of individualism and collectivism is also evidenced in a study of college students in Northern India (Sinha & Tripathi, 1994). Students were presented with a set of 22 situations or dilemmas (e.g., career choice and health concern), and were asked to select what they considered to be a desirable behavioral response to each situation. Three behavioral options were offered for each situation, which aligned with an individualist, collectivist, or mixed orientation. Despite India being considered a highly collectivist culture, students preferred the response that blended both collectivistic and individualistic orientations for virtually every situation.

In our own work with middle-class mothers from Taiwan, Greece, and the USA, many mothers embraced both autonomy and relatedness when speaking about the qualities they wished to instill in their four-year-old children (Tamis-LeMonda, Wang, Koutsouvanou, & Albright, 2002; Wang & Tamis-LeMonda, 2003). Mothers in all three societies endorsed developmental goals of assertiveness, independence, curiosity, sharing, and getting along with others, although the Anglo mothers from the USA were especially likely to endorse developmental goals of both autonomy and relatedness. Similarly, parents of Mexican, Dominican, Chinese-American, and African-American descent in our studies in NYC highlighted *both* autonomy and relatedness. Specifically, the mothers that we interviewed endorsed over 20 specific qualities that they hoped to see in their children, including being affectionate, co-operative, well-mannered, and obedient as well as being assertive, diligent, a leader, and attaining personal success. The additive coexistence of autonomy and relatedness is illustrated in the following four quotes by mothers of infants and toddlers who were asked to describe the qualities they would like to see in their very young children:

MOTHER #1:   '[I wish for him to be able] to talk with everybody … [and be sociable]. [Also] that in the future he can have a career, that he can be independent'.

MOTHER #2:   'She needs to respect other people and if she believes in something, she needs to stand up for it'.

MOTHER #3:   'As long as he always respects his elders and trusts his instincts, and know when something is wrong and you know be a leader, not a follower'.

MOTHER #4:   '[I want her to] respect people, and respect humanity. Um, know her spirit, you know, love herself'.

In each of these statements, mothers simultaneously emphasized qualities that have traditionally been classified at opposite ends of the individualistic-collectivistic or autonomy–relatedness spectrum. The juxtaposition of the goals of sociability and independence (mother #1), respect and assertiveness (mother #2), respect and leadership (mother #3), and respect and self-esteem (mother #4) within single statements suggests that parents indeed view developmental goals as harmoniously coexisting. In summary, although social science scholars

have represented the developmental goals of autonomy and relatedness as separate, the reflections of parents from diverse communities suggest that parents do not perceive a contradiction between encouraging both autonomy and relatedness in their children.

Functional dependence

Patterns in which developmental goals are viewed as additive can be contrasted with patterns in which the developmental goals of autonomy and relatedness are viewed as causally connected or *functionally dependent* on one another. Functional dependence refers to a type of means–end relationship in which one value system or developmental goal is thought to serve the function of promoting the other. Parents may view relatedness as a path to autonomy and/or view autonomy as a path to relatedness. Specifically, positive relationships with others (relatedness) might be viewed as promoting individual success (autonomy), just as individual success (autonomy) might be viewed as promoting positive relations with others (relatedness). To date, there has been little consideration of the functional connections between parents' developmental goals.

In terms of *pathways from relatedness to autonomy*, although closeness to the family, connection to others, and respect or obedience may be end goals in themselves, they may also be viewed as foundational to individual achievement and personal growth. Our research with both middle-income European-American mothers and immigrant families in the USA supports the idea that goals of relatedness may be viewed as promoting goals of autonomy. One area in which this functional dependence was especially evident concerned connection to the family *vis-à-vis* personal acheivement and success. Parents noted that promotion of family values enables children to work hard and ultimately become successful. This functional dependence is illustrated in the sentiments of a Dominican-American father of an adolescent girl who spoke about the importance of family respect and support as a way for his child to excel as an individual:

Well it's important for me to know that she recognize already that she's respecting the background that she has because if she don't respect where she's coming from, I don't think she could respect what she could become.

I'm her mentor because if you don't ... assure them that you are there for them whether it's good or bad, the kid won't succeed in life ... and just be yourself. Then you're going to do well.

Parents also expressed the view that the developmental goal of family obligation (relatedness) serves to promote personal development and success (autonomy). One Chinese mother in our study required her 13-year-old to assist her with small tasks, such as stringing beads, as a way to teach her child the skills necessary for individual achievement:

INTERVIEWER (upon seeing young child on mother's bed stringing beads): 'Always does that for you?'
MOTHER: 'Yeah. Since he has nothing to do, so I asked him to help. ... My friends open their own restaurants, their kids always help in restaurants. Since I don't have a restaurant, they help what I am doing now. We must teach them to work, so that they will understand life is not easy and they will study harder.'

Connection to social networks outside the family, especially friends, was also viewed by many parents as promoting individual autonomy and success. In our study of parents' childrearing goals among Taiwanese and US mothers of preschoolers (Wang & Tamis-LeMonda, 2003), one US mother noted that it was important for her preschooler to share, display compassion, and get along with others. At first glance, this set of goals reflected a relationship-oriented stance. However, she subsequently noted that if her daughter displayed these qualities, she would have many friends, which would in turn foster the development of her self-esteem—an autonomy-oriented stance. The sentiment that by having friends and being connected to groups children would develop as individuals was expressed by mothers in all the ethnic groups we studied, as reflected in the following two statements:

And why [do] we bring them to the parks? Because we want them to get in touch with other kids, so that they won't be afraid of other kids, so that they have confident personality, and get to know more stuff. (Chinese mother of a two-year-old boy)
So I was like, maybe if she's around kids. More so her age, but you know, be around more kids. She might pick up on things she's supposed to pick up faster. You know,

now she's learning the shapes. And how to put them into the right slots. (African-American mother of a 17-month-old girl)

These perspectives highlight the benefits of social relationships and connection to others, a core pillar of collectivism and the developmental goal of relatedness, for individual development. These mothers of preschoolers believed that contact with other children would facilitate cognitive development and learning (e.g., 'knowing more stuff' and 'learning the shapes') and self-development (e.g., 'confident personality' and 'better adaptational skills').

Connection to others and friendship was seen as important to personal achievement well beyond the preschool years. Parents of adolescent children in our studies often spoke about the importance of children's selection of appropriate friendships for children's ultimate success.

If he has good friends the friends could help him. [They] could speak with him and communicate with him ... [The friends] could help him learn to be good. (Chinese mother of a 13-year-old boy)

Parents may also view *autonomy as a pathway to relatedness*. For example, parents might feel that by letting children express themselves (autonomy goals), children will in turn confide with their parents and remain close to the family (relatedness goals). One Dominican parent of an adolescent girl noted '[Because] I let her voice her thoughts, I believe she trusts me more and speaks with me about anything'. Parents also often noted that children's self-esteem (autonomy) promoted children's social skills (relatedness). In their words, by feeling good about themselves, children would become more aware of how to treat others and would also in turn receive respect from others:

I think that ... once you learn how to be good to yourself, love yourself you will definitely learn how to treat others. (African-American mother of an adolescent girl)
It depends on you, what you want, but always have the pride of who you are. You are unique for what you are and it depends on how you project yourself to people. That's the kind of respect you're going to get back [from others]. (Dominican father of an adolescent girl)

In these examples, relatedness was founded on principles of individual growth and self-maximization.

Finally, individual achievement may be regarded as an important, and perhaps necessary, part of collective success, and personal success may feed back to the family in the form of family obligations, financial support, and responsibility. Children who achieve in school and the workplace bring pride to the family and are able to support their family financially in the future. Chinese parents, for example, have been described as encouraging their children's high levels of individual achievement as a means for giving back to or sharing success within their family, group, or society (Wilson & Pusey, 1982; Yu & Yang, 1994).

Parents may view children's unique skills and competencies as enabling children to contribute meaningfully to family tasks and fostering independence. Parents of adolescents in our study noted proudly that they let their children cook meals, and so forth, and noted how these steps toward independence in turn assisted the family:

> Mmhm, she already makes eggs … She makes her eggs. Um, on Saturday she wanted to make a 'cake' But there weren't any eggs. She went to get the eggs, but didn't find them here or there. Later I went out for them. I left her alone. She takes good care of [her little brother], um, I just go and do what I have to do, and then I come back. I don't take long. (Mexican mother of an 11-year-old girl)

For many of the parents in our studies, fostering independence in children was thought to lead to the enhancement of relational skills and to ultimately feed back into benefits for the family.

Summary

Current scholarship acknowledges that the value systems of individualism and collectivism, and developmental goals such as autonomy and relatedness, albeit distinct can coexist within communities and individuals. Thus far, however, efforts to document the precise nature of associations among these goals is absent. We suggest that parents' goals for their children can be conflicting, additive, or functionally dependent. Qualitative interviews with participants in our studies lend support to each of these patterns of association. Although these forms of coexistence were discussed at the individual level, similar forms of association might also be observed at a broader, cultural level, a point that

is addressed below. This final section of the article builds on these patterns of coexistence by exploring the dynamics of cultural value systems and parents' developmental goals across settings and time. As such, the assumption that cultural value systems and parents' developmental goals are static or homogeneous is directly challenged.

Dynamic and Changing Values

An implicit assumption of much of the literature on individualism and collectivism is that parents' goals for children are uniform across settings and time. This static treatment of value systems and associated developmental goals has recently come under scrutiny (Fiske, 2002). Fiske notes that a person may be individualistic at work or while playing chess, but highly collectivistic at home or in church. Triandis (1988) states that an individual's responses to questionnaires probing for individualistic vs. collectivistic values depend on the situation, the specific behavior, and the group that is present. These works underscore the dynamic, changing nature of individualism and collectivism, and of autonomy and relatedness. Missing from this work, however, is a discussion of how the *coexistence* of individualism and collectivism or autonomy and relatedness changes over time and context.

There are at least two types of change that may occur in the coexistence of societal-level value systems and individual-level developmental goals. Firstly, the *relative balance* of autonomy and relatedness may shift over settings and/or time. For example, parents may endorse both autonomy and relatedness (additive coexistence), yet change in the extent to which one or the other developmental goal is prioritized. Secondly, the *form of coexistence* may change over settings and/or time, that is, in whether relations between autonomy and relatedness are additive, conflicting or functionally dependent. These two types of changes in the coexistence of autonomy and relatedness may occur at micro levels in response to different settings and children's development or at macro levels in response to changes in political and economic contexts.

Change across settings

Changes in the *balance* of autonomy and relatedness within a particular form might be especially evident across public vs. private settings (e.g., school vs. home) or across settings that contain adults vs. peers. For example, parents who endorse both individualistic and collectivistic goals in an additive manner might stress goals associated with collectivism in public settings (e.g., being well-mannered and deferent to authority in school) yet emphasize goals associated with individualism in private settings (e.g., expressing personal choices and assertiveness at home). Here, individualistic and collectivistic goals are both considered important albeit unrelated goals, but their relative importance shifts across settings.

In our study, participants who discussed autonomy and relatedness in additive ways indicated that the balance of the two goals continually shifted across settings. One Mexican mother of an 18-month-old boy and an 11-year-old girl noted that she often asked teachers about her children's behaviors at childcare and at school, to be sure they were well-behaved. This mother endorsed obedience and respect for others at school but noted that it was okay for her children to be somewhat disobedient at home, suggesting that expectations for behavior conducive of relatedness shifted across these settings:

> At school they behave. They don't fight over there. Well, I say, on the one hand it's all right for them to misbehave here at home. It's not so bad.

Another African-American mother of an adolescent boy also noted that her expectations of her child's behaviors depended on the situation:

> A kid's place is supposed to be his place. You know, if something is wrong and he knows something about it, then he's supposed to speak up. Otherwise, if your family is having some visitors or whatever, you know, don't interrupt them.

Mothers in each of the examples above were consistent in maintaining an additive view of autonomy and relatedness in that both goals were present. For the first mother, relational goals were preeminent in public settings (school) but not in private ones (home). For the second mother, whether or not her child should assert his individuality vs. respect others varied across situations.

In addition to the relative importance of different priorities shifting across situations, the *form of coexist-*

ence between developmental goals may change across situations. Parents might shift from endorsing multiple goals (additive) to viewing different goals as conflicting or functionally related. For example, in a peer context, parents might encourage their children to both assert their personal interests (autonomy) and to share with and help their peers (relatedness), expressing an additive view of autonomy and relatedness. However, in school situations where children are exposed to unfamiliar children from diverse backgrounds and neighborhoods, parents may shift to viewing relatedness as conflicting with autonomy. Peers who are unknown to parents may be considered 'risky' because they may impede the chances of their own children's individual accomplishments. It is also possible, however, that parents will shift from an additive or conflicting perspective to a functional one when their children have opportunities to mingle with other children who are deemed to be more knowledgeable or 'connected'. Under such circumstances, parents may believe that relatedness will enhance their children's possibilities for individual success.

The relative emphases placed on autonomy vs. relatedness might change across macro contexts, such as country of residence. For example, Pessar (1995) found that in couples who had moved to the USA from the Dominican Republic, women took on more independent or autonomous roles outside the family (specifically, employment) and, as a result, men took on more household duties. Here, the relative balance of autonomy and relatedness-oriented activities were adapted to the demands of the new country. Similarly, the statements of a Ghanaian mother in our study suggest that the balance between autonomy and relatedness shifted toward autonomy and personal choice with her move to the USA from Ghana. As a result, she sought to promote collectivist values through her children's contact with their Ghanaian heritage so that the two developmental goals might be equalized. In the following quote, this mother notes the differences she observed in her children after they had returned from a visit to relatives in Ghana:

> With the kids being away, they, they, they come back good. They still kids, but they come back with respect. Everything is 'thank you much, Aunt Efua. Okay, Auntie.

Please, Auntie Efua. Excuse me, Auntie Efua.' You know, everything is so, he has manners. He has lots of manners … please and thank yous, and all the time.

Although this mother spoke admiringly of the emphasis within Ghanaian culture on manners and respect for elders as powerful influences on her daughter (and, at other points of the interview, on herself as a child), she also noted that her kids were 'still kids', alluding to the fact that they should have the freedom to act like children. She valued both autonomy and relatedness and wanted her daughter to strive to attain both these goals.

The *forms* of coexistence between autonomy and relatedness may also shift in new, unfamiliar contexts. For example, immigrant families may endorse both autonomy and relatedness in an additive manner in their home country, but be more likely to view these goals as conflicting upon arrival to the USA. Researchers, for example, have observed that parents of immigrant youth often send their children back to their native country when they are perceived as acting too 'selfishly', or as making the wrong personal choices about their friends, similar to the Ghanaian example above. Parents in these situations feel that their children should learn manners or respect in their larger extended families and country of origin (Smith, 2005; Suarez-Orozco, Todorova, & Louie, 2002). They may explicitly or implicitly believe that the goals of collectivism are being subverted or challenged by the goals of personal choice and individualism. Although these parents might not have experienced conflicts between autonomy and relatedness in their home country, the values and behavior of the host country might highlight such conflict.

One Dominican–American father spoke of the tension between the two goals of autonomy and relatedness that he experiences as a result of living in the USA:

We [Dominicans] are very friendly people. We like to bring joy to other peoples' life. We like to brighten up the day of somebody who is probably having a hard time … We like to touch and give hugs to someone. We express ourselves with our hands and I think that is unique… As a Dominican we are giving, showing what we are to this person with food, music, the way we speak, the way we laugh. It gives us that part of where we are coming from [Dominican Republic] and this is what we offer … Respectful, caring. We want to continue in the same way, but in the new society that we live in you have to be a little more flexible, be a little more understanding and let the kids be themselves… To be in the US you have to be number one.

Implicitly, this father suggests that the goals of being respectful and caring are not always consistent with the goals of flexibility, personal choice, and 'being number one'. Although his statements suggest that he hopes to promote both sets of values, he views them as conflicting with one another. However, over time, as immigrant families acculturate to the host country, goals once viewed to be in conflict may come to be viewed as complementary.

Change across developmental time

Changes in the balance and form of coexistence between autonomy and relatedness are rendered even more complex in the context of developmental time. Parents' developmental goals are constructed, negotiated, and renegotiated not only from situation to situation, but also as children develop (Tamis-LeMonda, 2003). If developmental goals coexist in all parents, the salience of individualistic vs. collectivistic goals might shift in balance at different periods in children's growth. Some families may shift from emphasizing relatedness in infancy to promoting autonomy as their children develop; other families will show less relative change in their emphases over time; still others might emphasize increasing interdependence with children's age—expecting older children to take on greater family responsibilities as they move beyond the 'selfish' tendencies of childhood. Thus, both the *relative balance* between autonomy and relatedness as well as *forms* of coexistence might change with development.

One example of the *relative balance* of autonomy and relatedness changing over time includes changes in the expression of warmth in East Asian parents over the course of early childhood (Rothbaum & Trommsdorff, 2007). Although personal responsibility and hard work are core Confucian principles that are stressed at all ages by Chinese parents, early childhood is also a time when individualistic values are blended with high levels of closeness and warmth in parent–child relationships. Parents exert little control in response to young children's dependency. Yet, these patterns change as children enter school, with parents exhibiting a decline in displays of warmth and increased authoritarian control with older children (e.g., Rothbaum & Trommsdorff, 2007; Rothbaum, Weisz, Pott, Miyake, & Morelli 2000).

Research on Turkish families also illustrates shifts in the balance of autonomy and relatedness in parents' goals across children's development (Kagitcibasi, 1996). In the Turkish language, the word *uslu* refers to a combination of highly valued characteristics, including the display of good manners, obedience, and being quiet rather than boisterous. This term is reserved for young children and shifts to a more inclusive term— *akilli-uslu*—when referring to adolescents and young adults. *Akilli* adds the quality of 'intelligence' to the construct of *uslu*, thereby indicating a shifting emphasis toward qualities that are associated with personal and cognitive growth with age. Here, the form of coexistence does not necessarily change, but the relative balance of autonomy and relatedness changes in response to the development of the child.

Similarly, the popular US term—'terrible twos'— captures the child's change from a coddled dependent infant to an autonomous, incorrigible child. As children transition from infancy to toddlerhood, parents often remark on the need to let their children make more choices and assert themselves. Moreover, the notion that two years of age is a turning point in children's independence is not limited to US mothers. As one Chinese mother of a two-year-old boy observed:

> I found that in this half month, he started, 'Mommy. I eat by myself'. He must have learned that from the nanny, 'Now you are big, you are no longer a little baby. Little babies need people to feed them because they are so little. But you are (a) big (boy), you should eat by yourself'.

Adolescence presents another period during which mothers observe their children's growing autonomy and may shift in their emphasis toward individualistic goals. Parents often define their early role as one in which they are guides to children's development, but by adolescence they remark that children are now 'on their own'. One Chinese mother of a 13-year-old boy noted that once you are older (a big boy), the choice to obey or not becomes the purview of the child, 'He will listen to me if he wants to but if he doesn't,

there is nothing I can do about it. He is a big boy now'. Similarly, a Mexican mother of an 18-month-old boy noted that although her role is currently to guide her young child, she recognized that by adolescence, her influence would be diminished as her son come to make his own choices: 'Our purpose is to teach and guide them along a good path. If they want to get lost, that is their problem'. Each of these examples reveals the ways in which the relative balance between relatedness and autonomy changes over developmental time.

The *form of coexistence* between autonomy and relatedness may also change with children's development. Parents may view the developmental goals of autonomy and relatedness as additive early in children's development and begin to view them as conflicting during adolescence. For example, parents increasingly encourage toddlers' autonomy with the emergence of developmental milestones such as walking and talking, but also foster toddlers' social skills (relatedness) through play interactions with peers and participation in organized group activities such as music classes, gymnastics, and sports. However, as children enter adolescence and the choice of friends is no longer the purview of parents, relatedness may be viewed as a threat to their adolescents' individual achievement. Friends may be seen as influencing choices and fears that children will become 'followers' heighten, as reflected in the following quotes from mothers in our study:

> I want him to be himself, to take his own decisions, to not get carried away by others.

> I don't want her to feel like she's doing it because somebody wants her to do it. Don't be easily misled or persuaded to do things. If anything else is to be a leader and not a follower.

> She's her own person. She don't let nobody influence her to do anything.

These statements reflect views of autonomy and relatedness as being in conflict among these parents of adolescents, and the question that remains is whether these views have shifted from an earlier emphasis on more balanced forms of coexistence. Although researchers have suggested that the relative balance of parents' emphases on autonomy and relatedness shifts over the course of development, no research has longitudinally explored how the form of coexistence may change over time. Research on dynamics to forms of coexistence between value systems and parents' developmental goals is needed to adequately understand how both the balance *and* form of coexistence between autonomy and relatedness in parents' socialization beliefs and practices change over the course of children's development.

Change across political and economic contexts

The relative balance of autonomy and relatedness and their forms of coexistence are also shaped by larger macro-level contexts such as political and economic trends (Bronfenbrenner & Morris, 1998). One example of macro-level influences on the coexistence of autonomy and relatedness is evidenced in Kagitcibasi and Ataca's (2005) historical account of the developmental goals of Turkish parents over the past three decades. When comparing Turkish families in the present to those in 1975, they found that high-income, urban Turkish parents valued autonomy more so than did their similar counterparts in prior generations. However, these parents simultaneously exhibited an increase in the 'psychological value of the child', which comprised expectations of joyfulness and closeness with their child (Kagitcibasi & Ataca, 2005). The authors ascribe these changes in parents' values for children to the economic growth and educational opportunities in Turkey that arose over the three decades of the study. As children in Turkey spend more time in school and as parents no longer rely on children for the material and economic sustenance of the household, there is a decline in children's utilitarian value and a concomitant increase in their psychological value.

Research on social and economic transformations in Eastern European countries and China more specifically offer another example of macro-level influences on the value systems of individualism vs. collectivism as well as the developmental goals of autonomy and relatedness. Over time, as countries transform from planned to market economies, workers' beliefs about autonomy and relatedness, and the balance and forms of coexistence between these goals, change as well (Chen et al., 2005; Guthrie, 1999, 2006).

An example of this process is reflected in the transformation of the Chinese concept of *guanxi* over the past two decades (Guthrie, 1998, 1999, 2006). The construct of *guanxi* emphasizes the functionally dependent coexistence between autonomy and relatedness. *Guanxi* is a form of social connection or relationship that is mutually beneficial to each partner in the dyad or network. Thus, relationships or connections serve, in essence, a utilitarian function to enhance individual success or achievement (i.e., relatedness as a path to autonomy). According to scholars (e.g., Guthrie, 1998; Walder, 1986), conceptions of relationships that rely heavily on social networking as a means for meeting individual needs (i.e., *guanxi*) are evident in shortage economies with weak legal infrastructures. In such economies, workers will rely on their social connections to address their individual needs as they believe it is their only route to meeting their individual needs. In our own research with Chinese-American immigrant youth in NYC (see Way et al., 2005; Way et al., 2007), we have seen evidence of the belief in *guanxi* in adolescents' descriptions of their parents' views about friendships (most of their parents immigrated to the USA during or before the early 1990s):

> My dad thinks friends use each other to get benefits from each other.

> My mom thinks its good to have lots of friends cause it's like connections with people ... like benefits you can have from having friends ... She told me that when she was small she had some friends that were like poor like she was and right now that one of those friends has a Porsche and she like makes a lot of money. And like they still talk to each other and now she's trying to help my mom start her own business.

Recently, however, social scientists have noted that this understanding of relationships or social connections as primarily utilitarian is losing significance in business and personal transactions as the economy in China moves from a planned to a market economy (Guthrie, 1998, 1999, 2006). With the emergence of a western-style legal infrastructure (a fundamental aspect of market economies), the reliance on *guanxi* becomes less necessary. In its place, our pilot studies in China over the past year suggest that Chinese workers have begun to view autonomy and relatedness as additive or conflicting, rather than as functionally dependent.

In interviews with parents during the winter of 2006, parents of infants in Nanjing, China spoke of the importance of *both* autonomy and relatedness in the socialization of their children. Their statements indicated that their beliefs about autonomy and relatedness were changing from being functionally dependent (that in which relationships with others promote individual ends) to viewing interpersonal relationships and individual achievement as both valuable in their own rights (additive). Mothers often not only indicated that they valued individual academic accomplishments and wanted their children to be leaders, but also strongly valued their children having good social skills so that they would be able to get along, have a lot of friends, and feel emotionally supported. Their narratives suggested that they sought both relatedness and autonomy for their children, but that one was not necessarily dependent on the other. A young Chinese mother of a two-year-old indicated that friendships are as important as academic achievement because in 'friendships you are learning as much about the world as you are in school'. This mother valued her child's learning about relationships as much as she valued her child's academic achievement.

Middle-school principals in our studies in Nanjing, China, however, discussed the conflicting nature of the goals of autonomy and relatedness. They noted that students who have a lot of friends are often those who do the least well in school. The principals often felt conflicted about the extent to which they should emphasize quality relationships (a key part of the government's current five-year education plan) vs. high academic achievement. In this example, the form of coexistence between relatedness and autonomy in China appears to be changing from viewing relationships as necessary for individual success (*guanxi*) to viewing relationships as potentially interfering with individual success (from the perspectives of principals).

Developmental psychologists studying Chinese children and parents have also indicated that the *relative balance* of autonomy and relatedness is dynamic, with changes in parents' views resulting from economic and political transitions. Chen and colleagues (2005) conducted a multiple cohort study of elementary school children in China in 1991, 1998, and 2002. In each cohort, parents', teachers', and peers' evalua-

tions of shy children were obtained in classrooms in Shanghai and Bejing. In 1991, shy children (as assessed by observations of children's behaviors in the classroom) were rated as extremely competent, popular, and as having the greatest potential to become leaders. At that time, because accommodating to the group was highly valued, shy children were considered to be particularly good 'citizens'. In 1998, as China was fully entering the transition to a market economy, in a new cohort of elementary school children from the same districts, shy children were ranked by their teachers, parents, and peers as neither highly competent nor incompetent. By 2002, when China was fully embedded in market economy that strongly valued individual initiative, in a third cohort of elementary school children, shy children were ranked by teachers, peers, and parents as incompetent, the least likely to become leaders, and the least popular among their peers (Chen et al., 2005). Thus, by 2002, students who distinguished themselves from others by taking initiative in positive ways were strongly valued, reflecting a shift in the balance between autonomy and relatedness.

The implications of dynamic values and developmental goals for parenting practices

In light of the dynamic nature of cultural value systems and parents' developmental goals, what are the implications for parenting practices and children's development? There is a growing body of empirical evidence connecting cultural value systems, parents' goals, and parents' everyday practices, yet much of this work is grounded in the assumption that cultural differences in parenting practices are stable across time and settings. For example, US mothers endorse self-feeding and infants sleeping in their own rooms at earlier ages than Puerto Rican mothers (Feng, Harwood Leyendecker, & Miller, 2001). German mothers respond more frequently to infant smiles than do mothers of the Cameroonian Nso, in efforts to promote infants' displays of positive emotions. In contrast, mothers of the Cameroonian Nso vigorously stimulate their infants' motor development so as to prepare children for manual labor within the family (relatedness goals; Keller, 2003). Japanese mothers more often encourage their five-month-old infants to look at them and engage in dyadic interactions (behaviors associated with relatedness), whereas US middle-income mothers encourage extra-dyadic interactions by pointing out features of the environment to their infants (behaviors associated with autonomy) (Bornstein, Miyake, & Tamis-LeMonda, 1985–1986). With infants of slightly older ages, Japanese mothers are more likely to engage their toddlers in other-directed pretend play (behaviors associated with relatedness) (e.g., by prompting their children to feed a baby doll) whereas US mothers are more likely to promote independent, concrete forms of play such as placing shapes in shape-sorters (behaviors associated with autonomy) (Tamis-LeMonda et al., 1992). Similarly, Chinese mothers engage in proportionally more elicitations of affiliation and connection when their toddlers confront unfamiliar challenge tasks in a laboratory setting (behaviors associated with relatedness) whereas Canadian mothers engage in proportionally more behaviors that encourage initiation and exploration (behaviors associated with autonomy) (Liu et al., 2005).

Together, these findings suggest that parenting practices are shaped by cultural values and developmental goals. However, what is missing from these accounts is a dynamic perspective of the changing nature of both parenting goals and practices across situations and time. If parents' goals and the associations between goals are dynamic, it is reasonable to expect *discontinuities* in parenting practices across situations and time. Parents most likely alter their expectations and behaviors in line with the current situation, selecting the appropriate times to emphasize the needs of the group vs. the needs of the child. Moreover, these shifting parenting practices are likely to be evidenced at nested time frames, with parents varying in their views and practices from moment-to-moment, within the course of a day, and across weeks, months, years, and decades. Consequently, discontinuities in parenting across settings and time might reflect adaptive reactions to environmental demands, rather than random noise. Thus, in revisiting parenting practices surrounding feeding, play, and sleep discussed above, researchers might begin to document when and how parents *change* their practices to align with their dynamic value systems and developmental goals.

Summary

Both the balance and forms of coexistence between individualism and collectivism, autonomy and relatedness, are dynamic. The salience of autonomy and relatedness in parents' developmental goals varies across settings and immigration as well as across developmental time in response to situational demands and children's growing abilities and expanding social relationships. Narratives from parents in our studies consistently underscore the ways in which the forms of coexistence between autonomy and relatedness changed as a result of immediate and larger context (e.g., from additive to conflicting), and immigrant parents in particular spoke of the need to adjust to the unequal balance between autonomy and relatedness in the host country. The dynamic nature of parents' developmental goals will likely be reflected in discontinuities in actual parenting practices across situations and developmental time, and if so, researchers should reconceptualize parenting discontinuities as potentially adaptive responses to changing task demands rather than as inconsistent ways of acting.

At macro levels, social, economic, and political changes might lead to shifts in the balance and forms of coexistence between autonomy and relatedness across generations. As one example, our ongoing research in Nanjing, China highlights these changes by suggesting that the functional associations between relatedness and individual success are shifting toward additive associations as relationships come to be esteemed in their own right in new market economies. However, these shifts are also producing conflicting associations in some instances, as reflected in the expressed wariness that strong friendships might interfere with the academic achievement of Chinese children.

Conclusions

Current scholarship on the value systems of individualism and collectivism has moved beyond grand divide theories to emphasize the coexistence of these values or developmental goals within individuals, families, and cultures. Our aim was to present a theoretical framework of the ways in which the values of individualism and collectivism, and developmental goals of autonomy and relatedness may coexist within individuals and within and across cultural contexts, and the ways in which these forms of coexistence may change over time. Drawing upon our work with parents from different ethnic and cultural groups, we identified a typology of three patterns of association between individualism and collectivism, autonomy and relatedness. Specifically, developmental goals that have largely been classified at opposite ends of a collectivism–individualism continuum might be conflicting, additive, or functionally dependent. Moreover, these forms of association are not static, but rather change from situation to situation, with children's development, and in response to social, political and economic contexts.

What factors might explain these dynamic patterns of association? At the most general level, trends of increased globalization, immigration, and technology expose parents and children to different values and behavioral systems in unprecedented ways. Some scholars have proposed that societies are converging toward greater individualism as a function of these global changes (Ghoshal & Bartlett, 1998), but it is also likely that changes in forms of coexistence between individualism and collectivism are heightened during periods of rapid change. As parents are faced with a multitude of options about the behaviors and attitudes that might help their children function in local and extended communities, traits that they deem to be important (or threatening) are likely to shift from situation to situation. At times, parents may interpret autonomy vs. relatedness as conflicting with family traditions and values, and these threats may become more salient as children expand their social networks, transition to adolescence, or when parents move to new countries or communities. At other times, parents may embrace both individualistic and collectivistic value systems, and view children who are autonomous, successful, maintain ties to the family, respect others, and display good manners to reflect the ideal. Finally, parents may view different developmental goals as functionally related, and consider certain goals as the means to other end goals. This latter form of association is reflected in widespread beliefs that children who are kind to others will in turn benefit from others' friendship, feel good about themselves, and be successful (relatedness as a path to autonomy); as well as beliefs that children who attain personal success will be better able to give back to the family and larger group both emotionally and instrumentally (autonomy as a path to relatedness). At the more macro level, periods of rapid social, political, and economic change, as occurred in the case of China, might lead to shifts in the balance of developmental goals and patterns of associations in workplace and family, in ways that highlight both benefits (functionality) and costs (conflicts) of new ways of thinking and acting.

Our discussion of the dynamic patterns of association between autonomy and relatedness sheds light on the limitations of current scholarship. Although a growing body of research acknowledges that autonomy and relatedness coexist in some form, there is a clear need to examine the precise nature of these forms of coexistence. To what extent do parents endorse different goals for their children? How and why do parents shift in their relative emphases on autonomy and relatedness across situations, time, and macro-structural change? How do the patterns of association change in response to both micro and macro contexts? We contend that parents are continually shifting in their developmental goals (and associated parenting practices) from day-to-day, week-to-week, and year-to-year. On a given day, the demands for individual achievement in a school setting might evoke conflicting or functional dependencies between relatedness and autonomy (e.g., peers at school may be viewed as harming or helping chances at individual success) that might be absent in the family setting. Across developmental time, as children transition from home to childcare settings, collectivistic goals might become subordinate to individualistic goals, as parents seek to support children's independence and ability to separate from the comforts of attachment figures. Some years later, there may be yet another shift toward greater emphasis on autonomy as children become adolescents and then young adults. Across historical time, changes to economic opportunity and market economies (as in the cases of China and Turkey discussed previously) might lead to shifts in the balance of autonomy-related goals as well as the form of association between autonomy and relatedness.

Finally, what might the dynamic coexistence of developmental goals (and associated parenting practices) mean for children? As a start, it is time to acknowledge that children are unlikely to be reared in environments that uniformly endorse individualistic or collectivistic ways of thinking and acting. Rather, children will be expected to be quiet, assertive, respectful, curious, humble, self-assured, independent, dependent, affectionate, or reserved depending on the situation, people present, children's age, and social–political and economic climates. Children will be told that friends are impediments to achievement and that friends are instrumental to learning and personal growth; that they should know that their parents will always be there for them, yet learn how to fend for themselves; that they should feel confident and proud of who they are, but that boasting is to be avoided and humility is a virtue; that they should always make their own choices, but be sure to respect others' wishes. This exposure to multiple ways of acting and thinking, and seemingly contradictory expectations, is what enables children to adapt to changing situations, lifestyles, people, and times. In short, the dynamic coexistence of autonomy and relatedness means that children are socialized to flexibly respond to the daily demands of their ever-changing cultural communities.

In closing, although research has moved beyond dichotomous characterizations of individualism/collectivism, autonomy/relatedness, there continues to be a relatively static portrayal of these value systems and developmental goals. As we have argued, not only are cultural values and developmental goals dynamic in and of themselves, but also the form of their coexistence is dynamic and depends on both micro and macro contexts. Exploring the ways in which these values or goals coexist and how their coexistence changes over time is critical to advancing a richer and more nuanced understanding of child development and parenting in diverse cultural contexts.

References

Bakan, D. (1966). *The duality of human existence.* Chicago: Rand Mcnally.

Bornstein, M. H., Miyake, K., & Tamis-LeMonda, C. S. (1985–1986). A cross-national study of mother and infant activities and interactions: Some preliminary compari-sons between Japan and the United States. *Research & Clinical Center for Child Development, 9*, 1–12.

Bornstein, M. H., Venuti, P., & Hahn, C-S. (2002). Mother-child play in Italy: Regional variation, individual stability and mutual dyadic influence. In. C. S. Tamis-LeMonda, & R. Harwood (Guest Editors), Special Issue of *Parenting: Science & Practice: Parental Ethnotheories: Cultural Practices and Normative Development, 2*, 273–301.

Brewer, M. B. (1991). The social self: On being the same and different at the same time. *Personality and Social Psychology Bulletin, 17*, 475–482.

Brewer, M. B., & Chen, Y.-R. (2007) Where (Who) are collectives in collectivism? Toward conceptual clarification of individualism and collectivism. *Psychological Review, 114*, 133–151.

Bridges, L. J. (2003). Autonomy as an element of developmental well-being. In M. H. Bornstein, L. Davidson, C. M. Keyes, & K. A. Moore (Eds.), *Well being: Positive development across the life course* (pp. 167–189). Mahwah, NJ: Erlbaum.

Bronfenbrenner, U., & Morris, P. A. (1998). The ecology of developmental processes. In W. Damon (Series Ed.) & R. M. Lerner (Vol. Ed.), *Handbook of child psychology: Theoretical models of human development* (5th ed., Vol. 1, pp. 993–1028). New York: Wiley.

Bugental, D. B., & Goodnow, J. J. (1998). Socialization processes. In W. Damon (Series Ed.) & N. Eisenberg (Vol. Ed.), *Handbook of child psychology: Social, emotional, and personality development* (5th ed., vol. 3, pp. 389–462). Hoboken, NJ: John Wiley & Sons, Inc.

Cha, J. (1994). Aspects of individualism and collectivism in Korea. In U. Kim, H. C. Triandis, C. Kagitcibasi, S. Choi, & G. Yoon (Eds.), *Individualism and collectivism: Theory, method, and applications* (vol. 18, pp. 157–174). Thousand Oaks, CA: Sage Publications, Inc.

Chao, R., & Tseng, V. (2002). Parenting of Asians. In M. H. Bornstein (Ed.), *Handbook of parenting: Social conditions and applied parenting* (2nd ed., Vol. 4, pp. 59–93). Mahwah, NJ: Lawrence Erlbaum Associates.

Chen, X., Cen, G., Li, D., & He, Y. (2005). Social functioning and adjustment in Chinese children: The imprint of historical time. *Child Development, 76*, 182–195.

Cortes, D. E. (1995). Variations in familism in two generations of Puerto Ricans. *Hispanic Journal of Behavioral Sciences, 17*, 249–255.

Deci, E. L., Ryan, R. M., & Koestner, R. (1999). A meta-analytic review of experiments examining the effects of extrinsic rewards on intrinsic motivation. *Psychological Bulletin, 125*, 627–668.

Dennis, T. A., Cole, P. M., Zahn-Waxler, C., & Mizuta, I. (2002). Self in context: Autonomy and relatedness in Japanese and U.S. mother-preschooler dyads. *Child Development, 73*, 1803–1817.

Feng, X., Harwood, R. L., Leyendecker, B., & Miller, A. M. (2001). Changes across the first year of life in infants' daily activities and social contacts among middle-class Anglo and Puerto Rican families. *Infant Behavior & Development*, *24*, 317–339.

Fiske, A. P. (2002). Using individualism and collectivism to compare cultures—A critique of the validity and measurement of the constructs: Comment on Oyserman et al. (2002). *Psychological Bulletin*, *128*, 78–88.

Fuligni, A. J., Tseng, V., & Lam, M. (1999). Attitudes toward family obligations among American adolescents from Asian, Latin American, and European backgrounds. *Child Development*, *70*, 1030–1044.

Ghoshal, S., & Bartlett, C. (1998). *The individualized corporation*. London: Random House.

Gilligan, C. (1982). *In a different voice: Psychological theory and women's development*. Cambridge, MA: Harvard University Press.

Gonzalez-Ramos, G., Zayas, L. H., & Cohen, E. (1998). Child-rearing values of low-income, urban Puerto Rican mothers of preschool children. *Professional Psychology Research and Practice*, *29*, 377–382.

Grotevant, H. D. (1998). Adolescent development in family contexts. In W. Damon (Series Ed.) & N. Eisertberg (Vol. Ed.), *Handbook of child psychology: Social, emotional, and personality development* (5th ed., Vol. 3, pp. 1097–1149). New York: John Wiley & Sons.

Guthrie, D. (1998). The declining significance of guanxi in China's economic transition. *The Chinese Quarterly*, *154*, 254–282.

Guthrie, D. (1999). *Dragon in a three-piece suit: The emergence of capitalism in China*. Princeton, NJ: Princeton University press.

Guthrie, D. (2006). *China and globalization: The social, economic, and political transformation of Chinese society*. Great Britain: Routledge Press.

Harkness, S., Super, C. M., & van Tijen, N. (2000). Individualism and the 'western mind' reconsidered: American and Dutch parents' ethnotheories of the child. In S. Harkness, C. Raeff, & C. M. Super (Eds.), *Variability in the social construction of the child. New Directions for Child and Adolescent Development*, *87*, 23–29.

Harwood, R. L., Miller, J. G., & Irizarry, N. L. (1995). *Culture and attachment: Perceptions of the child in context*. New York: Guilford Press.

Harwood, R. L., Schoelmerich, A., Schulze, P. A., & Gonzalez, Z. (1999). Cultural differences in maternal beliefs and behaviors: A study of middle-class Anglo and Puerto Rican mother–infant pairs in four everyday situations. *Child Development*, *70*, 1005–1016.

Hofstede, G. H. (1980). *Culture's consequence: International differences in work-related values*. Beverly Hills, CA: Sage.

Iyengar, S. S., & Lepper, M. R. (1999). Rethinking the value of choice: A cultural perspective on intrinsic motivation. *Journal of Personality and Social Psychology*, *76*, 349–366.

Johnson, D., & Johnson, R. (1989). *Cooperation and competition: Theory and research*. Edina, MN: Interaction Books.

Jones, H. B. (1997). The Protestant ethic: Weber's model and the empirical literature. *Human Relations*, *50*, 757–778.

Kagitcibasi, C. (1996). *Family and human development across cultures: A view from the other side*. Mahwah, NJ: Erlbaum.

Kagitcibasi, C. (2005). Autonomy and relatedness in cultural context: Implications for self and family. *Journal of Cross-Cultural Psychology*, *36*, 403–422.

Kagitcibasi, C., & Ataca, B. (2005). Value of children and family change: A three-decade portrait from Turkey. *Applied Psychology: An International Review*, *54*, 317–337.

Keller, H. (2003). Socialization for competence: Cultural models of infancy. *Human Development*, *46*, 288–311.

Killen, M., McGlothlin, H., & Lee-Kim, J. (2002). Between individuals and culture: Individuals' evaluation of exclusion from social groups. In H. Keller, Y. H. Porringa, & A. Schoelmerich (Eds.), *Between culture and biology: Perspectives on ontogenetic development* (pp. 159–190). Cambridge: Cambridge University Press.

Kohlberg, L. (1981). *The meaning and measurement of moral development*. Worcester, MA: Clark University Press.

Kohn, M. L. (1969). *Class and conformity: A study in values*. Chicago, IL: The University of Chicago Press.

Lieber, E., Yang, K. S., & Lin, Y. C. (2000). An external orientation to the study of causal beliefs: Application to Chinese populations and comparative research. *Journal of Cross-Cultural Psychology*, *3*, 160–186.

Lin, C. C., & Fu, V. R. (1990). A comparison of child-rearing practices among Chinese, immigrant Chinese, and Caucasian-American parents. *Child Development*, *61*, 429–433.

Liu, M., Chen, X., Rubin, K., Zheng, S., Cui, L., Li, D., et al. (2005). Autonomy- vs. connectedness-oriented parenting behaviours in Chinese and Canadian mothers. *International Journal of Behavioral Development*, *29*, 489–495.

Markus, H. R., & Kitayama, S. (1991). Culture and the self: Implications for cognition, emotion, and motivation. *Psychological Review*, *98*, 224–253.

Maslow, A. H. (1943). A theory of human motivation. *Psychological Review*, *50*, 370–396.

Maslow, A. H. (1948). 'Higher' and 'lower' needs. *Journal of Psychology: Interdisciplinary and Applied*, *25*, 433–136.

McGillicuddy-De Lisi, A. V., & Sigel, I. E. (1995). Parental beliefs. In M. H. Bornstein (Ed.), *Handbook of parenting* (Vol. 3, pp. 333–358). Mahwah, NJ: Lawrence Erlbaum Associates.

Mesquita, B., & Walker, R. (2003). Cultural differences in emotions: A context for interpreting emotional experiences. *Behavior Research and Therapy, 41*, 777–793.

Miller, P. J., Wang, S., Sandel, T., & Cho, G. E. (2002). Self-esteem as folk theory: A comparison of European American and Taiwanese mothers' beliefs. In C. S. Tamis-LeMonda, & R. Harwood (Guest Editors), Special Issue of *Parenting: Science & Practice: Parental Ethnotheories: Cultural Practices and Normative Development, 2*, 209–239.

Ogbu, J. U. (1988). Cultural identity and human development. *New Directions for Child Development, 42*, 11–28.

Oyserman, D., Coon, H. M., & Kemmelmeier, M. (2002). Rethinking individualism and collectivism: Evaluation of theoretical assumptions and meta-analyses. *Psychological Bulletin, 128*, 3–72.

Parsons, T., & Shils, E. A. (1951). Values, motives, and systems of action. In T. Parsons, & E. A. Shils (Eds.), *Toward a general theory of action*. Cambridge, MA: Harvard University Press.

Pessar, P. R. (1995). *A visa and a dream: Dominicans in the United States*. Boston: Allyn and Bacon.

Rothbaum, F., & Trommsdorff, G. (2007). Do roots and wings complement or oppose one another: The socialization of relatedness and autonomy in cultural context. In J. Grusec, & P. Hastings (Eds.), *Handbook of socialization* (2nd ed., pp. 461–489). New York: Guilford Press.

Rothbaum, F., Weisz, J., Pott, M., Miyake, K., & Morelli, G. (2000). Attachment and culture: Security in the United States and Japan. *American Psychologist, 55*, 1093–1104.

Ryan, R. M., & Deci, E. L. (2000a). Intrinsic and extrinsic motivations: Classic definitions and new directions. *Contemporary Educational Psychology, 25*, 54–67.

Ryan, R. M., & Deci, E. L. (2000b). Self-determination theory and the facilitation of intrinsic motivation, social development, and well-being. *American Psychologist, 55*, 68–78.

Sabogal, F., Marin, G., Otero-Sabogal, R., & Marin, B. V. (1987). Hispanic familism and acculturation: What changes and what doesn't? *Hispanic Journal of Behavioral Sciences, 9*, 397–412.

Sampson, E. E. (1977). Psychology and the American ideal. *Journal of Personality and Social Psychology, 35*, 767–782.

Shweder. R. A., Goodnow, J., Hatano, G., LeVine, R., Markus, H., & Miller, P. (1998). The cultural psychology of development: One mind, many mentalities. In W. Damon (Series Ed.) & R. M. Lemer (Vol. Ed.), *Handbook of child psychology: Theoretical models of human development* (5th Ed., Vol. 1, pp. 865–938). New York: Wiley.

Sinha, D., & Tripathi, R. C. (1994). Individualism in a collectivist culture: A case of coexistence of opposites. In U. Kim, H. C. Triandis, C. Kagitcibasi, S. Choi, & G. Yoon (Eds.), *Individualism and collectivism: Theory, method, and applications* (Vol. 18, pp. 123–136). Thousand Oaks, CA: Sage Publications, Inc.

Smetana, J. (2002). Culture, autonomy, and personal jurisdiction. In R. Kail, & H. Reese (Eds.), *Advances in child development and behavior* (Vol. 29, pp. 52–87). Amsterdam, The Netherlands: Academic Press.

Smith, P., & Schwartz, S. (1997). Values. In J. Berry, M. Segall, & C. Kagitcibasi (Eds.), *Handbook of cross-cultural psychology: Social behavior and applications* (2nd ed., Vol. 3, pp. 78–118). Needham Heights, MA: Allyn and Bacon.

Smith, R. (2005). *Mexican New York: Transnational lives of new immigrants,* Berkeley: University of California Press.

Spencer, M. B., & Dornsbusch, S. M. (1990). Challenges in studying minority youth. In S. Feldman, & G. R. Elliott (Eds.), *At the threshold: The developing adolescent* (pp. 123–146). Cambridge, MA: Harvard University Press.

Stevenson, H. W., Lee, S., Chen, C., Stigler, J. W., Hsu, C., & Kitamura, S. (1990). Contexts of achievement: A study of American, Chinese, and Japanese children. *Monographs of the Society for Research in Child Development, 55*, i–119.

Suarez-Orozco, C., Todorova, I. L., & Louie, J. (2002). Making up for lost time: The experience of separation and reunification among immigrant families. *Family Process, 41*, 625–643.

Super, C. M., & Harkness, S. (2002). Culture structures the environment for development. *Human Development, 45*, 270–274.

Tamis-LeMonda, C. S. (2003). Cultural perspectives on the 'Whats?' and 'Whys?' of parenting. *Human Development, 46*, 319–327.

Tamis-LeMonda, C. S., Bornstein, M. H., Cyphers, L., Toda, S., & Ogino, M. (1992). Language and play at one year: A comparison of toddlers and mothers in the United States and Japan. *International Journal of Behavioral Development, 15*, 19–42.

Tamis-LeMonda, C. S., Wang, S., Koutsouvanou, E., & Albright, M. (2002). Chitdrearing values in Greece, Taiwan, and the United States. *Parenting Science and Practice, 2*, 185–208.

Triandis, H. C. (1988). Collectivism and development. In D. Sinha, & H. S. R. Kao (Eds.), *Social values and development: Asian perspectives* (pp. 285–303). Thousand Oaks, CA: Sage Publications, Inc.

Triandis, H. C. (1994). Theoretical and methodological approaches to the study of collectivism and individualism. In U. Kim, H. C. Triandis, C. Kagitcibasi, S. Choi, & G. Yoon (Eds.), *Individualism and collectivism: Theory, method, and applications* (Vol. 18, pp. 41–51). Thousand Oaks, CA: Sage Publications, Inc.

Triandis, H. C. (1995). *Individualism & collectivism*. Boulder, CO: Western Press.

Triandis, H. C. (2000). Culture and conflict. *International Journal of Psychology*, *35*, 145–152.

Triandis, H. C., McCusker, C., & Hui, C. H. (1990). Multimethod probes of individualism and collectivism. *Journal of Personality and Social Psychology*, *59*, 1006–1020.

Vygotsky, L. S. (1978). *Mind in society: The development of higher psychological processes.* Cambridge, MA: Harvard University Press.

Walder, A. (1986). *Community neo-traditionalism: Work and authority in Chinese industry.* Berkeley and Los Angeles: University of California Press.

Wang, S., & Tamis-LeMonda, C. S. (2003). Do child-rearing values in Taiwan and the United States reflect cultural values of collectivism and individualism? *Journal of Cross-Cultural Psychology*, *34*, 629–642.

Way, N., Becker, B., & Greene, M. (2005). Friendships among African American, Latino, and Asian American adolescents in an urban context. In C. Tamis-Lemonda, & L. Baiter (Eds.), *Child Psychology: A Handbook of Contemporary Issues* (2nd ed., pp. 415–443). New York: Psychology Press.

Way, N., Greene, M., & Pandey, P. (2007). Parental peer-related attitudes and practices and their link to friendship quality among Chinese American and Puerto Rican youth. In B. Brown, & N. Mounts (Eds), *Links between parents and peers.* New Directions in Child Development.

Weber, M. (1958). *The Protestant ethic and the spirit of capitalism* (Talcott Parsons, Trans.). New York: Charles Scribner's Sons. (Originally published as two separate essays 1904–1905).

Weisner, T. (2002). The American dependency conflict: Continuities and discontinuities in behaviours and values of countercultural parents and their children. *Ethos*, *29*, 271–295.

Whiting, B. B. (1974). Folk wisdom and child rearing. *Merrill-Palmer Quarterly*, *20*, 9–19.

Whiting, B. B. (1978). The dependency hang-up and experiments in alternative life styles. In M. J. Yinger, & S. J. Cutler (Eds.), *Major social issues: A multidisciplinary view* (pp. 217–226). New York: The Free Press.

Wilson, R. W., & Pusey, A. W. (1982). Achievement motivation and small-business relationship patterns in Chinese society. In S. L. Greenblatt, R. W. Wilson, & A. A. Wilson (Eds.), *Social interaction in Chinese society* (pp. 195–208). New York: Praeger.

Witken, H. A., & Berry, J. W. (1975). Psychological differentiation in cross-cultural perspective. *Journal of Cross-Cultural Psychology*, *6*, 4–87.

Yu, A., & Yang, K. (1994). The nature of achievement motivation in collectivist societies. In U. Kim, H. C. Triandis, C. Kagitcibasi, S. Choi, & G. Yoon (Eds.), *Individualism and collectivism: Theory, method, and applications* (Vol. 18, pp. 239–250). Thousand Oaks, CA: Sage Publications, Inc.

....

Muslim and Non-Muslim Adolescents' Reasoning About Freedom of Speech and Minority Rights

Maykel Verkuyten and Luuk Slooter

Freedoms and rights are of concern to people all over the world. These issues are increasingly important today due to several decades of increased migration and the growing acknowledgment that many societies are now religiously, linguistically, ethnically, and culturally diverse. Within democratic societies, the development of adolescents' judgments about free speech and religious minority rights is an issue of particular salience. This is because such societies commonly see the teaching of tolerant reactions to dissenting others as an important part of the socialization of their youth.

Adolescence is both a salient and critical period for the learning of civil liberties and political tolerance

(e.g., Avery, 1989; Berti, 2005). This learning takes place within the interpretations and representations circulating within a given society. Current debates in many Western societies focus on religious diversity and the position of Islam in particular. Commentators and politicians, for example, often argue that freedoms and rights characterize Western democratic societies and are of minimal concern to Muslims or even contradictory to Islam. It is suggested and claimed that the rights-based morality of Western societies differs from the duty-based morality of Islam. This difference would be symbolized by the debate on the Danish cartoons of the Prophet Mohammed, *the fatwa* against the British novelist Salman Rushdie, and the murder of the Dutch filmmaker Theo van Gogh. Hence, according to some commentators, there is an ongoing "West–Muslim" cultural war, especially over issues of free speech and religious minority rights (e.g., Scroggins, 2005). Islam has moved to the center of immigration and diversity debates and politics in European countries (Zolberg & Long, 1999).

Thus, the development of reasoning about free speech and Muslim minority rights among both non-Muslim and Muslim adolescents is a key issue for understanding intergroup relations in Western countries. To address this issue, we conducted a study with majority group non-Muslim and minority group Muslim participants between 12 and 18 years of age. Various aspects of free speech and religious minority rights were investigated, such as agent, social implications, and belief type. We used an experimental questionnaire design to examine these aspects as well as the effects of ethnic group, age, and gender. We conducted our study in the Netherlands, one of the most secular countries in the world (Te Grotenhuis & Scheepers, 2001). Theoretically, the research aims to combine social-cognitive domain theory and intergroup theories. The research seeks to make a contribution to recent efforts to integrate these two theoretical frameworks. The work of Killen and colleagues (Killen, Margie, & Sinno, 2006; Killen, Sinno, & Margie, 2007), for example, has shown that ethnic and racial stereotypes and prejudices enters into the social reasoning behind exclusion and that children's own ethnicity influences how they evaluate social exclusion.

Freedom of speech and minority rights

Freedom of speech and minority rights are necessary for a diverse, equal, and democratic society. A limited number of studies have examined the development of judgments about freedom and rights in different contexts. In two studies among children, adolescents, and young adults in North America, Helwig (1995, 1997) examined freedom of speech and freedom of religion in contexts of conflicting considerations, such as psychological and physical harm, and equality of opportunity. Helwig found a fair amount of variation in the judgments and younger participants were more likely

than the older ones to subordinate each freedom to preventing harm and inequalities. Further, children were more concerned with psychological needs involved in freedom of speech, whereas there was growing recognition of the societal and democratic functions of free speech during adolescence.

In another study in Canada, Helwig and Prencipe (1999) examined children's judgments about flag-burning scenarios. Children found flag burning offensive and 6-year-olds more than 8-year-olds and 10-year-olds said that there should be a law in Canada and in other countries prohibiting flag burning. In evaluating the scenarios, children were also found to take the intentions of agents and the possible negative consequences for others into account.

Turiel and Wainryb (1998) examined a non-Western traditional cultural group: the Islamic Druze community in northern Israel. As with the Helwig studies, this community also endorsed freedom of speech and religion, and the exercising of these rights was evaluated in relation to moral, societal, and psychological considerations. Further, cross-national studies have shown that adolescents in different countries endorse human rights but also evaluate these in relation to different considerations and concerns, such as community welfare and social order (Clemence, Doise, de Rosa, & Gonzalez, 1995).

The findings of these and other studies (see Helwig & Turiel, 2002; Neff & Helwig, 2002; Ruck, Abramovitch, & Keating, 1998; Ruck, Peterson-Badali, & Day, 2002) demonstrate the complex nature of adolescents' judgments and reasoning about civil liberties. Endorsement of free speech and religious minority rights appears to be contextual and dependent on the ways that individuals coordinate and weigh different sorts of knowledge. The theoretical implication is that the social-cognitive domain model (see Smetana, 2006; Turiel, 2002) seems more adequate for understanding the development of social and political judgments than a cognitive developmental framework that proposes increasingly advanced stages of endorsement of civil liberties (e.g., Enright & Lapsey, 1981; Enright, Lapsey, Franklin, & Streuck, 1984).

The social-cognitive domain model emphasizes that children and adolescents apply different domains of knowledge in their social reasoning and judgments. Not only moral considerations (fairness, others' welfare) but also social-conventional (group norms, traditions) and psychological ones (self-understanding, personal choices) are used for the evaluation of a range of social events. This model has been applied to complex issues and for understanding how individuals differ in the ways that they categorize and evaluate social events. The enactment of free speech and minority rights, for example, might be seen as producing harm to people, as going against conventional standards, or as threatening the position and identity of one's group.

However, social-cognitive domain investigations into the endorsement of freedom of speech and religious minority rights have not taken the intergroup context into account. That is to say, the existing research has not systematically examined and compared the views of majority and minority group members living in a religiously and culturally diverse Western society such as the Netherlands. Social psychological research has demonstrated that the context of intergroup relationships affects children's and adolescents' perceptions and evaluative judgments (see Bennett & Sani, 2004). Many studies have shown that negative stereotypes, prejudice, and discrimination are pervasive in the lives of ethnic minority youth (e.g., Fisher, Wallace, & Fenton, 2000; McKown & Weinstein, 2003). For example, in a large-scale national study in the Netherlands, Verkuyten and Thijs (2002) found that ethnic minority group early adolescents are more likely than Dutch children to become the victims of ethnic name calling and social exclusion. The highest level of experienced ethnic name calling was found for the Islamic Turkish children. Research has shown that these kinds of experiences can have an impact on children's moral reasoning (see Killen et al., 2007).

In the Netherlands, as in other countries, the problems of a multicultural society are increasingly discussed in relation to Islam. In the media, Islam has become a symbol of problems related to ethnic minorities and immigration (see Ter Wal, 2004). As a result, public discussion focuses on the need to compel Islamic groups to assimilate and to reject or seriously limit Muslim minority rights. Appealing to the right of free speech, leading politicians have publicly described Islam as a "backward religion" that seriously threatens Dutch secularized society and culture and

have defined Muslims as a "fifth column" and argued for the need for a "cold war" against Islam (see Scroggins, 2005; Verkuyten & Zaremba, 2005). Furthermore, in 2005, the Pew Global Project Attitudes found that 51% of the Dutch population declared unfavorable opinions about Muslims. This was the highest percentage of all countries examined. In France, for example, the percentage was 36%, and in Great Britain, it was 14%. In addition, of all groups in the Netherlands, Muslims have on average the poorest academic results, irrespective of how academic performance is defined, and the weakest labor market position.

It is likely that this intergroup context affects how Muslim minority and non-Muslim majority adolescents evaluate issues of freedom of speech and Muslim minority rights, and the ways in which they evaluate the different considerations and concerns. Social identity theory (Tajfel & Turner, 1979) and optimal distinctiveness theory (Brewer, 1991) argue that under identity threatening circumstances, people will try to restore and reassert their threatened collective identity. Furthermore, realistic group conflict theory emphasizes the role of group interest in the dynamics of intergroup relations (e.g., Bobo, 1999; Sherif, 1966). For minority groups, minority rights offer the possibility of maintaining one's own distinctive culture and identity and obtaining a more equal social status in society. Because of this, we expected that when compared to non-Muslim participants, Muslim participants would, on the whole, be less in favor of free speech that negatively portrays religions in general (and Islam in particular) and that they would be more in favor of Muslim minority rights. We did not, however, think it would necessarily mean that Muslim participants would be less in favor of freedom of speech in general and of other (non-Muslim) group rights. When no intergroup concerns are involved, Muslim and non-Muslim participants were expected to give similar judgments.

Examining judgments about freedom of speech and minority rights

People can be both accepting and rejecting of civil liberties because judgments seem to depend on many factors, such as what and who people are asked to accept, the way in which they are asked to be accepting, and the underlying belief they are asked to accept. Our study has four aspects for examining judgments about freedom of speech and minority rights. These aspects relate to political rights, to the social consequences of effectuating rights, to the role of underlying belief type, and to dimensions of acceptance.

The first that we deal with here focuses on the endorsement of political rights. The great majority of existing research examines levels of political tolerance, particularly the endorsement of freedoms and civil liberties. There are various studies on adolescents' political thinking and behavior (see Berti, 2005, for a review). Among other things, these studies show that adolescents tend to support democratic rights in the abstract. However, similar to adults and in agreement with the social-cognitive domain model, adolescents often do not endorse the same rights in concrete circumstances (Helwig, 1995). It is one thing to endorse the freedom of speech in general, and another thing to apply this freedom to, for example, Muslim groups living in a secular country (Turiel, 2002). We focused on two concrete examples of freedom of speech, namely the freedom to offend others and the freedom to incite a war. Thus, we presented freedom of speech as in conflict with psychological harm and physical harm, respectively. Additionally, we examined two specific minority rights, namely, the right to found one's own schools and the right to demonstrate and protest. Both rights are guaranteed by the Dutch constitution but were presented as in conflict with the importance of social integration in society and the importance of valuing national identity. We used a between-subjects design to compare the judgments toward Muslim and non-Muslim groups claiming these freedoms and rights. We expected that the non-Muslim majority participants would be less accepting toward the Muslim than the non-Muslim group, whereas the Muslim minority participants would be more accepting toward the Muslims than the non-Muslims.

The second aspect we examined was the social implications of particular acts performed by Muslims. Civil liberties always have limits and should be evaluated in relation to other principles and values. Most people do not support freedoms and rights when they are in serious conflict with other considerations and

concerns. For example, one's own freedom ends when it threatens the freedom of others. Also, the right to act differently is limited by principles of equality and by operative public norms that govern the civic relations between people (Parekh, 2000). In our research, we contrasted the freedom of speech with the norm of not offending others. Furthermore, the freedom of religious expression (wearing of a headscarf) was contrasted with, respectively, democratic principles and the operative public norm of interpersonal communication. For all three contrasts, we used a between-subjects design in order to make a distinction between "minimal" and "maximal" social implications. This distinction refers to the extent to which the act contradicts the other principle or norm; for example, freedom of speech in contrast to ridiculing (minimal) or deeply offending (maximal) people. It was expected that both Muslim and non-Muslim participants would be less accepting in the maximal compared to the minimal conditions. In addition, we expected that compared to non-Muslims, Muslim minority participants would be less in favor of free speech that offends religious beliefs and more in favor of Muslim minority rights.

The third aspect we examined was how adolescents' judgments can depend on the underlying belief type. A basic distinction in belief type is between what one believes to be true and what one believes to be right. The former are beliefs about matters of fact and the latter are value judgments. Across a broad age range, developmental studies have found that children and adolescents distinguish between informational and moral beliefs and use this distinction in their judgments of social practices. For example, in a study among an ethnically mixed sample from the San Francisco Bay area, Wainryb (1993) showed that children and adolescents (9–23 years) contextualized their own judgments when they apply them to unknown cultural out-groups ("a country") with different informational beliefs (what they believe to be true) but not when they apply them to out-groups with different moral beliefs (what they believe to be right). In another study among European Americans, Wainryb, Shaw, and Maianu (1998) found that children and early adolescents (7–14 years) are more tolerant when the underlying dissenting beliefs were informational as opposed to moral.

Hence, the distinction between what one believes to be true and what one believes to be right seems to be important for judgments about minority rights. One reason for this is that the type of underlying belief can be used to infer intentions behind the practice that one dislikes or rejects but is asked to accept. Ignorance and misinformation can be inferred from informational dissent, whereas badness or immorality is a more likely inference from moral dissent. Following previous studies, we expected participants to be more accepting of Muslim and non-Muslim "harmful" practices based on informational beliefs than on moral beliefs. We used a between-subjects design to examine this expectation. Further, we examined the evaluation of practices of Muslim parents (female circumcision and gender differentiation) and of non-Muslim parents (home education and child vaccination) and we expected that non-Muslim majority participants would be less accepting toward the former than Muslim participants. However, both groups of participants were not expected to differ in their evaluation of practices of non-Muslim parents because in that case no intergroup concerns are at stake.

In addition to examining the effects of varying the content of the underlying beliefs, the fourth aspect we focused on was the different ways in which people may be asked to endorse minority rights. Accepting that people have a right to *hold* dissenting beliefs does not have to imply that one tolerates the *public expression* of such beliefs or the *actual practices* based on such beliefs (Vogt, 1997). These dimensions of tolerance can trigger different levels of endorsement. In their study, Wainryb et al. (1998) found, for example, that European American children and early adolescents were more accepting of dissenting speech than practices (see also Witenberg, 2002). In the present study, we focused on the judgment of actual dissenting practices by Muslim and non-Muslim parents toward their children and of the public expression aimed at trying to convince other parents to act similarly. In general, we expected that adolescents of both groups of participants would be relatively accepting toward public expressions because this is linked to freedom of speech, can be thought to stimulate debate, and does not directly cause harm or injustice to other people (see Wainryb et al., 1998). In contrast, actual practices

based on dissenting beliefs can involve harmful and unfair consequences and therefore we expected less acceptance for this dimension.

Age and gender

Enright and Lapsey (1981) have described a developmental progression from a generally intolerant attitude during the childhood years through to increasingly tolerant judgments during adolescence (see also Enright et al., 1984). The sequence they proposed runs parallel with changes in perspective taking and Kohlberg's stages of moral development. Other studies have found similar age-related changes, which are attributed to increasingly complex and principled forms of reasoning (e.g., Bobo & Licardi, 1989; Thalhammer, Wood, Bird, Avery, & Sullivan, 1994).

However, there are also studies that do not find age differences in moral judgments (e.g., Wainryb, 1993) or find that older adolescents are less tolerant than younger ones (e.g., Witenberg, 2002). In developmental stage studies, tolerance is typically examined as a single, global construct and dimensions of tolerance and types of dissenting beliefs and practices are not considered. Studies that do take different aspects of tolerance into account give a more complex picture of age differences with tolerance and intolerance coexisting at all ages (e.g., Wainryb et al., 1998). More importantly, studies on children's and adolescents' reasoning about civil liberties do not find support for a global stage interpretation (e.g. Helwig, 1995, 1997; Ruck et al., 1998). Rather, with age, early-developed concepts of rights and freedoms are increasingly assessed with other considerations and concerns, including the intergroup context. In contrast to young children (early), adolescents tend to make more context-sensitive judgments about freedoms and rights. The context dependence of the endorsement of civil liberties makes it unlikely that there is an age-related global developmental trend in our adolescent sample. Hence, we did not expect a consistent positive effect for age.

Killen and colleagues have found gender differences in children's reasoning about ethnic and racial exclusion. Compared to girls, boys find exclusion more acceptable and more often use conventional reasoning and stereotypes in justifying their evaluations

(Killen et al., 2007). Other research from the cognitive domain approach, however, has found few gender differences (Smetana, 2006). Further, studies on the development of judgments of freedoms and rights have either not examined gender differences (e.g., Helwig & Prencipe, 1999; Ruck et al., 2002) or found no differences between females and males (e.g., Helwig, 1995, 1997; Sigelman & Toebben, 1992). However, females may experience greater restrictions in their choices, freedoms, and opportunities, and these experiences can affect moral and social judgments (Turiel, 2002). Analyses and perceptions of differences between the Western and the Muslim world emphasize differential gender relationships. The ideal of egalitarian gender arrangements in Western societies is contrasted with the patriarchal and unequal gender relations in Muslim communities. Obedience to the father and the placing of various restrictions on the activities of females (e.g., regarding leisure time, sexuality, marriage, and the distribution of household tasks) is more common in some of these communities. Endorsement of Muslim minority rights involving women's clothing and gender arrangements and practices were considered in our study, and we explored whether male and female participants differ in their judgments of these practices.

Current study

To summarize, the main purpose of this investigation was to examine the contextual nature and development of reasoning about freedom of speech and minority rights among Muslim minority and non-Muslim majority adolescents. The study focuses on different forms and aspects of this reasoning by examining types of freedom of speech and types of minority rights, contrasting values, belief type, and dimensions of acceptance. In general, we expected that compared to non-Muslims, Muslim participants would be less endorsing of freedom of speech when it involves offending religious beliefs and to be more endorsing of Muslim minority rights. In addition, both Muslim and non-Muslim adolescents were expected to be less accepting of practices that are more difficult to reconcile with other values, to be less accepting of practices based on dissenting moral beliefs than informational beliefs, and to be less

accepting toward actual acts as opposed to public speech. We also examined age and gender differences. Gender differences were explored, and we did not expect a consistent effect for age.

Research on freedoms, rights, and tolerance often lacks relevance and ecological validity. Studies have examined, for example, the endorsement of abstract principles such as freedom of speech and freedom of religion. However, principle considerations differ from support for practical implications and situations. Most debates on freedoms, rights, and diversity are not about principles per se but rather about whether a principle is appropriate for a specific case at hand and how exactly it should be interpreted. Furthermore, studies that do use concrete examples, for example, in dilemmas and vignettes, tend to use rather unfamiliar and hypothetical scenarios. In our study, we tried to maximize the relevance and validity of the research by using cases and situations that currently are, or recently were, debated in Dutch society.

In this study, we are interested in the endorsement of free speech and minority rights among non-Muslim majority adolescents and Muslim minority group peers. Our focus is on the status difference between the majority and the minority group. In examining this difference, we considered it important to consider religiousness. It is likely that the Muslim participants are much more religious than the Dutch non-Muslims. Therefore, we assessed participants self-report of their own religiousness and took this variable into account in the analyses.

Method

Participants

The sample included 557 participants between 12 and 18 years of age ($M = 14.99$, $SD = 1.72$) from three schools. In total, 49.9% were females and 50.1% were males. Females and males did not differ significantly for age. All participants followed upper general secondary education (HAVO/VWO: "Higher General Secondary Education"/"Preparatory Scientific Education"). The non-Muslim group consisted of 324 adolescents (49.6% females, mean age = 14.57 years; 50.4% males, mean age = 14.66) with two ethnically Dutch parents. The mean age of females and males within this group did not differ significantly. The Muslim group was composed of 231 Muslim adolescents (53.7% females, mean age = 15.23 years; 46.3% males, mean age = 15.14 years) with Dutch citizenship, but whose parents came to the Netherlands as immigrants from countries such as Turkey, Morocco, Iran, Iraq, and Bosnia. The mean age of females and males within this group did not differ significantly. The gender distribution was similar in both groups, $\chi^2(1, 556) = 2.62$, $p > .10$. However, the Muslim group was somewhat older ($M = 15.19$, $SD = 1.77$) than the non-Muslim group ($M = 14.61$, $SD = 1.46$), $t(556) = 4.28$, $p < .001$. The two groups attended the same ethnically heterogeneous schools and took classes together. The adolescents were asked to participate in a study on current societal issues. They participated on a voluntary basis and the anonymous paper-and-pencil questionnaire was administered in separate class sessions and under supervision. All students in the different classes agreed to participate in the study. There was no information available on the socioeconomic backgrounds of the students.

Design and measures

For examining the contextual nature of adolescents' judgments about free speech and Muslim minority rights, an experimentally questionnaire design with different types of scenarios was used. Because we expected the different judgments to be relatively independent, the measures were not counterbalanced but given in a fixed order. Several of these scenarios have been used in a previous study (Verkuyten & Slooter, 2007).

First, two scenarios measured the *endorsement of free speech*. For the first scenario, there were two conditions (between subjects): (a) ridiculing religion ("Should it be allowed that a magazine uses drawings and words to make God and religion ridiculous?") and (b) racist views ("Should it be allowed that racist groups express their views in the media?"). Two statements followed the scenario in each condition: (a) offensive content ("No, because this is offending to some groups in society") and (b) free speech ("Yes, because there is always the right of free speech"). Responses to these statements were scored using 5-point scales ranging from *totally do not agree* (−2) to *totally agree* (2).

The second scenario also had two conditions (between subjects): (a) incite war against Islam ("Should it be allowed that on the Internet people can incite a war against Islam?") and (b) call for Jihad ("Should it be allowed that on the Internet people can call for the Jihad?"). In each condition, two statements (with 5-point scales) followed the scenario: (a) inciting violence ("No, because this incites violence") and (b) free speech ("Yes, because there is free speech"). For both scenarios, the level of agreement with the two statements was strongly related ($r = -.72$ and $r = -.64$, respectively). Therefore, we reversed the score of one of the two questions and computed two average scores whereby a higher score indicates a stronger endorsement of free speech.

Second, two scenarios were used to measure the *endorsement of Muslim minority rights*. The first scenario, with two conditions (between subjects), concerned the founding of separate schools: (a) Islamic schools ("Should people have the right to found Islamic schools to which only Muslims can go?") and (b) elite schools ("Should people have the right to found expensive elite schools to which only children of very rich parents can go?"). Two statements (with 5-point scales) followed the scenario in each condition: (a) social cohesion ("No, because this is bad for social cohesion in society") and (b) right of education ("Yes, because one should always respect the right of freedom of education").

The second scenario was concerned with the right to demonstrate and protest. There were again two conditions (between subjects): (a) Muslim demonstration ("A group of Muslims wants to hold a demonstration against the anti-Muslim feelings in the Netherlands. Is it ok when they burn the Dutch flag during the demonstration?") and (b) Surinamese demonstration ("A group of Surinamers wants to hold a demonstration against the Dutch history of slavery. Is it ok when they burn the Dutch flag during the demonstration?"). The Surinamese are one of the largest minority groups and they originate from the former Dutch colony of Surinam in South America. The two statements (with 5-point scales) following both versions were (a) Dutch identity ("No, because that is a lack of respect for Dutch identity") and (b) right to protest ("Yes, because every group has the right to demonstrate and protest"). For both scenarios, the level of agreement with the two state-ments was strongly related ($r = -.70$ and $r = -.61$, respectively). Thus, we reversed the score of one of the two questions and computed two average scores whereby a higher score was indicative of a stronger endorsement of Muslim minority rights.

Third, to examine whether judgments toward free speech and Muslim minority practices depended on the *social implications* or the degree to which these are contradictory with other values and norms (minimal and maximal), we used three scenarios. One about free speech and two about women's clothing (in this case, a headscarf). Each scenario had either a "mini-mal" version in which the practice had rather modest implications or a "maximal" version in which the practice had more far-reaching consequences. Participants were presented with either the minimal or the maximal versions for all three scenarios (between subjects).

The first scenario was on freedom of speech: (a) minimal condition ("Freedom of speech is an important value in our society. Another important value is that you should not offend people. Imagine that a film director makes a film in which he makes a fool of religious people") and (2) maximal condition ("... makes a film in which he causes deep offence to those of religious persuasion"). Following the sce-nario in each condition, the participants were asked, "What should the film company do with this film?" There were four response categories: (a) "Definitely not release the film"; (b) "Try to convince the director to change the film, but not release the film when he does not agree"; (c) "Try to convince the director to change the film, but release it when he does not agree"; and (d) "Do nothing and release the film."

The second scenario was on politics and religious expression (clothing) and there were two conditions: (a) minimal ("Democracy and people's freedom to make their own choices are central values in Dutch society. Imagine that an Islamic political party gets the majority vote in a local election in a Dutch city or village. This party can then decide to make the area more Islamic by asking women to wear a headscarf") and (b) maximal ("... to make the area more Islamic by making the wearing of a headscarf obligatory"). The level of acceptance was judged by asking the participants, "What should the Dutch government do

about this party's decision?" There were four response categories: (a) "Simply not accept this decision"; (b) "Try to convince the party to reconsider the decision, but forbid it when they do not agree"; (c) "Try to convince the party to reconsider the decision, but allow it when they do not agree"; and (d) "Do noth-ing and accept it."

The third scenario was about clothing at school. There were again two conditions: (a) minimal ("It is important in Dutch society that people can commu-nicate with each other in an open way. Another important value is that people themselves can decide which clothes they like to wear. Imagine that there is a group of pupils at your school that voluntarily decides to wear a headscarf that covers only their hair") and (b) maximal ("... that not only covers their hair but also their face"). The participants were asked what the school should do about this: (a) "Simply not accept it"; (b) "Try to convince them, but expel them from school when they do not agree"; (c) "Try to convince them, but allow it when they do not agree"; and (d) "Do nothing and accept it."

Fourth, to examine *two dimensions* and participants' acceptance of minority practices based on *different beliefs,* four scenarios were used. Two were related to perceived Muslim practices and two others were not. All four were similar in that they involved the behav-ior of parents toward their children based on either an informational belief or a moral belief (between subjects). The two Muslim stories described parents who (from a Western point of view) engage in harmful or unfair practices. The first story was on female circumcision that is taken to refer to Islam because it is understood in this way in public dis-course and debate. The practice, however, originated long before the spread of Islam and is also conducted in societies that are not Muslim (Gregg, 2005). The female circumcision story had two conditions: (a) informational belief ("A very light form of female circumcision is sometimes compared with male cir-cumcision. Some parents practice this light form because they think it is good for the healthy physical development of girls") and (b) moral belief ("... because they think it is required by their religion and culture"). The second story was on gender differen-tiation: (a) informational belief ("A Muslim father allows his sons to go out as often as they like, but he forbids his daughters to do the same. The father does this because of the fact that girls run more risks and are more vulnerable") and (b) moral belief ("... because he finds it good and right that boys have more freedom than girls").

The two non-Muslim stories also described parents who engage in practices that are uncommon in Dutch society. One was on home education: (a) informational belief ("Some parents prefer to educate their children at home rather than send them to school. These parents think that with home-education, children learn better and much more than at school") and (b) moral belief ("... that they have the right to raise their children the way they want to"). The other story was on vaccination: (a) informational belief ("There are parents that do not let their young children be vaccinated against all kinds off diseases. They do this because they think that vaccination hampers the development of the natural body resistance") and (2) moral belief ("... that vaccination goes against their convictions about life").

For each of the four scenarios, two dimensions of acceptance were tapped by assessing participants' judgments about the act itself (*act*) and parents campaigning to convince other parents to do the same (*public speech*). For the "act," the questions were, respectively, "Should it be allowed that parents have their daughters circumcised in this way?" "Should it be allowed that the father treats his sons and daughters differently?" "Should it be allowed that parents do not send their children to school?" and "Should it be allowed that these parents do not vaccinate their young children?" There were 5-point scales ranging from *no, certainly not* (1) to *yes, certainly* (5). For "public speech," the questions, with the same 5-point scales, asked whether it should be allowed that these parents campaign in order to try to convince other parents to do the same.

Finally, for measuring the adolescents' self-reported *religiousness*, two statements were presented and the participants were asked to indicate their level of agreement with each using a 5-point scale ranging from *totally do not agree* to *totally agree*. The two items were "God and religious rules are the most important guidelines in my life" and "I find it very important to be religious." The responses for both statements were highly correlated and Cronbach's alpha was .91.

Results

After examining differences in adolescents' self-reported religiousness, the results for the adolescents' reasoning about freedom of speech and minority rights are divided into four sections: (a) freedom of speech, (b) Muslim minority rights, (c) social implications (minimal and maximal), and (d) beliefs and dimensions of minority practices. The different judgments were examined using general linear model (GLM) univariate and multivariate procedures (Tabachnick & Fidell, 2001). Between-subjects analyses were conducted, in which experimental condition, participant group, and gender were included as factors, and age and (the covariate) religiousness as continuous variables. Significant interaction effects where examined using simple slope analysis and post hoc tests (Tukey's honestly significant difference [HSD]).

We first examined whether there were differences in adolescents' self-reported religiousness between the two groups of participants (non-Muslims vs. Muslims), between males and females, and for age. The GLM univariate procedure indicated a strong effect for participant group, $F(1, 551) = 99.89, p < .001, \eta_p^2 = .02$. The mean score for the Muslim minority group ($M = 4.22, SD = 0.93$) indicated high religiousness, whereas the mean score for the non-Muslim majority group was on the "disagree" side of the scale ($M = 2.15, SD = 1.05$). For the Muslim group, 83% of the participants scored above the neutral midpoint of the scale, whereas for the non-Muslim, 81.5% scored below the midpoint, indicating that the majority had a secular orientation. There was also a significant effect for age, $F(1, 551) = 11.74, p = .001, \eta_p^2 = .02$. Older adolescents were more religious than younger adolescents ($B = .15$). There was also a significant interaction effect between participant group and gender, $F(1, 551) = 6.58, p = .011, \eta_p^2 = .01$. Post hoc analysis showed that there was no gender difference for the non-Muslim group, but Muslim females scored significantly higher than Muslim males ($M = 4.38, M = 4.05$, respectively). No other significant effects were found.

Freedom of speech

The participants were asked to what extent people should have freedom of speech in the media. There

Table 12.1 Adjusted means (controlling for religiousness) and standard deviations (between brackets) for freedom of speech and Muslim minority rights for the non-Muslim and Muslim participants

	Non-Muslims	Muslims	Total
Freedom of speech			
Free speech			
Secular	−.41 (1.32)	−1.05 (0.95)	−.71 (1.35)
Racist	−.50 (1.18)	−.68 (1.12)	−.56 (1.21)
Free speech			
War on Islam	−1.22 (1.08)	−1.50 (0.73)	−1.39 (0.97)
Jihad	−.93 (1.06)	−.82 (1.15)	−.85 (1.09)
Minority rights			
Founding schools			
Islamic schools	−.47 (1.26)	.84 (1.18)	.16 (1.38)
Elite schools	.06 (1.33)	−.71 (1.23)	−.33 (1.34)
Demonstration			
Muslims	−1.21 (0.93)	.21 (1.34)	−.77 (1.21)
Surinamese	−.67 (1.13)	−.48 (1.27)	−.59 (1.19)
Social implications			
Minimal–maximal			
Free speech			
Minimal	2.31 (1.01)	2.05 (1.01)	2.15 (1.02)
Maximal	1.95 (1.05)	1.99 (0.99)	1.99 (1.04)
Headscarf			
Minimal	2.74 (0.88)	3.32 (0.79)	3.03 (0.90)
Maximal	2.43 (0.87)	3.16 (.0.72)	2.79 (0.91)

Note. For freedom of speech and minority rights, 5-point scales (−2 to 2). For minimal–maximal, 4-point scales (1 to 4).

were two scenarios: making religious offensive statements and rallying for war. The mean scores for both freedoms were below the neutral midpoint of the scales ($M = -0.61$, $SD = 1.28$, and $M = -1.12$, $SD = 1.05$, respectively) indicating that the participants tended to reject the affirmation of both freedoms. A paired sample t test indicated that the rejection was stronger for rallying for war than for making offensive statements, $t(556) = 7.55$, $p < .001$. The two measures were also unrelated ($r = .08$, $p > .05$).

For the freedom to make offensive statements, there were two conditions (between subjects): ridiculing religion and racist statements. The GLM procedure indicated that the full model accounted for 22% of the variance. The results indicated a significant negative effect for the covariate religiousness, $F(1, 551) = 21.11$, $p < .001$, $\eta_p^2 = .04$. Religious participants were

more strongly against freedom of speech than non-religious participants. In addition, there was a main effect for participant group. This effect was qualified, however, by a significant interaction effect with condition, $F(1, 551) = 9.79$, $p = .002$, $\eta_p^2 = .02$. Table 12.1 indicates that compared to non-Muslim participants, the Muslims were more strongly against freedom of speech that involves the ridiculing or offending of God and religion.

There were also two conditions for the second scenario on the freedom to incite or rally for war: war against Islam and the Jihad. The full model explained 9.2% of the variance. The GLM procedure indicated that the covariate religiousness was not significant. There was a significant main effect for condition and this effect was qualified by two significant interaction effects: between condition and participant group,

$F(1, 551) = 4.68, p = .031, \eta_p^2 = .01$, and between condition and gender, $F(1, 551) = 9.47, p = .002, \eta_p^2 = .02$. For the former interaction effect, Table 12.1 shows that both the Muslim and the non-Muslim participants rejected rallying for a war against Islam more strongly than they rejected calling for the Jihad, but the rejection was strongest among the Muslims. The latter interaction effect indicated that compared to males, females were more strongly against a call for war against Islam ($M = +1.23$, and $M = -1.49$, respectively) and less strongly against mobilizing for the Jihad ($M = -1.01$, and $M = -.72$, respectively).

Muslim minority rights

The participants were asked to what extent people have the right to establish separate schools and to demonstrate and protest. The mean scores for both rights were below the neutral midpoint of the scales ($M = -0.15, SD = 1.37$, and $M = -0.75, SD = 1.20$, respectively) indicating that the participants tended to reject the effectuation of both rights. A paired sample t test indicated that the rejection was stronger for the right to demonstrate than the right to establish separate schools, $t(556) = 8.54, p < .001$. The two measures were positively related ($r = .17, p < .01$) but the association was low indicating a limited amount of shared variance ($< 4\%$).

For the right to found separate schools, there were two conditions: Islamic and elite schools. The full model explained 18.5% of the variance. The GLM procedure indicated a main effect for condition that was, however, qualified by an interaction effect between condition and participant group, $F(1, 551) = 58.12, p < .001, \eta_p^2 = .01$, and between condition and gender, $F(1, 551) = 8.01, p = .002, \eta_p^2 = .02$. As shown in Table 12.1, the non-Muslim participants rejected this right more strongly for the Islamic schools than for the elite schools. In contrast, the Muslim participants endorsed the right to found separate schools more strongly for Muslims than for very rich parents. Additionally, females were more in favor of the right to found separate schools in the case of Muslim actors ($M = 0.37$) compared to nonreligious actors ($M = -0.49$), whereas males were equally rejecting toward both actors ($M = -0.15$ and $M = -0.17$, respectively).

There were no other significant effects, also not for the covariate religiousness.

The right to demonstrate had also two conditions: Muslims and Surinamers. The GLM procedure indicated that the full model explained 12.4% of the variance. There was a main effect for age, $F(1, 549) = 8.94, p = .002, \eta_p^2 = .03$. The age effect was negative ($B = -.14$) indicating that older adolescents rejected the right to demonstrate more strongly than the younger ones. There was also a significant main effect for participant group that was, however, qualified by an interaction effect between participant group and condition, $F(1, 549) = 12.75, p < .001, \eta_p^2 = .02$. As shown in Table 12.1, for the non-Muslim participants, the rejection was stronger for the Muslim condition than for the Surinamers condition. In contrast, the Muslim participants endorsed this right more strongly for the Muslim condition.

Social implications: minimal and maximal

The participants were asked to make judgments on a story about the freedom of speech and on two stories about Muslim minority rights involving the clothing (headscarf) of women. There were two conditions of each scenario that were varied in a between-subjects design: minimal implications and maximal implications.

Examining the free speech score as a dependent variable indicated that the full model accounted for 11.3% of the variance. The GLM procedure showed that there was a main negative effect for religiousness, $F(1, 551) = 8.12, p = .005, \eta_p^2 = .02$. There was also a main effect for gender, $F(1, 551) = 9.24, p < .003, \eta_p^2 = .03$. Compared to females, males were less against free speech in which religious people are offended ($M = 1.92, M = 2.23$, respectively). Age was also found to have a significant main effect, $F(1, 551) = 6.96, p = .009, \eta_p^2 = .03$. Younger adolescents were more rejecting than older ones ($B = -.12$). Additionally, we found a main effect for condition that was qualified by a significant interaction effect between condition and participant group, $F(1, 551) = 5.44, p = .020, \eta_p^2 = .01$. As shown in Table 12.1, non-Muslim participants were more in favor of free speech in the minimal compared to the maximal condition, whereas there was no difference between both conditions for the Muslim participants.

The judgments for the two stories on Muslim minority rights (headscarf) were strongly correlated ($r = .64$), therefore, an average score was used. For this score, the full model explained 32.2% of the variance. There was a positive effect for the covariate religiousness, $F(1, 551) = 7.76$, $p = < .006$, $\eta_p^2 = .02$. The main effect for condition was also significant, $F(1, 551) = 11.31$, $p < .001$, $\eta_p^2 = .04$. As shown in Table 12.1, the participants were more accepting in the minimal compared to the maximal condition. This effect was found for both the Muslim and the non-Muslim participants because the interaction between condition and participant group was not significant. There were two other significant main effects: for participant group and for age. These effects were qualified, however, by a significant interaction effect among participant group, age, and gender, $F(3, 551) = 8.33$, $p < .001$, $\eta_p^2 = .03$. Simple slope analysis showed a positive age effect for non-Muslim males ($B = .16$, $p < .001$). Thus, older non-Muslim males were less accepting than non-Muslim younger males. Further, there was a positive age effect for Muslim females ($B = 19.4$, $p < .001$). Muslim older females were less accepting than Muslim younger females. Age did not have a significant effect for non-Muslim females and for Muslim males.

Beliefs and dimensions of minority practices

The participants were asked to judge four scenarios, two of which were concerned with non-Muslim minority practices and two with Muslim minority practices. For the four scenarios, two dimensions of practices were tapped: performing the actual *act* and seeking *public support* by campaigning for it. In addition, the type of belief forming the basis of the act was varied in a between-subjects design by presenting half of the participants with a moral argument and the other half with an informational argument.

Repeated measures analyses with dimension as within-subjects measures and belief type, participant group, gender, and age as variables indicated for all four scenarios that the participants were more accepting of campaigning for public support than for performing the actual act itself ($ps < .001$, r^2 between .13 and .24). Hence, we found a clear dimension effect for all four scenarios. This effect was similar for Muslim and non-Muslim participants, for males and females, and for the different ages.

Act performance

The highest correlation between the four judgments about performing the act in the four scenarios was 0.17. This pattern of associations was similar for the non-Muslim and Muslim participants and independent of age. An initial one-way analysis contrasting the four scenarios revealed a significant effect, $F(3, 554) = 25.75$, $p < .001$, $\eta_p^2 = .11$. Participants accepted female circumcision the least ($M = 1.90$), followed by non-vaccination ($M = 2.04$), and then by home education ($M = 2.33$) and differential treatment ($M = 2.35$). Except for the latter two scores, all pair-wise mean differences were statistically significant (paired samples t tests, $ps < .01$). All the mean scores were also below the neutral midpoint of the scale (3), indicating that, in general, the participant did not support any of the actions.

The four "act performance" judgments were analyzed as multiple dependent variables. The multivariate effects (Pillai's) were significant for belief type, participant group, gender, age, and religiousness. In addition, there were significant multivariate interaction effects between participant group and gender, $F(4, 552) = 6.03$, $p = .002$, $\eta_p^2 = .06$, and between gender and age, $F(4, 551) = 2.64$, $p = .032$, $\eta_p^2 = .02$.

The univariate results indicated that religiousness was positively and significantly related to accepting three of the four acts: The effect for female circumcision was the exception.

The univariate results further indicated that belief type only made a difference for home education, $F(1, 551) = 4.86$, $p = .038$, $\eta_p^2 = .01$, and for differential treatment, $F(1, 551) = 11.25$, $p < .001$, $\eta_p^2 = .03$, but not for female circumcision and for nonvaccination. Participants found it more acceptable when home education was based on informational beliefs compared to moral beliefs ($M = 2.46$ and $M = 2.21$, respectively). In addition, participants found differential gender treatment more acceptable when this was based on informational beliefs rather than on moral beliefs ($M = 2.56$ and $M = 2.19$, respectively). There were no significant interaction effects between belief type and age, gender, or participant group.

Table 12.2 Adjusted mean scores (controlling for religiousness) and standard deviations (between brackets) for the four parental practices for religious group by gender

	Non-Muslims		Muslims	
	Females	Males	Females	Males
Female circumcision	1.96 (1.02)	2.19 (1.04)	1.35 (0.90)	2.09 (1.14)
Differential gender treatment	2.01 (1.13)	2.25 (1.12)	2.09 (1.23)	3.15 (1.31)
Home education	2.44 (1.15)	2.43 (1.14)	2.03 (1.15)	2.43 (1.23)
Nonvaccination	1.93 (1.03)	2.14 (1.22)	1.94 (1.09)	2.12 (1.11)

Note. 5-point scales (1 to 5).

The univariate results indicated effects of participant group for female circumcision and differential gender treatment. Both these effects were qualified by significant interaction effects between participant group and gender: for female circumcision, $F(1, 551) = 9.81, p = .002, \eta_p^2 = .02$, and for differential treatment, $F(1, 551) = 11.39, p < .001, \eta_p^2 = .04$. The results for this interaction are presented in Table 12.2. The table indicates that there is a clear gender difference among the Muslim participants but not among the non-Muslims. Compared to Muslim males, Muslim females were less accepting toward female circumcision and differential gender treatment, $F(1,231) = 21.35, p < .001$. For the non-Muslims, the gender difference was not significant, $F(1, 334) = 3.69, p > .05$.

For female circumcision, there was a further interaction effect between age and gender, $F(1, 551) = 8.92, p < .003, \eta_p^2 = .02$. Simple slope analysis indicated that older females were less accepting toward female circumcision than younger females ($B = -.09, p < .007$). There was no significant age effect for males ($B = -.01, p > .10$).

For home education, the univariate results showed a significant negative effect for age, $F(1, 551) = 4.91, p = .027, \eta_p^2 = .01$ ($B = -.13$). There was also a significant interaction effect between participant group and gender, $F(1, 551) = 4.75, p = .039, \eta_p^2 = .01$. As shown in Table 12.2, female Muslims were less supportive of this practice than the other participants.

Campaigning for public support

For the four scenarios, the judgments about parents seeking public support by campaigning for it were significantly related ($r > .43$). Therefore, we used an average score for analyzing these responses, and Cronbach's alpha was 0.78. The GLM procedure indicated that there was a significant positive effect for religiousness, $F(1, 551) = 3.67, p = .048, \eta_p^2 = .01$. There was also a significant effect for participant group, $F(1, 551) = 4.89, p = .032, \eta_p^2 = .01$, with non-Muslim participants accepting the campaigning for public support more strongly than Muslim participants ($M = 2.63$ and $M = 2.47$, respectively). In addition, there was a gender difference, $F(1, 551) = 7.40, p < .001, \eta_p^2 = .02$. Males were more accepting ($M = 2.75$) than females ($M = 2.37$). No other effects were significant. The full model accounted for 6.8% of the variance.

Discussion

This research examines how non-Muslim and Muslim adolescents living in the Netherlands reason about free speech and Muslim minority rights. In trying to maximize the relevance and ecological validity of the research, we focused on concrete cases rather than abstract principles, used realistic and currently debated issues instead of unfamiliar and hypothetical scenarios, and presented the participants with conflicting issues.

In general, the participants expressed low to moderate levels of acceptance and endorsement of freedom of speech and minority rights in the various conflicting situations. In agreement with social-cognitive domain theory and research (e.g., Helwig, 1995; Helwig & Turiel, 2002; Wainryb, 1993), these civil liberties were not applied absolutely across the

550   PART V   FAMILY, COMMUNITY, AND CULTURE

various conflicts. Further, the different judgments were not strongly associated, indicating that no single construct of acceptance or endorsement emerged. The low associations also suggest that it is unlikely that the fixed order in which the measures were presented affected the findings. In addition, we found that the endorsement of free speech and minority rights was sensitive to the context of beliefs and group memberships. Adolescents take into account various aspects of what they are asked to accept and who's freedom of speech and rights they are expected to endorse. The content and the nature of the social implications, the dimension of acceptance, and the underlying beliefs, all made a difference to the judgments.

The group membership of the actor and of the participants also was important. The rejection of freedom of speech was stronger among the Muslim than the non-Muslim participants when it involved offending God and religion and when it concerned Islam. For the endorsement of Muslim minority rights, the non-Muslim Dutch participants rejected the right to found separate schools and to burn the national flag in a demonstration, and this rejection was stronger for Muslim than for non-Muslim actors. In contrast, Muslim minority participants endorsed these rights more strongly when Muslim actors were involved. Furthermore, participants were less accepting of Muslim practices (the wearing of a headscarf) that contrasted more strongly with other values and operative public norms (maximal vs. minimal condition) and therefore had more far-reaching societal consequences. This was found for both groups of participants. However, in general, Muslim participants accepted these practices more strongly than non-Muslims.

There were also differences between female Muslim participants on the one hand and male Muslims and male and female non-Muslims on the other. Compared to the other three groups, Muslim females more strongly rejected female circumcision, differential gender treatment, and home education. This further indicates that decisions over whether something should be accepted is influenced by group memberships: Muslim females are less accepting when the harm or injustice ensuing from specific practices affects them as females. This result is in agreement

with intergroup theories (e.g., Tajfel & Turner, 1979) and with stigma approaches (e.g., Swim & Stangor, 1998) but, for example, not with the idea that females are more likely to use a care or welfare perspective, whereas males would reason more from a rights perspective (Gilligan, 1982). The responses of the non-Muslim females did not differ from the non-Muslim males and the Muslim males. The practices presented in the scenarios have implications for Muslim females in particular and therefore caused Muslim female participants to reject these practices more strongly.

Existing research on freedom of speech and rights has not examined the role of, for example, religious, gender and national identity (see Helwig & Turiel, 2002; Neff & Helwig, 2002). However, intergroup research and the present findings indicate that it is important to consider these social identities. The group memberships that are at stake and the existing intergroup context influence how majority and minority group children and adolescents evaluate practices and claims of different groups (see Bennett & Sani, 2004). The differences found between the Muslim and non-Muslim participants are in agreement with their specific group positions in Dutch society and do not support the idea that freedoms and rights are of little concern to Muslims or contradictory to Islam (see also Turiel & Wainryb, 1998). Muslims are less in favor of freedom of speech when it involves offending religion and they are more in favor of Muslim minority rights. Their judgments are quite similar to non-Muslims, however, when their group membership is not at stake. Hence, it seems important for future studies on the reasoning about freedom of speech and minority rights to examine the intergroup context and to include measures of, for example, national, religious, and ethnic group identification.

In addition to the differences between the participant groups, there were also similarities. For example, all participants rejected freedom of speech when it involved psychological and physical harm, and the rejection was stronger for the latter than the former type of harm (see also Helwig, 1995). Furthermore, in agreement with other studies (e.g., Wainryb et al., 1998; Witenberg, 2002), adolescents made a clear distinction between dimensions of acceptance in the four scenarios about parental practices. They were more accepting of parents campaigning for public support for these practices than for the actual act itself. This was found for all groups of participants. Not only is the higher acceptance of the public expression of the dissenting beliefs consistent with the idea of free speech but also can be seen as stimulating debate and as causing less direct harm or injustice than the actual act.

Participants were also more accepting of practices based on dissenting informational beliefs than on dissenting moral beliefs. This result is also in agreement with other studies (e.g., Wainryb, 1993; Wainryb et al., 1998) but was only found for two of the four scenarios. For female circumcision and nonvaccination no difference for belief type was found. This might be due to the fact that these two cases are about physical integrity and well-being, which are clear moral issues. These two practices were also the most strongly rejected by the participants. In addition, the effects for belief type were found for both non-Muslim and Muslim participants, for males and females, and for all age groups. These results are in agreement with the social-cognitive domain model and with research that has found that children and adolescents identify moral considerations as general and generalizable to a variety of contexts and groups (Smetana, 2006; Turiel, 2002). In contrast, informational beliefs are similar to social-conventional issues that are seen as group and context specific and that are applied when no clear moral issues are at stake.

The pattern of results demonstrates that adolescents use different forms of social reasoning to evaluate complex social issues of free speech and minority rights. In contrast to the idea of an age-related progression from less to more principled reasoning, the present results show few and no consistent age effects (see also Helwig, 1995, 1997; Ruck et al., 1998). Younger participants endorsed freedom of speech more strongly in the case of the film director, yet older participants rejected the right to demonstrate more strongly than younger participants did. In addition, we found that age made a difference in combination with other characteristics, such as participant group and gender (see also Helwig, 1997). There was a complex age effect, for example, for the endorsement of Muslim minority rights involving the wearing of a headscarf. For non-Muslim males, age was negatively related to the endorsement of these rights, whereas for Muslim females a positive effect for age was found. These results might be related to adolescents' growing political awareness involving religious and gender group relations and interests. Overall, the findings strongly suggest that judgments about free speech and minority rights do not develop through a stage-like sequence where a less accepting attitude is followed by a more accepting one. A decision of whether a particular expression or practice should be accepted always involves a variety of considerations, and the results show that adolescents weigh different aspects of behaviors and their contexts and consequences.

There are some limitations of the current research that should be considered and that give additional suggestions for further study. For example, the cross-sectional design of the current study does not allow to determine whether the age differences found are due to developmental differences in social reasoning or to some other factor such as context and cohort effects. A domain-specific perspective does not imply that developments in reasoning about rights and civil liberties do not occur in adolescence (see Helwig & Turiel, 2002). There are age-related changes in the ability to conceptualize and assess the information of complex situations and in coordinating different domains of knowledge. These changes do not, however, necessarily lead to different judgments. Younger and older adolescents can make the same judgment, although for different reasons.

It also seems pertinent for future studies to assess other types of belief. Social-cognitive domain theory makes a distinction between moral considerations, social-conventional issues, and psychological concerns. We examined the difference between moral and informational beliefs (Wainryb et al., 1998). However, the distinction between the two may not always be straightforward and can also be operationalized in different ways. For example, religious and cultural expectations do not have to indicate moral considerations but may also involve social-conventional concerns (Turiel, 2002). In addition, there are different kinds of moral principles, such as fairness and equality, and different kinds of social-conventional issues, such as group functioning and tradition. Furthermore, psychological concerns can be involved in judgments because what one is asked to accept or endorse may affect personal freedoms and interests (e.g., Helwig, 1997).

Furthermore, the research has examined only a restricted number of instances of freedom of speech and minority rights. Questions of freedom of speech and minority rights, however, involve many situations and issues and might also depend on the national context. Hence, it would be interesting to systematically conduct cross-national research among both majority and minority groups on the development of conceptions of different freedoms and rights.

Despite these qualification and limitations, we think that the present research makes a contribution to our understanding of the development of the reasoning about free speech and minority rights and by doing so also of our understanding of intergroup relations in diverse societies. There is a large body of research into ethnic and racial stereotypes and prejudice, including studies in European countries such as the Netherlands (e.g., Verkuyten & Thijs, 2001, 2002). This research, however, does not focus on religious differences, whereas religion, and Islam in particular, has emerged as the focus of immigration and diversity debates in Europe (Zolberg & Long, 1999). Furthermore, this research examines group perceptions and evaluations and not the social reasoning about civil liberties and minority practices. These latter topics, however, are at the heart of what is perceived as a "crisis of multiculturalism" (Modood & Ahmad, 2007).

Little is known about adolescents' attitudes toward out-groups, about their intergroup social reasoning, and about the development of their views on civil liberties. However, understanding these views is an important research goal both theoretically and practically. Theoretically, we used social-cognitive domain theory and intergroup theories and we tried to show that it is important to examine questions of civil liberties, and morality more generally, in the context of intergroup relations. We agree with Killen et al. (2006) that cognitive domain theory has tended to ignore the intergroup context, whereas intergroup theories have tended to ignore issues revolving around morality. Practically, a diverse, equal, and peaceful society does not require that we all like each other, but it does necessarily mean that people have learned to accept one another and endorse equal civil liberties. We need to understand how children and adolescents

think about free speech and minority rights and develop less or more accepting judgments. The present research has tried to make a contribution to this understanding.

References

Avery, P. G. (1989). Adolescent political tolerance: Findings from the research and implications for educators. *High School Journal*, *72*, 168–174.

Bennett, M., & Sani, F. (Eds.) (2004). *The development of the social self*. Hove, UK: Psychology Press.

Berti, A. E. (2005). Children's understanding of politics. In M. Barrett & E. Buchanan-Barrow (Eds.), *Children's understanding of society* (pp. 69–104). Hove, UK: Psychology Press.

Bobo, L. D. (1999). Prejudice as group position: Microfoundations of a sociological approach to racism and race relations. *Journal of Social Issues*, *55*, 445–472.

Bobo, L. D., & Licardi, F. C. (1989). Education and political tolerance. *Public Opinion Quarterly*, *53*, 285–308.

Brewer, M. B. (1991). The social self: On being the same and different at the same time. *Personality and Social Psychology Bulletin*, *17*, 475–482.

Clemence, A., Doise, W., de Rosa, A. S., & Gonzalez, L. (1995). Le representation sociale de droites de l'homme: Une recherché internationale sur l'entendue et les limites de l'universite. *Journal International de Psychologie*, *30*, 181–212.

Enright, R. D., & Lapsey, D. K. (1981). Judging others who hold opposite beliefs: The development of belief-discrepancy reasoning. *Child Development*, *52*, 1053–1063.

Enright, R. D., Lapsey, D. K., Franklin, C. C., & Streuck, K. (1984). Longitudinal and cross-cultural validation of belief-discrepancy reasoning construct. *Developmental Psychology*, *20*, 143–149.

Fisher, C. B., Wallace, S. A., & Fenton, R. E. (2000). Discrimination distress during adolescence. *Journal of Youth and Adolescence*, *29*, 679–695.

Gilligan, C. (1982). *In a different voice*. Cambridge, MA: Harvard University Press.

Gregg, G. S. (2005). *The middle east: A cultural psychology*. Oxford, UK: Oxford University Press.

Helwig, C. C. (1995). Adolescents' and young adults' conceptions of civil liberties: Freedom of speech and religion. *Child Development*, *66*, 152–166.

Helwig, C. C. (1997). The role of agent and social context in judgments of freedom of speech and religion. *Child Development*, *68*, 484–495.

Helwig, C. C., & Prencipe, A. (1999). Children's judgments of flags and flag-burning. *Child Development, 70*, 132–143.

Helwig, C. C., & Turiel, E. (2002). Civil liberties, and democracy: Children's perspectives. *International Journal of Law and Psychiatry, 25*, 253–270.

Killen, M., Margie, N. G., & Sinno, S. (2006). Morality in the context of intergroup relations. In M. Killen & J. Smetana (Eds.), *Handbook of moral development* (pp. 155–183). Mahwah, NJ: Erlbaum.

Killen, M., Sinno, S., & Margie, N. G. (2007). Children's experiences and judgments about group exclusion and inclusion. In R. Kail (Ed.), *Advances in Child Psychology* (Vol. 35, pp. 173–218). New York: Elsevier.

McKown, C., & Weinstein, R. S. (2003). The development and consequences of stereotypes consciousness in middle childhood. *Child Development, 78*, 498–515.

Modood, T., & Ahmad, F. (2007). British Muslim perspectives on multiculturalism. *Theory, Culture and Society, 24*, 187–213.

Neff, K. D., & Helwig, C. C. (2002). A constructivist approach to understanding the development and reasoning about rights and authority within cultural contexts. *Cognitive Development, 17*, 1429–1450.

Parekh, B. (2000). *Rethinking multiculturalism: Cultural diversity and political theory*. London: MacMillan.

Ruck, M. D., Abramovitch, R., & Keating, D. P. (1998). Children's and adolescent's understanding of rights: Balancing nurturance and self-determination. *Child Development, 64*, 404–417.

Ruck, M. D., Peterson-Badali, J., & Day, L. (2002). Adolescents' and mothers' understanding of children's rights in the home. *Journal of Research on Adolescence, 12*, 373–398.

Scroggins, D. (2005, June 27). The Dutch-Muslim cultural war. *The Nation*, 21–25.

Sherif, M. (1966). *Group conflict and co-operation: Their social psychology*. London: Routledge and Kegan Paul.

Sigelman, C. K., & Toebben, J. L. (1992). Tolerant reactions to advocates of disagreeable ideas in childhood and adolescence. *Merrill-Palmer Quarterly, 38*, 542–557.

Smetana, J. G. (2006). Social domain theory and social justice. In M. Killen & J. Smetena (Eds.), *Handbook of moral development* (pp. 117–153). Mahwah, NJ: Erlbaum.

Swim, J. K., & Stangor, C. (1998). *Prejudice: The target's perspective*. San Diego, CA: Academic Press.

Tabachnick, B. G., & Fidell, L. S. (2001). Using *multivariate statistics* (4th ed.). Boston: Allyn & Bacon.

Tajfel, H., & Turner, J. (1979). An integrative theory of intergroup conflict. In W. G. Austin & S. Worchel (Eds.), *The social psychology of intergroup relations* (pp. 33–47). Monterey, CA: Brooks/Cole.

Te Grotenhuis, M., & Scheepers, P. (2001). Churches in Dutch: Causes of religious disaffiliation in the Netherlands, 1937–1995. *Journal for the Scientific Study of Religion, 40*, 591–606.

Ter Wal, J. (2004). *Moslim in Nederland: Publieke Discussie Over de Islam in Nederland*. The Hague: Sociaal en Cultureel Planbureau.

Thalhammer, K., Wood, S., Bird, K., Avery, P. G., & Sullivan, J. L. (1994). Adolescents and political tolerance: Lip-synching to the tune of democracy. *Review of Education, Pedagogy, Cultural Studies, 16*, 325–347.

Turiel, E. (2002). *The culture of morality*. Cambridge, UK: Cambridge University Press.

Turiel, E., & Wainryb, C. (1998). Concepts of freedoms and rights in a traditional, hierarchically organized society. *British Journal of Developmental Psychology, 16*, 375–395.

Verkuyten, M., & Slooter (2007). Tolerance of Muslim beliefs and practices: Age related differences and context effects. *International Journal of Behavioral Development, 31*, 467–477.

Verkuyten, M., & Thijs, J. (2001). Ethnic and gender bias among Dutch and Turkish children in late childhood: The role of social context. *Infant and Child Development, 10*, 203–217.

Verkuyten, M., & Thijs, J. (2002). Racist victimization among children in the Netherlands: The effect of ethnic group and school. *Ethnic and Racial Studies, 25*, 310–331.

Verkuyten, M., & Zaremba, K. (2005). Inter-ethnic relations in a changing political context. *Social Psychology Quarterly, 68*, 375–386.

Vogt, W. P. (1997). *Tolerance and education: Learning to live with diversity and difference*. London: Sage.

Wainryb, C. (1993). The application of moral judgments to other cultures: Relativism and universality. *Child Development, 64*, 924–933.

Wainryb, C., Shaw, L. A., & Maianu, C. (1998). Tolerance and intolerance: Children's and adolescents' judgments of dissenting beliefs, speech, persons, and conduct. *Child Development, 69*, 1541–1555.

Witenberg, R. T. (2002). Reflective racial tolerance and its development in children, adolescents and young adults: Age related difference and context effects. *Journal of Research in Education, 12*, 1–8.

Zolberg, A. R., & Long, L. W. (1999). Why Islam is like Spanish: Cultural incorporation in Europe and the United States. *Politics and Society, 27*, 5–38.

Chinese Adolescents' Reasoning About Democratic and Authority-Based Decision Making in Peer, Family, and School Contexts

Charles C. Helwig, Mary Louise Arnold, Dingliang Tan, and Dwight Boyd

Recent research has advanced our understanding of children's and adolescents' conceptions of their own autonomy and their judgments about the fairness of social organization in various social contexts. A large body of research (summarized in Turiel, 1998) conducted mostly, but not exclusively, in Western cultural contexts, has found that children identify a domain of personal issues composed of matters considered to be up to the individual's personal choice and outside the legitimate jurisdiction of adults or other authorities. For example, issues such as choice of friends, recreational activities, and appearance have been found to be judged as up to the child to decide in the United States (Nucci, 1981), Brazil (Nucci, Camino, & Milnitsky-Sapiro, 1996), and Hong Kong (Yau & Smetana, 1996). Children in these societies have been found to use concepts such as individual rights and personal autonomy in support of their judgments of personal jurisdiction over decision making regarding these matters.

Conceptions of personal choice and autonomy are often seen as forming the foundation for democratic social organization, that is, group decision making in which individuals are given a voice or a say in decisions that affect them (Kurtines, Berman, Ittel, & Williamson, 1995). Individuals in modern Western societies encounter both democratic and authority-based systems of social organization in various aspects of their daily lives. Depending on the social context (peer group, family, workplace, school), social organization may be structured more or less according to authority, hierarchy, or tradition, or in a more democratic fashion in which individual participation in decision making is fostered or solicited (Levin, 1990). As well as varying across social contexts, the appropriateness of democratic or authority-oriented decision making may also be seen to vary within social contexts depending on the type of decision made. For example, in a school setting, children may be given autonomy in making some types of decisions (e.g., about where a class should go on a field trip) but not other types of decisions (e.g., matters of curriculum).

Most of the prior research on personal jurisdiction (e.g., Nucci, 1981) has examined judgments about specific acts, rather than features of social organization itself, such as procedures for making decisions in social groups or organizations. However, recent research has examined Canadian children's, adolescents', and young adults' reasoning about democratic and authority-based decision-making procedures for decisions involving 8-year-olds in the social context of the peer group, family, and school (Helwig, 2002; Helwig & Kim, 1999). This research examined judgments regarding a range of specific examples, including those that were expected to "pull for" children's direct involvement in decision making, such as decisions about what game a group of children would play, where a family would go on vacation, and where a school class would go on a field trip, as well as examples expected to be more likely to favor decision making by adult authorities, such as decisions about what movie a group of children would see, what school they would attend, or a decision about the content of the curriculum. Examples of the latter type were expected to raise issues such as the competence of children to make informed decisions or the potential harm that might ensue if children were given full decision-making autonomy in these instances. Participants were asked to evaluate three decision-making procedures that might be used to make decisions in these contexts, including two democratic procedures (majority rule and consensus) and decision making by adult authorities alone.

Helwig (2002) and Helwig and Kim (1999) found that children and adolescents distinguished the different types of decisions and social contexts in the manner expected, although these distinctions became more pronounced with increasing age. For example, most older children and adolescents believed that curriculum decisions should be left up to teachers, because of their greater competence and experience. However, for other decisions, such as school field trips or peer games, democratic decision-making procedures such as majority rule were seen as more appropriate, and consensus was seen as especially suitable for decisions made in the family context. Canadian children, adolescents, and adults appealed to concepts of fairness based on majority rule or consensus in justifying their preferences for democratic decision-making procedures, as well as to the importance of granting children a voice or say in decision making.

An important question is the extent to which the patterns found in this research extend to other— especially non-Western—cultural contexts. No other research has included direct comparisons among procedures such as majority rule, consensus, and authority; however, a small body of research has examined children's conceptions of majority rule (Kinoshita, 1989; Mann & Greenbaum, 1987; Mann, Tan, MacLeod-Morgan, & Dixon, 1984; Moessinger, 1981). These studies, conducted in Geneva, Israel, Japan, and Australia, have found that children endorse and support the principle of majority rule for several decisions, including, for example, field trip decisions in the school context. The findings of these studies suggest that democratic notions of fairness based on majority rule are found in various countries in the West and in at least one Asian culture. However, all of these societies share similarities in their political structures (Western-style democracy) and in their degree of openness to Western influences in the form of cultural and economic exchanges and free access to information. We know little, however, about the development of judgments of group decision-making procedures in societies with fundamentally different political systems and social structures from those typically found in the West, and especially whether concepts of democratic decision making exist in these societies or what form they might take. Accordingly, the current study is a beginning investigation of these questions in the cultural context of mainland China.

Several features of Chinese society make it an especially appropriate environment in which to investigate these issues. China has a communist political system, interpreted, at least by many in the West, as one in which individual rights and autonomy are often subordinated to group goals, centralized planning, and the authority of the Communist Party elite (Mackerras, 2001; Worden, Savada, & Dolan, 1988). China's general cultural orientation has been described as collectivist, in contrast to the individualist orientation believed by some to characterize Western societies (e.g., Triandis, 1989). Consistent with its collectivist characterization, the educational and family systems in China have been described as highly hierarchical and oriented to obedience to authority. For example, the educational system in China includes, among its salient features, a uniform nationwide curriculum, standardized college entrance exams, and an emphasis on rote learning, group routines, and respect for the authority of teachers (Breiner, 1980; Chen & Su, 2001; Wu, 1996). As well, Chinese family life is often described as modeled after traditional Confucian notions of filial piety, or the fostering of strict obedience and respect for parents and elders (Dien, 1982; Pye, 1992). In some characterizations of Confucian philosophical perspectives, the family is portrayed as a fixed hierarchy, with elders—especially fathers or other male adults—held in high esteem, and obedience toward parental injunctions viewed as "an absolute requirement that exists without regard to the quality of parental behavior" (Pye, 1992, p. 93).

Some theorists have proposed that differences such as these lead to radically different conceptions of self and morality in collectivist and individualist cultures (Markus & Kitayama, 1991; Shweder & Bourne, 1982; Shweder, Mahapatra, & Miller, 1987). In collectivist societies, including Asian societies such as China, it is maintained that a sociocentric or interdependent self-concept is held, in contrast to the independent or egoistic self-concept found in individualist cultures such as Western democracies and especially in North America. According to these theorists, different construals of the self are tied to different systems of social organization, producing culturally dependent and varying moral systems. Moral systems in hierarchical collectivist societies revolve around strict adherence to duties and role obligations, maintenance of the existing social order, and inequality among persons based on status. In contrast, social organization in individualist societies is more egalitarian and democratic, leading to moral systems focusing on individual rights and autonomy, consensus and contract, and equality among persons (Shweder, 1990; Shweder et al., 1987). Portrayals of Chinese social life, psychology, and culture as collectivist suggest little support for democratic or autonomous decision making, especially for children who are conceived to be in subordinate positions.

However, the validity of these dichotomous categorizations as a general means of characterizing cultures, and as applied to China in particular, has been challenged by recent conceptual and empirical critiques. Some social theorists, both Chinese and non-Chinese, have argued that the construal of Chinese philosophical perspectives such as Confucianism solely in terms of strict obedience to authority and rigid adherence to social roles and duties may be one-sided and inaccurate. For example, Sen (1999) identified a duty to oppose a bad or unjust government in the writings of Confucius, and others (see de Bary & Weiming, 1998) have argued that fundamental Confucian values of human dignity, self-cultivation, and justice may be compatible in several important respects with modern notions of human rights and individual autonomy. Developmental and social psychologists have raised conceptual issues such as the insufficiency of broad categories such as individualism and collectivism to capture important differences in judgments pertaining to different social contexts within cultures, and even within individuals (Helwig, 2005; Schwartz, 1990; Turiel, 2002; Wainryb, 1997). Endorsements of individualist values, such as freedom, autonomy, and personal choice, or collectivist values such as commitment to social duties and expectations, deference to authority, and social harmony, have been found to vary by the social context under consideration in studies of social reasoning in Western and non-Western cultures (e.g., Neff, 2001; Turiel, Hildebrandt, & Wainryb, 1991; Wainryb & Turiel, 1994). It also has been argued that global characterizations such as individualism and collectivism may fail to account for divergences in perspectives among individuals holding different positions in social hierarchies, including disagreements and opposition to cultural practices by

those in subordinate positions (Neff & Helwig, 2002; Turiel, 2002).

The empirical foundation of research that draws on the individualism-collectivism construct to distinguish Asian and Western cultures also recently has come under question (Bond, 2002; Takano & Osaka, 1999). A large scale meta-analysis (Oyserman, Coon, & Kemmelmeier, 2002) has found that purported differences between cultures on this dimension are often more exaggerated than is warranted by the data, and the interpretation of these differences is frequently unclear. For example, the meta-analysis revealed that Japanese respondents were sometimes more individualist and less collectivist than those from the United States—ostensibly the quintessential individualist culture (Bond, 2002; see also Takano & Osaka, 1999). Some studies conducted in the Chinese context have reached similarly paradoxical conclusions. Lau (1992), in a study of values preferences among college students using the Rokeach values survey (Rokeach, 1973), found that although Chinese individuals were high on locus of control (reflecting their perception of greater external restrictions on their personal autonomy), they nonetheless rated some individualist values, such as freedom, higher than their American counterparts, who in turn rated some collectivist values, such as family security, higher than Chinese students. Lau suggests that these findings show that individuals interpret existing cultural conditions in making judgments about values, such that some things may be valued more highly when they are perceived to be out of reach or insufficiently realized within one's social milieu.

Studies of parent–child relations in China also are beginning to raise doubts about some of the traditional characterizations of Chinese family structure as based on strong notions of filial piety and rigid obedience to adult authority. A review of research by Chinese scholars has suggested that Chinese children "do resent strict and authoritarian parenting" (Lau & Yeung, 1996, p. 33). Lau, Lew, Hau, Cheung, and Berndt (1990) found that family harmony in mainland Chinese families was related to greater warmth and less control by parents over children, paralleling findings on socialization outcomes in Western cultural contexts. In addition, a recent study on parent–child conflict among adolescents in mainland China (Yau &

Smetana, 2003) has found that Chinese adolescents experience conflicts with their parents over similar sorts of issues as North American adolescents (Smetana, 1988, 1989), and they likewise appeal to notions of personal choice and autonomy to support their perspectives in disputes.

The recently emerging evidence suggests that conceptions of personal autonomy and freedom are present and meaningful to Chinese adolescents—concepts that may aid in the development of notions of democratic decision making. Little research, however, has investigated directly the different ways social organization may be construed by individuals in the Chinese context, and especially their judgments about ideal or preferred procedures for organizing social life. Accordingly, the present study sought to investigate one aspect of Chinese adolescents' social reasoning and judgment: their evaluations of democratic and authority-oriented decision making in various social contexts.

Chinese adolescents' judgments of democratic and authority-oriented decision making were investigated in the social contexts of the peer group, school, and family to examine the role of variables such as social context, type of decision, and age in adolescents' social judgments and reasoning. The research also examined the role played by differences in degree or level of socioeconomic development through comparisons of judgments of adolescents from a modern urban environment with those from more traditional regions in China. The research was, in part, exploratory, given the absence of any prior studies conducted in China on this topic, but several general expectations were derived from findings of research on related topics conducted in both Western and Chinese cultural contexts. We expected that adolescents' social judgments and reasoning would be sensitive to features of situations, such as the social context and type of decision under consideration, as found in research conducted in the Canadian context (Helwig, 2002; Helwig & Kim, 1999). Specifically, we expected that adolescents would be more likely to endorse procedures that give children a considerable degree of autonomy in decision making (such as consensus or majority rule) in the peer context, as opposed to more hierarchical contexts such as school or family. We also expected that, for all social contexts, the judgments of Chinese adolescents would be responsive to the spe-

cific decision being considered, such that they would be more likely to endorse autonomous procedures over those based on adult authority when important social goals, such as educational considerations (e.g., in curriculum decisions) were not at issue. In supporting preferences for autonomous procedures, we expected that adolescents would apply concepts of personal jurisdiction and choice, given findings from recent research (e.g., Yau & Smetana, 2003) suggesting that adolescents in China have access to and use these concepts in support of their own autonomy in disputes with parents. It was not possible to predict beforehand, however, the exact distribution of support for each procedure or whether Chinese adolescents would have a preference for one of the autonomous procedures (either consensus or majority rule) over the other, either across or within social contexts.

Although we expected that Chinese adolescents would sometimes show support for autonomy in judgments about children's decision making, we also expected that, given the more hierarchical familial structure and historical tradition of filial piety in China, a stronger support for adult authority might be found in the family context than has been found in the West. Likewise, we expected that degree or level of modernization would have some impact, with more endorsement of adult authority expected in traditional locations of China than in urban areas, and conversely more support for autonomous procedures expected in urban areas than in traditional areas. However, it was not possible to predict the extent to which any regional effects might override those due to different decisions or social contexts, because it was not known to what degree adolescents even from highly traditional social environments would show acceptance or nonacceptance of particular hierarchical social structures or decision making based on adult authority that they may have experienced.

Method

Participants and research sites

The total sample included 574 Chinese participants approximately evenly distributed across gender in each of three age and grade groups: 13-year-olds or

Chinese Junior 1 (M = 12 years, 11 months; *range* = 11 years, 6 months to 13 years, 11 months; n = 193), 15- to 16-year-olds or Chinese Senior 1 (M = 15 years, 8 months; *range* = 14 years, 3 months to 17 years, 0 months; n = 190), and 18-year-olds or Chinese Senior 3 (M = 18 years, 1 month; *range* = 17 years, 0 months to 19 years, 11 months; n = 191). Participants were drawn from schools in three sites in China, providing a range of environments from which to sample judgments and reasoning that varied in degree of modernization or traditionalism and exposure to Western influences.

One subsample included students drawn from classrooms in two schools (referred to here as Nanjing 1 and Nanjing 2) located in the modern city of Nanjing, the capital of Jiangsu province, an economically developed area of China. Nanjing 1 is a high school associated with a university in the region, and Nanjing 2 is a separate secondary school. Students in these schools generally come from families whose parents are employed in professional, managerial, or business occupations. Although the curriculum is highly standardized across the country and content is controlled by the government, students at Nanjing 1 tend to be given a little more autonomy in choosing some of their courses than those from other schools in the sample.

A second subsample was drawn from a school in Taizhou, a small city in Jiangsu province. Taizhou is in an area that is less economically developed and more traditional than Nanjing, with a lower general standard of living (Jiangsu Statistical Yearbook, 2001). Taizhou is an ancient city of great historical significance; the area around Taizhou is associated with the development of Buddhist and Taoist philosophies and contains many temples and sites of religious and cultural importance. Taizhou and the surrounding area is currently undergoing economic development. Most of the students in the Taizhou school are from families residing in the surrounding rural areas of the province whose parents are employed in agriculture (mostly) or local industry.

The third subsample was drawn from a school located in the countryside in Hebei province in a more isolated, traditional, and less developed part of China, and its economic base is largely agricultural. The standard of living is lower in this part of China

than in the other areas (Hebei Economic Yearbook, 2001). As well, the quality of the educational facilities and teaching at this school is comparatively lower than the schools in the other areas, as is generally the case for schools in rural regions of China.

The sample was balanced such that approximately half the participants (again almost exactly evenly distributed by grade and gender) came from the modern urban environment (Nanjing city, n = 286), and the other half came from the more traditional environments (Taizhou city, n = 145, and Hebei province, n = 143). For the two schools drawn from the traditional environments (Taizhou and Hebei), each of the three grades was evenly represented (47–49 students per grade) at each school. However, because Nanjing 1 does not have a Junior 1 grade, all of the urban Junior 1 students (n = 96) came from Nanjing 2, the other urban school.

Design and procedure

A written version of the interview instrument used in previous research (Helwig & Kim, 1999) was developed for use with adolescents. We believed use of a pen-and-paper version of the instrument in the current project had distinct advantages for meeting the study's research objectives. First, it permitted data to be obtained from a larger number of participants than by interview methodologies, ensuring better representativeness and allowing for more extensive comparisons to be conducted among samples from the different regions. Second, because participants did not give their names, they may have expressed themselves more freely on these topics than they might have in face-to-face interviews. Social desirability, which may have been generated in face-to-face situations, also may have been reduced, given that Chinese people have been found to be more sensitive to social expectations in interactional situations than some other ethnic groups (Bond, 1991).

Data collection was administered in group classroom settings by graduate student research assistants trained by the Chinese coauthor. The assistants distributed the written instrument within classrooms and informed students that their participation was voluntary and that they may refuse to answer any question. The assistants read out loud a set of general instructions in the written instrument describing what was to be asked of students and the 5-point scale used in ratings (see later discussion). Participants were explained the use of the scale with appropriate examples and worked individually in answering the questions. At the completion of the session, participants were asked to place the instrument packets into a nondescript envelope provided for this purpose and to seal the envelope. The only descriptive information about participants requested was approximate age (in years and months) and gender. The envelopes were then collected from students. A complete set of data was sent to the first author's research lab in Canada for translation and analyses. Translation of both the research instrument and written protocols was carried out by a Chinese graduate student enrolled at the Ontario Institute for Studies in Education at the University of Toronto who was fluent in Chinese and English and who grew up in a region of China near Jiangsu province. Accuracy of the translation of the research instruments and protocols was verified by a second Chinese translator and by the Chinese coauthor during his visits to Canada.

The design follows closely Helwig and Kim (1999). The study examined adolescents' judgments and reasoning about various ways of making decisions in the peer group, the family, and the school classroom, presented in the form of scenario examples. Two types of decision-making procedures were presented: autonomous and authority-based. For autonomous decision making, two forms were presented: consensus based (where all must agree to arrive at a decision) and majority rule (voting). Authority-based decision making consists of cases in which adult authorities appropriate to each context make decisions for the children.

Within each social context, two types of decisions were contrasted: (a) one expected to pull for authority-based decision making because it may implicate issues of knowledge, social organizational goals, and the best interests of child agents, and (b) another expected to pull for children's autonomous decision making (or personal jurisdiction) because it may be less likely to implicate any of these issues. Decisions expected to pull for autonomous or democratic decision making in the peer, family, and school contexts, respectively, were: the selection of a game for children

to play (game), decisions about where a family should go on a weekend family outing (outing), and decisions about where a school class should go on a field trip (field trip). Decisions expected to pull for adult authority in these contexts were: the selection of a movie for children to view (movie), a decision about whether a child in a family should receive special tutoring during the weekend to boost his or her grades (tutoring), and decisions about what an elementary school class—equivalent to North American third-grade level—would learn in school each week (curriculum). See the Appendix for the six decision examples. These items largely paralleled those used in Helwig and Kim (1999), with some minor changes to make them more appropriate to the Chinese cultural context. Because families in China are not allowed to choose their children's school, a family decision used in Helwig and Kim regarding which school a child should attend was changed to the special tutoring example. Also, a decision about a family vacation in Helwig and Kim was changed to a decision about a family day outing because vacations are not common in rural environments in China. Moreover, all descriptions of the family context included a family with a single child, in accordance with China's official one-child policy.

The selection of specific examples used in the current study was guided by previous research conducted in Western and non-Western cultural contexts investigating children's conceptions of personal issues and decision making, majority rule, and surveys of children's involvement in various family decisions, including information from studies on common practices related to these issues conducted in the Chinese cultural context. Guiding the selection of examples expected to pull for child autonomy were findings from previous research in both Western and non-Western cultural contexts showing, for example, that children reject adult authority in choices about their recreational activities (e.g., Nucci, 1981, for the United States; Nucci et al., 1996, for Brazil), that they endorse majority rule in decisions such as school field trips in studies conducted in Japan (Kinoshita, 1989) and in Geneva (Moesinger, 1981), and that in the family context—at least in Western cultures—children are involved more in decisions about family recreational activities (such as vacations) than other types of decisions (e.g., Belch, Belch, & Ceresino, 1985; Jenkins, 1978). Based on findings from previous research (Helwig & Kim, 1999), we expected that decisions pulling for adult authority would implicate beliefs about issues such as the competence of adults to make better decisions or concerns about institutional goals or functions (e.g., as in choice of curriculum in school settings). In addition, these decisions were also expected to have the potential to raise concerns over children's welfare and well-being if, for example, children themselves were allowed to make imprudent decisions over educational matters or to choose an age-inappropriate movie. The tutoring example in the family context (new to the current study) was chosen in light of research findings showing that parents in China exert considerable pressure and control over children's educational choices and are highly concerned about academic achievement (Chao & Sue, 1996; Wu, 1996), leading to the expectation that this example would be more likely to pull for adult decision making over procedures that grant children more autonomy.

Because age may be an important factor in judgments of competency, and therefore in the tendency to grant autonomous decision-making capacity, age was kept constant across examples, with all child characters in each social context scenario described as 8 years old. This age was chosen to provide comparability of findings between the current study and Helwig and Kim (1999), as well as other research investigating the rights of children of this age group in Western contexts (e.g., Helwig, 1997). Order of presentation of the decision-making procedures, social contexts, and types of decision was counterbalanced, with 12 orders.

Assessments were made of three types of responses: (a) participants' evaluations and ratings (good vs. bad) of each decision-making procedure (i.e., consensus, majority rule, and adult authority) for each decision in each social context using a 5-point rating scale, (b) participants' written justifications for their evaluations, and (c) participants' choice of the procedure they liked best for each decision. The rating scale was presented following descriptions of each example to be evaluated and included two levels of discrimination labeled accordingly (e.g., "really bad" or "really good"; "a little bad" or "a little good"), with positive and negative poles of the scale separated by a neutral

midpoint. Participants circled the point on the scale that corresponded to their evaluation of each decision-making procedure for each decision. Participants were also invited to provide written justifications to support their evaluations, with appropriate space provided for comments after each rating assessment. Finally, they were asked to provide their choice of the best decision-making procedure (preference) for each decision by circling on the form the procedure that they thought was best.

Coding and reliability

A justification coding system (Table 12.3) was developed from a randomly selected portion (50%) of the protocols evenly distributed across grades and regions. The coding system was then used to code the remaining 50% of the data. Both portions were combined for analysis. The development of the coding system was conducted in consultation with the Chinese coauthor during one of his visits to Canada. The coding system includes justification categories similar to those used in previous research (e.g., Helwig & Kim, 1999), such as references to child rights and to autonomy and democratic principles such as majority rule and voice, as well as more culturally specific references to collectivist notions such as preserving group harmony or concepts reflecting Communist belief systems (see Table 12.3). Two Canadian research assistants (one of European and one of Chinese ethnic background) coded the data. Reliability analyses were conducted on a randomly selected set of 60 protocols (12% of 520 participants who provided written justification responses), balanced according to grade (20 at each grade level) and school (i.e., 5 participants from each grade at each school, except for Junior 1 at Nanjing 2, which included 10 participants to reflect that all of the urban Junior 1 participants came from this school). Inter-rater reliability between the two coders, calculated as Cohen's kappa, was .79.

Results

Results are presented separately for evaluations (ratings), preferences (best choice), and justifications. Evaluation ratings and justifications were analyzed

Table 12.3 Justification categories

Category	Description (and examples)
Child autonomy and rights	References to children's desires, personal choice, autonomy, and individual rights ("Everyone has his or her own right. The freedom of us children shouldn't be controlled by our parents," "Leaving a suitable space to let children make their own decisions is helpful for the formation of an independent spirit").
Democratic principles	Reference to democratic principles such as voice or having a say, majority rule or voting, and protection of the rights of minorities ("Voting is the best and most reasonable way," "The participants of a field trip are students and it should be democratically decided by them," "Views of the majority don't represent those of all. Why should others have to agree unwillingly with some people's private desires?").
Consensus	Reference to the principle of consensus or agreement ("Only if all the friends can agree can we play the game," "They should choose somewhere everyone wants to go").
Knowledge and ability	Reference to the knowledge, ability, or competence of agents to make informed decisions ("People in the Ministry of Education are usually knowledgeable and know what is good for us to learn," "Children are too young to make the right decision").
Positive welfare	Reference to positive consequences of various types ("They will be happy," "Everyone will feel good and benefit").
Harm	Reference to negative psychological or physical effects or effects on educational or academic interests ("If it's not a proper film for children, it'll have a bad influence on children," "The children may play an unsafe game," "This may handicap the development of students' own abilities").
Practicality	Reference to practical consequences of efficiency and expediency associated with decision making practices ("Everyone has his or her own idea. It is impossible for everyone to agree").
Authority	Simple reference to desires or prerogatives of authorities ("The educational authorities will deal with it. I trust them").
Collectivism	References to collectivist concepts, including Marxist political concepts or ideology ("Today's society is a society of cooperation. The spirit of cooperation should be cultivated from an early age," "It will help the children acquire such good qualities as caring about group harmony and following the group").
Approval or disapproval	Simple, unelaborated positive or negative judgments ("This way is good").
Other	Miscellaneous.

using ANOVAS on major variables of interest. All post hoc tests were conducted using Tukey's HSD test, with the critical value set at $p < .05$.

Evaluations

A 3 (age group) × 4 (school) × 2 (gender) × 3 (context) × 2 (decision type) × 3 (procedure) ANOVA was conducted on ratings, with context (peer, family, school), procedure (consensus, majority rule, adult authority), and decision type (decision expected to pull for autonomy vs. decision expected to pull for adult authority) as repeated measures. Several main effects and two-way interactions were found: decision type, $F(1, 493) = 98.47$, $p < .001$; procedure, $F(2, 492) = 504.51$, $p < .001$; context, $F(2, 492) = 13.32$, $p < .001$; Context × Decision Type, $F(2, 492) = 110.34$, $p < .001$; Context × Procedure, $F(4, 490) = 93.84$, $p < .001$; Decision Type × Procedure, $F(2, 492) = 88.86$, $p < .001$; Age Group × Procedure, $F(4, 986) = 7.16$, $p < .001$; and Age Group × Decision Type, $F(2, 493) = 4.33$, $p < .05$, all of which were qualified by three significant three-way interactions of Context × Decision Type × Procedure, $F(4, 490) = 18.42$, $p < .001$;

Age Group × Context × Procedure, $F(8, 982) = 2.74$, $p < .01$; and Age Group × Decision Type × Procedure, $F(4, 986) = 2.67$, $p < .05$. In addition, two- and three-way interactions of School × Procedure, $F(6, 986) = 8.8$, $p < .001$; School × Context × Procedure, $F(12, 1476) = 2.54$, $p < .01$; and School × Context × Decision Type, $F(6, 986) = 2.64$, $p < .05$, were qualified by a significant four-way interaction of School × Context × Decision Type × Procedure, $F(12, 1476) = 2.55$, $p < .01$.

The Context × Decision Type × Procedure interaction was explored by comparisons of decision types (those expected to pull for child autonomy vs. those expected to pull for adult authority) within procedures for each social context. We expected that the autonomous decision-making procedures of majority rule and consensus would be rated more positively in decisions expected to pull for child autonomy than in those expected to pull for adult authority. Conversely, we expected that the adult authority procedures would be more positively rated in decisions expected to pull for adult authority than in those expected to pull for child autonomy. Support for these expectations was found in significant comparisons indicating that majority rule was rated more positively in decisions expected to pull for child autonomy than in decisions expected to pull for adult authority in all three contexts ($M = 4.07$, $SD = .98$, for peer game > $M = 3.78$, $SD = 1.05$, for peer movie; $M = 3.87$, $SD = 1.06$, for family outing > $M = 2.98$, $SD = 1.20$, for family tutoring; $M = 3.99$, $SD = 1.02$, for school field trip > $M = 3.49$, $SD = 1.16$, for school curriculum). In addition, for the family context, consensus was rated more positively in the decision expected to pull for child autonomy ($M = 3.30$, $SD = 1.41$, for family outing) than in the decision expected to pull for adult authority ($M = 3.12$, $SD = 1.31$, for family tutoring). Conversely, and according to expectation, the procedure of adult authority was rated more positively in decisions expected to pull for adult authority than in those expected to pull for child autonomy in both peer and school contexts ($M = 2.55$, $SD = 1.23$, for peer movie > $M = 1.91$, $SD = 1.04$ for peer game; $M = 2.83$, $SD = 1.25$, for school curriculum > $M = 2.57$, $SD = 1.18$, for school field trip). Results for the authority procedure in the family context, however, were contrary to expectations. Adult authority was

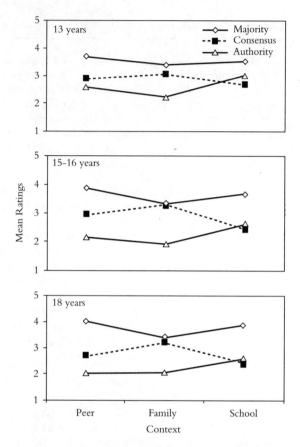

Figure 12.1   Mean ratings of procedures as a function of age and context.

rated more positively in the family outing decision ($M = 2.38$, $SD = .98$) than in the family tutoring decision ($M = 1.79$, $SD = .93$). Taken together, these findings indicate that the manipulation of decision type worked as expected for peer and school contexts, but not for the family, where participants tended to reject strongly decision making based on adult authority for the family tutoring example.

Figure 12.1 presents means for the Age Group × Context × Procedure interaction. The figure reveals that authority was rated more positively in the school context than in the peer or family (post hoc comparisons were significant for all three age groups). The figure also shows age differences in the types of decision-making procedures seen as more appropriate for each context. With increasing age, majority rule was seen as more appropriate to peer and school contexts and consensus was seen as more appropriate to the family context. Specifically, comparisons among contexts within each age group revealed that the youngest age group (13-year-olds) rated majority rule equivalently across contexts, the intermediate age group (15- to 16-year-olds) rated majority rule more positively in the peer than in the family context, and the oldest age group (18-year-olds) rated majority rule more positively in both the peer and school contexts than in the family (no other comparisons involving majority rule were significant). Conversely, with increasing age, consensus was rated as a more appropriate procedure for making decisions in the family context than in the peer or school contexts. Post hoc comparisons revealed that the youngest age group rated consensus equivalently across contexts, the intermediate age group rated consensus more positively in both family and peer contexts than in the school context, and the oldest age group rated consensus more positively in the family context than in both peer and school contexts.

Post hoc tests comparing decision-making procedures within contexts at each age group revealed that majority rule was rated more positively than other procedures (consensus and adult authority) by all age groups in all contexts except for the family, where majority rule and consensus were not distinguished (Figure 12.1). Consensus was rated more positively than adult authority by all age groups in the family context, and by the two older age groups (but not the youngest age group) in the peer context. Consensus and adult authority were not distinguished in the school context by any age group. No other comparisons were significant.

Post hoc tests exploring the Age Group × Decision Type × Procedure interaction revealed that the youngest age group evaluated the decision-making procedure of authority more positively in decisions expected to pull for child autonomy than the two older age groups ($M = 2.56, SD = .85$, for 13-year-olds > $M = 2.22, SD = .70$, for 15- to 16-year-olds, and $M = 2.18, SD = .75$, for 18-year-olds; no other comparisons were significant).

The significant four-way interaction of School × Context × Decision Type × Procedure was explored through comparisons between schools for each of the six decisions within each of the three decision-making procedures. The expectation that participants from more traditional environments would be more supportive of decision making based on adult authority received support. Of the 10 significant comparisons found, all of them involved differences between the urban schools (Nanjing 1 and Nanjing 2) and the schools from more traditional environments (Hebei and Taizhou), with participants from schools in traditional environments rating adult authority more positively than those from the urban schools, and participants from urban schools rating autonomous procedures such as majority rule and consensus more positively than those from traditional environments. Specifically, for peer game decisions, adult authority was rated more positively in Taizhou ($M = 2.17, SD = 1.12$) than in Nanjing 1 ($M = 1.61, SD = .85$), and for peer movie decisions, adult authority was rated more positively in Hebei ($M = 3.11, SD = 1.22$) than in Nanjing 1 ($M = 2.20, SD = 1.09$) and Nanjing 2 ($M = 2.37, SD = 1.19$). Similarly, for school field trip decisions, adult authority was rated more positively in Hebei ($M = 3.00, SD = 1.19$) than in Nanjing 1 ($M = 2.48, SD = 1.21$) and Nanjing 2 ($M = 2.27, SD = 1.12$), and in Taizhou ($M = 2.80, SD = 1.20$) than in Nanjing 2, and for school curriculum decisions, adult authority was rated more positively in Taizhou ($M = 3.05, SD = 1.22$) than in Nanjing 2 ($M = 2.65, SD = 1.32$). Conversely, for family tutoring decisions, consensus was rated more positively in Nanjing 1 ($M = 3.61, SD = 1.27$) than in Taizhou ($M = 3.10, SD = 1.42$) and Hebei ($M = 2.81, SD = 1.27$), and for school curriculum decisions, majority rule was rated more positively in Nanjing 2 ($M = 3.67, SD = 1.15$) than in Taizhou ($M = 3.16, SD = 1.27$).

Overall preference

Participants were also asked to select the best procedure for making each decision within the three social contexts. Participants' selections (percentages) for each procedure are found in Table 12.4 by age, region, decision, and social context. The patterns found in the table generally confirm those seen for the ratings. For example, majority rule was preferred across many decisions in all three social contexts, consensus was preferred most in the family, and adult authority was preferred most for school curriculum decisions.

Table 12.4   Preferences (best choice) for decision-making procedures by region, age, context, and decision

	Peer context						Family context						School context					
	Game			Movie			Outing			Tutoring			Field trip			Curriculum		
Region/age	M	C	A	M	C	A	M	C	A	M	C	A	M	C	A	M	C	A
Nanjing																		
13 years	71	25	4	67	16	17	64	28	8	55	41	4	66	19	14	58	16	26
15–16 years	74	25	1	58	31	12	59	39	2	38	60	2	79	8	14	49	21	30
18 years	78	20	2	78	16	5	61	34	5	47	49	4	88	8	3	65	10	25
Taizhou																		
13 years	49	40	12	37	34	29	41	51	8	41	50	9	28	41	30	40	26	34
15–16 years	67	26	6	51	28	21	56	42	4	37	54	9	66	17	17	45	15	40
18 years	75	18	7	68	18	14	63	33	5	45	48	7	80	9	11	47	13	40
Hebei																		
13 years	54	34	12	46	17	37	54	31	15	45	37	18	60	11	30	55	10	35
15–16 years	67	30	2	66	25	9	56	44	0	51	42	7	64	26	10	36	30	34
18 years	70	28	2	46	20	35	67	31	2	63	32	5	82	7	11	54	12	34

Note. Table gives percentage of adolescents judging each procedure as best. For decision-making procedures: M = majority rule (voting), C = consensus, and A = authority based. Percentage may not sum to 100 because of rounding.

A statistical analysis of participants' best choice responses was also performed, but because the results of this analysis are largely redundant with those given earlier for ratings and add little additional information, and given space constraints, these findings are not reported here (this analysis is available from the corresponding author on request).

Justifications

Participants were invited to provide written responses justifying their ratings for each decision-making procedure for each decision within peer, family, and school contexts. A total of 520 participants (or 91%) provided written responses to at least some portion of the instrument. To conduct valid statistical analyses on repeated-measures variables central to the aims of the current study (i.e., context, procedure, and decision type) the quantitative analysis of justifications was restricted to the subset of the overall sample (194 participants) who provided justifications for all 18 rating questions on the instrument. This criteria of inclusion, although most conservative, had the advantage of ensuring that there was no missing data in any cell. Examination of incomplete data in the unanalyzed

remainder of the sample revealed that missing responses were distributed evenly across assessment questions (a function of the counterbalancing); incompleteness in responding thus probably reflects participants' reactions to fatigue factors or time constraints rather than selectivity in responding to any particular question or scenario. To examine further whether the subsample used in the quantitative data analysis differed from the overall sample, frequency distributions of justification usage in the analysis subsample were compared with that of the total sample. This comparison revealed virtually identical percentages and patterns of justification usage for all justification categories between these samples.

To achieve adequate cell sizes for analysis across age groups and region variables, and because the only significant differences found in the evaluation analysis were between the urban (Nanjing) and traditional (Hebei and Taizhou) environments, data from the two urban schools (Nanjing 1 and Nanjing 2) and the two schools from the more traditional environments (Hebei and Taizhou) were collapsed, yielding an environment or setting variable with two levels (urban and traditional). The composition of the sample used in the quantitative justification analysis was as follows:

Table 12.5 Percentage usage of justifications by context, decision, and procedure

| Justification | Peer context | | | | | | Family context | | | | | | School context | | | | | |
| | Game | | | Movie | | | Outing | | | Tutoring | | | Field trip | | | Curriculam | | |
	M	C	A	M	C	A	M	C	A	M	C	A	M	C	A	M	C	A
Child autonomy/rights	8	4	48	6	5	30	2	2	37	31	36	46	4	5	32	7	7	21
Democratic principles	41	26	3	41	27	4	51	21	9	29	17	5	52	21	9	39	25	7
Consensus	5	14	1	7	16	0	10	17	1	3	4	1	4	10	1	3	8	1
Knowledge/ability	1	1	20	2	4	32	0	1	15	4	5	13	1	4	26	4	2	26
Positive welfare	19	12	7	11	7	12	15	20	6	6	9	5	11	10	9	11	10	9
Harm	5	5	6	7	7	4	5	8	8	5	7	12	5	7	5	8	9	6
Practicality	4	18	0	5	18	1	3	19	0	2	6	1	5	23	2	3	15	4
Authority	1	1	6	2	1	11	1	1	13	8	2	5	2	3	9	2	4	6
Collectivism	4	5	0	5	4	0	2	1	0	0	1	0	6	6	0	3	3	0
Approval/disapproval	4	2	2	4	2	1	4	4	2	3	4	1	3	4	1	4	4	3
Other	7	11	7	8	8	4	5	6	7	8	8	9	8	5	6	16	12	16

Note. For decision-making procedures, M = majority rule, C = consensus, A = authority based. Percentages may not sum to 100 because of rounding.

For the traditional setting, 13-year-olds or Junior 1 ($n = 44$; 19 males, 25 females), 15- to 16-year-olds or Senior 1 ($n = 30$; 13 males, 17 females), 18-year-olds or Senior 3 ($n = 25$; 15 males, 10 females); for the urban environment, 13-year-olds or Junior 1 ($n = 54$; 23 males, 31 females), 15- to 16-year-olds or Senior 1 ($n = 31$; 14 males, 17 females), 18-year-olds or Senior 3 ($n = 10$; 2 males, 8 females).

Table 12.5 presents the percentages of justifications, given by participants by context, decision, and procedure. ANOVA by age group, gender, setting (urban or traditional), context, procedure, and decision type (with context, procedure, and decision type as repeated measures) were conducted on a arcsin transformed proportions of justification usage (Winer, Brown, & Michels, 1991). The following justification categories constituting 10% or more of total justifications were analyzed: democratic principles (24%), child autonomy and rights (18%), and knowledge and ability (10%). Although the positive welfare category also constituted 10% of total responses, these were mostly simple references to general positive consequences (e.g., "They would be happy") often mentioned alongside other justifications; results for this category are not reported as they were largely uninformative and did not fall into any clearly meaningful patterns.

Democratic principles tended to be used more in justifying autonomous procedures such as majority rule and consensus (Table 12.5). Main effects of context, $F(2, 181) = 4.86, p < .01$; decision type, $F(1, 182) = 10.54, p < .01$; and procedure, $F(2, 181) = 109.67, p < .001$, and two-way interactions of Context × Decision Type, $F(2, 181) = 10.68, p < .001$; Context × Procedure, $F(4, 179) = 2.89, p < .05$; and Decision Type × Procedure, $F(2, 181) = 6.01, p < .01$, were qualified by a three-way Context × Decision Type × Procedure interaction, $F(4, 179) = 3.34, p < .05$. Post hoc exploration of the three-way interaction revealed that, for majority rule only, there was greater use of democratic principles in decisions expected to pull for child autonomy than in decisions expected to pull for adult authority for the family and school contexts, but not for the peer context.

In addition, a main effect of setting, $F(1, 182) = 13.53, p < .001$, and a two-way interaction of Age Group × Setting, $F(2, 182) = 3.24, p < .05$, were qualified by a three-way Age Group × Procedure × Setting interaction, $F(4, 364) = 2.90, p < .05$. Post hoc exploration of the three-way interaction revealed a single significant finding: There was greater use of democratic principles by 18-year-olds from urban than traditional environments when justifying majority rule.

Children appealed to child autonomy and rights to support autonomous procedures such as majority rule and consensus, and to reject decision making by adult authority (Table 12.5). References to child autonomy were particularly frequent in the family context. For child autonomy and rights, significant effects of context, $F(2, 181) = 44.90$, $p < .001$; decision type, $F(1, 182) = 35.35$, $p < .001$; and procedure, $F(2, 181) = 62.81$, $p < .001$, were found, qualified by significant Context × Decision Type, $F(2, 181) = 50.35$, $p < .001$; Context × Procedure, $F(4, 179) = 5.23$, $p < .01$; and Decision Type × Procedure, $F(2, 181) = 22.11$, $p < .001$, interactions. Post hoc tests exploring the Context × Decision Type interaction revealed that references to child autonomy and rights were more frequent in the family tutoring decision than in the family outing decision and, for decisions expected to pull for adult authority, were more frequent in the family context than in peer or school contexts. Post hoc tests exploring the Context × Procedure interaction revealed that, for majority rule and consensus, child autonomy and rights was used more in the family than in the peer and school contexts, and for the adult authority procedure, child autonomy and rights was used more in both family and peer contexts than in the school context. Post hoc tests exploring the Decision Type × Procedure interaction revealed that, for consensus and majority rule, child autonomy and rights was more frequently used in decisions expected to pull for adult authority than it was in decisions expected to pull for child autonomy (this appears to be largely a reflection of the high frequency of references to child autonomy and rights found in the family tutoring decision—see Table 12.5). Taken together, these findings indicate that the highly positive ratings and preferences for autonomous procedures such as consensus and majority rule found in the family context tended to be grounded on the perception that these procedures support children's exercise of their own autonomy and rights.

Knowledge and ability was used more in justifying adult authority procedures than in consensus or majority rule, more in school and peer contexts than in the family context, and more in justifying decisions expected to pull for adult authority than those expected to pull for child autonomy (Table 12.5). Significant main effects of context, $F(2, 181) = 5.65$, $p < .01$; decision type, $F(1, 182) = 6.22$, $p < .05$; and procedure, $F(2, 181) = 65.72$, $p < .001$, were found, along with a two-way Context × Procedure interaction, $F(4, 179) = 3.93$, $p < .01$, all of which were qualified by 2 three-way interactions: Age Group × Context × Procedure, $F(8, 360) = 2.11$, $p < .05$, and Context × Decision Type × Procedure, $F(4, 179) = 3.67$, $p < .01$. Post hoc comparisons exploring the Age Group × Context × Procedure interaction indicated that the two younger age groups used knowledge and ability more when justifying the adult authority procedure than consensus or majority rule in both peer and school contexts, but no differences between procedures were found in these age groups for the family context. For the oldest age group, however, the same pattern of differences between procedures in usage of knowledge and ability found in the younger age groups was significant only for the school context. In addition, the oldest age group was more likely to refer to knowledge when justifying adult authority in the school than in the family. Exploration of the Context × Decision Type × Procedure interaction indicated that there was more use of knowledge and ability in the adult authority procedure in the movie decision (the decision expected to pull for adult authority in the peer context) than in the peer game decision, and more use of knowledge for adult authority procedures in the peer context than in the family context, for decisions expected to pull for adult authority only. No other comparisons were significant.

In addition, a significant Context × Decision Type × Procedure × Setting × Gender interaction was found, $F(4, 179) = 3.31$, $p < .05$. Post hoc comparisons revealed a single significant comparison involving gender, with urban males more likely to refer to knowledge and ability than urban females when reasoning about the adult authority procedure for the family outing decision.

Discussion

The findings of this study suggest that concepts of rights, individual freedom and autonomy, and democratic norms (e.g., majority rule) are salient elements of Chinese adolescents' social reasoning. Chinese adolescents applied these concepts in evaluating procedures for making decisions involving children in various contexts, such as peer group, school, and family. In some cases, Chinese adolescents also appealed to adult authority and hierarchical decision making, especially in the school context for decisions about curriculum. The results reveal that reasoning about decision making varied by social context and by the specific decision under consideration, as found in research on these issues in Western cultural contexts (Helwig, 1998; Helwig & Kim, 1999).

In general, strong support was found for decision making based on majority rule. Chinese adolescents frequently judged majority rule to be the most "democratic" procedure in meeting the needs and interests of the majority of individuals. Majority rule was especially preferred for decisions in the peer context, and for family outing and school field trip decisions. Chinese adolescents did not, at least for these decisions, draw distinctions between children and adults, giving children the same rights as adults to input in decision making (indeed, some adolescents explicitly mentioned that children should be consulted and their input treated on a par with those of adults for decisions about these matters). The findings indicate that individuals in China develop notions of democratic fairness based on the norm of majority rule, as found in previous research conducted in both Western and Asian democracies (Kinoshita, 1989; Mann & Greenbaum, 1987; Moes-singer, 1981).

The judgments of Chinese adolescents were subtly discriminative, revealing a consideration of factors such as the social context and the type of decision being made. Even though there was a high degree of support for majority rule across situations, consensus was more likely to be seen as appropriate in the family than in other social contexts, and adult authority was seen as more appropriate in the school context than in other social contexts. In addition, Chinese adolescents, like Canadian children and adults in prior research, distinguished among the particular decisions made in each social context. Although the manipulation of decision type did not work in the anticipated direction for the family context (special tutoring was not more likely to elicit positive evaluations of authority-oriented decision making), for the peer and school contexts, decisions

that were expected to pull more for adult authority did in fact do so. In the peer context, Chinese adolescents evaluated adult authority more positively for movie decisions than for game decisions, and adult authority was evaluated more positively for curriculum than for field trip decisions in the school. Reasons used to support adult authority in these cases were highly similar to those found in the Canadian context, such as concern over the potentially harmful influence of violent or age-inappropriate content in movies and concern over children's competence to make curriculum decisions in the school (Helwig & Kim, 1999). These findings show that Chinese adolescents attempt to balance children's autonomy and the goals supported by hierarchical adult decision making, taking into account similar issues such as concern over children's welfare and their competence to make informed decisions when justifying limits on children's autonomy.

The developmental patterns found in the present study are in accord with models of social reasoning emphasizing the development of increasing sensitivity to social context in applications of social and moral judgments (Helwig, 1995a, 2005). Chinese adolescents' judgments of decision-making procedures became more differentiated by social context and decision type with age, as found in other studies on these and related concepts conducted in Western settings (Helwig, 1997; Helwig & Kim, 1999; Prencipe & Helwig, 2002). For example, consensus was seen as more appropriate to the family context with increasing age, whereas majority rule was seen as more appropriate with age to peer contexts and to classroom field trip decisions. These findings are consistent with those of other research, suggesting that consensus is more likely to be seen as appropriate to small group settings, such as the family, in which members share perspectives and values and in which informal methods such as negotiation may be used to resolve differences (e.g., Gentry, 1982; Helwig & Kim, 1999). In other situations, however, differences in perspectives may be more prevalent or less easily resolved, leading to the need for formal decision-making mechanisms such as majority rule to reconcile differences within groups. This interpretation suggests that common features of situations encountered by individuals in any society may drive the developmental convergence toward preferences for majority rule or consensus evident across diverse cultures.

Indeed, one of the more surprising findings of the current study was the similarity in responses across the three regions sampled. As expected, participants from the more traditional regions (Hebei and Taizhou) were more supportive of decision making by adult authorities. However, these differences between regions were small, and autonomous procedures such as majority rule or consensus were still favored by participants from traditional environments, even for decisions in hierarchical contexts such as curriculum decisions in the school and tutoring decisions in the family. Differences among the social contexts and particular decisions being contemplated appeared to be more important in accounting for patterns of judgments than broader environmental factors such as modernity or degree of traditionalism.

Overall, these findings present a picture of Chinese adolescents' social reasoning that is not consistent with global construals of Chinese psychology and culture as oriented toward collectivism, filial piety, and rigid adherence to authority (Dien, 1982; Pye, 1992; Triandis, 1989). References to collectivist concerns, such as maintaining social harmony, or simple appeals to adult authority, represented only a small proportion of justification responses. Instead, Chinese adolescents asserted children's autonomy to make decisions in the peer context, they often viewed children as having (or ought to have) equal rights to contribute to familial decision making and school curriculum decisions, and they rejected the imposition of hierarchical, adult-oriented decision making for most decisions across all three social contexts. Judgments supporting children's autonomous decision making were justified by direct appeals to children's freedom from adult interference, their rights as persons, and statements reflecting the importance of allowing children a sphere of decision making that would facilitate the development of their autonomy and independence. As the justification data indicate, Chinese adolescents applied concepts of personal jurisdiction (Nucci, 1981) and individual freedom and rights (Helwig, 1995b) to evaluate procedures of social organization.

Our findings are consistent with perspectives on social reasoning in which it is proposed that individuals take into account the features of situations when making moral and social judgments in ways that may, at times, reveal opposition to (or disagreement with) prevailing cultural characterizations or practices (Neff & Helwig, 2002; Turiel, 2002). The critical orientation held by many Chinese adolescents toward existing cultural practices is best seen in judgments about two cases: special tutoring in the family and curriculum in the school. Many Chinese participants were openly critical of existing practices that they believed gave authorities and parents too much control over children's decision making. Adolescents generally rejected adult authority in these instances, preferring democratic procedures such as majority rule for curriculum decisions in the classroom, or either consensus or majority rule for tutoring decisions in the family. Preferences for consensus in the family (given by approximately half of participants) tended to be justified by references to the necessity of securing the child's agreement, irrespective of the parents' wishes. The following examples illustrate some of the ways Chinese adolescents criticized the status quo in support of children's greater say in decisions about educational matters in the family and school:

> Tutoring is an extra-curricular activity. Imposing it on the child without her agreement will not produce good results. She is not willing to take it. Such a family is not democratic at all.

> Many things, such as natural inclination, creativity, and freedom, are strangled because of this.

> Education authorities' decisions are only based on examinations, and make us learn the boring texts. As to today's quality education, it develops one's interest. No to education authorities' decision!

In addition to appealing to general notions of fairness based on consensus or majority rule, Chinese adolescents also mentioned the importance of fostering individual interest and motivation through the involvement of children in educational decisions. The findings of the present study are consistent with those of recent research examining Chinese children's and adolescents' concepts of learning in educational settings. Li (2002) found evidence for conceptions of knowledge and learning among Chinese students that emphasize individual motivation and agency and the role of active learning. It is interesting that the views of Chinese adolescents regarding children's educational autonomy articulated in the current study contrast with those held by some Chinese educational authorities, including teachers. Wang, Elicker, McMullen, and Mao (2001), in a study of Chinese and American preschool teachers' beliefs about the curriculum, found that Chinese teachers were more likely to endorse teacher-centered or top-down educational practices emphasizing hierarchy, respect for authority, and highly structured routines, whereas American teachers were more likely to endorse child-centered practices emphasizing students' autonomy and choice. The findings of the present study suggest that there may be tension between the perspectives on learning held by Chinese students and those held among authorities and education officials, an area requiring further research. More generally, these findings illustrate how individuals at different levels of social hierarchies may hold contradictory goals and perspectives (Turiel & Wainryb, 1994), and they highlight the need to examine judgments of social practices from different perspectives in social hierarchies within cultures.

Similar findings that individuals contest and disagree with cultural practices have been found in other traditional cultures labeled as collectivist, such as the Druze, a traditional Muslim society in Israel (Wainryb & Turiel, 1994), and in India (Neff, 2001). The findings of the present study add to a growing body of research on moral and social reasoning conducted in various cultures suggesting that individuals' social reasoning is multifaceted and reflects concerns with individual autonomy, rights, and participation in decision making, along with the maintenance of hierarchical social arrangements and norms (Helwig & Turiel, 2002; Killen, Crystal, & Watanabe, 2002; Neff & Helwig, 2002; Nucci et al., 1996; Turiel & Wainryb, 1998; Yau & Smetana, 2003). These findings have more general implications for research on social and moral judgments in that they suggest that reasoning needs to be examined in more local contexts and situations, rather than at the general level of culture, and that provision needs to be made within theoretical models and research methodology for the detection and explanation of the diverse orientations individuals hold toward cultural belief systems and ideology,

including relations characterized by dissent, disagreement, and opposition to existing social and cultural practices. The complexities in social judgments and reasoning found in the current study, and in other research, may be obscured by attempts to characterize social reasoning within broad, all-encompassing cultural orientations, such as individualism and collectivism.

Some differences between the findings of the current study for the curriculum example and those of prior research with Canadian samples (Helwig, 2002; Helwig & Kim, 1999) further point to ways in which the responses of adolescents departed from presumed cultural orientations of individualism and collectivism. The majority of Canadian children and adolescents from about 11 years and older endorsed the hierarchical decision-making procedure of adult authority for school curriculum decisions, whereas the majority of Chinese adolescents endorsed procedures such as majority rule that gave children equal rights as those of adults. In their justifications, Canadian adolescents tended to defer to the greater expertise and knowledge of adults and to question children's competence to make educational decisions, whereas Chinese adolescents advocated greater involvement by children in educational decisions, often questioning the ability of adults to discern Children's intellectual interests and to make good decisions on their behalf.

A full explanation of these intriguing cultural differences awaits further research. One possibility, supported by the justification data, is that they may stem from differences in how educational practices in each culture are perceived to affect children's developing needs for autonomy and personal choice. Features such as the more rigid, hierarchical educational system in China, and the academic success orientation stressed by Chinese families, may lead Chinese adolescents to perceive authorities as having too much control over these aspects of children's lives, producing a corresponding desire for greater freedom and decision-making autonomy for children. Many of the statements made by Chinese adolescents in our research have been echoed by some Chinese policy makers and academics who have also criticized such cultural practices, expressing concern over what they see as parental overinvolvement in children's lives

(Wu, 1996) or the detrimental effects of a rigid, hierarchical educational system that fails to recognize children's rights and decision-making capacity in schools (Chen & Su, 2001). In addition, because of their relatively limited experience with autonomy in educational contexts, Chinese adolescents may be less likely to consider some of the negative implications resulting from children having too much control over educational matters such as the curriculum. In contrast, Western adolescents, who are customarily granted more freedom over educational choices, may be less inclined to perceive adult control over curriculum as involving a serious threat to their developing sense of autonomy. Indeed, debates in North America over issues that affect the rights and autonomy of children in school settings have largely centered on concerns over collectivist issues such as safety and school discipline, as reflected in controversies over school dress codes and uniforms, mandatory drug testing, and locker inspections and weapon searches. The responses of adolescents in each culture may be a reflection, in part, of areas over which they view encroachment on their developing autonomy by adult authorities. This interpretation is in line with that of Lau (1992) regarding the tendency of individuals to value more highly those values that are perceived as contested or insufficiently realized in their cultural environments. It is also consistent with models of social reasoning that propose that the emergence of autonomy in adolescence is marked by negotiation over areas of contention, disagreement, and conflict with rules and practices imposed by adults—a process that may be universal although its manifestation may take different forms in different cultural contexts (Nucci, 2001; Smetana, 2002; Yau & Smetana, 2003).

Some limitations of the current study's methods should be acknowledged. This study examined judgments and reasoning using a written measure assessing responses to hypothetical situations. It is possible that adolescents' judgments in actual situations may differ. Other situations need to be explored, even within social contexts, to get a more complete picture of Chinese adolescents' reasoning. For example, in assessing judgments about the curriculum example, the present study included a general case examining adolescents' judgments about who should determine what children would learn in class, with the findings

showing a high degree of support for greater student involvement. It is possible, however, that investigations of judgments and reasoning about specific curriculum decisions in contextualized situations may reveal less support for children's choice and autonomy, or may otherwise qualify some of the current study's findings. In addition, to provide comparability with previous research (Helwig & Kim, 1999), adolescents in this study made judgments about younger children (8-year-olds); it is possible that adolescents' judgments about their own educational experiences might differ in unknown ways. However, it is reasonable to expect that adolescents would express a desire for even more involvement with regard to their own academic decision making, given the general developmental pattern toward an increasing desire for autonomy with age found in research in several cultural contexts (Nucci et al., 1996; Smetana, 2002).

Further avenues of research are suggested by the results of this study. It would be of interest to examine whether Chinese adolescents' judgments of children's autonomy in decision making change over historical time, especially as Chinese students gain more autonomy over decisions about educational issues and presumably become more familiar with the consequences (both positive and negative) of expanded decision-making autonomy for children (assuming, of course, that such changes do occur within Chinese educational institutions and practices). It would also be informative to explore these issues further by including judgments about younger agents to determine whether and at what point Chinese adolescents would give more weight to issues such as children's possible lack of competence in making such decisions. As well, although the present study examined judgments of democratic decision making in contexts close to everyday life, such as the peer group, family, and school, it did not examine judgments in more distal or complex contexts, such as that of large social institutions, including the workplace or government. Differences in social organization between Western and Chinese societies may be greater for these contexts than for those examined in the current study, perhaps leading to more divergence in whether democratic concepts are seen as relevant to these settings or in how they are applied. Nonetheless, the finding that conceptions of democracy, individual autonomy, and rights are not restricted to Western societies, and are applied by Chinese adolescents to evaluate existing practices in several social contexts, suggests that a basis exists within Chinese social and moral reasoning for the extension of these concepts to judgments about justice in other social and institutional settings.

References

Belch, G. E., Belch, M. A., & Ceresino, G. (1985). Parental and teenage child influences in family decision making. *Journal of Business Research, 13,* 163–176.

Bond, M. H. (1991). *Beyond the Chinese face: Insights from psychology.* New York: Oxford University Press.

Bond, M. H. (2002). Reclaiming the individual from Hofetede's ecological analysis—A 20 year odyssey: Comment on Oysennan et aL (2002). *Psychological Bulletin, 128,* 73–77.

Breiner, S. J. (1980). Early child development in China. *Child Psychiatry and Human Development, 11,* 87–95.

Chao, R. K., & Sue, S. (1996). Chinese parental influence and their children's school success: A paradox in the literature on parenting styles. In S. Lau (Ed.), *Growing up the Chinese way: Chinese child and adolescent development* (pp. 93–120). Hong Kong: The Chinese University Press.

Chen, H., & Su, L. (2001). Child protection and development in China. *International Society for the Study of Behavioral Development Newsletter, 2,* 7–8.

de Bary, W. T., & Weiming, T. (Eds.). (1998). *Confucianism and human rights.* New York: Columbia University Press.

Dien, D. S. (1982). A Chinese perspective on Kohlberg's theory of moral development. *Developmental Review, 2,* 331–341.

Gentry, M. (1982). Consensus as a form of decision making. *Journal of Sociology and Social Welfare, 9,* 233–244.

Hebei economic yearbook. (2001). Beijing: China Statistics Press.

Helwig, C. C. (1995a). Social contexts in social cognition: Psychological harm and civil liberties. In M. Killen & D. Hart (Eds.), *Morality in everyday life: Developmental perspectives* (pp. 166–200). Cambridge, England: Cambridge University Press.

Helwig, C. C. (1995b). Adolescents' and young adults' conceptions of civil liberties: Freedom of speech and religion. *Child Development, 66,* 152–166.

Helwig, C. C. (1997). The role of agent and social context in judgments of freedom of speech and religion. *Child Development, 68,* 484–495.

Helwig, C. C. (1998). Children's conceptions of fair government and freedom of speech. *Child Development, 69,* 518–531.

Helwig, C. C. (2002). [Canadian adolescents' and young adults' judgments of decision making procedures]. Unpublished raw data.

Helwig, C. C. (2005). Culture and the construction of concepts of personal autonomy and democratic decision making, hi J. E. Jacobs & P. A. Klaczynski (Eds.), *The development of judgment and decision making in children and adolescents* (pp. 181–212). Mahwah, NJ: Erlbaum.

Helwig, C. C., & Kim, S. (1999). Children's evaluations of decision making procedures in peer, family, and school contexts. *Child Development, 70,* 502–512.

Helwig, C. C, & Turiel, E. (2002). Civil liberties, autonomy, and democracy: Children's perspectives. *International Journal of Law and Psychiatry, 25,* 253–270.

Jenkins, R. L. (1978). The influence of children in family decision making: Parents' perceptions. *Advances in Consumer Research, 6,* 413–419.

Jiangsu statistical yearbook. (2001). Beijing: China Statistics Press.

Killen, M., Crystal, D., & Watanabe, H. (2002). Japanese and American children's evaluations of peer exclusion, tolerance of differences, and prescriptions for conformity. *Child Development, 73,* 1788–1802.

Kinoshita, Y. (1989). Developmental changes in understanding the limitations of majority decisions. *British Journal of Developmental Psychology, 7,* 97–112.

Kurtines, W. M., Berman, S. L., Ittel, A., & Williamson, S. (1995). Moral development: A co-constructivist perspective. In W. M. Kurtines & J. L. Gewirtz (Eds.), *Moral development: An introduction* (pp. 337–376). Needham Heights, MA: Allyn & Bacon.

Lau, S. (1992). Collectivism's individualism: Value preference, personal control, and the desire for freedom among Chinese in mainland China, Hong Kong, and Singapore. *Personality and Individual Difference, 13*(3), 361–366.

Lau, S., Lew, W. J. F., Hau, K. T., Cheung, P. C., & Berndt, T. J. (1990). Relations among perceived parental control, warmth, indulgence, and family harmony of Chinese in mainland China. *Developmental Psychology, 26,* 674–677.

Lau, S., & Yeung, P. W. (19%). Understanding Chinese child development: The role of culture in socialization. In S. Lau (Ed.), *Growing up the Chinese way: Chinese child and adolescent development* (pp. 29–44). Hong Kong: The Chinese University Press.

Levin, H. (1990). Political socialization for workplace democracy. In O. Ichilov (Ed.), *Political socialization, citizenship education, and democracy* (pp. 158–176). New York: Teachers College Press.

Li, J. (2002). Learning models in different cultures. In J. Bempechat & J. G. Elliot (Eds.), Learning in culture and context. *New Directions for Child Development,* (No. 96, pp. 45–63). San Francisco: Jossey-Bass.

Mackerras, C. (2001). *The new Cambridge handbook of contemporary China.* Cambridge, England: Cambridge University Press.

Mann, L., & Greenbaum, C. W. (1987). Cross-cultural studies of children's decision rules. In C. Kagitcibasi (Ed.), *Growth and progress in cross-cultural psychology* (pp. 130–137). Berwyn, PA: Swets North America.

Mann, L., Tan, C., MacLeod-Morgan, C., & Dixon, A. (1984). Developmental changes in application of the majority rule in group decisions. *British Journal of Developmental Psychology, 2,* 275–281.

Markus, H. R., & Kitayama, S. (1991). Culture and the self: Implications for cognition, emotion, and motivation. *Psychological Review, 98,* 224–253.

Moessinger, P. (1981). The development of the concept of majority decision: A pilot study. *Canadian Journal of Behavioral Science, 13,* 359–362.

Neff, K. D. (2001). Judgements of personal autonomy and interpersonal responsibility in the context of Indian spousal relationships: An examination of young people's reasoning in Mysore, India. *British Journal of Developmental Psychology, 19,* 233–257.

Neff, K. D., & Helwig, C. C. (2002). A constructivist approach to understanding the development of reasoning about rights and authority within cultural contexts. *Cognitive Development, 17,* 1429–1450.

Nucci, L. P. (1981). The development of personal concepts: A domain distinct from moral and social concepts. *Child Development, 52,* 114–121.

Nucci, L. P. (2001). *Education in the moral domain.* Cambridge, England: Cambridge University Press.

Nucci, L. P., Camino, C., & Milnitsky-Sapiro, C. (1996). Social class effects on northeastern Brazilian children's conceptions of areas of personal choice and social regulation. *Child Development, 67,* 1223–1242.

Oyserman, D., Coon, H. M., & Kemmelmeier, M. (2002). Rethinking individualism and collectivism: Evaluation of theoretical assumptions and meta-analysis. *Psychological Bulletin, 128,* 3–72.

Prencipe, A., & Helwig, C. C. (2002). The development of reasoning about the teaching of values in school and family contexts. *Child Development, 73,* 841–856.

Pye, L. W. (1992). *The spirit of Chinese politics.* Cambridge, MA: Harvard University Press.

Rokeach, M. (1973). *The nature of human values.* New York: Free Press.

Schwartz, S. H. (1990). Individualism–collectivism: Critique and proposed refinements. *Journal of Cross-Cultural Psychology, 21*(2), 139–157.

Sen, A. (1999). *Development as freedom.* New York: Random House.

Shweder, R. A. (1990). In defense of moral realism: Reply to Gabennesch. *Child Development, 61,* 2060–2067.

Shweder, R. A., & Bourne, E. J. (1982). Does the concept of the person vary cross-culturally? In A. J. Marsella & G. M. White (Eds.), *Cultural conceptions of mental health and therapy* (pp. 97–137). Boston: Reidel.

Shweder, R. A., Mahapatra, M., & Miller, J. G. (1987). Culture and moral development. In J. Kagan & S. Lamb (Eds.), *The emergence of morality in young children* (pp. 1–83). Chicago: University of Chicago Press.

Smetana, J. G. (1988). Adolescents' and parents' conceptions of parental authority. *Child Development, 59,* 321–335.

Smetana, J. G. (1989). Adolescents' and parents' reasoning about actual family conflict. *Child Development, 60,* 1052–1067.

Smetana, J. G. (2002). Culture, autonomy, and personal jurisdiction in adolescent–parent relationships. In H. W. Reese & R. Kail (Eds.), *Advances in child development and behavior* (Vol. 29, pp. 51–87). New York: Academic Press.

Takano, Y., & Osaka, E. (1999). An unsupported common view: Comparing Japan and the U.S. on individualism/collectivism. *Asian Journal of Social Psychology, 2,* 311–341.

Triandis, H. C. (1989). The self and social behavior in differing cultural contexts. *Psychological Review, 96,* 506–520.

Turiel, E. (1998). The development of morality. In W. Damon (Series Ed.) & N. Eisenberg (Vol. Ed.), *Handbook of child psychology: Vol. 3. Social, emotional, and personality development* (5th ed., pp. 863–932). New York: Wiley.

Turiel, E. (2002). *The culture of morality: Social development, context, and conflict.* Cambridge, England: Cambridge University Press.

Turiel, E., Hildebrandt, C., & Wainryb, C. (1991). Judging social issues: Difficulties, inconsistencies, and consistencies. *Monographs of the Society for Research in Child Development, 56*(2).

Turiel, E., & Wainryb, C (1994). Social reasoning and the varieties of social experience in cultural contexts. In H. W. Reese (Ed.), *Advances in child development and behavior* (Vol 25, pp. 289–326). New York Academic Press.

Turiel, E., & Wainryb, C. (1998). Concepts of freedoms and rights in a traditional hierarchically organized society. *British Journal of Developmental Psychology, 16,* 375–395.

Wainryb, C. (1997). The mismeasure of diversity: Reflections on the study of cross-cultural differences. In H. Saltzstein

(Ed.), *Culture as a context for moral development: New perspectives on the particular and the universal. New Directions for Child Development* (No. 76, pp. 51–65). San Francisco: Jossey-Bass.

Wainryb, C., & Turiel, E. (1994). Dominance, subordination, and concepts of personal entitlement in cultural contexts. *Child Development, 65*, 1701–1722.

Wang, J., Elicker, J., McMullen, M., & Mao, S. (2001, April). *American and Chinese teachers' beliefs about early childhood curriculum.* Poster presented at the biennial meeting of the Society for Research in Child Development, Minneapolis, MN.

Winer, B. J., Brown, D. R., & Michels, K. M. (1991). *Statistical principles in experimental design.* New York: McGraw-Hill.

Worden, R. L., Savada, A. M., & Dolan, R. E. (Eds.). (1988). *China: A country study.* Washington, DC: Library of Congress.

Wu, D. Y. H. (1996). Parental control: Psychocultural interpretations of Chinese patterns of socialization. In S. Lau (Ed.), *Growing up the Chinese way: Chinese child and adolescent development* (pp. 1–28). Hong Kong: The Chinese University Press.

Yau, J., & Smetana, J. G. (1996). Adolescent–parent conflict among Chinese adolescents in Hong Kong. *Child Development, 67*, 1262–1275.

Yau, J. & Smetana, J. G. (2003). Adolescent-parent conflict in Hong Kong and Mainland China: A comparison of youth in two cultural contexts. *International Journal of Behavioral Development, 27*, 201–211.

Appendix

The Six Decision Examples

Peer context (game). Suppose there is a group of friends, all around the age of 8. Every day after school, they get together and play games. So, each day, they have to decide what game they are going to play.

Peer context (movie). Suppose there is a group of friends, all around the age of 8. The kids in this group wanted to see a movie. So, they were trying to decide which movie they should go see.

Family (outing). Suppose there is a family. In the family, there is an 8-year-old child and his/her parents. Suppose the family wanted to go on a weekend day outing. So, they were trying to decide where they should go to have fun during the weekend.

Family (tutoring). Suppose there is a family. In the family, there is an 8-year-old child and his/her parents. Suppose the family is trying to decide whether the child should get some special after school tutoring to help the child get really high grades in school. This tutoring would last almost the entire day on Saturday. But suppose the child did not want to spend his/her Saturday that way. The child wanted to do something that she/he wanted to do, not to work on more school work during the weekend.

School (field trip). Suppose there is a class of third-grade students, all around 8 years of age. Every Friday afternoon, the whole class would go on a field trip. Suppose they were trying to decide where they should go for one of their field trips.

School (curriculum). Suppose there is a class of third-grade students, all around 8 years of age. At the beginning of each week, a decision has to be made about what they are going to learn in school that week.

A Closer Look 11   African-American Culture: Understanding the Past
to Make Predictions About Development

In an essay about race and culture, McLoyd (2004) traces the cultural characterizations of African-Americans, who represent an ethnic minority group with a unique history in the United States. She identifies the complexities of being an ethnic minority member in a culture, which generalize to many "cultures within cultures." McLoyd cites studies which have identified the different realms of experience of African-Americans: (1) mainstream (beliefs and values shared with most individuals in the United States); (2) minority (coping strategies developed by minority groups to face life in oppressive environments); and (3) Afro-cultural (links between contemporary African descendants and traditional African belief systems). She then describes how membership in an ethnic minority group does not mean that the same cultural experience exists for all in the group, contrary to what the majority viewpoint might expect. This thoughtful essay provides new insights into culture, race, and ethnicity.

McLoyd, V. C. (2004). Linking race and ethnicity to culture: Steps along the road from inference to hypothesis testing. *Human Development*, 47, 185–191.

Classroom Exercises, Debates, and Discussion Questions

- *Classroom exercise: What is culture?* Students divide up into two different groups. In one group, the task is to list all of the attributes that are associated with individualism (such as self-reliance, autonomy, independence) and identify how these values and beliefs emerge in college life. In a second group, the task is to list all of the attributes of collectivism (group identity, duty, and interdependence) and to identify how these values and beliefs are part of their everyday life. Then both groups get together and discuss whether they identify more with individualistic or collectivistic values, or both. The discussion can focus on whether individualism and collectivism are separate ways of characterizing groups or coexist within groups.
- *Classroom exercise.* Discuss what cultural groups each person identifies with as an adult. How many cultural groups do most adults belong to, and how does this change over time? Ask each person to recall the cultural groups and categories that were meaningful to them as children growing up. Which groups were important and why?

- *Classroom discussion.* Children from immigrant families are bicultural in their newly arrived culture. What strategies best enable children to function well in the new cultural context? What is the role of parents and schools to help facilitate a positive transition?
- *Classroom discussion.* Multiculturalism is the recognition of the coexistence of different cultural groups in a society and full recognition of multiple cultures. Some countries have long histories of a strong national identity and find the notion of multiculturalism antagonistic to their traditions and way of life. Research shows different developmental periods for the acceptance and rejection of conventions in the home. How might this translate into how children and adolescents accept the conventions of a new culture?
- *Classroom discussion.* The United Nations Convention on the Rights of the Child was passed in 1989. The bill includes the rights of dignity and expression, development (good education, health care and clean environment), and care and protection (to live without violence, corporal punishment and a safe home). How does social developmental research bear on the UN Bill of Rights for Children?

- *Classroom discussion.* Cultures exist at multiple levels, beginning in the family, extending to school contexts and then to broader communities. How does the notion of culture change from early childhood to adulthood?
- *Classroom discussion: Culture and identity.* Discuss the different cultural groups that individuals belong to (including gender, race, ethnicity, music clubs, hobbies) and define what makes these groups "cultures." What are the criteria that create a cultural category? When is cultural identity important? When is it not important? The discussion can focus on how culture is both measured and defined.

Additional Resources

For more about culture, ethnicity, and rights, see:

Oyserman, D., Coon, H. M., & Kemmelmeier, M. (2002). Rethinking individualism and collectivism: Evaluation of theoretical assumptions and meta-analyses. *Psychological Bulletin, 128*, 3–72.

Ruck, M. D., Abramovitch, R., & Keating, D. P. (1998). Children's and adolescents' understanding of rights: Balancing nurturance and self-determination. *Child Development, 64*, 404–417.

Shweder, R. A., & Bourne, E. J. (1982). Does the concept of the person vary cross-culturally? In J. Marsella & G. M. White (Eds.), *Cultural conceptions of mental health and therapy* (pp. 97–137). Boston, MA: Reidel.

Super, C. M., & Harkness, S. (2002). Culture structures the environment for development. *Human Development, 45*, 270–274.

Triandis, H. C. (1995). *Individualism and collectivism.* Boulder, CO: Western Press.

Wainryb, C., Smetana, J. G., & Turiel, E. (2008). *Social development, social inequalities, and social justice.* Mahwah, NJ: Lawrence Erlbaum Associates.

ACKNOWLEDGMENTS

The editors and publisher gratefully acknowledge the permission granted to reproduce the copyright material in this book:

Chapter 2

Mary K. Rothbart, Stephan A. Ahadi, and Karen L. Hershey, "Temperament and Social Behavior in Childhood," pp. 21–39 from *Merrill-Palmer Quarterly* 40:1. © 1994 by Wayne State University Press, Detroit. Reprinted by permission of Wayne State University Press.

Paul D. Hastings, Carolyn Zahn-Waxler, JoAnn Robinson, Barbara Usher, and D. Bridges, "The development in concern for others in children with behavior problems," pp. 531–546 from *Developmental Psychology* 36:5. [Public domain]

Amrisha Vaish, Malinda Carpenter, and Michael Tomasello, "Sympathy Through Affective Perspective Taking and Its Relation to Prosocial Behavior in Toddlers," pp. 534–543 from *Developmental Psychology* 45:2. © 2009 by the American Psychological Association. Reprinted by permission of the American Psychological Association.

Chapter 3

Jude Cassidy, "The Nature of the Child's Ties," pp. 3–22 from *Handbook of Attachment: Theory, Research,* *and Clinical Applications*, 2nd edn, ed. J. Cassidy and P. R. Shaver (New York: Guilford Press, 2008). Reprinted by permission of Guilford Press.

Everett Waters, Susan Merrick, Dominique Treboux, Judith Crowell, and Leah Albersheim, "Attachment Security in Infancy and Early Adulthood: A Twenty-Year Longitudinal Study," pp. 684–689 from *Child Development* 71:3. © 2000 by the Society for Research in Child Development, Inc. All rights reserved. Reprinted by permission of the Society for Research in Child Development, Inc.

NICHD Early Child Care Research Network, "The Effects of Infant Child Care on Infant–Mother Attachment Security: Results of the NICHD Study of Early Child Care," pp. 860–879 from *Child Development* 68:5. © 1997 by the Society for Research in Child Development, Inc. All rights reserved. Reprinted by permission of the Society for Research in Child Development, Inc.

Chapter 4

Judy Dunn, "Mind-Reading, Emotion Understanding, and Relationships," pp. 142–144 from *International Journal of Behavioral Development* 24:2. © 2000 The International Society for the Study of Behavioural Development. Reprinted by permission of The International Society for the Study of Behavioural Development.

Amanda L. Woodward and Jessica A. Sommerville, "Twelve-Month-Old Infants Interpret Action in Context," from *Psychological Science* 11:1. © 2000 American Psychological Society. Reprinted by permission of the American Psychological Society.

Henry M. Wellman and David Liu, "Scaling of Theory-of-Mind Tasks," pp. 523–541 from *Child Development* 75:2. © 2004 by the Society for Research in Child Development, Inc.

All rights reserved. Reprinted by permission of the Society for Research in Child Development, Inc.

Chapter 5

Ernest V. E. Hodges, Michel Boivin, Frank Vitaro, and William M. Bukowski, "The Power of Friendship: Protection Against an Escalating Cycle of Peer Victimization," pp. 94–101 from *Developmental Psychology* 35:1. © 1999 by the American Psychological Association, Inc. Reprinted by permission of the American Psychological Society.

A. Michele Lease and Charlotte A. Kennedy, and Jennifer L. Axelrod, "Children's Social Constructions of Popularity," pp. 87–109 from *Social Development* 11:1. © 2002 by Blackwell Publishers Ltd. Reprinted by permission of Blackwell Publishers Ltd.

Stacey S. Horn, "Group status, group bias, and adolescents' reasoning about the treatment of others in school contexts," pp. 208–218 from *International Journal of Behavioral Development* 30:3. © 2006 by The International Society for the Study of Behavioural Development. Reprinted by permission of The International Society for the Study of Behavioural Development.

Chapter 6

Elliot Turiel, "The Development of Children's Orientations toward Moral, Social, and Personal Orders: More than a Sequence in Development," pp. 21–39 from *Human Development* 51. © 2008 S. Karger AG, Basel. Reprinted by permission of S. Karger AG.

Nancy Eisenberg, Ivanna K. Guthrie, Bridget C. Murphy, Stephanie A. Shepard, Amanda Cumberland, and Gustavo Carlo, "Consistency and Development of Prosocial Dispositions: A Longitudinal Study," pp. 1360–1372 from *Child Development* 70:6. © 1999 by the Society for Research in Child Development, Inc. Reprinted by permission of the Society for Research in Child Development, Inc.

Cecilia Wainryb, Leigh A. Shaw, Marcie Langley, Kim Cottam, and Renee Lewis, "Children's Thinking About Diversity of Belief in the Early School Years: Judgments of Relativism, Tolerance, and Disagreeing Persons," pp. 687–703 from *Child Development* 75:3. © 2004 by the Society for Research in Child Development, Inc. Reprinted by permission of the Society for Research in Child Development, Inc.

Chapter 7

Janis E. Jacobs, Stephanie Lanza, D. Wayne Osgood, Jacquelynne S. Eccles, and Allan Wigfield, "Changes in Children's Self-Competence and Values: Gender and Domain Differences across Grades One Through Twelve," pp. 509–527 from *Child Development* 73:2. © 2002 by the Society for Research in Child Development, Inc. Reprinted by permission of the Society for Research in Child Development, Inc.

Lisa Kiang, Tiffany Yip, Melinda Gonzales-Backen, Melissa Witkow, and Andrew J. Fuligni, "Ethnic Identity and the Daily Psychological Well-Being of Adolescents from Mexican and Chinese Backgrounds," pp. 1338–1350 from *Child Development* 77:5. © 2006 by the Society for Research in Child Development, Inc. Reprinted by permission of the Society for Research in Child Development, Inc.

Dominic Abrams, Adam Rutland, and Lindsey Cameron, "The Development of Subjective Group Dynamics: Children's Judgments of Normative and Deviant In-Group and Out-Group Individuals," pp. 1840–1856 from *Child Development* 74:6. © 2003 by the Society for Research in Child Development, Inc. Reprinted by permission of the Society for Research in Child Development, Inc.

Chapter 8

Robert J. Coplan, Kimberley A. Arbeau, and Mandana Armer, "Don't Fret, Be Supportive! Maternal Characteristics Linking Child Shyness to Psychosocial and School Adjustment in Kindergarten," pp. 359–371 from *Journal of Abnormal Child Psychology* 36. © 2008 Springer Science + Business Media, LLC. Reprinted by permission of Springer Science + Business Media, LLC.

Wonjung Oh, Kenneth H. Rubin, Julie C. Bowker, Cathryn Booth-LaForce, Linda Rose-Krasnor, and Brett Laursen, "Trajectories of Social Withdrawal from Middle Childhood to Early Adolescence," pp. 553–566 from *Journal of Abnormal Child Psychology* 36. © 2008 Springer Science + Business Media, LLC. Reprinted by permission of Springer Science + Business Media, LLC.

Xinyin Chen, Guozhen Cen, Dan Li, and Yunfeng He, "Social Functioning and Adjustment in Chinese Children: The Imprint of Historical Time," pp. 182–195 from *Child Development* 76:1. © 2005 by the Society for Research in Child Development, Inc. Reprinted by permission of the Society for Research in Child Development, Inc.

Chapter 9

Elizabeth A. Lemerise and William F. Arsenio, "An Integrated Model of Emotion Processes and Cognition in Social Information Processing," pp. 107–118 from *Child Development* 71:1. © 2000 by the Society for Research in Child Development, Inc. Reprinted by permission of the Society for Research in Child Development, Inc.

Dianna Murray-Close, Jamie M. Ostrov, and Nicki R. Crick, "A Short-Term Longitudinal Study of Growth of Relational Aggression during Middle Childhood: Associations with Gender, Friendship Intimacy, and Internalizing Problems," pp. 187–203 from *Development and Psychopathology* 19. © 2007 by Cambridge University Press. Reprinted by permission of Cambridge University Press.

Debra J. Pepler and Wendy M. Craig, "A Peek Behind the Fence: Naturalistic Observations of Aggressive Behavior with Remote Audiovisual Recording," pp. 548–553 from *Developmental Psychology* 31:4. © 1995 by the American Psychological Association, Inc. Reprinted by permission of the American Psychological Association, Inc.

Chapter 10

Melanie Killen and Charles Stangor, "Children's Reasoning about Social Inclusion and Exclusion in Gender and Race Peer Group Contexts," pp. 174–186 from *Child Development* 72:1. © 2001 by the Society for Research in Child Development, Inc. Reprinted by permission of the Society for Research in Child Development, Inc.

Clark McKown and Rhona S. Weinstein, "The Development and Consequences of Stereotype Consciousness in Middle Childhood," pp. 498–515 from *Child Development* 74:2. © 2003 by the Society for Research in Child Development, Inc. Reprinted by permission of the Society for Research in Child Development, Inc.

Judith A. Griffiths and Drew Nesdale, "In-group and Out-group Attitudes of Ethnic Majority and Minority Children," pp. 735–749 from *International Journal of Intercultural Relations* 30. © 2006 by Elsevier Ltd. Reprinted by permission of Elsevier Ltd.

Chapter 11

Anne C. Fletcher, Nancy F. Darling, Laurence Steinberg, and Sanford M. Dornbusch, "The Company They Keep: Relation of Adolescents' Adjustment and Behavior to their Friends' Perceptions of Authoritative Parenting in the Social Network," pp. 300–310 from *Developmental Psychology* 31:2. © 1995 by the American Psychological Association, Inc. Reprinted by permission of the American Psychological Association, Inc.

Nancy Darling, Patricio Cumsille, and M. Loreto Martínez, "Individual Differences in Adolescents'

Beliefs about the Legitimacy of Parental Authority and Their Own Obligation to Obey: A Longitudinal Investigation," pp. 1103–1118 from *Child Development* 79:4. © 2008 by the Society for Research in Child Development, Inc. Reprinted by permission of the Society for Research in Child Development, Inc.

Judith G. Smetana and Christopher Daddis, "Domain-Specific Antecedents of Psychological Control and Parent Monitoring: The Role of Parenting Beliefs and Practices," pp. 563–580 from *Child Development* 73:2. © 2002 by the Society for Research in Child Development, Inc. Reprinted by permission of the Society for Research in Child Development, Inc.

Chapter 12

Catherine S. Tamis-LaMonda, Niobe Way, Diane Hughes, Hirokazu Yoshikawa, Ronit Kahana Kalman, and Erika Y. Niwa, "Parents' Goals for Children: The Dynamic Coexistence of Individualism and Collectivism in Cultures and Individuals," pp. 183–209 from *Social Development* 17:1. © 2007 by Blackwell Publishing Ltd. Reprinted by permission of Blackwell Publishing Ltd.

Maykel Verkuyten and Luuk Slooter, "Muslim and Non-Muslim Adolescents' Reasoning about Freedom of Speech and Minority Rights," pp. 514–528 from *Child Development* 79:3. © 2008 by the Society for Research in Child Development, Inc. Reprinted by permission of the Society for Research in Child Development, Inc.

Charles C. Helwig, Mary Louise Arnold, Dingliang Tan, and Dwight Boyd, "Chinese Adolescents' Reasoning about Democratic and Authority-Based Decision Making in Peer, Family, and School Contexts," pp. 783–800 from *Child Development* 74:3. © 2003 by the Society for Research in Child Development, Inc. Reprinted by permission of the Society for Research in Child Development, Inc.

Every effort has been made to trace copyright holders and to obtain their permission for the use of copyright material. The publisher apologizes for any errors or omissions in the above list and would be grateful if notified of any corrections that should be incorporated in future reprints or editions of this book.

NAME INDEX

Aboud, F. E. 292, 293, 408, 419, 422
  ethnic attitudes 443, 444, 449
Aboud, F. E. and Amato, M. 292
Aboud, F. E. and Levy, S. R. 451–452
Aboud, F. E. and Skerry, S. A. 422
Abrams, D. 292–311
Abrams, D., Rutland, A., and Cameron, L.
  (2003) 255, 292–311
Abrams, D. et al. (2000) 293, 295,
  307, 308
Abrams, D. et al. (2002) 293, 295,
  303, 307
Abrams, D. et al. (2003) 294–295, 299,
  303, 307, 308
Abrams, D. et al. (2004) 293
Abu-Lughod, L. 210
Achenbach, T. M. 30, 44, 358
Achenbach, T. M. and Edelbrock, C. S.
  30, 348
Adler, P. A. and Adler, P. 165–168, 170,
  171, 173–174, 180–182
Ahadi, S. A. 15–26
Ahadi, S. A. and Rothbart, M. K. 15, 23
Ahadi, S. A. et al. (1993) 15, 18
Ahnert, L. et al. (2006) 78
Aiken, L. S. and West, S. G. 37, 305, 324,
  325, 501, 504
  victimization 160, 164
Ainsworth, M. D. S. 65, 66–67, 71–73,
  75–81, 86, 111
Ainsworth, M. D. S. and Wittig, B. A. 71,
  87, 92

Ainsworth, M. D. S. et al. (1971) 71
Ainsworth, M. D. S. et al. (1978) 86, 90,
  95, 98, 109
  attachment 70, 71, 76, 81
Akaike, H. 338
Albersheim, L. 86–91
Alexander, K. and Entwisle, D. 257
Allen, J. P. et al. (2006) 200
Almeida, D. M. and Kessler, R. C. 280
Alvarez, J. M. et al. (2001) 294
Ambady, N. et al. (2001) 424, 437
American Psychiatric Association 26, 41
Andrich, D. 140, 143
Arbeau, K. A. 317–332
Arbeau, K. A. and Coplan, R. J. 318
Arbuckle, J. 338
Archer, J. and McDonald, M. 258
Arcus, D. 318
Armer, M. 317–332
Arnold, M. L. 554–573
Aronfreed, J. 206, 209
Arsenio, W. F. 208, 367–379, 375, 376
Arsenio, W. F. and Lover, A. 367, 372,
  374, 375
Arsenio, W. F. et al. (2000) 372
Asendorpf, J. 333, 349, 360
Asendorpf, J. and Meier, G. H. 363–364
Asher, S. and Coie, J. 167, 407
Asher, S. et al. (1990) 358
Astington, J. W. 118, 134
Astington, J. W. and Jenkins, J. M.
  130, 144

Astington, J. W. et al. (1988) 233, 236
Augoustinos, M. and Rosewarne,
  D. L. 441, 444
Averhart, C. J. and Bigler, R. S. 422
Avery, P. G. 537
Axelrod, J. L. 165–183

Babad, E. 424
Baillargeon, R. et al. (1990) 126, 127
Bakan, D. 517
Bakermans-Kranenburg, M. J. and Van
  IJzendoorn, M. H. 62
Baldwin, D. A. and Baird, J. A. 122
Baldwin, J. M. 205
Baldwin, M. W. 70
Baltes, P. B. and Nesselroade, J. R. 259
Bandura, A. 5, 8, 256
Bandura, A. and Walters, R. H. 5
Banks, W. C. 442
Barber, B. and Olsen, J. 335
Barber, B. K. 493, 495
Barber, B. K. and Harmon, E. L. 493,
  494, 495, 496, 506, 507
Barber, B. K. et al. (1994) 493, 494, 495,
  497, 506
Barber, B. K. et al. (2002) 493, 494, 497,
  498, 509, 510
Barber, B. K. et al. (2005) 476
Barenboim, C. 294
Barglow, P. (1987) 92, 111
Barnes, G. M. and Farrell, M. P.
  497, 508

Social Development in Childhood and Adolescence: A Contemporary Reader, First Edition. Edited by Melanie Killen
and Robert J. Coplan.
Editorial material and organization © 2011 Blackwell Publishing Ltd. Published 2011 by Blackwell Publishing Ltd.

Baron, R. M. and Kenny, D. A. 227, 304, 434
Baron, R. M. et al. (1985) 423
Baron-Cohen, S. 144
Barrett, M. and Short, J. 292
Bar-Tal, D. and Raviv, A. 219
Bartsch, K. 131
Bartsch, K. and Estes, D. 119
Bartsch, K. and Wellman, H. M. 119, 129
Bates, J. E. 15
Batson, C. D. 17, 48, 57, 58, 59, 218–220
Batson, C. D. et al. (1997) 48, 58
Baumrind, D. 28, 319, 458, 459, 462, 463
Bearison, D. and Zimiles, H. 367
Bechara, A. et al. (1993) 370
Bechara, A. et al. (1994) 370
Behar, L. and Stringfield, S. 30
Belch, G. E. et al. (1985) 560
Bell, R. Q. 16
Belsky, J. 79, 93
Belsky, J. and Braungart, J. 94
Belsky, J. and Cassidy, J. 109
Belsky, J. and Rovine, M. 80, 92, 109, 110, 111
Belsky, J. and Steinberg, L. 91
Belsky, J. et al. (1984) 78
Belsky, J. et al. (1995) 109
Benedict, R. F. 348
Bennett, M. and Sani, F. 539, 550
Bennett, M. et al. (1998) 410
Bennett, W. J. 209
Bergeman, C. S. et al. (1993) 219
Berger, S. et al. (1995) 94
Berkowitz, J. 372
Berndt, T. J. 464
Berndt, T. J. and Heller, K. A. 294
Berndt, T. J. et al. (1999) 334
Berti, A. E. 537, 540
Biernat, M. 294
Bigler, R. S. 292, 294, 299, 422
Bigler, R. S. and Liben, L. S. 292
Bigler, R. S. et al. (1997) 422
Billingsley, A. 509
Bischof-Köhler, D. 57
Black, J. B. and Bower, G. H. 122
Black-Gutman, D. and Hickson, F. 294, 441, 444
Blair, R. J. R. 48, 58
Blasi, A. 206
Block, J. and Block, J. H. 219
Block, J. H. 28, 31, 86
Blyth, D. et al. (1982) 459, 465

Bobo, L. D. 423, 539
Bobo, L. D. and Licardi, F. C. 541
Bock, R. D. 140
Boivin, M. 154, 155–165
Boivin, M. and Hymel, S. 155, 157, 158, 162, 163, 332
Boivin, M. et al. (1995) 155, 156, 162, 163, 332, 349
Bok, S. 209
Bolger, N. and Zuckerman, A. 280, 282, 283
Bond, M. H. 556, 558
Bond, T. G. and Fox, C. M. 141, 142
Booth-LaForce, C. 332–348
Booth-LaForce, C. and Oxford, M. L. 333, 335, 343
Bornstein, M. H. 348, 350
Bornstein, M. H. et al. (1985) 532
Bornstein, M. H. et al. (2002) 518
Bowker, A. et al. (1998) 332
Bowker, J. C. 332–348
Bowlby, J. 7, 8, 65, 367
    attachment theory 66–82, 86, 87, 89, 90, 91
Bowman, P. J. and Howard, C. 423, 430
Boyd, D. 554–573
Branscombe, N. R. and Ellemers, N. 437
Branscombe, N. R. et al. (1999) 278
Bransford, J. and Johnson, M. 122
Brattesani, K. A. et al. (1984) 424
Braun, C. 424
Brazelton, T. B. 73, 92
Breiner, S. J. 555
Brendgen, M. et al. (2000) 334
Bretherton, I. 70, 73, 76–78, 80, 81
Bretherton, I. and Ainsworth, M. D. S. 72, 76, 81
Bretherton, I. et al. (1990) 367
Bretherton, I. et al. (1991) 81
Brewer, M. B. 410, 442, 443, 523, 539
Brewer, M. B. and Chen, Y.–R. 520, 523
Bridges, D. 26–47
Bridges, L. J. 519
Bronfenbrenner, U. 110, 459
Bronfenbrenner, U. and Morris, P. A. 350, 358, 530
Bronson, G. 72
Brown, B. 407
Brown, B. et al. (1993) 472
Brown, B. B. and Lohr, M. J. 184
Brown, B. B. et al. (1994) 184, 185, 187
Brown, R. 441, 442
Brown, T. 367, 370

Bruininks, R. H. 261–262
Bruininks, V. L. and Bruininks, R. H. 262
Brush, L. R. 273
Bryant, B. K. 15, 32, 223, 227
Bryk, A. S. and Raudenbush, S. W. 259, 262–263, 283
Bugental, D. B. and Goodnow, J. J. 521
Bukowski, W. M. 154, 155–165
Bukowski, W. M. et al. (1993) 352
Bukowski, W. M. et al. (1994) 156, 157, 336
Bukowski, W. M. et al. (1995) 155
Burgess, K. B. et al. (2005) 318
Burks, V. S. et al. (1999) 376
Burlingham, D. and Freud, A. 78
Burr, J. E. and Hofer, B. K. 234
Byrne, B. M. 256

Cai, X. and Wu, P. 349, 360
Cairns, R. B. et al. (1988) 155
Caldwell, B. M. and Bradley, R. H. 95
Calkins, S. D. and Fox, N. A. 328
Cameron, L. 292–311
Campbell, D. T. 441
Campbell, J. R. et al. (2000) 259, 273
Campos, J. J. et al. (1994) 368
Carey, S. 127, 234, 244
Carey, W. and McDevitt, S. 95
Carlo, G. 218–232
Carlson, S. M. and Moses, L. J. 144
Carpendale, J. I. and Chandler, M. J. 233, 235, 422, 429
Carpenter, M. 48–61
Carpenter, M. et al. (1998) 122
Carr, J. et al. (1975) 71
Carrothers, P. and Smith, P. K. 118
Carter, D. B. and Patterson, C. J. 407, 409, 412, 418
Carver, C. S. 319, 327, 328
Carver, C. S. and Scheier, M. F. 17, 24
Case, A. and Katz, L. 460
Casey, R. J. 374, 376
Casey, R. J. and Schlosser, S. 374, 376
Casiglia, A. C. et al. (1998) 348, 353, 359
Caspi, A. et al. (1988) 352
Cassidy, J. 65, 66–85
Cassidy, J. and Asher, S. R. 33, 321
Cassidy, J. and Berlin, L. J. 70, 81
Cassidy, J. and Kobak, R. 70
Cassidy, J. et al. (2005) 73
Cauce, A. M. et al. (1996) 508
Cen, G. 348–363
Cha, J. 523

Chandler, M. J. 233, 234
Chandler, M. J. and Carpendale, J. I. 422, 429
Chandler, M. J. and Lalonde, C. 233, 235
Chandler, M. J. and Moran, T. 27
Chandler, M. J. et al. (2000) 247
Chang, L. 349, 351, 361
Chao, R. and Tseng, V. 520
Chao, R. K. and Sue, S. 560
Cheah, C. L. and Rubin, K. H. 349, 351, 360, 361
Chen, H. and Su, L. 555, 570
Chen, X. 348–363
Chen, X. and Li, B. 354, 355, 358
Chen, X. et al. (1992) 348, 349, 351, 352, 353
Chen, X. et al. (1995a) 328, 348, 351, 352, 358
Chen, X. et al. (1995b) 348, 352, 353, 354
Chen, X. et al. (1997) 348, 354
Chen, X. et al. (1998) 43
Chen, X. et al. (2005) 348–363, 520, 530, 531
Clark, K. B. and Clark, M. P. 442
Clark, M. S. and Isen, A. M. 372
Clarke-Stewart, K. A. 92, 93, 109, 111
Clarke-Stewart, K. A. and Fein, G. G. 94
Clarke-Stewart, K. S. et al. (1994) 108
Clemence, A. et al. (1995) 538
Clinchy, B. and Mansfield, A. 245
Cochran, M. 459, 460, 465
Cochran, M. and Bo, I. 459, 473
Cohen, D. and Strayer, J. 27, 374, 375
Cohen, J. 134
Coie, D. et al. (1995) 348, 354, 359
Coie, J. D. and Dodge, K. A. 168, 180, 182, 348, 358, 360
Coie, J. D. et al. (1982) 170
Coie, J. D. et al. (1988) 43
Coie, J. D. et al. (1990) 167
Colby, A. and Damon, W. 206
Colby, A. and Kohlberg, L. 209
Cole, D. A. 350, 351
Cole, P. M. et al. (1990) 31
Cole, P. M. et al. (1996) 30
Coleman, J. 459, 473
Coleman, J. and Hoffer, T. 459, 460, 473
Colin, V. L. 78, 79, 86
Collins, W. A. 487
Collins, W. A. et al. (2000) 493, 510, 513
Compas, B. 279
Cook, W. L. and Goldstein, M. J. 495

Cooper, C. R. et al. (2002) 279
Coplan, R. J. 317–332
Coplan, R. J. and Armer, M. 318
Coplan, R. J. and Prakash, K. 318
Coplan, R. J. et al. (1994) 317
Coplan, R. J. et al. (2001) 317, 321
Coplan, R. J. et al. (2004) 317, 318, 319–321, 326, 348, 349, 360
Corsaro, W. A. 166
Corsaro, W. A. and Fingerson, L. 279
Cortes, D. E. 520
Costa, P. T. and McCrae, R. R. 95
Costanzo, P. R. and Dix, T. H. 375
Cottam, K. 233–250
Coull, A. et al. (2001) 295
Covington, M. V. 256
Cowan, P. 367
Cox, M. J. et al. (1992) 163
Craig, W. 366, 395–402
Crain, R. M. 258
Crick, N. R. 197, 379–395
Crick, N. R. and Dodge, K. A. 367, 368, 369, 372–376
Crick, N. R. and Grotpeter, J. K. 163, 168, 170
Crick, N. R. and Ladd, G. W. 374
Crockenberg, S. C. and Leerkes, E. M. 318
Cross, W. E. 278
Cross, W. E. and Fhagen-Smith, P. 278, 290
Cross, W. E. et al. (1998) 278
Crouter, A. and Head, M. R. 476, 488, 489, 491
Crouter, A. et al. (2005) 476–477
Crowell, J. 86–91
Crowell, J. and Treboux, D. 86, 90
Crozier, W. R. and Hostettler, K. 317
Crozier, W. R. and Perkins, P. 317
Crystal, D. et al. (2008) 452
Cumberland, A. 218–232
Cummings, E. M. et al. (1986) 27
Cumsille, P. 476–493
Cumsille, P. et al. (2002) 478
Cumsille, P. et al. (2006) 489
Cusick, P. A. 184
Cutting, A. L. and Dunn, J. 135
Cutting, A. et al. (2000) 119

Daddis, C. 493–512
D'Agostino, R. B. 250
Damasio, A. R. 212–213
Damasio, A. R. 368, 370, 371, 372, 374, 375

Damasio, A. R. et al. (1991) 370
Damasio, H. et al. (1994) 370
Damon, W. 206, 234, 244, 407, 410, 412, 419
Damon, W. and Hart, D. 255
Darley, J. and Fazio, R. 424
Darling, N. 458, 459–475, 476–493
Darling, N. and Steinberg, L. 476, 479, 488, 493, 497, 510
Darling, N. et al. (2005) 477, 479, 481, 487, 491
Darling, N. et al. (2006) 477, 478, 488, 489
Darling, N. et al. (2007) 476, 477, 478, 479–480, 487–489
Darwin, C. 7, 65, 67, 80, 203
Davidson, P. et al. (1983) 236, 238
Davis, M. H. 219, 223–224, 227, 230
Davis, M. H. and Franzoi, S. 219
Davison, M. L. 170
de Bary, W. T. and Weiming, T. 556
de Waal, F. 7
de Wolff, M. S. and van IJzendoorn, M. H. (1997) 70
Deater-Deckard, K. et al. (1996) 43
Decety, J. and Jackson, P. L. 48
Decety, J. and Sommerville, J. A. 57
Deci, E. L. and Ryan, R. M. 256, 258, 268, 271
Deci, E. L. et al. (1999) 519
Deeks, J. J. et al. (2001) 133
Dekovic, M. and Janssens, J. M. A. M. 28
Denham, S. A. 58, 135, 367, 370, 372
Denham, S. A. and Holt, R. W. 167
Denham, S. A. et al. (1990) 372
Denham, S. A. et al. (2000) 31, 37, 43
Dennis, T. A. et al. (2002) 523
DerSimonian, R. and Laird, N. 133
Desai, S. et al. (1989) 111
Deyhle, D. 184
Diamond, A. 127
Dien, D. S. 555, 568
Dienstbier, R. A. 15, 16, 23
Digman, J. M. 15
Dishion, T. J. et al. (1996) 43, 334, 344
Dodge, K. A. 121, 367, 368
Dodge, K. A. and Somberg, D. 33, 374
Dodge, K. A. et al. (2006) 327
Donelan-McCall, N. and Dunn, J. 119
Dong, Q. et al. (1994) 355
Donovan. J. and Jessor, R. 463
Dornbush, S. M. 459–475

Dornbush, S. M. et al. (1985) 462, 498, 500
Dornbush, S. M. et al. (1987) 463, 473
Doyle, A. B. and Aboud, F. E. 292, 294, 422, 441, 443, 448
Doyle, A. B. et al. (1988) 422, 443, 444
Dunn, J. 117, 118–122
Dunn, J. and Cutting, H. 120
Dunn, J. and Hughes, C. 48
Dunn, J. et al. (1991) 130, 144
Dunn, J. et al. (2000) 119
Dusek, J. B. and Joseph, G. 423
Dutke, S. and Stroebber, J. 431
Dworkin, R. 209

Early, D. M. et al. (2002) 318, 328
Easterbrooks, A. and Goldberg, W. 80
Eberhardt, J. L. and Fiske, S. T. 423
Eccles, J. S. 256–277
Eccles, J. S. and Harold, R. D. 256, 257, 272
Eccles, J. S. and Midgely, C. 257, 271
Eccles, J. S., Midgely, C. et al. (1993) 257, 259, 261, 271, 272
Eccles, J. S. and Wigfield, A. 256, 258, 261, 268
Eccles, J. S. et al. (1983) 256–261, 268, 269, 271–274
Eccles, J. S. et al. (1984) 256, 257, 258, 261, 272
Eccles, J. S. et al. (1989) 257, 259, 272
Eccles, J. S. et al. (1990) 273
Eccles, J. S. et al. (1993) 256, 257, 258, 29, 261, 279
Eccles, J. S. et al. (1998) 256, 257
Eckert, P. 184, 185, 187
Eder, D. 167, 184, 194, 197
Eder, D. et al. (1995) 166, 167
Egan, S. K. and Perry, D. G. 155, 156, 157, 158, 162, 163
Eisenberg, J. F. 72
Eisenberg, N. 15, 28, 59, 218–232
Eisenberg, N. and Fabes, R. A. 27–28, 58, 206, 360, 367, 371–372, 375
    prosocial disposition 218, 219, 220, 229
Eisenberg, N. and Hand, M. 220, 221, 222, 225, 229
Eisenberg, N. and Lennon, R. 48, 49, 59
Eisenberg, N. and Miller, P. 48, 49, 57, 59, 412
Eisenberg, N. and Mussen, P. H. 26

Eisenberg, N. and Shell, R. 42, 221, 229
Eisenberg, N. et al. (1981) 220
Eisenberg, N. et al. (1983) 42, 221
Eisenberg, N. et al. (1984) 220, 229
Eisenberg, N. et al. (1985) 221
Eisenberg, N. et al. (1987) 27, 219, 221, 222, 223, 224
Eisenberg, N. et al. (1988) 17, 220, 230
Eisenberg, N. et al. (1989) 49
Eisenberg, N. et al. (1990) 220, 230
Eisenberg, N. et al. (1991) 48, 57, 58, 219, 220, 230
    prosocial disposition 221, 222, 223, 224
Eisenberg, N. et al. (1992) 28
Eisenberg, N. et al. (1994) 372, 375
Eisenberg, N. et al. (1995) 28, 44, 219, 221, 222, 223, 224
Eisenberg, N. et al. (1996) 28, 44, 219, 229, 372, 374
Eisenberg, N. et al. (1997) 367, 371, 372, 373, 374
Eisenberg, N. et al. (1999) 27, 203, 218–232
Eisenberg, N. et al. (2006) 48, 57, 59
Ekman, P. 369
Ekman, P. and Davidson, R. J. 367
Elder, G. H. 350, 358
Elder, G. H. and Conger, R. D. 350
Ellis, P. L. 27
Embretson, S. E. and Reise, S. P. 140
Emde, R. N. et al. (1992) 219
England, E. M. and Petro, K. D. 185, 187
Enright, R. D. and Lapsey, D. K. 233, 234, 236, 245, 538, 541
Enright, R. D. et al. (1984) 538, 541
Epstein, J. 472
Epstein, S. 86
Epstein, Y. M. et al. (1976) 444
Erikson, E. H. 4, 5, 8, 255, 278
Escalona, S. K. 15–16
Evans, M. A. 317
Eyberg, S. M. and Robinson, E. A. 30
Eysenck, H. J. 15, 16, 22, 24
Eysenck, H. J. and Eysenck, M. W. 15

Fabes, R. A. et al. (1990) 28
Fabricus, W. V. and Khalil, S. L. 131
Feather, N. T. 256
Feng, X. et al. (2001) 531
Feng, Y. L. 35
Ferguson, R. F. 424
Feshbach, N. D. 26, 48, 57, 58

Feshbach, N. and Feshbach, S. 27
Feshbach, N. D. and Roe, K. 48
Festinger, L. 140, 211
Fischer, C. S. et al. (1996) 423
Fisher, C. B. 400
Fisher, C. B. et al. (2000) 539
Fiske, A. P. 526
Flammer, A. et al. (1999) 257, 271
Flanagan, C. A. 350, 358
Flavell, J. H. 143, 422, 429
Flavell, J. H. and Miller, P. H. 129, 134
Flavell, J. H. et al. (1990) 129, 131, 133, 135, 234, 244
Flavell, J. H. et al. (1992) 234, 244
Fletcher, A. C. 458, 459–475
Fonagy, P. et al. (1997) 120
Fordham, K. and Stevenson-Hinde, J. 317
Foster, D. 442
Foster, M. D. 437
Fox, N. A. and Fein, G. 91
Fox, N. A. and Field, T. M. 28
Fox, N. A. et al. (1991) 80
Frederickson, N. L. and Furnham, A. E. 166, 182
Freeman, V. G. et al. (1999) 210
Freire, P. 437
French, D. C. 352
Freud, A. and Dann, S. 78
Freud, S. 4–5, 7, 8, 66, 68, 86
    morality 203, 205, 211
    parent–child attachment 65, 69, 70
Friedman, O. et al. (2001) 131–132
Fuligni, A. J. 278–292, 477, 495
Fuligni, A. J. and Witkow, M. 279
Fuligni, A. J. et al. (1999) 279, 520
Furman, W. 337
Furman, W. and Buhrmester, D. 337

Gaines, S. O. 437
Gaito, J. 250
Garcia Coll, C. et al. (1995) 497, 510
Garcia Coll, C. et al. (1996) 423, 430
Garton, A. F. and Pratt, C. 256
Gazelle, H. and Ladd, G. 318, 326, 332, 333, 346
Gazelle, H. and Rudolph, K. 332, 333, 343, 345
Gelman, S. A. 234, 244
Genesee, F. et al. (1978) 442
Gentry, M. 567
George, C. and Solomon, J. 73
George, C. et al. (1985) 87

Gerald, D. E. and Hussar, W. J. 274
Gergen, K. J. et al. (1972) 218
Gewirth, A. 209
Ghoshal, S. and Bartlett, C. 533
Gilligan, C. 517, 550
Gold, M. 464
Golden, P. 473
Goldsmith, H. H. et al. (1987) 15
Gonzales, N. A. et al. (1996) 495
Gonzales, N. A. et al. (2001) 279
Gonzales-Backen, M. 278–292
Gonzales-Ramos, G. et al. (1998) 520
Goodman, L. A. 304
Goodman, R. 321
Goodwin, R. D. et al. (2004) 326
Goossens, F. A. and van IJzendoorn, M. 80
Gopnik, A. and Meltzoff, A. N. 127, 422, 429
Gopnik, A. and Slaughter, V. 129, 131, 133
Gopnik, A. et al. (1994) 131
Gosling, S. D. et al. (2003) 320
Gottman, J. et al. (1997) 371–372
Graham, S. 497
Gralinski, H. H. and Kopp, C. B. 494
Gray, J. A. 16, 17, 22, 319
Gray-Little, B. and Hafdahl, A. R. 278, 280
Graziano, W. G. 219
Graziano, W. G. and Eisenberg, N. 219
Greco, L. A. and Morris, T. L. 328
Green, B. F. 138
Greenberg, M. and Marvin, R. S. 72, 81
Greenberger, E. and Bond, L. 473
Greenberger, E. et al. (1974) 464
Greenberger, E. et al. (1981) 464
Greenberger, E. et al. (1988) 95
Greenfield, P. M. et al. (2003) 279
Gregg, G. S. 544
Griffiths, J. A. 406, 441–451
Grinder, R. E. 209
Grossman, K. and Grossman, K. E. 78
Grossman, K. et al. (1981) 80
Grossman, K. et al. (1985) 15
Grotevant, H. D. 519
Grusec, J. E. 26, 28, 42
Grusec, J. E. and Goodnow, J. J. 493
Grusec, J. E. et al. (1996) 26, 27
Guilford, J. P. 140
Guthrie, D. 530
Guthrie, I. 218–232
Guttman, L. 136, 138

Hagendoorn, L. H. and Henke, R. 184
Haidt, J. 211–212
Haidt, J. et al. (1993) 212
Hall, V. C. et al. (1986) 424
Halverson, C. et al. (1994) 15
Hamalaimen, M. and Pulkkinen, L. 29
Hamre, B. K. and Pianta, R. C. 321, 326
Happé, F. G. E. 129, 144, 422, 429
Harkness, S. et al. (2000) 518
Harlow, H. F. 66, 72
Harlow, H. F. and Harlow, M. K. 72
Harlow, H. F. et al. (1963) 75
Harpur, T. J. and Hare, R. D. 23
Harris, J. R. 163
Harris, P. L. 57, 144
Harris, P. L. et al. (1986) 149
Harris, P. L. et al. (1989) 131, 148
Hart, C. A. et al. (2000) 318, 349, 361
Harter, S. 256–257, 259, 268–269, 271–272, 274, 411, 464
    ethnic identity 280, 287, 288
Harter, S. and Pike, R. 321
Hartshorne, H. and May, M. A. 209
Hartup, W. W. 155
Hartup, W. W. and Stevens, N. 162
Harwood, M. D. and Farrar, J. 48
Harwood, R. L. et al. (1995) 517, 519, 520
Harwood, R. L. et al. (1999) 517
Hasebe, Y. et al. (2004) 477, 488
Haselager, G. et al. (1998) 334, 344
Hastings, P. D. 14, 26–47
Hastings, P. D. and Rubin, K. 28, 31
Hastings, P. D. et al. (2006) 58
Hatchett, S. J. and Jackson, J. S. 509
Hawley, P. H. 170
Hazan, C. and Shaver, P. 114
Hazan, C. and Zeifman, D. 77
He, Y. 348–363
Hebei Economic Yearbook 558
Hedges, L. V. and Nowell, A. 273
Heider, F. 122
Heinicke, C. and Westheimer, I. 78
Heller, K. A. and Berndt, T. J. 70
Helwig, C. C. 209, 407, 408, 417, 516, 538, 540–542, 549–552, 554–573
    Chinese children 554–555, 556, 557, 560, 567, 568, 569
Helwig, C. C. and Kim, S. 554–555, 557, 558, 559–560, 567, 569, 570
Helwig, C. C. and Prencipe, A. 538, 542
Helwig, C. C. and Turiel, E. 538, 549, 550, 551, 569

Henderson, H. A. et al. (2004) 317, 318
Hershey, K. L. 15–26
Hightower, A. D. et al. (1986) 33, 354
Hill, J. P. and Lynch, M. E. 258, 272
Hinde, R. A. 7, 72, 76, 77 81, 333, 343
Hirschfield, L. 422
Ho, D. YF. 351, 352, 359
Hobson, J. A. et al. (2006) 48–49, 57
Hobson, J. A. et al. (2009) 49
Hobson, J. A. et al. (in press) 57
Hodges, E. V. E. 154, 155–165
Hodges, E. V. E. and Perry, D. G. 156
Hodges, E. V. E. et al. (1995) 155, 156
Hodges, E. V. E. et al. (1997) 155–156, 157, 158, 161–163
Hodges, E. V. E. et al. (1999) 162, 163, 334
Hofer, B. K. and Pintrich, P. R. 234, 245
Hoff-Ginsberg, E. and Tardif, T. 496, 497, 501, 508
Hoffman, M. L. 15, 26, 27, 206, 219, 220, 372, 374
    sympathy 48, 57, 59
Hofstede, G. H. 517, 519
Hogg, M. A. and Abrams, D. 442
Hogrefe, G. J. et al. (1986) 131, 135
Hogue, A. and Steinberg, L. 162, 334
Hollander, E. P. 181
Holmes, R. 422
Holmgren, R. A. et al. (1998) 49
Horn, S. S. 154, 184–199
Horn, S. S. et al. (1999) 184, 185, 187, 189, 197
Horn, S. S. et al. (2001) 185
Horowitz, E. L. and Horowitz, R. E. 442
Howes, C. 108
Howes, C. and Hamilton, C. E. 110
Howes, C. et al. (1988) 80
Hraba, J. and Grant, G. 442
Huang, M. 349, 351, 360
Hubbard, J. A. and Coie, J. D. 367
Hughes, C. and Dunn, J. 118, 120, 135, 233
Hughes, C. et al. (1998) 121, 135
Hughes, D. 517–537
Hume, D. 220
Huntingford, F. 72
Huston, A. 259
Hutchison, P. and Abrams, D. 295
Hyde, J. S. and Linn, M. C. 272, 273
Hyde, J. S. et al. (1990) 272
Hymel, S. et al. (1990) 332, 333

Hymel, S. et al. (1993) 332
Hyun, J. H. 431

Iannotti, R. J. 48
Instituto Nacional de la Juventud
    479, 480
Isen, A. et al. (1978) 372
Iyengar, S. S. and Lepper, M. R. 519
Izard, C. E. 367, 369

Jaccard, J. et al. (1990) 40
Jacobs, J. E. 255, 256–277
Jacobs, J. E. and Eccles, J. S. 258, 259,
    271, 272
Jacobs, J. E. et al. (1998) 258
Jaeger, E. and Weinraub, M. 92
Janssens, J. and Dekovic, M. 28
Jencks, C. and Phillips, M. 422
Jenkins, R. L. 560
Jessor, R. and Jessor, S. 479, 489
Jiangsu Statistical Yearbook 558
Johnson, D. and Johnson, R. 517
Jones, H. B. 518
Jőreskog, K. 356
Jorm, A. F. et al. (2000) 319, 327
Judd, C. M. and McClelland, G. H.
    432, 433
Judd, C. M. et al. (2001) 299
Jussim, L. et al. (1996) 424
Juvonen, J. et al. (2004) 343

Kagan, J. 317
Kagan, J. et al. (1978) 78
Kagitcibasi, C. 517, 520, 521, 523, 529
Kagitcibasi, C. and Ataca, B. 530
Kahneman, D. et al. (1982) 211
Kalish, C. W. 235, 247
Kalish, C. W. et al. (2000) 244
Kalman, R. K. 517–537
Kandel, D. 472
Kandel, E. R. and Kupferman, I. 370
Kant, I. l 5
Karen, R. 91
Karniol, R. 58
Katz, P. A. 292, 293
Katz, P. A. and Kofkin, J. A. 422
Katz, P. A. et al. (1975) 294
Keil, F. C. 127, 234, 244
Keller, H. 517, 518, 520, 531
Kendler, K. S. et al. (1997) 319
Kennedy, C. A. 165–183
Keppel, G. and Zedeck, S. 432
Kerr, M. and Stattin, H. 476, 509

Kerr, M. et al. (1999) 476, 479
Kestenbaum, R. et al. (1989) 220
Kiang, L. 255, 278–292
Killen, M. 406, 407–421
Killen, M. and Smetana, J. 213
Killen, M. and Stangor, C. 185, 189, 197,
    292, 407–421
Killen, M. and Turiel, E. 409, 419
Killen, M. et al. (2002) 184, 185, 195,
    209, 292, 518, 569
Killen, M. et al. (2006) 184, 185, 195,
    538, 552
Killen, M. et al. (2007) 209, 538,
    539, 542
King, A. and Bond, M. 349
King, P. and Kitchener, K. S. 233, 234
Kinney, D. 187
Kinoshita, Y. 555, 559, 567
Kirchler, E. et al. (1994) 184, 185, 186,
    194, 195
Kistner, J. et al. (1993) 181
Kitchener, R. F. 234, 245
Kleinman, A. 350, 361
Knight, G. P. and Hill, N. E. 498
Kobak, R. R. and Duemmler, S. 70
Kobak, R. et al. (2005) 78
Kobak, R. et al. (2007) 78
Kochanska, G. 15, 16–17, 23
    concern for others 27, 29, 31, 32, 41
Kochanska, G. et al. (1989) 28, 31
Kochanska, G. et al. (1994) 32
Kochankska, G. et al. (1996) 229
Kochanska, G. et al. (1997) 229, 328
Kochenderfer, B. J. and Ladd, G. W. 155,
    162, 163, 334
Koenigs, M. et al. (2007) 212
Koestner, R. et al. (1990) 220
Kohlberg, L. 203, 236, 252, 517, 541
    morality 204–205, 206–210, 212,
    214, 215
Kohn, M. L. 517
Kohnstamm, G. et al. (1989) 15
Komatsu, L. K. and Galotti, K. M. 236
Kovacs, M. 354–355, 358
Kowalski, K. 443, 448
Krebs, D. and Russell, C. 58
Krevans, J. and Gibbs, J. C. 28
Kuhn, D. and Weinstock, M. 234
Kuhn, D. et al. (1988) 233, 234
Kuhn, D. et al. (2000) 235, 245, 249
Kuklinski, M. and Weinstein, R. S. 424
Kurtines, W. M. et al. (1995) 554
Kurzban, R. and Leary, M. R. 306

Ladd, F. W. et al. (2000) 322
Ladd, G. W. and Profilet, S. M. 321
Ladd, G. W. and Troop-Gordon, W. 334
Lafreniere, P. J. and Capnano, F. 328
Lahey, B. B. et al. (1993) 28
Lalonde, C. E. and Chandler, M. J.
    130, 144
Lamb, M. 78
Lamb, M. and Sternberg, K. 92
Lamb, M. et al. (1985) 81
Lambert, W. E. and Klineberg, O. 293
Lamborn, S. et al. (1991) 319
Lamborn, S. D. et al. (1996) 496
Langley, M. 233–250
Lanza, S. 256–277
Larkin, R. W. 184
Larrieu, J. and Mussen, P. 220
Larson, R. W. 256, 257, 349
Larson, R. W. and Verma, S. 257, 258
Lau, S. 556, 570
Lau, S. and Yeung, P. W. 556
Lau, S. et al. (1990) 556
Laupa, M. and Turiel, E. 236, 249
Laursen, B. 332–348
Lazarus, R. S. 369
Lease, A. M. 154, 165–183
Lease, A. M. and Axelrod, J. L. 170
Lease, A. M. et al. (2001) 182
LeDoux, J. E. 368, 370, 374
Lemerise, E. A. 366, 367–379
Lemerise, E. A. and Dodge, K. A. 376
Lemerise, E. A. et al. (1998) 372
Lemerise, E. A. et al. (1999) 374
Lenin, S. et al. (2003) 442
Leslie, A. M. 144
Leve, L. D. et al. (2005) 318
Levenson, R. W. and Ruef, A. M. 27
Levin, H. 554
Levine, J. M. 293
Levy, S. R. and Dweck, D. S. 422
Levy, S. R. et al. (1998) 422
Lewis, M. 210
Lewis, M. et al. (1975) 73
Lewis, R. 233–250
Li, D. 348–363
Li, J. 568
Liben, L. S. and Signorella, M. L. 407
Lieb, R. et al. (2000) 318
Lieber, E. et al. (2000) 517
Lillard, A. 118
Lillard, A. S. and Flavell, J. H. 122
Lin, C. C. and Fu, V. R. 523
Linacre, J. M. 141

Linacre, J. M. and Wright, B. D. 141
Linn, M. C. and Hyde, J. S. 272
Little, R. J. A. 338
Liu, D. 117, 129–149
Liu, M. et al. (2005) 532
Livesley, W. J. and Bromley, D. B. 294
Loehlin, J. C. and Nichols, R. 219
Lohman, B. J. and Jarvis, P. A. 279
Loomis, C. P. 442
Lord, P. N. and Novick, M. R. 140
Lorenz, K. E. 7, 8, 66
Lorr, M. and McNair, D. M. 282
Losoyo, S. et al. (1997) 319
Lunney, G. H. 250
Lytton, H. 15, 17
Lytton, H. and Romney, D. M. 273

Maass, A. et al. (2000) 448
Maccoby, E. E. 258, 272, 359, 408
Maccoby, E. E. and Martin, J. 460, 471
Maccoby, E. E. and Masters, J. C. 17, 23
Mackerras, C. 555
Mackie, D. M. et al. (1996) 410
MacKinnon, D. P. and Dwyer, J. H. 227
MacKinnon, D. P. et al. (1995) 304
MacLeod, J. 187
MacQuiddy, S. L. et al. (1987) 27, 41
Macrae, C. et al. (1996) 407
Magai, C. and McFadden, S. 370, 374
Main, M. 70, 74, 87, 98
Main, M. and Goldwyn, R. 87
Main, M. and Solomon, J. 87, 98
Main, M. and Weston, D. 80
Main, M. et al. (1985) 70, 80, 86
Main, M. et al. (2005) 73
Mak, A. and Nesdale, D. 441
Malatesta, C. 369, 370
Malatesta, C. and Wilson, A. 370
Mann, L. and Greenbaum, C. W. 555, 567
Mann, L. et al. (1984) 555
Mansfield, A. F. and Clinchy, B. M. 233, 234, 235, 245
Markus, H. R. and Kitayama, S. 517, 519, 555
Marques, J. M. and Pàez, D. 293
Marques, J. M. et al. (1988) 293, 307
Marques, J. M. et al. (1998) 293, 295
Marques, J. M. et al. (2001) 293, 308
Marsh, H. W. 256, 257, 258, 259, 271, 272
Marsh, H. W. and Young, A. S. 258, 260, 272, 273, 274

Marsh, H. W. et al. (1984) 257, 271
Martin, C. L. 294, 299
Martinez, M. L. 476–493
Martinez, M. L. et al. (2006) 479, 480, 488
Marvin, R. S. et al. (1977) 78
Mash, E. and Barkley, R. 332
Maslow, A. H. 519
Mason, C. A. et al. (1996) 507
Masten, A. S. and Coatsworth, J. 351
Masten, A. S. et al. (1985) 170, 171, 336, 353
Masters, J. and Wellman, H. 86
Matthews, K. A. et al. (1981) 27, 219
McCandless, B. and Hoyt, J. 442
McCarthy, D. 30
McCartney, K. 108
McCartney, K. and Phillips, D. 94
McClelland, G. H. and Judd, C. M. 433
McCord, J. 461, 473
McGillicuddy-De Lisi, A. V. and Sigel, I. E. 517
McKown, C. 406, 421–440
McKown, C. and Weinstein, R. S. 406, 421–440, 539
McLellan, J. A. and Youniss, J. 184, 185, 195, 196
McLoyd, V. C. 108, 497, 510, 574
Mead, G. H. 6–7, 8
Mead, M. 81
Mealey, L. 26
Meece, J. L. et al. (1982) 256
Meece, J. L. et al. (1990) 256
Meins, E. 119
Melhuish, E. C. et al. (1991) 108
Meltzoff, A. M. 122
Menard, S. 259
Merrick, S. 86–91
Merton, R. K. 424
Mesquita, B. and Walker, R. 519
Metsäpelto, R. L. and Pulkkinen, L. 319, 327, 328
Meyer, B. et al. (2005) 319
Michell, L. 167, 181
Michell, L. and Amos, A. 167
Miller, C. T. and Kaiser, C. R. 437
Miller, C. T. and Major, B. 437
Miller, D. B. and MacIntosh, R. 423, 430
Miller, P. A. and Eisenberg, N. 27, 28, 48
Miller, P. J. et al. (2002) 519, 522
Miller, R. and Wright, D. W. 336
Miller, R. et al. (1967) 72
Mills, C. W. 350

Mischel, W. 86
Mitchell, P. 129
Miyake, K. et al. (1985) 15
Modood, T. and Ahmad, F. 552
Moessinger, P. 555, 559, 567
Moffitt, T. E. 476, 479, 489
Moore, B. et al. (1984) 372
Moore, C. 119
Moore, H. A. and Johnson, D. R. 424
Morgan, G. A. and Riccinti, H. N. 72
Morison, P. and Masten, A. 348, 351, 352
Moscowitz, D. and Schwarz, J. 473
Mossakowski, K. N. 278, 288, 289
Mott, F. L. 111
Mroczek, D. K. and Almeida, D. M. 280
Murphy, B. C. 218–232
Murphy, B. C. and Eisenberg, N. 376
Murray, H. A. 72
Murray-Close, D. 366, 379–395
Muthén, B. 340
Muthén, B. and Shedden, K. 338
Myrdal, G. 426

National Center for Education Statistics 273
Neff, K. D. 556, 569
Neff, K. D. and Helwig, C. C. 538, 550, 556, 568, 569
Nelson, D. A. et al. (2005) 317
Nelson, D. A. et al. (2006) 321
Nesdale, D. 292, 441–451
Nesdale, D. et al. (1997) 441
Nesdale, D. et al. (2003) 441, 442, 443, 444, 445, 448, 449
Nesdale, D. et al. (2004) 441, 442, 443
Nesdale, D. et al. (2005) 441, 442
Nesse, R. M. 27
Newcomb, A. F. et al. (1993) 165, 166, 167, 170
Newton, P. 118, 120
NICHD. Early Childcare Research Network 65, 91–114
NICHD. Study of Early Child Care 111
Nicholls, J. G. 257
Nicholls, J. G. and Miller, A. T. 257, 271
Nicholls, J. G. and Thorkildsen, T. A. 236
Niwa, E. Y. 517–537
Nottelmann, E. D. 259, 271
Nucci, L. P. 185–187, 189, 197, 207, 208, 252, 494, 495, 499, 506
  Chinese children 554, 568, 570
Nucci, L. P. and Lee, J. 236, 495
Nucci, L. P. and Nucci, M. S. 208

Nucci, L. P. and Smetana, J. G. 495
Nucci, L. P. and Turiel, E. 207, 208
Nucci, L. P. and Weber, E. 208
Nucci, L. P. et al. (1981) 559
Nucci, L. P. et al. (1991) 478, 479, 489
Nucci, L. P. et al. (1996) 477, 485, 487, 490, 554, 559, 569, 570
Nucci, L. P. et al. (2004) 186
Nunnally, J. and Bernstein, J. H. 140
Nussbaum, M. C. 206, 215

Oatley, K. and Jenkins, J. M. 367, 368, 370, 372, 374
O'Connor, T. and Hirsch, N. 118, 120
Ogbu, J. U. 517
Oh, W. 332–348
Ollendick, T. et al. (1990) 344
Olson, S. L. et al. (2003) 135
Olweus, D. 26, 155, 156
Onishi, K. H. and Baillargeon, R. 58
Osgood, D. W. 256–277
Osgood, D. W. et al. (1996) 269
Ostrov, J. M. 379–395
Otten, S. et al. (1996) 184
Owen, M. R. and Henderson, B. K. 108
Owen, M. T. and Cox, M. J. 92
Oyserman, D. et al. (2002) 517, 556

Parekh, B. 540
Parke, R. D. and Buriel, R. 476, 497, 509
Parke, R. D. and Walters, R. 209
Parker, E. H. and Hubbard, J. A. 376
Parker, J. and Asher, S. 334, 336, 337
Parker, J. G. and Gottman, J. M. 165, 374, 375
Parkhurst, S. T. and Hopmeyer, A. 165–166, 167, 168–169, 170, 179, 182
Parsons, J. E. et al. (1982) 261
Parsons, T. and Shils, E. A. 517
Passman, R. H. and Erck, T. W. 72
Passman, R. H. and Weisberg P. 72
Patterson, G. and Stouthamer-Loeber, M. 462
Patterson, G. R. et al. (1967) 155
Patterson, G. R. et al. (1989) 476, 489
Peevers, B. H. and Secord, P. E. 294, 422, 429
Penner, L. A. and Finkelstein, M. A. 218, 223
Penner, L. A. et al. (1995) 219, 222, 223
Pepler, D. J. 366, 395–402

Perkins, S. A. and Turiel, E. 210
Perner, J. 129, 135
Perner, J. and Wimmer, H. 422, 129, 429–430
Perner, J. et al. (1987) 135
Perner, J. et al. (1989) 149
Perren, S. and Alsaker, F. D. 318
Perry, D. G. et al. (1988) 155, 157, 163
Perry, D. G. et al. (1990) 155, 375
Perry, D. G. et al. (1992) 155, 162
Perry, W. G. 233, 234, 236
Pessar, P. R. 527
Peterson, C. C. and Siegal, M. 145
Pettit, G. S. and Laird, R. D. 494, 496, 508
Pettit, G. S. et al. (2001) 476, 493–497, 506, 507, 508
Phinney, J. S. 255, 278, 280
Phinney, J. S. and Chavira, V. 423, 430, 437
Phinney, J. S. and Cobb, N. J. 423, 430
Piaget, J. 5–6, 8–10, 68, 117, 120, 127
  morality 203, 205, 207, 209
  social information processing 367, 368, 371
Pianta, R. C. 318, 321
Piliavin, J. A. et al. (1981) 218
Pillow, B. H. 148, 234, 245, 422, 429
Pillow, B. H. and Henrichon, A. H. 422, 429
Pillow, B. H. and Weed, S. T. 422, 429
Pinel, E. 422
Plutchik, R. 369, 370
Porges, S. W. 31
Porges, S. W. and Byrne, E. A. 28
Poulin, E. and Boivin, M. 168
Powlishta, K. K. 299
Powlishta, K. K. et al. (1994) 292
Pratt, C. and Bryant, P. E. 148
Prencipe, A. and Helwig, C. 567
Prior, M. et al. (2000) 317
Programa de Naciones Unidas Para el Desarrollo 479
Protho, J. W. and Grigg, C. M. 208
Pugh, G. 370
Pye, L. W. 555, 568

Quay, H. C. 17, 22
Quay, H. C. et al. (1987) 15, 17, 22
Quintana, S. M. 294, 295, 422, 423, 430
Quintana, S. M. and Baessa, Y. 423, 430
Quintana, S. M. and Vera, E. M. 423, 430

Radke-Yarrow, M. and Zahn-Waxler, C. 59, 229
Radke-Yarrow, M. et al. (1983) 206, 229
Radloff, L. S. 95, 464
Raine, A. et al. (1997) 28, 43
Rapee, R. M. 319
Rapee, R. M. et al. (2005) 317, 328
Rasch, G. 140
Raudenbush, S. W. 424
Raudenbush, S. W. and Bryk, A. S. 482
Renninger, K. A. 271
Repacholi, B. M. and Gopnik, A. 134, 147
Rheingold, H. 71, 76
Rholes, W. S. and Ruble, D. N. 422, 429
Rickle, A. V. and Biasatti, L. I. 31
Rist, R. C. 424
Rizzo, T. A. 155
Roberts, R. et al. (1990) 473
Robertson, J. 66
Robertson, J. and Bowlby, J. 66
Robins, R. W. et al. (in press) 23
Robinson, C. C. et al. (2001) 321
Robinson, J. 26–47
Robinson, J. et al. (1994) 28
Rodgers, R. 462
Rodkin, P. C. et al. (2000) 165–166, 167, 168, 170, 182
Roggman, L. et al. (1994) 92, 109
Rokeach, M. 556
Rose, A. 345
Rose, A. et al. (2004) 344
Rose-Krasnor, L. 332–348
Rosenberg, M. 282, 464
Rosenthal, R. 133
Rosenthal, R. and Jacobson, L. 422
Rosenthal, R. and Rubin, D. E. 424
Ross, R. T. 170
Roth, D. and Leslie, A. 132
Rothbart, M. K. 14, 15–26
Rothbart, M. K. and Ahadi, S. A. 318
Rothbart, M. K. and Bates, J. E. 219, 229, 318, 371
Rothbart, M. K. and Derryberry, D. 15, 372
Rothbart, M. K. and Mauro, J. A. 24
Rothbart, M. K. and Posner, M. 17, 22
Rothbart, M. K. et al. (1994) 18, 219, 229
Rothbart, M. K. et al. (1995) 16
Rothbart, M. K. et al. (in preparation) 18
Rothbaum, F. and Trommsdorff, G. 517, 519, 528–529

Rothbaum, F. et al. (2000) 529
Rowley, S. et al. (1998) 280, 289
Rubin, K. H. 321, 332–348
Rubin, K. H. and Asendorpf, J. 332, 348, 349
Rubin, K. H. and Burgess, K. B. 318, 327
Rubin, K. H. and Coplan, R. J. 317, 332, 335
Rubin, K. H. and Mills, R. SL. 328
Rubin, K. H. et al. (1989) 332
Rubin, K. H. et al. (1993) 332
Rubin, K. H. et al. (1995) 332, 333, 335, 327, 348, 352
Rubin, K. H. et al. (1998) 167, 168, 182
Rubin, K. H. et al. (2002a) 317, 318, 348, 352, 359
Rubin, K. H. et al. (2002b) 318
Rubin, K. H. et al. (2003) 332, 333, 334, 343
Rubin, K. H. et al. (2006a) 318, 333, 343, 344, 346
Rubin, K. H. et al. (2006b) 334, 336, 337, 344
Ruble, D. N. and Dweck, S. 294
Ruble, D. N. and Martin, C. L. 259
Ruble, D. N. et al. (2004) 292, 295
Ruby, P. and Decety, J. 48
Ruck, M. D. et al. (1998) 538, 541, 551
Ruck, M. D. et al. (2002) 542
Ruffman, T. et al. (2002) 131
Ruggiero, M. 464
Rushton, J. P. 218
Rushton, J. P. et al. (1981) 219, 222, 223, 227
Rushton, J. P. et al. (1986) 27, 219
Rustemli, A. et al. (2000) 442
Rutland, A. 292–311
Rutland, A. et al. (2003) 499
Rutter, M. 78, 91, 157
Ryan, K. 209
Ryan, R. M. ad Deci, E. L. 519
Rydell, A. M. et al. (1997) 321
Rydell, A. M. et al. (2005) 318
Ryff, C. D. et al. (2003) 278, 289

Saarni, C. 367, 370, 374, 375, 376
Saarni, C. et al. (1998) 369, 370
Sabbagh, M. A. and Callanan, M. A. 233
Sabogal, F. et al. (1987) 520
Sachdev, I. B. and Bourhis, R.Y. 184
Saffran, J. R. et al. (1996) 125
Sagi, A. and Hoffman, M. L. 48

Sagi-Schwartz, A. and Aviezer, O. 80
Salmivalli, C. and Isaacs, J. 343, 345
Sampson, E. E. 519
Sampson, R. and Groves, W. 472
Sanders, M. G. 423, 430
Sani, F. and Bennett, M. 311
Sansone, C. and Harackiewicz, J. M. 258, 268
Sarason, I. G. 431
Sarat, A. 208
Schachter, S. 293
Schacter, S. and Latane, B. 26
Schaefer, E. S. 462, 493, 498
Schaffer, H. R. and Emerson, P. E. 77, 78
Schank, R. C. and Abelson, R. P. 122, 126
Scheier, M. E. et al. (1989) 24
Schiefele, U. 271
Schmader, T. et al. (2001) 437
Schmidt, L. A. and Tasker, S. L. 317
Schneider, B. 334
Schneider, A. et al. (1998) 332, 335
Schwartz, C. E. et al. (1999) 317
Schwartz, D. and Merten, D. 184, 185, 187
Schwartz, D. et al. (1993) 155
Schwartz, S. H. 223, 556
Schwarz, G. 338
Schweder, R. A. et al. (1987) 206
Schweder, R. A. et al. (1997) 206
Schwedinger, H. and Schwedinger, J. 184, 187
Scroggins, D. 538, 539
Searle, J. R. 122, 126
Sears, R. R. 17, 23
Sears, R. R. et al. (1957) 66
Seeman, T. E. 279
Seligman, M. E. P. and Csikszentmihalyi, M. 290
Sellers, R. M. et al. (1998) 280, 290
Sellers, R. M. et al. (2003) 278, 289
Selman, R. L. 294, 422, 423, 429
Sen, A. 556
Serbin, L. A. and Sprafkin, C. 294
Shams, M. 442
Sharon, T. and Wynn, K. 122
Shavelson, R. J. et al. (1976) 256
Shaw, L. A. 233–250
Shaw, S. M. et al. (1995) 258
Sheffield Morris, A. et al. (2007) 327
Shelton, J. N. et al. (2005) 278, 280
Shelton, J. N. et al. (in press) 278
Shepard, S. A. 218–232

Sherif, M. 539
Shih, M. et al. (1999) 424
Short, G. 407
Shweder, R. A. 556
Shweder, R. A. and Bourne, E. J. 555
Shweder, R. A. et al. (1987) 555, 556
Shweder, R. A. et al. (1998) 518
Siegal, M. and Beattie, K. 148
Sigelman, C. K. and Toebben, J. L. 233, 542
Signorella, N. 273
Silbereisen, R. K. 349, 350, 358, 360
Silbereisen, R. K. et al. (2002) 350, 361
Simon, H. A. 367, 370
Simons, R. L. et al. (2002) 423
Singer, P. 215
Sinha, D. and Tripathi, R. C. 523
Skinner, B. F. 5, 8, 211, 215
Skinner, E. A. et al. (1998) 257, 260, 271
Slooter, L. 537–553
Slosson, R. L. et al. (1991) 261
Smetana, J. G. 189, 236, 247, 253, 458, 493–512
    Chinese children 557, 570
    exclusion 407, 412, 417
    individualism and collectivism 519, 521
    minority rights 538, 542, 551
    morality 207, 209
    parental authority 476–478, 482, 485, 487–489, 491
    psychological control 494, 495, 496, 499
Smetana, J. G. and Asquith, P. 494–496, 499, 507, 510
Smetana, J. G. and Bitz, B. 494, 495
Smetana, J. G. and Braeges, J. L. 236, 247
Smetana, J. G. and Chuang, S. 491
Smetana, J. G. and Daddis, 458, 476, 477, 488, 493–512
Smetana, J. G. and Gaines, C. 500
Smetana, J. G. and Turiel, E. 185, 186
Smetana, J. G. et al. (1991) 485, 487, 490
Smetana, J. G. et al. (1993) 236, 247
Smetana, J. G. et al. (2000) 494
Smetana, J. G. et al. (2003) 488
Smetana, J. G. et al. (2005) 477, 487
Smetana, J. G. et al. (2006) 476, 478, 488–489, 490
Smith, A. 48
Smith, P. and Schwartz, S. 519, 523
Smith, P. B. and Bond, M. H. 308
Smith, R. 528

Snyder, E. E. and Spreitzer, E. 257, 271
Soher, E. and Wilson, D. S. 27
Solomon, J. and George, C. 73, 81
Sommers, C. H. 274
Sommerville, J. A. 117, 122–128
Sorce, J. and Emde, R. 71, 72, 74
Southgate, V. et al. (2007) 58
Spencer, M. and Dornbusch, S. M. 497, 510, 520
Spencer, M. and Dupree, D. 508, 510
Spencer, S. J. et al. (1999) 424, 435
Spieker, S. J. and Booth, C. L. 108, 109
Spinrad, T. L. et al. (2004) 318
Sroufe, L. A. 92, 111
Sroufe, L. A. and Waters, E. 68, 76
Sroufe, L. A. et al. (1984) 375
Stangor, C. 407–421
Stangor, C. and Ruble, D. N. 407
Stangor, C. and Schaller, M. 422
Stattin, H. and Kerr, M. 509
Staub, E. 218, 220
Steele, C. M. 423, 435, 437
Steele, C. M. and Aronson, J. 422, 423, 424, 425, 435
Steele, H. et al. (1996) 80
Stein, A. H. 273
Steinberg, L. 459–475, 506, 507, 509
Steinberg, L. and Fletcher, A. C. 510
Steinberg, L. and Silk, J. S. 479
Steinberg, L. and Silverberg, S. 477
Steinberg, L. et al. (1989) 462
Steinberg, L. et al. (1991) 463, 465, 474, 493, 498
Steinberg, L. et al. (1992) 463
Steinberg, L. et al. (1994) 463, 473
Stevenson, H. W. et al. (1990) 519
Stevenson-Hinde, J. and Glover, A. 318
Stevenson-Hinde, J. and Shouldice, A. 349
Stewart, R. and Marvin, R. S. 78
Stewart, S. L. and Rubin, K. 344
Stipek, D. J. 271
Stipek, D. J. and Daniels, D. H. 423
Stipek, D. J. and McIver, D. 257, 271
Stoddart, T. and Turiel, E. 407, 409, 418
Stone, M. and Brown, B. B. 185, 187
Strayer, F. F. and Strayer, J. 7
Suarez-Orozco, C. et al. (2002) 528
Sullivan, H. S. 156, 162, 163, 333
Sullivan, K. and Winner, E. 132, 135
Super, C. M. and Harkness, S. 517
Surian, L. and Leslie, A. M. 132
Swim, J. K. and Stangor, C. 423, 550

Tabachnick, B. G. and Fidell, L. S. 545
Tajfel, H. 278, 288, 293
Tajfel, H. and Forgas, J. P. 278
Tajfel, H. and Turner, J. C. 194, 255, 293, 442, 539, 550
Tajfel, H. et al. (1971) 410
Takano, Y. and Osaka, E. 556
Tamis-LeMonda, C. S. 516, 517–537
Tamis-LeMonda, C. S. et al. (1992) 532
Tamis-LeMonda, C. S. et al. (2002) 524
Tan, D. 554–573
Tatum, B. D. 423, 430
Taylor, M. C. 424
Te Grotenhuis, M. and Scheepers, P. 538
Tellegen, A. 15, 22
Ter Wal, J. 539
Terry, R. 182
Terry, R. and Coie, J. D. 166
Teti, D. and Ablard, K. 78
Thalhammer, K. et al. (1994) 541
Theimer, C. E. et al. (2001) 197, 407, 409, 418
Thomas, A. and Chess, S. 14, 16, 317, 318, 476
Thompson, R. A. 48, 371
Thompson, R. A. and Meyer, S. 70
Thorkildsen, T. A. 206
Thorkildsen, T. A. et al. (2002) 187
Tisak, M. 189, 249, 494, 506, 510
    exclusion 407, 408, 412, 417
Tomasello, M. 48–61
Tomasello, M. and Barton, M. 122
Trabasso, T. et al. (1992) 122
Treboux, D. 86–91
Tremblay, R. E. et al. (1992) 27, 29
Triandis, H. C. 308, 517, 519–521, 526, 555, 567
Triandis, H. C. et al. (1990) 517
Trivers, R. L. 74, 79, 81
Tsai, J. L. et al. (2001) 278
Turiel, E. 203, 204–218, 234, 252, 368, 407, 477
    China 554, 556, 568
    diversity of beliefs 235, 236, 244, 247
    exclusion 407, 408, 418
    group status and bias 184–187, 189, 196–197
    minority rights 538, 540, 542, 551
    psychological control 494, 506, 510
Turiel, E. and Davidson, P. 235
Turiel, E. and Perkins, S. A. 210
Turiel, E. and Wainryb, C. 538, 550, 569
Turiel, E. et al. (1987) 407

Turiel, E. et al. (1991) 556
Turner, J. C. et al. (1987) 184

Umaña-Taylor, A. J. 278
Umaña-Taylor, A. J. et al. (2002) 278
Underwood, B. and Moore, B. 220
Underwood, M. K. 376
Usher, B. 26–47
Utsey, S. O. et al. (2000) 437
Utsey, S. O. et al. (2002) 278

Vaish, A. 14, 48–61
Valk, A. and Karu, K. 442, 444, 445
Van Ameringen, M. et al. (1998) 317
Van Avermaet, E. and McClintock, L. G. 410
Van den Boom, D. 15
Van der Mark, I. L. et al. (2002) 58, 59
Van IJzendoorn, M. and De Wolff, M. S. 78, 80
Van IJzendoorn, M. and Kroonenberg, P. M. 108
Vandell, D. L. 72, 95
Vandiver, B. J. et al. (2002) 289
Vaughan, G. M. 442, 444
Vaughn, B. et al. (1979) 86, 90
Vaughn, B. et al. (2006) 70
Verkuyten, M. 516, 537–553
Verkuyten, M. and Slooter, L. 543
Verkuyten, M. and Thijs, J. 539, 552
Verkuyten, M. and Zaremba, K. 539
Vitaro, F. 154, 155–165
Vitaro, F. et al. (1991) 158
Vogt, W. P. 541
Vorauer, J. D. and Kumhyr, S. M. 422
Vorauer, J. D. et al. (1998) 422
Vorauer, J. D. et al. (2000) 422
Vygotsky, L. S. 6, 8, 519

Wachs, T. D. and Gandour, M. J. 15
Wade, N. 215
Wainryb, C. 233–251, 540, 541, 549, 551, 556
Wainryb, C. and Ford, S. 247
Wainryb, C. and Turiel, E. 186, 187, 196, 556, 569
Wainryb, C. et al. (1998) 236, 238, 247, 540, 541, 550, 551
Wainryb, C. et al. (2001) 233, 235, 236, 238, 247, 250
Walder, A. 530
Walters, R. H. 5
Walton, M. D. 233

Wang, J. et al. (2001) 569
Wang, S. and Tamis-LeMonda, C. S.
   524, 525
Wankel, L. M. and Berger, B. G. 257, 271
Waters, E. 65, 86–91
Waters, E. et al. (1991) 90
Watson, J. B. 5, 211
Way, N. 517–537
Way, N. et al. (2005) 522, 530
Way, N. et al. (2007) 522, 530
Weber, M. 166, 518
Wehlage, G. et al. (1989) 464
Weinberger, D. A. 222–223, 227
Weinberger, D. A. et al. (1990) 461
Weinberger, S. L. and Goldberg, K. P. 174
Weiner, B. 256
Weinraub, M. et al. (1977) 78
Weinstein, R. S. 421–440
Weinstein, R. S. and McKown, C. 424
Weinstein, R. S. et al. (1987) 423, 424
Weinstock, L. M. and Whisman, M. A. 319
Weisner, T. 521
Weiss, R. S. 76
Wellman, H. M. 117, 129–149
Wellman, H. M. and Bartsch, K. 131,
   132, 147 148
Wellman, H. M. and Hickling, A. K. 129
Wellman, H. M. and Woolley, J. D. 129,
   131, 132, 134, 147
Wellman, H. M. et al. (1996) 131, 147
Wellman, H. M. et al. (2000) 48, 58
Wellman, H. M. et al. (2001) 130, 134,
   137, 148
Wellman, H. M. et al. (2004) 144

Wentzel, K. and Erdley, C. 409, 419
Werner, E. E. and Smith, R. S. 110
Werner, H. 205, 207
Wheeler, C. S. and Petty, R. E. 424,
   425, 430
Whiting, B. H. and Whiting, J. W. M. 516
Whiting, J. and Whiting, B. 523
Wigfield, A. 256–277
Wigfield, A. and Eccles, J. S. 269, 272, 274
Wigfield, A. et al. (1991) 256, 257,
   259, 272
Wigfield, A. et al. (1997) 257, 258, 259,
   260 271, 272
Wikan, U. 210
Williams, J. E. et al. (1975) 442, 443, 445
Wilson, E. O. 212, 219
Wilson, M. 140
Wilson, R. W. and Pusey, A. W. 526
Winer, B. J. 190, 413
Winer, B. et al. (1991) 190, 565
Witenberg, R. T. 541, 550
Witken, H. A. and Berry, J. W. 517
Witkow, M. 278–292
Wojslawowicz Bowker, J. C. et al.
   (2006) 336, 337
Wolfe, C. T. and Spencer, S. J. 424
Wong, C. A. et al. (2003) 278
Wood, J. J. et al. (2003) 319
Woodward, A. L. 117, 122–128
Woolley, J. and Wellman, H. M. 135
Worden, R. L. et al. (1988) 555
Wright, B. D. and Masters, G. N.
   140, 141
Wright, B. D. and Stone, M. H. 140

Wu, D. YH. 555, 560, 570
Wynn, K. 122
Wynne, E. A. 209

Xu, X. and Peng, L. 350, 351

Yang, K. S. 349, 359
Yau, J. and Smetana, J. G. 477, 487, 554,
   556–557, 569, 570
Yee, M. D. and Brown, R. J. 292,
   299, 410
Yip, T. 278–292
Yip, T. and Cross, W. E. 278, 290
Yip, T. and Fuligni, A. J. 280, 283
Yoshikawa, H. 517–537
Young, S. K. et al. (1999) 49, 57, 58, 59
Youniss, J. et al. (1994) 184, 185
Yu, A. and Yang, K. 526
Yu, R. 350, 351, 360

Zahn-Waxler, C. 17, 26–47
Zahn-Waxler, C. et al. (1979) 17, 28
Zahn-Waxler, C. et al. (1992) 27, 33, 36,
   49, 52, 53, 57–59, 219, 229
Zahn-Waxler, C. et al. (1995) 27, 28, 30,
   33, 34, 39, 41, 43, 409
Zahn-Waxler, C. et al. (2001) 27, 33
Zarbatany, L. et al. (1996) 407, 409, 419
Zaslow, M. S. and Hayes, C. D. 93, 111
Zdaniuk, B. and Levine, J. M. 306
Zelazo, P. D. et al. (1999) 118
Zeller, M. et al. (2003) 336
Zhang, W. W. 349, 350
Zolberg, A. R. and Long, L. W. 538, 552

SUBJECT INDEX

absolutism 234, 235
abuse 68, 70, 87
academic achievement 154, 155, 255, 279, 366, 539
    authoritative parenting 460, 463–470, 472–473
    Chinese children 348, 350–353, 354, 355–359, 560
    individualism and collectivism 526, 531
    popularity 167, 168, 171, 173–174
    self-competence 257–270, 271–274
    shyness 317, 320–321, 323, 326–327
    stereotypes 406, 423–426, 435, 437
Academic Skills Checklist 323
Acceptance–Involvement 462–463
action interpretation 122–128
active inhibitory control 17
activity level 18, 19, 21–22
admiration 171, 178, 179
Adolescent Self-Perception Profile 464
adult attachment assessment classification 87, 88–91
adult authority-based decisions 559–570
affect 367–368, 370, 371, 374–375
affectional bonds 75
affective responses 14, 63
affiliative behavioral systems 72, 81
age-related differences in group status 196–197
agreeableness 23, 219, 319–320, 322–323, 326–327

aggression 5, 7, 62, 154, 366, 496
    Chinese children 348, 351, 353, 355–359
    concern for others 26–29, 42–44
    observation 395–401
    popularity 166, 167–168, 171, 173, 175, 179–182
    reactive 171, 173
    relational 163, 171, 173, 366, 379–392
    suppression and prosocial disposition 223, 225, 227, 229
    sympathy 48, 56
    temperament 15–23
    victimization 155–156, 161–163
    withdrawal 333, 337
Akaike Information Criterion (AIC) 338–339, 342
alphabet task 426, 430, 432–437
altruism 218–222, 319, 344
amplification 460, 465, 468, 473
anger 14, 31, 33, 42–43, 98
    parent–child attachment 65, 66, 69–70
    temperament 18, 19–24
antisocial behavior 48, 121, 180, 366, 494
    authoritative parenting 459, 464, 469, 471
    concern for others 26, 27, 28, 44
antisocial personality 23, 41
anxiety 121, 154, 155–156, 205, 363, 493
    authoritative parenting 464, 472

Chinese children 348–349, 351–353, 359
    ethnic identity 280, 282–284, 285–287, 288–289
    parent–child attachment 65, 69, 74
    popularity 171, 173
    shyness 316, 317–321, 323, 326–329
    social information processing 374–375
    stereotypes 425, 426, 430–431, 435
    temperament 16, 17
    withdrawal 332, 333, 334, 337
approach 14, 16–19, 22, 76, 349
    avoidance 316, 317
argumentativeness 155, 156
assertiveness 167
Assessment of School Behavior 32–33
athleticism 167, 168, 171, 173–174, 180
attachment 5, 7, 15, 66–85, 333, 367
    assessment classification 94, 98–104, 108
    behavior 67, 68–69, 70–77, 80, 86
    bond 75–77, 80, 81
    exercises 115
    five criteria 76, 96, 99–100, 103–104, 110, 114
    hierarchies 76, 78–79
    security 65, 86–91, 220
    security and infant childcare 91–114
    theory 66–70, 517
    theory of mind 117, 119–120
attentional focusing 18, 19

attentional self-regulation 23, 24
Attitude Toward Maternal Employment
    Questionnaire 95–96
Australia 406, 441–450
authoritarianism 458, 488, 496–497, 513
    concern for others 28–29, 31,
        40–41, 43
authoritative parenting 458, 459–474,
    488, 513
    concern for others 28–29, 31
    shyness 318–319, 321, 322–323,
        326–327
autism 48, 57, 149
    theory of mind 117, 120, 129,
        144–145, 149
autonomy 6, 7, 9, 458
    Chinese children 516, 554, 555–571
    Individualism and
        collectivism 517–533
    parental authority 476, 477, 487, 491
    psychological control 494–495, 507
avoidance 33

Bayesian Information Criterion
    (BIC) 338–339
behavior problems 5, 62, 321, 358
    authoritative parenting 460, 463–467,
        469–471, 472–473
    concern for others 26–47
    conduct disorders 15, 17, 121,
        154, 374
    parental authority 476, 479–480,
        481–482, 485–487, 489–490
    victimization 156, 157, 159, 161–163
    see also antisocial behavior
behavioral activation system (BAS) 319,
    320, 322–323, 328
behavioral control 493–497, 498,
    500–501, 506
Behavioral Inhibition System (BIS) 17,
    319–320, 322–323, 326–327
behaviorism 5, 8, 205, 210–211, 212
belief–emotion 117, 136–138,
    142, 148
beliefs 5, 233–250, 255, 458
    China 358–359, 560, 569
    coefficients 265
    diversity 131–132, 136–139, 141–142,
        144, 147, 233–250
    exclusion 407–409, 418
    growth curves 264
    individualism and collectivism 51,
        530–531

mind-reading 117, 118–119
minority rights 540–545, 548,
    550–551
parental authority 476–491
parenting 493–510
scaling of tasks 129–144, 147–149
self-competence 256–260, 261,
    262–270, 271–274
stereotypes 422–423, 427, 429, 436
Berkeley Adult Attachment
    Interview 86, 87–89
best friends 194
    victimization 156, 157–163
    withdrawal 334, 335–338, 341–346
bias 156, 406, 410, 450, 452–453,
    490–491
    group dynamics 292–295, 299–301,
        303–304, 306–308
biological bases of attachment 67–70
black sheep effect 293, 296, 302, 307
bonding to teachers 463–468
brain damage 368, 370, 371
brightness 173–174, 175, 177, 179–180
Bruinicks–Osertsky Test of Motor
    Proficiency 261–262
Bryant Empathy Scale 32, 35, 37
bullying 3, 309, 366, 395–401, 403
    popularity 168, 171, 173–175, 177,
        179–180
    shyness 321
    social information processing 374
    victimization 155, 156, 157
    withdrawal 343

caregiving behavior 90, 91–114, 115, 203
    attachment 67, 71, 73–5, 77, 79–80, 81
Center for Epidemiologic Studies
    Depression Scale (CES-D) 95, 96,
    464
cheerleaders 184–185, 188–189,
    192–193, 199
Child Behavior Checklist (CBCL) 30,
    32, 33
Child Behavior Scale (CBS) 321, 323
Child Rearing Practices Report
    (CRPR) 31
Child Social Preference Scale
    (CSPS) 320, 323
childcare 14, 65, 91–114
    variables 95–96, 97–98, 99–100,
        103–104, 110, 114
Childhood Depression Inventory
    (CDI) 354–355

Child-rearing practices see parenting
    styles
Children's Behavioral Questionnaire
    (CBQ) 18–19
    victimization 157, 158, 163
Children's Report of Parent's Behavior
    Inventory (CRPBI) 498
Chile 458, 478, 479–491
China and Chinese children 18, 255,
    348–361, 516, 554–571
    ethnic identity 278–290
    social functioning 348–361
choices 442–444, 539, 554, 556–557
    exclusion 410–412, 415–416, 418
    individualism and collectivism
        518–520, 521–522, 527–528
cliques 154, 167
    dirties 188
    druggies 184, 185, 188
    gothics 184–186, 188–189
    jocks 184–185, 186, 188
    preppies 184, 185, 188, 189
    punkers 184, 185
cognition and cognitive ability 4, 5, 166
    attachment 67, 70
    social information processing
        367–368, 370, 373–375
    stereotypes 422, 425, 430, 431, 433,
        435
    sympathy 57–59, 60
    theory of mind 118–119, 120, 121,
        129, 130
Cognitive Development Society 130
cognitive developmental theories 5–6, 8
    group dynamics 293, 294, 307, 308
collectivism 516, 517–534
    China 555–556, 560–561, 565,
        568–570
comforting 49, 203, 222
companionship 156, 157–158, 162
concern for others 14, 26–47, 62–63,
    184–199
    development of morality 206–207
    popularity 171, 173
    prosocial disposition 218–220,
        223–226
    sympathy 49, 52–59
conduct disorders 15, 17, 121, 154, 374
    see also behavior problems
confidence see self-confidence
conflict resolution 157–158, 162,
    252–253, 366
Confucianism 520, 521, 528, 555–556

confusion 493
connection to family 518, 519, 520
conscience 15–17, 23, 27, 32, 205
conscientiousness 23
consensus decision-making 554–557, 559–568
control systems approach 68–69, 86
conventions 207, 213, 236, 477, 488
  exclusion 407–409, 412–418
  group status and bias 185–186, 187, 193–194
  psychological control 494–496, 499–500, 506–507, 509–510
coolness 165, 167–168, 171, 173–174, 181
countermanding 460, 465, 473
criminality 29
crowds 154
crying 67, 68, 74–75, 76, 77
culture 3–4, 6, 8–9, 154, 406, 516, 574
  attachment 73–75, 78
  Chinese children 348–353, 358–361
  communication theories 6–7, 8
  development of morality 205–206, 209–215
  ethnic attitudes 441, 450
  ethnic identity 279, 290
  exercises 115, 150, 312, 364, 574–575
  group dynamics 308
  group status and bias 184, 186–187, 195–196
  individualism and collectivism 517–534
  mind-reading 118, 121
  minority rights 537–538, 539, 540
  parental authority 479, 480, 487, 490
  psychological control 496, 510
  self-competence and gender 273
  shyness 316
  social development in China 554–560, 567–569
  sympathy 59
cyber-bullying 403

daily diary 279, 280–289
Davis's Interpersonal Reactivity Index 223, 227
day care 78
deception 117, 118, 120, 209–210
  lying and cheating 209, 233
defiance 167, 168, 171, 173

delinquency 154, 366, 458, 489
  authoritative parenting 459, 461, 464–467, 469, 471–472
demonstrations 538–540, 543, 546–547
depression 154, 366, 464, 493
  Chinese children 348–351, 353, 354–358, 361
  shyness 316, 317, 319
  victimization 155, 156
  withdrawal 332, 333
derisiveness 33
descriptive statistics 100–101
desires 117, 118–119, 129–144, 147, 149
  diversity 117, 132, 136–139, 141–142, 144, 147
determinism 65, 205, 214–215
developmentalism 459
differential evaluation 294–296, 301–308
differential inclusion 294–296, 301–308
differentiation 207, 208, 210
disagreements 233, 237–241, 242–243, 244, 248–249
discomfort 19, 23, 24, 28
discrimination 278–279, 289, 406, 419–420, 451–452, 539
  stereotypes 423, 427, 430, 436
dishonesty 156, 157
disobedience 27
dispositional optimism 24
disregard for others 27, 29, 33–37, 40–41, 44
disruptive behavior 155
  Chinese children 348, 351, 353, 356–357, 359
  popularity 166–167, 168, 171, 173–175, 177, 180
  withdrawal 333, 337
distress 48, 62, 114
  attachment behavior 66, 67, 69, 75
  attachment bond 76, 77
  concern for others 26, 28–29, 30–34, 41–44
  insecure attachment 94, 96–97, 98, 99
  internalized 463–464, 466–469, 471–473
  multiple attachments 78
  prosocial disposition 219–220, 223–224, 225–230
  sympathy 48, 52–53, 55–57, 59
  temperament 16–17, 23
dominance hierarchy 7

donating 219, 221, 222, 225–226
dual risk effects 104, 105–107, 110, 111, 112
duties 206

effort situations 50–53, 59
effort withdrawal 426, 431, 434–436
effortful control 15–24
ego 4
Electra conflict 4
embarrassment 316
embedded-action condition 123–126, 128
emotional contagion 48, 49, 57, 58
emotional prioritizing 370
emotionality 15, 371–372, 376
emotions 3, 4, 8, 14, 203, 352, 366
  attachment 67, 69–70, 74
  development of morality 205–208, 210–214
  prosocial disposition 219, 220, 229
  shyness 319–323, 327
  social information processing 367–376
  sympathy 48–61
  temperament 16, 17, 20–21
  theory of mind tasks 117, 118–122, 129, 134–143, 148–149
empathy 14, 62–63, 205, 374–375, 406
  concern for others 26, 27, 28–29, 32–37, 40–43
  sympathy 48, 49, 57, 59
  temperament 15, 17, 19–24
entropy 338–339
environment 62, 90, 219–220
  attachment 69–72, 74
  authoritative parenting 459, 460
  concern for others 27, 42
  development of morality 205, 207, 211
  temperament 14, 16, 62
epistemology 234–235, 244–245, 248–248
  development of morality 204–206, 210, 212
equal access 407, 412, 417–419
equal qualifications 408–409, 411, 413, 415–418, 420
equal treatment 407, 409, 412, 417, 418
ethnic centrality 280, 283–290
ethnic perspective-taking theory 423
ethnic regard 280, 283–290

ethnicity and race 8, 237, 452–453,
    516, 574
  authoritative parenting 460, 462, 465,
    472, 474
  Chinese children 554–571
  development of morality 209
  exclusion 406, 407–420
  group dynamics 294, 308, 309, 311, 312
  group status and bias 185, 187–188
  identity 255, 278–290
  individualism and
    collectivism 517–534
  in-group and out-group
    attitudes 441–450
  insecure attachment 94–95
  minority rights 537–540, 543,
    550, 552
  parental authority 477, 478, 479
  popularity 169, 181
  prosocial dispositions 230
  psychological control 495, 497–500,
    509–510
  reduction of prejudice 451–452
  stereotypes 422–423, 424–428, 430,
    435–437
  theory of mind 137
ethology 7, 8, 68, 74, 80, 86
evolution 66, 67, 69, 74, 80–81
exclusion and rejection 4, 366, 406,
    407–420
  Chinese children 349–351, 359–360
  group dynamics 292
  group identity 255
  group status and bias 184–185, 187,
    195, 196–197
  minority rights 538, 539–541
  morality 203, 209
  popularity 168, 173–175, 177,
    179–180, 182
  shyness 318, 320–321, 323, 326
  withdrawal 332, 333–334, 335–337,
    340–346
executive function expression
    accounts 144
exploratory behavior 67, 71, 74–76, 94
expressive equipment 173–175, 177,
    179–180
Extended Class Play (ECP) 336–337
externalizing problems 154, 348,
    327, 366
  concern for others 26–27, 29, 30,
    36–39, 41–44
  psychological control 493–494, 496

victimization 155–162, 163
  withdrawal 334, 346
extraversion 18, 319, 322, 323, 328
extraversion/positive emotionality 15
exuberance 14
Eyberg Child Behavior Inventory
    (ECBI) 30

fact beliefs 235, 237–249
fairness 6, 236, 240, 406, 568
  exclusion 407, 412, 417–419
  minority rights 538–539
  morality 203, 206–210, 212–215
false beliefs 129–145, 148, 150, 234,
    246–247
  autism 144–145
  contents 117, 137–142, 148
  explicit 117, 131–132, 137–138,
    142–143, 148
father attachment 78–82
fear 14, 65, 205, 333, 349
  attachment 67, 71–72, 74
  shyness 316, 317–318
  temperament 16–24
  victimization 157
feeding 66, 67–68, 70, 73, 74
female circumcision 541, 544–545,
    548–549, 550–551
flag-burning 538, 550
forced choice 443
freedom of speech 537–552
fretful parenting 320, 322–325,
    326–327, 328
friends 154, 155–165, 233, 436, 452–453
  authoritative parenting 459–474
  China 353, 354, 554
  ethnic attitudes 442, 444
  ethnic identity 282
  individualism and collectivism 522,
    525, 529–534
  parental authority 513
  popularity 165–182
  prosocial disposition 223–227, 229
  relational aggression 379–392
  social information processing
    374, 375
  withdrawal 316, 333–334, 335–38,
    340–346
Friendship Qualities Scale 157
Friendship Quality Questionnaire-
    Revised (FQQ) 337
frustration 14, 17–23
functionalist theories 369–370, 371, 374

gender 4–5, 8, 24, 255, 452–453
  action interpretation 123, 126
  authoritative parenting 459–460, 462,
    465–473
  childcare and attachment 93, 95,
    101–104, 106–111
  Chinese children 352, 354–355,
    358–359, 559, 566
  concern for others 27, 29–30, 34–36,
    40–42
  development of morality
    209, 215
  diversity of beliefs 238, 239
  ethnic attitudes 442, 445, 446
  ethnic identity 280–288, 290
  exclusion 406, 407–420
  group dynamics 295, 299, 308, 309,
    311, 312
  group status and bias 185, 189–192,
    194, 196–197
  minority rights 538, 541–542,
    544–545, 547–551
  parental authority 480, 482, 486
  popularity 167–172, 174–181
  prosocial behavior 225, 409, 412
  psychological control 494, 497,
    501–506, 508
  relational aggression 379–392
  self-competence 256–274
  shyness 322, 364
  stereotypes 422, 424–426,
    430, 436
  sympathy 49, 54, 55–56, 59
  theory of mind tasks 138
  victimization 163, 164
  withdrawal 335–336, 340, 341
General Growth Mixture Modeling
    (GGMM) 335–338, 341, 343
General Linear Modelling (GLM)
    545–547, 549
genetics 27, 43, 63
  attachment 67, 79, 80
  development of morality
    211, 215
  prosocial disposition 219–220, 229
gestures 18, 20, 22, 23
Global Self-Esteem 464
Goodness-of-fit 14, 16, 317, 318
gossip 168
grasp latency 20, 22, 23–24
grasping 122–128
Group Activity Knowledge
    assessment 413

group bias 184–199, 200
group dynamics 292–309, 311, 312
group functioning 407–409, 412, 416,
    418–419
group identification 304–305,
    307–308, 312
group identity 154, 184–199, 255,
    292–311, 442
  ethnicity 278–290
  exclusion 407–409, 412, 416–417
  minority rights 539
group status 184–199, 200
groups 3–4, 9, 184–199, 200
  ethnic attitudes 441–450
  exclusion 407–420
guanxi 530
guilt 5, 205, 212
  psychological control 493, 507
  temperament 15–17, 19–24
Guttman analysis 204
  Five-item scale 138–140,
    141–143, 145

happiness 280, 282–288
headscarves 540, 544, 546–548,
    550–441
heart rate and concern for others 28–31,
    39–40, 43
helping and helpfulness 33, 62, 206,
    335, 353
  prosocial disposition 219–227, 230
  sympathy 48–49, 52–53, 55–57, 60
help-seeking 15, 17–24
heuristics 211
hierarchical general linear modelling
    (HGLM) 482–486, 491
hierarchical linear modelling
    (HLM) 259, 262–264, 268, 269
  ethnic identity 283, 284, 286, 288
high intensity pleasure 19
Hollingshead Index 30
home education for Muslims 545–550
homework 463–468, 470, 472, 496, 522
honesty 209–210
hyperactivity 121

id 4
identification 205, 304–305,
    307–308, 312
identity 3, 9, 203
  ethnic 255, 278–290
  moderation hypothesis 305, 307
  see also group identity

ignorance 129–136
imagination 117, 118–120
imitation 205
immigration 441, 516
  ethnic identity 279, 281
  individualism and collectivism
    517–518, 522, 524, 527–528, 532
  minority rights 537–538, 539,
    543, 552
impulsivity 18, 19
incest 212
independence 65, 319, 458, 493
  individualism and collectivism
    522–524, 526, 528–529, 532
indifference 65
individual differences 118, 119–120,
    156, 294
  attachment 67, 70, 73
  prosocial disposition 219, 229, 230
individualism 516, 517–534,
    555–556, 569
Infant Temperament Questionnaire
    (ITQ) 95, 97
Infant/Toddler HOME Scale 95–97,
    100–105, 107, 110, 112
influence 3, 5, 171, 178–179, 181–182
in-group favoritism 410, 419
in-group members 292–309
inhibitory control 17–19
insecure avoidance 87–88, 91–94,
    98–99, 107, 111
insecure resistance 87–88, 98
integration 207
intentions and intentionality 5, 117,
    118, 129
  action interpretation 122, 127–129
interactive effect hypothesis 93
intergroup relationships 184, 185–186,
    195–196, 197
internal representations 65
internal working models 65, 70, 80
internalized distress 463–464, 466–469,
    471–473
internalizing problems 154, 348, 493
  relational aggression 379–392
  shyness 316, 317–319, 322–327
  victimization 155–163
  withdrawal 332, 334, 346
interpersonal expectancy effects 422
interpersonal responsibility 26, 32,
    34–37, 40–41
intrinsic motivation 518, 519, 520
Islam 516, 537–552, 569

Jihad 543, 546, 547
judgments 5–8, 117, 203, 255, 406, 510
  China 350–351, 554, 556–559,
    569–571
  diversity of beliefs 233–249
  exclusion 408–416, 417, 418–420
  group dynamics 292–309
  minority rights 538–543, 545,
    547–548, 550–551
  morality 204, 206–210, 213–215, 252
justice *see* fairness

knowledge 129, 130–142, 147–148
  access 117, 137–142, 147–148

language arts 256, 257–259, 261,
    264–267, 269–274
language delay 121
Latent Growth Curve Modeling
    (LGCM) 336, 342
leadership 521–522, 524, 531
  Chinese children 348, 353, 354,
    355–360
  national conference 193, 199
  popularity 167, 171, 178–179, 182
learning disabilities 48, 57
Lo-Mendell-Rubin (LMR) likelihood
    ratio test 338
loneliness 154, 332, 333, 348, 355, 493
  shyness 316, 317, 320–321, 323, 327
  victimization 155, 157
Loneliness and Social Dissatisfaction
    Questionnaire for Young
    Children 321, 323
low intensity pleasure 19
lying and cheating 209, 233
  deception 117, 118, 120, 209–210

majority rule decision making 554–555,
    557, 559–569
maternal deprivation 91–114
maternal factors and shyness 317–329
maternal negative control 29
mathematics 354, 424,
  exclusion 409–411, 413, 415, 419
  self-competence 256–259, 261,
    264–267, 269–274
McCarthy Scales of Children's
    Abilities 30
mental health 5, 460, 464–469,
    471–473
mind-reading 117, 118–122
mistrust 65

monotropy 78–79
mood states 282, 372, 374, 376
moral identity 203
moral judgment 117
morals and morality 3–9, 14, 16, 203,
    252, 517, 555–556
  development 204–215
  diversity of beliefs 234–244, 246, 248
  exclusion 407–409, 412–418
  exercises 62, 252–253
  minority rights 537–542, 545
  parental authority 477, 488
  prosocial disposition 222
  psychological control 494–496,
    499–500, 506–507, 509–510
mother–child attachment 5, 7, 65,
    66–85
motivation 5, 256–257, 258
  intrinsic 518, 519, 520
multiculturalism 516, 539, 552, 574
Multi-dimensional Inventory of Black
    Identity (MIBI) 282
Multigroup Ethnic Identity
    Measure 280
multiple attachments 67, 77–80
multiple beliefs 233, 236, 239, 242,
    244–245, 248
Multi–response Racial Attitude Measure
    (MRA) 443, 444
Muslim religion 516, 537–552, 569
My Child measure 32, 37

National Assessment of Educational
    Progress (NAEP) 273
National Educational Longitudinal
    Study (NELS) 273
negative affect 28, 29, 31, 41, 44
  temperament 15–24
negative life events 87–91
negativity 19–22, 24
neighbors 442, 447–449, 459
NEO Personality Inventory 95, 96
Network of Relationship Inventory
    (NRI) 337
neurophysiology 370, 374
neuroscience 9, 203, 212–215
neuroticism 15, 18
  shyness 319–320, 322–323, 326–327
neuroticism/negative emotionality 15
NICHD Study of Early Child
    Care 91–114
nonauthoritative parenting 463,
    465, 472

obedience 542, 555, 556
  individualism and collectivism
    518–520, 523–524, 527, 529
  parental authority 476–491
objectivism 234, 235, 245, 246
Observational Record of the Caregiving
    Environment (ORCE) 95, 97–98
Oedipal conflict 4
Opposite-sex relations 481–482, 484,
    486–489
optimism 519
out-group individuals 292–309
over-controlling parenting 332, 458
over-protectiveness 318–319, 320–323,
    326–328

parent–child attachment 65, 66–85
  childcare 91–114
  security 86–91
parental authority 458, 476–491
  psychological control 495, 497, 499,
    501, 506–507, 510
parental expectations 481, 484, 487, 488
parental monitoring 458, 462, 472,
    493–510
  authority 476–482, 484–491
Parental Styles and Dimensions
    Questionnaire (PSDQ)
    320–321, 323
parenting styles 5, 62, 65, 458
  concern for others 28–29, 31,
    40–43
  development of morality 205, 210
  fretful 320, 322–325, 326–327, 328
  individualism and
    collectivism 531–534
  minority rights 544–545
  nonauthoritative 463, 465, 472
  over-controlling 332, 458
  permissive 458, 488
  precision 507
  prosocial disposition 220
  restrictive 499–501, 503–510
  shyness 317, 318–319, 320–328
  temperament 15, 16, 24
  uninhibited 320, 322–324, 325, 328
  warm/supportive 320, 322–327
  withdrawal 333
  see also authoritarianism; authoritative
    parenting
passive control 17
Peer Relationships and Social Skills
    Ratings 33

peers 3, 5–6, 8, 14, 154, 200, 366
  authoritative parenting 459–474
  Chinese children 348–354, 358–361,
    554–571
  ethnic identity 279, 289
  exclusion 406, 407–420
  exercises 364, 452–453
  individualism and collectivism 527,
    529, 531
  parental authority 477
  popularity 165–182
  shyness 316, 317–318, 320–327
  social information processing 369,
    372–374, 376
  unsociability 363–364
  victimization 155–165
  withdrawal 316, 332–337, 340–346
perceived popularity 166, 168, 169–170,
    172–182
permissive parenting 458, 488
personal issues 477–478, 481, 483–486,
    488–489
  psychological control 495–496, 499,
    501–503, 505–508
personality 5, 9, 14, 15, 95–96, 280, 458
  maternal 317–320, 322
  paternal 328
  prosocial disposition 218–230
perspective taking 3, 6–7, 26, 117, 406
  prosocial disposition 220–221,
    223–227, 230
  stereotypes 423, 430
  sympathy 48–61
physical attractiveness 167, 171, 173, 180
Pictorial Scale of Perceived Competence
    and Social Acceptance for Young
    Children (PSPCSA) 321, 323
Play Observation Scale (POS) 321, 323
playing alone 171, 173
popularity 154, 165–183, 184, 337, 344
possession situations 50–53, 59
precision parenting 507
preconscious 5
prejudice 3, 406, 451–452
  exercises 452–453
  minority rights 538, 539, 552
  race and gender 408, 418, 419
  stereotypes 423, 427, 430, 436
Preschool Behavior Questionnaire
    (PBQ) 30
Preschool Racial Attitude Measure II
    (PRAM II) 443, 445
Profile of Mood States (POMS) 282

promoting healthy parent–adolescent relationship 513
prosocial behavior 14, 15, 24, 48–61
 Chinese children 348
 concern for others 26–29, 32–37, 40–44
 disposition 218–232
 gender 225, 409, 412
 morality 203
 popularity 165–166, 168, 173–175, 177, 179–180
 withdrawal 333, 335–337, 340–344
Prosocial Behaviors with Peers at School 33–37, 40–42
protection 155–165
provocative victims 155
proximity to parent 66–69, 71–74, 81
 attachment bond 75–76
prudential issues 477–479, 481–484, 486–489
psychoanalysis 4, 8, 66
 development of morality 205, 210–211, 212
psychological adjustment of mother 93, 96, 100–103, 107, 109–110
Psychological Autonomy Granting 462–463
psychological control 458, 493–510, 513
psychophysiology 27–31, 39–40, 43–44, 316, 317
psychosocial competence 460, 463, 464, 467, 469–470, 473
Psychosocial Maturity Inventory 464
psychoticism 15, 24

racism 543, 546
Rasch analyses 140–143
 five item model 141
 seven item model 142–143
reactivity 15–16, 19
real–apparent emotion 117, 136–142, 148–149
reinforcement 5, 16, 205, 211
rejection *see* exclusion and rejection
relatedness 517–533
relational aggression 163, 171, 173, 366, 379–392
relativism 205, 206, 207
 diversity of beliefs 233–240, 242, 243–249
religion 248, 442, 537–552, 558
 Islam 516, 537–552, 569
representational models 70, 75

respect 6, 205, 555
 individualism and collectivism 518–520, 523–525, 527–528, 533–534
restrictive parenting 499–501, 503–510
reticence 317–318
retrieval 73, 81
Revised Class Play (RCP) 170–171, 336–337, 353
rights 203, 218, 248, 516, 537–552
 China 556, 560–561, 565–571
 exclusion 407, 412, 417
 morality 206–209, 212, 214–215
risk difference (RD) 133–134, 135
romantic relationships 114
Rosenberg Self-Esteem Scale 282
rules 203, 236, 407, 458, 517, 522
 morality 205, 207, 213, 252
 parental authority 476–491
 psychological control 494, 498, 500, 508

sadness 26, 29, 31, 69, 75, 157
 temperament 19, 21, 22, 24
Sample Size Adjusted BIC (SSA) 338–339
scholarship 188–189, 192–193, 199
school adjustment 316, 317–329
 Chinese children 351, 358–60
school avoidance 155
school field trips 554–555
school liking 322, 323, 326
School Liking and Avoidance scale (SLAS) 322, 332
school orientation 463–468
secure avoidant attachment 107
security 70, 76–77, 78, 80, 91–114
 attachment 65, 86–91, 220
 friendship 157–158, 162
self-competence 255, 256–274
 growth curves 264
self-concept 6–7, 255, 278, 555
self-confidence 65, 167, 349–351
self-consciousness 316, 317
self-control 205
self-development 6–7
self-efficacy 255
self-esteem 154, 155, 255, 282, 332, 480
 authoritative parenting 464–467, 470, 472–473
 ethnic identity 280–283, 287–288
 individualism and collectivism 518–520, 522, 524–525

self-competence 256, 258
 shyness 316, 317–318
self-identity 255, 256–274, 278–290, 311
self-maximization 518–520, 522, 523, 525
self-regulation 15, 23, 24
 concern for others 27–28, 42–44
self-reliance 464–467, 470, 472–473
self-system 4, 255
sensitivity of mother 96–98, 100–111
sensitivity in play 96–97
separation from mother 66, 91–114
sexual attachments 79–80
shame 15, 19–22, 24
sharing 203, 206, 220–222, 224–230
shyness 19, 316, 363, 364, 531
 Chinese children 348–361
 maternal 317–329
 moderator 325–326
 popularity 171, 173
 withdrawal 316, 318, 332–346
siblings 58, 78, 79, 120
singing 410, 413
single-action condition 123–126, 128
six decision examples 559, 563, 573
Slossen Intelligence Test–Revised 261
sociability 15–26, 337, 343
 Chinese children 348–361, 554–571
sociable behavioral system 67, 71, 72–73, 81
social approach 333
social avoidance 333
social-cognitive development theory 154, 444, 449, 494
 exclusion 407, 417–418
social-cognitive domain theories 5–6, 8–9, 489
 minority rights 538–540, 542, 551–552
social competence 33, 321, 323, 373, 464–467, 470
 Chinese children 348, 353
 Withdrawal 332, 334
Social Competence Inventory (SCI) 321, 323
social control 167, 170, 171, 178, 179
social–cultural developmental theories 6–7, 8–9
social dissatisfaction 320–327
social dominance 169, 170, 171, 172–175, 179–180
social hierarchy 184, 186–187, 194, 196

social identity theory (SIT) 255, 293, 305, 406, 442, 539
social information processing 366, 367–376
social interaction 316, 317
social leaning theory 5, 8, 66
social prerogatives 178–179, 180, 181
social reasoning 184, 185–186, 189, 194–197
social relationships 117, 118–122
social skills 154, 155, 327, 350
  popularity 171, 173–175, 182
social understanding 118, 119–120
social visibility 166, 173–175, 177, 179–180, 182
socialization 15–26, 351, 537
  authoritative parenting 459, 463, 471, 472
  concern for others 28–29, 31, 34, 40–43
  individualism and collectivism 518, 521, 523, 531
  parental authority 476, 488, 489, 491
  self-competence and gender 259, 272, 273
  shyness 316, 318–319
  stereotypes 423, 436
Society for Research in Child Development 130
sociobiological theories 7
sociometric controversial subtype 182
sociometric popularity 165–182
solitude 363–364
somatic markers 370
soothability 19
soothing behaviors 75
spending power 171, 173, 180
sports 292–309, 521
  self-competence 256–259, 261, 264–267, 269–272
status 154, 166, 184–199
stereotypes 203, 273, 406, 421–437, 441
  exclusion 408–409, 411–419
  group status and bias 184–196
  minority rights 539, 552
  reduction of prejudice 451–452
  threat 422, 424–425, 432–437
stigmatization 422–426, 428–437
straightforward exclusion context 408, 411, 413–414, 417, 419–420
Strange Situation 67, 76, 86–88, 90, 115
  infant childcare 92–95, 97–98, 99–100, 109, 111

Strategic Disclosure Questionnaire 480–481
Strengths and Difficulties Questionnaire (SDQ) 321, 323
stress 327, 351
  ethnic identity 278–280, 282, 283–284, 285–289
strictness–supervision 462–463
student council 186–188, 192–193, 199
Student–Teacher Relationship Scale (STRS) 321, 323
subconscious 5, 211–212, 215
subjective group dynamics (SGD) model 293–296, 298–299, 302–303, 305–309
subjective task values 257–274
substance use 366, 458, 494
  authoritative parenting 459, 461, 464–467, 469, 471–472
  parental authority 477–481, 489
superego 4–5, 8
surgency 15, 18–24
sympathy 14, 17, 48–61, 62–63
  concern for others 28, 29, 33
  morality 205, 212
  prosocial disposition 218–221, 223–230

target evaluation 296, 299, 302–303, 307
target typicality 299, 302, 306
taste (value beliefs) 235, 237–249
Teacher Child Rating Scale 33
teacher expectancy 424
Teacher Report Form (TRF) 30, 32–33, 44
teasing 120, 366, 372, 374
temper-tantrums 14
temperament 5, 7, 14, 15–26, 62–63, 371
  infant childcare 93, 95, 97, 101–104, 107, 109
  prosocial disposition 219, 229
  shyness 318, 326, 328
  sympathy 59
  withdrawal 333
Ten Item Personality Inventory (TIPI) 320, 323
theory of mind 6, 7, 117, 118–122, 129–149, 150
  action interpretation 127
  diversity of beliefs 233
  relational aggression 366
  sympathy 58

tolerance 203, 240–242, 406
  diversity of beliefs 233–234, 236–249
  minority rights 537, 540–542
trolley car problem 213–214
truancy 366, 494
truth–telling 233, 235–237, 239–241
Tucker–Lewis Index (TLI) 342

unconscious 4–5, 8
undercontrol problems 332
unequal qualification exclusion context 408–409, 411, 413, 415–418, 420
uninhibited parenting 320, 322–324, 325, 328
unsociability 363–364

vaccination 545, 548, 549, 551
vagal tone 28, 30–31, 40, 44
values school 171, 173
van Gogh, Theo 538
victimization 3, 155–165, 366, 395–401
  antecedents 159–160, 161, 163
  individual risk factors 156, 161, 162
  outcomes 160–161, 163
  shyness 316, 318
  social risk factors 156, 161, 63
  withdrawal 316, 332–337, 340–346
vocabulary 18, 20, 22, 23, 67
  stereotypes 427–429, 432–435

wariness 14, 18
warm/supportive parenting 320, 322–327
well-being 278–290
Wechsler Intelligence Scale for Children III (WISC-III) 427, 428
Weinberger's Adjustment Inventory (WAI) 222, 223, 227, 230
withdrawal 33, 156, 316, 332–346
  Chinese children 349, 351, 361
  popularity 166–167, 173–175, 177, 179–180
  shyness 316, 318, 332–346
work orientation 464–465, 467, 470, 472–473

Youth Self-Perception Profile 464

zone of proximal development 6, 8

SOCIAL DEVELOPMENT IN CHILDHOOD AND ADOLESCENCE

With joyful love and affection to Rob, Sasha, and Jacob,
and with enduring love and gratitude to Marcia,
David, and Sean (M.K.)

With all my love to Vanessa, Adam, and Jaimie,
and with love and gratitude to my parents Barbara and Stephen,
primary contributors to my own social development (R.C.)